Contemporary Authors®

NEW REVISION SERIES

Explore your options!

Gale databases are offered in a variety of formats

ISSN 0275-7176

Contemporary

Authors®

A Bio-Bibliographical Guide to
Current Writers in Fiction, General Nonfiction,
Poetry, Journalism, Drama, Motion Pictures,
Television, and Other Fields

DANIEL JONES
JOHN D. JORGENSON
Editors

NEW REVISION SERIES
volume **59**

GALE

DETROIT • NEW YORK • TORONTO • LONDON

STAFF

Daniel Jones and John D. Jorgenson, *Editors, New Revision Series*

Thomas Wiloch, *Sketchwriting Coordinator and Online Research Specialist*

Tim Akers, Pamela S. Dear, Jeff Hunter, Jerry Moore, Deborah A. Stanley, Polly A. Vedder, Tim White and Kathleen Wilson, *Contributing Editors*

Greg Barnhisel, Marjorie Burgess, Charles Charbon, Daniel Feldstein, Mary Gillis, Lane A. Glen, Michael Goldman, Joan Goldsworthy, George Hynes, Anne Janette Johnson, Rena Korb, Jane Kelly Kosek, Joseph Kovack, David Kroeger, Ronald Lewandowski, Philip Lunde, Meg MacDonald, Robert Miltner, Julie Monahan, Stanley Olson, Trudy Ring, Dennis Ryle, Sue Salter, Pamela L. Shelton, Kenneth R. Shepherd, Denise Wiloch, and Tim Winter-Damon, *Sketchwriters*

Tracy Arnold-Chapman, Emily J. McMurray, and Pamela L. Shelton, *Copyeditors*

James P. Draper, *Managing Editor*

Victoria B. Cariappa, *Research Manager*

Julia C. Daniel, Tamara C. Nott, Tracie A. Richardson Norma Sawaya, and Cheryl L. Warnock, *Research Associates*

Talitha Dutton, *Research Assistant*

This book is printed on acid-free paper that meets the minimum requirements of American National Standard for Information Sciences-Permanence Paper for Printed Library Materials, ANSI Z39.48-1984.

Library of Congress Catalog Card Number 81-640179
ISBN 0-7876-1201-4
ISSN 0275-7176

Printed in the United States of America

10 9 8 7 6 5 4 3 2 1

Contents

Preface

The *Contemporary Authors New Revision Series* (*CANR*) provides updated information on authors listed in earlier volumes of *Contemporary Authors* (*CA*). Although entries for individual authors from any volume of *CA* may be included in a volume of the *New Revision Series, CANR* updates only those sketches requiring significant change. However, in response to requests from librarians and library patrons for the most current information possible on high-profile writers of greater public and critical interest, *CANR* revises entries for these authors whenever new and noteworthy information becomes available.

Authors are included on the basis of specific criteria that indicate the need for a revision. These criteria include a combination of bibliographical additions, changes in addresses or career, major awards, and personal information such as name changes or death dates. All listings in this volume have been revised or augmented in various ways and contain up-to-the-minute publication information in the Writings section, most often verified by the author and/or by consulting a variety of online resources. Many sketches have been extensively rewritten, often including informative new Sidelights. As always, a *CANR* listing entails no charge or obligation.

The key to locating an author's most recent entry is the *CA* cumulative index, which is published separately and distributed with even-numbered original volumes and odd-numbered revision volumes. It provides access to all entries in *CA* and *CANR*. Always consult the latest index to find an author's most recent entry.

For the convenience of users, the *CA* cumulative index also includes references to all entries in these Gale literary series: *Authors and Artists for Young Adults, Authors in the News, Bestsellers, Black Literature Criticism, Black Writers, Children's Literature Review, Concise Dictionary of American Literary Biography, Concise Dictionary of British Literary Biography, Contemporary Authors Autobiography Series, Contemporary Authors Bibliographical Series, Contemporary Literary Criticism, Dictionary of Literary Biography, Dictionary of Literary Biography Documentary Series, Dictionary of Literary Biography Yearbook, DISCovering Authors, DISCovering Authors: British, DISCovering Authors: Canadian, DISCovering Authors: Modules* (including modules for Dramatists, Most-Studied Authors, Multicultural Authors, Novelists, Poets, and Popular/Genre Authors), *Drama Criticism, Hispanic Literature Criticism, Hispanic Writers, Junior DISCovering Authors, Major Authors and Illustrators for Children and Young Adults, Major 20th-Century Writers, Native North American Literature, Poetry Criticism, Short Story Criticism, Something about the Author, Something about the Author Autobiography Series, Twentieth-Century Literary Criticism, World Literature Criticism, World Literature Criticism Supplement,* and *Yesterday's Authors of Books for Children.*

A Sample Index Entry:

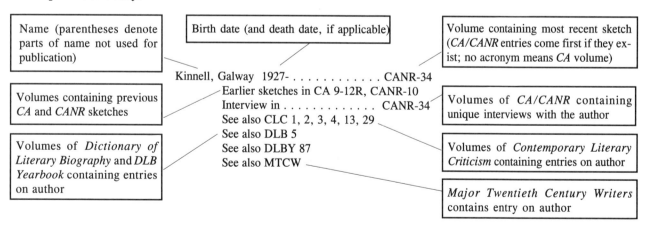

For the most recent *CA* information on Kinnell, users should refer to Volume 34 of the *New Revision Series,* as designated by "CANR-34"; if that volume is unavailable, refer to CANR-10. If CANR-10 is also unavailable, refer to CA 9-12R, published in 1974, for Kinnell's first revision entry.

How Are Entries Compiled?

The editors make every effort to secure new information directly from the authors. Copies of all sketches in selected *CA* and *CANR* volumes previously published are routinely sent to listees at their last-known addresses, and returns from these authors are then assessed. For deceased writers, or those who fail to reply to requests for data, we consult other reliable biographical sources, such as those indexed in Gale's *Biography and Genealogy Master Index,* and biobliographical sources, such as *Magazine Index, Newspaper Abstracts, LC MARC,* and a variety of online databases. Further details come from published interviews, feature stories, book reviews, online literary magazines and journals, author web sites, and often the authors' publishers supply material.

* Indicates that a listing has been compiled from secondary sources but has not been personally verified for this edition by the author under review.

What Kinds of Information Does an Entry Provide?

Sketches in *CANR* contain the following biographical and bibliographical information:

- **Entry heading:** the most complete form of author's name, plus any pseudonyms or name variations used for writing

- **Personal information:** author's date and place of birth, family data, ethnicity, educational background, political and religious affiliations, and hobbies and leisure interests

- **Addresses:** author's home, office, or agent's addresses, plus e-mail and fax numbers, as available

- **Career summary:** name of employer, position, and dates held for each career post; resume of other vocational achievements; military service

- **Membership information:** professional, civic, and other association memberships and any official posts held

- **Awards and honors:** military and civic citations, major prizes and nominations, fellowships, grants, and honorary degrees

- **Writings:** a comprehensive, chronological list of titles, publishers, dates of original publication and revised editions, and production information for plays, television scripts, and screenplays

- **Adaptations:** a list of films, plays, and other media which have been adapted from the author's work

- **Work in progress:** current or planned projects, with dates of completion and/or publication, and expected publisher, when known

- **Sidelights:** a biographical portrait of the author's development; information about the critical reception of the author's works; revealing comments, often by the author, on personal interests, aspirations, motivations, and thoughts on writing

- **Biographical and critical sources:** a list of books and periodicals in which additional information on an author's life and/or writings appears

Related Titles in the *CA* Series

Contemporary Authors Autobiography Series complements *CA* original and revised volumes with specially commissioned autobiographical essays by important current authors, illustrated with personal photographs they provide. Common topics include their motivations for writing, the people and experiences that shaped their careers, the rewards they derive from their work, and their impressions of the current literary scene.

Contemporary Authors Bibliographical Series surveys writings by and about important American authors since World War II. Each volume concentrates on a specific genre and features approximately ten writers; entries list works written by and about the author and contain a bibliographical essay discussing the merits and deficiencies of major critical and scholarly studies in detail.

Available in Electronic Formats

CD-ROM. Full-text bio-bibliographic entries from the entire *CA* series, covering approximately 101,000 writers, are available on CD-ROM through lease and purchase plans. The disc combines entries from the *CA, CANR,* and *Contemporary Authors Permanent Series* (*CAP*) print series to provide the most recent author listing. It can be searched by name, title, subject/genre, nationality/ethnicity, personal data, and as well as advanced searching using boolean logic. The disc is updated every six months. For more information, call 1-800-877-GALE.

Online. The *Contemporary Authors* database is made available online to libraries and their patrons through online public access catalog (OPAC) vendors. Currently, *CA* is offered through Ameritech Library Services' Vista Online (formerly Dynix), and is expected to become available through CARL Systems and The Library Corporation. More OPAC vendor offerings will soon follow.

GaleNet. *CA* is available on a subscription basis through GaleNet, a new online information resource that features an easy-to-use end-user interface, the powerful search capabilities of the BRS/Search retrieval software, and ease of access through the World Wide Web. For more information, call 1-800-877-GALE.

Magnetic Tape. *CA* is available for licensing on magnetic tape in a fielded format. Either the complete database or a custom selection of entries may be ordered. The database is available for internal data processing and nonpublishing purposes only. For more information, call 1-800-877-GALE.

Suggestions Are Welcome

The editors welcome comments and suggestions from users on any aspects of the *CA* series. If readers would like to recommend authors for inclusion in future volumes of the series, they are cordially invited to write: The Editors, *Contemporary Authors New Revision Series* , 835 Penobscot Bldg., 645 Griswold St., Detroit, MI 48226-4094; call toll-free at 1-800-347-GALE; or fax at 1-313-961-6599.

CA Numbering System and Volume Update Chart

Occasionally questions arise about the *CA* numbering system and which volumes, if any, can be discarded. Despite numbers like "29-32R," "97-100" and "157," the entire *CA* print series consists of only 144 physical volumes with the publication of *CA* Volume 158. The following charts note changes in the numbering system and cover design, and indicate which volumes are essential for the most complete, up-to-date coverage.

CA **First Revision**
- 1-4R through 41-44R (11 books)
  Cover: Brown with black and gold trim.
  There will be no further First Revision volumes because revised entries are now being handled exclusively through the more efficient *New Revision Series* mentioned below.

CA **Original Volumes**
- 45-48 through 97-100 (14 books)
  Cover: Brown with black and gold trim.
- 101 through 158 (58 books)
  Cover: Blue and black with orange bands.
  The same as previous *CA* original volumes but with a new, simplified numbering system and new cover design.

CA **Permanent Series**
- *CAP*-1 and *CAP*-2 (2 books)
  Cover: Brown with red and gold trim.
  There will be no further *Permanent Series* volumes because revised entries are now being handled exclusively through the more efficient *New Revision Series* mentioned below.

CA **New Revision Series**
- *CANR*-1 through *CANR*-59 (59 books)
  Cover: Blue and black with green bands.
  Includes only sketches requiring significant changes; **sketches are taken from any previously published *CA*, *CAP*, or *CANR* volume.**

If You Have:	You May Discard:
CA First Revision Volumes 1-4R through 41-44R **and** *CA Permanent Series* Volumes 1 and 2	*CA* Original Volumes 1, 2, 3, 4 Volumes 5-6 through 41-44
CA Original Volumes 45-48 through 97-100 **and** 101 through 158	**NONE:** These volumes will not be superseded by corresponding revised volumes. Individual entries from these and all other volumes appearing in the left column of this chart may be revised and included in the various volumes of the *New Revision Series*.
CA New Revision Series Volumes *CANR*-1 through *CANR*-59	**NONE:** The *New Revision Series* does not replace any single volume of *CA*. Instead, volumes of *CANR* include entries from many previous *CA* series volumes. All *New Revision Series* volumes must be retained for full coverage.

A Sampling of Authors and Media People Featured in This Volume

Margaret Atwood

A critically acclaimed poet, short story writer, and novelist, Atwood has been described as a Canadian nationalist, a feminist, and a gothic writer, but transcends these categories by incorporating universal concerns into her work. Her novels include *Surfacing, Cat's Eye,* and *The Robber Bride.*

Alan Ayckbourn

Ayckbourn has developed an international reputation as Great Britain's most successful living playwright. A prolific writer, Ayckbourn has won numerous awards for his plays, which are typically domestic comedies that focus on the dull rituals of English middle-class life.

Todhunter Ballard

A prolific writer of mysteries and Western novels, Ballard's many hard-boiled detective stories contributed greatly to the development of the typical Hollywood murder mystery.

David Cornwell

Better known as John le Carre, Cornwell is famous for his collection of espionage fiction that presents a world of deceit, corruption, and moral decay. Typically set within the context of the Cold War, le Carre's novels are compelling thrillers that examine themes of betrayal, loyalty and love.

John Creasey

The author of nearly six hundred books, Creasey was the most prolific writer of crime fiction in English. Two of Creasey's most popular characters were Inspector Roger West, a detective in Scotland Yard, and Richard Rollison—known as the Toff—a nickname for a wealthy gentleman who helped police solve crimes.

Gerald Durrell

A naturalist and zoologist, Durrell wrote many humorous and poignant books telling of his adventures with animals. A protector of wildlife, Durrell's books are noted for their honest, straightforward, and compassionate tone.

Ian Fleming

Ian Fleming is renowned for his collection of espionage tales featuring the flamboyant British secret agent James Bond. Bond has become a cultural icon as a result of the many film adaptations of Fleming's novels, which feature Bond in tales filled with action, adventure, sex and violence.

Garrison Keillor

Winner of a Grammy Award for best non-musical recording in 1987, Keillor is the author of witty and wistful stories presented in his *Lake Wobegon Days,* originally presented on his radio program entitled *A Prairie Home Companion.* Compared to such American humorists as Ring Lardner and Mark Twain, Keillor's wit appeals to audiences across the nation.

Jamaica Kincaid

Employing a highly poetic literary style, Kincaid presents tales about life on the Caribbean island of Antigua. Her novels are noted for their highly detailed descriptions of the ordinary, their vivid characterizations, and lyrical, hypnotic style. Titles include *Annie John, Lucy,* and *The Autobiography of My Mother.*

Nelson Mandela

Perhaps the world's most famous political prisoner, Mandela was elected President of South Africa in 1994. Following his release from prison in 1990, Mandela embarked on a successful world tour in which he spoke in eight major cities. His writings include *No Easy Walk to Freedom, The Struggle Is My Life,* and collections of his speeches made both during and after his incarceration.

Katherine Paterson

A two-time Newbery Medal winner, Paterson writes tales that examine familial relationships, adolescent crises, and spiritual triumph. Noted for her skillful, compassionate, and humorous narrative, Paterson combines a light touch with serious themes. Her compelling works achieve power through understatement and a pithy style.

Bill Pronzini

Winner of the Private Eye Writers of America award for best novel in 1981 with his book *Hoodwink,* Pronzini has established himself as a successful mystery writer. With his "Nameless Detective" series, Pronzini has developed a reputation as a writer of taut, engrossing thrillers.

Janet Quin-Harkin

Quin-Harkin is the author of over one hundred books, most of which appear as part of a series, such as her "Sweet Dreams" collection. Geared towards young readers, Quin-Harkin's books are infused with fast-paced plots and humor. Her works include *Peter Penny's Dance, Wanted: Date for Saturday Night,* and *The Boyfriend Wars.*

David Rabe

Rabe received the New York Drama Critics Circle Award for best American play in 1972 with *Streamers*. Noted for his lyrical language and dark humor, Rabe writes plays that examine issues of race, drug addiction, and war. Several of his plays have included characters who return home from the Vietnam War, and much of his work focuses on alienation, desperation, and death.

Thomas Eugene Robbins

Tom Robbins gained a large audience for his work with the paperback editions of his two novels, *Another Roadside Attraction* and *Even Cowgirls Get the Blues*. Known for his California style, Robbins' works emphasize a quest for freedom, a break from confining traditions, and the pursuit of a higher state of being.

Julian Symons

A biographer, historian, and poet, Symons was best known as a novelist and critic of the crime and detective novel genres. Regarded as a master of both the crime novel and the detective story, Symons often commented on the decaying state of society in his novels. His works included *The Color of Murder, The Progress of a Crime,* and *Bloody Murder.*

Emma Tennant

Tennant is an English novelist, critic and editor. Her wide-ranging body of fiction offers a satirical but penetrating vision of modern England. Critics have praised Tennant's style, lauding her sense of the absurd, and measured graceful prose. Her works include *The Magic Drum, Pemberley; or, "Pride and Prejudice" Continued,* and *Eleanor and Marianne.*

Colin Thubron

Winner of the Booker Prize in 1991 for the novel *Turning Back the Sun,* Thubron is the author of several travel books that have been acclaimed for their descriptive passages, sense of history, and personal observations. Critics laud Thubron's ability to create distinct characters and his skill in combining the personal with a sense of adventure. His works also include *A Cruel Madness,* and *Behind the Wall: A Journey through China.*

Judith Viorst

Described by one critic as "among the finest living authors for children," Viorst is also known for her wryly humorous poetry and her irreverent autobiographical works. She received an Emmy Award for poetic monologues in 1970 and a Christopher Award in 1988 for *The Good-bye Book.*

A

ABERCROMBIE, Nicholas 1944-

PERSONAL: Born April 13, 1944, in Birmingham, England; son of Michael (a university professor) and Jane (a university professor; maiden name, Johnson) Abercrombie; married Brenda Patterson (a publisher), January 2, 1969; children: Robert Benjamin, Joseph Edward. *Education:* Queen's College, Oxford, B.A., 1966; London School of Economics and Political Science, London, M.Sc., 1968; University of Lancaster, Ph.D., 1980. *Politics:* Socialist. *Religion:* None.

ADDRESSES: Home—1A Derwent Rd., Lancaster LA1 3ES, England. *Office*—Department of Sociology, University of Lancaster, Bailrigg, Lancaster, England. *Email*—n.abercrombie@lancaster.ac.uk.

CAREER: University College, London, research officer in town planning, 1968-70; University of Lancaster, Bailrigg, England, lecturer, 1970-83, senior lecturer, 1983-88, reader, 1988-90, professor of sociology, 1990—, pro vice chancellor, 1995—. Chair of Framework Press; active in local political organizations and Campaign for Nuclear Disarmament.

MEMBER: British Sociological Association.

AWARDS, HONORS: Morris Ginsberg fellow at London School of Economics and Political Science, London, 1983.

WRITINGS:

Class, Structure, and Knowledge, Basil Blackwell, 1980.

(With Stephen Hill and Bryan S. Turner) *The Dominant Ideology Thesis,* Allen & Unwin, 1980.

(With John Urry) *Capital, Labour, and the Middle Classes,* Allen & Unwin, 1983.

(With Hill and Turner) *The Penguin Dictionary of Sociology,* Penguin, 1984, third edition, 1994.

(With Hill and Turner) *Sovereign Individuals of Capitalism,* Allen & Unwin, 1986.

(With Alan Warde, Keith Soothill, John Urry, and Sylvia Walby) *Contemporary British Society,* Polity Press, 1988, second edition, 1994.

(Editor with Hill and Turner) *Dominent Ideologies,* Unwin Hyman, 1990.

(Editor with Russell Keat) *Enterprise Culture,* Routledge, 1991.

(Editor with Warde) *Social Change in Contemporary Britain,* Polity Press, 1992.

(Editor with Keat and Nigel Whiteley) *The Authority of the Individual,* Routledge, 1994.

(Editor with Warde) *Family, Household, and Life-Course,* Framework Press, 1994.

(Editor with Warde) *Stratification and Inequality,* Framework Press, 1994.

Television and Society, Polity Press, 1996.

(With Brian Longhurst) *The Diffused Audience,* Sage, in press.

WORK IN PROGRESS: "Further editions of *The Penguin Dictionary of Sociology* and *Contemporary British Society*; a book on Britain in the year 2000; a study of money."

SIDELIGHTS: Nicholas Abercrombie once told *CA:* "I am an academic interested in the sociological analysis of culture. My primary interest lies in the impact of cultural values on a society. *The Dominant Ideology Thesis,* for instance, is an examination of the idea that there are dominant beliefs in a society which become widely shared and help to perpetuate the particular social order. My co-authors and I showed, to the contrary, that in historical societies, and contemporary ones, there is either no dominant culture or, if there is, it makes remarkable little impact on subordinate groups, mainly because the machinery for transmitting it is relatively inefficient.

"In other work, past or projected, I examine the relationship of individualistic values to economic life, the impact of television on audiences, particularly in the way that viewers talk about television and the manner in which a consumer culture affects the book publishing industry.

"I also try to write introductory books on sociology, books that are accessible to the general reader. This accessibility is very important to sociology, as is a method of teaching that is student centered not teacher centered. The latter consideration has dictated my involvement with a firm that publishes teaching materials for use in schools in the United Kingdom."

BIOGRAPHICAL/CRITICAL SOURCES:

PERIODICALS

Times Literary Supplement, September 11, 1981.

* * *

ADCOCK, Thomas 1947-

PERSONAL: Born January 5, 1947, in Detroit, MI; son of Thomas Ross (an accountant) and Ava Doretta (a homemaker; maiden name, Bradshaw) Adcock; married Mary Templeton, June 18, 1966 (divorced, July, 1972); married Kim Sykes (an actress), August 13, 1984; children: Elizabeth Anne, Jessica Leah. *Education:* Attended Michigan State University, 1965-67. *Politics:* Socialist. *Religion:* None.

ADDRESSES: Home—484 West 43 St., No. 5N, New York, NY 10036. *Agent*—Gloria Loomis, Watkins/Loomis Agency, 133rd East 35th St., New York, NY 10016.

CAREER: Oakland Press, Pontiac, MI, reporter, 1968-69; *Detroit Free Press,* Detroit, MI, reporter, 1969-71; *St. Paul Pioneer Press,* St. Paul, MN, re-

porter, 1971-74; Sun Newspapers, Minneapolis, MN, editor, 1974-78; freelance writer, 1978—. Active with Students for a Democratic Society and Student Non-Violent Coordinating Committee, 1965-66, and Student Mobilizing Committee to End the War in Vietnam, 1966-70.

MEMBER: International Association of Crime Writers, National Writers Union, PEN American Center, Mystery Writers of America, Czech Writers Union.

AWARDS, HONORS: Edgar Scroll, Mystery Writers of America, 1987, for the story "Christmas Cop"; Readers Award, *Ellery Queen's Mystery,* 1987, for the story "Thrown-Away Child"; Edgar Award for best original paperback, Mystery Writers of America, 1991, for *Dark Maze.*

WRITINGS:

Precinct Nineteen, Doubleday (New York City), 1984.
Sea of Green, Warner Books (New York City), 1988.
Dark Maze, Pocket Books (New York City), 1991.
Drown All the Dogs, Pocket Books, 1994.
Devil's Heaven, Pocket Books, 1995.
Thrown-Away Child, Pocket Books, 1996.
Grief Street, Pocket Books, 1997.

Contributor of stories to periodicals, including *Alfred Hitchcock's Mystery* and *Ellery Queen's Mystery* magazines. Contributing editor, *Minneapolis-St. Paul* and *Twin Cities.*

WORK IN PROGRESS: A novel tentatively titled *Paraguay,* a tale of three true, unsolved mysteries linked by a fictional character who guides the reader through a country that Adcock says has been called "the last place on earth for the worst people in the world."

ADAPTATIONS: Thrown-Away Child is being developed as a film by Arena Pictures.

SIDELIGHTS: Crime and its many different forms is a central theme for mystery novelist Thomas Adcock. Adcock's novels feature Neil Hockaday, a New York City detective with a drinking problem. In *Drown All the Dogs,* Hockaday confronts the mysterious death of his Irish-born father, who died in London during World War II. When his dying uncle asks to see him, Hockaday visits Dublin and lands in the middle of the conflict between England and the Irish Republican Army. As he investigates his own past, he also contemplates the history of a country torn by centuries of civil strife. The novel draws together the cities of London, Dublin and New York in what Charles Champlin of the *Los Angeles Times Book Review* calls a "fine and tangled yarn."

Adcock's ear for language comes across in his dialogue and characterizations. Champlin notes that Adcock's "dialogue lets you hear by turns the soft brogue of Eire or the nasal snarl of pure Manhattan." Marilyn Stasio of the *New York Times Book Review* notes that while the book is "lively and literate," it is also an "improbable adventure." Stasio adds that Adcock's dialogue can sometimes go overboard but that it "is sure to please readers who feel cheated if they don't get a lot of windy conversation."

In *Devil's Heaven,* Hockaday is forced to take a break from the New York Police Department because of his drinking problem. His hiatus is interrupted when his wife's boss is found butchered. Meanwhile, a serial killer who targets homosexuals terrorizes the city's gay population. Unable to resist his sleuthing impulses, Hockaday acts as an unofficial aide to a fellow detective. A review in *Publishers Weekly* observes that the mystery is "well-plotted but Adcock's prose . . . is less effectively lyrical than over-the-top." Like *Drown All the Dogs, Devil's Heaven* is violent and contains graphic details that "might be too specific for some sensibilities," writes *Chicago Tribune* reviewer Dick Adler, who also notes that Adcock's attention to detail also provides "unsparing and acute . . . descriptions of lunches at the Four Seasons, client meetings and searches for love in tawdry and dangerous gay bars."

In *Thrown-Away Child,* Hockaday takes another holiday from his police job to visit his wife's parents in New Orleans. The murder of an ex-con puts an end to his leisurely visit, especially since the main suspect is Ruby's cousin, Perry DuClat. The murder is followed by a killing spree by a brutal sociopath. A *Publishers Weekly* reviewer comments that Adcock's depiction of New Orleans is "voodoo and murder [mixed] with hot spices," altogether "lavish and very effectively applied." But a *Washington Post Book World* reviewer observes that Adcock's New Orleans setting was a gamble, given that the city has been described "with more nuance" by other mystery writers. Yet the story has its moments, the reviewer writes, especially the "squirming semi-comic passages" concerning Hockaday and his African-Ameri-

can in-laws. Wes Lukowsky comments in *Booklist* that *Thrown-Away Child* is a mystery that tackles serious issues. The story, Lukowsky says, "is about growing up black and poor, and white and poor, and never quite being able to shake the stigma."

In *Grief Street* Detective Hockaday is up to his elbows in his own neighborhood of Hell's Kitchen doing battle with rogue cops and a murderer who thinks of himself as the devil. A reviewer for *Kirkus Reviews* describes the novel as a detective story filled "to the bursting point with Catholic guilt, self-laceration, and spiritual crisis, with a magnificent starring role for Hell's Kitchen.

Adcock once told *CA:* "Where does a burned-out journalist turn but to novels, to the writing of truth, as opposed to fact? For readers who care to know, the story of America at this time is contained in fiction—largely, I find, in crime fiction, as our society is rather top-heavy with the criminal element (the presidency, the corporations, the Central Intelligence Agency and National Security Council, for example). Serious journalism is on the wane as the media become more and more the agents of the military-industrial complex. In my work, I try to accomplish two important things: first, to provide my readers a good, solid entertainment, and second, to illuminate the essential sameness of criminals in pinstripes and politician suits and fine educations—and those with no education and no hope who become our nation's growing army of street criminals. My literary mentors are Lincoln Steffens, Upton Sinclair, William Saroyan, A. J. Liebling, and Norman Mailer."

Beyond writing novels, Adcock is heavily involved in several film and television projects. He divides his time between New York and Los Angeles but considers New York his true home.

BIOGRAPHICAL/CRITICAL SOURCES:

PERIODICALS

Booklist, March 15, 1996, p. 1242.
Chicago Tribune, January 1, 1995, p. 4.
Chicago Tribune Books, January 1, 1995, p. 7.
Kirkus Reviews, July 15, 1997.
Library Journal, January, 1994, p. 157.
Los Angeles Times Book Review, May 8, 1994, p. 11.
New York Times Book Review, February 6, 1994, p. 31.

Publishers Weekly, December 5, 1994, p. 68; February 19, 1996, p. 207.
Washington Post Book World, April 21, 1996, p. 7.

*   *   *

AGAR, Brian
   See BALLARD, (Willis) Todhunter

*   *   *

ALLEN, Roland
   See AYCKBOURN, Alan

*   *   *

AMOR, Anne Clark 1933-
   (Anne Clark)

PERSONAL: Born February 4, 1933, in London, England; daughter of John (an engineer) and Violetta (Bird) Ryan; married Norman Victor Clark (a telephone engineer), July 14, 1956 (divorced January, 1981); married Abdallah Amor (a gymnasium proprietor), February 23, 1982; children: (first marriage) Peter Norman, Miranda Anne. *Ethnicity:* "English." *Education:* Birkbeck College, London, B.A. (with honors), 1968.

ADDRESSES: Home—16 Parkfields Ave., London NW9 7PE, England. *Agent*—A.M. Heath, 79 St. Martin's Ln., London WC2N 4AA, England.

CAREER: Greater London Council, London, administrative officer for Department of Housing, 1951-81; writer, 1975—.

MEMBER: Lewis Carroll Society (chairperson), Lewis Carroll Society of North America, Lewis Carroll Society of Japan, Royal Society of the Arts (fellow), Oscar Wilde Society, Pre-Raphaelite Society, William Morris Society, Beatrix Potter Society.

WRITINGS:

UNDER NAME ANNE CLARK

Beasts and Bawdy (a study of medieval animal lore), Taplinger, 1975.
Lewis Carroll: A Biography, Shocken, 1979.

The Real Alice: Lewis Carroll's Dream Child (biography), Stein & Day, 1981.

UNDER NAME ANNE CLARK AMOR

Mrs. Oscar Wilde: A Woman of Some Importance (biography), Sidgwick & Jackson, 1983.
William Holman Hunt: The True Pre-Raphaelite (biography), Constable & Co., 1989.
(Editor and author of introduction) *The Letters of Archdeacon Charles Dodgson to His Son Skeffington,* Lewis Carroll Society, 1989.
Lewis Carroll: Child of the North, White Stone Publishing, 1995.
Wonderland Come True to Alice in Lyndhurst, White Stone Publishing, 1995.

OTHER

Contributor of book reviews to periodicals, including *Literary Review* and *Books and Bookmen.* Editor of *Jabberwocky* (journal of the Lewis Carroll Society), 1969-75.

WORK IN PROGRESS: A Victorian biography; a novel; work for the "The Genius of Lewis Carroll" and "The Carroll Companion."

SIDELIGHTS: Anne Clark's 1979 biography, *Lewis Carroll,* traces the life of the Reverend Charles Lutwidge Dodgson, best known under the Carroll pseudonym as the author of *Alice's Adventures in Wonderland* and *Through the Looking-Glass.* In the *Times Literary Supplement* Humphrey Carpenter observes that of the "endless stream" of biographies of Lewis Carroll, "Miss Clark's book is not only the most readily available at the moment, but also one of the best." Carpenter further notes that the work offers fresh information unknown to earlier biographers and that it is "particularly enlightening on the relationship between Dodgson/Carroll and Alice Liddell" (the little girl for whom *Wonderland* was written). While Clark's biography makes no judgment concerning the nature of their relationship, Carpenter believes that some of Clark's findings "would seem to support those who believe that [thirty-year-old Carroll] was really 'in love' with [ten-year-old] Alice . . . and perhaps even hoped to marry her one day."

Washington Post Book World reviewer Elizabeth Sewell considers two other areas of the book noteworthy. She mentions the discussion of Carroll's photography and the "expanded account given here of his connections with that other great Victorian photographer, Julia Cameron, of their personalities and work." In addition, Sewell commends Clark's attention to Carroll's religious views, particularly "his unwillingness to proceed from the diaconate to the priesthood, backing this up with careful and detailed work on his clerical father and the relations between father and son; also Carroll's strict segregation of religion and laughter."

Clark's *The Real Alice* follows Alice Liddell from her childhood meeting with Carroll through her marriage and the births of her three sons to her death in 1934 at the age of eighty-two. In a *Washington Post Book World* review, Reid Beddow comments that *The Real Alice* "paints a charming portrait of Victorian family life." Carpenter, in the *Times Literary Supplement,* lauds Clark's tracing of "a family tree that would surely have delighted Dodgson, showing as it does that Alice Liddell was almost a royal 'Queen Alice'" because of her distant relationship with the present royal family.

Mrs. Oscar Wilde: A Woman of Some Importance, the author's third biography, written as Anne Clark Amor, details the life of Constance Wilde, wife of the Irish poet, playwright, and humorist. According to *Times Literary Supplement* critic John Stokes, the very reticent Constance Wilde "eludes even a novelist's imagination." Amor's biography, Stokes notes, "endeavors to release another woman from the imprisoning male view." In a London *Times* review Bevis Hillier observes, "The more one reads, the more one's admiration for [Constance] grows." Hillier further states that Amor's portrayal of Constance explodes "convincingly the canard that she was stupid" and conveys "her beauty, charm and tenderness, her wonderful loyalty and courage in a situation which few women in history have to face" (the disgrace ensuing from the discovery of her husband's homosexuality and his resulting subsequent imprisonment). Hillier's review also credits Amor for maintaining the focus on "Constance Wilde's life, not Oscar's: He is only allowed on scene when his life impinges on hers." William French in the Toronto *Globe & Mail* sums up Amor's achievement with this book: "In this poignant biography . . . Amor restores Constance Wilde to her rightful place with an enthusiasm and reverence that stops just short of elevating her to sainthood. The respect seems deserved."

Anne Clark Amor once described for *CA* her fourth biography: "*William Holman Hunt: The True Pre-Raphaelite* traces Hunt's childhood and early struggle against parental opposition to become an artist, his founding of the Pre-Raphaelite Brotherhood with Millais and Rossetti, the hostility of the Royal Academy, and his success in the face of adverse criticism. The second part of the book concentrates on his adventures in Syria, the death of his wife after a year of marriage, and his struggle to bring up his infant son. His second marriage, to his deceased wife's sister, was illegal in England until the law was changed in 1907."

About her writing background, Amor once told *CA:* "Although I knew from the age of eight that I had a vocation for writing, I was hustled into the first steady job that presented itself, and found myself trapped by economic necessity. When my compulsion to write re-asserted itself, I turned, not to the detective fiction that had been the focus of my childish imagining, but to a serious study of mediaeval animal lore. I strayed accidentally into the field of biography at the suggestion of my publisher and found it greatly to my liking. Now, after four successful biographies, I find myself turning in the direction of the novel."

BIOGRAPHICAL/CRITICAL SOURCES:

PERIODICALS

Globe & Mail (Toronto), May 12, 1984.
Times (London), July 14, 1983.
Times Literary Supplement, November 13, 1981; June 24, 1983.
Washington Post Book World, December 23, 1979; October 10, 1982.

*   *   *

ANSTRUTHER, Ian 1922-

PERSONAL: Born May 11, 1922, in England; son of Douglas (in business) and Enid (a painter; maiden name, Campbell) Anstruther; married Susan Paten (an architect), November, 1963; children: Sebastian, Toby, Rachel, Harriet, Eleanor. *Education:* Attended New College, Oxford. *Politics:* None. *Religion:* None.

ADDRESSES: Home—Barlavington, Petworth, Sussex, England; fax: 01798 869401.

CAREER: Worked for British Diplomatic Service, London, 1944-49; farmer and writer, 1949—. *Military service:* British Army, Signals Corps, 1939-44; served in European theater; became captain.

MEMBER: Society of Antiquaries of London (fellow).

WRITINGS:

"I Presume": A Study of H. M. Stanley, Bles, 1956, published in the U.S. as *"Dr. Livingstone, I Presume",* Dutton, 1957.
The Knight and the Umbrella (Book Society selection), Bles, 1963.
The Scandal of the Andover Workhouse, Bles, 1973.
Oscar Browning: A Biography, John Murray, 1983.
Coventry Patmore's Angel, Haggerston Press, 1992.
(With Patricia Aske) *The Angel in the House* (collated edition), Haggerston Press, 1997.

SIDELIGHTS: Ian Anstruther once told *CA:* "In 1950 I inherited enough money to be able to retire from the Diplomatic Service. I bought a farm, which I run; at the same time, and every day, I work on my current book. My background is a literary one, the most successful member of the family since the war being the late Jan Struther (Mrs. Miniver). So it was natural for me to take to literature when I had the opportunity, and it was natural for me to live in the country, having been brought up in Scotland, in Argyll, and being of a rather solitary nature."

BIOGRAPHICAL/CRITICAL SOURCES:

PERIODICALS

Times Literary Supplement, November 25, 1983.

* * *

ARCHER, Nuala 1955-

PERSONAL: Given name is pronounced *New-la;* born June 21, 1955, in Rochester, NY; daughter of Charles Leslie Stewart (a physician) and Naomi June Therese (a physician; maiden name, Barry) Archer. *Education:* Wheaton College, Wheaton, IL, B.A., 1976; Trinity College, Dublin, Diploma in Anglo-Irish Literature, 1977; University of Wisconsin—Milwaukee, M.A., 1978, Ph.D., 1983.

CAREER: Dun Laoghaire College of Art and Design, Dublin, Ireland, lecturer in English, 1981-83; Oklahoma State University, Stillwater, visiting poet in residence, 1984-85, assistant professor of English, 1985—. Lecturer at College of Marketing and Design, Dublin, 1981-83. Photographer, with solo and group exhibitions in Ireland; gives workshops and poetry readings.

MEMBER: Modern Language Association of America, Poetry Society of America, Poetry Ireland Society, South Central Modern Language Association.

AWARDS, HONORS: First place award from Midwestern Regional Poetry Competition, 1978; first place awards from Ireland's Listowel Poetry Contest and Patrick Kavanagh National Poetry Competition, both 1980, both for *Whale on the Line;* Brendan Behan Memorial fellowship, 1983; grants from State Arts Council of Oklahoma, 1986.

WRITINGS:

Whale on the Line (poems), Gallery Press (Dublin, Ireland), 1981.
The Hour of Pan/ama, Salmon Publishing (Galway, Ireland), 1992.
From a Mobile Home, Salmon Publishing, 1995.

Work represented in anthologies, including *Anthology of Magazine Verse and Yearbook of American Poetry,* Monitor Book, 1981; *Nijinsky/Nijinska,* Kopernik Press, 1984; and *Unlacing: An Irish-American Women's Anthology.* Contributor of articles, stories, photographs, and more than fifty poems to magazines, including *Confrontation, Adrift, Cream City Review, Rubicon, American Poetry Review, Times Literary Supplement, Phoenix, Nimrod,* and *Pequod.* Editor in chief of *Midland Review,* 1984—; poetry co-editor of *Cimarron Review,* 1986—.

SIDELIGHTS: Nuala Archer enjoyed a multinational upbringing as an Irish-American who was raised in Panama, educated in Ireland and North America, and now lives in the United States. Her poetry captures some of the alienation and feeling of "otherness" such a background has created. She is, as Patricia Monaghan writes in *Booklist,* "an outsider everywhere . . . never fully at home." In *The Hour of Pan/ama,* Archer addresses her own childhood in the country of Panama; her life in Ireland and her present-day career as an academic in Oklahoma figure into other poems.

Archer's poetry expresses her sense of being the outsider not only in subject matter but through the kind of self-invented words and expressions she employs in her work. "She invents usages, slices words into constituent syllables, and deploys punctuation marks like firecrackers," Monaghan writes. M. P. White in *Choice* characterizes Archer's poetic language as "a quickly changing, seemingly random explosion of images, languages, and unusual or invented words." This language is meant, Archer explains in *The Hour of Pan/ama,* to prompt within the reader "a breakthrough in listening." White notes that Archer takes risks not only with her language, but "with the content, particularly in the poems about lesbian relationships." The *Publishers Weekly* critic thinks Archer's linguistic experimentations, although "making excellent use of alliteration and wordplay," fail in the poem "SheelaNaGigging ArOund," where they "distract from what's otherwise an excellent hymn to female sexuality."

BIOGRAPHICAL/CRITICAL SOURCES:

PERIODICALS

Booklist, February 1, 1996, p. 913.
Choice, March, 1993, p. 1142.
Publishers Weekly, January 22, 1996, p. 70.

* * *

ARDIES, Tom 1931-

PERSONAL: Born August 5, 1931, in Seattle, WA; son of John (in sales) and Irene (Nutt) McIntyre; married Sharon Bernard, April 27, 1963; children: Robyn, Sarita. *Education:* Attended Daniel McIntyre Collegiate Institute, Winnepeg, Canada. *Avocational interests:* Travel.

CAREER: Vancouver Sun, Vancouver, British Columbia, reporter, columnist, and editorial writer, 1950-64; *Honolulu Star Bulletin,* Honolulu, Hawaii, telegraph editor, 1964-65; special assistant to governor of Guam, 1965-67; writer. *Military service:* U.S. Air Force; received Commendation ribbon.

WRITINGS:

Kosygin Is Coming, Doubleday (New York City), 1974, published in England as *Russian Roulette,* Panther (London), 1975.

In a Lady's Service, Doubleday, 1976.
Palm Springs, Doubleday, 1978.

"CHARLIE SPARROW" SERIES

Their Man in the White House, Doubleday, 1971.
This Suitcase Is Going to Explode, Doubleday, 1972.
Pandemic, Doubleday, 1973.

OTHER

Also author, with Stanley Mann, of a screenplay, *Russian Roulette,* based on his novel *Kosygin Is Coming.*

ADAPTATIONS: Kosygin Is Coming was filmed in 1975 as *Russian Roulette.*

SIDELIGHTS: Tom Ardies's first three novels all fit the classic spy-story formula. *Their Man in the White House, This Suitcase Is Going to Explode,* and *Pandemic* follow the exploits of Charlie Sparrow, a tough, smart-aleck spy who is irresistible to women. The novels all feature lots of action and a dramatic, suspenseful climax. According to Carol Simpson Stern in the *St. James Guide to Crime & Mystery Writers,* Sparrow is "always the victor, be it pitting his will against his superiors, the CIA, and the fanatical enemy to save the nation from World War III, as in one book, or preventing the outbreak of a flu-virus pandemic, as in another. Sparrow descends from the chivalric and outlaw traditions, a kind of modern knight errant. . . . Capable of ball-breaking when he needs valuable information fast, a stud with women, he is, nonetheless, the democratic hero, an individualist, crude, but governed by a moral code that demands that fanatics who use cloning, lobotomies, or nuclear reactions for evil ends be defeated." Reviewing *This Suitcase Is Going to Explode,* Newgate Callendar stated in the *New York Times Book Review* that although the story is highly improbable, "if it's escape reading you want, *Suitcase* will hold you spellbound."

Stern ranks *Kosygin Is Coming* and *In a Lady's Service,* as Ardies's best works. *Kosygin* is a spy story that uses the Warren Commission report on the assassination of John F. Kennedy as its background. *In a Lady's Service* is a spoof of the spy genre. Stern observed that the author's "journalistic tidbits yield a Dip Threat, Mission-Impossible-like directives, and a ludicrous parody of his own plots." She concludes that in both these novels, "the plots are tighter, complications more zany, and characters more convincing" than in the Charlie Sparrow books.

BIOGRAPHICAL/CRITICAL SOURCES:

BOOKS

St. James Guide to Crime & Mystery Writers, St. James Press (Detroit), 1996.

PERIODICALS

Library Journal, September 1, 1972; October 15, 1972.
New York Times Book Review, July 23, 1972, p. 22.
Times Literary Supplement, October 13, 1972, p. 1235.*

*　　*　　*

ARMOUR, Peter 1940-

PERSONAL: Born November 19, 1940, in Fleetwood, England; son of James (a clerk) and Anne Mary (Monaghan) Armour. *Ethnicity:* "White." *Education:* Victoria University of Manchester, B.A., 1966; University of Leicester, Ph.D., 1980.

ADDRESSES: Office—Department of Italian, Royal Holloway, University of London, Egham, Surrey TW20 0EX, England. *Email*—p.armour@rhbnc.-ac.uk; fax: 01784 439196.

CAREER: University of Sheffield, Sheffield, England, lecturer in Italian, 1966-72; University of Leicester, Leicester, England, lecturer in Italian, 1972-79; University of London, London, England, lecturer in Italian at Bedford College, 1979-84, lecturer in Italian at University College, 1984-89, professor of Italian, Royal Holloway, 1989—.

MEMBER: Modern Humanities Research Association, Association for Language Learning, Society for Italian Studies, London Medieval Society, Societa Dantesca Italiana, Dante Society of America.

WRITINGS:

The Door of Purgatory: A Study of Multiple Symbolism in Dante's "Purgatorio," Clarendon Press, 1983.

Dante's Griffin and the History of the World: A Study of the Earthly Paradise ("Purgatorio," Cantos XXIX-XXXIII), Clarendon Press, 1989.
Dante Alighieri, *The Divine Comedy,* translated by Allen Mandelbaum with an introduction by Eugenio Montale and notes by Peter Armour, Everyman's Library, 1995.

Contributor of articles and translations to history and Italian studies journals.

SIDELIGHTS: Peter Armour once told *CA:* "Dante's *Comedy* is a fascinating story with various levels of reference and meaning. I have attempted some detective work on puzzling or apparently inconsistent passages. I try to be objective, tracing an image or symbol through medieval sources and following wherever its logic leads. The research becomes a journey (often a long one too), with unforeseen turns and forays into new areas. The writing, though, has become increasingly difficult. Why? Mainly because Dante is the real author, and his poetry and its meanings and impact cannot be put into any other words. I just hope that, having read my studies, people go on to read him with some fresh interest and enjoyment."

BIOGRAPHICAL/CRITICAL SOURCES:

PERIODICALS

Italian Studies, Volume 40, 1985; Volume 46, 1991.
Medium Aerum, Volume 54, 1985; Volume 60, 1991.
Modern Language Review, Volume 80, 1985; Volume 86, 1991.
Romance Philology, Volume 42, 1988-89.
Times Higher Education Supplement, February 3, 1984.
Times Literary Supplement, May 25, 1984.

*　　*　　*

ASHE, Gordon
See CREASEY, John

*　　*　　*

ATTICUS
See FLEMING, Ian (Lancaster)

ATWOOD, Margaret (Eleanor) 1939-

PERSONAL: Born November 18, 1939, in Ottawa, Ontario, Canada; daughter of Carl Edmund (an entomologist) and Margaret Dorothy (Killam) Atwood; married Graeme Gibson (a writer); children: Jess (daughter). *Education:* University of Toronto, B.A., 1961; Radcliffe College, A.M., 1962; Harvard University, graduate study, 1962-63 and 1965-67. *Politics:* "William Morrisite." *Religion:* "Immanent Transcendentalist."

ADDRESSES: Agent—Phoebe Larmore, 2814 Third St., Santa Monica, CA 90405; *Office*—c/o Oxford University Press, 70 Wynford Drive, Don Mills, ON, M3C 1J9, Canada.

CAREER: Writer. University of British Columbia, Vancouver, lecturer in English literature, 1964-65; Sir George Williams University, Montreal, Quebec, lecturer in English literature, 1967-68; York University, Toronto, Ontario, assistant professor of English literature, 1971- 72; House of Anansi Press, Toronto, editor and member of board of directors, 1971-73; University of Toronto, writer-in-residence, 1972-73; University of Alabama, Tuscaloosa, writer-in-residence, 1985; New York University, New York City, Berg Visiting Professor of English, 1986; Macquarie University, North Ryde, Australia, writer-in-residence, 1987. Worked variously as camp counselor and waitress.

MEMBER: PEN International, Amnesty International, Writers' Union of Canada (vice-chairperson, 1980-81), Royal Society of Canada (fellow), Canadian Civil Liberties Association (member of board, 1973-75), Canadian Centre, American Academy of Arts and Sciences (honorary member), Anglophone (president, 1984-85).

AWARDS, HONORS: E. J. Pratt Medal, 1961, for *Double Persephone;* President's Medal, University of Western Ontario, 1965; YWCA Women of Distinction Award, 1966 and 1988; Governor General's Award, 1966, for *The Circle Game,* and 1986, for *The Handmaid's Tale;* first prize in Canadian Centennial Commission Poetry Competition, 1967; Union Prize for poetry, 1969; Bess Hoskins Prize for poetry, 1969 and 1974; D.Litt., Trent University, 1973, Concordia University, 1980, Smith College, 1982, University of Toronto, 1983, Mount Holyoke College, 1985, University of Waterloo, 1985, University of Guelph, 1985, Victoria College, 1987, University of Montreal, 1991, and University of Leeds, 1994; LL.D., Queen's University, 1974; City of Toronto Book Award, Canadian Booksellers' Association Award, Periodical Distributors of Canada Short Fiction Award, all 1977, all for *Dancing Girls and Other Stories;* St. Lawrence Award for fiction, 1978; Radcliffe Medal, 1980; *Life before Man* selected as a notable book of 1980, American Library Association; Molson Award, 1981; Guggenheim fellowship, 1981; named Companion of the Order of Canada, 1981; International Writer's Prize, Welsh Arts Council, 1982; Book of the Year Award, Periodical Distributors of Canada and the Foundation for the Advancement of Canadian Letters, 1983, for *Bluebeard's Egg and Other Stories;* Ida Nudel Humanitarian Award, 1986; Toronto Arts Award for writing and editing, 1986; *Los Angeles Times* Book Award, 1986, for *The Handmaid's Tale;* named Woman of the Year, *Ms.* magazine, 1986; Arthur C. Clarke Award for Best Science Fiction and Commonwealth Literature Prize, both 1987, both for *The Handmaid's Tale;* Council for the Advancement and Support of Education silver medal, 1987; Humanist of the Year award, 1987; named Fellow of the Royal Society of Canada, 1987; named *Chatelaine* magazine's Woman of the Year; City of Toronto Book Award, Coles Book of the Year Award, Canadian Booksellers' Association Author of the Year Award, Book of the Year Award Foundation for Advancement of Canadian Letters citation, Periodical Marketers of Canada Award, and Torgi Talking Book Award, all 1989, all for *Cat's Eye;* Harvard University Centennial Medal, 1990; Order of Ontario, 1990; Trillium Award for Excellence in Ontario Writing and Book of the Year Award from the Periodical Marketers of Canada, both 1992, both for *Wilderness Tips and Other Stories;* Commemorative Medal for the 125th Anniversary of Canadian Confederation; Trillium Award for Excellence in Ontario Writing, Canadian Authors' Association Novel of the Year Award, Commonwealth Writers' Prize for Canadian and Caribbean Region, *Sunday Times* Award for Literary Excellence, all 1994, all for *The Robber Bride;* Government of France's Chevalier dans l'Ordre des Arts et des Lettres, 1994; Swedish Humour Association's International Humourous Writer Award, 1995, for *The Robber Bride.*

WRITINGS:

POETRY

Double Persephone, Hawkshead Press, 1961.
The Circle Game, Cranbrook Academy of Art (Bloomfield Hills, MI), 1964, revised edition, Contact Press, 1966.

Kaleidoscopes Baroque: A Poem, Cranbrook Academy of Art, 1965.

Talismans for Children, Cranbrook Academy of Art, 1965.

Speeches for Doctor Frankenstein, Cranbrook Academy of Art, 1966.

The Animals in That Country, Little, Brown (Boston), 1968.

The Journals of Susanna Moodie, Oxford University Press (Toronto), 1970.

Procedures for Underground, Little, Brown, 1970.

Power Politics, House of Anansi Press (Toronto), 1971, Harper (New York City), 1973.

You Are Happy, Harper, 1974.

Selected Poems, 1965-1975, Oxford University Press, 1976, Simon & Schuster (New York City), 1978.

Marsh Hawk, Dreadnaught, 1977.

Two-Headed Poems, Oxford University Press, 1978, Simon & Schuster, 1981.

Notes toward a Poem That Can Never Be Written, Salamander Press, 1981.

True Stories, Oxford University Press, 1981, Simon & Schuster, 1982.

Snake Poems, Salamander Press, 1983.

Interlunar, Oxford University Press, 1984.

Selected Poems II: Poems Selected and New, 1976-1986, Oxford University Press, 1986.

Morning in the Burned House, Houghton (Boston), 1995.

Also author of *Expeditions,* 1966, and *What Was in the Garden,* 1969.

NOVELS

The Edible Woman, McClelland & Stewart (Toronto), 1969, Little, Brown, 1970.

Surfacing, McClelland & Stewart, 1972, Simon & Schuster 1973.

Lady Oracle, Simon & Schuster, 1976.

Life before Man, Simon & Schuster, 1979.

Bodily Harm, McClelland & Stewart, 1981, Simon & Schuster, 1982.

Encounters with the Element Man, Ewert (Concord, NH), 1982.

Unearthing Suite, Grand Union Press, 1983.

The Handmaid's Tale, McClelland & Stewart, 1985, Houghton, 1986.

Cat's Eye, McClelland & Stewart, 1988, Doubleday (Garden City, NY), 1989.

The Robber Bride, Doubleday, 1993.

Alias Grace, Doubleday, 1996.

STORY COLLECTIONS

Dancing Girls and Other Stories, McClelland & Stewart, 1977, Simon & Schuster, 1982.

Bluebeard's Egg and Other Stories, McClelland & Stewart, 1983, Fawcett (New York City), 1987.

Murder in the Dark: Short Fictions and Prose Poems, Coach House Press (Toronto), 1983.

Wilderness Tips and Other Stories, Doubleday, 1991.

Good Bones, Coach House Press, 1992, published as *Good Bones and Simple Murders,* Doubleday, 1994.

OTHER

The Trumpets of Summer (radio play), Canadian Broadcasting Corporation (CBC-Radio), 1964.

Survival: A Thematic Guide to Canadian Literature, House of Anansi Press, 1972.

The Servant Girl (teleplay), CBC-TV, 1974.

Days of the Rebels, 1815-1840, Natural Science Library, 1976.

The Poetry and Voice of Margaret Atwood (recording), Caedmon, 1977.

Up in the Tree (juvenile), McClelland & Stewart, 1978.

(Author of introduction) Catherine M. Young, *To See Our World,* GLC Publishers, 1979, Morrow (New York City), 1980.

(With Joyce Barkhouse) *Anna's Pet* (juvenile), James Lorimer, 1980.

Snowbird (teleplay), CBC-TV, 1981.

Second Words: Selected Critical Prose, House of Anansi Press, 1982.

(Editor) *The New Oxford Book of Canadian Verse in English,* Oxford University Press, 1982.

(Editor with Robert Weaver) *The Oxford Book of Canadian Short Stories in English,* Oxford University Press, 1986.

(With Peter Pearson) *Heaven on Earth* (teleplay), CBC-TV, 1986.

(Editor) *The Canlit Foodbook,* Totem, 1987.

(Editor with Shannon Ravenal) *The Best American Short Stories, 1989,* Houghton, 1989.

For the Birds, illustrated by John Bianchi, Firefly Books, 1991.

(Editor with Barry Callaghan and author of introduction) *The Poetry of Gwendolyn MacEwen,* Exile Editions (Toronto), Volume 1: *The Early Years,* 1993, Volume 2: *The Later Years,* 1994.

Princess Prunella and the Purple Peanut (juvenile), illustrated by Maryann Kovalski, Workman (New York City), 1995.

Strange Things: The Malevolent North in Canadian Literature (collection of lectures), Clarendon/ Oxford University Press, 1996.

Contributor to anthologies, including *Five Modern Canadian Poets,* 1970, *The Canadian Imagination: Dimensions of a Literary Culture,* Harvard University Press, 1977, and *Women on Women,* 1978. Contributor to periodicals, including *Atlantic, Poetry, New Yorker, Harper's, New York Times Book Review, Saturday Night, Tamarack Review,* and *Canadian Forum.*

ADAPTATIONS: The Handmaid's Tale was filmed by Cinecom Entertainment Group, 1990.

SIDELIGHTS: As a poet, novelist, story writer, and essayist, Margaret Atwood holds a unique position in contemporary Canadian literature. Her books have received critical acclaim in the United States, Europe, and her native Canada, and she has been the recipient of numerous literary awards. Ann Marie Lipinski, writing in the *Chicago Tribune,* described Atwood as "one of the leading literary luminaries, a national heroine of the arts, the *rara avis* of Canadian letters." Atwood's critical popularity is matched by her popularity with readers. She is a frequent guest on Canadian television and radio, her books are best-sellers, and "people follow her on the streets and in stores," as Judy Klemesrud reported in the *New York Times.* Atwood, Roy MacGregor of *Maclean's* explained, "is to Canadian literature as Gordon Lightfoot is to Canadian music, more institution than individual." Atwood's popularity with both critics and the reading public has surprised her. "It's an accident that I'm a successful writer," she told MacGregor. "I think I'm kind of an odd phenomenon in that I'm a serious writer and I never expected to become a popular one, and I never did anything in order to become a popular one."

Atwood first came to public attention as a poet in the 1960s with her collections *Double Persephone,* winner of the E. J. Pratt Medal, and *The Circle Game,* winner of a Governor General's Award. These two books marked out the terrain that all of Atwood's later poetry would explore. *Double Persephone* concerns "the contrast between the flux of life or nature and the fixity of man's artificial creations," as Linda Hutcheon explained in the *Dictionary of Literary Biography. The Circle Game* takes this opposition further, setting such human constructs as games, literature, and love against the instability of nature. Human constructs are presented as both traps and

shelters, the fluidity of nature as both dangerous and liberating. Sherrill Grace, writing in her *Violent Duality: A Study of Margaret Atwood,* identified the central tension in all of Atwood's work as "the pull towards art on one hand and towards life on the other." This tension is expressed in a series of "violent dualities," as Grace terms it. Atwood "is constantly aware of opposites—self/other, subject/object, male/female, nature/man—and of the need to accept and work within them," Grace explained. "To create, Atwood chooses violent dualities, and her art reworks, probes, and dramatizes the ability to see double."

Linda W. Wagner, writing in *The Art of Margaret Atwood: Essays in Criticism,* asserted that in Atwood's poetry "duality [is] presented as separation." This separation leads her characters to be isolated from one another and from the natural world, resulting in their inability to communicate, to break free of exploitative social relationships, or to understand their place in the natural order. "In her early poetry," Gloria Onley wrote in the *West Coast Review,* " . . . [Atwood] is acutely aware of the problem of alienation, the need for real human communication and the establishment of genuine human community—real as opposed to mechanical or manipulative; genuine as opposed to the counterfeit community of the body politic." Speaking of *The Circle Game,* Wagner wrote that "the personae of those poems never did make contact, never did anything but lament the human condition. . . . Relationships in these poems are sterile if not destructive."

Atwood's sense of desolation, especially evident in her early poems, and her use of frequently violent images moved Helen Vendler of the *New York Times Book Review* to claim that Atwood has a "sense of life as mostly wounds given and received." About *The Circle Game* and *Procedures for Underground,* Peter Stevens noted in *Canadian Literature* that both collections contain "images of drowning, buried life, still life, dreams, journeys and returns." In a review of *True Stories* for *Canadian Forum,* Chaviva Hosek stated that the poems "range over such topics as murder, genocide, rape, dismemberment, instruments of torture, forms of torture, genital mutilation, abortion, and forcible hysterectomy," although Robert Sward of *Quill and Quire* explained that many reviewers of the book have exaggerated the violence and give "the false impression that all 38 poems . . . are about torture." Yet, Scott Lauder of *Canadian Forum* spoke of "the painful world we have come to expect from Atwood."

Suffering is common for the female characters in Atwood's poems, although they are never passive victims. In more recent works they take active measures to improve their situations. Atwood's poems, the *West Coast Review*'s Onley maintained, concern "modern woman's anguish at finding herself isolated and exploited (although also exploiting) by the imposition of a sex role power structure." Atwood explained to Klemesrud in the *New York Times* that her suffering characters come from real life: "My women suffer because most of the women I talk to seem to have suffered." By the early 1970s, this stance had made Atwood into "a cult author to faithful feminist readers," as the *Chicago Tribune*'s Lipinski commented. Atwood's popularity in the feminist community was unsought. "I began as a profoundly apolitical writer," she told Lindsy Van Gelder of *Ms.,* "but then I began to do what all novelists and some poets do: I began to describe the world around me."

Atwood's 1995 book of poetry, *Morning in the Burned House,* "reflects a period in Atwood's life when time seems to be running out," observed John Bemrose in *Maclean's.* Noting that many of the poems address grief and loss, particularly in relationship to her father's death and a realization of her own mortality, Bemrose added that the book "moves even more deeply into survival territory." Bemrose further suggested that in this book, Atwood allows the readers greater latitude in interpretation than in her earlier verse: "Atwood uses grief . . . to break away from that airless poetry and into a new freedom."

Atwood's feminist concerns also emerge clearly in her novels, particularly in *The Edible Woman, Surfacing, Life before Man, Bodily Harm,* and *The Handmaid's Tale.* These novels feature female characters who are, Klemesrud reported, "intelligent, self-absorbed modern women searching for identity. . . . [They] hunt, split logs, make campfires and become successful in their careers, while men often cook and take care of their households." Like her poems, however, Atwood's novels "are populated by pained and confused people whose lives hold a mirror to both the front page fears—cancer, divorce, violence—and those that persist quietly, naggingly— solitude, loneliness, desperation," Lipinski wrote.

The Edible Woman tells the story of Marian Mc-Alpin, a young woman engaged to be married, who rebels against her upcoming marriage. Her fiance seems too stable, too ordinary, and the role of wife too fixed and limiting. Her rejection of marriage is accompanied by her body's rejection of food; she cannot tolerate even a spare vegetarian diet. Eventually Marian bakes a sponge cake in the shape of a woman and feeds it to her fiance because, she explains, "You've been trying to assimilate me." After the engagement is broken off, she is able to eat some of the cake herself.

Reaction to *The Edible Woman* was divided, with some reviewers pointing to the flaws commonly found in first novels. John Stedmond of *Canadian Forum,* for example, believed that "the characters, though cleverly sketched, do not quite jell, and the narrative techniques creak a little." Linda Rogers of *Canadian Literature* found that "one of the reasons *The Edible Woman* fails as a novel is the awkwardness of the dialogue." But other critics note Atwood's at least partial success. Tom Marshall, writing in his *Harsh and Lovely Land: The Major Canadian Poets and the Making of a Canadian Tradition,* called *The Edible Woman* "a largely successful comic novel, even if the mechanics are sometimes a little clumsy, the satirical accounts of consumerism a little drawn out." Millicent Bell of the *New York Times Book Review* termed it "a work of feminist black humor" and claimed that Atwood's "comic distortion veers at times into surreal meaningfulness." And Hutcheon described *The Edible Woman* as "very much a social novel about the possibilities for personal female identity in a capitalistic consumer society."

Surfacing, Atwood's second novel, is "a psychological ghost story," as Marshall described it, in which a young woman confronts and accepts her past during a visit to her rural home. She comes to realize that she has repressed disturbing events from her memory, including an abortion and her father's death. While swimming in a local lake, she has a vision of her drowned father which "drives her to a healing madness," Marshall stated. Hutcheon explained that "*Surfacing* tells of the coming to terms with the haunting, separated parts of the narrator's being . . . after surfacing from a dive, a symbolic as well as a real descent under water, where she has experienced a revealing and personally apocalyptic vision."

Many of the concerns found in Atwood's poetry reappear in *Surfacing.* The novel, Roberta Rubenstein wrote in *Modern Fiction Studies,* "synthesizes a number of motifs that have dominated [Atwood's] consciousness since her earliest poems: the elusiveness and variety of 'language' in its several senses; the continuum between human and animal, human being and nature; the significance of one's heritage . . . ; the search for a location (in both time and place); the brutalizations and victimizations of love; drowning and surviving." Margaret Wimsatt of *Commonweal* agreed with this assessment. "The novel," Wimsatt wrote, "picks up themes brooded over in the poetry, and knits them together coherently." Marshall asserted that both *The Edible Woman* and *Surfacing* "are enlargements upon the themes of [Atwood's] poems. In each of them a young woman is driven to rebellion against what seems to be her fate in the modern technological 'Americanized' world and to psychic breakdown and breakthrough."

In *Life before Man,* Atwood dissects the relationships between three characters: Elizabeth, a married woman who mourns the recent suicide of her lover; Elizabeth's husband, Nate, who is unable to choose between his wife and his lover; and Lesje, Nate's lover, who works with Elizabeth at a museum of natural history. All three characters are isolated from one another and unable to experience their own emotions. The fossils and dinosaur bones on display at the museum are compared throughout the novel with the sterility of the characters' lives. As Laurie Stone noted in the *Village Voice, Life before Man* "is full of variations on the theme of extinction." Similarly, Rubenstein wrote in the *Chicago Tribune* that the novel is a "superb living exhibit in which the artifacts are unique (but representative) lives in progress."

Although *Life before Man* is what Rosellen Brown of *Saturday Review* called an "anatomy of melancholy," MacGregor pointed out a tempering humor in the novel as well. *Life before Man,* MacGregor wrote, "is not so much a story as it is the discarded negatives of a family album, the thoughts so dark they defy any flash short of Atwood's remarkable, and often very funny, insight." Comparing the novel's characters to museum pieces and commenting on the analytical examination to which Atwood subjects them, Peter S. Prescott of *Newsweek* wrote that "with chilly compassion and an even colder wit, Atwood exposes the interior lives of her specimens." Writing in the *New York Times Book Review,* Marilyn French made clear that in *Life before Man,* Atwood "combines several talents—powerful introspection, honesty, satire and a taut, limpid style—to create a splendid, fully integrated work."

The novel's title, French believes, relates to the characters' isolation from themselves, their history, and from one another. They have not yet achieved truly human stature. "This novel suggests," French wrote, "that we are still living life before man, before the human—as we like to define it—has evolved." Prescott raised the same point. The novel's characters, he wrote, "do not communicate; each, in the presence of another, is locked into his own thoughts and feelings. Is such isolation and indeterminacy what Atwood means when she calls her story 'Life before Man'?" This concern is also found in Atwood's previous novels, French argued, all of which depict "the search for identity . . . a search for a better way to be—for a way of life that both satisfies the passionate, needy self and yet is decent, humane and natural."

Atwood further explores this idea in *Bodily Harm.* In this novel Rennie Wilford is a Toronto journalist who specializes in light, trivial pieces for magazines. She is, Anne Tyler explained in the *Detroit News,* "a cataloguer of current fads and fancies." Isabel Raphael of the London *Times* called Rennie someone who "deals only in surfaces; her journalism is of the most trivial and transitory kind, her relationship with a live-in lover limited to sex, and most of her friends 'really just contacts.'" Following a partial mastectomy, which causes her lover to abandon her, Rennie begins to feel dissatisfied with her life. She takes on an assignment to the Caribbean island of St. Antoine in an effort to get away from things for a while. Her planned magazine story focusing on the island's beaches, tennis courts, and restaurants is distinctly facile in comparison to the political violence she finds on St. Antoine. When Rennie is arrested and jailed, the experience brings her to a self-realization about her life. "Death," Nancy Ramsey remarked in the *San Francisco Review of Books,* "rather than the modern sense of ennui, threatens Rennie and the people around her, and ultimately gives her life a meaning she hadn't known before."

Bodily Harm, Frank Davey of the *Canadian Forum* asserted, follows the same pattern set in Atwood's earlier novels: "Alienation from natural order . . . , followed by descent into a more primitive but healing reality . . . , and finally some reestablishment of order." Although Davey was "troubled" by the similarities between the novels and stated that "Atwood doesn't risk much with this book," he concluded that "these reservations aside, *Bodily Harm* is still a pleasure to read." Other critics have few such reservations about the book. Anatole Broyard of the *New York Times,* for example, claimed that "the only way to describe my response to [*Bodily Harm*] is to say that it knocked me out. Atwood seems to be able to do just about everything: people, places, problems, a perfect ear, an exactly-right voice and she tosses off terrific scenes with a casualness that leaves you utterly unprepared for the way these scenes seize you." Tyler called Atwood "an uncommonly skillful and perceptive writer," and went on to state that, because of its subject matter, *Bodily Harm* "is not always easy to read. There are times when it's downright unpleasant, but it's also intelligent, provocative, and in the end—against all expectations—uplifting."

In *The Handmaid's Tale* Atwood turns to speculative fiction, creating the dystopia of Gilead, a future America in which Fundamentalist Christians have killed the president and members of Congress and imposed their own dictatorial rule. In this future world, polluted by toxic chemicals and nuclear radiation, few women can bear children; the birthrate has dropped alarmingly. Those women who can bear children are forced to become Handmaids, the official breeders for society. All other women have been reduced to chattel under a repressive religious hierarchy run by men.

The Handmaid's Tale is a radical departure from Atwood's previous novels. Her strong feminism was evident in earlier books, but *The Handmaid's Tale* is dominated by the theme. As Barbara Holliday wrote in the *Detroit Free Press,* Atwood "has been concerned in her fiction with the painful psychic warfare between men and women. In 'The Handmaid's Tale,' a futuristic satire, she casts subtlety aside, exposing woman's primal fear of being used and helpless." Atwood's creation of an imaginary world is also new. As Mary Battiata noted in the *Washington Post, The Handmaid's Tale* is the first of Atwood's novels "not set in a worried corner of contemporary Canada."

Atwood was moved to write her story only after images and scenes from the book had been appearing to her for three years. She admitted to Mervyn Rothstein of the *New York Times,* "I delayed writing it . . . because I felt it was too crazy." But she eventually became convinced that her vision of Gilead was not far from reality. Some of the anti-female measures she had imagined for the novel actually exist. "There is a sect now, a Catholic charismatic spinoff sect, which calls the women handmaids," Atwood told Rothstein. "A law in Canada," Battiata reported, "[requires] a woman to have her husband's permission before obtaining an

abortion." And Atwood, speaking to Battiata, pointed to repressive laws in the totalitarian state of Romania as well: "No abortion, no birth control, and compulsory pregnancy testing, once a month." *The Handmaid's Tale,* Elaine Kendall explained in the *Los Angeles Times Book Review,* depicts "a future firmly based upon actuality, beginning with events that have already taken place and extending them a bit beyond the inevitable conclusions. *The Handmaid's Tale* does not depend upon hypothetical scenarios, omens, or straws in the wind, but upon documented occurrences and public pronouncements; all matters of record." Stephen McCabe of the *Humanist* called the novel "a chilling vision of the future extrapolated from the present."

Yet, several critics voiced a disbelief in the basic assumptions of *The Handmaid's Tale.* Mary McCarthy, in her review for the *New York Times Book Review,* complained that "I just can't see the intolerance of the far right . . . as leading to a super-biblical puritanism." And although agreeing that "the author has carefully drawn her projections from current trends," McCarthy asserted that "perhaps that is the trouble: the projections are too neatly penciled in. The details . . . all raise their hands announcing themselves present. At the same time, the Republic of Gilead itself, whatever in it that is not a projection, is insufficiently imagined." Richard Grenier of *Insight* objected that the Fundamentalist-run Gilead does not seem Christian: "There seems to be no Father, no Son, no Holy Ghost, no apparent belief in redemption, resurrection, eternal life. No one in this excruciatingly hierarchized new clerical state . . . appears to believe in God." Grenier also found it improbable that "while the United States has hurtled off into this morbid, feminist nightmare, the rest of the democratic world has been blissfully unaffected." Writing in the Toronto *Globe and Mail,* William French stated that Atwood's "reach exceeds her grasp" in *The Handmaid's Tale,* "and in the end we're not clear what we're being warned against." Atwood seems to warn of the dangers of religious fanaticism, of the effects of pollution on the birthrate, and of a possible backlash to militant feminist demands. The novel, French stated, "is in fact a cautionary tale about *all* these things . . . but in her scenario, they interact in an implausible way."

Despite this flaw, French saw *The Handmaid's Tale* as being "in the honorable tradition of *Brave New World* and other warnings of dystopia. It's imaginative, even audacious, and conveys a chilling sense of fear and menace." Prescott also compared *The*

Handmaid's Tale to other dystopian novels. It belongs, he writes, "to that breed of visionary fiction in which a metaphor is extended to elaborate a warning. . . . Wells, Huxley and Orwell popularized the tradition with books like 'The Time Machine,' 'Brave New World' and '1984'—yet Atwood is a better novelist than they." Christopher Lehmann-Haupt identified *The Handmaid's Tale* as a book that goes far beyond its feminist concerns. Writing in the *New York Times,* Lehmann-Haupt explained that the novel "is a political tract deploring nuclear energy, environmental waste, and antifeminist attitudes. But it [is] so much more than that—a taut thriller, a psychological study, a play on words." Van Gelder agreed. The novel, she wrote, "ultimately succeeds on multiple levels: as a page-turning thriller, as a powerful political statement, and as an exquisite piece of writing." Lehmann-Haupt concluded that *The Handmaid's Tale* "is easily Margaret Atwood's best novel to date."

In *The Robber Bride,* her 1993 novel, Atwood explores women's issues and feminist concerns, this time concentrating on women's relationships with each other—both positive and negative. Inspired by the Brothers Grimm's fairy tale "The Robber Bridegroom," the novel chronicles the relationships of college friends Tony, Charis, and Roz with their backstabbing classmate Zenia. Now middle-aged women, the women's paths and life choices have diverged, yet Tony, Charis, and Roz have remained friends. Throughout their adulthood, however, Zenia's manipulations have nearly destroyed their lives and cost them husbands and careers. Lorrie Moore, writing in the *New York Times Book Review,* called *The Robber Bride* "Atwood's funniest and most companionable book in years," adding that its author "retains her gift for observing, in poetry, the minutiae specific to the physical and emotional lives of her characters." About Zenia, Moore commented, "charming and gorgeous, Zenia is a misogynist's grotesque: relentlessly seductive, brutal, pathologically dishonest," postulating that "perhaps Ms. Atwood intended Zenia, by the end, to be a symbol of all that is inexplicably evil: war, disease, global catastrophe." Judith Timson commented in *Maclean's* that *The Robber Bride* "has as its central theme an idea that feminism was supposed to have shoved under the rug: there are female predators out there, and they will get your man if you are not careful," adding, "As a sort of grown-up sequel to Atwood's 1988 novel, *Cat's Eye,* the book seems to be saying that if you think little girls can be mean to each other, you should see what big ones can accomplish."

Atwood, however, maintained that she had a feminist motivation in creating Zenia. The femme fatale all but disappeared from fiction in the 1950s, due to that decade's sanitized ideal of domesticity; and in the late 1960s came the women's movement, which in its early years encouraged the creation of only positive female characters, Atwood asserted in interviews. "I think we're now through with all that, and we can put the full cast of characters back on the stage," she told Lauri Miller in an interview in the *San Francisco Review of Books.* "Because to say that women can't be malicious and intentionally bad is to say that they're congenitally incapable of that, which is really very limiting." Atwood also commented that "there are a lot of women you have to say are feminists who are getting a big kick out of this book," according to interviewer Sarah Lyall in the *New York Times.* "People read the book with all the wars done by men, and they say, 'So, you're saying that women are crueler than men,'" the novelist added. "In other words, that's normal behavior by men, so we don't notice it. Similarly, we say that Zenia behaves badly, and therefore women are worse than men, but that ignores the helpfulness of the other three women to each other, which of course gives them a power of their own."

Francine Prose, reviewing *The Robber Bride* for the *Washington Post Book World,* made a similar point, recommending the book "to those well-intentioned misguided feminists or benighted sexists who would have us believe that the female of the species is 'naturally' nicer or more nurturing than the male." Prose found the book "smart and entertaining" but not always convincing in its blend of exaggerated and realistic elements. *New York Times* critic Michiko Kakutani also thought Atwood had not achieved the proper balance in this regard: "Her characters remain exiles from both the earthbound realm of realism and the airier attitudes of allegory, and as a result, their story does not illuminate or entertain: it grates."

Alias Grace represents Atwood's first venture into historical fiction, but the book has in much common with her other works in its contemplation of "the shifting notions of women's moral nature" and "the exercise of power between men and women," *Maclean's* contributor Diane Turbide noted. Based on a true story that Atwood previously had explored in a television script entitled *The Servant Girl, Alias Grace* centers on Grace Marks, a servant who was found guilty of murdering her employer and his mistress in northern Canada in 1843. Some people doubt Grace's guilt, however, and as she serves out her sentence of life in prison, she claims not to remember the murders. Eventually, reformers begin to agitate for clemency for Grace. In a quest for evidence to support their position, they assign a young doctor, versed in the new science of psychiatry, to evaluate her soundness of mind. Over many meetings, Grace tells the doctor the harrowing story of her life—a life marked by extreme hardship. Much about Grace, though, remains puzzling; she is haunted by flashbacks of the supposedly forgotten murders and by the presence of a woman who died from a mishandled abortion. The doctor, Simon Jordan, does not know what to believe in Grace's tales.

Several reviewers found Grace a complicated and compelling character. "Sometimes she is prim, naive, sometimes sardonic; sometimes sardonic because observant; sometimes observant because naive," commented Hilary Mantel in the *New York Review of Books. Los Angeles Times Book Review* critic Richard Eder lauded Atwood for making Grace "utterly present and unfathomable" and her story "pure enchantment." Eder continued, "We are as anxious as Jordan to know what [Grace] is, yet bit by bit it seems to matter less. What matters is that she becomes more and more distinct and unforgettable." Turbide added that Grace is more than an intriguing character: she is also "the lens through which Victorian hypocrisies are mercilessly exposed."

Mantel also remarked upon the novel's portrait of Victorian life. "We learn as much about Grace's daily routine . . . as if Atwood had written a manual of antique housewifery, and yet the information neither intrudes nor slows the action," she observed. Atwood's use of period detail goes beyond mere background, Mantel asserted: "Other authors describe clothes; Atwood feels the clothes on her characters' backs." Francine Prose, however, writing in the *New York Times Book Review*, thought the historical trivia excessive. "The book provides, in snippets, a crash course in Victorian culture . . . Rather than enhancing the novel's verisimilitude, these mini-lessons underline the distance between reader and subject," she contended. Prose added that "Some readers may feel that the novel only intermittently succeeds in transcending the burden of history, research and abstraction . . . Others will admire the liveliness with which Ms. Atwood toys with both our expectations and the conventions of the Victorian thriller."

Atwood has remained a noted writer of short stories as well as novels. *Wilderness Tips and Other Stories,* published in 1991, is a collection of "10 neatly constructed, present-tense narratives," reported Merle Rubin in the *Christian Science Monitor.* While finding Atwood's writing style drab and unappealing, Rubin nevertheless praised the author for her "ability to evoke the passing of entire decades . . . all within the brief compass of a short story." The tales in Atwood's 1992 collection *Good Bones,* published in 1994 as *Good Bones and Simple Murders,* "occupy that vague, peculiar country between poetry and prose," stated John Bemrose in *Maclean's.* Describing Atwood as "storyteller, poet, fabulist and social commentator rolled into one," Bemrose claimed that "the strongest pieces in *Good Bones* combine a light touch with a hypnotic seriousness of purpose." In the *New York Times Book Review,* Jennifer Howard labeled *Good Bones and Simple Murders* a "sprightly, whimsically feminist collection of miniatures and musings, assembled from two volumes published in Canada in 1983 and 1992." A *Publishers Weekly* reviewer, who characterized the entries as "postmodern fairy tales, caustic fables, inspired parodies, witty monologues," declared each piece to be "clever and sharply honed."

Survival: A Thematic Guide to Canadian Literature is Atwood's most direct presentation of her strong belief in Canadian nationalism. In this work she discerns a uniquely Canadian literature, distinct from its American and British counterparts, and discusses the dominant themes to be found in it. Canadian literature, she argues, is primarily concerned with victims and with the victim's ability to survive. Atwood, Onley explained, "perceives a strong sado-masochistic patterning in Canadian literature as a whole. She believes that there is a national fictional tendency to participate, usually at some level as Victim, in a Victor/Victim basic pattern." But "despite its stress on victimization," Hutcheon wrote "this study is not a revelation of, or a reveling in, [masochism]." What Atwood argues, Onley asserted, is that "every country or culture has a single unifying and informing symbol at its core: for America, the Frontier; for England, the Island; for Canada, Survival."

Several critics find that Atwood's own work exemplifies this primary theme of Canadian literature. Her examination of destructive sex roles and her nationalistic concern over the subordinate role Canada plays to the United States are variations on the victor/victim theme. As Marge Piercy explained in the *American Poetry Review,* Atwood believes that a writer must consciously work within his or her nation's literary tradition. Atwood argues in *Survival,* Piercy wrote, "that discovery of a writer's tradition may be of use, in that it makes available a conscious choice of how to deal with that body of themes. She suggested that exploring a given tradition consciously can lead to writing in new and more interesting ways." Because Atwood's own work closely parallels the themes she sees as common to the Canadian literary tradition, *Survival* "has served as the context in which critics have subsequently discussed [Atwood's] works," Hutcheon stated.

Atwood's prominent stature in Canadian letters rests as much on her published works as on her efforts to define and give value to her nation's literature. "Atwood," Susan Wood wrote in the *Washington Post Book World,* "has emerged as a champion of Canadian literature and of the peculiarly Canadian experience of isolation and survival." Hutcheon noted the writer's "important impact on Canadian culture" and believes that her oeuvre, "internationally known through translations, stand as testimony to Atwood's significant position in a contemporary literature which must deal with defining its own identity and defending its value."

Although she has been labelled a Canadian nationalist, a feminist, and even a gothic writer, Atwood incorporates and transcends these categories. Writing in *Saturday Night* of Atwood's several perceived roles as a writer, Linda Sandler concluded that "Atwood is all things to all people . . . a nationalist . . . a feminist or a psychologist or a comedian . . . a maker and breaker of myths . . . a gothic writer. She's all these things, but finally she's unaccountably Other. Her writing has the discipline of a social purpose but it remains elusive, complex, passionate. It has all the intensity of an act of exorcism." Atwood's work finally succeeds because it speaks of universal concerns. Piercy wrote, "Atwood is a large and remarkable writer. Her concerns are nowhere petty. Her novels and poems move and engage me deeply, can matter to people who read them."

BIOGRAPHICAL/CRITICAL SOURCES:

BOOKS

Beran, Carol L., *Living over the Abyss: Margaret Atwood's Life before Man,* ECW Press (Toronto), 1993.

Bouson, J. Brooks, *Brutal Choreographies: Oppositional Strategies and Narrative Design in the Novels of Margaret Atwood,* University of Massachusetts Press (Amherst), 1993.

Contemporary Literary Criticism, Gale (Detroit), Volume 2, 1974, Volume 3, 1975, Volume 4, 1975, Volume 8, 1978, Volume 13, 1980, Volume 15, 1980, Volume 25, 1983, Volume 44, 1987.

Cooke, John, *The Influence of Painting on Five Canadian Writers: Alice Munro, Hugh Hood, Timothy Findley, Margaret Atwood, and Michael Ondaatje,* Edwin Mellen (Lewiston, NY), 1996.

Davidson, Arnold E., and Cathy N. Davidson, editors, *The Art of Margaret Atwood: Essays in Criticism,* House of Anansi Press, 1981.

Dictionary of Literary Biography, Volume 53: *Canadian Writers since 1960,* Gale, 1986.

Gibson, Graeme, *Eleven Canadian Novelists,* House of Anansi Press, 1973.

Grace, Sherrill, *Violent Duality: A Study of Margaret Atwood,* Vehicule Press, 1980.

Grace, Sherrill, and Lorraine Weir, editors, *Margaret Atwood: Language, Text and System,* University of British Columbia Press, 1983.

Hengen, Shannon, *Margaret Atwood's Power: Mirrors, Reflections and Images in Select Fiction and Poetry,* Second Story Press (Toronto), 1993.

Howells, Coral Ann, *Margaret Atwood,* St. Martin's (New York City), 1996.

Irvine, Lorna, *Collecting Clues: Margaret Atwood's Bodily Harm,* ECW Press (Toronto), 1993.

Lecker, Robert, and Jack David, editors, *The Annotated Bibliography of Canada's Major Authors,* ECW Press, 1980.

Marshall, Tom, *Harsh and Lovely Land: The Major Canadian Poets and the Making of a Canadian Tradition,* University of British Columbia Press, 1978.

McCombs, Judith, and Carole L. Palmer, *Margaret Atwood: A Reference Guide,* G. K. Hall (Boston), 1991.

Michael, Magali Cornier, *Feminism and the Postmodern Impulse: Post-World War II Fiction,* State University of New York Press (Albany), 1996.

Nicholson, Colin, editor, *Margaret Atwood: Writing and Subjectivity: New Critical Essays,* St. Martin's, 1994.

Rao, Eleanora, *Strategies for Identity: The Fiction of Margaret Atwood,* P. Lang (New York City), 1993.

Sandler, Linda, editor, *Margaret Atwood: A Symposium,* University of British Columbia (Vancouver), 1977.

Twigg, Alan, *For Openers: Conversations with Twenty-Four Canadian Writers,* Harbour, 1981.
Woodcock, George, *The Canadian Novel in the Twentieth Century,* McClelland & Stewart, 1975.

PERIODICALS

American Poetry Review, November/December, 1973:, March/April, 1977; September/October, 1979.
Atlantic, April, 1973.
Book Forum, Volume 4, number 1, 1978.
Books in Canada, January, 1979; June/July, 1980: March, 1981.
Canadian Forum, February, 1970; January, 1973; November/December, 1974; December/January, 1977-78; June/July, 1981; December/January, 1981-82.
Canadian Literature, autumn, 1971; spring, 1972; winter, 1973; spring, 1974; spring, 1977.
Chicago Tribune, January 27, 1980; February 3, 1980; May 16, 1982; March 19, 1989.
Chicago Tribune Book World, January 26, 1986.
Christian Science Monitor, June 12, 1977; December 27, 1991, p. 14; November 19, 1993, p. 19.
Commonweal, July 9, 1973.
Communique, May, 1975.
Detroit Free Press, January 26, 1986.
Detroit News, April 4, 1982.
Essays on Canadian Writing, spring, 1977.
Globe and Mail (Toronto), July 7, 1984; October 5, 1985; October 19, 1985; February 15, 1986; November 15, 1986; November 29, 1986; November 14, 1987.
Hudson Review, autumn, 1973; spring, 1975.
Humanist, September/October, 1986.
Insight, March 24, 1986.
Journal of Canadian Fiction, Volume 1, number 4, 1972.
Los Angeles Times, March 2, 1982; April 22, 1982; May 9, 1986; January 12, 1987.
Los Angeles Times Book Review, October 17, 1982; February 9, 1986; December 23, 1987; November 14, 1993, pp. 3, 11; December 15, 1996, p. 2.
Maclean's, January 15, 1979; October 15, 1979; March 30, 1981; October 5, 1992; October 4, 1993; February 6, 1995; September 23, 1996, pp. 42-45; October 14, 1996, p. 11.
Malahat Review, January, 1977.
Manna, Number 2, 1972.
Meanjin, Volume 37, number 2, 1978.
Modern Fiction Studies, autumn, 1976.
Ms., January, 1987.

New Leader, September 3, 1973.
New Orleans Review, Volume 5, number 3, 1977.
Newsweek, February 18, 1980; February 17, 1986.
New York Times, December 23, 1976; January 10, 1980; February 8, 1980; March 6, 1982; March 28, 1982; September 15, 1982; January 27, 1986; February 17, 1986; November 5, 1986; October 26, 1993, p. C20; November 23, 1993, pp. C13, C16.
New York Times Book Review, October 18, 1970; March 4, 1973; April 6, 1975; September 26, 1976; May 21, 1978; February 3, 1980; October 11, 1981; February 9, 1986; October 31, 1993, pp. 1, 22; December 11, 1994; April 28, 1996, p. 22; December 29, 1996, p. 6.
Observer, June 13, 1982.
Ontario Review, spring/summer, 1975.
Open Letter, summer, 1973.
Parnassus: Poetry in Review, spring/summer, 1974.
People, May 19, 1980.
Poetry, March, 1970; July, 1972; May, 1982.
Publishers Weekly, August 23, 1976; October 3, 1994; August 28, 1995, pp. 107-08; October 7, 1996, p. 58.
Quill and Quire, April, 1981; September, 1984.
Room of One's Own, summer, 1975.
San Francisco Review of Books, January, 1982; summer, 1982; February/March, 1994, pp. 30-34.
Saturday Night, May, 1971; July/August, 1976; September, 1976; May, 1981.
Saturday Review, September 18, 1976; February 2, 1980.
Saturday Review of the Arts, April, 1973.
Shenandoah, Volume 37, number 2, 1987.
Studies in Canadian Literature, summer, 1977.
This Magazine Is about Schools, winter, 1973.
Time, October 11, 1976.
Times (London), March 13, 1986; June 4, 1987; June 10, 1987.
Times Literary Supplement, March 21, 1986; June 12, 1987.
Tribune Books (Chicago), November 21, 1993, p. 1.
University of Toronto Quarterly, summer, 1978.
Village Voice, January 7, 1980.
Vogue, January, 1986.
Washington Post, April 6, 1986.
Washington Post Book World, September 26, 1976; December 3, 1978; January 27, 1980; March 14, 1982; February 2, 1986; November 7, 1993, p. 1.
Waves, autumn, 1975.
West Coast Review, January, 1973.*

AYCKBOURN, Alan 1939-
(Roland Allen)

PERSONAL: Surname is pronounced Ache-born; born April 12, 1939, in Hampstead, London, England; son of Horace (a concert musician) and Irene (Worley) Ayckbourn; married Christine Roland, May 9, 1959; children: Steven Paul, Philip Nicholas. *Ethnicity:* "White." *Education:* Attended Haileybury and Imperial Service College, Hertfordshire, England, 1952-57.

ADDRESSES: Office—Stephen Joseph Theatre, Westborough, Scarborough, North Yorkshire, YO11 1JW, England. *Agent*—Casarotto Ramsay Ltd., National House, 60-66 Wardour St., London W1R 4ND, England.

CAREER: Stephen Joseph Theatre-in-the-Round Company, Scarborough, England, stage manager and actor, 1957-59, writer and director, 1959-61; Victoria Theatre, Stoke-on-Trent, England, actor, writer, and director, 1961-64; British Broadcasting Corporation (BBC), Leeds, Yorkshire, England, drama producer, 1965-70; Stephen Joseph Theatre, writer and artistic director, 1970—; professor of contemporary theatre, St. Catherine's College, Oxford University, 1992. Visiting playwright and director, Royal National Theatre, London, 1977, 1980, 1986-88. Also acted with several British repertory companies.

AWARDS, HONORS: London Evening Standard best comedy award, 1973, for *Absurd Person Singular,* best play awards, 1974, for *The Norman Conquests,* 1977, for *Just Between Ourselves,* 1987, for *A Small Family Business; Plays and Players* 1989, for *Henceforward . . . Vaudeville,* and 1990, for *Man of the Moment,* best new play awards, 1974, for *The Norman Conquests,* and 1985, for *A Chorus of Disapproval;* named "playwright of the year" by Variety Club of Great Britain, 1974; D.Litt, University of Hull, 1981, University of Keele, 1987, and University of Leeds, 1987; *London Evening Standard* Award, Olivier Award, and *Drama* Award, all 1985, all for *A Chorus of Disapproval;* appointed Commander of the British Empire, 1987; Director of the Year Award, *Plays and Players,* 1987, for production of Arthur Miller's *A View from the Bridge;* Drama-Logue Critics Award, 1991, for *Henceforward . . . Vaudeville;* TMA/Martini Regional Theatre Award for Best Show for Children & Young People, 1993, for *Mr. A's Amazing Maze Plays;* lifetime achievement award, Writers' Guild of Great Britain, Birmingham Press Club Personality of the Year

Award, and the John Ederyn Hughes Rural Wales Award for Literature, all 1993; named Yorkshire Man of the Year award, and the Mont Blanc de la Culture Award for Europe, both 1994; Best West End Play award, Writers' Guild of Great Britain, 1996, for *Communicating Doors;* knighted, 1997.

WRITINGS:

PLAYS

(Under pseudonym Roland Allen) *The Square Cat,* first produced in Scarborough at Library Theatre, June, 1959.

(Under pseudonym Roland Allen) *Love after All,* first produced in Scarborough at Library Theatre, December, 1959.

(Under pseudonym Roland Allen) *Dad's Tale,* first produced in Scarborough at Library Theatre, December 19, 1960.

(Under pseudonym Roland Allen) *Standing Room Only,* first produced in Scarborough at Library Theatre, July 13, 1961.

Xmas v. Mastermind, first produced in Stoke-on-Trent, England at Victoria Theatre, December 26, 1962.

Mr. Whatnot, first produced in Stoke-on-Trent at Victoria Theatre, November 12, 1963, revised version produced in London at Arts Theatre, August 6, 1964.

The Sparrow, first produced in Scarborough at the Library Theatre, July 13, 1967.

Relatively Speaking (first produced as *Meet My Father* in Scarborough at Library Theatre, July 8, 1965, produced on the West End at Duke of York's Theatre, March 29, 1967), Samuel French, 1968.

We Who Are About To . . . (one-act; includes *Countdown*; first produced in London at Hampstead Theatre Club, February 6, 1969; also see below), published in *Mixed Doubles: An Entertainment on Marriage,* Methuen, 1970.

Mixed Doubles: An Entertainment on Marriage (includes *Countdown,* and *We Who Are About to . . . ;* first produced on the West End at Comedy Theatre, April 9, 1969), Methuen, 1970.

How the Other Half Loves (first produced in Scarborough at Library Theatre, July 31, 1969, produced on the West End at Lyric Theatre, August 5, 1970), Samuel French, 1971.

The Story So Far, produced in Scarborough at Library Theatre, August 20, 1970, revised version as *Me Times Me Times Me,* produced on tour March 13, 1972, second revised version as *Fam-*

ily Circles, produced in Richmond, England at Orange Tree Theatre, November 17, 1978.

Ernie's Incredible Illucinations (first produced in London, 1971), Samuel French, 1969.

Time and Time Again (first produced in Scarborough at Library Theatre, July 8, 1971, produced on the West End at Comedy Theatre, August 16, 1972), Samuel French, 1973.

Absurd Person Singular (first produced in Scarborough at Library Theatre, June 26, 1972, produced on the West End at Criterion Theatre, July 4, 1973), Samuel French, 1974.

Mother Figure (one-act; first produced in Horsham, Sussex, England at Capitol Theatre, 1973, produced on the West End at Apollo Theatre, May 19, 1976; also see below), published in *Confusions,* Samuel French, 1977.

The Norman Conquests (trilogy; composed of *Table Manners, Living Together,* and *Round and Round the Garden;* first produced in Scarborough at Library Theatre June, 1973, produced on the West End at Globe Theatre, August 1, 1974), Samuel French, 1975.

Absent Friends (first produced in Scarborough at Library Theatre, June 17, 1974, produced on the West End at Garrick Theatre, July 23, 1975), Samuel French, 1975.

Service Not Included (television script), produced by British Broadcasting Corporation (BBC), 1974.

Confusions (one-acts; includes *Mother Figure, Drinking Companion, Between Mouthfuls, Gosforth's Fete,* and *A Talk in the Park;* first produced in Scarborough at Library Theatre, September 30, 1974, produced on the West End at Apollo Theatre, May 19, 1976), Samuel French, 1977.

(Author of book and lyrics) *Jeeves* (musical; adapted from stories by P. G. Wodehouse), music by Andrew Lloyd Webber, first produced on the West End at Her Majesty's Theatre, April 22, 1975.

Bedroom Farce (first produced in Scarborough at the Library Theatre, June 16, 1975, produced on the West End at Prince of Wales's Theatre, November 7, 1978, produced on Broadway at Brooks Atkinson Theatre, 1979; also see below), Samuel French, 1977.

Just Between Ourselves (first produced in Scarborough at Library Theatre, January 28, 1976, produced on the West End at Queen's Theatre, April 22, 1977; also see below), Samuel French, 1978.

Ten Times Table (first produced in Scarborough at Stephen Joseph Theatre-in-the-Round, January 18, 1977, produced on the West End at Globe Theatre, April 5, 1978; also see below), Samuel French, 1979.

Joking Apart (first produced in Scarborough at Stephen Joseph Theatre-in-the-Round, January 11, 1978, produced on the West End at Globe Theatre, March 7, 1979), Samuel French, 1979.

(Author of book and lyrics) *Men on Women on Men* (musical), music by Paul Todd, first produced in Scarborough at Stephen Joseph Theatre-in-the-Round, June 17, 1978.

Sisterly Feelings (first produced in Scarborough at Stephen Joseph Theatre-in-the-Round, January 10, 1979, produced on the West End at Olivier Theatre, June 3, 1980; also see below), Samuel French, 1981.

Taking Steps (first produced in Scarborough at Stephen Joseph Theatre-in-the-Round, September 27, 1979, produced on the West End at Lyric Theatre, September 2, 1980), Samuel French, 1981.

(Author of book and lyrics) *Suburban Strains* (musical; first produced in Scarborough at Stephen Joseph Theatre-in-the-Round, January 20, 1980, produced in London at Round House Theatre, February 2, 1981), music by Todd, Samuel French, 1981.

Season's Greetings (first produced in Scarborough at Stephen Joseph Theatre-in-the-Round, September 24, 1980, revised version first produced in Greenwich, England at Greenwich Theatre, January 27, 1982, produced on the West End at Apollo Theatre, March 29, 1982), Samuel French, 1982.

(Author of book and lyrics) *Me, Myself, and I* (musical), music by Todd, first produced in Scarborough at Stephen Joseph Theatre-in-the-Round, June, 1981.

Way Upstream (first produced in Scarborough at Stephen Joseph Theatre-in-the-Round, October, 1981, produced in London at National Theatre, October 4, 1982), Samuel French, 1983.

(Author of book and lyrics) *Making Tracks* (musical), music by Todd, first produced in Scarborough at Stephen Joseph Theatre-in-the-Round, December 16, 1981.

Intimate Exchanges (first produced in Scarborough at Stephen Joseph Theatre-in-the-Round, June 3, 1982, produced on the West End at the Ambassadors Theatre, August 14, 1984), Samuel French, 1985.

It Could Be Any One of Us, first produced in Scarborough at Stephen Joseph Theatre-in-the-Round, October 9, 1983.

A Chorus of Disapproval (first produced in Scarborough at Stephen Joseph Theatre-in-the-Round, May 3, 1984, produced on the West End at the

Lyric Theatre, June 11, 1986), Samuel French, 1985, screenplay adaptation by Ayckbourn and Michael Winner, Southgate Entertainment, 1989.

Woman in Mind (first produced in Scarborough at Stephen Joseph Theatre-in-the-Round, June 3, 1985, produced on the West End at Vaudeville Theatre, September 3, 1986), Faber, 1986, Samuel French, 1987.

The Westwoods, first produced in Scarborough at Stephen Joseph Theatre-in-the-Round, May 1984, produced in London at Etcetera Theatre, May 31, 1987.

A Small Family Business (first produced at the Royal National Theatre, June 5, 1987), Faber, 1987, Samuel French, 1988.

Henceforward . . . (first produced in Scarborough at Stephen Joseph Theatre-in-the-Round, July 30, 1987, produced on the West End at Vaudeville Theatre, November 21, 1988), Faber, 1989.

Man of the Moment, first produced in Scarborough at Stephen Joseph Theatre-in-the-Round, August 10, 1988.

Mr. A's Amazing Maze Plays (first produced in Scarborough at Stephen Joseph Theatre-in-the-Round, November 30, 1988), Faber, 1989.

The Revengers' Comedies, first produced in Scarborough at Stephen Joseph Theatre-in-the-Round, June 13, 1989.

Wildest Dreams, first produced in Scarborough, May 6, 1991.

Time of My Life, first produced in Scarborough, April 21, 1992.

Dreams from a Summer House, first produced in Scarborough, August 26, 1992.

Communicating Doors, first produced in Scarborough, February 2, 1994.

Haunting Julia, first produced in Scarborough, April 20, 1994.

The Musical Jigsaw Play, first produced in Scarborough, December 1, 1994.

A Word from Our Sponsor, first produced in Scarborough, April 20, 1995.

By Jeeves, first produced in Scarborough, May 1, 1996.

The Champion of Paribanou, first produced in Scarborough, December 4, 1996.

Things We Do for Love, first produced in Scarborough, April 24, 1997.

OMNIBUS VOLUMES

Three Plays (contains *Absurd Person Singular, Absent Friends,* and *Bedroom Farce*), Grove, 1979.

Joking Apart and Other Plays (includes *Joking Apart, Just Between Ourselves,* and *Ten Times Table*), Chatto & Windus, 1979.

Sisterly Feelings and Taking Steps, Chatto & Windus, 1981.

Alan Ayckbourn: Plays 1, Faber, 1995.

ADAPTATIONS: A Chorus of Disapproval was produced as a feature film in Great Britain in 1989.

SIDELIGHTS: Alan Ayckbourn is generally considered Great Britain's most successful living playwright. For well over two decades Ayckbourn comedies have been appearing regularly in London's West End theatres, earning the author handsome royalties as well as an international reputation. London *Times* reviewer Anthony Masters observes that Ayckbourn's work since the mid-1960s "is rich in major and minor masterpieces that will certainly live and are now overdue for revival." A prolific writer who often crafts his dramas just shortly before they are due to be staged, Ayckbourn extracts wry and disenchanted humor from the dull rituals of English middle-class life. To quote *Nation* contributor Harold Clurman, the dramatist is "a master hand at turning the bitter apathy, the stale absurdity which most English playwrights now find characteristic of Britain's lower-middle-class existence into hilarious comedy." *Dictionary of Literary Biography* essayist Albert E. Kalson describes a typical Ayckbourn play as an "intricately staged domestic comedy with a half-dozen intertwined characters who reflect the audience's own unattainable dreams and disappointments while moving them to laughter with at least a suggestion of a tear." In the London *Times,* Andrew Hislop comments that the plays, translated into two dozen languages, "are probably watched by more people in the world than those of any other living dramatist."

Kalson suggests that Ayckbourn's work "is rooted in the Home Counties, his characters' speech patterns reflecting his upbringing." Indeed, although Ayckbourn was born in London, he was raised in a succession of small Sussex towns by his mother and her second husband, a provincial bank manager. Ayckbourn told the *New York Times* that his childhood was not comfortable or cheery. "I was surrounded by relationships that weren't altogether stable, the air was often blue, and things were sometimes flying across the kitchen," he said. *New York Times* contributor Benedict Nightingale finds this youthful insecurity reflected in Ayckbourn's writings, since the characters "often come close to destroying each other, though more commonly through insensitivity than obvious malice." At seventeen Ayckbourn determined that he wanted to be an actor. After several years with small repertory companies, during which he learned stage managing as well as acting techniques, he took a position with the Stephen Joseph Company in Scarborough. According to Kalson, his continuing association with that group "eventually turned a minor actor into a major playwright." Nightingale is philosophical about Ayckbourn's creative development. "If he had been a happier man," the critic writes, ". . . he wouldn't have wanted to write plays. If he had been a more successful actor, he would have had no need to do so. If he'd known happier people in his early life, his plays wouldn't be so interesting. And if he had not been an actor at all, it would have taken him much longer to learn how to construct his plots, prepare his effects and time his jokes."

Ayckbourn began his tenure at Scarborough as an actor and stage manager. He has described the company as "the first of the fringe theatres," with interests in experimental theatre-in-the-round work and other so-called underground techniques. As he gained experience, Ayckbourn began to agitate for larger roles. The group leader, Stephen Joseph, had other ideas, however. In *Drama,* Ayckbourn reminisced about his earliest attempts at playwrighting. Joseph told him, "If you want a better part, you'd better write one for yourself. You write a play, I'll do it. If it's any good. . . . Write yourself a main part." Ayckbourn appreciated the latter advice especially, calling it "a very shrewd remark, because presumably, if the play had not worked at all, there was no way I as an actor was going to risk my neck in it." Ayckbourn actually wrote several plays that were staged at Scarborough in the early 1960s—pseudonymous works such as *The Square Cat, Love after All, Dad's Tale,* and *Standing Room Only.* According to Ian Watson in *Drama,* these "belong to Ayckbourn's workshop period, and today he is careful to ensure that nobody reads them, and certainly nobody produces them."

Eventually Ayckbourn gave up acting when he discovered his particular muse—the fears and foibles of Britain's middle classes. As he began to experience success outside of Scarborough, however, he continued to craft his work specifically for that company and its small theatre-in-the-round. A large majority of his plays have debuted there, despite the lure of the West End. "My plays are what one would expect from someone who runs a small theater in a community such as Scarborough," Ayckbourn told the *Chi-*

cago Tribune. "That means the cost for the play is about the budget for one production in the company's season, and the subject matter offers the audience a chance to see something they know, to laugh at jokes they've heard before." Kalson likewise notes that the playwright "bears in mind the requirements of the Scarborough audience, many of them his neighbors, upon whom he depends for the testing of his work. He will neither insult nor shock them, respecting their desire to be entertained. He provides them with plays about the life he observes around him, sometimes even his own." *Los Angeles Times* correspondent Sylvie Drake writes: "Alan Ayckbourn is a blithe spirit. He has been writing plays for actors he knows in a theater in Scarborough, England, without much concern for the rest of the world. Since that 'rest of the world' admires nothing more than someone with the audacity to pay it no attention, it promptly embraced his idiosyncratic comedies and totally personal style."

Ayckbourn's early plays "succeeded in resuscitating that most comatose of genres, the 'farcical comedy,'" according to Nightingale in *New Statesman.* In *Modern Drama,* Malcolm Page similarly characterizes the early works as "the lightest and purest of comedies, giving [Ayckbourn] the reputation of being the most undemanding of entertainers." Plays such as *Relatively Speaking, How the Other Half Loves,* and *Absurd Person Singular* "abound with the basic element of theatrical humor, that is incongruity, the association of unassociable elements," to quote Guido Almansi in *Encounter.* Typically revolving around extramarital affairs or class conflicts, the comedies begin with a peculiar situation that grows inexorably out of control, with mistaken identities, unclarified misunderstandings, and overlooked clues. *New York Times* commentator Walter Goodman writes: "How Mr. Ayckbourn contrives to get his people into such states and persuade us to believe that they are reasonable is a secret of his comic flair." With the enthusiastic reception for *Relatively Speaking,* concludes Oleg Kerensky in *The New British Drama: Fourteen Playwrights since Osborne and Pinter,* Ayckbourn established himself "as a writer of ingenious farcical comedy, with an ear for dialogue and with a penchant for complex situations . . . and ingenious plots." That reputation led some critics to question Ayckbourn's lasting contribution to the theatre, but subsequent plays have clarified the author's more serious intentions. Kalson concludes: "Beyond the easy jokes, the mistaken identities, the intricate staging, Ayckbourn was learning a craft that would enable him, always within the framework of bourgeois comedy, to illuminate the tedium, the pain, even the horror of daily life recognizable not only in England's Home Counties, . . . or in gruffer, heartier northern England, . . . but all over the world."

Throughout his years of playwrighting, Ayckbourn has taken risks not easily reconciled with popular comedy. Some American critics have labeled him "the British Neil Simon," but in fact his characters often must contend with an undercurrent of humiliation, mediocrity, and embarrassment that Simon does not address. In the *Chicago Tribune,* Howard Reich writes: "The best of Ayckbourn's work . . . is funny not only for what its characters say but because of what they don't. Between the wisecracks and rejoinders, there breathe characters who are crumbling beneath the strictures of British society." Ayckbourn may pillory the manners and social conventions of the middle classes, but he also concerns himself with the defeats that define ordinary, often hopeless, lives. According to Alan Brien in *Plays and Players,* the author "shows . . . that what is funny to the audience can be tragic to the characters, and that there is no lump in the throat to equal a swallowed laugh which turns sour." *New York* magazine contributor John Simon suggests that Ayckbourn "extends the range of farce, without cheating, to cover situations that are not farcical—the fibrillations of the heart under the feverish laughter. And he keeps his characters characters, not walking stacks of interchangeable jokebooks." As Guido Almansi notes in *Encounter,* the playwright "knows how to operate dramatically on what seems to be utterly banal: which is certainly more difficult than the exploitation of the sublime."

A favorite Ayckbourn theme is the pitfalls of marriage, an institution in which the playwright finds little joy. *New Yorker* correspondent Brendan Gill contends that the author "regards human relationships in general and the marriage relationship in particular as little more than a pailful of cozily hissing snakes." Richard Eder elaborates in the *New York Times:* "His characters are simply people for whom the shortest distance between two emotional points is a tangle; and who are too beset by doubts, timidities and chronic self-complication to have time for anything as straightforward as sex." Harold Hobson also observes in *Drama* that behind Ayckbourn's foolery "he has this sad conviction that marriage is a thing that will not endure. Men and women may get instant satisfaction from life, but it is not a satisfaction that will last long. . . . It is when

Ayckbourn sees the tears of life, its underlying, ineradicable sadness, that he is at his superb best." *Bedroom Farce* and *Absurd Person Singular* both tackle the thorny side of marriage; the two plays are among Ayckbourn's most successful. In *New Statesman,* Nightingale concludes that in both works Ayckbourn "allows his people to have feelings, that these feelings can be hurt, and that this is cause for regret. . . . There are few sadder things than the slow destruction of youthful optimism, not to mention love, trust and other tender shoots: Mr. Ayckbourn makes sure we realise it."

Throughout his career Ayckbourn has demonstrated a reluctance to be limited by conventional staging techniques. This tendency, born in the Scarborough theatre-in-the-round atmosphere, has become an abiding factor in the playwright's work. "Alan Ayckbourn's comedies have become such money-spinners and he himself has won such general critical acclaim that it is difficult to think of him as an experimental dramatist," writes Shorter. "He has however probably done as much as any other living playwright to use the stage with an original sense of its scope—to stretch its scenic and dramatic possibilities." Some Ayckbourn plays juxtapose several floors of a house—or several different houses—in one set; others offer alternative scenes decided at random by the actors or by a flip of a coin. According to J. W. Lambert in *Drama,* Ayckbourn's "ingenuity in thus constructing the plays positively makes the head spin if dwelt upon; but of course it should not be dwelt upon, for however valuable the challenge may have been to his inventive powers, it is to us only an incidental pleasure. The value of the work lies elsewhere—in its knife-sharp insights into the long littleness of life and in its unflagging comic exhilaration." Page likewise insists that while his staging skills "are frequently dazzling, Ayckbourn claims our attention for his insights about people: he prompts us to laugh, then to care about the character and to make a connection with ourselves, our own behavior, and possibly beyond to the world in which we live."

The Norman Conquests, first produced in 1973, combines Ayckbourn's theme of the frailty of relationships with an experimental structure. The piece is actually a trilogy of plays, any one of which can be seen on its own for an understanding of the story. Together, however, the three parts cover completely several hours in the day of an unscrupulous character named Norman, whose "conquests" are generally restricted to the seduction of women. In the *Chicago Tribune,* Richard Christiansen suggests that the three plays "fit together like Chinese boxes. Each comedy has the same cast of characters, the same time frame and the same house as a setting; but what the audience sees on stage in the dining room in one play may happen off stage in the living room in another, and vice versa. Though each play can be enjoyed on its own, much of the fun relies on the audience knowing what is going on in the other two plays." Almansi writes: "As we view the second and then the third play of the trilogy, our awareness of what is going on in the rest of the house and likewise the satisfaction of our curiosity grow concurrently. We enjoy guessing what preceded or what will follow the entrance or the exit of the actor from the garden to the lounge, or from the latter to the kitchen, and we slowly build up a complete picture of the proceedings, as if we were Big Brother enjoying a panoptic and all-embracing vision. I dare surmise that this innovation will count in the future development of theatrical technique." Gill comments that despite its length, the farce "is likely to make you laugh far more often than it is likely to make you look at your watch."

Page, among others, sees a gradual darkening of Ayckbourn's vision over the years. The author's plays, writes Page, "challenge an accepted rule of contemporary comedy: that the audience does not take home the sorrows of the characters after the show. This convention—a matter of both the dramatist's style and the audience's expectations—verges on breakdown when Ayckbourn shifts from farce to real people in real trouble." London *Times* reviewer Bryan Appleyard similarly contends that in recent Ayckbourn dramas "the signs are all there. Encroaching middle age and visionary pessimism are beginning to mark [his] work." This is not to suggest that the author's plays are no longer funny; they simply address such themes as loneliness, adultery, family quarrels, and the twists of fate with candor and sincerity. "Up to now, we have thought of Ayckbourn as the purveyor of amusing plays about suburban bumblers," writes Dan Sullivan in a *Los Angeles Times* review of Ayckbourn's futuristic comedy *Henceforward.* "Here we see him as a thoughtful and painfully honest reporter of the crooked human heart—more crooked every year, it seems." Appleyard observes that Ayckbourn "appears to be entering a visionary middle age and the long-term effect on his plays is liable to be stronger polarization. Villains will really be villains . . . and heroes may well at last begin to be heroes." Indeed, Ayckbourn seems to have become interested in the acceleration of moral decay in his country; plays

such as *Way Upstream, A Chorus of Disapproval,* and *A Small Family Business* explore small communities where extreme selfishness holds sway. In the *Chicago Tribune,* for instance, Matthew Wolf calls *A Small Family Business* "a strong study of one man's seduction into a milieu of moral filth." Christiansen concludes that the cumulative effect of these plays puts Ayckbourn "into his rightful place as an agile and insightful playwright in the front ranks of contemporary theatre."

Drama essayist Anthony Curtis declares that Ayckbourn's career "is shining proof that the well-made play is alive and well." Now entering his fourth decade as a playwright, Ayckbourn continues to craft at least one full-length work a year; he also directs his own and others' works in Scarborough and at London's National Theatre. In *Drama,* Michael Leech writes: "There are those who compare [Ayckbourn] to a latterday Moliere, those who say he is a mere play factory, others who might opine that he veers violently between the two extremes. Certainly he is one of our most prolific and gifted writers of comedy, with characters pinned to the page with the finesse and exactness of a collector of unusual butterflies. . . . And he can look back on a body of work that for most writers would be a life-time's effort." London *Times* commentator Andrew Hislop finds Ayckbourn "at the summit of his career. . . . The security of his Scarborough nest has enabled him to continue his work remarkably unaffected by those who have over-praised him, comparing him to Shakespeare, and those who have unjustly reviled him, regarding him as a vacuous, right-wing boulevardier." Certainly Ayckbourn has more champions than critics, both in England and abroad. Hobson, for one, concludes that the public responds to Ayckbourn's work "because he is both a highly comic writer and, dramatically speaking, a first-class conjuror. The tricks he plays in some of his work are stupendous. They are miracles of human ingenuity." Shorter also observes that as a playwright, Ayckbourn is "homely," "comforting," "immediately accessible," and "easily enjoyed." The critic adds: "Witness the crowded audiences of laughing shirt-sleeved holiday-makers. . . . They are never made to frown or allowed to yawn. . . . They are too busy . . . recognizing themselves, or at any rate each other. They are in fact what Mr. Ayckbourn calls his 'source material,' and he means to stick close to it, despite his popular success and the wealth it has brought him."

Ayckbourn told the *Los Angeles Times* that his ambition is to write "totally effortless, totally truthful, unforced comedy shaped like a flawless diamond in which one can see a million reflections, both one's own and other people's." He also commented in the London *Times* that the best part of his work "is not the clapping, it's the feeling at the end of the evening, that you have given the most wonderful party and those five hundred strangers who came in are feeling better. . . . I don't know, but they are sort of unified into a whole and that is marvelous. That's really like shutting the door on a good party and thinking—that went well!"

BIOGRAPHICAL/CRITICAL SOURCES:

BOOKS

Contemporary Literary Criticism, Gale, Volume 5, 1976; Volume 8, 1978; Volume 18, 1981; Volume 33, 1985.
Elsom, John, *Post-War British Theatre,* Routledge & Kegan Paul, 1976.
Hayman, Ronald, *British Theatre since 1955: A Reassessment,* Oxford University Press, 1979.
Joseph, Stephen, *Theatre in the Round,* Barrie & Rockcliff, 1967.
Kerensky, Oleg, *The New British Drama: Fourteen Playwrights since Osborne and Pinter,* Hamish Hamilton, 1977.
Taylor, John Russell, *The Second Wave: British Drama for the Seventies,* Methuen, 1971.
Taylor, John Russell, *Contemporary English Drama,* Holmes & Meier, 1981.
Watson, Ian, *Alan Ayckbourn: Bibliography, Biography, Playography, Theatre Checklist, No. 21,* T.Q. Publications, 1980.
Watson, Ian, *Conversations with Ayckbourn,* Macmillan (London), 1981.
White, Sidney Howard, *Alan Ayckbourn,* Twayne, 1985.

PERIODICALS

Chicago Tribune, July 17, 1982; July 15, 1983; August 2, 1987.
Commonweal, May 3, 1991.
Drama, autumn, 1974; spring, 1979; summer, 1979; January, 1980; October, 1980; first quarter, 1981; second quarter, 1981; autumn, 1981; spring, 1982; summer, 1982; Volume 162, 1986.
Encounter, December, 1974; April, 1978.
Guardian, August 7, 1970; August 14, 1974.
Listener, May 23, 1974.

Los Angeles Times, January 20, 1983; March 6, 1984; March 30, 1987; October 28, 1987.
Modern Drama, March, 1983.
Nation, March 8, 1975; December 27, 1975; April 21, 1979; April 8, 1991; June 8, 1992.
New Leader, June 1, 1992.
New Republic, November 9, 1974; September 11, 1989.
New Statesman, May 31, 1974; July 5, 1974; December 1, 1978; June 13, 1980.
Newsweek, October 21, 1974.
New York, October 28, 1974; December 22, 1975; April 16, 1979; April 2, 1984; November 13, 1989; February 25, 1991; March 4, 1991; May 18, 1992.
New Yorker, October 21, 1974; December 22, 1975; April 9, 1979; February 25, 1991; May 11, 1992.
New York Times, October 20, 1974; February 16, 1977; April 4, 1977; March 25, 1979; March 30, 1979; March 31, 1979; May 1, 1979; October 16, 1981; May 29, 1986; June 15, 1986; June 25, 1986; October 3, 1986; October 29, 1986; November 26, 1986; July 20, 1987; April 15, 1988; June 5, 1988.
Observer, February 13, 1977; March 4, 1979.
Plays and Players, September, 1972; September, 1975; January, 1983; May, 1983; April, 1987.
Sunday Times (London), June 3, 1973; June 8, 1980.
Sunday Times Magazine, February 20, 1977.
Time, May 9, 1979; August 13, 1984; June 11, 1990; March 4, 1991; November 11, 1991; February 7, 1994; June 13, 1994.
Times (London), January 5, 1976; January 19, 1980; February 4, 1981; February 2, 1982; June 7, 1982; August 18, 1982; October 6, 1982; October 10, 1983; May 4, 1984; June 4, 1985; April 9, 1986; September 5, 1986; November 5, 1986; December 15, 1986; June 1, 1987; June 8, 1987; June 27, 1987; February 10, 1988; November 23, 1988.
Tribune, February 13, 1981.
Variety, February 18, 1991; May 4, 1992; August 3, 1992; August 16, 1993; November 8, 1993; December 27, 1993.
Wall Street Journal, August 2, 1994.
Washington Post, July 10, 1977.

* * *

AYDY, Catherine
See TENNANT, Emma (Christina)

B

BAKER, Jean H(ogarth Harvey) 1933-

PERSONAL: Born February 9, 1933, in Baltimore, MD; daughter of F. Barton (an insurance agent) and Rose Lindsay (Hopkins) Harvey; married Ralph Robinson Baker (a physician), September 12, 1953; children: Susan Dixon, Robinson Scott, Robert Walker, Jean Harvey. *Education:* Goucher College, A.B., 1961; Johns Hopkins University, M.A., 1965, Ph.D., 1971. *Politics:* Democrat.

ADDRESSES: Home—8717 McDonogh Rd., Baltimore, MD 21208-1021. *Office*—Department of History, Goucher College, Towson, MD 21204.

CAREER: Notre Dame College, Baltimore, MD, instructor of history, 1967-69; Goucher College, Towson, MD, instructor, 1969, assistant professor, 1969-75, associate professor of history, 1975-78, professor of history, 1979-82, Elizabeth Todd professor of history, 1981—. *Maryland Historical Magazine*, editor, 1979.

MEMBER: Organization of American Historians, American Historical Association, Berkshire Conference of Women Historians, Phi Beta Kappa.

AWARDS, HONORS: American Council of Learned Societies fellow, 1976; Goucher College Faculty Teaching prize recipient, 1979; National Endowment for the Humanities fellow, 1982; Berkshire Prize in History, 1983, for *Affairs of Party: The Political Culture of Northern Democrats in the Mid-Nineteenth Century;* Willie Lee Rose prize in Southern history, 1989; Newberry Library fellow, 1991.

WRITINGS:

The Politics of Continuity, Johns Hopkins University Press (Baltimore, MD), 1973.
Ambivalent Americans, Johns Hopkins University Press, 1976.
Affairs of Party: The Political Culture of Northern Democrats in the Mid-Nineteenth Century, Cornell University Press (Ithaca, NY), 1983.
Mary Todd Lincoln: A Biography, Norton (New York City), 1987.
The Stevensons: A Biography of an American Family, Norton, 1996.

Also author of *Maryland: A History;* author of lecture "Not Much of Me: Abraham Lincoln as a Typical American," Louis A. Warren Lincoln Library and Museum (Fort Wayne, IN), 1988, part of the Alfred Whital Stern Collection of Lincolniana, Library of Congress, delivered at the 11th Annual R. Gerard McMurtry Lecture, Fort Wayne Museum of Art, 1988.

SIDELIGHTS: A respected feminist historian and history professor at Goucher College in Maryland, Jean H. Baker is an acclaimed writer of historical biographies. Her in-depth approach displays comprehensive research as she discerns cultural and sociological influences to support feminist interpretations of the consequences of a male-dominated order in history. Although critics sometimes discount her feminist interpretations as limited in deciphering the complexities of historical personalities, many commend her accomplished prose which recounts the sights and sounds of each era gracefully.

Mary Todd Lincoln: A Biography, published in 1987, investigates the work of Baker's predecessors in assessing the life of this puzzling woman. Baker includes meticulously collected letters by scholars to further understanding of the First Lady as a gifted woman whose life was constricted by her times and whose personage was damaged by male-dominated historical interpretation.

Her telling story of the life of Mary Todd Lincoln is considered a comprehensive, but not wholly definitive work by critics. *American Historical Review* writer Anne Firor Scott in her analysis of Baker's book, argues that "Feminist historians can find many better cases than this to illuminate the real (as opposed to the self-imposed) consequences of a male-dominated social order." She nonetheless claims that *Mary Todd Lincoln* will "undoubtedly become the accepted interpretation of Mary Todd Lincoln's troubled life," and lauds Baker's prose and comprehensive research.

The Stevensons: A Biography of an American Family, Baker's 1996 chronicle of the Stevenson family, spans two centuries in relating the lineage of a clan who exemplified American liberalism in Illinois. The eldest, Adlai Stevenson, was Grover Cleveland's second vice president and Adlai Stevenson III was a senator. The lives of the Stevenson women mirror emerging societal patterns. Commendatory but unbiased is her tone, Baker focuses especially on the figure of Adlai Stevenson II. Baker's presentation of the one-time governor and failed presidential candidate who confronted McCarthyism in the Red scare era and the Soviets during the Cuban Missile crisis heightens her familial theme.

Opinions of reviewers are compatible about Baker's saga of the Stevensons. Richard Norton Smith reflects in the *Chicago Tribune,* "Baker's sweeping narrative, beautifully written and scrupulously even-handed, does full justice to Stevenson and his people. . . ." Smith's assessment of Baker's workmanship is representative of other reviewers' appraisals of her biography of the Stevensons. Allen D. Boyer in *The New York Times Book Review* lauds Baker's "sharp eye for theme and irony."

BIOGRAPHICAL/CRITICAL SOURCES:

PERIODICALS

American Historical Review, February, 1989, p. 221.
Chicago Tribune, February 25, 1996, p. 47.

Christian Science Monitor, April 8, 1996.
Los Angeles Times, August 7, 1987.
National Review, July 31, 1987.
New York Times, August 25, 1987.
New York Times Book Review, September 13, 1987; April 14, 1996, p. 20.
Washington Post, February 25, 1996.

*   *   *

BAKER, Russell (Wayne) 1925-

PERSONAL: Born August 14, 1925, in Loudoun County, VA; son of Benjamin Rex (a stonemason) and Lucy Elizabeth (a schoolteacher; maiden name, Robinson) Baker; married Miriam Emily Nash, March 11, 1950; children: Kathleen Leland, Allen Nash, Michael Lee. *Education:* Johns Hopkins University, B.A., 1947.

ADDRESSES: Office—c/o *New York Times,* 229 West 43rd St., New York, NY 10036.

CAREER: Baltimore *Sun,* Baltimore, MD, member of staff, 1947-53, London bureau chief, 1953-54; *New York Times,* member of Washington, DC, bureau, 1954-62, author of nationally syndicated "Observer" column for the *New York Times,* 1962—. Host of PBS television series "Masterpiece Theatre," 1993—. *Military service:* U.S. Naval Reserve, 1943-45.

MEMBER: American Academy and Institute of Arts and Letters (elected 1984); American Academy of Arts and Sciences (fellow).

AWARDS, HONORS: Frank Sullivan Memorial Award, 1976; George Polk Award, 1979, for commentary; Pulitzer Prize, 1979, for distinguished commentary (in "Observer" column), and 1983, for *Growing Up;* Elmer Holmes Bobst prize, 1983, for nonfiction; American Academy and Institute of Arts and Letters, 1984; Howland Memorial Prize, Yale University, and Fourth Estate Award, National Press Club, all 1989; H.L.D., Hamilton College, Princeton University, Johns Hopkins University, Franklin Pierce College, Yale University, Long Island University, and Connecticut College; LL.D., Union College; D.Litt, Wake Forest University, University of Miami, Rutgers University, Columbia University; H.H.D., Hood College.

WRITINGS:

COLLECTIONS

No Cause for Panic, Lippincott (Philadelphia), 1964.
Baker's Dozen, New York Times (New York City), 1964.
All Things Considered, Lippincott, 1965.
Poor Russell's Almanac, Doubleday (New York City), 1972.
So This Is Depravity, Congdon & Lattes (New York City), 1980.
The Rescue of Miss Yaskell and Other Pipe Dreams, Congdon & Weed (New York City), 1983.

AUTOBIOGRAPHY

Growing Up, Congdon & Weed, 1982.
The Good Times, Morrow (New York City), 1989.

OTHER

(Author of text) *Washington: City on the Potomac,* Arts, 1958.
An American in Washington, Knopf (New York City), 1961.
Our Next President: The Incredible Story of What Happened in the 1968 Elections (fiction), Atheneum (New York City), 1968.
The Upside-Down Man (children's book), McGraw (New York City), 1977.
(Editor) *The Norton Book of Light Verse,* Norton (New York City), 1986.
(Editor) *Russell Baker's Book of American Humor,* Norton, 1993.
(With William Knowlton Zinsser) *Inventing the Truth: The Art and Craft of Memoir,* Houghton (Boston), 1995.

Also coauthor of musical play *Home Again,* 1979. Contributor to periodicals, including *Saturday Evening Post, New York Times Magazine, Sports Illustrated, Ladies Home Journal, Holiday, Theatre Arts, Mademoiselle, Life, Look,* and *McCalls.*

ADAPTATIONS: One of Baker's columns, "How to Hypnotize Yourself into Forgetting the Vietnam War," was dramatized and filmed by Eli Wallach for *The Great American Dream Machine,* PBS, 1971.

SIDELIGHTS: Noted humorist Russell Baker has charmed readers for years with his witty, literate observations of the foibles and follies of contemporary life. Baker began his career as a journalist for the Baltimore *Sun* and the *New York Times,* where he enjoyed a reputation as a skilled reporter and astute political commentator. The author is perhaps best known for his "Observer" column, which has appeared in the *New York Times* since 1962 and in syndication in hundreds of other papers across the country. Regarded by *Washington Post Book World* critic Robert Sherrill as "the supreme satirist of this half century," Baker has been credited with taking newspaper humor and turning it into "literature— funny, but full of the pain and absurdity of the age," according to *Time*'s John Skow.

Armed with a sense of humor described by *Washington Post* writer Jim Naughton as "quick, dry, and accessibly cerebral," Baker has taken aim at a wide range of targets, including the presidency, the national economy, and the military. In one "Observer" column, Baker spoofed the government's MX-missile plan, a proposal to transport nuclear weapons around the country using the nation's railroads. Baker took the idea even further by proposing the MX-Pentagon plan, a system of mobile Pentagon replicas, complete with a phony president and secretary of defense, that would criss-cross the United States and confuse the nation's enemies. In another essay, Baker suggested that the reason Congress voted against a bill requiring truth-in-advertising labels on defective used cars was the politicians' fear that the same fate would someday befall them: "Put yourself in your Congressman's shoes. One of these days he is going to be put out of office. Defeated, old, tired, 120,000 miles on his smile and two pistons cracked in his best joke. They're going to put him out on the used-Congressman lot. Does he want to have a sticker on him stating that he gets only eight miles on a gallon of bourbon? That his rip-roaring anti-Communist speech hasn't had an overhaul since 1969? That his generator is so decomposed it hasn't sparked a fresh thought in 15 years?"

Though many of Baker's columns concern themselves with the dealings of pompous politicians and the muddled antics of government bureaucrats, not all of the author's essays are political in nature. All manner of human excesses, fads, and trendy behavior have come under Baker's scrutiny; among the topics he has satirized are Super Bowl Sunday, the Miss America pageant, television commercials, and the jogging craze. Other selections have touched on the author's anger over the physical and moral decay of urban America. In "Such Nice People," Baker examined his fellow New Yorkers' reactions to the deterioration of their city, finding a thin veneer of civility masking their barely-suppressed rage. "In a city like this," he wrote, "our self-control must be tight. Very tight. So we are gentle. Civilized. Quivering with self-control. So often so close to murder, but always so self-controlled. And gentle." *Spectator* critic Joe Mysak applauded this type of essay, judging its significance to be "closer to the grain of American life" than Baker's politically-tinged writings, and columns of this sort moved Sherrill to write: "when it comes to satire of a controlled but effervescent ferocity, nobody can touch Baker." In addition to having his column appear in newspapers, Baker has published several compilations of selected "Observer" columns.

Baker has also written a fictional story of the 1968 presidential election, *Our Next President,* as well as a children's book, *The Upside-Down Man.* In *Russell Baker's Book of American Humor,* published in 1993, Baker edited a collection of humorous literary pieces, both fiction and nonfiction, from the past 200 years. The book includes one-line snippets as well as poems, short stories, and excerpts from longer essays from the likes of Mark Twain, Garrison Keillor, Mae West, Tom Wolfe, Fran Lebowitz, Abraham Lincoln, Annie Szmanski, and P. J. O'Rourke, among others. Christopher Buckley, writing in the *New York Times Book Review,* called the collection "mostly funny . . . generous and big-hearted," while *Washington Post Book World* contributor Burling Lowrey remarked that the pieces in the book "prove the validity of two familiar axioms: (1) We should always treat light things seriously and serious things lightly; and (2) All first-rate humor is subversive." Baker has also edited *The Norton Book of Light Verse* and co-authored *Inventing the Truth: The Art and Craft of Memoir.*

Along with his writings in "Observer" and his other humorous literary endeavors, Baker is known for his memoirs, *Growing Up* and *The Good Times.* The former chronicles Baker's adventures as a youngster in Depression-era Virginia, New Jersey, and Baltimore, while the latter recounts his career as a journalist, from his early work on the crime beat at the Baltimore *Sun* to his days as a Washington correspondent with the *New York Times.* Both books earned critical and popular acclaim for their gentle humor and warm, retrospective narratives.

Described by Mary Lee Settle of the *Los Angeles Times Book Review* as "a wondrous book, funny, sad, and strong," *Growing Up* explores the often difficult circumstances of Baker's childhood with a mix of humor and sadness. His father, a gentle, blue-collar laborer fond of alcohol, died in an "acute diabetic coma" when Baker was five. Baker's mother, Lucy Elizabeth, suddenly widowed and impoverished, accepted her brother's offer to live with his family in New Jersey. Before moving, Lucy left her youngest daughter Audrey in the care of wealthier relatives who could provide the infant with a more comfortable existence than she. In *Growing Up,* Baker bore witness to his mother's pain and ambivalence over the decision: "It was the only deed of her entire life for which I ever heard her express guilt. Years later, in her old age, she was still saying, 'Maybe I made a terrible mistake when I gave up Audrey.'"

The family lived off the kindness of relatives for years, finally settling in Baltimore, where Lucy eventually remarried. Baker got his first taste of journalistic life at a young age when, at his mother's insistence, he began selling copies of *The Saturday Evening Post.* Lucy exerted a strong influence over Baker's life, serving as "goad, critic, and inspiration to her son," in the words of *New York Times Book Review* critic Ward Just. The loving but tempestuous relationship that existed between mother and son threaded its way through the work, so that *Growing Up* becomes as much the mother's story as the son's. Baker portrays Lucy as a driven woman, haunted by her life of poverty and obsessed with the idea that her son would achieve success. "I would make something of myself," Baker wrote in *Growing Up,* "and if I lacked the grit to do it, well then she would make me make something of myself." *Spectator* critic Peter Paterson saw the work as "a tribute" to the women in Baker's life, first and foremost to Lucy, "who dominates the book as she dominated her son's existence."

Baker's fully-drawn portraits of his mother and other relatives were a result of his extensive research efforts. To gather information for his book, Baker interviewed dozens of family members, collecting a trove of facts about historical America in the process. In a *Washington Post* interview, Baker said, "I was writing about a world that seemed to have existed 200 years ago. I had one foot back there in this primitive countrylife where women did the laundry running their knuckles on scrub boards and heated irons on coal stoves. That was an America that was completely dead." In a review of *Growing Up,* *Washington Post Book World* reviewer Jonathan Yardley wrote that Baker "passed through rites that for our culture are now only memories, though cherished ones, from first exposure to the miracle of indoor plumbing to trying on his first pair of long pants," and Settle found Baker's descriptions of such scenes "as funny and as touching as Mark Twain's."

Many critics also lauded Baker's ability to translate his personal memories into a work of universal experience. *New Statesman* critic Brian Martin admired the author's "sharp eye for the details of ordinary life," while Yardley offered even stronger praise, affirming that Baker "has accomplished the memorialist's task: to find shape and meaning in his own life, and to make it interesting and pertinent to the reader. In lovely, haunting prose, he has told a story that is deeply in the American grain, one in which countless readers will find echoes of their own, yet in the end is very much his own."

The Good Times, the sequel to *Growing Up,* continued Baker's story, recounting the author's coming of age as a journalist during the 1950s and 1960s. Hired in 1947 as a writer for the Baltimore *Sun,* Baker developed a reputation as a fast, accurate reporter, eventually earning a promotion to the post of London bureau chief. In the opinion of *New York Times* reviewer Frank Conroy, the time spent in London made Baker a better reporter and a better writer. Conroy determined that Baker's "ability to take the best from the Brits—who in general write better than we do . . . was perhaps the key event in his growth as a writer." Though Baker enjoyed London, he moved on to become the *Sun's* White House correspondent, a decision he soon regretted. Once in Washington, Baker found the work boring, the atmosphere stifling, and his writing style unappreciated. Writing in *The Good Times,* Baker acknowledged: "I had swapped the freedom to roam one of the world's great cities and report whatever struck my fancy. And what had I got in return? A glamorous job which entitled me to sit in a confined space, listening to my colleagues breathe."

Frustrated at the *Sun,* Baker jumped at an offer to write for the *New York Times* Washington bureau, although he insisted on covering the Senate, hoping to capture the human side of the country's leaders. But in time even Congress, with its fawning politicians and controlled press briefings, proved disappointing. Recalling his dissatisfaction with the work, Baker told *Time,* "I began to wonder why, at the age of thirty-seven, I was wearing out my hams waiting for somebody to come out and lie to me." When the *Sun* attempted to regain Baker's services with the promise of a column, the *Times* promptly countered

the offer with its own column, a proposal which convinced Baker to stay.

The Good Times is filled with Baker's portrayals of political heavyweights like John Kennedy, Lyndon Johnson, and Richard Nixon. Baker also profiled some of his fellow journalists, saving his harshest criticisms for those reporters who compromised their professional integrity by letting themselves become seduced by savvy politicians. Complimenting Baker on his balanced characterizations, Just reported that the author's "level gaze is on full display here in the deft, edged portraits" of his Congressional contacts, while William French of the Toronto *Globe and Mail* stated that "Baker's thumbnail sketches of the Washington movers and shakers of his time are vivid."

Many critics viewed *The Good Times* favorably, including Just who wrote: "*The Good Times* is a superb autobiography, wonderfully told, often hilarious, always intelligent and unsparing." Some reviewers, however, felt that Baker's trademark sense of modesty was used to excess in the book. In Conroy's opinion, Baker took too little credit for his early success, "ascribing much to luck and his ability to touch-type." Naughton was more critical of Baker's style, asserting that "his humility weakens the book." Other reviewers observed that, because of its subject matter, *The Good Times* necessarily evoked different feelings from its predecessor, *Growing Up.* "Some readers may find that this sequel lacks the emotional tug of the original," Robert Shogan stated in the *Los Angeles Times Book Review,* "what *The Good Times* offers instead is an insider's view of modern American journalism that illuminates both the author and his trade." Along those lines, Yardley added that "Baker seems to understand that it is one thing to write for public consumption about the distant years of childhood, and quite another to write about the unfinished stories of marriage and parenthood. . . ." He concluded, "In the end, though, *The Good Times* is every bit as much a personal document as was *Growing Up.*"

Describing his success to Naughton, Baker downplayed his talents, stating, "I've just had the good luck to escape the meaner reviewers." Readers of his work attribute Baker's success to things altogether different. Skow noted that while Baker most often uses humor to make his point, he "can also write with a haunting strain of melancholy, with delight, or . . . with shame and outrage." In addition, Baker's consistency and clarity are mentioned as strengths. "There is just a lucidity and a sanity about him that is so distinctive," U.S. Senator Daniel Patrick Moynihan told *Time.* "He writes clearly because he thinks clearly." Finally, summarizing the opinions of many critics, Mysak declared: "For a look at how we live now . . . Baker has no superiors, and few peers."

BIOGRAPHICAL/CRITICAL SOURCES:

BOOKS

Baker, Russell, *So This Is Depravity,* Congdon & Lattes, 1980.
Baker, *Growing Up,* Congdon & Weed, 1982.
Baker, *The Rescue of Miss Yaskell and Other Pipe Dreams,* Congdon & Weed, 1983.
Baker, *The Good Times,* Morrow, 1989.
Contemporary Literary Criticism, Volume 31, Gale, 1985.

PERIODICALS

Chicago Tribune, January 16, 1987.
Detroit Free Press, June 27, 1989.
Detroit News, November 7, 1982; July 9, 1989.
Economist, January 22, 1994, p. 97.
Entertainment Weekly, December 31, 1993, p. 62.
Globe and Mail (Toronto), January 19, 1985; June 24, 1989.
Library Journal, May 1, 1989.
Los Angeles Times, December 7, 1980; January 22, 1984; March 17, 1988.
Los Angeles Times Book Review, October 10, 1982; November 30, 1986; June 11, 1989.
New Statesman, March 16, 1984.
Newsweek, September 29, 1980; November 8, 1982.
New Yorker, March 8, 1993, p. 33.
New York Times, January 30, 1972; October 6, 1982; May 23, 1989.
New York Times Book Review, January 30, 1972; October 18, 1982; May 28, 1989; July 8, 1990; February 20, 1994, p. 22.
New York Times Magazine, September 12, 1982.
People, December 20, 1982; October 4, 1993, p. 12.
Publishers Weekly, January 24, 1972; April 28, 1989.
Spectator, February, 1984; March, 1984.
Time, January 19, 1968; January 17, 1972; June 4, 1979; November 1, 1982; October 4, 1993, p. 81.
Times Literary Supplement, April 6, 1984.
Tribune Books (Chicago), January 16, 1987; May 21, 1989.

Washington Post, July 25, 1989.
Washington Post Book World, October 5, 1980; October 3, 1982; October 9, 1983; January 18, 1987; May 28, 1989; December 5, 1993, p. 3.

*   *   *

BALDWIN, Faith 1893-1978
(Amber Lee)

PERSONAL: Born October 1, 1893, in New Rochelle, NY; died March 19, 1978; daughter of Stephen Charles (a lawyer) and Edith Hervey (Finch) Baldwin; married Hugh H. Cuthrell (president, Brooklyn Union Gas Co.), November 6, 1920 (died August 31, 1953); children: Hugh H. (deceased), Hervey (Mrs. Chester A. Moores, Jr.), Stephen, Ann. *Education:* Educated in New York. *Politics:* Republican. *Religion:* Protestant. *Avocational interests:* Reading, book collecting, walking in the woods, and swimming.

ADDRESSES: Home—Route 2, Weed Ave., Norwalk, CT *Agent*—Harold Ober Associates, 40 East 49th St., New York, NY 10017.

CAREER: Novelist. Founder, director, and lecturer, Famous Writers School, Westport, CT

MEMBER: National League of Penwomen, Pen and Brush.

WRITINGS:

Mavis of Green Hill, Small, Maynard, 1921.
Laurel of Stonystream, Small, Maynard, 1923.
Magic and Mary Rose, Small, Maynard, 1924.
Sign Posts (poetry) Small, Maynard, 1924.
Thresholds, Small, Maynard, 1925.
Those Difficult Years, Small, Maynard, 1925.
Three Women, Dodd, 1926.
Departing Wings, Dodd, 1927.
Rosalie's Career, Clode, 1928.
Betty, Clode, 1928.
Alimony, Dodd, 1928, reprinted, Amereon, 1976.
The Incredible Year, Dodd, 1929.
Garden Oats, Dodd, 1929, reprinted, Amereon, 1976.
(With Achmed Adullah) *Broadway Interlude,* Harcourt, 1929.

Judy: A Story of Divine Corners (children's), Dodd, 1930, reprinted, Amereon, 1976.

Make-Believe, Dodd, 1930.

The Office Wife, Dodd, 1930, reprinted, Amereon, 1976.

Babs: A Story of Divine Corners (children's), Dodd, 1931.

Skyscraper, Cosmopolitan, 1931, reprinted, Amereon, 1976.

Today's Virtue, Dodd, 1931.

Mary Lou: A Story of Divine Corners (children's) Dodd, 1931.

Self-Made Woman, Farrar & Rinehart, 1932.

Week-End Marriage, Farrar & Rinehart, 1932.

(With Adullah) *Girl on the Make,* Smith, 1932.

District Nurse, Farrar & Rinehart, 1932.

Myra: A Story of Divine Corners (children's), Dodd, 1932.

White Collar Girl, Farrar & Rinehart, 1933, reprinted, Amereon, 1976.

Beauty, Farrar & Rinehart, 1933.

Love's a Puzzle, Farrar & Rinehart, 1933.

Innocent Bystander, Farrar & Rinehart, 1934.

Within a Year, Farrar & Rinehart, 1934.

Wife vs. Secretary (short stories), Grosset, 1934.

Honor Bound, Farrar & Rinehart, 1934.

American Family, Farrar & Rinehart, 1935, reprinted, Holt, 1972, published in England as *Conflict,* Low, 1935.

The Puritan Strain, Farrar & Rinehart, 1935.

The Moon's Our Home, Farrar & Rinehart, 1936, reprinted, Amereon, 1976.

Men Are Such Fools!, Farrar & Rinehart, 1936, reprinted, Amereon, 1976.

Private Duty, Farrar & Rinehart, 1936.

Girls of Divine Corners, Farrar & Rinehart, 1936.

The Heart Has Wings, Farrar & Rinehart, 1937.

That Man Is Mine, Farrar & Rinehart, 1937, reprinted, Aeonian Press, 1975.

Twenty-Four Hours a Day, Farrar & Rinehart, 1937, reprinted, Amereon, 1976.

Manhattan Nights, Farrar & Rinehart, 1937.

(With Samuel Ornitz and E. E. Paramore) *Portia on Trial* (screenplay), Republic, 1937.

Hotel Hostess, Farrar & Rinehart, 1938, reprinted, Amereon, 1976.

Enchanted Oasis, Farrar & Rinehart, 1938.

Rich Girl, Poor Girl, Farrar & Rinehart, 1938.

White Magic, Farrar & Rinehart, 1939, reprinted, Amereon, 1976.

Station Wagon Set, Farrar & Rinehart, 1939, reprinted, Amereon, 1976.

The High Road, Farrar & Rinehart, 1939, reprinted, Aeonian Press, 1974.

Career by Proxy, Farrar & Rinehart, 1939.

Letty and the Law, Farrar & Rinehart, 1940, reprinted, Amereon, 1976.

Medical Center, Farrar & Rinehart, 1940.

(Contributor) Elizabeth L. Gilman, editor, *Picnic Adventures,* Farrar & Rinehart, 1940.

Rehearsal for Love, Farrar & Rinehart, 1940, reprinted, Amereon, 1976.

Something Special, Farrar & Rinehart, 1940.

Temporary Address: Reno, Farrar & Rinehart, 1941.

And New Stars Burn, Farrar & Rinehart, 1941.

The Heart Remembers, Farrar & Rinehart, 1941.

Blue Horizon, Farrar & Rinehart, 1942, reprinted, Amereon, 1976.

Breath of Life, Farrar & Rinehart, 1942, reprinted, Amereon, 1976.

Five Women in Three Novels (includes *Star on Her Shoulder, Detour,* and *Let's Do the Town*), Farrar & Rinehart, 1942.

. . . The Rest of My Life with You, Farrar & Rinehart, 1942.

You Can't Escape, Farrar & Rinehart, 1943, reprinted, Amereon, 1976.

Washington, USA, Farrar & Rinehart, 1943.

Change of Heart, Farrar & Rinehart, 1944, reprinted, Aeonian Press, 1974.

He Married a Doctor, Farrar & Rinehart, 1944.

Romance Book, World Publishing, 1944.

A Job for Jenny, Farrar & Rinehart, 1945, published in England as *Tell Me My Heart,* R. Hale, 1950.

Second Romance Book, World Publishing, 1945.

Arizona Star, Farrar & Rinehart, 1945, reprinted, Amereon, 1976.

No Private Heaven, Farrar & Rinehart, 1946.

Woman on Her Way, Rinehart, 1946.

Give Love the Air, Rinehart, 1947.

Sleeping Beauty, Rinehart, 1947, reprinted, Amereon, 1976.

They Who Love, Rinehart, 1948.

Marry for Money, Rinehart, 1948, reprinted, Amereon, 1978.

The Golden Shoestring, Rinehart, 1949.

Look Out for Liza, Rinehart, 1950.

The Whole Armor, Rinehart, 1951.

The Juniper Tree, Rinehart, 1952.

Widow's Walk: Variations on a Theme (poetry), Rinehart, 1954.

Face toward the Spring, Rinehart, 1956.

Three Faces of Love, Rinehart, 1957.

Many Windows: Seasons of the Heart, Rinehart, 1958.

Blaze of Sunlight, Rinehart, 1959.

Testament of Trust, 1960.
Harvest of Hope, 1962.
The West Wind, 1962.
The Lonely Man, 1964.
Living by Faith (nonfiction), 1964.
There Is a Season, 1966.
Evening Star, 1966.
The Velvet Hammer, 1969.
Take What You Want, 1970.
Any Village, 1971.
One More Time, 1972.
No Bed of Roses, 1973.
Time and the Hour, 1974.
New Girl in Town, 1975.
Thursday's Child, 1976.
Adam's Eve, 1977.

Also author of two books under pseudonym Amber Lee. Has ghostwritten three books. Author of column published in *Woman's Day*, 1958-65. Contributor of numerous short stories and articles to various magazines.

ADAPTATIONS: Week-End Marriage was filmed by First National in 1932; *Skyscraper* was filmed as *Skyscraper Souls* by Metro-Goldwyn-Mayer (MGM) in 1932; *Beauty* was filmed as *Beauty for Sale* by MGM in 1933; *The Moon's Our Home* was filmed as *The Moon Is Our Home*, by Paramount in 1936; *Portia on Trial* was filmed by Republic in 1937; *Men Are Such Fools* was filmed by Warner Bros. in 1938. Other film titles adapted from works by Baldwin include *August Week-End*, filmed by Chesterfield Motion Pictures Corp. in 1936; *Love Before Breakfast*, filmed by Universal in 1936; *Comet Over Broadway*, filmed by Warner Bros. in 1938; *Apartment for Peggy*, filmed by Twentieth Century-Fox in 1948; *Horsie*, filmed by Robert Stillman Productions in 1951; and *Queen for a Day*, filmed by United Artists in 1951.

SIDELIGHTS: "There ought to be some sort of literary or at least book prize for Faith Baldwin," a *New York Times* critic wrote in 1939. "She can turn them out a mile a minute, all readable . . . all tops in her field."

Baldwin, one of the eminent romance novelists of the first half of the twentieth century, knew what her audience wanted and gave it to them. Baldwin's

novels typically presented a young, successful woman whose career conflicted with marriage, as in *Self-Made Woman* or *White Collar Girl*. Given the tenor of the times, marriage always won out. Taken from a more modern perspective, the author's novels "are neither predatory nor manipulative," Nancy Regan remarked in *Twentieth-Century Romance and Historical Writers*. "In that sense, they are old-fashioned. Most contemporary romances prey on their readers' needs and insecurities, perhaps on their need for insecurity, their mostly unconscious desire to prolong adolescence, that uncertain, indeterminate state where—despite probability—one might indeed turn out to be beautiful. . . . Baldwin's books appeal to the obverse of this romantic fantasy, to the need for stability, lifelong sharing, patient familiarity."

Perhaps it is no coincidence that Baldwin, who began publishing in 1921, reached her artistic and commercial peak during the Great Depression, when many women longed for relief from the worries of real life. Baldwin once explained her success during those years of hardship: "People had to have some escape hatch, some way to get out of themselves, especially during the Depression. . . . When we got into the war nothing was more exciting than the headlines. After that I was still successful, but it was all different, because the world was different. Escape wasn't as important then."

While critical reaction to her books was mixed, the author often peppered her love stories with realism. Office politics sparked conflict in *Office Wife*, in which a secretary falls in love with her boss, and *District Nurse* presented a woman who aided the poor people of a large city.

"The folk who populate [her] novels are usually rich, solid (if sometimes troubled), and almost never dull," noted Regan. "They are, fancifully, the burghers of Dutch painting come out of their dark counting houses into sunlit American suburbs. Ministers, country doctors, district nurses, lawyers . . . aviators, real estate agents, and . . . a movie star, the idle rich: this is the litany of Baldwin's saints."

In 1933 a critic in the *Boston Transcript* referred to one of Baldwin's books as "movie fare," and indeed they were. From the 1930s through the 1950s, a number of films were made based on her stories and novels. But her formulaic plotting continued to strengthen its grip on romance readers. She turned out as many as three books a year through the mid 1950s, when television began to assert its power over readers. Nevertheless, Baldwin continued publishing until a year prior to her death in 1978.

In Regan's view, the essence of Baldwin's work is "the cosy adolescent fantasy of proximity and protection, as when the young heroines of *The Heart Has Wings* and *Enchanted Oasis* are compelled by 'accidents' to spend innocent nights with the men of their dreams. Baldwin's novels are less romances than comedies: ripe, full of sunlight, crowded with people making do with each other. Comedies in the classical sense, her books are pledges of our willingness to live life with other no better than they might be and certainly no better than ourselves."

According to a writer for the *New York Times,* "the key to her popularity was that [Baldwin] enabled lonely working people, young and old, to identify with her glamorous and wealthy characters. She told them that certain problems and preoccupations, about love and friendship, are shared by everybody. . . . Her books were meant not only to interest readers but also to encourage them. Women found in them solace as well as entertainment."

BIOGRAPHICAL/CRITICAL SOURCES:

BOOKS

Twentieth-Century Romance and Historical Writers, 3rd edition, edited by Aruna Vasudevan, St. James Press, 1994.

PERIODICALS

New York Times, February 8, 1942; September 12, 1954; March 20, 1978.
Saturday Review, September 18, 1954; October 13, 1956.
Cosmopolitan, August, 1959.
Cincinnati Enquirer, January 20, 1974.
American Way, June, 1974.
Authors in the News, Volume 1, 1976.
Washington Post, March 21, 1978.
Time, April 3, 1978.*

*   *   *

BALDWIN, Margaret
  See WEIS, Margaret (Edith)

BALLARD, P. D.
  See BALLARD, (Willis) Todhunter

*   *   *

BALLARD, (Willis) Todhunter 1903-1980
  (W. T. Ballard, Willis T. Ballard; pseudonyms: Brian Agar, P. D. Ballard, Parker Bonner, Sam Bowie, Nick Carter, Hunter D'Allard, Brian Fox, Harrison Hunt, George Hunter, John Hunter, Neil MacNeil, Clint Reno, John Shepherd, Jack Slade, Clay Turner)

PERSONAL: Born December 13, 1903, in Cleveland, OH; died December 27, 1980; son of Fredrick Wayne (an electrical engineer) and Cordelia (Todhunter) Ballard; married Phoebe Dwiggins (a writer), February 5, 1936; children: Wayne. *Education:* Wilmington College, B.S., 1926 *Avocational interests:* Western history, metals, oil deposits, mining, fishing, travel.

CAREER: Writer, 1927-80. F. W. Ballard & Co., Cleveland, OH, draftsman, 1926-28; employed by various magazines, newspapers, and film studios, 1929-34; Wright Paterson Field, OH, member of production control staff in maintenance division, 1942-45.

MEMBER: Western Writers of America (past vice president), Writers Guild of America West.

AWARDS, HONORS: Spur Award for best historical novel, Western Writers of America, 1965, for *Gold in California!.*

WRITINGS:

(Under name W. T. Ballard) *Say Yes to Murder,* Putnam (New York City), 1942, published under pseudonym John Shepherd as *The Demise of a Louse,* Belmont (New York City), 1962.
Murder Can't Stop, McKay (Philadelphia), 1946.
(Under name W. T. Ballard) *Dealing Out Death,* McKay, 1948.
Two-Edged Vengeance (appeared serially in *Esquire* under title "Red Horizon"), Macmillan (New York City), 1951.
The Circle C Feud, Sampson Low (London), 1952.
Incident at Sun Mountain, Houghton (New York City), 1952.

(Under name W. T. Ballard) *Walk in Fear,* Gold Medal Books (New York City), 1952.
West of Quarantine, Houghton, 1953.
High Iron, Houghton, 1953.
(With James Charles Lynch) *Showdown,* Popular Library (New York City), 1953.
Rawhide Gunman, Popular Library, 1954.
Trigger Trail (appeared serially in *Ranch* under title "Empire West"), Popular Library, 1955.
Blizzard Range, Popular Library, 1955.
Gunman from Texas, Popular Library, 1956.
Guns of the Lawless, Popular Library, 1956.
(Under name Willis T. Ballard) *The Package Deal,* Appleton (New York City), 1956.
Roundup, Popular Library, 1957.
Trail Town Marshal, Popular Library, 1957.
Saddle Tramp, Popular Library, 1958.
(Under name W. T. Ballard) *Chance Elson,* Pocket Books (New York City), 1958.
Trouble on the Massacre, Popular Library, 1959.
(Under name W. T. Ballard) *Fury in the Heart,* Monarch Books (New York City), 1959.
The Long Trail Back, Doubleday (New York City), 1960.
The Night Riders, Doubleday, 1961.
(Under name W. T. Ballard) *Pretty Miss Murder,* Pocket Books, 1961.
(Under name W. T. Ballard) *The Seven Sisters,* Pocket Books, 1962.
Gopher Gold, Doubleday, 1962 (published in England as *Gold Fever in Gopher,* Jenkins, 1962).
Westward the Monitors Roar, Doubleday, 1963, published as *Fight or Die,* Tower Books, 1977.
(Under name W. T. Ballard) *Three for the Money,* Pocket Books, 1963.
Gold in California!, Doubleday, 1965.
(Under name W. T. Ballard) *Murder Las Vegas Style,* Tower (New York City), 1967.
The Californian, Doubleday, 1971.
Nowhere Left to Run, Doubleday, 1972.
Outlaw Brand, Avon, 1972.
Loco and the Wolf, Doubleday, 1973.
Home to Texas, Dell, 1974.
Trails of Rage, Doubleday, 1975.
(Under name W. T. Ballard) *This Range Is Mine,* Doubleday, 1975.
Sheriff of Tombstone, Doubleday, 1977.

UNDER PSEUDONYM BRIAN AGAR

Have Love, Will Share, Monarch Books, 1961.
The Sex Web, Soft Cover Library, 1967.
Land of Promise, Universal Publishing & Distributing, 1967.

UNDER PSEUDONYM P. D. BALLARD

Age of the Junkman, Fawcett (New York City), 1963.
End of a Millionaire, Fawcett, 1964.
Brothers in Blood, Fawcett, 1972.
Angel of Death, Fawcett, 1972.
The Death Brokers, Fawcett, 1973.

UNDER PSEUDONYM PARKER BONNER

Superstition Range, Popular Library, 1952.
Outlaw Brand, Popular Library, 1954.
Tough in the Saddle, Monarch Books, 1964.
Modoc Indian Wars, Monarch Books, 1965.
Plunder Canyon, Avon, 1967.
The Man from Yuma, Berkley Publishing, 1967.
The Town Tamer, Paperback Library, 1968.
Applegate's Gold, Avon, 1969.
Borders to Cross, Paperback Library, 1969.
Look to Your Guns, Paperback Library, 1969.

UNDER PSEUDONYM SAM BOWIE

Thunderhead Range, Monarch Books, 1959.
Chisum, Ace Books, 1970.
The Train Robbers, Ace Books, 1973.
Canyon War, G & D, 1980.

UNDER PSEUDONYM BRIAN FOX

A Dollar to Die For, Award (New York City), 1968.
The Wild Bunch, Award, 1969.
Outlaw Trail, Award, 1969.
Unholy Angel, Award, 1969.
Sabata, Award, 1970.
Dead Ringer, Award, 1971.
Apache Gold, Award, 1971.
Dragooned, Award, 1971.
Return of Sabata, Award, 1972.
Bearcats!, Award, 1973.

UNDER PSEUDONYM JOHN HUNTER

West of Justice, Ballantine, 1954.
Ride the Wind South, Pocket Books, 1957.
Badlands Buccaneer, Pocket Books, 1959.
Marshal from Deadwood, Pocket Books, 1960.
Desperation Valley: A Novel of the Cherokee Strip, Macmillan, 1964.
Duke, Paperback Library, 1965.
Death in the Mountain, Ballantine, 1969.
Lost Valley, Ballantine, 1971.
Hell Hole, Ballantine, 1971.

The Burning Land, Ballantine, 1973.
Gambler's Gun, Ballantine, 1973.
The Higraders, Ballantine, 1974.
Death in the Mountain, Ballantine, 1974.

Also author of *Trouble Range.*

UNDER PSEUDONYM NEIL MacNEIL

Death Takes an Option, Gold Medal Books, 1958.
Third on a Seesaw, Gold Medal Books, 1959.
Two Guns for Hire, Gold Medal Books, 1959.
Hot Dam, Gold Medal Books, 1960.
The Death Ride, Gold Medal Books, 1960.
Mexican Slay Ride, Gold Medal Books, 1962.
The Spy Catchers, Gold Medal Books, 1965.

Also author of memoir "The Highland Heart of Nova Scotia."

UNDER PSEUDONYM JACK SLADE

Bandito, Tower, 1968.
Lassiter, Tower, 1968.

UNDER PSEUDONYM CLAY TURNER

Give a Man a Gun, Paperback Library, 1971.
Go West Ben Gold!, Warner, 1974.
Gold Goes to the Mountain, Warner, 1974.

OTHER

(Under pseudonym Harrison Hunt, with Norbert Davis) *Murder Picks the Jury,* S. Curl for Mystery House, 1947.
The Outcast (screenplay; adapted from Ballard's novel *Two-Edged Vengeance* and short story "Red Horizon," published in *Esquire*), Republic Pictures, 1954.
(Under pseudonym John Shepherd) *Lights, Camera, Murder,* Belmont, 1960.
(Under pseudonym Hunter D'Allard) *The Long Sword,* Avon, 1962.
(Under pseudonym Nick Carter) *The Kremlin File,* Universal Publishing & Distributing, 1963.
(With Phoebe Ballard) *The Man Who Stole a University* (juvenile), Doubleday, 1967.
(Under pseudonym George Hunter) *How to Defend Yourself, Your Family, and Your Home: A Complete Guide to Self-Protection,* McKay, 1967.
(Editor) *A Western Bonanza: Eight Short Novels of the West,* Doubleday, 1969.

(Under pseudonym Clint Reno) *Sierra Massacre,* Fawcett, 1974.
(Under pseudonym Clint Reno) *Sun Mountain Slaughter,* Fawcett, 1974.

Also author of about fifty motion picture and television scripts. Contributor of over one thousand stories to magazines, including *Saturday Evening Post, Esquire, This Week, Collier's, Liberty, McCall's,* and *Black Mask.* Ballard's manuscripts are collected at the University of Oregon Library in Eugene.

ADAPTATIONS: Film rights to *Applegate's Gold* were sold to Solar Productions in 1969.

SIDELIGHTS: Todhunter Ballard was a prolific writer of mysteries and Western novels. His books contributed to the development of the contemporary mystery genre. As James L. Traylor noted in *St. James Guide to Crime and Mystery Writers,* Ballard's "*Say Yes to Murder* set the standard for the Hollywood murder mystery" while his other mystery novels "played an unacknowledged role in the development of the hard-boiled detective tradition."

Ballard's first published story appeared in *Hunter Trader Trapper* magazine when he was twelve years old. He continued to submit work to magazines while working as a draftsman for his father's electrical engineering firm. With the bankruptcy of the family business in the Great Depression of the 1930s, Ballard moved to the West Coast. Chancing upon a Hollywood cigar store newsstand carrying an issue of *Detective Dragnet* in which one of his stories appeared, Ballard also encountered an old acquaintance from his hometown of Cleveland whose family manufactured movie trailers. Queried by the friend as to what he was doing in Hollywood, Ballard told Stephen Mertz in *Armchair Detective* that he produced a copy of the magazine and lied: "'I'm freelancing, working for magazines. . . .' Why [he] was impressed by a dime pulp I'll never know, but he was. The meeting culminated in his offering me a job writing for the studio at seventy-five bucks a week. A bonanza at that time."

Ballard continued to write for the pulp magazines, however. According to Mertz, Ballard's "importance to the mystery field is that he was one of the original contributors to *Black Mask,* that famous detective pulp which, during the thirties . . . , pioneered the then-revolutionary American hard-boiled detective form." Approximating his average output for the pulps at about a million words per year, Ballard described to Mertz the lifestyle of a pulp writer living in Los Angeles during the thirties and forties: "We all worked hard, played hard, lived modestly, drank but only a few to excess, gambled some when we had extra cash. Most of our friends were other writers. In the Depression when any of us got a check he climbed in his jalopy and made the rounds to see who was in worse straits than he and loaned up to half what he had just received."

Ballard's novel *Say Yes to Murder* introduced his character Bill Lennox, a "troubleshooter" for a film studio. The character was based on Ballard's friend Jim Lawson who, in his job with one of the major film companies, was assigned to keeping a watchful eye on the troublesome son of a studio boss. Lennox appeared in four novels altogether, with *Dealing Out Death* "the best," according to Traylor. "It is more mysterious in execution, more believable because of its finely honed dialogue, and has the never-never land of Las Vegas as an appropriate background for mirth and murder."

When the market for detective fiction, especially for the studios, weakened, Ballard began to write Westerns, using his middle name Todhunter. "But unlike the detective publications the westerns would not absorb enough copy under a single byline to support me . . . ," Ballard related to Mertz. "The houses would take only one a year and a name was tied up solely by one house. Therefore the shift to a long series of pseudonyms under which I could work for several houses at once."

Writing in *Twentieth-Century Western Writers,* J. Fraser Cocks, III, explained that Ballard's "best writing occurs when he . . . expresses his fundamental belief that law and order and moral community will triumph over the near anarchy that was the frontier." Acknowledging a preference for Westerns over detective fiction, Ballard told Mertz that his most satisfying book was the Spur Award-winning *Gold in California!,* a young boy's episodic tale of growing up in California: "It's a good book. It sold over 30,000 copies, which is a huge sale for a western and I am proud of it." Cocks praised *Gold in California!* for Ballard's description of "how the wagon trains organized themselves for the trip across the plains and [identified] the social organization best suited to ensure the survival of the travellers." Cocks also found much to admire about *Incident at Sun Mountain,* a novel based on actual history. It is, Cocks claimed, "the well-researched story of the Golden Circle, a group of Southern sympathizers, who planned to seize the silver mines of Sun Mountain, Utah and use the wealth to finance the Rebellion. Ballard effectively interweaves the political intrigue accompanying the formation of Lincoln's first administration into the narrative to give the story a convincing historical context."

Traylor concluded that "Ballard wrote convincingly in many styles and from different viewpoints. He was extremely prolific. . . . His crime novels are always rewarding; he had the ability to engage the reader with his characters, making the reader care what happened to them—crook, cop, or PI [private investigator]." Speaking of Ballard's work as a Western writer, Cocks noted that "Ballard's staple subject was the conflict engendered by disputes over land and cattle. These stories contain his best plots and most believable characters. Their subtext is the gradual replacement of the rule of force by that of law and order."

Ballard once told *CA* that all his books, "no matter what name they carry, are collaborations with Phoebe Ballard."

BIOGRAPHICAL/CRITICAL SOURCES:

BOOKS

St. James Guide to Crime and Mystery Writers, fourth edition, St. James Press (Detroit), 1996.

Traylor, James L., editor, *Hollywood Troubleshooter: W. T. Ballard's Bill Lennox,* Popular Press (Bowling Green, OH), 1984.

Twentieth-Century Western Writers, second edition, St. James Press, 1991.

PERIODICALS

Armchair Detective, winter, 1979.

Books, October 18, 1942, p. 22.

Chicago Sun, January 23, 1948.

Kirkus, February 1, 1956, p. 24.

Library Journal, March 15, 1956, p. 81.

New York Times, October 18, 1942, p. 10; January 25, 1948, p. 30; April 8, 1956, p. 36.

San Francisco Chronicle, April 2, 1956, p. 19.

Time, October 24, 1969.

Writer's Digest, August, 1969.*

BALLARD, W. T.
See BALLARD, (Willis) Todhunter

* * *

BALLARD, Willis T.
See BALLARD, (Willis) Todhunter

* * *

BEDFORD, Donald F.
See FEARING, Kenneth (Flexner)

* * *

BELFORD, Barbara 1935-

PERSONAL: Born November 23, 1935, in Oakland, CA; daughter of Harold Graef (a professor) and Veronica (an actress; maiden name, Burns) Belford; married Frank G. de Furia (a physician), December 23, 1963 (died June 25, 1973); children: Deborah. *Education:* Vanderbilt University, B.A. (cum laude), 1957; Columbia University, M.A. (cum laude), 1962; attended University of Edinburgh, 1955-56, and Columbia University, 1972-73.

ADDRESSES: Home—350 Central Park West, New York, NY 10025. *Agent*—Elaine Markson Agency, 44 Greenwich Ave., New York, NY 10011.

CAREER: Columbia University, Graduate School of Journalism, New York City, assistant professor, beginning 1978, professor of journalism, 1989—. Former editor and reporter for *New York Herald Tribune, Quincy Patriot Ledger, St. Petersburg Times, Scotsman,* and *Redbook.*

MEMBER: PEN American Center, Authors Guild.

AWARDS, HONORS: Literature on Media Award, San Francisco State University, 1987, for *Brilliant Bylines: A Biographical Anthology of Notable Newspaperwomen in America.*

WRITINGS:

The Young Mothers (nonfiction), Warner Books (New York City), 1977.
Brilliant Bylines: A Biographical Anthology of Notable Newspaperwomen in America, Columbia University Press (New York City), 1986.
Violet: The Story of the Irrepressible Violet Hunt and Her Circle of Lovers and Friends—Ford Madox Ford, Somerset Maugham, H. G. Wells, and Henry James, Simon & Schuster (New York City), 1990.
Bram Stoker: A Biography of the Author of "Dracula", Knopf (New York City), 1996.

Contributor to periodicals.

WORK IN PROGRESS: Biography of Sir Arthur Conan Doyle.

SIDELIGHTS: Barbara Belford has written two critically-praised biographies of literary figures. In *Violet: The Story of the Irrepressible Violet Hunt and Her Circle of Lovers and Friends—Ford Madox Ford, Somerset Maugham, H. G. Wells, and Henry James,* Belford focuses on the career and relationships of Violet Hunt, a London writer born in 1862 and known for her tumultuous friendships and scandalous affairs with famous authors. In *Bram Stoker: A Biography of the Author of "Dracula,"* Belford provides a chronicle of the creator of one of fiction's most enduring characters.

In *Violet,* Belford describes Hunt as a strong-willed woman who had a flair for sustaining unhealthy attachments. Her own literary contributions—overshadowed by her tempestuous social life and the illustrious company she kept—have received little attention since her death in 1942. Belford discovered ten years of Hunt's missing diaries and, through these, attempts to present a comprehensive picture of Hunt's character, relationships, and achievements.

The first of Hunt's disastrous relationships, beginning in 1890, was with Oswald Crawfurd, a married diplomat and publisher who was nearly thirty years older than Hunt. Their affair lasted seven years, but when Crawfurd's wife died, he promptly left Hunt to marry someone else. His abandoned mistress, however, soon found a new beau in writer Somerset Maugham. A novelist and playwright, Maugham would later model the character of Rose Waterford in his 1919 novel *The Moon and Sixpence* on Hunt. Four years later, the forty-four-year-old Hunt began a year-long liaison with writer and historian H. G. Wells. Wells's 1909 work *Tono-Bungay,* a novel about English life, included a character based on Hunt.

Hunt's longest and, according to Belford, most dramatic affair, was with a married writer, Ford Madox Hueffer, who would later be known as Ford Madox Ford. The biography characterizes their relationship as volatile; in fact, Hunt's alleged violent streak inspired the evil Sylvia Tietjens character in Ford's novel *Parade's End.* After Ford and Hunt had traveled to Germany, newspapers reported that they had been married there, prompting a successful libel case from Ford's enraged wife. Because Hunt and Ford were well known in London's literary circles, the scandal was widely publicized, and though some were amused by the incident, there was enough outrage to damage Hunt's reputation.

Belford states that while Hunt's romantic relationships were stormy, her literary career was stable, and she was able to earn a living by writing. Hunt published seventeen novels, two collections of short stories, two translations, a biography, poems, memoirs of her years with Ford, and critical articles. None of her work, however, remains in print, and few libraries house her volumes in their collections. Many critics consider Belford's account of Hunt's career an important chronicle. *Washington Post Book World* contributor Ann Waldron refers to *Violet* as "an entirely appropriate book about Violet Hunt: lively, splendidly revealing the bizarre facts of Hunt's life." Moira Hodgson, writing in the *New York Times Book Review,* calls the book "a vivid and entertaining portrayal of a woman one would have liked to know. Ms. Belford makes her abundantly alive."

Belford's next biography was of another resident of late-nineteenth-century London, Bram Stoker. Athough he wrote eighteen books in all, Stoker would probably have remained an obscure figure if not for his classic vampire novel, *Dracula.* Belford's book examines the autobiographical elements in Stoker's novel, and each chapter starts with a quotation from the famous novel. Richard Jenkyns, a reviewer for *New Republic,* believes that Belford makes too much of the parallels between Stoker's life and his classic book. Yet he comments favorably on the portions of *Bram Stoker* that describe the novelist's work as the manager of the famous Lyceum Theatre in London. The theater was owned by Henry Irving, a "mesmeric and exploitative genius,"

according to *New York Times Book Reivew* contributor Margot Peters. Irving also served as one of the lead actors in the theater company.

"The story of Irving and the Lyceum has been told before, but Belford tells it well," advises Jenkyns. "Her descriptive passages show her at her best. She has an especially keen nose for smells: the aroma of polished brass and oiled wood in the lobby of the Shelbourne Hotel in Dublin and the fragrances of the local theater. . . . Perhaps she is imagining some of this, but it is well imagined." Peters also finds that the sections on life at the Lyceum are the high point of Belford's biography, stating that the book "succeeds chiefly in showcasing some of the most fascinating characters ever to gather on the same stage"—including Irving's leading lady, Ellen Terry; Walt Whitman; Albert Tennyson; Mark Twain; and George Bernard Shaw.

Karl Beckson, a reviewer for *Washington Post Book World,* takes the theme of the autobiographical elements in *Dracula* more seriously than did Jenkyns; yet he too found that the description of life at the Lyceum was the best part of an excellent book: "Belford's rich evocation of the London theatrical scene is engrossing and informative." Beckson further praises Belford's "skillful handling of the biographical material" involving Irving, Terry, and the other acting notables. Beckson concludes: "In Belford's highly readable account, Stoker achieves new life, as does his masterpiece."

Belford told *CA:* "Now that biography has become an appreciated art form, it is a wonderful time to write lives. I enjoy spending five or more years in an intensely personal relationship with a subject, trying to sift out truth from myth, fact from propaganda. I have chosen Victorian literary figures because they are a prism into what I feel is the most fascinating period—sexually, politically, culturally—in English literature. To create a living portrait in words is the difficult goal of the biographer. Or as Virginia Woolf put it, 'Yes—writing lives is the devil!'"

BIOGRAPHICAL/CRITICAL SOURCES:

PERIODICALS

Booklist, April 15, 1996, p. 1408.
Kirkus Reviews, March 1, 1996, p. 344.
Library Journal, May 1, 1996, p. 93.
Los Angeles Times Book Review, October 7, 1990, p. 10.

New Republic, August 5, 1996, pp. 39-40.
New York Review of Books, May 30, 1991, p. 28.
New York Times Book Review, October 21, 1990, p. 16; April 7, 1996, p. 20.
Publishers Weekly, August 3, 1990, p. 68; February 12, 1996, p. 64.
Times Literary Supplement, November 23, 1990, p. 1258.
Tribune Books (Chicago), April 14, 1996, p. 1.
Washington Post Book World, September 9, 1990, p. 5; April 21, 1996, pp. 4-5.

* * *

BELL, Marvin (Hartley) 1937-

PERSONAL: Born August 3, 1937, in New York, NY; son of Saul and Belle (Spector) Bell; married Mary Mammosser, 1958 (marriage ended); married Dorothy Murphy; children: Nathan Saul, Jason Aaron. *Education:* Alfred University, B.A., 1958; attended Syracuse University, 1958; University of Chicago, M.A., 1961; University of Iowa, M.F.A., 1963.

ADDRESSES: Home—1416 E. College St., Iowa City, IA 52245; fax: 319-337-5217; (May through August) P.O Box 1759, Port Townsend, WA 98368; fax: 360-385-7999. *Office*—Writers' Workshop, University of Iowa, Iowa City, Iowa 52242. *Email*—marvin-bell@uiowa.edu; fax.

CAREER: University of Iowa, Writers' Workshop, Iowa City, visiting lecturer, 1965, assistant professor, 1967-69, associate professor, 1969-75, professor of English, 1975—; University of Iowa, Flannery O'Connor Professor of Letters, 1986—. Visiting lecturer, Oregon State University, 1969, Goddard College, 1972, University of Hawaii, 1981, and University of Washington, 1982; University of the Redlands, Lila Wallace-*Reader's Digest* writing fellow, 1991-92, 1992-93; Woodrow Wilson visiting fellow, St. Mary's College of California, 1994-95, Nebraska-Wesleyan University, 1996-97, and Pacific University, 1996-97. Judge for various writing competitions. *Military service:* U.S. Army, 1964-65; first lieutenant.

AWARDS, HONORS: Lamont Award from the Academy of American Poets, 1969, for *A Probable Volume of Dreams;* Bess Hokin Award, *Poetry* (magazine), 1969; Emily Clark Balch Prize, *Virginia Quar-*

terly *Review,* 1970; Guggenheim fellowship, 1976; National Book Award finalist, 1977, for *Stars Which See, Stars Which Do Not See;* National Endowment for the Arts Fellowship, 1978, 1984; Prize, *American Poetry Review,* 1981; Senior Fulbright Scholar to Yugoslavia, 1983, to Australia, 1986; LH.D., Alfred University, 1986; Literature Award, American Academy of Arts and Letters, 1994.

WRITINGS:

POETRY

Poems for Nathan and Saul (pamphlet), Hillside Press (Vista, CA), 1966.
Things We Dreamt We Died For, Stone Wall Press (Washington, DC), 1966.
A Probable Volume of Dreams, Atheneum (New York City), 1969.
Woo Havoc (pamphlet), Barn Dream Press, 1971.
The Escape into You, Atheneum, 1971.
Residue of Song, Atheneum, 1974.
Stars Which See, Stars Which Do Not See, Atheneum, 1978.
These Green-Going-to-Yellow, Atheneum, 1981.
(With William Stafford) *Segues: A Correspondence in Poetry,* David Godine (Boston), 1983.
Drawn by Stones, by Earth, by Things that Have Been in the Fire, Atheneum, 1984.
New and Selected Poems, Atheneum, 1987.
Iris of Creation, Copper Canyon Press, 1990.
A Marvin Bell Reader: Selected Poetry and Prose, Middlebury College Press/University Press of New England, 1994.
The Book of the Dead Man, Copper Canyon Press (Port Townsend, WA), 1994.
Ardor: The Book of the Dead Man, Volume 2, Copper Canyon Press, 1997.
Poetry for a Midsummer's Night, Seventy Fourth Street Productions (Seattle), 1997.
Wednesday: Selected Poems, 1966-1997, Salmon Publishing (Ireland), 1998.

OTHER

Old Snow Just Melting: Essays and Interviews, University of Michigan Press (Ann Arbor), 1983.
(Author of introduction) Earl S. Braggs, *Hat Dancer Blue,* Anhinga (Tallahassee, FL), 1992.
(Author of preface) David H. Bain and Mary S. Duffy, editors, *Whose Woods These Are: A History of the Bread Loaf Writers' Conference, 1926-1990,* Ecco Press (New York City), 1993.

Also contributor of poems to various anthologies, including *Contemporary American Poets,* edited by Mark Strand, New American Library (New York City), 1969; *New Yorker Book of Poems,* Viking (New York City), 1969; *Major Young Poets,* edited by Al Lee, World Publishing, 1971; *New Voices in American Poetry,* edited by David Allan Evans, Winthrop Publishing, 1973; *Preferences,* edited by Richard Howard, Viking, 1974; *American Poetry Anthology,* edited by Daniel Halpern, Avon (New York City), 1975; *Fifty Poets,* edited by Alberta Turner, McKay (New York City), 1977; *Fifty Years of American Poetry,* Academy of American Poets, Abrams (New York City), 1984; *The Vintage Book of Contemporary American Poetry,* edited by J. D. McClatchy, Random House (New York City), 1990; *Poems for a Small Planet: Contemporary American Nature Poetry,* edited by Robert Pack and Jay Parini, Middlebury College Press/University Press of New England, 1993; *Voices on the Landscape,* edited by Michael Carey and Bob Neymeyer, Loess Hills Press, 1996; and *The Invisible Ladder,* edited by Liz Rosenberg, Holt (New York City), 1996.

Writer of column, "Homage to the Runner," for *American Poetry Review,* 1975-78, 1990-92. Editor and publisher, *Statements,* 1959-64; poetry editor, *North American Review,* 1964-69, and *Iowa Review,* 1969-71.

WORK IN PROGRESS: Sounds of the Resurrected Dead Man's Footsteps, for Sutton Hoo Press, 1998.

SIDELIGHTS: American poet and critic Marvin Bell "is a poet of the family. He writes of his father, his wives, his sons, and himself in a dynamic interaction of love and loss, accomplishment, and fear of alienation. These are subjects that demand maturity and constant evaluation. A complete reading of Bell's canon shows his ability to understand the durability of the human heart. Equally impressive is his accompanying technical sophistication," comments William M. Robins in the *Dictionary of Literary Biography.* The son of a Jew who immigrated from the Ukraine, Bell writes of distance and reconciliation between people, often touching on his complex relationship to his heritage.

For example, *A Probable Volume of Dreams* opens with a poem addressed to the poet's father, initiating a dialogue that continues throughout Bell's works. "Although Bell is never narrowly confessional, it is important to note just how much the death of the father—his profound absence and presence—helps

shape Bell's poetry and create possible worlds. *The father:* Bell's own dead father, and his growing sense of himself as a father who has sons and who, like him, will someday die," writes Arthur Oberg in *The American Poetry Review.* In addition to this motif, the poems "tell how unlinear life and art are, how 'progress' is a deception of the nineteenth century, how increasingly distant the finishing line for the poet-runner proves to be," Oberg observes. *A Probable Volume of Dreams* won the Lamont Award from the Academy of American Poets in 1969.

Concern with the self and its relationships in the earlier poetry has given way to reflections on the self in relation to nature in later books, such as *Stars Which See, Stars Which Do Not See.* Speaking of this development to Wayne Dodd and Stanley Plumly in an *Ohio Review* interview, Bell said that attention to nature has always been an integral part of his life. He grew up among farmers, so the rural life that so fascinated other writers during the 1960s back-to-nature movement was not Bell's inspiration. His first work came from his interest "in what language could make all by itself. . . . And I was interested in relationships between people. I wrote one whole book of poems-in-series about the relationships between a couple of people, or among several people. But now, for whatever good reasons, I *am* interested in allowing nature to have the place in my poems that it always had in my life," he said.

Bell also said the change in subject matter signalled a change in attitude—personal and cultural. "That is," he said, "contemporary American poetry has been tiresome in its discovery of the individual self, over and over and over, and its discovery of emotions that, indeed, we all have: loneliness, fear, despair, ennui, etcetera. I think it can get tiresome when the discovery of such emotions is more or less all the content there is to a poem. We know these things. . . . So I sort of write poetry nowadays from some other attitudes, I think, that came upon me without my ever really thinking about them. I think, for example, that it's ultimately pleasanter and healthier and better for everyone if one thinks of the self as being very small and very unimportant. . . . And I think, as I may not always have thought, that the only way out of the self is to concentrate on others and on things outside the self."

Bell sometimes refers to this development as an achievement of poetic modesty. He told Dodd and Plumly, "There is a kind of physical reality that we all share a sense of. I mean, we might argue about what reality is, but we all know how to walk across a bridge—instead of walking across the water, for instance. And it seems to me that one definition of modesty in poetry would be a refusal to compromise the physical facts of what it is that is showing up in one's poems," Bell explained.

Speaking of his personal aesthetic, he told the interviewers, "I would like to write poetry which finds salvation in the physical world and the here and now and which defines the soul, if you will, in terms of emotional depth, and that emotional depth in terms of the physical world and the world of human relationships." Regarding style, he added, "I'd like to write a poetry which has little if any insistence about it, as little as possible. I would like to write a poetry which doesn't seem either to button-hole the reader, or demand too much allegiance, or demand that too much of the world be given up for the special world of the poem."

Reviewers comment that Bell's later poems fulfill these aspirations. G. E. Murray, writing in the *Georgia Review,* declares, "I am impressed by this poet's increasing ability to perceive and praise small wonders. There is life and health in this book, and if sometimes Bell's expression is quiet and reserved, his talent is not. Altogether, *Stars Which See, Stars Which Do Not See* demonstrates an important transitional phase for the poet—a subdued, graceful vein that enables him to 'speak of eyes and seasons' with an intimacy and surehandedness that informs and gratifies. . . . I believe Marvin Bell is on a track of the future—a mature, accessible and personalized venture into the mainstream of contemporary American verse." Of the same book, David St. John writes in *Parnassus,* "Many poets have tried to appropriate into their poems a gritty, tough-talking American character, and to thereby earn for themselves some . . . 'authenticity'. . . . In *Stars Which See, Stars Which Do Not See,* Bell has found within his *own* voice that American voice, and with it the ability to write convincingly about the smallest details of a personal history."

Bell's subsequent works have elicited from critics an appreciation of the poet's blending of precise descriptive powers with deceptively simple grammar and syntax. In reviewing *These Green-Going-to-Yellow,* Richard Jackson comments in the *American Book Review* that Bell's strategy of deploying words and phrases in unusual contexts has resulted in "an increasingly expansive and colloquial language that is willing to gather in larger fragments of the world

without the 'new critical' necessity of neatly tying each bit together on the surface of the text." The poet's linguistic maturity is similarly singled out in discussions of the 1987 anthology *New and Selected Poems.* For several critics, the less private and self-referential later poetry contained in this volume has made Bell one of the most arresting of contemporary writers. A *Poetry* reviewer noted that Bell "is a discreet master of withheld information. His writing has a distinctive enough flavor to make us feel we know him well after turning the last page of this book; but . . . [o]f the events and circumstances of his life the poems say very little directly." And a contributor for *American Poetry Review* comments: "It is Bell's later poetry, far less private and solipsistic, and far more abundantly intelligent and astonishing [than his earlier poetry,] that has made him one of the best poets now working."

In 1994 Bell published what many reviewers regard as his most radical work, *The Book of the Dead Man,* which consists of a sequence of thirty-three poems on various facets of life that are narrated by the anonymous title character. Stan Sanvel Rubin asserts in *Prairie Schooner* that Bell has fashioned in this work "a dazzling linguistic Chinese box, at once alluring and elusive, which shows up for once and for all (maybe) the emptiness of 'Language Poetry' and, in fact, much recent experimental and postmodern writing." Meanwhile, Bruce Murphy, writing in *Poetry,* notes that "Bell is really out there—trying to invent a new kind of poetry, something like an epic with only one character."

Bell's volume of essays, *Old Snow Just Melting: Essays and Interviews,* is judged by critics as concerned with themes typical of the author's poetic works, particularly mutability and decay. *Virginia Quarterly Review* contributor Thomas Swiss commends Bell's prose, averring that Bell "writes with style: clean, metaphoric prose that's readable and instructive. He writes simply without condescending and without ignoring the complexity of the issues he examines." The volume also presents valuable insights into the author's poetic process. Bell writes, as quoted by Swiss, "I'll tell you right now the secrets of writing poetry. . . . First, one learns to write by reading. . . . Number two, I believe that language, compared to the materials of other art forms, has only one thing going for it: the ability to be precise. . . . And the third and most important secret is that, if you do anything seriously for a long time, you get better at it."

BIOGRAPHICAL/CRITICAL SOURCES:

BOOKS

Contemporary Literary Criticism, Gale (Detroit), Volume 8, 1978, Volume 31, 1985.
Dictionary of Literary Biography, Volume 5: *American Poets since World War II,* Gale, 1980.
Malkoff, Karl, *Crowell's Handbook of Contemporary American Poetry,* Crowell (New York City), 1973.

PERIODICALS

American Book Review, September, 1982, p. 20.
American Poetry Review, May-June, 1976; September, 1985; January-February, 1989.
Antaeus, spring/summer, 1982.
Antioch Review, spring, 1982; spring, 1995.
Booklist, March 15, 1994, p. 1322.
Chicago Review, Volume 28, number 1, 1976.
Georgia Review, fall, 1982, pp. 675-79.
Hudson Review, August, 1985.
Iowa Review, winter, 1981.
Missouri Review, summer, 1982.
Nation, February 2, 1970.
New Republic, March 29, 1975.
New York Times Book Review, April 8, 1984; November 11, 1984.
North American Review, January/February, 1995.
Ohio Review, Volume 17, number 3, 1976.
Parnassus, fall/winter, 1972.
Poetry, March, 1985, p. 349; April, 1988, pp 35-7; August, 1991, pp. 280-95; December, 1995, pp. 159-61.
Prairie Schooner, spring, 1996, pp. 181-84.
Shenandoah, summer, 1971.
Stand, Volume 13, number 4, 1972.
Virginia Quarterly Review, summer, 1982, p. 94; winter, 1986, pp. 173-85; spring, 1988, p. 62.

*   *   *

BENTLEY, Phyllis Eleanor 1894-1977

PERSONAL: Born November 19, 1894, in Halifax, England; died June 27, 1977, in Halifax, England; daughter of Joseph Edwin (a textile manufacturer) and Eleanor (Kettlewell) Bentley. *Education:* Attended Cheltenham Ladies' College; University of London, B.A., 1914.

CAREER: Teacher; government secretary during World War I and World War II; library cataloger; freelance writer. Council and committee member, Royal Literary Fund. Lecturer.

MEMBER: PEN (vice-president of English centre), Authors Society, Royal Society of Literature (fellow), Halifax Thespians, Halifax Authors' Circle (president), Halifax Antiquarian Society (vice-president), English-Speaking Union Club.

AWARDS, HONORS: D.Litt., University of Leeds, 1949; Officer, Order of the British Empire, 1970.

WRITINGS:

The World's Bane and Other Stories, Unwin (London), 1918.
Pedagomania; Or, the Gentle Art of Teaching, Unwin, 1918.
Environment (novel), Sidgwick & Jackson (London), 1922, Hillman-Curl (New York City), 1935.
Cat-in-the-Manger (novel), Sidgwick & Jackson, 1923.
The Spinner of the Years (novel), Benn (London), 1928, Rae D. Henkle, 1929.
The Partnership (novel), Benn, 1928, Little, Brown (Boston), 1929, reprinted, Chivers, 1977.
Carr: The Biography of Philip Joseph Carr, Benn, 1929, Macmillan (New York City), 1933.
Trio, Gollancz, 1930, reprinted, Chivers, 1976.
Inheritance (novel), Macmillan, 1932, reprinted, Pan Books, 1967.
A Modern Tragedy (novel), Macmillan, 1934.
The Whole of the Short (short story collection), Gollancz, 1935.
Freedom, Farewell (novel), Macmillan, 1936, reprinted, Gollancz, 1968.
Sleep in Peace (novel), Macmillan, 1938.
The Power and the Glory (novel), Macmillan, 1940 (published in England as *Take Courage,* Gollancz, 1940).
Manhold, Macmillan, 1941.
Here Is America (nonfiction), Gollancz, 1941.
The English Regional Novel (nonfiction), Allen & Unwin, 1941, reprinted, Arden, 1978.
The Rise of Henry Morcar (novel), Macmillan, 1946, reprinted, Gollancz, 1967.
Some Observations on the Art of Narrative (nonfiction), Home & Van Thal, 1946, Macmillan, 1947, reprinted, Arden, 1978.
Colne Valley Cloth from the Earliest Times to the Present Day (nonfiction), Huddersfield and District Woollen Export Group, 1947.

The Brontes (nonfiction), Home & Van Thal, 1947, A. Swallow, 1948, new edition, Pan Books, 1973.

Life Story (novel), Macmillan, 1948.

Quorum, Gollancz, 1950, Macmillan, 1951, reprinted, Chivers, 1972.

Panorama: Tales of the West Riding, Gollancz, 1952, reprinted, Chivers, 1974.

The House of Moreys (novel), Macmillan, 1953, reprinted, Ace Books (New York City), 1976.

Noble in Reason, Macmillan, 1955.

Love and Money: Seven Tales of the West Riding, Macmillan, 1957.

Crescendo (novel), Macmillan, 1958.

The New Apprentice (play), Samuel French (New York City), 1959.

Kith and Kin: Nine Tales of Family Life, Macmillan, 1960, reprinted, Chivers, 1977.

The Young Brontes (nonfiction), Roy, 1961.

O Dreams, O Destinations (autobiography), Macmillan, 1962.

Committees (nonfiction), Collins, 1962.

Public Speaking (nonfiction), Collins, 1964.

Enjoy Books: Reading and Collecting (nonfiction), Gollancz, 1964.

The Adventures of Tom Leigh (juvenile), Macdonald, 1964, Doubleday, 1966.

Tales of the West Riding, Gollancz, 1965.

A Man of His Time (novel), Macmillan, 1966.

Ned Carver in Danger (juvenile), Macdonald, 1967.

Oath of Silence, Doubleday, 1967.

Forgery (juvenile), Doubleday, 1968 (published in England as *Gold Pieces,* Macdonald, 1968).

Ring in the New, Gollancz, 1969.

The Brontes and Their World, Viking, 1969.

Sheep May Safely Graze (juvenile), Gollancz, 1972.

The New Venturers (juvenile), Gollancz, 1973.

More Tales of the West Riding, Gollancz, 1974.

(With John Ogden) *Haworth of the Brontes,* Dalton, 1977.

Also author of television plays for children and of various pamphlets for the Bronte Society and the British Council. Contributor of articles and short stories to magazines.

SIDELIGHTS: Phyllis Bentley, a prominent English regional novelist, devoted her career to writing almost exclusively about the West Riding country of Yorkshire, her lifelong home. In particular, her books focused on the rise and fall of the local weaving industry; both her father and grandfather were textile manufacturers. Within the confines of this strict regionalism, Bentley's literary specialty was the chronicle, a form which allowed her to trace the flow of historical events through several generations of one or more families. "Bentley was proud to call herself a regional novelist," Angela Bull wrote in *Twentieth-Century Romance and Historical Writers.* "Her region was the old West Riding of Yorkshire. Its landscape of rocky hillsides, heathery moors, tumbling streams, and bustling towns provides a constant backdrop to her stories; her characters—strong-willed, stubborn, passionate, and uncompromising—are seen as the natural products of their setting." Bentley also wrote several studies of Charlotte and Emily Bronte, nineteenth-century British novelists who were also from the Yorkshire countryside.

Bentley regarded her trilogy—*Inheritance, The Rise of Henry Morcar,* and *A Man of His Time*—as her most significant accomplishment. Although the first novel in the series (*Inheritance*) was very well-received, the sequels did not meet with as much success. Commenting on *Inheritance,* a *Christian Science Monitor* critic wrote: "The bleak, brusque and raw Yorkshire scene of industrial town and moorland is a fine setting for such an iron drama of the generations. Provincial as the book is, peculiar to their soil as the characters are, these conflicts go to the roots of a sizable part of human nature, and Miss Bentley presents them with a humanity and a realism not often found. . . . [The book] is generous, powerful, clear-headed without illusions, and most skillfully controlled." A *New Statesman* reviewer felt that "*Inheritance* is written with great intelligence and dramatic power. It cannot be said that [Bentley] breaks new ground, or that she illuminates life for us at unexpected points; but this is perhaps more than one has a right to demand of a novelist who has the courage to be obvious, and the gift of holding one's attention, not only by her narrative skill, but by her own honest absorption in the lives of her dramatis personae."

Some critics, while they enjoyed the book, felt that it tended to "unravel" toward the end. "Miss Bentley's earlier chapters are richer and more realistic than those which bring the recital across the threshold of the twentieth century," observed a *Books* reviewer, "and there is an inevitable loosening of the dramatic fabric. . . . In the scenes of a hundred years ago the author is notably at home. . . . [Nevertheless,] the book has an eloquence which escapes classification." A *New Republic* critic wrote: "If for no other reason, Phyllis Bentley ought to be commended for having gotten new blood out of that terrible old turnip, the English family chronicle. . . . But what is extraordinary about *Inheritance* is the way the story suddenly collapses in the last few chapters, those covering the developments after the War. It is a real collapse. . . . The result is a forced, uncongenial ending tacked on to a work which otherwise has dignity and power."

Bentley's problems with the depiction of more-or-less current events surfaced again in reviewers' comments on *The Rise of Henry Morcar,* the second novel of the trilogy. For example, a *New York Times* critic observed that "Miss Bentley is at her best in the early scenes. . . . Here is a solidity of engrossing detail. . . . [But] the episodes of the recent war . . . have not been assimilated so well. As a lover, Henry Morcar is stilted; as a patriot, he sounds as if his sentiments had been strained through the British Ministry of Information." A *Times Literary Supplement* reviewer also noticed "a rather sudden change of emphasis" (from an examination of Morcar's private life to a more general view of the war years in England) in the second half of the novel, but he feels that the shift "is inherent in the twofold purpose of the story."

Depicting contemporary characters apparently was still a problem for Bentley in the last volume of the trilogy as well, at least according to a *Times Literary Supplement* reviewer. "In this volume Dr. Bentley seems less sure of her characters than in earlier ones. Morcar himself is real enough but the younger generation seems somewhat conceptual, consistent in theory but in practice speaking with no contemporary voice. The background, however, . . . is intimately observed and lovingly described, and the sometimes pedestrian narrative and occasionally sentimental characterization are compensated for by the fact that the problems dealt with are real ones." A *Library Journal* critic agreed with this latter point, but not with the charge that her characters were "sentimental" and lacked a contemporary flavor. "Dr. Bentley's awareness of our time and its difficulties is impressive; her characters compel belief and sympathy. Realistic but never pessimistic, [*A Man of His Time*] should appeal especially to readers tired of sensationalism, absurdity, and futility."

In addition to her fiction, Bentley also wrote several books about the Bronte sisters, nineteenth-century British novelists best known for such titles as *Jane Eyre* and *Wuthering Heights.* The Brontes were from Bentley's own Yorkshire and so, as Abbott Martin wrote in *New York Times,* Bentley was "exceptionally well qualified" to write about them as "she understands the world of the Brontes."

In her study *The Brontes* Bentley provided a narrative of the sisters' lives, a description of their major works and an evaluation of their standing in British literature. B. R. Redman in *Saturday Review of Literature* found *The Brontes* to be "an entirely worthy telling of a tale which must always fascinate and move those who read it." Eric Forbes-Boyd in *Christian Science Monitor* praised Bentley's "ability and discernment."

In *The Brontes and Their World* Bentley examines the two authors in the context of the historical period in which they lived. She sees their novels as expressions of the conflict between the rural lifestyle of the sisters' childhood and the rising Industrial Revolution of their mature years. The critic for *Christian Science Monitor* called *The Brontes and Their World* "a highly readable account" and "an excellent work."

Bentley wrote a third account of the Brontes' lives in *The Young Brontes,* a book for younger readers which focuses on the childhood of the famous sisters. Since the Brontes began writing stories at a remarkably early age, Bentley's look at their formative years was of real value, according to Philippa Pearce in *New Statesman.* "So much of the Brontes' childhood is directly relevant to their adult literary work," Pearce noted, adding that "Bentley is the right person to write such a book." The critic for *Saturday Review* called it "a fascinating study," while the *Times Literary Supplement* critic belived that "Bentley can be trusted . . . to give us *The Young Brontes* in true character."

BIOGRAPHICAL/CRITICAL SOURCES:

BOOKS

Bentley, Phyllis, *O Dreams, O Destinations* (autobiography), Macmillan, 1962.
Twentieth-Century Romance and Historical Writers, third edition, St. James Press (Detroit), 1994.

PERIODICALS

Books, September 18, 1932; July 2, 1933, p. 4.
Book World, May 5, 1968.
Christian Science Monitor, April 16, 1932; October 4, 1947, p. 11; November 28, 1969, p. B5.
Commonweal, December 28, 1932; October 6, 1933, p. 18.

Forum, October, 1933, p. 90.
Library Journal, October 1, 1966.
Listener, November 14, 1968.
Nation, August 23, 1933, p. 137.
New Republic, October 26, 1932.
New Statesman, April 16, 1932; November 19, 1960, p. 60; April 13, 1962, p.63; November, 1968.
New Statesman and Nation, October 18, 1947, p. 34.
New Yorker, December 28, 1946.
New York Herald Tribune Books, May 13, 1962, p. 10.
New York Times, September 18, 1932; December 15, 1946; January 9, 1949, p.24.
Saturday Review, April 2, 1932; May 12, 1962, p. 45.
Saturday Review of Literature, January 29, 1949, p. 32.
Spectator, April 2, 1932; November 28, 1947, p. 179.
Springfield Republican, July 16, 1933, p. 7E.
Times Literary Supplement, April 7, 1932; May 25, 1946; November 25, 1960, p. xxvi; April 13, 1962, p. 247; March 10, 1966; May 25, 1967.
Weekly Book Review, December 22, 1946.
Young Readers' Review, May, 1966.*

* * *

BERNE, Leo
  See DAVIES, L(eslie) P(urnell)

* * *

BEVAN, Gloria (Isabel) 1911-
  (Fiona Murray)

PERSONAL: Born July 20, 1911, in Kalgoorlie, Western Australia; married Thomas Henry Bevan, 1937 (deceased); children: three daughters.

ADDRESSES: Home—1 Hoberia Rd., Onehunga, Auckland, New Zealand.

CAREER: Writer. Watkin & Wallis, Auckland, New Zealand, typist, 1926-36.

WRITINGS:

ROMANCE AND GOTHIC NOVELS

The Distant Trap, Mills & Boon (London), 1969, Harlequin (Toronto), 1970.
The Hills of Maketu, Harlequin, 1969.
Beyond the Ranges, Mills & Boon, 1970, Harlequin, 1971.
Make Way for Tomorrow, Harlequin, 1971.
It Began in Te Rangi, Mills & Boon, 1971, Harlequin, 1972.
Vineyard in a Valley, Harlequin, 1972.
Flame in Fiji, Harlequin, 1973.
The Frost and the Fire, Harlequin, 1973.
Connelly's Castle, Harlequin, 1974.
High-Country Wife, Mills & Boon, 1974, Harlequin, 1975.
Always a Rainbow, Harlequin, 1975.
Dolphin Bay, Harlequin, 1976.
Bachelor Territory, Harlequin, 1977.
Plantation Moon, Mills & Boon, 1977, J. Curley, 1983.
Fringe of Heaven, Harlequin, 1978, J. Curley, 1984.
Kowhai Country, Mills & Boon, 1979.
Half a World Away, Mills & Boon, 1980, Harlequin, 1981.
Master of Mahia, Harlequin, 1981.
Emerald Cave, Mills & Boon, 1981, Harlequin, 1982.
Greek Island Magic, Mills & Boon, 1983.
The Rouseabout Girl, Harlequin, 1983.
Southern Sunshine, Mills & Boon, 1985.
Golden Bay, Mills & Boon, 1987, Harlequin, 1991.
Pacific Paradise, Mills & Boon, 1989.
Summer's Vintage, Mills & Boon, 1992.

UNDER PSEUDONYM FIONA MURRAY

Invitation to Danger, R. Hale (London), 1965.
Gold Coast Affair, Horowitz (Sydney, Australia), 1967.
A Nice Day for Murder, R. Hale, 1971.

SIDELIGHTS: Gloria Bevan began her career as a mystery writer but quickly changed to romance novels. Bevan explains in *Twentieth-Century Romance and Historical Writers* that she has been "fascinated with [the romance genre] ever since."

Writing in *Twentieth-Century Romance and Historical Writers,* P. Campbell notes that Bevan's novels are marked by the author's careful attention to both realistic characters and vivid locations. Bevan, writes

Campbell, "pays considerable detail to creating credible and interesting characters. The exotic settings of her books also help to attract readers—and her characters may find themselves falling in love in Australia, Fiji, or the author's native New Zealand."

Bevan's characters are ordinary people who live in real places which are meticulously described. "Bevan's heroes and heroines," writes Campbell, "are the sort of people the reader might encounter in everyday life." The settings reflect Bevan's love for her native land. "Bevan is obviously proud of New Zealand and most of her books reflect this love, whether it be through descriptions of the landscape or in her attention to the most minute detail of clothing or custom," writes Campbell.

The plots of Bevan's romance novels follow a traditional formula in which a misunderstanding or secret spurs the action, with a resolution in which the leading characters find love. In *Summer's Vintage,* for example, Sarah inherits a vineyard but when she arrives to reluctantly claim her property, she is mistaken for a new laborer, a mistake she goes along with until she discovers how much running the estate means to the man she loves. "Luckily—as in the way in old good formula romances—everything is resolved in the end," Campbell notes.

BIOGRAPHICAL/CRITICAL SOURCES:

BOOKS

Twentieth-Century Romance and Historical Writers, third edition, St. James Press (Detroit, MI), 1994.

*   *   *

BISSON, Terry (Ballantine) 1942-

PERSONAL: Born February 12, 1942, in Hopkins County, KY; son of Max and Martha (Ballantine) Bisson; married Deirdre Holst, 1962 (divorced 1966); married Judy Jensen; children: (first marriage) Kristen, Gabriel, Welcome; (second marriage) Nathaniel, Peter, Zoe. *Education:* Attended Grinnell College, 1960-62; University of Louisville, B.A., 1964.

ADDRESSES: Home—Box 416, Van Brunt Station, Brooklyn, NY 11215. *Agent*—Susan Ann Protter, 110 West 40th St., New York, NY 10018.

CAREER: Writer. Magazine comic writer, 1964-72; automotive mechanic, 1972-77; editor and copywriter with Berkley Books, New York, NY, and Avon Books, New York, NY, 1976-85; consultant to HarperCollins, 1994-95.

MEMBER: Science Fiction Writers of America, Authors Guild.

AWARDS, HONORS: World Fantasy Award nomination, 1987, for *Talking Man;* Nebula Award, Science Fiction Writers of America, Hugo Award, World Science Fiction Convention, and Theodore Sturgeon Award, all 1991, all for story "Bears Discover Fire; " Phoenix Award, 1993.

WRITINGS:

SCIENCE FICTION

Wyrldmaker (novel), Pocket Books (New York City), 1980.
Talking Man (novel), Arbor House (New York City), 1986.
Fire on the Mountain (novel), Arbor House, 1988.
Voyage to the Red Planet (novel), Morrow (New York City), 1990.
Bears Discover Fire and Other Stories, Tor Books (New York City), 1993.
Johnny Mnemonic: A Novel (novelization of screenplay by William Gibson), Pocket Books (New York City), 1995.
Pirates of the Universe (novel), Tor Books, 1996.

OTHER

Nat Turner (biography for young adults), Chelsea House (New York City), 1987.
(With Tom and Ray Magliozzi) *Car Talk with Click and Clack, the Tappet Brothers,* Dell (New York City), 1991.
(With Elizabeth Ballantine Johnson) *A Green River Girlhood,* Green River (Owensboro, KY), 1991.

Contributor to *Washington Post, Omni, Playboy, Magazine of Fantasy and Science Fiction* and *Harper's.*

ADAPTATIONS: The stories "Two Guys from the Future," "They're Made Out of Meat," "Next," "Are There Any Questions?," "Partial People," and "The Toxic Donut," were all adapted for the stage and produced at the West Bank Theatre, New York, 1992-93.

SIDELIGHTS: Terry Bisson has written science fiction novels and short stories marked by what Paul Kincaid in the *St. James Guide to Science Fiction Writers* calls "the importance of home and the sense of nostalgia." This sense of nostalgia, which Kincaid believes "places Bisson firmly in the tradition of Southern writers," is expressed in an often humorous manner. Bisson's fiction, Kincaid explains, "like the stories of Howard Waldrop or the cartoons of Gary Larson, is as much ironic commentary on the genre as it is a fresh work of science fiction." Bisson's short stories have won particular praise. As a *Publishers Weekly* critic puts it, Bisson "is one of science fiction's most promising short story practitioners."

Bisson's novel *Talking Man* follows a rural eccentric nicknamed the Talking Man, though he never speaks, on a cross-country journey. As the trip unfolds, the Talking Man finds that the nation is changing drastically the farther he travels. By the time he returns home to rural Kentucky, society has undergone a radical alteration into a near-utopia. Jesus Salvador Trevino in the *Los Angeles Times Book Review* calls *The Talking Man* "an action-filled romp through a surreal landscape of ever-changing America." According to Trevino, the theme of the novel is an exploration of the question "If someone is changing our reality from moment to moment, how do we know it?"

Fire on the Mountain explores another kind of American utopia. The novel posits an alternate history in which John Brown's raid on Harper's Ferry in 1859 was successful, leading to a national slave revolt and the establishment of an independent black country in the Southern United States. A *Publishers Weekly* critic claims that the novel displays Bisson's "talent for evoking the joyful, vertiginous experiences of a world at fundamental turning points." John Clute in the *Washington Post Book World* explains that *Fire on the Mountain* creates "an America magically cleansed and calm and rich; the remoteness of that world from ours only increases the pathos of the fable. But within its exceedingly frail pages, the dream obtains. Within its pages, we can be joyous, for a space."

In *Voyage to the Red Planet* Bisson turns to satire, creating a future world where, following a great depression, government services have been sold to private corporations. In this privatized society, a movie producer named Markson leaves for Mars to make a film. During the long voyage, the corporation running mission control back on Earth has cash flow problems. They must focus their efforts on more lucrative activities. According to Gerald Jones in the *New York Times Book Review,* the film crew knows "something is wrong when their requests for course corrections are routed to an answering machine and [they are called] back collect." Kincaid calls *Voyage to the Red Planet* "a comedy of ramshackled adventure, and there are the predictable disasters and problems along the way, most of them casting a satirical light on the Earth left behind." Jonas believes that Bisson shows a "genuine affection for his characters" and has an "ability to remind us of the excitement and wonder of space travel even while poking fun at the conventions of space fiction."

Bisson creates another satirical future in *Pirates of the Universe.* In this society, Space Ranger Gunther Ryder is close to winning his coveted place in the retirement theme park Pirates of the Universe. But when he returns from his latest mission, Gunther "finds himself entangled in a Kafkaesque conundrum," as the critic for *Publishers Weekly* explains. Unable to e-mail anyone or use computer systems because of a bureaucratic snafu, Gunther is thus also unable to contact the proper bureaucracy to fix the problem. "It is all very funny," Gregory Feeley writes in the *Washington Post Book World.* The critic for the *New York Times Book Review* admires Bisson's "knack for capturing a reality that is never as simple as we would like to believe."

After publishing several novels, Bisson only turned to writing short stories in 1990. Since that time he has enjoyed acclaim from critics who count him among the science fiction genre's best short-story writers. In 1991, Bisson won a Hugo Award, Nebula Award, and Theodore Sturgeon Award for "Bears Discover Fire," a short story that manages to combine the nonsensical with the ordinary to good effect. Martha Soukup in the *Washington Post Book World* calls the story "a gentle, wise tale of a man whose mother is dying, whose nephew wants to learn how to mount tires, and of bears who discover fire and now sit around campfires instead of hibernating." The collection *Bears Discover Fire and Other Stories* displays what the *Publishers Weekly* critic calls Bisson's "seemingly effortless control and precision." Soukup believes that the stories "that will stay with the reader are Bisson's homier tales. . . . There's a warmth in them, and a respect for ordinary folk. . . . There is also a sharpness and wit that is quite Bisson's own."

BIOGRAPHICAL/CRITICAL SOURCES:

BOOKS

St. James Guide to Fantasy Writers, St. James Press (Detroit), 1996.
St. James Guide to Science Fiction Writers, 4th edition, St. James Press, 1996.

PERIODICALS

Analog, December 15, 1988, p. 179; December 15, 1990, p. 181.
Atlanta Journal and Constitution, July 29, 1990, p. N8.
Locus, April, 1990, p. 35; February, 1994, p. 39.
Los Angeles Times Book Review, November 9, 1986; August 8, 1990, p. E8.
Magazine of Fantasy and Science Fiction, April, 1989, p. 38; February, 1994, p. 39.
New York Times Book Review, November 13, 1988, p. 26; September 2, 1990, p. 18; May 12, 1996, p. 27.
Publishers Weekly, June 3, 1988, p. 73; November 1, 1993, p. 70; March 25, 1996, p. 67.
School Library Journal, February, 1989, p. 104.
Science Fiction Chronicle, June, 1988, p. 50.
Washington Post Book World, November 27, 1988, p. 8; November 28, 1993, p. 8; March 31, 1996, p. 8.

*   *   *

BLACK, Mansell
  See TREVOR, Elleston

*   *   *

BLAKE, Robert
  See DAVIES, L(eslie) P(urnell)

*   *   *

BLOOM, Claire   1931-

PERSONAL: Born February 15, 1931, in London, England; daughter of Edward Max and Elizabeth (Grew) Bloom; married Rod Steiger (an actor), Sep-

tember 19, 1959 (divorced, 1969); married Philip Roth (a writer), April 29, 1990 (divorced March, 1993); children (first marriage): Anna-Justine. *Education:* Attended public and private schools in England and the United States; studied acting with Eileen Thorndike, 1946-48.

ADDRESSES: Agent—Marion Rosenberg Agency, 8428 Melrose Place West, Hollywood, CA 90060-5308.

CAREER: Actress, 1946—. Repertory actress associated with Oxford Repertory Theatre, 1946, and the Stratford-on-Avon Memorial Theatre, 1948. Actress in stage productions, including *The Lady's Not for Burning,* 1949, *Ring Round the Moon,* 1950, *Romeo and Juliet,* 1952, *King Lear,* 1955, *The Trojan Women,* 1963, *A Doll's House,* 1971 and 1973, *Hedda Gabler,* 1971, *Vivat! Vivat Regina!,* 1972, *A Streetcar Named Desire,* 1974, *The Innocents,* 1976, *Rosmersholm,* 1977, and in one-woman shows featuring the works of Shakespeare and others. Actress in films, including *The Blind Goddess,* 1948, *Limelight,* 1952, *The Man Between,* 1953, *Richard III,* 1956, *The Brothers Karamazov,* 1956, *Look Back in Anger,* 1959, *The Outrage,* 1964, *The Spy Who Came in From the Cold,* 1965, *Charly,* 1968, *Three into Two Won't Go,* 1969, *A Doll's House,* 1973, *Islands in the Stream,* 1977, *The Cherry Orchard,* 1981, *These Are Women,* 1982, *When We Dead Awaken,* 1990, *Daughters, Wives and Mothers,* 1991, *Silenced Voices,* 1992, *Women in Love,* 1993, *The Cherry Orchard,* 1994, and *Long Days Journey into Night,* 1996. Actress in television productions in England and the United States, including *Brideshead Revisited,* 1982, *Henry VIII,* 1979, *Cymebeline,* 1983, *The Mirror Crack'd,* 1992, *Village Affairs,* 1994, and *Family Money,* 1996. Appeared at the Old Vic Theatre, London, in various Shakespearean roles, 1952-54; toured with the Old Vic Theatre Co., in *Romeo and Juliet,* throughout the United States and Canada, 1956-57.

AWARDS, HONORS: Plays and Players Award, best actress awards from the *Evening Standard* (London) and the Variety Club, all 1974, for performance as Blanche du Bois in *A Streetcar Named Desire;* British Film and TV Award, 1984; fellow of Guildhall School of Music.

WRITINGS:

Limelight and After: The Education of an Actress (autobiography), Harper (New York), 1982.

Leaving a Doll's House: A Memoir, Little, Brown (Boston), 1996.

SIDELIGHTS: Claire Bloom has been called one of the most beautiful, sensitive actresses of the twentieth century. At a very young age, she won fame for her interpretation of the great Shakespearean roles for women. Over the years, she proved her range and her staying power by performing with equal success on stage, in films, and for television, in productions that ranged from the classics to popular entertainment. Bloom has also written two volumes of memoirs. The first, *Limelight and After: The Education of an Actress,* was started after a play in which she had a leading role closed prematurely in Boston. Bloom retreated to take a hiatus in Connecticut, where she then shared a house with noted novelist Philip Roth. As she told Roderick Mann of the *Los Angeles Times:* "After a while I became restless and started putting down odd memories on paper. I showed them to a friend I live with, a writer, and he encouraged me to continue." In fact, Bloom credited Roth with helping her throughout the writing of her autobiography, *Limelight and After.* "As a result," she volunteered to Mann, "when I submitted the book to Harper & Row, there didn't have to be many changes. Philip had been my editor."

Bloom spent three years on the manuscript. "I wanted to see what it had all been about and write it down and see how much I remembered really," she explained to *Chicago Tribune* reporter Connie Lauerman. "I thought my childhood and young years in the theater were interesting and what happened to me. . . between 17 and 22 was really quite unique." And so it was to her early life and to the two roles that elevated her to international recognition that Bloom devoted most of her book.

By naming her autobiography *Limelight and After* Bloom acknowledged the importance of the 1952 film *Limelight* to her career. How she came to star in the film is primary among the events the actress felt distinguished her youth. She was just beginning to achieve some renown as a stage actress in England when American playwright Arthur Laurents told her that he had suggested her for the lead in Charlie Chaplin's new Hollywood film. "If he had told me Shakespeare was interested in me, I would have found it equally believable," Bloom recollected. "I did nothing. I forgot the whole thing, so overwhelmed by the idea that I put it out of my mind." Nevertheless, when Chaplin heard nothing from Bloom, the silent screen great followed up on

Laurents's suggestion himself, cabling Bloom to send photographs for consideration. The pictures led to a screen test in New York and a summons to Hollywood followed a few months later.

In her memoirs Bloom recounts in detail the making of the film and the development of her close relationship with Chaplin. Because her father, who had failed to provide security for his wife and children throughout Bloom's childhood, left the family to seek his fortune in South Africa, Bloom began acting professionally at age fifteen to help support her mother and younger brother. After she started working with Chaplin, she recalled, "Without regret I abandoned what little loyalty I had left for the natural father who disappointed me, and adopted, on the spot, the father I felt I'd had every right to expect: a father brilliant, worldly, charming, handsome, rich, and strong." Moreover, Lauerman pointed out, "It was Charlie Chaplin who brought her international fame."

Bloom returned to London before the release of *Limelight.* There, without even auditioning, she won the role of Juliet in the Old Vic Theatre's production of *Romeo and Juliet.* It was a role she had coveted since childhood. Likening her attainment of the part to the way she was swept into *Limelight,* Bloom commented, "The irony has always been that however hard I have pursued my career, then or now, the roles meaning most to me have seemingly fallen from nowhere." The night the play opened the audience applauded through fourteen curtain calls. A month later *Limelight* premiered and the cover of *Time* magazine featured a picture of Bloom over the caption, "A star is born."

Bloom recognized this double achievement as a watershed: "After twenty-two, my private and my professional life began to conform somewhat more to the norm: Trial and error, success and failure, obstruction and breakthrough, and then again obstruction." So, in the final section of her book Bloom only briefly chronicled the professional experiences she regards as pivotal, offered glimpses of fellow performers she esteems, and commented generally on acting techniques. She also noted the special difficulties female performers face, such as the need to balance career and motherhood or the paucity of roles available for mature actresses.

"These are not your average actress' memoirs—littered with show-business anecdotes and the names of bed partners," judged interviewer Roderick Mann. "I knew the kind of book I wanted to write," Bloom told him, "and I wrote it. After all, who you have or have not been to bed with is not the most revealing aspect of your life. And it's simply not my nature to discuss that sort of thing."

Fourteen years later, Bloom reconsidered these words to an extent with the second volume of her memoirs, *Leaving a Doll's House: A Memoir.* In this autobiography, she wrote extensively about her romantic relationships, including liasions with actors Richard Burton, Yul Brynner, and Anthony Quinn. She called her adulterous affair with Burton the greatest love of her life, but after many years, they went their separate ways. She married actor Rod Steiger, of whom she spoke well in her book, but eventually left him for Hillard Elkins, a theatrical producer who also served as her manager for a time. When Elkins deserted Bloom for another woman, she experienced crises in both her personal and professional life. It was at this juncture that she met Philip Roth in Manhattan. The course of their relationship forms a large amount of *Leaving a Doll's House.* They cohabitated for some fifteen years before she asked him to marry her; their legal union lasted only three years before Roth threw Bloom out of their shared home. By the terms of a prenuptial agreement he had insisted upon, he was able to divorce her without leaving her anything, and in fact, he presented her with a bill for billions of dollars owed for wrongs he felt she had committed over the years. In *Leaving a Doll's House,* she paints Roth as a brilliant, cruel, controlling man whom she loved too much for her own good.

Reviewers differed widely in their opinions of Bloom's second book. Assessing it in the *New Yorker,* Daphne Merkin found it difficult to become emotionally involved with the story told in its pages. She termed the quality of the prose "lacklustre" and the emotions described as "almost canned." She further stated, "The real problem with Bloom's book is that it asks readers to do more than feel sympathy and outrage on behalf of its put-upon heroine: beginning with the portentous title, it asks us to take her plight as paradigmatic of something larger than her own misbegotten amorous choices. She presents her book as a classic drama of captivity and release. . . . Indeed, this glamorous and determined and resourceful woman . . . wants to play another emotionally battered wife with a horrific tale to tell. She is badly miscast." *New York Times Book Review* contributor Patricia Bosworth also found that Bloom "too often portrays herself as a victim, which is exasperating:

she obviously is very strong; otherwise, she would not have survived."

Other reviewers were pleased with Bloom's book, however. Among their number was Jonathan Yardley of *Washington Post Book World,* who called *Leaving a Doll's House* an "exceptional memoir." He found that "her candor is impressive" and concluded: "Though her life has not been easy, she is quick to acknowledge its pleasures and rewards, including those that were hard-earned. But in the end what she leaves us with is a renewed understanding that talent, beauty and fame, just like money, can't buy you love." And Bettina Drew recounted in *Tribune Books* that Bloom "recounts a rich and committed professional life and provides a detailed and harrowing account of the disintegration of her . . . relationship with writer Philip Roth. . . . She doesn't seem to air their considerable dirty laundry for cruelty or revenge. With journal entries and letters adding depth, she writes with sadness rather than anger, and it has the ring of honesty."

BIOGRAPHICAL/CRITICAL SOURCES:

BOOKS

Bloom, Claire, *Leaving a Doll's House: A Memoir,* Little, Brown (Boston), 1996.
Bloom, *Limelight and After: The Education of an Actress,* Harper, 1982.

PERIODICALS

Atlanta Journal-Constitution, November 3, 1996, p. L11.
Booklist, October 15, 1996, p. 378.
Chicago Tribune, February 11, 1982; October 20, 1991, section 6, p. 4; March 28, 1994, section 5, p. 3.
Drama: The Quarterly Theatre Review, autumn, 1982.
Harper's Bazaar, October, 1996, p. 172.
Horn Book, October, 1982, p. 552.
Library Journal, November 15, 1996, p. 63.
Los Angeles Times, March 4, 1982; September 27, 1989, section VI, p. 1.
Los Angeles Times Book Review, October 13, 1996, p. 3.
Madamoiselle, July, 1982, p. 51.
Newsweek, September 30, 1996, p. 78.
New York, September 9, 1996, p. 119; October 21, 1996, p. 26.
New Yorker, November 4, 1996, p. 102.

New York Times, February 21, 1989, p. C17; September 17, 1996, pp. C11, C15.
New York Times Book Review, October 13, 1996, p. 7.
Observer, March 28, 1982.
People, March 1, 1982, p. 16.
Publishers Weekly, September 2, 1996, p. 104.
Time, November 17, 1952; October, 1983, p. 530; Septebmer 30, 1996, p. 75.
Tribune Books (Chicago), October 20, 1996, p. 3.
Vogue, June, 1982, p. 51.
Washington Post Book World, October 20, 1996, p. 3.

* * *

BOLTON, Evelyn
  See BUNTING, Anne Evelyn

* * *

BONNER, Parker
  See BALLARD, (Willis) Todhunter

* * *

BORDEN, Mary 1886-1968
  (Mary Borden-Turner, Bridget Maclagan)

PERSONAL: Born May 15, 1886, in Chicago, IL; died December 2, 1968; daughter of William and Mary (Whiting) Borden; married George Douglas Turner; married Sir Edward Spears (a major general, British Army, member of Parliament, and historian), 1918; children: (first marriage) Joyce Comfort Hart-Davis, Mary Hamilton Hall; (second marriage) Michael (deceased). *Education:* Vassar College, B.A., 1907. *Politics:* Conservative. *Religion:* Protestant.

CAREER: Author. Organizer and director of field hospitals for the French in both World Wars. Official hostess at British legations in Beirut and Damascus when husband was minister plenipotentiary to Syria and Lebanon, 1942-44.

MEMBER: Society of Authors.

AWARDS, HONORS: British medals for war service, 1914-18; French Legion of Honor and Croix de Guerre with bar and palm.

WRITINGS:

The Tortoise, Knopf (New York City), 1921.
Jane—Our Stranger, Knopf, 1923.
Three Pilgrims and a Tinker, Knopf, 1924.
The Technique of Marriage, Heinemann (London), 1924, Doubleday, Doran (New York City), 1933.
Jericho Sands, Heinemann, 1925, Knopf, 1926.
Four O'Clock, and Other Stories, Doubleday, Page, 1927.
Flamingo, or the American Tower, Doubleday, Page, 1927.
Jehovah's Day, Heinemann, 1928, Doubleday, Doran, 1929.
The Forbidden Zone, Heinemann, 1929, Doubleday, Doran, 1930.
A Woman with White Eyes, Doubleday, Doran, 1930.
Sarah Defiant, Doubleday, Doran, 1931.
Sarah Gay, Heinemann, 1931.
(With E. M. Delafield and Susan Ertz) *Man, Proud Man,* Hamilton, 1932.
Mary of Nazareth, Doubleday, Doran, 1933.
The King of the Jews, Little, Brown (Boston), 1935.
Action for Slander, Heinemann, 1936, Harper (New York City), 1937.
The Black Virgin, Heinemann, 1937, published as *Strange Week-end,* Harper, 1938.
Passport for a Girl, Harper, 1939.
Journey Down a Blind Alley, Harper, 1946.
No. 2 Shovel Street, Heinemann, 1949.
Catspaw, Longmans, Green, 1950 (published in England as *For the Record,* Heinemann, 1950).
You, the Jury (Book-of-the-Month Club selection), Longmans, Green, 1952 (published in England as *Martin Merriedew,* Heinemann, 1952).
Margin of Error, Longmans, Green, 1954.
The Hungry Leopard, Longmans, Green, 1956.

UNDER PSEUDONYM BRIDGET MACLAGAN

The Mistress of Kingdoms; or Smoking Wax, Duckworth, 1912.
Collision, Duckworth, 1913.
The Romantic Lady, Constable, 1916, (under name Mary Borden), Knopf, 1920, (under name Mary Borden-Turner), Heinemann, 1924.

Adapted novel, *Action for Slander,* for motion picture of the same title. Writer of scripts for British Broadcasting Corp.'s *Saturday Night Theatre.*

SIDELIGHTS: Mary Borden served as a director of French field hospitals in both World Wars, for which she received military medals for bravery, and was married to a British army general and member of Parliament. She drew upon these experiences for the backgrounds in several of her novels. "Borden wrote in a tightly scripted style, every word carefully chosen to evoke the right feeling and atmosphere," wrote P. Campbell in *Twentieth-Century Romance and Historical Writers.*

Many of Borden's novels concern illicit love affairs. In *Action for Slander,* Major Daviot is accused of cheating at cards and takes his accuser to court. But Daviot is secretly having an affair with his accuser's wife and this is the underlying reason the charge of cheating was made. D. L. Mann in *Boston Transcript* praised the "understanding of human nature" exhibited by Bentley in her novel, and called *Action for Slander* "a remorselessly moral story."

Sarah Gay deals with the love affair between a young English woman working, as did Borden herself, for the French Red Cross during World War I, and a Frenchman she meets at the hospital. Sarah gives up her husband and children back home to live in Paris with her new lover. But when one of her children becomes ill, Sarah returns to England.

In *A Woman with White Eyes,* Borden wrote a more impressionistic novel that explored new stylistic techniques than did her usual work. Telling the retrospective stories of two female friends nearing sixty, the novel details their relationships with husbands, lovers and family members over a sometimes-stormy lifetime. Calling *A Woman with White Eyes* "perhaps the most complex novel of the year," Fanny Butcher of the *Chicago Daily Tribune* found the profusion of memories a bit overwhelming, saying "if *A Woman with White Eyes* had been a little less diffused, technically, it would have been a much more powerful book." Margaret Wallace in the *New York Evening Post* thought the novel "lacks the homely virtues of clarity and simplicity" although being a "brilliant and subtle piece of writing." L. A. G. Strong in *Spectator* concluded that *A Woman with White Eyes* "is a most impressive and moving book, full of scenes that haunt the memory."

After her death, the *London Times* commented, "Miss Borden was a writer of very real and obvious gifts. Intelligent, resourceful, and accomplished, not seldom impressive in their sustained narrative power, most of her novels were nevertheless somewhat narrowly confined to the experience of the very rich and exalted and in the result were stamped by a certain conventionality of outlook. She tried in time to broaden the field of her observation and imaginative sympathy, but continued for the most part to make the best use of her talents in keeping to the type of wealthy and fashionable milieu which for many years she knew best."

BIOGRAPHICAL/CRITICAL SOURCES:

BOOKS

Twentieth-Century Romance and Historical Writers, third edition, St. James Press (Detroit), 1994.

PERIODICALS

Boston Transcript, March 6, 1937, p. 2.
Chicago Daily Tribune, November 8, 1930, p. 13; March 20, 1937, p. 19.
New York Evening Post, December 6, 1930, p. 4D.
Spectator, October 25, 1930, p. 145.

OBITUARIES:

PERIODICALS

London Times, December 3, 1968.
New York Times, December 3, 1968.
Publishers Weekly, December 30, 1968.
Washington Post, December 4, 1968.*

* * *

BORDEN-TURNER, Mary
  See BORDEN, Mary

* * *

BOWIE, Sam
  See BALLARD, (Willis) Todhunter

BOYLE, Mark
  See KIENZLE, William X(avier)

*   *   *

BRANDT, Tom
  See DEWEY, Thomas B(lanchard)

*   *   *

BRAUN, Lilian Jackson 1916(?)-

PERSONAL: Born c. 1916, in MA; married first husband (deceased); married Earl Bettinger, 1979.

ADDRESSES: Agent—Blanche C. Gregory, Inc., 2 Tudor Pl., New York, NY 10017. *Office*—Putnam Berkeley Group, 200 Madison Ave., New York, NY 10016.

CAREER: Mystery writer. Crowley Knower Company, Detroit, MI, freelance advertising copywriter; Ernst Kern Department Store, Detroit, began as advertising copywriter, became public relations director; *Detroit Free Press,* Detroit, editor, 1948-78.

AWARDS, HONORS: Edgar Award nomination, Mystery Writers of America, 1986, for *The Cat Who Saw Red.*

WRITINGS:

"THE CAT WHO. . ." MYSTERY SERIES

The Cat Who Could Read Backwards, Dutton (New York City), 1966.
The Cat Who Ate Danish Modern, Dutton, 1967.
The Cat Who Turned On and Off, Dutton, 1968.
The Cat Who Saw Red, Jove (New York City), 1986.
The Cat Who Played Brahms, Jove, 1987.
The Cat Who Played Post Office, Jove, 1987.
The Cat Who Knew Shakespeare, Jove, 1988.
The Cat Who Had Fourteen Tales (stories), Jove, 1988.
The Cat Who Sniffed Glue, Putnam (New York City), 1988.
The Cat Who Went Underground, Putnam, 1989.
The Cat Who Talked to Ghosts, Putnam, 1990.
The Cat Who Lived High, Putnam, 1990.
The Cat Who Knew a Cardinal, Putnam, 1991.

The Cat Who Wasn't There, Putnam, 1992.
The Cat Who Moved a Mountain, Putnam, 1992.
The Cat Who Went into the Closet, Putnam, 1993.
The Cat Who Came to Breakfast, Putnam, 1994.
The Cat Who Blew the Whistle, Putnam, 1995.
Lilian Braun: Three Complete Novels (contains *The Cat Who Knew Shakespeare, The Cat Who Sniffed Glue,* and *The Cat Who Went Underground*), Putnam, 1994.
The Cat Who Said Cheese, Putnam, 1996.
Three Complete Novels (contains *The Cat Who Wasn't There, The Cat Who Went into the Closet,* and *The Cat Who Came to Breakfast*), Putnam, 1996.

OTHER

Work represented in anthologies, including *Mystery Cats: Feline Felonies by Modern Masters of Mystery,* Dutton, 1991, and *More Mystery Cats,* Dutton, 1993. Regular columnist, *Lilian Jackson Braun Newsletter;* contributor to *Ellery Queen's Mystery Magazine.*

SIDELIGHTS: Lilian Jackson Braun is author of "The Cat Who. . ." mystery series featuring amateur sleuth Jim Qwilleran (known to his friends as Qwill). Of particular assistance to Qwilleran is the enterprising Koko, a Siamese cat whose seemingly psychic abilities often help the reporter as he attempts to solve the mystery. Qwilleran and Koko, as well as Qwilleran's other cat Yum Yum, are the main characters in each of the novels. The cats, according to Carol Barry in the *St. James Guide to Crime and Mystery Writers,* "are likable and smart but not supernatural. [They] are not depicted as cloyingly sweet but as elegant and intelligent. The use of cats as Qwilleran's companions and co-sleuths adds wit, atmosphere, and interest that even a non-cat-lover can relate to and enjoy." Most of the Qwilleran novels are set in the northern Midwest where Qwilleran has worked for several local newspapers, first in a large city and then in a rural community. "The way Braun pictures Qwilleran, he's your next door neighbor or your favorite uncle," according to Catherine A. Nelson in *Armchair Detective..* "She has a way of telling a story that keeps you reading and turning the pages. . . . You'll never tire of reading Braun's Cat Who books."

Braun began her writing career as an advertising copywriter, then switched to journalism with the *Detroit Free Press.* During her thirty years at the *Free Press* Braun wrote short mystery stories involving cats, many of which appeared in *Ellery Queen's*

Mystery Magazine. Eventually, two of these stories were selected to appear in the *Best Detective Stories of the Year* anthology. When E. P. Dutton, publisher of the yearly anthology, asked Braun to write a mystery novel involving her cat character, she couldn't refuse.

In an interview with Nelson in *Armchair Detective* magazine, Braun explained why she chose cats as the focus of her writing: "I was forty years old when my first husband gave me a Siamese kitten for a birthday present. I really flipped over the cat. I named him Koko, after a character in Gilbert and Sullivan's Mikado. I adored him and he adored me. When he was ten years old, he was killed in a fall from a tenth-floor window. Our neighbors seemed to think he was pushed. I was not only grief-stricken, but angry. I started having nightmares about friends and relatives falling out of tenth-story windows, so I knew I had to do something to get it off my mind. So I wrote a short story, 'The Sin of Madame Phloi.' It was not a re-enactment of the incident, but it was inspired by what happened."

"The Cat Who. . ." series began in 1966 with *The Cat Who Could Read Backwards,* in which Qwilleran, a respected journalist, investigates treachery and murder within the art community of a Midwest town. Although Anthony Boucher in the *New York Times Book Review* claimed Braun "has a great deal to learn about the construction of the mystery novel," he nonetheless concluded that *The Cat Who Could Read Backwards* was "a highly rewarding first novel" and that Koko was "probably the New Detective of the Year."

Braun soon followed up her initial success with two more entries in the series, *The Cat Who Ate Danish Modern* (taking Qwill into the world of interior decorating) and *The Cat Who Turned On and Off* (involving antique dealers). But after her fourth novel was abandoned by her publisher, Braun focused on her career as an editor at the *Detroit Free Press.* She retired from the paper in 1978 and, eight years later, she revived her mystery series with *The Cat Who Saw Red.* Here Qwilleran, who has become a newspaper restaurant reviewer, comes to suspect that a former lover has met with foul play. As the amateur sleuth once again tries to uncover the truth, he suspects that someone is trying to poison Koko and Yum Yum. The popularity of *The Cat Who Saw Red* proved that Braun's work had lost none of its appeal, and the novel earned an Edgar Award nomination from the Mystery Writers of America in 1986.

In the ensuing years Braun has produced more works in the series. "Braun's ability to introduce and sustain a strong cast of supporting characters," Barry writes, "keeps the reader eagerly awaiting the next book. . . . The murders are both surprising and shocking, but the dialogue, the local color, and the characters make up more of the story than the act of murder itself."

In 1988 Braun published *The Cat Who Knew Shakespeare,* in which Qwilleran, who has inherited a substantial fortune and moved to a mansion, investigates the mysterious suicide of a newspaper publisher. As is usual in the series, the profoundly intuitive Koko proves of considerable use to Qwilleran in his sleuthing. *The Cat Who Went Underground,* the tenth entry in Braun's series, finds Qwilleran and his cats immersed in considerable intrigue when their vacation is disrupted by the suspicious disappearance of a handyman.

The succeeding mystery, *The Cat Who Talked to Ghosts,* involves peculiar circumstances at a historical museum in Qwilleran's isolated hometown. The action begins when the institution's curator informs Qwilleran of supernatural events at the museum. Her death soon afterward serves as further motivation for Qwilleran to investigate, and he soon uncovers secrets about one of the town's prominent families. *The Cat Who Lived High* concerns Qwilleran's efforts to help a friend spare an old building from demolition. Attempting to determine the structure's usefulness, Qwilleran decides to live there for the winter, and is soon investigating the murder of a previous tenant. He is assisted by Koko, who uses a board game to help catch the killer.

In *The Cat Who Came to Breakfast* Qwilleran and the cats investigate strange accidents, including a drowning, an explosion, and a hotel food poisoning, at an island resort built near Pickax City. When it seems as if the accidents have been caused by locals intent on stopping development in their community, Qwilleran uncovers the truth. In his review of the novel, the critic for *Kirkus Reviews* claims that "Like Agatha Christie resolutely keeping up British standards in the face of a shrinking Empire, Braun maintains the forms of the American cozy [mystery story]."

Braun's 1995 book *The Cat Who Blew the Whistle* shows the result of her research into railroading. In the book, the model railroad buff president of the Lumbertown Credit Union disappears after an embezzlement is discovered at the credit union. Qwilleran, Koko and Yum Yum investigate the mystery while Qwilleran continues his long-standing relationship with librarian Polly Duncan. The critic for *Publishers Weekly* calls *The Cat Who Blew the Whistle* the "best of [the] series," and Barbara Duree in *Booklist* adds that "the author provides enough background information to make new readers feel at home, and devotees of the series will applaud the added interest of railroading language and lore." *The Cat Who Said Cheese* follows Qwilleran and his cats as they uncover who planted a bomb at a hotel during Pickax City's Great Food Expo. "As always Lilian Jackson Braun spins an amazing tale with her remarkable cats," according to Nelson.

Barry concludes: "Braun's *Cat Who . . .* series succeeds not only because of the dialogue, which flows easily and is never superfluous or boring. Braun is able to grasp the reader's attention quickly and keep it fully engaged throughout the book. Readers can enjoy BRaun's books not only for their mystery plots but as stories of witty and entertaining characters, local color, and, of course, the antics of the cats."

BIOGRAPHICAL/CRITICAL SOURCES:

BOOKS

St. James Guide to Crime and Mystery Writers, St. James Press (Detroit), 1996

PERIODICALS

Armchair Detective, fall, 1991, pp. 388-398; spring, 1996, p. 233.
Booklist, August, 1992, p. 1997; February 15, 1993, p. 1038; May 15, 1993, p. 1716; December 1, 1994, p. 635.
Cat Fancy, November, 1994, pp. 40-43; December 1, 1994, p. 635.
Globe & Mail (Toronto), December 17, 1988.
Kirkus Reviews, January 1, 1994, p. 18.
Library Journal, May 1, 1991, p. 123; November 15, 1992, p. 120; March 1, 1993, p. 112; May 1, 1993, p. 130; December, 1994, p. 138.
Lilian Jackson Braun Newsletter, 1990—.
New York Times Book Review, March 6, 1966, p. 38; June 18, 1967, p. 37; January 12, 1969, p. 43; April 2, 1989, p. 33; May 19, 1991, p. 45.
Observer, July 16, 1967, p. 21; March 16, 1968, p. 29; March 24, 1968, p. 29; July 27, 1969, p. 25.

Publishers Weekly, July 8, 1988, p. 29; March 22, 1991, p. 73; October 11, 1991, p. 52; January 25, 1993, p. 80; January 17, 1994, p. 412; January 16, 1995, p. 40.
Saturday Review, March 26, 1966, p. 35.
Times Literary Supplement, September 21, 1967, p. 844; June 6, 1968, p. 603; September 18, 1969, p. 1018.
Tribune Books (Chicago), October 19, 1986, p. 5; January 7, 1990, p. 6.

*   *   *

BRIDGE, Ann
    See O'MALLEY, Mary Dolling (Sanders)

*   *   *

BRIDGEMAN, Richard
    See DAVIES, L(eslie) P(urnell)

*   *   *

BRISTOW, Gwen 1903-1980

PERSONAL: Born September 16, 1903, in Marion, SC; died August 16, 1980, in New Orleans, LA; daughter of Louis Judson (a minister) and Caroline Cornelia (Winkler) Bristow; married Bruce Manning, January 14, 1929 (deceased). *Education:* Judson College, A.B., 1924; attended Columbia University School of Journalism, 1924-25, and Anderson College.

CAREER: Times-Picayune, New Orleans, LA, reporter, 1925-34; freelance writer, beginning 1934.

MEMBER: Authors League of America, PEN International (Los Angeles center president, 1969-71; international corresponding secretary, beginning 1971), Pen and Brush.

WRITINGS:

The Alien and Other Poems, Badger (Boston), 1926.
(With husband, Bruce Manning) *The Invisible Host,* Mystery League (New York City), 1930, published as *The Ninth Guest,* Popular Library (New York City), 1975.

(With Manning) *Gutenberg Murders,* Mystery League, 1931.

(With Manning) *Two and Two Make Twenty-Two,* Mystery League, 1932.

(With Manning) *The Mardi Gras Murders,* Mystery League, 1932.

Deep Summer, Crowell (New York City), 1937, reprinted, Buccaneer Books, 1979.

The Handsome Road, Crowell, 1938, reprinted, Buccaneer Books, 1979.

This Side of Glory, Crowell, 1940, reprinted, Buccaneer Books, 1979.

Gwen Bristow: A Self Portrait, Crowell, 1940.

Tomorrow Is Forever, Crowell, 1943, reprinted, Buccaneer Books, 1976.

Jubilee Trail (Literary Guild selection), Crowell, 1950.

Celia Garth (Literary Guild selection), Crowell, 1959, reprinted, Popular Library, 1974.

Plantation Trilogy (includes *Deep Summer, The Handsome Road, This Side of Glory,* and additional historical material to preface each book), Crowell, 1962.

Calico Palace, Crowell, 1970.

Golden Dreams, Crowell, 1980.

Bristow's novels were translated into numerous languages, including German, French, Spanish, Dutch, and Swedish.

ADAPTATIONS: The Invisible Host was dramatized by Owen Davis under the title *The Ninth Guest,* and filmed by Columbia with the latter title in 1931; *Tomorrow Is Forever* was filmed by RKO in 1946; and *Jubilee Trail* was filmed by Republic in 1953.

SIDELIGHTS: Gwen Bristow, who began her fiction-writing career by working with her husband, Bruce Manning, on mystery stories, became well known for her "Plantation Trilogy"—*Deep Summer, The Handsome Road,* and *This Side of Glory.* Susan Quinn Berneis in *Twentieth-Century Romance and Historical Writers* noted: "History takes precedence over romance in the novels of Gwen Bristow. Her plots are detailed and neatly resolved and her characters are sharply drawn, if with broad strokes; but she reserves her greatest skill for the unfolding of American history as displayed around the lives of the people who created it."

Each volume of the "Plantation Trilogy" takes place on a different Louisiana plantation and concerns a heroine character finding love in tumultuous historical periods. In *Deep Summer* Bristow writes of a young girl in the late 18th century who marries an aristocratic Southerner. Margaret Wallace in *New York Times* found that "whatever its faults—and they are trivial in comparison with its virtues—*Deep Summer* is a grand job of story telling." Lisle Bell in *Books* called *Deep Summer* "a rich, colorful and charmingly written story."

The Handsome Road is set during the Civil War and Reconstruction periods of American history and tells of two women—one from the landed aristocracy, the other from dire poverty. L. M. Field in *New York Times* called *The Handsome Road* "very rich, very fully and carefully detailed," while the critic for *Springfield Republican* found it to be "dramatic from start to finish." "Bristow," wrote Eugene Armfield in *Saturday Review of Literature,* "belongs among those Southern novelists who are trying to interpret the South and its past in critical terms."

The trilogy ends with *This Side of Glory,* the story of a marriage between a wealthy woman and a poor man and the resulting clashes between their respective families. The *Times Literary Supplement* critic called *This Side of Glory* "a vigorous and thoughtful piece of work, done with an admirably firm sense of character and a loving eye for the landscape of the Mississippi valley in the neighborhood of New Orleans." Margaret Wallace in the *New York Times* wrote: "There can be no question any longer of Gwen Bristow's solid and versatile talent as a novelist. . . . [*This Side of Glory* is] the most expert piece of straight story telling Miss Bristow has given us yet."

BIOGRAPHICAL/CRITICAL SOURCES:

BOOKS

Twentieth-Century Romance and Historical Writers, third edition, St. James Press (Detroit), 1994.

PERIODICALS

Atlantic Monthly, January, 1944.

Books, April 11, 1937, p. 13.

Book Week, November 21, 1943, p. 4.

Chicago Sunday Tribune, May 24, 1959, p. 3.

Christian Science Monitor, February 9, 1950, p. 11; May 21, 1959, p. 13.

New York Times, April 4, 1937, p. 6; May 1, 1938, p. 7; March 31, 1940, p. 7; December 26, 1943, p. 8; February 5, 1950, p. 30; May 31, 1959, p. 18.

New York Times Book Review, May 31, 1959.
Saturday Review, July 25, 1959, p. 42.
Saturday Review of Literature, May 7, 1938, p. 18;
 April 6, 1940, p. 21; February 11, 1950, p. 33.
Springfield Republican, May 22, 1938, p. 7E.
Times Literary Supplement, October 29, 1938, p.
 697; July 13, 1940, p. 337.
Weekly Book Review, November 21, 1943, p. 22.

OBITUARIES:

PERIODICALS

Chicago Tribune, August 19, 1980.*

* * *

BROWN, Fredric (William) 1906-1972

PERSONAL: Born October 29, 1906, in Cincinnati, OH; died March 11 (some sources say March 12 or 13), 1972, in Tucson, AZ; son of Karl Lewis (a journalist) and Emma Amelia (Graham) Brown; married Helen Ruth, 1929 (divorced, 1947); married Elizabeth Charlier, October 11, 1948; children: (first marriage) James Ross, Linn Lewis. *Education:* Attended Hanover College and University of Cincinnati. *Avocational interests:* Chess, music, poker, reading.

CAREER: Office worker, 1924-36; *Milwaukee Journal,* Milwaukee, WI, proofreader and writer, beginning in 1936; writer, 1947-72.

MEMBER: Mystery Writers of America, Writers Guild of America.

AWARDS, HONORS: Edgar Allan Poe Award for best first mystery novel from Mystery Writers of America, 1948, for *The Fabulous Clipjoint.*

WRITINGS:

Murder Can Be Fun (mystery; first published in a condensed version as *The Santa Claus Murders* in *Detective Story,* October, 1942), Dutton (New York City), 1948, published as *A Plot for Murder,* Bantam (New York City), 1949.
The Screaming Mimi (mystery; first published in a shortened version in *Mystery Book,* October, 1949), Dutton, 1949.

What Mad Universe (science fiction), Dutton, 1949, reprinted, introduction by Phil Klass, Bantam, 1978.
Here Comes a Candle: A Novel, Dutton, 1950.
Night of the Jabberwock (mystery), Dutton, 1950.
The Case of the Dancing Sandwiches, Dell (New York City), 1951.
The Far Cry (detective novel), Dutton, 1951.
The Deep End (mystery), Dutton, 1952.
We All Killed Grandma (mystery), Dutton, 1952.
The Lights in the Sky Are Stars (science fiction), Dutton, 1953 (published in England as *Project Jupiter,* Boardman [London], 1954).
Madball, Dell, 1953.
(Editor with Mack Reynolds, and author of introduction) *Science-Fiction Carnival: Fun in Science-Fiction,* Shasta Publishers, 1953.
His Name Was Death (mystery), Dutton, 1954.
Martians, Go Home (science fiction; first published in a short version in *Astonishing Science-Fiction,* September, 1954), Dutton, 1955.
The Wench Is Dead (mystery), Dutton, 1955.
The Lenient Beast (mystery), Dutton, 1956.
Rogue in Space (first published in *Super Science Stories,* 1949), Dutton, 1957.
The Office (novel), Dutton, 1958.
One for the Road (mystery; first published in a shortened version as *The Army Waggoner Murder* in *The Saint,* February, 1958), Dutton, 1958.
Knock Three-One-Two (mystery), Dutton, 1959.
The Mind Thing (science fiction), Bantam, 1961.
The Murderers, Dutton, 1961.
The Five-Day Nightmare (mystery), Dutton, 1962.
Mitkey Astromouse (juvenile), illustrations by Heinz Edelmann, Harlin Quist, 1971.
It's Only Everything, published in *A Key to Fredric Brown's Wonderland: A Study and an Annotated Bibliographical Checklist,* by Newton Baird, Talisman Literary Research, 1981.

Also author of "Star Spangled Night" and "Madman's Holiday." Stories represented in anthologies, including *Nightmares and Geezenstacks,* Bantam, 1961; *How Like an Angel,* edited by Margaret Millar, Black, 1962; *Crimes and Misfortunes: The Anthony Boucher Memorial Anthology of Mysteries,* edited by J. Francis McComas, Random House, 1970; *Science Fiction Hall of Fame: The Greatest Science Fiction Stories of All Time,* edited by Robert Silverberg, Doubleday, 1970; *And the Gods Laughed: A Collection of Science Fiction and Fantasy,* Phantasia Press, 1987; *Brother Mouse,* McMillan, 1987; *Happy Ending,* McMillan, 1990; *The Walter-Walker,* McMillan, 1990.

AMBROSE AND ED HUNTER DETECTIVE SERIES

The Fabulous Clipjoint (first published in a condensed version as "Dead Man's Indemnity" in *Mystery Book,* 1946), Dutton, 1947, reprinted, new introduction by Ron Goulart, Gregg, 1979.
The Dead Ringer, Dutton, 1948.
The Bloody Moonlight, Dutton, 1949 (published in England as *Murder in the Moonlight,* Boardman, 1950).
Compliments of a Fiend, Dutton, 1950.
Death Has Many Doors, Dutton, 1951.
The Late Lamented, Dutton, 1959.
Mrs. Murphy's Underpants, Dutton, 1963.

"FREDRIC BROWN IN THE DETECTIVE PULPS" SERIES

Homicide Sanitarium, Dennis McMillan, 1985.
Before She Kills, Dennis McMillan, 1986.
The Freak Show Murders, Dennis McMillan, 1986.
Thirty Corpses Every Thursday, Dennis McMillan, 1986.
Pardon My Ghoulish Laughter, Dennis McMillan, 1986.
Red Is the Hue of Hell, Dennis McMillan, 1986.

OTHER

Also author of television plays for "Alfred Hitchcock" series.

ADAPTATIONS: Short story "Madman's Holiday" was adapted as the film *Crack-Up,* RKO, 1946; *The Screaming Mimi* was released as a film by Columbia, 1958.

SIDELIGHTS: Fredric Brown first appeared on the literary scene during the golden age of "pulp fiction"—those thrillers, sci-fi and crime novels produced at low cost in mass numbers and embraced by an audience not yet surrendered to television. Distinguishing himself from his pulp peers, Brown—who won the Edgar Award for best first mystery novel and a place in the *Science Fiction Hall of Fame* anthology—became known as a writer of depth and perception; his novels often explored deep themes and challenged readers to think for themselves. "Using many of the conventions of science fiction, including bug-eyed monsters, time-travel, and alternate worlds, Brown created situations in which he could probe human foibles with a humorous or ironic twist," averred Amelia A. Rutledge in *Dictionary of Literary Biography;* in the best of his fiction "one finds intensity, psychological perception, and a true grasp of the fantastic mode."

After proving his hand at crime and science fiction short stories, Brown made an auspicious feature-length debut with *The Fabulous Clipjoint.* The 1948 mystery was the first in a series that featured the uncle-and-nephew detective team of Ambrose and Ed Hunter. The book seemed "refreshingly unhackneyed" to *Chicago Sun Book Week* reviewer James Sandoe. Brown followed it with numerous short stories in the genre and other mystery novels—many unrelated to the Hunter series—demonstrating an ingenuity in plotting and a combination of violence and wry humor that became hallmarks of his work.

The Lights in the Sky Are Stars is considered among Brown's most penetrating psychological studies. In a characterization deemed exceptionally rich and mature for the science fiction of its time, the novel portrays a man obsessed by space travel yet denied it because he was handicapped in an accident. Battling alcoholism and bureaucracy, he helps arrange an exploratory flight to Jupiter only to see the ship leave without him. According to Rutledge, the novel "best represents all of [Brown's] qualities as an author: the probing of motivation, concealed hints of the true story, and the depiction of human love, determination, and belief in the stars as man's destiny."

It was in 1958 that Brown produced his first "straight" (non-genre) novel. *The Office* presents the recollections of 35 years in the front office of Conger & Way. The workplace is staffed by an array of character types: salesmen, bookkeepers, secretaries, and the office boy who matured into the story's narrator. Their interactions and changing relationships over the years propel the plot.

The Office garnered the author some of his best reviews. The *San Francisco Chronicle,* for example, noted that while the characters are intentionally portrayed as "dull," it is through Brown's skill that "drama is made of ordinary human beings' emotions. . . .What he has made of his remembered knowledge is a fine story, homely in its basic quality and filled with sympathetic perception." Further, the novel "is a new direction for Brown. It will not surprise anyone who knows his great ability in storytelling that he has made such a rich human document of 'The Office'."

Armchair Detective writer Newton Baird gave an overall assessment of Brown, noting that in the author's best works he "fought the paradox that would seem to exist between naturalism and romanticism. He never conquered this dilemma, he was pulled on the one hand by determinism, on the other by human volition, and he never created a hero who was complete and confident in the real world." A common denominator in Brown stories, Baird continued, "is that the worst horrors are not those in reality (which are difficult enough to deal with), but those in the unreality of our delusions, in our fantasies and irrational imaginations—in our nightmares."

Baird gave another assessment of Brown, this time in the *St. James Guide to Crime and Mystery Writers.* In this article Baird singled out the novel *The Far Cry* as Brown's "tour de force. It probes a love/hate perplex to one of mystery writing's most startling endings, but the horror almost spoils the achievement." At the same time, Baird remarked that "the best expressions of his ingenuity and imagination are in some of his short stories, particularly the collection *Nightmares and Geezenstacks,* a delightful potpourri of innocent and ribald humor, expectation and surprise."

Brown's vast literary output sometimes diluted his inventiveness, with "everyday characters and conventional villainy [dominating] his lesser work, like *Murder Can Be Fun* or a failed experiment, *Here Comes a Candle,*" added Baird. But in the long run, "Brown is really one of a kind. . . .[He] portrayed a world that always betrayed and terrified idealists, making them yearn for a place that inspired rather than suppressed freedom and adventure. In his detective novels and mysteries his characters sometimes found that what they had hoped for proved more horrifying than what they had to begin with. In his fantasies, through 'loopholes in reality,' happiness is achieved. So this unique writer wrote from his own time and the future."

BIOGRAPHICAL/CRITICAL SOURCES:

BOOKS

Baird, Newton, *A Key to Fredric Brown's Wonderland: A Study and an Annotated Bibliographical Checklist,* Talisman, 1981.
Dictionary of Literary Biography, Volume 8:*Twentieth-Century American Science Fiction Writers,* Gale, 1981.

St. James Guide to Crime and Mystery Writers, St. James Press, 1996.

PERIODICALS

Armchair Detective, July, 1977.
Chicago Sun, April 2, 1948; December 2, 1949, p. 61; December 23, 1949, p. 40.
Chicago Sun Book Week, March 2, 1947, p. 9.
New Yorker, April 28, 1951, p. 27; January 12, 1952, p. 27.
New York Herald Tribune Book Review, April 6, 1947, p. 19; December 4, 1949, p. 42; May 21, 1950, p. 19; August 27, 1950, p. 11; September 23, 1951, p. 22; December 23, 1951, p. 9; December 6, 1953, p. 50; June 6, 1954, p. 12; February 22, 1959, p. 11.
New York Times, November 7, 1948, p. 40; April 16, 1950, p. 39; August 13, 1950, p. 22; December 30, 1951, p. 14; June 14, 1953, p. 19; October 24, 1954, p. 36; December 4, 1955, p. 52; April 15, 1956, p. 20; February 22, 1959, p. 31.
New York Times Book Review, August 16, 1959, p. 24.
San Francisco Chronicle, January 7, 1951, p. 18; December 25, 1955, p. 15; April 24, 1958, p. 33; March 8, 1959, p. 23; September 20, 1959, p. 25.
Saturday Review of Literature, September 9, 1950, p. 33.

OBITUARIES:

PERIODICALS

New York Times, March 14, 1972.
Washington Post, March 14, 1972.*

* * *

**BROWN, Morna Doris 1907-1995
(Morna Doris MacTaggart; pseudonyms: E. X. Ferrars, Elizabeth Ferrars)**

PERSONAL: Born September 6, 1907, in Rangoon, Burma, died March 30, 1995; daughter of Peter Clouston and Marie (Ferrars) MacTaggart; married Robert Brown, 1940. *Education:* University College, London, diploma in journalism, 1928.

CAREER: Writer.

AWARDS, HONORS: Silver Dagger Award, Crime Writers Association, 1981.

MEMBER: Crime Writers Association, Mystery Writers of America, Detection Club, Edinburgh Soroptimists Club.

WRITINGS:

(Under name Morna Doris MacTaggart) *Turn Single,* Nicholson, 1932.
(Under name Morna Doris MacTaggart) *Broken Music,* Dutton, 1934.
(Editor and contributor) *Planned Departures,* Hodder, 1958.

ALL PUBLISHED BY HODDER (LONDON) AS ELIZABETH FERRARS AND BY DOUBLEDAY (NEW YORK CITY) AS E. X. FERRARS, EXCEPT AS INDICATED

Give a Corpse a Bad Name, Hodder, 1940.
Remove the Bodies, Hodder, 1940, published as *Rehearsals for Murder,* Doubleday, 1941.
Death in Botanist's Bay, Hodder, 1941, published as *Murder of a Suicide,* Doubleday, 1941.
Don't Monkey with Murder, Hodder, 1942, published as *The Shape of a Stain,* Doubleday, 1942.
Your Neck in a Noose, Hodder, 1942, published as *Neck in a Noose,* Doubleday, 1943.
I, Said the Fly, Hodder, 1945, Doubleday, 1945.

ALL PUBLISHED BY COLLINS (LONDON) AS ELIZABETH FERRARS AND BY DOUBLEDAY, HARPER (NEW YORK CITY), AND WALKER (NEW YORK CITY) AS E. X. FERRARS, EXCEPT AS INDICATED

Murder among Friends, Collins, 1946, published as *Cheat the Hang Man,* Doubleday, 1946.
With Murder in Mind, Collins, 1948.
The March Hare Murders, Collins, 1949, Doubleday, 1949.
Hunt the Tortoise, Collins, 1950, Doubleday, 1950.
Milk of Human Kindness, Collins, 1950.
The Clock that Wouldn't Stop, Collins, 1952, Doubleday, 1952.
Alibi for a Witch, Collins, 1952, Doubleday, 1952.
Murder in Time, Collins, 1953.
The Lying Voices, Collins, 1954.
Enough to Kill a Horse, Collins, 1955, Doubleday, 1955.
Always Say Die, Collins, 1956, published as *We Haven't Seen Her Lately,* Doubleday, 1956.
Murder Moves In, Collins, 1956, published as *Kill or Cure,* Doubleday, 1956.

Furnished for Murder, Collins, 1957.
Count the Cost, Doubleday, 1957 (published in England as *Unreasonable Doubt,* Collins, 1958).
Depart This Life, Doubleday, 1958 (published in England as *A Tale of Two Murders,* Collins, 1959).
Fear the Light, Collins, 1960, Doubleday, 1960.
The Sleeping Dogs, Collins, 1960, Doubleday, 1960.
The Busy Body, Collins, 1962, published as *Seeing Double,* Doubleday, 1962.
The Wandering Widows, Collins, 1962, Doubleday, 1962.
The Doubly Dead, Collins, 1963, Doubleday, 1963.
A Legal Fiction, Collins, 1964, published in the U.S. as *The Decayed Gentlewoman,* Doubleday, 1963.
Ninth Life, Collins, 1965.
No Peace for the Wicked, Collins, 1966, Harper, 1966.
Zero at the Bone, Collins, 1967, Walker, 1968.
The Swaying Pillars, Collins, 1968, Walker, 1969.
Skelton Staff, Collins, 1969, Walker, 1969.
The Seven Sleepers, Collins, 1970, Walker, 1970.
A Stranger and Afraid, Collins, 1971, Walker, 1971.
Breath of Suspicion, Collins 1972, Doubleday, 1972.
Foot in the Grave, Doubleday, 1972, Collins, 1973.
The Small World of Murder, Collins, 1973, Doubleday, 1973.
Hanged Man's House, Collins, 1974, Doubleday, 1974.
Alive and Dead, Collins, 1974, Doubleday, 1975.
Drowned Rat, Collins, 1975, Doubleday, 1975.
The Cup and the Lip, Collins, 1975, Doubleday, 1976.
Blood Flies Upward, Collins, 1976, Doubleday, 1977.
The Pretty Pink Shroud, Collins, 1977, Doubleday, 1977.
Murders Anonymous, Collins, 1977, Doubleday, 1978.
Last Will and Testament, Collins, 1978, Doubleday, 1978.
In at the Kill, Collins, 1978, Doubleday, 1979.
Witness before the Fact, Collins, 1979, Doubleday, 1980.
Designs on Life, Collins, 1980, Doubleday, 1980.
Frog in the Throat, Doubleday, 1980.
Experiment with Death, Collins, 1981, Doubleday, 1981.
Thinner than Water, Collins, 1981, Doubleday, 1982.
Skeleton in Search of a Cupboard, Collins, 1982, published in the U.S. as *Skeleton in Search of a Closet,* Doubleday, 1982.

Death of a Minor Character, Collins, 1983, Doubleday, 1983.

Something Wicked, Collins, 1983, Doubleday, 1984.

Root of All Evil, Collins, 1984, Doubleday, 1984.

The Crime and the Crystal, Collins, 1985, Doubleday, 1985.

I Met Murder, Collins, 1985, Doubleday, 1986.

The Other Devil's Name, Collins, 1986, Doubleday, 1987.

Come and Be Killed, Collins, 1987, Doubleday, 1987.

A Murder Too Many, Collins, 1988, Doubleday, 1989.

Trial by Fury, Collins, 1989, Doubleday, 1989.

Woman Slaughter, Collins, 1989, Doubleday, 1990.

Smoke Without Fire, Collins, 1989, Doubleday, 1990.

Sleep of the Unjust, Collins, 1990, Doubleday, 1991.

Danger from the Dead, Collins, 1991, Doubleday, 1992.

Beware of the Dog, HarperCollins, 1992, Doubleday, 1993.

Answer Came There None, HarperCollins, 1992, Doubleday, 1993.

Thy Brother Death, HarperCollins, 1993, Doubleday, 1993.

A Hobby of Murder, HarperCollins, 1994, Doubleday, 1994.

Seeing Is Believing, HarperCollins, 1994, Doubleday, 1996.

A Choice of Evils, HarperCollins, 1995, Doubleday, 1997.

A Thief in the Night, HarperCollins, 1995.

CONTRIBUTOR

Raymond Postgate, editor, *Detective Stories of Today,* Faber, 1940.

Choice of Weapon, Hodder, 1958.

George Hardinge, editor, *Winter's Crimes 2,* Macmillan, 1970.

Hardinge, editor, *Winter's Crimes 4,* Macmillan, 1972.

Hardinge, editor, *Winter's Crimes 6,* Macmillan, 1974.

Ellery Queen's Giants of Mystery, Davis Publications, 1976.

Hardinge, editor, *Winter's Crimes 9,* Macmillan, 1977.

Crime on the Coast and No Flowers By Request, Gollancz, 1984, Berkeley, 1987.

Contributor of short stories to *Ellery Queen's Mystery Magazine.*

SIDELIGHTS: According to Professor B.J. Rahn in *Armchair Detective,* Morna Brown (who published as Elizabeth Ferrars in England and E. X. Ferrars in America) was perhaps the "best qualified of all living authors to comment on the [British detective fiction] genre in England because she has been an observer of and an active participant in the crime scene for over fifty years." H.R.F. Keating, in *Murder Must Appetize* (1975), wrote that Ferrars belonged among "that quite large and much-to-be-thanked band of crime authors who were writing in the good old days and are writing still in today's yet better ones." This enduringly prolific and popular writer maintained the attention of English and American mystery readers from World War II until her death in 1995.

For Anthony Boucher of the *New York Times Book Review,* Ferrars was a "consistently admirable craftswoman who combine[d] neat puzzles with a fine feeling for people." Ferrars's mysteries usually revolve around the tangled domestic relationships of a group of English villagers. L. G. Offord of the *San Francisco Chronicle* called Ferrars "one of the top practitioners of the nice, quiet English-village mystery" and found her novel *Kill or Cure* to be "the 'domestic' mystery in its highest form." Agreeing with this appraisal, Connie Fletcher wrote in *Booklist* that "Ferrars is a master at disrupting cozy village life with crimes." "Domestic malice," Leo Harris of *Books and Bookmen* commented, "seems to me to be a . . . fruitful source of really interesting crime, and few are more malicious, in the nicest Jane Austenish way, or more domestic (ditto) than Elizabeth Ferrars."

Although at times her settings range abroad as far as Africa or Australia, the majority of her fiction takes place in England or Scotland. Most of Ferrars's characters are English, middle-class, and academically employed. *St. James Guide to Crime and Mystery Writers* contributor Mary Helen Becker commented that "her female characters are politely feminist, independent young women who do not submerge their work or their professional identity in a quest for romance, although romantic liaisons often figure in her tales." A reviewer for the *Times Literary Supplement* described Ferrars' most convincing characters as "in all senses of the word, very ordinary people—concerned, but not too curious, about their neighbours." Ferrars' novels often contain as much mystery as character study. Boucher found *We Haven't Seen Her Lately* "a novel of suspense and character, with subtle and adroit exposure of personalities." Isaac Anderson of the *New York Times* wrote of *Cheat the Hangman,* "as a mystery story this book is very good indeed. As a novel of tangled human relations in wartime London it is even better than that."

Given her status as a prominent woman writer, Ferrars was often asked about which strong female role models she had had while growing up. "My mother was the center of the family. . . . And it certainly was a matriarchal family." Like Ferrars herself, Ferrars' mother was born in Burma, and learned early how to take care of herself. "You had to deal with everything yourself," Ferrars explained, and added that her mother had passed this determination on to her daughter. Ferrars also attended England's first important co-educational school, Bedales, where she interacted with boys in a way that few English girls of her age did. "[I] had no feeling," she commented, "of being second-rate to boys. . . . I never think about being a feminist. . . . [But in Bedales] one did absolutely grow up on equal terms with boys and never felt in the least bit that one had to compete."

After completing her secondary education at Bedales, she attended London's University College, where she received a degree in journalism. Immediately upon finishing her university days, Ferrars began to write novels--first, under her given name (Morna Doris MacTaggart), then, with *Give a Corpse a Bad Name,* as Elizabeth Ferrars. This novel, according to Becker in the *Dictionary of Literary Biography,* was "an auspicious beginning." Set in Devonshire, the novel tells the story of Anna Milne, a successful author who runs over a drunken man who is later discovered to be her husband. Toby Dyke, a former journalist, and his companion George aid the local constable in investigating the death. Toby and George are featured in *Remove the Bodies, Death in Botanist's Bay, Don't Monkey With Murder* and *Your Neck in a Noose.* All of these novels feature an eccentric cast of supporting characters.

After using the customary model, requiring a sleuth or detective to solve the crime, for her first five novels, Ferrars made what she called a "rather revolutionary" break with tradition in 1944. "I remember asking Doubleday and also Hodder and Stoughton, who were my publishers, if it would be all right without the detective," she reminisced to Rahn. *I, Said the Fly* (1945) was her first novel that did not utilize a detective character, and she felt that it was "much the best thing I'd written" up to that time. Until the mid-1980's, Ferrars continued to use what

Rahn described as "an omniscient narrator as the dominant voice telling the story . . . [she] focuses this impersonal viewpoint on the thoughts and feelings of an intelligent, liberal, independent female character in the center of the action." 1948's *With Murder in Mind,* although a departure from Ferrars' customary style, utilized this type of female character. The novel consists of a young woman's conversations with her therapist.

Dictionary of Literary Biography contributor Becker marked Ferrars' "middle period" as beginning with *Milk of Human Kindness* (1950), a perfect example of her domestic murder mysteries. 1952 saw the publication of *The Clock That Wouldn't Stop* and *Alibi for a Witch.* The first book recounts the story of a London advice columnist accused of blackmail; the second, set among British expatriates in Southern Italy, was called "interesting . . . and highly ingenious" by the *New York Times Book Review.* *The Lying Voices* (1954) juxtaposed the "lying voices" of inaccurate clocks with the unreliable statements of the characters. In a review of 1956's *Always Say Die,* Leo Harris of *Books and Bookmen* paid Ferrars perhaps the highest compliment possible for a mystery writer, comparing her to Agatha Christie: "Miss Ferrars uses the Christie technique of shoving great clues under your very nose disguised as idle chit-chat or semi-relevant description." With *Depart This Life* (1958) and *Fear the Light* (1960), Ferrars honed her skills at the domestic mystery, focusing these novels on intrafamily problems.

In the 1960s and the 1970s, Ferrars continued to reliably produce fine mysteries. According to Becker in the *Dictionary of Literary Biography,* "*Sleeping Dogs* (1960), featuring a writer who does a story about a housekeeper tried for murdering a child, and *The Busy Body* (1962), which has an especially intriguing opening, are examplary Ferrars novels." Anthony Boucher of the *New York Times Book Review* called Ferrars "one of England's steadily most reliable pros" in a review of 1963's *The Doubly Dead.*

In the late 1960s and early 1970s, Ferrars set many of her books away from the familiar London settings. *The Small World of Murder* takes place on a trip around the world; *Skeleton Staff* and *Breath of Suspicion* are set in Madeira; *The Seven Sleepers* has its locale in Scotland. The environs of Helsington, England, are the settings for a number of Ferrars' mysteries, including *Foot in the Grave* (1972), *Alive and Dead* (1974), *Blood Flies Upwards* (1976) and *A*

Stranger and Afraid (1972). The last of these novels introduces Inspector Ditteridge, one of Ferrars' recurring characters.

In a number of novels after 1978, Ferrars used the characters of Felix and Virginia Freer (who, though married, live apart) in her books. Virginia, a physiotherapist, narrates the books and assists Felix, who solves the crimes. Felix is a difficult and not entirely sympathetic character, a pathological liar and petty kleptomaniac. "He must be dreadful to live with. I can trace certain of his characteristics to people I've known," Ferrars told Rahn in the *Armchair Detective* interview. "Oddly, there's one particular man we used to know, but he wasn't a person who was very important to me. He was a shoplifter, and often he used to get the morning tea. Those were his two activities."

The first Freer novel, *Last Will and Testament* (1978), establishes the relationship of the two characters--Virginia is both pleased and apprehensive at the arrival of her sometime-con-man husband at her provincial home, but begins to appreciate his presence after a number of murders in the neighborhood. *Frog in the Throat* (1980) brings Felix and Virginia together with a pair of sisters who jointly write novels. When one of the sisters is murdered, Felix solves the crime. The Freers also appear in *Thinner Than Water* (1981), *Death of a Minor Character* (1983), *I Met Murder* (1985), and others. Of the last novel, the *New Yorker* wrote that "the character who solves [the murder]--Felix Freer, a petty thief and chronic liar who commutes between a Fox & Grapes and a Rose & Crown; who is not above sharing his estranged wife's roof, joint of lamb, and tea when it suits him; and who compares their alliance unfavorably with that of the Macbeths--is English to the core."

Elizabeth Ferrars continued to write until her death in 1995. By any reckoning a major figure among twentieth-century British mystery writers, Ferrars left her mark on the mystery-writing world, and her "splendidly civilized traditional mysteries," as Becker wrote in the *St. James Guide to Crime and Mystery Writers*, "will undoubtedly continue to please readers for years to come."

BIOGRAPHICAL/CRITICAL SOURCES:

BOOKS

Dictionary of Literary Biography, Volume 87, *British Mystery and Thriller Writers since 1940*, Gale (Detroit), 1989.

St. James Guide to Crime and Mystery Writers, fourth edition, St. James Press (Detroit), 1996.
Writers Directory, St. James Press, 1994.

PERIODICALS

Armchair Detective, fall, 1990.
Best Sellers, May 15, 1966.
Booklist, May 1, 1975; October 15, 1977; February 15, 1979.
Books, December 14, 1941.
Books and Bookmen, April, 1956; July, 1970; August, 1972; June, 1973.
Chicago Tribune, June 11, 1950.
Listener, August 3, 1978.
New Republic, June 10, 1946.
New Yorker, May 25, 1946; February 1, 1964; August 6, 1979; August 18, 1986.
New York Herald Tribune Book Review, October 9, 1949; January 13, 1957; August 31, 1958.
New York Times, May 26, 1946.
New York Times Book Review, July 8, 1956; August 31, 1958; June 5, 1960; June 16, 1963; December 22, 1963; September 12, 1971; September 3, 1972; January 7, 1973.
San Francisco Chronicle, December 28, 1952; January 29, 1956; February 10, 1957; June 19, 1960.
Saturday Review, July 11, 1942; July 21, 1945.
Spectator, June 29, 1945; June 10, 1972.
Times (London), April 3, 1995, p. 19.
Times Literary Supplement, August 4, 1966; June 11, 1970; November 8, 1974; December 12, 1975; April 22, 1977.
Washington Post Book World, April 27, 1975; June 20, 1976; February 20, 1977; February 18, 1979.
Weekly Book Review, June 9, 1946.*

*   *   *

BUNTING, A. E.
  See BUNTING, Anne Evelyn

*   *   *

BUNTING, Anne Evelyn 1928-
  (Evelyn Bolton, A. E. Bunting, Eve Bunting)

PERSONAL: Born December 19, 1928, in Maghera, Northern Ireland; came to the United States in 1960;

became U.S. citizen; daughter of Sloan Edmund (a merchant) and Mary (Canning) Bolton; married Edward Davison Bunting (a medical administrator), April 26, 1951; children: Christine, Sloan, Glenn. *Education:* Graduated from Methodist College, Belfast, 1945; also attended Queen's University. *Politics:* Democrat. *Religion:* Protestant.

ADDRESSES: Home and office—1512 Rose Villa St., Pasadena, CA 91106.

CAREER: Freelance writer, 1969—. University of California, Los Angeles, teacher of writing, 1978 and 1979; writing instructor at writing conferences.

MEMBER: PEN International, California Writer's Guild, Southern California Council on Writing for Children and Young People, Society of Children's Book Writers (board member).

AWARDS, HONORS: Barney the Beard was named an Honor Book by the Chicago Book Clinic; Golden Kite Award, Society of Children's Book Writers, for best fiction book, Outstanding Science Trade Book for Children, and Outstanding Social Science Book for Children from National Council for Social Studies and the Children's Book Council, all 1976, all for *One More Flight;* Children's Book of the Year awards from Child Study Association of America, 1976, for *One More Flight,* 1979, for *The Big Red Barn,* 1981, for *Goose Dinner* and *The Waiting Game,* 1986, for *The Valentine Bears,* and 1987, for *The Mother's Day Mice* and *Sixth Grade Sleepover; Winter's Coming* was named one of the *New York Times* Top Ten Books of 1977; Golden Kite award, 1977, for *Ghost of Summer,* which was also named Best Fiction Book for Children by Southern California Council on Literature for Children and Young People, 1977; *Skateboards: How to Make Them, How to Ride Them* was named Classroom Choice '78 by Scholastic Paperbacks; *If I Asked You, Would You Stay?* was selected one of American Library Association's Best Books for Young Adults, 1984; PEN Special Achievement Award, 1984, for her contribution to children's literature; Nene Award from the Hawaii Association of School Librarians and the Hawaii Library Association, 1986, for *Karen Kepplewhite Is the World's Best Kisser; School Library Journal*'s Best Books of the Year selections, 1986, for *The Mother's Day Mice,* and 1989, for *The Wednesday Surprise;* Southern California Council on Literature for Children and Young People Award for Excellence in a Series, 1986, for "Lippincott Page Turners" series; Parents' Choice Award from the

Parents' Choice Foundation, 1988, for *The Mother's Day Mice;* Virginia Young Readers Award, 1988-89, California Young Readers Medal from the California Reading Association, 1989, and South Carolina Young Adult Book Award from the South Carolina Association of School Librarians, 1988-89, all for *Face at the Edge of the World;* Southern California Council on Literature for Children and Young People Award for Outstanding Work of Fiction for Young Adults, 1989, for *A Sudden Silence;* Sequoyah Children's Book Award from the Oklahoma Library Association, Mark Twain Award from the Missouri Association of School Librarians, and Sunshine State Young Readers Award from the Florida Association for Media in Education, all 1989, all for *Sixth Grade Sleepover;* Caldecott Medal, 1995, for *Smoky Night.*

WRITINGS:

UNDER NAME EVE BUNTING; JUVENILES

The Once-a-Year Day, Golden Gate, 1974.
The Wild One, Scholastic Book Services (New York City), 1974.
Barney the Beard, Parents' Magazine Press (New York City), 1975.
The Skateboard Four, Albert Whitman (Niles, IL), 1976.
One More Flight, illustrated by Diane De Groat, Warne (New York City), 1976.
Blacksmith at Blueridge, Scholastic (New York City), 1976.
Josefina Finds the Prince, illustrated by Jan Palmer, Garrard (Eastman, MD), 1976.
Skateboard Saturday, Scholastic, 1976.
(With Glenn Bunting) *Skateboards: How to Make Them, How to Ride Them,* Harvey House (New York City), 1977.
The Big Cheese, illustrated by Sal Murdocca, Macmillan (New York City), 1977.
Winter's Coming, illustrated by Howard Knotts, Harcourt (San Diego, CA), 1977.
Ghost of Summer, illustrated by W. T. Mars, Warne, 1977.
Cop Camp, Scholastic, 1977.
The Haunting of Kildoran Abbey, Warne, 1978.
Magic and the Night River, Harper (New York City), 1978.
Going against Cool Calvin, Scholastic, 1978.
The Big Find, Creative Education (Mankato, MN), 1978.
Yesterday's Island, Warne, 1979.
The Big Red Barn, illustrated by Knotts, Harcourt, 1979.

Blackbird Singing, illustrated by Steven Gammell, Macmillan, 1979.

The Sea World Book of Sharks, with photographs by Flip Nicklin, Sea World Press, 1979, Harcourt, 1984.

The Sea World Book of Whales, Sea World Press, 1979, Harcourt, 1980.

Terrible Things, Harper, 1980, revised edition published as *Terrible Things: An Allegory of the Holocaust,* Jewish Publication Society, 1989.

St. Patrick's Day in the Morning, illustrated by Jan Brett, Houghton (Boston, MA), 1980.

Demetrius and the Golden Goblet (Book-of-the-Month Club selection), illustrated by Michael Hague, Harcourt, 1980.

The Robot Birthday, illustrated by Marie DeJohn, Dutton (New York City), 1980.

The Skate Patrol, Albert Whitman, 1980.

The Skate Patrol Rides Again, illustrated by Don Madden, Albert Whitman, 1981.

Goose Dinner, illustrated by Knotts, Harcourt, 1981.

The Empty Window, illustrated by Judy Clifford, Warne, 1981.

The Happy Funeral, illustrated by Mai Vo-Dinh, Harper, 1981.

Rosie and Mr. William Star, Houghton, 1981.

Jane Martin, Dog Detective, illustrated by Amy Schwartz, Garrard, 1981.

Jane Martin and the Case of the Ice Cream Dog, Garrard, 1981.

The Spook Birds, illustrated by Kathleen Tucker, Albert Whitman, 1981.

The Giant Squid, Messner (New York City), 1981.

The Great White Shark, Messner, 1982.

The Skate Patrol and the Mystery Writer, illustrated by Madden, Albert Whitman, 1982.

Karen Kepplewhite Is the World's Best Kisser, Clarion (New York City), 1983.

The Traveling Men of Ballycoo, illustrated by Kaethe Zemach, Harcourt, 1983.

The Valentine Bears, illustrated by Brett, Clarion, 1983.

Ghost behind Me, Archway (New York City), 1984.

The Man Who Could Call Down Owls, illustrated by Charles Mikolaycak, Macmillan, 1984.

Monkey in the Middle, illustrated by Lynn Munsinger, Harcourt, 1984.

Someone Is Hiding on Alcatraz Island, Clarion, 1984.

Surrogate Sister, Lippincott (Philadelphia, PA), 1984.

Clancy's Coat, Clarion, 1984.

Face at the Edge of the World, Clarion, 1985.

Sixth Grade Sleepover, Harcourt, 1986.

Scary, Scary Halloween, Clarion, 1986.

The Mother's Day Mice, Clarion, 1986.

Janet Hamm Needs a Date for the Dance, Clarion, 1986.

Will You Be My POSSLQ?, Harcourt, 1987.

Ghost's Hour, Spook's Hour, Clarion, 1987.

Happy Birthday, Dear Duck, Clarion, 1988.

A Sudden Silence, Harcourt, 1988.

How Many Days to America?: A Thanksgiving Story, Clarion, 1988.

Is Anybody There?, Lippincott, 1988.

The Ghost Children, Clarion, 1989.

No Nap, Clarion, 1989.

The Wednesday Surprise, Clarion, 1989.

In the Haunted House, Clarion, 1990.

Our Sixth-Grade Sugar Babies, Lippincott, 1990.

Such Nice Kids, Clarion, 1990.

The Wall, Clarion, 1990.

Night Tree, Harcourt, 1991.

A Turkey for Thanksgiving, Clarion, 1991.

Fly Away Home, Clarion, 1991.

The Hideout, Harcourt, 1991.

Jumping the Nail, Harcourt, 1991.

Sharing Susan, HarperCollins, 1991.

A Perfect Father's Day, Clarion, 1991.

The Mask, Child's World (Mankato, MN), 1992.

Summer Wheels, Harcourt, 1992.

Our Teacher's Having a Baby, Clarion, 1992.

The Bicycle Man, Harcourt, 1992.

Coffin on a Case, Harper, 1992.

The Day before Christmas, Clarion, 1992.

Someday a Tree, Clarion, 1993.

Survival Camp, Child's World, 1993.

Red Fox Running, Clarion, 1993.

Night of the Gargoyles, Clarion, 1994.

A Day's Work, Clarion, 1994.

Sunshine Home, Clarion, 1994.

Nasty Stinky Sneakers, HarperCollins, 1994.

The In-Between Days, HarperCollins, 1994.

Flower Garden, Harcourt, 1994.

Smoky Night, Harcourt, 1994.

Dandelions, Harcourt, 1995.

Cheyenne Again, Clarion, 1995.

Once upon a Time, R. C. Owen (Katonah, NY), 1995.

Spying on Miss Muller, Clarion, 1995.

Sunflower House, Harcourt, 1996.

Going Home, HarperCollins, 1996.

Train to Somewhere, Clarion, 1996.

Trouble on the T-ball Team, Clarion, 1996.

The Blue and the Gray, Scholastic, 1996.

SOS Titanic, Harcourt, 1996.

Market Day, HarperCollins, 1996.
I Am the Mummy Heb-Nefer, Harcourt, 1997.
Moonstick, HarperCollins, 1997.
Secret Place, Clarion, 1997.

UNDER NAME EVE BUNTING; "MAGIC CIRCLE" SERIES

The Two Giants, Ginn (Lexington, MA), 1972.
A Gift for Lonny, Ginn, 1973.
Box, Fox, Ox and the Peacock, Ginn, 1974.
Say It Fast, Ginn, 1974.
We Need a Bigger Zoo!, Ginn, 1974.

UNDER NAME EVE BUNTING; "DINOSAUR MACHINE" SE-
RIES

The Day of the Dinosaurs, EMC Corp., 1975.
Death of a Dinosaur, EMC Corp., 1975.
The Dinosaur Trap, EMC Corp., 1975.
Escape from Tyrannosaurus, EMC Corp., 1975.

UNDER NAME EVE BUNTING; "NO SUCH THINGS?" SERIES

The Creature of Cranberry Cove, EMC Corp., 1976.
The Demon, EMC Corp., 1976.
The Ghost, EMC Corp., 1976.
The Tongue of the Ocean, EMC Corp., 1976.

UNDER NAME EVE BUNTING; "EVE BUNTING SCIENCE FIC-
TION" SERIES

The Day of the Earthlings, Creative Education, 1978.
The Followers, Creative Education, 1978.
Island of One, Creative Education, 1978.
The Mask, Creative Education, 1978.
The Mirror Planet, Creative Education, 1978.
The Robot People, Creative Education, 1978.
The Space People, Creative Education, 1978.
The Undersea People, Creative Education, 1978.

UNDER NAME EVE BUNTING; "EVE BUNTING YOUNG RO-
MANCE" SERIES

Fifteen, Creative Education, 1978.
For Always, Creative Education, 1978.
The Girl in the Painting, Creative Education, 1978.
Just Like Everyone Else, Creative Education, 1978.
Maggie the Freak, Creative Education, 1978.
Nobody Knows but Me, Creative Education, 1978.
Oh, Rick, Creative Education, 1978.
A Part of the Dream, Creative Education, 1978.

Survival Camp!, Creative Education, 1978.
Two Different Girls, Creative Education, 1978.

UNDER NAME EVE BUNTING; "LIPPINCOTT PAGE TURN-
ERS" SERIES

The Cloverdale Switch, Lippincott, 1979, published
    as *Strange Things Happen in the Woods,* Harper,
    1984.
The Waiting Game, Lippincott, 1981.
The Ghosts of Departure Point, Lippincott, 1982.
If I Asked You, Would You Stay?, Lippincott, 1984.
The Haunting of SafeKeep, Lippincott, 1985.

UNDER NAME A. E. BUNTING; JUVENILES

High Tide for Labrador, Golden Gate (Chicago),
    1975.

UNDER NAME A. E. BUNTING; "HIGH POINT" SERIES

Pitcher to Center Field, Elk Grove Books (Chicago),
    1974.
Surfing Country, Elk Grove Books, 1975.
Springboard to Summer, Elk Grove Books, 1975.

UNDER NAME EVELYN BOLTON; "EVELYN BOLTON HORSE
BOOK" SERIES

Stable of Fear, Creative Education, 1974.
Lady's Girl, Creative Education, 1974.
Goodbye Charlie, Creative Education, 1974.
Ride When You're Ready, Creative Education, 1974,
    republished under name Eve Bunting, Child's
    World, 1992.
The Wild Horses, Creative Education, 1974, repub-
    lished under name Eve Bunting, Child's World,
    1992.
Dream Dancer, Creative Education, 1974.

OTHER

Also author of stories for basal readers published by
several educational houses, including Heath, Laidlaw
Brothers, Lyons & Carnahan, and Rand McNally.
Contributor to anthologies, including *Cricket's
Choice,* 1975, and *Scribner's Anthology for Young
People.* Contributor of adult and juvenile stories to
magazines.

ADAPTATIONS: How Many Days to America? was
adapted into a film, Coronet/MTI Film and Video,
1991.

SIDELIGHTS: One of juvenile fiction's most highly regarded and prolific writers, Anne Evelyn Bolton (also known as Evelyn Bolton, A. E. Bunting and Eve Bunting) has published some one hundred books since her debut work, *The Two Giants,* in 1972. This expatriate Irishwoman who settled in the United States in 1960 draws from a wide range of experience, with a result that her young protagonists are a diverse group—Irish, Japanese, Chinese-American, Inuit, Puerto Rican, Hawaiian-Irish, African-American and Caucasian among them. Also wide-ranging is the audience for an Eve Bolton book; she writes for everyone from preschooler to high-schooler.

"Reviewers generally praise Bunting books," according to Allen Raymond in his article for *Early Years.* "Whether it is due to the clarity and liveliness of the dialogue, to the real-life situations in which the author puts her characters, or whether it is the moral approach to difficult choices, there is something about her books which brings praise [from major periodicals]."

Bunting characteristically imbues her fiction with understanding and tolerance, respect for the environment, and a penchant for winding subtle facts into fiction to enhance the young reader's learning experience. For example, in her middle-graders' nonfiction, according to *Children's Literature Review,* the author "writes about sea creatures—sharks, whales, and squids—in works that address the evolution, physical characteristics, and habits of her subjects while including interesting background information about them." Middle-school and older children are exposed to introductory-level science fiction and suspense, as well as such issue-oriented fiction topics as divorce, teen suicide and terrorism, and (in *Smoky Night*) the reality of the Los Angeles riots of 1992. Bunting also creates fiction aimed at scholastic niche markets, such as the "high-interest, low vocabulary fourth-fifth grade" in the "Creative Science Fiction" series, and "reluctant readers" in the "Young Romance" books.

Many of Bunting's books are set in her native Ireland, to great success even with American audiences. In *Clancy's Coat,* notes *Horn Book* reviewer Mary Burns, the author "captured the sense of metaphor and the lilting cadence" of Irish speech in her fable about a feud that develops between neighbors Tippitt and Clancy when Tippett's cow ruins Clancy's garden. It takes all winter to do it, but eventually the two come to reconcile in a "strong message about working out differences," *Booklist* critic Ilene Cooper claims.

Bunting does not hesitate to write about differences of a more serious sort. Her 1995 novel, *Smoky Night*—a Caldecott Medal winner—examines the 1992 Los Angeles riot as seen through a child's eyes. This "troubling and curiously affectless picture book," *New York Times* critic Selma G. Lanes comments, attempts to make the chaos and confusion of those turbulent days more comprehensible to children. In the words of the book's young narrator, "Mama explains about rioting. It can happen when people get angry. They want to smash and destroy. They don't care anymore what's right and what's wrong." But in *Smoky Night,* says Lanes, "evil goes unpunished, undefined and almost unacknowledged. True, the author would have us believe that because two feuding pet cats—one belonging to the story's black narrator, the other to a Korean storekeeper—have become friends as a result of a horrific trial by fire, then so too will their owners. This is likely to seem a dubious triumph to young listeners, who will be worrying that the book's victims have been left temporarily homeless, their neighborhood in ruins." A *Los Angeles Times* contributor, however, expressed appreciation for the work, noting that *Smoky Night*'s author and illustrator "deserve honor not just as artists but also as healers."

Helping young readers understand the changes that occur when one grows to maturity also provides a subtext in many of Bunting's books. An entire "Young Romance" series (*Fifteen; For Always; The Girl in the Painting; Just Like Everyone Else; Maggie the Freak; Nobody Knows But Me; Oh, Rick!; A Part of the Dream; Survival Camp;* and *Two Different Girls*) is targeted to the reluctant-reader market with brief, sparsely illustrated tales of budding love and peer pressure. Two reviewers brought mixed reaction to this series; while *School Library Journal* reviewer Cyrisse Jaffee dismisses the books as "uniformly trite and superficial, *Booklist* critic Judith Goldberg thinks the tales have more to offer as a result of the author's "lively writing style and depth of characterization."

"There is no special secret to writing for all age levels," Bunting told *Top of the News* in 1986. "You climb inside the head and the heart of the young person in your story. You think like that child. You feel like that child. You are that child."

BIOGRAPHICAL/CRITICAL SOURCES:

BOOKS

Children's Literature Review, Volume 28, Gale (Detroit), 1992.

PERIODICALS

Booklist, June 15, 1978; March 1, 1984, p. 966.
Early Years, October, 1986.
Horn Book, April, 1984, p. 181.
Los Angeles Times, February 20, 1995, p. 4.
New York Times, May 21, 1995, p. 25.
Publishers Weekly, February 5, 1996, p. 89.
School Library Journal, September, 1978.
Top of the News, winter, 1986, p. 132-134.*

* * *

BUNTING, Eve
  See BUNTING, Anne Evelyn

* * *

BURFORD, Eleanor
  See HIBBERT, Eleanor Alice Burford

* * *

BURGESS, Trevor
  See TREVOR, Elleston

* * *

BURNETT, W(illiam) R(iley) 1899-1982
  (John Monahan, James Updyke)

PERSONAL: Born 1899, in Springfield, OH; died of heart failure, April 25, 1982, in Santa Monica, CA; buried at Forest Lawn, Glendale, CA; son of Theodore Addison and Emily Upson Colwell (Morgan) Burnett; married first wife, Marjorie Louise

Bartow, 1921; married second wife, Whitney Forbes Johnstone, 1943; children: (second marriage) James Addison, William Riley III. *Education:* Miami Military Institute, graduate, 1919; attended Ohio State University, 1919-20. *Politics:* Democrat. *Religion:* Episcopalian.

CAREER: Former shop steward in a factory and an insurance salesman; State of Ohio, Department of Labor Relations, statistician, 1921-27; novelist and screenwriter, 1927-82. Consultant to Warner Brothers, Inc., beginning 1930, and to other film companies.

MEMBER: International Screenwriters Guild, PEN, Academy of Motion Picture Arts and Sciences, Writers Club (Hollywood), The Players (New York City).

AWARDS, HONORS: O. Henry Memorial Award for best short story of 1930, for "Dressing Up"; *High Sierra* was named one of the ten best films of 1941 by the National Board of Review; Academy Award nomination for best screenplay, 1942, for *Wake Island,* and 1963, for *The Great Escape;* Writers Guild of America Award, 1949, for *Yellow Sky,* and 1963, for *The Great Escape; The Asphalt Jungle* was named one of the ten best films of 1950 by the *New York Times;* Edgar Allan Poe Award, 1951, and Grand Masters Award for contributions to the genre of crime writing and for originating the subgenre of the gangster novel, 1980, both from Mystery Writers of America; Screenwriters Award for best drama, 1963, for *The Great Escape.*

WRITINGS:

NOVELS

Little Caesar (Literary Guild selection; also see below), Dial (New York City), 1929, reprinted with new introduction by the author, 1958.
Iron Man (Book-of-the-Month Club selection), Dial, 1930.
Saint Johnson, Dial, 1930.
The Silver Eagle, Dial, 1931.
The Giant Swing, Harper (New York City), 1932.
Dark Hazard (Book-of-the-Month Club selection), Harper, 1933.
Goodbye to the Past: Scenes from the Life of William Meadows, Harper, 1934.
The Goodhues of Sinking Creek, with woodcuts by J. J. Lankes, Harper, 1934.
King Cole: A Novel, Harper, 1936 (published in England as *Six Days' Grace,* Heinemann, 1937).

The Dark Command: A Kansas Iliad, Knopf, 1938.
High Sierra (also see below), Knopf, 1940.
The Quick Brown Fox, Knopf, 1942.
Nobody Lives Forever, Knopf, 1943.
Tomorrow's Another Day, Knopf, 1945.
Romelle, Knopf, 1946.
The Asphalt Jungle (also see below), Knopf, 1949, reprinted and edited by Otto Penzler, Morrow, 1984.
Stretch Dawson, Fawcett, 1950.
Little Men, Big World, Knopf, 1951.
Vanity Row (also see below), Knopf, 1952.
Adobe Walls: A Novel of the Last Apache Rising, Knopf, 1953.
(Under pseudonym John Monahan) *Big Stan,* Fawcett, 1953.
Captain Lightfoot, Knopf, 1954, reprinted, American Reprint (Mattituck, NY), 1978.
(Under pseudonym James Updyke) *It's Always Four O'Clock,* Random, 1956.
Pale Moon, Knopf, 1956.
Underdog, Knopf, 1957.
Bitter Ground, Knopf, 1958.
Mi Amigo: A Novel of the Southwest, Knopf, 1959.
Conant, Popular Library, 1961.
Round the Clock at Volari's, Fawcett, 1961.
The Goldseekers, Doubleday, 1962.
The Widow Barony, Macdonald, 1963.
The Abilene Samson, Pocket Books, 1963.
The Winning of Mickey Free, Bantam, 1965.
The Cool Man, Fawcett, 1968.
Goodbye Chicago: 1928, End of an Era, St. Martin's, 1981.
Little Caesar, The Asphalt Jungle, High Sierra, Vanity Row, Zomba Books, 1984.

SCREENPLAYS

(With John Monk Saunders and Robert Lord) *The Finger Points,* First National, 1931.
(With Ben Hecht, Seton I. Miller, John Lee Mahin, and Fred Pasley) *Scarface: Shame of a Nation,* United Artists, 1932.
(With Lester Cole) *Some Blondes Are Dangerous* (based on Burnett's novel *Iron Man*), Universal, 1937.
(With Wells Root) *The Getaway,* Metro-Goldwyn-Mayer, 1941.
(With Huston) *High Sierra* (based on Burnett's novel of the same title; produced by Warner Brothers, 1941), edited and with an introduction by Douglas Gomery, University of Wisconsin Press for Wisconsin Center for Film and Theatre Research, 1979.

(With Albert Maltz) *This Gun for Hire,* Paramount, 1942.
(With Frank Butler, and contributor of story) *Wake Island,* Paramount, 1942.
(Co-author) *Background to Danger,* Warner Brothers, 1943.
(With John Howard Lawson and A. I. Bezzerides) *Action in the North Atlantic,* Warner Brothers, 1943.
(With Alan le May) *San Antonio,* Warner Brothers, 1945.
Nobody Lives Forever (based on his novel of the same title), Warner Brothers, 1946.
(Co-author) *Belle Starr's Daughter* (based on Burnett's story of the same title), Twentieth Century-Fox, 1949.
(Co-author) *Vendetta,* RKO, 1950.
(With William Wister Haines) *The Racket,* RKO, 1951.
(Co-author) *Dangerous Mission,* RKO, 1954.
I Died a Thousand Times (based on Burnett's novel *High Sierra*), Warner Brothers, 1955.
(With Oscar Brodney) *Captain Lightfoot* (based on Burnett's novel of the same title), Universal-International, 1955.
(With James R. Webb) *Illegal,* Warner Brothers, 1955.
(With Robert Creighton Williams) *Accused of Murder* (based on Burnett's novel *Vanity Row*), Republic, 1956.
(With Ted Berkeman and Raphael Blau) *Short Cut to Hell,* Paramount, 1957.
September Storm, Twentieth Century-Fox, 1960.
Sergeants Three, United Artists, 1962.
(With James Clavell) *The Great Escape,* United Artists, 1963.

Also author of the screenplay for *The Lawbreakers,* 1962, and of television play *Debt of Honor.* Writer of other scripts for the adventure series "Naked City," 1958-62, "The Untouchables," "77 Sunset Strip," and "Bonanza." Also worked as an uncredited contributor of various material and as a consultant for numerous films, including *Law and Order,* Universal, 1932, *The Whole Town's Talking,* Columbia, 1935, *The Westerner,* Samuel Goldwyn, 1940, *The Man I Love,* Warner Brothers, 1946, *The Walls of Jericho,* Twentieth Century-Fox, *The Asphalt Jungle,* Metro-Goldwyn-Mayer, 1950, *Night People,* Twentieth Century-Fox, 1954, *The Hangman,* Paramount, 1959, *Four for Texas,* Warner Brothers, 1963, *Ice Station Zebra,* Metro-Goldwyn-Mayer, 1968, and *Stiletto,* Avco, 1969.

OTHER

The Roar of the Crowd: Conversations with an Ex-Big-Leaguer (on baseball), foreword by Frank Frisch, illustrations by Russell Hoban, C. N. Potter, 1964.

(Author of afterword) Ben Maddow and Huston, *The Asphalt Jungle: A Screenplay,* Southern Illinois University Press, 1979.

Also contributor of short stories to numerous magazines, including *Esquire, Harper's, Scribner's, Collier's, Liberty, Redbook,* and *Saturday Evening Post.*

ADAPTATIONS: A film version of *Little Caesar* was produced by Warner Brothers in 1930 under the same title and featured the then little-known Edward G. Robinson in the role of Rico—a character type he defined and went on to play several other times. *Iron Man* became a 1931 film of the same title starring Lew Ayres and Jean Harlow by Universal, who remade it in 1937 as *Some Blondes Are Dangerous;* in 1951, it was again remade under the original title by Universal-International. *Dark Hazard* was filmed by First National in 1941 under the same title and was remade in 1937 by Warner Brothers as *Wine, Women and Horses.* In addition to serving as the basis for the film on which Burnett did uncredited work, *Saint Johnson* became a thirteen-part serialization in 1937 entitled *Wild West Days;* it was filmed a second time under the title *Law and Order* in 1940, and again in a sequel of the same title produced by Universal-International in 1953 featuring Ronald Reagan. *The Dark Command* was filmed in 1940 by Republic under the same title starring John Wayne, Walter Pidgeon, Roy Rogers, and George "Gabby" Hayes. *The Giant Swing* was filmed as *Dance Hall* in 1941. *High Sierra,* in addition to serving as the basis for two films on which Burnett worked, was filmed by Warner Brothers in 1949 as *Colorado Territory.* A film version of *Adobe Walls* entitled *Arrowhead* was produced by Paramount in 1953 starring Charlton Heston. Besides serving as the basis for the film on which Burnett did uncredited work, and which featured Sterling Hayden, Sam Jaffee, and Marilyn Monroe, *The Asphalt Jungle* was remade in 1958 by Metro-Goldwyn-Mayer as *The Badlanders* starring Alan Ladd, again in 1963 as *Cairo* starring George Sanders, and once more in 1972 as an all-black version entitled *A Cool Breeze;* in 1961, it was Converted by Metro-Goldwyn-Mayer into thirteen programs for the *Asphalt Jungle* television series. In addition to the film on which Burnett worked, *Captain Lightfoot* was adapted for the screen in 1974 as *Thunderbolt and Lightfoot.* Several of Burnett's stories were also filmed. "Beast of the City" became a film of the same title produced by Warner Brothers in 1934. "Jail Break" was filmed in 1935 by Columbia as "The Whole Town's Talking" and was released in England as "Passport to Fame." "Dr. Socrates" served as the basis for a film of the same title produced by Warner Brothers in 1935, and was remade as "King of the Underworld" in 1939; it was again remade in 1942 as "Bullet Scars." "Across the Aisle" was filmed by Twentieth Century-Fox in 1936 as "Thirty-six Hours to Kill." "Crash Dive" was filmed by Twentieth Century-Fox in 1943 and starred Tyrone Power. "Yellow Sky" served as the basis for a film of the same title starring Gregory Peck and Anne Baxter produced by Twentieth Century-Fox in 1949; in 1967, it was remade as "The Jackals." A sound recording of *High Sierra* was made by American Forces Radio and Television Service in 1973.

SIDELIGHTS: "If his novels were to be judged solely for their influence," noted George Grella in *St. James Guide to Crime and Mystery Writers,* "W. R. Burnett would undeniably be numbered among the most important writers of his time." The death of Burnett in 1982 closed a prolific writing career of more than half a century in which he published 36 novels and accumulated more than 60 screen credits. In the process Burnett saw 17 stories adapted to film and others serialized in popular magazines.

Burnett is remembered primarily for his genre-defining "tough-guy" fiction. Daniel Barry wrote in the *Dictionary of Literary Biography* that Burnett "distinguished himself by writing several prototypical works on the American underworld and gangsters." In Grella's view, the novelist "established the dominant iconography of sleek cars and flashy clothes, bootleg liquor and tommy guns, the atmospheres of dance halls and saloon, brothels and speakeasies, the gilded seediness of city life in what used to be called the underworld."

Three Burnett novels [*Little Caesar, High Sierra* and *The Asphalt Jungle*] especially fit those descriptions, and are particularly well remembered today for their motion-picture adaptations. "Most of all," says Grella, *Little Caesar* made the gangster one of the generative symbols of the 1930s—the small, dark, menacingly self-controlled man whose parabolic trajectory and anarchic rebellion against the existing social order ironically reflected the aspirations and dissatisfactions of Americans everywhere in a harsh and difficult time."

Burnett was very much a product of that time. After briefly studying journalism and playing football at Ohio State University, he left college and was variously employed until his father, an aide to the governor, secured him a position as a statistician with the State of Ohio. Burnett commented to Cook that "it was one of those political jobs, so I started writing then just to keep from getting bored." He frequented the library during his lunch breaks and wrote late into the night—a practice he maintained throughout his lifetime. During this early period, Burnett also read extensively, but "absolutely indiscriminately . . . ," he remarked to Mate and McGilligan. "I didn't know good from bad."

In 1927, Burnett left Ohio for the big-city excitement of Chicago, and from the vantage point of a hotel desk clerk, he observed an alien and appalling world. At once jolted but curiously fascinated by the Chicago underworld, this self-dubbed "hick from Ohio" was made privy to it by a gangster acquaintance, and *Little Caesar* evolved. "What I got from him was a viewpoint," Burnett explained to Mate and McGilligan. "I had the old-fashioned Ohio ideas about right and wrong, remorse and all that stuff, which to him was nonsense. . . . To him it was a war." Burnett originally submitted the novel to Scribner's but Maxwell Perkins returned it for rewriting; unwilling to comply, Burnett took it instead to Dial where it was unhesitatingly published in 1929. Immediately successful, the novel was named a Literary Guild selection and garnered Burnett a vast readership.

In a fast-paced narrative of endemic dialogue and few descriptive passages, *Little Caesar* records the internal gangland struggle for power by the ambitious, ruthless, and ill-fated Rico Cesare Bandello, who ultimately falls from power and dies a nobody. David Madden wrote in *Tough Guy Writers of the Thirties* that the characterization of Rico represents the novel's "greatest achievement. . . . He inspired all the imitations of the gunman which proliferate in fiction, motion pictures, and television programs. Rico is the tough guy in his purest form, a totally disinterested killer who cares about nothing but power. . . . His very lack of the ordinary interests of men and his 'motiveless malignity' make him a figure of pure menace and evil." Burnett described to

Mate and McGilligan his intentions for the characterization of Rico: "I was reaching for a gutter Macbeth. . . . He was doomed from the first. . . . He is the picture of overriding ambition."

An early *New York Herald Tribune Books* review by Herbert Asbury credited Burnett with having written "not only the most exciting book of the year but the most important novel of the post-war underworld that has ever been published." G. T. Hellman wrote in the *New Republic:* "For the most part *Little Caesar* bears the stamp of authenticity; it is exciting, moves rapidly, has humor. It is not literature, but it is a good deal more than journalism." Madden found nearly forty years later that "although it certainly fails to be a really good novel by any standards, *Little Caesar* . . . remains the classic gangster story." Burnett attributed the novel's enormous success—"The smack in the face it was"—to the fact that the story is told from the unique perspective of the gangster, and he added to Mate and McGilligan, "It's a commonplace now, but it had never been done before." The novel was quickly purchased by the motion picture industry, and while Burnett was personally displeased with the resultant "conventionalized" film version, the movie was immensely popular and, aided by Edward G. Robinson's star turn in the title role, affected the genre of the gangster film as indelibly as *Little Caesar* had the crime novel.

Burnett journeyed to Hollywood in 1930 as a consultant and screenwriter for Warner Brothers at the prodigious salary of one thousand dollars per week. Mate and McGilligan observe that "Burnett had the Irishman's gift of gab and a natural wit that was to stand him well in Hollywood, as well as a certain way of looking at the world: realistic, pragmatic, hard-bitten." He eventually worked for all the major studios and never left southern California. Although he became one of the highest paid in his profession, earning $3500 weekly in the midst of the Great Depression, Burnett expressed to Cook that he did not esteem his film work very highly: "The most I could say for myself is that I did the best possible work under the circumstances. . . . Writing for pictures isn't writing. It's rewriting. And that's not my way of doing things."

From the 1930s through the 1950s, Burnett continued to publish novels on various topics almost annually. Asked by Mate and McGilligan whether there was ever a point during his career at which he wrote novels with the intention of converting them to motion pictures, Burnett responded: "Never. Some of them just fell into movies, and some of them didn't. . . . Novel writing was what I was interested in—not pictures" Added the author: "I was actually subsidizing myself so I could write novels." However, Mate and McGilligan remarked that a "plunge into bankruptcy, brought on by one day too many at the track, forced Burnett into a more active screenwriting career."

According to Cook, Burnett perhaps anticipated a film version of *High Sierra* when he first conceived the novel: "About the time [Burnett] struck bottom, he went off on a trip to the mountains to sort things out. He looked at all the natural beauty around him and thought, 'What an incongruous setting this would be for a violent film—and what a place for a chase'." The subsequent best-selling novel, which did produce a memorable film, relates the story of the last surviving member of the Dillinger gang, Roy Earle, who is released from prison to commit one last robbery. The attempt fails and he flees the police to the mountains of California where he is killed. In the *Saturday Review of Literature,* B. R. Redman praised Burnett for his effective restraint in the novel: "In his description of violent physical action, Mr. Burnett's dramatic sense stops him short of melodrama; in his delineation of character his sympathy stops short of sentimentality." And a *Times Literary Supplement* contributor wrote, "The story has all the thrills one can want, much brilliant hard wit in the creamiest American vernacular and more than a little of the common touch that no good novelist in America despises."

Barry found that both American and British reviewers recognized the novel as "an excellent work of gangster fiction, mostly because of the characterization of Roy Early. . . . He was a man who happened to be a gangster, a man holding to the traditional sense of right and wrong." Unlike the stoically sinister Rico in *Little Caesar,* Earle falls in love with, but is later rejected by, a woman whose physical impediment he corrects. Barry considered the character to be one whose values no longer conform to those of the society into which he is released. Burnett perceived the character, based in part upon his own research on John Dillinger, as less of a "gangster" than a nostalgic "reversion to the Western bandit," and he indicated further to Mate and McGilligan that those of his characters most out of their element, like Earle, are symbolic to him of "Old America, rural America, and a simpler time."

The novel translated well to the screen in a film that was named by the National Board of Review as one of the ten best of 1941. "Its mood, imaginative scenery, and dialogue have made it a movie classic," wrote Barry. Burnett collaborated on the film with John Huston, who according to Mate and McGilligan once called Burnett "one of the most neglected American writers. There are moments of reality in his books that are quite overpowering. More than once they've had me breaking into a sweat."

The Asphalt Jungle, published twenty years after *Little Caesar* and nine after *High Sierra,* reflects Burnett's continued influence upon the genres of crime writing and the gangster film. Burnett indicated to Mate and McGilligan that the novel is the first part of a trilogy, including *Little Man, Big World* and *Vanity Row,* that studies the "corruption of a whole city in three stages: status quo, imbalance, and anarchy." *The Asphalt Jungle* traces an elaborately wrought jewel heist and reveals from several perspectives the internecine aspect of criminality. But Barry noted that "the various criminals forming the gang are not necessarily bad. They participate in crime, which Burnett sees as a 'left-handed form of human endeavor.' And they all hope to fulfill individual dreams with this heist." "For myself," wrote V. P. Hass in the *Saturday Review of Literature,* "I should place it behind *Little Caesar* for sheer drive but ahead of it for its subtle probing of the criminal mind. However you rank it, *The Asphalt Jungle* is a corking yarn." The novel served as the basis for four films, the first and most eminent of which was chosen by the *New York Times* as one of the ten best films of 1950.

Although Burnett published less frequently during the last decades of his life, he continued to write plays and short stories, and when he died, he left five novels in varied stages of completion. Though he had built a reputation on the strengths of his gangster stories, Burnett chafed at the tough-guy distinction and indicated to Bruce Cook in a *Detroit News Magazine* article that no more than one-third of his work could be categorized as such. "Burnett also wrote Westerns, historical novels and novels of character," noted Cook. Ken Mate and Pat McGilligan interviewed Burnett for *Film Comment* and suggested that "ironically, Burnett's inexhaustible virtuosity may have reduced his critical stature. Had he stuck to writing crime novels, he might now have a reputation similar to those of James M. Cain, Raymond Chandler, and Dashiell Hammett."

Throughout his career, Burnett was recognized for having influenced both the genre of the crime novel and, at the very outset of the sound era in motion pictures, the gangster film as well. Burnett's achievements were recognized throughout his career by several awards. In 1980, he received the Grand Masters Award from the Mystery Writers of America for his contribution not only to the genre of crime writing, but for originating the subgenre of the gangster novel as well. His works were popular in England for decades, and two of his novels have been translated into twelve other languages, including French and Italian. Although Barry acknowledged Burnett as "one of the early hard-boiled writers," he also believed that Burnett's influence extends much farther: "Three of his novels were firsts of their kind in dealing with criminals: *Little Caesar*'s clipped narrative has been imitated often but never surpassed; *High Sierra* provides a memorable psychological study; and *The Asphalt Jungle* shows the impact of one crime on the lives of people on both sides of the law. Though his plots sometimes seem corny, Burnett's dialogue is refreshing; his coinage of phrases like 'pumping lead' illustrates American phraseology in the twentieth century." And though he died in relative obscurity, Burnett continues to be the focus of students of fictional genres as one of the leading influences of the mass culture of his time.

"Beyond everything else," wrote a *Boston Transcript* critic in 1933, Burnett "knows the drifter, the gambler, the race track, thoroughly." The author "does not rise to dramatic heights. His most intense situations are presented in language such as his persons are in the habit of using, sometimes descending to the vernacular, at other times using the ordinary language of the man on the street—never the conventional language of most novels."

BIOGRAPHICAL/CRITICAL SOURCES:

BOOKS

Dictionary of Literary Biography, Volume 9, Gale (Detroit), 1981.
Madden, David, editor, *Tough Guy Writers of the Thirties,* Southern Illinois University Press, 1968.
St. James Guide to Crime and Mystery Writers, fourth edition, St. James Press (Detroit), 1996.

PERIODICALS

Boston Transcript, September 9, 1933.
Detroit News Magazine, November 8, 1981.
Film Comment, February, 1983.
New Republic, July 10, 1929.
New Statesman and Nation, August 3, 1940.
New York Herald Tribune Books, June 2, 1929.
New York Times, June 2, 1929; August 21, 1949.
New York Times Book Review, June 24, 1984.
Reprint Bulletin, Volume XXIX, number 2, 1984.
Saturday Review of Literature, June 15, 1929; March 30, 1940; October 15, 1949.
Times Literary Supplement, July 27, 1940.

OBITUARIES:

PERIODICALS

Chicago Tribune, May 1, 1982.
London Times, April 30, 1982.
Newsweek, May 10, 1982.
New York Times, April 29, 1982.
Time, May 10, 1982.
Washington Post, April 29, 1982.*

C

CARR, Philippa
See HIBBERT, Eleanor Alice Burford

* * *

CARRUTH, Hayden 1921-

PERSONAL: Surname accented on final syllable; born August 3, 1921, in Waterbury, CT; son of Gorton Veeder (an editor) and Margery Tracy Barrow (maiden name, Dibb) Carruth; married Sara Anderson, March 14, 1943; married Eleanore Ray, November 29, 1952; married Rose Marie Dorn, October 28, 1961; married Joe-Anne McLaughlin, December 29, 1989; children: (first marriage) Martha Hamilton; (third marriage) David Barrow. *Education:* University of North Carolina, A.B., 1943; University of Chicago, M.A., 1948. *Politics:* Abolitionist.

ADDRESSES: Home— RD 1, Box 128, Munnsville, NY 13409.

CAREER: Poet; free-lance writer and editor. Editor-in-chief, *Poetry,* 1949-50; associate editor, University of Chicago Press, 1951-52; project administrator, Intercultural Publications, Inc., 1952-53; poetry editor, *Harper's* magazine, 1977—. Poet-in-residence, Johnson State College, 1972-74; adjunct professor, University of Vermont, 1975-78; visiting professor, St. Michael's College, Winooskie, VT; professor of English, Syracuse University, 1979-85; professor, Bucknell University, 1985-86; professor, Syracuse University, 1986-91, professor emeritus, 1991—. Owner and operator, Crow's Mark Press, Johnson, VT. *Military service:* U.S. Army Air Forces, World War II; became staff sergeant; spent two years in Italy.

MEMBER: New York Foundation for the Arts (senior fellow, 1993).

AWARDS, HONORS: Bess Hokin Prize, 1954, Vachel Lindsay Prize, 1956, Levinson Prize, 1958, and Morton Dauwen Zabel Prize, 1967, all from *Poetry* magazine; Harriet Monroe Poetry Prize, University of Chicago, 1960, for *The Crow and the Heart;* grant-in-aid for poetry, Brandeis University, 1960; Bollingen Foundation fellowship in criticism, 1962; Helen Bullis Award, University of Washington, 1962; Carl Sandburg Award, *Chicago Daily News,* 1963, for *The Norfolk Poems;* Emily Clark Balch Prize, *Virginia Quarterly Review,* 1964, for *North Winter;* Eunice Tietjens Memorial Prize, 1964; Guggenheim Foundation fellow, 1965 and 1979; National Endowment for the Humanities fellow, 1967; National Foundation on the Arts and Humanities grant, 1967 and 1974; Governor's Medal, State of Vermont, 1974; Shelley Memorial Award, Poetry Society of America, 1978; Lenore Marshall Poetry Prize, 1978, for *Brothers, I Loved You All; The Voice That Is Great within Us: American Poetry of the Twentieth Century* was selected as one of the New York Public Library's Books for the Teen Age, 1981 and 1982; Whiting Writers Award, Whiting Foundation, 1986; Sarah Josepha Hale award, 1988; senior fellowship, National Endowment for the Arts, 1988; Ruth Lilly Poetry Prize, 1990; honorary degrees from New England College, 1987, Syracuse University, 1993; National Book Critics Circle Award in Poetry, 1993; National Book Award in poetry, 1996, for *Scrambled Eggs and Whiskey: Poems 1991-1996.*

WRITINGS:

POETRY

The Crow and the Heart, 1946-1959, Macmillan (New York City), 1959.
In Memorium: G. V. C., privately printed, 1960.
Journey to a Known Place (long poem), New Directions (New York City), 1961.
The Norfolk Poems: 1 June to 1 September 1961, Prairie Press, 1962.
North Winter, Prairie Press, 1964.
Nothing for Tigers; Poems, 1959-1964, Macmillan, 1965.
Contra Mortem (long poem), Crow's Mark Press, 1967.
(Contributor) *Where Is Vietnam?: American Poets Respond,* Anchor Books (New York City), 1967.
For You: Poems, New Directions, 1970.
The Clay Hill Anthology, Prairie Press, 1970.
From Snow and Rock, From Chaos: Poems, 1965-1972, New Directions, 1973.
Dark World, Kayak (Santa Cruz, CA), 1974.
The Bloomingdale Papers, University of Georgia Press (Athens), 1975.
Loneliness: An Outburst of Hexasyllables, Janus Press (Rogue River, OR), 1976.
Aura, Janus Press, 1977.
Brothers, I Loved You All, Sheep Meadow (New York City), 1978.
Almanach du Printemps Vivarois, Nadja, 1979.
The Mythology of Dark and Light, Tamarack (Madison, WI), 1982.
The Sleeping Beauty, Harper (New York City), 1983, revised edition, Copper Canyon Press (Port Townsend, WA), 1990.
If You Call This Cry a Song, Countryman Press (Woodstock, VT), 1983.
Asphalt Georgics, New Directions, 1985.
Lighter Than Air Craft, edited by John Wheatcroft, Press Alley, 1985.
The Oldest Killed Lake in North America, Salt-Works Press, 1985.
Mother, Tamarack Press, 1985.
The Selected Poetry of Hayden Carruth, Macmillan, 1986.
Sonnets, Press Alley, 1989.
Tell Me Again How the White Heron Rises and Flies Across the Nacreous River at Twilight toward the Distant Islands, New Directions, 1989.
Collected Shorter Poems, 1946-1991, Copper Canyon Press, 1992.
Collected Longer Poems, Copper Canyon Press, 1993.

Selected Essays and Reviews, Copper Canyon Press, 1995.
Scrambled Eggs and Whiskey: Poems, 1991-1995, Copper Canyon Press, 1996.

EDITOR

(With James Laughlin) *A New Directions Reader,* New Directions, 1964.
The Voice That Is Great within Us: American Poetry of the Twentieth Century, Bantam (New York City), 1970.
The Bird/Poem Book: Poems on the Wild Birds of North America, McCall, 1970.
The Collected Poems of James Laughlin, Moyer Bell (Wakefield, RI), 1994.

OTHER

Appendix A (novel), Macmillan, 1963.
After "The Stranger": Imaginary Dialogues with Camus, Macmillan, 1964.
(Contributor) *The Art of Literary Publishing,* Pushcart Press (Wainscott, NY), 1980.
Working Papers: Selected Essays and Reviews, edited by Judith Weissman, University of Georgia Press, 1981.
Effluences from the Sacred Caves: More Selected Essays and Reviews, University of Michigan Press (Ann Arbor), 1984.
Sitting In: Selected Writings on Jazz, Blues, and Related Topics (includes poetry), University of Iowa Press (Iowa City), 1986, expanded edition, 1993.
Suicides and Jazzers, University of Michigan Press, 1992.

Contributor to periodicals, including *Poetry, Hudson Review, New Yorker,* and *Partisan Review.* Editor-in-chief, *Poetry,* 1949-50; member of editorial board, *Hudson Review,* 1971—; poetry editor, *Harper's,* 1977-83.

SIDELIGHTS: Though known primarily as a critic and editor, Hayden Carruth is also, according to the *Virginia Quarterly Review,* "a poet who has never received the wide acclaim his work deserves and who is certainly one of the most important poets working in this country today. . . . [He is] technically skilled, lively, never less than completely honest, and as profound and deeply moving as one could ask." Characterized by a calm, tightly controlled, and relatively "plain" language that belies the intensity of feeling behind the words, Carruth's poetry elicits praise from those who admire its wide variety of verse forms and criticism from those who find its precision and restraint too impersonal and academic.

Commenting in his book *Babel to Byzantium,* James Dickey speculates that these opposing views of Carruth's work may result from the occasionally uneven quality of his poetry. In a discussion of *The Crow and the Heart,* for example, Dickey notes "a carefulness which bursts, once or twice or three times, into a kind of frenzied eloquence, a near-hysteria, and in these frightening places sloughing off a set of mannerisms which in the rest of the book seems determined to reduce Carruth to the level of a thousand other poets. . . . [He] is one of the poets (perhaps all poets are some of these poets) who write their best, pushing past limit after limit, only in the grip of recalling some overpowering experience. When he does not have such a subject at hand, Carruth amuses himself by being playfully skillful with internal rhyme, inventing bizarre Sitwellian images, being witty and professionally sharp."

American Poetry Review critic Geoffrey Gardner, who characterizes Carruth as "a poet who has always chosen to make his stand just aside from any of the presently conflicting mainstreams," says that such linguistic playfulness is typical of the poet's early work. He attributes it to Carruth's struggle "to restore equilibrium to the soul [and] clarity to vision, through a passionate command of language," a struggle that gives much of his poetry "a Lear-like words-against-the-storm quality." Continues Gardner: "I won't be the first to say Carruth's early work is cumbered by archaisms, forced inversions, sometimes futile extravagances of vocabulary and a tendency of images and metaphors to reify into a top heavy symbolism. . . . But the courage of [his] poems can't be faulted. From the earliest and against great odds, Carruth made many attempts at many kinds of poems, many forms, contending qualities of diction and texture. . . . If the struggle of contending voices and attitudes often ends in poems that don't quite succeed, it remains that the struggle itself is moving for its truthfulness and intensity. . . . Carruth uniformly refuses to glorify his crazies. They are pain and pain alone. What glory there is—and there are sparks of it everywhere through these early poems—he keeps for the regenerative stirrings against the storm of pain and isolation."

Like many poets, Carruth turns to personal experience for inspiration; however, with the possible exception of *The Bloomingdale Papers* (a long poetic

sequence Carruth wrote in the 1950s while confined to a mental hospital for treatment of alcoholism and a nervous breakdown), he does not indulge in the self-obsessed meditations common among some of his peers. Instead, Carruth turns outward, exploring such "universal opposites" as madness (or so-called madness) and sanity or chaos and order. He then tries to balance the negative images—war, loneliness, the destruction of the environment, sadness—with mostly nature-related positive images and activities that communicate a sense of stability—the cycle of the seasons, performing manual labor, contemplating the night sky, observing the serenity of plant and animal life. But, as Gardner points out, "Carruth is not in the least tempted to sentimentality about country life. . . . [He recognizes] that it can be a life of value and nobility in the midst of difficult facts and chaos." Nor is he "abstractly philosophical or cold," according to the critic. "On the contrary," Gardner states, "[his poems] are all poems about very daily affairs: things seen and heard, the loneliness of missing friends absent or dead, the alternations of love for and estrangement from those present, the experiences of a man frequently alone with the non-human which all too often bears the damaging marks of careless human intrusion." Furthermore, he says, "Carruth comes to the politics of all this with a vengeance. . . . [His poems] all bear strong public witness against the wastes and shames of our culture that are destroying human value with a will in a world where values are already hard enough to maintain, in a universe where they are always difficult to discover. Carruth does not express much anger in [his] poems. Yet one feels that an enormous energy of rage has forced them to be."

Concludes Alastair Reid in the *Saturday Review:* "[Carruth's] poems have a sureness to them, a flair and variety. . . . Yet, in their dedication to finding an equilibrium in an alien and often cruel landscape, Vermont, where the poet has dug himself in, they reflect the moods and struggles of a man never at rest. . . . His work teems with the struggle to live and to make sense, and his poems carve out a kind of grace for us."

In the 1990s, the appearance of anthologies and collections of Carruth's verse and prose have allowed critics to assess his career as a whole. In reviewing *Collected Shorter Poems,* which appeared in 1992, *Poetry* contributor David Barber calls attention to the rich diversity of the poet's oeuvre: "Hayden Carruth is vast; he contains multitudes. Of the august order of American poets born in the Twenties, he is undoubtedly the most difficult to reconcile to the convenient branches of classification and affiliation, odd man out in any tidy scheme of influence and descent." Somewhat deceptively titled, *Collected Shorter Poems,* which won the 1992 National Book Critics' Circle Award, is not a comprehensive volume, but is comprised of selections from thirteen of Carruth's previously published volumes, together with many poems appearing for the first time. Writing in the *Nation,* Ted Solotaroff finds the volume to be a welcome opportunity for giving a "full hearing" to "a poet as exacting and undervalued as Carruth generally has been." Solotaroff highlights two characteristics typifying Carruth's poetic achievement. First, he describes him as a "poet's poet, a virtuoso of form from the sonnet to free verse, from medieval metrics to jazz ones." Secondly, Solotaroff draws attention to the moral seriousness of Carruth's work as a critic of contemporary poetry, claiming that the poet "has also been, to my mind, the most catholic, reliable and socially relevant critic of poetry we have had in an age of burgeoning tendencies, collapsing standards and a general withdrawal of poets from the public to the private sector of consciousness." The 1993 volume *Collected Longer Poems* received similar praise from the majority of critics, who felt that this collection contained much of the poet's best work. Anthony Robbins, commenting in *American Book Review,* characterizes Carruth's poetry as being "grounded in the traditions of Romance, in *entre-les-guerres* modernism revised in light of mid-century existentialism, and in his own personal forms of nonviolent anarchism." Both Robbins and *Bloomsbury Review* contributor Shaun T. Griffin call attention to the importance of the volume's opening selection, "The Asylum," which details the poet's experiences of being hospitalized for a breakdown. Griffin judges these "among the most honest and harrowing in the volume," maintaining that "they ring with the compelling voice of despair; the wind floats through them, and the reader finds himself staring at the November landscape, leafless, dark, and dormant."

Carruth's prose discussions of poets and poetry was anthologized in the 1995 volume *Selected Essays and Reviews.* Spanning thirty years of his critical writing, this collection was enthusiastically received by critics, who singled out for particular praise the essays on Alexander Pope, Edwin Muir, and Paul Goodman. In the following year, Carruth published his most recent collection of verse, *Scrambled Eggs and Whiskey: Poems 1991-1995,* a volume that cen-

ters on meditations of such themes as politics, history, aging, nostalgia, guilt, and love.

Carruth once told *CA:* "I have a close but at the same time uncomfortable relationship with the natural world. I've always been most at home in the country probably because I was raised in the country as a boy, and I know something about farming and woodcutting and all the other things that country people know about. That kind of work has been important to me in my personal life and in my writing too. I believe in the values of manual labor and labor that is connected with the earth in some way. But I'm not simply a nature poet. In fact, I consider myself and I consider the whole human race fundamentally alien. By evolving into a state of self-consciousness, we have separated ourselves from the other animals and the plants and from the very earth itself, from the whole universe. So there's a kind of fear and terror involved in living close to nature. My poems, I think, exist in a state of tension between the love of natural beauty and the fear of natural meaninglessness or absurdity.

"I think there are many reasons for poets and artists in general to be depressed these days. . . . They have to do with a lot . . . [of] things that are going on in our civilization. They have to do with the whole evolution of the sociology of literature during the last fifty years. Things have changed; they've turned completely around. I don't know if I can say it briefly but I'll try. When I was young and starting to write poetry seriously and to investigate the resources of modern poetry, as we called it then, we still felt beleaguered; modern poetry was still considered outrageous by most of the people in the publishing business and in the reading audience at large. We still spoke in terms of the true artists and the philistines. We felt that if we could get enough people to read T. S. Eliot and Wallace Stevens and e. e. cummings and William Carlos Williams and other great poets of that period, then something good would happen in American civilization. We felt a genuine vocation, a calling, to try and make this happen. And we succeeded. Today thousands of people are going to colleges and attending workshops and taking courses in twentieth-century literature. Eliot and Stevens are very well known, very well read; and American civilization has sunk steadily, progressively, further and further down until most of the sensible people are in a state of despair. It's pretty obvious that good writing doesn't really have very much impact on social events or national events of any kind. We hope that it has individual impact, that readers here and there are made better in some way by reading our work. But it's a hope; we have no proof."

BIOGRAPHICAL/CRITICAL SOURCES:

BOOKS

Contemporary Literary Criticism, Gale (Detroit), Volume 4, 1975, Volume 7, 1977, Volume 10, 1979, Volume 18, 1981, Volume 84, 1994.
Dickey, James, *Babel to Byzantium,* Farrar, Straus (New York City), 1968.
Dictionary of Literary Biography, Volume 5: *American Poets since World War II,* Gale, 1980.

PERIODICALS

American Book Review, September, 1995, p. 23.
American Poetry Review, May, 1979; January, 1981.
Bloomsbury Review, January/February, 1996, p. 18.
Chicago Tribune Book World, December 26, 1982.
Current Biography, April, 1992, p. 10.
Library Journal, September 1, 1990, p. 263; November 1, 1993, p. 95; March 1, 1996, p. 4.
Los Angeles Times, December 12, 1986.
Los Angeles Times Book Review, June 3, 1984.
Nation, February 15, 1965; October 25, 1971; November 16, 1992, p. 600; December 27, 1993, p. 810.
New York Times, January 3, 1976.
New York Times Book Review, May 12, 1963; April 6, 1975; September 2, 1979; May 23, 1982; August 21, 1983; January 22, 1984; July 14, 1985; May 11, 1986; December 27, 1992, p. 2.
Poetry, August, 1963; May, 1974; July, 1993, p. 237; March, 1996, p. 343.
Publishers Weekly, January 31, 1994, p. 82; October 9, 1995, p. 80; February 26, 1996, p. 101.
Saturday Review, October 27, 1979.
Seneca Review, spring, 1990.
Times Literary Supplement, July 23, 1971.
Virginia Quarterly Review, summer, 1963; summer, 1971; summer, 1979.
Washington Post Book World, January 1, 1984; April 13, 1986.

*   *   *

CARSON, Rosalind
   See CHITTENDEN, Margaret

CARTER, Nick
   See BALLARD, (Willis) Todhunter

*   *   *

CASPARY, Vera 1899-1987

PERSONAL: Born November 13, 1899, in Chicago, IL; died of a stroke June 13, 1987, in New York, NY.; daughter of Paul (a department store buyer) and Julia (Cohen) Caspary; married I. G. Goldsmith (a film producer), October 5, 1949 (deceased). *Education:* Educated in Chicago public schools. *Politics:* Independent Democrat.

CAREER: Freelance writer of books, plays, and films. *Dance* (magazine), New York, NY, editor, 1925-27.

MEMBER: Authors Guild, Authors League of America, Dramatists Guild, Writers Guild of America West.

AWARDS, HONORS: Awards from Screen Writers Guild for *A Letter to Three Wives* and *Les Girls.*

WRITINGS:

The White Girl, Sears (New York City), 1929.
Ladies and Gents, Century (New York City), 1929.
Music in the Streets Sears, 1930.
Thicker than Water, Liveright (New York City), 1932.
Laura, Houghton (Boston), 1942.
Bedelia, Houghton, 1944.
The Murder in the Stork Club, Black (New York City), 1946, published as *The Lady in Mink,* Gordon Martin (London), 1946.
Stranger than Truth, Random House (New York City), 1946.
The Weeping and the Laughter, Little, Brown (Boston), 1950.
Thelma, Little, Brown, 1952.
False Face, W. H. Allen (London), 1954.
The Husband, Harper (New York City), 1957.
Evvie, Harper, 1960.
A Chosen Sparrow, Putnam (New York City), 1964.
The Man Who Loved His Wife, Putnam, 1966.
The Rosecrest Cell, Putnam, 1967.
Final Portrait, W. H. Allen, 1971.
Ruth, Pocket Books (New York City), 1972.
The Dreamers, Pocket Books, 1975.

The Secret of Elizabeth, Pocket Books, 1978, published as *Elizabeth X,* W. H. Allen, 1978.
The Secrets of Grown-Ups (autobiography), McGraw (New York City), 1979.

SCREENPLAYS

Scandal Street, Paramount, 1931.
The Night of June 13, Paramount, 1932.
I'll Love You Always, Columbia, 1935.
Easy Living, Paramount, 1937.
Lady from Louisiana, Republic, 1941.
Claudia and David, Twentieth Century-Fox, 1946.
Bedelia (based on her novel), General Film Distributors, 1946.
Out of the Blue, Eagle Lion, 1947.
A Letter to Three Wives, Twentieth Century-Fox, 1949.
Three Husbands, United Artists, 1950.
I Can Get It for You Wholesale, Twentieth Century-Fox, 1951.
The Blue Gardenia, Warner Bros., 1953.
Give a Girl a Break, Metro-Goldwyn-Mayer, 1954.
Les Girls, Metro-Goldwyn-Mayer, 1957.
Bachelor in Paradise, Metro-Goldwyn-Mayer, 1961.

Also author of *Such Women Are Dangerous.* Author of plays *Blind Mice,* with Winifred Lenihan, 1931, *Laura* (based on her novel of the same title), with George Sklar, *Wedding in Paris,* and *Geraniums in My Window.*

SIDELIGHTS: A freelancer by nature and a storyteller at heart, Vera Caspary came into her profession at an opportune time—the labor shortage of World War I opened doors to the young woman in business. For years, she churned out copy for advertisements and correspondence courses (on subjects she knew little about, "including a notoriously successful dance course," according to *Library Journal*), before breaking into book publishing with her first novel, *The White Girl,* in 1929.

That work, with its plot reminiscent of Fannie Hurst's potboiler classic *Imitation of Life,* concerns a young woman of mixed race who moves from her native South to Chicago in search of a better life. There she passes for white, but lives in fear of someone uncovering the truth about her black heritage. A love affair ends in tragedy. Typical of critics' reaction at the time was a comparison of Caspary's style to that of Hurst and Edna Ferber, plus praise for the author's handling of a controversial subject. "Tense, but never hysterical, the novel is especially notable for the lack of sensationalism with which it handles a difficult theme," remarked the critic for the *New York Times.*

Caspary explores societal themes again with her 1932 novel, *Thicker Than Water,* which presents four decades in the lives of a Portuguese Jewish family in Chicago. While acknowledging problems with plot pacing, critics were quick to laud Caspary's approach to her subject. As a *Books* critic pointed out, "The subtle alterations in Jewish and family life, the slow fading of orthodox observances, the swift infiltration of materialistic attitudes—these things are integral parts of the novel. They give Miss Caspary's book a definite social value."

"In all her fiction," noted Jane S. Bakerman in the *St. James Guide to Crime and Mystery Writers,* Caspary "employs a taut, gritty style and an even, unjudgemental tone that is almost Naturalistic. All her novels reveal her ear for clipped, brisk dialogue, one of her strongest techniques, for this device conveys clearly and without burdensome modifiers the tone, mood and tension of men and women under threat." In the mystery/thriller genre, Caspary had several successes. Her best-known work in this category, *Laura,* began as a novel, evolved into a stage play co-adapted by the author, and blossomed as a hit motion picture with Gene Tierney in the title role. (So well-received was the picture, in fact, that director Otto Preminger afterwards declared *Laura* to be his first film, effectively dismissing the five features he directed prior to it.)

With *Laura*—in which a detective finds himself falling in love with the title character, a crime victim with secrets of her own—Caspary created a mystery that is also a personality study, noted Bakerman. The novel "is brilliantly constructed, and the reader shares the characters' fascination with Laura's vivid, appealing personality. Actually, Laura examines the American Dream from a new, revealing angle. The unreality of the dream is clearly symbolized by the novel's cleverly constructed double climax. Deservedly, *Laura* is a mystery classic."

At the time of its publication, *Books* reviewer Will Cuppy said of *Laura,* "If you have no room for 'psychothriller' in your vocabulary, just think of it as a superior mystery, done with a novel twist and much skill." A *Springfield Republican* critic called *Laura* "a difficult book to classify; it carries a triple threat as a mystery, a love story, and a character study." And Isaac Anderson of the *New York Times* concluded that, whatever label is applied to the book, "it is something quite different from the run-of-the-mill detective story, and Vera Caspary deserves thanks for providing it."

Other Caspary mysteries that gained critical and popular notice included *Bedelia, The Man Who Loved His Wife,* and *False Face.* In the latter novel a seemingly competent teacher, Nina Redfield, is revealed to be "emotionally adolescent" as Bakerman commented. The character "has remained entranced with her school beau, [now] a dangerous criminal whom she romanticizes."

Fifty years of writing novels and screenplays led Caspary to publish her autobiography, *The Secrets of Grown-Ups,* in 1979. *Washington Post Book World* reviewer Faiga Levine called Caspary's life "a Baedeker of the 20th century. An independent woman in an unliberated era, she collided with or was touched by many of its major historical and cultural events: wars, the Depression, the Spanish Civil War, the Leopold/Loeb . . . murder case, Hollywood in its romantic heyday, Hollywood in the grip of McCarthyism [which the author experienced firsthand once word of her onetime affiliation with the Communist Party came to light], the footloose life of the artistic rich, publishing, Broadway." A *New York Times Book Review* critic wrote that "despite the coy title, this is a lively, tough account of how a woman born into a conservative Jewish family broke conventions by plunging into the world of journalism and screenwriting at a time when women's liberation was still a faint rumble in the underground." Mary Ann Callan, in a *Los Angeles Times* piece, remarked on how, "against stifling odds, [Caspary] breaks from tradition, defies prejudice."

BIOGRAPHICAL/CRITICAL SOURCES:

BOOKS

St. James Guide to Crime and Mystery Writers, St. James Press (Detroit), 1996.

PERIODICALS

Books, August 21, 1932; January 31, 1943.
Los Angeles Times Book Review, December 23, 1979.
New York Times, January 20, 1929; January 31, 1943.
New York Times Book Review, January 20, 1980.

Springfield Republican, February 7, 1943.
Washington Post Book World, August 18, 1979.

OBITUARIES:

PERIODICALS

Chicago Tribune, June 19, 1987.
Los Angeles Times, June 19, 1987.
New York Times, June 17, 1987.
Times (London), June 22, 1987.
Washington Post, June 18, 1987.*

*   *   *

CHANCE, John Newton 1911-1983
    (Jonathan Chance, John Drummond, John Lymington, David C. Newton)

PERSONAL: Born in 1911 in London, England; died August 3, 1983, in Cornwall, England; son of Richard Newton Chance (a comic strip editor); married Shirley Savill; children: three sons. *Education:* Attended Streatham Hill College.

CAREER: Writer. *Military service:* Served in the Royal Air Force during World War II.

WRITINGS:

Wheels in the Forest, Gollancz (London), 1935.
Murder in Oils, Gollancz, 1935.
The Devil Drives, Gollancz, 1936.
Rhapsody in Fear: A Crime Novel, Gollancz, 1937.
Maiden Possessed, Gollancz, 1937.
Death of an Innocent, Gollancz, 1938.
The Devil in Greenlands: A Small Matter of Life and Death, Gollancz, 1939.
The Ghost of Truth: A Scandal in Two Parts, Gollancz, 1939.
Screaming Fog, MacDonald & Co. (London), 1944, published as *Death Stalks the Cobbled Square,* R. M. McBride (New York City), 1946.
The Red Knight, MacDonald & Co., 1945.
The Knight and the Castle: A deHavilland Story, MacDonald & Co., 1946.
The Eye in Darkness, MacDonald & Co., 1946.
The Black Highway: A deHavilland Story, MacDonald & Co., 1947.
Coven Gibbet, MacDonald & Co., 1948.
The Brandy Pole, MacDonald & Co., 1949.

The Night of the Full Moon, Macdonald & Co., 1950.

Aunt Miranda's Murder, Macdonald & Co., 1951.

The Man in My Shoes, Macdonald & Co., 1952.

The Twopenny Box, Macdonald & Co., 1952.

The Randy Inheritance, Macdonald & Co., 1953.

The Jason Affair, Macdonald & Co., 1953, published in the United States as *Up to Her Neck: A Novel of Suspense*, Popular Library (New York City), 1955.

The Jason Murders, Macdonald & Co., 1954.

Jason and the Sleep Game, Macdonald & Co., 1954.

Jason Goes West, Macdonald & Co., 1955.

A Shadow Called Janet, Macdonald & Co., 1956.

The Last Seven Hours, Macdonald & Co., 1956.

Dead Man's Knock, R. Hale (London), 1957.

The Little Crime, R. Hale, 1957.

Man with Three Witches, R. Hale, 1958.

Affair with a Rich Girl, R. Hale, 1958.

The Fatal Fascination, R. Hale, 1959.

The Man with No Face, R. Hale, 1959.

Yellow Belly (nonfiction), R. Hale, 1959.

Lady in a Frame, R. Hale, 1960.

Alarm at Black Brake, R. Hale, 1960.

The Night of the Settlement, R. Hale, 1961.

The Crimes at Rillington Place: A Novelist's Reconstruction (nonfiction), Hodder & Stoughton (London), 1961.

Import of Evil, R. Hale, 1961.

Triangle of Fear, R. Hale, 1962.

The Forest Affair, R. Hale, 1963.

The Man behind Me, R. Hale, 1963.

Commission for Disaster, R. Hale, 1964.

Death under Desolate, R. Hale, 1964.

Stormlight, R. Hale, 1965.

The Double Death, R. Hale, 1966.

The Affair at Dead End, R. Hale, 1966.

The Case of the Death Computer, R. Hale, 1967.

The Case of the Fear Makers, R. Hale, 1967.

The Death Women, R. Hale, 1967.

The Hurricane Drift, R. Hale, 1967.

The Mask of Pursuit, R. Hale, 1967.

The Thug Executive, R. Hale, 1967.

The Rogue Aunt, R. Hale, 1968.

Mantrap, R. Hale, 1968.

The Halloween Murders, R. Hale, 1968.

Fate of the Lying Jade, R. Hale, 1968.

Death of the Wild Bird, R. Hale, 1968.

Dead Men's Shoes, R. Hale, 1968.

The Abel Coincidence, R. Hale, 1969.

The Ice Maidens, R. Hale, 1969.

Involvement in Austria, R. Hale, 1969.

The Killer Reaction, R. Hale, 1969.

The Killing Experiment, R. Hale, 1969.

Three Masks of Death, R. Hale, 1970.

A Ring of Liars, R. Hale, 1970.

The Mists of Treason, R. Hale, 1970.

The Mirror Train, R. Hale, 1970.

The Faces of a Bad Girl, R. Hale, 1971.

A Wreath of Bones, R. Hale, 1971.

The Cat Watchers, R. Hale, 1971.

A Bad Dream of Death, R. Hale, 1972.

The Dead Tale-Tellers, R. Hale, 1972.

Last Train to Limbo, R. Hale, 1972.

The Man with Two Heads, R. Hale, 1972.

The Love-Hate Relationship, R. Hale, 1973.

The Grab Operators, R. Hale, 1973.

The Farm Villains, R. Hale, 1973.

Canterbury Killgrims, R. Hale, 1974.

Girl in the Crime Belt, R. Hale, 1974.

The Starfish Affair, R. Hale, 1974.

Hill Fog, R. Hale, 1975.

The Shadow of the Killer, R. Hale, 1975.

The Monstrous Regiment, R. Hale, 1975.

A Fall-Out of Thieves, R. Hale, 1976.

The Devil's Edge, R. Hale, 1976.

The Murder Makers, R. Hale, 1976.

Return to Death Valley, R. Hale, 1976.

Motive for a Kill, R. Hale, 1977.

The House of the Dead Ones, R. Hale, 1977.

The Frightened Fisherman, R. Hale, 1977.

End of an Iron Man, R. Hale, 1978.

Ducrow Folly, R. Hale, 1978.

Drop of Hot Gold, R. Hale, 1979.

The Guilty Witness, R. Hale, 1979.

Thieves' Kitchen, R. Hale, 1979.

A Place Called Skull, R. Hale, 1980.

The Death Watch Ladies, R. Hale, 1980.

The Mayhem Madchen, R. Hale, 1980.

The Black Widow, R. Hale, 1981.

The Death Importer, R. Hale, 1981.

The Mystery of Enda Favell, R. Hale, 1981.

Madman's Will, R. Hale, 1982.

The Hunting of Mr. Exe, R. Hale, 1982.

The Shadow in Pursuit, R. Hale, 1982.

The Traditional Murders, R. Hale, 1983.

The Death Chemist, R. Hale, 1983.

Terror Train, R. Hale, 1983.

Looking for Samson, R. Hale, 1984.

Nobody's Supposed to Murder the Butler, R. Hale, 1984.

The Bad Circle, R. Hale, 1985.

The Time Bomb, R. Hale, 1985.

The Woman Hater, R. Hale, 1986.

The Psychic Trap, R. Hale, 1986.

Spy on a Spider, R. Hale, 1987.

The Hit Man, R. Hale, 1987.

The Hiller Weapon, R. Hale, 1987.

The Smiling Cadaver, R. Hale, 1987.
The Reluctant Agent, R. Hale, 1988.
The Shadow Before, R. Hale, 1988.
The Offshore Conspiracy, R. Hale, 1988.
The Man on the Cliff, R. Hale, 1988.
A Confusion of Eyes, R. Hale, 1989.
The Running of the Apies, R. Hale, 1989.
A Tale of Tangled Ladies, R. Hale, 1989.

UNDER PSEUDONYM JONATHAN CHANCE

The Light Benders, R. Hale, 1968.

UNDER PSEUDONYM JOHN DRUMMOND

The Essex Road Crime, Amalgamated Press (London), 1944.
The Manor House Menace, Amalgamated Press, 1944.
The Painted Dagger, Amalgamated Press, 1944.
The Riddle of the Leather Bottle, Amalgamated Press, 1944.
The Tragic Case of the Station Master's Legacy, Amalgamated Press, 1944.
At Sixty Miles an Hour, Amalgamated Press, 1945.
The House on the Hill, Amalgamated Press, 1945.
The Riddle of the Mummy Case, Amalgamated Press, 1945.
The Mystery of the Deserted Camp, Amalgamated Press, 1948.
The Town of Shadows, Amalgamated Press, 1948.
The Case of the "Dead" Spy, Amalgamated Press, 1949.
The Riddle of the Receiver's Hoard, Amalgamated Press, 1949.
The Secret of the Living Skeleton, Amalgamated Press, 1949.
The South Coast Mystery, Amalgamated Press, 1949.
The Case of L. A. C. Dickson, Amalgamated Press, 1950.
The Mystery of the Haunted Square, Amalgamated Press, 1950.
The House in the Woods, Amalgamated Press, 1950.
The Secret of the Sixty Steps, Amalgamated Press, 1951.
The Case of the Man with No Name, Amalgamated Press, 1951.
Hated by All!, Amalgamated Press, 1951.
The Mystery of the Sabotaged Jet, Amalgamated Press, 1951.
The House on the River, Amalgamated Press, 1952.
The Mystery of the Five Guilty Men, Amalgamated Press, 1954.

The Case of the Two-Faced Swindler, Amalgamated Press, 1955.
The Teddy-Boy Mystery, Amalgamated Press, 1955.

UNDER PSEUDONYM JOHN LYMINGTON

Night of the Big Heat, Hodder & Stoughton, 1959, Dutton (New York City), 1960.
The Giant Stumbles, Hodder & Stoughton, 1960.
The Grey Ones, Hodder & Stoughton, 1960, Macfadden-Bartell, 1970.
A Sword above the Night, Hodder & Stoughton, 1961.
The Coming of the Strangers, Hodder & Stoughton, 1961, Macfadden-Bartell, 1971.
The Screaming Face, Hodder & Stoughton, 1963, Macfadden-Bartell, 1970.
The Sleep Eaters, Hodder & Stoughton, 1963, Macfadden-Bartell, 1969.
Froomb!, Hodder & Stoughton, 1964, Doubleday (New York City), 1966.
The Night Spiders (stories), Corgi, 1964, Doubleday, 1967.
The Green Drift, Hodder & Stoughton, 1965.
The Star Witches, Hodder & Stoughton, 1965.
Ten Million Years to Friday, Hodder & Stoughton, 1967, Doubleday, 1970.
The Nowhere Place, Hodder & Stoughton, 1969, Doubleday, 1971.
Give Daddy the Knife, Darling, Hodder & Stoughton, 1969.
The Year Dot, Hodder & Stoughton, 1972.
The Hole in the World, Hodder & Stoughton, 1974.
A Spider in the Bath, Hodder & Stoughton, 1975.
The Laxham Haunting, Hodder & Stoughton, 1977.
Starseed on Eye Moor, Hodder & Stoughton, 1978.
The Waking of the Stone, Hodder & Stoughton, 1978.
The Grey Ones [and] *A Sword above the Night,* Manor (New York City), 1978.
A Caller from Overspace, Hodder & Stoughton, 1979.
Voyage of the Eighth Mind, Hodder & Stoughton, 1980.
The Power Ball, R. Hale, 1981.
The Terror Version, R. Hale, 1982.
The Vale of the Sad Banana, R. Hale, 1984.

UNDER PSEUDONYM DAVID C. NEWTON

The Black Ghost, Oxford University Press (London), 1947.
The Dangerous Road, Oxford University Press, 1948.

OTHER

Bunst and the Brown Voice (children's book), Oxford University Press, four volumes, 1950-53.

(With wife, Shirley Newton Chance) *The Jennifer Jigsaw* (children's book), Oxford University Press, 1951.

Yellow Belly (autobiography), R. Hale, 1959.

The Crimes at Rillington Place: A Novelist's Reconstruction, Hodder & Stoughton, 1961.

Contributor of several hundred articles to newspapers.

ADAPTATIONS: The film *Crosstrap,* 1961, was adapted from one of Chance's novels.

SIDELIGHTS: John Newton Chance was known for his many mystery novels written under a variety of pseudonyms and for his science fiction novels written as John Lymington. He was, according to Jack Adrian in the *St. James Guide to Crime and Mystery Writers,* "one of the more prolific detective-thriller writers of the mid-20th century."

Chance's mystery novels were marked by their propensity for the gothic and gruesome. "Eerie and bizarre situations abound," as Adrian remarked. Among the most macabre moments in Chance's fiction, Adrian believed, are "the flight through the plague-pits in *Screaming Fog;* the entrance of the garrulous vicar through the French windows in *The Red Knight;* the discovery of a body among the dismembered figures in a waxworks modeling-room at night in *The Eye in Darkness.*"

The twenty-five novels written by Chance under the John Drummond pseudonym were part of the Sexton Blake Library, a long-running British adventure series written over the years by a number of pseudonymous authors. Chance's contributions to the saga, Adrian wrote, are "probably his most sustained creative effort. . . . Especially good are *The Manor House Menace, The Town of Shadows, The Mystery of the Haunted Square,* and *The House on the River*—though all are worth reading."

Under the pseudonym John Lymington, Chance wrote a number of science fiction novels which earned critical praise for their tense pace and psychological suspense. *Ten Million Years to Friday* tells of the reawakening of an ancient monstrous creature and a scientist's efforts to save the beast from destruction by humankind. A *Publishers Weekly* critic found that "the reader is caught up immediately, and finds himself reading on compulsively." In *The Nowhere Place,* a small English town is beset by a wave of unexplained phenomena. Some of the townspeople blame a nearby government laboratory, while others believe it could be hallucinogens or the work of the devil. The story, Frederick Patten wrote in *Library Journal,* "builds to an eerie climax." Adrian described Chance's books under the Lymington name as "excellent psychological SF novels."

BIOGRAPHICAL/CRITICAL SOURCES:

BOOKS

St. James Guide to Crime and Mystery Writers, 4th edition, St. James Press (Detroit), 1996.

PERIODICALS

Best Sellers, February 15, 1970, p. 430.

Books and Bookmen, November, 1965, p. 56.

Kirkus Reviews, February 15, 1946, p. 14; November 15, 1965, p. 1170.

Library Journal, December 15, 1969, p. 4539; September 15, 1971, p. 2795.

Magazine of Fantasy and Science Fiction, July, 1966, p. 34; December, 1967, p. 34; August, 1970, p. 58.

National Review, April 5, 1966, p. 320.

New York Times, May 12, 1946, p. 34.

Observer, August 22, 1965, p. 21.

Publishers Weekly, December 8, 1969, p. 43.

Punch, August 25, 1965, p. 289; September 27, 1967, p. 485.

Spectator, August 16, 1975, p. 218.

Springfield Republican, July 28, 1946, p. 4D.

Weekly Book Review, May 5, 1946, p. 22.

OBITUARIES:

PERIODICALS

London Times, August 8, 1983.*

*   *   *

CHANCE, Jonathan
See CHANCE, John Newton

CHESLER, Phyllis 1940-

PERSONAL: Born October 1, 1940, in Brooklyn, NY; daughter of Leon and Lillian (Hammer) Chesler; children: Ariel David (son). *Education:* Bard College, B.A., 1962; New School for Social Research, M.A., 1967, Ph.D., 1969; New York Medical College, graduate study, 1968-69. *Religion:* Jewish.

ADDRESSES: Office—Department of Psychology, College of Staten Island of the City University of New York, Staten Island, NY 10301. *Agent*—Lois de la Haba, 133 Broadway, Suite 810, New York, NY 10010.

CAREER: New York University, New York City, intern in psychotherapy at Washington Square Institute for Psychotherapy and Mental Health, 1968-69; Metropolitan Hospital, New York City, clinical research associate, 1968-69; College of Staten Island of the City University of New York, Staten Island, NY, assistant professor of psychology, 1969—; Research Assoiciate, International Research Institute on Jewish Women (founded by Hadassah), Brandeis University, Waltham, MA, 1997—. Lecturer at institutions, including Institute for Developmental Studies and New School for Social Research, City University of New York; psychotherapist in private practice. Cofounder, Association for Women in Psychology, 1970; cofounder, National Women's Health Network, 1976. Member of board of directors of Women's Action Alliance, 1972—, and Center for the Study of Psychiatry, 1974—.

MEMBER: American Association for the Abolition of Involuntary Mental Hospitalization, American Association for the Advancement of Science, American Psychological Association, Association for Women in Psychology (founder), American Association of University Professors, National Organization for Women, Eastern Psychological Association, New York State Psychological Association.

WRITINGS:

Women and Madness, Doubleday (Garden City, NY), 1972, twenty-fifth anniversary edition, Four Walls Eight Windows Press (New York City), 1997.
(Author of interpretive essay) *Wonder Woman,* introduction by Gloria Steinem, Holt (New York City), 1972.

(With Emily Jane Goodman) *Women, Money and Power,* Morrow (New York City), 1976.
About Men, Simon & Schuster (New York City), 1978.
With Child: A Diary of Motherhood, Lippincott-Crowell (New York City), 1979, revised edition including a new introduction by Ariel Chesler, Four Walls Eight Windows Press, 1998.
Mothers on Trial: The Battle for Children and Custody, McGraw-Hill (New York City), 1986, revised edition, Four Walls Eight Windows Press, 1998.
Sacred Bond: The Legacy of Baby M, Times Books (New York City), 1988, published in England as *Sacred Bond: Motherhood under Siege,* introduction by Ann Oakley, Virago (London), 1990.
Patriarchy: Notes of an Expert Witness, Common Courage Press (Monroe, ME), 1994.
(Editor with Esther D. Rothblum and Ellen Cole) *Feminist Foremothers in Women's Studies, Psychology, and Mental Health,* Haworth Press (New York City), 1995.
Letter to a Young Feminist, Four Walls Eight Windows Press, 1997.

Contributor to numerous publications, including *The Radical Therapist Collective Anthology,* edited by Jerome Agel, Ballantine (New York City), 1971; *Women in Sexist Society: Studies in Power and Powerlessness,* edited by Vivian Gornick and Barbara K. Moran, Basic Books (New York City), 1971; *Psychology for Our Times: Readings,* edited by Philip Zimbardo and Christina Maslach, Scott, Foresman (Glenview, IL), 1973; and *Psychology of Adjustment,* edited by James F. Adams, Holbrook, 1973.

Also contributor to periodicals, including *New York Magazine, Ms., Psychology Today, Radical Therapist,* and *Village Voice.* Editor-at-large and columnist for *On the Issues* magazine.

SIDELIGHTS: Radical feminist Phyllis Chesler has been "an articulate and consistent critic of American culture for over 27 years," according to *Feminist Writers* contributor Mary A. Hess. "Her candor and incisive prose style have [provided her with] a reputation as one of America's most articulate and thoughtful feminist writers, while her activism in representing women who are marginalized by illness, poverty, and exploitation has not diminished despite personal hardship." In her writings, Chesler has sought to expose what she believes to be the unfair and unequal treatment of women in the health care and criminal justice systems; her 1972 book *Women* and Madness was "instrumental in initiating reforms in the mental health establishment," states Hess. In other books, she has focused on motherhood and society's changing attitudes toward women and children. In addition, she has written books and essays in defense of controversial female figures such as Mary Beth Whitehead—the surrogate mother in the Baby M case—and Aileen Wuolnos, a prostitute who killed four men in self-defense.

Chesler documented her mixed feelings about pregnancy and motherhood in *With Child: A Diary of Motherhood.* Linda B. Osborne writes in *Washington Post Book World:* "At 37, Phyllis Chesler gave birth to a son, and *With Child* is a diary of her pregnancy, the birth and her first year of motherhood. It is an informal, very personal narrative, charged with nervous energy, enthusiasm and anxiety, and marked by the ambivalence towards motherhood that grew out of the feminist movement over the last 15 years." Chesler's pregnancy also led her to write *Mothers on Trial: The Battle for Children and Custody.* While awaiting the birth of her child, she began exploring the assault on women's custody rights. Because of that book, relates Hess, Chesler is now "often approached by women seeking her advocacy, as she was by numerous mothers whose experiences as both traditional and non-traditional mothers were challenged on the basis of their fitness as caregivers and as a result of the non-custodial parent claiming rights to the child." Hess further reports that whenever possible, Chesler uses "oral histories to grant silenced women their own voice, believing strongly in their power to persuade the reader."

Chesler continued her exploration of the oppression of women in *Patriarchy: Notes of an Expert Witness.* In this collection of previously published essays, she documents the effects of what she sees as the patriarchal bias in the health care and criminal justice systems. Included are stories of women in custody battles, women on trial, and women imprisoned in psychiatric institutions. Reviewing the book in the *New York Times Book Review,* Anndee Hochman rates it "provocative but uneven" and explains that the essays are bound together by "Chesler's contention that the media, the court systems, and the mental health system "all operate on a sexist double standard that punishes women." Therese Stanton, a reviewer for *Ms.,* calls *Patriarchy* "thrilling and devastating reading—thrilling because of the explosion created when truth is spoken, and devastating because of the harshness of that truth."

BIOGRAPHICAL/CRITICAL SOURCES:

BOOKS

Feminist Writers, St. James Press (Detroit), 1996.

PERIODICALS

Chicago Tribune Book World, October 28, 1979.
Library Journal, October 15, 1994, p. 75.
Ms., January, 1995, p. 72.
New York Times, March 9, 1978.
New York Times Book Review, October 21, 1979; February 26, 1995, p. 16.
Publishers Weekly, April 3, 1978.
Signs: Journal of Women and Culture in Society, Volume 14, number 1, 1988.
Washington Post Book World, December 23, 1979.

*   *   *

CHITTENDEN, Margaret 1935- (Rosalind Carson)

PERSONAL: Born January 31, 1935, in London, England; naturalized U. S. citizen, 1962; daughter of James F. (a production supervisor) and Jenny (an accountant; maiden name, Huthert) Barrass; married James C. Chittenden (a manager of technicians), October 4, 1958; children: Stephen John, Sharon Lynne. *Education:* Educated in England. *Avocational interests:* Working out at the gym, beachcombing, canoeing, hiking the rainforest, surfing the net, reading, and travel.

ADDRESSES: Home—6101 Nyanza Park Dr. S.W., Tacoma, WA 98499; website—www.techline.com/ ~megc. *Agent*—Curtis Brown Ltd., 10 Astor Place, New York, NY 10003.

CAREER: Freelance writer. Ministry of Works, London, England, clerical officer, 1951-53; J. Arthur Rank Productions, Denham, Buckinghamshire, England, accountant for Pinewood Studios, 1953-54, and Denham Film Laboratories, 1954-59; doctor's secretary in Sacramento, CA, 1959-60. Member, Pacific Northwest Writers Conference Literary Council.

MEMBER: Romance Writers of America, Mystery Writers of America, American Crime Writers

League, International Association of Crime Writers, Novelists Inc.

AWARDS, HONORS: Pacific Northwest Writers Conference Literary Council Achievement Award.

WRITINGS:

NOVELS

Findlay's Landing, Ace Books (New York City), 1975.
Song of Dark Water, Pinnacle Books (New York City), 1978.
House of the Twilight Moon, Pinnacle Books, 1979.
The Other Child, Pinnacle Books, 1979.
The Face in the Mirror, Pinnacle Books, 1980.
Beyond the Rainbow, Worldwide Library, 1986.
Forever Love, Worldwide Library, 1988.
Until October, Harlequin, 1989.
This Time Forever, Harlequin, 1990.
The Scent of Magic, Harlequin, 1991.
The Wainwright Secret, Harlequin, 1992.
Shadow of a Doubt, Harlequin, 1993.
Double Take, Harlequin, 1993.
When the Spirit Is Willing, Harlequin, 1993.
As Years Go By, Harlequin, 1995.
Dying to Sing, Kensington (New York City), 1996.
Dead Men Don't Dance, Kensington, 1997.
Dead Beat and Deadly, Kensington, 1998.

UNDER PSEUDONYM ROSALIND CARSON

This Dark Enchantment, Harlequin, 1982.
Song of Desire, Harlequin, 1982.
Such Sweet Magic, Harlequin, 1983.
Love Me Tomorrow, Harlequin, 1984.
Lovespell, Harlequin, 1984.
To Touch the Moon, Harlequin, 1985.
The Marrying Kind, Harlequin, 1987.
Close to Home, Harlequin, 1988.
The Moon Gate, Harlequin, 1988.

OTHER

When the Wild Ducks Come (juvenile), Follett, 1972.
Merrymaking in Great Britain (juvenile), Garrard, 1974.
The Mystery of the Missing Pony (juvenile), Garrard, 1980.
(Contributor of novel to four-novel anthology) *Marriage by Design,* Harlequin, 1994.
How to Write Your Novel, The Writer (Boston), 1995.

Contributor of short stories and articles to children's and women's magazines, including *Good Housekeeping, Ladies' Homes Journal* and *Boys' Life.*

WORK IN PROGRESS: Another mystery novel.

SIDELIGHTS: After publishing some twenty romance novels under her own name and the pseudonym Rosalind Carson, Margaret Chittenden turned to mysteries with her 1996 novel *Dying to Sing.* Although several of her romance novels had featured suspenseful plots and detective work, it was only with *Dying to Sing* that Chittenden wrote a straight detective story.

Dying to Sing introduces amateur sleuth Charlie Plato, a thirty-year-old divorcee and owner of the San Francisco country bar CHAPS, and her partner Zack Hunter, a former television actor now living on residuals. Following an earthquake that opens a fissure in the CHAPS' flowerbed, a skeleton is uncovered. When the police show little interest in the body, and the bar starts getting threatening phone calls, Charlie and Zack work to discover its identity. The story, writes the *Library Journal* reviewer, has "easy pacing, solid plotting, and well-oiled prose." Emily Melton in *Booklist* finds the novel to be "fun, fresh, entertaining, and original." Charlie, according to the critic for *Publishers Weekly,* possesses "a wry tone and a good heart" and "demonstrates an appealing, lightweight charm." Charlie reappears in Chittenden's 1997 outing *Dead Men Don't Dance,* in which Zack decides to run for city council. When his opponents begin to turn up dead, the police focus their attention on Zack's campaign and Charlie swings into action to save her friend's reputation.

Commenting at her website on the Charlie Plato mysteries, Chittenden notes: "All twenty-six years of my writing life, I've wanted to write a mystery series that featured a young female amateur sleuth. In her own words, Charlie Plato is a 'thirty year old divorcee with an attitude,' which makes her, depending on your point of view, a cliche, or a nineties woman."

BIOGRAPHICAL/CRITICAL SOURCES:

PERIODICALS

Booklist, July 1, 1978, p. 1669; July, 1996, p. 1807.
Good Housekeeping, November, 1981.
Library Journal, May 15, 1973, p. 1695; October 15, 1974, p. 2738; June 1, 1996, p. 155.
Locus, October, 1990, p. 51; May, 1991, p. 46.

Publishers Weekly, February 5, 1973, p. 89; February 10, 1984; May 27, 1996, p. 69.
School Library Journal, December, 1980, p. 72.

*   *   *

CHODOROW, Nancy (Julia) 1944-

PERSONAL: Born January 20, 1944, in New York, NY; daughter of Marvin (a professor of applied physics) and Leah Ruth (Turitz) Chodorow; married Michael Reich (a professor of economics), June 19, 1977 (separated); children: Rachel, Gabriel. *Education:* Radcliffe College, A.B. (summa cum laude), 1966; attended London School of Economics and Political Science, London, 1966-67, Harvard University, 1967-68, and San Francisco Psychoanalytic Institute, 1985-93; Brandeis University, M.A., 1972, Ph.D., 1975.

ADDRESSES: Office—Department of Sociology, University of California, Berkeley, 410 Barrows Hall, Berkeley, CA.

CAREER: Wellesley College, Wellesley, MA, instructor in women's studies, 1973-74; University of California, Santa Cruz, lecturer, 1974-76, assistant professor, 1976-79, associate professor of sociology, 1979-86; Institute for Personality Assessment and Research, University of California, Berkeley, associate research sociologist, 1981-83; University of California, Berkeley, associate professor, beginning 1986-89, professor of sociology, 1989—. Member of faculty, San Francisco Psychoanalytic Institute, beginning 1994; psychoanalyst in private practice, in Oakland, CA.

MEMBER: International Psychoanalytic Association, American Psychoanalytic Association, Sociological Research Association, Phi Beta Kappa.

AWARDS, HONORS: National Institutes for Mental Health fellowship, 1966-68, 1972-73; Brandeis University fellowship, 1969-70; National Science Foundation fellowship, 1970-72; Jessie Bernard Award, American Sociological Association, 1979, for *The Reproduction of Mothering: Psychoanalysis and the Sociology of Gender;* Center for Advanced Study in the Behavioral Sciences fellow, 1980-81; Russell Sage Foundation grant, 1981-86; National Endowment for the Humanities grant, 1982-85, 1985-86, and fellowship, 1995-96; Editions Iichiko prize (To-

kyo), 1991; American Council of Learned Societies fellowship, 1991-92; Guggenheim fellowship, 1995-96.

WRITINGS:

The Reproduction of Mothering: Psychoanalysis and the Sociology of Gender, University of California Press (Berkeley), 1978.
Feminism and Psychoanalytic Theory, Yale University Press (New Haven, CT), 1989.
Femininities, Masculinities, Sexualities: Freud and Beyond, University Press of Kentucky (Lexington), 1994.

OTHER

Contributor to numerous anthologies, including *Advances in Psychoanalytic Sociology,* edited by Jerome Rabow, Gerald M. Platt, and Marion S. Goldman, Krieger (Malabar, FL), 1987; *Theoretical Perspectives on Sexual Difference,* edited by Deborah L. Rhode, Yale University Press, 1990; and *Cambridge Companion to Freud,* edited by Jerome Neu, Cambridge University Press (New York City), 1991. Also contributor to various periodicals, including *Annual of Psychoanalysis, Women and Therapy, Journal of the American Psychoanalytic Association, The Psychoanalytic Quarterly,* and *Signs.* Consulting editor for *Feminist Studies.*

SIDELIGHTS: Nancy Chodorow is a sociologist, educator, and psychoanalyst whose books break new ground on the subject of the psychology of gender. She has made significant contributions to feminist theory with "her reappraisal of the ways in which the psychological dynamics of the sex-gender system is systematically reproduced and subject to historical change and development," according to *Feminist Writers* contributor Gerri McNenny. *The Reproduction of Mothering: Psychoanalysis and the Sociology of Gender* is perhaps Chodorow's most influential book. In it, she challenges the traditional view that females are biologically predisposed toward nurturing infants. Mothering, she argues, fulfills a woman's psychological need for reciprocal intimacy that begins during her babyhood when she and her mother perceive each other as extensions of themselves. Mothers are also close to their infant sons, says Chodorow, but they view their male children as different and do not share with them the same sense of "oneness" that they experience with their daughters. The author therefore contends that mature males, unaccustomed to a psychologically intimate relationship are, therefore, content to leave mothering to women.

Discussing *The Reproduction of Mothering*, McNenny explains: "Drawing on object-relations theory and the work of Talcott Parsons and the Frankfurt school, Chodorow contends that gender identity formation is largely a result of the dynamics of family relationships. . . . In the 'preoedipal' stage, Chodorow points out, the infant experiences a "primary identification' with the mother and forms a primary love for the mother that makes no differentiation between the child's needs and desires and the ability of the mother to fulfill them. Gradually the child goes on to establish a sense of self through an expanded awareness of its own physical being. It begins to differentiate from the mother as it becomes less dependent upon her."

Sigmund Freud believed that once a girl entered the "oedipal" stage, forming an attachment to her father, her relationship with her mother became a hostile one because the mother was then seen as a rival. Chodorow does not agree with this classic theory, arguing instead that a girl's preoedipal bond with her mother can continue even after she develops a fascination with her father. "To establish her gender identity, a girl need not dissociate herself from the mother as radically as a boy does; a boy must establish his gender identity in contradistinction to his mother," McNenny elaborates. "Chodorow emphasizes the impact of same-gendered mothering on the psychosocial development of girls as well as boys." Chodorow critiques Freudian psychoanalytic theory in many other ways as well. "She argues that psychoanalysis cannot make universal claims concerning psychological development; they must take into account the cultural and historical conditions of the time, including the awareness of the fact that the nuclear family is the model from which most hypotheses and theories about psychological development are constructed," notes McNenny.

Chodorow's analysis of the failings of Freudian theory continues in *Femininities, Masculinities, Sexualities: Freud and Beyond*. According to *Choice* contributor R. H. Balsam, it includes "an excellent critique of Freud's views about women. . . . Chodorow's book will interest feminists, cultural theorists, and psychoanalysts, especially those following her thought since the seventies." Adam Phillips also responds favorably to the book, describing it as "concise," "informative," and "timely" in

his *London Review of Books* assessment. And in *The Women's Review of Books,* Terri Apter declares that *Femininities, Masculinities, Sexualities* displays Chodorow's greatest strengths: "careful listening, revealing hidden images, high-lighting connections."

BIOGRAPHICAL/CRITICAL SOURCES:

BOOKS

Chisholm, D., and others, editors, *Feminism in Psychoanalysis: A Critical Dictionary,* Blackwell, 1992.
Doane, Janice L., and Devon L. Hodges, *From Klein to Kristeva: Psychoanalytic Feminism and the Search for the "Good Enough" Mother,* University of Michigan Press (Ann Arbor), 1992.
Feminist Writers, St. James Press (Detroit), 1996.

PERIODICALS

Choice, January, 1995, p. 874.
Contemporary Sociology, July, 1979.
Journal of the American Academy of Psychoanalysis, summer, 1994.
London Review of Books, March 9, 1995, p. 10.
Ms., October, 1978.
New Statesman, April 4, 1980.
New York Times Book Review, October 30, 1994, p. 49.
North American Review, fall, 1978.
Psychoanalytic Dialogues, 5(2), 1995.
Social Science Quarterly, September, 1980.
Time, February 26, 1979.
Women's Review of Books, January, 1995, p. 21.

*   *   *

CHURCHILL, Joyce
See HARRISON, M(ichael) John

*   *   *

CLARK, Anne
See AMOR, Anne Clark

COLE, Adrian 1949-

PERSONAL: Born July 22, 1949, in Plymouth, England; son of Frederick Terence (an army officer) and Ruth (Littlewood) Cole; married Judith Rose Nixon, May 25, 1977; children: Samuel, Katia. *Education:* Attended grammar school in the rural county of Cornwall, 1961-66.

ADDRESSES: Home—The Old Forge, 35 Meddon St., Bideford, Devon EX39 2EF, England. *Agent*—Abner Stein, 10 Roland Gardens, London SW7 3PH, England.

CAREER: Birmingham Public Libraries, Birmingham, England, librarian, 1967-76; local government officer, Decon County Council, 1977-91; Bideford College, Devon, England, school administrator, 1991—.

WRITINGS:

Madness Emerging, R. Hale (London), 1976.
Paths in Darkness, R. Hale, 1977.
The Coming of the Voidal (stories), Spectre Press (Burton-on-Trent, Staffordshire), 1977.
Longborn the Inexhaustible (stories), British Fantasy Society (Dagenham, Exxes), 1978.
Wargods of Ludorbis, R. Hale, 1981.
The LUCIFER Experiment, R. Hale, 1981.
Moorstones, Spindlewood (Barnstaple, Devon), 1982.
The Sleep of Giants, Spindlewood, 1984.
A Place among the Fallen, Allen & Unwin (London), 1986, Avon (New York City), 1987.
Throne of Fools, Unwin Hyman (London), 1987, Avon, 1990.
The King of Light and Shadows, Unwin Hyman, 1988, Avon, 1990.
The Gods in Anger, Unwin Hyman, 1988, Avon, 1991.
Mother of Storms, Unwin Hyman, 1989, Avon, 1992.
Thief of Dreams, Unwin Hyman, 1989, Avon, 1993.
Warlord of Heaven, Unwin Hyman, 1990, Avon, 1993.
Labyrinth of Worlds, Unwin Hyman, 1990, Avon, 1993.
Blood Red Angel, Avon, 1993.

DREAM LORDS TRILOGY

A Plague of Nightmares, Zebra (New York City), 1975.

Lord of Nightmares, Zebra, 1975.
Bane of Nightmares, Zebra, 1976.

SIDELIGHTS: Adrian Cole's novels combine fantasy with elements from horror and science fiction. Despite the difficulty of classifying his work by genre, Cole's "strengths lie in his ability to tell a pacey, action-packed story," writes Pauline Morgan in the *St. James Guide to Fantasy Writers.*

Cole's novel *A Place among the Fallen* has drawn considerable critical commentary. The novel tells the story of "Korbillian, a man who has Power," Morgan explains. Korbillian must stop a distant evil released by power-hungry men and enlists the help of a number of associates to assist him. "They go reluctantly at first," Morgan writes, "but gradually are won to his cause. This is a good-versus-evil quest fantasy with a lot of familiar elements such as underground races, bad lands, hostile vegetation." A *Booklist* critic points out that *A Place among the Fallen* has "vivid atmosphere, a large cast of interesting characters, and a gripping if relentlessly grim plot." Stuart Hannabuss in *British Book News* calls the novel "credible and plausible, with memorable characters and vivid set-pieces, clearly structured from its stark opening on a storm-tossed beach."

Cole told *CA:* "I have always had a fundamental drive, a basic need to write (my earliest ventures were at the age of about ten), but I began writing with serious intent to sell at about age twenty. If any one book acted as the touchstone that set me off, it was *Lord of the Rings,* and at that time my diet consisted almost entirely of escapist literature. Hence my early works were purely escapist, with the emphasis on the action and the sets rather than characters.

"My later books, such as the related *Moorstones* and *Sleep of Giants,* retain strong fantasy elements, but deal in more detail with human predicaments, especially the evaluation of good and evil. My earlier works had very clearly defined, one-dimensional heroes and villains, whereas the later books introduce the element of doubt, the questioning of self, of faith, of what is and what is not evil. I have also paralleled the grey areas of the inner self with the hazy borderland between real and imaginary landscapes, setting my books in actual places (i.e., Southwest England) which have very tangible otherworldly aspects. In the books, a physical journey across strange, uncertain terrains corresponds with an inner journey. On reflection, my own journey as a writer is also bound up on the struggles of the protagonists.

"The book *A Place among the Fallen* is really a return to the traditional fantasy novel. A large work (some 150,000 words), it is an adventure that is firmly rooted in Tolkien, Burroughs, and many contemporary fantasy writers. Primarily escapist, it does introduce, less prominently than its predecessors, questions of faith, of values, moral and religious, and I would hope that its many characters are better drawn and developed than those of my early works.

"I have also written a number of stories about a particularly bizarre character, the Voidal. These stories, which are hybrid black fantasies, were really a reaction to the stagnation of certain aspects of heroic fantasy. I have attempted to stretch out the boundaries of this, as I see it, limited sub-genre of sword-and-sorcery, although I now question my own stamina and commitment to such a challenge.

"My target is not, I realize, to explore fantastic settings at the expense of character, and while I want primarily to develop character and dialogue in my work, I have come to the conclusion that my chosen field is the uncertain borderland between reality and fantasy. This borderland is within us, and our environment is an extension of what lies there."

BIOGRAPHICAL/CRITICAL SOURCES:

BOOKS

St. James Guide to Fantasy Writers, St. James Press (Detroit), 1996.

PERIODICALS

Booklist, July, 1987, p. 1655.
British Book News, July, 1987, p. 569.
Locus, August, 1990, p. 47; December, 1990, p. 52; April, 1991, p. 41.
Observer, January 24, 1982, p. 30.
Publishers Weekly, February 3, 1975, p. 76.*

* * *

COOKE, M. E.
See CREASEY, John

COOKE, Margaret
See CREASEY, John

* * *

COONTS, Stephen (Paul) 1946-

PERSONAL: Born July 19, 1946, in Morgantown, WV; son of Gilbert Gray (an attorney) and Violet (a teacher; maiden name, Gadd) Coonts; married Nancy Quereau, February 19, 1971 (divorced, 1984); married Deborah Buell, April 12, 1995; children: Rachael, Lara, David. *Education:* West Virginia University, A.B., 1968; University of Colorado, J.D., 1979.

ADDRESSES: Home—Denver, CO. *Agent*—Robert Gottlieb, William Morris Agency, 1350 Avenue of the Americas, New York, NY 10019.

CAREER: Cab driver and police officer, 1977-81; Hymes & Coonts Attorneys, Buckhannon, WV, private practice, 1980-81; Petro-Lewis Corporation (oil and gas company), Denver, CO, in-house counsel, 1981-86; fulltime writer, 1986—. *Military service:* U.S. Navy, 1968-77, served as aviator in Vietnam, 1971-73; became lieutenant; worked as flying instructor; received Distinguished Flying Cross.

MEMBER: Trustee, West Virginia Wesleyan College, Naval Institute Foundation.

AWARDS, HONORS: Author award of merit, U.S. Naval Institute, 1986, for *Flight of the Intruder;* inducted into Academy of Distinguished Alumni, West Virginia University, 1992.

WRITINGS:

Flight of the Intruder (novel), U.S. Naval Institute Press, 1986.
Final Flight (novel), Doubleday (New York City), 1988.
The Minotaur (novel; Book-of-the-Month Club selection), Doubleday, 1989.
Under Siege (novel; Book-of-the-Month Club alternate selection), Pocket Books (New York City), 1990.
The Cannibal Queen: An Aerial Odyssey across America (nonfiction), Pocket Books, 1992.
The Red Horseman (novel), Pocket Books, 1993.
The Intruders (novel), Pocket Books, 1994.

War in the Air: True-Life Accounts of the 20th Century's Most Dramatic Air Battles—by the Men Who Fought Them, Pocket Books, 1996.

All of Coons's novels and *The Cannibal Queen: An Aerial Odyssey across America,* were recorded in full by Books on Tape, and in abridged versions by Bantam and Simon & Schuster.

ADAPTATIONS: Flight of the Intruder was adapted into a Paramount film starring Willem Dafoe, Danny Glover, and Brad Johnson in 1991, and the novel was made into a computer video game.

SIDELIGHTS: Stephen Coonts is the best-selling author of a series of thriller novels—*Flight of the Intruder, Final Flight, The Minotaur,* and *Under Siege*—that feature naval aviator Jake Grafton. Like the fictional Grafton, Coonts has flown sophisticated planes for the U.S. Navy, such as the A-6 Intruder. Coonts's nearly ten years of military service included two years in Vietnam, the setting of his first novel, *Flight of the Intruder.* But Coonts insists that Grafton is not his fictional counterpart. "I intentionally tried to make Jake Grafton into Everyman in Vietnam," Coonts said in *People.* "Not handsome, not wise, not witty, not smart. Just average. The book . . . [is] not my story. I had to be there to write it, but I'm not Jake Grafton."

Flight of the Intruder was a surprise best-seller. Coonts started writing the book after his divorce in 1984. He remembered in *People,* "All of a sudden I had the time to write the story. Like every newly divorced guy, I had tons of time and no money." At first, Coonts could not persuade any New York publisher to print the book. Then he read Tom Clancy's *The Hunt for Red October,* a best-selling submarine thriller, and decided to send his manuscript to the same publisher, the U.S. Naval Institute Press. The timing was right, and in 1986 the Institute published *Flight of the Intruder*—only the second work of fiction (Clancy's was the first) ever released by the Naval Institute Press during its more than 100 years of publishing history. The novel achieved best-seller status even sooner than *The Hunt for Red October,* and it went on to become one of the longest running best-sellers in 1987, according to *Publishers Weekly.*

Flight of the Intruder presents a realistic portrayal of naval aviators who fought in the Vietnam War. Jake Grafton, the book's hero, is an average pilot who tires of the seemingly pointless and dangerous missions of hitting minor targets, such as mud huts and bombed-out barracks. Convinced that military leaders are not making the right decisions to quickly end the war, Grafton decides to fly off on his own and attack what he thinks may be the communist headquarters in Hanoi. He struggles with this decision because it represents an act of disobedience similar to the antiwar protests—which he hates—going on at home.

Reviewers praised *Flight of the Intruder* for its vivid descriptions of life in the cockpit. "When Grafton is at the controls of his Intruder, the novel comes alive with a jolt," remarked Reid Beddow in *Washington Post Book World.* Some critics, however, felt the novel had its weak moments. For example, David Holahan in Chicago *Tribune Books* faulted the "obligatory 'love interest' chapters, which are unconvincing and distracting." Holahan nonetheless applauded the author's "compelling tale of aerial warfare" and affirmed that "Coonts' accounts of the riveting drama of combat flights are first rate, as are the scenes of wisecracking camaraderie aboard ship and on leave ashore." Beddow, moreover, concluded that "Coonts . . . has written a first novel of impressive power and authority."

Protagonist Jake Grafton returns to action in Coonts's next three novels, *Final Flight, The Minotaur,* and *Under Siege.* The first concerns Grafton's attempt to thwart an international terrorist plot led by an Arab named Colonel Qazi, whose followers converge on an Italian harbor to hijack a U.S. aircraft carrier containing nuclear missiles. The second is set in the United States and revolves around Grafton's efforts to prevent a Pentagon double agent from learning about the "Athena" stealth bomber. And *Under Siege* finds Grafton countering an attack on top officials in Washington, D.C., by Colombian terrorists who want to free an imprisoned drug kingpin. Critics generally praised the intensity of the flight and battle scenes in these books but found other portions less engaging. Still, George C. Wilson commented in *Washington Post Book World,* "If you liked the authentic flying and carrier scenes in *The Flight of the Intruder,* you will find enough fresh ones in *Final Flight* to make you glad you bought the book." In addition, *Washington Post Book World* contributor Rory Quirk found considerable merit in *The Minotaur:* "What unfolds is a fast-paced, graphic thriller that combines equal parts high tech and high adventure, laced with harrowing insights into the thankless, razor-edge world of the Navy test pilot and the labyrinth of superpower espionage." Quirk also affirmed in a review for the

Washington Post that "*Under Siege* is a disquieting story, told by a first- rate storyteller who, so far, has resisted grinding out formulaic bestsellers."

Later books that feature Jake Grafton include *The Red Horseman*—in which Jake and his assistant, Toad Tarkington, dismantle the nuclear weapons of the former Soviet Union as well as a cabal of evil CIA agents—and *The Intruders,* which is set in 1973 and deals with Jake's disillusionment with the Vietnam War. A reviewer in *Publishers Weekly* concluded that with "its dominant question about Jake's future a foregone conclusion, [*The Intruders*] stands as one of the weakest in the series."

With *The Cannibal Queen: An Aerial Odyssey Across America,* Coonts ventures into nonfiction to recount his summer-long journey to each of the contiguous forty-eight American states in a fifty-year-old open-cockpit biplane. Most critics responded positively to his obvious enthusiasm and love of flying. Some commentators, however, sensed the book was a bit self indulgent, and a few were put off by the author's frequent discourses on political issues. A writer in *Kirkus Reviews* concluded: "Middle-class, upbeat to a fault, and unmeditative. Yet the descriptions of flight and the portrait of an America seemingly trapped in a time-warp are arresting."

An interview with Coonts can be found in *Contemporary Authors,* Volume 133.

BIOGRAPHICAL/CRITICAL SOURCES:

PERIODICALS

Booklist, May 1, 1992, p. 1562; April 15, 1993, p. 1470.
Detroit Free Press, September 25, 1988.
Detroit News, November 27, 1988.
Entertainment Weekly, October 21, 1994, p. 60.
New York Times, November 1, 1986.
New York Times Book Review, October 22, 1989, p. 37; November 18, 1990, p. 41; May 23, 1993, p. 21; October 30, 1994, p. 26.
People, January 19, 1987.
Publishers Weekly, January 8, 1988; August 22, 1994, p. 41.
School Library Journal, February, 1991, p. 104.
Tribune Books (Chicago), November 23, 1986.
Wall Street Journal, October 8, 1990.
Washington Post, October 29, 1990.

Washington Post Book World, October 5, 1986; October 23, 1988; October 12, 1989; July 4, 1993.

* * *

COOPER, Henry St. John
See CREASEY, John

* * *

CORNWELL, David (John Moore) 1931-
(John le Carre)

PERSONAL: Born October 19, 1931, in Poole, Dorsetshire, England; son of Ronald Thomas Archibald and Olive (Glassy) Cornwell; married Alison Ann Veronica Sharp, November 27, 1954 (divorced, 1971); married Valerie Jane Eustace, 1972; children: (first marriage) Simon, Stephen, Timothy; (second marriage) Nicholas. *Education:* Attended Bern University, Switzerland, 1948-49; Lincoln College, Oxford, B.A. (with honours), 1956.

ADDRESSES: Agent— Bruce Hunter, David Higham Ltd., 5-8 Lower John St., Golden Sq., London W1R 4HA, England.

CAREER: Writer. Millfield Junior School, Galstonbury, Somerset, England, teacher, 1954-55; Eton College, Buckinghamshire, England, tutor, 1956-58; British Foreign Office, second secretary in Bonn, West Germany (now Germany), 1960-63, consul in Hamburg, West Germany (now Germany), 1963-64. *Military service:* British Army Intelligence Corps, beginning 1949.

AWARDS, HONORS: Gold Dagger, Crime Writers Association, 1963, Somerset Maugham Award, 1964, and Edgar Allan Poe Award, Mystery Writers of America, 1965, all for *The Spy Who Came in from the Cold;* James Tait Black Memorial Prize, 1977, and Gold Dagger, 1978, both for *The Honourable Schoolboy;* Gold Dagger, 1980; honorary fellow, Lincoln College, Oxford, 1984; Grand Master Award, Mystery Writers of America, 1986; Malparte prize, 1987; Diamond Dagger, Crime Writers Association, 1988; honorary doctorates, University of

Exeter, 1990, University of St. Andrews, 1996, and University of Southampton, 1997.

WRITINGS:

NOVELS; ALL WRITTEN UNDER THE PSEUDONYM JOHN LE CARRE

Call for the Dead, Gollancz (London), 1960, Walker (London), 1962, published as *The Deadly Affair,* Penguin (New York City), 1966.
A Murder of Quality, Gollancz, 1962, Walker, 1963.
The Spy Who Came in from the Cold, Gollancz, 1963, Coward, 1964.
The Incongruous Spy: Two Novels of Suspense (contains *Call for the Dead* and *A Murder of Quality*), Walker, 1964.
The Looking Glass War, Coward, 1965.
A Small Town in Germany, Coward, 1968.
The Naive and Sentimental Lover, Knopf (New York City), 1971.
Tinker, Tailor, Soldier, Spy, Knopf, 1974.
The Honourable Schoolboy, Knopf, 1977.
Smiley's People, Knopf, 1980.
The Quest for Karla (contains *Tinker, Tailor, Soldier, Spy, The Honourable Schoolboy,* and *Smiley's People*), Knopf, 1982.
The Little Drummer Girl, Knopf, 1983.
A Perfect Spy, Knopf, 1986.
The Russia House, Knopf, 1989.
The Secret Pilgrim, Knopf, 1991.
The Night Manager, Knopf, 1993.
Our Game, Knopf, 1995.
John Le Carre: Three Complete Novels (includes *Tinker, Tailor, Soldier, Spy, Honourable Schoolboy,* and *Smiley's People*), Wings (Avenel, NY), 1995.
The Tailor of Panama, Knopf, 1996.

OTHER; ALL WRITTEN UNDER THE PSEUDONYM JOHN LE CARRE

Dare I Weep, Dare I Mourn (teleplay), produced on *Stage 66,* American Broadcasting Corp. (ABC), 1966.
(Author of introduction) Bruce Page, Phillip Knightley, and David Leitch, *The Philby Conspiracy,* Doubleday (New York City), 1968.
(With John Hopkins) *Smiley's People* (teleplay; based on his novel), British Broadcasting Corp. (BBC), 1982.
The Clandestine Muse, Seluzicki (Portland, OR), 1986.

(With Gareth H. Davies) *Vanishing England,* Salem House, 1987.

Contributor to periodicals, including *Saturday Evening Post.*

ADAPTATIONS: The Spy Who Came in from the Cold was filmed by Paramount in 1965; *Call for the Dead* was filmed as *The Deadly Affair* by Columbia in 1967; *The Looking Glass War* was filmed by Columbia in 1970; *Tinker, Tailor, Soldier, Spy* was filmed for television by the BBC in 1980; *The Little Drummer Girl* was filmed by Warner Brothers; *A Perfect Spy* was a seven-hour BBC-TV series and was shown on public television's *Masterpiece Theatre* in the United States; a film version of *The Russia House,* written by Tom Stoppard, directed by Fred Schepisi, and starring Sean Connery and Michelle Pfeiffer, was released in 1990.

SIDELIGHTS: The novels of David Cornwell, written under the pseudonym John le Carre, depict the clandestine world of Cold War espionage as a morally ambiguous realm where treachery, deceit, fear, and betrayal are the norm. The atmosphere in a le Carre novel, writes a reviewer for the *Times Literary Supplement,* is one of "grubby realism and moral squalor, the frazzled, fatigued sensitivity of decent men obliged to betray or kill others no worse than themselves." Le Carre uses his fiction to dramatize what he sees as the moral bankruptcy of the Cold War. In an open letter published in *Encounter,* le Carre writes: "There is no victory and no virtue in the Cold War, only a condition of human illness and a political misery." Leonard Downie, Jr., quotes le Carre in a *Washington Post* article as saying, "We are in the process of doing things in defense of our society which may very well produce a society which is not worth defending." It is this paradox, and the moral ambiguity which accompanies it, that informs le Carre's espionage novels and makes them, many critics believe, among the finest works of their genre. Le Carre's novels are believed by some critics to have raised the entire espionage genre to a more respectable and serious level of literature. "The espionage novel," writes Joseph McClellan in the *Washington Post Book World,* for example, "has become a characteristic expression of our time . . . and John le Carre is one of the handful of writers who have made it so." "More than any other writer," George Grella states in the *New Republic,* "[le Carre] has established the spy as an appropriate figure and espionage as an appropriate activity for our time, providing both symbol and metaphor to explain contemporary history."

Le Carre began writing espionage fiction in the early 1960s while working as a diplomat with the British Foreign Office in London. He had earlier worked for an undisclosed length of time with the British Secret Service, and there is some speculation among reviewers that le Carre's work as a diplomat was also espionage-related, a speculation le Carre dismisses as untrue. Nevertheless, his novels reveal an intimate knowledge of the workings of the British government's espionage bureaucracy. "Le Carre's contribution to the fiction of espionage," writes Anthony Burgess in the *New York Times Book Review,* "has its roots in the truth of how a spy system works. . . . The people who run Intelligence totally lack glamour, their service is short of money, [and] they are up against the crassness of politicians. Their men in the field are frightened, make blunders, grow sick of a trade in which the opposed sides too often seem to interpenetrate and wear the same face." Geoffrey Stokes, writing in the *Village Voice,* goes so far as to claim that in le Carre's novels, "bureaucracy [is] transformed into poetry." Because of his diplomatic position when he first began writing, Cornwell was not permitted to publish anything under his real name, and so the pseudonym John le Carre was born. "Le Carre" is French for "the square." "I've told so many lies about where I got the name from," Downie quotes le Carre as explaining, "but I really don't remember. The one time I did the celebrity circuit in America, I was reduced to inventing the fiction that I'd been riding on a bus to the foreign office and abstracted the name from a shoeshop. But that was simply because I couldn't convince anybody it came from nowhere."

Although the source for his pseudonym is now forgotten, the initial inspiration for le Carre's fiction is easily found. It comes from the sensational disclosures in the 1950s that several high-ranking members of the British Secret Service and Foreign Office were actually Soviet agents. These deep-penetration agents, called "moles," had infiltrated the British espionage establishment during the Second World War and had, over a period of years, risen to extremely sensitive positions. Of the several spies discovered, the most highly placed was Kim Philby, a man generally acknowledged to be the greatest traitor in British history. Philby had been in charge of British counter-intelligence against the Soviet Union while secretly working for the Soviets, and was responsible for betraying hundreds of British agents to

their deaths. These real-life espionage revelations caught the interest of the British reading public and such books as Ian Fleming's "James Bond" spy series became best-sellers. Le Carre, too, because of his own intelligence work, was intrigued and disturbed by the discovery of traitors in the British Secret Service. Grella states that le Carre has an "obsession with the relationship between love and betrayal" and has consistently explored this theme in all of his fiction.

Le Carre wrote his first two novels, *Call for the Dead* and *A Murder of Quality,* while working for the Foreign Office, first in London and then in Bonn. At that time, the German capital was a center for intelligence operations. "You couldn't have been [in Germany] at that period," le Carre tells Miriam Gross of the *Chicago Tribune Magazine,* "without being aware of the shadow of an enormous intelligence apparatus." Le Carre introduced George Smiley, an intelligence agent featured in many of his later novels, in *Call for the Dead.* Smiley is an "improbable spy master," writes Richard W. Noland in *Clues: A Journal of Detection.* "[He is] short, fat, quiet and wears 'really bad clothes, which hung about his squat frame like skin on a shrunken toad,'" Noland quotes from *Call for the Dead.* Though physically unimposing, Smiley is a brilliant espionage agent who has served in the British Secret Service for more than thirty years. In *Call for the Dead,* Smiley investigates the suicide of a Foreign Office clerk who had just been given a security clearance, while in *A Murder of Quality* he tracks down the murderer of a schoolmaster's wife.

It wasn't until the publication of *The Spy Who Came In from the Cold* in 1963 that le Carre's work attracted widespread critical and popular acclaim. An immediate world-wide best-seller (the book has sold over twenty million copies since it first appeared), *Spy* enabled le Carre to leave his position with the Foreign Office to write full time. He tells Nicholas Wapshott of the London *Times:* "I had said to my accountant, if my assets reach 20,000 pounds, would you let me know?. . . When he told me I had reached that amount, with *The Spy Who Came In from the Cold,* it was a great relief. . . . I gave in my resignation." The novel tells the story of Alec Leamas, a fifty-year old British intelligence agent who wishes to retire from active duty and "come in from the cold," as he describes it. He is persuaded to take on one last assignment before leaving the Secret Service: a pretended defection behind the Iron Curtain to give false information to the East Germans implicating one of their high-ranking intelligence officers as a British agent. It is thought that the officer will then be imprisoned, thereby removing him from effective espionage work against the British. Leamas's real mission, and the treachery of his superiors, only gradually becomes clear to him as the plot unfolds.

Le Carre's pessimism about East-West relations is clearly evident in *Spy,* where both sides in the Cold War conflict are depicted as amoral and murderous. "The bureaucracies of East and West," writes Noland, describing the situation as related in *Spy,* "wage the Cold War by one simple rule—operational convenience. . . . In the name of operational convenience and alliances of expediency, any and all human values—including love and life itself—are expendable." In *Spy,* writes a *Times Literary Supplement* critic, le Carre puts forth the ideas that "the spy is generally a weak man, the tool of bureaucrats who are neither scrupulous nor particularly efficient, and that there is nothing to choose between 'us' and 'them' in an ethical sense." This is underlined when Leamas and his girlfriend are pitted against the intelligence agencies of both Britain and East Germany, "the two apparently opposed organizations on one side and helpless human beings . . . on the other," as Julian Symons writes in *Mortal Consequences: A History from the Detective Story to the Crime Novel.* Symons believes that *Spy* is the best of le Carre's novels because in *Spy* "the story is most bitterly and clearly told, the lesson of human degradation involved in spying most faithfully read."

Many of the qualities in le Carre's writing that are most praised by critics were first displayed in *Spy.* One of these is an authenticity and realism not usually found in espionage fiction. "Here is a book," Anthony Boucher writes in the *New York Times Book Review,* "a light year removed from the sometimes entertaining trivia which have (in the guise of spy novels) cluttered the publishers' lists." A reviewer for the *Times Literary Supplement* believes that, in *Spy,* "the technicalities of [spy] network organization carry a stamp of authenticity seldom found in stories of this nature," although the critic decries the "basically sensational" subject matter.

To make his work seem as authentic as possible, le Carre introduces a number of slang terms peculiar to the espionage underworld. Words like "mole," borrowed from the Soviet KGB, and "circus," a nickname for the British Secret Service, are used throughout *Spy.* Some of these terms are actual espionage jargon, but many were invented by le Carre

himself. "I thought it very important," le Carre tells Gross, "to give the reader the illusion of entering the secret world, and to that end I invented jargon that would be graphic and at the same time mysterious. Some people find it irritating. I rather like it." Le Carre, Downie reports, "borrowed 'mole' from the KGB and is pleased that it has quickly become part of the real spy language of the West."

Graham Greene sets the tone for most critical commentary about *The Spy Who Came In from the Cold* when he calls it, as K. G. Jackson of *Harper* quotes Greene, "the best spy novel I have ever read." D. B. Hughes of *Book Week* also praises *Spy* as "a beautifully written, understated and immensely perilous story. . . . Only rarely does a book of this quality appear—an inspired work and one in which the author's own inner excitement kindles the page." Several critics feel that with this novel le Carre transcends the espionage genre entirely, writing not category fiction but literature. Noland finds, for example, that with *The Spy Who Came In from the Cold* le Carre's "spy fiction became something more than most conventional spy fiction. It became, in fact, a political statement about the moral confusion and bankruptcy of the Cold War." Boucher also sees something more to le Carre's novel. "The author develops his story superbly," he writes, "both as a compelling and dazzlingly plotted thriller, and as a substantial and penetrating novel of our time. [Le Carre is one of] the small rank of [espionage] writers who can create a novel of significance, while losing none of the excitement of the tale of sheer adventure."

This high critical praise has continued with each succeeding espionage novel le Carre has published. *The Looking Glass War,* for example, is described by Hughes as "a superb spy story, unflawed, a bitter, cruel, dispassionate—yet passionate—study of an unimportant piece of espionage and the unimportant little men who are involved in it." A group of British agents mount an operation into East Germany that is doomed to failure under present political conditions, a fact which the agents refuse to see. Symons argues in *New Review* that in both *Spy* and *The Looking Glass War,* betrayal is the primary theme. In the first, an agent is betrayed to further the career of a more highly placed agent. In the second, an entire operation is abandoned and the people involved in it are left to die. It is possible, Symons writes, "to see espionage activities as brave and patriotic. . . , and yet to view them also as basically disgusting, outrages to the human personality. From such a point of view these two books seem to say an ultimate word about the nature of spying."

Le Carre draws heavily upon his time at the British Foreign Office in writing *A Small Town in Germany,* a novel set in Bonn, West Germany. The novel relates the story of a British diplomat who disappears with very sensitive documents which may damage Britain's chances of joining the Common Market. Speaking of the novel in a *Nation* review, John Gliedman states that le Carre "has long been a master of the essential machinery of the spy and detective novel. He has also shown himself to be a sensitive observer of character and manner, within the limits of the genre. But nothing which has come before quite prepares us for the literary distinction of this effort—the quality of its prose, the complexity of its construction, the cunning of some of its dialogue. . . . It represents something of a breakthrough in the use of the spy genre for serious purposes. *A Small Town in Germany* is that rarest of all things in contemporary fiction—good art which is also popular art." Robert Ostermann, writing in *National Observer,* agrees that *A Small Town in Germany* is better than le Carre's previous fiction. He calls it "broader in scope and more confidently crafted; tuned with exquisite fineness to the sliding nuances of its characters; shot through with the physical presence of Bonn, . . .and conveyed in a tough, precise prose that matches the novel's mordant tone down to the smallest metaphor."

Tinker, Tailor, Soldier, Spy, le Carre's next espionage novel, begins a loosely connected trilogy in which George Smiley is pitted against the Russian master spy "Karla." Writing in *Newsweek,* Alexis Gelber and Edward Behr report that "with *Tinker, Tailor* and Smiley, [le Carre] hit his stride." *Tinker, Tailor* is a fictionalized treatment of the Kim Philby spy case in which Smiley goes after a Soviet mole in British intelligence, a mole placed and directed by Karla. The novel's structure "derives from the action of Smiley's search," writes Noland. "[Smiley] must pursue his man through the maze of official documents." Knowing that the mole must be a highly placed agent, Smiley goes back through the records of intelligence operations, seeking a pattern of failure which might be attributed to the machinations of a particular agent. His investigation finally becomes, Noland believes, "a moral search . . . a quest for some kind of truth about England."

As in previous novels, le Carre examines the ramifications of betrayal, but this time in greater depth than he had previously attempted. The mole Smiley uncovers has not only betrayed his country and friends but has seduced Smiley's wife as well. The critic for the *Times Literary Supplement* sees a "moral dilemma" at the center of the book: "Smiley gets his man. In doing so he removes from another man his last illusions about friendship, loyalty and love, and he himself is left drained in much the same way. It is a sombre and tragic theme, memorably presented." Similarly, Richard Locke writes in the *New York Times Book Review* of the "interlocking themes of sexual and political betrayal" to be found in *Tinker, Tailor.* Writing in *Clues: A Journal of Detection,* Holly Beth King sees a deeper significance to the novel's title, which is derived from a children's nursery rhyme. King sees a "whole intricately woven set of relationships between adults and children, between innocence and disillusionment, between loyalty and betrayal that gives the novel's title a deeper resonance."

Although the complexity of *Tinker, Tailor* is praised by many critics, Pearl K. Bell writes in *New Leader* that "it is myopic and unjust to link le Carre with high art." Bell believes that a more correct evaluation of le Carre would see him as "a master craftsman of ingeniously plotted suspense, weaving astoundingly intricate fantasies of discovery, stealth, surprise, duplicity, and final exposure." Similarly, Locke finds that "le Carre belongs to the select company of such spy and detective story writers as Arthur Conan Doyle and Graham Greene in England and Dashiell Hammett, James M. Cain, Raymond Chandler, and Ross Macdonald in America. There are those who read crime and espionage books for the plot and those who read them for the atmosphere . . . le Carre's books . . . offer plenty for both kinds of readers." Bell concludes that le Carre is "unarguably the most brilliantly imaginative practitioner of the [espionage] genre today." Writing in *Newsweek,* Peter S. Prescott defines what sets le Carre's espionage fiction apart from many other works in the genre. "Le Carre's work is above all plausible," he writes, "rooted not in extravagant fantasies of the cold war but in the realities of the bureaucratic rivalry summoned up through vapors of nostalgia and bitterness, in understated pessimism, in images of attenuation and grinding down." In *Tinker, Tailor,* Stokes argues, "Smiley is merely the protagonist; bureaucracy itself is the hero. . . . Without the structure bureaucracy imposes on the random accumulation of facts that assail us on a daily basis, there is indeed only 'perpetual chaos.'"

Smiley's running battle with the Soviet spy master Karla continues in *The Honourable Schoolboy,* a novel set in Hong Kong, where British intelligence is investigating a prosperous businessman who seems to be working for the Soviets. Several critics point out a similarity between le Carre's novel and Joseph Conrad's novel, *Lord Jim.* The character Jerry Westerby, a British intelligence officer and friend of Smiley, is very similar to Conrad's character Jim. "Le Carre," Noland states, "obviously has Conrad's romantic protagonist in mind in his portrait of Westerby and in many of the events of the story." This "huge and hugely engrossing new thriller. . . ," writes David Ansen in *Newsweek,* "keeps opening out, like a Conrad adventure, into ever-widening pools of moral and emotional complexity."

Again concerned with one of Karla's moles, this one working inside Communist China, *The Honourable Schoolboy* traces Smiley's diligent efforts to discover and capture the agent for the West. As in previous novels, *Schoolboy* depicts an agent, this time Westerby, who is at odds with the amorality of espionage work and who, because of his belief in human values, loses his life in the course of an espionage operation. "The point, surely," writes Noland, "is that such romantic heroism is not very useful in the world of Cold War espionage." "It is difficult not to overpraise [*The Honourable Schoolboy*]," Mollie Panter-Downes writes in her *New Yorker* review. Although believing the novel too long, the plot "essentially thin," and le Carre's "fondness for stylistic mocking" embarrassing, Panter-Downes nonetheless praises *The Honourable Schoolboy.* "It has a compelling pace," she states, "a depth beyond its genre, a feeling for even the least of its characters, a horrifying vision of the doomed and embattled Southeast Asian left in the wake of the Vietnam War, and a dozen set pieces—following, fleeing, interrogating—that are awesomely fine."

Not all critics are as impressed with the novel. Louis Finger, writing in the *New Statesman,* believes that "the things that are wrong with le Carre, at the level of seriousness he no doubt feels he's aimed for here, totally debilitate the book's appeal as a run-of-the-mill espionage yarn." Responding to critics who classify le Carre's work as literature, Clive James of the *New York Review of Books* states that "raising le Carre to the plane of literature has helped rob him of his more enviable role as a popular writer who could take you unawares."

Le Carre brings his trilogy to a close with *Smiley's People,* the last confrontation between George Smiley and the Soviet master spy Karla. No longer content to thwart Karla's agents, Smiley works in this novel to force Karla himself to defect to the West. This operation is done off the record because the British Secret Service, due to political pressure, cannot engage in an offensive intelligence operation. It becomes instead a personal mission involving the retired Smiley and the friends and espionage contacts he has gathered over the years. "Smiley and his people," Noland states, "carry it out by personal choice and commitment, not for the British (or American) establishment. The whole operation is a victory for personal human loyalty and skill."

Despite the success of the operation, there is an ambiguity about it which brings into question the morality of espionage. "Smiley and his people are fighting for decency," writes Michael Wood in the *New York Times Book Review,* "but there is more blood on their hands than they or anyone else care to contemplate." Julian Moynihan clarifies this in *New Republic.* "We know," Moynihan writes, "that Smiley has ruined many lives, some innocent, in his tenacious pursuit of Karla; . . . and we just don't believe that the dirty tricks of one side are OK because they were ordered up by a decent little English guy with a disarming name." "If this is the end of the Smiley stories. . . ," writes Joseph McClellan in the *Washington Post Book World,* "it is an appropriately ambiguous conclusion to a series that has dealt splendidly in ambiguities from the beginning."

"In *Smiley's People,*" Tom Buckley states in *Quest/80,* "le Carre has done what no sensible person would have thought possible. He has written a novel at least as good as, and in some respects better than, his masterpiece, *The Spy Who Came In from the Cold.*" Jonathan Yardley agrees in an article for the *Washington Post,* calling it "the best of the le Carre's novels." Yardley goes on to evaluate le Carre's achievement as a writer by stating that he "has produced a body of work that is notable for technical brilliance, depth, and consistency of themes, and absolute verisimilitude."

In *The Little Drummer Girl,* le Carre turns to a different world arena for his setting—the Middle East refugee camps of the Palestinians. "It is as if Mr. le Carre," writes Anatole Broyard of the *New York Times,* "has had enough of British politics, as if he feels that neither Britain nor the Soviet Union is at the hot center of things anymore." Le Carre had originally planned to write a Smiley story set in the Middle East but could not find a convincing plot for his character. Because the espionage activity in this novel is of an active and open variety, unusual for le Carre, there is a great deal more action in *Drummer Girl* than is usual for a le Carre novel. There is also a female protagonist, le Carre's first, who is recruited by the Israelis to infiltrate a Palestinian terrorist group and set up its leader for assassination. "The Israelis triumph in the novel," William F. Buckley, Jr., writes in *National Review,* "even as they do in life. But Mr. le Carre is careful to even up the moral odds. . . . He permits the Palestinian point to be made with rare and convincing eloquence." Writing in *Esquire,* Martin Cruz Smith gives the opinion that *The Little Drummer Girl* is "the most balanced novel about Jews and Arabs, outrage for outrage and tear for tear, I've read." "Without condoning terrorism," Gelber and Behr write, "the book makes the reasons for it understandable—perhaps the first popular novel to do so."

Because of this insistence upon looking at both sides in the Middle East conflict as having valid reasons for waging war, le Carre succeeds, many critics believe, in presenting the situation in its complexity. It is through the character of Charlie, an actress recruited by the Israelis for the mission, that le Carre presents the arguments of both the Arabs and Jews. Charlie is first converted to the Israeli position by Israeli Intelligence and then, in order to play the part of a Palestinian sympathizer convincingly, she is indoctrinated in the Palestinian position. "In the course of the story," Hope Hale Davis states in the *New Leader,* "we have a chance, with Charlie, to become passionately partisan on one side and then the other, and also—with less risk to the psyche than Charlie suffers—both sides at once." According to Mark Abley, writing in *Maclean's,* le Carre "is resigned to the fact that neither side will be pleased by his controversial new novel." This is because le Carre portrays both sides as amoral killers, much the way he portrays both sides in the Cold War. Le Carre tells *Newsweek:* "There was no way of telling the story attractively unless one accepted certain premises—that terrible things were being done to the Jews. I began with the traditional Jewish hero looking for a Palestinian 'baddie.' Once into the narrative, the reader, I believed, would be prepared to consider more ambiguous moral preoccupations."

Some reviewers, however, see le Carre as an apologist for the Palestine Liberation Organization (PLO) and *The Little Drummer Girl* as lacking the moral ambiguity that characterizes his earlier books. "Here, one might have thought, is an ideal subject for moral ambiguity," David Pryce-Jones writes in the *New Republic.* "Le Carre finds it clear-cut. To him, the Palestinians are good, the Israelis bad." In their review of the book for *Chronicles of Culture,* Rael Jean Isaac and Erich Isaac acknowledge that le Carre does introduce the kind of moral ambiguities and correspondences between adversaries that he uses in other novels, "but these suggestions of ambiguity and correspondence are deceptive, for le Carre sets Israel up as the villain of this novel. . . . Le Carre employs meretricious techniques to make Israel appear guilty of the vicious practices that the PLO has made famous."

In his novels since *The Little Drummer Girl,* le Carre has featured stories that reflect the dissolution of the former Soviet Union and the end of the Cold War while continuing to portray flawed protagonists caught up in sinister circumstances. In *The Russia House,* which is set in a decaying Soviet Union, an aging publisher is recruited by British Intelligence to secure a top-secret manuscript from a Soviet engineer. After falling in love with the engineer's former girlfriend, however, the publisher must use his wits to keep himself and the woman alive while British and American spies pursue national interests not concerned with such individual freedoms. The novel was made into a movie starring Sean Connery and Michelle Pfeiffer.

The Night Manager, on the other hand, leaves behind Cold War settings altogether as a hotel manager in Switzerland struggles against international arms dealers funded by wealthy British businessmen. And *Our Game*, which is set in the warring republics of the former Soviet Union-Ossetia, Ingushetia, and Chechnia—again features a troubled central character caught up in socio-political forces beyond his control.

In *The Tailor of Panama,* published in 1996, le Carre explores his usual terrain of spy games and intrigue, this time against the tropical backdrop of Panama. Harry Pendel, a clothes tailor to the powerful and wealthy of Panama, is coerced into spying for British Intelligence in the midst of a plot to undo the Panama Treaty that will give control of the Panama Canal back to Panama in 1999. Although he does his duty by supplying information to his British recruiter, Pendel finds his life--and the lives of his family--in jeopardy in part because of the falsehoods he makes up to embellish his information. Writing in the *New*

York Times, Michiko Kakutani praises le Carre's refined storytelling prowess and his "colorful and deft" depiction of Panama. Kakutani, however, avers that the author is less successful in creating a plausible story line. *Times Literary Supplement* reviewer Frederic Raphael concurs, remarking that le Carre "does not seem to finish his button-holes, or fashion his concealed pockets, with quite the old finesse." Still, Kakutani notes, "the result is a riotous, readable novel."

Speaking of the relationship between his life and writings to Fred Hauptfuhrer of *People,* le Carre reveals: "If I write knowledgeably about gothic conspiracies, it's because I had knowledge of them from earliest childhood." In several published interviews, le Carre has spoken of his personal life and how the business dealings and political ambitions of his father colored his own views of the world. Because his father often found himself in legal or financial trouble due to his sometimes questionable business deals, the family found itself, le Carre tells Gross, "often living in the style of millionaire paupers. . . . And so we arrived in educated, middle-class society feeling almost like spies, knowing that we had no social hinterland, that we had a great deal to conceal and a lot of pretending to do." In an interview with Melvyn Bragg in the *New York Times Book Review,* le Carre states: "From early on, I was extremely secretive and began to think that I was, so to speak, born into occupied territory." He tells *Newsweek* that "there is a correlation, I suppose, between the secret life of my father and the secret life I entered at a formative age." Le Carre fictionalized his relationship with his father in the 1986 novel, *A Perfect Spy.*

"As for my own writing," le Carre tells Gross, "the real fun is the fun of finding that you've enchanted people, enchanted them in the sense that you've admitted them to a world they didn't know about. And also that you've given them a great deal of relief, in a strange way, because they've discovered a bit of life interpreted for them in ways that, after all, they find they understand."

BIOGRAPHICAL/CRITICAL SOURCES:

BOOKS

Barley, Tony, *Taking Sides: The Fiction of John le Carre,* Open University Press, 1986.
Bestsellers 89, Issue 4, Gale (Detroit), 1989.
Contemporary Literary Criticism, Gale, Volume 3, 1975, Volume 5, 1976, Volume 9, 1978, Volume 15, 1980, Volume 28, 1984.
Dictionary of Literary Biography, Volume 87: *British Mystery and Thriller Writers since 1940, First Series,* Gale, 1989.
Harper, Ralph, *The World of the Thriller,* Press of Case Western University (Cleveland, OH), 1969.
Homberger, Eric, *John le Carre,* Ungar (New York City), 1985.
Monaghan, David, *The Novels of John le Carre: The Art of Survival,* Blackwell (Oxford), 1985.
Monaghan, David, *Smiley's Circus: A Guide to the Secret World of John le Carre,* Orbis (London), 1986.
Palmer, Jerry, *Thrillers: Genesis and Structure of a Popular Genre,* St. Martin's (New York City), 1979.
Symons, Julian, *Mortal Consequences: A History from the Detective Story to the Crime Novel,* Harper (New York City), 1972.
Wolfe, Peter, *Corridors of Deceit: The World of John le Carre,* Bowling Green University Popular Press (Bowling Green, OH), 1987.

PERIODICALS

Armchair Detective, spring, 1980.
Book Week, January 26, 1964.
Chicago Tribune, June 19, 1989.
Chicago Tribune Book World, March 6, 1983.
Chicago Tribune Magazine, March 23, 1980.
Christian Science Monitor, January 14, 1980.
Chronicles of Culture, August, 1983.
Clues: A Journal of Detection, fall/winter, 1980; fall/winter, 1982.
Commentary, June, 1983.
Detroit News, August 29, 1982.
Economist, July 1, 1989, p. 75.
Esquire, April, 1983.
Globe and Mail (Toronto); June 10, 1989.
Harper, January, 1964; November, 1965; December, 1968.
Life, February 28, 1964.
Listener, July 4, 1974.
Los Angeles Times, May 31, 1989; October 16, 1989.
Los Angeles Times Book Review, June 18, 1989.
Maclean's, March 7, 1983.
Nation, December 30, 1968.
National Observer, October 28, 1968.
National Review, March 13, 1983.
New Leader, June 24, 1974; March 7, 1983.

New Republic, July 31, 1976; January 19, 1980; April 18, 1983; August 21, 1989, p. 30; August 9, 1993.

New Review, July, 1974.

New Statesman, July 12, 1974; September 23, 1977.

Newsweek, October 28, 1968; June 17, 1974; September 26, 1977; March 7, 1983; June 5, 1989, p. 52; July 5, 1993; p. 54.

New York, December 24, 1979; October 25, 1982.

New Yorker, October 3, 1977; August 23, 1993; p. 165.

New York Review of Books, October 27, 1977; February 7, 1980; April 14, 1983; September 28, 1989, p. 9; March 28, 1991; p. 8; August 12, 1993; p. 20.

New York Times, January 28, 1969; September 22, 1977; February 25, 1983; May 18, 1989, p. C28; December 1, 1991; July 8, 1993; October 18, 1996, p. B16.

New York Times Book Review, January 12, 1964; June 5, 1965; March 11, 1966; January 27, 1967; June 30, 1974; September 25, 1977; January 6, 1980; March 13, 1983; June 7, 1987, p. 34; May 21, 1989, p. 3; January 6, 1991, p. 3; June 27, 1993.

New York Times Magazine, September 8, 1974.

People, August 19, 1974; September 13, 1993, p. 63.

Publishers Weekly, September 19, 1977.

Quest/80, January, 1980.

Salmagundi, summer, 1970.

Saturday Review, July 24, 1965.

Spectator, July 6, 1974.

Time, January 17, 1964; May 29, 1964; September 29, 1980; January 14, 1991, p. 61.

Times (London); September 6, 1982; June 24, 1989.

Times Literary Supplement, September 13, 1963; June 24, 1965; September 24, 1971; July 19, 1974; September 9, 1977; August 4, 1989; October 18, 1996, p. 22.

Tribune Books (Chicago); May 21, 1989.

U.S. News and World Report, June 19, 1989, p. 59.

Village Voice, October 24, 1977; January 14, 1980.

Washington Post, September 29, 1980; November 29, 1982; May 25, 1989; October 14, 1989.

Washington Post Book World, December 8, 1974; December 23, 1979; June 4, 1989.

Yale Review, January, 1994, p. 150.

*   *   *

CORNWELL, Smith
See SMITH, David (Jeddie)

COTT, Nancy F(alik) 1945-

PERSONAL: Born November 8, 1945, in Philadelphia, PA; daughter of Max E. (a textile manufacturer) and Estelle (Hollander) Falik; married Leland Cott (an architect), August 31, 1969; children: Joshua, Emma. *Education:* Cornell University, B.A. (magna cum laude), 1967; Brandeis University, Ph.D., 1974.

ADDRESSES: Home—172 Hancock St., Cambridge, MA 02139. *Office*—P.O. Box 208236, American Studies Program, Yale University, New Haven, CT 06520. *E-mail*—nancy.cott@yale.edu.

CAREER: Wheaton College, Norton, MA, parttime instructor in history, 1971; Clark University, Worcester, MA, parttime instructor in history, 1972; Wellesley College, Wellesley, MA, parttime instructor in history, 1973-74; Yale University, New Haven, CT, assistant professor, 1975-79, associate professor, 1979-86, professor, 1986-90, Stanley Woodward professor of history and American Studies, 1990—, chair of women's studies program, 1980-87, 1992-93, chair of American studies program, 1994-97. Lecturer at Boston Public Library, spring, 1975, and at colleges and universities.

MEMBER: American Antiquarian Society, American Historical Association, American Studies Association, Society of American Historians, Massachusetts Historical Society, Berkshire Conference of Women Historians, Coordinating Committee of Women in the Historical Profession, Phi Beta Kappa, Phi Kappa Phi.

AWARDS, HONORS: Rockefeller Foundation humanities fellow, 1978-79; Harvard Law School fellowship, 1978-79, 1993-94; Radcliffe Visiting Research scholar, 1982, 1991, 1997; Whitney Humanities fellowship, Yale University, 1983-84, 1987; A Whitney Griswold Grant, Yale University, 1984, 1987, 1988, 1991, 1993; Guggenheim fellowship, and Charles Warren fellowship, Harvard University, both 1985; American Council of Learned Societies grant, 1988; National Endowment of the Humanities fellowship, 1993-94; Radcliffe College Graduate Alumnae Award, 1997.

WRITINGS:

(Editor) *Root of Bitterness: Documents of the Social History of American Women,* Dutton (New York City), 1972, revised edition, with others, Northeastern University Press (Boston), 1996.

The Bonds of Womanhood: "Woman's Sphere" in New England, 1780-1835, Yale University Press (New Haven, CT), 1977, revised edition, 1997.

(Editor with Elizabeth H. Pleck) *A Heritage of Her Own: Families, Work, and Feminism in America,* Simon & Schuster (New York City), 1979.

The Grounding of Modern Feminism, Yale University Press, 1987.

A Woman Making History: Mary Ritter Beard through Her Letters, Yale University Press, 1991.

Contributor of articles and reviews to history and women's studies journals. Member of editorial board of *American Quarterly,* 1977-80, *Feminist Studies,* 1977-85, *Journal of Social History,* 1978—, *Yale Review,* 1980-88, 1991—, *Reviews in American History,* 1981-85, *Women's Studies Quarterly,* 1981—, *Gender and History,* 1993-96, *Journal of Women's History,* 1987—, and *Yale Journal of Law and the Humanities,* 1988—; member of editorial advisory board of *The Correspondence of Lydia Maria Child,* University of Massachusetts, 1977-80. General editor, *History of Women in the United States: Historical Articles on Women's Lives and Activities,* twenty volumes, K. G. Saur, 1993-94, and *The Young Oxford History of Women,* eleven volumes, Oxford University Press (New York City), 1995.

WORK IN PROGRESS: Research on the history of marriage as a public institution in the United States.

SIDELIGHTS: Feminist historian and educator Nancy F. Cott is recognized even beyond the academic discipline of women's studies as an influential scholar in the field of women's history in the United States. Through works such as *The Bonds of Womanhood: "Woman's Sphere" in New England, 1780-1835,* 1987's *The Grounding of Modern Feminism,* as well as her editorship of books including *Root of Bitterness: Documents of the Social History of American Women,* Cott has contributed significantly to the growing body of work substantiating women's role in social and political progress throughout two centuries of U.S. history.

Cott's feminism was inspired by the Women's Liberation movement that promoted the ratification of the Equal Rights Amendment by the States during the ten years following 1972. Pursuing her interests in family history while a student at Brandeis University, Cott conducted the research that would eventually culminate in 1977's *The Bonds of Womanhood.* Graduating from Brandeis in 1974, Cott accepted

several lectureships before joining Yale University's American studies program in 1975. In the years since, she has been instrumental in the establishment of that university's women's studies program, and has attained the rank of professor of both history and American studies.

Published in 1987, *The Grounding of Modern Feminism* provides the modern feminist movement with an historical context. Feminism is an ideology distinct from that behind the suffrage movement; developing shortly before the outbreak of World War I, "it was both broader and narrower: broader in intent, proclaiming revolution in all the relations of the sexes, and narrower in the range of its willing adherents," according to Cott. Discussing the development of factionalism within the modern women's movement, Cott explains that such factionalism between conservative and radical adherents predated the passage of the 19th Amendment and continues to characterize the movement as we approach the millennium.

In addition to her historical works, Cott has served as editor of several collections of women's historical documents in the United States. *A Heritage of Her Own: Families, Work, and Feminism in America* includes articles by many pioneers in women's history, while *A Woman Making History: Mary Ritter Beard through Her Letters* provides an intimate glimpse of the woman who Cott characterizes as "the only historian [of the pre-World War II era] who paid serious attention to women's lives . . . and examined women as actors and agents."

In addition to her continued writing and teaching responsibilities, Cott is the author of numerous articles published in such journals as *Feminist Studies, Journal of Social History,* and the *Journal of American History.* Her continued research in the once ignored area of women's history continues to shed new light on Americans' collective past and illuminate the possibilities implicit within their future.

BIOGRAPHICAL/CRITICAL SOURCES:

BOOKS

Cott, Nancy F., *The Bonds of Womanhood: "Woman's Sphere" in New England, 1780-1835,* Yale University Press, 1977.

Cott, editor, *A Woman Making History: Mary Ritter Beard through Her Letters,* Yale University Press, 1991.

Feminist Writers, St. James Press (Detroit), 1996.

PERIODICALS

Ms., March/April, 1995, pp. 68-71.

*   *   *

COVINGTON, Vicki 1952-

PERSONAL: Born October 22, 1952, in Birmingham, AL; daughter of Jack (a metallurgical engineer) and Katherine (a teacher; maiden name, Jennings) Marsh; married Dennis Covington (a writer), December 24, 1977; children: Ashley, Laura. Education: University of Alabama, B.A., 1974, M.S.W., 1976.

ADDRESSES: Home—Birmingham, AL. Agent—Amanda Urban, International Creative Management, 40 West 57th St., New York, NY 10019.

CAREER: University of Alabama in Birmingham, social worker in substance abuse programs, 1978-88; writer, 1988—.

AWARDS, HONORS: Fellow of National Endowment for the Arts, 1988.

WRITINGS:

NOVELS

Gathering Home, Simon & Schuster (New York City), 1988.
Bird of Paradise, Simon & Schuster, 1990.
Night Ride Home, Simon & Schuster, 1992.
The Last Hotel for Women, Simon & Schuster, 1996.

SIDELIGHTS: Through the prism of family life in the American South, Vicki Covington's novels reflect the upheaval of social and political change, from world war to the civil rights battle at home. She is frequently noted for her realistic portrayals that eschew romanticism with a keen yet compassionate eye.

In Bird of Paradise, her second book, Covington creates the memorable Honey Shugart, an open-hearted woman who has had her fair share of hard times, including life with her now-deceased alcoholic husband and the death of her sister. Honey worries as much about what to feed a visitor as she does about the possible commercial development of her childhood home. She makes sense of the world around her with common-sense aphorisms that reveal the flavor of her roots in rural Alabama. "Honey's story provides the enormous pleasure of a small world skillfully, gracefully and gently observed," writes Regina Weinreich in her review for the New York Times Book Review.

Perseverance in a claustrophobic mining town is a key theme of Night Ride Home. The cast of characters include a father who could well be expected to express opposition to his daughter's wedding by showing up with a gun, a kleptomaniacal mother with a singing voice like velvet, the two newlyweds, and the eyes and the ears of the town, the prostitute Bolivia Ivey. "Without getting all sappy about it, Vicki Covington manages to convey a community too brave to admit defeat, even when it smacks them in the face," comments Joyce R. Slater in the Chicago Tribune.

Her 1996 novel, The Last Hotel for Women, was widely reviewed and generally well received. This "strange hybrid of politics and longing," as described by Alice Truax of the New York Times Book Review, is set in Alabama, as are all of Covington's stories. Covington takes on one of the most contentious periods in Southern history: the battle over African-American civil rights in the 1960s. The protagonist, Dinah Fraley, has close ties to both sides of the battle. The first is with one of the South's most excoriated officials, public safety commissioner "Bull" Connor; the other is with Angel, an injured freedom rider.

Connor was close to Dinah's mother, a madam who operated her business in the house the Fraley family have transformed into a hotel. This intimate view of a troubling historical figure highlights Covington's skill at characterization. Without whitewashing Connor's racial hatred, the author paints a picture of an emotionally hobbled man. Humanizing "Bull" Connor is a "bit of a feat," observes Bettina Drew in the Washington Post. "[Covington] has written a novel where the larger problem of segregation is seen as a society's emotional response gone awry."

How the Fraley family survives the turmoil of the 1960s depicts the South's own struggle to answer the question of whether to keep living in the past or move on to a new future. In Bookpage, an online book review page found at www.bookpage.com, Laurie Parker notes that Covington "is a master of undercurrent, telling one story on the surface while tapping into something deeper and more powerful underneath."

BIOGRAPHICAL/CRITICAL SOURCES:

PERIODICALS

Bookpage, February, 1996.
Chicago Tribune, September 14, 1992, section 5, p. 3.
Los Angeles Times, June 18, 1990.
New York Times Book Review, July 8, 1990, p. 16; April 7, 1996, p. 9.
Publishers Weekly, January 1, 1996, p. 58; January 8, 1996, p. 26.
Washington Post Book World, June 2, 1996, p. 9.

*   *   *

COX, William R(obert) 1901-1988
    (Willard d'Arcy, Mike Frederic, John Parkhill, Joel Reeve, Wayne Robbins, Roger G. Spellman, Jonas Ward)

PERSONAL: Born April 14, 1901, in Peapack, NJ; died August 7, 1988, in Sherman Oaks, CA, of congestive heart failure; son of William and Marion Grace (Wenz) Cox; married second wife, Casey Collins; children: Douglas Campbell (stepson).

CAREER: Professional writer.

MEMBER: Writers Guild of America, Western Writers of America (past committeeman, director, and vice-president; president, 1965-66, 1971-72).

WRITINGS:

NOVELS

Make My Coffin Strong, Fawcett (New York), 1954.
The Lusty Men, Pyramid (New York), 1957.
The Tycoon and the Tigress, Fawcett, 1958.
Hell to Pay, New American Library (New York), 1958.
Comanche Moon: A Novel of the West, McGraw (New York), 1959.
Murder in Vegas, New American Library, 1960.
Death Comes Early, Dell (New York), 1961.
Death on Location, New American Library, 1962.
The Duke, New American Library, 1962.

The Outlawed, New American Library, 1963, published as *Navajo Blood,* 1973.
Bigger than Texas, Fawcett, 1963.
(Under pseudonym Roger G. Spellman) *Tall for a Texan,* Fawcett, 1965.
The Gunsharp, Fawcett, 1965.
Way to Go, Doll Baby!, Avon (New York), 1966.
Black Silver, Profit Press, 1967.
Day of the Gun, Belmont (New York), 1967.
Firecreek (based on screenplay by Calvin Clements), Bantam (New York), 1968.
Moon of Cobre, Bantam, 1969.
Law Comes to Razor Edge, Popular Library (New York), 1970.
The Sixth Horseman, Ballantine (New York), 1972.
Jack o'Diamonds, Dell, 1972.
Chicano Cruz, Bantam, 1972.
Hot Times, Fawcett, 1973.
The Gunshop, Gold Lion (London), 1973.
The Fourth-of-July Kid, Tower (New York), 1981.
Cemetery Jones, Fawcett, 1985.
Cemetery Jones and the Maverick Kid, Fawcett, 1986.

NOVELS UNDER PSEUDONYM JONAS WARD

Buchanan's War, Fawcett, 1970.
Trap for Buchanan, Fawcett, 1971.
Buchanan's Gamble, Fawcett, 1972.
Buchanan's Siege, Fawcett, 1973.
Buchanan on the Run, Fawcett, 1973.
Get Buchanan!, Fawcett, 1974.
Buchanan Takes over, Fawcett, 1975.
Buchanan Calls the Shots, Fawcett, 1975.
Buchanan's Big Showdown, Fawcett, 1976.
Buchanan's Texas Treasure, Fawcett, 1977.
Buchanan's Stolen Railway, Fawcett, 1978.
Buchanan's Manhunt, Fawcett, 1979.
Buchanan's Range War, Fawcett, 1979.
Buchanan's Big Fight, Fawcett, 1980.
Buchanan's Black Sheep, Fawcett, 1985.
Buchanan's Stage Line, Fawcett, 1986.
Buchanan's Gun, Fawcett, 1986.

YOUNG ADULT NOVELS

Five Were Chosen: A Basketball Story, Dodd (New York), 1956.
Gridiron Duel, Dodd, 1959.
The Wild Pitch, Dodd, 1963.
Tall on the Court, Dodd, 1964.
Third and Eight to Go, Dodd, 1964.

(Under pseudonym Mike Frederic) *Frank Merriwell, Freshman Quarterback,* Award (New York), 1965.
(Under pseudonym Mike Frederic) *Frank Merriwell, Freshman Pitcher,* Award, 1965.
(Under pseudonym Mike Frederic) *Frank Merriwell, Sports Car Racer,* Award, 1965.
Big League Rookie, Dodd, 1965.
Trouble at Second Base, Dodd, 1966.
(Under pseudonym Joel Reeve) *Goal Ahead,* S. G. Phillips (New York), 1967.
The Valley Eleven, Dodd, 1967.
Jump Shot Joe, Dodd, 1968.
Rookie in the Backcourt, Dodd, 1970
Big League Sandlotters, Dodd, 1971.
Third and Goal, Dodd, 1971.
Gunner on the Court, Dodd, 1972.
Playoff, Bantam, 1972.
The Backyard Five, Dodd, 1973.
The Running Back, Bantam, 1974.
The Unbeatable Five, Dodd, 1974.
Game, Set, and Match, Dodd, 1977.
Battery Mates, Dodd, 1978.
Home Court Is Where You Find It, Dodd, 1980.

OTHER

The Veils of Bagdad (screenplay), Universal, 1953.
Tanganyika (screenplay), Universal, 1954.
Luke Short and His Era, Doubleday (New York), 1961, published in England as *Luke Short, Famous Gambler of the Old West: A Biography,* Foulsham for Fireside Press (London), 1962.
The Mets Will Win the Pennant (nonfiction), Putnam (New York), 1964.
(Editor) *Rivers to Cross* (collection of stories by members of Western Writers of America), Dodd, 1966.

Also author of more than one hundred television scripts for *Fireside Theater, Broken Arrow, Zane Grey Theater, General Electric Theater, Wells Fargo, Bonanza, The Grey Ghost, Route 66, Alcoa Theater, Wagon Train, Rawhide, Adam-12, The Virginian,* and other programs. Contributor of more than one thousand stories, including many under the pseudonyms Willard d'Arcy, John Parkhill, Joel Reeve, and Wayne Robbins, to crime and western publications and to such magazines as *Saturday Evening Post, Collier's, This Week, Argosy, American, Pic, Blue Book,* and *Cosmopolitan.* Cox's manuscripts are collected at the University of Oregon and the University of Wyoming.

SIDELIGHTS: William R. Cox was in many ways "the classic pulp writer," asserted James L. Traylor in *St. James Guide to Crime and Mystery Writers.* After launching his writing career as a sports reporter in the early 1920s, he moved into short fiction. Eventually he sold more than 1000 short stories, many to the great pulp magazines such as *Argosy, Detective Tales, Blue Book,* and *Black Mask.* He continued writing short stories until 1972, but by the 1950s his primary emphasis was on novels—mostly crime novels, westerns, and young adult sports stories.

Although most of his plots were quite formulaic, they were rendered in a professional, readable style. Reviews of the 1960 western *Commanche Moon: A Novel of the West* are typical of critical reaction to Cox's work. *Library Journal* contributor G. M. Gressley said of that book: "While the plot is not particularly inventive, Cox has deftly handled his narrative. Especially well done is the element of suspense which is maintained throughout the book." Reviewing *Commanche Moon* in the *New York Times Book Review,* Nelson Nye called it "well told and thoroughly engrossing. . . . An unusually gripping . . . account. . . . All the ingredients for first-class drama are here, and Cox certainly makes the most of them. This is a book you'll want to tell your friends about."

Traylor mused that Cox's writing style "is more representative of character study than of pure plot development." Discussing several books that featured a character named Tom Kincaid, a professional gambler and troubleshooter, Traylor rated them "solid examples of the action/adventure subgenre of the crime story." He pointed out that these books, and Cox's other crime stories too, "have fast movement and human interest, stressing character motivation." Traylor also expressed the opinion that "Cox might well have become much more appreciated had he received better support from the packagers of his novels. *Hell to Pay* has an atrocious cover, which in no way reveals the humanitarian nature of Tom Kincaid. Similarly, *Way to Go, Doll Baby!* is such a terrible title that it had little chance of success even though it is an entertaining and thoughtful character study of a middle-aged police inspector."

In an interview with Traylor published in *Armchair Detective,* Cox once declared: "I am a professional and proud of it. I was one since I first started on the magazine page of the Newark *Sunday Call,* under the watchful eye of my mentor, Edward Sothern Hipp, later one of the four top theatrical critics in New York. I make no claim to authorial talent or great wisdom. My job is to entertain as in the days of the minstrels. James Branch Cabell, Ernest Hemingway, Scott Fitzgerald, John O'Hara, and Stephen Crane are my idols . . . and some William Faulkner."

BIOGRAPHICAL/CRITICAL SOURCES:

BOOKS

St. James Guide to Crime and Mystery Writers, St. James Press (Detroit), 1996.

PERIODICALS

Armchair Detective, fall, 1982, pp. 253-66.
Booklist, February 1, 1960; May 15, 1961.
Chicago Sunday Tribune, April 30, 1961, p. 7.
Kirkus Reviews, January 15, 1961.
Library Journal, February 1, 1960; October 15, 1964.
New York Times Book Review, January 3, 1960, p. 21; September 20, 1964, p. 26.
San Francisco Chronicle, May 15, 1961, p. 35.
Springfield Republican, April 9, 1961, p. 5D.

OBITUARIES:

PERIODICALS

Armchair Detective, winter, 1989, pp. 92-93.
Chicago Tribune, August 12, 1988.
Los Angeles Times, August 12, 1988.
New York Times, August 12, 1988.*

*   *   *

COXE, George Harmon 1901-1984

PERSONAL: Born April 23, 1901, in Olean, NY; died January 30, 1984; son of George H. and Harriet C. (Cowens) Coxe; married Elizabeth Fowler, May 18, 1929; children: Janet, George III. *Education:* Attended Purdue University, 1919-20, and Cornell University, 1920-21. *Politics:* Republican.

CAREER: Worked as a reporter, 1922-27, with *Santa Monica Outlook,* Santa Monica, CA, *Los Angeles Express,* Los Angeles, CA, *Utica Observer Dispatch,* Utica, NY, *Commercial & Financial Chronicle,* New York City, and *Elmira Star-Gazette,* Elmira, NY;

Barta Press, Cambridge, MA, advertising salesperson, 1927-32; Metro-Goldwyn-Mayer, Hollywood, CA, writer, 1936-38, 1944; novelist.

MEMBER: Mystery Writers of America (member of board of directors, 1946-48, 1969-70; president, 1952), Authors Guild, Sigma Nu, Phi Zeta, Old Lyme Country Club, Cornell Club (New York City), Plantation Club, Sea Pines Golf Club.

AWARDS, HONORS: Grand Master Award from Mystery Writers of America, 1964.

WRITINGS:

NOVELS; ALL PUBLISHED BY KNOPF, EXCEPT AS INDICATED

Murder with Pictures, 1935.
The Barotique Mystery, 1936.
The Camera Clue, 1937.
Four Frightened Women, 1939.
Murder for the Asking, 1939.
The Glass Triangle (also see below), 1940.
The Lady Is Afraid, 1940.
Mrs. Murdock Takes a Case, 1941.
No Time to Kill, 1941.
Assignment in Guiana, 1942.
Silent Are the Dead, 1942.
The Charred Witness, 1942.
Alias the Dead, 1943.
Murder for Two, 1943.
Murder in Havana, 1943.
The Groom Lay Dead, 1944.
The Jade Venus (also see below), 1945.
Woman at Bay, 1945.
Dangerous Legacy, 1946.
Flash Casey: Detective, Avon, 1946.
Fashioned for Murder, 1947.
The Fifth Key (first published in *American Magazine,* 1945; also see below), 1947.
The Hollow Needle, 1948.
Venturous Lady, 1948.
Inland Passage, 1949.
Lady Killer, 1949.
Eye Witness, 1950.
The Frightened Fiances, 1950.
The Man Who Died Twice, 1951.
The Widow Had a Gun, 1951.
Never Bet Your Life, 1952.
The Crimson Clue, 1953.
Uninvited Guest (first published in the *Chicago Tribune* as "Nobody Wants Julia"), 1953.
Death at the Isthmus, 1954.

Focus on Murder, 1954.
Top Assignment, Knopf, 1955.
Suddenly a Widow, 1956.
Murder on Their Minds, 1957.
One Minute Past Eight, 1957.
The Impetuous Mistress, 1958.
Man on a Rope, 1958.
The Big Gamble, 1958.
Slack Tide (condensed version published in *American Magazine* as *The Captive-Bride Murders*), 1959.
Triple Exposure (includes *The Glass Triangle, The Jade Venus, The Fifth Key*), 1959.
The Last Commandment, 1960.
One Way Out, 1960.
Error of Judgment, 1961.
Moment of Violence, 1961.
Mission of Fear, 1962.
The Man Who Died Too Soon, 1962.
One Hour to Kill, 1963.
The Hidden Key, 1963.
Deadly Image, 1964.
The Reluctant Heiress, 1965.
With Intent to Kill, 1965.
The Ring of Truth, 1966.
The Candid Imposter, 1968.
An Easy Way to Go, 1969.
Double Identity, 1970.
Fenner, 1971.
Woman with a Gun, 1972.
The Silent Witness, 1973.
The Inside Man, 1974.
No Place for Murder, 1975.

Creator of television and radio series, "Crime Photographer," 1943-52. Contributor of short stories, novellas, and serials to magazines.

SIDELIGHTS: Called "the professional's professional" by the *New York Times Book Review*'s Anthony Boucher and "a master of the art of the detective novel" by William Lyon Phelps, George Harmon Coxe was an American master of the classic detective novel, and created a number of memorable characters in his long writing career. Coxe, who worked on newspapers for a number of years before he started writing full-time, wrote mysteries for forty years, publishing at a rate of more than a novel a year throughout that time period. Erle Stanley Gardner referred to his multitudinous books as "uniformly entertaining, gripping, and exciting."

Coxe's first great fictional character was Flash Casey, a newspaper photographer who doubled as a sleuth. Casey appeared in Coxe's stories for the

Black Mask detective magazine. According to J. Randolph Cox in the *St. James Guide to Crime and Mystery Writers*, "Jack (Flashgun, or Flash) Casey is a large, rumpled man with a touch of gray at the temples. He may curse at being dragged out of bed in the morning, but will do anything to help a colleague or anyone in genuine trouble. . . . A Casey plot can be summed up as a triple conflict: Casey is after a news story in pictures, the opposition (the criminals) don't want him to get those pictures, and the police don't want him to interfere. Casey's interference, of course, delivers the criminals to the police."

As he shifted from writing stories to writing novels, Coxe developed another photographer character, Kent Murdock. Cox wrote that "Murdock is more sophisticated than Casey and is more socially at ease. . . . There is a certain amount of pleasant predictability about the Murdock stories. . . . Murdock was expected to stumble over bodies in closets; it was part of his job and part of his character. Murdock's colleague in some of the novels was Jack Fenner, who, in 1971, branched out on his own." Casey disappeared in Coxe's first novel, *Murder with Pictures,* a book called by C. W. Morton, Jr. in the *Boston Transcript* "a plausible, well put-together, decently written yarn." Isaac Anderson in the *New York Times* was even more enthusiastic, stating that Coxe "has hit the bullseye with his first shot, and we can see no good reason why he should not repeat."

Barotique Mystery, Coxe's next effort, was again positively reviewed by Anderson in the *New York Times,* who said that "this story confirms us in the opinion that George Harmon Coxe is a rising star in the mystery fiction firmament." Coxe's 1939 duo of novels, *Four Frightened Women* and *Murder for the Asking,* were both well-received; the first was called "a fast and fairly tough example of the younger fleshly school" of mysteries by Will Cuppy of *Books,* and the second's "well-oiled plot, some fancy sleuthing, crisp conversation, good characters--especially the thugs and cops--and extra super-charged conclusion" were complimented by the *Saturday Review of Literature.* Another novel, *The Glass Triangle* (1940), was called "one of the best of Mr. Coxe's stories about Kent Murdock" by Anderson in the *New York Times.*

Throughout the 1940s and 1950s, Coxe continued to produce well-received mysteries. *New York Times* critic Anderson again appreciated Coxe's work, calling 1947's *Fashioned for Murder* "closely integrated and full of action and suspense." Coxe, Anderson opined in a review of that same year's *Fifth Key,* "tells the story with a narrative skill which even makes his red herrings seem not in the least fishy." 1949's *Lady Killer* garnered the following praise from *New York Times* critic Dom Frasca: "An intricate, deftly handled plot. Fans of George Herman Coxe will not be disappointed." Another Murdock novel, *Eye Witness* (1950), was applauded for its "good plot, speedy action, customary crisp Coxe conversation, and well-concealed solution" by the *Saturday Review of Literature,* and 1954's *Focus on Murder* was called, by the *New York Times'* Boucher "the best case for photographer Kent Murdock in some three years and one of his best ever."

Coxe occasionally took Murdock out of Boston, as he did for 1957's *One Minute Past Eight.* *New York Times* reviewer Boucher enthusiastically evaluated this novel: "Exotic settings usually stimulate Coxe to his best efforts, and he gets full value here out of Caracas, Venezuela, with emphasis on its food, its boom-culture, and its threatening Segurnal (national secret police). The plot neatly entwines local passions with the complications of a will in Boston and a $120,000 gambling debt in Las Vegas, to make a story as readable as it is ingenious."

Cox explained in the *St. James Guide to Crime and Mystery Writers* that "Coxe's third major series centers on the medical examiner Paul Standish. The medical background is as authentic in this series as the newspaper background in the Casey and Murdock series. Coxe also wrote books about Sam Crombie (a large man in a seersucker suit and Panama hat, who plods along and does his job) and Maxfield Chauncey Hale (detective in spite of himself)."

"To some readers Coxe may seem dull," continued Cox. "There is little explicit violence, just tales of people caught up in webs of their own spinning, told in deceptively simple formal style." Reviewers often pointed out the similarities of Coxe's novels, and their reliability: "pretty much the same pattern as its admirable predecessors" was the *Saturday Review of Literature*'s verdict on *The Lady Is Afraid;* "Mr. Coxe always delivers the goods," commented E. D. Doyle in the *San Francisco Chronicle.* Although critics at times complained about an element of predictability in Coxe's works, there was an almost universal critical opinion that Coxe was never less than capable, and often extremely appealing. *New York Times* critic Boucher's opinion of 1958's *Impetuous*

Mistress is emblematic of critical judgment on Coxe's work as a whole: it is characterized by "pure professional storytelling."

Coxe's manuscripts and personal papers are housed and available for study at the Beinecke Rare Book and Manuscript Library at Yale University.

BIOGRAPHICAL/CRITICAL SOURCES:

BOOKS

St. James Guide to Crime & Mystery Writers, fourth edition, St. James Press (Detroit), 1996.

PERIODICALS

Books, January 1, 1939.
Boston Transcript, November 30, 1935.
New York Times, November 24, 1935; January 4, 1942; March 9, 1947; September 21, 1947; March 20, 1949; March 23, 1954; September 29, 1957; March 30, 1958.
San Francisco Chronicle, September 21, 1947.
Saturday Review of Literature, December 14, 1935; December 30, 1939; August 5, 1939; March 25, 1950.*

*   *   *

CREASEY, John 1908-1973
(Gordon Ashe, M. E. Cooke, Margaret Cooke, Henry St. John Cooper, Credo, Norman Deane, Elise Fecamps, Robert Caine Frazer, Patrick Gill, Michael Halliday, Charles Hogarth, Brian Hope, Colin Hughes, Kyle Hunt, Abel Mann, Peter Manton, J. J. Marric, James Marsden, Richard Martin, Rodney Mattheson, Anthony Morton, Ken Ranger, William K. Reilly, Tex Riley, Jeremy York)

PERSONAL: Born September 17, 1908, in Southfields, Surrey, England; died of congestive heart failure, June 9, 1973, in Bodenham, Salisbury, England; buried in Bodenham churchyard; son of Joseph (a cabinet maker and coach builder) and Ruth (Creasey) Creasey; married Margaret Elizabeth Cooke, 1935 (divorced, 1939); married (Evelyn) Jean Fudge, February 16, 1941 (divorced, 1970); married Jeanne Williams (a writer), October, 1970 (divorced, 1973); married Diana Hamilton Farrell,

May, 1973; children: (first marriage) Colin John; (second marriage) Martin John, Richard John. *Education:* Attended London elementary and secondary schools. *Politics:* Liberal.

CAREER: Writer. Held various clerical jobs, London, England, 1926-35. Publisher, Jay Books, 1957-59; editor and publisher, *John Creasey Mystery Magazine,* 1956-65; director of Robert Sommerville Ltd. (literary agency) and of Salisbury Arts Theatre. Member of governing body of Liberal Party, 1945-50; Liberal Party candidate for Parliament, 1950; founder of All Party Alliance Movement, 1967; All Party Alliance Movement candidate for Parliament, 1967-68. Chairman of fund-raising committees for famine relief and refugee organizations, including National Savings Movement, United Europe, and Oxford Committee for Famine Relief.

MEMBER: Crime Writers Association (co-founder; chairman, 1953-57), Mystery Writers of America (chairman, 1966-67), Western Writers of America, Authors' League, Society of Authors (London), P.E.N., National Liberal Club, Paternosters (chairman, 1967), Rotary International, Westerners Club (Tucson, Arizona), Royal Automobile Club (London).

AWARDS, HONORS: Member, Order of the British Empire (M.B.E.), 1946; Mystery Writers of America, Edgar Allan Poe Award, 1962, for *Gideon's Fire,* and Grand Master Award, 1969, for outstanding contributions to the mystery novel genre.

WRITINGS:

Seven Times Seven (mystery novel), Melrose (London), 1932.
Men, Maids, and Murder (mystery novel), Melrose, 1933, revised edition, Long (London), 1973.
(Contributor) *The Evening Standard Detective Book,* Gollancz (London), 1950.
Four of the Best (also see below; contains *The Department of Death, Inspector West Alone, The Prophet of Fire,* and *Hunt the Toff*), Hodder & Stoughton (London), 1955.
(Contributor) Rex Stout, editor, *Eat, Drink, and Be Buried,* Viking (New York City), 1956, published in England as *For Tomorrow We Die,* Macdonald & Evans (London), 1958.
(Contributor) Elizabeth Ferrars, editor, *Planned Departures,* Hodder & Stoughton, 1958.
(Editor and contributor) *Mystery Bedside Book,* six volumes, Hodder & Stoughton, 1960-65.

The Mountain of the Blind (mystery novel), Hodder & Stoughton, 1960.
The Foothills of Fear (mystery novel), Hodder & Stoughton, 1961, Walker & Co. (New York City), 1966.
(Editor) *Crimes across the Sea: The 19th Annual Anthology of the Mystery Writers of America, 1964* (anthology), Harper (New York City), 1964.
The Masters of Bow Street (mystery novel), Hodder & Stoughton, 1972, Simon & Schuster (New York City), 1974.

JUVENILE FICTION

The Men Who Died Laughing, Thompson (Dundee, England), 1935.
The Killer Squad, George Newnes (London), 1936.
Blazing the Air Trail, Low (London), 1936.
The Jungle Flight Mystery, Low, 1936.
The Mystery 'Plane, Low, 1936.
Murder by Magic, Amalgamated Press (London), 1937.
The Mysterious Mr. Rocco, Mellifont Press (London), 1937.
The S.O.S. Flight, Low, 1937.
The Secret Aeroplane Mystery, Low, 1937.
The Treasure Flight, Low, 1937.
The Air Marauders, Low, 1937.
The Black Biplane, Low, 1937.
The Mystery Flight, Low, 1937.
The Double Motive, Mellifont Press, 1938.
The Doublecross of Death, Mellifont Press, 1938.
The Missing Hoard, Mellifont Press, 1938.
Mystery of Manby House, Northern News Syndicate, 1938.
The Fighting Flyers, Low, 1938.
The Flying Stowaways, Low, 1938.
The Miracle 'Plane, Low, 1938.
Dixon Hawke: Secret Agent, Thompson, 1939.
Documents of Death, Mellifont Press, 1939.
The Hidden Hoard, Mellifont Press, 1939.
The Blue Flyer, Mellifont Press, 1939.
The Jumper, Northern News Syndicate, 1939.
The Mystery of Blackmoor Prison, Mellifont Press, 1939.
The Sacred Eye, Thompson, 1939.
Mottled Death, Thompson, 1939.
Peril by Air, George Newnes, 1939.
The Flying Turk, Low, 1939.
The Ship of Death, Thompson, 1939.
The Monarch of the Skies, Low, 1939.
Dazzle—Air Ace No. One, George Newnes, 1940.
Five Missing Men, George Newnes, 1940.

The Poison Gas Robberies, Mellifont Press, 1940.
The Cinema Crimes, T. A. & E. Pemberton (Manchester, England), 1945.
The Missing Monoplane, Low, 1947.

NONFICTION

(Ghost writer) *Jimmy Wilde: Fighting Was My Business,* M. Joseph (London), 1938.
(Compiler and editor) *Action Stations!: An Account of the H.M.S. Dorsetshire and Her Earlier Namesakes,* John Long, 1942.
(With Walter Hutchinson) *The Printer's Devil: The History of a Printer's Charity,* Hutchinson (London), 1943.
Heroes of the Air: A Tribute to the Courage, Sacrifice and Skill of the Men of the R.A.F., Dorset "Wings for Victory" Campaign Committee (Dorchester, England), 1943.
(With John Lock) *Log of a Merchant Airman,* Stanley Paul (London), 1943.
(Under pseudonym Credo) *Man in Danger,* Hutchinson, 1948.
(With Jean Creasey) *Round the World in 465 Days,* R. Hale (London), 1953.
Round the Table: The First Twenty-Five Years of the English Goodwill Association, National Association of Round Tables of Great Britain and Ireland (London), 1953.
(With Jean Creasey and sons, Martin and Richard Creasey) *Let's Look at America,* R. Hale, 1956.
They Didn't Mean to Kill: The Real Story of Road Accidents, Their Cause, Costs, and Cure, Hodder & Stoughton, 1960.
(With Jean, M., and R. Creasey) *Optimists in Africa,* Howard Timmins (Capetown), 1963.
African Holiday, illustrations and captions by M. Creasey, Howard Timmins, 1963.
Good, God, and Man: An Outline of the Philosophy of Self-ism, illustrations by M. Creasey, Hodder & Stoughton, 1968, Walker & Co., 1971.
Evolution to Democracy, Hodder & Stoughton, 1969, revised edition, White Lion, 1972.

"DEPARTMENT Z" MYSTERIES

The Death Miser, Melrose, 1933.
Redhead, Hurst & Blackett (London), 1933, revised edition, Arrow Books (London), 1971.
First Came a Murder, Melrose, 1934, revised edition, John Long, 1969, McKay (New York City), 1972.

Death round the Corner, Melrose, 1935, revised edition, Popular Library (New York City), 1970.
The Mark of the Crescent, Melrose, 1935, revised edition, John Long, 1970, Popular Library, 1972.
Thunder in Europe, Melrose, 1936, revised edition, John Long, 1970, Popular Library, 1972.
The Terror Trap, Melrose, 1936, revised edition, Arrow Books, 1969, Popular Library, 1972.
Carriers of Death, Melrose, 1937, revised edition, Popular Library, 1968.
Days of Danger, Melrose, 1937, revised edition, John Long, 1970, Popular Library, 1972.
Death Stands By, John Long, 1938, revised edition, Arrow Books, 1966, Popular Library, 1972.
Menace!, John Long, 1938, revised edition, Popular Library, 1971.
Murder Must Wait, Melrose, 1939, revised edition, John Long, 1969, Popular Library, 1972.
Panic!, John Long, 1939, Popular Library, 1972.
Death by Night, John Long, 1940, revised edition, Arrow Books, 1970, Popular Library, 1972.
The Island of Peril, John Long, 1940, revised edition, John Long, 1970, Popular Library, 1976.
Sabotage, John Long, 1941, revised edition, Arrow Books, 1971, Popular Library, 1976.
Go away Death, John Long, 1941, revised edition, 1969, Popular Library, 1976.
The Day of Disaster, John Long, 1942, revised edition, John Long, 1969.
Prepare for Action, Stanley Paul, 1942, revised edition, Arrow Books, 1966, Popular Library, 1975.
No Darker Crime, Stanley Paul, 1943, Popular Library, 1976.
Dangerous Quest, John Long, 1944, revised edition, Arrow Books, 1965, Walker & Co., 1974.
Dark Peril, Stanley Paul, 1944, revised edition, John Long, 1969, Popular Library, 1975.
The Peril Ahead, Stanley Paul, 1946, revised edition, John Long, 1969, Popular Library, 1974.
The League of Dark Men, Stanley Paul, 1947, revised edition, John Long, 1968, Popular Library, 1975.
The Department of Death, Evans Brothers (London), 1949, Popular Library, 1979.
The Enemy Within, Evans Brothers, 1950, Popular Library, 1977.
Dead or Alive, Evans Brothers, 1951, Popular Library, 1974.
A Kind of a Prisoner, Hodder & Stoughton, 1956, Popular Library, 1975.
The Black Spiders, Hodder & Stoughton, 1957, Popular Library, 1975.

"SEXTON BLAKE" MYSTERIES

The Case of the Murdered Financier, Amalgamated Press (London), 1937.
The Great Air Swindle, Amalgamated Press, 1939.
The Man from Fleet Street, Amalgamated Press, 1940.
The Case of the Mad Inventor, Amalgamated Press, 1942.
Private Carter's Crime, Amalgamated Press, 1943.

"THE TOFF" MYSTERIES

Introducing the Toff, John Long, 1938, revised edition, 1954.
The Toff Goes On, John Long, 1939, revised edition, 1955.
. . . Steps Out, John Long, 1939, revised edition, 1955.
Here Comes . . . , John Long, 1940, Walker & Co., 1967, revised edition, Sphere Books (London), 1969.
. . . Breaks In, John Long, 1940, revised edition, 1955.
Salute the Toff, John Long, 1941, Walker & Co., 1971.
. . . Proceeds, John Long, 1941, Walker & Co., 1968.
. . . Goes to Market, John Long, 1942, Walker & Co., 1967.
. . . Is Back, John Long, 1942, revised edition, Corgi Books (London), 1971, Walker & Co., 1974.
. . . Among Millions, John Long, 1943, revised edition, Panther Books, 1964, Walker & Co., 1976.
Accuse . . . , John Long, 1943, revised edition, Corgi Books, 1972, Walker & Co., 1975.
. . . and the Curate, John Long, 1944, Walker & Co., 1969, published in England as *. . . and the Deadly Parson,* Lancer Books (London), 1970.
. . . and the Great Illusion, John Long, 1944, Walker & Co. 1967.
Feathers for . . . , John Long, 1945, revised edition, Hodder & Stoughton, 1964, Walker & Co., 1970.
. . . and the Lady, John Long, 1946, Walker & Co., 1975.
. . . on Ice, John Long, 1946, revised edition, Corgi Books, 1976, published as *Poison for . . . ,* Pyramid Publications (London), 1976.
Hammer . . . , John Long, 1947.
. . . in Town, John Long, 1948, revised edition, Walker & Co., 1977.

. . . Takes Shares, John Long, 1948, revised edition, Corgi Books, 1971, Walker & Co., 1972.
. . . and Old Harry, John Long, 1949, revised edition, Hodder & Stoughton, 1964, Walker & Co., 1970.
. . . on Board, Evans Brothers, 1949, revised edition, Corgi Books, 1971, Walker & Co., 1973.
Fool . . . , Evans Brothers, 1950, Walker & Co., 1966.
Kill . . . , Evans Brothers, 1950, Walker & Co., 1966, revised edition, Corgi Books, 1972.
A Knife for . . . , Evans Brothers, 1951, Pyramid Publications, 1964, revised edition, Corgi Books, 1971.
. . . Goes Gay, Evans Brothers, 1951, published as *A Mask for . . . ,* Walker & Co., 1966.
Hunt . . . , Evans Brothers, 1952, Walker & Co., 1969, revised edition, Corgi Books, 1972.
Call . . . , Hodder & Stoughton, 1953, Walker & Co., 1969.
. . . Down Under, Hodder & Stoughton, 1953, Walker & Co., 1969, published in England as *Break . . . ,* Lancer Books, 1970.
Murder out of the Past, and Under-Cover Man (short stories), Barrington Gray (Leighton-Sea, Essex, England), 1953.
. . . at Butlin's, Hodder & Stoughton, 1954, Walker & Co., 1976.
. . . on the Trail (short stories), Everybody's Books, c. 1954.
. . . at the Fair, Hodder & Stoughton, 1954, Walker & Co., 1968.
A Six for . . . , Hodder & Stoughton, 1955, Walker & Co., 1969, published in England as *A Score for . . . ,* Lancer Books, 1972.
. . . and the Deep Blue Sea, Hodder & Stoughton, 1955, Walker & Co., 1967.
Make-Up for . . . , Hodder & Stoughton, 1956, Walker & Co., 1967, published in England as *Kiss . . . ,* Lancer Books, 1971.
. . . in New York, Hodder & Stoughton, 1956, Pyramid Publications, 1964.
Model for . . . , Hodder & Stoughton, 1957, Pyramid Publications, 1965.
. . . on Fire, Hodder & Stoughton, 1957, Walker & Co., 1966.
. . . and the Stolen Tresses, Hodder & Stoughton, 1958, Walker & Co., 1965.
. . . on the Farm, Hodder & Stoughton, 1958, Walker & Co., 1964, published as *Terror for . . . ,* Pyramid Publications, 1965.
Double for . . . , Hodder & Stoughton, 1959, Walker & Co., 1965.
. . . and the Runaway Bride, Hodder & Stoughton, 1959, Walker & Co., 1964.

A Rocket for . . . , Hodder & Stoughton, 1960, Pyramid Publications, 1964.

. . . and the Kidnapped Child, Hodder & Stoughton, 1960, Walker & Co., 1965.

Follow . . . , Hodder & Stoughton, 1961, Walker & Co., 1967.

. . . and the Teds, Hodder & Stoughton, 1961, published as *. . . and the Toughs,* Walker & Co., 1968.

A Doll for . . . , Hodder & Stoughton, 1963, Walker & Co., 1965.

Leave It to . . . , Hodder & Stoughton, 1963, Pyramid Publications, 1965.

. . . and the Spider, Hodder & Stoughton, 1965, Walker & Co., 1966.

. . . in Wax, Walker & Co., 1966.

A Bundle for . . . , Hodder & Stoughton, 1967, Walker, 1968.

Stars for . . . , Walker & Co., 1968.

. . . and the Golden Boy, Walker & Co., 1969.

. . . and the Fallen Angels, Walker & Co., 1970.

Vote for . . . , Walker & Co., 1971.

. . . and the Trip-Trip-Triplets, Walker & Co., 1972.

. . . and the Terrified Taximan, Walker & Co., 1973.

. . . and the Sleepy Cowboy, Hodder & Stoughton, 1974, Walker, 1975.

The Toff and the Crooked Copper, Hodder and Stoughton, 1977.

The Toff and the Dead Man's Finger, Hodder and Stoughton, 1978.

"ROGER WEST" MYSTERIES

Inspector West Takes Charge, Stanley Paul, 1942, revised edition, Pan Books (London), 1963, Scribner (New York City), 1972.

. . . Leaves Town, Stanley Paul, 1943, published as *Go Away Murder,* Lancer Books, 1972.

. . . at Home, Stanley Paul, 1944, Scribner, 1973.

. . . Regrets, Stanley Paul, 1945, revised edition, Hodder & Stoughton, 1965, Lancer Books, 1971.

Holiday for Inspector West, Stanley Paul, 1946.

Battle for . . . , Stanley Paul, 1948.

Triumph for . . . , Stanley Paul, 1948, published as *The Case against Paul Raeburn,* Harper, 1958.

. . . Kicks Off, Stanley Paul, 1949, published as *Sport for . . . ,* Lancer Books (New York City), 1971.

. . . Alone, Evans Brothers, 1950, Scribner, 1975.

. . . Cries Wolf, Evans Brothers, 1950, published as *The Creepers,* Harper, 1952.

A Case for . . . , 1951, published as *Figure in the Dusk,* Harper, 1952.

Puzzle for . . . , Evans Brothers, 1951, published as *The Dissemblers,* Scribner, 1967.

. . . at Bay, Evans Brothers, 1952, published as *The Blind Spot,* Harper, 1954, published as *The Case of the Acid Throwers,* Avon (New York City), 1960.

A Gun for . . . , Hodder & Stoughton, 1953, published as *Give a Man a Gun,* Harper, 1954.

Send . . . , Hodder & Stoughton, 1953, revised edition, Coronet Books, 1972, Scribner, 1976, published as *Send Superintendent West,* Pan Books, 1965.

A Beauty for . . . , Hodder & Stoughton, 1954, published as *The Beauty Queen Killer,* Harper, 1956, published as *So Young, So Cold, So Fair,* Dell (New York City), 1958.

. . . Makes Haste, Hodder & Stoughton, 1955, published as *The Gelignite Gang,* Harper, 1956, published as *Night of the Watchman,* Berkley Publishing (New York City), published as *Murder Makes Haste,* Lancer Books.

Two for . . . , Hodder & Stoughton, 1955, published as *Murder: One, Two, Three,* Scribner, 1960, published as *Murder Tips the Scales,* Berkley Publishing, 1962.

Parcels for . . . , Hodder & Stoughton, 1956, published as *Death of a Postman,* Harper, 1957.

A Prince for . . . , Hodder & Stoughton, 1956, published as *Death of an Assassin,* Scribner, 1960.

Accident for . . . , Hodder & Stoughton, 1957, published as *Hit and Run,* Scribner, 1959.

Find . . . , Hodder & Stoughton, 1957, published as *The Trouble at Saxby's,* Harper, 1959, published as *Doorway to Death,* Berkley Publishing, 1961.

Murder, London—New York, Hodder & Stoughton, 1958, Scribner, 1961.

Strike for Death, Hodder & Stoughton, 1958, published as *The Killing Strike,* Scribner, 1961.

Death of a Racehorse, Hodder & Stoughton, 1959, Scribner, 1962.

The Case of the Innocent Victims, Hodder & Stoughton, 1959, Scribner, 1966.

Murder on the Line, Hodder & Stoughton, 1960, Scribner, 1963.

Death in Cold Print, Hodder & Stoughton, 1961, Scribner, 1962.

The Scene of the Crime, Hodder & Stoughton, 1961, Scribner, 1963.

Policeman's Dread, Hodder & Stoughton, 1962, Scribner, 1964.

Hang the Little Man, Scribner, 1963.

Look Three Ways at Murder, Hodder & Stoughton, 1964, Scribner, 1965.

Murder, London—Australia, Scribner, 1965.

Murder, London—South Africa, Scribner, 1966.

The Executioners, Scribner, 1967.

So Young to Burn, Scribner, 1968.

Murder, London—Miami, Scribner, 1969.

A Part for a Policeman, Scribner, 1970.

Alibi, Scribner, 1971 (published in England as *Alibi for . . . ,* Coronet Books, 1973).

A Splinter of Glass, Scribner, 1972.

The Theft of Magna Carta, Scribner, 1973.

The Extortioners, Hodder & Stoughton, 1974, Scribner, 1975.

A Sharp Rise in Crime, Hodder & Stoughton, 1977, Scribner, 1978.

"DR. PALFREY" MYSTERIES

Traitors' Doom, John Long, 1942, Walker & Co., 1970.

The Valley of Fear, John Long, 1943, published as *The Perilous Country,* 1949, revised edition, Arrow Books, 1966, Walker & Co., 1973.

The Legion of the Lost, John Long, 1943, Steven Daye (New York City), 1944, revised edition, John Long, 1968, Walker & Co., 1974.

Death in the Rising Sun, John Long, 1945, revised edition, 1970, Walker & Co., 1976.

The Hounds of Vengeance, John Long, 1945, revised edition, 1969.

Shadow of Doom, John Long, 1946, revised edition, 1970.

The House of Bears, John Long, 1946, revised edition, 1962, Walker & Co., 1975.

Dark Harvest, John Long, 1947, revised edition, Arrow Books, 1962, Walker & Co., 1977.

The Wings of Peace, John Long, 1948, revised edition, 1969, Walker & Co., 1978.

Sons of Satan, John Long, 1948, revised edition, 1972.

The Dawn of Darkness, John Long, 1949.

The League of Light, Evans Brothers, 1949, revised edition, 1969.

The Man Who Shook the World, Evans Brothers, 1950, revised edition, John Long, 1972.

The Prophet of Fire, Evans Brothers, 1951, Walker & Co., 1978.

The Children of Hate, Evans Brothers, 1952, published as *The Children of Despair,* Jay Books (New York City), 1958, revised edition, John Long, 1970, published as *The Killers of Innocence,* Walker & Co., 1971.

The Touch of Death, Hodder & Stoughton, 1954, Walker & Co., 1968.

The Mists of Fear, Hodder & Stoughton, 1955, Walker & Co., 1977.

The Flood, Hodder & Stoughton, 1956, Walker & Co., 1969.

The Plague of Silence, Hodder & Stoughton, 1958, Walker & Co., 1968.

The Drought, Hodder & Stoughton, 1959, Walker & Co., 1967, published in England as *Dry Spell,* New English Library (London), 1967.

The Terror: The Return of Dr. Palfrey, Hodder & Stoughton, 1963, Walker & Co., 1966.

The Depths, Hodder & Stoughton, 1963, Walker & Co., 1966.

The Sleep, Hodder & Stoughton, 1964, Walker & Co., 1968.

The Inferno, Hodder & Stoughton, 1965, Walker & Co., 1968.

The Famine, Hodder & Stoughton, 1967, Walker & Co., 1968.

The Blight, Walker & Co., 1968.

The Oasis, Hodder & Stoughton, 1969, Walker & Co., 1970.

The Smog, Hodder & Stoughton, 1970, Walker & Co., 1971.

The Unbegotten, Hodder & Stoughton, 1971, Walker & Co., 1972.

The Insulators, Hodder & Stoughton, 1972, Walker & Co., 1973.

The Voiceless Ones, Hodder & Stoughton, 1973, Walker & Co., 1974.

The Thunder-Maker, Walker & Co., 1976.

The Whirlwind, Hodder & Stoughton, 1979.

PLAYS

Gideon's Fear (adaptation of his novel *Gideon's Week* [see below under pseudonym J. J. Marric]; first produced in Salisbury, England, 1960), Evans Brothers, 1967.

Strike for Death, first produced in Salisbury, 1960.

The Toff: A Comedy Thriller in Three Acts, Evans Brothers, 1963.

Hear Nothing, Say All, first produced in Salisbury, 1964.

MYSTERIES UNDER PSEUDONYM GORDON ASHE

Who Was the Jester?, George Newnes, 1940, published as *The Masked Gunman: The Man Who Stayed Alive,* John Long, 1955.

No Need to Die, John Long, 1956, Ace (New York City), 1957.

*"PATRICK DAWLISH" MYSTERIES UNDER ASHE PSEUD-
ONYM*

The Speaker, John Long, 1939, published as *The
Croaker,* Holt (New York City), 1972.
Death on Demand, John Long, 1939.
Terror by Day, John Long, 1940.
The Secret Murder, John Long 1940, revised edition,
Corgi Books, 1972.
'Ware Danger!, John Long, 1941.
Murder Most Foul, John Long, 1942, revised edi-
tion, Corgi Books, 1973.
There Goes Death, John Long, 1942, revised edition,
Corgi Books, 1973.
Death in High Places, John Long, 1942, revised
edition, Corgi Books, 1973.
Death in Flames, John Long, 1943, revised edition,
Corgi Books, 1973.
Two Men Missing, John Long, 1943, revised edition,
Corgi Books, 1971.
Rogues Rampant, John Long, 1944, revised edition,
Corgi Books, 1973.
Death on the Move, John Long, 1945.
Invitation to Adventure, John Long, 1945.
Here Is Danger, John Long, 1946.
Give Me Murder, John Long, 1947.
Murder Too Late, John Long, 1947.
Engagement with Death, John Long, 1948.
Dark Mystery, John Long, 1948.
A Puzzle in Pearls, John Long, 1949, revised edi-
tion, Corgi Books, 1971.
Kill or Be Killed, Evans Brothers, 1950, reprinted,
Lythway Press (Bath, England), 1973.
The Dark Circle, Evans Brothers, 1950, Curley
(South Yarmouth, MA), 1991.
Murder with Mushrooms, Evans Brothers, 1950, re-
vised edition, Corgi Books, 1971, Holt, 1974.
Death in Diamonds, Evans Brothers, 1951.
Missing or Dead, Evans Brothers, 1951.
Death in a Hurry, Evans Brothers, 1952.
The Long Search, John Long, 1953, published as
Drop Dead, Ace Books, 1954.
Sleepy Death, John Long, 1953.
Double for Death, John Long, 1954, Holt, 1969.
Death in the Trees, John Long, 1954, published as
You've Bet Your Life, Ace Books, 1957.
The Kidnapped Child, John Long, 1955, Holt, 1971,
published as *The Snatch,* Corgi Books, 1965.
Day of Fear, John Long, 1956, Holt, 1978.
Wait for Death, John Long, 1957, Holt, 1972.
Come Home to Death, John Long, 1958, published
as *The Pack of Lies,* Doubleday (New York
City), 1959.
Elope to Death, John Long, 1959, Holt, 1977.

The Man Who Laughed at Murder, Doubleday, 1960,
published in England as *Don't Let Him Kill,*
1960.

*"CRIME HATERS" MYSTERIES (CONTINUATION OF
"DAWLISH" MYSTERIES); UNDER ASHE PSEUDONYM*

The Crime Haters, Doubleday, 1960.
Rogue's Ransom, Doubleday, 1961.
Death from Below, John Long, 1963, Holt, 1968.
The Big Call, John Long, 1964, Holt, 1975.
A Promise of Diamonds, Dodd (New York City),
1964.
A Taste of Treasure, Holt, 1966.
A Clutch of Coppers, John Long, 1967, Holt, 1969.
A Shadow of Death, John Long, 1968, Holt, 1976.
A Scream of Murder, John Long, 1969, Holt, 1970.
A Nest of Traitors, John Long, 1970, Holt, 1971.
A Rabble of Rebels, Long, 1971, Holt, 1972.
A Life for a Death, Holt, 1973.
A Herald of Doom, John Long, 1974, Holt, 1975.
A Blast of Trumpets, Holt, 1975.
A Plague of Demons, John Long, 1976, Holt, 1977.

*MYSTERIES UNDER PSEUDONYM M. E. COOKE; PUBLISHED
BY MELLIFONT PRESS, EXCEPT AS NOTED*

Fire of Death, Fiction House (London), 1934.
The Black Heart, Gramor Publications (London),
1935.
The Casino Mystery, 1935.
The Crime Gang, 1935.
The Death Drive, 1935.
Number One's Last Crime, Fiction House, 1935.
The Stolen Formula Mystery, 1935.
The Big Radium Mystery, 1936.
The Day of Terror, 1936.
The Dummy Robberies, 1936.
No One's Last Crime, Fiction House, 1936.
The Hypnotic Demon, Fiction House, 1936.
The Moat Farm Mystery, Fiction House, 1936.
The Secret Fortune, Fiction House, 1936.
The Successful Alibi, 1936.
The Hadfield Mystery, 1937.
The Moving Eye, 1937.
The Raven, Fiction House, 1937.
The Mountain Terror, 1938.
For Her Sister's Sake, Fiction House, 1938.
The Verrall Street Affair, George Newnes, 1940.

*ROMANCE NOVELS UNDER PSEUDONYM MARGARET
COOKE; PUBLISHED BY FICTION HOUSE, EXCEPT AS
NOTED*

For Love's Sake, Northern News Syndicate, 1934.
Troubled Journey, 1936.
False Love or True?, Northern News Syndicate, 1937.
Fate's Playthings, 1938.
Web of Destiny, 1938.
Whose Lover?, 1938.
A Mannequin's Romance, 1938.
Love Calls Twice, Northern News Syndicate, 1938.
The Road to Happiness, 1938.
The Turn of Fate, 1939.
Love Triumphant, 1939.
Love Comes Back, 1939.
Crossroads of Love, Mellifont Press, 1939.
Love's Journey, 1940.

ROMANCE NOVELS UNDER PSEUDONYM HENRY ST. JOHN COOPER; PUBLISHED BY LOW

Chains of Love, 1937.
Love's Pilgrimage, 1937.
The Tangled Legacy, 1938.
The Greater Desire, 1938.
Love's Ordeal, 1939.
The Lost Lover, 1940.

MYSTERIES UNDER PSEUDONYM NORMAN DEANE

Play for Murder, Hurst & Blackett, 1946, revised edition, Arrow Books, 1975.
The Silent House, Hurst & Blackett, 1947, revised edition, Arrow Books, 1973.
Why Murder?, Hurst & Blackett, 1948, revised edition, Arrow Books, 1975.
Intent to Murder, Hurst & Blackett, 1948, revised edition, Arrow Books, 1973.
The Man I Didn't Kill, Hurst & Blackett, 1950, reprint published under pseudonym Michael Halliday (see below), revised edition, Arrow Books, 1972.
No Hurry to Kill, Hurst & Blackett, 1950, revised edition, Arrow Books, 1973.
Double for Murder, Hurst & Blackett, 1951, revised edition, Arrow Books, 1972.
Golden Death, Hurst & Blackett, 1952.
Look at Murder, Hurst & Blackett, 1952, revised edition, Arrow Books, 1974.
Murder Ahead, Hurst & Blackett, 1953, revised edition, Arrow Books, 1974.
Death in the Spanish Sun, Hurst & Blackett, 1954, reprint published under name Michael Halliday (see below).
Incense of Death, Hurst & Blackett, 1954.

"BRUCE MURDOCH" MYSTERIES UNDER DEANE PSEUDONYM

Secret Errand, Hurst & Blackett, 1939, revised edition published under author's own name, New English Library, 1968, McKay, 1974.
Dangerous Journey, Hurst & Blackett, 1939, revised edition published under author's own name, Arrow Books, 1971, McKay, 1974.
Unknown Mission, Hurst & Blackett, 1940, revised edition, McKay, 1972.
The Withered Man, Hurst & Blackett, 1940, revised edition published under author's own name, Arrow Books, 1971.
I Am the Withered Man, Hurst & Blackett, 1941, revised edition published under author's own name, Arrow Books, 1971, McKay, 1973.
Where Is the Withered Man?, Hurst & Blackett, 1942, revised edition, McKay, 1972.

"LIBERATOR" MYSTERIES UNDER DEANE PSEUDONYM

Return to Adventure, Hurst & Blackett, 1943, revised edition, John Long, 1974.
Gateway to Escape, Hurst & Blackett, 1944, revised edition, Arrow Books, 1973.
Come Home to Crime, Hurst & Blackett, 1945, revised edition, John Long, 1974.

ROMANCE NOVELS UNDER PSEUDONYM ELISE FECAMPS; PUBLISHED BY FICTION HOUSE

Love of Hate, 1936.
Love's Triumph, 1936.
True Love, 1937.

"MARK KIRBY" MYSTERIES UNDER PSEUDONYM ROBERT CAINE FRAZER; PUBLISHED BY POCKET BOOKS (NEW YORK CITY), EXCEPT AS NOTED

Mark Kirby Solves a Murder, 1959, published in England as *R.I.S.C.,* Collins (London), 1962, reprinted as *The Timid Tycoon,* Fontana Books (London), 1966.
. . . and the Secret Syndicate, 1960, published in England as *The Secret Syndicate,* Collins, 1963.
. . . and the Miami Mob, 1960, published in England as *The Miami Mob* with *Mark Kirby Stands Alone* (also see below), Collins, 1965.
The Hollywood Hoax, 1961.

. . . Stands Alone, 1962, published with *The Miami Mob,* Collins, 1965, published in England as *. . . and the Manhattan Murders,* Fontana Books, 1966.
. . . Takes a Risk, 1962.

JUVENILE FICTION UNDER PSEUDONYM PATRICK GILL; PUBLISHED BY MELLIFONT PRESS

The Fighting Footballers, 1937.
The Laughing Lightweight, 1937.
The Battle for the Cup, 1939.
The Fighting Tramp, 1939.
The Mystery of the Centre-Forward, 1939.
The 10,000-Pound Trophy Race, 1939.
The Secret Supercharger, 1940.

MYSTERIES UNDER PSEUDONYM MICHAEL HALLIDAY

Four Find Danger, Cassell (London), 1937.
Three for Adventure, Cassell, 1937, revised edition, Corgi Books, 1976.
Two Meet Trouble, Cassell, 1938.
Murder Comes Home, Stanley Paul, 1940.
Heir to Murder, Stanley Paul, 1940.
Murder by the Way, Stanley Paul, 1941.
Who Saw Him Die?, Stanley Paul, 1941.
Foul Play Suspected, Stanley Paul, 1942.
Who Died at the Grange?, Stanley Paul, 1942.
Five to Kill, Stanley Paul, 1943.
Murder at Kings's Kitchen, Stanley Paul, 1943.
Who Said Murder?, Stanley Paul, 1944.
No Crime More Cruel, Stanley Paul, 1944.
Crime with Many Voices, Stanley Paul, 1945.
Murder Makes Murder, Stanley Paul, 1946.
Mastery Motive, Stanley Paul, 1947, revised edition published under pseudonym Jeremy York in "Superintendent Folly" series (see below).
Lend a Hand to Murder, Stanley Paul, 1947.
First a Murder, Stanley Paul, 1948, revised edition published under pseudonym Jeremy York in "Superintendent Folly" series (see below).
No End to Danger, Stanley Paul, 1948.
Who Killed Rebecca?, Stanley Paul, 1949.
The Dying Witnesses, Evans Brothers, 1949.
Dine with Murder, Evans Brothers, 1950.
Murder Week-End, Evans Brothers, 1951.
Quarrel with Murder, Evans Brothers, 1951, revised edition, Corgi Books, 1975.
Murder at End House, Hodder & Stoughton, 1955.
Murder Assured, Hodder & Stoughton, 1958.
The Man I Didn't Kill, Hodder & Stoughton, 1961.
Hate to Kill, Hodder & Stoughton, 1962.
The Guilt of Innocence, Hodder & Stoughton, 1964.

Death in the Spanish Sun, reprinted, Mayflower Dell, 1968.

MYSTERIES UNDER HALLIDAY PSEUDONYM (PUBLISHED IN UNITED STATES UNDER PSEUDONYM JEREMY YORK)

Death out of Darkness, Hodder & Stoughton, 1954, World Publishing (Cleveland, OH), 1971.
Out of the Shadows, Hodder & Stoughton, 1954, World Publishing, 1971.
Cat and Mouse, Hodder & Stoughton, 1955, published as *Hilda, Take Heed,* Scribner, 1957.
Death of a Stranger, Hodder & Stoughton, 1957, published as *Come Here and Die,* Scribner, 1959.
Runaway, Hodder & Stoughton, 1957, World Publishing, 1971.
Missing from Home, Hodder & Stoughton, 1959, published as *Missing,* Scribner, 1960.
Thicker than Water, Hodder & Stoughton, 1959, Doubleday, 1962.
Go ahead with Murder, Hodder & Stoughton, 1960, published as *Two for the Money,* Doubleday, 1962.
How Many to Kill?, Hodder & Stoughton, 1960, published as *The Girl with the Leopard Skin Bag,* Scribner, 1961.
The Edge of Terror, Hodder & Stoughton, 1961, Macmillan (New York City), 1963.
The Man I Killed, Hodder & Stoughton, 1961, Macmillan, 1963.
The Quiet Fear, Hodder & Stoughton, 1963, Macmillan, 1968.

"FAME BROTHERS" MYSTERIES UNDER HALLIDAY PSEUDONYM

Take a Body, Evans Brothers, 1951, revised edition, Hodder & Stoughton, 1964, World Publishing, 1972.
Lame Dog Murders, Evans Brothers, 1952, World Publishing, 1972.
Murder in the Stars, Hodder & Stoughton, 1953, World Publishing, 1973.
Man on the Run, Hodder & Stoughton, 1953, World Publishing, 1972.

"DR. EMMANUEL CELLINI" MYSTERIES UNDER HALLIDAY PSEUDONYM (PUBLISHED IN UNITED STATES UNDER PSEUDONYM KYLE HUNT)

Cunning as a Fox, Hodder & Stoughton, 1965, Macmillan, 1965.

Wicked as the Devil, Hodder & Stoughton, 1966, Macmillan, 1966.
Slick as a Serpent, Hodder & Stoughton, 1967, Macmillan, 1967.
Too Good to Be True, Hodder & Stoughton, 1969, Macmillan, 1969.
A Period of Evil, Hodder & Stoughton, 1970, World Publishing, 1971.
Cruel as a Cat, Hodder & Stoughton, 1971.
As Lonely as the Damned, Hodder & Stoughton, 1971, World Publishing, 1972.
As Empty as Hate, Hodder & Stoughton, 1972, World Publishing, 1972.
As Merry as Hell, Hodder & Stoughton, 1973, Stein & Day (New York City), 1974.
This Man Did I Kill?, Stein & Day, 1974.
The Man Who Was Not Himself, Stein & Day, 1976.

OTHER MYSTERIES UNDER HUNT PSEUDONYM

Kill Once, Kill Twice, Simon & Schuster, 1956.
Kill a Wicked Man, Simon & Schuster, 1957.
Kill My Love, Simon & Schuster, 1958.
To Kill a Killer, Random House (New York City), 1960.

MYSTERIES UNDER PSEUDONYM BRIAN HOPE

Four Motives for Murder, George Newnes, 1938.

MYSTERIES UNDER PSEUDONYM COLIN HUGHES

Triple Murder, George Newnes, 1940 (also published as *What Dark Motive?*).

MYSTERIES UNDER PSEUDONYM ABEL MANN

Danger Woman, Pocket Books, 1966.

MYSTERIES UNDER PSEUDONYM PETER MANTON; PUB-
LISHED BY WRIGHT & BROWN (LONDON), EXCEPT AS
NOTED

Murder Manor, 1937. *The Grey Vale School Mystery* (juvenile fiction), Low, 1937.
Stand by for Danger, 1937.
The Circle of Justice, 1938, revised edition, New English Library, 1959.
Three Days' Terror, 1938.
The Crime Syndicate, 1939, revised edition, New English Library, 1969.
Death Looks On, 1939.
Murder in the Highlands, 1939.

The Midget Marvel (juvenile fiction), Mellifont Press, 1940.
Policeman's Triumph, 1949.
Thief in the Night, 1950.
No Escape from Murder, 1953.
The Crooked Killer, 1954.
The Charity Murders, 1954.

"GIDEON" MYSTERIES UNDER PSEUDONYM J. J. MARRIC;
PUBLISHED BY HARPER, EXCEPT AS NOTED

Gideon's Day (also see below), 1955, published as *Gideon of Scotland Yard,* Berkeley Publishing, 1958.
Gideon's Week (also see below), 1956.
. . . *Night* (also see below), 1957.
. . . *Month,* 1958, . . . *Staff,* 1959.
. . . *Risk,* 1960.
. . . *Fire,* 1961.
. . . *March* (also see below), 1962.
. . . *Ride,* 1963.
Gideon at Work (contains *Gideon's Day, Gideon's Week,* and *Gideon's Night*), 1964, published in England as *The Gideon Omnibus,* Hodder & Stoughton, 1964.
. . . *Vote,* 1964.
. . . *Lot,* 1964.
. . . *Badge,* 1966.
. . . *Wrath* (also see below), 1967.
. . . *River* (also see below), 1968.
. . . *Power,* 1969.
. . . *Sport,* 1970.
. . . *Art,* 1971.
. . . *Men,* 1972.
. . . *Press,* 1973.
London Omnibus (contains *Gideon's March, Gideon's Wrath,* and *Gideon's River*), Hodder & Stoughton, 1973.
. . . *Fog,* 1974.
. . . *Drive,* 1976.

JUVENILE FICTION UNDER PSEUDONYM JAMES MARSDEN

Ned Cartwright—Middleweight Champion, Mellifont Press, 1935.

UNDER PSEUDONYM RICHARD MARTIN

Keys to Crime (mystery), William Earl & Co. (Bournemouth, England), 1947.
Vote for Murder (mystery), William Earl & Co., 1948.
Adrian and Jonathon, Hodder & Stoughton, 1954.

*MYSTERIES UNDER PSEUDONYM ANTHONY MORTON; PUB-
LISHED BY LOW*

Mr. Quentin Investigates, 1943.
Introducing Mr. Brandon, 1944.

"BARON" MYSTERIES UNDER MORTON PSEUDONYM

The Man in the Blue Mask, Lippincott (Philadelphia),
1937, published in England as *Meet the Baron,*
Harrap (London), 1937.
The Return of Blue Mask, Lippincott, 1937, pub-
lished in England as *The Baron Returns,* Harrap,
1937.
Salute Blue Masks!, Lippincott, 1938, published in
England as *The Baron Again,* Low, 1938.
Blue Mask at Bay, Lippincott, 1938, published in
England as *The Baron at Bay,* Low, 1938.
Alias Blue Mask, Lippincott, 1939, published in
England as *Alias the Baron,* Low, 1939.
Challenge Blue Mask!, Lippincott, 1939, published
in England as *The Baron at Large,* Low, 1939,
revised edition published as *The Baron at Large,*
Corgi Books, 1972, Walker & Co., 1975.
Blue Mask Strikes Again, Lippincott, 1940, published
in England as *Versus the Baron,* Low, 1940.
Blue Mask Victorious, Lippincott, 1940, published in
England as *Call for the Baron,* Low, 1940, re-
vised edition published as *Call for the Baron,*
Walker & Co., 1976.
The Baron Comes Back, Low, 1943.
A Case for the Baron, Low, 1945, Duell, Sloan &
Pearce (New York City), 1949.
Reward for the Baron, Low, 1945.
Career for the Baron, Low, 1946, Duell, Sloan &
Pearce, 1950.
The Baron and the Beggar, Low, 1947, Duell, Sloan
& Pearce, 1950.
Blame the Baron, Low, 1948, Duell, Sloan &
Pearce, 1951.
A Rope for the Baron, Low, 1948, Duell, Sloan & Pearce,
1949.
Books for the Baron, Low, 1949, Duell, Sloan &
Pearce, 1952.
Cry for the Baron, Low, 1950, Walker & Co., 1970.
Trap . . . , Low, 1950, Walker & Co., 1971.
Attack . . . , Low, 1951, revised edition, Corgi
Books, 1972.
Shadow . . . , Low, 1951.
Warn . . . , Low, 1952.
The Baron Goes East, Low, 1953.
. . . in France, Hodder & Stoughton, 1953, Walker
& Co., 1976.

Danger for . . . , Hodder & Stoughton, 1953 Walker
& Co., 1974.
. . . Goes Fast, Hodder & Stoughton, 1954, Walker
& Co., 1972.
Nest-Egg for . . . , Hodder & Stoughton, 1954,
published as *Deaf, Dumb, and Blonde,*
Doubleday, 1961.
Help from . . . , Hodder & Stoughton, 1955, Walker
& Co., 1977.
Hide . . . , Hodder & Stoughton, 1956, Walker &
Co., 1978.
Frame . . . , Hodder & Stoughton, 1957, published
as *The Double Frame,* Doubleday, 1961.
Red Eye for . . . , Hodder & Stoughton, 1958,
published as *Blood Red,* Doubleday, 1960.
Black for . . . , Hodder & Stoughton, 1959, pub-
lished as *If Anything Happens to Hester,*
Doubleday, 1962.
Salute for . . . , Hodder & Stoughton, 1960, Walker
& Co., 1973.
A Branch for . . . , Hodder & Stoughton, 1961,
published as *. . . Branches Out,* Scribner, 1967.
Bad for . . . , Hodder & Stoughton, 1962, published
as *. . . and the Stolen Legacy,* Scribner, 1967.
A Sword for . . . , Hodder & Stoughton, 1963,
published as *. . . and the Mogul Swords,*
Scribner, 1966.
. . . on Board, Hodder & Stoughton, 1964, Walker
& Co., 1968.
. . . and the Chinese Puzzle, Hodder & Stoughton,
1965, Scribner, 1966.
Sport for . . . , Hodder & Stoughton, 1966, Walker
& Co., 1969.
Affair for . . . , Hodder & Stoughton, 1967, Walker
& Co., 1968.
. . . and the Missing Old Masters, Hodder &
Stoughton, 1968, Walker & Co., 1969.
. . . and the Unfinished Portrait, Hodder &
Stoughton, 1969, Walker & Co., 1970.
Last Laugh for . . . , Hodder & Stoughton, 1970,
Walker & Co., 1971.
. . . Goes A-Buying, Hodder & Stoughton, 1971,
Walker & Co.,1972.
. . . and the Arrogant Artist, Hodder & Stoughton,
1972, Walker & Co., 1973.
Burgle . . . , Hodder & Stoughton, 1973, Walker &
Co., 1974.
. . . , King-Maker, Walker & Co., 1975.
Love for . . . , Hodder & Stoughton, 1979.

WESTERNS UNDER PSEUDONYM KEN RANGER

One-Shot Marriott, Low, 1938.
Roaring Guns, Low, 1939.

WESTERNS UNDER PSEUDONYM WILLIAM K. REILLY

Range War, Stanley Paul, 1939.
Two Gun Texan, Stanley Paul, 1939.
Gun Feud, Stanley Paul, 1940.
Stolen Range, Stanley Paul, 1940.
War on Lazy-K, Stanley Paul, 1941, Phoenix Press (New York City), 1946.
Outlaw's Vengeance, Stanley Paul, 1941.
Guns over Blue Lake, Jenkins (London), 1942.
Riders of Dry Gulch, Jenkins, 1943.
Long John Rides the Range, Jenkins, 1944.
Miracle Range, Jenkins, 1945.
The Secret of the Range, Jenkins, 1946.
Outlaw Guns, William Earl & Co., 1949.
Range Vengeance, Ward, Lock (London), 1953.

WESTERNS UNDER PSEUDONYM TEX RILEY; PUBLISHED BY WRIGHT & BROWN, EXCEPT AS INDICATED

Two-Gun Girl, 1938.
Gun-Smoke Range, 1938.
Gunshot Mesa, 1939.
The Shootin' Sheriff, 1940.
Rustler's Range, 1940.
Masked Riders, 1940.
Death Canyon, 1941.
Guns on the Range, 1942.
Range Justice, 1943.
Outlaw Hollow, 1944.
Hidden Range, William Earl & Co., 1946.
Forgotten Range, William Earl & Co., 1947.
Trigger Justice, William Earl & Co., 1948.
Lynch Hollow, William Earl & Co., 1949.

MYSTERIES UNDER PSEUDONYM JEREMY YORK

By Persons Unknown, Bles (London), 1941.
Murder Unseen, Bles, 1943.
No Alibi, Melrose, 1943.
Murder in the Family, Melrose, 1944, revised edition published in "Superintendent Folly" series (see below).
Yesterday's Murder, Melrose, 1945.
Wilful Murder, McNaughton (Los Angeles), 1946.
Death to My Killer, Melrose, 1950, Macmillan, 1966.
Sentence of Death, Melrose, 1950, Macmillan, 1964.
Voyage with Murder, Melrose, 1952.
Safari with Fear, Melrose, 1953.
So Soon to Die, Stanley Paul, 1955, Scribner, 1957.
Seeds of Murder, Stanley Paul, 1956, Scribner, 1958.
Sight of Death, Stanley Paul, 1956, Scribner, 1958.

My Brother's Killer, John Long, 1958, Scribner, 1959.
Hide and Kill, John Long, 1959, Scribner, 1960.
To Kill or to Die, John Long, 1960, Macmillan, 1966, published as *To Kill or Die,* Panther Books, 1965.

"SUPERINTENDENT FOLLY" MYSTERIES UNDER YORK PSEUDONYM

Find the Body, Melrose, 1945, revised edition, Macmillan, 1967.
Murder Came Late, Melrose, 1946, revised edition, Macmillan, 1969.
Let's Kill Uncle Lionel, Melrose, 1947, revised edition, Corgi Books, 1973, McKay, 1976.
Run Away to Murder, Melrose, 1947, Macmillan, 1970.
Close the Door on Murder, Melrose, 1948, revised edition, Corgi Books, 1971, McKay, 1973.
The Gallows Are Waiting, Melrose, 1949, revised edition, Corgi Books, 1972, McKay, 1973.
First a Murder, revised edition, Corgi Books, 1970, McKay, 1972.
Mystery Motive, revised edition, Corgi Books, 1970, published in United States under author's own name, McKay, 1974.
Murder in the Family, revised edition, McKay, 1976.

MYSTERIES, WITH IAN BOWEN, UNDER JOINT PSEUDONYM CHARLES HOGARTH

Murder on Largo Island, Selwyn & Blount, 1944.

OTHER

Also author of juvenile fiction *One Glorious Term* and *The Captain of the Fifth,* published by Low in 1930s; *The Fear of Felix Corder, John Brand: Fugitive,* and *The Night of Dread,* published by Fleetway Press; and *Dazzle and the Red Bomber,* published by George Newnes. Also author, under pseudonym Rodney Mattheson, of *The Dark Shadow,* and *The House of Ferrars,* both published by Fiction House. Contributor to numerous magazines, including *Ellery Queen's Mystery Magazine* and *Armchair Detective.* Editor of *John Creasey Mystery Magazine,* 1956-65.

ADAPTATIONS: John Creasey's books have been adapted for two British television series, *The Baron,* 1966, and *Gideon.* A number of his novels have also been adapted for films, including *Salute the Toff,* 1951, and *Hammer the Toff,* 1952, Butcher; *Gideon's*

Day, by Columbia Production Ltd., 1958; and *Cat and Mouse,* by Eros, 1958.

SIDELIGHTS: "If such a man were created in a novel, no one could possibly believe in him. In real life he is almost unbelievable; it is hardly surprising that his English publishers call him 'a legend in his own lifetime.'" John Creasey thus summarized his career in an autobiographical article which he wrote in the third person for *Armchair Detective.*

Creasey had reason to speak in superlatives; a retelling of his life actually sounds like a not-too-believable work of fiction. Facts concerning his literary output are astonishing: The author of nearly six hundred books, Creasey was the world's most prolific writer of crime fiction in English. He once estimated that between three and four thousand different editions of his books had appeared in a total of twenty-six languages. At the time of his death nearly sixty million copies of his books had been sold worldwide.

Creasey's popular success allowed him to live a life as colorful as that of one of his characters. He lived in a forty-two room manor, virtually commuted between England and the United States, traveled twice around the world, married four times, started his own political party, ran for the British Parliament several times, and owned a Rolls-Royce marked with the symbol of his "Toff" character—a monocled gentleman sporting a top hat.

His success, while based on reader acceptance of his novels, was largely a product of his own determination. For example, although Creasey began submitting articles for publication when only ten, by age seventeen he had also collected an amazing total of 743 rejection slips from publishers. Although he had his first novel published by the time he was twenty-seven, it was actually the tenth he had written, and during the same period of time he had been fired from twenty-five jobs—often for writing on his employer's time. But Creasey did not believe in defeat. *Armchair Detective* editor Allen J. Hubin once wrote: "I was greatly struck with [Creasey's] confidence and determination. 743 rejection slips without a sale! the imagination boggles. . . . But as John says, 'It was never a question of *if,* it was only a question of *when.*'"

This determined attitude remained with Creasey throughout his life; he did not accept setbacks, he fought them. When told by many acquaintances that he would "never be able to sell" in the United States,

Creasey responded by personally visiting nineteen U.S. publishers and editors in an attempt to discover the reason for lack of positive reader response to the previous U.S. editions of his books. Unsatisfied with the various explanations he received, he developed his own theory. Unlike their British counterparts, American readers of crime novels, he believed, needed a protagonist with whom they could more readily identify. He purposely set out to change his style, making his novels more acceptable to the American audience.

In 1951, Creasey spent six months in the United States attempting to convince American companies to accept his books for publication. Again, he received rejection slips—sixty-eight—but finally obtained a contract from Harper to publish *Inspector West Cries Wolf* (appearing under the U.S. title *The Creepers*). As in the past, Creasey's persistence led to success. The novel was well received in the United States, and the entire collection of Inspector West books became one of his most popular series among U.S. readers.

Creasey's own favorite character was Richard Rollison, otherwise known as the Toff—a nickname, the author once explained, that means "someone who behaves handsomely." The Toff is a wealthy gentleman who frequently helps the police to solve crimes, but who also has many strong contacts on the wrong side of the law. He is, according to Melvyn Barnes in *St. James Guide to Crime & Mystery Writers,* "a larger-than-life character who encounters more than his share of damsels in distress and is a stickler for fair play. The stories are fast-moving, with a succession of twists and crises. . . . The Toff is portrayed as a glamorous adventurer on the lines of Charteris's The Saint." Writing in *Dictionary of Literary Biography,* Marvin S. Lachman noted that "plots are minimal in the Toff series, and only many false starts and contrived complications drag them out to novel length. The books frequently start out with Rollison doing a good deed for someone only to find himself involved in a major crime. . . . The Toff books never broke new ground in mystery fiction, but they gained great popularity because they were fast-moving thrillers about likable characters. If the Toff and the people he tried to help were very good, the villains he confronted were extremely evil, and that, too, was part of the attraction of the series."

Barnes observed that the Toff and Inspector West "present an interesting contrast. Rollison, rich and gentlemanly, is . . . , in a series of books entirely unpretentious, typically British, thoroughly readable, apparently seeking only to entertain yet being prepared to wrestle with the occasional social problem." In the Roger West series, Barnes contended, "we find something more solid, not only a competent picture of life and relationships at Scotland Yard, but good examples of detection and pursuit. West may be a little too much the romantic figure, and his domestic life may be somewhat intrusive in those books where it has little bearing upon the investigation in hand. Nevertheless Creasey produced some quite excellent West books in structure *(Look Three Ways at Murder)*, in topicality *(Strike for Death)*, and in variety of background. Although most of West's cases are set in London, those with international connections and titles are particularly good."

"Inspector West" and "The Toff" were among Creasey's longest-running and popular series, but his "Gideon" books—written under the pseudonym J. J. Marric—most favorably impressed reviewers. Under this pseudonym, according to a *London Times* article, "[Creasey] received far better reviews than he was accustomed to get under his own name." In the *Detroit News,* for example, Richard Werry noted, "Marric's characters have real personal problems which make them more substantial than the papier-mache stereotypes common in most mystery fiction." Julian Symons also commented on the high quality of Marric's writing. In *Mortal Consequences* Symons wrote: "Creasey's Gideon books, written as J. J. Marric, are his best work. . . . His stories are notable for the ingenuity of the ideas with which he overflows." The *New York Times Book Review*'s Anthony Boucher added: "[Creasey's 'Gideon' books] are marked by the technically dazzling handling of a large number of plots in small compass. . . . All of the Creasey avatars are skilled at telling an exciting story; Marric, in addition, can *write.*"

Not all reviewers, however, had such high regard for Creasey's work. A *New York Times* writer observed: "Mr. Creasey had his detractors among professional critics, some of whom described his writings as undistinguished." Critics, believing that quick production diminished the quality of his writing, belittled Creasey for his rapid rate of publication. A *New York Times Book Review* writer, for example, described Creasey as "a sort of homicide computer—punch a button and out comes a book." Lewis Nichols, also writing in the *New York Times Book Review,* saw Creasey more as a business concern than as an author and referred to him as "Syndicate C."

Creasey, later in life, was able to shrug off such criticism. In *Writer,* he once jokingly called himself "a hackneyed old professional . . . suspected . . . by so many to have invented the computer first and Creasey and pen-names later." Early in his career, however, a critic who accused him of being more interested in quickly-completed than well-written prose caused Creasey to re-evaluate his writing method. Claiming in a *Newsweek* article, "I need to write with speed or it's no good," Creasey had attempted to write two books a week, with one day off between for playing cricket. After realizing the truth behind the critic's comments, Creasey decided to slow his pace to a pattern consistently followed until his death.

He began to take greater care in the production of his books. Each was written in longhand first, then scrutinized and revised five or six times before going to the publisher—often up to twelve months after being originally written. Creasey also began the practice of revising his earlier novels to make them more contemporary as well as to polish his style. He had a staff of readers instructed to "tear to bits" each of the novels due to be revised. Using these critical reports, Creasey made the necessary revisions and then had the book retyped and reread by other assistants. Some books were so extensively rewritten that the original detective was completely replaced by another character.

At times, revision also meant that a novel would appear under a different Creasey pseudonym than the one under which it had originally appeared. While several of his early pen names were chosen for him by his publishers, others, like J. J. Marric, originated with Creasey. J. J. Marric was chosen deliberately for the "Gideon" series; the name derived from the initials of the given names of Creasey and his second wife, Jean, combined with the first syllables of the given names of their two sons: *Mar*tin and *Rich*ard. Creasey once gave the reason for both his use of pseudonyms and his enormous number of books in *Newsweek.* He explained: "When I began writing, I discovered that the only way to make a living at the craft was to publish more than two books a year. Since, at that time, no publishers wanted to print more than two books a year from one author, I just changed names; then, too, different pen names permit me to write in different tones."

No matter which pseudonym was used, there was always a "special stamp" of a Creasey book, according to Hubin in the *New York Times Book Review.*

These distinguishing characteristics, as Hubin saw them, were "uncluttered plotting, and emphasis . . . on the basic goodness of most people involved." Newgate Callendar referred to "the Creasey formula" in a *New York Times Book Review* article. In Callendar's analysis, a typical Creasey novel had "a fairly rat-tat-tat style—short sentences, lots of padding, emphasis on plot gimmicks, [and] very little in the way of characterization." William Vivian Butler had yet another enumeration of Creasey literary characteristics. He listed the following points in a *Spectator* review: "The driving narrative, the subtly understated heroics, the simple humanity, the strident small-l liberalism, the all-embracing love of London—and, above all, the dogged vulnerable heroes."

Creasey devoted the last year of his life to the production of a novel telling the history of London's Metropolitan Police. "He meant this . . . to be," according to the London *Times,* "a vindication of his claim to be a serious writer." Creasey's avid readers never doubted this claim. A London *Times* writer noted, "His business, he believed, was to sell books and to entertain." Creasey accomplished both these aims. As reviewer Butler stated in *Spectator,* "[His career was an] incredible forty-year, six hundred book feast . . . [for] his fans." Barnes concluded: "No attempt need be made to examine Creasey's huge output for philosophical messages or sociological import, although these can be found if one feels them to be essential attributes before deeming a crime novelist respectable. Suffice it to say that his reported belief, that the crime novel is almost the only novel worth reading today, was amply justified by the tremendous public response to the sheer entertainment value of his books."

BIOGRAPHICAL/CRITICAL SOURCES:

BOOKS

Contemporary Literary Criticism, Volume 11, Gale (Detroit), 1979.
Creasey, John, and Robert E. Briney, *John Creasey—Fact or Fiction? A Candid Commentary in Third Person, with a Bibliography,* Armchair Detective Press (White Bear Lake, MN), 1968, revised edition, 1969.
Dictionary of Literary Biography, Volume 77: *British Mystery Writers, 1920-1939,* Gale, 1989.
St. James Guide to Crime & Mystery Writers, St. James Press (Detroit), 1996.
Symons, Julian, *Mortal Consequences: A History— From the Detective Story to the Crime Novel,* Harper, 1972.

PERIODICALS

Armchair Detective, October, 1968.
Detroit News, November 28, 1971; June 4, 1972.
Life, April 27, 1962.
Newsday, December 12, 1970.
Newsweek, February 2, 1958.
New York Times, July 22, 1972.
New York Times Book Review, November 28, 1958; January 22, 1961; March 18, 1962; July 28, 1968; September 1, 1968; November 3, 1968; January 19, 1969; June 1, 1969; April 11, 1976.
Publishers Weekly, February 8, 1965.
Spectator, March 22, 1975.
Times Literary Supplement, September 18, 1969; January 22, 1970; October 22, 1971.
Variety, June 10, 1970.
Writer, September, 1972.

OBITUARIES:

PERIODICALS

AB Bookman's Weekly, October 1, 1973.
Newsweek, June 25, 1973.
New York Times, June 10, 1973.
Publishers Weekly, June 18, 1973.
Times (London), June 11, 1973.*

* * *

CREDO
See **CREASEY, John**

* * *

CRISP, Quentin 1908-

PERSONAL: Birth-given name, Denis Pratt; name legally changed, 1977; born December 25, 1908, in Sutton, Surrey, England; immigrated to the United States, 1977.

*ADDRESSES: Home—*46 East Third St., New York, NY 10003.

CAREER: Writer. Worked as commercial artist and artist's model; actor in stage productions, including *The Naked Civil Servant, An Evening With Quentin Crisp,* and *The Importance of Being Earnest,* and in films, including *The Bride,* 1985, *Orlando,* 1993, and *Naked in New York,* 1994.

AWARDS, HONORS: Special Drama Desk Award for unique theatrical experience, 1979.

WRITINGS:

Color in Display, Blandford Press (London), 1938.
The Naked Civil Servant (autobiography), J. Cape (London), 1968, Holt (New York), 1977, revised edition, New American Library (New York), 1983.
How to Have a Life-style (nonfiction), Cecil Woolf (London), 1975, Methuen (New York), 1979.
Love Made Easy (novel), Duckworth (London), 1977.
Chog: A Gothic Fable, Methuen, 1979.
(With Donald Carroll) *Doing It With Style* (nonfiction), F. Watts (New York City), 1981.
How to Become a Virgin (autobiography), St. Martin's (New York City), 1981.
The Wit and Wisdom of Quentin Crisp, edited by Guy Kettlehack, Harper (New York City), 1984.
(With John Hofsess) *Manners From Heaven: A Divine Guide to Good Behavior,* Hutchinson (London), 1984, Harper, 1985.
How to Go to the Movies: A Guide for the Perplexed (film criticism), St. Martin's, 1989.
Quentin Crisp's Book of Quotations: 1000 Observations on Life and Love by, for, and about Gay Men and Women, Macmillan (New York City), 1989.
Resident Alien: The New York Diaries, HarperCollins, 1996.

OTHER

An Evening With Quentin Crisp (autobiographical stage production; also see below), first produced in New York City at Players Theatre, 1978.

Also author of *The Return of Quentin Crisp* (autobiographical stage production), which toured the country in 1990. Contributor to periodicals, including *Christopher Street, Listener, New York Times,* and *New York.*

ADAPTATIONS: The Naked Civil Servant was adapted as a television play in 1975; *An Evening With Quentin Crisp* was recorded by DRG, 1979.

SIDELIGHTS: Quentin Crisp "clearly . . . has to be seen as a forerunner of twentieth-century homosexual activism," declared Jon Hodge in *Gay & Lesbian Biography.* Crisp adopted a flamboyantly effeminate style years before homosexuality was accepted in any way by the general public. This made his early years in England difficult indeed, and in his 1968 autobiography, *The Naked Civil Servant,* he recounted the psychological and social hardships he endured during his youth. The book is marked by Crisp's perception—sometimes shocking, sometimes absurd—of life, and is related in a manner both candid and witty. Although he has written other books, editorials, and articles, appeared on stage and in films, and even served as the subject of a documentary film and a song by Sting ("Englishman in New York"), *The Naked Civil Servant* remains "Crisp's most important contribution to literature," affirmed Hodge.

Crisp, whose given name was Denis Pratt, was born in England in 1908. His family struggled with debt throughout his youth, but he was able to attend a small boarding school. He maintains, however, that the only thing he learned there was that he was very unpopular. He briefly attended King's College and studied journalism, but soon left the world of formal education behind. At that time he "felt the pressures of both finding a job and confronting his sexuality," related Hodge, "two issues that simultaneously found resolution via each other while Crisp was wandering through the streets of London's West End. There he saw men, some of whom were prostitutes, who adopted a campy style of flamboyant dress and cosmetics as an expression of their homosexuality. Crisp immediately followed suit. He sat with these men at the Black Cat at Compton Street in Soho, compared lipstick and chatted the nights away." He enjoyed his new appearance and kept it up even when he left prostitution behind to work at various arts-related occupations. He was at one time or another an artist's model, an architectural copier, a commercial artist, a critic, an actor, and a writer and artist in the advertising field. "All center on the world of images and representation," Hodge pointed out, "which, arguably, laid the groundwork for his life profession" as an advocate of personal style.

Crisp's life changed dramatically following the 1968 publication of *The Naked Civil Servant.* The book, whose title refers to Crisp's work as a model, "was, at the time of its initial publication in London, virtually the only such work by a homosexual who was open about his sexual identity," stated Robert B. Marks Ridinger in *Gay & Lesbian Literature.* "Covering his (often violent) experiences with the working class population of London from 1926 until the late 1960s, it presents a virtually unparalleled account of the social atmosphere of Depression-era England, the Blitz and World War II years, and post-war recovery, from the perspective of a deliberately marginalized individual. Of particular interest to the student of gay and lesbian history are the descriptions of attitudes and fashions of speech and behavior among some homosexuals" over the four decades covered in the book.

The Naked Civil Servant also firmly established Crisp's reputation as a unique—and often extravagant—wit, with an acute sense of the absurd. Paul Bailey, reviewing the book in *Observer Review,* called Crisp a "professional eccentric" and added that "Crisp states his alarming case wittily and gracefully." A reviewer for *Punch* expressed similar views, writing that Crisp "makes his outrageous life sound tremendously amusing." The reviewer added, however, that *The Naked Civil Servant* is a rather "egocentric display" of Crisp's wit.

When the book was aired as a television production in 1975, Crisp became an overnight sensation. He was invited to the United States by Michael Bennett, director of the Broadway show *A Chorus Line.* Bennett was interested in making a musical version of Crisp's book. Crisp was enthusiastic about the idea, but it never came to pass. The visit still changed his life forever, though. He declared in a *Contemporary Authors* interview that in the United States, "happiness rains down from the skies," and he made up his mind to stay in his new country.

He soon developed an autobiographical stage show, *An Evening with Quentin Crisp,* which further enhanced his newfound fame—or, as he describes it, notoriety. Before long, he was a spokesperson on style, culture, art, and homosexuality. He wrote more autobiographical books, including *How to Have a Life-style, How to Become a Virgin,* and *Resident Alien: The New York Diaries.* These subsequent writings maintained his reputation as an extravagant humorist whose primary subject is himself. Reviewing *How to Have a Life-style,* a writer for the *New York Times Book Review* declared that Crisp "is his own best advertisement, and his book is another witty, aphoristic, outrageous and often very acute description" of himself. In *How to Become a Virgin,* he formally resumed the narrative of *The Naked Civil Servant* and detailed his newfound fame. Jennifer Uglow, writing in the *Times Literary Supplement,*

deemed *How to Become a Virgin* a "less flamboyant and acerbic book" than *The Naked Civil Servant* but added that it too was "full of ridiculous anecdotes" and "nicely calculated extravagances." In *Resident Alien,* written in his eighth decade, he comes across as "the Queen Mother . . . implausibly combined with . . . Andy Warhol," according to *Spectator* reviewer Adam Mars-Jones.

Crisp has written books on other subjects besides himself, although they all bear his unique stamp and many personal reflections. In *Manners From Heaven,* he applies his keen wit and sense of the absurd to etiquette. "The lie is the basic building block of good manners," he writes, insisting that one should never tell the truth to one's friends. Cal Burnett, writing in the Detroit *Metro Times,* called *Manners From Heaven* "delightful reading: thoughtful and brisk, witty and brash, elegant but never marred by the faintest trace of stuffiness or self-importance." In *How to Go to the Movies: A Guide for the Perplexed,* he presents a collection of his film reviews. Chris Savage King, writing in *New Statesman & Society,* found that "his criticism is idiosyncratic rather than impassioned—the precedent is Colette, not Pauline Kael—but as an organic aesthete and a great outsider, his insights are thrilling to read and typically accurate." King noted with approval the "glitter" in Crisp's prose, and concluded: "There is much on Life in General, and when the dazzle threatens to blind us he eases the reader through with some cosy and utterly apt personal anecdotes. He remains a very fine and distinguished sage of our age, and we should heed his words."

Although Crisp is singled out by many as one of the first homosexual activists, he has often found himself at odds with the modern gay movement because he advises against militant action. He commented on this issue in his *CA* interview: "Of course partly, like everybody else, I believe what my nature inclines me to believe rather than anything that could be proved to me by logic. I am naturally an extremely passive person; therefore it's not in my nature to demand anything. But I think it is also true that the gay people now seem to have deliberately separated themselves from the rest of the world. They *want* gay bars; they *want* gay clubs. They want to write gay books and gay plays. I just want to live in the world. So I feel the deliberate separation is not much help. You can't get integration—if that's the final object—by demanding it and by labeling yourself gay, by only going to gay restaurants and gay bars and gay clubs. What help is that? What one wants is to creep out into the world. And I think this is more easily done, not by retreating, by any means, but by not threatening the world."

Asked by *Chicago Tribune* interviewer Cheryl Lavin about his secret for remaining vital even as an octogenarian, Crisp informed her that "the main thing is to never, ever work. I just sit around all day doing what Americans call hanging out. . . . I sit in a room all day. I answer the phone. I do crossword puzzles. I write letters. I open a tin of soup or fry an egg. I wash my socks. I file my nails. I do all the things that other people do on their day off. Except I do them every day." He concluded that "I'm ready now to die. I've done and been and said what I can, so as far as I'm concerned, I can die quite tidily at any minute."

BIOGRAPHICAL/CRITICAL SOURCES:

BOOKS

Crisp, Quentin, *The Naked Civil Servant,* Duckworth, 1968.
Crisp, Quentin, *How to Become a Virgin,* St. Martin's, 1981.
Crisp, Quentin, *Resident Alien: The New York Diaries,* HarperCollins, 1996.
Gay and Lesbian Biography, St. James Press (Detroit), 1997, pp. 133-34.
Gay and Lesbian Literature, St. James Press, 1994, pp. 96-97.

PERIODICALS

Advocate, March 8, 1979, pp. 33-35; October 1, 1985, pp. 8-9.
Chicago Tribune, June 19, 1990, section 5, p. 3.
Film Comment, November/December, 1990.
Listener, January 25, 1968.
Los Angeles Times, July 19, 1993, p. F1.
Metro Times (Detroit), April 24, 1985.
New Leader, February 11, 1980, p. 19.
New Statesman & Society, April 27, 1990, p. 39.
New York Times Book Review, September 18, 1977; February 3, 1980.
Observer Review, January 14, 1968.
Punch, January 31, 1968.
Smithsonian, April, 1980, p. 148.
Spectator, June 22, 1996, pp. 33-34.
Time, January 25, 1982, p. 81.
Times (London), May 18, 1981.
Times Literary Supplement, March 17, 1968; May 29, 1981.

Washington Post, October 25, 1978.
Washington Post Book World, February 17, 1980; November 8, 1981; February 14, 1982; March 17, 1985.

OTHER

An Evening With Quentin Crisp (recording of stage production; also see above), DRG, 1979.
Resident Alien (documentary film about Crisp), released in 1992.

*   *   *

CRONE, Moira 1952-

PERSONAL: Born August 10, 1952, in Goldsboro, NC; daughter of James Clarence (an accountant) and Ethel (an executive assistant; maiden name, Donnelly) Crone; married Rodger L. Kamentz (a poet and writer), October 14, 1979; children: Anya Miriam, Kezia Vida. *Education:* Smith College, B.A. (with high honors), 1974; Johns Hopkins University, M.A., 1977.

ADDRESSES: Office—Department of English, Louisiana State University, Allen Hall, Baton Rouge, LA 70808.

CAREER: Enoch Pratt Free Library, Baltimore, MD, tutor in reading and English as a second language, 1977-78; Goucher College, Towson, MD, lecturer in English, 1979-81; Louisiana State University, Baton Rouge, instructor, 1981-83, assistant professor, 1983-86, associate professor, beginning 1986, currently professor of English. Lecturer at Johns Hopkins University, 1979-81; member of board of directors of Bethesda Writers' Center, 1981, and Fiction Collective, New York City.

MEMBER: Authors Guild, Associated Writing Programs, Phi Kappa Phi.

AWARDS, HONORS: Fellow at Mary Ingraham Bunting Institute, Radcliffe College, 1987-88; Collin C. Diboll award, Pirates Alley Faulkner Society, 1993, for *Dream State: Stories;* Ragdale Foundation fellow, 1995.

WRITINGS:

The Winnebago Mysteries and Other Stories, Fiction Collective (New York City), 1982.

The Life of Lucy Fern, Part One (novel), Adult Ficiton (Cambridge, NY), 1983.

The Life of Lucy Fern, Part Two (novel), Adult Fiction, 1983.

A Period of Confinement (novel), Putnam (New York City), 1986.

Dream State: Stories, University of Mississippi Press (Jackson), 1995.

Work represented in anthologies, including *American Made,* Fiction Collective, 1986. Contributor of stories to magazines, including *New Yorker, Gettysburg Review, North American Review, Negative Capability, Boston Sunday Globe Magazine, American Voice, Mademoiselle, Western Humanities Review,* and *Southern Review.*

Also coeditor of *City Lit,* 1980, and editor and founder of *The New Delta Review,* 1983-86.

SIDELIGHTS: In her stories and novels, Moira Crone "emphasizes that most people are scared of human relationships because so much can and does go wrong," as Paul A. Doyle writes in *Contemporary Novelists.* Crone's stories tell of a college-aged daughter who leaves school to wander the country in a Winnebago, of a woman whose father has abandoned the family only to call for help whenever he is broke and drunk, and of a young father cheating on his wife with a teenaged girl.

"The strength of Crone's short fiction," writes a critic for *Publishers Weekly,* "is the realism that the author grants to her characters and their situations." Although, as Gary Krist writes in the *New York Times Book Review,* "many of Ms. Crone's characters are . . . adrift, as confused as they are self-aware, as uncertain of what they want to say as they are forthcoming," Crone "presents her characters and themes with much sensitivity and perception," according to Doyle. "Even when we become exasperated with a character's behavior, we usually understand the reasons—often totally illogical and perverse—for the actions."

In *Dream State* Crone sets her stories in the Deep South of Louisiana, writing of the Cajuns, Creoles and French Quarter characters in what Krist describes as "arguably . . . patronizing" and reminiscent of "well-meaning anthropology." Still, Krist believes, the collection "successfully presents a fresh version of the Deep South, one that is exotic without being either grotesque or romanticized."

Crone once told *CA:* "I was born in the tobacco country of North Carolina in 1952. My father was a native of the region, and my mother was from Brooklyn, New York. I spent my childhood in the same house where my father was born, with frequent visits to New York City to visit my grandmother and other relatives. In 1970 I entered Smith College, where I worked with V.S. Pritchett.

"After graduation, I lived in Boston and studied with another British author, Penelope Mortimer. In 1976 I was offered a fellowship for the Johns Hopkins Writing Seminars, where John Barth and Leslie Epstein taught. From 1977 to 1980 I worked as a teacher of English as a second language to Spanish-speaking adults in the Fells Point section of Baltimore and as a fiction workshop teacher. I also began publishing in literary magazines. Since 1981 I have lived in Louisiana, with extended stays out of the country—in France in 1983 and Jerusalem in 1986.

"My first book, *The Winnebago Mysteries and Other Stories,* was accepted for publication in 1980. It is a novella and a collection of stories I wrote during the late seventies. The strong reception of my book of stories helped me find a place for my novel, *A Period of Confinement,* a book about pregnancy and motherhood, and art.

"My next book is about the way a second generation absorbs the intentional and unintentional inflictions they receive as children and how their parents' losses and disappointments are transmuted into their own. It is a coming-of-age novel, concerning the attachments that threaten people and the need for separation, and for betrayal, as well as for forgiveness.

"My primary concerns as a writer have always been the questions of separation—questions about difference and individuation. I am centrally obsessed with motherhood and the conundrum of identity motherhood presents to mothers and children."

BIOGRAPHICAL/CRITICAL SOURCES:

BOOKS

Contemporary Novelists, sixth edition, St. James Press (Detroit), 1996.

PERIODICALS

Kirkus Reviews, July 15, 1995, p. 965.
New York Times Book Review, October 29, 1995, p. 35.
Publishers Weekly, August 28, 1995, p. 103.
Short Story, fall, 1995, pp. 81-90.*

*   *   *

CROWTHER, Brian
  See GRIERSON, Edward

D-E

D'ALLARD, Hunter
See BALLARD, (Willis) Todhunter

*   *   *

D'ARCY, Willard
See COX, William R(obert)

*   *   *

DAS, Kamala 1934-
(Madhavi Kutty)

PERSONAL: Born March 31, 1934, in the district of Malabar (now Kerala), India; daughter of V. M. (an editor) and Balamani Amma (a poet; maiden name, Nalapat) Nair; married K. Madhava Das (a banker), February 4, 1949; children: Monu Nalapar, Chinnen, Jaisurya (sons). *Education:* Educated privately in Calcutta. *Politics:* "Once upon a time believed in the Indian National Congress." *Religion:* Hindu. *Avocational interests:* Tree-planting.

ADDRESSES: Home—Nalapat House, Nalapat Rd., Punnayurkulam, Kerala, India. *Office*—*Times* of India, Chittoor Rd., Cochin, India.

CAREER: Writer and activist. Book Point, Bombay, India, director; Bahutantrika Group (artist collective), Bombay, founder and president. Member of governing council, Indian National Trust for Cultural Heritage, New Delhi; vice president, State Council for Child Welfare, Trivandrum, India; chair, For-

estry Board, Kerala, India, and chair of committee for environmental education. Independent candidate for Parliament, 1984. Former president, Jyotsha Art and Education Academy; former president, Kerala Children's Film Society; former member, State Planning Board Committee on Art, Literature, and Mass Communications. Conducts seminars on environmental protection for rural groups. Artist, exhibiting works in Cochin, India.

MEMBER: International PEN, World Poetry Society (Orient editor).

AWARDS, HONORS: Asian Poetry Prize, International PEN, 1963; Kerala Sahitya Academy awards, 1969 and 1970, both for *Thanuppu;* Chimanlal Award for Journalism, 1971; honorary doctorate in literature, World Academy of Arts and Culture (Taiwan), 1984; Asian World Prize for Literature, 1985; Kamala Das Research Centre, St. Berkmans College, Changasasseery, Kerala, named in her honor.

WRITINGS:

IN ENGLISH

Summer in Calcutta: Fifty Poems, Everest Press (Delhi, India), 1965, InterCulture (Chicago), 1975.

The Descendants (poems), Writers Workshop (Calcutta), 1967, Ind-US (East Glastonbury, CT), 1975.

The Old Playhouse and Other Poems, Orient Longman (Madras, India), 1973.

The Alphabet of Lust (novel), Orient Paperback (New Delhi), 1976.

My Story (autobiography), Sterling (Jullundur, India), 1976, Ind-US, 1977.

A Doll for the Child Prostitute (stories), India Paperbacks (New Delhi), 1977.

Tonight, This Savage Rite: The Love Poetry of Kamala Das and Pritish Nandy, Arnold-Heinemann (New Delhi), 1979.

The Heart of Britain (nonfiction), Firma KLM (Calcutta), 1983.

Kamala Das: A Collage (collection of one-act plays), compiled by Arum Kuckreja, Vidja Prakashan Mandir (New Delhi), 1984.

Collected Poems, privately printed, 1984.

Kamala Das: A Selection, with Essays on Her Work (poetry), edited by S. C. Harrex and Vincent O'Sullivan, Centre for Research in the New Literatures in English (Adelaide, Australia), 1986.

Padmavati, the Harlot and Other Stories, Sterling (New Delhi), 1992.

Also author of *Best of Kamala Das,* Bodhi Books (Calcutta); *Selections from Kamala Das,* D. C. Books (Kottayam, India); *Towards the Twenty-first Century; Collected Stories;* and *The Smell of the Bird.*

IN MALAYALAM; AS MADHAVI KUTTY

Tharisunilam (stories; title means "Fallow Fields"), Current Books (Trissur, India), 1962.

Tanuppa (stories), Current Books, 1967. *Pathu kathakal* (stories), Current Books, 1968.

Thanuppu (stories; title means "Cold"), Current Books, 1970.

Premathinte vilapa kavyam (stories; title means "Requiem for a Love"), Current Books, 1971.

Draksakshi Panna (juvenile; title means "Eyewitness"), Orient Longman, 1973.

Munnu novalukal (three novels), Navadhara (Trivandum, India), 1977.

Kisah sacabies hati (stories), Choice (Singapore), 1978.

Asrita (novel), Odisa (Kataka), 1980.

Tvamasi mama (novel), Natha Pabalisim (Calcutta), 1983.

Amrtam Bibbhati (novel), Niu Bengala (Calcutta), 1984.

Anoraniyan (novel), Paribesaka Natha Bradarsa (Calcutta), 1985.

Ente cerukathakal (stories), Matrbhumi (Calcutta), 1985.

Manomi (novel), Paribesaka Natha Bradarsa, 1985.

Bhayam ente nisavasthram (stories), Matrbhumi, 1986.

Swatantrasenaniyude makal (stories), Purna (Calcutta), 1991.

Neermatalam poothakalam (stories), D. C. Books, 1993.

Also author of *Narachirukal parakkumbol* (stories; title means "When the Bats Fly"); *Ente snehita Aruna* (stories; title means "My Friend Aruna"); *Chuvanna pavada* (stories; title means "The Red Skirt"); *Rajavinte premabajanam* (stories; title means "The King's Beloved"); and *Mathilukal* (stories; title means "Walls"), all published by Current Books.

OTHER

Contributor of stories, plays, and political commentaries to journals. Poetry editor, *Illustrated Weekly of India,* 1971-72 and 1978-79.

WORK IN PROGRESS: A book on herbs and medicinal plants used as cures in ancient India; research on witchcraft for a book on sorcery in Malabar; poems.

SIDELIGHTS: Poet, artist, activist, and fiction writer Kamala Das is one of India's most prolific female authors. Composing her fictions in both her native Malayalam and the English she learned while attending Catholic schools as a child, Das's writing reflects the cultural inheritance of a woman reared in a family that included noted poets and philosophers and an upbringing spent in the company of the steady stream of artists, writers, and thinkers that would visit her family's home in Malabar, India. This childhood would be followed by an adult life that included an unfulfilling marriage at age fifteen, a series of extramarital affairs, illnesses, and other personal experiences, all of which have combined to create the framework for her written works.

Beginning to write in earnest during her twenties, Das's early writing was controversial due to its focus on sexuality. Poetry collections such as *Summer in Calcutta* and short story collections such as *Thanuppu,* written in her native Malayalam under the name Madhavi Kutty, exhibit a candor and courage unusual for a woman with her tradition-steeped upbringing. As Dorothy Jones commented in *Kamala Das: A Selection with Essays on Her Work,* "To write frankly about sexuality in a society which expects women to be modest, submissive and unobtrusive is in itself an act of rebellion which imparts energy and vigour to much of [her]. . . writing." But Das's rebellion consisted of more than angry words. "Das's principal achievement has been to define and expose the prison in which a woman finds herself trapped, rather than proclaiming an escape route out of it," continued Jones, "although she also records the urge to escape and a desperate longing for freedom."

In 1974, when Das was only forty years old, she suffered a heart attack. The shock of her illness and the period of extended convalescence that followed gave her the opportunity to scrutinize her past. This period of introspection resulted in the autobiography *My Story,* first serialized in Bombay's *Current Weekly.* Far more candid in portraying the author's private life than her poetry had been, *My Story* "reveals the powerful link between [Das's] marriage and her need to write poetry," maintained Devindra Kohli in *Contemporary Women Poets.* Through its figurative language, the work also exposed the dual nature of the inner poet to the world: while appearing as a strong, staunchly independent Indian woman, she is also submissive in her relationships with men, particularly within the social and financial constraints imposed by marriage. As Das would later reflect in her poem, "Loud Posters" from *Summer in Calcutta,* through the experience of publishing such a candid work, "I've stretched my two-dimensional / Nudity on sheets of weeklies, monthlies, / Quarterlies, a sad sacrifice."

Despite the fact that she never embraced the Movement for Women's Liberation during the 1970s, Das's writings of the period depict strong, female protagonists, survivors amid a corrupt, male-dominated society. Most revealing is 1977's *Doll for a Child Prostitute.* While told in a simple fashion, this is the story of a preteen girl who is sold by her family to a house of prostitution after being raped by her stepfather renders her unmarriageable. The girl catches the eye of a man old enough to be her grandfather; Das's depiction of the young girl playing with her new doll—a gift from this elderly admirer—before being summoned to have sex with this old man both shocks and saddens the reader. In the young girl's short life, the one who most uses her is also the only one to show her affection.

Although her outlook regarding the status of women expressed in her writing is often described as forward thinking, Das's fictions are also deeply influenced by her traditional Hindu beliefs. Many of her female protagonists bear the names of Hindu goddesses and elements from Indian mythology can be discerned in many of her works. Also crucial to a complete understanding of her writing is the effect of

India's post-colonial culture. "I am Indian, very brown, born in Malabar," Das wrote in her 1965 poem, "Introductions." She continues: "speak three languages, write in two, dream in one/. . . the language I speak becomes mine/. . . it is half English, half Indian/. . . it is as human as I am human." Indeed, Das "defies categorizations that are not heavily qualified," commented Kohli. "While she empathizes with the rebel, she can also celebrate her rootedness in her tradition; outspoken about her womanhood, she does not, however, typecast genders."

Deeply committed to a host of social issues throughout her life, Das has worked actively in support of ecological causes and on behalf of the preservation of her native culture. She ran as an independent candidate for the Indian Parliament in 1984. Regarding her interest in politics, she once commented: "I believe that the strength accumulated over the years by a writer should be utilized in public service, ultimately. Merely writing cannot change the social system." Das writes that she is also "interested in producing children's films in order to draw the young ones' attention from terrorist-attitudes now so prevalent in our country." Das has served as president of the Kerala Children's Film Society, a group which screens films at schools free of cost.

Das once told *CA:* "I believe in the ancient religion of Love which is the root of the tree of religions. If a branch is severed and removed it must soon wither and die. This is the reason why I oppose religious revivals. Like drugs, religions and political systems too have an expiry date. If they outlive that date they become poisonous. The prevalent religions and political systems have outlived their expiry dates."

BIOGRAPHICAL/CRITICAL SOURCES:

BOOKS

Dwivedi, A. N., *Kamala Das and Her Poetry,* Doaba (New Delhi), 1983.
Feminist Writers, St. James Press (Detroit), 1996.
Jussawalla, Feroza F., *Family Quarrels: Towards a Criticism of Indian Writing in English,* Peter Lang (London), 1985.
Kohli, Devindra, *Kamala Das,* Arnold-Heinemann, 1975.
Nabar, Vrinda, *The Endless Female Hungers: a Study of Kamala Das,* Sterling, 1993.

Rahman, Anisur, *Expressive Form in the Poetry of Kamala Das,* Abhinav (New Delhi), 1981.
Contemporary Women Poets, St. James Press, 1997.

PERIODICALS

Commonwealth Quarterly, Volume 3, number 10, 1973.
Journal of Commonwealth Literature, spring, 1994.
New Literatures Review, summer, 1991.
Times Literary Supplement, February 3, 1978.
World Literature Written in English, Volume 25, number 2, 1985.*

* * *

DAVIES, L(eslie) P(urnell) 1914-
(Leo Berne, Robert Blake, Richard Bridgeman, Morgan Evans, Ian Jefferson, Lawrence Peters, Thomas Philips, G. K. Thomas, Leslie Vardre, Rowland Welch)

PERSONAL: Born October 20, 1914, in Cheshire, England; son of Arthur (a gardener) and Annie (Sutton) Davies; married Wynne Tench, November 13, 1940. *Education:*Manchester College of Science and Technology, University of Manchester, qualified as optometrist (F.B.O.A.), 1939. *Avocational interests:* Reading about the unusual; painting.

ADDRESSES: Home—Apartment K-1, Edificio Alondra, El Botanico, Puerto de la Cruz, Tenerife, Canary Islands. *Agent*—Howard Moorepark, 444 East 82nd St., New York, NY 10028; and Carl Routledge, Charles Lavell Ltd., Mowbray House, 176 Wardour St., London WIV 3AA, England.

CAREER: Assistant dispensing pharmacist in Crewe, England, 1930-39; optometrist in private practice, beginning 1939; freelance writer. Professional artist in Rome, Italy, 1945-46; postmaster in Birmingham, England, 1947-57. *Military service:* British Army, Royal Army Medical Corps, World War II; served in France, and with 8th Army in North Africa and Italy; became staff sergeant.

WRITINGS:

The Paper Dolls, Jenkins (London), 1964, Doubleday (New York City), 1966.
Man Out of Nowhere, Jenkins, 1965, published as *Who Is Lewis Pinder?,* Doubleday, 1966.

The Artificial Man, Jenkins, 1965, Doubleday, 1967.
Psychogeist, Jenkins, 1966, Doubleday, 1967.
The Lampton Dreamers, Jenkins, 1966, Doubleday, 1967.
(Under pseudonym Leslie Vardre) *Tell It to the Dead,* Long (London), 1966, published as *The Reluctant Medium,* Doubleday, 1967.
Twilight Journey, Jenkins, 1967, Doubleday, 1968.
(Under pseudonym Leslie Vardre) *The Nameless Ones,* Jenkins, 1967, published as *A Grave Matter,* Doubleday, 1968.
The Alien, Jenkins, 1968.
Dimension A, Doubleday, 1969.
Stranger to Town, Doubleday, 1969.
Adventure Holidays, Ltd., Doubleday, 1970.
Genesis Two, Doubleday, 1970.
The White Room, Doubleday, 1969.
The Shadow Before, Doubleday, 1970.
Give Me Back Myself, Doubleday, 1971.
What Did I Do Tomorrow, Barrie & Jenkins, 1971, Doubleday, 1973.
The Silver Man (in Swedish), Wahlstroms Bokforlag (Stockholm), 1972.
Assignment Abacus, Doubleday, 1975.
Possession, Doubleday, 1976.
The Land of Leys, Doubleday, 1979.
Morning Walk, R. Hale (London), 1983.

Contributor of more than 250 short stories published under various pseudonyms in United Kingdom and other countries.

ADAPTATIONS: The Artificial Man was filmed as *Project X,* Paramount, 1968; *The Alien* was filmed as *The Groundstar Conspiracy,* Universal, 1970. The film rights to *Psychogeist* have been sold.

SIDELIGHTS: L. P. Davies combines elements from the science fiction and mystery genres to produce thrillers concerning psychic powers and supernatural phenomena. In *The Paper Dolls,* for example, a schoolboy falls from a building in an apparent accident which, when investigated, reveals malevolent psychics who can force others to do their bidding. In other stories, Davies writes of disoriented characters who awake to find themselves in situations they cannot explain. Mary Helen Becker in the *St. James Guide to Crime and Mystery Writers* calls Davies "the master of the suspenseful identity crisis—one character after another must confront reality (or apparent reality) with a disordered perception. The author is proficient at sketching English villages and rural scenes for background, and adroitly constructs thrillers which are unusual and entertaining."

The Paper Dolls was Davies' first novel and it set the tone for many later ones by combining a mystery with a bit of science fiction. When schoolmaster Gordon Seacombe begins to investigate the apparent accidental death of one of the boys at the school he runs, he uncovers much more than he expected, discovering that two brothers at the school have dangerous psychic abilities. John Dickson Carr, writing in *Harper,* calls *The Paper Dolls* "a kind of updated, more devilish *Dr. Jekyll and Mr. Hyde.* You won't believe the solution, but you must be dead and buriable if you haven't enjoyed yourself." Anthony Boucher in the *New York Times Book Review* finds *The Paper Dolls* to be "a vigorous man-against-the-unknown adventure story, with touches of horror, all the more effective for their being underplayed."

In such novels as *Man Out of Nowhere, The Shadow Before,* and *Give Me Back Myself,* Davies presents characters who are confused about their individual identity. In *Man Out of Nowhere,* an amnesiac finds himself variously identified as four different individuals, all of whom are dead and buried. In *The Shadow Before,* a London pharmacist awakening from brain surgery discovers himself to be the wealthy owner of a country estate. In his review of *The Shadow Before,* A. J. Hubin in the *New York Times Book Review* states that "the terror inherent in dis-orientation [is treated] in the suspenseful Davies fashion." "Since the late 1960s," Becker explains, "Davies has turned out some dozen thrillers, each dealing with some aspect of psychic disturbance—caused by drugs, brain tumor, amnesia, hypnosis, or deception. The depersonalization or disorientation of the hero, or the seemingly supernatural goings-on are satisfactorily—sometimes ingeniously—explained."

BIOGRAPHICAL/CRITICAL SOURCES:

BOOKS

St. James Guide to Crime and Mystery Writers, fourth edition, St. James Press (Detroit), 1996.

PERIODICALS

Best Sellers, December 1, 1968, p. 28.
Harper, July, 1966, p. 233.
New York Times Book Review, May 8, 1966, p. 20; December 31, 1967, p. 16; September 6, 1970, p. 24.
Saturday Review, January 27, 1968, p. 51.
Times Literary Supplement, April 30, 1971, p. 511.

DeANDREA, William L(ouis) 1952-1996
(Philip DeGrave; Lee Davis Willoughby, a house pseudonym)

PERSONAL: Born July 1, 1952, in Port Chester, NY; died October 9, 1996, of a blood infection; son of William Nicholas (an engineering assistant) and Mary Agnes (a registered nurse; maiden name, Morabito) DeAndrea; married Orania Papazoglou (a writer), January 1, 1984; children: Matt. *Education:* Syracuse University, B.S., 1974. *Religion:* Roman Catholic.

ADDRESSES: Agent—Meg Ruley, Jane Rotrosen Literary Agency, 318 East 51st St., New York, NY 10022.

CAREER: Reporter for Westchester-Rockland Newspapers, New York, 1969-70; factory worker, Electrolux Corporation, Old Greenwich, Connecticut, 1975-76; writer, 1976-96.

MEMBER: Mystery Writers of America.

AWARDS, HONORS: Edgar Allan Poe Award from Mystery Writers of America, for Best First Novel, 1978, for *Killed in the Ratings,* 1979, for Best Paperback Original, for *The HOG Murders,* 1994, for Best Critical/Biographical Book, for *Encyclopedia Mysteriosa: A Comprehensive Guide to the Art of Detection in Print, Film, Radio, and Television.*

WRITINGS:

MYSTERY NOVELS

The HOG Murders, Avon (New York City), 1979.
The Lunatic Fringe, M. Evans (New York City), 1980.
Five O'Clock Lightning, St. Martin's (New York City), 1982.
Cronus, Mysterious Press (New York City), 1984.
(Under pseudonym Philip DeGrave) *Unholy Moses,* Doubleday (New York City), 1985.
Snark, Farrar, Straus (New York City), 1985.
(Under pseudonym Philip DeGrave) *Keep the Baby, Faith,* Doubleday, 1986.
Azrael, Mysterious Press, 1987.
Atropos, Mysterious Press, 1990.
The Werewolf Murders, Doubleday, 1992.
The Manx Murders, Otto Penzler Books (New York City), 1994.
Written in Fire, Walker (New York City), 1995.

"MATT COBB" MYSTERY SERIES

Killed in the Ratings (Mystery Guild main selection), Harcourt (New York City), 1978.
Killed in the Act, Doubleday, 1981.
Killed with a Passion, Doubleday, 1983.
Killed on the Ice, Doubleday, 1984.
Killed in Paradise, Mysterious Press, 1988.
Killed on the Rocks, Mysterious Press, 1990.
Killed in Fringe Time, Simon & Schuster (New York City), 1995.

OTHER

(Under pseudonym Lee Davis Willoughby) *The Voyageurs* (novel), Dell (New York City), 1983.
Encyclopedia Mysteriosa: A Comprehensive Guide to the Art of Detection in Print, Film, Radio, and Television, Prentice Hall (New York City), 1994.

A collection of DeAndrea's manuscripts is housed at the Mugar Memorial Library, Boston University.

ADAPTATIONS: The film rights to *The Lunatic Fringe* have been optioned.

SIDELIGHTS: William L. DeAndrea was considered by many critics to be one of the most talented and entertaining of contemporary mystery writers. Jon L. Breen, a contributor to *St. James Guide to Crime and Mystery Writers,* called him "one of the best of the writers . . . to set up shop on detective fiction's Main Street, long occupied by . . . Queen, Christie, and Carr." Reviewers praised DeAndrea's ability to create fast-paced mystery stories filled with engaging characters and authentic dialogue and set in exciting locales. In a *New York Times Book Review* article on *Killed in the Ratings,* Newgate Callendar summed up the traits of a DeAndrea mystery in this manner: "His characters are cleanly outlined, the dialogue sounds natural, the backgrounds are authentic and the pace is expertly kept." A critic wrote in the *Library Journal* of *Five O'Clock Lightning:* "This book is a lot of fun. It skillfully weaves real people with fictional ones in a light-hearted way while managing to be suspenseful, exciting, and inventive." And Callendar wrote in an article on *Killed with a Passion* published in the *New York Times Book Review* that DeAndrea had great "stylistic competence. . . . His characters are believable. . . . Mr. DeAndrea does not force; his writing is always natural."

DeAndrea once explained to *CA* his thoughts on writing mystery novels: "I have concentrated on crime fiction for several reasons. The most basic is that it's what I find most entertaining, and it's my opinion that if a work of fiction hasn't entertained, it hasn't done anything. I'm very suspicious of anyone who says he's going to sit down and produce a work of art. All you can do is write a story—when it's *finished,* then it's art or it's not.

"At the same time, it's possible in crime fiction to deal with any important question—the form, in fact, imposes important questions on the writer. Any crime story is automatically concerned with good versus evil, order versus chaos, and illusion versus reality, whether the writer chooses to stress them or not."

Many of DeAndrea's mysteries have been described as topical in that they are set in modern situations. For example, DeAndrea's Matt Cobb series features behind-the-scenes action in the television industry. The author's main character—"city-wise, tough-talking [and] shrewd" Matt Cobb, to quote the description of *Publishers Weekly*'s Barbara A. Bannon—works for a major network as a head of special projects. In *Killed in the Ratings,* DeAndrea's first novel, a murder takes place amid the milieu of network television, and Cobb sets out to solve it. In a review of this book, Jean M. White wrote in the *Washington Post Book World* that DeAndrea "gives us a 21-inch picture of the machinations of the TV world—the ruthless rivalry between networks, the jockeying for executive position, the frantic programming that turns on a percentage point in ratings rather than the merits of a show."

DeAndrea's *Killed in the Act* is also set in the television industry but encompasses movie stars, Hollywood, and the motion picture business as well. Callendar remarked in the *New York Times Book Review* that *Killed in the Act* is "an adventure that is as lively as its predecessor. A bunch of superstars descend on New York for an anniversary show. That means show biz. That means temperaments, jealousies, hatreds. That means a murder takes place on television during a live show." And White commented in a *Washington Post Book World* review of *Killed in the Act* that DeAndrea "enlivens his mystery show with flip dialogue, zany media types, and behind-the-camera peeps at the frenetic television industry." A reviewer for *Library Journal* praised the author's writing style and close attention to detail, noting that "despite its modern tone, this story's clues and red herrings are planted as carefully as in any classic mystery. The writing is smooth."

Breen commented at length on the Cobb books. Of *Killed in the Act,* he noted that "the relatively fresh background is humorously but sympathetically observed, and there is some genuinely witty writing, including much fun with similes and metaphors. . . . The time-honored gathering-of-the-suspects at the end of the book reveals DeAndrea's affinity with the Golden Age masters of puzzle-making, and there are some excellent clues and plot gimmicks. The choice of quotes from old TV shows as epigraphs to the chapters is a nice touch." In *Killed with a Passion,* "the narration is smoother and funnier than ever, and DeAndrea's reliable sense of fair play makes him showcase his clues so audaciously some readers may actually solve the case on the evidence provided," while *Killed in Paradise* is rated by Breen as "one of the best of the recent spate of mystery-game-interrupted-by-real-murder novels, exploiting the comic possibilities of sorting out the real mystery from the manufactured one."

DeAndrea also wrote several espionage-oriented mysteries, featuring a protagonist whose name changed in each volume. In *Cronus* the agent was known as Clifford Driscoll; in *Snark* he was Jeffrey Bellman; and in *Azrael* and *Atropos* he was Allan Trotter. Breen remarked of these books: "Though far from the classical plots of the Cobb and Benedetti novels, the spy books reveal the same skeptical but uncynical worldview as well as the same talent for manipulating story elements in surprising ways." The author also wrote two historical mysteries: *The Lunatic Fringe* was set in 1896 New York and featured Theodore Roosevelt, who was the Police Commissioner in the city at that time; and *Five O'Clock Lightning* features real-life baseball players in a fictional mystery. Breen opined: "The two historicals are more action and suspense thrillers than pure detective stories, but in each DeAndrea displays his reader-bamboozling proclivities."

DeAndrea had a long time interest in communicating arts, as evidenced in his frequent use of the television industry as a backdrop for his mysteries. DeAndrea once explained to *CA:* "I was born just after television, and I've never lived in a place without one. I can't perceive TV as the monster the PTA and various nervous others say it is. I always have watched a lot of TV, and I have never committed a violent crime. For this I thank my parents, who were kind enough to accept the responsibility for me them-

selves, and not foist it off on an electric appliance. When we'd see a violent or antisocial act committed on the tube, my parents would say, 'See that? That's bad. If you ever do anything like that, I'll beat you senseless.' Voila! With the addition of one parental admonition, the monster became a fount of moral instruction.

"Similarly, I don't believe television keeps children from reading. It didn't keep me from reading. And authors know (and have known for generations) that so pitifully few *adults* read anything more profound than Ann Landers that it's silly to blame anything other than the comforts of ignorance. To sum up this part of the program: If thine eye offends thee, pluck out the plug, and leave the rest of us alone. Better yet, let them go read a book, especially mine."

BIOGRAPHICAL/CRITICAL SOURCES:

BOOKS

St. James Guide to Crime and Mystery Writers, St. James Press (Detroit), 1996.

PERIODICALS

Best Sellers, July, 1978; January, 1982.
Booklist, April 15, 1978; March 15, 1984.
Chicago Tribune Book World, March 20, 1983.
Kirkus Reviews, January 15, 1978; September 15, 1984.
Library Journal, May 1, 1978; November 1, 1981; May 1, 1982; September 15, 1984.
New York Times Book Review, April 2, 1978; April 22, 1979; April 25, 1982; May 22, 1983; September 30, 1984; December 2, 1984.
Observer, August 5, 1979.
Publishers Weekly, January 16, 1978; August 29, 1980; October 9, 1981; April 16, 1982; December 24, 1982; April 13, 1984; August 10, 1984.
School Library Journal, November, 1980.
Washington Post Book World, March 19, 1978; September 7, 1980; November 15, 1981; August 19, 1984.
West Coast Review of Books, May, 1978.

OBITUARIES:

PERIODICALS

Armchair Detective, winter, 1997, p. 9.*

DEANE, Norman
See CREASEY, John

* * *

DeGRAVE, Philip
See DeANDREA, William L(ouis)

* * *

DEWEY, Thomas B(lanchard) 1915-1981
(Tom Brandt, Cord Wainer)

PERSONAL: Born March 6, 1915, in Elkhart, IN; died in 1981; son of Henry Evert and Elizabeth (Blanchard) Dewey; married Maxine Morley Sorensen, 1951; married Doris L. Smith, 1972; children: (previous marriage) Thomas B., Deborah. *Education:* Kansas State Teachers College (now Emporia State University), B.S. in Ed., 1936; State University of Iowa, graduate study, 1937-38; University of California, Los Angeles, Ph.D., 1973.

CAREER: Harding Market Co., Chicago, IL, clerical worker, 1936-37; Storycraft, Inc. (correspondence school), Hollywood, CA, editor, 1938-42; U.S. Department of State, Washington, DC, administrative and editorial assistant, 1942-45; worked for advertising agency, Los Angeles, CA, 1945-52; Arizona State University, Tempe, assistant professor of English, 1971-77.

MEMBER: Mystery Writers of America (director-at-large, 1960-62).

WRITINGS:

Hue and Cry, Morrow (New York City), 1944, published as *Room for Murder,* New American Library (New York City), 1950, published as *The Murder of Marion Mason,* Dakers (London), 1951.
As Good as Dead, Morrow, 1946.
Draw the Curtain Close, Morrow, 1947, published as *Dame in Danger,* New American Library, 1958.
Mourning After, Mill (New York City), 1950.
Handle with Fear, Mill, 1951.
Murder of Marion Mason, Dakers, 1952.
Every Bet's a Sure Thing, Simon & Schuster (New York City), 1953.

Prey for Me, Simon & Schuster, 1954, published as *The Case of the Murdered Model,* Avon (New York City), 1955.
The Mean Streets, Simon & Schuster, 1955.
My Love is Violent, Popular Library (New York City), 1956.
The Brave, Bad Girls, Simon & Schuster, 1956.
And Where She Stops, Popular Library, 1957, published as *I.O.U. Murder,* Boardman, 1958.
You've Got Him Cold, Simon & Schuster, 1958.
(With Harold M. Imerman) *What Women Want to Know,* Crown, 1958.
The Case of the Chased and the Unchaste, Random House, 1959.
The Girl Who Wasn't There, Simon & Schuster, 1960, published as *The Girl Who Never Was,* Mayflower (New York City), 1962.
Go to Sleep, Jeannie, Popular Library, 1959.
Too Hot for Hawaii, Popular Library, 1960.
Hunter at Large, Simon & Schuster, 1961.
The Golden Hooligan, Dell (New York City), 1961, published as *Mexican Slay Ride,* T. V. Boardman, 1961.
How Hard to Kill, Simon & Schuster, 1962.
Go, Honeylou, Dell, 1962.
The Girl with the Sweet Plump Knees, Dell, 1963.
A Sad Song Singing, Simon & Schuster, 1963.
Don't Cry for Long, Simon & Schuster, 1964.
The Girl in the Punchbowl, Dell, 1964.
Can a Mermaid Kill?, Tower (New York City), 1965.
Portrait of a Dead Heiress, Simon & Schuster, 1965.
Only on Tuesdays, Dell, 1965.
Nude in Nevada, Dell, 1965.
Deadline, Simon & Schuster, 1966.
(Editor) *Sleuths and Consequences,* Simon & Schuster, 1966.
A Season for Violence, Gold Medal (New York City), 1966.
Death and Taxes (Detective Book Club selection), Putnam (New York City), 1967.
The King Killers, Putnam, 1968, published as *Death Turns Right,* R. Hale (London), 1969.
The Love-Death Thing, Simon & Schuster, 1969.
The Taurus Trip, Simon & Schuster, 1970.

UNDER PSEUDONYM CORD WAINER

Mountain Girl, Gold Medal, 1953.

UNDER PSEUDONYM TOM BRANDT

Kiss Me Hard, Popular Library, 1954.
Run, Brother, Run!, Popular Library, 1954.

ADAPTATIONS: Every Bet's a Sure Thing and *A Sad Song Singing,* have been adapted for television.

SIDELIGHTS: Thomas B. Dewey wrote hardboiled mystery novels featuring a Chicago detective known only as Mac. Combining the tough approach of the hardboiled school with Mac's overwhelming decency, Dewey's novels "are among the best modern representatives of the authentic 'tough' tradition: hardboiled, human, humane," wrote Anthony Boucher in the *New York Times.* L. G. Offord in the *San Francisco Chronicle* found that "Mac combines toughness with integrity as well as its every been done." D. B. Hughes in *Book Week* wrote: "There isn't a private eye extant more satisfying than Thomas B. Dewey's Mac."

"Mac," wrote John M. Muste in the *St. James Guide to Crime and Mystery Writers,* "is very much in the Sam Spade/Philip Marlowe/Lew Archer tradition of private eyes. He is always, if sometimes reluctantly, on the side of the underdog; he tells his own stories, and he seems to have no life apart from his activities as a detective; he lives alone, and his existence is spartan; he is tough, but partial to children; gorgeous women throw themselves, or are thrown, into his path, but with rare exceptions he is chaste; and he always solves his cases before the police do."

Among the best of the novels featuring Mac is *The Girl Who Wasn't There,* a story that, Boucher explained, "hooks the reader strongly with the callous murder of a sympathetic character and holds him with the restrained but forceful narration of the 'hard-boiled' school at its genuine best." James Sandoe, reviewing the novel for the *New York Herald Tribune Book Review,* claimed: "Dewey has built in a couple of pretty surprises and a nice crash of nervous-wry finale that all in all brings it off neatly."

In *A Sad Song Singing,* Mac goes in search of a missing folksinger in what Boucher called "essentially a gentle and likable story about youth, folksinging and the coming of age of an artist." Sandoe found the novel to be "told with tenderness" and warned that it was "a tough tale that will tackle your tear ducts soundly."

Speaking of Dewey's mysteries, A. L. Rosenzweig in *Book World* explained that "in these flip days of easy morals and sticky-fingered operatives, Mac shines for his ungrudging decency. . . . Dewey's prose is among the crispest in the business, stripped of frills and shot from guns." According to Muste, "Dewey's

novels are interesting and successful, and Mac is a memorable private eye, even if he too often exemplifies the "White Knight" referred to in several of these stories. Dewey is less tough than Hammett, and his stories lack both the pungent local color which makes Chandler's and Ross Macdonald's novels distinctive and the moral ambiguity which tantalizes Philip Marlowe and Lew Archer. But Dewey belongs at the head of the second rank of the hard-boiled writers."

BIOGRAPHICAL/CRITICAL SOURCES:

BOOKS

St. James Guide to Crime and Mystery Writers, fourth edition, St. James Press (Detroit), 1996.

PERIODICALS

Best Sellers, November 1, 1970.
Book Week, September 29, 1963, p. 26.
Book World, July 21, 1968, p. 14.
Library Journal, September 1, 1963, p. 88.
New York Herald Tribune Book Review, May 22, 1960, p. 12.
New York Times, February 28, 1954, p. 28.
New York Times Book Review, September 28, 1958, p. 47; May 29, 1960, p. 21; September 29, 1963, p. 52; July 28, 1968.
San Francisco Chronicle, March 13, 1955, p. 13; May 29, 1960, p. 23; June 24, 1962, p. 38.*

* * *

DRUMMOND, John
See CHANCE, John Newton

* * *

DUDLEY-SMITH, T.
See TREVOR, Elleston

* * *

DURRELL, Gerald (Malcolm) 1925-1995

PERSONAL: Surname accented on the first syllable; born January 7, 1925, in Jamshedpur, India; died

January 30, 1995, on the Channel Island of Jersey, off the coast of England; son of Lawrence Samuel (a civil engineer) and Louisa Florence (Dixie) Durrell; married Jacqueline Sonia Rasen, 1951 (divorced); married Lee Wilson McGeorge, 1979. *Education:* Educated privately in France, Italy, Switzerland, and Greece. *Avocational interests:* Reading, photography, drawing, and swimming.

CAREER: Whipsnade Zoological Park, Whipsnade, Bedfordshire, England, student animal keeper, 1945-46; leader and underwriter of zoological expeditions to various parts of the world, including Cameroon, 1947, 1948, and 1956, Nigeria, 1948, Guyana, 1949, Argentina, 1953 and 1958, Paraguay, 1953, Australia, New Zealand, and Malaya, 1961, Sierra Leone, 1964, Mexico, 1968, Mauritius, 1976 and 1977, Assam, India, 1978, Malagasy Republic, 1981, and the Soviet Union, 1986; Jersey Wildlife Preservation Trust, Trinity, Jersey, Channel Islands, founder, 1958, director, 1964-95. Founder and chairman, Wildlife Preservation Trust International, Philadelphia, Penn., 1972-95; founder and president, Wildlife Preservation Trust Canada, Toronto, 1986-95. Conductor of film expedition to Australia and New Zealand for British Broadcasting Corporation (BBC) television series "Two in the Bush," 1962; host of television series "The Stationary Ark," "Ark on the Move," "The Amateur Naturalist," "Durrell in Russia," and "Ourselves and Other Animals."

MEMBER: International Institute of Arts and Letters (fellow), Royal Society of Literature (fellow), Royal Geographical Society (fellow), Fauna Preservation Society, American Zooparks Association, British Ornithologists Union, Australian Mammal Society, Nigerian Field Society, Malayan Nature Society, Zoological Society of London (fellow), Bombay Natural History Society.

AWARDS, HONORS: National Association of Independent Schools award, 1956, for *Three Tickets to Adventure*; D.H.L., Yale University, 1977; honorary D.Sc., University of Durham, 1988, University of Kent, 1989; Officer of the Order of the British Empire.

WRITINGS:

The Overloaded Ark, Viking, 1953.
Three Singles to Adventure, Hart-Davis, 1954, published as *Three Tickets to Adventure*, Viking, 1955.
The Bafut Beagles, Viking, 1954.

The New Noah (juvenile; also see below), Collins, 1955, Viking, 1964.
The Drunken Forest, Viking, 1956.
My Family and Other Animals (memoirs), Hart-Davis, 1956, Viking, 1957.
Encounters with Animals, Hart-Davis, 1958, Avon, 1970.
A Zoo in My Luggage, Viking, 1960.
Island Zoo, Collins, 1961, published as *Island Zoo: The Animals a Famous Collector Couldn't Part With*, Macrae Smith, 1963.
The Whispering Land, Hart-Davis, 1961, Viking, 1962.
Look at Zoos, Hamish Hamilton, 1961.
Menagerie Manor, Hart-Davis, 1964, Viking, 1965.
Two in the Bush (story of the filming of the BBC television series of the same title), Viking, 1966.
Birds, Beasts and Relatives (memoirs), Viking, 1969.
Fillets of Plaice (memoirs), Viking, 1971.
Catch Me a Colobus, Viking, 1972.
A Bevy of Beasts (memoirs), Simon & Schuster, 1973 (published in England as *Beasts in My Belfrey*, Collins, 1973).
The Stationary Ark, Simon & Schuster, 1976.
Golden Bats and Pink Pigeons, Simon & Schuster, 1977.
The Garden of the Gods (memoirs), Collins, 1978, published as *Fauna and Family*, Simon & Schuster, 1979.
(With wife, Lee Durrell) *The Amateur Naturalist: A Practical Guide to the Natural World*, Hamish Hamilton, 1982, Knopf, 1983.
Ark on the Move (story of the filming of the nature series of the same title), Coward-McCann, 1983.
How to Shoot an Amateur Naturalist (story of the filming of the television series "The Amateur Naturalist," starring Durrell), Little, Brown, 1984.
(With Lee Durrell) *Gerald and Lee Durrell in Russia* (story of the filming of the nature series "Durrell in Russia"), Simon & Schuster, 1986.
(With Peter Evans) *Ourselves and Other Animals*, Pantheon, 1987.
The Aye-Aye and I: A Rescue Mission in Madagascar, Simon & Schuster (New York City), 1994.

FICTION

(Compiler) *My Favourite Animal Stories*, Butterworth, 1961, McGraw, 1962.
Rosy Is My Relative (novel), Viking, 1968.
The Donkey Rustlers (juvenile novel), Viking, 1968.

The Talking Parcel (juvenile fantasy), Collins, 1974, Lippincott, 1975.

The Picnic and Suchlike Pandemonium (short stories), Collins, 1979, published as *The Picnic and Other Inimitable Stories*, Simon & Schuster, 1980.

The Mockery Bird (novel), Collins, 1981, Simon & Schuster, 1982.

The Fantastic Flying Journey (juvenile fantasy), Conran Octopus, 1987.

OTHER

(Author of introduction) Bernard Heuvelmans, *On the Track of Unknown Animals*, Hill & Wang, 1958.

(Contributor) *Three Great Animal Stories* (includes *The New Noah*), Collins, 1966.

(Author of notes) Jacquie Durrell, *Beasts in My Bed*, Atheneum, 1967.

Elephant Country (television script), National Broadcasting Company (NBC), 1971.

(Contributor) Martin Boddey, editor, *The Twelfth Man*, Cassell, 1971.

(Author of introduction) Theodore Stephanides, *Island Trails*, Macdonald & Co., 1973.

(Author of foreword) *The Encyclopedia of Natural History*, Smith Publishers, 1978.

Contributor to *Encyclopedia of Natural History* and to newspapers and magazines in England, Canada, the United States, Australia, and New Zealand, including the *New York Times*, *Harper's*, *Mademoiselle*, *Atlantic*, *Holiday*, and *Show*.

ADAPTATIONS: The Amateur Naturalist: A Practical Guide to the Natural World was made into a BBC television series, featuring Durrell searching for animal life in a variety of locations. *My Family and Other Animals*, his most popular book, was filmed for a 12-part series by BBC television, and was screened in the U.K. in 1987.

SIDELIGHTS: Gerald Durrell was "famous for his work in preserving real wild animals and for his humorous and poignant books on the subject," said Brigitte Weeks in the *Washington Post Book World*. The youngest brother of novelist and poet Lawrence Durrell, and a respected naturalist and zoologist, he was "one of the best writers around for capturing the spirit of nature and travel," according to Jack Imes, Jr., in *Best Sellers*. His books about his travels in search of specimens for zoos, his chronicles of his own youth spent on the Greek island of Corfu, and

his occasional revels in the realm of fiction "won him fame and readers in numbers surpassed perhaps only by James Herriott," in the opinion of London *Times* contributor Caroline Moorehead.

Although born in India, Gerald Durrell returned with his family to England in 1928. In 1933 the Durrells left for the continent, eventually settling on the Greek island of Corfu. There, under the instruction of Theodore Stephanides and others, Durrell developed the interest in zoology that was to become the consuming passion of his life. He described this life in *My Family and Other Animals, Birds, Beasts, and Relatives*, and *The Gardens of the Gods*, three books that combine "reminiscence and natural history in a highly individual fashion," according to a reviewer in *Choice*. August Derleth, writing for the *Chicago Sunday Times*, reported that *My Family and Other Animals* "is an amusingly nostalgic account of a childhood notably different from most, replete with sympathetic characters (not excluding the nonhuman) who are more than just types." *New York Times Book Review* contributor Gavin Maxwell called *Birds, Beasts, and Relatives* "a delightful book full of simple, long-known things: cicadas in the olive groves, lamp-fishing at night, the complexities of fish and animals—but, above all, childhood molded by these things and recalled intimately in middle age."

In 1939 the Durrells left Corfu, driven by the onset of World War II. After returning to England, Gerald spent some time working in a pet shop in London, then managed to obtain a position as a student animal keeper at the Whipsnade zoo, experiences which he chronicled in *Fillets of Plaice* and *A Bevy of Beasts*. *Fillets*, a title suggested by his brother Lawrence based on the latter's own book *Spirit of Place*, is a selection of five episodes from various points in Gerald's life. The stories are "not all zoological," according to Ronald Blythe in the *Listener*, "but it is a kind of decency learnt from animals which gives them their attractive flavour. They are youthful disasters and mystifications recollected in hilarity." *A Bevy of Beasts* tells of Durrell's year-long stint as a student keeper of animals in the Whipsnade Zoological Park. "Involved, and yet objective, Mr. Durrell combines his personal passion with keen humour and no illusions," stated Jean Stubbs in *Books and Bookmen*. "Gallivanting gnus, bumbling bears, looming giraffes, superior camels, and Billy the Goat," she continued, "come off the pages with all the engaging and lovely maddening qualities of Dickensian characters."

Durrell's first book, *The Overloaded Ark*, was written at the suggestion of his brother Lawrence. Telling of his adventures collecting animals in the British Cameroons, it broke with the genre's tradition of life-threatening situations and hair-raising thrills; lighthearted in tone and filled with humorous anecdotes, Durrell's work recounts not the dangers, but the delights of collecting animals. "There is nothing of the 'mighty hunter' in Durrell's book," declared M. L. J. Akeley in *Saturday Review*. "He carried a small gun, but never fired in self-defense." This book and its successors *The Bafut Beagles, Three Tickets to Adventure* and *The Drunken Forest*, all accounts of collecting trips to various exotic parts of the world, were well received by reviewers. For instance, *The Bafut Beagles* "is, first of all, a gay little book," remarked J. W. Krutch in the *New York Herald Tribune Book Review*, "—no charging rhinoceroses, no man-eaters lurking in the tall grass, no sinister drums subduing the sophisticated European with the hypnotism of Africa's dark beating heart." Similarly, he said of *The Drunken Forest*, "[Durrell's] books are as far as possible from either the earnestness of the I-am-a-humble-servant-of-science or the robustness of the bring-'em-back-alive schools." Marston Bates, writing in the *New York Times*, expressed the opinion that Durrell "has shown that an honest, straightforward account of such a trip [to British Guyana, in *Three Tickets to Adventure*], written by a person who likes words as well as animals, who can be amused at himself and the frustrations of his circumstances, is also never dull."

In 1958 Durrell established a zoological park on the channel island of Jersey for the purpose of breeding and caring for endangered species. *A Zoo in My Luggage, Menagerie Manor, Catch Me a Colobus*, and *The Stationary Ark* all tell of his efforts to begin and maintain populations of animals for other zoological gardens and for their eventual reintroduction into the wild. *Christian Science Monitor* contributor D. K. Willis called Durrell "a writer who sees animals as individuals demanding nothing less than man's utmost care and respect—as fellow sharers of the earth, not to be diminished on the one hand, or set up on pedestals." "He writes with good breeding about breeding," said Neil Millar in the *Christian Science Monitor*; "he tells how the captivating are made captive and the cagy are caged. His enthusiasm is as infectious as a chuckle in a church." Peter Canby of *Saturday Review* stated of *The Stationary Ark*, "On one level this book is about zoos, particularly the one that the renowned naturalist himself started on the island of Jersey. More profoundly,

however, *The Stationary Ark* is about the misuse of wild animals in captivity."

In his final nonfiction work before his death in 1995, *The Aye-Aye and I: A Rescue Mission in Madagascar,* Durrell recounted a trip to the island of Madagascar on behalf of the aye-aye, a rare lemur inhabiting the island. Critics noted that the book reveals Durrell's trademark sense of humor and his undeniable passion for protecting wildlife. Writing in the Chicago *Tribune Books,* Clarence Petersen commented that *The Aye-Aye and I* "combines masterly travel- and nature-writing."

Durrell also used his interest in animals as the basis of his fiction. *Rosy Is My Relative*, the author's first novel, tells the story of Adrian Rookwhistle's adventures while traveling across Edwardian England with Rosy, an elephant with an unfortunate penchant for alcohol. Peter Corodimas of *Best Sellers* described this work as "a descendant of the traditional rambling, good-natured British novel which goes back at least as far as Smollett." *The Mockery Bird*, a later effort, concerns animal preservation and the destruction of habitat. The action takes place on the tropical island of Zenkali, a paradise that has been chosen as the site of a new British military base. Construction of the base will involve building a dam and hydroelectric plant, which in turn will mean the flooding of virgin jungle and many small valleys. Peter Foxglove, the new assistant to the political advisor of Zenkali's king, discovers a valley in the backwoods filled with mockery birds, a species supposed to have been extinct for many years. Eventually it is shown that the economy of the entire island depends on this species, and the valley is preserved. Durrell's goal, declared Vic Sussman of the *Washington Post Book World*, is to emphasize the importance of species preservation: "Long before there was a vigorous environmental movement, in fact, people like Durrell were devoting their lives to reversing the trend of extinction and exploitation." *The Mockery Bird*, he concluded, is intended "to convey [Durrell's] message of conservation and compassion."

Durrell's later work in television and in the books based on his programs emphasized the need for education in the natural sciences, yet it still maintained the standards of his earlier work. *The Amateur Naturalist*, a handbook for the average animal collector, serves as an example. It inspired not only a television series, but another book as well: *How to Shoot an Amateur Naturalist*, based on Durrell's experiences while filming the series. *The Amateur Natural-

ist "provides astonishing amounts of information," wrote James Kaufmann in the *Christian Science Monitor*, "which goes down as easily as if sugar-coated." However, he continued, the information it provides is only part of the book's attraction; Durrell has "a seemingly unlimited capacity for the appreciation of any plant or animal. He treats the common and the arcane with equal enthusiasm. Durrell's sense of wonder, his delight in telling stories, his love of nature are contagious." *Los Angeles Times Book Review* contributor Barbara Salzman expressed similar feelings: "Durrell has put together the perfect book for the budding dabbler, youthful or not. [The volume is] a wonderful primer, a bounty of material for those ready to observe—and appreciate—the teeming life around us, and the delicate strands that weave it together." Imes, writing about *How to Shoot an Amateur Naturalist*, stated: "[Durrell] is an amateur only in the best sense of that word; a man with deep knowledge because of his vast interest in the magnificent mysteries of living things. [But] this book is no dull science documentary droning with a stern-voiced narrator. Instead, it is a romp." Although both *Washington Post Book World* contributor T. H. Watkins and *Times Literary Supplement* reviewer Stephen Mills charged Durrell with paying too much attention to people and not enough to the animals that are his subject, they both recommended the work; Watkins, for example, called it "natural history writing at its graceful and entertaining best."

Gerald Durrell never lost sight of his objective in spite of his efforts to entertain. In the "Tailpiece" to his novel *The Mockery Bird*, he stated that "the world and its wildlife [are] being steadily and ruthlessly decimated by what we call progress." At the Jersey Wildlife Trust, he continued, "we are endeavouring to build up colonies of almost extinct species, to save them, and to train people from different parts of the world in the arts of captive breeding, in order to help these animals that are being edged into oblivion by our unthinking rapaciousness. . . . We are pleading on behalf on behalf of these plants and creatures because they cannot plead for themselves, and it is, after all, your world which we are asking you to help preserve."

BIOGRAPHICAL/CRITICAL SOURCES:

BOOKS

Durrell, Gerald, *My Family and Other Animals*, Hart-Davis, 1956, Viking, 1957.

Durrell, Gerald, *Birds, Beasts and Relatives*, Viking, 1969.

Durrell, Gerald, *Fillets of Plaice*, Viking, 1971.

Durrell, Gerald, *A Bevy of Beasts*, Simon & Schuster, 1973 (published in England as *Beasts in My Belfrey*, Collins, 1973).

Durrell, Gerald, *The Garden of the Gods*, Collins, 1978, published as *Fauna and Family*, Simon & Schuster, 1979.

Durrell, Gerald, *The Mockery Bird*, Collins, 1981, Simon & Schuster, 1982.

PERIODICALS

Antioch Review, winter, 1980.

Atlantic, December, 1953, February, 1962, February, 1967, October, 1969, December, 1971.

Best Sellers, April 15, 1965, June 1, 1968, September 15, 1969, February 1, 1972, June 1, 1973, January, 1978, January, 1981, June, 1982, December, 1985.

Books and Bookmen, November, 1968, September, 1971, September, 1972, March, 1974, January, 1977, December, 1977.

Chicago Sunday Tribune, April 7, 1957, January 28, 1962.

Chicago Tribune Book World, October 3, 1982.

Children's Book World, November 3, 1968.

Choice, March, 1970.

Christian Science Monitor, September 24, 1953, October 13, 1955, November 7, 1960, January 25, 1962, November 5, 1964, April 27, 1965, December 28, 1967, October 3, 1968, May 1, 1969, September 11, 1969, December 30, 1971, October 25, 1972, June 6, 1973, September 2, 1983, December 2, 1983, April 6, 1984.

Commonweal, October 16, 1953, November 6, 1964.

Economist, November 20, 1971, December 28, 1974.

Harper's, September, 1969, November, 1974.

Listener, August 19, 1971.

Los Angeles Times Book Review, November 4, 1979, November 20, 1983, December 14, 1986, August 21, 1994, p. 7.

New Statesman, November 19, 1964, October 15, 1976.

New Statesman and Nation, October 20, 1956.

New Yorker, October 3, 1953, November 6, 1954, October 8, 1955, May 25, 1957, October 29, 1960, January 27, 1962, June 1, 1968, December 28, 1980, April 19, 1982, December 5, 1983.

New York Herald Tribune Book Review, November 7, 1954, October 9, 1955, October 28, 1956, May 26, 1957, November 6, 1960, February 11, 1962.

New York Review of Books, September 28, 1978.

New York Times, September 27, 1953, December 5, 1954, September 18, 1955, September 30, 1956, April 7, 1957, November 28, 1983.

New York Times Book Review, November 13, 1960, February 4, 1962, January 26, 1964, June 25, 1967, May 26, 1968, November 24, 1968, August 24, 1969, October 1, 1972, May 13, 1973, November 27, 1977, November 18, 1979, December 11, 1983, April 8, 1984, August 14, 1994, p. 28.

People, March 15, 1982.

Quill and Quire, April, 1986.

San Francisco Chronicle, November 16, 1954, September 16, 1955, October 2, 1956, April 11, 1957, October 26, 1960, January 25, 1962.

Saturday Review, September 26, 1953, September 29, 1956, November 7, 1964, December 3, 1966, October 7, 1972, December 10, 1977.

Spectator, July 6, 1956, October 28, 1960, December 11, 1976.

Time, April 15, 1957, December 5, 1960, February 2, 1962, September 12, 1969, September 24, 1973, October 9, 1978, April 12, 1982.

Times (London), November 12, 1981, November 24, 1984.

Times Literary Supplement, September 4, 1953, March 26, 1954, December 3, 1954, May 18, 1956, December 21, 1956, November 4, 1960, November 10, 1961, November 23, 1962, January 12, 1967, February 1, 1967, October 3, 1968, November 6, 1969, December 1, 1972, September 21, 1973, December 6, 1974, March 22, 1985.

Tribune Books (Chicago), August 7, 1994, p. 8.

Virginia Quarterly Review, winter, 1970.

Washington Post, November 6, 1979.

Washington Post Book World, December 24, 1972, May 6, 1973, May 4, 1975, June 14, 1982, September 17, 1985.

OBITUARIES:

PERIODICALS

Los Angeles Times, February 2, 1995, p. A20.

Times (London), January 31, 1995, pp. 1, 23.*

*   *   *

EGERTON, Lucy
  See MALLESON, Lucy Beatrice

*   *   *

ELLER, Scott
  See SHEPARD, Jim

*   *   *

EVANS, Morgan
  See DAVIES, L(eslie) P(urnell)

F

FAWCETT, Ron
See HARRISON, M(ichael) John

＊　　＊　　＊

FEARING, Kenneth (Flexner) 1902-1961
(Donald F. Bedford, a joint pseudonym)

PERSONAL: Born July 28, 1902, in Oak Park, IL; died June 26, 1961; son of Harry L. (an attorney) and Olive (Flexner) Fearing; married Nan Lurie, 1945; children: one son. *Education:* University of Wisconsin, B.A., 1924.

CAREER: Poet and novelist. Worked at various jobs, including newspaper reporter, salesman, mill hand, and clerk. Freelance writer and editor, 1927-61.

AWARDS, HONORS: Guggenheim fellowship, 1936 and 1939; American Academy award, 1945.

WRITINGS:

POETRY

Angel Arms, Coward McCann (New York City), 1929.
Poems, Dynamo (New York City), 1935.
Dead Reckoning: A Book of Poetry, Random House (New York City), 1938.
Collected Poems of Kenneth Fearing, Random House, 1940.
Afternoon of a Pawnbroker and Other Poems, Harcourt (New York City), 1943.

Stranger at Coney Island and Other Poems, Harcourt, 1948.
New and Selected Poems, Indiana University Press (Bloomington), 1956.

NOVELS

The Hospital, Random House, 1939.
Dagger of the Mind, Random House, 1941, as *Cry Killer!,* Avon (New York City), 1958.
Clark Gifford's Body, Random House, 1942.
The Big Clock, Harcourt, 1946, as *No Way Out,* Perennial (New York City), 1980.
(With Donald Friede and H. Bedford Jones under joint pseudonym Donald F. Bedford) *John Barry,* Creative Age Press (New York City), 1947.
Loneliest Girl in the World, Harcourt, 1951, as *The Sound of Murder,* Spivak (New York City), 1952.
The Generous Heart, Harcourt, 1954.
The Crozart Story, Doubleday, 1960.

ADAPTATIONS: The Big Clock was adapted into the films *The Big Clock,* 1948, and *No Way Out,* 1987.

SIDELIGHTS: Novelist and poet Kenneth Fearing's writings deal with the urban, mechanized society, a world wherein faith and love no longer have meaning. He portrays the everyday in a macabre light, simultaneously evoking what critic Dudley Fitts called "horror and delight." In discussing his 1938 work *Dead Reckoning: A Book of Poetry,* Louis Untermeyer wrote in *Saturday Review of Literature* that "Fearing's technique is more startling than any of his confrères. In this, the best of his [first] three volumes of poems, he has freed himself of a dependence on purely muscular, hard-boiled idioms which threatened to characterize him as the Ernest Hemingway of modern verse. In this book the tone is richer and the gamut is wider. The device—the free use of the newspaper headline, the comic strip, the clichés of advertising, the ticker-tape, the radio signal—are not only appropriate, they are convincing." And T. C. Wilson, in a *Poetry* review, said, "He has wit and sympathy and understanding; his best work possesses remarkable vigor and speed as well as sensitivity of rhythm and phrasing. As much can be said of very few poets writing today." T. C. Chubb commented in the *New York Times* that "the lyre of poetry has been ousted by the steam riveter. But it holds the intense, original and angry writing of a man who sees vividly and feels vividly and who has set down the things he has thus seen and thus felt with an angry and effective tongue. It is not pleasant, and it is not musical, but it may well be the way that vivid poetry will be written in the immediate." And Ruth Lechlitner likewise lauded in *Books:* "On all counts it seems to me that Fearing's 'American Rhapsodies' will stand among the best poems written during the last two decades. In 'Dead Reckoning'. . . he sees in terms that are simple, vital and recognizable to a contemporary. Like ideographs in a running telegraphic framework his poems flash the news of our time."

The then-experimental structure and imagery of Fearing's first novel, *The Hospital,* seem in many ways to have prefigured by some fifty-odd years the now-familiar, frenzied immediacy, the multi-layered storylines, rapid-fire jumpcuts, and pseudo-verité or hyperrealist visual approaches of the modern, television medical drama series. Written in brief chapters, each assigned the name of the relevant protagonist, Fearing covers a few, intensely focused hours in that individual's life—each one of a group of doctors, nurses, patients, and maintenance men in a large, urban hospital. The focus of the story deals with the impact on their lives, and the macrosystem of the hospital itself, by the accidental shutdown of power, for several minutes, by a drunken janitor. "Probably no hospital has ever known such concentrated drama as author Fearing packs in," noted a *Time* reviewer. "But the distortions of his pictures resemble far more those produced by a microscope than defective mirrors." Otis Ferguson, writing in *New Republic,* added that, "There is some good lean writing in the book, and something like a staccato prose poem in the sections leading up to the last delirium of Dr. Gavin. The people are likely, too—but they don't stay with you long, being swallowed up in numbers.

The hospital itself remains longer." And R. C. Feld, reviewing the work in the *New York Times,* commented: "Exciting and dramatic as is the story, it is Fearing's treatment which calls for highest praise. He has the poet's gift of expression and condensation and, within the compass of a few pages, creates the pattern of a life. While his sympathies are broad enough to take in all human weakness, he is particularly concerned with those whose lives, metaphorically speaking, are spent in the world's basement. For them he has tenderness and for those who keep them there a stinging bitterness. The end of the book is not happy, but it is a realistic tying up of human threads."

Fearing's second novel, *Dagger of the Mind,* is a somewhat offbeat mystery set in an artists' colony, possibly somewhere on Long Island. Isaac Anderson in his *New York Times* review asserted: "here are gathered some of the most eccentric and unconventional characters that can possibly be imagined. . . . Taken as a whole, this book is not so much a mystery story as a study in abnormal psychology—an absorbing one at that—although the mystery element is by no means negligible." Not all reviewers perceived Fearing's quirky cast of characters as the strength Anderson did, however; a critic in the *Saturday Review of Literature* noted that, "The resolution of the plot, if not altogether satisfactory, is pretty sound; certainly the basic gag is a very good one, and it is only regrettable that Mr. Fearing was more interested in caricaturing the establishment than in sticking close to the development of his central twist." But Dorothy Hillyer of the *Boston Transcript* lauded the work, noting that "Amateur psychologists—and this means practically everybody—will have a fine time interpreting this exciting book." And Will Cuppy wrote in *Books:* "Take it any way you like, the story is a novelty in the mystery field and the total effect is most impressive."

The third Fearing novel, *Clark Gifford's Body,* deals with an abortive revolution in a "mythical country, of no particular time." "As an experiment in discontinuity, the novel is of considerable interest," George Conrad stated in *Books,* "but most readers will keep hoping Mr. Fearing will quit hopping." A reviewer in *Nation* maintained that the novel is narrated "through the eyes of a dozen or more characters and skips back and forth in time over a period of thirty years before and after the 'attack'; it's a confusing technique that befuddles the reader, creates a sterile objectivity, and spares Mr. Fearing the necessity of committing himself on his own viewpoint, if any." However, in his

New York Times review, Isaac Anderson called *Clark Gifford's Body* "an oddly disturbing novel, and it is difficult to say whether the general effect of it is heightened by the curiously episodic manner in which it is told—a manner which begins by being annoying and ends by having a fascination of its own."

The Big Clock, which was produced as a motion picture in 1948, and produced thirty-nine years later as *No Way Out,* is Fearing's best-known work. In stark journalistic style, the book relates the events following a murder. Tired of his mistress, a publisher of a large metropolitan magazine kills her, pinning the crime on a stranger seen leaving her apartment that evening. He subsequently assigns the story to his ace crime reporter who, in fact, was the very stranger seen the night of the murder: the hunter and hunted are one.

In discussing *The Big Clock,* C. V. Terry wrote in the *New York Times:* "If you enjoy top-drawer detective fiction . . . we can recommend this one with no reservations whatsoever." Richard Match agreed in the *Weekly Book Review:* "It will be some time before chill-hungry clients meet again so rare a compound of irony, satire, and icy-fingered narrative." And Hamilton Basso lauded the work in the *New Yorker,* noting that "I have not developed the habit of reading thrillers, but I have read enough of them to know that from now on Mr. Fearing is my man."

BIOGRAPHICAL/CRITICAL SOURCES:

BOOKS

St. James Guide to Crime & Mystery Writers, fourth edition, St. James Press (Detroit), 1996.

PERIODICALS

Booklist, February 1, 1939, p. 35.
Books, April 2, 1939, p. 25; September 3, 1939, p. 4; February 2, 1941, p. 13; July 5, 1942, p. 8.
Book Week, October 20, 1946, p. 15.
Boston Transcript, September 16, 1939, p. 1; March 8, 1941, p. 2.
Christian Century, January 1, 1947, p. 64.
Kirkus, September 15, 1946, p. 467.
Nation, August 19, 1939, p. 201; September 30, 1939, p. 355; June 27, 1942, 743; October 26, 1946, p. 479; November 13, 1948; January 19, 1957.

New Republic, September 30, 1939, p. 195; October 7, 1946, p. 462.
New Statesman & Nation, December 20, 1941, p. 511.
New Yorker, January 7, 1939, p. 55; September 9, 1939, p. 77; February 8, 1941, p. 68; September 21, 1946, p. 116.
New York Times, July 30, 1939, p. 5; September 3, 1939, p. 6; February 2, 1941, p. 12; June 28, 1942, p. 22; September 22, 1946, p. 6; October 24, 1948; February 17, 1957.
Poetry, April 1939, p. 26; January 1941; December 1943; August 1957.
Time, December 26, 1938, p. 44; September 4, 1939, p. 52.
San Francisco Chronicle, September 22, 1946, p. 19.
Saturday Review, June 29, 1957.
Saturday Review of Literature, January 21, 1939, p. 18; February 15, 1941, p. 19; October 12, 1946, p. 50.
Spectator, November 28, 1941, p. 520.
Time, October 7, 1946, p. 116.
Weekly Book Review, September 22, 1948, p. 4.*

* * *

FECAMPS, Elise
   See CREASEY, John

* * *

FEIFFER, Jules (Ralph) 1929-

PERSONAL: Born January 26, 1929, in Bronx, New York; son of David (held a variety of positions, including dental technician and salesman) and Rhoda (a fashion designer; maiden name, Davis) Feiffer; married Judith Sheftel (a production executive with Warner Bros.), September 17, 1961 (divorced); married Jennifer Allen (a journalist); children: (first marriage) Kate; (second marriage) Halley, Julie. *Education:* Attended Art Students League, New York City, 1946, and Pratt Institute, 1947-48 and 1949-51.

ADDRESSES: Home—325 West End Ave., New York, NY 10023. *Office*—c/o Universal Press Syndicate, 4900 Main St., Kansas City, MO 64112.

CAREER: Assistant to cartoonist Will Eisner, 1946-51, and ghostwriter for Eisner's comic book "The Spirit," 1949-51; author of syndicated cartoon strip, "Clifford," 1949-51; held a variety of positions in the art field, 1953-56, including producer of slide films, writer for Columbia Broadcasting System, Inc.'s (CBS's) "Terry Toons," and designer of booklets for an art firm; author of cartoon strip (originally entitled "Sick, Sick, Sick," later changed to "Feiffer"), published in *Village Voice,* 1956-97, published weekly in London *Observer,* 1958-66, and 1972-82, and regularly in *Playboy,* 1959—, *New Yorker,* 1993—, and *New Statesman & Society,* 1994—; syndicated cartoonist, 1959—. Faculty member, Yale Drama School, 1973-74. Senior fellow, National Arts Journalism Program, Columbia University, 1997-98. *Military service:* U.S. Army, Signal Corps, 1951-53; worked in cartoon animation unit.

MEMBER: PEN, American Academy of Arts and Letters (board of directors), Authors League of America, Authors Guild (life member), Dramatists Guild (member of council), Writers Guild of America, East.

AWARDS, HONORS: Special George Polk Memorial Award, 1962; named most promising playwright of 1966-67 season by New York drama critics, London Theatre Critics Award, 1967, Outer Circle Critics Award, 1969, and Obie Award from the *Village Voice,* 1969, all for *Little Murders;* Outer Circle Critics Award, 1970, for *The White House Murder Case;* Pulitzer Prize, 1986, for editorial cartooning.

WRITINGS:

CARTOON COLLECTIONS

Sick, Sick, Sick, McGraw, 1958, published with introduction by Kenneth Tynan, Collins, 1959.
Passionella, and Other Stories (also see below), McGraw, 1959.
Boy, Girl, Boy, Girl, Random House, 1961.
Feiffer's Album, Random House, 1963.
The Penguin Feiffer, Penguin, 1966.
Feiffer's Marriage Manual, Random House, 1967.
Feiffer on Civil Rights, Anti-Defamation League of B'nai B'rith, 1967.
Pictures at a Prosecution: Drawings and Text from the Chicago Conspiracy Trial, Grove, 1971.
Feiffer on Nixon: The Cartoon Presidency, Random House, 1974.

(With Israel Horovitz) *VD Blues,* Avon, 1974.
Tantrum: A Novel in Cartoons, Knopf, 1979.
Jules Feiffer's America: From Eisenhower to Reagan, edited by Steve Heller, Knopf, 1982.
Marriage Is an Invasion of Privacy and Other Dangerous Views, Andrews & McMeel, 1984.
Feiffer's Children, Andrews & McMeel, 1986.
Ronald Reagan in Movie America: A Jules Feiffer Production, Andrews & McMeel, 1988.
The Complete Color Terry & the Pirates, Remco, 1990.

PUBLISHED PLAYS

The Explainers (satirical review; produced in Chicago at Playwright's Cabaret Theatre, May 9, 1961), McGraw, 1960.
Crawling Arnold (one act; first produced in Spoleto, Italy, at Festival of Two Worlds, June 28, 1961; first produced in United States in Cambridge, MA, at Poets' Theatre, 1961), Dramatists Play Service, 1963.
Hold Me! (first produced Off-Broadway at American Place Theatre, January, 1977), Random House, 1963.
The Unexpurgated Memoirs of Bernard Mergendeiler (one-act; first produced in Los Angeles, at the Mark Taper Forum, October 9, 1967), Random House, 1965.
Little Murders (two-act comedy; first produced on Broadway at Broadhurst Theatre, April 25, 1967; first American play produced on the West End by Royal Shakespeare Co. at Aldwych Theatre, 1967; also see below), Random House, 1968, reprinted, Penguin, 1983.
(Contributor) "Dick and Jane" (one act; produced in New York City at Eden Theatre as part of *Oh! Calcutta!,* devised by Tynan, June 17, 1969; also see below), published in *Oh! Calcutta!,* edited by Tynan, Grove, 1969.
Feiffer's People: Sketches and Observations (produced as *Feiffer's People* in Edinburgh, Scotland, at International Festival of Music and Drama, August, 1968), Dramatists Play Service, 1969.
The White House Murder Case: A Play in Two Acts [and] Dick and Jane: A One-Act Play (*The White House Murder Case* first produced Off-Broadway at Circle in the Square Downtown, February 18, 1970), Grove, 1970.
Knock Knock (first produced Off-Off-Broadway at Circle Repertory Theatre, January 18, 1976), Hill & Wang, 1976.

Elliot Loves (first produced on Broadway, 1989), Grove, 1989.
Anthony Rose, Dramatists Play Service, 1990.

UNPUBLISHED PLAYS

The World of Jules Feiffer, produced in New Jersey at Hunterdon Hills Playhouse, 1962.
God Bless, first produced in New Haven, CT, at Yale School of Drama, October 10, 1968; produced on the West End by Royal Shakespeare Co. at Aldwych Theatre, 1968.
Munro (adapted by Feiffer from story in *Passionella, and Other Stories*), first produced in Prospect Park, Brooklyn, August 15, 1971.
(With others) *Watergate Classics,* first produced at Yale School of Drama, November 16, 1973.
Grownups, first produced in Cambridge, MA, at Loeb Drama Center, June, 1981; produced on Broadway at Lyceum Theater, December, 1981.
A Think Piece, first produced Off-Off-Broadway at Circle Repertory Theatre, 1982.
Carnal Knowledge (revised version of play of same title originally written c. 1970; also see below), first produced in Houston, at Stages Repertory Theater, spring, 1988.

Also author of *Interview* and *You Should Have Caught Me at the White House,* both c. 1962.

SCREENPLAYS

Munro (animated cartoon; adapted by Feiffer from story in *Passionella, and Other Stories*), Rembrandt Films, 1961.
Carnal Knowledge (adapted from Feiffer's unpublished, unproduced play of same title written c. 1970), Avco Embassy, 1971.
Little Murders (adapted by author from play of same title), Twentieth Century-Fox, 1971.
Popeye, Paramount/Walt Disney Productions, 1980.

Also author of unproduced screenplays, *Little Brucie, Bernard and Huey,* and *I Want to Go Home.*

OTHER

(Illustrator) Robert Mines, *My Mind Went All to Pieces,* Dial, 1959.
(Illustrator) Norton Juster, *The Phantom Tollbooth,* Random House, 1961.
Harry, the Rat with Women (novel), McGraw, 1963.
(Editor and annotator) *The Great Comic Book Heroes,* Dial, 1965.

Silverlips (teleplay), Public Broadcasting Service (PBS), 1972.
(With Herb Gardner, Peter Stone, and Neil Simon) *Happy Endings* (teleplay), American Broadcasting Companies (ABC), 1975.
Akroyd (novel), Simon & Schuster, 1977.
(Author of introduction) Rick Marshall, editor, *The Complete E. C. Segar Popeye,* Fantagraphics (Stamford, CT), 1984.
Feiffer: The Collected Works, Vol. 1: Clifford, Fantagraphics, 1989.
Feiffer: The Collected Works, Vol. 2: Munro, Fantagraphics, 1989.
Feiffer: The Collected Works, Vol. 3: "Sick, Sick, Sick," Fantagraphics, 1991.
Feiffer: The Collected Works: Passionella, Fantagraphics, 1993.
The Man in the Ceiling (children's book), HarperCollins, 1993.
A Barrel of Laughs, A Vale of Tears (children's book), HarperCollins, 1995.

WORK IN PROGRESS: Feiffer's screenplay, *I Want to Go Home,* is being made into a film directed by Alain Resnais.

ADAPTATIONS: The Feiffer Film, based on Feiffer's cartoons, was released in 1965; *Harry, the Rat with Women* was made into a play and produced at Detroit Institute of Arts, 1966; *Passionella, and Other Stories* was adapted by Jerry Bock and Sheldon Harnick into "Passionella," a one-act musical produced on Broadway as part of *The Apple Tree,* 1967; *Jules Feiffer's America: From Eisenhower to Reagan* was adapted by Russell Vandenbroucke into a play entitled *Feiffer's America; What Are We Saying?,* a parody on Feiffer's cartoons, was produced in Rome.

SIDELIGHTS: On learning that *Hudson Review* contributor John Simon describes Jules Feiffer's play *Little Murders* as "bloody-minded," and makes reference to its "grotesque horror" and "hideous reality," those who only know Feiffer as a cartoonist and not as a playwright might be more than a little surprised. Such brutal words are unexpected when used to characterize the work of a cartoonist—whom we might imagine would only want to make us laugh—but, then, Feiffer comes to his work as a playwright from the perspective of someone, as Clive Barnes points out in the *New York Times,* who despite his profession "never makes jokes." Instead of looking for a laugh, Barnes observes, Feiffer "muses on urban man, the cesspool of urban man's mind, the beauty of his neurosis, and the inevitability of his wilting disappointment." The laughter Feiffer seeks centers on our willingness to find humor in some of life's darkest moments.

Feiffer reveals the origins of his somewhat black humor in a *Washington Post* interview with Henry Allen: "Back then [in the 1950s], comedy was still working in a tradition that came out of World War I. . . . Comedy was mired in insults and gags. It was Bob Hope and Bing Cosby, Burns and Allen, Ozzie and Harriet. There was no such thing as comedy about relationships, nothing about the newly urban and collegiate Americans. What I was interested in was using humor as a reflection of one's own confusion, ambivalence and dilemma, dealing with sexual life as one knew it to be." The *Chicago Tribune*'s Connie Lauerman notes that because his cartoons dealt with the social reality of the day, Feiffer became "the original satirist-spokesman for the urban, middle-class, newly educated, going-through-analysis, post World War II generation." His cartoons presented a mixture of social commentary and political satire previously reserved for the editorial page of the newspaper.

From the beginning of his career Feiffer avoided the silliness expected of a non-political cartoonist and created what Barnes calls "the magically peculiar and peculiarly magical world of Feiffer: a world full of the perils of rejection, the dangers of acceptance, the wild and perpetual struggles of ego for id, the dire discomfort of parenthood, [and] the unceasing wars between men and women." His characters include people who are odd enough to be humorous but who at the same time can elicit a painful, empathetic response from his readers: Passionella, who achieves movie stardom because she has the world's largest breasts; Bernard Mergeneiler, known for his romantic failures; and an inventor who creates a "Lonely Machine" that makes light conversation and delivers sympathetic remarks whenever necessary.

Feiffer's concerns as a cartoonist have followed him to the stage, as the *New York Times*'s Michiko Kakutani observes: "Clearly those cartoons . . . share with 'Grown Ups' and his earlier plays certain recognizable themes and preoccupations. The interest in adult responsibilities and the difficulty of 'growing up,' for instance, first surfaced in Mr. Feiffer's early cartoons about Munro, a 4-year-old boy who finds himself drafted into the Army; and it was developed further in such works as 'Tantrum,' the story of a husband and father who reverts to being a 2-year old." In the *Chicago Tribune,* Richard Christiansen

notes that "Hold Me!" is filled with "humorous Jules Feiffer sketches that deal with the . . . cartoonist's constant themes of anxiety, depression, rejection, disappointment, and other light matters."

Some critics fault Feiffer's plays for being too dependent on his cartoons for inspiration. In the *Village Voice* Carll Tucker, for example, comments: "Feiffer's genius as a cartoonist is for dramatic moments—establishing and comically concluding a situation in eight still frames. His characters have personality only for the purpose of making a point: They do not have, as breathing dramatic characters must, the freedom to develop, to grow away from their status as idea-bearers." A similar criticism is leveled by the *New York Times*'s Frank Rich, who writes: "As yet more cartoonist than dramatist, Mr. Feiffer presents his most inspired riffs as set pieces, often monologues."

Other critics voice their approval for what they see as the influence of Feiffer's cartoons in his work for the theater. In Alan Rich's *New York* magazine review of Feiffer's play, *Knock Knock,* for example, the critic notes: "What gives [*Knock Knock*] its humor—and a great deal of it is screamingly funny—is the incredible accuracy of [Feiffer's] language, and his use of it to paint the urban neurosis in exact colors. This we know from his cartoons, and we learn it anew from this endearing, congenial theater piece." Other commentators on New York's theatrical scene, such as *Dictionary of Literary Biography* contributor Thomas Edward Ruddick, are able to separate Feiffer's dramatic work from his other creative efforts. "Feiffer's plays show considerable complexity of plot, character, and idea, and command attention," Ruddick asserts, "not dependent upon Feiffer's other achievements. His plays, independently, constitute a noteworthy body of work."

Those who enjoyed Feiffer for his adults-only satire may have been surprised to see the cartoonist venture into the children's book market in the 1990s. For his part, Feiffer is the father to essentially three generations of girls; in 1993, when *Man in the Ceiling* was published, he had 31-year-old Kate, 11-year-old Halley (to whom that book is dedicated) and 15-month-old Julie. "I'm glad they're girls," the author tells *Publishers Weekly* writer John F. Baker. "Boys are terribly active and geared toward just the sort of sports I was never any good at."

Feiffer's attraction to the youth market arose "from a combination of his fond recollections of reading to

Halley as a small child . . . and an illustrator friend's interest in doing a book," according to Baker. With *The Man in the Ceiling,* Feiffer writes and illustrates the tale of Jimmy, a little boy who dreams of being a cartoonist. His aptitude for drawing underscores the fact that the boy is "not much good at anything else, including such boyish but unFeiffer-like pastimes as sports," Baker continues.

"Yes, I did cartoons as a kid, just like Jimmy," Feiffer admits in the *Publishers Weekly* piece. "And I rediscovered some of them while I was working on [the book]. But those drawings of Jimmy's were the toughest part; I had to get the tone just right—they mustn't be too satirical—and it terrified me for a long time. I left them right to the end."

Feiffer's caution was rewarded by the favorable reviews that greeted *The Man in the Ceiling.* Jonathan Fast, in fact, singles out "Jimmy's" artwork, noting in his *New York Times Book Review* piece, "the adventures of Mini-Man, Bullethead and The Man in the Ceiling, Jimmy's *magnum opus,* are reprinted in glorious pencil and run as long as six pages." Evidently Feiffer's efforts also reached a younger audience: Nine-year-old reviewer Erin Smith tells the *San Francisco Review of Books* that the work "has great pictures. The story is just as funny. The best pictures are the comics that Jimmy drew."

In 1995 Feiffer released his second children's book, *A Barrel of Laughs, A Vale of Tears.* The volume is comprised of fairy tales with a slightly acerbic air meant to appeal to children and parents alike. Featuring King Whatchamacallit, who speaks in spoonerisms: "My son, when you're around, no till gets soiled—er, no soil gets tilled; no noo gets shailed—that is, no shoe gets nailed." Another urbane character, J. Wellington Wizard, amuses children's author Daniel Pinkwater. "Written with conviction, not to say innocence, Mr. Feiffer's ebullient story renders the reader capable of maximum suspension of disbelief—and what would be corny is touching instead," Pinkwater declares in the *New York Times Book Review.*

As Feiffer reveals to Baker, the best part of being a children's author is the honest response from his young readers: "It's much more direct even than in the theatre, so much more heartening. You create something out of love and devotion, and when you get it back, you can't believe it."

BIOGRAPHICAL/CRITICAL SOURCES:

BOOKS

Anobile, Richard J., *Popeye: The Movie Novel,* Avon, 1980.
Cohen, Sarah Blacher, editor, *From Hester Street to Hollywood: The Jewish-American Stage and Screen,* Indiana University Press, 1983.
Contemporary Dramatists, 4th edition, St. James Press, 1988.
Contemporary Literary Criticism, Gale (Detroit), Volume 2, 1974, Volume 8, 1978; Volume 64, 1991.
Corliss, Richard, *Talking Pictures: Screenwriters in the American Cinema,* Overlook, 1974.
Dictionary of Literary Biography, Gale, Volume 7: *Twentieth-Century American Dramatists,* 1981, Volume 44: *American Screenwriters, Second Series,* 1986.

PERIODICALS

American Cinematographer, January 1971, p. 37.
American Film, December, 1980; July-August, 1987, p. 36.
Chicago, April, 1988, p. 32.
Chicago Tribune, June 29, 1979; November 2, 1982.
Commonweal, December 1, 1989, p. 676; August 10, 1990, p. 455.
Harper's, September, 1961, pp. 58-62.
Hudson Review, summer, 1967.
Los Angeles Times, November 13, 1988.
Newsweek, June 18, 1990, p. 58.
New York, February 2, 1976; December 21, 1981, pp. 81-2; May 25, 1987, p. 108; November 26, 1990, p. 33; December 3, 1990, p. 148.
New Yorker, May 18, 1987, p. 87; November 2, 1992, p. 55.
New York Times, January 21, 1977; December 15, 1981; May 7, 1987.
New York Times Book Review, December 19, 1982, p. 8; November 14, 1993, p. 57; December 31, 1995, p. 12.
New York Times Magazine, May 16, 1976.
Publishers Weekly, October 25, 1993, p. 62; November 20, 1995.
San Francisco Review of Books, April/May 1994.
School Library Journal, February, 1994, p. 102.
Time, June 18, 1990, p. 85.
Village Voice, February 2, 1976.
Washington Post, August 17, 1979.*

FERRARS, E. X.
See BROWN, Morna Doris

*   *   *

FERRARS, Elizabeth
See BROWN, Morna Doris

*   *   *

FERRIDGE, Philippa 1933-
   (Philippa Wiat)

PERSONAL: Born October 2, 1933, in London, England; daughter of Henry Edmund (a civil servant) and Anne (Turner) Wyatt; married Dennis Ferridge (an accountant); children: Elaine, Teresa, Francesca. *Education:* Attended grammar school in Wimbledon, England. *Religion:* Roman Catholic.

ADDRESSES: Home—19 Normandale, Bexhill-on-Sea, East Sussex TN39 3LU, England.

CAREER: Writer, 1972—.

WRITINGS:

UNDER NAME PHILIPPA WIAT

NOVELS

Like as the Roaring Waves, R. Hale (London), 1972.
The Master of Blandeston Hall, R. Hale, 1973.
The Heir of Allington, R. Hale, 1973.
The Knight of Allington, R. Hale, 1974.
The Rebel of Allington, R. Hale, 1974.
Lord of the Black Boar, R. Hale, 1975.
Sword of Woden, R. Hale, 1975.
Tree of Vortigern, R. Hale, 1976.
The Queen's Fourth Husband, R. Hale, 1976.
Lion without Claws, R. Hale, 1976, St. Martin's (New York City), 1977.
The Atheling, R. Hale, 1977.
Sound Now the Passing-Bell, R. Hale, 1977.
My Lute Be Still, R. Hale, 1977.
Raven in the Wind, R. Hale, 1978.
Maid of Gold, R. Hale, 1978.
Yet a Lion, R. Hale, 1978.
Westerfalca, R. Hale, 1979.
The Golden Chariot, R. Hale, 1979.

The Four-Poster, R. Hale, 1979.
Lord of the Wolf, R. Hale, 1980.
Shadow of Samain, R. Hale, 1980.
The King's Vengeance, R. Hale, 1981.
The Mistletoe Bough, R. Hale, 1981.
Bride in Darkness, R. Hale, 1982.
Wynchwood, R. Hale, 1982.
Five Gold Rings, R. Hale, 1983.
Children of the Spring, R. Hale, 1983.
Cartismandua, R. Hale, 1984.
Prince of the White Rose, R. Hale, 1984.
Queen-Gold, R. Hale, 1985.
Fair Rosamond, R. Hale, 1985.
The Grey Goose Wing, R. Hale, 1986.
The Whyte Swan, R. Hale, 1986.
Wear a Green Kirtle, R. Hale, 1987.
The Cloister and the Flame, R. Hale, 1988.
Phantasmagoria, R. Hale, 1988.
The Kingmaker's Daughter, R. Hale, 1989.
One Child Bride, R. Hale, 1990.
The Lady Editha, R. Hale, 1991.
The Hammer and the Sword: A Novel of Wat Tyler, R. Hale, 1992.
The Lovers, R. Hale, 1993.

OTHER

Editor, *The Law List,* 1953-67. *The Golden Chariot* has been translated into Serbo-Croatian.

SIDELIGHTS: Philippa Ferridge was first drawn to writing historical novels after researching her own family history, especially her notable ancestor the poet Sir Thomas Wyatt. Writing under the pseudonym Philippa Wiat, a variation on her maiden name of Wyatt, Ferridge usually sets her novels in sixteenth-century England. "Wiat is happiest when writing of the 16th century," Judith Rhodes comments in *Twentieth-Century Romance and Historical Writers,* "and it is in this era that the bulk of her novels are set. Her approach varies—in some novels actual historical personages form the pivot of the story, in others the characters are wholly fictional."

Rhodes finds that when Wiat focuses on developing characters based on actual figures, her novels are at their best: "Where she does allow the personalities to develop, the novels at once become more interesting and more believable." Rhodes cites *The Whyte Swan* as a case in point. It is, Rhodes believes, "one of her better novels. . . . One particular scene in this book, between Edward and his mother Isabelle . . . , is especially successful because the strength of the personalities, and the interplay between them, are allowed free rein."

Wiat's *Lion Without Claws* also received critical praise. Telling a dramatized version of the real-life Philip Howard's rise to prominence during the reign of Elizabeth I, the novel details Philip's seduction of the queen as well as "sundry lords and ladies on the side," as the critic for *Kirkus Reviews* explains. Philip's libertine lifestyle is cut short when he experiences a mystical vision which returns him to the Church. This return to a moral life ironically led him to be imprisoned by his enemies at court. Andrea Lee Shuey in *Library Journal* calls *Lion Without Claws* "a well-written historical novel."

Ferridge told *CA:* "From Sir Thomas Wyatt, the sixteenth-century poet, onward, my family has produced more than its fair share of writers and poets, though I myself did not start writing professionally until the youngest of my three daughters had reached school age. It did not occur to me until the day I started writing that I would be a writer, although many people find that difficult to believe. I simply woke up one morning with an urge to write. I can only assume that my writing genes had started working, for it was then I had the idea of writing a saga of my family, writing under my maiden name, but using the archaic spelling, Wiat.

"I had grown up with the knowledge that I came from a literary family, which included Sir Thomas, his grandson George Wyatt, who was the first biographer of Anne Boleyn, and his great-grandson, Sir Francis Wyatt, who became governor of Virginia in the early days of colonization, and also wrote poetry.

"I spent many days at the British Museum, researching that large collection of family papers known as 'The Wyatt Manuscripts,' and at home I wrote and rewrote almost unceasingly until my first novel was completed.

"It is generally agreed amongst authors that everyone thinks writing is easy—except authors! In my experience nothing is more true. I next started writing my Allington trilogy and for the three years following worked with feverish intensity, making up for lost time as it were, writing for twelve hours a day, seven days a week.

"The Allington trilogy was centered around Sir Thomas Wyatt who, born at Allington Castle in 1503, became a favorite of Henry VIII and ambassador to Spain. Sir Thomas was reputedly the lover of Anne Boleyn, the second wife of King Henry VIII. Both research and family tradition have convinced me that not only was Sir Thomas Anne's lover, he was moreover the father of her daughter, Queen Elizabeth I."

BIOGRAPHICAL/CRITICAL SOURCES:

BOOKS

Twentieth-Century Romance and Historical Writers, third edition, St. James Press (Detroit, MI), 1994.

PERIODICALS

Books and Bookmen, May, 1983, p. 31.
Eastbourne Herald, October 27, 1973; December 10, 1977; April 15, 1978.
Kent Messenger, May, 1976.
Kirkus Reviews, January 1, 1978, p. 21.
Library Journal, April 1, 1978, p. 778.
Sunday Telegraph, July 16, 1978.
Times Literary Supplement, January 1, 1982, p. 12.
Wimbledon News, September 17, 1976.

    *   *   *

FINKEL, Donald 1929-

PERSONAL: Born October 21, 1929, in New York, NY; son of Saul Aaron (an attorney) and Meta (Rosenthal) Finkel; married Constance Urdang (a writer), August 14, 1956; children: Liza, Thomas Noah, Amy Maria. *Education:* Columbia University, B.S., 1952, M.A., 1953

ADDRESSES: Home—2051 Park Ave., #D, St. Louis, MO 63104.

CAREER: University of Iowa, Iowa City, instructor, 1957-58; Bard College, Annandale-on-Hudson, NY, instructor, 1958-60; Washington University, St. Louis MO, poet in residence, 1960-91. Visiting professor, Bennington College, 1966-67; visiting lecturer, Princeton University, 1985.

MEMBER: Cave Research Foundation, Phi Beta Kappa.

AWARDS, HONORS: Helen Bullis Prize, 1964, for *Simeon;* Guggenheim fellow, 1967; National Book Award nomination, 1970, for *The Garbage Wars;* Ingram Merrill Foundation grant, 1972; National Endowment for the Arts grant, 1973; Theodore Roethke Memorial Award, 1974, for *Adequate Earth;* National Book Critics Circle Award nomination, 1975, for *A Mote in Heaven's Eye,* and 1981, for *What Manner of Beast;* Morton Dauwen Zabel Award, 1980, for *Endurance: An Antarctic Idyll* [and] *Going Under.*

WRITINGS:

POETRY

The Clothing's New Emperor, edited by John Hall Wheelock, Scribner (New York City), 1959.
Simeon, Atheneum (New York City), 1964.
A Joyful Noise, Atheneum, 1966.
Answer Back, Atheneum, 1968.
The Garbage Wars, Atheneum, 1970.
Adequate Earth, Atheneum, 1972.
A Mote in Heaven's Eye, Atheneum, 1975.
Endurance: An Antarctic Idyll [and] *Going Under,* Atheneum, 1978.
What Manner of Beast, Atheneum, 1981.
The Detachable Man, Atheneum, 1984.
(With others) *Reading Ourselves to Sleep,* Pterodactyl Press, 1985.
Selected Shorter Poems, Atheneum, 1987.
The Wake of the Electron, Atheneum, 1987.
Beyond Despair, Garlic Press (St. Louis), 1994.

OTHER

The Jar (play), produced in Boston, 1961.
(Translator) *A Splintered Mirror: Chinese Poetry from the Democracy Movement,* North Point Press (San Francisco), 1991.

Contributor to *Poetry, New Yorker,* and other publications. A collection of Finkel's manuscripts is housed at Washington University Library, St. Louis.

WORK IN PROGRESS: Vexed Questions: The Wild Child, Jean-Marc Itard, and Other Quandaries, a book-length poem; *The Analects of Bone,* "a long poem dealing with prehistoric cave painting and related reflections on the beginnings of the aesthetic impulse."

SIDELIGHTS: Donald Finkel is a poet who uses a collage style to bring together fragments of text into

a whole. "Finkel's collages," writes Dennis Lynch in *Contemporary Poets,* "are daring attempts to bring unity to the world's chaos through art. At his worst he can be obscure and pedantic; at his best he can produce works of startling resonance." Finkel's forte, in the opinion of *Nation* contributor Mary Kinzie, is "finding eloquent and credible language for the speechless and the alien"—a feat accomplished by "extraordinary leaps of insight." *Saturday Review* critic Chad Walsh applauds Finkel's "impressive sense of poetic architecture," noting that "an unsolemn but not frivolous vitality charges through much of his verse."

This vitality is evident in Finkel's 1966 publication, *A Joyful Noise,* which reveals the author to be "a creator of comic extravagance, of an imagination which responds to the seemingly chance, grotesque and unreal nature of present-day life in its own terms," according to *Poetry* reviewer R. J. Mills. Finkel's poems are grimly and outrageously funny, bawdy, satirical, and dreamlike. His characters comprise "a Jewish-French-Irish stew whose chefs might be [Yiddish storyteller] Isaac Singer, [surrealist poet] Andre Breton, and [theater-of-the-absurd playwright] Samuel Beckett," Mills says.

Finkel's 1968 collection, *Answer Back,* is, according to Lynch, "an astonishing book arranged around the metaphor of cave exploration. . . . Speleology, though, is only one of Finkel's concerns here: his other topics include Vietnam, the relation of the sexes, the nature of religion, the function of poetry, the origins of the universe, and much more. His voice modulates from biblical tones to satiric ones, and his verse ranges from lyrics to doggerel. . . . Needless to say, the whole effect is rather staggering." Speaking of the collage technique used in *Answer Back,* Walsh calls Finkel "T. S. Eliot reborn, so far as much of the technique is concerned." The book is one long poem which, "zig-zagging between the neolithic past and the napalm present, creates a sense of the human condition in which all times are blended into a dimension of external experience. This poet is worthy grist for the scholarly commentators, but meanwhile I pause to celebrate his extraordinary sense of language and acuteness of observation," Walsh says. Robert Pack in the *Saturday Review* believes that the quotes and allusions in the poem are carried "by its own strong rhythm, its discrete images, and above all, by its courage to make affirmations seem possible and true in a difficult world." Lynch concludes that "while Finkel's erudition is impressive and the clever juxtaposition he creates amusing, he also seems too unrestrained and has produced a poem too fragmented."

In the poetry collection *Adequate Earth,* Finkel turns his attention to the continent of Antarctica, a place he visited in 1970 as a member of a scientific expedition. Finkel's vision of the remote continent's alien landscape reveals its beauty and mystery. Lynch describes the collection as a "masterpiece" and finds Finkel to be "daring in his choice of subject." Louis Coxe in a *New Republic* review recommends *Adequate Earth,* calling it "a splendid piece of work . . . rich, complex, resonant and—simple, in the best sense." Lynch concludes that "*Adequate Earth* is one of the few fine contemporary epic poems. It has a vast sweep: part of it is mythmaking, . . . part of it is devastating satire, . . . part of it is tragedy in its accounts of ill-fated attempts to explore the polar regions; and all of it is a tribute to man's ability to endure in even the harshest of worlds."

Finkel records another view of arctic wastelands in *Endurance: An Antarctic Idyll* [and] *Going Under,* two long poems about "the inhospitality of the earth." The first poem describes the shipwreck and rescue of a 1914 expedition to Antarctica led by Ernest Shackleton, notes John Fuller in the *Times Literary Supplement;* in the second, Finkel borrows the voices of two men who explored Kentucky's Mammoth Caves. Finkel uses the narrative to search "the dark beyond the dark," as it is named in the poem. An encounter with "moral conflict" or "the external verities" such as is available in similar works is lacking here, says Fuller, since the book casts man as "nothing more than a kind of biological rust clinging to the surface of our small planet." But G. E. Murray, writing in the *Nation,* feels that *Endurance* is the stronger of the two poems, since its story "of shipwreck and blind treks across glaciers build to an incantation of survival." Murray concludes, "Finkel's detailed pacing and breadth of voice make this a poetry of considerable scope and spirit."

In *A Mote in Heaven's Eye,* "Finkel has, as he has always had, an authentic rhythm, a colloquial and jeering tone, a surrealist humor and a gift for child-like diminution of life to cartoon dimensions. But these tricks are laid aside for a harsher outline in his . . . poems about Mexico, beautiful and clearly seen," writes Helen Vendler in the *New York Times Book Review.* Finkel's far-reaching surreal imagery at times requires more imagination than the *Western Humanities Review* contributor could muster; but

when successful, says the reviewer, those images make the poems "memorable." The same reviewer comments, "[Finkel's] tone is often absurdly grave and gravely ironic . . . . He controls a mixed style with a faultless ear."

For the poems in *What Manner of Beast,* Finkel returns to the collage method of organization. Using quotes from "a bizarre miscellany of sources," Finkel concentrates on the relationships between animals and humans to reflect on the perhaps arbitrary distinctions between the two forms of life, says Jay Parini in the *Times Literary Supplement.* "The boundaries between humans and the other creatures, he seems to be saying, grow ever hazier," observes Phoebe Pettingell. In the *New Leader,* she continues, "Ultimately humans and animals communicate affection and need—a universal connective according to [Finkel]. He sees all creatures as sojourners in a strange land, wandering bewildered and delighted among half-understood objects." Kinzie summarizes in the *Nation:* "Owing to the correspondence between these two realms, every cruel act by a beast (for example, rival apes tearing each other's infants to bits) is matched with equally gratuitous acts committed by men. . . . For every dark intention within primitive men alluded to in his sources, he excerpts yet more chilling and indefensible motives on the part of men presumed civilized."

In *A Splintered Mirror: Chinese Poetry from the Democracy Movement,* Finkel translated the works of seven poets of the Misty Poetry school, "so called for the blurriness of the poems' themes, a vagueness intended to subvert the social realist aesthetic enforced by the Chinese state," as the critic for *Publishers Weekly* states. "Through apparently personal themes," Kitty Chen Dean writes in *Library Journal,* "the poems offer a political message that is simply a call for freedom to write poetry." The *Publishers Weekly* critic finds that "these poems effectively capture various moods and feelings," but the strongest of them "ponder the loss of love."

Coxe places Finkel among those poets who "know their craft and . . . have something to say." According to Richard Howard in *Alone with America: The Art of Poetry in the United States since 1950,* "Finkel's purpose is to establish the poem in a world without myth, on the surface. . . . The poem becomes Finkel's direct experience of what surrounds him—imperfect, but continuing—without his being able to shield himself by a mythology or a metaphysic in his combat with the damages of a lifetime, the disgraces of a death." His creed, concludes Howard, is stated in these lines from *Answer Back:* "My angel is mortal, for which, by the gods, / I believe in him the more."

BIOGRAPHICAL/CRITICAL SOURCES:

BOOKS

Contemporary Poets, 6th edition, St. James Press (Detroit), 1996.
Howard, Richard, *Alone with America: The Art of Poetry in the United States since 1950,* Atheneum, 1969, enlarged edition, 1980.

PERIODICALS

Best Sellers, March, 1982.
Booklist, April 1, 1973, p. 738; September 15, 1975, p. 111.
Georgia Review, winter, 1976, p. 1021; fall, 1979, p. 699.
Hudson Review, autumn, 1970, p. 565; spring, 1976, p. 115.
Library Journal, February 15, 1991, pp. 197-198.
Nation, May 19, 1979, p. 578; December 12, 1981, p. 647.
New Leader, March 8, 1982, p. 14.
New Republic, February 3, 1973, p. 30.
New York Times, March 1, 1966.
New York Times Book Review, December 20, 1964; September 4, 1966, p. 4; November 22, 1970, p. 30; September 7, 1975, p. 6.
Parnassus, fall/winter, 1973; spring/summer, 1979.
Poetry, July, 1965, p. 309; November, 1966, p. 114; February, 1969, p. 344; November, 1971, p. 99; September, 1973, p. 351; February, 1976, p. 292; December, 1982, p. 170.
Prairie Schooner, summer, 1972, p. 176.
Publishers Weekly, January 18, 1991, p. 53.
St. Petersburg Times, April 3, 1988.
Saturday Review, January 2, 1965, p. 30; May 21, 1966, p. 31; August 24, 1968, p. 40.
Times Literary Supplement, January 18, 1980, p. 65; July 2, 1982, p. 720.
Village Voice, December 15, 1975, p. 73.
Virginia Quarterly Review, winter, 1967, p. XVII; autumn, 1968, p. CL; autumn, 1982, p. 133.
Washington Post Book World, July 28, 1968, p.4.
Western Humanities Review, winter, 1969, p. 93; autumn, 1976, p. 364.
Yale Review, March, 1976, p. 425.

FISCHER, Bruno 1908-
(Russell Gray)

PERSONAL: Born June 29, 1908, in Germany; came to the United States in 1913, naturalized citizen, 1919; son of Herman (a grocer) and Sarah (Metzger) Fischer; married Ruth Miller (a school secretary), March 20, 1934; children: Adam, Nora Fischer Ernst. *Education:* Graduated from Rand School of Social Science. *Politics:* Social Democrat. *Religion:* Jewish.

ADDRESSES: Home and office—19 Twin Pines Rd., Putnam Valley, NY 10579.

CAREER: Long Island Daily Press, Long Island City, NY, reporter, 1929-31; editor of *Labor Voice,* 1931-32, and *Socialist Call,* 1934-36; Macmillan Publishing Co., Inc., New York City, executive editor, 1961-65; Arco Publishing Co., Inc., New York City, education editor, 1965-70; writer, 1970—.

MEMBER: Authors Guild of Authors League of America, Mystery Writers of America, Social Democrats, Workmen's Circle.

WRITINGS:

MYSTERY NOVELS

So Much Blood, Greystone Press (New York City), 1939, published as *Stairway to Death,* Pyramid (New York City), 1951.
The Hornet's Nest, Morrow (New York City), 1943.
Quoth the Raven, Doubleday (New York City), 1944, published as *Croaked the Raven,* Quality Press (London), 1947, published as *The Fingered Man,* Ace Books (New York City), 1953.
The Dead Men Grin, McKay (Philadelphia), 1945.
The Spider Lily, McKay, 1946.
The Pigskin Bag, Ziff-Davis (New York City), 1946.
Kill to Fit, Green (New York City), 1946.
More Deaths Than One, Ziff-Davis, 1947.
The Bleeding Scissors, Ziff-Davis, 1948, published as *The Scarlet Scissors,* Foulsham (London), 1950.
The Restless Hands, Dodd (New York City), 1948.
The Angels Fell, Dodd, 1950.
(Under pseudonym Russell Gray) *The Lustful Ape* Lion (New York City), 1950, published under name Bruno Fischer, Fawcett (New York City), 1959.
The Silent Dust, Dodd, 1950.
The House of Flesh, Fawcett, 1950.

The Lady Kills, Fawcett, 1951.
The Paper Circle, Dodd, 1951, published as *Stripped for Murder,* New American Library (New York City), 1953.
Fools Walk In, Fawcett, 1951.
The Fast Buck, Fawcett, 1952.
(Editor) *Crook's Tour,* Dodd, 1953.
Run for Your Life, Fawcett, 1953.
So Wicked My Love, Fawcett, 1954.
Knee-Deep in Death, Fawcett, 1956.
Murder in the Raw, Fawcett, 1957.
Second-Hand Nude, Fawcett, 1959.
The Girl Between, Fawcett, 1960.
The Evil Days, Random House (New York City), 1974.

OTHER

Work appears in anthologies, including *Best Detective Stories of the Year 1945,* edited by David Coxe Cooke, Dutton (New York City), 1946, *Rue Morgue No. 1,* edited by Rex Stout and Louis Greenfield, Creative Age Press (New York City), 1946, *Best Detective Stories of the Year 1950,* edited by David Coxe Cooke, Dutton, 1950, *Dangerous Dames,* edited by Brett Halliday, Dell (New York City), 1955, *Best Detective Stories of the Year, 17th Annual Collection,* edited by David Coxe Cooke, Dutton, 1962, and *The Hard-Boiled Detective: Stories from Black Mask Magazine 1920-1950,* edited by Herbert Ruhm, Vintage (New York City), 1977. Contributor of about five hundred stories, some under pseudonym Russell Gray, and several hundred articles to magazines, including *Black Mask.* Fischer's books have been translated into eleven languages.

SIDELIGHTS: Beginning as a prolific writer for the pulp magazines of the 1930s, often under his pseudonym of Russel Gray, Bruno Fischer turned in the 1940s to writing mystery novels. By the 1950s, Fischer was writing original paperback mysteries for Fawcett, one of the leading paperback houses of the time. Specializing in stories about what Bill Pronzini in the *St. James Guide to Crime and Mystery Writers* calls "shocking and gruesome crimes," Fischer nonetheless handles this material in a "deft and restrained" manner, Pronzini states. Fischer places the "emphasis on detection and characterization rather than on the lurid aspects," Pronzini writes. "One of his recurring themes is the morality play: ordinary people thrust into extraordinary situations in which their moral standards are tested and sometimes corrupted."

Many of Fischer's novels are set in the small towns of upstate New York and dealt with ordinary people confronting unusual crimes. Fischer's virtues as a writer, according to Anthony Boucher in the *New York Times,* include "a nice feeling for upstate New York, a fine sense of the impinging of crime and violence on ordinary life, [and] a biting handling of the economic factors in human motivation."

Fischer earned critical acclaim for several of his novels, including *Quoth the Raven* and *The Hornet's Nest.* In *The Hornet's Nest* Fischer tells an "action-filled tale of mysterious deaths, fortune-telling ladies, and super-tough gangsters," as the reviewer for *Saturday Review of Literature* writes. Will Cuppy in *Weekly Book Review* writes: "Fischer spins his amazing narrative with a straight face, but there can be no harm in taking it with a smile." *Quoth the Raven* contains what a *Saturday Review of Literature* reviewer calls "plentiful action, some good characters, and [a] sinuous plot," while Will Cuppy states that "customers who demand surprise at any cost should be satisfied." So twisted is the plot that Isaac Anderson in the *New York Times* claims "high marks for you if you can spot the guilty one."

Fischer was not adverse to experimenting with the structure of his novels. In *More Deaths Than One,* for instance, he presented eight different versions of a murder—one version per character. "This innovation," writes Jack Glick in the *New York Times,* "is both refreshing and successful in that it reveals the working of each suspect's mind yet still keeps the culprit a shrouded specter until the last chapter."

Fischer once wrote *CA:* "Though I've had my flings at editing and newspaper writing, I am essentially a free-lance writer—setting my own pace, working at home, being pretty much independent. I'm a storyteller, in particular, a recounter of mysteries, dedicated wholly to the printed word."

BIOGRAPHICAL/CRITICAL SOURCES:

BOOKS

St. James Guide to Crime and Mystery Writers, fourth edition, St. James Press (Detroit), 1996.

PERIODICALS

New Yorker, November 4, 1944, p. 20.
New York Times, October 29, 1944, p. 18; July 27, 1947, p. 19; October 7, 1951, p. 22.

Saturday Review of Literature, March 4, 1944, p. 27; October 28, 1944, p. 27.
Weekly Book Review, February 27, 1944, p. 10; October 22, 1944, p. 21.

*   *   *

FITZALAN, Roger
   See TREVOR, Elleston

*   *   *

FLEMING, Ian (Lancaster) 1908-1964
   (Atticus)

PERSONAL: Born May 28, 1908, in London, England; died August 12, 1964; son of Valentine (a major in the armed forces and a Conservative member of the British Parliament) and Evelyn Beatrice (Ste. Crois Rose) Fleming; married Anne Geraldine Charteris (formerly Lady Rothermere), March 24, 1952; children: Caspar. *Education:* Attended Eton, Royal Military Academy at Sandhurst, University of Munich, and University of Geneva. *Avocational interests:* Swimming, gambling, golf.

CAREER: Moscow correspondent for Reuters Ltd., London, England, 1929-33; associated with Cull & Co. (merchant bankers), London, England, 1933-35; stockbroker with Rowe & Pitman, London, England, 1935-39; returned to Moscow, 1939, officially as a reporter for *The Times,* London, unofficially as a representative of the Foreign Office; Kemsley (later Thomson) Newspapers, foreign manager, 1945-59; publisher of *The Book Collector,* 1949-64. *Military service:* Royal Naval Volunteer Reserve, 1939-45; lieutenant; did secret service work as a personal assistant to the director of Naval Intelligence, 1939-45.

MEMBER: Turf Club, Broodle's Club, Portland Club.

AWARDS, HONORS: Order of the Dannebrog, 1945; Young Reader's Choice Award, 1967, for *Chitty-Chitty-Bang-Bang.*

WRITINGS:

"JAMES BOND" SERIES

Casino Royale (also see below), J. Cape (London), 1953, Macmillan (New York City), 1954, published in paperback as *You Asked for It,* Popular Library (New York City), 1955.
Live and Let Die (also see below), J. Cape, 1954, Macmillan (New York City), 1955.
Moonraker (also see below), Macmillan, 1955, published as *Too Hot to Handle,* Perma Books (New York City), 1957.
Diamonds Are Forever (also see below), Macmillan, 1956.
From Russia, with Love (also see below), Macmillan, 1957.
Doctor No (also see below), Macmillan, 1958.
Goldfinger (also see below), Macmillan, 1959.
For Your Eyes Only: Five Secret Exploits of James Bond, Viking (New York City), 1960, published in England as *For Your Eyes Only: Five Secret Occasions in the Life of James Bond,* Cape, 1960.
Gilt-Edged Bonds: Casino Royale, From Russia, with Love, Doctor No, introduction by Paul Gallico, Macmillan, 1961.
Thunderball (also see below), Viking (New York City), 1961.
The Spy Who Loved Me (also see below), Viking, 1962.
On Her Majesty's Secret Service (also see below), New American Library (New York City), 1963.
You Only Live Twice (also see below), New American Library, 1964.
Bonded Fleming: A James Bond Omnibus (contains *Thunderball, For Your Eyes Only,* and *The Spy Who Loved Me*), Viking, 1965.
The Man with the Golden Gun (also see below), New American Library, 1965.
More Gilt-Edged Bonds (contains *Live and Let Die, Moonraker,* and *Diamonds Are Forever*), Macmillan, 1965.
Octopussy (also see below; includes story "The Living Daylights"), New American Library, 1965, published in England as *Octopussy, and The Living Daylights,* J. Cape, 1966.
A James Bond Quartet (contains *Casino Royale, Live and Let Die, Moonraker,* and *From Russia, with Love*), J. Cape, 1992.
A James Bond Quintet (contains *Diamonds Are Forever, Doctor No, Goldfinger, For Your Eyes Only,* and *The Spy Who Loved Me*), J. Cape, 1993.

The Essential James Bond (includes *Thunderball, On Her Majesty's Secret Service, You Only Live Twice, The Man with the Golden Gun, Octopussy,* and *The Living Daylights*), J. Cape, 1994.

Ian Fleming's James Bond (includes *Moonraker, From Russia with Love, Dr No, Goldfinger, Thunderball,* and *On Her Majesty's Secret Service*), Chancellor Press (London), 1994.

OTHER

The Diamond Smugglers (novel), J. Cape, 1957, Macmillan, 1958.

Thrilling Cities (essays), J. Cape, 1963, New American Library, 1964.

Chitty-Chitty-Bang-Bang: The Magical Car (juvenile), illustrations by John Burningham, Random House (New York City), 1964.

Fleming Introduces Jamaica (nonfiction), edited by Morris Cargill, Deutsch (London), 1965, Hawthorn (New York City), 1966.

Also author, with Kevin McClory and Jack Whittington, of screenplay adaptation of his novel *Thunderball,* 1965. Columnist, under pseudonym Atticus, for the *Sunday Times,* London, during the 1950s. Contributor to *Horizon, Spectator,* and other magazines.

A collection of Fleming's letters, manuscripts, and other papers and memorabilia is housed at Lilly Library, Indiana University, and additional material is owned by Glidrose Productions.

ADAPTATIONS: Films adapted from Fleming's works and/or based on his characters include *Dr. No,* 1962, *From Russia with Love,* 1963, *Goldfinger,* 1964, *Thunderball,* 1965, *The Poppy Is Also a Flower,* 1966, *Casino Royale,* 1967, *You Only Live Twice,* 1967, *Chitty-Chitty-Bang-Bang,* 1968, *On Her Majesty's Secret Service,* 1969, *Diamonds Are Forever,* 1971, *Live and Let Die,* 1973, *The Man with the Golden Gun,* 1974, *The Spy Who Loved Me,* 1977, *Moonraker,* 1979, *For Your Eyes Only,* 1981, *Never Say Never Again,* 1983, *Octopussy,* 1983, *A View to a Kill,* 1985, *The Living Daylights,* 1987, *Licence to Kill,* 1989, and *Goldeneye,* 1995. After Fleming's death, Kingsley Amis continued the James Bond novels under the pseudonym Robert Markham. *The Book of Bond; or, Every Man His Own 007,* by Lt. Col. William (Bill) Tanner, is a guide for gentlemen who would like to be as glamorous as Fleming's hero.

SIDELIGHTS: The success of Ian Fleming's espionage adventure tales about the fictional secret agent James Bond has been astounding, both in the English versions and in translations, even though the author himself called his works "trivial piffle." Bond, a special agent for British intelligence, is a cynical, cold man with a suave exterior, physically tough, endowed with numerous gadgets and luxury accouterments, and irresistible to women. Malcolm Muggeridge proposed that the Bond books became so wildly popular because "Fleming's squalid aspirations and dream fantasies happened to coincide with a whole generation's. He touched a nerve. The inglorious appetites for speed at the touch of a foot on the accelerator and for sex at the touch of a hand on the flesh, found expression in his books. We live in the Century of the Common Bond, and Fleming created him." William Plomer put forth another, loftier view of the stories: "They are brilliant, romantic fairy-tales in which a dragon-slaying maiden-rescuing hero wins battle after battle against devilish forces of destruction, and yet is indestructible himself: an ancient kind of myth skilfully re-created in a modern idiom. They are, like life, sexy and violent, but I have never thought them corrupting. Compared with some of the nasty stuff that gets into print, they have a sort of boyish innocence." Sarel Eimerl noted one difference between Fleming's stories and most espionage novels, a difference which may account for part of this success. Fleming, who had worked with British Intelligence, had, or gave the impression of having, "the inside dope." He sounded authentic.

Fleming and Bond often became confused in the public mind. John Pearson described Fleming as a modern-day Lord Byron, "tall, saturnine, hollow-cheeked, his face lopsided with its magnificently broken nose, his brow half-covered by that thoughtful comma of black hair which he was to pass on to his hero. . . ." Like Bond, Ian Fleming enjoyed travel and luxury. He was a "noted womanizer," related Joan DelFattore in *Dictionary of Literary Biography,* whose "attitude toward women is surely one of the reasons for the uneven quality of James Bond's relationships with the female characters in his novels." He had some training as a secret agent, but failed a key test designed to see whether or not he could kill in cold blood.

Plomer disagreed, however, that Bond was a reflection of Fleming: "There may be something Flemingish about Bond, but I didn't see much of Bond in Fleming, who was more perturbable. Let us admit, as Fleming himself did, that Bond and his adventures are something of an adolescent fantasy," or as Fleming later said, "a highly romanticized version of *anybody*." Fleming, who named his principal character after the ornithologist who wrote *Birds of the West Indies,* considered Bond to be "an extremely dull, uninteresting man to whom things happened," and in the end tired of him, calling him "a cardboard dummy," and seriously considered killing him off. A *Times Literary Supplement* writer still believed that Fleming and his character were undoubtedly related: "We are left with the image of a rather sad, middle-aged Mitty threatened with heart trouble, steering his Thunderbird through the London streets with decent care, brooding on his lucrative fantasies. Yet he had to have his material. He had to make a show of living dangerously. He had to keep up with James Bond, and Bond killed him in the end."

The writer referred to Fleming's own excessive habits, including heavy drinking and smoking. DelFattore reported that during the 1940s the author was "smoking between sixty and seventy cigarettes a day and drinking inordinate quantities of gin." His health gradually failed under such abuse; he developed kidney trouble and had repeated heart attacks. His production of books and stories declined along with his health, but by the time he was seriously affected, Fleming had already realized his dream of wealth through the sales of his books and the movies made from them. In 1990 Fleming himself was the subject of a made-for-television movie, *The Secret Life of Ian Fleming,* starring Jason Connery, the son of one of the best-known screen Bonds, Sean Connery.

Bond's genesis occurred during World War II, when, as Plomer reported, Fleming came to him "with a diffidence that came surprisingly from so buoyant a man, [and] said he had a wish to write a thriller. . . . I at once made it . . . plain how strongly I believed in his ability to write such a book, and in its probable originality. 'But,' I said, 'it's no good writing just *one*. With that sort of book, you must become regular in your habits. You must hit the nail again and again with the same hammer until it's driven into the thick head of your potential public.'" Muggeridge, who recalls discussing Fleming's writing with him when he was at work on *Casino Royale* remembers that Fleming "was insistent that he had no 'literary' aspiration at all, and that his only purpose was to make money and provide entertainment." By the time he died, Fleming reportedly had made 2.8 million

dollars from his books alone, to say nothing of what he earned from the many films made of them.

From *Casino Royale* to *The Man with the Golden Gun,* the Bond books evoked strong responses from critics, both positive and negative. Some reviewers described Bond's adventures as wonderful entertainment, others found them to be a significant reflection of modern culture and fantasies, while still others considered Fleming's books offensively bad, filled with racism, snobbery, misogynism, excessive violence, and poor writing. Discussing what he perceived to be a moral void in the Bond books, Bernard Bergonzi wrote in *Twentieth Century,* "Where the relations between the sexes are concerned, Mr Fleming's characteristic mode of fantasy seems to be that of a dirty-minded schoolboy." Bergonzi went on to decry the "strongly marked streak of voyeurism and sado-masochism" he found in Fleming's books, and remarked that the author "describes scenes of violence with uncommon relish. . . . It is these that really bring his books down to the horror-comic level. . . . In *Casino Royale,* for instance, Bond is captured by a Communist agent. . . . [He] is stripped naked and tied to a chair from which the seat has been removed; he is then systematically beaten on the genitals with a carpet-beater for about an hour."

Reviewing *Dr. No* for *New Statesman,* Paul Johnson called it "badly written to the point of incoherence" and "the nastiest book I have ever read." He found three basic ingredients in the story, "all unhealthy, all thoroughly English: the sadism of a schoolboy bully, the mechanical, two-dimensional sex-longings of a frustrated adolescent, and the crude, snob-cravings of a suburban adult. Mr. Fleming has no literary skill, the construction of the book is chaotic, and entire incidents and situations are inserted, and then forgotten, in a haphazard manner. But the three ingredients are manufactured and blended with deliberate, professional precision."

On the other end of the critical spectrum, Kingsley Amis held Bond up as the modern embodiment of the romantic heroes of Lord Byron. Like them, Amis suggested in his *The James Bond Dossier,* Bond is "lonely, melancholy, of fine natural physique, which has become in some way ravaged, of similarly fine but ravaged countenance, dark and brooding in expression, of a cold or cynical veneer, above all *enigmatic,* in possession of a sinister secret." He applauded Fleming's skill in bringing off "the unlikely feat of enclosing this wildly romantic, almost narcissistic, and (one would have thought) hopelessly out-of-date persona inside the shellac of a secret agent, so making it plausible, mentally actable, and, to all appearance, contemporary." Bond was also evaluated quite seriously by George Grella, who wrote in *The Critic as Artist: Essays on Books 1920-1970* that "James Bond is the Renaissance man in mid-century guise, lover, warrior, connoisseur. He fights the forces of darkness, speaks for the sanitary achievements of the age, enjoys hugely the fruits of the free enterprise economy. He lives the dreams of countless drab people, his gun ready, his honor intact, his morals loose: the hero of our anxiety-ridden, mythless age: the savior of our culture."

"Don't try to read any of the Bond adventures seriously!" warned Ann S. Boyd in *The Devil with James Bond!* "Bond was meant for fun, for escape." Still, she contended that in rereading Fleming's books, one may "discover that there is more to his series of thriller adventures than one originally might suspect." In Boyd's estimation, the Bond canon is really "the saga of a modern knight of faith whose adventures involve a gallery of modern demons which have been attacking contemporary mankind just as diabolically as Medusa and all the other legendary demons and dragons attacked mankind in ages past. Rather than casting pearls before swine, Fleming's genius has cast swine as the personifications of the devil before a hero who is willing to sacrifice all for the great pearl of life and faith."

Writing in *Dictionary of Literary Biography*, Joan DelFattore summed up the Bond novels: "Fleming's books are superficial, implausible, and erratically structured, and they have unquestionably been overshadowed in popularity by the Bond films, which are even more superficial, implausible, and erratically structured. On the other hand, Fleming's work is, for the most part, imaginative, readable, and, most important, outrageously entertaining."

"The phenomenon of James Bond [has] always troubled both his admirers and his detractors, who have great difficulty simply accounting for it," declared George Grella in *St. James Guide to Crime and Mystery Writers*. "The major sources of his appeal are not entirely obscure. For one thing, the James Bond novels are a perfect example of the right thing at the right time, as appropriate an expression and index of their age as, for example, the Sherlock Holmes stories or the novels of Dashiell Hammett." Evaluating Fleming's literary achievement, Grella found that the author "in his own way mastered one of the most enviable and admirable feats in all of literature—the mingling of the barely credible, the utterly incredible, and the specifically identifiable in an excitingly sustained narrative fiction. In literary circles the product of such a mixture is often referred to as the concrete universal; it is no mean accomplishment, and is shared by writers like Chaucer, Fielding, Dickens, Melville, and Faulkner."

Grella proposed that "whatever the final quality of Fleming's achievement, his undeniable popularity and financial success, his powerful influence over the writers who follow him, and his union of the fantastic and the absolutely real deserve serious and careful study. It may be a very long time before that study reaches its proper point, but it may eventually establish Ian Fleming as one of the most appropriate writers of his time." He summarized: "Ian Fleming accomplished an extraordinary amount in the history of the thriller. Almost singlehandedly, he revived popular interest in the spy novel, spawning legions of imitations, parodies, and critical and fictional reactions, thus indirectly creating an audience for a number of novelists who followed him in the form. . . . Bond became the best-known fictional personality of his time and Fleming the most famous writer of thrillers since Sir Arthur Conan Doyle. . . . Whatever Fleming's merit or defects, he created more than novels of action and adventure, sex and violence—he created a phenomenon. Such an achievement is eminently worthy of attention."

BIOGRAPHICAL/CRITICAL SOURCES:

BOOKS

Amis, Kingsley, *The James Bond Dossier,* New American Library, 1965.
Benson, Raymond, *The James Bond Bedside Companion,* Dodd (New York City), 1984.
Bond, Mary Wickham, *How 007 Got His Name,* Collins, 1966.
Boyd, Ann S., *The Devil with James Bond!,* John Knox, 1966.
Bruce, Ivar, *You Only Live Once: Memories of Ian Fleming,* Weidenfeld and Nicolson (London), 1975, University Publications of America (Frederick, MA), 1985.
Campbell, Ian, *Ian Fleming: A Catalogue of a Collection: Preliminary to a Bibliography,* privately printed, 1978.
Concise Dictionary of British Literary Biography, Volume 7: *Writers after World War II, 1945-1960,* Gale (Detroit), 1991.

Contemporary Literary Criticism, Gale, Volume 3, 1975, Volume 30, 1984.

Contosta, David R., *The Private Life of James Bond,* Sutter House (Lititz, PA), 1993.

del Buono, Oreste, and Umberto Eco, editors, *The Bond Affair,* translation by R. A. Downie, Macdonald, 1966.

Dictionary of Literary Biography, Volume 87: *British Mystery and Thriller Writers since 1940, First Series,* Gale, 1989.

Gant, Richard, *Ian Fleming: The Man with the Golden Pen,* Mayflower, 1966.

Gardner, John E., *Ian Fleming's James Bond,* Avenet (New York City), 1987.

Haining, Peter, *James Bond: A Celebration,* W. H. Allen (London), 1987.

Harrison, Gilbert A., editor, *The Critic as Artist: Essays on Books 1920-1970,* Liveright, 1972.

Lane, Sheldon, editor, *For Bond Lovers Only,* Panther, 1965.

Lycett, Andrew, *Ian Fleming: The Intimate Story of the Man Who Created James Bond,* Turner (Atlanta), 1996.

McCormick, Donald, *The Life of Ian Fleming,* P. Owen (London), 1993.

Panek, LeRoy L., *The Special Branch: The British Spy Novel, 1890-1980,* Bowling Green University Popular Press (Bowling Green, OH), 1981.

Pearson, John, *The Life of Ian Fleming,* McGraw (New York City), 1966.

Pearson, *007 James Bond,* Morrow (New York City), 1973.

Pearson, *James Bond: The Authorised Biography of 007,* Granada (London), 1985, Grove (New York), 1986.

Pelrine, Eleanor, and Dennis Pelrine, *Ian Fleming: Man with the Golden Pen,* Swan, 1966.

Playboy Interviews, Playboy Press, 1967.

Reference Guide to English Literature, second edition, St. James Press (Detroit), 1991.

Rosenberg, Bruce A., and Ann Steward, *Ian Fleming,* Twayne (Boston), 1989.

Rubin, Steven Jay, *The James Bond Films,* Arlington (London), 1982.

St. James Guide to Crime and Mystery Writers, St. James Press, 1996.

Sauerberg, Lars Ole, *Secret Agents in Fiction: Ian Fleming, John le Carre and Len Deighton,* St. Martin's (New York City), 1984.

Snelling, O. F., *007 James Bond: A Report,* Spearman (London), 1964, New American Library, 1965.

Starkey, Lycurgus M., *James Bond: His World of Values,* Abingdon (Nashville, TN), 1966.

Symons, Julian, *Mortal Consequences: From the Detective Story to the Crime Novel,* Harper, 1972.

Twentieth-Century Crime and Mystery Writers, third edition, St. James Press, 1991.

Twentieth-Century Young Adult Writers, St. James Press, 1994.

Van Dover, J. Kenneth, *Murder in the Millions: Erle Stanley Gardner, Mickey Spillane, Ian Fleming,* Ungar (New York City), 1984.

Zeiger, Henry A. *Ian Fleming: The Spy Who Came in with the Gold,* Duell, Sloan & Pearce (New York City), 1965.

PERIODICALS

Commentary, July, 1968.

Critic, October-November, 1965.

Encounter, January, 1965.

Life, August 10, 1962.

Nation, June 21, 1958, pp. 566-567.

National Review, September 7, 1965, pp. 776-777.

New Republic, July 2, 1966, p. 29.

New Statesman, April 5, 1958, pp. 430, 432; April 2, 1965, pp. 540-541.

Newsweek, June 15, 1964, p. 103.

New Yorker, April 21, 1962.

New York Times, February 16, 1967; April 25, 1967.

New York Times Book Review, July 4, 1961; November 5, 1961; April 1, 1962; December 11, 1966.

Reporter, July 13, 1967.

Spectator, April 17, 1953, p. 494; April 12, 1957, p. 493; December 13, 1957, pp. 844-845; April 4, 1958, p. 438.

South Atlantic Quarterly, winter, 1968, pp. 1-12.

Sunday Herald Tribune Book World, August 29, 1965, pp. 1, 17.

Times Literary Supplement, April 17, 1953, p. 249; October 27, 1966.

Twentieth Century, March, 1958, pp. 220-228; May, 1958, pp. 478-779.*

*   *   *

FORD, Elbur
See HIBBERT, Eleanor Alice Burford

*   *   *

FOX, Brian
See BALLARD, (Willis) Todhunter

FOXX, Jack
  See PRONZINI, Bill

*   *   *

FRAZER, Robert Caine
  See CREASEY, John

*   *   *

FREDERIC, Mike
  See COX, William R(obert)

*   *   *

FURST, Alan   1941-

PERSONAL: Born February 20, 1941, in New York, NY. *Education:* Oberlin College, A.B., 1962; Pennsylvania State University, M.A., 1967.

ADDRESSES: Home—Box 2345, Sag Harbor, NY 11963.

CAREER: Writer.

AWARDS, HONORS: Fulbright teaching fellowship, 1969-70; Edgar Award nomination, 1976.

WRITINGS:

NOVELS

Your Day in the Barrel, Atheneum (New York City), 1976.
The Paris Drop, Doubleday (New York City), 1980.
The Caribbean Account, Delacorte (New York City), 1981.
Shadow Trade, Delacorte, 1983.
Night Soldiers, Houghton (Boston), 1988.
Dark Star, Houghton, 1991.
The Polish Officer, Random House (New York City), 1995.
The World at Night, Random House, 1996.

OTHER

(With Debbi Fields) *One Smart Cookie: How a Housewife's Chocolate Chip Recipe Turned into a Multimillion-Dollar Business—The Story of Mrs. Field's Cookies,* Simon & Schuster (New York City), 1987.

Contributor to periodicals, including *Esquire, Architectural Digest, Elle, GQ,* and *International Herald Tribune.*

SIDELIGHTS: The European intelligence services—Soviet, German, French, and British—from 1933 and during World War II, are the domain of novelist Alan Furst. Furst creates factually accurate stories staged against historical events, from Polish battlefields to Parisian nightlife.

Shadow Trade features a former CIA agent, Guyer, now in business for himself after being downsized. Here Furst describes the complex and morally questionable habits and techniques of the spy world. In his review for the *Times Literary Supplement,* Reginald Hill notes that *Shadow Trade* "is intelligent, honest, gripping, and not much for our comfort." In *Shadow Trade,* everyone in the world has a double who can be tracked down and manipulated by darker forces to achieve their evil goals. "Out of this," Hill says, "Furst spins a compelling and original plot without any escapist pyrotechnics."

Furst's next novel, *Night Soldiers,* moves briskly from country to country to follow its hero, Khristo Stoianev. The story begins tragically when the rise of fascism in Bulgaria kills the teenaged Khristo's brother, and the grieving boy ends up in Moscow undergoing training by the NKVD, the KGB's precursor. As a tool of the Communists, he is dispatched to Spain to murder fellow party members Moscow considers turncoats. But Khristo escapes the dirty task and flees to France. By the end of World War II, Khristo has worked his way to a happier arrangement as a spy for the Western victors. Walter Goodman of the *New York Times* says "the characters tend to be personifications of their nations, and the book serves as something of a tour guide, especially to towns up and down the Danube." In sum, the reviewer finds *Night Soldiers* "absorbing," yet lacking tension because of its "episodic quality."

Night Soldiers is especially notable as a chronicle of European espionage, observes Anthony Levitas of the *Los Angeles Times Book Review,* because "the action unfolds not in the 1950s or 60s, but in the 1930s and 40s." In Levitas' view, Furst has wisely chosen his time frame "to show that it is here, before the war, that the modern lingua franca of diplomatic duplicity and international terror comes into its own."

The spy in *Dark Star* is Andre Szara, a Polish-born Russian Jew who serves the NKVD while working as a foreign correspondent for *Pravda* in Paris. Among the jittery French Jewry is the rich Joseph de Montfried, who appeals to Szara's heritage to pass along secrets about the German military to the British in exchange for British passports that would then be used to help Jews escape Germany. "The historical background and intelligence information are woven into the novel seamlessly," comments Herbert Mitgang of the *New York Times*. "It's as if Mr. Furst obtained documents under a Freedom of Information Act." Mitgang observes a slight leap of faith required by the reader as the novel approaches its end. This is also the observation of Josephine Wol in her review for the *Washington Post*. Wol laments that the last few chapters "ring more of tidy fictional endings than of open-ended reality." Yet she writes that the work is "stimulating and satisfying."

In *The Polish Officer*, Capt. Alexander de Milja accepts the daring job of underground spy for his exiled government after Poland falls to the Nazis. De Milja proves adept at varying his disguises, particularly with several European languages under his belt. His tasks include smuggling Poland's gold reserves out of the country as well as the hands of the Germans, bomb production, and propaganda. "Relying more on period detail than on the plot (which ultimately fizzles out) in depicting the tense life of a spy and the delicacy of maintaining one's cover, Furst writes like a confident crafter of the genre," observes Gilbert Taylor in his review for *Booklist*.

Furst's skill as a historian is also recognized by Robert Chatain in his review for the *Chicago Tribune*. Chatain writes: "What we see in Furst's novels is the birth of modern spying, the knotted habits of thinking, tradecraft and expediency that have led several generations of public servants down a path that arguably has done their governments more harm than good."

In *The World at Night*, Furst remains rooted in European history of the 1930s and 40s. Here his am-

bivalent hero is Jean-Claude Casson, a Grade B film producer whose world turns upside down after the Nazis invade his beloved France. Without funds, he comes close to collaboration with German film companies in Paris, but in the end he cannot make himself do it. Eventually he is caught up in the more serious decision of who to spy for, since both sides are actively recruiting him.

Lorraine Kreahling, in a profile of Furst for the *New York Times*, lauds the author's "careful portrayal of the banalities and the realities of everyday life [which] allows the reader to experience what it means to have not only one's freedom but also one's middle-class comforts suddenly swept away." Richard Eder of the *Los Angeles Times* notes that the novel has "an appreciation of France that is at once passionate, graceful and cold, an evocation of French virtues and vices under terrible testing."

Despite the seriousness of the times, Furst manages to give the novel a comic edge. As observed by Herbert Mitgang for the *Chicago Tribune*, "the novel is full of keen dialogue and witty commentary." But Richard Bernstein of the *New York Times* faulted the work for being "weak on the connections between events."

BIOGRAPHICAL/CRITICAL SOURCES:

PERIODICALS

Booklist, January 1, 1995, p. 802.
Chicago Tribune, February 26, 1995, section 14, p. 5. June 23, 1996, section 14, p. 4.
Chicago Tribune Books, May 26, 1991, p. 7.
Los Angeles Times Book Review, February 21, 1988; April 28, 1991, p. 2; June 2, 1996, p. 2.
New York Times, January 30, 1988, p. 16; June 12, 1991, section C, p. 17; June 5, 1996, section C, p. 18, July 21, 1996, p. 2.
New York Times Book Review, October 25, 1987; April 28, 1991, section 7, p. 24; September 8, 1996, p. 23.
Time, April 15, 1991, p. 65.
Times Literary Supplement, April 5, 1985, p. 394.
Washington Post, January 18, 1988; June 4, 1991, section B, p. 3; June 19, 1996, section C, p. 2.

G

GEARHART, Sally Miller 1931-

PERSONAL: Born April 15, 1931, in Pearisburg, VA; daughter of Kyle M. and Sarah Gearhart. *Education:* Sweet Briar College, B.A. (English), 1952; Bowling Green State University, M.A., 1953 (public address); University of Illinois, Ph.D. (theater), 1956; additional study at University of Kansas, 1969-70. *Politics:* "Lesbian-Feminist." *Religion:* "Philogyny."

ADDRESSES: Home—P.O. Box 1027, Willits, CA 95490.

CAREER: Stephen F. Austin State University, Nacogdoches, TX, assistant professor of speech, 1956-60; Texas Lutheran College, Seguin, associate professor of speech and drama and head of department, 1960-70; San Francisco State University, San Francisco, instructor, then associate professor, then professor of speech, 1972-92, chair of department, 1984-86, acting associate dean of School of Humanities, 1984-86, acting coordinator of women studies, 1989-90, professor emerita, 1992—. Member of board of directors of San Francisco Family Service Agency; cochair of Council on Religion and the Homosexual; member of San Francisco Women's Centers.

MEMBER: Speech Communication Association of America, American Civil Liberties Union (ACLU), National Center for Lesbian Rights, People for the Ethical Treatment of Animals (PETA).

WRITINGS:

(With William R. Johnson) *Loving Women/Loving Men: Gay Liberation and the Church,* Glide (San Francisco), 1974.

The Wanderground: Stories of the Hill Women, illustrated by Elizabeth Ross, Alyson (Los Angeles), 1978.
(With Susan Rennie) *A Feminist Tarot,* Alyson, 1981.

Contributor of short stories and essays to numerous anthologies.

SIDELIGHTS: Sally Miller Gearhart is among the most well-known authors of feminist-inspired utopian fiction. Most notable among her works is the collection of interlocking narratives titled *The Wanderground: Stories of the Hill Women.* Reflecting its author's deep commitment to both lesbian feminist politics and an ecologically inspired spirituality, *The Wanderground* is characteristic of Gearhart's published work, not only in its themes of what she terms "philogyny"—"the love of women"— and its publication by a small, women-run press. In addition to *The Wanderground,* Gearhart is the coauthor of both *Loving Women/Loving Men: Gay Liberation and the Church* and *A Feminist Tarot.* Her short fiction and essays have been included in numerous anthologies of lesbian and feminist writings.

The Wanderground is a set of interrelated short stories focusing on an environmentally aware, lesbian separatist commune. The women living in the hills of Wanderground maintain deep spiritual connections both to each other and to nature. Community rules in Wanderground include revolving leadership roles, equitable opportunities for addressing a group meeting, and the encouragement of self-expression. Group rule binds the members of Wanderground community, in contrast with the male-dominated hierarchical power structures common in most modern governments.

The Wanderground contains both an alternative to traditional hierarchicies, "but also to a linear narrative structure," according to Nancy Jesser in *Feminist Writers*. "The stories in the collection are discrete, yet interconnected. By reading them together it is possible to construct a history of the creation of the community, but that construction is left to the reader." The inhabitants of Wanderground maintain only an oral history, which is kept vital through the ritual of retellings in what are called "Remember Rooms." "It is in these 'rooms' that Gearhart makes her most pointed critiques of patriarchy and its violence against women," noted Jesser. "Through ritual accountings of rape and violence, the memories of why the Hill women have separated themselves from men is re-lived and re-affirmed. Gearhart promotes a well-guarded separatism from men."

Gearhart's utopian community embodies the division she sees as necessary between women and men: women are depicted as more environmentally atuned than the Gentles (men), who must live outside the Wanderground. While the Gentles may be necessary for procreation, it is clear that their aggressive, destructive tendencies make them unfit to enter the peaceful community of women. It is on this point that some critics have taken issue with Gearhart, arguing that her feminist utopia, based as it is on the continued separation between men and women, is pessimistic.

However, it is Gearhart's lack of belief that a successful truce will ever transpire in the ongoing war between the sexes that inspires both *The Wanderground* and her continued work. "My love of myself as a woman and my love of other women motivates all my writing (and my creative existance)," Gearhart once told *CA*. "In a society that hates women and the womanly, woman-love is a miracle and therefore a hefty motivation."

BIOGRAPHICAL/CRITICAL SOURCES:

BOOKS

Feminist Writers, St. James Press (Detroit), 1996.
Foss, Karen A., Sonja K. Foss, and Cingy L. Griffin, *Feminist Rhetorical Theory*, Sage, 1997.
Keulen, Margarete, *Radical Imagination: Feminist Conceptions of the Future in Ursula Le Guin, Marge Piercy, and Sally Miller Gearhart*, P. Lang (New York City), 1991.

PERIODICALS

Extrapolation, Volume 32, number 4, 1991.
Signs, summer, 1984.
Women and Language, winter, 1987.

* * *

GILBERT, Anthony
   See MALLESON, Lucy Beatrice

* * *

GILL, Patrick
   See CREASEY, John

* * *

GLENDINNING, Victoria 1937-

PERSONAL: Born April 23, 1937, in Sheffield, Yorkshire, England; daughter of Baron (a banker) and Evangeline (Hurst) Seebohm; married Oliver Nigel Valentine Glendinning (a professor), 1958 (marriage ended, 1981); married Terence de Vere White (a writer), 1982 (deceased, 1994); married Kevin O'Sullivan (a consulting engineer), 1996; children: (first marriage) Paul, Hugo, Matthew, Simon. *Education:* Somerville College, Oxford, B.A., 1959; Southampton University, diploma in social administration, 1969. *Avocational interests:* Gardening.

ADDRESSES: Agent—David Higham Associates, 5-8 Lower John Street, Golden Square, London W1R 4HA, England.

CAREER: Part-time teacher in Southampton, England, 1960-69; writer, 1969—. Part-time psychiatric social work in Southampton and in Dublin, Ireland, 1970-73; editorial assistant for *Times Literary Supplement* in London, 1974-78.

MEMBER: PEN, Society of Authors, National Union of Journalists, Royal Society of Literature (fellow).

AWARDS, HONORS: James Tait Black Prize and Duff Cooper Literary Award, both 1981, both for *Edith Sitwell: A Unicorn Among Lions;* Whitbread

Award in biography, 1984, for *Vita: The Life of V. Sackville-West,* and 1993, for *Trollope;* D.Litt., Southampton University, 1994.

WRITINGS:

BIOGRAPHIES

A Suppressed Cry: Life and Death of a Quaker Daughter, Routledge & Kegan Paul (London), 1969.

Elizabeth Bowen: Portrait of a Writer, Weidenfeld & Nicolson (London), 1977, published in the United States as *Elizabeth Bowen,* Knopf (New York City), 1978.

Edith Sitwell: A Unicorn Among Lions, Knopf, 1981.

Vita: The Life of V. Sackville-West, Knopf, 1983.

Rebecca West: A Life, Knopf, 1987.

Trollope, Hutchinson (London), 1992, published in the United States as *Anthony Trollope,* Knopf, 1993.

NOVELS

The Grown-Ups, Hutchinson, 1989, Knopf, 1990.

Electricity, Little, Brown (Boston), 1995.

OTHER

(Coeditor, with son Matthew Glendinning) *Sons & Mothers,* Virago, 1996.

Also author of introductions to numerous books. Contributor to periodicals, including *Times Literary Supplement, New Statesman, Irish Times,* London *Observer,* London *Times, Washington Post,* and *New York Times.*

ADAPTATIONS: Electricity has been read as a serial on BBC radio, adapted as a radioplay broadcast in 1997 on BBC radio, and has been optioned for adaptation as a film.

SIDELIGHTS: Victoria Glendinning is a British biographer esteemed for her accomplished profiles of literary women. Though "neither as psychoanalytical as most American literary biographers, nor as speculative or judgmental," wrote Jane Marcus in *Chicago Tribune Book World,* Glendinning excels at creating vivid human portraits of her subjects. In her examinations of the lives of Elizabeth Bowen, Edith Sitwell, Vita Sackville-West, and Rebecca West, reflected Fiona MacCarthy in a critique for the London *Times,* Glendinning demonstrates her facility for capturing "that interesting area where literary lady becomes flamboyant figure."

Elizabeth Bowen, author of numerous novels, short stories, essays, and travel books, is one of the biographer's earliest subjects. Though never very fashionable in the United States, Bowen has been ranked by some critics alongside such authors as Virginia Woolf, E. M. Forster, and Evelyn Waugh. According to *Time* reviewer Paul Gray, Glendinning "argues passionately that Bowen is important, not only for her writings but also for her timing." In the biographer's estimation, reported Gray, "Bowen was destined to be the last of the Anglo-Irish writers."

Bowen grew up in County Cork, Ireland, at Bowen's Court, the family home since the mid-seventeenth century. As a youth she suffered her mother's death and father's mental illness, then she married early and turned to writing, often focusing on relationships or emotional crises. Eventually becoming well-known in literary circles, Bowen taught in the States and in England; she also conducted a literary salon in London, made acquaintance with members of the Bloomsbury group, and became a popular hostess. Critiquing for *Saturday Review,* Lynne Sharon Schwartz praised Glendinning's *Elizabeth Bowen* as a "lively and sympathetic study link[ing] Bowen's childhood preoccupations with the major themes of her novels." Approval also came from Francis Wyndham in the *Times Literary Supplement,* who admired the biographer's "novelist's flair" and ability to go "beyond the artful assemblage of available material to construct a complex character and to hint at its essence."

After completing the Bowen biography, Glendinning turned her attention to Edith Sitwell. An English prose writer, experimental poet, and eccentric who died in 1964, Sitwell has held a fluctuating literary reputation. Her life story, however, has always commanded attention. Often regarded as a self-made celebrity, Sitwell presented a forbidding appearance to the world: six feet tall, bony, and angular with a long, "glorious" nose, Sitwell's figure was wholly unfashionable for her time. Daring to adorn herself with clothes befitting her stature—mantled gowns, headdresses, and magnificent jewels—the author is said to have cut a regal, gothic figure admired by both the public and her literary peers: apparently Gertrude Stein described her as "a grenadier," Elizabeth Bowen compared her to "a high altar on the move," and Virginia Woolf likened her to the Emperor Heliogabalus. Reviewing *Edith Sitwell: A Uni-*

corn Among Lions for *Time,* Melvin Maddocks speculated that "the Sitwell mystique centered on her extraordinary physical presence" but added that Glendinning "wholeheartedly . . . convince[s] her reader that the Sitwell persona could never have been created unless Edith deeply and passionately cared about poetry."

Glendinning's book fared well with the critics. It was commended by Alany Pryce-Jones in the *New York Review of Books* for being "perceptive about Edith's virtues: her generosity . . . her kindliness . . . her consideration . . . the inner humility which lay beneath a nervous aggressiveness." And in the *New York Times Book Review,* Michael Holroyd professed that Glendinning "writes from love and has produced a . . . sophisticated and penetrating work [that] orchestrates Edith Sitwell's notoriety, chronicles the rows, revenges and ripostes by which she came to afflict the public."

The biography is notable, as well, for contending Edith and her literary brothers, Osbert and Sacheverell, staged media events largely to keep their work in the public eye. Indeed, Glendinning counters critic F. R. Leavis's famous 1932 assertion that "the Sitwells belong to the history of poetry *and* the history of publicity." Evaluating for the *Washington Post Book World,* Nigel Nicholson estimated that this declaration, coupled with Glendinning's belief that Sitwell's twelve best poems give her "an unquestioned, uncategorized place on anyone's Parnassus," has the biographer ascribing Sitwell "a more dignified place in English life and letters than her reputation for spikiness and conceit has generally allowed her."

Glendinning's next work, *Vita: The Life of V. Sackville-West,* focuses on another literary maverick. Better known for her unconventional marriage and sexual liaisons with women than for her work as novelist, poet, and critic, Sackville-West, according to Glendinning, is best understood in the context of "an adventure story." Vita "was rather less of an achiever than she in fact appeared or would have liked to think herself," related Fiona MacCarthy in another review for the London *Times.* The critic added, "This central irony, faced squarely and with sympathy, gives Victoria Glendinning's book its great pathos and its strength."

"One reads this biography at once fascinated and appalled," remarked Michiko Kakutani, critiquing for the *New York Times.* According to Kakutani,

Vita—spoiled, willful, and determined to get what she wanted, including a romance with novelist Virginia Woolf—left her life well documented, particularly through journals and letters to her husband. With a wealth of information upon which to draw, Glendinning has rendered comments both "shrewd and percipient," reported the *Times Literary Supplement.* And in his review for the *Washington Post Book World,* Leon Edel judged that Glendinning "substantially enlarges [Vita's] legend and provides us with names, dates, passions, recriminations and griefs . . . of Vita's lesbian loves, an outpouring of faded intrigues and stale perfumes of yesteryear. The biography is briskly and professionally . . . written and is a mine of Edwardian and Georgian gossip."

Glendinning also has written a life of author and feminist Rebecca West. While in her twenties, West distinguished herself as a social and literary critic; then proceeded to become a celebrated journalist as well as a novelist. Although many critics believe that her work has too long been overshadowed by her notoriety as the bearer of H. G. Wells's illegitimate son Anthony, West is redeemed in Glendinning's biography. As Elaine Kendall noted in the *Los Angeles Times Book Review:* "Glendinning manages to rehabilitate Rebecca West's image in a work that succeeds both as a model of cool objectivity and as a capsule history of modern woman from 1892 to 1983, with West always in the vanguard of change." And in critic Dennis Drabelle's opinion, expressed in the *Washington Post Book World,* the book "evinces a rapport between biographer and subject that sets it above the others." Drabelle added, "As captured in this balanced, stylish biography, Rebecca West seems not only 'the most interesting woman of this century in England' but also the most vital."

Writing for the *New York Times Book Review,* Samuel Hynes remarked that "books about the lives of gifted women are inevitably also books about the restraints in women's lives—society, conventions, manners, class, men— and about the desires of those women to free their gifts from such restraints and to live their lives on their own terms." In her examinations of the lives of Elizabeth Bowen, Edith Sitwell, Vita Sackville-West, and Rebecca West, Glendinning has proven her ability to navigate these issues, presenting biographies that, in the words of *Ms.* contributor Catharine R. Stimpson, are "responsible, intelligent, serious, exhaustive." Glendinning, concluded Kendall, has established herself as a specialist "in biographies of extraordinary women, the more imposing the better."

In her next biography, Glendinning examines the life of Anthony Trollope, the popular British novelist noted for his keen insight into Victorian mores and the interior world of domestic life. Published soon after two other Trollope biographies, Glendinning's book was generally well-received, with commentators praising Glendinning for her thorough examination of Trollope's works for details about the author himself and for her re-creation of a lost era. Glendinning portrays Trollope as an abused and neglected child, who upon adulthood settled into what he expected would be a lifelong dedication to public service in the post office. But his accomplishments as a civil servant fueled a growing self-confidence that propelled him toward the completion of his first novel.

John Gross wrote in the *New York Review of Books* that "one of the book's great strengths is its weaving together of personal detail and social history." Writing for the *New York Times Book Review,* James R. Kincaid found the work "rich" and "sweet," and lauded Glendinning for her vivid portrait of a remote subject. Noting differences between Glendinning's work and that of other Trollope biographers, Kincaid commented that Glendinning's biography offers "a far more detailed and insistent image of Trollope's wife and family, the dark subtleties of his domestic life and his sustaining fantasies. Ms. Glendinning's Trollope is less bluff and boisterous than any we have seen, more unsettled, depressed and courageously dogged."

The work also appears to recast Trollope's image as a predictable novelist and "archetype of the beef-eating, fox-chasing, no nonsense male," remarked Andrew Motion of the London *Observer.* Instead, Motion argued, Glendinning places "[Trollope] at the centre of a large and complex family, emphasizing his sympathy with women, defining the way the book explores the balance of power between the sexes, and generally turning a red-faced old fogey into a surprisingly supple thinker."

To Bryan Cheyette of the *New Statesmen & Society,* Glendinning's portrait is still not convincing. "Trollope, as both civil servant and writer, attempted to locate himself at the centre of a nostalgic Englishness," Cheyette observed, one that the reviewer considered to be rife with racist, sexist and anti-Semitic attitudes. "But [Glendinning's] gushing enthusiasm makes it impossible for her to question the narrowness of Trollope's Little Englandism."

Glendinning's novels have received a mixed reception. Her first book, *The Grown-Ups,* featured a pompous, ego-centric author named Leo Ulm and the loving women whom he mistreats. To Jan Dalley of the London *Observer,* the story is "a good old-fashioned tale of the sex war—the men impossibly vain, the women infuriatingly masochistic—and of marriage." Donna Rifkind argued in her review for the *Wall Street Journal* that the story of women flocking to an abusive man would be more believable if Glendinning had "worked a little harder developing Leo's character." Joyce Slater commented in the *Chicago Tribune* that *The Grown-Ups* is "witty and insightful" but that one reads it "with a mixture of fascination and revulsion."

Electricity, Glendinning's second novel, is set in Victorian England and focuses on Charlotte Mortimer, who is ambitious and willful, yet constrained by an era of limited opportunities for women. To escape a wretched family life, Mortimer marries Peter, one of the country's first electrical engineers and a symbol of the promises and disappointments of a new age. After Peter is accidentally electrocuted, Charlotte supports herself by offering spiritual advice, but is ruined after accusations that she is a charlatan. At the story's conclusion, Charlotte is left with the choice of marrying one of two suitors or pursuing independence. Nicola Humble noted in the *Times Literary Supplement* that "it is a mark of the book's emotional and conceptual complexity that we have no idea which of the three she will select."

Kathryn Harrison, writing for the *New York Times Book Review,* found Glendinning's manipulation of the past uneven. "Sometimes *Electricity* is so graceful that we never question it; at other times . . . it loses that fine balance." Jan Marsh of the *New Statesmen & Society* argued that the lack of credibility lies "not in the unlikely happenings but the novel's conventional chronology."

Humble observed that Glendinning revisits common themes and interests in her writing. "The questions Victoria Glendinning asks about the period are motivated by modern curiosity: what did the average late-Victorian girl know about sex and her own body, how did family relationships work, what sort of sanitary arrangements were available?" "The answers," Humble noted, "are provided by Charlotte Mortimer."

BIOGRAPHICAL/CRITICAL SOURCES:

BOOKS

Contemporary Literary Criticism, Volume 50, Gale, 1988.
Glendinning, Victoria, *Edith Sitwell: A Unicorn Among Lions,* Knopf, 1981.

PERIODICALS

Chicago Tribune, January 28, 1990, p. 6; January 31, 1993.
Chicago Tribune Book World, June 14, 1981; January 8, 1984.
Christian Science Monitor, February 1, 1993.
Los Angeles Times, June 5, 1981; January 26, 1990; January 9, 1994.
Los Angeles Times Book Review, October 11, 1987.
Ms., March, 1978; December, 1983.
Nation, February 25, 1984.
National Review, September 21, 1984.
New Republic, March 11, 1978; October 19, 1987.
New Statesmen & Society, September 4, 1992, p. 41; April 14, 1995, p. 41.
New Yorker, May 24, 1981.
New York Review of Books, December 17, 1981; March 29, 1984; April 8, 1993, pp. 9-11.
New York Times, January 11, 1978; November 1, 1983; December 29, 1989.
New York Times Book Review, January 15, 1978; June 14, 1981; October 23, 1983; October 18, 1987; January 7, 1990; January 31, 1993, pp. 1, 23-24; October 22, 1995, p. 15.
Observer (London), August 2, 1981; October 2, 1983; March 19, 1989, p. 48; August 30, 1992, p. 50.
Saturday Review, January 21, 1978.
Time, January 16, 1978; June 5, 1981.
Times (London), July 30, 1981; September 29, 1983; April 9, 1987.
Times Literary Supplement, October 7, 1977; July 31, 1981; September 30, 1983; April 24, 1987; August 28, 1992, pp. 3-4; April 7, 1995, p. 24.
Village Voice, December 6, 1983; November 24, 1987.
Wall Street Journal, January 30, 1990; February 10, 1993.
Washington Post, January 10, 1990, p. A16; February 7, 1993.
Washington Post Book World, February 5, 1978; June 7, 1981; November 27, 1983; October 4, 1987.

GORDON, Jeffie Ross
See TESSLER, Stephanie Gordon

* * *

GRAY, Russell
See FISCHER, Bruno

* * *

GREEN, Hannah 1927(?)-1996

PERSONAL: Born in Cincinnati, OH, c. 1927; died October 16, 1996, in New York City, of lung cancer; daughter of Matthew Addy (a foreign patent and trademark agent) and Mary McAlpin (Allen) Green; married John Wesley (a painter), December, 1971. *Education:* Wellesley College, B.A., 1948; Stanford University, M.A., 1956.

CAREER: Church World Service Language Institute, teacher of English in Camp for Displaced Persons, Ulm, Germany, 1949-50; Stanford University, Stanford, CA, instructor in English composition and creative writing, 1954-57; research assistant to author Matthew Josephson, 1961-65; Columbia University, New York, NY, professor of fiction in School of the Arts, beginning 1970. Assistant to editor of *Pacific Spectator,* 1953-54.

MEMBER: PEN, Authors Guild, MacDowell Colony Fellows (president of executive committee, beginning 1976).

AWARDS, HONORS: MacDowell Colony fellow, 1960, 1964, 1967, 1969, 1970, 1975, 1978; Ohioana Library Award for the best novel by an Ohioan in 1972, 1973, for *The Dead of the House;* Creative Artists Public Service award from New York State Council on the Arts, 1973-74; Mary Elvira Stevens Traveling Fellowship from Wellesley College, 1974-75; National Endowment for the Arts grant, 1978.

WRITINGS:

(Contributor) Wallace Stegner and Richard Scowcroft, editors, *Stanford Short Stories,* Stanford University Press (Stanford, CA), Volume II: *1954,* 1954, Volume III: *1955,* 1955.

The Dead of the House, (novel), Doubleday (New York City), 1972, new edition, Turtle Point (New York City), 1996.
In the City of Paris (juvenile), Doubleday, 1985.

Contributor to periodicals, including *Mademoiselle, Unmuzzled Ox,* and *New Yorker.*

SIDELIGHTS: *The Dead of the House,* a novel more than ten years in the making, is rooted in Green's family and their lives and past in Cincinnati, Ohio. "Framed by the twenty years between the 1930's and the 1950's," wrote critic L. J. Davis, "it ranges as far back as the War of Austrian Succession and sketches whole lifetimes with what seems an effortless stroke of the pen. *The Dead of the House* is less a novel than a kind of dream, a protracted prose poem of singular delicacy, filled with generosity, love, and wisdom, and steeped in lore. [It] is a deeply felt, uniquely American fiction. . . . It is hard to remember a book as superbly balanced in all its parts."

New York Times reviewer Thomas Lask noted that Green's book was "not the usual family chronicle." He observed, "She writes under the eye of eternity. . . . Time flows in and around the events of her book like some tune that ties all meanings together. . . . Throughout the novel the wisdom of the blood takes over, almost, from the wisdom of the head. . . . It is a work of recovery, a love note to the past—something to shore the spirit against the ruins."

"In writing this book I began for the first time to write in my own way," Green recalled in an essay in the Hungarian Magazine *Nagyvilag.* "At the time (in the early fifties) it seemed to me that most of the women writers who were discussed in the writing courses of the period wrote as if they were bodiless; often they chose male narrators or heroes representing themselves as men, and I felt there was something basically false in this. I was very conscious from the start of wanting to write as a woman, to have my particular womanly sensuality and sensibility to be a part of the texture and life of the book."

Green also published a children's book, *In the City of Paris,* inspired by a trip made to France with her husband in the 1970s. A whimsical tale of the injustice done to French dogs who are, by law, kept out of city parks while other animals are allowed inside, *In the City of Paris* was called "a clever story that will engage readers" by the critic for *Publishers*

Weekly. Green's trip to France also inspired her to write *Golden Spark, Little Saint: My Book of the Hours of Saint Foy,* unpublished at the time of her death in 1996. Visiting a church in Conques in the south of France, Green viewed the bones of Saint Foy, martyred under the Romans centuries ago. The visit was a revelation for Green, who began, according to Robert McG. Thomas, Jr., in the *New York Times,* "writing—and rewriting—a book about the martyred 12-year-old girl who was betrayed by her father, refused to renounce her faith and [was] put to death, inspiring a cult that continues in France." The book, combining fiction with the known facts of St. Foy's life, is scheduled for posthumous publication.

Green's unfinished novels *College Days* and *Dreams and Early Memories* draw, as did *The Dead of the House,* on the history and lives of her Ohio family. "In life," Green once told *CA,* "time is my foe—I do not use it well—but in art I fall on my knees before its mysteries and transmute its secrets to the best of my abilities."

BIOGRAPHICAL/CRITICAL SOURCES:

BOOKS

Contemporary Literary Criticism, Volume 3, Gale (Detroit), 1974.

PERIODICALS

Atlantic Monthly, May, 1972.
Boston Globe, March 6, 1972.
Hudson Review, October, 1972, pp. 500-501.
New Republic, March 11, 1972.
New York Post, March 25, 1972.
New York Times, February 12, 1972.
New York Times Book Review, February 13, 1972, p. 5.
Publishers Weekly, September 13, 1985, p. 131.
Saturday Review, May 27, 1972.
Southern Review, summer, 1973, pp. 713-716.
Wall Street Journal, March 7, 1972.
Washington Post Book World, February 27, 1972, p. 4.

OBITUARIES:

PERIODICALS

New York Times, October 18, 1996, p. D21.
Washington Post, October 20, 1996, p. B4.*

GRIERSON, Edward 1914-1975
(Brian Crowther, John P. Stevenson)

PERSONAL: Born March 9, 1914, in Bedford, England; died May 24, 1975; son of Edward and Ruby Fort (Buckle) Grierson; married Helen Henderson, 1938; children: Anne Fort. *Education:* Exeter College, Oxford, honour school of jurisprudence, 1935. *Avocational interests:* Lawn tennis.

CAREER: Barrister-at-law, Bradford, England, 1938-39; Australian Broadcasting Commission, Sydney, New South Wales, Australia, announcer, 1948; novelist, 1952-75. Justice-of-the-peace, County of Northumberland, 1952-75. Chairman of petty sessions, Bellingham, Northumberland, 1960-75; deputy chairman, Northumberland Quarter Sessions, 1960-71; deputy traffic commissioner, Northern Traffic Area, 1974-75. *Military service:* British Army, West Yorkshire Regiment, Infantry, 1939-46; became lieutenant colonel.

MEMBER: Inner Temple (London), Northumberland Commission of the Peace, Bellingham Justices (chairman), PEN (London).

AWARDS, HONORS: Crime Writers Association award, 1956.

WRITINGS:

(Under pseudonym Brian Crowther) *Shall Perish with the Sword,* Quality Press (London), 1949.
Reputation for a Song (Book Society choice, England), Chatto & Windus (London), 1951, Knopf (New York City), 1953.
The Hastening Wind, Knopf, 1953 (published in England as *The Lilies and the Bees,* Chatto & Windus, 1953).
(With Raymond Lulham) *His Mother's Son* (play), produced in Harrogate, Yorkshire, 1953.
Far Morning, Knopf, 1955.
The Second Man, Knopf, 1956.
(Under pseudonym John P. Stevenson) *The Captain General,* Doubleday (New York City), 1956, (under name Edward Grierson), Chatto & Windus, 1958.
Storm Bird: The Strange Life of Georgina Weldon, Chatto & Windus, 1959.
Dark Torrent of Glencoe, Doubleday, 1960.
The Massingham Affair, Chatto & Windus, 1962, Doubleday, 1963.
A Crime of One's Own, Putnam (New York City), 1967.

The Fatal Inheritance: Philip II and the Spanish Netherlands, Doubleday, 1969.
The Death of the Imperial Dream, Doubleday, 1972 (published in England as *The Imperial Dream: The British Commonwealth and the Empire, 1775-1969,* Collins [London], 1972).
Confessions of a Country Magistrate, Gollancz (London), 1972.
King of Two Worlds: Philip II of Spain, Putnam, 1974.
The Companion Guide to Northumbria, Collins, 1976.

RADIO PLAYS

The Ninth Legion, 1956.
The Second Man, 1956.
Mr. Curtis's Chamber, 1959.

SIDELIGHTS: Edward Grierson's best-known book is *Reputation for a Song,* a novel Melvyn Barnes in *St. James Guide to Crime and Mystery Writers* calls "a supremely competent study of domestic murder and a perfect example of courtroom drama." Grierson also wrote historical novels, detective stories and nonfiction accounts of British history.

Reputation for a Song concerns the trial of Rupert Anderson, a young man accused of murdering his father. Beginning at Rupert's trial, the novel then flashes back to the evolution of the circumstances surrounding the murder. Grierson drew upon his own experience in the legal profession to present his dramatic courtroom story. He creates, the *New Yorker* critic believed, "a remarkably detailed portrait of an English suburban community." James Hilton in the *New York Herald Tribune Book Review* remarked: "Its background of English life and legal procedure is authentic." Grierson's deft narrative skill was also noted by critics. Margaret Eliason in *Library Journal* opined that the "mood and settings are excellent and suspense well sustained." Tangye Lean in *Spectator* stated that *Reputation for a Song* was "expertly arranged and extremely readable."

In *The Second Man* Grierson again drew upon his legal background to invent a story of a woman barrister trying to save her client. Barnes found that "the atmosphere of the courts can be positively felt." James Sandoe in the *New York Herald Tribune Book Review* went so far as to rank *The Second Man* "among the very best of that long, diverse series of detective stories set within the formalities of a trial." While Anthony Boucher in the *New York Times* called the novel "interesting as a detective story and as an analysis of the characters," he felt that "its all but unique quality lies in Mr. Grierson's minute and superb dissection of the legal process."

Among Grierson's nonfiction works that earned critical attention are *The Fatal Inheritance,* a study of Spain's doomed relationship with its colony in the Netherlands, and *The Death of the Imperial Dream,* an outline of England's decline as a colonial power. W. W. MacDonald in *Library Journal* called *The Fatal Inheritance* "the best popular account of the subject to date," while F. J. Gallagher in *Best Sellers* claimed that Grierson "tells the story in a lively dramatic style, the characters come alive and he has the artist's skill in depicting the action of battle or pageantry or daily living. It is an absorbing and thrilling story." Speaking of *The Death of the Imperial Dream,* the *New Yorker* critic found "intelligent, attractive history." J. A. Caseda in *Library Journal* called it "a witty, artfully written account" and "an entertaining introduction."

In his historical fiction Grierson ranged widely in period and setting. His *The Massingham Affair,* for example, is a mystery set in the late nineteenth century. While Sandoe in *Library Journal* found the novel to be "a most ingenious puzzle," Boucher in the *New York Times Book Review* praised Grierson's abilities strongly: "He seems unable to write less than a classic. . . . Grierson's quiet mastery of prose and narrative creates a full, rich novel, and an absorbing study of the law in action."

BIOGRAPHICAL/CRITICAL SOURCES:

BOOKS

St. James Guide to Crime and Mystery Writers, fourth edition, St. James Press (Detroit), 1996.

PERIODICALS

Best Sellers, October 15, 1967, p. 27; April 15, 1969, p. 29.
Chicago Sunday Tribune, February 8, 1953, p. 6; July 19, 1953, p. 4.
Economist, February 19, 1972, p. 242.
Horn Book, June, 1961, p. 37.
Library Journal, January 1, 1953, p. 78; August, 1960, p. 85; May 1, 1963, p. 88; March 15, 1969, p. 94; June 15, 1972, p. 97.
New Statesman, September 19, 1969, p. 78; February 18, 1972, p. 83.
New Yorker, January 31, 1953, p. 28; September 2, 1972, p. 48.
New York Herald Tribune Book Review, January 4, 1953, p. 5; June 17, 1956, p. 9.
New York Times, January 4, 1953, p. 5; July 19, 1953, p. 14; May 27, 1956, p. 16.
New York Times Book Review, April 14, 1963, p. 20; October 15, 1967, p. 57; May 17, 1981.
Saturday Review, January 17, 1953, p. 36.
Spectator, March 7, 1952, p. 188.
Times Literary Supplement, March 28, 1952, p. 226; May 15, 1953, p. 313; April 20, 1956, p. 235; February 23, 1967, p. 152.*

H-I

HALL, Adam
    See TREVOR, Elleston

*   *   *

HALLIDAY, Michael
    See CREASEY, John

*   *   *

HAMILTON, Donald (Bengtsson) 1916-

PERSONAL: Born March 24, 1916, in Uppsala, Sweden; immigrated to the United States in 1924; son of Bengt L. K. and Elise (Neovius) Hamilton; married Kathleen Stick, 1941 (died, October 1989); children: Hugo, Elise, Gordon, Victoria. *Education:* University of Chicago, B.S., 1938.

ADDRESSES: Home and office—P.O. Box 1045, Santa Fe, NM 87501; and Old Saybrook, CT.

CAREER: Self-employed writer and photographer, 1946—. *Military service:* U.S. Naval Reserve, four years; became lieutenant.

MEMBER: Mystery Writers of America, Outdoor Writers Association of America, Western Writers of America.

AWARDS, HONORS: Spur Short Story Award, Western Writers of America, 1967.

WRITINGS:

NOVELS; "MATT HELM" SERIES

Death of a Citizen, Gold Medal (New York City), 1960.
The Wrecking Crew, Gold Medal, 1960.
The Removers, Gold Medal, 1961.
Murderers' Row, Gold Medal, 1962.
The Silencers, Gold Medal, 1962.
The Ambushers, Gold Medal, 1963.
The Shadowers, Gold Medal, 1964.
The Ravagers, Gold Medal, 1964.
The Devastators, Gold Medal, 1965.
The Betrayers, Gold Medal, 1966.
The Menacers, Gold Medal, 1968.
The Interlopers, Gold Medal, 1969.
The Poisoners, Gold Medal, 1971.
The Intriguers, Gold Medal, 1972.
The Intimidators, Gold Medal, 1974.
The Terminators, Gold Medal, 1975.
The Retaliators, Gold Medal, 1976.
The Terrorizers, Gold Medal, 1977.
The Mona Intercept, Gold Medal, 1980.
The Revengers, Gold Medal, 1982.
The Annihilators, Gold Medal, 1983.
The Infiltrators, Gold Medal, 1984.
The Detonators, Gold Medal, 1985.
The Vanishers, Gold Medal, 1986.
The Demolishers, Gold Medal, 1987.
The Frighteners, Gold Medal, 1989.
The Threateners, Gold Medal, 1992.
The Damagers, Gold Medal, 1993.

MYSTERY NOVELS

Date with Darkness, Rinehart (Boulder, CO), 1947.
The Steel Mirror, Rinehart, 1948.
Murder Twice Told, Rinehart, 1950.
Night Walker, Dell (New York City), 1954, published as *Rough Company,* Wingate (London), 1954.
Line of Fire, Dell, 1955.
Assignment: Murder, Dell, 1956, published as *Assassins Have Starry Eyes,* Gold Medal, 1966.

WESTERN NOVELS

Smoky Valley, Dell, 1954.
Mad River, Dell, 1956.
The Big Country, Dell, 1957.
The Man from Santa Clara, Dell, 1960, published as *The Two-Shoot Gun,* Fawcett (New York City), 1971.
Texas Fever, Gold Medal, 1960.

OTHER

(Editor) *Iron Men and Silver Stars,* Gold Medal, 1967.
Donald Hamilton on Guns and Hunting (nonfiction), Gold Medal, 1970.
Cruises with Kathleen (collection of yachting stories), McKay (New York City), 1980.

Author of screenplay, *Five Steps to Danger,* with Henry S. Kesler and Turnley Walker, 1957.

Contributor of articles on hunting, yachting, and photography to popular magazines.

A manuscript collection of the author's works is housed at the University of California, Los Angeles.

ADAPTATIONS: Movies based on Hamilton's novels include *The Violent Men, Five Steps to Danger, The Big Country, The Silencers,* 1966, *Murderers' Row,* 1966, *The Ambushers,* 1967, and *The Wrecking Crew,* 1969, with the last four starring Dean Martin as Matt Helm.

SIDELIGHTS: One of the most popular secret agent characters ever created, the cynical and ruthless Matt Helm made his first appearance "in what I might call 'just another book,'" author Donald Hamilton once told *CA.* Having already written quite a few short stories and nonfiction articles as well as several novels, Hamilton detected nothing unusual about the manuscript he submitted to his editor in 1960—*Death of a Citizen.* The editor, however, "immediately saw it as a series. We had problems—like getting rid of the wife and children which might encumber his free-wheeling—but it all started from that." Though some people have compared Matt Helm to Ian Fleming's James Bond, Hamilton explains that he has read only one of Fleming's books, "and that was quite some time ago. I've deliberately avoided reading the James Bond novels for fear that I would unintentionally borrow something from him, or bend over too far backward to avoid any similarity."

Since the publication of *Death of a Citizen* in 1947, Hamilton, who resides, in part, on a thirty-eight-foot motorsailor on the Connecticut shoreline, has written nearly one Matt Helm adventure per year.

Hamilton's first novel, *Date with Darkness,* is a tale of espionage, in which a U.S. naval lieutenant on leave becomes involved with an attractive, mysterious French woman who is being pursued by a group who want revenge. The book met with mixed reviews. While a reviewer for *Saturday Review of Literature* termed it "Tough and torrid," and *Kirkus* deemed the book "Intricate intrigue, with some explicit amatory touches" and "a very good time passer," Anthony Boucher, writing in the *San Francisco Chronicle,* described it as "Underplayed harsh melodrama, written with an appalling contempt for the callousness of all its characters." B. V. Winebaum, in a *New York Times* review, lambasted the novel. "If it is Mr. Hamilton's purpose to suggest that the French underground was no better than the Nazis," stated the critic, "he had better try again, with a straight face, considerable documentation, and less attention to the works of Raymond Chandler, who is all too often aped these days." On a very positive note, however, James Sandoe's *Chicago Sun Book Week* review praised the work as, "The best thriller I have read since Eric Ambler's 'A Coffin for Dimitros'. . . . The novel's sea-borne finale and its acrid little postscript conclude the tale admirably."

Steel Mirror, Hamilton's second book, is a mystery novel. A *Kirkus* reviewer termed it a "Psycho-thriller, well paced and produced," and a critic for *Saturday Review of Literature* hailed it as "commendable." Philip Hewitt-Myring, in a *New York Times* review, said, "Though the story is not in the highest, or Eric Ambler, class of 'naturalistic' thriller, it is much more convincing than most of these tales of beauty on the run; and Emmett is an agreeably ordinary, though not an unheroic, hero. The ending of the story is positively cynical—and that is a change, too."

Murder Twice Told, Hamilton's third book, combines two stories, one of counter-espionage, the other a detective tale. James Sandoe, writing in the *Chicago Sun,* maintained that "a good many people have recommended a good many books as impossible to lay down once you've been so unwary as to pick them up. I don't much care for this adhesive definition of success but I'd be willing to let it stand for this pair." And a *New York Herald Tribune Weekly Book Review* critic praised the work: "Both stories are written with Mr. Hamilton's flair for hair-on-end suspense and in his hard-hitting yet literate prose."

Regarding Hamilton's western novels, essayist Robert E. Skinner commented in *St. James Guide to Crime & Mystery Writers:* "Hamilton scored some seminal triumphs as a western novelist in the 1950s. His *The Big Country,* an offbeat western about a Yankee ship captain who goes west to marry a rancher's daughter, is considered one of this century's great western novels, and was adapted into an award-winning film."

Skinner said of the Helm novels, "Donald Hamilton created Matt Helm at a time when secret agents were very much in vogue, thanks to the enormous popularity of Ian Fleming's Bond. This was, perhaps, encouraged by the fact that Helm, like Bond, is a professional assassin for a super-secret government agency. However, that is where the comparison ends. It is worthy of note, too, that Helm's popularity has far exceeded James Bond's as a literary character, and the series has enjoyed a longevity that is unusual in the annals of crime fiction."

Skinner described Matt Helm as "a curious amalgam of average guy, sportsman, patriot, and ruthless killer wrapped in the same personality. He can be pragmatic to a fault, hyperpatriotic, yet sentimental about dogs, and almost maudlin in love. Unlike many crime heroes, Helm does what he says he will do, and if he is ordered to kill, he lets nothing stand in the way of that order."

Skinner commented on a link between Hamilton's earlier Western novels and his later Helm novels: "One of the things that makes the Helm stories truly unique is the fact that Helm himself is a naturalistic hero who draws from the mystique of the American frontier. Many of Helm's most exciting confrontations occur in a wilderness setting, something that he

prefers. Helm idealizes the frontier hero, and his own rigid code is a blend of medieval chivalry and the Code of the West. He draws strength from it, and a sense of justification, as well. Often he calls up the names of Western heroes in his explanations of his sometimes sentimental, sometimes ruthless behavior."

"Unlike Bond, who utilized numerous gimmicks," Skinner noted, "Helm uses the tools of the frontiersman—no-frills pistols, rifles, knives, and sometimes bare hands—to carry out his missions. Although we know from his earliest appearance that his primary expertise is that of a long-range sniper, most of his kills are dealt out *mano-a-mano* in stand-up pistol duels or knife fights. Helm enjoys these contests, and as is typical of naturalistic heroes from Natty Bumppo on down, he can give a full measure of respect to a fellow professional, regardless of his politics."

As for the longevity of the series, Skinner commented, "Unlike other paperback heroes, Matt Helm has endured for almost four decades. Hamilton has tried, albeit semi-successfully, to have his hero grow emotionally and engage in adventures that were timely, and less concerned with the evils of communism. At the end of *The Terrorizers,* Helm is nearly killed exterminating a band of leftist American terrorists. For the first time in his career, he seems not only sickened by the killing, but by the person he has become. He ends the story unsure of his future, and at least entertaining the notion of taking a high-level desk job that [his boss] has offered him."

Skinner concluded: "Hamilton has adhered to a strict formula which, while often predictable, is unfailingly entertaining. His ability to create a fully realized protagonist, crisp, tough dialogue, and skillfully choreographed fight scenes make the Matt Helm series not only one of the most enduring, but certainly one of the all-time best series of original paperback thrillers."

BIOGRAPHICAL/CRITICAL SOURCES:

BOOKS

Newquist, Ray, *Conversations,* Volume 4, Rand McNally, 1967.
St. James Guide to Crime & Mystery Writers, fourth edition, St. James Press (Detroit), 1996.

PERIODICALS

Books and Bookmen, November 1968.
Book World, January 7, 1968.
Chicago Sun, November 12, 1948, p. N12; May 5, 1950, p. 5.
Chicago Sun Book Week, June 29, 1947, p. 6.
Kirkus, April 15, 1947; September 1, 1948; February 15, 1950, p. 117.
New Republic, July 21, 1947; July 26, 1975; November 27, 1976; November 26, 1977.
New Yorker, November 13, 1948, p. 152.
New York Herald Tribune Weekly Book Review, October 26, 1947, p. 32; November 21, 1948, p. 28; April 30, 1950, p. 16.
New York Times, July 6, 1947, p. 12; December 12, 1948, p. 22; June 4, 1950, p. 20.
New York Times Book Review, February 4, 1968.
San Francisco Chronicle, June 22, 1947, p. 16; May 21, 1950, p. 25.
Saturday Review of Literature, July 19, 1947; December 18, 1948, p. 30.

*   *   *

HARRIS, Geraldine (Rachel) 1951-

PERSONAL: Born October 17, 1951; adopted daughter of Leslie George (a company director) and Mary Edith (Wood) Harris; married Richard Gilmore Eric Pinch (a number theorist), January 7, 1978. *Education:* King's College, Cambridge University, B.A. (honors), 1977, M.A., 1980; Wadham College, Oxford University, 1977-84, D.Phil., 1985. *Politics:* Social Democrat. *Religion:* Anglican.

ADDRESSES: Home—Pyramid View, 65 Harpes Rd., Oxford, Oxfordshire OX2 7QJ, England. *Office*—Griffith Institute, Ashmolean Museum, Oxford University, Beaumont St., Oxford, England.

CAREER: Writer. Associated as Egyptologist with Griffith Institute, Ashmolean Museum, Oxford University, Oxford, England.

MEMBER: Society of Authors, Folklore Society, Egypt Exploration Society, Jomsborg (meadkeeper, 1975-77).

WRITINGS:

White Cranes Castle, illustrated by Lisa Jensen, Macmillan (London), 1979.

"SEVEN CITADELS" SERIES; NOVELS

Prince of the Godborn, Greenwillow (New York City), 1982.
The Children of the Wind, Greenwillow, 1982.
The Dead Kingdom, Greenwillow, 1983.
The Seventh Gate, Greenwillow, 1983.

OTHER

Gods and Pharaohs from Egyptian Mythology, illustrated by John Sibbick and David O'Connor, Lowe (London), 1982, Schocken (New York City), 1983, reprinted, P. Bedrick (New York City), 1996.
The Junior Atlas of Ancient Egypt, Lionheart (London), 1989.
New Kingdom Votive Offerings to Hathor, Griffith Institute (Oxford), 1989.

Contributor to journals, including *Folklore* and *Orientalia.*

SIDELIGHTS: Geraldine Harris has achieved recognition for her four-volume series "Seven Citadels." The protagonist of this four-part story is seventeen-year-old Kerish-lo-Taan, a Galkian prince. One of the Godborn, Kerish is sent on a quest to search for and free the Promised Saviour whose freedom is necessary for the future of the Galkian Empire. Each book describes the prince's encounters and confrontations as he and other helpers make their way across dangerous landscape in their quest for the goal of salvation. Assessing the "Seven Citadels," a *Booklist* reviewer praises the "dimensional characterizations, well-developed sociopolitical manipulations, and compelling adventure and action." Liz Holliday, in the *St. James Guide to Fantasy Writers,* commends that Harris "is afraid neither to show her protagonists as complex and faulty heroes at best, nor to allow them to grow as their quest—which takes many years—proceeds."

To rescue the Promised Saviour, Kerish is told that he must obtain seven golden keys that will open the gates to the Saviour's prison. These keys are kept by seven immortal sorcerers each located on a different citadel. In order to get the sorcerers to relinquish their keys, Kerish must convince each sorcerer to give up his or her immortality, an unlikely but not impossible task.

In the first book of the series, *Prince of the Godborn,* Kerish begins the journey for the keys accompanied by his half-brother and warrior, Lord Forollkin. The two are able to retrieve the first two keys, one from the Kingdom of Ellerinon, the other from an illusionist child sorcerer.

Part two of the series, *The Children of the Wind,* portrays Kerish and Forollkin, joined by the disfigured creature Gidjabolgo (who was the result of a wish by the second sorcerer), trying to locate the third key. They must cross a swamp filled with serpents and swarming with oversized insects in order to get to sorceress Sendaka. Successful in crossing the swamp, the search party confronts Sendaka, obtains the third key, becomes trapped by the children of the wind, and are eventually rescued. Reviewing the first two books of the "Seven Citadels," a *Voice of Youth Advocates* contributor lauds that as the story progresses "the characters continue to mature."

The Dead Kingdom, the third part of the "Seven Citadels," chronicles the confrontations with three more sorcerers and the retrieval of the fourth, fifth, and sixth keys. It also focuses on the romance that develops between Lord Forollkin and Kerish's cousin, Gwerith. This book leaves off with the capture of the penultimate key.

In the final installment, *The Seventh Gate,* Kerish obtains the final key and is faced with having to make a difficult decision at the seventh gate. At this final gate, or the gate of death, Kerish realizes that he is the Saviour and that he has the choice to either have peace in death or be reborn in his land of suffering to rebuild the Empire, offering salvation for his people. The book culminates with Kerish's fateful decision of being reborn. *Booklist* reviewer describes the fourth book as "a powerful, if enigmatic end to a satisfying fantasy saga."

Harris once told *CA:* "I divide my time between very dry academic work and creative writing and find that this balance suits me very well. My main interest as a writer is exploring religious questions through the medium of fantasy."

BIOGRAPHICAL/CRITICAL SOURCES:

BOOKS

Pringle, David, editor, *St. James Guide to Fantasy Writers,* St. James Press (Detroit), 1996.

PERIODICALS

Booklist, February 15, 1983, p. 770; November 1, 1983, p. 403; May 1, 1984, p. 1234.
Voice of Youth Advocates, August, 1984, p. 147; October, 1983, p. 215; April, 1984, p. 38.*

*   *   *

HARRISON, M(ichael) John 1945-
(Joyce Churchill, Ron Fawcett)

PERSONAL: Born July 26, 1945, in Warwickshire, England; son of Alan Spencer (an engineer) and Dorothy (a clerk; maiden name, Lee) Harrison. *Education:* Educated in England. *Politics:* None. *Religion:* Atheist. *Avocational interests:* Mountaineering, fell-walking in Scotland and in England's Lake District, playing guitar, riding horses.

ADDRESSES: Agent—Anthony Sheil Associates, 43 Doughty St., London WC1N 2LF, England.

CAREER: Atherstone Hunt, Atherstone, Warwickshire, England, groom, 1963; student teacher in Warwickshire, England, 1963-65; Royal Masonic Charity Institute, London, England, clerk, 1966; freelance writer, 1966—; *New Worlds* (Magazine), London, literary editor and reviewer, 1968-75.

WRITINGS:

The Committed Men (novel), Doubleday, 1971.
The Pastel City (novel), New English Library, 1971, Doubleday, 1972.
The Centauri Device (novel), Doubleday, 1974.
The Machine in Shaft Ten and Other Stories, Panther, 1975.

Contributor of articles, short stories, and reviews, sometimes under pseudonym Joyce Churchill, to *Transatlantic Review, New Worlds, New Worlds Quarterly, Fantasy and Science Fiction, New Writings in Science Fiction, Science Fantasy, It,* and *Frendz.* Literary editor of *New Worlds,* 1968—.

WORK IN PROGRESS: Editing *The Human Factor: Sympathy for the Devil;* research for a book on mountain rescue in Great Britain.

SIDELIGHTS: M. John Harrison is closely associated with the British New Wave science fiction that emerged in the 1960s. The New Wave opened the science fiction genre to experimental literary techniques from the avant-garde. Harrison's fiction is, according to John Mellors in the *Listener,* "elegantly written but uncomfortably disturbing." "Harrison first found his voice," Paul J. McAuley writes in *St. James Guide to Fantasy Writers,* "as a critic and short story writer in *New Worlds* magazine, in the late 1960s and early 1970s. Although his fictions were notable from the beginning for their finely worked surfaces, Harrison's precise evocations of the quiddity of the world should not blind us to the strong narrative structures underpinning them."

Harrison's interest in the innovative approach of New Wave science fiction is particularly evident in his short stories, where he uses disjointed narrative structures, plays with the nature of reality and creates characters whose moments of revelation are ambiguous. As Colin Greenland writes in *British Book News,* "It is the uncertainty, the tension between the perceived or imagined ideal and the shabby actuality, that gives [Harrison's] fiction its nervous edge; that, and the fierce clarity of his prose."

Harrison's short fiction is usually set against a drabby and rundown background. "Harrison excels," as Mellors explains, "in evoking bleak and threatening landscapes." Amid this sordid world, Harrison spins tales of hopeless characters who seek redemption but find only fresh misery. "His world," writes Roz Kaveney in *Books and Bookmen,* "is obsessively bleak, doomed and visually sordid. . . . Harrison is determined to bring entropy to every corner of his universe; there is no possibility of joy for his characters and little of survival."

Typical of Harrison's approach is the story "Engaro," which tells of a poverty-stricken bookstore owner who tracks down through oblique references and cryptic clues the secret country of Engaro, rumored to be the source and foundation of all the world's mysteries. When he finds the country, however, he discovers it to be depressingly ordinary and everyday, not at all the romantic paradise he had imagined.

A similar study of entropy appears in the novels *The Pastel City, A Storm of Wings* and *In Viriconium.* These novels envision a society suffering from "a plague of despair," according to McAuley. Harrison's characters, McAuley explains, are "so paralysed by their past that they fail to confront the present." In the city of Viriconium, the world is now so ancient and tired that time is confused and the past repeats itself over and over again. A kind of terminal wasteland where the cultural wreckage of the centuries lies scattered, Viriconium is home to "writers, inventors and painters [who] preside over unfinished designs, paintings, and writings, letters going nowhere, ambivalent performances, inexplicable events and recollections," as Valentine Cunningham writes in the *Observer.* This situation is, McAuley argues, a criticism of fantasy literature itself, especially "those decadent forms of high fantasy which initiate and heighten only selected aspects of the world."

Harrison writes: "I became a professional writer in 1966, living frugally in the bleak 'bedsitter' belt of London's Tufnell Park and Camden Town—an area of oneroomed cold water apartments full of Irish expatriots, junkies and broken gas meters. I still find the area fascinating. I believe, with the Hardy of *The Return of the Native,* that the landscape *is* the fiction; all else devolves from it. I use the science fiction and fantasy forms because they allow greatest latitude of image.

"I am antipolitical, and particularly opposed to 'ideological' politics as a rationale or substitute for administrative or economic (i.e., practical) politics. At the moment, two hemiglobal, implacably opposed, and totally outdated ideological systems are, in the person of various 'limited' wars, killing thousands of people who have never heard of the principles involved; and, in bolstering their own economic situations, starving millions more to death. I see no logical or humanistic reason why this state of affairs should exist, especially since it is based on precepts a hundred or more years old."

BIOGRAPHICAL/CRITICAL SOURCES:

BOOKS

St. James Guide to Fantasy Writers, St. James Press (Detroit), 1996.

PERIODICALS

Booklist, February 15, 1972, p. 489; March 1, 1973, p. 620; July 1, 1980, p. 1592; September 15, 1984, p. 109.

Books and Bookmen, September, 1983, p. 34.
British Book News, April, 1983, p. 260; March, 1984, p. 134.
Kirkus Reviews, July 1, 1971, p. 701; October 1, 1972, p. 1164.
Library Journal, August, 1971, p. 2550; December 1, 1972, p. 3932; April 15, 1980, p. 538.
Listener, February 2, 1984, p. 28.
London Review of Books, August 4, 1983, p. 20.
Magazine of Fantasy and Science Fiction, December, 1972, p. 39; October, 1980, p. 55; July, 1983, p. 31.
New Statesman, August 13, 1971, p. 212.
Observer, November 21, 1971, p. 32; October 31, 1982, p. 30.
Punch, July 13, 1983, p. 61.
Science Fiction Review, August, 1982, p. 55.
Times Literary Supplement, October 29, 1982, p. 1203.

*   *   *

**HIBBERT, Eleanor Alice Burford 1906-1993
(Eleanor Burford, Phillipa Carr, Elbur Ford,
Victoria Holt, Kathleen Kellow, Jean Plaidy,
Ellalice Tate)**

PERSONAL: Born 1906, in London, England; died January 18, 1993, on a cruise ship in the Mediterranean; daughter of Joseph and Alice (Tate) Burford; married G. P. Hibbert. *Education:* Privately educated.

WRITINGS:

UNDER NAME ELEANOR BURFORD

Daughter of Anna, Jenkins (London), 1941.
Passionate Witness, Jenkins, 1941.
The Married Lover, Jenkins, 1942.
When All the World Is Young, Jenkins, 1943.
So the Dreams Depart, Jenkins, 1944.
Not in Our Stars, Jenkins, 1945.
Dear Chance, Jenkins, 1947.
Alexa, Jenkins, 1948.
House at Cupid's Cross, Jenkins, 1949.
Believe the Heart, Jenkins, 1950.
Love Child, Jenkins, 1950.
Saint or Sinner?, Jenkins, 1951.
Dear Delusion, Jenkins, 1952.
Bright Tomorrow, Jenkins, 1952.
Leave Me My Love, Jenkins, 1953.

When We Are Married, Jenkins, 1953.
Castles in Spain, Jenkins, 1954.
Heart's Afire, Jenkins, 1954.
When Other Hearts, Jenkins, 1955.
Two Loves in Her Life, Jenkins, 1955.
Begin to Live, Mills & Boon (London), 1956.
Married in Haste, Mills & Boon, 1956.
To Meet a Stranger, Mills & Boon, 1957.
Pride of the Morning, Mills & Boon, 1958.
Dawn Chorus, Mills & Boon, 1959.
Red Sky at Night, Mills & Boon, 1959.
Blaze of Noon, Mills & Boon, 1960.
Night of the Stars, Mills & Boon, 1960.
Now That April's Gone, Mills & Boon, 1961.
Who's Calling?, Mills & Boon, 1962.

UNDER PSEUDONYM PHILIPPA CARR

The Miracle at St. Bruno's, Putnam (New York City), 1972.
The Lion Triumphant, Putnam, 1973.
The Witch from the Sea, Putnam, 1975.
Saraband for Two Sisters, Putnam, 1976.
Lament for a Lost Lover, Putnam, 1977.
The Love Child, Putnam, 1978.
Song of the Siren, Putnam, 1979.
Will You Love Me in September, Putnam, 1980.
The Adulteress, Putnam, 1981.
The Drop of the Dice, Putnam, 1981.
Knave of Hearts, Putnam, 1983; published in England as *Zipporah's Daughter,* Collins (London), 1983.
Voices in a Haunted Room, Putnam, 1984.
The Return of the Gypsy, Putnam, 1985.
Midsummer's Eve, Putnam, 1986.
The Pool of St. Branok, Putnam, 1987.
The Changeling, Putnam, 1989.
The Black Swan, Putnam, 1991.
A Time for Silence, Putnam, 1991.
The Gossamer Cord, Putnam, 1992.

UNDER PSEUDONYM ELBUR FORD

Poison in Pimlico, Laurie (London), 1950.
Flesh and the Devil, Laurie, 1950.
Bed Disturbed, Laurie, 1952.
Such Bitter Business, Heinemann (London), 1953, published as *Evil in the House,* Morrow (New York City), 1954.

UNDER PSEUDONYM VICTORIA HOLT

Mistress of Mellyn, Doubleday (New York City), 1960.

Kirkland Revels, Doubleday, 1962.

Bride of Pendorric, (also see below), Doubleday, 1963.

The Legend of the Seventh Virgin, Doubleday, 1965.

Menfreya in the Morning, Doubleday, 1966 (published in England as *Menfreya,* Collins, 1966).

The King of the Castle, Doubleday, 1967.

Queen's Confession: A Biography of Marie Antoinette, Doubleday, 1968, published as *The Queen's Confession,* Collins, 1968.

The Shivering Sands, Doubleday, 1969.

The Secret Woman, Doubleday, 1970.

The Shadow of the Lynx, Doubleday, 1971.

On the Night of the Seventh Moon, Doubleday, 1972.

The Curse of the Kings, Doubleday, 1973.

The House of a Thousand Lanterns, Doubleday, 1974.

Pride of the Peacock, Doubleday, 1974.

Lord of the Far Island, Doubleday, 1975.

The Devil on Horseback, Doubleday, 1977.

My Enemy the Queen, Doubleday, 1978.

The Spring of the Tiger, Doubleday, 1979.

The Mask of the Enchantress, Doubleday, 1980.

The Judas Kiss, Doubleday, 1981.

The Demon Lover, Doubleday, 1982.

The Time of the Hunter's Moon, Doubleday, 1983.

The Landowner Legacy, Doubleday, 1984.

Judas Loss, Fawcett (New York City), 1986.

The Road to Paradise Island, Fawcett, 1986.

Secret for a Nightingale, Fawcett, 1986.

The Silk Vendetta, Fawcett, 1987.

The India Fan, Fawcett, 1988.

The Captive, Doubleday, 1989.

Snare of Serpents, Doubleday, 1990.

Daughter of Deceit, Doubleday, 1991.

Seven for a Secret, Doubleday, 1992.

The Black Opal, Doubleday, 1993.

UNDER PSEUDONYM KATHLEEN KELLOW

Danse Macabre, R. Hale (London), 1952.

Rooms at Mrs. Oliver's, R. Hale, 1953.

Lilith, R. Hale, 1954, published under pseudonym Jean Plaidy, R. Hale, 1967.

It Began in Vauxhall Gardens (also see below), R. Hale, 1955.

Call of the Blood, R. Hale, 1956.

Rochester, the Mad Earl, R. Hale, 1957.

Milady Charlotte, R. Hale, 1959.

The World's a Stage, R. Hale, 1960.

UNDER PSEUDONYM JEAN PLAIDY

Together They Ride, Swan (London), 1945.

Beyond the Blue Mountains, Appleton (New York City), 1947, new edition, R. Hale, 1964.

Murder Most Royal, R. Hale, 1949, Putnam, 1972, published as *King's Pleasure,* Appleton, 1949.

The Goldsmith's Wife, Appleton, 1950, published as *The King's Mistress,* Pyramid (New York City), 1952.

Madame Serpent (first novel in *Catherine de Medici* trilogy; also see below), Appleton, 1951.

The Italian Woman (second novel in *Catherine de Medici* trilogy; also see below), R. Hale, 1952, Putnam, 1975.

Daughter of Satan, R. Hale, 1952, Putnam, 1973, as *The Unholy Woman,* Harlequin (Toronto), 1954.

Queen Jezebel (third novel in *Catherine de Medici* trilogy; also see below), Appleton, 1953.

The Spanish Bridegroom, R. Hale, 1954, Macrae Smith (Philadelphia), 1956.

St. Thomas's Eve, R. Hale, 1954, Putnam, 1970.

The Sixth Wife, R. Hale, 1953, Putnam, 1969.

Gay Lord Robert, R. Hale, 1955, Putnam, 1972.

Royal Road to Fotheringay, R. Hale, 1955, published as *Royal Road to Fotheringay: A Novel of Mary, Queen of Scots,* Putnam, 1956.

The Wandering Prince (first novel in *Charles II* trilogy; also see below), R. Hale, 1956, Putnam, 1971.

Health unto His Majesty (second novel in *Charles II* trilogy; also see below), R. Hale, 1956, published as *A Health unto His Majesty,* Putnam, 1972.

Flaunting, Extravagant Queen, R. Hale, 1957.

Here Lies Our Sovereign Lord (third novel in *Charles II* trilogy; also see below), R. Hale, 1957, Putnam, 1973.

Madonna of the Seven Hills, R. Hale, 1958, Putnam, 1974.

Light on Lucrezia, R. Hale, 1958, Putnam, 1976.

Louis, the Well-Beloved, R. Hale, 1959.

The Rise of the Spanish Inquisition (first novel in *The Spanish Inquisition: Its Rise, Growth, and End* trilogy; also see below), R. Hale, 1959.

Road to Compiegne, R. Hale, 1959.

Castile for Isabella (first novel in *Isabella and Ferdinand* trilogy; also see below), R. Hale, 1960.

The Growth of the Spanish Inquisition (second novel in *The Spanish Inquisition: Its Rise, Growth, and End* trilogy; also see below), R. Hale, 1960.

Spain for the Sovereigns (second novel in *Isabella and Ferdinand* trilogy; also see below), R. Hale, 1960.

Daughters of Spain (third novel in *Isabella and Ferdinand* trilogy; also see below), R. Hale, 1961.

The Young Elizabeth, Roy, 1961.

Meg Roper: Daughter of Sir Thomas More, Constable, 1961, Roy, 1964.

The End of the Spanish Inquisition (third novel in *The Spanish Inquisition: Its Rise, Growth, and End* trilogy; also see below), R. Hale, 1961.

Katharine, the Virgin Widow (first novel in *Katharine of Aragon* trilogy; also see below), R. Hale, 1961.

The Shadow of the Pomegranate (second novel in *Katharine of Aragon* trilogy; also see below), R. Hale, 1962.

The King's Secret Matter (third novel in *Katharine of Aragon* trilogy; also see below), R. Hale, 1962.

The Young Mary, Queen of Scots, Parrish, 1962, Roy, 1963.

The Captive Queen of Scots, R. Hale, 1963, Putnam, 1970.

The Thistle and the Rose, R. Hale, 1963, Putnam, 1973.

Mary, Queen of France, R. Hale, 1964.

The Murder in the Tower, R. Hale, 1964, Putnam, 1974.

Evergreen Gallant, R. Hale, 1965, Putnam, 1973.

The Three Crowns, R. Hale, 1965, Putnam, 1977.

The Haunted Sisters, R. Hale, 1966, Putnam, 1977.

The Queen's Favourites, R. Hale, 1966, Putnam, 1978.

Queen in Waiting, R. Hale, 1967, Putnam, 1985.

The Princess of Celle, R. Hale, 1967, Putnam, 1985.

The Spanish Inquisition: Its Rise, Growth, and End (trilogy; contains *The Rise of the Spanish Inquisition, The Growth of the Spanish Inquisition,* and *The End of the Spanish Inquisition*), Citadel, 1967.

The Prince and the Quakeress, R. Hale, 1968, Putnam, 1986.

Caroline, the Queen, R. Hale, 1968, Putnam, 1986.

It Began in Vauxhall Gardens (originally published under pseudonym Kathleen Kellow), R. Hale, 1968.

Katharine of Aragon (trilogy; contains *Katharine, the Virgin Widow, The Shadow of the Pomegranate,* and *The King's Secret Matter*), R. Hale, 1968.

The Scarlet Cloak (originally published under pseudonym Ellalice Tate; also see below), R. Hale, 1969.

The Third George, R. Hale, 1969, Putnam, 1987.

Perdita's Prince, R. Hale, 1969, Putnam, 1987.

Catherine de Medici (trilogy; contains *Madame Serpent, The Italian Woman,* and *Queen Jezebel*), R. Hale, 1969.

Sweet Lass of Richmond Hill, R. Hale, 1970, Putnam, 1988.

Indiscretions of the Queen, R. Hale, 1970, Putnam, 1988.

Isabella and Ferdinand (trilogy; includes *Castile for Isabella, Spain for the Sovereigns,* and *Daughters of Spain*), R. Hale, 1970.

The Regent's Daughter, R. Hale, 1971, Putnam, 1989.

Goddess of the Green Room, R. Hale, 1971, Putnam, 1989.

The Captive of Kensington Palace, R. Hale, 1972, Putnam, 1976.

Victoria in the Wings, R. Hale, 1972, Putnam, 1990.

Charles II (trilogy; contains *The Wandering Prince, Health unto His Majesty,* and *Here Lies Our Sovereign Lord*), R. Hale, 1972.

The Queen's Husband, R. Hale, 1973, Putnam, 1978.

The Queen and Lord M., R. Hale, 1973, Putnam, 1977.

The Widow of Windsor, R. Hale, 1974, Putnam, 1978.

The Bastard King, R. Hale, 1974, Putnam, 1979.

The Lion of Justice, R. Hale, 1975, Putnam, 1979.

Mary, Queen of Scots: The Fair Devil of Scotland, Putnam, 1975.

The Passionate Enemies, R. Hale, 1976, Putnam, 1979.

The Plantagenet Prelude, R. Hale, 1976, Putnam, 1980.

The Revolt of the Eaglets, R. Hale, 1977, Putnam, 1980.

The Heart of the Lion, R. Hale, 1977, Putnam, 1980.

The Prince of Darkness, R. Hale, 1978, Putnam, 1980.

The Battle of the Queens, R. Hale, 1978, Putnam, 1981.

The Queen from Provence, R. Hale, 1979, Putnam, 1981.

Edward Longshanks, R. Hale, 1979, published as *Hammer of the Scots,* Putnam, 1981.

The Follies of the King, R. Hale, 1980, Putnam, 1982.

The Vow on the Heron, R. Hale, 1980, Putnam, 1982.

Passage to Pontefract, R. Hale, 1981, Putnam, 1982.

The Star of Lancaster, R. Hale, 1981, Putnam, 1982.

Epitaph for Three Women, R. Hale, 1981, Putnam, 1983.

Red Rose of Anjou, R. Hale, 1982, Putnam, 1983.

The Sun in Splendour, R. Hale, 1982, Putnam, 1983.

Uneasy Lies the Head, R. Hale, 1982, Putnam, 1984.

Myself My Enemy, Hale, 1983, Putnam, 1984.

Queen of the Realm: The Story of Elizabeth I, Hale, 1984, Putnam, 1985.

Victoria Victorious, R. Hale, 1985, Putnam, 1986.

The Lady in the Tower, Putnam, 1986.

The Courts of Love, R. Hale, 1987, Putnam, 1988.

In the Shadow of the Crown, R. Hale, 1988, Putnam, 1989.

The Queen's Secret, R. Hale, 1989, Putnam, 1990.

The Reluctant Queen: The Story of Anne of York, R. Hale, 1990.

William's Wife, R. Hale, 1990.

The Pleasures of Love, R. Hale, 1991.

Kisses of Death, R. Hale, 1993.

UNDER PSEUDONYM ELLALICE TATE

Defenders of the Faith, Hodder & Stoughton (London), 1956.

The Scarlet Cloak, Hodder & Stoughton, 1957.

Queen of Diamonds, Hodder & Stoughton, 1958.

Madame du Barry, Hodder & Stoughton, 1959.

This Was a Man, Hodder & Stoughton, 1961.

OTHER

The Triptych of Poisoners, R. Hale, 1958.

(Contributor) *Three Great Romantic Stories* (contains *Bride of Pendorric*), Collins, 1972.

Contributor to newspapers and magazines, sometimes under undisclosed pseudonyms.

ADAPTATIONS: Mistress of Mellyn, Hibbert's first novel under her pseudonym Victoria Holt, was adapted for the stage by Mildred C. Kuner; *Daughter of Satan,* written under the pseudonym Jean Plaidy, is being filmed.

SIDELIGHTS: "I think people want a good story and this I give them," Eleanor Burford Hibbert once told *CA.* "They like something which is readable and you can't really beat the traditional for this. I write with great feeling and excitement and I think this comes over to the reader." Hibbert is perhaps best known for the pseudonyms Victoria Holt and Jean Plaidy, under which she has prolifically crafted most of her fiction. Kay Mussell in *Twentieth-Century Romance*

and Historical Writers found that "Hibbert was one of the most prolific and popular romance writers of the 20th century." Hibbert's gothic novels under the Holt pseudonym in the 1960s, particularly *Mistress of Mellyn,* sparked a renewed interest in the genre which continues to this day.

Doubleday kept the Holt pseudonym a well-guarded secret when it first appeared, and many thought that Holt was actually Daphne du Maurier. "I have heard her name mentioned in connection with mine," Hibbert once indicated to *CA,* "and I think it is because we have both lived in Cornwall and have written about this place. *Rebecca* is the atmospheric suspense type of book which mine are, but I don't think there is much similarity between her others and mine."

The first of the Holt gothics was 1960's *Mistress of Mellyn,* which tells of the Victorian governess Martha Leigh, who takes charge of the young Alvean at a great and gloomy manor house in the Cornwall countryside and earns the love of the manor's lord. "This gaslit, gothic novel with its labyrinthine mansion, its intimations of ghosts, its whispers of scandal and treachery, is a legitimate descendant of Jane Eyre," according to the *Kirkus* reviewer. Calling the novel "an unusually readable and likable book," Anthony Boucher in the *New York Times Book Review* believed that "Holt's touch is so assured, her presentation of late nineteenth-century Cornwall so loving, her heroine so (almost anachronistically) spirited that even a jaded curmudgeon like this reviewer has no objection to reading the old story once more."

Critics were often generous to the later Holt gothic novels as well. In the *Chicago Sunday Tribune,* for instance, Genevieve Casey said of *Kirkland Revels:* "Murder, intrigue, threats of insanity, family skeletons rattling in closets and ghosts who walk in the moonlight keep the reader credulous and turning pages fast in this absorbing story." Reviewing *The Legend of the Seventh Virgin* for *Best Sellers,* Casey wrote: "Among the clamour of novels by angry young men, among the probings and circumlocution of psychological novels, the works of Victoria Holt stand out, unpretentious, sunny, astringent, diverting." Even about work not as critically well-received as others, reviewers still praised the author's ability to engage a reader's interest. In the *New York Times Book Review,* for example, Anthony Boucher said of *Menfreya in the Morning:* "It's hard to say objectively, just why . . . [this] is so intensely readable and enjoyable. . . . It is Holt's weakest and slightest plot to date, and equally certainly nothing much happens in the way of either action or character development for long stretches. But somehow the magic . . . is still there." And in a *Washington Post Book World* review of *The Landower Legacy,* Susan Dooley called the author "a very competent escape artist."

Hibbert's historical novels under the Plaidy pseudonym are also well regarded by critics. Writing about *The Captive of Kensington Palace* in *Books and Bookmen,* for instance, Jean Stubbs remarked that "Jean Plaidy never fails to provide what may be termed 'a good read,'" and referred to the novel as a "compulsive good read." In similar terms, a reviewer for *Kirkus* found that *Beyond the Blue Mountains* "richly peopled with lifelike and colorful characters, the story rolls on and on from one dilemma to the next, not quite to the point of reader exhaustion." Speaking of *Madame Serpent,* a novel concerning the 16th century monarch Catherine de Medici, Richard Blakesley in the *Chicago Sunday Tribune* praised Plaidy's ability to render realistic characters. "Plaidy,' opined Blakesley, "has brought this remarkably sinister woman into full focus in this historical thriller. Seldom has a character been brought to life with such clarity."

Mussell concluded that "Hibbert was prolific, probably too much so for her own good. Her last few years witnessed a significant decrease in the complexity and believability of her plots. . . . Her best work was probably her first five or six Victoria Holt novels, when she was setting the standards for the host of authors who imitated her formula, although few could match her in the evocation of terror. . . . *Mistress of Mellyn* . . . deserves a place among the most important gothic romances of the century, placing Hibbert . . . near the top of her field as heiress to Daphne du Maurier, whose *Rebecca* remains the premier gothic romance of the 20th century."

"Dickens, Zola, Brontes (particularly), and nearly all the Victorians" have influenced her writings, Hibbert says. "I write regularly every day. I think this is important. As in everything else, practice helps to make perfect. Research is just a matter of reading old records, letters, etc., in fact everything connected with the period one is researching. I can only say that I love writing more than anything else. I find it stimulating and I never cease to be excited about it."

BIOGRAPHICAL/CRITICAL SOURCES:

BOOKS

Contemporary Literary Criticism, Volume 7, Gale (Detroit), 1977.
Twentieth-Century Romance and Historical Writers, third edition, St. James Press (Detroit), 1994.

PERIODICALS

Atlanta Journal-Constitution, July 4, 1966.
Best Sellers, February 1, 1965, p. 24; May 15, 1966, p. 26; July 1, 1971; August 15, 1974.
Booklist, June 15, 1992; September 1, 1993.
Books and Bookmen, January, 1973.
Chicago Sunday Tribune, May 13, 1951, p. 4; January 14, 1962.
Chicago Tribune, January 24, 1993, sec. 2, p. 7.
Kirkus, August 15, 1947, p. 15; January 15, 1949, p. 17; July 1, 1960, p. 28.
Library Journal, December 1, 1961, p. 86; March 15, 1966, p. 91; August, 1988; October 15, 1989; April 1, 1990; June 1, 1990; October 1, 1991; August, 1992; May 15, 1993.
Los Angeles Times, January 22, 1993, p. A22.
Los Angeles Times Book Review, June 16, 1985.
New York Herald Tribune Books, January 7, 1962, p. 5.
New York Times, December 7, 1947, p. 24; June 26, 1949, p. 18.
New York Times Book Review, September 11, 1960, p. 36; April 17, 1966, p. 37; January 15, 1984; November 6, 1988.
People Weekly, September 20, 1993.
Publishers Weekly, July 10, 1987; June 24, 1988; August 11, 1989; June 29, 1990; July 5, 1991; July 20, 1992; July 12, 1993.
Saturday Review of Literature, June 4, 1949, p. 32.
School Library Journal, November, 1990; April, 1992.
Times (London), January 2, 1986; January 21, 1993, p. 19.
Washington Post, January 21, 1993, p. B7.
Washington Post Book World, November 7, 1982.

OBITUARIES:

PERIODICALS

Chicago Tribune, January 24, 1993, sec. 2, p. 7.
Los Angeles Times, January 22, 1993, p. A22.
Times (London), January 21, 1993, p. 19.
Washington Post, January 21, 1993, p. B7.*

HILL, Fiona
See PALL, Ellen Jane

*　*　*

HOGARTH, Charles
See CREASEY, John

*　*　*

HOLT, Victoria
See HIBBERT, Eleanor Alice Burford

*　*　*

HOOKE, Sylvia Denys
See MALLESON, Lucy Beatrice

*　*　*

HOPE, Brian
See CREASEY, John

*　*　*

HOROVITZ, Israel (Arthur) 1939-

PERSONAL: Born March 31, 1939, in Wakefield, MA; son of Julius Charles (a lawyer) and Hazel (Solberg) Horovitz; married second wife, Doris Keefe (an artist), December 25, 1959 (divorced December, 1972); married Gillian Adams, July 1981; children: (second marriage) Rachael Keefe, Matthew Keefe, Adam Keefe, (third marriage) Hannah Rebecca and Oliver Adams (twins). *Education:* Royal Academy of Dramatic Art, London, M.A., 1963; attended New School for Social Research, 1963-66; City University of New York, M.A., 1972. *Religion:* Jewish.

ADDRESSES: Office—The Actors Studio, 432 West 44th St., New York, NY 10036. *Agent*—Gloria Safier, 667 Madison Ave., New York, NY 10021; Margaret Ramsay Ltd., 14A Goodwin's Ct., London WC2N 4LL, England; and Les Editions de Minuit, 9 rue Bernard-Palissy, Paris, France.

CAREER: Playwright and director. Stagehand, Paper Mill Playhouse, Millburn, NJ, 1963-65; Playwright-in-residence, Royal Shakespeare Co., London, 1965; instructor in playwriting, Circle in the Square Theatre School, New York City, 1968-70; playwright-in-residence, City College of the City University of New York, New York City, 1969-74; part-time professor of playwriting, New York University, New York City, 1970-76; director of the playwrights unit of The Actors Studio, 1977—. Fannie Hurst Visiting Professor of Theatre Arts, Brandeis University, Waltham, MA, 1974-75. Founder and artistic director, Gloucester Stage Company, Gloucester, MA, 1980—. Founding member, Eugene O'Neill Memorial Theatre Foundation.

MEMBER: International P.E.N., Authors League of America, Societe de Compositeurs Dramatique (Paris), Dramatists Guild, New Dramatists, Inc., Actors Studio (member of playwrights unit), Players.

AWARDS, HONORS: Rockfeller fellowships in playwriting, 1968, 1969; Vernon Rice Award, 1968, for *The Indian Wants the Bronx;* Drama Desk Best Play award, 1968, for *The Indian Wants the Bronx* and *It's Called the Sugar Plum;* Obie awards for Best American Play, for *The Indian Wants the Bronx,* 1968, and *The Honest-to-God Schnozzola,* 1969; *Jersey Journal* Best Play award, 1968, for *The Indian Wants the Bronx; Plays and Players* Best Foreign Play award, 1969, for *It's Called the Sugar Plum; Show Business* award for best Off-Broadway play, 1969, for *Line* and *Rats; Village Voice* Off-Broadway award, 1969, for *The Honest-to-God Schnozzola;* Cannes Film Festival Prix de Jury, 1971, for *The Strawberry Statement;* American Academy of Arts and Letters Award in Literature, 1972; New York State Council on the Arts grant, 1972, 1974; co-recipient of Academy of Television Arts and Science (Emmy) award, for *VD-Blues;* Christopher Award, for *VD-Blues;* French Critics Prize, 1973, for *Line;* National Endowment of the Arts Award, 1974-75; Fulbright Foundation grant, 1975; Guggenheim fellowship, 1977-78; Eliot Norton Prize, 1986; Best Play award, *Boston,* magazine, 1987; honorary doctorate, Massachusetts State University, 1991.

WRITINGS:

FICTION

Cappella (novel), Harper (New York City), 1973.
Spider Poems and Other Writings (verse), Harper, 1973.
Nobody Loves Me, Editions de Minuit (Paris), 1975, Braziller (New York City), 1976.

PUBLISHED PLAYS

It's Called the Sugar Plum (one-act; produced with *The Indian Wants the Bronx,* Off-Broadway at Astor Place Theatre, 1968), Dramatists Play Service (New York City), 1968.
The Indian Wants the Bronx (one-act; produced with *It's Called the Sugar Plum,* Off-Broadway at Astor Place Theatre, 1968; produced with *Rats* in London at Open Space Theatre, 1969), Dramatists Play Service, 1968.
Line (produced as one-act Off-Off-Broadway at Cafe LaMama, 1967; produced as two-act in Los Angeles at Mark Taper Forum, 1969; produced as one-act with *Acrobats* Off-Broadway at Theatre De Lys, 1971), Dramatists Play Service, 1968.
Rats (one-act; produced with ten other one-acts Off-Broadway at Cafe Au Go Go, 1968; produced with *The Indian Wants the Bronx* in London at Open Space Theatre, 1969), Dramatists Play Service, 1968.
Morning (one-act; produced in Spoleto, Italy, at Festival of Two Worlds, directed by Horovitz as *Chiaroscuro,* 1968; produced with *Noon* by Terrence McNally and *Night* by Leonard Melfi on Broadway at Henry Miller's Theatre, 1968), Random House, 1968.
First Season (contains *The Indian Wants the Bronx, Line, It's Called the Sugar Plum,* and *Rats*), Random House, 1968.
The Honest-to-God Schnozzola (one-act; produced in Provincetown, MA, at Act IV Theatre, 1968; produced with *Leader,* Off-Broadway at Gramercy Arts Theatre, 1969), Breakthrough Press, 1971.
Acrobats (one-act; produced in Amsterdam at Mickery Theatre, 1968; produced with *Line* Off-Broadway at Theatre De Lys, 1971), Dramatists Play Service, 1971.
Clair-Obscur (produced in Paris at Theatre Lucernaire, 1970), Gallimard, 1972.

Dr. Hero (originally titled *The World's Greatest Play;* produced, under title *Hero,* in New York, 1971; produced under title *Dr. Hero,* Off-Broadway at New York Public Theatre, 1971), Dramatists Play Service, 1973.
Play for Trees [and] *Leader* (*Play for Trees* televised on National Educational Television (NET), 1969; *Leader,* one-act, produced with *The Honest-to-God Schnozzola,* Off-Broadway at Gramercy Arts Theatre, 1969), Dramatists Play Service, 1973.
Shooting Gallery [and] *Play for Germs* (*Shooting Gallery* produced at the WPA New Plays Festival; *Play for Germs* based on television play, *VD-Blues;* also see below), Dramatists Play Service, 1973.
The Primary English Class (produced Off-Off Broadway at The Cubicula, 1975; produced Off-Broadway at the Circle-in-the-Square Theatre, 1975), Dramatists Play Service, 1976.
Uncle Snake, Dramatists Play Service, 1976.
The Good Parts (produced in New York at the Actors Studio, 1979), Dramatists Play Service, 1990.
A Christmas Carol: Scrooge and Marley (adapted from Dickens' novel), Dramatists Play Service, 1979.
The Great Labor Day Classic and The Former One-on-One Basketball Champion, Dramatists Play Service, 1982.
Year of the Duck, Dramatists Play Service, 1988.
North Shore Fish, Dramatists Play Service, 1989.
Henry Lumper, Dramatists Play Service, 1990.
The Widow's Blind Date, Dramatists Play Service, 1990.
Israel Horovitz: Collected Works Volume I: Sixteen Short Plays (contains *Line, It's Called the Sugar Plum, The Indian Wants the Bronx, Rats, Morning, The Honest-to-God Schnozzola, Play for Germs, Shooting Gallery, Acrobats, The Great Labor Day Classic, The Former One-on-One Basketball Champion, Hopscotch, The 75th, Stage Directions, Spared,* and *Faith*), Smith & Kraus (Lyme, New Hampshire), 1994. *New England Blue: Plays of Working-Class Life* (contains *The Widow's Blind Date, Park Your Car in Harvard Yard, Henry Lumper, North Shore Fish, Strong Man's Weak Child,* and *Unexpected Tenderness*), Smith & Kraus, 1996.

Horovitz's plays have been anthologized in *Collision Course,* edited by Edward Parone, Random House, 1968; *The Waterford Plays,* edited by John Lahr, Grove, 1968; *The Best Short Plays,* edited by Stanley Richards, Chilton, 1968, 1969, 1970, 1975, 1977, and 1978; and *Famous American Plays of the 1960s,* edited by Harold Clurman, Dell, 1972.

UNPUBLISHED PLAYS

The Comeback, produced in Boston at Emerson College, 1958.

The Hanging of Emanuel, produced in South Orange, NJ, at Il Cafe Cabaret Theatre, 1962.

This Play Is about Me, produced at Il Cafe Cabaret Theatre, 1963.

The Killer Dove (two-act), produced in West Orange, NJ, at Theatre-on-the-Green, 1966.

Le Premiere, produced in Paris, directed by Horovitz, at Theatre de Poche, 1972.

The Reason We Eat, produced in Stamford, CT, at Hartman Theatre, 1976, produced in Boston at Boston Repertory Co., 1977.

The Former One-on-One Basketball Champion, produced in New York at the Actors Studio, 1977.

Man with Bags (an adaptation of Ionesco's *l'Homme Aux Valises*), produced in Towson, MD, at Towson State University Theatre, 1977.

Cappella (an adaptation of Horovitz's novel of the same title; see above), produced Off-Broadway at the Off-Center Theatre, 1978.

Strong-Man's Weak Child, produced in Los Angeles, 1990.

Fighting Over Beverly, produced in Gloucester, MA, 1993.

Lebensraum, produced in Gloucester, MA, 1996.

My Old Lady, produced in Gloucester, MA, 1996.

Also author of unproduced plays *The Death of Bernard the Believer, The Simon Street Harvest, Mackerel,* and *The Lounge Player,* author of *Sunday Runners in the Rain.*

PLAYS; "WAKEFIELD" SERIES

Alfred the Great (three-act; produced in Paris at American Center Theatre, directed by Horovitz, 1972; produced in Great Neck, NY, 1972; produced with *Our Father's Failing* and *Alfred Dies* under program title *The Wakefield Plays,* in New York at Actor's Studio, 1978), Harper, 1974.

Stage Directions [and] *Spared* (*Stage Directions* produced in New York at Actors Studio, produced with *Spared, Hopscotch,* and *The 75th,* under program title *The Quannapowitt Quartet,* at New York Shakespeare Festival, 1978; *Spared* produced with *Hopscotch* in Paris at Theatre du Centre Cultural Americain, directed by Horovitz, 1974), Dramatists Play Service, 1976.

Hopscotch, produced with *Spared* in Paris at Theatre du Centre Cultural American, 1974.

The 75th (produced with *Hopscotch, Stage Directions,* and *Spared* under program title *The Quannapowitt Quartet,* 1978), Dramatist Play Service, 1976.

Our Father's Failing, produced with *Alfred the Great* and *Alfred Dies* under program title *The Wakefield Plays,* 1978.

Alfred Dies, produced with *Alfred the Great,* and *Our Father's Failing,* under program title *The Wakefield Plays,* 1978.

SCREENPLAYS

The Strawberry Statement (based on the book by James Simon Kunen), Metro-Goldwyn-Mayer (M-G-M), 1970.

Line (adapted from his play of same title; see above), Kaleidoscope Films, 1970.

Believe in Me (originally titled *Speed Is of the Essence*), M-G-M, 1971.

Acrobats (adapted from his play of same title; see above), Walker Stuart Productions, 1972.

Also author of screenplays *Fast Eddie,* 1980; *Author! Author!; Fell,* 1982; *Berta,* 1982; *Firebird at Dogtown,* 1984; *Light Years,* 1985; *Wedlock,* 1985; *A Man in Love* (with Diane Kurys), 1987; *Payofski's Discovery,* 1987; *The Deuce* , 1988; *Strong-Man's Weak Child,* 1988; *Faith,* 1988; *Fighting over Beverley,* 1988; *The Pan,* 1989; *Letters to Iris,* 1989; *The Quiet Room,* 1990; *Park Your Car in Harvard Yard,* 1991; and *Strong Man,* 1991.

TELEVISION PLAYS

(With Jules Feiffer, and director and producer) *VD-Blues* (produced by NET, 1972), Avon, 1974.

Start to Finish, produced by Columbia Broadcasting System (CBS), 1977.

The Making and Breaking of Splinters Braun, produced by CBS, 1977-78.

Bartleby, the Scrivener (adapted from the Melville novel of same title), produced for Public Television, Baltimore, MD, 1978.

A Rosen by Any Other Name, Dramatists Play Service, 1987.

Today I Am a Fountain Pen, Dramatists Play Service, 1987.

The Chopin Playoffs, Dramatists Play Service, 1990.

Author of several television plays for British Broadcasting Corp. Also author of television plays *The*

Primary English Class (based on Horovitz's play of same title; see above), 1976, *The Deer Park* (adapted from Norman Mailer's novel), 1979, *Funny Books, D.C.A.C.,* and *The Indian Wants the Bronx* (based on his play of the same title; see above). *Today I Am a Fountain Pen, A Rosen by Any Other Name,* and *The Chopin Playoffs* were adapted for the stage in 1986.

OTHER

Contributor of poetry to various publications including *Village Voice, Poetry, Painted Bride Quarterly, Paris Review,* and others. Also contributor to Dramatist Guild *Quarterly,* 1976.

SIDELIGHTS: Israel Horovitz claims his two greatest influences as a dramatist have been Euripides, antiquity's foremost tragedian, and Samuel Beckett, progenitor of the darkly comic twentieth-century Theatre of the Absurd. Many of his plays do seem to combine tragic sensibilities with a distinctly modern ear for dialogue, satirical wit, and familiar, if not always personable, characters.

Critics have variously compared his work to that of Aeschylus and Eugene Ionesco, Aristophanes, and Harold Pinter. Horovitz's *Wakefield Plays* are a modern Greek epic: a cycle consisting of three full-length tragedies (*The Alfred Trilogy*) and four one-acts (*The Quannapowitt Quartet*), all of which take place in the playwright's native Wakefield, Massachusetts. Referring to the scale of the project and its reliance on Greek myth, *New Spectator* critic Martin Esslin dubbed the *Wakefield* cycle "an American Orestia." At the other end of the spectrum, a *Plays and Players* reviewer wrote of Horovitz' oeuvre, "Again and again, one sees the shadows of either Beckett or Ionesco falling across the stage—the lean but reverberating image of desolation, or the increasingly farcical insanity of logic."

This unique combination of the classical and the contemporary has made Horovitz one of America's most-produced playwrights, both at home—especially at universities and regional theatres—and abroad. His plays have been translated into nearly thirty languages, and in France, where the Irish-born Samuel Beckett is revered as the master of modern malaise, no American writer has had more plays translated and produced in the French language than Horovitz (Eugene O'Neill runs a close second).

Horovitz's first play, *The Comeback,* was produced in Boston when he was eighteen and a freshman at

Harvard University. A tremendous outpouring of work has followed ever since. In 1963 he completed graduate work at London's Royal Academy of Dramatic Art, then returned to England two years later to become the first playwright-in-residence at the Royal Shakespeare Company. Afterward, he returned to New York and the newest hotbed of theatrical activity: Off-Broadway.

During Horovitz's early New York years a host of well-known actors launched their careers with juicy parts in his plays. Richard Dreyfuss, Marsha Mason, Jill Clayburgh, Herve Villechaize, and even Sylvester Stallone (who played one of the giant, ferocious rodents in *Rats*) appeared in Horovitz works in churches, basements, converted garages, and living rooms scattered around the burgeoning Off-Broadway scene. In 1968 a relatively unknown Al Pacino won the Obie Award for Best Actor for his portrayal of the bullying hoodlum Murph in *The Indian Wants the Bronx.*

Diversity may be one of the keys to Horovitz's success. A myriad of quirky characters and unique settings populate his plays. *Rats* (1968) concerns a couple of playful rodents whose games turn deadly serious when they fight over a baby in a crib. Marital strife is the subject of *Acrobats* (1971), a brief one-act written specifically for a husband and wife acrobatic team. Sports figure prominently in at least two of Horovitz' plays, *The Great Labor Day Classic* (1979), about runners in a 25 kilometer race, and *The Former One-on-One Basketball Champion* (1978), in which a washed-up pro ballplayer on his way to commit suicide stops for a final game of hoops with an angry teenager. *Morning,* the first third of the *Morning, Noon, and Night* triptych Horovitz co-authored with Terrence McNally and Leonard Melfi in 1968, is an alarming serio-comedy about a black family who, seeking better opportunities, take pills to turn themselves white.

A tremendous variety of people and places appear in Horovitz's plays. Still, a handful of themes and stylistic traits recur, providing insight into the playwright's views on the American landscape. Competition, one-upmanship and a strong, sometimes maniacal desire to get ahead characterize many Horovitz creations. Life in the United States is often viewed as a game, sometimes a deadly one, in which opponents vie for real or imagined prizes. To win, they may play by the rules (if any exist), cheat, lie, threaten, cajole, or resort to physical or psychological violence. Like his contemporaries Edward Albee and Sam Shepard, Horovitz finds cutthroat American competition alternately humorous, frightening, and tragic.

He also seems especially interested in the way communication, or the lack of it, is at the root of many modern sociological ills. Like a linguist, Horovitz deconstructs and analyzes languages, dialects, slang, jargon, and even literary conventions. In *Stage Directions* (1976), a play that actually reflects some of the writer's own tragic family history, the characters speak no proper "dialogue." They only describe their actions and, occasionally, their emotions as they mourn the deaths of their parents. In another experiment with communication, *The Primary English Class* (1976), an instructor tries to teach her adult students the rudiments of English. No one in the group shares the same language and the confusion that ensues creates a microcosmic Tower of Babel for our times.

By his own estimation, Horovitz's professional career began in earnest with two New York productions, both Off-Broadway, in the late 1960s. *Line,* first presented at Cafe La Mama ETC in 1967, features one of the simplest sets ever imagined: a white, adhesive tape line fixed to the stage floor. The play revolves around the efforts of five characters who jockey for position behind the line. Fleming, the simplest and least cunning of the bunch, arrived early and has been waiting behind the line all night, drinking beer and eating potato chips. Almost immediately after the play begins his place is usurped by Stephen, a ranting lunatic who cracks sacrilegious jokes and sings the words on his credit card to Mozart tunes.

This odd couple is joined by the voluptuous Molly and her husband, Arnall. She is a young, coarse, cunning woman, used to getting what she wants, who tries to seduce her way to the front of the line. Meanwhile, the older and perennially cuckolded Arnall tries and tries but always winds up last. The final figure, Dolan, is a more restrained and determined man who covets second place, because from there he can glimpse the front and plan his attack.

The purpose of the line is never made clear, and it doesn't seem to matter. It is a metaphor, and therefore it might exist anywhere and for any purpose. What is important are the various characters' reactions to the line and each other, and what they reveal about human nature. As several critics pointed out, the lesson of the play is an obvious one. "There are

no real images here, only parallels," complained Clive Barnes in the *New York Times,* "The line itself, with its crazy changes of fortune encompassed by accident and mayhem, is a very obvious and nonpoetic parallel for life itself." Martin Gottfried wrote in *Women's Wear Daily* that Horovitz "wants to tell us that the rat race is absurd, that our competitiveness only feeds our own need for competition, that we are our own judges of those plastic battles with which we litter our lives."

Its lack of subtlety notwithstanding, *Line* managed to find both audiences and supportive reviewers. Jeremy Tallmer, critic for the *New York Post,* gave Horovitz his first New York review as a professional playwright. In it, he praised both Horovitz's writing and his acting (at the last minute the author had to step in and play the part of Stephen). The headline of the review read, "WELCOME MR. HOROVITZ." A later production, mounted at the 13th Street Repertory Theater, opened in 1975 and has been running ever since, making it Off-Broadway's longest-running (non-musical) play.

Horovitz' other great Off-Broadway success is probably his best-known work: *The Indian Wants the Bronx.* The Indian of the title is Gupta, a white-turbaned Hindu who speaks no English and has had the misfortune of being marooned at a bus stop on 5th Avenue in New York City one late September night. Gupta is searching for his son, Prem, who lives in the Bronx, when he encounters Joey and Murph, a couple of juvenile street toughs with a penchant for unprovoked violence. They toy with the hapless immigrant until, tiring of their game, they beat him, cut him with a knife, and leave him jabbering hysterically into the broken line of a pay phone.

The Indian Wants the Bronx seems, at first glance, to be an indictment of American xenophobia, urban violence, and juvenile delinquency. The idea for the play, however, actually originated in England in the early sixties where Horovitz was studying theatre at the Royal Academy of Dramatic Art. While waiting on line outside a cafeteria for an early breakfast, the budding young playwright witnessed a scene similar to the one he eventually wrote about. A car full of "teddy boys" (the 1960s version of skinheads) harassed a young Hindu student who, not understanding their language or their insults, laughed and waved congenially. The real-life version ended harmlessly; the rowdy aggressors, their game spoiled, sped away. but the incident haunted Horovitz. "So profound was the young Hindu's loneliness," the writer recalls, "he was thrilled to have human contact, even from cruel and dangerous aggressors."

The Indian Wants the Bronx premiered in New York on a double bill with *It's Called the Sugar Plum* on January 17, 1968. The latter play, another character-centered piece, concerns a Harvard boy who inadvertently kills a fellow student in a car accident, then must face the wrath of the dead boy's girlfriend. As the play develops, the victim recedes more and more into the background as the egocentric survivors quarrel over whose pain is more severe and which of them received more coverage in the press reports.

Horovitz, who has written more one-acts than full-length dramas and is used to seeing his works on double- or triple-bills, doubted the wisdom of pairing these two plays. "*It's Called the Sugar Plum* is a sweet, fragile play," he insists, "By contrast, *The Indian Wants the Bronx* has the sweetness and fragility of a sledgehammer."

Nevertheless, critical response was mostly positive. Dan Sullivan reported in the *New York Times* that "the theatrical power of *The Indian Wants the Bronx,* the abstract beauty, if you will, of the violence, cannot be denied." Gottfried praised the structure of the play, the way it built intensity, and called the conclusion, "frightening and pointed, as good a climax as any play might want." In the *New Yorker,* Edith Oliver wrote, "Both plays are frightening, and the aimlessness of the utterly believable characters—their aimless cruelty and their aimless, solemn fatuity—is the most frightening thing about them."

In 1979 Horovitz founded the Gloucester Stage Company (GSC) in Massachusetts as "a theatre for playwrights and new plays," and since then many of his works have premiered in this tiny New England town before taking off around the world. *Park Your Car in Harvard Yard, Strong Man's Weak Child, North Shore Fish,* and *Henry Lumper* are just a few Horovitz works that began at the GSC. "It just goes to show," the playwright told *American Theatre,* "you throw a pebble into the water in Gloucester and the ripples go a long way."

Horovitz' journey as a playwright has certainly taken him a long way: from small-town Massachusetts to London, Paris, New York, and back again, where he lives comfortably with his family and continues to write for the world's stages. In 1996 he began a new cycle of plays about Americans in Europe. The first

two installments, *Lebensraum* and *My Old Lady,* both premiered at the Gloucester Stage Company during their summer season. Horovitz is at home and doing what he loves best. "What is this business of playwriting, finally," he asks in *American Theatre,* "if not to create a record of what life was like, in our time, on our little dot on planet Earth? As serious playwrights, we can do no more. We can do no less."

BIOGRAPHICAL/CRITICAL SOURCES:

BOOKS

Contemporary Dramatists, 5th edition, St. James Press (Chicago), 1993.
Contemporary Literary Criticism, Volume 56, Gale (Detroit), 1989.
Dictionary of Literary Biography, Volume 7: *Twentieth-Century American Dramatists,* Gale, 1981.
Gottfried, Martin, *Opening Nights,* Putnam (New York City), 1970.
Horovitz, Israel, *Israel Horovitz: Sixteen Short Plays,* Smith & Kraus, 1994.
Kane, Leslie, editor, *Israel Horovitz: A Collection of Critical Essays,* Greenwood Press (Westport, CT), 1994.
Kerr, Walter, *Thirty Days Hath November: Pain and Pleasure in the Contemporary Theatre,* Simon & Schuster, 1970.
Little, Stuart, and Arthur Cantor, *The Playmakers,* Norton, 1970.

PERIODICALS

American Theatre, October 1992, p. 39.
Booklist, August 1994, p. 2016.
Christian Science Monitor, July 22, 1970.
Library Journal, March 15, 1996, p. 71.
Nation, February 12, 1968; December 18, 1989, p. 766; January 20, 1992, p. 66.
New Statesman, September 6, 1968.
New York, January 16, 1989, p. 80; November 20, 1989, p. 129; November 18, 1991, p. 95; November 7, 1994, p. 101.
New Yorker, January 27, 1968; May 3, 1969; November 20, 1989, p. 110; November 18, 1991, p. 126.
New York Times, January 18, 1968; June 30, 1968; November 29, 1968; February 16, 1971; January 28, 1972.
Plays and Players, July 1976.
Show Business, December 14, 1968.

Variety, August 5, 1970; July 15, 1987, p. 66;
August 26, 1987, p. 114; January 4, 1989, p.
82; October 7, 1991, p. 203; November 11,
1991, p. 58; August 30, 1993, p. 27; September
6, 1993, p. 45; September 13, 1993, p. 36;
September 5, 1994, p. 62; October 24, 1994, p.
78; September 18, 1995, p. 92.

Village Voice, December 5, 1968; April 24, 1969;
October 28, 1971.

Women's Wear Daily, January 18, 1968.

*   *   *

HUGHES, Colin
  See CREASEY, John

*   *   *

HUNT, Harrison
  See BALLARD, (Willis) Todhunter

*   *   *

HUNT, Kyle
  See CREASEY, John

*   *   *

HUNTER, George
  See BALLARD, (Willis) Todhunter

*   *   *

HUNTER, John
  See BALLARD, (Willis) Todhunter

*   *   *

INADA, Lawson Fusao 1938-

PERSONAL: Born May 26, 1938, in Fresno, CA;
son of Fusaji and Masako (Saito) Inada; married

Janet Francis, February 19, 1962; children: Miles
Fusao, Lowell Masao. *Education:* Attended University of California, Berkeley, 1956-57; Fresno State
College (now California State University, Fresno),
B.A., 1959; University of Iowa, graduate study,
1960-62; University of Oregon, M.F.A., 1966.

ADDRESSES: Home—2320 Morada Lane, Ashland,
OR 97520. *Office*—Department of English, Southern
Oregon State College, Ashland, OR 97520.

CAREER: University of New Hampshire, Durham,
instructor in English, 1962-65; Southern Oregon
State College, Ashland, associate professor, 1966-
77, professor of English, 1977—. Visiting lecturer at
Lewis and Clark College, 1969, Eastern Oregon
State College, 1975, and University of Hawaii, 1976;
King/Parks Scholar-in-Residence at Wayne State
University, 1987. Host of radio program, *Talk Story:
The Written Word,* on KSOR-FM, Ashland, OR.
Seminar leader at various poetry and creative writing
workshops, including Asian-Americans for a Fair
Media Conference, 1975, Siskiyou Writers Conference, 1977, and Iowa State Department of Education
Conference, 1978. Judge, Coordinating Council of
Literary Magazines College Contest, 1976. Chair,
Council of Literary Magazines, 1982-84; site evaluator, National Endowment for the Arts, 1987—;
member, Committee on Racism and Bias in the
Teaching of English, 1988—. Member of board of
directors, Southern Oregon Public Television,
1990—. Has given readings of his poetry at numerous universities and seminars, including University
of California, Berkeley, University of California,
Los Angeles, University of Michigan, University of
Oregon, San Francisco State University, University
of Washington, Oregon Poetry-in-the-Schools, Minnesota Poetry-in-the-Schools, Seattle Arts Commission Festival, and National Poetry Festival. Consultant to literary organizations, including Third World
Writers Festival, Central Washington State College,
1974, Society for the Study of Multi-Ethnic Literature of the United States, 1977, and Asian-American
Writers Conference, 1978.

MEMBER: Japanese American Citizens League.

AWARDS, HONORS: University of Iowa Writers
Workshop fellowship, 1960-62; National Endowment
for the Arts creative writing fellowship, 1972; Pioneer Writers Award from Asian-American Writers
Conference, 1975; Oregon State teaching excellence
award, 1984; National Endowment for the Arts poetry fellowship, 1985; Arizona Commission for the

Arts research fellowship, 1990; named Oregon State Poet of the Year, 1991; American Book Award for *Legends from Camp*, 1994.

WRITINGS:

Three Northwest Poets: Drake, Inada, Lawder, Quixote Press (Madison, WI), 1970.

Before the War: Poems As They Happen, Morrow (New York City), 1971.

(Co-editor) *Aiiieeeee!: An Anthology of Asian-American Writers,* Howard University Press (Washington, DC), 1974.

(With Garrett Kaoru Hongo and Alan Chong Lau) *The Buddha Bandits Down Highway 99,* Buddhahead Press (Mountain View, CA), 1978.

(With Patti Moran McCoy and Kathleen Bullock) *Hey Diddle Rock,* Kids Matter (Ashland, OR), 1986.

(With McCoy and Bullock) *Hickory Dickory Rock,* Kids Matter, 1986.

(With McCoy and Bullock) *Humpty Dumpty Rock,* Kids Matter, 1986.

(With McCoy and Bullock) *Rock-a-doodle-doo,* Kids Matter, 1986.

(Co-editor) *The Big Aiiieeeee!: An Anthology of Chinese American and Japanese American Literature,* Penguin (New York City), 1990.

In This Great Land of Freedom: The Japanese Pioneers of Oregon, Japanese-American National Museum (Los Angeles), 1993.

Legends from Camp, Coffee House Press (Minneapolis), 1993.

Drawing the Line, Coffee House Press, 1997.

Consultant/writer, *The Boys of Heart Mountain* and *Moving Memories,* video-documentaries, Japanese American National Museum. Work represented in numerous anthologies, including *Down At the Santa Fe Depot: Twenty Fresno Poets,* David Kherdian, editor, Giligia Press, 1970, *The Modern Idiom,* Lio Hamalian, editor, Crowell (New York City), 1972, *Settling America,* David Kherdian, editor, Macmillan (New York City), 1974, *Modern Poetry of Western America,* William Stanfford, editor, Brigham Young University Press (Provo, UT), 1975, *Focus on Forms,* Philip J. McFarland, editor, Houghton (Boston), 1977, *Dreamers and Desperadoes: Contemporary Short Fiction of the American West,* Craig Lesley, editor, Dell (New York City), 1993, and *Moment's Notice: Jazz in Poetry and Prose,* Art Lange and Nathaniel Mackey, editors, Coffee House Press, 1993. Contributor of poetry to periodicals,

including *Amerasia Journal, Bridge, Carleton Miscellany, Chicago Review, Evergreen Review, Kayak, Massachusetts Review, English Journal, Mother Jones, Northwest Review, San Francisco Review,* and *Southwest Review.* Member of editorial board, *Directory of American Poets and Fiction Writers* 1976—, and *Contemporary Poetry,* 1977—. Assistant editor, *Northwest Review,* 1965-66; editor, *Rogue River Gorge,* 1970—; contributing editor, *Dues: Third World Writing,* 1972-74; contributing editor, *Northwest Review,* 1987—; guest editor, *Hawaii Review,* summer, 1978.

SIDELIGHTS: In 1993, Lawson Fusao Inada published *Legends from Camp,* a set of poems that reflects on life in the World War II-era internment camps for Japanese Americans. Himself an internee at a camp, Inada "carries a reader into a child's world behind barbed wire," as R. C. Doyle explains in *Choice. Legends from Camp* won an American Book Award in 1994.

Legends from Camp is divided into five sections, beginning with Inada's time in the internment camp, then moving to "Fresno," "Jazz," "Oregon," and "Performance." As Andrew J. Dephtereos writes in *American Book Review,* the collection creates "a decidedly personal history of Inada, told in chapters that represent significant stages in his persona's life."

Inada's poems embody his conviction that poetry must be accessible to all readers, not just to those who are most knowledgeable about the genre. "Poetry happens—whenever, wherever it wants," Inada asserts in the preface to *Legends from Camp,* "and the poet simply has to be ready to follow through on the occasion." Reviewing the collection for *Amerasia Journal,* Lonny Kaneko explains that Inada "writes a kind of popular poem, built for the listener's ear, aware, like jazz, of the need to capture in sound the spirit of his theme, of letting it build and reverberate in repeated phrases, little riffs and refrains that play through the poems." While the critic for *Publishers Weekly* finds Inada's work to be "unsophisticated in tone, technique and conceptual structure," Jessica Grim of the *Library Journal* judges the book to be "playful, full of life, and easy to understand, even when the subject is somber—as in the first section, 'Camp,' which recounts the author's experience as a boy in the Japanese internment camps." Doyle comments that the powerful "Camp" section "will add a fresh dimension to a growing body of literature that remembers, humanizes, and shares the Japanese American internment experience for new generations."

BIOGRAPHICAL/CRITICAL SOURCES:

PERIODICALS

Amerasia Journal, winter, 1993, p. 167.
American Book Review, December, 1993, p. 22.
Choice, May, 1993, p. 1465.
Library Journal, January, 1993, p. 121.

Los Angeles Times Book Review, September 5, 1993, p. 6.
Nation, August 28, 1995, p. 204.
Publishers Weekly, May 31, 1991, p. 67; November 16, 1992, p. 57.
Small Press, summer, 1993, p. 85.
Western American Literature, spring, 1994, p. 85.

OTHER

I Told You So: Lawson Fusao Inada (documentary film), Visual Communications, 1975.

J

JAMES, Norah C(ordner) ?-1979

PERSONAL: Born in London, England; died in 1979; daughter of John H. Cordner-James (a consulting mining engineer). *Education:* Attended Francis Holland School for Girls, London, and Slade School of Art. *Politics:* Labour. *Religion:* Church of England.

CAREER: Former designer of book jackets, organizing secretary for the Civil Service Clerical Association in England, and advertising and publicity manager for Jonathan Cape Ltd. (publishers), London, England; novelist, 1929-79. Borough councillor for Finsbury, 1945-46. *Military service:* Auxiliary Territorial Service, World War II.

MEMBER: National Book League.

WRITINGS:

NOVELS

Sleeveless Errand, Morrow (New York City), 1929.
Hail! All Hail!, Scholartis Press (London), 1929.
Shatter the Dream, Constable (London), 1930, Morrow, 1931.
To the Valiant, Morrow, 1930.
The Wanton Way, Morrow, 1931 (published in England as *Wanton Ways,* Duckworth [London], 1931).
Hospital, Duckworth, 1932.
Nurse Adriane, Covici, Friede (New York), 1933.
Jealousy, Covici, Friede, 1933.
Sacrifice, Covici, Friede, 1934 (published in England as *Strap-Hangers,* Duckworth, 1934).
The Return, Duckworth, 1935.
The Lion Beat the Unicorn, Duckworth, 1935.

By a Side Wind, Jarrolds (London), 1936.
Two Divided by One, Macaulay (New York City), 1936.
Sea View, Jarrolds, 1936.
The Stars Are Fire, Cassell (London), 1937.
Women Are Born to Listen, Macaulay, 1937.
As High as the Sky, Macaulay, 1938.
The House by the Tree, Cassell, 1938.
Mighty City, Cassell, 1939.
The Gentlewoman, Cassell, 1940.
The Hunted Heart, Cassell, 1941.
The Long Journey, Cassell, 1941.
Two Selfish People, Cassell, 1942.
Enduring Adventure, Cassell, 1944.
One Bright Day, Cassell, 1945, modernized edition, Hurst & Blackett (London), 1964.
The Father, Cassell, 1946.
There Is Always To-morrow, Macdonald & Co. (London), 1946.
Penny Trumpet, Macdonald & Co., 1947.
Brittle Glory, Macdonald & Co., 1948.
Swift to Sever, Macdonald & Co., 1949.
Pay the Piper, Macdonald & Co., 1950.
Pedigree of Honey, Macdonald & Co., 1951.
So Runs the River, Macdonald & Co., 1952.
A Summer Storm, Macdonald & Co., 1953.
Silent Corridors, Hutchinson (London), 1953, McGraw (New York City), 1955.
Over the Windmill, Hutchinson, 1954.
Wed to Earth, Hutchinson, 1955.
Mercy in Your Hands, Hutchinson, 1956.
The Flower and the Fruit, Hutchinson, 1957.
The True and the Tender, Hutchinson, 1958.
Portrait of a Patient, Hutchinson, 1959.
The Uneasy Summer, Hutchinson, 1960.
The Wind of Change, Hurst & Blackett, 1961.
A Sense of Loss, Hutchinson, 1962.

The Green Vista, Hurst & Blackett, 1963.
Sister Veronica Greene, Hurst & Blackett, 1963.
Small Hotel, Hurst & Blackett, 1965.
Hospital Angeles, Hurst & Blackett, 1966.
Double Take, Hurst & Blackett, 1967.
Point of Return, Hurst & Blackett, 1968.
There Is No Why, Hurst & Blackett, 1970.
Ward of Darkness, Hurst & Blackett, 1971.
The Doctor's Marriage, Hurst & Blackett, 1972.
If Only, Hurst & Blackett, 1972.
The Bewildered, Hurst & Blackett, 1973.
Love, Hurst & Blackett, 1975.

JUVENILES

Tinker the Cat: An Animal Story, Dent (London), 1932.
Jake the Dog: An Animal Story, Dent, 1933.
Mrs. Piffy, Dent, 1934.

NONFICTION

Cottage Angles, with engravings by Gwendolyn Raverat, Dent, 1935.
I Live in a Democracy (autobiography), Longmans, Green (New York City), 1939.
(With Barbara Beauchamp) *Greenfingers and the Gourmet* (cookbook), Nicholson & Watson (London), 1949.
Cooking in Cider (cookbook), World's Work (London), 1952.

OTHER

Short stories have been published in *Women's Realm, Woman's Own, Sunday Mirror,* and other magazines and newspapers in England.

SIDELIGHTS: Norah James's first novel, *Sleeveless Errand,* became a bestseller despite being banned in Great Britain for its depiction of alternate lifestyles and use of blasphemous language. The 1929 title, in which both main characters contemplate suicide over broken relationships, established James as a romance/realist writer with an eye for the neurotic London society of her day. Through the next half-century James turned out book after book—at least one, sometimes two per year—in which sexual and romantic matters were dealt with frankly yet tenderly, and in which women's issues were portrayed from a feminist perspective. According to M. C. Dawson in *Books,* "Miss James has a respect for the small lives that makes her handling of them very gentle."

Sleeveless Errand concerns the final days in the life of Paula, a bohemian who has been discarded by her lover. A chance encounter in a coffee shop leads her to the more conventional Bill, who is despondent over his wife's infidelity. Together Paula and Bill explore the fringes of London society, and the staid Bill is introduced to bisexuals, whores, and the disenchanted women of the post-World War I generation—Paula among them.

The book caused a sensation when it was first published in 1929, and it catapulted James to success. A *Bookman* reviewer praised the work for its "sustained vitality that would seem to guarantee a certain amount of truth behind the depressing picture it presents." Likewise, F. Van de Water in the *New York Evening Post* commented on James: "Her style is spare and strong; her character drawing clear, if implausible; her sense of beauty vividly tender." On the other hand, the decidedly moralist *Christian Century* reviewed *Sleeveless Errand* as "about as dismal a picture of a degenerate society as our present crop of disillusioned novels has produced."

From her publishing debut in 1979 James went on to write numerous titles, her last appearing in 1975, just four years prior to her death. Among her favorite topics were hospital dramas and love stories that did not necessarily tie up with happy endings. Whatever her topic, she was especially popular in her native Britain. William Plomer concluded in *The Spectator:* "The world [James] presents has a life of its own, true within its own limits, and managing to catch some reflections of universal truth."

BIOGRAPHICAL/CRITICAL SOURCES:

BOOKS

Twentieth-Century Romance and Historical Writers, third edition, St. James Press (Detroit, MI), 1994, pp. 345-47.

PERIODICALS

Bookman, September 1929, p. 99.
Books, June 9, 1929, p. 4; September 6, 1931, p. 2; January 29, 1933, p. 8; May 21, 1933, p. 9; February 25, 1934, p. 12.
Christian Century, February 12, 1930, p. 243.
Christian Science Monitor, February 15, 1930, p. 7.
New Republic, March 29, 1933, p. 193; May 9, 1934, p. 372.
New York Evening Post, June 8, 1929, p. 5.

New York Times, June 9, 1929, p. 8; September 6, 1931, p. 6; September 27, 1936, p. 17.
Saturday Review, February 11, 1933, p. 143.
Spectator, January 18, 1935, p. 96.
Times Literary Supplement, November 19, 1931, p. 917; February 1, 1934, p. 77; July 9, 1938, p. 467.*

* * *

JARMAN, Rosemary Hawley 1935-

PERSONAL: Born April 27, 1935, in Worcester, England; daughter of Charles (a master butcher) and Josephine (Hawley) Smith; married David C. Jarman, 1958 (divorced, 1970). *Education:* Until the age of eleven was educated solely by maternal grandmother, a former headmistress at British schools; Alice Ottley School, Worcester, 1946-52; studied opera in London, 1952-55.

ADDRESSES: Home—Llanungar Cottage, Whitchurch, Solva, Haverfordwest, Dyfed SA62 6UD, Wales. *Agent*—A. M. Heath, 79 St. Martin's Lane, London WC2N 4AA, England.

CAREER: Worcestershire (England) County Council, local government officer, 1962-68; Midlands Electricity, Worcestershire, receptionist, 1969; Rural District Council, Upton on Severn, Worcestershire, secretary, 1970. Singer, specializing in lieder and oratorio work, and cellist. Writer.

MEMBER: Society of Authors, Richard III Society.

AWARDS, HONORS: First Novel Award of Silver Quill (author's club), 1971, for *We Speak No Treason;* nominated Esteemed Daughter of Mark Twain by Cyril Clemens, 1973.

WRITINGS:

We Speak No Treason (novel; Literary Guild alternate selection), Little, Brown (Boston, MA), 1971.
The King's Grey Mare (novel), Little, Brown, 1973.
Crown in Candlelight (novel; Literary Guild selection), Little, Brown, 1978.
Crispin's Day: The Glory of Agincourt (nonfiction; History Book Club choice), Little, Brown, 1979.
The Courts of Illusion, Little, Brown, 1983.

Contributor of short stories to *Woman* and other periodicals.

WORK IN PROGRESS: A research project on the fall of the Inca empire in the 16th century.

SIDELIGHTS: Rosemary Hawley Jarman writes novels about the rulers of 15th-century England, the period better known as the Wars of the Roses. Jarman has been fascinated with that era of British history since she "fell totally and irrevocably in love with King Richard III" a quarter of a century ago. The author recalled in *Twentieth-Century Romance and Historical Writers* that her interest in Richard III brought history to life, "the characters fully fleshed, the climate of the times oddly familiar as if I drew upon past experience." She added: "To me the 15th century, in which all my work to date is set, was a time for flowers and blood, swords and viols, when courtly manners rode in tandem with dreadful punishments."

Jarman's *We Speak No Treason* presents a fictional portrait of Richard III; *The King's Grey Mare* recounts the life of Elizabeth Woodville, wife of Edward IV; *Crown in Candlelight* depicts Henry V, his wife Katherine, and her lover Owen Tudor; and *The Courts of Illusion* follows the fortunes of Perkin Warbeck, who claims to be King Edward VI's son and heir. All four novels have been praised by critics both for their art and for their historical accuracy.

In *We Speak No Treason,* the much-maligned Richard III is portrayed in a new light through the observations of three different narrators. One of these narrators is Patch, a court jester who makes a subsequent appearance in *The Courts of Illusion.* First published in 1971, *We Speak No Treason* won the Silver Quill award for a first novel and received plaudits from the critics. *Best Sellers* reviewer W. R. Evans, for instance, termed the book a "fine historical novel" and "a readable and worthwhile work of art." In addition, a *Times Literary Supplement* reviewer added that "the historical background is very good indeed. Every major source has been used to add verisimilitude to the tale, and the facts and the details are introduced with such lightness of touch that they drop into place almost unnoticed."

Crown and Candlelight provides a fictional panorama of the Wars of the Roses and its principle provocateurs: Richard II, Henry Bolingbroke, and Bolingbroke's son and daughter-in-law, Henry V and Katherine of France. Thomas Lask of the *New York*

Times remarked that the chapters of *Crown in Candlelight* "are a series of resplendent pageants; even the bedroom scenes have a Technicolor finish." Jarman, Lask continued, "is master of the small expressive detail whether it be the military means of reducing a besieged city in the 15th century or the cut of my lady's gown."

The civil war between the Plantagenets and Tudors also forms the backbone of *The King's Grey Mare* and *The Courts of Illusion.* In the latter title, Jarman explores the possibility that a man named Perkin Warbeck—styled by the Tudors as a penniless fisherman—was indeed who he claimed to be, the legitimate son of King Edward IV. A reviewer in the *British Book News* cited the work for its meticulous research but added: "It is the vitality of the characters and the vivid reconstruction of the world they inhabit that make the most lasting impressions." In *Library Journal*, Lydia Burruel concluded that *The Courts of Illusion* "offers the reader a vivid and expertly crafted recreation of 15th-century England."

Jarman's nonfiction book *Crispin's Day: The Glory of Agincourt* describes the events leading up to Henry V's surprising victory at the Battle of Agincourt in 1415. A *Kirkus Reviews* critic deemed the work "unoriginal and unambitious" but went on to declare that it "gathers up grittily detailed momentum [and is] . . . gorily compelling." A *British Book News* reviewer likewise praised Jarman's use of detail, concluding: "The account of the battle itself lacks only television colour cameras."

Jarman places a great deal of importance on writing. As she once told *CA:* "It is almost impossible to explain the amount of spiritual preparation necessary before any attempt at writing. A positive consecration which should culminate in the classical 'whitening of thought.' I am not speaking of character or even of plot, these are gratuitous, rather of the *form* of the work, not only the timing and points of high emphasis but the psychic materialization which has to do with the powers of the spirit, the opening of the mind and the release of Browning's 'imprisoned splendour.' Or the life-force such as Kundalini uncoiling to fill the empty space. A great man once said to me: 'Never forget, we are the elect, we writers, we are sublime.' This may sound arrogant but it is truth. Every time we achieve the impossible, building towers out of smoke, capturing illusion by allowing ourselves to be captured. How closely linked are art and religion! Thus writing is the true transubstantiation, and the

possible is not what you can do but what you want to do!"

BIOGRAPHICAL/CRITICAL SOURCES:

BOOKS

Twentieth-Century Romance and Historical Writers, third edition, St. James Press, 1994, pp. 349-350.

PERIODICALS

Best Sellers, September 1, 1971; August 1978.
Books and Bookmen, October, 1983, p. 29.
British Book News, March, 1980, p. 189; September, 1983, p. 580.
Christian Science Monitor, July 18, 1973.
Kirkus Reviews, September 15, 1979, p. 1111.
Library Journal, November 15, 1979, p. 2458; June 15, 1983, p. 1274.
New York Times, March 17, 1978.
Time, January 3, 1972; August 27, 1973.
Times Literary Supplement, May 14, 1971; October 27, 1978.

*　　*　　*

JAYAWARDENA, Kumari
   See JAYAWARDENA, Visakha Kumari

*　　*　　*

JAYAWARDENA, Visakha Kumari 1931-
   (Kumari Jayawardena)

PERSONAL: Born June 16, 1931; daughter of A. P. and Eleanor de Zoysa; married Lal Jayawardena; children: Rohan (son). *Education:* London School of Economics and Political Science, University of London, B.Sc., 1955, Ph.D., 1964; Ecole de Sciences Politiques, diploma, 1956; Bar-at-Law, Lincoln's Inn, 1958.

ADDRESSES: Office—Department of Women's Studies, Colombo University, Sri Lanka.

CAREER: University of Sri Lanka (formerly University of Ceylon), Colombo, Sri Lanka, associate professor in political science, Colombo University, 1969-85; Institute of Social Studies, the Hague, member of faculty of Women's Studies Programme, 1981-82; director, Workers Education Programme; currently professor of Women's Studies, Colombo University, Sri Lanka. Author of numerous publications in Sinhalese.

WRITINGS:

UNDER NAME KUMARI JAYAWARDENA

The Rise of the Labor Movement in Ceylon, Duke University Press (Durham, NC), 1972.

The Rise of the Working Class in Sri Lanka and the Printers Strike of 1893, Wesley Press (Wellawatte), 1974.

(With Maria Mies) *Feminism in Europe: Liberal and Socialist Strategies, 1789-1919,* Institute of Social Studies (The Hague), 1981.

Feminism and Nationalism in the Third World, Zed (London), 1982, revised edition, 1986.

Ethnic and Class Struggles in Sri Lanka, Colombo University Press (Colombo, Sri Lanka), 1985.

The White Woman's Other Burden: Western Women and South Asia during British Colonial Rule, Routledge (New York City), 1995.

SIDELIGHTS: Through her written works covering the advance of feminism during the wave of nationalism that spread through the colonized world during the early twentieth century, Visakha Kumari Jayawardena argues that female figures should be added to the list of people involved in the de-colonization process. "Like histories of other areas at other times, the history of de-colonization usually overlooks the contributions of women, and Jayawardena wants to acknowledge a tradition of feminism in the Third World," explained Amy Caiazza in *Feminist Writers.* "She also wants to encourage Western and non-Western feminists to recognize their differences and similarities, so that they can build a cross-national sense of sisterhood without ignoring distinctions among women."

Trained in the study of economic systems at the London School of Economics and Political Science, Jayawardena spent the early part of her career as an educator teaching at the University of Ceylon (now the University of Sri Lanka). While the social and economic inequities of colonial rule were central to her work, such inequities as they related to women would quickly begin to occupy her study. In 1981, after joining the Women's Studies Programme at the Institute of Social Studies in the Hague, Jayawardena worked with co-author Maria Mies to produce *Femi-*

nism in Europe: Liberal and Socialist Strategies, 1789-1919. This study of the rise of the European Feminist movement would be followed in 1982 by one of the scholar's most significant works, *Feminism and Nationalism in the Third World.*

In *Feminism and Nationalism in the Third World,* the author contends that Third World women, organized in support of various political movements, have significantly aided many fledgling nationalization and democratization processes. With the gains in education made during colonial rule in the nineteenth century, middle-class women began to rally around such political issues as the vote, the ability of men to take more than one wife, and other issues oppressive to women. This early organized political action would be the touchstone out of which female participation in the nationalization process would occur.

"Consequently," noted Caiazza, "for Jayawardena feminism is not just a Western phenomenon." While the form of oppression visited upon Third World women takes radically different forms than that battled by European and American women during the late-nineteenth and the early-twentieth centuries, influences of white female missionaries, among others, provided women in Third World countries an example of social alternatives to matriarchal domination. As Caiazza added, "Jayawardena [also] argues that women are not the same everywhere, and differences such as class, race, and ethnicity matter." As Jayawardena maintains in her feminist-inspired written works, such differences may change the face of feminism, but they do not eliminate the possibility of its emergence within the Third World.

In addition to her work as a writer and scholar at Sri Lanka's Colombo University, Jayawardena is an active supporter of both civil rights and feminist causes in her native Sri Lanka. Supplementing her works published in English, she is the author of numerous works in her native Sinhalese.

BIOGRAPHICAL/CRITICAL SOURCES:

BOOKS

Feminist Writers, St. James Press (Detroit), 1996.

PERIODICALS

Choice, February 1996, p. 1001.*

JEFFERSON, Ian
   See DAVIES, L(eslie) P(urnell)

* * *

JEFFREY, William
   See PRONZINI, Bill

* * *

JENNINGS, Gary (Gayne) 1928-
   (Gabriel Quyth)

PERSONAL: Born September 20, 1928, in Buena Vista, VA; son of Glen Edward (a printer) and Vaughnye May (Bays) Jennings. *Ethnicity:* "Hillbilly." *Education:* Studied with New York Art Students League, 1949-51.

ADDRESSES: Agent—McIntosh & Otis, Inc., 310 Madison Ave., New York, NY 10017.

CAREER: Writer. Copywriter and account executive for advertising agencies, New York City, 1947-58; newspaper reporter in California and Virginia, 1958-61; managing editor, *Dude* and *Gent,* 1962-63. *Military service:* U.S. Army, Infantry, 1952-54; served as correspondent in Korea; awarded Bronze Star, citation from Republic of Korea Ministry of Information.

MEMBER: PEN International, Authors Guild, Authors League of America, Screenwriters Guild, Pocaliers Club.

WRITINGS:

Personalities of Language, Crowell (New York City), 1965, revised and updated edition published as *World of Words: The Personalities of Language,* Atheneum (New York City), 1984.
The Treasure of the Superstition Mountains (nonfiction), Norton (New York City), 1973.
The Terrible Teague Bunch (novel), Norton, 1975.
Sow the Seeds of Hemp (novel), Norton, 1976.
The Rope in the Jungle (young adult novel), Lippincott (Philadelphia), 1976.
Aztec (novel; Literary Guild selection), Atheneum, 1980.
The Journeyer (novel; Literary Guild selection), Atheneum, 1984.

Spangle (novel; Literary Guild selection), Atheneum, 1987.
(Under pseudonym Gabriel Quyth) *The Lively Lives of Crispin Mobey* (novel), Atheneum, 1987.
Raptor (novel), Doubleday (New York City), 1992.
Aztec Autumn, Forge (New York City), 1997.

NONFICTION FOR YOUNG ADULTS

March of the Robots, Dial (New York City), 1962.
The Movie Book, Dial, 1963.
Black Magic, White Magic, Dial, 1964.
Parades!, Lippincott, 1966.
The Killer Storms: Hurricanes, Typhoons, and Tornadoes, Lippincott, 1970.
The Shrinking Outdoors, Lippincott, 1972.
The Earth Book, Lippincott, 1974.
March of the Heroes, Association Press, 1975.
March of the Gods, Association Press, 1976.
March of the Demons, Association Press, 1978.

Contributor to numerous anthologies and textbooks. Contributor of articles, short stories, and essays to periodicals, including *American Heritage, Cosmopolitan, Fantasy & Science Fiction, Harper's, National Geographic, New York Times Book Review, Reader's Digest, Redbook,* and *Ellery Queen's Mystery Magazine.*

SIDELIGHTS: Gary Jennings is a well-known author of epic historical novels, each one set in a different period but all sharing the theme of survival by wit and chance in violent times. Previously a writer for young adults, Jennings usually structures his historical novels around a narrator who comes of age in the vicissitudes of the story and then takes his or her life lessons into an adulthood fraught with danger and sexual escapade. Carefully researched and possessing a wealth of period detail, Jennings's novels have earned him praise as "a historical novelist of the first order," according to Christian H. Moe in *Twentieth-Century Romance and Historical Writers.*

One of Jennings's best-known historicals is *Aztec,* a multi-layered story about the native response to the Spanish conquest of Mexico. "In rubbing the myths of each race to their common bones, Gary Jennings has produced in *Aztec* a monumental novel," noted Nicholas Shakespeare in the London *Times.* Jennings unfolds the story of the overthrow of the Native Mexicans through the voice of an amiable but wry Aztec adventurer named Mixtli. Judith Matloff observed in the *Saturday Review:* "In picaresque fashion, Mixtli travels the length and breadth of Mexico, working as scribe, merchant, warrior, and ambassador to Montezuma," thus becoming involved in various aspects of the war against the conquistadors. In addition, the novel contains an abundance of details about the Aztecs—their culture, their religion, their customs, their daily life.

In preparing to write the novel, Jennings lived for twelve years in Mexico while conducting research on Aztec culture and the Spanish conquest. He read many accounts about the wars, but found many of them biased against the Indians. So, as Jennings told John F. Baker in a *Publishers Weekly* interview, "I began to study the Nahuatl language [of the Aztecs], and it shows them as people who had a sense of the bawdy, and who had all sorts of human reactions. I wanted to bring them alive as flesh-and-blood people." The author traveled about the country, seeking primary sources and "trying to get a sense, from living Indians, of their legendary past," recounted Baker. Jennings's research paid off, for the voice of his narrator Mixtli is filled with resonance of the Nahuatl speech. As *Times Literary Supplement* contributor Gordon Brotherston commented, "Much of the novel's power stems from Nahua sources transcribed into the alphabet after the Spanish invasion, not just the direct quotations from Nahua poems and of set pieces . . . but the whole range of devices used by Mixtli to keep his audience alert."

"Historical novels are most often praised or dismissed as novels," observed Thomas M. Disch in the *Washington Post Book World,* "but surely it is their power as narrative history that is their main strength, the power to evoke the *feel* of ages lost to memory. . . . So it is with Gary Jennings's *Aztec.*" The novel "has everything that makes a story vulgarly appealing, in the best sense of the phrase," remarked Christopher Lehmann-Haupt of the *New York Times.* "It has sex—my goodness, does it have sex! . . . [and] it has violence." While these elements may be appealing, "the violence usually serves a constructive storytelling purpose . . . and the sexual passages almost always relate to the book's most fascinating and subtle aspect, which is the way the hero, Mixtli, unconsciously re-enacts the life of the Indian god Quetzalcoatl," continued Lehmann-Haupt. "It is this particular dimension of *Aztec* which raises it above the level of a mere historical potboiler."

In *The Journeyer,* Jennings relates the "other half" of Marco Polo's adventures, the half the famous explorer supposedly withheld so as not to offend European sensibilities. The author recreated much of Polo's route for his research, traveling through Italy, the Middle East, and Central and Southeast Asia by various modes of transport—including camel and elephant. "Thus he enlivens his picaresque story with wonderfully detailed descriptions of the landscape, climate, flora and fauna Polo encountered along the way," wrote Gene Lyons in *Newsweek.* "As Jennings did for pre-Hispanic Mexico in *Aztec,*" commented Grover Sales in the *Los Angeles Times Book Review,* "he has enriched *The Journeyer* with an anthropologist's knowledge of diverse lands and cultures." Added the critic: "Jennings combines inexhaustible research with the yarn-spinner's art, drawing indelible portraits of Marco and his companions on the long journey."

Chicago Tribune Book World contributor Jack Dierks similarly found the novel engrossing, explaining that "employing both great sweep and meticulous detail, Jennings has produced an impressively learned gem of the astounding and the titillating. As pure travelogue it is impeccable, and the adventures that befall our heroes come like tales spun out by some erudite and prurient Scheherazade, heaping wonder onto oddity." Lehmann-Haupt however, expressed some reservations about the work: "For all the wonders of *The Journeyer*—its sweep, its humor, its vivid scenery, its sustained narrative drive—I found it ever so faintly disappointing after the brilliance of *Aztec.* Part of the problem may be the predictability [of the novel, for] many of the deeper patterns of *Aztec* are repeated in *The Journeyer.*" But Sales offered the opinion that "with astonishing speed and consummate skill, novelist Gary Jennings has capped his 1980 *Aztec,*" while Dierks considered the book an "even more compelling work of derring-do."

For *Spangle,* his third major historical work, Jennings traveled with nine different circuses in America and Europe. The novel follows the adventures of "Florian's Flourishing Florilegium," a 19th-century performing troupe, and Zachary Edge, a Southern Civil War veteran who joins it after the war. Like the author's previous works, *Spangle* contains the same elements of the spectacle, sex, violence, and detail that mark most of his historical fiction. "Yet for Gary Jennings," noted Lehmann-Haupt, "the formula seems to work uniquely. There is something mesmerizing about the world he creates." *Los Angeles Times Book Review* contributor MacDonald Harris felt that *Spangle* "is impressive in its sheer mass and richness, in the enthusiasm and energy of its telling, in the obvious pleasure the author takes in the work." This enthusiasm, asserted Harris, "is contagious. Before the novel is over we develop, along with the characters, a contempt for non-circus people and a conviction that the only sensible and reasonable thing to do . . . is to run away and join a circus."

While some critics have considered the amount of detail and breadth of scope in Jennings's work enriching, Donna Olendorf found it distracting. Writing in the *Detroit Free Press,* Olendorf remarked that "if only [Jennings] had restricted his focus to the performing arena, *Spangle* might have shone. Instead, Jennings changes gears as the caravan rumbles along, shifting from history into romantic tragedy. . . . This tangled tale has more contortions than the Florilegium's acrobat." And Lehmann-Haupt pointed out that one "disappointment about *Spangle* is that, like *The Journeyer,* it lacks the multiple layers of meaning that made *Aztec,* with its reenactment by the hero of the life of the god Quetzalcoatl, so unusual." But Harris thought that the setting, more contemporary than Jennings's previous work, makes it "a realistic novel, not a romance. . . . It is also the great strength of *Spangle* and its superiority over his first two books." Similarly, H. J. Kirchhoff stated in the Toronto *Globe and Mail* that the protagonists "are picaresque triumphs, and the supporting cast . . . is strong from top to bottom." Kirchhoff concluded by commenting that any faults "that blemished the earlier books seem to have been overcome; Spangle is simply excellent."

For his 1992 title *Raptor,* Jennings pressed further into the past than ever before. Set in the fifth century A.D.—and framed by Theodoric the Great's conquest of Rome—*Raptor* tells the story of a wily hermaphrodite named Thorn and his/her adventures in Theodoric's employ. Styling the work "a ripping yarn," *New York Times Book Review* contributor Joe Queenan noted: "In 'Raptor,' Mr. Jennings successfully demonstrates that a person who could make a very fine living in Las Vegas in the 20th century really had to have both his and her wits about him and her if he and she wanted to survive in the sixth." Thorn's response to his/her situation is to become a predator—a raptor like the hawk he has tamed—in order to protect himself and his interests. "Thorn is a memorable character, and unique outside of science fiction," wrote Judith Tarr in the *Washington Post Book World.* ". . . Raptor is a splendid entertainment: a historical novel of the old school, impressively researched and remarkably accurate—and above all, a roaring good read." In the *New York Times,* Lehmann-Haupt declared that Jennings's "latest bois-

terously imaginative historical extravaganza . . . recaptures some of the magic of 'Aztec.'" The critic concluded: "If you loved 'Aztec,' then you'll at least enjoy 'Raptor.' And if you haven't read 'Aztec,' then prepare yourself for astonishment."

Aztec, The Journeyer, Spangle, and *Raptor* have been published in twelve countries abroad.

BIOGRAPHICAL/CRITICAL SOURCES:

BOOKS

Twentieth-Century Romance and Historical Writers, third edition, St. James Press (Detroit, MI), 1994, pp. 350-351.

PERIODICALS

Chicago Tribune Book World, November 30, 1980; March 25, 1984.
Detroit Free Press, January 10, 1988.
Detroit News and Free Press, July 13, 1997.
Globe and Mail (Toronto), February 25, 1984; April 16, 1988.
Kirkus Reviews, April 15, 1992, p. 487; June 1, 1997.
Los Angeles Times, March 26, 1985.
Los Angeles Times Book Review, January 29, 1984; November 1, 1987.
Newsweek, January 9, 1984.
New York Times, February 5, 1981; January 10, 1984; November 16, 1987; June 22, 1992, p. C15.
New York Times Book Review, December 14, 1980; May 31, 1992, p. 15.
Publishers Weekly, December 12, 1980; April 13, 1992, p. 41.
Saturday Review, November, 1980.
Times (London), July 9, 1981.
Times Literary Supplement, July 24, 1981.
Washington Post, November 30, 1987.
Washington Post Book World, November 30, 1980; November 29, 1984; May 24, 1992, p. 7.

*   *   *

**JOHNS, Janetta
See QUIN-HARKIN, Janet**

JOLLEY, (Monica) Elizabeth 1923-

PERSONAL: Born June 4, 1923, in Birmingham, Warwickshire, England; immigrated to Australia, 1959, naturalized citizen, 1978; daughter of Charles (a science teacher) and Margarethe (a teacher; maiden name, von Fehr) Knight; married Leonard Jolley (a university librarian); children: Sarah Nelson, Richard, Ruth Radley. *Education:* Studied nursing at St. Thomas Hospital, London, 1940-43, and at Queen Elizabeth Hospital, Birmingham, 1943-46. *Avocational interests:* Orchards, goose farming.

ADDRESSES: Home—28 Agett Rd., Claremont, Western Australia 6010, Australia. *Agent*—Caroline Lurie, Australian Literary Management, 2 Armstrong St., Middle Park, Victoria 3206, Australia.

CAREER: Writer, 1964—. Worked as a nurse, domestic, and salesperson in Australia; part-time tutor in creative writing and literature at Fremantle Arts Centre in Fremantle, Western Australia, 1974-85; writer in residence at Western Australian Institute of Technology (now Curtin University of Technology), 1978—, and at Western Australian College of Advanced Education, Nedlands, 1983—; part-time teacher; lecturer; and workshop coordinator.

MEMBER: International PEN, Australian Society of Authors (president, 1985-86), Fellowship of Australian Writers.

AWARDS, HONORS: State of Victoria Short Story Award, 1966, for "Hedge of Rosemary," 1981, for "The Libation," and 1982, for "Running on the Spot"; Sound Stage Radio Drama Special Prize, 1975, for "Night Report"; co-recipient of Con Wieckhard Prize for, 1975, for *Palomino;* co-recipient of short story prize from University of Queensland, 1981, for "Hep Duck and Hildegard the Meat"; Australian Writers Guild Award for original radio drama, 1982, for "Two Men Running"; Western Australia Week Award for fiction and the Melbourne *Age* Book of the Year Award, both 1983, both for *Mr. Scobie's Riddle; Miss Peabody's Inheritance* shortlisted for the New South Wales Premier's Prize, 1984; senior fellow of the Literature Board of the Australia Council, 1984-86; New South Wales Premier's Prize for fiction, 1985, for *Milk and Honey;* Citizen of the Year in Arts, Culture, and Entertainment, 1987; Australian Bicentennial Authority National Literary commission to write novel *The Sugar Mother;* Miles Franklin Award, 1987, and Book of the Year Award, Barbara Ramsdell Plaque, from Fellowship of Australian

Writers (FAW) Victorian Branch, 1988, and Booker Prize nomination, 1988, all for *The Well;* Officer of the Order of Australia for services to Australian literature, 1988; Imaginative Writing Section, *Age* Book of the Year Award, 1989, for *My Father's Moon;* FAW Australian Natives Association Literature Award, 1991, for *Cabin Fever;* Gold Medal Award from Australian Literary Society, 1991, for *Cabin Fever* and general contribution to Australian literature; France-Australia Award, 1993, for translation of *The Sugar Mother;* Premier of Central Australia's Prize and Prize for Historical and Critical Writing, 1993, for *Central Mischief;* Age Book of the Year Award for Fiction, 1993, and National Book Council Banjo Award, 1994, both for *The Georges' Wife;* Australian Unity Literature Award from FAW (Victoria), 1995, for *The Orchard Thieves;* honorary doctorates from Western Australia Institute of Technology, 1986, and Macquarie University, 1995.

WRITINGS:

NOVELS

Palomino, Outback Press, 1980, Persea Press, 1987.
The Newspaper of Claremont Street, Fremantle Arts Center Press (Fremantle, W.A., Australia), 1981, Penguin (New York City), 1988.
Mr. Scobie's Riddle, Penguin, 1983, Viking, 1984.
Miss Peabody's Inheritance, University of Queensland Press (Saint Lucia, Queensland, Australia), 1983, Viking, 1984.
Milk and Honey, Fremantle Arts Centre Press, 1984, Persea Press, 1986.
Foxybaby, University of Queensland Press, 1984, Viking, 1985.
The Well, Viking Penguin, 1986.
The Sugar Mother, Fremantle Arts Center Press, 1988, Harper (New York City), 1988.
My Father's Moon, Viking (Ringwood, Victoria, Australia), Harper (New York City), 1989.
Cabin Fever (sequel to *My Father's Moon*), Penguin (Ringwood, Victoria, Australia), 1990, HarperCollins (New York City), 1991.
The Georges' Wife, Viking (Ringwood, Victoria, Australia), 1993.
The Orchard Thieves, Viking (Ringwood, Victoria, Australia), 1995.

SHORT STORY COLLECTIONS

Five Acre Virgin and Other Stories, Fremantle Arts Centre Press, 1976.

The Travelling Entertainer, Fremantle Arts Centre Press, 1979.
Woman in a Lampshade, Penguin, 1983.

RADIO PLAYS: BROADCAST BY ABC AND BBC WORLD SERVICE

"Night Report," 1975.
"The Performance," 1976.
"The Shepherd on the Roof," 1977.
"The Well-Bred Thief," 1977.
"Woman in a Lampshade," 1979.
"Two Men Running," 1981.
"Paper Children," 1988.
"Little Lewis Has Had a Lovely Sleep," 1988.
"The Well," 1992.
"Lorelei in the Wheat," 1993.
"The Silver Apples of the Moon" and repeat of "Lorelei," 1994.

RADIO PLAYS: COLLECTIONS

Off the Air: Nine Plays for Radio, edited by Delys Bird, Penguin, 1995.

OMNIBUS VOLUMES

Stories (contains *Five Acre Virgin* and *The Travelling Entertainer*), Fremantle Arts Centre Press, 1984, Viking, 1988.

OTHER

Central Mischief: Elizabeth Jolley on Writing, Her Past and Herself, edited and with an introduction by Caroline Lurie, Viking, 1992.
Diary of a Weekend Farmer (diary and poems), Fremantle Arts Center Press, 1993.

Also author of stories and poems broadcast on radio, 1966-82. Work represented in more than twenty anthologies, including *Summer Tales 2, Sandgropers, Australian New Writing,* and *A Taste of Cockroach.* Work also represented in the biographical film *The Nights Belonged to the Novelist.* Fiction editor for literary journal *VOICES,* 1993-94. Contributor to periodicals, including *New Yorker* and *Grand Street.*

ADAPTATIONS: *The Newspaper of Claremont Street* was adapted for the stage by Alan Becher and David Britton and produced in various cities in Australia.

SIDELIGHTS: Elizabeth Jolley is "an Australian original who deserves a wide American audience,"

declared Bob Halliday in the *Washington Post Book World.* Since the long overdue publication of her first novel in 1980, the British-born novelist, short story writer, and dramatist has produced a body of work that confounds critics. Attempts have been made to compare her achievement with that of Barbara Pym and Flannery O'Connor, with D. H. Lawrence and Edgar Allan Poe, but none wholly succeed. She remains, as Elizabeth Ward described in her *Washington Post Book World* critique, "a profoundly iconoclastic writer."

Jolley has established a place for herself both in Australian and world letters with stories devoted to society's misfits. Portrayed with wit and compassion, her characters are quirky and unpredictable, prompting critics to headline reviews of her work with phrases such as "Dotty and Disorderly Conduct," "Aussie Oddities," and "Jolley Aussies." Although Jolley has been lauded for invigorating Australian fiction with a new comic vein, her high humor is often a means for revealing profound feeling. Much of her work, in fact, deals with loneliness, loss, and attempts to establish relationships, even if unconventional.

It was just one such unconventional relationship that for many years made Jolley, in the words of *Time* reviewer Paul Gray, "one of Australia's best-kept literary secrets." The author, who immigrated to Australia with her husband and three children in 1959, held numerous jobs during the 1960s and 1970s. She wrote during those years, publishing in periodicals and anthologies, but had little luck securing a book publisher. The latter seventies saw the publication of two collections of short stories, *Five Acre Virgin and Other Stories* and *The Travelling Entertainer,* as well as the broadcast of several of her radio plays, but it was not until 1980 that a small Australian press agreed to release her first novel, *Palomino.*

Palomino was originally drafted in the late fifties and early sixties, then reworked in the seventies (a typical pattern for Jolley, whose stories often evolve from one another as they are repatterned). The novel explores the lesbian relationship between sixty-year-old Laura, a deregistered obstetrician and gynecologist, and a much younger woman, Andrea. Andrea, it also happens, is pregnant with her own brother's child, thus adding an incestuous motif to the book. Prior to 1980, Australian publishers considered the book too controversial. As Jolley told Ward in a 1986 interview for the *Washington Post Book World:* "I've gotten rejection letters which say that nowhere in

Australia is there an audience for this kind of material. . . . Other countries were publishing those kinds of books and stories; nobody would look at them here, they just didn't want to know, they were terrified. . . . Most people like to live comfortably within certain little boundaries. . . . That's the clue, the idea of being threatened."

Mixed reviews greeted *Palomino*'s publication. Some critics had sentiments similar to Ward's assessment that "considered as a first novel, *Palomino* is remarkably assured and distinctive, stating clearly . . . the preoccupations which shape all of Jolley's writing." Others saw it as a somewhat anomalous work, claiming it lacks much of the absurd quality now associated with the author's vintage writing.

Jolley's second published novel, however, *The Newspaper of Claremont Street,* has been generally regarded as classic Jolley. As Gray described: "It is brief, deceptively simple, eccentric and entirely in keeping with the comic, macabre nature of her best fiction." The book's protagonist is Margarite Morris, a cleaning lady referred to as Newspaper, or Weekly, because she spreads news from one home to another as she makes her cleaning rounds. Although she wears her employers' hand-me-down clothes and is often the object of derision, Weekly—called "a bit barmy" by a *New York Times Book Review* critic—is saving her money to fulfill a secret dream: the purchasing of a house in the country where she can retire, escaping her present life.

Weekly's dream is threatened, however, when a widowed former employer, Nastasya Torben—"Narsty," Weekly dubs her—moves in with the domestic and begins to dominate her life. The ensuing struggle between the two "has all the classic elements of comedy and tragedy," wrote Judith Freeman in the *Los Angeles Times Book Review*. And in an interview with James Idema recounted in the *Chicago Tribune,* Jolley herself called the book "a metaphor for taking on more than one can manage." Also, "I have dealt frequently in my writing with overdevotion," she explained, "the dependence that sometimes grows between people, the fear in one of hurting and losing the other. That can be a strangling fear." Weekly, however, overcomes her problem in an ending, according to Freeman, that "is swift and black- humored."

With the publication of her third and fourth novels, Jolley began attracting attention outside of Australia. The third, *Mr. Scobie's Riddle,* won the 1983 Western Australia Week Award for fiction and the 1983

Melbourne *Age* Book of the Year Award, while the fourth, *Miss Peabody's Inheritance,* garnered acclaim for making the New South Wales Premier's Prize shortlist. The books, suggested Thomas M. Disch in a critique for the *New York Times Book Review,* should be "read in tandem" if their self-reflexive narratives are to be most appreciated.

Mr. Scobie's Riddle, set in St. Christopher and St. Jude's Hospital for the Aged, features a variety of characters destined to live out their days in an institution whose personnel are more concerned with schedules and efficiency than meeting individual needs. The home, contended A. P. Riemer in a *Southerly* review, is "a place of dislocation." Most of its residents are demented or senile, and all of them are trapped. They are neither able to function independently outside the facility nor allowed to live normally within it.

Mr. Scobie, a retired music teacher, and Miss Hailey, a former school teacher and unpublished novelist, are two residents who through their dreams and memories try to make life tenable. They are also the vehicles by which Jolley gives voice to her sentiments about the condition of the artist. Riemer observed: "We may recognize in *Mr. Scobie's Riddle* not merely some of the preoccupations of recent Australian fiction, but also an allusive, parodistic image of the novelist who, through the very pursuit of an 'art' which finds its inception, and perhaps, proper milieu in another world, is as 'crazy' as Miss Hailey herself."

Like *Mr. Scobie's Riddle, Miss Peabody's Inheritance* uses the novelist-within-a-novel device. The story divides its attention between Miss Dorothy Peabody, a London typist living a very circumscribed life, and Australian novelist Diana Hopewell whose lesbian romance, *Angels on Horseback,* Miss Peabody admires. Miss Peabody writes a venerative letter to Diana, who not only writes back but also sends pages from her work in progress. Awakened to the possibilities of life through Diana's work, Miss Peabody begins to confuse fiction and reality, ultimately leaving her job and flying to Australia. She arrives only to find that her idol has died. Miss Peabody was not forgotten, however. Diana left her devoted fan her unfinished manuscript, Miss Peabody's "inheritance." Disch suggested that the novel is more "artfully self-reflecting" than *Mr. Scobie's Riddle.* In his opinion, Jolley's purpose in examining the relationships among novelist, reader, and fictional characters has less to do with literary theory than with "an old-fashioned concern for morality, in [Miss Peabody's] case the morality of imaginative experience."

Foxybaby is another novel presenting a fiction-within-a-fiction. This time the setting is a summer weight-loss school for women run by Miss Josephine Peycroft, who believes in a "Better Body Through the Arts." The pivotal character, Miss Alma Porch, is a teacher and writer—the sort of "goofy lady novelist" Robert Coover identified in the *New York Times Book Review* as a "Jolleyean archetype." Her job is to direct a drama workshop, and the text she selects is her own, not yet complete, *Foxybaby*. As Miss Porch's pupils begin to relate to the characters in her play they reveal, according to Michiko Kakutani's *New York Times* critique, how Jolley has used "overall narrative structure to reflect and refract the relationships that exist between the author of a work of fiction, its characters and its audience." *Foxybaby*, summarized a *Times Literary Supplement* reviewer, is "an unusual novel about the genderless erotic adventure of writing."

Many critics have maintained that the author's sixth novel, *Milk and Honey*, represents a bit of a departure in the Jolley canon. In this tale of a cellist, his wife, and his obsession with another woman, Jolley abandons her typical third-person narrative for a monologue, producing a work that is "darker, richer and more complicated" in tone, according to Peter Ackroyd's *New York Times Book Review* appraisal. The reviewer also acknowledged it as a "more haunting and ultimately more profound" novel than its predecessors.

In its successor, *The Well,* Jolley recapitulates some of the themes and techniques for which she is best known. Nevertheless, "nothing in Jolley's previous work prepares one for *The Well*," contended reviewer William H. Pritchard in the *New Republic*. The novel centers on Hester Harper, a lame spinster living on her dying father's farm, and her relationship with the younger Katherine, an orphan Hester brings to live with them. After Hester's father dies, the two women continue to live a companionable if somewhat bizarre life together. Then one evening, returning from a dance with Katherine at the wheel of the car, they strike a man down.

Panicking, the two women decide to dump the deceased down a disused well, a repository for other unwanted objects in their lives. With "a psychological precision verg[ing] on the relentless," in the words of *Los Angeles Times* reviewer Richard Eder, Jolley details the women's mounting hysteria. Hester believes the dead man is the thief who stole her money and insists that Katherine descend into the well and recover it. Katherine refuses, claiming that the man is alive—and that he has conversed with her, proposing marriage. The story, opined Eder, dissolves into "a dreamlike blackness in which reality and hallucination are undistinguishable."

Jolley's subsequent novel, *The Sugar Mother,* was published in 1988. Although its protagonist, the stuffy middle-aged literature professor Dr. Edwin Page, is obsessed with his bodily functions, he "is less obviously a misfit than some other Jolley characters," according to *Washington Post Book World* contributor Elizabeth Ward. When Edwin's obstetrician wife, Cecilia, goes abroad on a yearlong research fellowship, the dependent Edwin is left to fend for himself. On the evening after Cecilia leaves, Edwin's neighbors, Mrs. Bott and her twenty-year-old daughter Leila, come to Edwin for help, having locked themselves out of their home. Learning that Cecilia is away and that she and Edwin are childless, Mrs. Bott converses with Edwin, extolling the surrogate motherhood trend ("sugared mothers," she pronounces), and eventually invites herself and her daughter to live with the not inhospitable Edwin.

Subsequently, Edwin falls in love with Leila, who later reveals that she is pregnant, and Mrs. Bott convinces Edwin that Cecilia, upon her return, will welcome Edwin's baby, carried by a surrogate mother. "It is at this point that the novel begins to disturb," contended Ward. By the eve of Cecilia's return Edwin is uncertain of what he wants, and the novel's conclusion, according to Stephen McCauley in the *New York Times Book Review,* "sustained over the last forty pages, is almost unbearably tense." The critic added that *The Sugar Mother* is Jolley's "warmest novel, her most moving and possibly the best introduction to her fiction."

In *My Father's Moon,* Jolley tells the story of a young Englishwoman, Vera Wright, who becomes a nursing student during World War II and falls in love with a married doctor. Soon, she is pregnant by him, but he is killed during military training, and she has to bring up their daughter alone. The sequel, *Cabin Fever,* shows Vera forty years later, a successful psychologist, recalling, in no particular order, her wartime experiences, postwar privation, unsatisfying jobs, and other aspects of her life.

"The fascinating thing about "Cabin Fever" is that it tells essentially the same story [as *My Father's Moon*], but the main difference is one of perspective," commented *Los Angeles Times Book Review* contributor Elizabeth Ward. Added *Times Literary Supplement* critic Patricia Craig: "It is as if the author can't get this theme out of her head until she has had another go at probing it." Craig found *Cabin Fever* as much about the nature of memory as anything else: "It is not so much the story that interests [Jolley] as the act of recalling, and the effect on the page of certain recollections." The recollections do not form a complete story of Vera's life; there is no information about the fate of her daughter, or about how Vera attained her professional status. Craig, though, termed Jolley's "studied reticence" effective: "If she seems unduly economical with the facts, and if her selection of incidents is somewhat fitful, she nevertheless succeeds in communicating the oddity and pungency of the period in question (the late 1940s)." Vera's memories, Ward remarked, show the character trying to "make sense of a life full . . . of 'pain and trouble, disorder and sorrow' and yet constantly hopeful." Frederick Busch, writing in the *New York Times Book Review,* praised Jolley's style and tone: "Although her prose seems direct, there is a complexity that simmers beneath it." He asserted that "to read 'Cabin Fever' is to come in contact with an interesting, wounded, somber mind" and called the novel "a poignant celebration and farewell."

In her short fiction, as in her novels, Jolley frequently deals with quirky, unconventional characters and displays an offbeat sense of humor. "Her sympathies lie with obscure and eccentric individuals who construct a world for themselves in a hostile, categorically-minded society," noted Bruce Williams in a *Westerly* review of *The Travelling Entertainer.* Stories in this collection include "The Long Distant Lecture," concerning a professor's panic as he loses his way to a speaking engagement, and "The Performance," about a man in a mental hospital telling his life story to a fellow patient. Hospitals are a recurrent setting in Jolley's writing, providing a venue for "the meeting of sinister and absurd," as Helen Daniel put it in the book *LIARS: Australian New Novelists.* A surreal marriage ceremony takes place in a hospital in "Hilda's Wedding," in the collection *Woman in a Lampshade;* in "Surprise! Surprise! from Matron," from *Five Acre Virgin and Other Stories,* a nursing

home is the prize in a poker game. Other recurrent subjects in Jolley's stories include recent immigrants to Australia and the desire for land ownership.

Some of Jolley's short stories have a strong relationship to her novels. Several critics have found the germ of *Mr. Scobie's Riddle* in "Surprise! Surprise! from Matron." "The Libation" from *Woman in a Lampshade* is "virtually a sequel" to *Palomino,* Daniel commented; this story features a woman visiting the room where her female lover has died the week before. The title character of *The Newspaper of Claremont Street* is featured in the story "Pear Tree Dance," also from *Woman in a Lampshade.* Commenting on Jolley's tendency to revisit characters and themes, Daniel observed that the author "disrupts the narrative line and interweaves rival fictions to draw forth the possibilities of time and place and consciousness that intersect within a given moment. The continuum of her work is extraordinary, each component of it setting up reverberations of others and revealing its dynamic character, such that a later work may cause us to see an earlier one in a new light." In an essay for *Meanjin* on Jolley's body of work, Helen Garner noted that the author's "repetitions and re-usings, conscious but not to the point of being orchestrated, set up a pattern of echoes which unifies the world, and is most seductive and comforting."

Jolley's offbeat creations have their detractors. "Uneven as a novelist . . . Jolley is if anything less impressive" in the stories in *Woman in a Lampshade,* asserted Anne Laren in *Kirkus Reviews.* Laren found that Jolley's "pathos too often slips over into mawkishness—while the dollops of quirkiness seem self-conscious and strained." Garner, however, contended that even when Jolley's stories are overly facile or sentimental, they have something to recommend them. "Even a clumsy, flustered, amateurish story will have a nugget of sense at its centre, an image that surprises, a simple—even a crude—stroke that almost saves it," Garner maintained.

Jolley told *CA:* "I am always deeply touched that people have read my work and commented on it. I think, as a writer, I have learned a great deal about writing from these comments." In the *Contemporary Authors Autobiography Series,* she noted, "My fiction is not autobiographical but, like all fiction, it springs from moments of truth and awareness, from observation and experience. I try to develop the moment of truth with the magic of imagination."

BIOGRAPHICAL/CRITICAL SOURCES:

BOOKS

Bird, Delys, and Brenda Walker, editors, *Elizabeth Jolley: New Critical Essays,* Angus & Robertson (Moss Vale, N.S.W., Australia), 1991.
Contemporary Authors Autobiography Series, Volume 13, Gale (Detroit), 1991.
Contemporary Literary Criticism, Volume 46, Gale, 1988.
Daniel, Helen, *LIARS: Australian New Novelists,* Penguin, 1988.
Jolley, Elizabeth, *Central Mischief: Elizabeth Jolley on Writing, Her Past and Herself,* edited and with an introduction by Caroline Lurie, Viking (Ringwood, Victoria, Australia), 1992.
Jolley, *Diary of a Weekend Farmer* (diary and poems), Fremantle Arts Center Press (Saint Lucia, Queensland, Australia), 1993.
Salzman, Paul, *Elizabeth Jolley's Fictions: Helplessly Tangled in Female Arms and Legs,* University of Queensland Press, 1993.
Short Story Criticism, Volume 19, Gale, 1995.

PERIODICALS

Chicago Tribune, June 8, 1986; May 12, 1988; May 20, 1988; July 22, 1988.
Detroit News, February 2, 1986.
Kirkus Reviews, September 1, 1986, pp. 1313-14.
Los Angeles Times, January 28, 1986; May 26, 1986; November 19, 1986.
Los Angeles Times Book Review, December 9, 1984, p. 1; January 3, 1988, pp. 3, 9; August 7, 1988, p. 3; July 21, 1991, p. 3, 9.
Meanjin, June, 1983, pp. 153-57.
New Republic, February 23, 1987.
New Yorker, September 23, 1991, p. 115.
New York Times, November 16, 1985.
New York Times Book Review, November 18, 1984, p. 14; November 24, 1985, pp. 1, 36; June 15, 1986, p. 12; November 16, 1986, p. 1; July 19, 1987, p. 11; December 20, 1987, p. 16; July 10, 1988; July 7, 1991, p. 9.
Observer (London), January 27, 1991, p. 58.
Time, December 7, 1987, p. 87.
Times (London), March 31, 1988.
Times Literary Supplement, October 18, 1985, p. 1173; June 13, 1986; August 15, 1986, p. 894; January 25, 1991, p. 20.

Washington Post Book World, July 1, 1984; January 1, 1986; November 2, 1986 August 16, 1987; July 31, 1988.
Westerly, June, 1980, pp. 104-107.*

* * *

JOSEPH, Marie

PERSONAL: Born in Blackburn, Lancashire, England; married Frank Joseph (a chartered engineer), December, 1942; children: Marilyn Joseph Hampton, Kathryn Joseph Stevenson. *Education:* Attended girls' high school in Blackburn, Lancashire, England. *Religion:* Protestant.

ADDRESSES: Home—Studio, Green Lane, Stanmore, Middlesex, England. *Agent*—Mary Irvine, 4 Coombe Gardens, Wimbledon, London, England.

CAREER: Civil servant. Post Office Telephones, Blackburn, England, clerical officer, 1938-44.

MEMBER: Romantic Novelists Association, Society of Women Writers and Journalists, Byron Ladies' Club.

AWARDS, HONORS: Romantic Novelists Association award, 1987, for *A Better World Than This.*

WRITINGS:

The House Through the Trees (juvenile), Nelson (London), 1964.
One Step at a Time (autobiography), St. Martin's (New York City), 1977.
Maggie Craig, St. Martin's, 1980.
A Leaf in the Wind, St. Martin's, 1981.
Emma's Sparrow, St. Martin's, 1982.
The Listening Silence, Arrow (London), 1982, St. Martin's, 1983.
Footsteps in the Park, Arrow, 1982.
Gemini Girls, Arrow, 1983.
Lisa Logan, Arrow, 1984.
Polly Pilgrim, Arrow, 1984.
Clogger's Child, Arrow, 1986.
A Better World Than This, Century (London), 1986.
A World Apart, Century, 1988.
Passing Strangers and Other Stories, Arrow, 1989.
Ring-a-Roses, Chivers (Bath, England), 1990.
Travelling Man, Arrow, 1990.

When Love Was Like That and Other Stories, Century, 1991.
Since He Went Away, Century, 1992.

Contributor of stories to magazines.

SIDELIGHTS: At one time a prolific writer of short stories for British women's magazines—W. H. Bradley in *Twentieth-Century Romance and Historical Writers* explains that "hardly a week went by without her by-line appearing in one magazine or another"— Marie Joseph belatedly turned to writing novels in the 1980s. Since her change in genre, Joseph has enjoyed success with her novels of ordinary people finding love in their everyday lives. As Bradley states, Joseph is "a writer whose work is always comforting, reassuring and often amusing, as well as being thought provoking."

In her award-winning novel *A Better World Than This,* Joseph tells the story of Daisy Bell, who works with her mother at the family bakery. When a handsome customer visits the shop, Daisy fantasizes a romance with the man. Even learning that he is married and the father of two children does not dissuade her from dreaming. Set in the Lancashire mill towns of the 1930s, the novel recreates the period successfully. "Throughout the story," notes Bradely, "the indomitable courage and determined cheerfulness of Daisy shines through like a beacon. Few readers could fail to feel great affection for the sometimes naive, but always loveable, Daisy Bell."

In other novels Joseph has chronicled the lives of other working-class women who have overcome adversity in their lives. *Maggie Craig,* set in a nineteenth-century industrial town, follows the title heroine as she faces her mother's early death, her father's subsequent breakdown, and a loveless marriage. Marylaine Block in *Library Journal* finds "the characters are well drawn and the relationships are believable." *The Listening Silence* is set during World War II and tells of a deaf woman's romance with an RAF flyer. Andrea Lee Shuey in *Library Journal* calls the novel "a touching book that shows real feeling for what it must be like to be deaf in a world of war and death."

Speaking of Joseph's approach to writing, Bradley explains that her stories are "never depressing. Her characters always look for the brighter side, rarely complain about their lot. This quality has no doubt made a contribution to the popularity of her writing."

Joseph told *CA:* "My novels are all set in the north of England, in periods ranging from the turn of the century to the present day. I try to show the social history of the time, for instance the poverty of workers in Lancashire cotton mills, as opposed to the comparative affluence of the mill owners.

"I set my novels in the north of England because I was born there and have an in-depth knowledge of the area. My own mother, who died giving birth to me, was a weaver in a cotton mill, as were her four sisters, so my background is authentic. I lived as a child in the kind of house described in *Maggie Craig,* and the tight-knit community of near poverty and strict Methodism was my own. I was brought up by my maternal grandmother until the age of seven, and when she died, I lived with an uncle who was a magistrate, a teetotaler, a Trades Union secretary, and a Methodist, as well as being an idealistic socialist of the old school! So, it is obvious why my novels all have a strong leaning towards the conditions of the time.

"Although I have lived in the south of England for almost thirty years, I am still a Lancashire woman at heart and can never forget the hardships of those days. I grew up during the Thirties Depression and vividly remember the way women coped to bring up families on very little money. I remember too their sense of humor and their courage, and these qualities I hope to show in my novels."

BIOGRAPHICAL/CRITICAL SOURCES:

BOOKS

Twentieth-Century Romance and Historical Writers, third edition, St. James Press (Detroit, MI), 1994.

PERIODICALS

Booklist, May 15, 1982, p. 1225; July, 1983, p. 1389.
Books and Bookmen, August, 1983, p. 31; April, 1984, p. 28.
Kirkus Reviews, October 1, 1977, p. 1076; March 1, 1982, p. 294; June 15, 1982, p. 692; February 15, 1983, p. 200; September 15, 1984, p. 870.
Library Journal, April 1, 1982, p. 745; August, 1982, p. 1481; April 15, 1983, p. 840.
Publishers Weekly, April 9, 1982, p. 42; June 18, 1982, p. 59; March 4, 1983, p. 86; September 7, 1984, p. 73.

K

KEILLOR, Garrison
  See KEILLOR, Gary (Edward)

* * *

KEILLOR, Gary (Edward) 1942-
  (Garrison Keillor)

PERSONAL: Known professionally as Garrison Keillor; born August 7, 1942, in Anoka, MN; son of John Philip (a railway mail clerk and carpenter) and Grace Ruth (a homemaker; maiden name, Denham) Keillor; married Mary C. Guntzel, September 1, 1965 (divorced May, 1976); married Ulla Skaerved (a social worker), December 29, 1985; children: (first marriage) Jason. *Education:* University of Minnesota, B.A., 1966, graduate study, 1966-68. *Politics:* Democrat. *Religion:* Plymouth Brethren.

ADDRESSES: Agent—American Humor Institute, 80 Eighth Ave., No. 1216, New York, NY 10011.

CAREER: Writer. KUOM-Radio, Minneapolis, MN, staff announcer, 1963-68; Minnesota Public Radio, St. Paul, MN, producer and announcer, 1971-74, host and principal writer for weekly program *A Prairie Home Companion,* 1974-87; host of *Garrison Keillor's American Radio Company of the Air,* 1989—.

AWARDS, HONORS: George Foster Peabody Broadcasting Award, 1980, for *A Prairie Home Companion;* Edward R. Murrow Award from Corporation for Public Broadcasting, 1985, for service to public radio; *Los Angeles Times* Book Award nomination,

1986, for *Lake Wobegon Days;* Grammy Award for best nonmusical recording, 1987, for *Lake Wobegon Days;* Ace Award, 1988; Best Music and Entertainment Host Award, 1988; Gold Medal for spoken English, American Academy of Arts and Letters, 1990; inducted into Museum of Broadcast Communications and Radio Hall of Fame, 1994.

WRITINGS:

UNDER NAME GARRISON KEILLOR

G.K. the DJ, Minnesota Public Radio, 1977.
The Selected Verse of Margaret Haskins Durber, Minnesota Public Radio, 1979.
Happy to Be Here: Stories and Comic Pieces, Atheneum (New York City), 1982, expanded edition, Penguin (New York City), 1983.
Lake Wobegon Days (novel), Viking (New York City), 1985.
Leaving Home: A Collection of Lake Wobegon Stories, Viking, 1987.
We Are Still Married: Stories and Letters, Viking, 1989.
WLT: A Radio Romance, Viking, 1991.
The Book of Guys, Viking, 1993.
Cat, You Better Come Home, illustrated by Steve Johnson, Viking, 1995.
The Old Man Who Loved Cheese, illustrated by Anne Wilsdorf, Little, Brown (Boston), 1996.

RECORDINGS

A Prairie Home Companion Anniversary Album, Minnesota Public Radio, 1980.
The Family Radio, Minnesota Public Radio, 1982.

News from Lake Wobegon, Minnesota Public Radio, 1982.

Prairie Home Companion Tourists, Minnesota Public Radio, 1983.

Ten Years on the Prairie: A Prairie Home Companion 10th Anniversary, Minnesota Public Radio, 1984.

Gospel Birds and Other Stories of Lake Wobegon, Minnesota Public Radio, 1985.

A Prairie Home Companion: The Final Performance, Minnesota Public Radio, 1987.

More News from Lake Wobegon, Minnesota Public Radio, 1988.

Lake Wobegon Loyalty Days: A Recital for Mixed Baritone and Orchestra, Minnesota Public Radio, 1989.

Local Man Moves to City, Highbridge, 1991.

(With Frederica von Stade) *Songs of the Cat,* Highbridge, 1991.

Keillor has also recorded his book *Lake Wobegon Days.*

OTHER

(Author of foreword) Bob Eliott and Ray Goulding, *The New Improved! Bob and Ray Book,* McGraw (New York City), 1986.

(Author of foreword) A. J. Liebling, *The Honest Rainmaker: The Life and Times of Colonel John R. Stingo,* North Point Press (Berkeley, CA), 1989.

Contributor of articles and stories to periodicals, including *New Yorker, Harper's* and *Atlantic Monthly.*

WORK IN PROGRESS: A novel; more stories.

SIDELIGHTS: With the words "It's been a quiet week in Lake Wobegon, my hometown," radio humorist and author Garrison Keillor introduced his monologue on his long-running Minnesota Public Radio program *A Prairie Home Companion.* The stories he told over the air, based partly on his memories of growing up in semi-rural Anoka, Minnesota, were among the highlights of the live-broadcast show—an eclectic mixture of comedy and music (including bluegrass, blues, ethnic folk, choral, gospel, opera, and yodeling)—which reached an audience of about 4 million listeners per week by the time it went off the air in 1987. It reached a great many more people in its last year when the Disney Channel obtained cable television broadcasting rights.

As principal writer and host of the show, Keillor also revealed his humor in the commercials he wrote for the sponsors of his program, including Ralph's Pretty Good Grocery ("If you can't find it at Ralph's, you can probably get along without it"), Bertha's Kitty Boutique ("For persons who care about cats"), the Chatterbox Cafe ("Where the coffeepot is always on, which is why it always tastes that way"), Bob's Bank ("Neither a borrower nor a lender be; so save at the sign of the sock"), the Sidetrack Tap ("Don't sleep at our bar; we don't drink in your bed"), and especially those Powdermilk Biscuits ("Heavens, they're tasty") that "give shy persons the strength to get up and do what needs to be done."

Many critics place Keillor in the tradition of such American humorists as Ring Lardner, James Thurber, and Mark Twain. Like Twain, who gained a reputation traveling on the American lecture circuit in the last years of the nineteenth and first years of the twentieth century, Keillor's audience originally came from his live performances. Roy Blount, Jr., writing in the *New York Times Book Review* about *A Prairie Home Companion,* states that it was "*impossible* to describe. Everyone I have met who has heard it has either been dumbfounded by it, or addicted to it, or both." "The same is true of Keillor's prose," Blount continues, referring to a series of pieces written for the *New Yorker* and collected in *Happy to Be Here: Stories and Comic Pieces.* However, "many of these pieces," writes Peter A. Scholl in the *Dictionary of Literary Biography Yearbook: 1987,* "show the witty and urbane Keillor rather than the wistful, wandering storyteller in exile from Lake Wobegon, where 'smart doesn't count for very much.'"

In 1985, the publication of *Lake Wobegon Days* brought Keillor's small town to national prominence. Beginning with the first explorations of the French traders in the eighteenth century, Keillor goes on to describe the town's history up to the present day. But Lake Wobegon is, according to Mary T. Schmich in the *Chicago Tribune,* "a town that lies not on any map but somewhere along the border of his imagination and his memory." Keillor describes it in *Lake Wobegon Days:* "Bleakly typical of the prairie, Lake Wobegon has its origins in the utopian vision of nineteenth-century New England Transcendentalists, but now is populated mainly by Norwegians and Germans. . . . The lake itself, blue-green and sparkling in the brassy summer sun and neighbored by the warm-colored marsh grasses of a wildlife-teeming slough, is the town's main attraction, though the view is spoiled somewhat by a large grain elevator by the railroad track."

Lake Wobegon, in Keillor's stories, becomes a sort of American Everytown, "the ideal American place to come from," writes Scholl. "One of the attributes of home in Keillor's work is evanescence. . . . Dozens of his stories concern flight from Lake Wobegon, and the title of his radio show gains ironic force with the realization that it was adapted from the Prairie Home Lutheran cemetery in Moorhead, Minnesota; we are permanently at home only when we are gone." Yet "the wonderful thing about Keillor's tone in detailing life as it is lived in Lake Wobegon is not derived from his pathos knowing he can never go home again," Scholl continues. "He refuses to emphasize his status as exile in the novel [*Lake Wobegon Days*]. The wonder flows from his understanding that the complicated person he has become . . . is truly no step up from the guy down in the Sidetrack Tap he might have been had he never left home in the first place."

Keillor left *A Prairie Home Companion* in June of 1987, deciding that he needed more time to devote to his writing, and, suggests Schmich, in order to escape the unwanted fame that dogged his heels in Minnesota. His next book, *Leaving Home,* consisted of edited versions of his monologues from the last months of the show—many of them about people leaving Lake Wobegon. "Every once in a while," declares Richard F. Shepard in the *New York Times,* "the author slips into a poetic mood and you know he is saying goodbye to a world that was, a goodbye he makes clear as he goes along." The book, Shepard concludes, "says what it has to say with a rare, dry humor that is in what we like to believe is the very best American tradition." "His humor," says Scholl, "is sustained by his comic faith, which like Powdermilk Biscuits, helps readers and listeners 'get up and do what needs to be done.'"

Keillor lived briefly in Denmark with his Danish wife Ulla Skaerved, then returned to the United States and set up a residence in New York City. In 1989 he began a new radio program, *Garrison Keillor's American Radio Company of the Air.* Although one of his latest books, *We Are Still Married,* mostly reprints pieces that appeared originally in the *New Yorker,* he has not yet exhausted his stories about the denizens of his quiet hometown. "In some hidden chamber of our hearts," writes David Black in *Rolling Stone,* "most of us, no matter where we

live, are citizens of Lake Wobegon"—the place where, as Keillor has told us, "all the women are strong, all the men are good-looking, and all the children are above average."

Keillor made another foray into the world of novel writing with his 1992 release, *WLT: A Radio Romance.* The book is about Ray and Roy Soderbjerg, two brothers who establish a radio station during the glory days of radio in 1926. They bumble through their new enterprise, booking acts small and smaller as they explore the frontier of radio broadcasting. Acts such as the Shepherd Boys (a gospel group), Lily Dale (a wheelchair-bound woman with a seductive voice), and the Shoe Shine Boys (a folk group) compete with radio melodramas like *Adventures in Homemaking* and *Noontime Jubilee.* Brother Ray is a lecherous man who chases after any female who comes within his realm, whereas Roy craves the country life. The station "adopts" boy broadcaster Francis With, whose parents have either died or gone mad, and he is molded into the ubiquitous announcer Frank White, who becomes the station's top draw. The novel chronicles decades of the station's rise until television becomes the draw of the day.

The novel shows the appeal of radio during its golden days, the struggling personalities involved, the backstage hijinks, and the listeners' loyalties. Critical reaction to the book was mixed. Anne Bernays, writing in the *New York Times Book Review,* claims that the work, unusual for the man so known for his humor, "is a much darker book than one would expect. . . . Mr. Keillor's famous grin now covers a grimace." She relates that this undertone is one of her main problems with the work: "Funny and energetic as *WLT* is, the book's subtext of what can only be described as disappointment disappoints. I ended up wishing Mr. Keillor had let me laugh more; he still has the humorist's singular and worthy touch." Elizabeth Beverly of *Commonweal* criticizes Keillor's style in writing the book, claiming that the chapters are too short and choppy: "They seriously hinder his ability to tell a story from the inside. There's not enough room to move, not enough time to fill in background information." Beverly concludes that "Keillor the novelist doesn't know what he wants. He cannot hear what he wants. He is learning to work in a medium which, in this case, has resisted him. This novel is a failed venture, but bespeaks a great hope." While Michael Ratcliffe, writing in the London *Observer,* remarks that Keillor's novel is "very funny," he finds fault with its structure, claiming that it is "not really a novel at all. Keillor is an intensive miniaturist, but he is driving a stretched limo here. . . . *Radio Romance* is like a brilliant bedding plant: it flowers as floribundantly as promised in the photograph, but puts down no roots to grow."

Keillor's next work was a book of short stories and vignettes called *The Book of Guys*. A comic spinoff of the work of Robert Bly, the poet who wrote best-selling works about male bonding in the wilderness, *The Book of Guys* tracks the struggles with manhood experienced by such diverse protagonists as Dionysus and Buddy the Leper. Roy Bradley, Boy Broadcaster, for example, hails from the tongue-twisting village Piscacatawamaquoddymoggin, and his tale is as much one of a broken heart as of his radio vocation. Lonesome Shorty, a cowboy who takes to collecting china, ends up in conflict over how his hobby has created conflict in his previously conventional life. "Keillor puts on the mantle of guyness, with its repeating pattern of male bonding and rugged manly embraces, and camps around in it," comments Susan Jeffreys of *New Statesman & Society.*

Jeffreys claims that the book "is the best thing he has done since *Lake Wobegon Days*; maybe even better." Lisa Zeidner praises the work in the *New York Times Book Review,* calling it "an endearingly acerbic collection." Zeidner, however, finds that Keillor is not necessarily at his peak when he is pointing out the differences between the sexes: "The most substantial tales aren't really about manhood at all, but about the arbitrariness and absurdity of modern success, especially in show business," she comments. "He drags his heroes through the mud of contemporary culture and teaches them the essential tongue-in-cheek Lake Wobegon lesson . . . 'not to imagine we *are* someone but to be content being who we are.'"

Keillor's two books for children, *Cat, You Better Come Home* and *The Old Man Who Loved Cheese,* feature Keillor's trademark sense of the absurd. In *Cat, You Better Come Home,* Keillor fictionalizes the life of a feline who wants more than she gets in her own house, so she runs away to a life of show business, only to return broken down to the man who loves her. *The Old Man Who Loved Cheese* features Wallace P. Flynn, a man whose love for the dairy product causes him to lose his wife and his family. However, after he realizes that the joys of human companionship are much more satisfying than his favorite food, he gives it up and his life is restored.

BIOGRAPHICAL/CRITICAL SOURCES:

BOOKS

Contemporary Literary Criticism, Volume 40, Gale (Detroit), 1986.
Dictionary of Literary Biography Yearbook: 1987, Gale, 1988.
Keillor, Garrison, *Lake Wobegon Days,* Viking, 1985.
Lee, Judith Tavoss, *Garrison Keillor: A Voice of America,* University Press of Mississippi (University), 1991.

PERIODICALS

Booklist, June 1 and 15, 1996, p. 1732.
Chicago Tribune, March 15, 1987.
Chicago Tribune Book World, January 24, 1982.
Children's Book Review Service, Inc., June, 1995, p. 124; July, 1996, p. 147.
Christian Century, July 21-28, 1982; November 13, 1985.
Commonweal, April 10, 1992, p. 26.
Country Journal, January, 1982.
Detroit Free Press, September 8, 1985.
Detroit News, September 1, 1985.
Esquire, May, 1982.
Kirkus Reviews, April 1, 1996, p. 532.
New Statesman & Society, January 14, 1994, p. 40.
New York Times, October 31, 1982; August 20, 1985; October 31, 1985; October 21, 1987.
New York Times Book Review, February 28, 1982; August 25, 1985; November 10, 1991, p. 24; December 12, 1993, p. 13; May 21, 1995, p. 20.
Observer (London), January 19, 1992, p. 53; December 3, 1995, p. 16.
Publishers Weekly, September 13, 1985; May 8, 1995, p. 294; April 1, 1996, p. 74.
Rolling Stone, July 23, 1981.
Saturday Review, May-June, 1983.
School Library Journal, July, 1995, p. 78; May, 1996, p. 93.
Time, November 9, 1981; February 1, 1982; September 2, 1985; November 4, 1985; November 22, 1993, p. 82; December 11, 1995, p. 77.
Washington Post, August 23, 1989.
Washington Post Book World, January 18, 1982; November 28, 1993, p. 1.
Yale Review, January, 1993, p. 148.*

KEITH, J. Kilmeny
See MALLESON, Lucy Beatrice

*   *   *

KELLOW, Kathleen
See HIBBERT, Eleanor Alice Burford

*   *   *

KENT, Alexander
See REEMAN, Douglas Edward

*   *   *

KERNS, Daniel R.
See LICHTENBERG, Jacqueline

*   *   *

KEYES, Frances Parkinson 1885-1970

PERSONAL: Surname rhymes with "prize"; born July 21, 1885, in Charlottesville, VA; died July 3, 1970, in New Orleans, LA; buried at "The Oxbow," the Keyes family plot in Newbury, VT; daughter of John Henry (a professor of Greek) and Louise (Johnson) Wheeler; married Henry Wilder Keyes (a governor and senator), June 8, 1904 (died, 1938); children: Henry W., John P., Francis. *Education:* Educated privately; attended Miss Carroll's School and Winsor School in Boston, MA, and Mlle. Dardelle's School in Switzerland. *Politics:* "Republican by inheritance; frequently independent." *Religion:* Converted to Roman Catholicism, 1939.

CAREER: Writer, 1921-70. *Good Housekeeping* magazine, New York City, associate editor, 1923-35; *National Historical Magazine,* Daughters of American Revolution, Washington, DC, editor, 1937-39.

MEMBER: National Society of Colonial Wars, National Society of Colonial Dames, American Society of the French Legion of Honor, National Women's Press Club, National Society of Women's Geographers, Sulgrave Club (Washington, DC), Orleans Club (New Orleans), Fragment Society (Boston).

AWARDS, HONORS: Litt.D., George Washington University, 1921, and Bates College, 1934; named "Outstanding Catholic Woman in the U.S." and awarded Siena Medal by Theta Phi Alpha, 1946; Diploma of Amis de Saumur, 1948; Medal of Honor, General Council of the Seine, 1950, for "work as a novelist and journalist and friendship for France"; Silver Medal of French Recognition, 1951, "in recognition of aid in the reconstruction of the Abbey of the Benedictines at Lisieux, France"; L.H.D., University of New Hampshire, 1951; Christopher Award, 1953, for *Bernadette of Lourdes: Shepherdess, Sister and Saint;* Order of Isabella the Catholic, 1959, "in recognition of work in Spain"; Legion of Honor, 1962, for work in France.

WRITINGS:

The Old Gray Homestead (also see below), Houghton (Boston), 1919, published as *Sylvia Cary,* Paperback Library, 1962.

The Career of David Noble (also see below), F. A. Stokes (New York City), 1921.

Letters from a Senator's Wife, Appleton (New York City), 1924.

Queen Anne's Lace (also see below), Liveright (New York City), 1930.

Silver Seas and Golden Cities: A Joyous Journey through Latin Lands, Liveright, 1931, published as *Silver Seas and Golden Cities,* Pyramid Books, 1964.

Lady Blanche Farm: A Romance of the Commonplace (also see below), Liveright, 1931.

Senator Marlowe's Daughter (also see below), Messner (New York City) 1933, published in England as *Christian Marlowe's Daughter,* Eyre & Spottiswoode (London), 1935.

The Safe Bridge, Messner, 1934.

The Happy Wanderer (poems), Messner, 1935, 2nd edition, 1954.

Honor Bright, Messner, 1936.

Capital Kaleidoscope: The Story of a Washington Hostess, Harper (New York City), 1937.

Written in Heaven: The Life on Earth of the Little Flower of Lisieux, Messner, 1937, revised edition published as *Therese, Saint of a Little Way,* 1950, 3rd edition, 1962.

Pioneering People in Northern New England (biographical sketches), Judd & Detweiler (Washington, DC), 1937.

Parts Unknown, Messner, 1938, published in England as *Ambassadress,* Eyre & Spottiswoode, 1938.

The Great Tradition (also see below), Messner, 1939.

Along a Little Way, Kenedy (New York City), 1940, revised edition, Hawthorn (New York City), 1962.

Bernadette, Maid of Lourdes, Messner, 1940, also published as *The Sublime Shepherdess* (also see below), Messner, 1940, revised edition published as *Bernadette of Lourdes: Shepherdess, Sister and Saint,* Messner, 1953.

Fielding's Folly, Messner, 1940.

The Grace of Guadalupe (also see below; Catholic Book Club selection), Messner, 1941.

All That Glitters, Messner, 1941.

Crescent Carnival, Messner, 1942, published in England as *If Ever I Cease to Love You,* Eyre & Spottiswoode, 1943.

Also the Hills, Messner, 1943.

The River Road (also see below), Messner, 1945, part one published in England as *River Road,* Eyre & Spottiswoode, 1946, part two published separately as *Vail il d'Alvery,* Messner, 1947.

Once on Esplanade: A Cycle between Two Creole Weddings, Dodd, 1947.

Came a Cavalier, Messner, 1947.

Dinner at Antoine's, Messner, 1948.

Joy Street, Messner, 1950, abridged edition, Eyre & Spottiswoode, 1956, Fawcett, 1959.

All This Is Louisiana, Harper, 1950.

The Cost of a Best Seller, Messner, 1950.

Steamboat Gothic (also see below), Messner, 1952, published in England by Eyre & Spottiswoode in two volumes; Volume 1: *Larry Vincent,* 1952, Volume 2: *Steamboat Gothic,* 1953, abridged edition, Fawcett, 1959.

The Royal Box, Messner, 1954.

The Frances Parkinson Keyes Cookbook, Doubleday (New York City), 1955.

St. Anne: Grandmother of Our Saviour, Messner, 1955, revised edition, Hawthorn, 1962.

Blue Camellia, Messner, 1957.

The Land of Stones and Saints, Doubleday, 1957.

Guadalupe to Lourdes (contains *The Grace of Guadalupe* and *The Sublime Shepherdess*), Catechetical Guild Educational Society, 1957.

Victorine, Messner, 1958, published in England as *The Gold Slippers,* Eyre & Spottiswoode, 1958.

Station Wagon in Spain, Farrar, Straus (New York City), 1959, published in England as *The Letter from Spain,* Eyre & Spottiswoode, 1959.

Christmas Gift, Hawthorn, 1959.

Mother Cabrini, Missionary to the World, Farrar, Straus, 1959.

(Translator and author of foreword) Maria Vela, *The Third Mystic of Avila,* Farrar, Straus, 1960.

Roses in December (autobiography), Doubleday, 1960, revised edition, Liveright, 1966.

The Chess Players, Farrar, Straus, 1960.

The Rose and the Lily: The Lives and Times of Two South American Saints, Hawthorn, 1961.

Madame Castel's Lodger, Farrar, Straus, 1962.

(Compiler) *A Treasury of Favorite Poems,* Hawthorn, 1963.

The Restless Lady, and Other Stories, Liveright, 1963.

Three Ways of Love (also see below), Hawthorn, 1963.

The Explorer, McGraw (New York City), 1964.

Saint Catherine of Siena (excerpted from *Three Ways of Love*), Catholic Family Book Club, 1965.

I, the King, McGraw, 1966.

Tongues of Fire, Coward (New York City), 1966.

The Heritage, McGraw, 1968.

All Flags Flying (memoirs), McGraw, 1972.

Also author of *We Three Kings of Orient Are,* 1956, and *Keeping Christmas,* 1957. Author of monthly column in *Good Housekeeping.* Contributor to periodicals, including *Writer's Digest.*

SIDELIGHTS: While Frances Parkinson Keyes was "the favourite novelist of many American readers during the middle third of this century," according to Warren French in *Twentieth-Century Historical and Romance Writers,* the author "received only a few sympathetic and understanding criticisms during her lifetime." An avid traveler who spoke Spanish, French, and German fluently, Keyes wrote novels that were rich in local color and concerned with people of wealth and refinement. She also wrote nonfiction, much of it influenced by her conversion to Catholicism and concerned with the lives of the saints.

Born into an intellectual family (her father was a professor of Greek) and educated at private schools in Boston and abroad, Keyes entered the public eye even before she was first published. She was the First Lady of New Hampshire, having married Henry Wilder Keyes in 1904, who became governor in 1917. By the time he was elected a U.S. Senator in 1919, Keyes had released her first novel, *The Old Gray Homestead.*

A score of romances followed, many staying true to Keyes's penchant for local color, descriptions of life among the upper classes, and generation-spanning sagas. The author's "legends," as French puts it, "to the delight of her lending-library readers and the despair of fashionable reviewers, were richly decorated with the fruits of long and careful research into the culture—in both the artistic and anthropological sense—of the regions that intrigued her."

Chief among those regions was the French Quarter of New Orleans. Beginning with *Crescent Carnival,* Keyes developed a pattern of alternating books about Louisiana with those in other settings, spending the late winter in New Orleans, the summer in Europe, and the rest of the year in New England or South America. Keyes's son, Henry, says in the afterword of *All Flags Flying* that his mother's move to Louisiana was "perhaps the most important change in [her] life, next to her 'gradual growth to Catholicism.'" She took up residence in the New Orleans French Quarter at Beauregard House, which had been built by the maternal grandfather of chess master Paul Morphy. The house was later owned by the Confederate General Pierre Gustave Toutant Beauregard, the man who had ordered the bombardment of Fort Sumter near Charleston, South Carolina, launching the Civil War. Keyes restored the house and used the renovated slave quarters as a place to write. Two of her books involve real individuals connected with the house: Morphy is the leading character in *The Chess Players,* and Beauregard in *Madame Castel's Lodger.* The house was eventually acquired by the Keyes Foundation, a charitable trust established by Frances Keyes in 1948 to help potential writers and to preserve historic buildings.

One of the most popular New Orleans titles was *Dinner at Antoine's,* a mystery as well as a novel of manners centering on a murder that takes place during Mardi Gras. While reviewers found the mystery elements lacking in thrills, they lauded Keyes's use of detail on the food and dress of Louisiana.

In the scope of her popular romances, Keyes is often mentioned in the same breath as her contemporaries Edna Ferber and Taylor Caldwell; indeed, in a 1959 *Life* article entitled "Queens of Fiction," the three are profiled as equals. But decades later, while Ferber and Caldwell books remain potboiler classics, Keyes is virtually forgotten. "How could a popular favourite so soon lose her place in readers' affections?" wonders French. "The mystery of this 'gen-

eration gap' poses an important problem in changing tastes, much like the elusive problems that often provide the leisurely momentum for [Keyes's] tales."

To French, "length and detail alone do not distinguish Keyes's novels from Ferber's and Caldwell's. The reason for the comparative impermanence of Keyes's fabrications is most likely that the societies she portrayed have faded with the passing years. Although neither Keyes nor her readers would probably have thought of themselves as decadent, they were profoundly so; and this fascination with decadence suggest the reason that Creole Louisiana and its hothouse culture provided the ideal vehicle for rewarding their tastes."

Even as readers embraced the worldly writer, critics were less enthusiastic. A typical *New York Times Book Review* article commented that a Keyes novel is "carefully worked out, but lacking the spark of a single compelling character." But "reviewers who faulted her indifferent plotting, rambling narratives, flabby style . . . and long, confidential prefaces shaping her struggles in creating the books and acknowledging the help of those who befriended her missed altogether the source of her appeal," argued French. "Reading a novel by Keyes was not a way to pass the time restlessly on idle days, it was rather like a chatty visit from an old and welcoming friend who had just returned from fabulous places, brimming over with their quaint lore and exciting gossip."

Martin Weil said in the *Washington Post* that "although they generally failed to win the enthusiasm of literary critics or Hollywood producers, . . . Keyes's books, carefully researched and vividly described, won the attention of the reading public, selling more than twenty million copies." *Honor Bright,* for example, her first novel to make the best-seller list, was followed by eighteen others, including *Came a Cavalier, Steamboat Gothic, Dinner at Antoine's, Joy Street,* and *The River Road.*

R. Wernick, writing in *Life,* attributed Keyes's success to her ability "to evoke a rich, full-flavored atmosphere of aristocratic living on a grand, complicated scale." Wernick believed that to read a Keyes novel was "to enter an enormous ballroom decorated with expensive good taste, where a number of generally kindly people (a few, however, a positive swine) rotate in elegant costumes and whisper to each other interminable stories of family entanglements." Keyes herself admitted in a *Writer's Digest* interview with Peggy Ann Brock that the key to her success was researching the scene of the story: "People will discover what isn't authentic. They have a sort of sixth sense, and a feeling about whether or not the author's been there and how well he knows his scene. . . . The writer must know the customs of the area or the period he's writing about, and the kind of furniture to use for his story. He must dress his character correctly and feed him properly."

BIOGRAPHICAL/CRITICAL SOURCES:

BOOKS

Breit, Harvey, *The Writer Observed,* World, 1956.
Heyn, Ernest, editor, *My Most Inspiring Moment: Encounters with Destiny Relived by Thirty-eight Best-Selling Authors,* Doubleday, 1965.
Keyes, Frances Parkinson, *Along a Little Way,* Kenedy, 1940.
Keyes, *The Cost of a Best Seller,* Messner, 1950.
Keyes, *All Flags Flying,* McGraw, 1972.
Twentieth-Century Historical and Romance Writers, 3rd edition, St. James Press, 1994.

PERIODICALS

English Journal, June, 1951.
Life, April 6, 1959.
New York Times, November 8, 1942; December 9, 1945; June 5, 1968.
New York Times Book Review, December 10, 1950.
Time, December 26, 1960.
Times Literary Supplement, September 5, 1952.
Writer's Digest, October, 1969.

*   *   *

KIENZLE, William X(avier) 1928-
  (Mark Boyle)

PERSONAL: Born September 11, 1928, in Detroit, MI; son of Alphonzo and Mary Louise (Boyle) Kienzle; married Javan Herman Andrews (an editor and researcher), 1974. *Education:* Sacred Heart Seminary College, B.A., 1950; also attended St. John's Seminary, 1950-54, and University of Detroit, 1968. *Politics:* Independent. *Religion:* Roman Catholic. *Avocational interests:* Playing piano, reading, yard work.

ADDRESSES: Home and office—P.O. Box 645, Keego Harbor, MI 48320-0645.

CAREER: Ordained Roman Catholic priest, 1954; left priesthood, 1974; Roman Catholic Archdiocese of Detroit, Detroit, MI, archdiocesan priest in five parishes, 1954-74, editor-in-chief of *Michigan Catholic,* 1962-74; *MPLS.* magazine, Minneapolis, MN, editor-in-chief, 1974-77; Western Michigan University, Kalamazoo, associate director of Center for Contemplative Studies, 1977-78; University of Dallas, Irving, TX, director of Center for Contemplative Studies, 1978-79; writer, 1979—.

MEMBER: International Association of Crime Writers, Authors Guild, Authors League of America.

AWARDS, HONORS: Michigan Knights of Columbus journalism award, 1963, for general excellence; honorable mention from Catholic Press Association, 1974, for editorial writing.

WRITINGS:

MYSTERY NOVELS

The Rosary Murders, Andrews & McMeel (Fairway, KS), 1979.
Death Wears a Red Hat, Andrews & McMeel, 1980.
Mind over Murder, Andrews & McMeel, 1981.
Assault with Intent, Andrews & McMeel, 1982.
Shadow of Death, Andrews & McMeel, 1983.
Kill and Tell, Andrews & McMeel, 1984.
Sudden Death, Andrews, McMeel & Parker, 1985.
Deathbed, Andrews, McMeel & Parker, 1986.
Deadline for a Critic, Andrews, McMeel & Parker, 1987.
Marked for Murder, Andrews & McMeel, 1988.
Eminence, Andrews & McMeel, 1989.
Masquerade, Andrews & McMeel, 1990.
Chameleon, Andrews & McMeel, 1991.
Body Count, Andrews & McMeel, 1992.
Dead Wrong, Andrews & McMeel, 1993.
Bishop as Pawn, Andrews & McMeel, 1994.
Call No Man Father, Andrews & McMeel, 1995.
Requiem for Moses, Andrews & McMeel, 1996.
The Man Who Loved God, Andrews & McMeel, 1997.

OTHER

Campaign Capers (play), produced in Detroit, 1960.
(Contributor) *Homocide Host Presents,* Write Way, 1996.

Contributor under pseudonym Mark Boyle to *MPLS.* magazine.

ADAPTATIONS: The Rosary Murders was produced as a motion picture starring Donald Sutherland by Take One Productions, 1987.

WORK IN PROGRESS: The Greatest Evil, Andrews & McMeel, anticipated publication in 1998.

SIDELIGHTS: Though he no longer delivers the sermons that often captivated his parishioners, William X. Kienzle is still writing for others. After leaving the priesthood in 1974, he "exchanged his pulpit for a typewriter," as Bill Dunn describes in *Publishers Weekly,* and began writing the tales that have made him a best-selling mystery author. The twenty years he spent in the clergy now provide the raw material for his popular series involving Father Robert Koesler, an amateur sleuth and sharply defined priest who resembles Kienzle in several ways. "The fictitious Father Koesler divides his time between his pastoral duties within the Detroit archdiocese and his journalistic duties as an editor of the area's Catholic newspaper, just as Kienzle spent his time during the 1960's," *Detroit News Magazine* writer Andrea Wojack observes.

Despite these similarities, Wojack does not envision Koesler as Kienzle in disguise. Rather, she sees him as a product of both Kienzle's background and "the tradition of clerical detectives in fiction, like [G. K.] Chesterton's Father Brown and Harry Kemelman's Rabbi Small." Andrew M. Greeley similarly observes in the *Los Angeles Times Book Review:* "William Kienzle is the Harry Kemelman of Catholicism, and his priest detective, Robert Koesler . . . is the Detroit response to Rabbi Small." The critic adds: "I am not suggesting that Kienzle is consciously imitating Kemelman—though there would be nothing wrong with such imitation. Rather I am arguing that religio-ethnic subcultures are fertile seedbeds for mystery stories. Kienzle's sensitivity to pathos and foolishness, shallow fads and rigid ideologies, mindless nonsense and deep faith of the contemporary Catholic scene compares favorably with Kemelman's vivid description of suburban Jewish life."

A native Detroiter, Kienzle also uses the city and its Catholic parishes as a backdrop for his fiction, reportedly drawing many of his characters from people he has known. "Kienzle's portrayals of various priests obviously [are] an insider's (or ex-insider's) work," a *Detroit News* contributor comments. "He seems accurate, yet relaxed, in his depictions of the clergy, and his genuine affection for many of them

far outruns any tendency toward satiric thrust." In addition, Father Koesler's solutions rely on his knowledge of the Church and its workings; in *Eminence,* for example, "Koesler's command of ecclesiastical detail is full and fascinating," *Los Angeles Times Book Review* critic Charles Champlin states, and "the uses of Latin and points of Canon law are significant clues."

Despite Kienzle's assertion that his novels are, as Dunn reports, "first of all thrillers," many critics find a deeper meaning in his work. In his review of *Mind over Murder,* for example, *Detroit Free Press* managing editor Neal Shine observes: "There has always been the sense that there's as much message as mystery in Kienzle's books. Kienzle is a former Detroit priest whose feelings about some of the ways in which the Catholic Church deports itself can hardly be called ambivalent. In *Mind over Murder* he goes to the heart of the matter for a lot of Catholics—marriage and the Church. The people with the clearest motives for rubbing out the monsignor are those who have run up against his incredibly inflexible rulings on marriage." *Chicago Tribune* writer Peter Gorner likewise remarks that in *Deadline for a Critic* "Kienzle addresses serious modern issues"; nevertheless, the author also "stops to digress and tell us his wonderful stories." The critic concludes that "Kienzle's books are more small morality plays than classic mysteries. He always is welcomed to my shelves."

Although Kienzle includes philosophical inquiries and religious asides in his books, many critics contend that his primary strength lies in the development of the mystery. In *Kill and Tell,* for example, "we're back to basics with a fascinating cast of three-dimensional characters who *act* like people caught up in a baffling case, a protagonist in Father Koesler who is both wry and intelligent, and an honest-to-badness murder at a tension-filled cocktail party that is truly puzzling," Don G. Campbell recounts in the *Los Angeles Times Book Review. Best Sellers* contributor Tony Bednarczyk likewise asserts that in *The Rosary Murders,* which he calls a "well paced, tightly written novel," the author, "more importantly, creates well defined characters that inhabit his story rather than decorate it." *"The Rosary Murders* quickly established Father Koesler as among the most likable and authentic of all recent sleuths and gave his wise and compassionate creator a midlife career and a new pulpit," Gorner concludes. "Since then, few mystery series have been more cozy and persuasive."

The series's more recent installments have found Father Koesler and his cohorts in the press and the police department in the midst of a plot involving a Mafia hitman who has confessed to murdering a priest in *Body Count;* investigating a thirty-year-old murder in *Dead Wrong;* and working to find the killers of several priests in advance of a visit by the Pope in *Call No Man Father.* As always, Kienzle mixes in numerous anecdotes from his own experience as a priest and sets the stories in the urban setting of Detroit. "Kienzle's novels are longer and more leisurely than most mysteries, more discursive, and with shorter episodic scenes than in tightly plotted action stories of confrontation and violence," notes Jane Gottschalk in *Crime and Mystery Writers.* Gottschalk adds, "But in the bizarre plots, the sharp delineation of even the most minor characters (with more warts than beauty spots), and the sophisticated urbanity of the telling make them first-rate literate reading."

BIOGRAPHICAL/CRITICAL SOURCES:

BOOKS

Contemporary Authors Autobiography Series, Volume 1, Gale (Detroit), 1984.
Contemporary Literary Criticism, Volume 25, Gale, 1983.
St. James Guide to Crime & Mystery Writers, St. James Press (Detroit), 1996.

PERIODICALS

Best Sellers, July, 1979.
Booklist, April 15, 1992, p. 1506; May 1, 1995, p. 1555.
Chicago Tribune, May 29, 1985; April 8, 1987; May 3, 1989.
Chicago Tribune Book World, July 11, 1982.
Detroit Free Press, February 22, 1980; April 26, 1981.
Detroit News, July 15, 1979; April 5, 1981.
Detroit News Magazine, March 16, 1980.
Library Journal, May 1, 1987; April 1, 1989.
Los Angeles Times, April 24, 1981; May 7, 1987.
Los Angeles Times Book Review, June 22, 1980; May 23, 1982; August 5, 1984; May 7, 1987; April 9, 1989; April 11, 1993, p. 8.
Michigan Magazine, August 11, 1985.
National Catholic Reporter, July 15, 1988; May 26, 1995, p. 25.
New York Times Book Review, June 15, 1980; June 21, 1981; May 23, 1982; May 20, 1990.

Publishers Weekly, April 18, 1980; March 11, 1988; February 3, 1989; March 9, 1990; March 15, 1991; March 2, 1992, p. 52; March 8, 1993, p. 70; March 21, 1994; March 6, 1995, p. 63; March 18, 1996, p. 61.
Rapport, Volume 16, number 6, 1992, p. 21.
Tribune Books (Chicago), November 7, 1993, p. 10.

* * *

KINCAID, Jamaica 1949-

PERSONAL: Born Elaine Potter Richardson, May 25, 1949, in St. Johns, Antigua; daughter of a carpenter/cabinet maker and Annie Richardson; married Allen Shawn (a composer and professor at Bennington College); children: Annie Shawn and Harold. *Education:* Studied photography at the New School for Social Research in New York; attended Franconia College, NH. *Religion:* Jewish.

ADDRESSES: Home—P.O. Box 822, North Bennington, VT 05257.

CAREER: Writer. *New Yorker,* New York City, staff writer, 1976-95. Visiting Professor, Harvard University, Cambridge, MA.

AWARDS, HONORS: Morton Dauwen Zabel Award, American Academy and Institute of Arts and Letters, 1983, for *At the Bottom of the River;* honorary degrees from Williams College and Long Island College, both in 1991, Colgate University, Amherst College, and Bard College; Lila Wallace-*Reader's Digest* Fund annual writer's award, 1992; *The Autobiography of My Mother* was a finalist for the National Book Critics Circle Award for fiction and the PEN Faulkner Award, both 1997.

WRITINGS:

At the Bottom of the River (short stories), Farrar, Straus (New York City), 1983.
Annie John (novel), Farrar, Straus, 1985.
A Small Place (essays), Farrar, Straus, 1988.
Annie, Gwen, Lilly, Pam and Tulip, illustrations by Eric Fischl, Knopf (New York City) and Whitney Museum of American Art, 1989.
Lucy (novel), Farrar, Straus, 1990.
The Autobiography of My Mother (novel), Farrar, Straus, 1995.

Also contributor to periodicals. *At the Bottom of the River* has been recorded by the Library of Congress Archive of Recorded Poetry and Literature.

SIDELIGHTS: Jamaica Kincaid gained wide acclaim with her first two works, *At the Bottom of the River* and *Annie John.* In these and other books about life on the Caribbean island of Antigua, where she was born, Kincaid employs a highly poetic literary style celebrated for its rhythms, imagery, characterization, and elliptic narration. As Ike Onwordi wrote in *Times Literary Supplement:* "Jamaica Kincaid uses language that is poetic without affectation. She has a deft eye for salient detail while avoiding heavy symbolism and diverting exotica. The result captures powerfully the essence of vulnerability."

"Everyone thought I had a way with words, but it came out as a sharp tongue. No one expected anything from me at all. Had I just sunk in the cracks it would not have been noted. I would have been lucky to be a secretary somewhere," Kincaid told Leslie Garis in the *New York Times Magazine.* When she was seventeen, Kincaid, whose given name was Elaine Potter, left the rural island to become an *au pair* in New York City. By the time she returned, almost twenty years later, she had become a successful writer for the *New Yorker* magazine under her chosen name.

In her first collection of stories, *At the Bottom of the River,* Kincaid shows an imposing capacity for detailing life's mundane aspects. This characteristic of her writing is readily evident in the oft-cited tale "Girl," which consists almost entirely of a mother's orders to her daughter: "Wash the white clothes on Monday and put them on the stone heap; wash the color clothes on Tuesday and put them on the clothesline to dry; don't walk barehead in the hot sun; cook pumpkin fritters in very hot sweet oil . . . ; on Sundays try to walk like a lady, and not like the slut you are so bent on becoming." Anne Tyler, in a review for *New Republic,* declared that this passage provides "the clearest idea of the book's general tone; for Jamaica Kincaid scrutinizes various particles of our world so closely and so solemnly that they begin to take on a nearly mystical importance."

"The Letter from Home," also from *At the Bottom of the River,* serves as further illustration of Kincaid's style of repetition and her penchant for the mundane. In this tale a character recounts her daily chores in such a manner that the story resembles an incantation: "I milked the cows, I churned the butter, I stored the cheese, I baked the bread, I brewed the tea," Kincaid begins. In *Ms.,* Suzanne Freeman cited this tale as evidence that Kincaid's style is "akin to hymn-singing or maybe even chanting." Freeman added that Kincaid's "singsong style" produces "images that are as sweet and mysterious as the secrets that children whisper in your ear."

With the publication of *At the Bottom of the River,* Kincaid was hailed as an important new voice in American fiction. Edith Milton wrote in the *New York Times Book Review* that Kincaid's tales "have all the force of illumination, and even prophetic power," and David Leavitt noted in the *Village Voice* that they move "with grace and ease from the mundane to the enormous." He added that "Kincaid's particular skill lies in her ability to articulate the internal workings of a potent imagination without sacrificing the rich details of the external world on which that imagination thrives." Doris Grumbach expressed similar praise in a review for the *Washington Post Book World.* She declared that the world of Kincaid's narrators "hovers between fantasy and reality," and she asserted that Kincaid's prose "results not so much in stories as in states of consciousness." Grumbach also noted that Kincaid's style, particularly its emphasis on repetition, intensifies "the feelings of poetic jubilation Kincaid has . . . for all life."

That exuberance for life is also evident in Kincaid's second book, *Annie John,* which contains interrelated stories about a girl's maturation in Antigua. In *Annie John* the title character evolves from a young girl to an aspiring nurse and from innocent to realist: she experiences her first menstruation, buries a friend, gradually establishes a life independent of her mother, and overcomes a serious illness. She is ultimately torn by her pursuit of a career outside her life in Antigua, and Kincaid renders that feeling so incisively that, as Elaine Kendall noted in her review for the *Los Angeles Times,* "you can almost believe Kincaid invented ambivalence."

Critically acclaimed as a coming-of-age novel, *Annie John* was praised by a number of reviewers for expressing qualities of growing up that transcend geographical locations. "Her work is recollections of childhood," Paula Bonnell remarked in the *Boston Herald.* "It conveys the mysterious power and intensity of childhood attachments to mother, father and friends, and the adolescent beginnings of separation from them." Susan Kenney, writing in the *New York Times Book Review,* noted Annie John's ambivalence about leaving behind her life in Antigua and declared that such ambivalence was "an inevitable and un-avoidable result of growing up." Kenney concluded that Kincaid's story is "so touching and familiar . . . so inevitable [that] it could be happening to any of us, anywhere, any time, any place. And that's exactly the book's strength, its wisdom, and its truth."

Kincaid's second novel, *Lucy,* is a first-person narrative in which nineteen-year-old Lucy not only expresses feelings of rage, but struggles with separation from her homeland and especially her mother. *Lucy* is about a young woman from Antigua who comes to an unnamed American city to work as an *au pair* girl. She is employed by a wealthy, white couple—Mariah and Lewis—to take care of their four young daughters. In the *Washington Post Book World,* Susanna Moore commented: "Lucy is unworldly. She has never seen snow or been in an elevator. . . . Written in the first person, [the novel] is Lucy's story of the year of her journey—away from her mother, away from home, away from the island and into the world." Richard Eder mused in the *Los Angeles Times Book Review* that "The anger of Lucy . . . is an instrument of discovery, not destruction. It is lucid and cool, but by no means unsparing."

The novel ends with Lucy writing in a journal given to her by Mariah, the woman for whom she works, and weeping over the very first line: "'I wish I could love someone so much that I would die from it.' And then as I looked at this sentence a great wave of shame came over me and I wept and wept so much that the tears fell on the page and caused all the words to become one great blur." Eder ended his review saying, "she will turn the page and go on writing."

Derek Walcott, a West Indian poet, talked with Garis in the *New York Times Magazine* about Kincaid's identification with issues that thread through all people's lives: "That relationship of mother and daughter—today she loves her mother, tomorrow she hates her, then she admires her—that is so true to life, without any artificiality, that it describes parental and filial love in a way that has never been done before. [Kincaid's] work is so full of spiritual contradictions clarified that it's extremely profound and courageous." Thulani Davis, writing in the *New York Times Book Review* said, "Ms. Kincaid is a marvelous writer whose descriptions are richly detailed; her sentences turn and surprise even in the bare context she has created, in which there are few colors, sights or smells and the moments of intimacy and confron-

tation take place in the wings, or just after the door closes. . . . Lucy is a delicate, careful observer, but her rage prevents her from reveling in the delicious-ness of a moment. At her happiest, she simply says, 'Life isn't so bad after all.'"

The Autobiography of My Mother, Kincaid's third novel, follows her previous fictional efforts in its West Indies setting and vivid, poetic prose. The book's narrator, Xuela, is an elderly woman who recounts her difficult life, beginning with the death of her mother at Xuela's birth. In what reviewers termed a chilling, unsparing tone, Xuela describes her childhood abuse at the hands of a stepmother; the corruption of her father, a policeman; and the abor-tion of her unborn child, after she realizes that the baby is intended for the baby's father and his barren wife. At the end of the novel, the narrator calls her account a story of the mother she never knew, of her unborn baby, and of "the voices that should have come out of me, the faces I never allowed to form, the eyes I never allowed to see me," as quoted by Dale Peck in the *London Review of Books.*

As with the author's earlier works, *The Autobiogra-phy of My Mother* received significant critical praise, especially for Kincaid's lyrical writing style. "Kincaid has written a truly ugly meditation on life in some of the most beautiful prose we are likely to find in contemporary fiction," averred Cathleen Schine in the *New York Times Book Review.* *Maclean's* reviewer Diane Turbide concurred, not-ing, "Kincaid employs an almost incantatory tone, using repetition and unusual syntax to give the book a hypnotic rhythm." Several reviewers commented that Kincaid's striking prose was not matched by the novel's thematic development. Schine wrote that "there is . . . something dull and unconvincing about Xuela's anguish." And according to Peck, "The prose is lovely . . . and, I would argue, distinctly, beautifully American, yet the sentiments expressed by the words themselves are trite, falsely universalising, and often just muddled." However, *Time* reviewer John Skow stated, "The reward here, as always with Kincaid's work, is the reading of her clear, bitter prose." The novel was a finalist for the National Book Critics Circle Award for fiction in 1997.

Henry Louis Gates, Jr., a distinguished critic and black studies scholar, told Emily Listfield in *Harper's Bazaar* that he felt comfortable comparing Kincaid's work to that of Toni Morrison and Wole Soyinka: "There is a self-contained world which they explore with great detail. Not to chart the existence of that world, but to show that human emotions manifest themselves everywhere." Gates said that an important contribution of Kincaid is that "she never feels the necessity of claiming the existence of a black world or a female sensibility. She assumes them both. I think it's a distinct departure that she's making, and I think that more and more black American writers will assume their world the way that she does. So that we can get beyond the large theme of racism and get to the deeper themes of how black people love and cry and live and die. Which, after all, is what art is all about."

BIOGRAPHICAL/CRITICAL SOURCES:

BOOKS

Black Literature Criticism, Volume 2, Gale (Detroit), 1991.
Contemporary Literary Criticism, Gale, Volume 43, 1987, Volume 68, 1991.
Cudjoe, Selwyn R., editor, *Caribbean Women Writers: Essays from the First International Conference,* Callaloo, 1990.
Dance, D. Cumber, editor, *Fifty Caribbean Writers,* Greenwood (Westport, CT), 1986.
Ferguson, Moira, *Jamaica Kincaid: Where the Land Meets the Body,* University Press of Virginia (Charlottesville), 1994.
Kincaid, Jamaica, *At the Bottom of the River,* Farrar, Straus, 1983.
Kincaid, *Lucy,* Farrar, Straus, 1990.
Kincaid, *The Autobiography of My Mother,* Farrar, Straus, 1995.
Simmons, Diane, *Jamaica Kincaid,* Macmillan (New York City), 1994.

PERIODICALS

Atlantic, May, 1985.
Boston Herald, March 31, 1985.
Christian Science Monitor, April 5, 1985.
Essence, March, 1996, p. 98.
Harper's Bazaar, October, 1990; January, 1996, p. 66.
Library Journal, December 1, 1989.
Listener, January 10, 1985.
London Review of Books, February 6, 1997, p. 25.
Los Angeles Times, April 25, 1985.
Los Angeles Times Book Review, October 21, 1990.
Maclean's, May 20, 1985; April 8, 1996, p. 72.
Ms., January 1984.
Nation, June 15, 1985; February 5, 1996, p. 23.

New Republic, December 31, 1983.
New Statesman, September 7, 1984.
New York Times Book Review, January 15, 1984; April 7, 1985; July 10, 1988; October 28, 1990; February 4, 1996, p. 5.
New York Times Magazine, October 7, 1990.
People, February 19, 1996, p. 27.
Time, February 5, 1996, p. 71.
Times Literary Supplement, November 29, 1985.
Village Voice, January 17, 1984.
Virginia Quarterly Review, summer, 1985.
Voice Literary Supplement, April 1985; February 1996, p. 11.
Washington Post, April 2, 1985.
Washington Post Book World, October 7, 1990.
World Literature Today, autumn, 1985.

OTHER

Interview with Jamaica Kincaid, conducted by Kay Bonetti, recorded for American Audio Prose Library (Bennington, VT), 1991.

*   *   *

KNOWLES, Valerie (J.) 1934-

PERSONAL: Born August 2, 1934, in Montreal, Quebec, Canada; daughter of Trevor Durnford (an insurance company official) and Margaret Jean (a homemaker; maiden name, Mackay) Ross; married David Clifford Knowles (a civil servant), March 11, 1961. *Ethnicity:* "Scottish-Canadian." *Education:* Smith College, B.A. (with honors), 1956; McGill University, M.A., 1957; Carleton University, B.J., 1964. *Religion:* Anglican.

ADDRESSES: Home—554 Piccadilly Ave., Ottawa, Ontario, Canada K1Y 0J1. *Agent*—Joanne Kellock, 11017 80th Ave., Edmonton, Alberta, Canada T6G 0R2. *Email*—knowles@istar.ca.

CAREER: Prince of Wales College (now University of Prince Edward Island), Charlottetown, Prince Edward Island, instructor in history, 1958-59; teacher of history at a school in Rockcliffe Park, Ontario, 1959-60; Carleton University, Ottawa, Ontario, instructor in history, 1961; Public Archives of Canada, Ottawa, archivist, 1961-63; Carleton University, discussion group leader and bibliographer in department of history, 1964-72; freelance writer, 1972—.

MEMBER: Media Club of Ottawa (member of executive committee), Zonta Club of Ottawa (chair of publicity, program, and education fund committees).

AWARDS, HONORS: Grant from Ontario Arts Council, 1988.

WRITINGS:

(Contributor) *The Canadian Family Tree,* Corpus Information Services Ltd., 1979.

Leaving with a Red Rose, edited by Jonathan Williams, Deneau Publishers, 1981.

First Person: A Biography of Cairine Wilson, Canada's First Woman Senator, edited by Jonathan Williams, Janet Keith, and Peggy Blackstock, Dundurn Press, 1988.

Strangers at Our Gates: Canadian Immigration and Immigration Policy, 1540-1990, Dundurn Press, 1992, revised and expanded edition, 1997.

Through the Chateau Door: A History of the Zonta Club of Ottawa, 1929-1989, Zonta Club, 1994.

Making Waves: A History of the Riverside Hospital of Ottawa, Riverside Hospital of Ottawa, 1997.

Author of newsletters for Capital Visitors and Convention Bureau, Canadian Public Personnel Management Association, Office of Equal Opportunities for Women, and Canadian Department of Indian and Northern Affairs. Contributor to magazines, including *Canadian Geographic, Legion, Foodservice and Hospitality, Horizon Canada,* and *North/Nord,* and to newspapers.

WORK IN PROGRESS: Research on Canadian immigration and immigration policies.

SIDELIGHTS: Valerie Knowles once told *CA:* "Although I had written countless articles for newspapers and magazines, I never had any intention of writing a book until I was commissioned to write a history of Ottawa Civic Hospital's school of nursing. The resulting work, *Leaving with a Red Rose,* whetted my appetite for more long-term projects utilizing my background in history, and I began to consider possible topics. After giving the matter considerable thought, I decided to undertake a book-length biography of Cairine Wilson, the first woman to be appointed to Canada's unelected upper house, the Senate. I chose this subject for a number of reasons, not the least of which was my admiration for her and the fact that no book-length biography had ever been done of her. Indeed, Canadian feminist historians

have, until very recently, ignored Cairine Wilson, despite her lengthy and rich career.

"Cairine Wilson (1885-1962) was raised in one of Montreal's most affluent and influential Scots-Canadian families in an atmosphere of strict Presbyterianism, tempered by Scots liberalism. The daughter of Robert Mackay, a wealthy businessman and later senator, she displayed an early interest in politics. However, it wasn't until 1921, twelve years after her marriage to Norman Wilson, that she ventured into politics, taking on the sort of jobs that had hitherto been the preserve of men. In 1930 she was appointed to the Canadian Senate by her friend, Mackenzie King, then leader of the Liberal Party and Canadian prime minister. The appointment followed some four months after the Judicial Committee of the Imperial Privy Council in London, England, ruled that the British North America Act's reference to 'qualified persons' in section twenty-four applied to both men and women and that as a consequence women could be summoned to the Canadian Senate.

"Although she could have rested on her laurels, Cairine Wilson worked extremely hard as a senator, embracing a wide range of causes and placing herself firmly in the progressive ranks of her party. It is her work with refugees, however, that perhaps more than anything else justifies a book-length biography of her. At a time when refugees were not popular in Canada (1938-1946), she tried hard to persuade the government to lower immigration barriers and worked tirelessly to have individual refugees and their families admitted to this country. She served in the Senate for over thirty years, earning a reputation as a great humanitarian and a woman of exemplary dedication and integrity. With all her pursuits, she still found the time to raise a family of eight children.

"Shortly after *First Person* was published, my publisher asked me if I would be interested in working on a manuscript relating to Canadian immigration patterns and policies. Since the topic has long interested me and is now very topical, I have taken up his challenge. Just where it will lead me, however, I do not yet know."

BIOGRAPHICAL/CRITICAL SOURCES:

PERIODICALS

Canadian Historical Review, December, 1994.
Globe and Mail (Toronto), October 29, 1988.
Ottawa Citizen, December 10, 1988.

KONIGSBURG, E(laine) L(obl) 1930-

PERSONAL: Born February 10, 1930, in New York, NY; daughter of Adolph (in business) and Beulah (Klein) Lobl; married David Konigsburg (a psychologist), July 6, 1952; children: Paul, Laurie, Ross. *Education:* Carnegie Institute of Technology (now Carnegie-Mellon University), B.S., 1952; graduate study, University of Pittsburgh, 1952-54. *Religion:* Jewish.

ADDRESSES: Agent—c/o Atheneum Books for Young Readers, 1230 Avenue of the Americas, New York, NY 10022.

CAREER: Writer. Shenango Valley Provision Co., Sharon, PA, bookkeeper, 1947-48; Bartram School, Jacksonville, FL, science teacher, 1954-55, 1960-62. Worked as manager of a dormitory laundry, playground instructor, waitress, and library page while in college; research assistant in tissue culture and organic chemistry lab at the University of Pittsburgh.

AWARDS, HONORS: Jennifer, Hecate, Macbeth, William McKinley, and Me, Elizabeth was chosen as an honor book in *Book Week* Children's Spring Book Festival, 1967, and as a Newbery Honor Book, 1968; Newbery Medal, 1968, and William Allen White Award, 1970, both for *From the Mixed-Up Files of Mrs. Basil E. Frankweiler;* Carnegie-Mellon Merit Award, 1971; American Library Association (ALA) Notable Children's Book and National Book Award nomination, both 1974, both for *A Proud Taste for Scarlet and Miniver;* ALA Best Book for young adults, for *The Second Mrs. Giaconda,* and *Father's Arcane Daughter;* ALA Notable Children's Book and American Book Award nomination, 1980, both for *Throwing Shadows; Jennifer, Hecate, Macbeth, William McKinley, and Me, Elizabeth, About the B'nai Bagels, A Proud Taste for Scarlet and Miniver,* and *Journey to an 800 Number* were all chosen Children's Books of the Year by the Child Study Association of America; Newbery Medal, 1997, for *The View from Saturday;* special recognition award, Cultural Council of Greater Jacksonville, 1997.

WRITINGS:

JUVENILE; SELF-ILLUSTRATED

Jennifer, Hecate, Macbeth, William McKinley, and Me, Elizabeth, Atheneum (New York City), 1967, published as *Jennifer, Hecate, MacBeth, and Me,* Macmillan (London), 1968.

From the Mixed-up Files of Mrs. Basil E. Frankweiler, Atheneum, 1967.
About the B'nai Bagels, Atheneum, 1969.
(George), Atheneum, 1970, published as *Benjamin Dickenson Carr and His (George),* Penguin (London), 1974.
A Proud Taste for Scarlet and Miniver, Atheneum, 1973.
The Dragon in the Ghetto Caper, Atheneum, 1974.
Samuel Todd's Book of Great Colors, Macmillan (New York City), 1990.
Samuel Todd's Book of Great Inventions, Atheneum, 1991.
Amy Elizabeth Explores Bloomingdale's, Atheneum, 1992.

JUVENILE

Altogether, One at a Time (short stories), illustrated by Gail E. Haley, Mercer Meyer, Gary Parker, and Laurel Schindelman, Atheneum, 1971, second edition, Macmillan, 1989.
The Second Mrs. Giaconda, illustrated with museum plates, Atheneum, 1975.
Father's Arcane Daughter, Atheneum, 1976.
Throwing Shadows (short stories), Atheneum, 1979.
Journey to an 800 Number, Atheneum, 1982, published as *Journey by First Class Camel,* Hamish Hamilton (London), 1983.
Up from Jericho Tel, Atheneum, 1986.
T-Backs, T-Shirts, COAT, and Suit, Atheneum, 1993.
The View from Saturday, Atheneum, 1996.

OTHER

TalkTalk: A Children's Book Author Speaks to Grown-Ups, Atheneum, 1995.

Also author of promotional pamphlets for Atheneum. Some of Konigsburg's works have been recorded on audiocassette, and *From the Mixed-up Files of Mrs. Basil E. Frankweiler* is also available in Braille.

Collections of E. L. Konigsburg's manuscripts and original art are held at the University of Pittsburgh, Pennsylvania.

ADAPTATIONS: From the Mixed-up Files of Mrs. Basil E. Frankweiler was adapted as a motion picture starring Ingrid Bergman, Cinema 5, 1973, which was later released as *The Hideaways,* Bing Crosby Productions, 1974, and as a television film starring Lauren Bacall, ABC-TV, 1995; *Jennifer, Hecate, Macbeth, William McKinley, and Me, Elizabeth* was adapted for television as *Jennifer and Me,* NBC-TV, 1973; *The Second Mrs. Giaconda* was adapted as a play and first produced in Jacksonville, FL, 1976; *Father's Arcane Daughter* was adapted for television as *Caroline?,* Hallmark Hall of Fame, 1990.

SIDELIGHTS: E. L. Konigsburg is best known as an award-winning author and illustrator of humorous juvenile novels and stories. Konigsburg's books are not simply amusing, however; almost every story contains an element of seriousness, usually in the form of a child's search for identity. The volumes "have grown out of the material closest to hand, the events of her own life," declared Perry Nodelman in the *Dictionary of Literary Biography.* "Her writing is a witty distillation of complex experience, and she always tells her stories from an interesting point of view."

Konigsburg was born in New York City, the second of three daughters, and reared in small Pennsylvania towns. "Growing up in a small town gives you two things," she commented in her 1968 Newbery Award acceptance speech, printed in *Horn Book:* "a sense of your place and a feeling of self-consciousness—self-consciousness about one's education and exposure, both of which tend to be limited. On the other hand, limited possibilities also means creating your own options. A small town allows you to grow in your own direction, without a bombardment of outside stimulation. You can get a sense of yourself in relation to yourself not to a host of accomplished others."

As a child Konigsburg did much of her reading in the bathroom. "It was the only room in our house that had a lock on the door," she wrote in *Saturday Review,* "and I could run water in the tub to muffle the sounds of my sobbing over Rhett Butler's leaving Scarlett. Reading was tolerated in my house, but it wasn't sanctioned like dusting furniture or baking cookies. My parents never minded what I read, but they did mind *when* (like before the dishes were done) and *where* (there was only one [bathroom] in our house)." "There was no one to guide my reading," she recalled in her Newbery speech: "consequently I read a lot of trash along the *True Confessions* line. I have no objection to trash. I've read a lot of it and firmly believe it helped hone my taste."

In the *Third Book of Junior Authors* Konigsburg discussed her education: "I drew a lot as a child and was an excellent student for as long as I can remember. I graduated valedictorian from Farrell High

School and wanted to go away to college. My high school had no guidance department and no one in my family had ever gone to university. I devised a plan whereby I would work for a year, earn enough for two semesters of tuition and board, go back to work to finance another academic year, and so on until I finished my degree. No one had ever told me about scholarships. Right after high school, I got a job as a bookkeeper in a wholesale meat plant," the Shenango Valley Provision Company. It was while working there that she met her future husband, David Konigsburg, the brother of one of the owners of the business.

"The following year I enrolled at Carnegie Institute of Technology in Pittsburgh as a chemistry major. If I had in mind eventually to be a writer and artist, the notion was so deeply submerged that I was unaware of it. Besides, if you were the first person in your family to go to college, you didn't say you were going away to become a writer. You said you were going away to become a *something*—a librarian, a teacher, a chemist, a *something.* I chose chemistry because I was good at it and there would be jobs waiting when I finished. In Farrell, I never met anyone who made his living from the arts.

"One day late in my freshman year as I was walking across campus, my English professor stopped me and inquired about my plans. When I told him that I would be returning to my job for another year, he said, '*Miss* Lobl, I think that this school would not choose to lose students of your *ilk.*' Thanks to his intervention, I was able to get a scholarship. I had jobs all through school—in the library, managing a laundry service in the dormitory—and I remained *enrolled.*" "College was a crucial 'opening up' for me," she later reflected. "I worked hard and did well. However, the artistic side of me was essentially dormant. My close college friends never even knew that I could write and loved to draw. Chemistry majors spend long hours in the lab; some of our courses were full-day labs, and there was not a lot of time for much besides work and school work."

Graduating with honors, she married David Konigsburg and studied chemistry at the graduate school of the University of Pittsburgh while he prepared himself for a career as an industrial psychologist. "I'm convinced that, had I not been such a disaster in the lab, I could have made a contribution to chemistry, something creative," she once told *CA.* "I had the mind for it, but not the temperament.

There was all that awful lab work to get through. And there was no one to tell me that it is only in the higher reaches that science and art are one."

When her husband obtained a post as an industrial psychologist in Jacksonville, Florida, Konigsburg accompanied him, obtaining a position of her own as a teacher of science at Bartram, a private all-girls school. "I began to suspect that chemistry was not my field," she admitted in the *Third Book of Junior Authors*. "Not only did I always ask my students to light my Bunsen burner, having become match-shy, but I became more interested in what was going on inside them than what was going on inside the test tubes." "Going to teach in this private girls' school gave me remarkable insight into girls," she explained to *CA*. "I had gone to the school with a prejudice against private schools, thinking that they catered to spoiled young women who had it all. They *had* all the creature comforts of the world, but I soon learned that they were just as uncomfortable inside as I was when I was growing up."

Konigsburg left teaching in 1955, shortly before the birth of her son Paul and took up painting after her daughter, Laurie, was born a year later. In 1959, she gave birth to her youngest child, Ross. She returned to Bartram in 1960 and continued to teach until 1962, when she moved with her family to New York. She began writing when her youngest child started school. "I decided that I would take the mornings—not make a bed, not do the dishes—and write," she recalled in her Newbery speech. "This turned out to be easier than I expected. We had just moved to Port Chester, New York, where I knew no one, so I was spared the endless round of telephone calls from friends, neighbors and acquaintances. I kept my writing a secret except from my family. When my kids came home for lunch, I would often read them what I'd written and watch their reactions."

"When I realized that my kids' growing up was very different from my own but was related to this middle-class kind of child that I had seen when I had taught at the private girls' school," Konigsburg told *CA*, "I wanted to write something that reflected their kind of growing up, something that addressed the problems that come about even though you don't have to worry if you wear out your shoes whether your parents can buy you a new pair, something that tackles the basic problems of who am I? What makes me the same as everyone else? What makes me different?"

Konigsburg's original intention to write books that reflected the middle-class background of her own children led to her first two books. *Jennifer, Hecate, Macbeth, William McKinley, and Me, Elizabeth*, for example, was inspired by her daughter's efforts to make friends in Port Chester. It tells of two girls, one of whom regards herself as a witch, who choose to revel in their own personal oddness rather than conform to normal patterns of behavior. Her Newbery Award-winning novel *From the Mixed-up Files of Mrs. Basil E. Frankweiler* was directly influenced by her children's behavior on a family picnic. Konigsburg wrote in *Forty Percent More Than Everything You Want to Know about E. L. Konigsburg* that after listening to her children complain about ants, warm milk, and melted cupcake icing, "I thought to myself that if my children ever left home, they would never become barbarians even if they were captured by pirates. Civilization was not a veneer to them; it was a crust. They would want at least all the comforts of home plus a few dashes of extra elegance. Where, I wondered, would they ever consider running to if they ever left home? They certainly would never consider any place less elegant than the Metropolitan Museum of Art."

From the Mixed-up Files of Mrs. Basil E. Frankweiler tells the story of two children who do just that. Claudia, tired of being big sister to three siblings and bored with suburbia, decides to run away from home. She takes along Jamie, her thrifty brother, for financial assistance. Their temporary home is the New York Metropolitan Museum of Art, where they bathe in the fountain and sleep in a musty, sixteenth-century bed. While exploring the museum, they become intrigued by an angel reputed to have been sculpted by Michelangelo. Claudia is convinced that discovering the identity of the statue will help her determine her own. Their search leads them to Mrs. Frankweiler, the narrator and original owner of the statue, who helps Claudia come to an understanding about herself.

Konigsburg's first two books were published within a few months of each other. In the meantime, the Konigsburgs left Port Chester to return to Jacksonville. "In the midst of moving," wrote Nodelman, "Elaine Konigsburg learned of her astonishing coup." *From the Mixed-up Files of Mrs. Basil E. Frankweiler* had won the Newbery Medal, and *Jennifer, Hecate, Macbeth, William McKinley, and Me, Elizabeth* was a Newbery runner-up—the first time an author had ever had two books on the Newbery list in one year. "The Newbery list," Nodelman concluded, "has not included two books by the same author before or since."

In *(George)*, one of Konigsburg's later books, the protagonist's identity crisis is much more serious than that of the average child. Ben has had an alter ego, George, since he was a young boy. Until Ben's twelfth year, George had been known only to Ben and his immediate family. But when Ben, an exceptional student, is placed in a high school chemistry class, George begins to vocalize, thus disturbing the class. Consequently, Ben is sent to a psychiatrist who helps him merge the two personalities. George's presence has prompted some reviewers to label Ben as schizophrenic. Konigsburg told *CA*, however, that she thinks of George as Ben's "inner self."

Other books have followed, among them *T-Backs, T-Shirts, COAT, and Suit, The View from Saturday*, and *TalkTalk: A Children's Book Author Speaks to Grown-Ups*, a work of nonfiction published in 1995. In characteristic Konigsburg fashion, *T-Backs, T-Shirts, COAT, and Suit* depicts the lives of adolescents, this time through the eyes of twelve-year-old Chloe as she tries to make sense of the adult world around her. Spending the summer with her Aunt Bernadette in Florida, Chloe becomes involved in the growing controversy over whether or not food service vendors working the beach near her aunt's home should be allowed to wear revealing thong-backed bathing suits. The controversy soon mushrooms into a debate about individual freedom versus conformity to the religious standards of a minority. Gradually, the pre-teen comprehends her aunt's seemingly contradictory position: While Bernadette has refused to join her coworkers in donning the revealing beachwear, she has also refused to take a stand against others' right to wear it. Her reason is discovered to be that a recent mastectomy has made her personally uncomfortable about revealing her body. While noting that *T-Backs, T-Shirts* "belabors the politics and reexamines some 1960s issues" in her review for *Booklist*, Hazel Rochman maintained that "although [Bernadette's] shame may not be politically correct feminism, it does humanize the wise strong mentor, who turns out to be as vulnerable as she is nonconformist." "Some valuable lessons will be learned by the students reading this book," adds Rachel Axelrod in *Voice of Youth Advocates*.

The View from Saturday, published in 1996, once again put Konigsburg squarely in the winner's circle when it netted its author her second Newbery Medal.

In the novel, a group of precocious sixth-graders join together under the guidance of their coach, the wheelchair-bound Mrs. Olinski, to compete in a regional Academic Bowl competition. The four students surprise everyone by reaching the state finals and winning the Academic Bowl championship. No one is more surprised, and overjoyed, than Mrs. Olinski, who gradually comes to understand why she chose such an unlikely group of unusual young people. "Some of us have already read every book E. L. Konigsburg ever wrote. . . ," exclaimed Beth Gutcheon in her glowing review of *The View from Saturday* for the *New York Times Book Review*, "but others are going to begin with this book and will probably find it very hard to stop before going through the whole shelf."

TalkTalk: A Children's Book Author Speaks to Grown-ups is a collection of nine lectures and speeches in which Konigsburg expresses her thoughts on the importance of books in the lives of young readers. Framing the text of these speeches, which include her 1968 Newbery Award acceptance for *The Mixed-up Files* and her contributions to the Anne Carroll Moore Memorial Lectures in 1992, are Konigsburg's impressions of the changing climate of children's literature as it reflects a changing society. As Colleen Macklin wrote in *Voice of Youth Advocates, TalkTalk* is "a breath of fresh air, a reaffirmation of why [children's writers] do what they do, a celebration of the excellence of what children's literature can be."

Konigsburg is often praised for the depth, wit, and sophistication of her novels. Her protagonists exhibit an extraordinary capacity for growth, even when that growth cannot be achieved without pain. "I have serious reservations about the young adult genre," she once stated in a *Library Quarterly* article. "I think there's too much trash being published under that label, too much of the sort of thing I used to read in *True Confessions*—though, as I've said, I'm not against reading trash, but I do object to trash masquerading as literature. You might say I like my trash pure and simple. What bothers me most is that too many young adult novels are not extensions of a personal history or imagination but are 'novelizations' of television. They display sit-com humor, deal with the disease of the month or a current social disorder. I feel more at home in the category of 'children's books,' which is an older, more literary tradition."

"I can tell you," Konigsburg explained to *CA*, "that there is no greater compliment than having your work cherished by . . . someone who has read a lot and chooses your book out of a vast experience of reading. There is also no greater compliment than hearing from a young man in Pennsylvania, 'I never liked reading until I read you.' And . . . imagine the joy of being *chosen* by someone who otherwise reads only assignments. So I guess you could say that I love all my readers, for I do. I think they are wonderful, and I like it when they think that I am. Don't we all want to be wonderful to someone?"

BIOGRAPHICAL/CRITICAL SOURCES:

BOOKS

Children's Literature Review, Volume 1, Gale (Detroit), 1976.

de Montreville, Doris, and Donna Hill, editors, *Third Book of Junior Authors,* H. W. Wilson (Bronx, NY), 1972.

Dictionary of Literary Biography, Volume 52: *American Writers for Children since 1960: Fiction,* Gale, 1986, pp. 214-27.

Hanks, Dorrel Thomas, *E. L. Konigsburg,* Twayne (New York City), 1992.

Heins, Paul, editor, *Crosscurrents of Criticism: Horn Book Essays 1968-1977,* Horn Book (Boston), 1977.

Hoffman, Miriam, and Eva Samuels, *Authors and Illustrators of Children's Books: Writings on Their Lives and Works,* Bowker (New York City), 1972.

Hopkins, Lee Bennett, *More Books by More People,* Citation Press (New York City), 1974.

Kingman, Lee, editor, *Newbery and Caldecott Medal Books: 1966-1975,* Horn Book, 1975.

Konigsburg, E. L., *The Genesis of "A Proud Taste for Scarlet and Miniver"* (pamphlet), Atheneum (New York City), 1973.

Konigsburg, *Forty Percent More Than Everything You Want to Know about E. L. Konigsburg* (pamphlet), Atheneum, 1974.

Konigsburg, *How I Came to Love a Thief and Write "The Second Mrs. Giaconda"* (pamphlet), Atheneum, 1978.

Mainiero, Lina, *American Women Writers: A Critical Reference Guide from Colonial Times to the Present,* Volume 2, Ungar (New York City), 1980.

Roginski, Jim, compiler, *Newbery and Caldecott Medalists and Honor Book Winners,* Libraries Unlimited (Littleton, CO), 1982.

Townsend, John Rowe, *A Sounding of Storytellers: Essays on Contemporary Writers for Children,* Penguin Books (New York City), 1979.

Ward, Martha E., and Dorothy A. Marquardt, *Authors of Books for Young People,* second edition, Scarecrow (Metuchen, NJ), 1971.

PERIODICALS

Booklist, November 1, 1993, p. 515.

Chicago Tribune Book World, February 2, 1986.

Chicago Tribune Children's Book World, November 8, 1970.

Children's Literature Association Quarterly, spring, 1983, p. 6.

Christian Science Monitor, May 1, 1974, p. F1.

Horn Book, December, 1970, p. 619; August, 1971, p. 384; April, 1973, p. 179; June, 1976, pp. 253-61; February, 1978, p. 79; April, 1980; July/August, 1990, p. 468; January/February, 1992, p. 59; March/April, 1996, p. 229.

Language Arts, February, 1986; April, 1992, p. 299.

Learning Today, fall, 1981.

Library Journal, October 15, 1967; March 15, 1968; February 15, 1970; May 15, 1971, p. 1805.

Library Quarterly, Volume 51, number 1, 1981.

New York Times Book Review, November 5, 1967, p. 44; February 25, 1968, March 30, 1969, p. 30; November 8, 1970, May 30, 1971, p. 8; October 14, 1973, p. 8; November 4, 1973; October 5, 1975; November 7, 1976; December 9, 1979; May 30, 1982; May 25, 1986; November 10, 1996.

Publishers Weekly, February 26, 1968; July 6, 1992, p. 55; August 16, 1993, p. 105; May 8, 1995, p. 298.

Saturday Review, November 9, 1968, pp. 45-46; November 14, 1970.

School Library Journal, March, 1968; February, 1970; October, 1973, p. 117; November, 1986, p. 30; September, 1992, p. 206; October, 1993, p. 124; February, 1996, p. 42.

Times (London), June 16, 1983.

Times Literary Supplement, October 3, 1968; April 3, 1969; July 2, 1971; April 4, 1975; March 25, 1977; June 16, 1983.

Top of the News, April, 1968.

Voice of Youth Advocates, December, 1993, p. 294; December, 1995, p. 335.

Washington Post Book World, April 11, 1982; May 11, 1986.

KONWICKI, Tadeusz 1926-

PERSONAL: Born June 22, 1926, in Nowa Wilejka, Poland; son of Michal (a metal worker) and Jadwiga (Kiezun) Konwicki; married Danuta Lenica, April 25, 1949; children: Maria, Anna. *Education:* Attended University of Warsaw and Jagellonian University of Cracow, 1945-49.

ADDRESSES: Home—U1 Gorskiego, 1 m 68, 00-O33 Warsaw, Poland.

CAREER: Novelist, screenwriter, and film director. Director of films, including *Ostatni dzien lata,* 1960, *Zaduszki,* 1962, *Salto,* 1964, *Matura,* 1965, *Jak daleko stad, jak blisko,* 1972, *Dolina Issy,* 1982, and *Lawa,* 1989. *Wartime service:* Member of Polish underground during World War II.

MEMBER: Polish Writers' Union, Union of Polish Filmmakers.

AWARDS, HONORS: State Prize for Literature, 1950, for *Przy budowie,* and 1954, for *Wladza;* Venice Film Festival Grand Prix, 1958, for *Ostatni dzien lata;* special jury prize from Mannheim Film Festival, 1962, for *Zaduszki;* prize from San Remo Film Festival, 1972, for screenplay, *Jak daleko stad, jak blisko;* Mondello Prize for Literature, 1981.

WRITINGS:

NOVELS

Wladza (title means "The Power"), Czytelnik, 1954.
Godzina smutku (title means "The Hour of Sadness"), Czytelnik, 1954.
Rojsty (title means "The Marshes"), Czytelnik, 1956.
Z oblezonego miasta (title means "From the Besieged Town"), Iskry (Warsaw), 1956.
Dziura w niebie (title means "A Hole in the Sky"), Iskry, 1959.
Sennik wspolczesny, Iskry, 1963, translation by David Welsh published as *A Dreambook for Our Time,* MIT Press, 1969.
Wniebowstapienie (title means "Ascension") Iskry, 1967.
Nic albo Nic (title means "Nothing or Nothing"), Czytelnik, 1971.
Kronika wypadkow milosnych (title means "The Chronicle of Love Affairs"), Czytelnik, 1974.

Kalendarz i klepsydra (title means "A Calendar and an Hourglass"), Czytelnik, 1976.
Kompleks polski, Index on Censorship (London), 1977, translation by Richard Lourie published as *The Polish Complex,* Farrar, Straus (New York City), 1982.
Mala apokalipsa, Index on Censorship, 1979, translation by Lourie published as *A Minor Apocalypse,* Farrar, Straus, 1983.
Wschody i zachody kziezyca, Index on Censorship, 1982, translation by Lourie published as *Moonrise, Moonset,* Farrar, Straus, 1987.
Rzeka Podziemna, Podziemne Ptaki (title means "Underground River, Underground Birds"), Aneks, 1985.
Bohian, Czytelnik, 1987, translation by Lourie published as *Bohin Manor,* Farrar, Straus, 1990.
Czytadio, Niezalezna Oficyna, 1993.
Pamflet na siebie, Nowa, 1995.

SCREENPLAYS

Kariera (title means "The Career"), Film Polski, 1955.
Zimowy zmierzch (title means "Winter's Twilight"), 1956.
Ostatni dzien lata (title means "The Last Day of Summer"), Film Polski, 1958.
(With J. Kawalerowicz) *Matka Joanna od Aniolow* (title means "Mother Joan of the Angels"), Film Polski, 1961.
Zaduszki (title means "Halloween"), Film Polski, 1962.
(With J. Kawalerowicz) *Faraon* (title means "Pharaoh"), Film Polski, 1965.
Salto, Film Polski, 1965.
Matura (title means "Entrance Examination"), 1965.
Ostatni dzien lata (collected screenplays), Iskry, 1966, revised edition, 1973.
Jowita, Film Polski, 1967.
Jak daleko stad, jak blisko (title means "So Far, So Near"), Film Polski, 1972.
Dolina issy (title means "Issa Valley"), Film Polski, 1982.
Kronika wypadkow milosnych (title means "The Chronicle of Love Affairs"), 1986.
Lawa (title means "Lava"), Film Polski, 1989.

OTHER

Przy budowie (short stories; title means "At the Building Site"), Czytelnik, 1950.

Zwierzoczlekoupior (juvenile), illustrations by wife, Danuta Konwicki, Czytelnik, 1969, translation by George and Audrey Korwin-Rodziszewski published as *The Anthropos-Specter-Beast,* S. G. Phillips, 1977.

Dlaczego kot jest kotem (juvenile; title means "Why a Cat Is a Cat"), KAW (Warsaw), 1976.

Nowy swiat iokolice (memoirs), Czytelnik, 1986, translation by Walter Arndt published as *New World Avenue and Vicinity,* Farrar, Straus, 1991.

SIDELIGHTS: Tadeusz Konwicki is one of Poland's leading novelists. He is, Jackson Diehl notes in the *Washington Post,* "a major Polish artist whose comic, despairing portraits of the country have quickly been accepted as classics both at home and in the West."

It was not until the 1956 post-Stalinist political and cultural "thaw" in Poland that Konwicki and his contemporaries were able to have their major works published. Prior to that time, Konwicki published minor works, including a collection of short stories and a novel, both of which won his country's State Prize for Literature and are, in the opinion of Jerzy Krzyzanowski of *Books Abroad,* "cliches of socialist-realist fiction . . . modeled on Soviet novels" that demonstrate the results of severe state-imposed censorship.

The publication of *Rojsty* in 1956 is considered a turning point in Konwicki's literary career. The author had waited eight years to publish his somber and satirical account of a young man's desperate attempts to become a hero. *Rojsty* is based on Konwicki's own bitter experiences as a guerrilla fighter with the Home Army of the Polish underground, when the guerrillas successfully liberated the city of Wilno from Nazi occupation and were punished with arrest, deportation, and imprisonment by the advancing Soviet troops. Konwicki managed to escape the concentration camp roundup and join another group in fighting the Soviet invaders. The unit disbanded when the men realized that the situation was indeed hopeless. As Krzyzanowski observes, "The psychological wounds inflicted by those tragic events were to remain in his memory during the years to come, affecting, and to a great extent shaping, his artistic vision."

Sennik wspolczesny, translated as *A Dreambook for Our Time,* was Konwicki's first novel to appear in English translation and has been compared to the works of Albert Camus and Joseph Conrad. Writing in *World Literature Today,* Ruel K. Wilson theorizes that the novel's great overnight success was due to its "brutal frankness of subject matter and imagery." With this book Konwicki began a painful exploration into a world of tormented survivors where, in the words of Wilson, "the past holds them all prisoner, for their attitudes toward the present have been conditioned by their experiences before and during the German occupation."

Dreambook's protagonist, Oldster, is a former partisan consumed with guilt and seeking retribution for his wartime actions. As the novel opens, he "awakens after a suicide attempt, surrounded by inquisitive faces in the remote village to which he has drifted," relates Neal Ascherson in the *New York Review of Books.* "We understand," Ascherson continues, "that he is solitary, crushed and bewildered by memories of the war and the postwar years to which, although some fifteen years in the past, he can still give no meaning. But the other inhabitants are in the same pass. Nothing is happening in this somnolent place, malarial with sinister memories of violence and mystery." Oldster has returned to this valley and forest, the scene of his crime, to find forgiveness.

During the war he had been assigned to kill a fellow countryman who had betrayed partisans to the Germans. Carrying out the order, Oldster had fired his shot with his victim's young daughter as witness. But not having shot to kill, Oldster is convinced that the man has survived and is living in the valley. He also suspects that the partisan chief, who gave the execution order, is still hiding in the nearby forest. "Whether this is delusion, obsession, mania, is never made clear," states critic Abraham Rothberg in the *New York Times Book Review.*

After experiencing much torment and loneliness, Oldster meets a man who can give him some perspective. "During the war too, I kept to the political average," the man tells him. "Most of the nation neither fought at the front, nor hid in the forests, nor suffered in concentration camps. The ordinary majority stayed in their badly heated houses, ate frozen potatoes and dealt a little in the black market. I did the same. Nobody gave me a medal for what I did during the occupation, but nobody reproved me either. I didn't gain anything, but I didn't lose anything." Oldster finally realizes, Rothberg observes, "that the present, however unheroic and boring, must be lived in and endured. After giving up the nightmare of the past, both its horror and heroism, half-willing, half-pushed, half-knowing, half-duped, he is constrained to leave the valley, saying in the very last lines of the book: '. . . I would scramble with the remains of my strength out of these seething depths to the edge of reality, and would get up to an ordinary, commonplace day, with its usual troubles, its everyday toil, its so well-known familiar drudgery.'"

In *Dreambook,* Konwicki achieves a surrealistic quality with what Mark Schechner in the *Nation* calls "a blurring of perception." Schechner explains: "This is indeed a dreambook for not only does the past inhabit the present with inescapable recollections but present events themselves dissolve in a dreamlike haze of uncertainty. Here . . . the terrors of war lead to emotional anesthesia. . . . As in a play by Beckett, the simplest acts are performed with maddening difficulty, and the most routine thoughts and recollections are achieved only through a tedious grasping with the will to forget."

Wilson finds *Dreambook*'s vision of humanity "gloomy and nihilistic." He elaborates: "Konwicki's grim caricatures perturb and sometimes amuse the reader, although they evoke little sympathy. . . . the novel's message is highly symbolic. The dream atmosphere, visual, pungent, yet impressionistic, inclines us to accept the work for what it is: a montage of apocalyptic events seen and relived by an obsessive and guilty imagination." V. D. Mihailovich in *Saturday Review* draws a comparison between Konwicki's writing style and film technique: "The author, who is also a movie director, mixes dramatic episodes, flashbacks, nightmarish reveries, and inner monologues with abandon." He praises Konwicki's "wide use of metaphors, symbols, and irony," which he feels "enlivens the style." Mihailovich further states: "Though the characters are full-blooded eccentrics, their antics are in harmony with their inner mechanisms. A certain dreamlike quality, a gossamer of things long past yet somehow still clinging to life, pervades Konwicki's facile and poetic narration. As a result the reader is rewarded with illustrations of the consequences of indelible war experiences and with beautiful prose as well."

Delving further into the nightmarish world of the guilty survivor, Konwicki produced a subsequent novel, *Wniebowstapienie.* Here "the horrors of war memories give way to the torments of life in the corrupted post-war society," Krzyzanowski notes. *Wniebowstapienie*'s characters are ghost-like, creatures for whom the city of Warsaw serves as a purgatory. "Building the plot around a bank robbery,

Konwicki leads his characters through the streets, restaurants, parks and jails but most frequently gathers them together in the empty marble halls of the Palast [Warsaw's Palace of Culture], its basements and power stations, juxtaposing their enormous size and deserted spaces with the ugliness and pettiness of everyday life in contemporary Poland. Such an ironic twist," Krzyzanowski writes, "adds a grotesque flavor to that somber and masterfully written novel, in which realistic presentation of characters and scenery achieves another dimension of supernatural and symbolic vision." Because of its pessimistic depiction of Polish society, *Wniebowstapienie* was banned in that country. David Welsh recalled: "Gomulka, then First Secretary to the Party, is believed personally to have ordered the withdrawal of all 30,000 copies some months later, and a wall of silence descended on Konwicki, although he since has been allowed to publish a couple of innocuous novels. His 'editor' is said to have been degraded to 'editing' labels for bottles of mineral water, no doubt with a cut in her wages."

Like many of his earlier writings, Konwicki's unconventional tale *Zwierzoczlekoupior,* translated as *The Anthropos-Specter-Beast,* is woven with elements of the dreamworld. In a review of the original Polish edition Welsh calls it "even more comic and weird than [Konwicki's] previous work." He continues: "Ostensibly written for children . . . it is not meant for 'good children,' as they will not benefit from it (says Konwicki). The book exists on at least three levels: the narrative itself which can be related to *Winnie-the-Pooh* and *Alice in Wonderland;* the 'real world,' bearing in mind always that reality is something peculiarly ambiguous in Konwicki's fiction; and the narrator's dream. Konwicki's handling of these three levels is masterly."

Nic ablo Nic is considered by some critics to be Konwicki's most ambitious novel. According to Krzyzanowski, it "explores all the passions, obsessions, fears and complexes he has inherited from the violent past and which he sees in the present." Konwicki came from that portion of Poland which was lost to the Soviet Union during World War II, and his feelings of sorrow and estrangement from the loss of his homeland are intensely expressed in *Nic ablo Nic.* Although Konwicki made a "sentimental journey" to the land of his childhood in one of his minor novels, notes Krzyzanowski, only in the author's major works "does he transform it into an everpresent image of major importance."

When the Polish motion picture industry became somewhat liberated from rigid ideological standards in the late 1950's, Konwicki discovered a new mode of expression. His subsequent films, with themes of self-destructive guilt and deep sexual frustration, are closely related to his novels. One such film is *Ostatni dzien lata,* a melancholy story of two young lovers who meet on the beach. Krzyzanowski describes the film's poignant imagery: "In the fast-moving shadows of jet fighters screaming overhead like modern symbols of doom and destruction the lovers are able to enjoy just a brief moment of happiness, since neither their past experiences nor the uncertain future can provide them with any lasting relationship." The film ends as the young woman awakens to find only her lover's quickly disappearing footprints in the blowing sand. Krzyzanowski observes that "the image of water as a primordial source and a final grave for all things also appears in Konwicki's subsequent works." He also mentions that "the motifs of impending doom, the impossibility of sharing one's own past, and the futility of seeking lasting happiness—enhanced with images and visual symbols" found in the film, are forebears of the themes of *A Dreambook of Our Time.* Konwicki's next film, *Salto,* is considered "a visual postscript" to *Dreambook.*

Konwicki's novel *Kompleks polski,* translated as *The Polish Complex,* was first published by a semi-clandestine Polish publishing house founded by a small group of dissidents who were working against the communist regime. It was the first of his novels to appear from a non-government publisher in Poland and the first major Polish novel to be printed by an opposition press. Konwicki's action inspired a host of other major Polish writers to join dissident publishers, creating a subculture of hundreds of published books with tens of thousands of copies in print.

Translated and published in the United States in 1982, *The Polish Complex* ironically contrasts the Poland of 1863, a period of national rebellion against Czarist rule, with the pre-Solidarity Poland of the late 1970s, a period of hypocritical complacency. Speaking of the novel in the *New York Review of Books,* Jaroslaw Anders finds it "a powerful and engaging book, demonstrating how in the less fortunate parts of the world history becomes a private obsession, and how the collective subconscious can determine the fates of both individuals and nations." Eva Hoffman, writing in the *New York Times Book Review,* calls *The Polish Complex* "a powerful tract—an impassioned, furious polemic on Poland's impossible condition." Konwicki, Hoffman claims, "writes like a man who has nothing to lose—and who wants to use that freedom for the primary and urgent task of speaking the raw, unmediated truth."

Mala apokalipsa, which was translated as *A Minor Apocalypse,* is "a visceral jeer, a surreal yell at conditions in Warsaw," according to Andrew Sinclair in the London *Times.* A darkly humorous novel, it tells the story of a writer much like Konwicki who, as an act of defiance, is instructed by the dissident underground to set himself afire during a communist party congress. The immolation will be his "final story" or "absolute novella." Told within the space of a single day and following the narrator as he prepares for his symbolic death, the novel presents a view of an entire nation and its people caught in a mad system. "The grim, sardonically mocking humor that Konwicki employs," writes Douglas Hill in the Toronto *Globe and Mail,* "turns the whole misadventure into a savage joke. Scenes seem surreal. Warsaw is literally collapsing: a bridge gives way, a plane crashes, tomorrow's queues began yesterday. Public life is a drunken brawl; personal relations take place furtively, accidentally, amid the rubble and the clamor." Maciej Karpinski in the *New York Times Book Review* states: "*A Minor Apocalypse* offers readers a vision of slavery under a totalitarian system of government. . . . [Konwicki] has given us a grotesque parable that probes to the core of the absurd."

Despite its portrait of a communist society, several reviewers note that the novel also tells a highly personal story. "Polish literature," writes Gerard T. Kapolka in the *Polish Review,* "has rarely, if ever, produced so introspective a novel. . . . We are taken so deeply into the mind of the protagonist here that we begin to feel all of his annoyances and begin to believe in the impossibility of continuing to live in such a ludicrous manner." Michael Szporer in *Modern Fiction Studies* explains that "Konwicki portrays himself as an ideological burnout, weary of symbolism. And I would say that it is precisely this weariness, this fuzziness, this seemingly random and impulsive minoritarianism that makes him the most farsighted, the most thoroughly political writer in 'the other Europe.'" *A Minor Apocalypse* "lifted Mr. Konwicki to the stature of a prophet" in Poland, Ewa Kuryluk reports in the *New York Times Book Review.* Sinclair believes that the novel is "a minor masterpiece of rage and despair from Eastern Europe."

In *Wschody i zachody kziezyca,* translated as *Moonrise, Moonset,* Konwicki again mixes the personal with the public by combining fiction with memoir in a work that straddles the boundaries between the novel and the diary. Ascherson finds that *Moonrise, Moonset* "is a darting, constantly changing mixture of different elements: autobiography, criticism, self-criticism, fiction, gossip, both benevolent and malevolent, history, anecdote, and fierce moral polemic. It may appear shapeless but it is not."

The diary portion of the novel begins with the official recognition of Solidarity in the fall of 1980 and ends with the declaration of martial law in December of 1981. Within this time frame are interwoven remembrances of Konwicki's childhood, his years as a member of the anti-Nazi underground and as a member of the Home Army, the Polish anti-communist resistance movement, and his life in postwar communist Poland. Konwicki speaks of his one-time membership in the Polish communist party as a shameful period: "My friends dragged me into it, as if it were a beer house or a brothel." Walter Goodman in the *New York Times* notes that he is also "hard on the signers of the Yalta agreement and on 'the wonderful poetically inclined left in the West' which he condemns for writing off the Home Army as fascist and giving 'progressive terrorism a kiss on the lips' but never protesting the despotism that settled over the countries of Central Europe."

As in his previous novels, Konwicki ultimately speaks of the personal rather than the public life. Kuryluk believes the title of the novel, *Moonrise, Moonset,* "seems to evoke the tides as well as the cycles of a man's moody soul swinging back and forth between depression and exhilaration, boredom and irritation." According to Ascherson, "What is really taking place [in *Moonrise, Moonset*] is a complex but carefully planned process of self-exposure." Goodman argues that what holds the novel together is "the passion of a writer whose hopes seem to have died 40 years ago and who has had to live and work in a society that he despises. . . . Like him or not, it's hard to remain unshaken by the strength of his writing . . . or the depth of his pain over the horrors of his country's history."

In contrast to much of Konwicki's works, *Bohian,* translated as *Bohin Manor,* can be seen almost as a return to established literary conventions. A romance set on a Lithuanian manor farm in 1875, Konwicki's novel "presents the quintessential late-nineteenth-century dilemma of home versus the world," according to Julian Graffy in the *Times Literary Supplement.* His protagonist, thirty-year-old Helena Konwicka, begins to realize that her youth is passing from her. Resolving to marry the aging Count Broel-Plater to relieve her isolation and regain the standard of life to which she was accustomed prior to the Polish uprising against Tsarist Russia that had cost her family its wealth, Helena meets Elias Szyra. A Jew and a member of the lower class, Szyra insinuates himself into Helena's life, claiming that he wants to be taught to read; gradually he and Helena enter a romantic relationship that neither wants. Characteristic of its author, the novel ends in tragic, albeit mildly optimistic, circumstances.

Bohin Manor, however, is more than fiction; it is the story of Konwicki's grandmother, and throughout the course of most of the novel readers look for clues as to which of the two suitors will be the father of Konwicki's father. The novel "surprises" its readers, notes Stanislaw Beres in an article translated in *Review of Contemporary Fiction,* by eliminating the distinctions between authenticity and artifice. "Only minor signs . . . assure us that Konwicki is still at play; the authorial self-reflective handling of the romance element, the manipulation of tensions, and finally the appeal to anti- and pro-Semitic feelings and complexes still alive in Poland, . . . assure us that Konwicki is bent, more than formerly, on involving the reader in a fiction; he has made it his goal precisely to create a nearly complete illusion of reality, to deceive us into believing that his book is not repeating a convention but presenting genuine reality." Indeed, Konwicki fuses reality and illusion, truth and fiction, "past and future" throughout his novel, according to Sally Laird. Peppering his novel with characters linked to actual historic figures (Adolf Hitler, Vladimir Lenin, Josef Stalin), the author extends this fusion "not of this imagination only," Laird explains in the London *Observer,* "but of Lithuania itself, its landscape and atmosphere, its deep enclosure in endless woods, . . . in air so heavy that the past gets trapped and the future is infinitely long in gestation."

Konwicki has revisited his more immediate history in a collection of over fifty self-illustrated essays collectively titled *Nowy swiat iokolice* in its original publication and translated as *New World Avenue and Vicinity* in 1990. Alternating between childhood memories of growing up in prewar Wilno (the Eastern European setting of *Bohin Manor*) and his life in present-day Warsaw, the author's memoirs are perhaps the most accessible of his works, "reveal[ing] a complex mind chary of easy answers," contends Brooke Horvath in *Review of Contemporary Fiction,* "a mind that may find reality 'cobweb-thin' with nothing beyond but 'vacancy, the void'. . . . But it is a mind well worth attending to."

Speaking of his life in an article for the *Contemporary Authors Autobiography Series,* Konwicki explains: "I often look back at myself. Each time I do, shivers run down my spine. I have made many mistakes and could have made many more. I have written quite a few dead pages. I don't have a clean, bright biography. There were tumbles into the gutter and arduous efforts to get out of there. . . . But the strangest thing is that if I could live it all over again, I would choose the same way. . . . I have lived as the times wished—or rather a particle of the times, a small whirlpool which sprang out of nowhere and will end in nothingness. Why should I be wiser than my times, I from whom you have taken away belief in human genius?"

BIOGRAPHICAL/CRITICAL SOURCES:

BOOKS

Contemporary Authors Autobiography Series, Volume 9, Gale (Detroit, MI), 1989.
Contemporary Literary Criticism, Gale, Volume 8, 1978, Volume 28, 1984, Volume 54, 1989.

PERIODICALS

Best Sellers, September, 1983.
Books Abroad, winter, 1971; summer, 1974.
Christian Science Monitor, October 13, 1983.
Economist, July 18, 1992, p. 92.
Globe and Mail (Toronto), July 21, 1984.
London Review of Books, July 23, 1992, pp. 19-21.
Los Angeles Times Book Review, January 17, 1982; August 28, 1983; November 15, 1987; August 12, 1990.
Modern Fiction Studies, spring, 1986.
Nation, June 19, 1976.
New Republic, April 10, 1976; November 21, 1983.
Newsweek, August 8, 1983.
New Yorker, February 21, 1983; January 2, 1984.
New York Review of Books, May 27, 1976; March 4, 1982; October 13, 1983; December 17, 1987.
New York Times, August 13, 1987; July 15, 1990.
New York Times Book Review, May 17, 1970; January 10, 1982; October 23, 1983; August 30, 1987.
Observer (London), September 6, 1992, p. 50.

Polish Review, Volume 29, number 3, 1984.
Review of Contemporary Fiction, summer, 1992, p. 201; fall, 1994, pp. 189-96.
Saturday Review, June 20, 1970.
Sewanee Review, April, 1992, pp. 300-11.
Times (London), November 24, 1983; May 19, 1988.
Times Literary Supplement, October 1, 1982; November 25, 1983; July 22, 1988; July 17, 1992, p. 21.
Tribune Books (Chicago), July 29, 1990.
Village Voice, September 15, 1987.
Washington Post, September 5, 1986.
Washington Post Book World, January 17, 1982; November 18, 1990.
World Literature Today, summer, 1977; spring, 1980; autumn, 1991, p. 734.

*   *   *

KURYS, Diane 1948-

PERSONAL: Born in 1948; daughter of Daniel (a clothing store owner) and Lena Kurys. *Education:* Educated in France.

ADDRESSES: Office—c/o French Film Office, 745 Fifth Ave., New York, NY 10151.

CAREER: Screenwriter and director of motion pictures. Actress in stage productions, including *The Miser,* and motion pictures, including *Fellini's Casanova,* 1976. Co-producer of films, including *Coup de Sirocco* and *Le Grand Pardon.*

AWARDS, HONORS: Prix Louis Delluc, 1977, for *Diabolo menthe;* nomination for Academy Award for best foreign-language film from Academy of Motion Picture Arts and Sciences, 1983, for *Entre Nous.*

WRITINGS:

SCREENPLAYS (AND DIRECTOR)

Diabolo menthe, Gaumont, 1978, released in the United States as *Peppermint Soda,* New Yorker Films, 1979.
Cocktail Molotov, Alexandre Films/Antenne 2, 1980, released in the United States by Alexandre Films, 1981.

Coup de foudre (title means "Thunderclap"), Ariel Zietoun, 1983, released in the United States as *Entre Nous* (title means "*Between Us*"), United Artists Classics, 1983.

(With Oliver Schatzky) *A Man in Love* (also known as *Un Homme amoureux*), Cinecom Pictures, 1987.

C'est la vie, Samuel Goldwyn Company, 1990.

Pour Sacha, Alexandre Films, 1992.

Apres l'amour, released in the United States as *Love after Love,* Alexandre Films, 1994.

SIDELIGHTS: Diane Kurys is an acclaimed screenwriter-director whose films derive from her personal experiences. She was born in 1948 and was only six years old when her parents—Russian immigrants in France—separated, a break she chronicled in the 1983 film *Coup de foudre,* which was released in the United States as *Entre Nous.* She spent several years in the French public schools, where she experienced some of the same events she recounted in 1978's *Diabolo menthe,* released in the United States as *Peppermint Soda.*

In *Peppermint Soda* Kurys details one year in the life of Anne Weber, a thirteen-year-old schoolgirl whose world consists of fierce friendships, flirtations, and forbidden pantyhose. Kurys's alter ego, Anne lives in relative comfort with her divorced mother and a slightly older sister. She undergoes the usual traumas and trials of female adolescence, including her first romance and her first menstruation, and experiences her first acquaintance with the radical politics that were so instrumental in shaping Kurys's own life. "'Peppermint Soda' was conceived when I began thinking that there are . . . very few films about girls in high school and how they're raised," Kurys told the *New York Times* in 1979. "I decided to make this film out of my own memories."

Peppermint Soda was a substantial critical success upon its release in 1978. In France it received the coveted Prix Louis Delluc, and in the United States, where it was released in 1979, it earned recognition as an unexpectedly impressive filmmaking debut. Kurys's approach to her subject was sincere but nonjudgmental, with events ranging from the personal to the public and political all rendered in an equally low-key manner. It was Kurys's unassuming style that most enchanted American critics such as Richard Christiansen and Judith Martin. Christiansen, writing in the *Chicago Tribune,* praised Kurys's "taste and delicacy" and declared that *Peppermint Soda* was "shot, selected, and arranged with

the loving care lavished on a treasured family album." Similarly, Martin wrote in the *Washington Post* that the life of Anne Weber—specifically, one year: from fall 1963 to fall 1964—was "sensitively depicted." For Kurys, the success and acclaim was rather intimidating. "When I made 'Peppermint Soda,' I didn't know anything," she revealed to the *New York Times* in its 1979 profile. "Now I know a little—so I'm scared."

Despite reservations about her grasp of filmmaking, Kurys quickly followed *Peppermint Soda* with *Cocktail Molotov,* which recounts the life of a seventeen-year-old—also named Anne—during the hectic period of student unrest in 1968 Paris. Anne is a malcontent anxious to flee her dull, repressive home life, one which seems to epitomize middle-class values, and find a more meaningful, fulfilling existence. She eventually travels to Venice with intentions of departing for Israel and life on a kibbutz there. Once in Venice, however, Anne and her companions—her boyfriend and his affable, goofy best friend—learn of the disturbances in Paris. The three innocents, suddenly dedicated to radical politics, then hitchhike back to Paris hoping to participate in the melee.

Although *Cocktail Molotov* offers a perspective on French political activism in the late 1960s, it consistently balances the political with the personal and, like *Peppermint Soda,* rarely strays from focusing on its heroine. The *New York Times*'s Vincent Canby found Kurys's style "engaging" and called *Cocktail Molotov* an "appealing" work. He contended, though, that her carefree handling of the film's more comedic aspects sometimes undermined her critical depiction of bourgeois life. "The film," charged Canby, "is a nearly perfect example of the kind of French film that apotheosizes middle-class values while pretending to question them." Nonetheless, Canby praised Kurys's filmmaking and commended her more personalized perspective on the events of 1968 in Paris.

In 1983 Kurys completed her third film, *Entre Nous,* about her mother's friendship with another woman and how that bond ended her parents' marriage. As the film begins, Kurys's mother—here named Lena—awaits deportation to a German camp for Jews during World War II. A French camp worker becomes interested in Lena and proposes marriage, noting that such a union would exempt her from deportation. Lena accepts his offer, whereupon the couple embark from the camp and trek across mountainous terrain in winter. Meanwhile the other woman, Madeleine, is first seen married to a teacher, but that marriage ends abruptly when he is gunned down during a partisan attack. The narrative then skips forward several years and refocuses on Lena and her husband, now a successful garage mechanic, living with their two daughters in a Lyon flat. At an afternoon school presentation, Lena meets Madeleine, who is now remarried to an aspiring actor.

The two women quickly become friends, and as that friendship grows, Lena's husband, Michel, becomes increasingly resentful. Soon Lena's bond with Madeleine supersedes her marital relationship, much to the chagrin of Michel. And as Lena grows closer to the artistic—though weak-willed—Madeleine, she also becomes more self-confident and independent. Michel, well-meaning but ultimately patronizing and even inconsiderate, tries to tolerate his wife's bond with Madeleine, but his efforts only exacerbate his anxiety. Tensions finally explode when he finds the two women together at a boutique he has financed for Lena, who is the proprietor. Having earlier forbidden his wife to see the emotionally unstable Madeleine, Michel is incensed to find her there, and he responds by destroying the boutique. His destructive tantrum prompts a daring, but inevitable, decision from Lena, who takes her two daughters and leaves for Paris. The film ends with the tearful Michel realizing that he has lost his family, and as he weeps a note appears on-screen revealing the biographical nature of the film.

With *Entre Nous* Kurys achieved her greatest artistic triumph to date. The film proved popular both in Europe, where it won particular acclaim from French critics, and in the United States, where it was eventually nominated for an Academy Award for best foreign language film. American critics generally agreed that *Entre Nous* was a subtle, incisive exploration of the women's friendship and its effect on their marriages. Among the film's many supporters was Sheila Benson, who wrote in the *Los Angeles Times* that *Entre Nous* was an "astonishing" work. Benson was perhaps most impressed with Kurys's skill in fashioning fully realized characters, and she commended the screenwriter for creating "no absolute villains." Furthermore, Benson noted that *Entre Nous,* as the product of a relatively young filmmaker, was "an extraordinary signpost of what we may look forward to."

Similarly, the *New York Times*'s Canby declared that Kurys, on the merits of *Entre Nous,* had to be ranked in "the forefront of the commercial French cinema."

Like Benson, Canby acknowledged Kurys's impartial perspective and her ability to portray both women and men with equal candor. "Like all serious works of narrative film, [*Entre Nous*] examines people in particular situations and makes some speculation about what it finds," Canby wrote. "After that, it's for each of us to interpret according to his own circumstances." For Canby, *Entre Nous* was a "very personal, moving . . . film."

After completing *Entre Nous* Kurys coauthored and directed *A Man in Love,* her first film in English. It concerns the love affair of an actor and actress on the set of a movie in which they are also cast as lovers. The actor is Steve Elliott, a cold, disdainful American who shows little regard for those beneath him in the film profession. Although married—to a woman grown bitter by her husband's haphazard marital commitment—Steve falls in love with Jane Steiner, a French actress known for her stage work. The lovers meet after Steve arrogantly refuses an interview with Jane's father, an alcoholic journalist. Jane consequently berates Steve, who thus becomes intrigued with his upstart co-star. Much of *A Man in Love* details the folly of the affair as Steve, playing suicidal Italian writer Cesar Pavese in the film-within-the-film, manipulates his relationship with Jane to fit his needs as a creative actor. Jane, meanwhile, is also undergoing traumatic times with her mother, who may be dying. By film's end, the narrative emphasis has shifted from Steve to Jane. Neither of her key relationships—with Steve and with her mother—ends happily for Jane. When filming is done Steve returns to his wife, and Jane's mother dies. Jane then sits before her typewriter and begins writing the story that becomes, presumably, that of *A Man in Love.*

Among American critics, *A Man in Love* was considered inferior to Kurys's previous films. It earned particular ire from the *New York Times,* where Janet Maslin called it "an unaccountably bad film" and complained that it was both unconvincing and uncompelling. Less harsh was the *Los Angeles Times*'s Michael Wilmington, who found *A Man in Love* flawed but admirable. He conceded that the dialogue was rather stilted and that the film's romance was "not as dangerous or pathetic as it should be." But Wilmington also contended that Kurys's work contained "passion. . . and courage and intelligence," and he applauded the actors' performances. "If [*A Man in Love*] misses," he concluded, "it's an honorable miss, one made with humanity and love."

In 1990 Kurys released *C'est la vie,* which is something of a sequel to *Entre Nous.* Set in 1958, the film is the story of a summer vacation taken by Lena and her two daughters. During their time at the beach, Lena has a brief affair; later, her husband reappears, discovers the affair, becomes furious again, and then tries to reconcile one more time. Lena declines. Much of the film's substance comes from the small, daily adventures of the two girls and their cousins. "All the children go through a familiar range of adventures and caprices, from stupid pranks to a first kiss, from surprising perceptions to nerve-wearing silliness," commented a *New Republic* reviewer. Noting that nothing about the story was particularly original, the writer went on to say that the film makes viewers care "about the people, not about novelty of plot. . . . Kurys has become a cinematic connoisseur of family transitions, an ambience of troubled sexuality in adults juxtaposed with the opening of sexual realms in children. . . . Her directing in general has become wonderfully secure—swift in movement, acute in rhythm, precise in points of view."

Apres l'amour (titled *Love after Love* in its American release), Kurys's 1994 film, was celebrated as "wise and graceful," by *Los Angeles Times* critic Kevin Thomas. It is the story of a popular French novelist named Lola, her long-standing relationship with David, a successful architect, and the desultory affairs in which each indulges. Lola is struggling with writer's block and searching for a renewed sense of meaning. "Through Lola's quietly intensifying search for renewal, Kurys evokes an acute sense of contemporary urban life as it is lived in most major cities of the world. Lola and David may be more sophisticated in regard to the vicissitudes of amour than most couples, yet Kurys suggests that traditional French worldliness in affairs of the heart may be wearing a tad thin in the competitive, economically depressed '90s," wrote Thomas.

Hal Hinson, a writer for the *Washington Post,* was less charmed by the film's open-minded approach to love and commitment. In his opinion, if portrayed by another filmmaker, the situations in *Love after Love* would "give rise to a torrent of passion and guilt, but Kurys's people are portrayed as being too worldly and sophisticated for either. . . Her previous movies . . . seemed completely without a moral dimension. . . . In Kurys's world, affairs aren't bad because they're hurtful or dishonest, but because they create such sticky scheduling problems." But Kurys's lack of moralizing was praised by another reviewer, Michael Wilmington, who wrote in the *Chicago Tribune:* "Her characters breathe. Her sense of place seems unerring. Her situations believably recreate life in all its messiness and mischance." Thomas concluded: 'Love after Love' has the easy flow and intimacy typical of Kurys, who has always seemed the most natural and spontaneous of filmmakers. Indeed, this lovely and thoughtful film proceeds with so much effortlessness that you may be in danger of overlooking its considerable substance."

BIOGRAPHICAL/CRITICAL SOURCES:

PERIODICALS

Chicago Tribune, September 11, 1979; November 16, 1990, p. D7; October 14, 1994, p. M7.
Film Comment, July-August, 1983; October, 1987.
Library Journal, August, 1994, p. 152.
Los Angeles Times, February 16, 1984; July 18, 1987; August 14, 1987; July 8, 1994, p. F14.
New Republic, December 3, 1990, pp. 26-27.
New York Times, August 5, 1979; April 26, 1981; October 8, 1983; January 25, 1984; January 29, 1984; July 31, 1987; October 14, 1994, p. C10.
People, October 29, 1984.
Washington Post, September 21, 1979; September 12, 1987; November 16, 1990, p. D7; November 11, 1994, p. D6.

*   *   *

KUTTY, Madhavi
See DAS, Kamala

L

LACY, Donald Charles 1933-

PERSONAL: Born January 4, 1933, in Henry County, IN; son of Charles William (a clergyperson and plasterer) and Marian Marcille (Walradth) Lacy; married Dorothy Marie Thomas, November 6, 1959; children: Anne Marie, Donna Jean, Sharon Elizabeth, Martha Elaine. *Education:* Ball State University, B.S., 1954, M.A., 1958; Christian Theological Seminary, Indianapolis, IN, M.Div., 1961, D.Min., 1976.

ADDRESSES: Home—1078 Walkerton Trail, Walkerton, IN 46574. *Office*—1000 Georgia St., Walkerton, IN 46574.

CAREER: Teacher of social studies and English at the secondary level in the public schools of Jay County, IN; ordained United Methodist clergyperson, 1960 and 1962; pastor in North Indiana Conference, 1958-68, 1985—, pastor in South Indiana Conference, 1968-85; served major churches across Indiana, including First United Methodist Church in Hagerstown, IN, 1966-70, Union Chapel United Methodist Church in Indianapolis, 1970-73, First United Methodist Church in Seymour, IN, 1974-79, and Walkerton United Methodist Church, 1993—. Cochair of the Commission in South Indiana Conference, 1977-80; chair of the Department of Ecumenical Concerns of the Indiana Council of Churches, 1983-87; chair of Jewish-Christian Dialogue for the United Methodist Church at Hebrew Congregation in Indianapolis, 1984; chair of the commission of the North Indiana Conference, 1991-94; coordinator of Methodist/Lutheran Dialogue, 1991-95. *Military service:* U.S. Navy, 1955-56.

MEMBER: International Platform Association, International Order of Saint Luke the Physician, Marian Order of Priests (associate member), Scottish Rite of Indianapolis, York Rite of Muncie, Indiana, York Rite College of Fort Wayne, Society of Mary, National Association of Evangelicals, Emmaus Community, Ecumenical Society of the Blessed Virgin Mary, Jackson County (Indiana) Association of Clergy (president), Phi Delta Kappa, Pi Gamma Mu.

WRITINGS:

(Contributor) Cynthia Pearl Maus and Ronald E. Osborn, editors, *The Church and the Fine Arts,* Harper (New York City), 1960.

Gems from James, Dorrance (Bryn Mawr, PA), 1974, second edition, Adams Press (Minneapolis, MN), 1982.

Called to Be, C.S.S. Publishing (Lima, OH), 1978, second edition, 1980.

Mary and Jesus, C.S.S. Publishing, 1979, second edition, 1993.

Founding Fathers Religious Quiz, C.S.S. Publishing, 1982.

(Contributor) *Sound of a Sermon Division,* Parish Publications (Madison Heights, MI), 1982.

Methodist Mass, C.S.S. Publishing, 1983.

John Seventeen, C.S.S. Publishing, 1983.

Decalogue for Ecumenical Discipleship, C.S.S. Publishing, 1985.

Healing Echoes, C.S.S. Publishing, 1986.

Devotion to Mary Should Go Beyond Denominations, Our Sunday Visitor (Huntington, IN), 1987.

Daily Food for the Journey: Pastor's Morning Worship, Evangel Press (Nappanee, IN), 1988.

Synopsis, Logos, 1988-94.

Nourishment for the Day: Morning Worship for Laity, Evangel Press, 1989.
Come, Holy Spirit, Evangel Press, 1989.
Lakeside Devotions, Evangel Press, 1990.
Reactivating Acts, Brentwood Christian Press, 1991.
Jewels from John, C.S.S. Publishing, 1992.
A Plea for Christian Unity, Evangel Press, 1992.
A Mother and Her Infant Son, C.S.S. Publishing, 1994.
A Letter to a Roman Catholic, Evangel Press, 1996.

Author of "Lacy's Logic," a column in Rushville Republican, 1980-81. Contributor to theology and religious periodicals, including *Pulpit Digest, Good News, Science of Mind,* and *Interpreter.*

WORK IN PROGRESS: "Quality columns for newspapers and magazines, moving towards syndication with a distinctly identifiable form using my name, covering a wide range of subjects but emphasizing the need for Christian Unity and Interreligious Dialogue. A book on the Blessed Virgin Mary is a strong probability."

SIDELIGHTS: Lacy told *CA:* "It is difficult for me to remember back far enough to the point of not being interested in writing and publishing. Writing has been and is a very strong driving force in my life. I have considered it a ministry that I must do!

"When you get rejection slip after rejection slip, it is only a driven person that will continue. A fascination in all of this is that if one is convinced he really has something needing to be said, he will find a way to get that done.

"Certainly credit goes to those who continually ask about your next book. What is it about? When will it be published? Of course, I have never really felt deep-down that I needed to please anybody, except God, with my words. It is very important that I sense inspiration and creativity at work. Writing for money has never been a major interest. Writing to have my ideas spread as far as possible has always been a top priority.

"Living the lives of pastor, author, ecumenist, educator, and consultant virtually simultaneously has frequently been a struggle! They are so intertwined that it really is difficult to separate them. God has been very good to me and has enabled such a synthesis to take place. My superiors in the United Methodist Church have sometimes found me more of a liability than an asset in the sense I was not afraid

to publish what I believed. However, our system has far more things to commend it than it has to discredit it.

"Who can say which of one's writings will stand the test of time, finding a place in the hearts and minds of others year after year! After more than thirty-five years of being published, it seems a handful have ongoing appeal as I listen to others. *Called to Be,* that sought to bring to the surface essentials from sermons from the 'Sermon on the Mount,' provides an enduring commentary on our Lord's greatest teaching. The feature 'Preaching Is . . .' is a definition of preaching that others continually discover to be helpful and illuminating. *Mary and Jesus* has a way of winsomely taking the Blessed Virgin Mary and making her believable, plus necessary to understanding the Christian Faith. *A Mother and Her Infant Son* provides Christmas material that presents a unique perspective, especially for young mothers. *Methodist Mass* was the model for the newly revised United Methodist liturgy in the early 1970s and continues as a kind of landmark for liturgists; the *Indianapolis Star,* among others, did a feature on it. *Decalogue for Ecumenical Discipleship* is a teaching tool that has timeless quality about it and has provided the basis upon which Lacy and Associates was formed. *Devotion to Mary Should Go Beyond Denominations* remains the one writing that circulated among millions; the *Fort Wayne Journal Gazette,* among many others, published major articles. Interestingly, two publications *A Plea for Christian Unity* and *A Letter to a Roman Catholic* have made their way in controversy to large numbers.

"Of course, who knows the persons who have filed away copies from seemingly uneventful series' over the years? In the *Hagerstown Exponet* (Indiana) there was 'God Loves Us'; in the *Rushville Republican* (Indiana) there was 'Lacy's Logic'; and in the *Senior Times* was 'Mini-Meditations for Many Occasions' based in Argos, Indiana. During the Bicentennial I wrote a trio of features based on the religious faith of the Founding Fathers that circulated in newspapers and was used from pulpits across the State of Indiana; this project was based on a feature I did for the *Evansville Press. Hoosier United Methodist* published several features that dealt with ecumenical and interreligious concerns; the one that received the most attention was entitled 'Now Is the Time to Answer the Call.' *Emphasis* (C.S.S.), a regular publication containing sermonic helps, carried dozens of my contributions. Other magazines where my work appeared were *Church Management: The Clergy Jour-*

nal, Church School, Science of Mind, Sharing, Interpreter, New Oxford Review, and many others. Yes, and some may have tapes of the two guest appearances I made on *Sunday Morning in Chicago* over WGN Radio!

"Perhaps a feature in the *Vidette Messenger* of Valparaiso, Indiana, gives the best depiction of the way I ideally like to view myself: 'He's the religious equivalent of a Renaissance man.'

"The most serious and humbling problem for those of us driven to do what we do is our mortality. There is so much more to do! Maybe God will allow me the privilege of asking Him a few questions in the hereafter. Much of my published material has now been placed with the Indiana Historical Society in Indianapolis but I have every intention of writing and publishing until entering 'the way of all flesh.'

"What wisdom do I have for those younger who are driven to write? I offer only these insights: *One,* writing that offers something really significant is born from the wedding of the human and the Divine; *Two,* beware of writing solely for monetary gain and/or notoriety; *Three,* there are no uninteresting people; *Four,* always be forgiving of your enemies; *Five,* use computers sparingly; *Six,* always be humble but never weak; *Seven,* flee from that which is nominal and superficial; *Eight,* affirm and encourage other writers; *Nine,* virtually everything you write will already have been written; and *Ten,* be grateful for every moment of your life."

BIOGRAPHICAL/CRITICAL SOURCES:

PERIODICALS

Indianapolis News, December 6, 1980.
North Carolina Christian Advocate, October 26, 1978.

*   *   *

LARMINIE, Margaret Beda 1924-
   (Margaret Yorke)

PERSONAL: Born January 30, 1924, in Surrey, England; daughter of John Peel Alexander and Alison Yorke (Lyle) Larminie; married Basil Nicholson, 1945 (marriage dissolved, 1957); children: Diana Margaret, Ian Basil. *Avocational inter-*

ests: Reading, theater, travel, music, swimming, cooking, and trying to learn languages.

ADDRESSES: Home—Oriel Cottage, Long Crendon, Aylesbury, Buckinghamshire HP18 9AL, England. *Agent*—Curtis Brown Ltd., 4th Floor, Haymarket House, 28/29 Haymarket, London SW1 Y4SP, England.

CAREER: Writer. Oxford University, Oxford, England, assistant librarian at St. Hilda's College, 1959-61, library cataloger at Christ Church, 1963-65. *Military service:* Women's Royal Naval Service, 1942-45.

MEMBER: English-Speaking Union, Crime Writers' Association (vice-chairman, 1978; chairman, 1979-80), Mystery Writers of America, Society of Authors, Detection Club, PEN.

AWARDS, HONORS: Swedish Academy of Detection Award for best foreign crime novel, 1982, for a translation of *The Scent of Fear.*

WRITINGS:

UNDER PSEUDONYM MARGARET YORKE

Summer Flight, R. Hale (London), 1957.
Pray, Love, Remember, R. Hale, 1958.
Christopher, R. Hale, 1959.
Deceiving Mirror, R. Hale, 1960.
The China Doll, R. Hale, 1961.
Once a Stranger, Hurst & Blackett (London), 1962.
The Birthday, Hurst & Blackett, 1963.
Full Circle, Hurst & Blackett, 1965.
No Fury, Hurst & Blackett, 1967.
No Medals for the Major, Bles (London), 1974.
The Small Hours of the Morning, Walker & Co. (New York City), 1975.
The Cost of Silence, Hutchinson (London), 1977.
The Point of Murder, Hutchinson, 1978, published as *The Come-On,* Harper (New York City), 1979.
Death on Account, Hutchinson, 1979.
The Scent of Fear, Hutchinson, 1980, St. Martin's (New York City), 1981.
The Hand of Death, Hutchinson, 1981, St. Martin's, 1982.
Devil's Work, St. Martin's, 1982.
Find Me a Villain, St. Martin's, 1983.
The Smooth Face of Evil, St. Martin's, 1984.
Intimate Kill, St. Martin's, 1985.
Safely to the Grave, St. Martin's, 1986.
Evidence to Destroy, Viking (New York City), 1987.

Speak for the Dead, Viking, 1988.

Crime in Question, Viking, 1989.

Admit to Murder, Mysterious Press (London), 1990.

A Small Deceit, Mysterious Press (New York City), 1992.

Criminal Damage, Mysterious Press (New York City), 1992.

Dangerous to Know, Mysterious Press (New York City), 1993.

Serious Intent, Mysterious Press (New York City), 1995.

A Question of Belief, Mysterious Press (New York City), 1996.

UNDER PSEUDONYM MARGARET YORKE; "PATRICK GRANT" SERIES

Dead in the Morning, Bles, 1970.

Silent Witness, Walker & Co., 1973.

Grave Matters, Bles, 1973, Bantam (New York City), 1983.

Mortal Remains, Bles, 1974.

Cast for Death, Walker & Co., 1976.

UNDER PSEUDONYM MARGARET YORKE; STORY COLLECTIONS

Pieces of Justice, Warner Futura (London), 1994.

OTHER

Contributor to anthologies, including *Murder Ink: The Mystery Reader's Companion,* Workman (New York City), 1977. Contributor to magazines and radio broadcasts.

SIDELIGHTS: Margaret Beda Larminie is better known as the crime novelist Margaret Yorke, whose suspenseful stories often revolve around ordinary people thrust into harm's way either by chance or by choice. Yorke's favorite milieu is the small English village that is evolving into modernity, and her themes range from juvenile delinquency and marital strife to miscarriages of justice and the haphazard nature of violent crimes. According to Karl G. Fredriksson in the *St. James Guide to Crime and Mystery Writers,* the author's main thesis is "how coincidence maketh criminals of us all." Fredriksson added: "This ultimately is the strength of Yorke's novels. The plots are based on the small human weaknesses that we all have, and would like to get rid of but can't. This gives the reader a feeling of presence in the novels."

Yorke told Fredriksson that her earliest writing efforts were "family problem novels" of a conventional sort, but she was always tempted "to stir up their quiet plots with some violent action." She turned to crime fiction in 1970 and introduced her sleuth Patrick Grant, a decidedly unassuming Oxford don. Grant appears in five York novels—including *Cast for Death*—which more or less follow the classic lines of crime fiction. Once she departed ways with Grant, however, Yorke began to explore a variety of themes and characters, almost all of whom find their mundane lives changed by violence and chance.

One well-known example is *No Medals for the Major,* in which a retired military man finds himself implicated in the death of a little girl in the village where they both live. The reader knows the major is innocent, but the combination of his own chivalrous lies and the malicious gossip issued by the townspeople create an untenable situation for him. Circumstance also plays a role in Yorke's *The Point of Murder.* The novel's heroine, who is carrying on a quiet and secret love affair, suddenly finds herself the target of a murderer whose previous crime she happened to witness. In the *Washington Post Book World,* Jeam M. White cited Yorke as a writer "who can deal with subtleties of character, meanwhile building suspense to a breaking point."

Yorke is best known as an author of the "whydunit," rather than the "whodunit." Few of her plots revolve around discovering the criminal. Instead the reader watches as the criminal wreaks havoc—or tries to—on the other characters in the story. Nor are her works filled with gratuitous violence. As she herself noted in the *St. James Guide to Crime and Mystery Writers,* "I am more interested in the consequences of serious crime than in its description." Whatever her aims, she creates character studies that enliven her plots and help to keep the stories anchored in everyday life. *Spectator* contributor Patrick Cosgrave applauded Yorke for her "extraordinary gift for making prosaic human detail into adventure and romance."

BIOGRAPHICAL/CRITICAL SOURCES:

BOOKS

St. James Guide to Crime and Mystery Writers, fourth edition, St. James Press (Detroit, MI), 1996.

PERIODICALS

Spectator, August 21, 1976, p. 24; October 29, 1977, p. 23; March 10, 1979, p. 22.
Washington Post Book World, September 26, 1976, p. H2; February 18, 1979, p. E7.
Wilson Library Bulletin, May, 1979, p. 641.

*   *   *

LEAR, Peter
  See LOVESEY, Peter (Harmer)

*   *   *

LE CARRE, John
  See CORNWELL, David (John Moore)

*   *   *

LEE, Amber
  See BALDWIN, Faith

*   *   *

LEWIN, Michael Zinn 1942-

PERSONAL: Born July 21, 1942, in Springfield, MA; son of Leonard C. (a writer) and Iris (a social worker; maiden name, Zinn) Lewin; married Marianne Ruth Grewe (a social worker), August 11, 1965; children: Elizabeth, Roger. *Education:* Harvard University, A.B., 1964; further study at Cambridge University, 1964-65.

ADDRESSES: Home—32 Lansdown Place, Frome, Somerset, England. *Agent*—Wallace, Aitken & Sheil, Inc., 118 East 68th St., New York, NY 10021.

CAREER: Writer. Central High School, Bridgeport, CT, physics teacher, 1966-68; George Washington High School, New York, NY, science teacher, 1968-69; *Somerset Standard,* Frome, England, basketball columnist, 1972-89.

MEMBER: Mystery Writers of America, Crime Writers Association, West County Writers Association, Frome Revue Group.

AWARDS, HONORS: Falcon Award, 1987; Marlowe Award, 1992; Mystery Masters Award, Magna Cum Murder Annual Convention, 1994.

WRITINGS:

MYSTERY NOVELS

Ask the Right Question, Putnam (New York City), 1971.
The Way We Die Now, Putnam, 1972.
The Enemies Within, Knopf (New York City), 1974.
Night Cover, Knopf, 1976.
The Silent Salesman, Knopf, 1978.
Outside In, Knopf, 1980.
Missing Woman, Knopf, 1981.
Hard Line, Morrow (New York City), 1982.
Out of Season, Out of Time, Morrow, 1984, published as *Out of Time,* Macmillan (London), 1984.
Late Payments, Morrow, 1986.
And Baby Will Fall, Morrow, 1988, published as *Child Proof,* Macmillan, 1988.
Called by a Panther, Mysterious Press (New York City), 1991.
Underdog, Mysterious Press, 1993.
Family Business, Foul Play (Woodstock, VT), 1995.

RADIO PLAYS

The Way We Die Now, British Broadcasting Corp. (BBC), 1974.
The Loss Factor, BBC, 1975.
The Enemies Within, BBC, 1976.
Arrest Is as Good as a Change, BBC, 1982.
A Place of Safety, BBC, 1985.
Missing Woman, BBC, 1987.
Rainey Shines, BBC, 1987.
The Interests of the Child, BBC, 1988.
Ask the Right Question, BBC, 1989.
Wrong Number, BBC, 1989.
The Eyes Have It, BBC, 1989.
Cross, Rems of, BBC, 1993.
Keystone (from the novel by Peter Lovesey), BBC, 1993.
Rough Cider (from the novel by Peter Lovesey), BBC, 1994.
The Silent Salesman, BBC, 1994.
Who Killed Gnutley Almond?, BBC, 1995.

PLAYS

The Magnificent Seven, produced in Frome, Somerset, 1987.
Deadlock, produced in Stroud, Gloucestershire, 1990.

OTHER

How to Beat College Tests: A Practical Guide to Ease the Burden of Useless Courses, Dial (New York City), 1969.
(Editor with Liza Cody) *Culprit: An Annual of Crime Stories,* three volumes, Chatto & Windus (London), 1992-94, St. Martin's, 1993-95.
Telling Tails (stories), PawPaw Press (London), 1994.

Contributor of articles and stories to *Sport, Penthouse,* and other periodicals.

SIDELIGHTS: Michael Z. Lewin's detective character Albert Samson plies his trade in the author's childhood home of Indianapolis. Samson's cases are in the hard-boiled tradition of Raymond Chandler and Dashiell Hammett but are mitigated by a comic sense. "Lewin's world vision is fundamentally comic," Larry E. Grimes comments in the *St. James Guide to Crime and Mystery Writers.*

Critics have found Samson to be a unique creation in the detective genre, a detective who is drawn in the tough, cynical tradition of the hard-boiled school but tempered with enough warmth and hope to be realistic. "Samson," Newgate Callendar explains in the *New York Times Book Review,* "is the Galahad type, rather a mess in his personal life, but motivated by basic honesty and integrity. In that respect, he is in the classic tradition of the American detective." T. J. Binyon in the *Times Literary Supplement* believes that "of all the private eyes who chase panting after [Raymond Chandler's detective character] Philip Marlowe and [Ross Macdonald's] Lew Archer, Samson is undoubtedly up near the head of the field."

Samson solves his cases with a dogged determination that makes up for his limited financial resources and lack of high-profile connections. He takes what a *Library Journal* critic calls "a direct, no-nonsense approach to his work." Many of Samson's cases involve finding missing persons. In *Ask the Right Question,* he is hired by a 16-year-old girl to find her real father. "Halfway through [the story, Samson]

has the mystery solved to everyone's satisfaction—except his own," writes Haskel Frankel in *Saturday Review.* "It's then that the case really opens up." *Missing Woman* finds Samson out to locate a woman gone missing in a small Indiana town where the local playboy has just turned up dead. "The dialogue is authentic, the settings attractive, and the mystery real," Robin Winks notes in *New Republic.* Binyon finds that Lewin, "like Ross Macdonald, realizes that the causes for human behaviour may not necessarily lie around on the surface of life, but may be buried deep in the past."

Lewin once wrote *CA:* "I am gradually broadening the kinds of writing I do so that it keeps being hard and so I keep learning."

BIOGRAPHICAL/CRITICAL SOURCES:

BOOKS

St. James Guide to Crime and Mystery Writers, fourth edition, St. James Press (Detroit), 1996.

PERIODICALS

Christian Science Monitor, January 6, 1982, p. 17.
Library Journal, November 15, 1971, p. 96.
New Republic, March 4, 1978, p. 178; October 7, 1981, p. 185.
New York Times Book Review, November 21, 1971, p. 36; March 12, 1978, p. 49; November 15, 1981, p. 34.
Saturday Review, November 27, 1971, p. 54.
Times Literary Supplement, May 12, 1978, p. 517; July 2, 1982, p. 725.

*   *   *

LICHTENBERG, Jacqueline 1942-
(Daniel R. Kerns)

PERSONAL: Born March 25, 1942, in Flushing, NY; daughter of M. Kern and Mary Brice; married Salomon Lichtenberg; children: Naomi Gail, Deborah Ruth. *Education:* University of California, Berkeley, B.S., 1964.

ADDRESSES: Home—8 Fox Lane, Spring Valley, NY 10977. *E-mail*—xeyq30a@prodigy.com. *Agent*—Richard Curtis Literary Agency, 171 East 74th Street, New York, NY 10021.

CAREER: Worked as industrial chemist for two years, one of them in Israel; writer, 1968—; computer programmer, Chevron Corporation, 1993—. Policy advisor, Star Trek Welcommittee; former chairperson, Science Fiction Writers of America Speakers Bureau.

WRITINGS:

(With Sondra Marshak and Joan Winston) *Star Trek Lives!,* Bantam, 1975.
(Contributor) Alice Laurence, editor, *Casandra Rising,* Doubleday, 1978.
(Under pseudonym Daniel R. Kerns) *Hero,* Ace Books (New York City), 1993.
(Under pseudonym Daniel R. Kerns) *Border Dispute,* Ace Books, 1994.
The Biblical Tarot: Never Cross a Palm with Silver, Belfry Books, 1997.
The Biblical Tarot: The Not So Minor Arcana, The Magic of the Wands, Belfry Books, 1998.

"SIME/GEN" SERIES; SCIENCE FICTION NOVELS

House of Zeor, Doubleday (Garden City, NY), 1974, third edition, 1981.
Unto Zeor, Forever, Doubleday, 1978.
(With Jean Lorrah) *First Channel,* Doubleday, 1980.
Mahogany Trinrose: A Sime/Gen Novel. Doubleday, 1981.
(With Lorrah) *Channel's Destiny,* Doubleday, 1982.
RenSime, Doubleday, 1984.
(With Lorrah) *Zelerod's Doom: A Sime/Gen Novel,* DAW (New York City), 1986.

"DUSHAU" TRILOGY; SCIENCE FICTION NOVELS

Dushau, Popular Library (New York City), 1985.
Farfetch, Popular Library, 1985.
Outreach, Popular Library, 1986.

"KREN" SERIES; SCIENCE FICTION NOVELS

Molt Brother, Playboy Press (New York City), 1982.
City of a Million Legends, Berkley (New York City), 1985.

"LUREN" SERIES; SCIENCE FICTION NOVELS

Those of My Blood, St. Martin's Press (New York City), 1988.
Dreamspy, St. Martin's Press, 1989.

Reviewer of science fiction and fantasy in *The Monthly Aspectarian.* Fans of Lichtenberg's "Sime" series publish an amateur magazine, *Ambrov Zeor,* carrying fiction, poetry, and commentary.

SIDELIGHTS: "Jacqueline Lichtenberg," writes Susan Shwartz in the *St. James Guide to Science Fiction Writers,* "began her career in science fiction as the author of *Star Trek* fan fiction, and is the creator of one of the largest and most popular of the fannish 'universes' in which the cast of the *U.S.S. Enterprise* goes where no man (or woman) has gone before." *Star Trek Lives!,* cowritten with Sondra Marshak and Joan Winston, marked the beginning of the great explosion of "Star Trek" fandom that was partly responsible for bringing the cast of the original series to the large screen in the 1980s, and to the spinoffs "Star Trek: The Next Generation," "Star Trek: Deep Space Nine," and "Star Trek: Voyager." Lichtenberg has carried her devotion to the fan ideal into her own work; her science fiction novels have attracted fans of their own who enjoy Lichtenberg's vivid imagination and her willingness to allow them to participate in the creation of her worlds. "The audience for her work is among the most dedicated in the field," Shwartz explains, "and Lichtenberg is notable for her willingness to enter their lives as generously as she has opened her worlds to them."

Lichtenberg's earliest, and perhaps her most popular, series is the "Sime/Gen" series of novels. In the Sime/Gen books, humanity has split into two separate species. "The Simes," explains Gerald Jonas in the *New York Times Book Review,* "have developed special tentacles on their forearms which they use to draw life-energy—known as 'selyn'—from Gens." While Gens' bodies can manufacture their own selyn, Simes cannot, and without it they die; but the process of drawing selyn from a Gen usually kills the donor. A few Simes have found ways to draw selyn from Gens without killing, but the process must be done with complete trust by both parties. Lichtenberg uses this idea of mutual dependency to construct "a convincing view of two segments of humankind," declares Rosemary Herbert in *Library Journal,* "each living in need and fear of the other."

Lichtenberg explores both the vampiric metaphor in some of her other books, including *Those of My Blood* and *Dreamspy* (both about extraterrestrial vampires), and mutual dependency in the books of the "Kren" series, *Molt Brother* and *City of a Million Legends.* The Kren are a race of intelligent venomous reptiles who form close relationships only when they molt their old skins. "At that time, they choose molt brothers (or sisters) to guard them," explains Shwartz. "This bond, like the selyn transfer for Simes, is perilous, profound, and occasionally ecstatic." "All of Lichtenberg's books are marked by an extraordinary density of thought," Shwartz concludes. "She creates extremely dangerous characters: the sinister Simes, the venomous Kren whose pain somehow makes them vulnerable and understandable to her often fanatic readers."

The Zeor site on the World Wide Web is located at http://www.j51.com/~zeor and the Tecton Central web site is located at http://www.best.com/~shadorat/sg/sgfr.html.

BIOGRAPHICAL/CRITICAL SOURCES:

BOOKS

St. James Guide to Science Fiction Writers, fourth edition, St. James Press (Detroit), 1996.

PERIODICALS

Kirkus Reviews, October 15, 1988, p. 1498.
Library Journal, June 1, 1974, p. 1567; June 15, 1978, p. 1295; April 15, 1981, p. 906; April 15, 1982, p. 828; February 15, 1984, p. 289; November 15, 1988, p. 87; November 15, 1989, p. 108.
New York Times Book Review, July 24, 1977, p. 15; June 25, 1978, p. 22.
Publishers Weekly, March 4, 1974, p. 74; April 3, 1978, p. 72; March 20, 1981, p. 58; December 23, 1983, p. 55; October 14, 1988, p. 52; October 27, 1989, p. 60.
Voice of Youth Advocates, October, 1981, p. 43; June, 1984, p. 101; October, 1985, p. 268; February, 1986, p. 394; February, 1987, p. 292; June, 1990, p. 118.

* * *

LOVESEY, Peter (Harmer) 1936-
(Peter Lear)

PERSONAL: Born September 10, 1936, in Whitton, Middlesex, England; son of Richard Lear (a bank official) and Amy (Strank) Lovesey; married Jacqueline Ruth Lewis, May 30, 1959; children:

Kathleen Ruth, Philip Lear. *Education:* University of Reading, B.A. (honors), 1958.

ADDRESSES: Agent—Vanessa Holt Limited, 59 Crescent Road, Leigh-on-Sea, Essex SS9 2PF, England.

CAREER: Thurrock Technical College, Essex, England, senior lecturer, 1961-69; Hammersmith College for Further Education, London, head of general education department, 1969-75; currently full-time writer. *Military service:* Royal Air Force, 1958-61; served as education officer; became flying officer.

AWARDS, HONORS: Macmillan/Panther First Crime Novel award, 1970, for *Wobble to Death;* Silver Dagger, Crime Writers' Association, 1977, 1995, 1996, and Gold Dagger, 1983, Crime Writers' Association, for *The False Inspector Dew;* Veuve Clicquot/Crime Writers Association Short Story Award, 1985; Grand Prix de Litterature Policiere, 1985; Prix du Roman d'Aventures, 1987; finalist for Best Novel award, Mystery Writers of America, 1988, for *Rough Cider,* and 1996, for *The Summons;* Ellery Queen Readers award, 1991; Anthony Award, 1991; Mystery Writers of America Golden Mysteries Short Story prize, 1995.

WRITINGS:

CRIME NOVELS

Wobble to Death (Sergeant Cribb mystery), Dodd (New York City), 1970.
The Detective Wore Silk Drawers (Sergeant Cribb mystery), Dodd, 1971.
Abracadaver (Sergeant Cribb mystery), Dodd, 1972.
Mad Hatter's Holiday: A Novel of Murder in Victorian Brighton (Sergeant Cribb mystery), Dodd, 1973.
Invitation to a Dynamite Party (Sergeant Cribb mystery), Macmillan (New York City), 1974, published as *The Tick of Death,* Dodd, 1974.
A Case of Spirits (Sergeant Cribb mystery), Dodd, 1975.
Swing, Swing Together (Sergeant Cribb mystery), Dodd, 1976.
Waxwork (Sergeant Cribb mystery), Pantheon (New York City), 1978.
The False Inspector Dew, Pantheon, 1982.
Keystone, Pantheon, 1983.
Rough Cider, Bodley Head (New York City), 1986, Mysterious Press (New York City), 1987.
Bertie and the Tinman, Mysterious Press, 1988.

The Black Cabinet: Stories Based on True Crimes, Carroll & Graf (New York City), 1989.

On the Edge, Mysterious Press, 1989.

Bertie and the Seven Bodies, Mysterious Press, 1990.

The Last Detective, Doubleday (New York City), 1991.

Diamond Solitaire, Mysterious Press, 1992.

Bertie and the Crime of Passion, Little, Brown (Boston), 1993, reprinted, Mysterious Press, 1995.

The Summons, Mysterious Press, 1995.

Bloodhounds, Warner Books (New York City), 1996.

SHORT STORIES

Butchers and Other Stories of Crime, Macmillan, 1985, Mysterious Press, 1987.

The Staring Man and Other Stories, Eurographica (Helsinki), 1989.

The Crime of Miss Oyster Brown and Other Stories, Little Brown (London), 1994.

NONFICTION

The Kings of Distance: A Study of Five Great Runners, Eyre & Spottiswoode (London), 1968, published as *Five Kings of Distance,* St. Martin's Press (New York City), 1981.

(With Tom McNab) *The Guide to British Track and Field Literature 1275-1968,* Athletics Arena (London), 1969.

The Official Centenary History of the Amateur Athletic Association, Guinness Superlatives (London), 1979.

OTHER

(Under pseudonym Peter Lear) *Goldengirl,* Cassell (London), 1977, Doubleday, 1978.

(Under pseudonym Peter Lear) *Spider Girl,* Viking, 1980.

(Under pseudonym Peter Lear) *The Secret of Spandau,* M. Joseph (London), 1986.

Also author with wife, Jacqueline Ruth Lovesey, of "Sergeant Cribb" teleplays for Granada television and PBS's "Mystery!" program, including "The Last Trumpet," "Murder, Old Boy?" "Something Old, Something New," "The Horizontal Witness," and "The Choir That Wouldn't Sing." Contributor to periodicals, including *Armchair Detective, Ellery Queen's Mystery Magazine, Harper's,* and *Company.*

Contributor to numerous publications, including *Winter's Crimes 5,* edited by Virginia Whitaker, St. Martin's Press, 1973; *Murder Ink: The Mystery Reader's Companion,* edited by Dilys Winn, Workman, 1977; *Winter's Crimes 10,* edited by Hilary Watson, St. Martin's Press, 1978; *Mystery Guild Anthology,* edited by John Waite, Constable, 1980; *Best Detective Stories of the Year 1981,* edited by Edward D. Hoch, Dutton, 1981; *Winter's Crimes 14,* edited by Watson, St. Martin's Press, 1982; *Top Crime,* edited by Josh Pachter, St. Martin's Press, 1983; *Winter's Crimes 15,* edited by George Hardinge, St. Martin's Press, 1983; *The Best of Winter's Crimes,* edited by Hardinge, St. Martin's Press, 1986; *John Creasey's Crime Collection, 1986,* edited by Harris, St. Martin's Press, 1986; *The Year's Best Mystery and Suspense Stories, 1986,* edited by Hoch, Walker, 1986; *The New Adventures of Sherlock Holmes,* edited by Martin H. Greenberg and Carol-Lynn Waugh, Carroll & Graf, 1987; and *John Creasey's Crime Collection, 1988,* edited by Harris, St. Martin's Press, 1988.

ADAPTATIONS: Peter Lovesey's *Goldengirl,* written under the pseudonym Peter Lear, was filmed by the Avco Embassy Pictures Corp. in 1979. It starred James Coburn as Dryden, the shrewd sports agent, and Susan Anton as Goldengirl, the woman bred to win three gold medals in track events at the 1980 Moscow Olympics.

SIDELIGHTS: Peter Lovesey is the author of almost twenty novels of detective fiction as well as thrillers, short story collections, and plays. He is best known for his Sergeant Cribb series, novels set in Victorian England, although his work jumps continents and decades. His most famous novel, *The False Inspector Dew,* for which he won a Gold Dagger award, is not a Cribb novel but is set in England in the 1920s. All of Lovesey's fiction is remarkable for its vivid yet offbeat historical details—Ralph Spurrier, writing in the *St. James Guide to Crime & Mystery Writers,* notes that readers "revel in the author's obvious love for the etiquette, finery, and hypocrisy of the Victorian times." Lovesey portrays a clear understanding of the psychology of the societies he depicts. As James Hurt points out in the *Dictionary of Literary Biography,* "[Lovesey's] are modern novels about the past, not attempts to resuscitate past forms."

Lovesey's interest in sport led him to write his prize-winning first Victorian crime novel *Wobble to Death.* He told Diana Cooper-Clark in the *Armchair Detective,* "At this time, I didn't regard myself as an authority or expert on the Victorian period. But I had become interested in Victorian sport as a school boy because I wasn't a very good athlete and would have liked to have been. I was flat-footed and butter-fingered and couldn't really perform very well in any team game, so I tried to take up the more individual sports, like high jumping." While researching the life of a Native American athlete, he found a description of the Victorian "wobble," a walking endurance contest. Later, while "perusing the personals columns of the [London] *Times* as Sherlock Holmes used to do," he states, he discovered an advertisement for a crime novel contest. *Wobble to Death* was the result.

Wobble to Death is the first of a series of novels featuring Detective Sergeant Cribb and his assistant Constable Thackeray. Critics have praised these books for their authentic evocation of Victorian atmosphere and restrained characterization. Lovesey explains to Cooper-Clark: "I was looking in *Wobble to Death* for a realistic Victorian detective. I was conscious that the great detectives were super figures, the omniscient Sherlock Holmes, the sophisticated Lord Peter Wimsey, and even Hercule Poirot, with the little grey cells. These were not really for me. I wanted somebody who would have to struggle to solve a crime and have to work against the limitations of the period."

Marcel Berlins of the London *Times* states: "Peter Lovesey has written eight [Sergeant Cribb] detective novels set in late Victorian times, and not one has fallen short on factual accuracy or ratiocinative skill. . . . Mr. Lovesey's strength is to place those subdued characters into a meticulously researched historical reality, and produce a supremely satisfying novel of detection." All eight novels featuring Cribb and Thackeray proved very popular. They were adapted and broadcast in America on PBS's "Mystery!" program, and Lovesey later collaborated with his wife Jacqueline to produce six new "Sergeant Cribb" stories for the series. James Hurt says these novels "stand as a major achievement of modern British mystery fiction."

"For my own pleasure. . ." Lovesey says, "I vary the voices, forms, and styles of the novels, even within the series." He certainly has not limited himself to his Cribb stories. In an effort to "widen" his range as he embarked on the career of a fulltime writer, Lovesey wrote the first of his three non-mystery thrillers, all with contemporary settings. He has also published three collections of short stories. Writing short stories fulfills two goals for Lovesey: the sheer enjoyment of writing them and, Lovesey

says, they "give me the opportunity to take risks and try new things that may be used later in novels."

Yet Lovesey has kept returning to the detective novel. He left the Victorian period for *The False Inspector Dew,* bringing his evocative talents to a 1920s transatlantic cruise. A reviewer for the London *Times* reports, "Lovesey has researched his setting not merely just enough to have plenty of local colour to push in when there's some excuse, but so thoroughly that he had at his fingertips a dozen facts to choose from at any instant." This, along with a gripping story line, the reviewer adds, is part of "the charge that powers his book." Hurt further applauds the novel, declaring it to be "one of the best mysteries ever written, one that opens up new possibilities for the genre."

Lovesey continued to experiment with places and time periods. *Keystone,* a mystery set in Hollywood in 1915, appeared next. It involves the Keystone Cops and many of the period's actors, such as Fatty Arbuckle, Mabel Normand, and Mack Sennett. Hurt finds in this novel "historically accurate" characterizations and "[F]ascinating technical details of early moviemaking" mixed with a deeper message: that Keystone comedy masks the violence of America about to embark on World War I. In *Rough Cider,* a novel of psychological suspense, and *On the Edge,* in which two ex-WAAF plotters turn into murderesses, Spurrier sees a "much tougher centre . . . than anything the author produced before." Of the latter novel Spurrier says, "The setting, style, and feel of the writing is richly authentic and the cliche 'page-turning' is perfectly apt."

Lovesey again returned to the Victorian era with his "Bertie" books. This time, the author features a rather unusual detective—Albert Edward, Prince of Wales, Queen Victoria's son and heir, who later became Edward VII of England. In the first book, *Bertie and the Tinman,* Bertie, as he is known to his intimates, tells the story of the apparent suicide of his favorite jockey Fred Archer, popularly known as the Tinman. Doubting that Archer was suicidal, the Prince becomes suspicious and launches a personal investigation that takes him all over Victorian London, from the coarsest fleshpots to the most elegant salons. "The rueful, candid voice [Lovesey] gives to the fleshy prince rings true," declares *Time* magazine contributor William A. Henry III, and "the details of the horse-racing and music-hall worlds are vivid, and much of the tale is sweetly funny." "This is an affectionate look at Prince Albert, a likable chap even with his pomposities and one-sided view of life," reports Newgate Callendar in the *New York Times Book Review*. "And the race-track scenes and backgrounds crackle with authenticity. There is a great deal of humor in the book, even a strong dash of P. G. Wodehouse. *Bertie and the Tinman* is a delightful romp."

Most recently, Lovesey started yet another series, the Peter Diamond books, which have contemporary settings. Lovesey sees his movements through time as evidence of his having "evolved by stages." Recently Lovesey has experienced another evolution, from the written word and the page to the spoken word and the stage. In 1994, Lovesey, along with other British mystery writers Liza Cody and Michael Z. Lewin, toured eight American cities, performing a program filled with skits, dramatic readings, sound effects, and audience participation. Lovesey said in an *Armchair Detective* interview of the performance, "In this show we're still concerned with the craft of writing. There's a serious element even in something which appears to have entertainment value and laughter."

Lovesey and his critics recognize the great gift of this ability to entertain. Hurt credits Lovesey's development of "rich comic characterizations within a traditional puzzle framework" which "humaniz[es] a too often sterile form" as Lovesey's chief contribution to the genre of British mystery writing. Hurt continues, "At his best (and he is often at his best) Lovesey has brought a comic lightness to the mystery novel that has expanded its possibilities in new and unexpected ways." It is likely that Lovesey would agree with this analysis. "The aim of all my writing is to entertain and involve the reader," he says. "if successful, then I can be subversive, suggesting ironies, springing surprises, and now and then chilling the blood."

Lovesay told *CA:* "My first published work was sports journalism, a long series of pieces, mostly unpaid, on the history of track and field. I chose to write on sports because I wanted to participate, however remotely. I had discovered early in life that I was not cut out to be an athlete; I was pathetically inept at every kind of sport. So I cornered the market in track and field history. One magazine gave me the by-line 'The World's Foremost Authority on the History of Athletics'; in fact, I was the world's *only* authority. But eventually I had enough material for a book. *The Kings of Distance* was published in England in 1968 (1981 in the U.S.).

"I was drawn to mystery writing by the lure of money. In 1969 Macmillan and Panther Books announced a first crime novel competition with a thousand pound first prize. I was then a teacher, earning a salary of less than this. Using a Victorian long distance race as the background, I wrote *Wobble to Death*, won the prize, and was launched as a writer of historical mysteries. Seven more followed, featuring the detectives Sergeant Cribb and Constable Thackeray. They were all adapted for the TV series 'Sergeant Cribb,' made by Granada, and seen in America in the *Mystery!* series on PBS. A further six episodes were scripted by my wife Jacqueline and me.

"I was reluctant to write only historical mysteries, so I tried a modern thriller, *Goldengirl,* under the pen name Peter Lear. This was about a gifted American woman athlete's exploitation by various individuals as she tries to win a unique triple at the Olympics. It was filmed by Avco Embassy, starring Susan Anton and James Coburn, directed by Joseph Sargent.

"I was encouraged to venture out of the Victorian period in my mystery writing, and wrote several one-off novels set in more recent times. In recent years I have tended to alternate between Victorian and contemporary settings. The Victorian series features Bertie, the Prince of Wales, writing his detective memoirs and revealing to perceptive readers more than he intends. The modern novels are about a police sleuth, Peter Diamond, embattled against forensic scientists and computer operators, and, amazingly, coming out the winner."

BIOGRAPHICAL/CRITICAL SOURCES:

BOOKS

Barnes, Melvin, *Murder in Print: A Guide to Two Centuries of Crime Fiction,* Barn Owl Books, 1986.

Benstock, Bernard, editor, *Art in Crime Writing,* St. Martin's Press, 1983.

Burack, Sylvia K., *Writing Mystery and Crime Fiction,* The Writer, 1985.

Carr, John C., *The Craft of Crime: Conversations with Crime Writers,* Houghton, 1983.

Cooper-Clark, Diana, *Designs of Darkness: Interviews with Detective Novelists,* Bowling Green State University Popular Press, 1983.

Dictionary of Literary Biography, Volume 87: *British Mystery and Thriller Writers since 1940,* Gale (Detroit), 1989.

Dove, George N., and Earl F. Bargainner, *Cops and Constables: American and British Fictional Policemen,* Bowling Green State University Popular Press, 1986.

Keating, H. R. F., *Crime and Mystery: The One Hundred Best Books,* Carroll & Graf, 1987.

St. James Guide to Crime & Mystery Writers, fourth edition, St. James Press (Detroit), 1996.

PERIODICALS

Armchair Detective, summer, 1981; spring, 1995.
New Republic, March 3, 1982.
Newsweek, July 3, 1978; April 5, 1982.
New York Times, June 15, 1979; October 14, 1983.
New York Times Book Review, October 25, 1970; October 15, 1972; February 15, 1976; May 28, 1978; October 3, 1982; March 12, 1989, p. 24; January 20, 1990, p. 35; October 20, 1991, p. 40; October 24, 1993, p. 28; January 8, 1995, p. 26; October 8, 1995, p. 26.
Publishers Weekly, October 25, 1985; January 6, 1989, p. 92.
Saturday Review, October 28, 1972.
Spectator, March 28, 1970; April 10, 1982.
Times (London), March 1, 1980; March 18, 1982; December 31, 1987.
Times Literary Supplement, April 9, 1970; June 25, 1982.
Washington Post Book World, September 17, 1972; May 16, 1982; March 20, 1988.

* * *

LYALL, Gavin (Tudor) 1932-

PERSONAL: Born May 9, 1932, in Birmingham, England; son of Joseph Tudor (an accountant) and Ann (Hodgkiss) Lyall; married Katharine E. Whitehorn (a columnist, fashion editor, and associate editor), January 4, 1958; children: two sons. *Education:* King Edward VI School, Birmingham, 1951; Pembroke College, Cambridge, B.A. (with honors), 1956. *Religion:* Quaker. *Avocational interests:* Travel, cooking, military history, guns, model making, cats, and beer.

ADDRESSES: Home—14 Provost Rd., London NW3 4ST, England. *Agent*—Peters Fraser and Dunlop, 5th Floor, The Chambers, Chelsea Harbour, Lots Road, London SW 10, England.

CAREER: Freelance writer, 1963—. *Picture Post,* London, journalist, 1956-57; British Broadcasting Corp. (BBC), London, television film director, 1958-59; *Sunday Times,* London, began as journalist, became aviation editor, 1959-63. Lyall has travelled as a staff journalist in Europe, the United States, Libya, India, Pakistan, Nepal, and Australia. *Military service:* Royal Air Force, 1951-53; became pilot officer.

MEMBER: Crime Writers Association (chair 1967-68).

AWARDS, HONORS: Crime Writers Association Silver Dagger award 1964, 1965.

WRITINGS:

ADVENTURE NOVELS

The Wrong Side of the Sky, Scribner (New York City), 1961.
The Most Dangerous Game, Scribner, 1963.
Midnight Plus One, Scribner, 1965.
Shooting Script, Scribner, 1966.
Venus with Pistol, Scribner, 1969.
Blame the Dead, Viking (New York City), 1973.
Judas Country, Viking, 1975.

"MAJOR MAXIM" SPY NOVEL SERIES

The Secret Servant, Viking, 1980.
The Conduct of Major Maxim, Hodder & Stoughton (London), 1982, Viking, 1983.
The Crocus List, Hodder & Stoughton, 1985, Viking, 1986.
Uncle Target, Viking, 1988.

OTHER

(Editor) *The War in the Air, 1939-1945: An Anthology of Personal Experience,* Hutchinson (London), 1968, published as *The War in the Air: The Royal Air Force in World War II,* Morrow (New York City), 1969.
(With Frank Handman and Martin Davison) *Moon Zero Two* (screenplay), Hammer, 1969.

SIDELIGHTS: Gavin Lyall has made a name for himself as the author of thrillers—tales of adventure in which heroes undertake a difficult and dangerous mission and tales of espionage in the national and international arenas. These books have drawn the attention of critics over the years for their well-executed and suspenseful plots, complex characters, and finely drawn locations. Lyall began his writing career as a journalist, and he uses his experiences in foreign locales such as Libya, India, Pakistan, Persia, and Nepal to provide rich and exotic details for his novels. His works are also impeccably researched, providing a realistic yet subtle backdrop. All of this careful plotting and detail leads to a body of "literate novels," according to J. Randolph Cox of the *St. James Guide to Crime & Mystery Writers.* Cox further states, "Though the plots of these books build slowly, by the time the first bullet thuds home the reader knows the characters well enough to recognize them and, more importantly, to care about their fate on the downward plunge."

Lyall's early thrillers are all told from the first-person point of view. These "high-adventure novels," writes Carol Simpson Stern in the *Dictionary of Literary Biography,* "belong in the tradition of Geoffrey Household and Raymond Chandler," and Cox further sees Lyall's viewpoint as allowing "humor to lighten the grim path of high adventure. His heroes may adopt the flip Chandler style, but they don't overdo it." Most of Lyall's novels have received generally favorable reviews. R. C. Healey of the *New York Herald Tribune Books* declares Lyall's first novel, *The Wrong Side of the Sky,* to be "a model thriller" and a reviewer for *Kirkus Reviews* calls it "slick to spectacular." Lyall's sophomore effort, *The Most Dangerous Game,* was similarly lauded. *New York Times Book Review* critic Anthony Boucher writes, "The way in which all [the] diverse threads become one cord in the last few pages is one of the happy miracles of the season. Lyall . . . is a master of the rare art of storytelling."

Stern maintains that, while Lyall's first three novels relied "heavily for their success on his skillful and technically precise descriptions of how a series of obstacles is overcome," his next three novels show that "his control as a writer becomes more secure, his plots more complex, and his tone more cynical." Peter Parley of *Spectator* offers "all praise" for *Venus with Pistol,* Lyall's fifth novel, and recommends it "for those with a thirst for the find in the attic and a bottle of scotch in the third drawer down." Maurice Prior of *Books* comments that while the theme is "not . . . outrageously original," Lyall possesses a "nice lucid smooth style." Prior further

notes that "any thinness in story-content" is offset by "effortless and studious" narration and concludes that *Venus with Pistol,* with Lyall's "inimitable stamp," is "cogent, neatly devised, with nicely-contrived denouement."

Aside from being mere novels of adventure, Lyall's books also suggest deeper issues. They are filled with characters who face moral dilemmas, all of which further propels the plot. Of *Midnight Plus One* Brigid Brophy writes for the *New Statesman* that Lyall "very nearly fulfills its deeper purpose of being morally exciting." The character of British Army Major Henry Maxim "enables [Lyall] to offer elaborate moral and political commentary," contends Stern, while creating a "more subtle, less formulaic hero." Two things led him to create Maxim: coincidence—Lyall ended up with files of material about the inner workings of government; and the realization that he was typecasting himself—Lyall said, "Trying to sort out a plot, I once discarded an idea because 'You can't do that in a Gavin Lyall book,'" He also felt he was ready to write from the third person, or according to Lyall, "God-s-eye view."

Lyall's first Maxim and espionage novel was *The Secret Servant.* In the opinion of a London *Times* critic, *The Secret Servant* is "the richest [of all Lyall's books] yet, a new departure that has paid off handsomely." Although noting that the book lacks "steel-compressed intensity," this same reviewer applauds the book's "splendid readability" and proposes that it is "Le Carre made easy." Also pleased with Lyall's departure was *New York Times Book Review* contributor Peter Andrews. Andrews describes *The Secret Servant* as "neat, literate and deliciously cynical. . . . Lyall . . . knows how to lash a narrative from chapter to chapter pausing only for some judicious bloodletting along the way. . . . *The Secret Servant* is a first-class piece of work." However, *Times Literary Supplement* reviewer T. J. Binyon found Lyall's change of genre disconcerting: "Anything by Gavin Lyall is bound to be original, intelligent and well-written. *The Secret Servant* is certainly all these things. . . . But with the move into the field of Deighton and Le Carre has come the use of their kind of oblique, allusive dialogue, their kind of jargon. . . . *The Secret Servant* is exciting, very readable, and far better than most of its kind, but one still wishes that Gavin Lyall had stuck to his guns."

The Secret Servant evolved into a spy novel series with the reappearance of its trigger-happy protagonist

Maxim, first in *The Conduct of Major Maxim* and then in *The Crocus List*. In two succeeding *Times Literary Supplement* reviews, Binyon concedes that the quality of *The Conduct of Major Maxim* will silence any doubts about Lyall's genre switch and maintains that *The Crocus List* "is undoubtedly the best Harry Maxim yet. Brilliantly engineered and written with . . . elegance, it moves forward with the irresistible power of a Tiger tank." A few reviewers mention that *The Crocus List* starts off slow but that its pace quickens. The novel's opening scene describes a failed assassination attempt made on the President of the United States in Britain, the details of which Maxim must untangle. According to *Spectator* critic Harriet Waugh, "This is an exciting and well-plotted story and Harry Maxim is an odd, almost interesting hero—an honourable man who gets a kick out of killing."

Lyall enjoys the introduction of a serial character in his work. "The biggest [compensation]," Lyall says, "is the greater freedom to explore a wide range of characters, and let them develop more slowly." Many critics seem to agree with Lyall's development of his characters, particularly Maxim. Stern believes that the Maxim novels "reveal [Lyall's] strength as a writer of character . . . real people, not stereotypes" and Tim Heald of the London *Times* writes that Maxim is an "instantly recognizable character with warts we know to love." Stern further states, "Lyall's reputation as a writer of novels of suspense and of espionage is secure."

BIOGRAPHICAL/CRITICAL SOURCES:

BOOKS

Dictionary of Literary Biography, Volume 87: *British Mystery and Thriller Writers since 1940,* Gale (Detroit), 1989.

St. James Guide to Crime & Mystery Writers, fourth edition, St. James Press (Detroit), 1996.

PERIODICALS

Books, January, 1970.
Globe and Mail (Toronto), November 15, 1986.
Kirkus Reviews, May 1, 1961.
New Statesman, March 12, 1965; June 27, 1980.
New York Herald Tribune Books, September 3, 1961.
New York Times Book Review, October 13, 1963; November 16, 1980; March 13, 1983; February 9, 1986.
Spectator, November 22, 1969; August 17, 1985.
Times (London), June 19, 1980.
Times Literary Supplement, June 20, 1980; December 31, 1982; June 21, 1985.
Washington Post Book World, March 2, 1986.*

*   *   *

LYMINGTON, John
See CHANCE, John Newton

M

MacAVOY, Roberta Ann 1949-

PERSONAL: Surname is accented on first syllable; born December 13, 1949, in Cleveland, OH; daughter of Francis (a mechanic) and Helen (a secretary; maiden name, Macruski) MacAvoy; married Ronald Allen Cain (a computer programmer and analyst), June 10, 1978. *Education:* Case Western Reserve University, B.A., 1971. *Avocational interests:* Playing music, keeping horses.

ADDRESSES: Home—Underhill at Nelson Farm, 1669 Nelson Road, House 6, Scotts Valley, CA 95066. *Agent*— Richard Curtis Associates, 171 East 74th Street, New York, NY 10021.

CAREER: Columbia University, New York City, assistant to financial aid officer of Columbia College, 1975-78; SRI International, Menlo Park, CA, computer programmer, 1979-82; writer, 1982—.

MEMBER: American Connemara Pony Society, American Donkey and Mule Society, Folk Harpers Guild.

AWARDS, HONORS: John W. Campbell Best New Writer award, LOCUS award, and PKD memorial award, all 1984.

WRITINGS:

SCIENCE FICTION

The Third Eagle: Lessons along a Minor String, Doubleday (New York City), 1989.

FANTASY NOVELS

(With Sharon Devlin) *The Book of Kells,* Bantam (New York City), 1985.
The Grey Horse, Bantam, 1987.

"DAMIANO TRILOGY"; FANTASY

Damiano (also see below), Bantam, 1984.
Damiano's Lute (also see below), Bantam, 1984.
Raphael (also see below), Bantam, 1984.
A Trio for Lute (omnibus; includes *Damiano, Damiano's Lute, Raphael),* Nelson Doubleday (New York City), 1985.

"BLACK DRAGON" SERIES; FANTASY

Tea With the Black Dragon, Bantam, 1983.
Twisting the Rope: Casadh an t'Sugain, Bantam, 1986.

"NAZHUET OF SORDALING" SERIES; FANTASY

Lens of the World, Morrow (New York City), 1990.
King of the Dead, Morrow, 1991.
The Belly of the Wolf, Morrow, 1993, published in England as *Winter of the Wolf,* Headline (London), 1993.

SIDELIGHTS: R. A. MacAvoy is an author who belongs "in the top rank of the American fantasists' roster," according to Roland Green in *Booklist*. All but one of MacAvoy's books have been fantasies—the exception is a science fiction novel—but within the fantasy genre, she has demonstrated the ability to come up with many original approaches to her work. "She is an author who constantly strives to achieve something new," asserted Pauline Morgan in the *St. James Guide to Fantasy Writers.* She has created imaginary worlds, as most fantasists do, but she has also set novels in contemporary times, Renaissance Italy, and ancient Ireland. "I like to write," MacAvoy once told *CA.* "Language and character interest me. Plot does not, but I understand I'd better have one if anyone's to read my book."

Tea with the Black Dragon was MacAvoy's first published novel. Set in modern times, it features a few eccentric characters living in California's Silicon Valley. Martha Macnamara is a middle-aged player with an Irish-American band; Maryland Long is an ancient dragon who has assumed human form. Macnamara travels to San Francisco to visit her daughter, who subsequently vanishes. "In many ways this is a detective novel with a touch of fantasy, in which the principal characters are superbly portrayed," commented Morgan. The characters reappeared in *Twisting the Rope,* in which Long has become the manager of Macnamara's band. When one of the group's members is found dead, he begins to track down the killer. The fantasy in these books lies mostly in Long's secret identity as a dragon.

In the "Damiano" trilogy, MacAvoy played a little more freely with magic. The books are set in a parallel-world Renaissance Italy. There, magic is an everyday occurrence. The young protagonist, Damiano Delstrego, is the son of a wizard; his two closest friends are a talking dog and the archangel Raphael, who is visible only to him. "The first volume, *Damiano,* can almost stand alone," mused Morgan. "It is the skill of the writer, and the knowledge that there is more to be told that leads the reader to seek out the rest of the trilogy." By the end of volume one, Damiano has relinquished his magic powers and become a traveling musician. *Damiano's Lute* follows him through France during the time of the plague. *Raphael* features the angel as the main character; he has been tricked into becoming human by his wicked brother, Lucifer. "The trilogy is a very ambitious project, combining a number of complex themes," noted Morgan. "For Damiano first, then Raphael, it is a voyage of self-discovery. Linked with this is a battle of good versus evil as both characters fight the traps set for them by Lucifer. The historical background is well researched, with the subtleties of having magic working against this background carefully calculated. In a situation where it would be easy to descend into cliche or sentimentality, MacAvoy manages to tread lightly and balance the many strands so that often the result is unexpected."

Thorough research is also evident in *The Book of Kells.* Its setting is Ireland at a time when the Vikings were burning Christian settlements. The fantasy angle comes into play when a modern-day artist, John Thorburn, and an historian, Derval O'Keane, find themselves transported back into the past. The attitudes of ancient and modern people are skillfully contrasted in this book. Ireland is again the setting for *The Grey Horse.* The title character is a being who assumes human form to court one of the village women. It is a detailed portrait of village life in an earlier time.

In the "Nazhuret" series, MacAvoy constructed another imaginary world, but one without most of the usual trappings of fantasy. There are no mad sorcerers, enchanted weapons, or malevolent evil lords. The main character, Nazhuret of Sordaling, narrates the tale; he describes himself as a goblin-like creature, who entered the Royal Sordaling School as a child. He knows nothing of his ancestry, but guesses he must have some noble blood, because this is a requirement for entry into the school. Each of the three volumes—*Lens of the World, The King of the Dead,* and *The Belly of the Wolf*—can stand on its own, although they also work together to provide a smooth narrative. A *Publishers Weekly* reviewer declared that the Nazhuret books "may be one of the best fantasy series of the decade. . . . [MacAvoy's] prose is graceful, understated and vivid. Anyone who doubts that fantasy can be literary, artistic, thoughtful and genuinely moving need only follow Nazhuret's adventures to learn otherwise." A writer for *Kirkus Reviews* was similarly enthusiastic, stating that MacAvoy's prose is "quiet, unpretentious, vivid, understated, succinct: an object lesson for other, more verbose fantasists in how to produce more from less, and how to write an appealing and gratifying trilogy by offering a self-contained story each time out."

BIOGRAPHICAL/CRITICAL SOURCES:

BOOKS

St. James Guide to Fantasy Writers, St. James Press (Detroit), 1996.

PERIODICALS

Booklist, January 1, 1994, p. 811.
Kirkus Reviews, December 1, 1993, p. 1493.
Locus, February 14, 1984, p. 36.

New York Times Book Review, January 2, 1994, p. 22.
Publishers Weekly, December 20, 1993.*

*   *   *

MACLAGAN, Bridget
  See BORDEN, Mary

*   *   *

MacNEIL, Neil
  See BALLARD, (Willis) Todhunter

*   *   *

MacTAGGART, Morna Doris
  See BROWN, Morna Doris

*   *   *

MADDEN, Deirdre 1960-

PERSONAL: Born August 20, 1960, in Belfast, Northern Ireland. *Education:* Trinity College, Dublin, B.A. (with honors), 1983; University of East Anglia, M.A. (with distinction), 1985.

ADDRESSES: Home—County Antrim, Northern Ireland. *Agent*—A. P. Watt Ltd., 20 John St., London WC1N 2DR, England.

CAREER: Writer.

AWARDS, HONORS: Hennessy Literary Award, 1980; Rooney Prize for Irish Literature, 1987; Somerset Maugham Award from Society of Authors, 1989.

WRITINGS:

NOVELS

Hidden Symptoms, Atlantic Monthly Press (Boston), 1987.
The Birds of the Innocent Wood, Faber (London), 1988.

Remembering Light and Stone, Faber, 1992.
Nothing Is Black, Faber, 1994.
One by One in the Darkness, Faber, 1996.

Work also represented in anthologies, including *First Fictions: Introduction 9,* Faber, 1986.

WORK IN PROGRESS: A novel.

SIDELIGHTS: Deirdre Madden's first book, *Hidden Symptoms,* was published when she was still in her twenties. Many reviewers commented on the young author's polished prose and powerful story. *Hidden Symptoms,* set in Belfast in 1969, explores the consequences of familial and national loyalties and animosities. There are three central characters: Theresa, a university student who is embittered by the death of her twin brother at the hands of Protestant terrorists; Kathy, Theresa's best friend, and Robert, Kathy's lover, a journalist who rejects both politics and religion. All three have needs that are hidden behind carefully constructed facades. Laurel Graeber wrote in the *New York Times Book Review* that the connections between the protagonists sometimes seems "contrived," but she went on to say that "Ms. Madden writes movingly and often lyrically of the differences that lead these three to wound one another." She concluded that the novel possesses a "sorrowful impact." A writer for *Kirkus Reviews* voiced some reservations about the book, stating that "it flirts with the maudlin, takes some embarrassing shortcuts, and ends with a top-heavy dialogue on Catholicism"; but, the writer concluded, the novel is for the most part "effective . . . with the thematic ambitiousness of Joyce (there are allusions throughout); the eye for atmosphere and mood of the early Brian Moore; and, not least, with the fetching creation of the intelligent, uncompromisingly passionate Theresa. . . . Well above average, at moments exceptional." A *Publishers Weekly* reviewer expressed unreserved enthusiasm, calling *Hidden Symptoms* a "powerful" book, and concluding: "The beaten-down feelings of young Irish intellectuals whose faith is sorely tested, or lost completely, are eloquently voiced here."

Despite its overtones of fable, Madden's next novel, *The Birds of the Innocent Wood,* was praised by *London Review of Books* contributor John Lanchester for keeping the emotional framework of the story realistic and believable. It is a "dark, stoical and unyieldingly somber story" of a family's bleak life on an Irish farm. The reviewer found Madden's control and purpose "remarkable," but went on to say that "this very control is also the novel's difficulty. There is no humour in it. . . . The universe of the book has a predetermined quality to it, and its characters, because they can appear ciphers of the author's purpose, don't always engage the reader's emotion."

Madden's precise control is also mentioned by Andrea Ashworth in a *Times Literary Supplement* discussion of *Nothing Is Black.* "Maddens' sentences are carefully composed and executed to produce simple, sometimes starkly poetic prose," wrote Ashworth. "But the dialogue, although never monotonous, can be monochromatic. In framed discussions, her characters stop doing and start discoursing. . . . At such points, Madden's art is too abstract, obscuring the appeal of her most concrete and colourful scenes."

By the time of her fifth novel, *One by One in the Darkness,* Madden's voice was well-defined. Patricia Craig described it in *Times Literary Supplement* as "a lucid voice, but one that admits no note of bravado or gaiety. It creates a thinly populated world in which everyone is more or less fraught and unfulfilled. Bereavement, suffering, guilt and blame are Madden's subjects, and her books are overloaded with the miseries of life." In *One by One in the Darkness,* these miseries take the form of a terrorist killing and its aftermath. Craig notes that aside from the murder, "very little happens." She concludes, however, that "What saves [Madden] as a writer, and makes her novels likeable, despite their refusal of qualities such as charm, high spirits, robustness and aplomb, is a formidable descriptive gift which is harnessed to the small-scale and quotidian."

BIOGRAPHICAL/CRITICAL SOURCES:

PERIODICALS

Kirkus Reviews, November 15, 1986, p. 1680.
Library Journal, February 15, 1987, p. 161.
Listener, January 28, 1988, p. 25.
London Review of Books, February 4, 1988, p. 17.
Los Angeles Times Book Review, September 24, 1989, p. 14.
New York Times Book Review, February 15, 1987, p. 20.
Observer, January 31, 1988, p. 27; July 3, 1994, p. 24; July 17, 1994, p. 15.
Publishers Weekly, November 28, 1986, p. 66.
Punch, February 5, 1988, p. 45.
Times Literary Supplement, February 5, 1988, p. 133; October 2, 1992, p. 22; July 8, 1994, p. 20; May 24, 1996, p. 26.
Washington Post, January 14, 1987.*

MAITLAND, Sara (Louise) 1950-

PERSONAL: Born February 27, 1950, in London, England; daughter of Adam (a farmer) and Hope (Fraser-Campbell) Maitland; married Donald Hugh Thomson Lee (a priest), June 24, 1972; children: Mildred McNab Lee, Adam Maitland Lee. *Education:*Oxford University, B.A. (with honors), 1971. *Politics:* Feminist/Socialist. *Religion:* Roman Catholic.

ADDRESSES: Home—St. Chad's Vicarage, Dunloe St., London E2, England. *Agent*—Anne McDernird, Curtis Brown Ltd., 162-168 Regent St., London W1R 5TA, England.

CAREER: Freelance academic researcher in Oxford, England, 1972-73; freelance journalist, writer, and lecturer, 1973—.

MEMBER: National Union of Journalists.

AWARDS, HONORS: Somerset Maugham Award, 1979, for *Daughter of Jerusalem.*

WRITINGS:

(With Zoe Fairbairns, Valerie Miner, Michele Roberts, and Michelene Wandor) *Tales I Tell My Mother* (fiction), Journeyman (London), 1978, South End (Boston), 1980.
Daughter of Jerusalem (novel), Blond & Briggs (London), 1978, published as *Languages of Love,* Doubleday (Garden City, NY), 1981.
(Author of introduction) Antonia White, *The Hound and the Falcon,* Virago (London), 1982.
A Map of the New Country: Women and Christianity (nonfiction), Routledge (London), 1983.
Telling Tales (fiction), Journeyman, 1983.
(Editor with Jo Garcia) *Walking on the Water,* Virago, 1983.
(With Aileen La Tourette) *Weddings and Funerals* (fiction), Brilliance, 1984.
Virgin Territory (novel), M. Joseph (London), 1984, Beaufort Books (New York City), 1986.
Vesta Tilley (biography), Virago, 1986.
(With M. Wandor) *Arky Types* (novel), Methuen (London), 1987.
A Book of Spells (fiction), M. Joseph, 1987.
Very Heaven: Looking Back at the 60s, Virago, 1988.
(Editor with Lisa Appignanesi) *The Rushdie File,* ICA, Fourth Estate (London), 1989, Syracuse University Press (Syracuse, NY), 1990.

Three Times Table, Chatto & Windus (London), 1990, Holt, 1991.

Women Fly When Men Aren't Watching (fiction), Virago, 1993.

Home Truths (novel), Chatto & Windus, 1993, published as *Ancestral Truths,* Holt (New York City), 1994.

Angel and Me: Short Stories for Holy Week, Mowbray (London), 1995.

A Big-Enough God: A Feminist's Search for a Joyful Theology, Holt, 1995.

Angel Maker: The Short Stories of Sara Maitland, Holt, 1996.

Also contributor to anthologies, including *Happy Unicorns,* edited by S. Purcell and L. Purves, Sidgwick & Jackson (London), 1970; *Introduction 5,* Faber, 1973; *Best of Bananas,* edited by Emma Tennant, Quartet, 1977; *Why Children,* Women's Press, 1979; *Fathers,* edited by U. Owen, Virago, 1983; and *Gender and Writing,* edited by Michelene Wandor, Pandora (London), 1983.

Also contributor of articles and stories to journals, including *Critical Quarterly, Listener, New Society, Time Out, Spare Rib, Guardian, City Limits, Bananas,* and *New Statesman.*

SIDELIGHTS: Critically praised for her sophisticated use of language and her well-grounded story lines, Sara Maitland presents, according to Laurie Muchnick in the *Village Voice Literary Supplement,* "a heightened, changeable reality in which religion, mythology, feminism, and chaos theory are stirred together in a witches' brew of weirdness and possibility." Often compared by critics with the work of British writer Angela Carter, Maitland's novels and stories are characterized by the exploration of the historic relationship between orthodox Christianity and female empowerment, as well as by magic. While Maitland is quick to depart from New Age mysticism, she explained to Muchnick the relationship between magic and the craft of fiction: "What I'm really interested in is what I think fiction can do, which is to make magical changes happen in people's lives. . . . All fiction, however social realist . . . is in fact part fantasy."

Maitland's first novel, *Daughter of Jerusalem* (published in the United States as *Languages of Love*) foreshadows her later works through its reliance on Old Testament narratives as a reflection of its modern female protagonist. Liz, a staunch feminist, secretly wishes to retain some elements of traditional feminin-

ity in her life. Her inability to conceive the child she so fervently desires prompts her to undergo invasive medical procedures; her physician's intimation that her barrenness is somehow psychosomatic angers her to the point that she joins a group of radical feminists in backing a pro-choice campaign during a public protest, despite the stand's conflict with her own religious convictions. Critic Susan Kennedy, writing in the *Times Literary Supplement,* deemed *Daughter of Jerusalem* an "extremely intelligent and enjoyable first novel."

Virgin Territory finds missionary nun Sister Anna devastated after learning that a fellow nun has been raped; her horrified reaction to the situation causes her to come to terms with her relationship with God as well as with her growing belief that she is a lesbian. *Three Times Table,* published in 1990, contrasts the lives of three successive generations: a seventy-something paleontologist named Rachel, Rachel's hippie daughter Phoebe, and Phoebe's fifteen-year-old daughter Maggie, whose existence in a fantasy world threatens to prohibit her maturation into womanhood. 1993's *Ancestral Truths* (published in England as *Home Truths*) focuses on another family; this time the seven Kerslake siblings, their assorted husbands, wives, and children, and their parents as the entire group vacations in the Scottish Highlands. "Maitland brilliantly conveys the dynamics of a large family," noted *Commonweal* reviewer Daria Donnelly; "in particular, the combination of love, exasperation, and jealousy that these adult brothers and sisters feel for one another and their parents."

In addition to novels, Maitland is the author of several volumes of short fiction, including *A Book of Spells* and *Women Fly When Men Aren't Watching.* Her nonfiction works include *A Map of the New Country: Women and Christianity,* a biography of British socialite Vesta Tilley, and *A Big-Enough God: A Feminist's Search for a Joyful Theology,* which *Commonweal* reviewer Luke Timothy Johnson called "well worth reading for its invitation to a fearless and joyful embrace of the world as God's gift and of human existence as the joyful celebration of that gift."

"I am a feminist, a socialist, a catholic Christian, a wife and a mother," Maitland once told *CA.* "This seems to produce enough conflicts to give me writing material for years to come. Writing both fiction and nonfiction is a policy now; I would like to find a form that would bring the two modes together as theology once did and as the Women's Movement now struggles toward."

BIOGRAPHICAL/CRITICAL SOURCES:

BOOKS

Contemporary Literary Criticism, Volume 49, Gale (Detroit), 1988.
Feminist Writers, St. James Press (Detroit), 1996.

PERIODICALS

American Book Review, July/August, 1985, pp. 13-14.
Commonweal, August 19, 1994, pp. 24-26; November 3, 1995, pp. 22-24.
New Statesman, March 4, 1983, p. 25; September 4, 1987, p. 29.
New York Times Book Review, March 13, 1994, p. 12.
Publishers Weekly, January 30, 1981, p. 62.
Spectator, April 14, 1990.
Times Literary Supplement, December 1, 1978, p. 1404; April 15, 1983.
Village Voice Literary Supplement, March, 1994, pp. 28-29.*

*   *   *

MALLESON, Lucy Beatrice 1899-1973
(Lucy Egerton, Anthony Gilbert, Sylvia Denys Hooke, J. Kilmeny Keith, Anne Meredith)

PERSONAL: Born February 15, 1899, in London, England; died December 9, 1973. *Education:*Educated in England. *Avocational interests:* Theatre-going, amateur dramatics, travel.

CAREER: Writer. Secretary for Red Cross, Ministry of Food, and Coal Association; worked as journalist in England.

MEMBER: Detection Club (founding member and general secretary).

AWARDS, HONORS: Second prize from *Ellery Queen's Mystery* contest, 1946, for short story, "You Can't Hang Twice."

WRITINGS:

UNDER PSEUDONYM ANTHONY GILBERT; MYSTERY NOVELS

The Tragedy at Freyne, Dial (New York City), 1927.
The Murder of Mrs. Davenport, Dial, 1928.

Death at Four Corners, Dial, 1929.
The Mystery of the Open Window, Gollancz (London), 1929, Dodd (New York City), 1930.
The Night of the Fog, Dodd, 1930.
The Case Against Andrew Fane, Dodd, 1931.
The Long Shadow, Collins (London), 1932.
The Body on the Beam: A Detective Story, Dodd, 1932.
The Musical Comedy Crime, Collins, 1933.
Death in Fancy Dress, Collins, 1933.
The Man in Button Boots, Collins, 1934, Holt (New York City), 1935.
An Old Lady Dies, Collins, 1934.
The Man Who Was Too Clever, Collins, 1935.
Courtier to Death, Collins, 1936.
Murder by Experts, Collins, 1936, Dial, 1937.
Courtier to Death, Collins, 1936, published as *The Dover Train Mystery,* Dial, 1936.
Murder Has No Tongue, Collins, 1937.
The Man Who Wasn't There, Collins, 1937.
Treason in My Breast, Collins, 1938.
The Bell of Death, Collins, 1939.
The Clock in the Hat Box, Collins, 1939, Arcadia House (New York City), 1943.
Dear Dead Woman, Collins, 1940, Arcadia House, 1942, published as *Death Takes a Redhead,* Arrow Editions (New York City), 1944.
She Vanished in the Dawn, Arcadia House, 1941, published as *The Vanishing Corpse,* Collins, 1941.
The Woman in Red, Collins, 1941, Smith & Durrell (New York City), 1943, published as *The Mystery of the Woman in Red,* Quinn (New York City), 1944.
Mystery in the Woodshed, Smith & Durrell, 1942 (published in England as *Something Nasty in the Woodshed,* Collins, 1942).
The Case of the Tea-Cosy's Aunt, Collins, 1942, published as *Death in the Blackout,* Smith & Durrell, 1943.
The Mouse Who Wouldn't Play Ball, Collins, 1943, published as *Thirty Days to Live,* Smith & Durrell, 1944.
A Spy for Mr. Crook, A. S. Barnes (New York City), 1944.
The Scarlet Button, Collins, 1944, Smith & Durrell, 1945.
He Came by Night, Collins, 1944, published as *Death at the Door,* Smith & Durrell, 1945.
Don't Open the Door!, Collins, 1945, published as *Death Lifts the Latch,* Smith & Durrell, 1946.
The Black Stage, Collins, 1945, A. S. Barnes, 1946, published as *Murder Cheats the Bride,* Bantam (New York City), 1948.

The Spinster's Secret, Collins, 1946, published as *By Hook or Crook,* A. S. Barnes, 1947.

Die in the Dark, Collins, 1947, published as *The Missing Widow,* A. S. Barnes, 1948.

Death in the Wrong Room, A. S. Barnes, 1947.

Lift Up the Lid, Collins, 1948, published as *The Innocent Bottle,* A. S. Barnes, 1949.

Death Knocks Three Times, Collins, 1949, Random House (New York City), 1950.

A Nice Cup of Tea, Collins, 1950, published as *The Wrong Body,* Random House, 1951.

Murder Comes Home, Collins, 1950, Random House, 1951.

Lady-Killer, Collins, 1951.

A Case for Mr. Crook, Random House, 1952, published as *Miss Pinnegar Disappears,* Collins, 1952.

Black Death, Random House, 1953, published as *Dark Death,* Pyramid (New York City), 1963 (published in England as *Footsteps behind Me,* Collins, 1953).

Death Won't Wait, Random House, 1954, published as *Snake in the Grass,* Collins, 1954.

A Question of Murder, Random House, 1955 (published in England as *Is She Dead Too?,* Collins, 1955).

Riddle of a Lady, Collins, 1956, Random House, 1957.

And Death Came Too, Random House, 1956.

Give Death a Name, Collins, 1957.

Death against the Clock, Random House, 1958.

Prelude to Murder, Random House, 1959 (published in England as *Third Crime Lucky,* Collins, 1959).

Death Casts a Long Shadow, Random House, 1959, published as *Death Takes a Wife,* Collins, 1959.

Out for the Kill, Random House, 1960.

After the Verdict, Random House, 1961, published as *She Shall Die,* Collins, 1961.

Uncertain Death, Collins, 1961, Random House, 1962.

No Dust in the Attic, Collins, 1962, Random House, 1963.

(Under pseudonyms Anthony Gilbert and Anne Meredith) *Up Goes the Donkey,* Hodder & Stoughton, 1962.

Ring for a Noose, Collins, 1963, Random House, 1964.

Knock, Knock, Who's There?, Collins, 1964, published as *The Voice,* Random House, 1965.

The Fingerprint, Collins, 1964, Random House, 1965.

Passenger to Nowhere, Collins, 1965, Random House, 1966.

The Looking Glass Murder, Collins, 1966, Random House, 1967.

The Visitor, Random House, 1967.

Murder Anonymous, Random House, 1968 (published in England as *Night Encounter,* Collins, 1968).

Missing from Her Home, Random House, 1969.

Mr. Crook Lifts the Mask, Random House, 1970 (published in England as *Death Wears a Mask,* Collins, 1970).

Tenant for the Tomb, Random House, 1971.

Murder's a Waiting Game, Random House, 1972.

A Nice Little Killing, Random House, 1974.

(With others) *Crime on the Coast, and No Flowers by Request,* Gollancz, 1984.

Also author of *The Mills of God,* 1969.

UNDER PSEUDONYM ANNE MEREDITH

Portrait of a Murderer (mystery), Gollancz, 1933, Reynal & Hitchcock (New York City), 1934.

The Coward, Gollancz, 1934.

The Gambler, Gollancz, 1937.

The Showman, Faber (London), 1938.

The Stranger, Faber, 1939.

The Adventurer, Faber, 1940.

Three-A-Penny (autobiography), Faber, 1940.

There's Always Tomorrow, Faber, 1941, published as *Home Is the Heart,* Howell, Soskin (New York City), 1942.

Mrs. Boot's Legacy: A Sketch for Three Female Characters, Samuel French (London), 1941.

The Family Man: A Victorian Novel, Howell, Soskin, 1942.

Curtain, Mr. Greatheart, Faber, 1943.

The Beautiful Miss Burroughes, Faber, 1945.

The Rich Woman, Random House, 1947.

The Sisters, Faber, 1948, Random House, 1949.

The Unknown Path, Random House, 1950 (published in England as *The Draper of Edgecumbe,* Faber, 1950).

A Fig for Virtue, Faber, 1951.

Call Back Yesterday, Faber, 1952.

The Innocent Bride, Hodder & Stoughton (London), 1954.

The Day of the Miracle, Hodder & Stoughton, 1955.

Impetuous Heart, Hodder & Stoughton, 1956.

Christine, Hodder & Stoughton, 1957.

A Man in the Family, Hodder & Stoughton, 1959.

The Wise Child, Hodder & Stoughton, 1960.

Up Goes the Donkey, Hodder & Stoughton, 1962.

UNDER PSEUDONYM SYLVIA DENYS HOOKE

Nettle Harvest, Chapman & Hall (London), 1927, Doubleday, Doran, 1928.

Old Stars for Sale, Chapman & Hall, 1928.
Aubrey Dene, Longmans, Green (London), 1930.
Strange Guest, Murray (London), 1932.

RADIO PLAYS

The Plain Woman, British Broadcasting Corp. (BBC), 1940.
Death at 6:30, BBC, 1940.
A Cavalier in Love, BBC, 1940.
The Bird of Passage, BBC, 1941.
There's Always Tomorrow, BBC, 1941.
Calling Mr. Brown, BBC, 1941.
He Came By Night, BBC, 1941.
The Adventurer, BBC, 1941.
Footprints, BBC, 1941.
Thirty Years Is a Long Time, BBC, 1941.
A Bird in a Cage, BBC, 1942.
His Professional Conscience, BBC, 1942.
Find the Lady, BBC, 1942.
The Home-Coming, BBC, 1944.
Mystery Man of New York, BBC, 1945.
Of Brides in Baths, BBC, 1945.
Full Circle, BBC, 1946.
Hard Luck Story, BBC, 1947.
The Sympathetic Table, BBC, 1948.
A Nice Cup of Tea, BBC, 1948.
Profitable Death, BBC, 1950.
After the Verdict, BBC, 1952.
Now You Can Sleep, BBC, 1952.
My Guess Would Be Murder, BBC, 1954.
I Love My Love with an "A", BBC, 1957.
No One Will Ever Know, BBC, 1960.
Black Death, BBC, 1960.
And Death Came Too, BBC, 1962.

OTHER

(Under pseudonym J. Kilmeny Keith) *The Man Who Was London* (novel), Collins, 1925.
(Under pseudonym J. Kilmeny Keith) *The Sword of Harlequin* (novel), Collins, 1927.
(Under pseudonym Lucy Egerton) *Lady at Large* (novel), Cassell (London), 1936.
(Under pseudonym Lucy Egerton) *Courage in Gold,* Cassell, 1938.

Work represented in anthologies, including: Davis Dresser, editor, *The Blond Cried Murder,* Walter J. Black, 1956; Lionel White, editor, *A Grave Undertaking,* Walter J. Black, 1961; Hillary Waugh, editor, *End of a Party,* Walter J. Black, 1965; Judson Pentecost Philips, editor, *Thursday's Folly,* W. J. Black, 1967. Contributor to *Punch* and other magazines.

ADAPTATIONS: Malleson's novel, *The Woman in Red,* written under the Gilbert pseudonym, was made into the motion picture *My Name Is Julia Ross* and released by Columbia Pictures in 1945.

SIDELIGHTS: Lucy Beatrice Malleson was best known as a mystery writer under her pseudonym Anthony Gilbert. Under the Gilbert name, she chronicled the adventures of Arthur G. Crook, an English lawyer who also solves murder mysteries. In an article for the *Dictionary of Literary Biography,* Mary Helen Becker called Crook "a coarse but lovable lawyer with a particular concern for the weak and helpless, who spends more time detecting than practicing law." Crook, according to Jane S. Bakerman in the *St. James Guide to Crime and Mystery Writers,* is "one of the most interesting fictional detectives yet to solve a case."

Malleson first became interested in crime stories when she saw John Willard's play, *The Cat and the Canary.* Her first successful mystery, *The Tragedy at Freyne,* was published in 1927 under the pseudonym Anthony Gilbert. A *Boston Transcript* critic asserted that "it is a very good tale. The characters are so interesting that you might read it for them alone, and the murder is softened so that you do not have to lie awake nights shuddering over it." A critic for the *New York Times* added that the book "is an unusually well told mystery tale."

The early Gilbert stories featured detective Scott Egerton, a rising young politician. Egerton appeared in, among others, *Body on the Beam, Mystery of the Open Window,* and *Night of the Fog.* Reviewing *Body on the Beam,* Isaac Anderson observed that "the story does not move as rapidly as some detective stories, but it has the merit of being logical and very human." A *Times Literary Supplement* critic proclaimed *Mystery of the Open Window* "a capital, if decidedly gruesome, story, told with a sense of style, an eye for character, and even the saving grace of a humorous touch here and there." Concerning *Night of the Fog,* a *Bookman* critic succinctly declared it "a clever, clean-cut mystery." Malleson also featured French detective M. Dupuy in two novels, *The Man in Button Boots* and *Courtier to Death.* Will Cuppy praised the plot of *The Man in Button Boots* as "ingenious," adding that Gilbert's "characters [are] amusing, and his tale readable enough for an off evening."

In 1936, Malleson discarded both Egerton and Dupuy in favor of the wily sleuth, Arthur G. Crook. A Cockney lawyer, Crook defends his clients with formidable skill and inevitably solves the mystery. He first appeared in *Murder by Experts,* a novel which Nicholas Blake ventured to pronounce as having "everything—atmosphere and colour, engaging chapter-headings, originality of plot, good dialogue, varied and convincing characters, a brilliant double twist at the end, and a general air of distinction." Becker said that this first Crook adventure was "long, complicated, and slow moving. . . . Crook himself is much less endearing than the irrepressible figure of the later cases."

Bakerman found that the Crook novels exhibited several praiseworthy traits: "These books . . . reveal that Gilbert is adroit at both the conventionally ordered mystery and the 'inverted' mystery in which the criminal is known from the outset and the suspense depends on the reader's concern lest the murderer succeed. Another of Gilbert's strengths is splendid development of supporting characters. . . . For skillful plotting, lively characterization, and clever action, then, Gilbert can be highly ranked among mystery writers, and for the creation of Arthur Crook, she cannot be faulted." Becker called the Arthur Crook mysteries "lively and delightful." Crook's speech, she wrote, "is colorful and common, filled with aphorisms, homespun philosophy, and slang; he protects the weak and helpless and outwits the establishment. Even her minor characters are individuals with personality, wit, and strength."

Under the pseudonym Anne Meredith, Malleson wrote inverted detective stories in which the murderer is known from the beginning of the book and is finally brought to justice at the end. The first such book was *Portrait of a Murderer.* Critics were impressed with Malleson's technique. A *New York Times* reviewer asserted that "the reader's knowledge of the murderer's identity does not in the least detract from his interest in the working out of the story." Sylva Norman concurred: "The book suffers nothing in suspense and excitement. Miss Meredith has fine judgment and distinction of thought and style." Most of the Meredith nonmysteries are set in Victorian England, and reviewers were generally impressed with Malleson's historical knowledge. Regarding *The Unknown Path,* Joyce Geary declared, "the historical side of things is . . . handled beautifully by Miss Meredith. . . . Her knowledge of the sociological background of Victorian England is most rewarding."

Becker concluded that Malleson was "a sort of quintessential English mystery writer. . . . A solid, professional writer of enjoyable mysteries."

BIOGRAPHICAL/CRITICAL SOURCES:

BOOKS

Dictionary of Literary Biography, Volume 77: *British Mystery Writers, 1920-1939,* Gale (Detroit), 1989.
St. James Guide to Crime and Mystery Writers, 4th edition, St. James Press (Detroit), 1996.

PERIODICALS

Bookman, November, 1930.
Boston Transcript, August 10, 1927; March 26, 1930.
Chicago Sun Book Week, March 9, 1947.
Manchester Guardian, March 4, 1941.
New York Herald Tribune, April 7, 1935; March 1, 1942; September 27, 1942.
New York Times, March 29, 1927; April 24, 1932; April 29, 1934; May 9, 1937; March 1, 1942; October 11, 1942; November 9, 1947; March 27, 1949; July 9, 1950.
San Francisco Chronicle, August 7, 1949.
Saturday Review of Literature, December 27, 1947.
Spectator, November 3, 1933; June 12, 1936; April 4, 1947.
Springfield Republican, January 10, 1943; November 11, 1945.
Times Literary Supplement, October 17, 1929; March 1, 1941; April 18, 1942; March 8, 1947.

OBITUARIES:

PERIODICALS

AB Bookman's Weekly, January 14, 1974.*

*   *   *

MANCHESTER, William (Raymond) 1922-

PERSONAL: Born April 1, 1922, in Attleboro, MA; son of William Raymond and Sallie (Thompson) Manchester; married Julia Brown Marshall, March 27, 1948; children: John Kennerly, Julie Thompson, Laurie. *Education:* Massachusetts State College (now University of Massachusetts), A.B., 1946; University of Missouri, A.M., 1947. *Avocational interests:* photography

ADDRESSES: Office—Wesleyan University, 329 Wesleyan Station, Middletown, CT 06457. *Agent*—

Don Congdon Associates, Inc., 156 Fifth Ave., Suite 625, New York, NY 10010.

CAREER: Daily Oklahoman, Oklahoma City, OK, reporter, 1945-46; *Baltimore Sun,* Baltimore, MD, reporter, Washington correspondent, and foreign correspondent in the Middle East, India, and Southeast Asia, 1947-54; Wesleyan University, Middletown, CT, managing editor of Wesleyan University Publications, 1955-64, member of university faculty, 1968-69, member of faculty of East College, 1968—, writer in residence, 1975—, adjunct professor of history, 1979—, professor emeritus of history, 1992—. Friends of the University of Massachusetts Library, president of board of trustees, 1970-72, trustee, 1970-74. *Military service:* U.S. Marine Corps, 1942-45; became sergeant; awarded Purple Heart.

MEMBER: PEN, American Historical Association, Society of American Historians, Authors Guild, Authors League of America, Williams Club, Century Club.

AWARDS, HONORS: Guggenheim fellow, 1959-60; Wesleyan Center for Advanced Studies, fellow, 1959-60; L.H.D., University of Massachusetts, 1965; Prix Dag Hammarskjoeld au merite litteraire, 1967; Overseas Press Club citation for best book on foreign affairs, 1968; University of Missouri honor award for distinguished service in journalism, 1969; Connecticut Book Award, 1975; L.H.D., University of New Haven, 1979; National Book Award nomination, 1980, for *American Caesar: Douglas MacArthur, 1880-1964;* ALA Notable Book citation, 1980, for *Goodbye, Darkness: A Memoir of the Pacific War;* President's Cabinet Award, University of Detroit, 1981; Frederick S. Troy Award, University of Massachusetts, 1981; McConnaughty Award, Wesleyan University, 1981; *Los Angeles Times* Biography Prize nomination, 1983, and Union League/Abraham Lincoln Literary Award, 1984, both for *The Last Lion: Winston Spencer Churchill, Volume 1: Visions of Glory: 1874-1932;* Connecticut Bar Association Distinguished Public Service Award, 1985; D. Litt., University of Richmond, 1988; L.H.D., Russell Sage College, 1990; Pierson College, Yale University, fellow, 1992; Sarah Joseph Hale Award, 1993.

WRITINGS:

Disturber of the Peace: The Life of H. L. Mencken (originally serialized in *Harper's,* July-August, 1950), Harper (New York City), 1951, second

edition edited by Stephen B. Oates and Paul Mariani, University of Massachusetts Press (Amherst), 1986.

The City of Anger (novel), Ballantine (New York City), 1953, reprinted, Little, Brown (Boston), 1987.

Shadow of the Monsoon (novel), Doubleday (New York City), 1956.

Beard the Lion (novel), Morrow (New York City), 1958.

A Rockefeller Family Portrait: From John D. to Nelson, Little, Brown, 1959.

(Contributor) Bredemier and Toby, editors, *Social Problems in America,* Wiley (New York City), 1960.

The Long Gainer: A Novel, Little, Brown, 1961.

Portrait of a President: John F. Kennedy in Profile, Little, Brown, 1962, second edition, 1967.

(Contributor) Don Congdon, editor, *Combat World War I,* Dial (New York City), 1964.

(Contributor) Poyntz Tyler, *Securities Exchanges and the SEC,* Wilson (Bronx, NY), 1965.

The Death of a President: November 20-November 25, 1963 (originally serialized in *Look,* January 24-March 7, 1967; Book-of-the-Month Club selection), Harper, 1967, published with revised introduction, Arbor House (New York City), 1985, published with new addition by the author, Harper, 1988.

The Arms of Krupp, 1587-1968 (originally serialized in *Holiday,* November, 1964-February, 1965; Literary Guild selection), Little, Brown, 1968.

The Glory and the Dream: A Narrative History of America, 1932-1972 (Literary Guild selection), Little, Brown, 1974, reprinted, Bantam (New York City), 1989.

Controversy and Other Essays in Journalism, Little, Brown, 1976.

American Caesar: Douglas MacArthur, 1880-1964 (Book-of-the-Month Club selection), Little, Brown, 1978.

Goodbye, Darkness: A Memoir of the Pacific War (Book-of-the-Month Club selection), Little, Brown, 1980.

One Brief Shining Moment: Remembering Kennedy (Book-of-the-Month Club selection), Little, Brown, 1983.

The Last Lion: Winston Spencer Churchill, Volume 1: Visions of Glory: 1874-1932 (Book-of-the-Month Club selection), Little, Brown, 1983.

(Contributor) *A Sense of History: The Best Writing from the Pages of American Heritage,* American Heritage/Houghton (New York City/Boston), 1985.

The Last Lion: Winston Spencer Churchill, Volume 2: Alone: 1932-1940 (Book-of-the-Month Club selection), Little, Brown, 1987.

(Contributor) Annie Dillard and Robert Atwan, editors, *Best American Essays 1988,* Ticknor & Fields (New York City), 1988.

The Last Lion: Winston Spencer Churchill, Volume 3: Defender of the Realm: 1940-1965, Little, Brown, 1988.

(Author of text) *In Our Time: The World as Seen by the Photographers of Magnum,* Norton (New York City), 1989.

A World Lit Only by Fire: The Medieval Mind and the Renaissance: Portrait of an Age, Little, Brown, 1992.

Also author of introduction for *Thimblerigger: The Law v. Governor Marvin Mandel.* Contributor to *Encyclopaedia Britannica.* Contributor to *Atlantic, Harper's, Reporter, Saturday Review, Holiday, Nation, Esquire,* and *Saturday Evening Post.*

ADAPTATIONS: "The City of Anger," adapted from Manchester's novel of the same title, aired on NBC-TV in 1955. "American Caesar," a television miniseries based on Manchester's biography of Douglas MacArthur, was narrated by John Huston, produced by John McGreevey, aired on the Ted Turner cable network in 1985, and is presently available on videocassette.

SIDELIGHTS: William Manchester's oeuvre ranges from structured novels to massive biographies. But his books, the author tells Stefan Kanfer of *People* magazine, all share one common theme—the study of power: "What exactly is power? Where are its roots? How do some people get it and others miss it entirely?" Using what Kanfer calls the "Manchester trademarks: unflagging energy, hundreds of interviews, monuments of detail and pounds of manuscript," Manchester, states Kenneth Atchity in the *Los Angeles Times,* has made himself "the [James] Michener of biographers."

Manchester's first book focused on the power of words. He was first attracted to the writings of H. L. Mencken, the famous critic and literary curmudgeon, while an undergraduate in college. After serving with the Marines in World War II, Manchester entered the graduate school of the University of Missouri and completed a thesis on Mencken. The critic read the thesis, authorized Manchester's proposed biography, and invited the young writer to join the staff of the Baltimore *Evening Sun,* Mencken's newspaper.

Disturber of the Peace: The Life of H. L. Mencken helped establish Manchester's reputation as a talented writer. Although some reviewers felt that Manchester's devotion to Mencken interfered with the story, many praised the young biographer's effort. *Saturday Review* critic Charles Angoff declares that *Disturber of the Peace* "is probably the most fully documented" of all Mencken studies and added that some of Manchester's remarks "display a refreshing critical independence." George Genzmer, writing in *Nation,* calls the book "a generally well-proportioned narrative that . . . portrays [Mencken's] charm, vigor, and humor with notable effect." Manchester, Genzmer continues, "is slapdash in handling some details and in brushing in the background, but, such matters aside, the story is authentic."

Manchester then turned to fiction, and wrote four novels over the next few years. Many of these deal with the use and abuse of power and are based on Manchester's reporting experiences; for instance, *The City of Anger* traces corruption in an East Coast city very much like Baltimore, while *The Long Gainer* examines an academic and political scandal resembling one that "rocked the University of Maryland some years ago," reports Wirt Williams in the *New York Times Book Review. Beard the Lion* is a thriller involving politics in the Near East in the late 1950s, while *Shadow of the Monsoon* tells of post-Raj India, where Manchester served as a foreign correspondent.

Although they were generally favorably received, Manchester's novels are perhaps most significant because of the way they prefigure stylistic elements of his later nonfiction. The publisher's note that introduces the 1985 edition of *The City of Anger* explains, "The reviewers of each [of Manchester's four novels] commented on his skillful command of detail—accurate detail, for his eye has always been a lens, not a prism." "His use of detail is both Manchester's strength and his weakness," the publisher's note continues. "Those who dislike it, particularly in his nonfiction, criticize him as a collector of trivia. But to Manchester the skills of narration grow out of the mastery of detail. It is a matter of taste."

Manchester returned to biography in 1959 with *A Rockefeller Family Portrait: From John D. to Nelson,* and in 1962 with *Portrait of a President: John F. Kennedy in Profile.* Although different in many ways, the two books share several features: both were originally published as magazine articles, both reiterate Manchester's interest in power in their subjects (the family of then-governor Nelson Rockefeller of New

York and then-President Kennedy), and critics gave both mixed reviews while recognizing that the two volumes were highly approving of their subjects. "Those who are looking for material to criticize the Rockefeller family or its individual members," writes Leo Egan in the *New York Times* about *A Rockefeller Family Portrait,* "would be well advised to look somewhere else." Tom Wicker remarks in the *New York Times Book Review,* that *Portrait of a President* "is what its title says it is—a portrait, not dishonest, but smitten, one in which the dazzled artist has gazed upon the subject with loving eyes and found redeeming beauty in his every flaw."

Yet several critics admit that Manchester's depictions of the Rockefellers and of Kennedy are appealing; in *Saturday Review,* Cleveland Amory calls *A Rockefeller Family Portrait* "skillfully and carefully" composed, and adds, "At least the first three-quarters of this book is as capably written as anything that has passed this writer's desk in some time." "In sum," declares G. W. Johnson in the *New Republic,* "what Manchester gives us [in *Portrait of a President*] is a picture of a brave, honorable and resolute man struggling with problems that may well be beyond his, or any human capacity to solve."

It was partly on the basis of *Portrait of a President* that, early in 1964, Jacqueline Kennedy asked Manchester to write an account of President Kennedy's assassination, offering him exclusive interviews with family members. Manchester had met Kennedy shortly after World War II when both of them were disabled veterans living in Boston, and he had since become a family friend. He agreed to write the book, and signed an agreement with Senator Robert Kennedy providing that most of the volume's royalties would go to the new Kennedy Memorial Library, and that Senator Kennedy and the President's widow would have the right to review the manuscript. When Manchester finished the book after two years of exhaustive research and writing, however, both Kennedys felt unable to read it. They sent representatives to review the manuscript instead, and, after some changes, the representatives unanimously approved publication of *The Death of a President: November 20-November 25, 1963.*

Controversy followed close behind the book's approval. After *Look* magazine made a record-setting bid of $665,000 for serialization rights, Jacqueline Kennedy, on the advice of several associates, withdrew her permission to publish the story. Her action was based on fears that Manchester's representation of Johnson's government would damage Senator Kennedy's presidential aspirations in 1968. However, both Manchester's publishers, *Look* and Harper & Row, refused to stop publication and, in December of 1966, representatives of the Kennedy family filed suit. "We *couldn't* stop," Manchester told Gale. "Contracts had been signed in 17 countries, [and] we (Bobby [Kennedy] and me) would have been sued into penury." The matter was settled out of court when the publishers' representatives persuaded Mrs. Kennedy to read the book for herself, and, after superficial changes, *The Death of a President* went to press early in 1967.

Although much of the media attention the book received centered on Mrs. Kennedy's suit rather than on its substance, reviewers noted several important characteristics of the work: Manchester's massive accumulation of facts, and his subjective treatment of the subject. "Had the Kennedy family merely wanted to set the record straight," states Margaret L. Coit in *Saturday Review,* "they should have approached some cut-and-dried academician who would have marshaled the facts with cold objectivity. Instead, their choice fell upon a highly emotional and subjective writer who identified himself with John F. Kennedy, his time, and his generation. They should have foreseen that the facts would not remain inert under his fingers, that the whole horror would blaze forth again with compounded intensity."

Manchester himself lends credibility to this interpretation of his work. In the introduction to the 1985 edition of *The Death of a President,* he writes: "Here . . . I have attempted to lead the reader back through historical events by recreating the sense of immediacy people felt at the time, so that he sees, feels, and hears what was seen, felt, and heard—mourns, rejoices, weeps, or loves with mourners, rejoicers, weepers, or lovers long since vanished: figures whose present has become our past." Finally, Manchester concludes, "*The Death of a President* was not written for Jackie or any of the others. I wrote it for the one Kennedy I had known well and deeply loved, the splendid man who had been cruelly slain at 12:30 p.m. Texas time on Friday, November 22, 1963."

After the furor surrounding *The Death of a President* died down, Manchester returned to the work he had abandoned for the Kennedy project: a history of the Krupp family, chief of the steel and munitions makers in Germany until 1967. Although Manchester's investigation begins in Renaissance Germany, the major portion of his study concentrates on the Krupps' role in Hitler's Third Reich. Alfried Krupp, who ran the business during the Second World War, was convicted at the Nuremburg trials of war crimes, including the exploitation of citizens of occupied countries and Jews as slave labor; he received a sentence of twelve years' imprisonment and the confiscation of all his property. However, Alfried served only three years of his term before the American High Commissioner in Germany released him and restored his property to him.

Many reviewers were impressed by the scope of *The Arms of Krupp.* "In this monumental study," declares *Saturday Review* commentator Henry C. Wolfe, "William Manchester has written a melodramatic, often macabre account of the Krupp empire that fascinates from beginning to ironical end." Christopher Lehmann-Haupt, writing in the *New York Times,* comments, "As research alone, the book is impressive. Manchester has unearthed material not known to the public before, and pieced it together in patterns that were not seen before." "The Krupps story, as Mr. Manchester tells it," states Geoffrey Barraclough in the *New York Review of Books,* "is a paradigm of German history."

Manchester chose an even broader range for his next book, *The Glory and the Dream: A Narrative History of America, 1932-1972.* Manchester follows the generation that grew up during the Depression, chronicling its triumphs and tragedies, telling of its heroes and struggles: the Second World War, the loss of FDR, General MacArthur's resignation, Frank Sinatra and the Beatles, and the Bomb. Writing in the *New York Times Book Review,* Alfred Kazin calls *The Glory and the Dream* a "fluent, likeable, can't-put-it-down narrative history of America" that is "popular history in our special tradition of literary merchandising." "Reading Manchester," Kazin continues, "you run with the Bonus Army, lift up your chin like Roosevelt, put up the flag at Iwo Jima, and nervously dismiss MacArthur. You are against Communism and the Cold War. You participate!" "There is no fiction that can compare with good, gossipy, anecdotal history—the 'inside story' of who said or did what in moments of great tension or crisis," reports Anatole Broyard in the *New York Times.* "I think you ought to read this history and weep, read it and laugh, read it and make sure you don't repeat it."

The biography *American Caesar: Douglas MacArthur, 1880-1964,* Manchester's next book, brought wide acclaim from critics for its authoritative evocation of one of the most powerful and controversial figures in modern American history. Although MacArthur's military expertise defeated the Japanese in World War II's South Pacific theater with a minimum of casualties, his repeated disobedience of orders forced President Truman to remove him from command during the Korean War. "The personality and charisma of MacArthur are so successfully recreated in Manchester's biography that it is easy to forget that the book, unlike the man, had an author," remarks Orville Schell in *Saturday Review.* "This is to Manchester's credit. . . . [He] has written a thorough and spellbinding book. It is a dramatic chronicle of one of America's last epic heroes." Manchester's *American Caesar* "is exquisitely ambivalent," declares Broyard in the *New York Times,* "not so much torn as balanced between the two MacArthurs, whom he calls 'noble and ignoble, arrogant and shy, the best of men and the worst of men, the most protean, most ridiculous, and most sublime.'"

The author's own South Pacific experiences as a sergeant of Marines in World War II are the subject of *Goodbye, Darkness: A Memoir of the Pacific War.* Recalling his combat service, Manchester wonders what made his lightly wounded younger self leave the hospital and return to his unit, only to receive an almost fatal injury. He believes that his gesture was partly an act of solidarity with his men, partly a desire to uphold family tradition, and partly a pride of country—feelings that, Manchester believes, have atrophied in post-war America. While not all critics agree with the author's analysis of the situation, many extol the power of his book. "Those sections of the book that are about the war itself are very well done," declares Broyard in the *New York Times.* "Manchester's combat writing is one of his book's strengths and stands comparison with the best" of the genre, adds *New York Times Book Review* contributor Ted Morgan. Clay Blair, writing in the *Chicago Tribune Book World,* states, "The reviewer is hard put to describe this intelligent, beautifully crafted but complicated work in a nutshell."

Manchester returned to biography with his three-volume work examining the life of another important figure of the Second World War, Winston Churchill. The first two volumes of the biography *The Last Lion: Winston Spencer Churchill* trace Churchill's personal and political career from his early years to the time he became Prime Minister of Great Britain, while the final volume details Churchill's life during World War II, his rocky post-war political career, and the years leading up to his death in 1965. Since Manchester's volumes have been preceded by many other studies, including Martin Gilbert's official Churchill biography, which runs to more than nine million words in length, some reviewers, in the words of *New York Review of Books* contributor Norman Stone, "simply do not see any need for Manchester's book[s]." And Kenneth Harris, reviewing the second volume of the work for the *New York Times Book Review,* avers that the accuracy of Manchester's work pales in comparison to Gilbert's. Harris states, "So long as Mr. Manchester follows or parallels the trail laid down by the definitive Gilbert biography, his history is safe. When he explores on his own, it is sometimes at risk."

Others, however, recognize valuable elements in the author's work that sets his version of the Churchill epic apart from all others. Robert Conot writes in the *Chicago Tribune Book World* that "Churchill and Manchester were clearly made for each other." Manchester's "accumulated merits, of scrupulous research, sustained narrative lucidity, . . . [and] unabashed inquisitiveness, seem to me to outweigh most of the errors—of judgment, mainly—that [he] can be charged with," declares Alistair Cooke in the *New Yorker.* Reviewing the work's second volume in *Time,* Gerald Clarke notes that the work is "told with skill and vivid anecdotes." Finally, Cooke concludes, Manchester is able "to introduce us, by way of new and dramatic emphases, to many startling things we thought we knew."

Manchester turned his attention to earlier periods in European history with *A World Lit Only by Fire: The Medieval Mind and the Renaissance: Portrait of an Age.* Characteristically unafraid to draw strong conclusions, Manchester in this work bemoans the lack of civilization during the medieval age, a state he attributes in part to the change-resistant Catholic Church. Some reviewers were unsparing in their criticism of the work's accuracy. Norman F. Cantor, commenting in the *Washington Post Book World,* faults Manchester for an "extremely shallow" interpretation of the intellectual history of the Renaissance and a bias against the Catholic Church. "It is distressing to think that this anti-Christian diatribe, reviving the wildest and most ignorant 19th-century polemics against the Catholic Church, will with the publisher's heavy promotion make its way into thousands of middle-class households and school libraries." However, an *Observer* critic called the book "lively" and commended Manchester for telling a wide-ranging narrative of the times.

BIOGRAPHICAL/CRITICAL SOURCES:

BOOKS

Authors in the News, Volume 1, Gale (Detroit), 1976.
Bestsellers 89, Issue 2, Gale, 1989.
Corry, John, *The Manchester Affair,* Putnam (New York City), 1967.
Manchester, William, *The City of Anger* (novel), Ballantine, 1953, reprinted, Little, Brown, 1985.
Manchester, *The Death of a President: November 20-November 25, 1963,* revised edition, Arbor House, 1985.
Manchester, *In Our Time: The World as Seen by Magnum Photographers,* Norton, 1989.
Manchester, *A World Lit Only by Fire: The Medieval Mind and the Renaissance: Portrait of an Age,* Little, Brown, 1992.
Something about the Author, Gale, Volume 65.

PERIODICALS

Americana, March-April, 1990.
Atlantic, May, 1967.
Boston Sunday Globe, October 23, 1988.
Chicago Tribune Book World, September 28, 1980; May 15, 1983; November 20, 1983.
Detroit Free Press, January 1, 1989.
Detroit News, June 26, 1983.
Forbes, November 20, 1995.
Kirkus Reviews, March 15, 1992.
Los Angeles Times, November 6, 1983.
Los Angeles Times Book Review, May 8, 1983; November 27, 1983; December 11, 1988.
Nation, April 14, 1951; September 19, 1959; April 17, 1967.
National Review, May 30, 1967; January 27, 1989.
New Republic, October 8, 1962; April 22, 1967.
Newsday, September 18, 1988; October 2, 1988.
New Statesman, April 21, 1967.
Newsweek, November 25, 1974; September 11, 1978; December 12, 1988.
New Yorker, January 20, 1951; April 8, 1967; August 22, 1983.
New York Herald Tribune Book Review, January 7, 1951; July 19, 1953; August 2, 1959.
New York Review of Books, April 20, 1967; March 27, 1969; October 12, 1978; January 22, 1981; November 10, 1983.
New York Times, January 14, 1951; July 13, 1953; April 8, 1956; August 9, 1959; April 3, 1967; December 6, 1968; November 15, 1974; September 20, 1978; September 17, 1980; May 25, 1983.

New York Times Book Review, September 10, 1961; September 30, 1962; April 9, 1967; November 24, 1968; November 17, 1974; August 31, 1980; June 5, 1983; November 27, 1988.

New York Times Magazine, June 14, 1987.

Observer, March 20, 1994.

People, November 27, 1978.

Saturday Review, July 11, 1959; January 21, 1967; April 15, 1967; December 21, 1968; January 11, 1975; October 14, 1978.

Saturday Review of Literature, January 6, 1951.

Spectator, December 16, 1989.

Time, January 8, 1951; December 20, 1968; November 18, 174; September11, 1978; October 31, 1988.

Times (London), November 24, 1988.

Times Literary Supplement, December 14, 1967; February 20, 1969; August 19, 1983.

Tribune Books (Chicago), September 18, 1988; December 3, 1989; August 15, 1993.

U.S. News & World Report, October 25, 1993.

Washington Post Book World, October 30, 1983; November 10, 1985; October 16, 1988; May 3, 1992.

*   *   *

MANDELA, Nelson R(olihlahla) 1918--

PERSONAL: Born 1918 in Umtata, Transkei, South Africa; son of Henry Mandela (a Tembu tribal chief); married Edith Ntoko (a nurse; divorced); married Nomzamo Winnie Madikileza (a social worker and political activist; divorced), June 14, 1958; children: (first marriage) Makgatho, Thembi (deceased), Makaziwe Phumla Mandela; (second marriage) Zenani (married to Prince Thumbumuzi Dhlamini of Swaziland), Zindziswa. *Education:* Attended University College of Fort Hare and Witwatersrand University; University of South Africa, law degree, 1942.

CAREER: Mandela & Tambo law firm, Johannesburg, South Africa, partner, 1952-c. 1960; political organizer and leader of the African National Congress (ANC), Johannesburg, South Africa, 1944—, held successive posts as secretary and president of the Congress Youth League, deputy national president of the ANC, and commander of the Umkonto we Sizwe ("Spear of the Nation") paramilitary organization; sentenced to five years in prison for inciting Africans to strike and for leaving South Africa without a valid travel document, 1962; sentenced to life imprison-

ment for sabotage and treason, 1964; incarcerated in various penal institutions, including Robben Island and Pollsmoor prisons, South Africa, 1962-90. President of African National Congress, 1991—; President of South Africa, 1994—.

AWARDS, HONORS: Honorary doctor of law degrees from the National University of Lesotho, 1979, and City College of the City University of New York, 1983; Jawaharlal Nehru Award for International Understanding from the government of India, 1980; Bruno Kreisky Prize for Human Rights from the government of Austria, 1981; named honorary citizen of Glasgow, 1981, and Rome, 1983; Simon Bolivar International Prize from UNESCO, 1983; Litt. D University of Calcutta, 1986; nominated for 1987 Nobel Peace Prize; Human Rights Prize, European Parliament, 1988; Gaddafi International Prize for Human Rights, 1989; L.L.B., University of South Africa, 1989; Human Rights Award, American Jewish Committee, 1993; Nobel Peace Prize, 1993.

WRITINGS:

NONFICTION

No Easy Walk to Freedom, Basic Books, 1965.

Nelson Mandela Speaks, African National Congress Publicity and Information Bureau (London), c. 1970.

The Struggle Is My Life, International Defence and Aid Fund (London), 1978, revised and updated edition, Pathfinder Press, 1986, further revised and updated edition published as *Nelson Mandela: The Struggle Is My Life: His Speeches and Writings Brought Together with Historical Documents and Accounts of Mandela in Prison by Fellowprisoners,* International Defence and Aid Fund, 1990.

Nelson Mandela, Symbol of Resistance and Hope for a Free South Africa: Selected Speeches since His Release, edited by E. S. Reddy, Sterling, 1990.

Nelson Mandela, Speeches 1990: "Intensify the Struggle to Abolish Apartheid," edited by Greg McCartan, photographs by Margrethe Siem, Pathfinder Press, 1990.

(With Fidel Castro) *How Far We Slaves Have Come! South Africa and Cuba in Today's World,* Pathfinder Press, 1991.

A Better Life for All: Working Together for Jobs, Peace, and Freedom, ANC Department of Information and Publicity, 1994.

Long Walk to Freedom: The Autobiography of Nelson Mandela, Little Brown, 1994.

Nelson Mandela: The Struggle is My Life: His Speeches and Writings Brought Together with Historical Documents and accounts of Mandela in Prison by Fellow-Prisoners, Mayibuye Books, 1994.

OTHER

Contributor of articles to the South African political journal *Liberation,* 1953-59; author of introduction to *Oliver Tambo Speaks: Preparing for Power,* Braziller, 1988.

SIDELIGHTS: Nelson Mandela has been called both "the world's most famous political prisoner" and "South Africa's Great Black Hope," by journalist Tom Mathews in *Newsweek.* A leader of the banned African National Congress (ANC) insurgent movement during the 1950s and 60s, Mandela had been jailed by white governments for a quarter of a century for his efforts to enfranchise his fellow blacks. Through his leadership and personal sacrifices, Mandela has come to symbolize the struggle against apartheid, the system of enforced racial inequality that denied political rights to South Africa's black majority. Mandela's release from prison in February, 1990, was followed by a triumphant world tour that included eight major cities in the United States. Strong admiration for the former political prisoner provided a common bond for many Americans who were at odds over how to defeat racial injustice. "No leader since the Reverend Martin Luther King, Jr., has brought together such a diverse coalition in the fight against racial injustice," noted a writer for *Time.* After his release, Mandela engaged in negotiations on behalf of the ANC with then-South African president F. W. de Klerk over a settlement of power that resulted in democratic-styled elections. In these elections, held in 1994, Mandela was elected President of South Africa, completing his astonishing rise to power after decades of imprisonment.

Mandela is descended from Xhosa-speaking tribal chieftains from the Transkei region of South Africa. He left his ancestral home at a young age to avoid an arranged marriage and pursued a professional career in the commercial capital of Johannesburg. Obtaining his law degree from the University of South Africa in 1942, Mandela joined the ANC two years later at the age of twenty-six and helped found the Congress Youth League (CYL) with Walter Sisulu, Oliver Tambo, and others. With Mandela as its secretary, the CYL urged its parent organization, the ANC, to abandon the strictly constitutional approach to reform that it had fruitlessly pursued with successive white minority governments since its founding in 1912 in favor of a more militant and confrontational strategy.

Under strong youth pressure, the ANC adopted a new program of action in 1949 that recognized such non-violent—but sometimes illegal—tactics as electoral boycotts, "stay-at-homes" (general strikes), student demonstrations, and civil disobedience. In June, 1952, Mandela mounted the first major test of the new ANC program by organizing the Defiance Against Unjust Laws campaign, a coordinated civil disobedience of six selected apartheid laws by a multiracial group of some eighty-six hundred volunteers. The government's violent response to the Defiance Campaign generated a backlash of popular support for the ANC that helped thrust Nelson Mandela to national prominence; it also brought him a nine-month suspended jail sentence, a two-year government "banning" order that confined him to Johannesburg and prohibited him from attending public gatherings, and an order to resign his ANC leadership posts as deputy president of the national organization, president of the Transvaal branch, and president of the CYL. Mandela refused to do so, and as a result he was obliged to conduct most of his political organizing work under the cover of his Johannesburg law partnership with Oliver Tambo and to limit his public profile to writing articles for the pro-ANC journal *Liberation.*

In December, 1956, following a year of ANC-led mass protests against the Nationalists' proposal to create seven tiny tribal "homelands" in which to segregate South Africa's black population, the government brought charges against Mandela and 155 other anti-apartheid leaders under anti-Communist and treason statutes. During most of the four-and-one-half years that the "Treason Trial" lasted, Mandela remained free on bail, continuing to work at his law office during the evenings and discreetly engaging in political activities within the limitations of a new five-year banning order leveled on him in February, 1956.

In March of 1960, an action occurred that marked a historical watershed in the struggle for black rights in South Africa. Responding to a demonstration against "pass laws," which required black South Africans to carry government identification documents, the police in the Johannesburg suburb of Sharpeville turned their weapons on a group of unarmed protesters, killing sixty-nine people. The massacre sparked a wave of angry new protests and public pass-book burnings, to which Pretoria (the seat of the South African government) responded by declaring a state of national emergency. The government banned the ANC and PAC, and detained some eighteen hundred political activists without charges, including Mandela and the other "Treason Trial" defendants. This crackdown prompted the trial lawyers to withdraw from the case, declaring that the emergency restrictions prevented them from mounting an effective defense, and left Mandela, Duma Nokwe, Walter Sisulu, and several others to represent their sizable group of ANC leaders.

As an advocate for his group, Mandela distinguished himself with his legal ability and eloquent statements of the ANC's political and social philosophy. He defended the 1949 Programme of Action and the Defiance Campaign as necessary disruptive tactics when the government was indifferent to legal pressure; he also sought to assuage white fears of a black political takeover by insisting that the ANC's form of nationalism recognized the right of all South African racial groups to enjoy political freedom and nondiscrimination together in the same country. In a unique legal victory for South African black activists, the trial judge acquitted all the defendants for insufficient evidence in March, 1961, finding that the ANC did not have a policy of violence.

Among those anxiously awaiting the verdict was Nomzamo Winnie Madikileza, who had married Mandela during the early stages of the trial. The government's ban of the ANC meant an end to any normal home life for the Mandelas, however. Immediately after his release, Mandela went underground to avoid new government banning orders. He surfaced in late March to deliver the keynote speech at the All-In African Conference held in Pietermaritzburg, which had been organized by the ANC and other opposition political organizations to address the Nationalists' plan to declare a racialist South African republic in May of that year. The All-In Conference opposed this proposal with a demand that the government hold elections for a fully representative national convention empowered to draft a new and democratic constitution for all South Africans. Meeting no response to the assembly's demands from the H. F. Verwoerd government, Mandela helped organize a three-day general strike for the end of May to press for the convention. Verwoerd's security forces mobilized heavily against the strike by suspending civil liberties, making massive preemptive arrests, and deploying heavy military equipment, which succeeded in limiting public support for the action (although hundreds of thousands of Africans nationwide still stayed away from work).

Facing arrest, Mandela once again disappeared underground, this time for seventeen months, assuming numerous disguises in a cat-and-mouse game with the police during which he became popularly known as the "Black Pimpernel." The ANC leader was finally captured disguised as a chauffeur in the province of Natal by police acting on an informer's tip in August, 1962. Brought to trial in October on charges of inciting Africans to strike and leaving the country without a valid travel document, Mandela turned his defense into an indictment of the apartheid system. In an eloquent statement to the presiding judge, the ANC leader rejected the right of the court to hear the case on the grounds that—as a black man—he could not be given a fair trial under a judicial system intended to enforce white domination, and, furthermore, that he considered himself neither legally nor morally bound to obey laws created by a parliament in which he had no representation. Despite his impressive courtroom performance, Mandela was convicted of both charges and sentenced to five years in prison.

Unknown to the authorities at the time of his trial, Mandela and other ANC leaders had reluctantly decided to launch an underground paramilitary movement in 1961 for the first time in the ANC's history. In November of 1961, Mandela helped organize and assumed command of the Umkonto we Sizwe ("Spear of the Nation") guerrilla organization and began planning a sabotage campaign directed against government installations and the economic infrastructure. Umkonto's first military action occurred on December 16, 1961, when the organization simultaneously attacked government buildings in Johannesburg, Port Elizabeth, and Durban. The group went on to engage in many more acts of sabotage over the next year while Mandela traveled surreptitiously to England, Ethiopia, Algeria, and other African countries to meet political leaders, seek arms for the movement, and undergo military training.

Mandela's role in leading Umkonto came to light in June, 1963, when police raided the ANC's underground headquarters in the Johannesburg suburb of Rivonia and discovered documents relating to the armed movement. Nine top ANC leaders were arrested and brought to trial in early 1964 on charges of committing sabotage and conspiring to overthrow the government by revolution with the help of foreign troops. Mandela once again conducted his own defense, using the courtroom as a platform to explain and justify the ANC's turn to armed struggle and to condemn the apartheid regime. Mandela declared at the trial, "It would be unrealistic and wrong for African leaders to continue preaching peace and non-violence at a time when the Government met our peaceful demands with force." He fully acknowledged helping to found Umkonto and planning acts of sabotage, but he denied the government's contention that the ANC and Umkonto intended to subject the anti-apartheid struggle to revolutionary control, either foreign or domestic.

While he acknowledged being strongly influenced by Marxist thought, Mandela denied ever having been a member of the Communist party, insisting that he held a deep and abiding admiration for Western legal and political institutions and wished to "borrow the best from both East and West" to reshape South African society. As elaborated in the ANC's Freedom Charter (a 1955 manifesto that Mandela helped to draft that remains the basic statement of the group's political purpose), the ANC looked forward to a democratic, pluralist society with certain mildly socialistic reforms—including land redistribution, nationalization of the country's mines, and a progressive tax and incomes policy—intended to dilute the economic power of the white minority and raise the country's black majority out of poverty.

Mandela's trial ended in June, 1964, when he and eight other defendants were convicted of sabotage and treason and sentenced to life imprisonment. Confined to the Robben Island fortress for political prisoners seven miles offshore from Cape Town, the ANC leaders were kept rigidly isolated from the outside world. They were denied access to radio, television, and newspapers, and prohibited from publishing articles, giving public interviews, or even discussing politics with visitors. All Mandela's past speeches and published works were banned, and merely possessing his writings in South Africa was made a criminal offense. Despite these restrictions, two book-length collections of Mandela's best known political statements were published abroad and have since circulated widely among South African anti-apartheid activists.

No Easy Walk to Freedom, published in 1965, includes Mandela's 1953 presidential address to the Transvaal province ANC (in which he discusses the Defiance Campaign), his speech at the 1961 All-In African Conference, and excerpts from his testimony at his three political trials. A second collection, *The Struggle Is My Life,* contains material from 1944 to 1985, including four prison statements from Mandela; and a revised 1986 edition of the title incorporates the memoirs of two of Mandela's fellow prisoners from Robben Island prison who had been released. Six

speeches made by Mandela between February and May, 1990, during his first months of freedom, are collected in *Nelson Mandela, Speeches 1990: "Intensify the Struggle to Abolish Apartheid."* Published in 1990, the volume also includes Mandela's 1989 letter to South African president P. W. Botha stressing the need for negotiations between the government and the ANC.

Shortly after her husband's 1962 conviction, Winnie Mandela received her first government banning order restricting her to Johannesburg and preventing her from attending public or private meetings of any kind. In 1965, the government forced her out of her job with the Child Welfare Society by further restricting her to her home township of Orlando West and preventing her from engaging in essential fieldwork elsewhere in the Soweto district. She was then fired from a succession of low-paying jobs in the white commercial district after the security police pressured her employers, and she finally found herself reduced to supporting her two young daughters on the charity of friends and political associates. Despite this hardship, Winnie Mandela continued to work surreptitiously with the ANC during the 1960s by helping produce banned political pamphlets and newsletters in her home. During this period, the suspicious police ransacked the Mandela house repeatedly, but prosecutors could never find enough evidence to bring a court case against her.

In May, 1969, however, Winnie Mandela was arrested with other suspected ANC sympathizers under a new law that allowed the government to detain "terrorist" suspects indefinitely without charges. Taken to Pretoria Prison, she was interrogated virtually non-stop for five days and nights about her supposed links to ANC saboteurs. She was then jailed without charges for seventeen months, spending the first two hundred days of this period incommunicado and in solitary confinement. Finally, under pressure from Nelson Mandela's lawyers, the authorities improved Winnie's confinement conditions and brought her to trial on twenty-one political charges in September, 1970. The trial judge dismissed the case against her and all but one of her co-defendants for insufficient evidence, and Winnie Mandela was released that month.

Though freed from prison, Winnie Mandela was still subjected to close police vigilance in the early 1970s as South Africa's white minority government reacted to new challenges from a growing world anti-apartheid movement and the anti-colonial wars in nearby

Mozambique and Angola. Immediately upon her release, she was placed under a new five-year banning order that confined her to her home during the evenings and on weekends. She was subjected to frequent police home searches in ensuing years and was arrested and sentenced to six months in prison for talking to another banned person in 1974. The authorities eventually allowed her banning order to expire in October, 1975, and over the next ten months she was able to enjoy the rights of free association and movement for the first time in many years.

This period of relative freedom for Winnie Mandela coincided with the birth of a militant "Black Consciousness" youth movement led by Stephen Biko and other students in Soweto. The student revolt had as its immediate aim the annulment of the Bantu Education Act, which consigned blacks to inferior education and obliged them to learn Afrikaans, the language of South African whites of Dutch descent, instead of English. When police shot down a number of unarmed demonstrators in Soweto in June, 1976, however, the township's youth erupted in a fury of uncontrolled rioting and clashes with the security forces that left at least six hundred people dead. Many of the participants in the Soweto uprising who escaped being killed or imprisoned fled the country and made contact with ANC exile headquarters in Lusaka, Zambia. This militant young cadre helped to radicalize the Congress and substantially strengthen its military wing, allowing the ANC to reestablish both a political and military presence inside South Africa by the end of the decade.

The ebb in the popular struggle after the Soweto uprising lasted until 1984, when the townships exploded again over the adoption of a new South African constitution that gave parliamentary representation to "Coloureds" and Indians but not to blacks. The townships remained in a state of near-continuous political turmoil in succeeding years as anti-government youth clashed violently with the security forces and other blacks accused of collaborating with the regime. But, unlike the situation a decade earlier, when the township civilians stood unorganized and alone against the apartheid government, a number of powerful social and political forces joined the fray in the mid-1980s to mount the greatest challenge to white minority rule in South African history. The United Democratic Front (UDF), a coalition of some 680 anti-apartheid organizations that supports the political line of the ANC, organized large street demonstrations and protests by township squatters facing eviction that were harshly repressed by the govern-

ment in 1985. Meanwhile, the ANC itself stepped up its guerrilla campaign in South Africa and began targeting white residential areas and causing civilian casualties for the first time. The Nationalist government of P. W. Botha also came under mounting attack from abroad as the United States and other Western countries imposed limited trade and investment sanctions on South Africa in a bid to force reform. Finally, in 1987, the one-million-strong black trade union movement began to flex its powerful muscles with strikes by workers in the strategic transport and mining sectors.

A common demand voiced throughout the previous decade by the diverse forces seeking to change the apartheid system was that Nelson Mandela be released immediately. In 1985, Winnie Mandela managed to break her government restrictions and return to Soweto to join the fight for her husband's freedom (this turn of events occurred after her Brandfort house was firebombed and burned to the ground in August of that year while she was in Johannesburg for medical treatment). Accusing the security police of the attack and saying that she feared for her life, Winnie Mandela insisted on moving back to her Soweto house; amid much local and international publicity, the Botha government permitted her to do so. In succeeding months, Winnie Mandela took advantage of the government's weakened position to openly flout her banning orders by giving press interviews and speaking out militantly at public demonstrations and at the funerals of young township victims of government repression.

Speaking at a funeral on a return visit to Brandfort in April, 1986, for example, Winnie Mandela denounced the authorities as "terrorists" and called on blacks to take "direct action" against the government to free the imprisoned nationalist leaders. "The time has come where we must show that we are disciplined and trained warriors," she added in what some observers interpreted as a call to insurrection. In a bid to improve its international image and deflect criticism of a new state of emergency it had imposed the previous month, the Botha regime, in July, 1986, chose not to prosecute Winnie Mandela and instead lifted all banning restrictions on her. Among Winnie Mandela's first public actions once her right to free speech had been restored was to call for international economic sanctions against the apartheid government.

The Botha government met the current crisis with a "divide and rule" strategy combining harsh repression and isolated reforms that did not fundamentally alter the structure of apartheid. While repealing such symbols of apartheid as pass laws and long-standing bans on interracial sex and marriage, the government violently crushed the township uprisings and detained tens of thousands of antiapartheid protesters without trial under sweeping state-of-emergency powers. Fearing the popular reaction if Mandela were to die in prison, previous South African governments sought to find a way to free him as early as 1973, but the confined ANC leader had always rejected conditions that he accept exile abroad or in the Transkei "homeland" and that he renounce violence by the insurgent organization. In late 1987, the Botha regime began hinting at the possibility that it might finally release Nelson Mandela unconditionally in an attempt to mollify domestic and international public opinion. The advisability of releasing the ANC leader in terms of domestic politics reportedly stimulated a hot debate in the Botha cabinet, with those in favor of the move arguing that Mandela was now more conservative than much of the current ANC leadership and could therefore effect a split in the organization. Detractors contended that freeing South Africa's best-known political prisoner could further alienate hard-line whites and possibly stimulate a black insurrection. Reform-minded South Africans, on the other hand, believed Mandela was the only political leader prestigious enough to win the confidence of both liberal whites and the increasingly alienated black township youth, thereby delivering the country from the specter of race war.

In November, 1987, the authorities unconditionally freed Mandela's long-time comrade-in-arms Govan Mbeki (a top ANC and South African Communist party leader who was convicted at the Rivonia Trial and served twenty-four years on Robben Island), as a way of testing the political waters for Mandela's possible release. In August, 1988, Mandela was diagnosed with tuberculosis, and the announcement prompted a new round of demands from the international community that he should be set free. The next year brought the release of Walter Sisulu—considered by some to be the second most important figure in South Africa's fight against apartheid—along with the rest of the Rivonia prisoners with the exception of Mandela himself. South African president F. W. de Klerk, who succeeded Botha in 1989, came into power on a reform platform; with the Rivonia amnesties, de Klerk initiated the first conciliatory measures which soon included unconditional freedom for Mandela and the lifting of the ban on the ANC (the government had delayed Mandela's pardon with the stipulation that he formally renounce violence, but it fi-

nally relented, granting his freedom February 11, 1990). De Klerk was quoted in *Time* as saying, "I came to the conclusion that [Mandela] is committed to a peaceful solution and a peaceful process." Bruce W. Nelan of *Time* suggested that de Klerk intended to demystify Mandela and the antiapartheid movement by setting its "spiritual leader" free: "By legalizing the ANC, [de Klerk] removes its cloak of underground heroism and turns it into an ordinary political party. Both Mandela and his organization will then be forced by circumstance and expectation to make compromises. And compromises are expected to anger and disillusion segments of the black majority, giving the government opportunities to divide the opposition." Nelan further conjectured that the South African president looked for the end of international sanctions against South Africa by beginning talks with black leaders—and the longer the government dragged out negotiations, the more likely momentum behind the antiapartheid movement would falter.

Embarking on a thirteen country tour in June and July, 1990, Mandela was received in the United States as—in the words of Nelan—a "heroic superstar." His mission, however, was political; he wanted both assurances from governments that sanctions would remain in place until South Africa was committed to peaceful change, and donations to revitalize the ANC. In New York City, people jammed the streets to catch a glimpse of Mandela passing by in a ticker tape parade. Speaking at a crossroads in Harlem, Mandela told a crowd nearing 100,000, "I am here to claim you because . . . you have claimed our struggle." Mandela also appeared at rallies in seven other American cities, including Boston, Miami, Detroit, and Los Angeles. In Washington, D.C., President George Bush—who, as vice-president under Ronald Reagan, fought against the Comprehensive Anti-Apartheid Act of 1986—agreed to keep economic sanctions in place, at least for the short term. "I want to find a way to show our appreciation to de Klerk, and yet I don't want to pull the rug out from under Mr. Mandela," Bush was quoted as saying in *Time.*

Upon his return to South Africa, Mandela was faced with serious obstacles which threatened to disrupt any progress he made negotiating with the government. Bloody clashes between the ANC and its backers, and Inkatha, a Zulu organization of about 1.5 million members, had been flaring up since 1987 in Natal Province. Led by Chief Mangosuthu Buthelezi, who "opposes strikes, armed struggle and foreign sanctions against the country's white government," according to Jeffrey Bartholet in *Newsweek,* Inkatha had been targeting the United Democratic Front, an organization comprised of Zulus who support the ANC. While still in prison, Mandela had hoped for a reconciliation with Buthelezi, but his very release sparked two days of violence in Natal that killed fifty people. In March, 1990, Mandela agreed to hold a joint rally with Buthelezi in Durban, but canceled out when the venue appeared too potentially explosive. Two weeks after the ANC announced an end to armed struggle against apartheid in August, 1990, a raid by Inkatha supporters on train passengers at Soweto's Inhlazane Station resulted in a wave of violence that spread to other townships around Johannesburg, leaving more than two hundred people dead. Right-wing politicians exploited the turmoil, attempting to use the ethnic strife as proof of the unviability of a black South African government. "The rivalry plays on white fears that tribalism could rip apart a post-apartheid South Africa. While de Klerk's National Party ties its future to the ANC, the right-wing Conservative Party has seized on Buthelezi's demands for a role equal to Mandela's," commented Joseph Contreras in *Newsweek*. While de Klerk pressed Mandela to help quell the violence by meeting with Buthelezi, Mandela blamed Pretoria. "Under the noses of the police, Inkatha *impis* go places fully armed and attack and kill people," he reportedly said.

Black-on-black violence continued unabated, with the ANC withdrawing from talks in May, 1991, after the government refused to outlaw tribal weapons carried by Inkatha party members. In the same month, Winnie Mandela was convicted of kidnapping and being an accessory to assault and sentenced to six years in prison. The conviction stemmed from the actions of her bodyguards, who called themselves the Mandela United Football Club although—as John Bierman reported in *Maclean's*—"they never played a single organized game of soccer." In 1988, members of the club kidnapped four black youths from a hostel. According to Bierman, "evidence showed that [Winnie] Mandela's bodyguards took the victims to her Soweto home, where they tied them up and savagely beat them. One of the youths, fourteen year-old James (Stompie) Moeketsi Seipei, was later found dead." Winnie Mandela denied any involvement in the crime, stating in court she was in the Orange Free State—three hundred kilometers away—when it occurred; she has since appealed the decision. Mandela supported his wife throughout her trial. He appeared to observers to be devoted to the woman who supported him through the many years of his imprisonment with her visits and letters, who endured jail and police mistreatment on his behalf. "There have been moments

when conscience and a sense of guilt have ravaged every part of my being," Mandela once wrote his wife, agonized by separation from his family.

Mandela insisted that the negative publicity surrounding Winnie's court case had no effect on his negotiations with Pretoria. Although far from fully enfranchising the black population, the government did institute further reforms, including the repeal of the Population Registration Act in June, 1991, which required every South African baby to be documented by race. Although international response was positive, the South African government was far from eradicating apartheid; blacks still didn't have the right to vote. Mandela, whom political experts considered outmaneuvered by de Klerk, had become increasingly cynical of the president, stating, "What he has done is merely to bring about changes which maintain the status quo."

The ANC addressed their setbacks at a national conference in Durban during July, 1991—the first such gathering in South Africa in thirty years. The party had been splitting between young radicals who favored a more militant approach toward immediate change, and older, conservative leaders who recommended negotiating gradually with the government. The Durban conference reaffirmed the moderate philosophy within the ANC by electing Mandela president, Walter Sisulu deputy president, and Cyril Ramaphosa secretary general. "This is an overwhelming victory for the moderates and a crushing blow to the militants who were outpolled two-to-one," commented South African political expert Donald Simpson in *Maclean's*.

Mandela struggled to balance his group's objectives with assurances to white South Africans that the ANC did not wish to turn the country into a socialist state. "We would nationalize the mines, the banks and other monopolies, but the rest of the economy is based on private enterprise," Mandela informed *Newsweek* in an interview. "Not even the land is nationalized, which is normally the first sector of the economy which socialist [governments] nationalize."

A growing distrust of de Klerk among blacks soured into seething resentment in June, 1992, when about two hundred Inkatha supporters rampaged through the township of Boipatong with guns, machetes and spears, killing at least forty people. Witnesses claimed the Zulu attackers had been assisted by the police. Rejecting calls among militant members to reengage in armed struggle, ANC leaders instead displayed their frustration with the government's inability to control the violence—and the seeming insincerity within de Klerk's National Party in negotiating a new, nonracial constitution—by withdrawing from the talks. A campaign of mass-action (boycotts, strikes and sit-ins) was instituted while the ANC pressed Pretoria with a list of demands, including a full investigation of the Boipatong massacre.

Addressing a Pretoria rally comprised of 70,000 peaceful marchers in August, 1992, Mandela responded to the crowd's calls of "De Klerk must go!" with a statement indicating the true purpose of the march: not to overthrow de Klerk, but to prompt him into faster action towards creating a democratic government. Mandela and de Klerk finally met on September 26, 1992, for the first time since May, agreeing to resume negotiations on the constitution and to accelerate efforts in forging an interim government. Several conditions laid down by the ANC for the resumption of talks were met by de Klerk, namely the erection of fences around single-sex workers' hostels (often the origination point of Inkatha-inspired violence), a ban on carrying tribal weapons in public, and the release of close to five hundred blacks, deemed political prisoners by the ANC. In exchange for the amnesty, the ANC agreed to a general amnesty for white governmental officials accused of crimes during the years of apartheid. One day after Mandela's summit with de Klerk, Buthelezi walked out of negotiations, angered over the deals struck between the two leaders. Buthelezi made it clear that Inkatha would not participate in postapartheid elections, even though political experts suggested de Klerk's Nationalist Party was counting on Buthelezi's (and Inkatha's) support to bolster their showings at the polls against the ANC. De Klerk denied Buthelezi's charges of striking "illegitimate" deals and claimed the real impediment to progress was due to factionalism between the blacks. Addressing this setback on television, de Klerk said, "It appears to me more and more that we won't have peace until Mr. Mandela and Chief Buthelezi make their peace."

Despite his long imprisonment and personal suffering, political setbacks and the unrelenting strife between Inkatha and the ANC, Mandela's efforts to end institutional apartheid were finally realized in June, 1993, when South Africa's first free elections were announced. Scheduled for April 27, 1994, the election was agreed upon by a majority of the country's twenty-six parties as a measure to reassure blacks that change was coming. "And the voters will almost certainly reward Mandela's stoic struggle by conferring on him the leadership of his country," declared Scott MacLeod in *Time.* This prediction proved accurate, as Mandela was elected President, with the ANC capturing 63% of the popular vote.

Since becoming President, Mandela has worked to heal the racial divisions in South Africa; to achieve South Africa's readmittance to the world community of democratic nations; and to address the crushing poverty of the country's black citizens. Mandela has been successful in luring western private investment into South Africa, but economic progress for South Africa's poor black majority has been slow, prompting some criticism of Mandela's tenure. An increased crime rate is another difficult issue facing Mandela's government. In an interview with *Newsweek,* Mandela declared that "the previous government concentrated not on suppressing crime but on suppressing the liberation movement, and tended to ignore crime. So you could understand why crime in the black areas rocketed. We inherited that situation." In addition to his political challenges, Mandela went through a messy divorce with Winnie.

In his autobiography *Long Walk to Freedom,* published in 1994, Mandela recounts his remarkable life, including his childhood in the Transkei region; his political beginnings in the 1940s and 1950s with the ANC; his twenty-seven year imprisonment; and the period after his release in 1990. Reviewers greeted the book with praise, commending Mandela's lack of bitterness and thoughtful assessment of his achievements and shortcomings. Terming the book "one of the few political autobiographies that's also a page-turner," *Los Angeles Times Book Review,* contributor Chris Goodrich called *Long Walk to Freedom* "a monumental book, one that well matches its author." Chicago *Tribune Books* reviewer Penelope Mesic concurred, calling the work "a truly wonderful autobiography, sharp, literate, unpretentious and-surprisingly-as emotionally involving as it is informative." For his long struggle on behalf of South Africa's oppressed masses and his efforts toward a peaceful transfer of power from the white minority leadership, Mandela, along with F. W. de Klerk, was awarded the 1993 Nobel Peace Prize.

BIOGRAPHICAL/CRITICAL SOURCES:

BOOKS

Benson, Mary, *Nelson Mandela: The Man and the Movement,* Norton, 1986.

Cooper, Floyd, *Mandela: From the Life of the South African Statesman,* Philomel, 1996.

Harrison, Nancy, *Winnie Mandela* (biography), Braziller, 1986.

Holland, Gini, and Mike White, *Nelson Mandela,* Raintree Steck-Vaughn, 1997.

Juckes, Tim J., *Opposition in South Africa: The Leadership of Z. K. Matthews, Nelson Mandela, and Stephen Biko,* Praeger, 1995.

Mandela, Nelson R., *No Easy Walk to Freedom,* Basic Books, 1965.

Mandela, Nelson R., *The Struggle Is My Life,* Pathfinder Press, 1986.

Mandela, Nelson R., *Long Walk to Freedom: The Autobiography of Nelson Mandela,* Little Brown, 1994.

Mandela, Winnie, *Part of My Soul Went with Him* (autobiography), edited by Anne Benjamin and Mary Benson, Norton, 1985.

Newsmakers: 1990, Gale, 1990.

Roberts, Jack L., *Nelson Mandela: Determined to Be Free,* Millbrook Press, 1995.

Stefoff, Rebecca, *Nelson Mandela: Hero for Democracy,* Fawcett Columbine, 1994.

Strazzabosco, Jeanne, *Learning about Forgiveness from the Life of Nelson Mandela* (juvenile) Rosen, 1996.

PERIODICALS

Christianity Today, July 17, 1995, p. 33.

Crisis, February, 1983.

Detroit News, July 6, 1993, p. 2A.

Ebony, December, 1985; September, 1986; August, 1994, p. 28; January, 1995, p. 78.

Globe and Mail (Toronto), December 14, 1985.

Library Journal, December, 1986, p. 117; September 15, 1990, p. 61.

Los Angeles Times Book Review, January 8, 1995, p. 3

Maclean's, May 27, 1991, pp. 22-23; July 15, 1991, p. 23.

Ms., November, 1985; January, 1987.

Nation, July 1, 1991, pp. 15-18.

National Review, April 30, 1990, pp. 37-39, January 23, 1995, p. 72.

New Republic, October 19, 1992, pp. 16-19.

New Statesman & Society, June 7, 1985; September 25, 1992, pp. 26-27, January 20, 1995, p. 39.

Newsweek, September 9, 1985; February 24, 1986; February 19, 1990, pp. 44-51; March 5, 1990, p. 31; July 2, 1990, pp. 16-20; August 27, 1990, pp. 41-42; May 27, 1991, p. 33; July 1, 1991, p. 37; March 2, 1992, p. 42; July 6, 1992, p. 47; November 6, 1995, p. 51; April 8, 1996, p. 84.

New York Review of Books, May 8, 1986, February 2, 1995, p. 10.

New York Times, July 19, 1978; July 7, 1985; July 29, 1986; June 21, 1992, sec. 1, pp. 1, 14; October 25, 1992, p. E5; July 7, 1993, p. A3; May 10, 1996, p. A14; May 16, 1996, sec. 4 p. E2.

New York Times Book Review, December 8, 1985; December 18, 1994, p. 1.

People, February 26, 1990, p. 77-79.

Time, January 5, 1987; August 29, 1988, p. 43; May 29, 1989, p. 77; October 23, 1989, p. 49; December 25, 1989, p. 28; January 29, 1990, p. 49; February 19, 1990, p. 42-44; June 25, 1990, pp. 20-21; December 17, 1990, p. 25; July 1, 1991, pp. 38-39; August 17, 1992, p. 15; June 14, 1993, pp. 34-38; January 3, 1994, p. 34; May 16, 1994, p. 65.

Tribune Books (Chicago), December 18, 1994, p. 1.

U.S. News & World Report, February 27, 1989, p. 13; April 9, 1990, p. 15; May 9, 1994, p. 10; October 17, 1994, p. 92.*

*   *   *

MANN, Abel
See CREASEY, John

*   *   *

MANTON, Peter
See CREASEY, John

*   *   *

MARLOWE, Derek 1938-

PERSONAL: Born May 21, 1938, in London, England; son of Frederick William (an electrician) and Helene (Alexandroupolos) Marlowe; married Sukie Phipps, 1968; children: three sons and two daughters. *Education:* Attended Cardinal Vaughan School, 1949-57, University of London, 1957-60. *Politics:* Socialist. *Religion:* Humanist.

ADDRESSES: Home—8 Holland Park Rd., London W. 14, England. *Agent*—Tim Corrie, Peters, Fraser & Dunlop, 5th Floor, The Chambers, Chelsea Harbour, Lots Rd., London SW10 0XF, England.

CAREER: Writer.

AWARDS, HONORS: Foyle Award, best play of 1961-62, for *The Scarecrow;* Writers Guild Award and Emmy Award, both 1972, for television writing.

WRITINGS:

A Dandy in Aspic (also see below), Putnam (New York City), 1966.
The Memories of Venus Lackey, Viking (New York City), 1968.
A Single Summer with L.B.: The Summer of 1816, J. Cape (London), 1969, published as *A Single Summer with Lord B.,* Viking, 1970.
Echoes of Celandine, Viking, 1970, published as *The Disappearance,* Penguin (London), 1978.
Do You Remember England?, Viking, 1972.
Somebody's Sister, Viking, 1974.
Nightshade, Weidenfeld & Nicolson (London), 1975, Viking, 1976.
The Rich Boy from Chicago, St. Martin's (New York City), 1979.
Nancy Astor, the Lady from Virginia: A Novel (also see below), Weidenfeld & Nicolson, 1982, Dell (New York City), 1984.

PLAYS

(Adapter) *The Seven Who Were Hanged* (based on the novel by Andreyev), produced in Edinburgh, Scotland, 1961, produced in London as *The Scarecrow,* 1964.
(Adapter) *The Lower Depths* (based on a play by Gorki), produced in London, 1962.
How Disaster Struck the Harvest, produced in London, 1964.
How I Assumed the Role of a Popular Dandy for Purposes of Seduction and Other Base Matters, produced in London, 1965.

Author of screenplays *A Dandy in Aspic,* produced in 1968, (with Joseph Massot) *The Universal Soldier,* 1972, *A Single Summer,* 1979, and *The Knight,* 1979. Also author of television plays *Requiem for Modigliani,* 1970, *The Search for the Nile,* 1971, *The Knight,* 1978, *Nancy Astor,* 1982, *Jamaica Inn,* 1983, *A Married Man,* 1984, *First among Equals,* 1986, and *Jack the Ripper,* 1988.

ADAPTATIONS: The Disappearance was filmed by World Northal Corporation in 1981.

SIDELIGHTS: Although Derek Marlowe's novels range from the romantic (*A Single Summer with L.B.*) to the biographical (*Nancy Astor*), he is best known as an author of crime and espionage thrillers. Marlowe's thrillers are described by John S. Whitley in *St. James Guide to Crime and Mystery Writers* as "highly literate (and literary), stylistically most elegant, and with a well-researched, totally credible background."

Marlowe's first espionage thriller, *A Dandy in Aspic,* is the story of a Russian spy inside British intelligence who, after assassinating a number of British agents, is himself assigned to catch the killer. Whitley calls the plot an "excellent, intriguing notion." Richard Schickel in *Book Week* admits that the idea is "an arresting one," but finds that the lead character "is seriously flawed" and "a very superficial fellow." But the novel was favorably received by Guy Davenport in *National Review:* "Marlowe is an accomplished master of the [spy novel], and before one is halfway through his Byzantine plot anything at all has become plausible."

Echoes of Celandine again concerns an assassin, this time assigned to kill a woman who turns out to be his estranged wife. The novel "is a very superior thriller," writes Clive Jordan in *New Statesman.* Although Jordan faults the hero for being "so cool about everything that the reader gets a bit glacial too," he nonetheless judges the book to be "beautifully written, riddling references to Magritte with allusions to Vita Sackville-West and the bad Lord Byron."

In *Somebody's Sister,* Marlowe writes a detective tale about the supposedly accidental death of a young girl in a crash on the Golden Gate Bridge. Peter Prince notes in *New Statesman* that the novel is "a kind of realistic critique of the whole school of romantic/idealistic detective fiction as exemplified by the Philip Marlowe series." Although not liking the story's ending, Newgate Callendar in the *New York Times Book Review* admits that Marlowe handles the plot details of the case "very well." The critic for *Library Journal* calls the book a "gripping literate thriller" with a "splendid understated ending."

Nightshade is a thriller set on a Caribbean island where a vacationing English couple find themselves embroiled with voodoo and murder. It presents, Whitley explains, "a vision of what happens when civilized man steps outside the controls of civilization and finds himself face to face with his deepest fears and desires." The critic for *Time* finds that "what starts out as a thin, sinister tale ends as a psychological chiller finely wrought." "Marlowe," Callendar writes, "keeps tension at a quiet but very high level. . . . When the reader puts down the book, he has been through an experience."

BIOGRAPHICAL/CRITICAL SOURCES:

BOOKS

St. James Guide to Crime and Mystery Writers, fourth edition, St. James Press (Detroit), 1996.

PERIODICALS

Book Week, October 30, 1966, p. 22.
Library Journal, March 15, 1970, p. 95; October 1, 1974, p. 99.
Listener, February 14, 1980.
National Review, October 4, 1966, p. 18.
New Statesman, May 29, 1970, p. 79; November 8, 1974, p. 88; January 23, 1976.
New York Times Book Review, February 15, 1970, p. 47; November 24, 1974, p. 39; July 18, 1976, p. 32.
Punch, March 10, 1982.
Spectator, March 15, 1980.
Time, July 26, 1976, p. 108.
Times Literary Supplement, November 13, 1969, p. 1297.

*   *   *

MARRIC, J. J.
  See CREASEY, John

*   *   *

MARSDEN, James
  See CREASEY, John

*   *   *

MARTIN, Richard
  See CREASEY, John

MASSON, David I(rvine) 1915-

PERSONAL: Born on November 6, 1915, in Edinburgh, Scotland; married Olive Masson in 1950; children: one daughter. *Education:* Oundle School, Northamptonshire, 1929-34; Oxford University, Merton College, B.A. (honours), 1937, M.A., 1941.

ADDRESSES: Office—c/o Faber and Faber Ltd., 3 Queen Sq., London WC1N 3AU, England.

CAREER: Assistant Librarian, University of Leeds, 1938-40, and University of Liverpool, 1945-55; Sub-Librarian, in charge of Brotherton Collection, University of Leeds, 1956-79. *Military service:* Served in the Royal Army Medical Corps, 1940-45.

MEMBER: Modern Humanities Research Association.

WRITINGS:

The Caltraps of Time (seven stories), Faber (London), 1968.

Stories have appeared in several anthologies. Contributor of articles, mainly on the sound of various languages in poetry, to American, British, and European periodicals; also contributor to symposia and encyclopedias.

OTHER

Hand-List of Incunabula in the University Library, Liverpool, privately printed, 1948, supplement, 1955.
Catalogue of the Romany Collection . . . University of Leeds, Nelson (Edinburgh), 1962.
Poetic Sound-Patterning Reconsidered, Leeds Philosophical and Literary Society (Leeds, England), 1976.
Keith Douglas's Phonetic Rhetoric and Phonetic Lyricism: A Study of Three Poems, Leeds Philosophical and Literary Society, 1991.

SIDELIGHTS: David I. Masson is best known for his compilation of science fiction short stories, *The Caltraps of Time.* Of these seven stories, some depict the degradation of the world and linguistic changes through time. In the *St. James Guide to Fantasy Writers,* Masson reveals that "several stories reflect my conviction that the human race is insane." Masson's most acclaimed story, "Traveller's Rest," uses differential time in a war setting. In the South, a land of peace, decades pass while during the same period only minutes pass in the war-torn North. Another tale "The Two Timer" features a look at the 20th century through the eyes of an upper-class man from the 17th century, who traveled through time in a time machine. In his own earlier form of the English language, the gentleman provides a satirical assessment of life in the 20th century. In "The Transfinite Choice" the protagonist, a 1980s researcher, is accidentally transported into the 24th century, a time when English has become unrecognizable to the researcher. "Not So Certain" portrays another expedition, this time to another planet. In this tale, the travelers run into difficulty when they must try to understand the native language. Explorers in the tale "Mouth of Hell," instead of dealing with linguistic obstacles, must handle a vast cleft that drops forty kilometers to molten magma.

Masson describes his writing in the *St. James Guide to Fantasy Writers:* "My science fiction . . . explores bizarre assumptions for the sake—or so it seems to me—of mythopoeia, fable, satire, ridicule, scorn, or indignation, and perhaps inner truth about experience and feeling."

BIOGRAPHICAL/CRITICAL SOURCES:

BOOKS

St. James Guide to Fantasy Writers, St. James Press (Detroit), 1996.

PERIODICALS

Times Literary Supplement, April 4, 1968, p. 356.

*   *   *

MATTHESON, Rodney
   See CREASEY, John

*   *   *

McCLELLAND, Diane Margaret 1931-
   (Diane Pearson)

PERSONAL: Born November 5, 1931, in Croyden, England; daughter of William Holker and Miriam Harriet Youde; married Richard Leeper McClelland

(an actor and physician), 1975. *Education:* Attended secondary school in Croyden, England.

ADDRESSES: Agent—Curtis Brown Ltd., 1 Craven Hill, London W2 3EP, England.

*CAREER:*Jonathan Cape Ltd., London, England, book production assistant, 1948-52; associated with local government, 1952-64; Corgi Books Ltd., London, editor, 1964—.

WRITINGS:

UNDER PSEUDONYM DIANE PEARSON

The Loom of Tancred, R. Hale (London), 1967, published as *Bride of Tancred,* Corgi (London), 1976.
The Marigold Field, Lippincott (Philadelphia), 1969.
Sarah, Lippincott, 1971, published as *Sarah Whitman,* Macmillan (London), 1971.
Csardas, Macmillan, 1975, Fawcett (Greenwich, CT), 1985.
the Summer of the Barshinskeys, Crown (New York City), 1984.
Voices of Summer, Bantam (London), 1992.

SIDELIGHTS: Diane McClelland writes historical romance novels under the pseudonym Diane Pearson. Her works are set in a range of historical periods and in such diverse geographical locations as India, Russia and the English countryside. Despite their diversity, Pearson's books deal with recurring themes. As Marina Oliver writes in *Twentieth-Century Romance and Historical Writers,* Pearson writes "of strong women rising above sorrows and disadvantages, and the importance of religion." All of Pearson's books, Oliver writes, "have the page-turning quality of a born storyteller's work."

Bride of Tancred, Pearson's first novel, is a gothic story in which Miriam, a young Victorian girl, is sent to work in a gloomy mansion where her employer's family is obsessed by memories of the late domineering father who brought ruin to their good name. Oliver writes: "The atmosphere created is one of immense tension, fear, and ominous foreboding."

In *The Mamrigold Field* Pearson weaves a tale of an ambitious woman determined to marry a local village man. The *Times Literary Supplement* critic thinks that although the author aims "at integrating romantic inventiveness with historical verisimilitude, Miss Pearson achieves neither." But A. C. Ringer in *Library Journal* calls *The Marigold Field* an "absorbing chronicle of English village life" and praises Pearson for her "gift for characterization."

Pearson's sequel to *The Marigold Field, Sarah,* follows the tribulations of the daughter from the earlier novel. Sarah, a London schoolteacher, marries an eccentric scholar and moves to India with him. L. M. Pritchard in *Best Sellers* praised Pearson's "prowess in enlightening us about social struggles and class structures" of the early twentieth century. Lucy Cadogan of *New Statesman* calls *Sarah* "a fast-moving, well-documented and undemanding historical novel." Ringer found *Sarah* to be "as rich in characterization and as absorbing to read as its predecessor."

Several of Pearson's novels tell sweeping stories. For example, *Csardas* "is a book of enormous scope," Oliver maintains, "following the fortunes of the Ferenc sisters from the glittering days of the Austro-Hungarian Empire to the totalitarianism of communist rule." *The Summer of the Barshinskeys* tells of a Russian exile who takes an English wife and settles in the English countryside. Their daughters become entangled in the Russian Revolution as Galina, trapped in St. Petersburg with an aged lover and a young admirer, strives to escape the violent turmoil and Daisy volunteers to assist escaping refugees. *Voices of Summer* concerns an operetta company in Austria and their tangled interpersonal relationships and backstage manueverings. Oliver calls *Voices of Summer* "a romance par excellance, in much lighter mood than Pearson's other novels."

Oliver concludes that "Pearson creates marvellously memorable characters, she establishes them indelibly in a few lines of dialogue, with great expertise. She conveys the deepest emotions of both men and women equally well, and tackles both tragedy and comedy superbly."

McClelland told *CA:* "I have never actively thought about why I write or what I am trying to say. I firmly believe that too much dissection of motive destroys the instinct to write. I suppose, however, if I look at what I have written, my intention has unwittingly been to represent the 'little' people of the world, those who are unlauded and unknown but who frequently have just as much courage and sensitivity as the world's giants."

BIOGRAPHICAL/CRITICAL SOURCES:

BOOKS

Twentieth-Century Romance and Historical Writers, 3rd edition, St. James Press (Detroit), 1994.

PERIODICALS

Best Sellers, October 1, 1968, p. 29; October 1, 1971, p. 31.
Library Journal, July, 1969, p. 94; October 1, 1971, p. 96.
New Statesman, July 9, 1971, p. 82.
New Yorker, October 25, 1969, p. 45.
New York Times Book Review, October 3, 1971, p. 34.
Times Literary Supplement, July 10, 1969, p. 759.

* * *

MEREDITH, Anne
    See MALLESON, Lucy Beatrice

* * *

MILLER, Sue 1943-

PERSONAL: Born November 29, 1943; daughter of James Hastings (a minister and educator) and Judith Beach Nichols; married second husband Doug Bauer (a writer), in the mid-1980s; children: (first marriage) Ben. *Education:* Radcliffe College, B.A., 1964; received master's degrees from Harvard University, Boston University, and Wesleyan University.

ADDRESSES: Home—Boston, MA. *Agent*—Maxine Groffsky, Maxine Groffsky Literary Agency, 2 Fifth Ave., New York, NY 10011.

CAREER: Writer. Teacher of creative writing courses at universities. Worked variously as a day-care worker, high school teacher, waitress, model, and researcher.

AWARDS, HONORS: Boston University creative writing fellowship, 1979; Pushcart Press honorable mention, 1984; National Book Critics Circle Award nomination, 1991, for *Family Pictures;* Bunting Institute fellowship, Radcliffe College; grant from Massachusetts Artists Foundation; MacDowell fellowship; Guggenheim fellowship.

WRITINGS:

The Good Mother, Harper (New York City), 1986.
Inventing the Abbotts, and Other Stories (contains "Leaving Home" and "Appropriate Affect"), Harper, 1987.
Family Pictures, Harper, 1990.
For Love, Harper, 1993.
The Distinguished Guest, Harper, 1995.

Contributor of short stories to periodicals, including *Atlantic, Mademoiselle,* and *Ploughshares.*

ADAPTATIONS: The Good Mother was adapted as a motion picture, written by Michael Bortman, directed by Leonard Nimoy, starring Diane Keaton and Liam Neeson, Buena Vista, 1988; *Family Pictures* was adapted as a television movie, written by Jennifer Miller, directed by Philip Saville, starring Anjelica Huston and Sam Neill, 1993; *Inventing the Abbotts* was adapted as a motion picture, written by Ken Hixon, directed by Pat O'Connor, 20th-Century-Fox, 1997.

SIDELIGHTS: Fiction writer Sue Miller earned immediate acclaim with her first novel, *The Good Mother.* In her appraisal of the book for the *New York Times Book Review,* Linda Wolfe asserted, "Every once in a while, a first novelist rockets into the literary atmosphere with a novel so accomplished that it shatters the common assumption that for a writer to have mastery, he or she must serve a long, auspicious apprenticeship." Such profuse praise surprised Miller, who did not begin writing seriously until she was thirty-five (she took a writing course and her first story was published). Since deciding to pursue a writing career, Miller has distinguished herself by producing works fraught with bittersweet emotion that provide insight into family life, particularly nontraditional families with divorced mothers. *Publishers Weekly* contributor Rosemary Herbert lauded the author's rendition of such scenes, calling Miller "an extraordinarily accomplished writer who is particularly skilled in the use of visual images and homey detail."

Miller explained to Herbert that her inspiration for *The Good Mother* was her dissatisfaction with "a number of postfeminist novels which suggested that all you need to do is shed your husband and then you

enter this glorious new life of accomplishment and ease." *The Good Mother* is the saga of a divorced woman embroiled in a custody battle. This fight is based on her lover's alleged improper sexual contact with her daughter. At the story's beginning, narrator Anna Dunlap realizes her dissatisfaction with her role as a dutiful wife and extricates herself from an apathetic marriage. She then attempts to create a new life for herself and her four-year-old daughter, Molly. With this move, Anna hopes to focus on self-fulfillment and continue to build an open, loving relationship with her daughter. Soon she meets Leo, a sculptor, and embarks upon a fervent love affair that offers the passion and spontaneity that her marriage lacked. The relationship progresses and Leo becomes a fixture in the household, even helping care for Molly. Anna's domestic bliss is shattered, however, when her ex-husband serves court papers citing an improper relationship—with sexual overtones—between Molly and Leo and charging Anna with negligence.

The remainder of *The Good Mother* addresses the trial and its outcome. Crediting Miller's rendering of suspense, *USA Today*'s Robert Wilson noted that she "makes the court case both dramatic and convincing, and effectively interweaves the impersonal legal machinations with the almost devastatingly intense emotions Anna feels for Molly and Leo." In the book Anna explains her alleged remissness to the court-appointed social worker: "I was very caught up in my feelings about Leo, and I just didn't give enough thought to Molly, to what might be confusing or difficult for her in all of it." Ultimately Anna loses custody of Molly, but earns her title as a "good mother" by accepting the painful ruling for the sake of her child's well-being. In a *Publishers Weekly* interview, Miller commented that her narrator was "a person who thought she could make her life like someone else's, who thought she could be in control of her life. And that seems to me to be a false thing to believe in this world."

The Good Mother rested atop the bestseller lists for six months and Miller earned widespread acclaim for the book. *New York Times* contributor Michiko Kakutani deemed the work "a remarkably assured first novel" and added, "Thanks to Sue Miller's gift for precise psychological detail, her sure sense of narrative and her simple compassion for ordinary lives, this powerful novel proves as subtle as it is dramatic, as durable—in its emotional afterlife—as it is instantly readable." Catherine Petroski, writing in *Chicago Tribune,* remarked that the "story mesmerizes the reader till the last page is turned."

A few critics, however, charged that in *The Good Mother* Miller needlessly makes her protagonist a victim. She betrays Leo by agreeing with the court that he acted irresponsibly. Confronting these criticisms, Josephine Humphreys, writing in *Nation,* countered, "Because . . . Anna is, in the end, human rather than heroic, the novel is all the more disturbing and powerful." The author, however, did view Anna as a heroic character. She told Beth Austin of the *Chicago Tribune* that with *The Good Mother* "I was trying . . . to establish what I regard as a very female notion of heroism and, I think, a very feminist notion of heroism." Miller noted that her character's choices may be more valiant than what she believes is the typical male response of fighting despite the consequences. Anna realized how her battle might adversely effect her daughter and instead chose to protect her child from that emotional trauma.

Miller followed *The Good Mother* with a collection of short fiction titled *Inventing the Abbotts, and Other Stories.* Ellen Lesser, in her *Village Voice* appraisal, stated, "The new volume demonstrates that Miller doesn't need the breadth of a novel to chart the complex and confusing topography of families after divorce." In "Leaving Home," Leah, a divorced mother, realizes that the behavior she prompted from her son while he was growing up corresponds to his present problem of standing up to his wife. Observing his marital problems, she regrets that he no longer turns to her for advice. Another story, "Appropriate Affect," documents a quiet grandmother with a sad, sweet smile who turns surly after suffering a stroke. This unexpected—though truthful—behavior drives her family away. In the title piece of the volume, Doug narrates his older brother Jacey's romantic liaisons with three sisters from a higher socio-economic class in a dull, midwestern town. In this story, noted *Times Literary Supplement* reviewer Roz Kaveney, "Miller writes with genuine power."

Miller's second novel, *Family Pictures,* was also a bestseller. Using third-person narration, the author chronicles the history of an upper-middle-class family living in Chicago from the end of World War II to the mid-1980s. The author told Laura Shapiro of *Newsweek* that she wanted the book "to be about a whole family almost as a character, and to trace the way everybody contributes to this mutual reality." *Family Pictures* concerns David and Lainey Eberhardt and their six children. The couple's early marital happiness is tested after learning that their third child, son Randall, is autistic. David is a psychiatrist who sides with other experts in the medical field to blame Lainey for her son's autism, citing some form of subconscious rejection. Lainey feels betrayed by her husband's charges, but subdues her anger. Instead, in an attempt to prove that Randall's autism is not her fault, she bears three more healthy children against David's wishes.

Based on this undercurrent of anger and blame, *Family Pictures* describes how Randall defines the family and how the directions of the other family members have been altered because of his plight. Fourth child Nina, a photographer, serves as a frequent narrator. She likens her family's situation to that of a photograph in which the main subject is shown in sharp detail while the background remains a blur. As he grows older, Randall's behavior becomes less predictable, and when he demonstrates abusive tendencies, the family is forced to institutionalize him. Previously held together by the tragedy of his condition and the strain of caring for him, the family begins to crumble and David and Lainey separate.

Shapiro called *Family Pictures* "a big, wonderful, deeply absorbing novel that retains the vivid domestic focus of *The Good Mother* while spiraling far beyond it." Michael Dorris, writing in the *Detroit News* judged that "the entire novel, in fact, is packed with . . . moments of wisdom and insight, and suffused with terrific writing," and added, "*Family Pictures* is rich with complexity and paradox. It makes no easy judgments of right and wrong about its embattled protagonists." "Miller is particularly good at dramatizing scenes of domestic chaos and the complex interplay of adults and children," according to Christopher Lehmann-Haupt in the *New York Times.* Praising the author's adept handling of several narrative shifts in *Family Pictures, Chicago Tribune* contributor Anne Tyler noted, "in tone it is absolutely flawless. It captures perfectly the sass and grit of family life." In a *New York Times Book Review* article, Jane Smiley concluded that *Family Pictures* is "profoundly honest, shapely, ambitious, engrossing, original and true, an important example of a new American tradition that explores what it means . . . to make a home, live at home and learn what home is."

Miller's third novel, titled simply *For Love,* explores the complexity of emotion faced by a woman approaching her middle years. In youth, protagonist Lottie Gardner had specialized in reinventing herself—changing her name from Char to Charlotte to Lottie, marrying and divorcing and marrying again. In her forties, Lottie realizes that through what Ron Carlson, in a *New York Times Book Review* piece, called "the many lenses of her life: daughter, sister, mother, lover and wife" she must continually try "to understand the rules of love, even as they appear to be changing."

Carlson found that Miller writes with the kind of realism "that takes us by the shoulders and says, '*Look at this!*'" Similarly, *Chicago Tribune* critic Madison Smartt Bell praised Miller for a body of work that is "remarkably free of politically motivated distortion. She is in no sense an ideologue but a strong believer in reality." Bell, however, added that the realism in *For Love* is marred by the lack of a central plot point. Calling the novel "cloudy and hard to grasp," Gail Pool, a *Women's Review of Books* writer, similarly saw insufficient power in Lottie's character to carry a whole novel. Still, Pool admitted, *For Love,* "despite its problems, is a very readable book, largely because Miller is a good storyteller."

Bringing out private conflicts in a public forum sets the stage for Miller's fourth novel, *The Distinguished Guest.* The title character is Lily Maynard—in her eighties, frail and ill, but with her detailed (and perhaps embellishing) memory intact. Ten years before the start of the narrative, Lily has authored a feminist bestseller based on her marriage to a civil rights activist in the 1960s. Now, divorced, debilitated, and estranged from her two eldest children, she takes refuge in the home of her resentful youngest, Alan, and his family. Alan and his wife, Gaby, have only begun to work out their own marital difficulties; the presence of Lily only exacerbates the tension. The small circle is joined by a journalist, Linnett, who has arrived to write Lily's life story for a magazine. In relating her life to Linnett, Lily dredges all manner of family conflict. It is in the character of Linnett that Miller—so often lauded for her realistic portrayals— hits a false note, in the view of Kakutani. Writing in the *New York Times,* Kakutani opined that the author's creation of Linnett "must surely rank as one of the more unbelievable depictions of a journalist to appear in a novel in a long time." Kakutani also faulted the novel for "[diluting the] portrait of a mother and her middle-aged son with lots of extraneous talk about race relations and middle-class guilt." "Where Miller fumbles a bit is in her effort to plop the issue of racism into her characters' hands," agreed *Detroit Free Press*'s Susan Hall-Balduf. The author, she continued, "doesn't speak plainly of the issue until she brings in the book's only black character."

But the parallels drawn between the conflict between the races, and the conflicts within a single family, are just what critic Roxana Robinson found compelling. In her *Los Angeles Times Book Review* article, she noted that both issues "are complex and highly charged, both provoke public debate and private anguish. Both raise the question of personal debt: what one owes, and is owed." To Robinson, *The Distinguished Guest* presents "no simple resolutions to these conflicts between idealism and realism, parent and child, black and white. But Miller's compassionate narrative explores the problems and reveals the possibilities for change."

One powerful moment in the novel was noted by several reviewers. In this scene, a dinner-table discussion reveals Lily's offhanded cruelty when, in the presence of Alan and Alan's grown son, the matriarch says, "There's no surer or shorter route to heartbreak than having high expectations for your children." This remark, *Chicago Tribune* critic Penelope Mesic averred, "amounts to indicting Alan both as an overfond parent and a failure himself." "The various responses . . . form a sort of paradigm for the novel's larger construction," wrote Richard Bausch in his *New York Times Book Review* assessment. "We move through the moment, and its aftermath, with all sorts of insights that lend weight and richness to what glides by on the surface."

Overall, Miller's fourth novel was well received for its gripping—if uncomfortable—take on the strained dynamics between adult children and their aging parents. Praising the author's ability to avoid "flattering" her audience, Mesic summarized that reading *The Distinguished Guest* is "a rueful pleasure—akin to poking a sore tooth with an exploratory tongue, or trying on clothes, fearing they're unflattering from behind, and backing up to a three-fold mirror. In such cases the best we can feel is that we know the worst." *The Distinguished Guest,* concluded Bausch, "is a very moving book about—and for—grown-ups who are willing to consider, with honesty and intelligence, some unavoidable grown-up predicaments."

In her fictional works, Miller presents poignant and authentic portraits of family life. Reviewers credit the author with matching the promise she showed in her first book. In addition, some critics singled out Miller's rendering of female characters for special praise. The author, though, objects to being tagged a women's writer because of the inherent limitations and suggestion that her work would not appeal to men. Miller explained to Shapiro, "Women are beginning to use the experience of being female, of being a mother, and they're using it metaphorically. I don't want to let men off the hook. They need to learn how to read women's metaphors just the way women have learned to read men's metaphors."

BIOGRAPHICAL/CRITICAL SOURCES:

BOOKS

Bestsellers 90, Issue 3, Gale (Detroit), 1990.
Contemporary Literary Criticism, Gale, Volume 44, 1987.

PERIODICALS

America, November 17, 1990.
Booklist, January 1, 1993.
Boston Globe, March 28, 1993, p. B38.
Boston Magazine, August, 1990.
Chatelaine, September, 1990; June 1993.
Chicago Tribune, April 27, 1986; July 19, 1989.
Christian Century, June 13, 1990; April 28, 1993.
Christian Science Monitor, April 30, 1986.
Commonweal, October 12, 1990; December 7, 1990.
Cosmopolitan, March, 1987; April, 1993.
Detroit Free Press, April 23, 1995, p. 7F.
Detroit News, August 8, 1986; April 25, 1990.
Economist, April 17, 1993.
Globe and Mail (Toronto), November 22, 1986.
Library Journal, May 1, 1987; April 15, 1990; October 15, 1990; February 15, 1993.
Los Angeles Times, April 14, 1986; May 4, 1990.
Los Angeles Times Book Review, May 7, 1995, p. 2.
Maclean's November 14, 1988; August 6, 1990; June 7, 1993.
Nation, May 10, 1986.
National Catholic Reporter, November 9, 1990.
New Statesman and Society, November 23, 1990.
Newsweek, April 30, 1990; April 19, 1993.
New York, May 14, 1990; March 22, 1993.
New York Review of Books, August 16, 1990.
New York Times, April 23, 1986; September 15, 1986; April 30, 1990; April 5, 1993; April 21, 1995.
New York Times Book Review, April 27, 1986; April 19, 1987; May 24, 1987; April 22, 1990; April 11, 1993, p. 7; May 7, 1995.
Publishers Weekly, May 2, 1986; March 27, 1987; February 23, 1990; September 7, 1990; May 3, 1993.
Time, June 25, 1990; January 11, 1993; May 3, 1993.
Times Literary Supplement, July 17, 1987; December 21, 1990; March 22, 1996, p. 23.

Tribune Books (Chicago), April 22, 1990; April 11, 1993, p. 3; April 16, 1995, p. 5.
USA Today, April 4, 1986.
Village Voice, June 23, 1987.
Washington Post, June 19, 1986; May 15, 1990.
Washington Post Book World, May 4, 1986; May 17, 1987.
Wilson Library Bulletin, November, 1990.
Women's Review of Books, July, 1993, p. 33.

*   *   *

MINER, Valerie 1947-

PERSONAL: Born August 28, 1947, in New York, NY; daughter of John Daniel (a sailor) and Mary (a restaurant hostess; maiden name, McKenzie) Miner. *Education:* University of California, Berkeley, B.A., 1969, M.J., 1970; attended University of Edinburgh, 1968, and University of London, 1974-75.

CAREER: Daily Review, Hayward, CA, reporter, 1964-65; *Castro Valley Vista,* Castro Valley, CA, reporter, 1965; freelance writer and editor in London, 1974-76; University of California, Berkeley, lecturer in field studies program, beginning 1977. Instructor at Centennial College, Toronto, Ontario, and University of Toronto, both 1972-74, and York University, 1973; lecturer at California State University, Hayward, 1977, and San Francisco State University, 1977-78; guest lecturer at City Literary Institute, London, 1975, University of Alberta, 1976, Mills College and Contra Costa Press Institute, 1977, and Stanford University, 1979. Broadcaster in Toronto, Ontario, 1973.

MEMBER: National Feminist Writers Guild (founding member), San Francisco Media Alliance, Women against Violence in Pornography and Media (member, board of directors), Theta Sigma Phi.

WRITINGS:

(With M. Kostash, M. McCracken, E. Paris, and H. Robertson) *Her Own Woman* (nonfiction), Macmillan (New York City), 1975.
(With Zoe Fairbairns, Sara Maitland, Michele Roberts, and Michelene Wandor) *Tales I Tell My Mother* (stories), Journeyman (London), 1978, South End (Boston), 1980.
Blood Sisters: An Examination of Conscience, St. Martin's (New York City), 1982.

Murder in the English Department, St. Martin's Press, 1982.

Movement: A Novel in Stories, Crossing Press (Trumansburg, NY), 1982.

Winter's Edge, Methuen (London), 1984, Crossing Press, 1987.

(With Fairbairns, Maitland, Roberts, and Wandor) *More Tales I Tell My Mother,* Journeyman, 1987.

All Good Women, Crossing Press (Freedom, CA), 1987.

(Editor with Helen E. Longino) *Competition: A Feminist Taboo?* (nonfiction), Feminist Press (New York City), 1987.

Trespassing and Other Stories, Crossing Press, 1989.

Rumors from the Cauldron: Selected Essays, Reviews, and Reportage, University of Michigan Press (Ann Arbor), 1992.

A Walking Fire, State University of New York Press (Albany), 1994.

Work represented in anthologies, including *Modern Commonwealth Literature,* 1976; *Canadians All,* 1979; *Take Back the Night: First Feminist Papers on Pornography,* 1980; and *Old Maids to Radical Spinsters: Unmarried Women in the Twentieth-Century Novel,* University of Illinois Press, 1991.

Also contributor to periodicals, including *Mademoiselle, Saturday Night, New Society, Maclean's, New Statesman, Economist, Ploughshares, Virginia Quarterly Review,* and *Feminist Review.* Past member of editorial staff of *Listener, Time Out,* and the Writers and Readers Publishing Cooperative.

SIDELIGHTS: Journalist and fiction writer Valerie Miner is the author of several novels and short story collections that reflect her less-than-optimistic belief that we are entering a post-feminist era. Through such novels as *Blood Sisters: An Examination of Conscience* and *A Walking Fire,* Miner draws the reader into fictions that focus on such woman-centered issues as sexual violence, social advocacy, abortion, divorce, and lesbianism as they become manifested in the changing circumstances of her independent female protagonists. The author of numerous journalistic pieces, Miner's *Rumors from the Cauldron: Selected Essays, Reviews, and Reportage* was collected, as the author writes in the 1992 volume's introduction, as "my own small resistance to cultural amnesia. We can continue to imagine as feminists only if we can remember."

Blood Sisters, Miner's debut novel, focuses on the adult relationship between two Irish-born cousins.

Attempting to follow the path of their grandmother, an Irish patriot, the two women commit themselves to different political causes. Liz, a lesbian living a carefree existence in California, enacts her pacifism through her New Age religion; meanwhile Beth, a London schoolteacher, is active in groups fighting for an end to the British occupation of Northern Ireland. Personality conflicts between the two ensue after free-spirited Californian Liz arrives in rain-soaked London in response to a job offer.

In 1982's *Movement,* the cultural upheavals of the late 1960s and early 1970s underlie Susan Campbell's efforts to break from her closeted position as a homemaker and gain independence. Miner punctuates the novel with vignettes about the lives of a multitude of women, thereby showing women's common experience. Describing the novel as a collection of short stories, Joel Drucker noted in the *San Francisco Review of Books* that "you can hear Miner's camera eye clicking away as she crafts these vignettes, striving above all to show women as people, not victims or heroines. Dignity and integrity, central features of political action, are vital aspects of *Movement.*"

Murder in the English Department, unlike the promise of its title, was considered by critics to be a feminist statement rather than a work of detective fiction. In the novel, women's studies professor Nan Weaver is accused of the murder of a sexist male colleague named Angus Murchie; she cannot prove her innocence except by revealing the confidence made her by a beautiful student: that Murchie was stabbed to death in self defense after attempting to rape the young woman. Noting that the male characters in the novel are portrayed negatively, and that protagonist Nan, "admirable as she may be," does not capture the affections of the reader, *Washington Post Book Review* critic Jean M. White noted of *Murder in the English Department* that "Miner writes crisply and has a good ear for dialogue. Maybe she'll be satisfied to write a good story the next time out without stacking the deck to make her point and burdening her tale with editorializing."

Winter's Edge, which Miner published in 1985, describes the declining relationship between two elderly women wishing to remain in their home instead of moving into a colorless retirement home. Calling the novel "Depressing at times, and certainly no lightweight," a *Publishers Weekly* reviewer added that *Winter's Edge* "takes a thought-provoking look at human nature."

Miner's other novels include *All Good Women* and *A Walking Fire,* a portrayal of the extended aftereffects of the Vietnam War. She is also the author of the short story collection *Trespassing and Other Stories,* and several essays on feminist topics that have appeared in published anthologies.

BIOGRAPHICAL/CRITICAL SOURCES:

BOOKS

Backtalk: Women Writers Speak Out, Rutgers University Press (New Brunswick, NJ), 1993.
Contemporary Literature Criticism, Volume 40, Gale (Detroit), 1988.
Feminist Writers, St. James Press (Detroit), 1996.
Miner, Valerie, *Rumors from the Cauldron: Selected Essays, Reviews, and Reportage,* University of Michigan Press, 1992.

PERIODICALS

Belles Lettres, summer, 1992, p. 26; fall, 1994, pp. 88-89.
Choice, February, 1988, p. 940.
Los Angeles Times Book Review, January 26, 1986, p. 10; September 6, 1987, p. 8.
New York Times Book Review, January 19, 1986, p. 20; October 11, 1987, p. 57; September 4, 1994, p. 16.
Publishers Weekly, September 27, 1985, p. 95.
San Francisco Review of Books, November/December, 1982, pp. 16, 27.
Times Literary Supplement, July 19, 1985, p. 800; July 21, 1989, p. 803.
Washington Post Book World, March 20, 1983, p. 11.
Women's Review of Books, April, 1986, p. 11; November, 1987, p. 18; September, 1992, p. 24; February, 1995, p. 88.*

*   *   *

MOERS, Ellen 1928-1979

PERSONAL: Born December 9, 1928, in New York, NY; died of cancer, August 25, 1979, in New York, NY; daughter of Robert (a lawyer) and Celia Lewis (a teacher; maiden name, Kauffman) Moers; married Martin Mayer (a writer), June 23, 1949; children: Thomas, James. *Education:* Vassar College, B.A., 1948; Radcliffe College, M.A., 1949; Columbia University, Ph.D., 1954.

CAREER: Hunter College (now Hunter College of the City University of New York), New York City, lecturer in English, 1956-57; Columbia University, New York City, lecturer in English, 1957-58, senior research associate, 1966-68; Barnard College, New York City, associate professor of English, beginning 1968.

MEMBER: American Studies Association, Phi Beta Kappa.

AWARDS, HONORS: Guggenheim fellowship, 1962-63; National Endowment for the Humanities senior fellowship, 1972-73.

WRITINGS:

The Dandy: Brummell to Beerbohm, Viking (New York City), 1960.
Two Dreisers, Viking, 1969.
Literary Women: The Great Writers, Doubleday (Garden City, NY), 1976.
Harriet Beecher Stowe and American Literature, Stowe-Day Foundation (Hartford, CT), 1978.

Contributor of critical and scholarly articles to *Commentary, Harper's, Columbia Forum, American Scholar, Victorian Studies, New York Review of Books,* and other publications.

SIDELIGHTS: Prior to her untimely death in 1979, scholar and literary critic Ellen Moers significantly advanced the study of women's literature, an area of research that finally came into its own during the mid-1970s. "As long-neglected women authors were restored to print and to the canon, Moers's seminal work *Literary Women: The Great Writers* inspired numerous students to write on women's fiction and to be literary detectives," according to Mary A. Hess in *Feminist Writers.* Moers herself described her chosen area of scholarship—the nineteenth-century novel—as "the only intellectual field to which women, over a long stretch of time, have made an indispensable contribution." She characterized the scholarly activity on behalf of forgotten female authors undertaken during the 1970s as a "golden harvest of memoirs to thicken the air with women's voices, to bring the old and young together in testimony to a woman's life."

The author of several works of literary criticism, including *Two Dreisers,* which critic Herbert Kupferberg deemed "an illuminating voyage of discovery into the life of one of the most important and influential American novelists," Moers began preparing her groundbreaking *Literary Women* during a two-year National Endowment for the Humanities senior fellowship. Upon publication, Moers's work was hailed by critics; characteristic response included Renee Winegarten's summation of the work as "a witty, provocative, stimulating, and entertaining 'celebration of the great women who have spoken for us all'" in *American Scholar*. Even decades after its publication, *Literary Women* remains an important reference for students of women's writing and other women's studies disciplines.

While some reviewers took issue with Moers's prose style, "on nearly every page one can see where some concept of Moers's has borne fruit; literary researchers followed her lead and countless studies can be traced back to her insights," according to Hess. In *Literary Women* Moers coined the term "heroinism" for "literary feminism" and focused on both written works and the many obstacles that existed for their female authors. The threat of poverty and the social ridicule of women writers as "scribblers" combined with society's inherent sexism to make the writing life a difficult, if not impossible goal for most women to pursue. Moers cites the Bronte sisters, George Eliot, Sylvia Plath, and Virginia Woolf, among others, as examples of the few women whose talents and social standing were such that they were able to overcome such obstacles.

Focusing on the life of the author of *Uncle Tom's Cabin, Harriet Beecher Stowe and American Literature,* published two years after *Literary Women,* continued Moers's efforts to showcase the contributions of undervalued female novelists in light of new research and understanding of the role of nineteenth-century women. In addition to her works of literary criticism, Moers was the author of *The Dandy: From Brummell to Beerbohm,* a historical work on dandyism in Great Britain and France based on her dissertation written at Columbia University. In addition to her book-length works, Moers contributed reviews to a variety of periodicals and academic journals.

BIOGRAPHICAL/CRITICAL SOURCES:

BOOKS

Feminist Writers, St. James Press (Detroit), 1996.

PERIODICALS

Book World, July 6, 1969.
Commentary, January, 1970.
National Observer, August 4, 1969.
New Republic, July 19, 1969.
New Yorker, August 30, 1969.
Observer Review, August 20, 1970.
Virginia Quarterly Review, autumn, 1969.

OBITUARIES:

PERIODICALS

AB Bookman's Weekly, September 24, 1979.
Publishers Weekly, September 17, 1979.*

*   *   *

MONAHAN, John
  See BURNETT, W(illiam) R(iley)

*   *   *

MORTON, Anthony
  See CREASEY, John

*   *   *

MURRAY, Fiona
  See BEVAN, Gloria (Isabel)

N

NAMJOSHI, Suniti 1941-

PERSONAL: Born April 20, 1941, in Bombay, India; daughter of Manohar (a test pilot) and Sarojini (an agriculturist; maiden name, Naik Nimbalkar) Namjoshi; companion of poet Gillian Hanscombe since 1984. *Education:* University of Poona, B.A., 1961, M.A. (English literature), 1963; University of Missouri, M.S. (public administration), 1969; McGill University, Ph.D. (English literature), 1972. *Politics:* Feminist.

ADDRESSES: Home—Grindon Cottage, Combpyne Lane, Rousdon near Lyme Regis, England DT7 3XW. *E-mail*—s.m.namjoshi@exeter.ac.uk.

CAREER: University of Poona, Fergusson College, Poona, India, lecturer in English literature, 1963-64; Government of India, Indian Administrative Service, New Delhi, India, officer, 1964-69; University of Toronto, Scarborough College, Scarborough, Ontario, lecturer, 1972-73, assistant professor, 1973-78, associate professor of English literature, 1978-89.

MEMBER: League of Canadian Poets, Writers' Guild of Great Britain.

AWARDS, HONORS: Grants from Ontario Arts Council, 1976, 1977, 1987-88, 1992, for poetry; Canada Council short term grant, 1981, 1990, 1993 for poetry; Canada Council Travel Grant, 1993, 1994.

WRITINGS:

POETRY

Poems, Writers Workshop (Calcutta), 1967.

(Translator with mother, Sarojini Namjoshi) Ram Ganesh Gadkari, *Poems of Govindagraj,* Writers Workshop, 1968.

More Poems, Writers Workshop, 1971.

Cyclone in Pakistan, Writers Workshop, 1971.

The Jackass and the Lady, Writers Workshop, 1980.

The Authentic Lie, Fiddlehead (Fredericton, New Brunswick, Canada), 1982.

From the Bedside Book of Nightmares, Fiddlehead, 1984.

Flesh and Paper, Ragweed Press (Charlottetown), 1986.

Because of India: Selected Poems and Fables, Onlywomen Press (London), 1989.

PROSE

Feminist Fables, Sheba (London), 1981.

The Conversations of Cow, Women's Press (London), 1985.

Aditi and the One-Eyed Monkey (for children), Sheba, 1986, Beacon Press (Boston), 1989.

The Blue Donkey Fables, Women's Press, 1988.

The Mothers of Maya Diip, Women's Press, 1989.

Saint Suniti and the Dragon, Spinifex (Melbourne), 1993, Virago (London), 1994.

Building Babel, Spinifex, 1996.

OTHER

(With Gillian Hanscombe) *Kaliyug: Circles of Paradise* (play), performed in 1993.

Work also represented in numerous anthologies, including *Modern Indian Poetry in English,* edited by P. Lal, Writers Workshop, 1978; *Aurora: New Canadian Writing, 1980,* edited by Morris Wolfe, Doubleday

(Garden City, NY), 1980; *The Maple Laugh Forever: An Anthology of Canadian Comic Poetry,* edited by Douglas Barbour and Stephen Scobie, Hurtig, 1981; and *New Lesbian Writing,* edited by Margaret Cruikshank, Grey Fox Press (San Francisco), 1984.

SIDELIGHTS: Poet and feminist Suniti Namjoshi speaks to both her feminism and her identity as a lesbian through mythical creatures drawn from sources as diverse as fairy tales, the plays of William Shakespeare, and the fiction of Lewis Carroll. These creatures constantly transmute, under Namjoshi's pen, to refract a diversity of beings, emotions, and genders, showing the poet's vision of personal "identity" to be far from static.

Born in Bombay, India in 1941, Namjoshi attended English boarding schools. Attending universities in her native India, the United States, and Canada, Namjoshi ultimately chose to remain in Canada, where she taught at the University of Toronto from 1972 until 1989. Her first published book of poetry, simply titled *Poems,* was followed by several other poetry collections, including *The Jackass and the Lady, The Authentic Lie,* and *From the Bedside Book of Nightmares,* all written in English. The collaboration, with her mother, Sarojini Namjoshi, of Ram Ganesh Gadkari's *Poems of Govindagraj* early in her career garnered positive reviews. K. S. Narayana Rao of *Books Abroad* cited the women's translation of Gadkari's verse from the Marathi as "an excellent service to the Indian literary community" and added that the Namjoshis "must be congratulated upon a wise choice and a commendable execution of a literary task."

In reviewing Namjoshi's 1982 volume of poetry, *The Authentic Lie,* as well as in Namjoshi's poetry in general, Mary Meigs in *Room of One's Own* identified "something more complicated than rational meaning" at the basis of her works. As an example of the "shimmering complexity" of Namjoshi's poetry, the critic singled out "Discourse with the Dead," the first section of *The Authentic Lie,* in which the poet, by imagining a conversation with her deceased father, confronts the paradox "that the dead often live in us more fully than the living." Other critics were equally impressed by Namjoshi's language, stressing her singular blend of complexity and lucidity. The poet's voice, Meigs asserted, is "like a dream language." However, the critic added, Namjoshi's "elaborate imagery, her ironies and paradoxes are not used as a disguise or a shield, but as a way of clarifying."

The collection *From the Bedside Book of Nightmares* echoes *The Tempest* as Namjoshi retells Shakespeare's story of Prospero, Miranda, and Caliban. In Namjoshi's feminist version of the classic tale, Caliban is transformed into a woman, eventually becoming like a sister to Prospero's daughter. Remarking on Namjoshi's other woman-centered works, Jacquelyn Marie noted in *Feminist Writers* that the writer's poems "view families and social institutions in all their power struggles, though they avoid didacticism through [Namjoshi's] use of innuendo, humor, and realism."

Although raised in a British culturation, elements of Namjoshi's Hindu tradition can often be seen joined with her feminism throughout her work. Evaluating Namjoshi's oeuvre as a fellow Indian, Harveen Sachdeva Mann stated in the *Journal of Commonwealth Literature* that the author is able to create "a 'nation' that has hitherto been totally ignored in modern Indian nationalist discourse, one underwritten by egalitarian lesbian sexual politics." Despite the portrayal of Hindu elements in a feminist light, Namjoshi's matriarchies are not always benign; as Marie explained, "there are hierarchies and power plays and cruelty even in feminist paradises."

Calling Namjoshi "an innovative, creative poet who captures the universal, personal, and social experiences fabulistically," Angelina Paul noted in *Contemporary Women Poets* that the poet "uses metaphors and similes, myths and fables to suggest various layers of meanings on life." *Canadian Literature* reviewer Ian Sowton also acknowledged the "pronounced intertextuality" of such works as *The Authentic Lie* and discerned an "elaborate substructure of literary allusions" in Namjoshi's poems. Among these allusions, Sowton explained, "are retellings of myths, nursery rhymes, and fairy stories as well as an effective continuation of an *Alice in Wonderland* conversation that's nearly as zany-but-shrewd as its original."

In Namjoshi's work, *Feminist Fables,* the author combines her poetic and interpretive talents in a feminist rendition of ninety-five traditional fables, including such familiar stories as "Bluebeard," "Beauty and the Beast," and "Red Riding Hood." Eileen Manion of the Montreal *Gazette* remarked that "the reader is constantly surprised by the freshness of an imagination liberated rather than constrained through the adopting of a feminist perspective." Yet for Namjoshi, as Meigs explained, retelling a fable from a woman's point of view does not mean restoring "myth to a pre-patriarchal state of non-sexism." According to the critic, Namjoshi intervenes "with her own humorous ideal—of the common-sense woman who resists the injustice inherent in the old story." Although in the original fable the woman often figures as a victim of violent acts, Namjoshi, in Meigs's opinion, is able to make "ironic use, in her alternative versions, of the intractable original." While praising Namjoshi's imagination, critics also noted her keen awareness of reality. Like all good fables, declared Yvonne M. Klein in *RFR-DFR,* the author's stories "contain an element of mystery, a prod to the unconscious, an enigma to be puzzled over." Klein nonetheless saw these fables as "rooted in the real experience of women."

Violence, which appears frequently in *Feminist Fables,* is a recurrent theme throughout Namjoshi's work—the poet's "most important theme," as Meigs commented. However, if Namjoshi, as critics observed, perceives violence as all-pervasive, her belief in love is crystallized in poems that Meigs praised as "exuberant and delicate," celebrating "those magic times with other women when the mind ceases to observe and suffer."

Namjoshi once told *CA:* "I work four hours a day, six days a week. I think I write in order to give pleasure, to celebrate the fact that however appalling we are, we're human, we're alive. I wrote my thesis on Ezra Pound, I admire Adrienne Rich, but for some reason the two books that seem to have entered my imagination most are Lewis Carroll's *Alice in Wonderland* (and *Through the Looking Glass*) and Jonathan Swift's *Gulliver's Travels.*"

BIOGRAPHICAL/CRITICAL SOURCES:

BOOKS

Aaron, Jane and Sylvia Walby, editors, *Out of the Margins,* Falmer Press (London), 1991.
A Study of Indian Women Poets in English, Sterling (New Delhi), 1984.
Chedgzoy, Kate, *Shakespeare's Queer Children: Sexual Politics and Contemporary Culture,* Manchester University Press, 1995.
Contemporary Women Poets, St. James Press (Detroit), 1997.
Feminist Writers, St. James Press, 1996.
Kanaganayakam, Chelva, *Configurations of Exile: South Asian Writers and Their World,* TSAR (Toronto), 1995.
Writers of the Indian Diaspora: A Bio-Bibliographical Source, Greenwood Press, 1993.

PERIODICALS

Books Abroad, winter, 1970.
Canadian Literature, summer, 1983.
Canadian Woman Studies, winter, 1982; fall, 1983.
Fiddlehead, autumn, 1985.
Gazette (Montreal), March 3, 1984.
Indian Review of Books, December 16, 1993-January 15, 1994, pp. 264-67; January 16-February 15, 1996, p. 31.
Journal of Commonwealth Literature, Volume 29, number 2, 1994.
Pink Ink, December-January, 1984.
RFR-DFR, March, 1983.
Room of One's Own, February, 1984.
Times Literary Supplement, April 24, 1981; September 14 1990.
World Literature Today, winter, 1991, pp. 72-80.

* * *

NAYLOR, Phyllis (Reynolds) 1933-

PERSONAL: Born January 4, 1933, in Anderson, IN; daughter of Eugene S. and Lura (Schield) Reynolds; married second husband, Rex V. Naylor (a speech pathologist), May 26, 1960; children: Jeffrey Alan, Michael Scott. *Education:* Joliet Junior College, diploma, 1953; American University, B.A., 1963. *Politics:* Independent. *Religion:* Unitarian Universalist. *Avocational interests:* Music, drama, hiking, swimming.

ADDRESSES: Home—9910 Holmhurst Rd., Bethesda, MD 20817.

CAREER: Elementary school teacher in Hazel Crest, IL, 1956; Montgomery County Education Association, Rockville, MD, assistant executive secretary, 1958-59; National Education Association, Washington, DC, editorial assistant with *NEA Journal,* 1959-60; full-time writer, 1960—. Active in civil rights and peace organizations.

MEMBER: Society of Children's Book Writers, Authors Guild, Authors League of America, Children's Book Guild (president, 1974-75, 1983-84).

AWARDS, HONORS: Golden Kite Award for nonfiction, Society of Children's Book Authors, 1978, and International Reading Association (IRA) Children's Choice citation, 1979, both for *How I Came to Be a*

Writer; IRA Children's Choice citation, 1980, for *How Lazy Can You Get?;* American Library Association (ALA) Young Adult Services Division (YASD) Best Book for Young Adults citation and Notable Children's Book in the Field of Social Studies citation from National Council for Social Studies, both 1982, and, South Carolina Young Adult Book Award, 1985-86, all for *A String of Chances;* Child Study Award, Bank Street College, 1983, for *The Solomon System;* ALA Notable Book citation, 1985, and IRA Children's Choice Citation, 1986, both for *The Agony of Alice;* Edgar Allan Poe Award, Mystery Writers of America, 1985, for *Night Cry;* Notable Children's Book in the Field of Social Studies citation, 1985, for *The Dark of the Tunnel;* ALA YASD Best Book for Young Adults Citation, 1986, for *The Keeper;* creative writing fellowship, grant, National Endowment for the Arts, 1987; ALA YASD Best Book for Young Adults citation, 1987, and Best Young Adult Book of the Year from Michigan Library Association, 1988, both for *Year of the Gopher;* Society of School Librarians International Book Award, 1988, for *Maudie in the Middle;* Christopher Award from the Christophers, 1989, for *Keeping a Christmas Secret;* ALA Notable Book for Young Adults Citation, 1989, for *Send No Blessings;* John Newbery Medal from Association for Library Service to Children, 1992, for *Shiloh.*

WRITINGS:

Crazy Love: An Autobiographical Account of Marriage and Madness (nonfiction; Literary Guild selection), Morrow (New York City), 1977.
In Small Doses (humorous fiction), Atheneum (New York City), 1979.
Revelations (novel), St. Martin's (New York City), 1979.
Unexpected Pleasures (fiction), Putnam (New York City), 1986.
The Craft of Writing the Novel, Writer (Boston), 1989.

FOR CHILDREN AND YOUNG ADULTS; NONFICTION

How to Find Your Wonderful Someone, How to Keep Him/Her if You Do, How to Survive if You Don't, Fortress (Philadelphia), 1972.
An Amish Family, J. Philip O'Hara (Merrick, NY), 1974.
Getting Along in Your Family, Abingdon (Nashville, TN), 1976.
How I Came to Be a Writer, Atheneum, 1978, revised edition, Aladdin Books (New York City), 1987.

Getting Along with Your Friends, Abingdon, 1980.
Getting Along with Your Teachers, Abingdon, 1981.

FOR CHILDREN AND YOUNG ADULTS; FICTION

The Galloping Goat and Other Stories (short stories), Abingdon, 1965.
Grasshoppers in the Soup: Short Stories for Teenagers, Fortress, 1965.
Knee Deep in Ice Cream and Other Stories (short stories), Fortress, 1967.
What the Gulls Were Singing, Follett (Chicago), 1967.
Jennifer Jean, the Cross-Eyed Queen, Lerner (Minneapolis), 1967.
To Shake a Shadow, Abingdon, 1967.
The New Schoolmaster, Silver Burdett (Morristown, NJ), 1967.
A New Year's Surprise, Silver Burdett, 1967.
When Rivers Meet, Friendship (New York City), 1968.
The Dark Side of the Moon (short stories), Fortress, 1969.
Meet Murdock, Follett, 1969.
To Make a Wee Moon, Follett, 1969.
The Private I and Other Stories (short stories), Fortress, 1969.
Making It Happen, Follett, 1970.
Ships in the Night, Fortress, 1970.
Wrestle the Mountain (Junior Literary Guild selection), Follett, 1971.
No Easy Circle, Follett, 1972.
To Walk the Sky Path (Weekly Reader Book Club selection), Follett, 1973.
Witch's Sister (first volume of Witch trilogy), Atheneum, 1975.
Walking through the Dark (Junior Literary Guild selection), Atheneum, 1976.
Witch Water (second volume of Witch trilogy), Atheneum, 1977.
The Witch Herself (third volume of Witch trilogy), Atheneum, 1978.
How Lazy Can You Get? (Weekly Reader Book Club selection), Atheneum, 1979.
A Change in the Wind, Augsburg Press (Minneapolis), 1980.
Eddie, Incorporated, Atheneum, 1980.
Shadows on the Wall (first volume of York trilogy), Atheneum, 1980.
All Because I'm Older, Atheneum, 1981.
Faces in the Water (second volume in York trilogy), Atheneum, 1981.
Footprints at the Window (third volume of York trilogy), Atheneum, 1981.

The Boy with the Helium Head, Atheneum, 1982.

A String of Chances, Atheneum, 1982.

Never Born a Hero, Augsburg Press, 1982.

The Solomon System, Atheneum, 1983.

The Mad Gasser of Bessledorf Street (first volume in Bessledorf series), Atheneum, 1983.

A Triangle Has Four Sides, Augsburg Press, 1984.

Night Cry, Atheneum, 1984.

Old Sadie and the Christmas Bear, Atheneum, 1984.

The Dark of the Tunnel, Atheneum, 1985.

The Agony of Alice (first volume in Alice series), Atheneum, 1985.

The Keeper (Junior Literary Guild selection), Atheneum, 1986.

The Bodies in the Bessledorf Hotel (second volume in Bessledorf series), Atheneum, 1986.

The Baby, the Bed, and the Rose, Atheneum, 1987.

The Year of the Gopher, Atheneum, 1987.

Beetles, Lightly Toasted, Atheneum, 1987.

(With Lura Schield Reynolds) *Maudie in the Middle,* Atheneum, 1988.

One of the Third Grade Thonkers, Atheneum, 1988.

Alice in Rapture, Sort Of (second volume in Alice series), Atheneum, 1989.

Keeping a Christmas Secret, Atheneum, 1989.

Bernie and the Bessledorf Ghost (third volume in Bessledorf series), Atheneum, 1990.

Send No Blessings, Atheneum, 1990.

The Witch's Eye (first volume in second Witch trilogy), Delacorte (New York City), 1990.

King of the Playground, Atheneum, 1991.

Reluctantly Alice (third volume in Alice series), Atheneum, 1991.

Shiloh, Atheneum, 1991.

Witch Weed (second volume in second Witch trilogy), Delacorte, 1991.

All but Alice (fourth volume in Alice series), Atheneum, 1992.

Josie's Troubles, Atheneum, 1992.

The Witch Returns (third volume in second Witch trilogy), Delacorte, 1992.

Alice in April (fifth volume in Alice series), Atheneum, 1993.

The Face in the Bessledorf Funeral Parlor (fourth volume in Bessledorf series), Atheneum, 1993.

The Boys Start the War, Delacorte, 1993.

The Girls Get Even (sequel to *The Boys Start the War*), Delacorte, 1993.

The Grand Escape, Atheneum, 1993.

Alice In-Between (sixth volume in Alice series), Atheneum, 1994.

Boys Against Girls (sequel to *The Girls Get Even*), Delacorte, 1994.

The Fear Place, Atheneum, 1994.

Alice the Brave (seventh volume in Alice series), Atheneum, 1995.

Being Danny's Dog, Atheneum, 1995.

Alice in Lace (eighth volume in Alice series), Atheneum, 1996.

The Bomb in the Bessledorf Bus Depot (fifth volume in Bessledorf series), Atheneum, 1996.

Ducks Disappearing, Atheneum, 1996.

Ice, Atheneum, 1996.

Shiloh Season (sequel to *Shiloh*), Atheneum, 1996.

I Can't Take You Anywhere, Atheneum, 1997.

Outrageously Alice (ninth volume in Alice series), Atheneum, 1997.

ADAPTATIONS: The Keeper was adapted into the ABC Afterschool Special *My Dad Can't Be Crazy; Shiloh* was adapted into a feature film and released in 1997.

SIDELIGHTS: Phyllis Naylor's extensive output of novels for children and young adults displays great diversity of subject and tone. She has dealt with many serious issues—mental illness in *The Keeper;* crib death and a crisis of faith in *A String of Chances;* difficult moral choices in *Shiloh.* Her body of work, however, also includes the comic mysteries of the Bessledorf series, the supernatural tales of the Witch trilogies, and a broad range of other stories. Additionally, she has written nonfiction for young people; her subjects here include writing as a career and advice on relationships. Her work for adults likewise comprises fiction and nonfiction; among the latter is an account of her troubled first marriage, to a paranoid schizophrenic.

Several critics have praised Naylor as an author who creates believable and sympathetic characters in stories that appeal to young readers. "Prolific and talented children's writer Phyllis Reynolds Naylor does more than understand the adolescent heart—she eloquently expresses it in all its bittersweet complexity," observed Linda Barrett Osborne in a *Washington Post Book World* review of two of Naylor's novels, *Ice* and *Being Danny's Dog.* "Poised between childhood and adulthood, her young characters survive loss, discover strength in crisis, and meet the challenges of 'broken' homes and bruised psyches with honesty, humor and determination."

Naylor has featured single-parent families in a number of her juvenile novels. The protagonists of *Ice* and *Being Danny's Dog* both have absent fathers; the main character in Naylor's Alice series is a girl coping with adolescence after her mother's death. *The Agony of Alice,* the first of the series, finds Alice longing for a woman's guidance as she enters puberty; subsequent entries show her falling in love for the first time, learning about adult responsibilities, and contending with all the ups and downs of her teenage years. Critiquing *The Agony of Alice* for *School Library Journal,* Caroline Ward Romans commented that Naylor "exhibits a deft touch at capturing the essence of an endearing heroine growing up without a mother." In *Booklist,* Hazel Rochman termed the novel "a wonderfully funny and touching story that will make readers smile with wry recognition."

In a different vein is the Bessledorf series, which centers on a young boy, Bernie Magruder, whose father manages the Bessledorf Hotel in Middleburg, Indiana. The hotel is the scene of many humorous mysteries; for instance, the second book in the series, *The Bodies in the Bessledorf Hotel,* deals with corpses that unexpectedly appear and disappear at the hostelry. "The subject of bodies, which I feared might be a bit touchy, is treated comically," noted *Washington Post Book World* contributor Carolyn Banks, who went on to praise the deadpan humor of the book's opening dialogue between Bernie and a police officer. Critics have sometimes found the series' comedic topics inappropriate or distasteful, though. *School Library Journal* reviewer John Sigwald called *The Bomb in the Bessledorf Bus Depot* "unfortunately untimely," given real-life tragedies; he noted that "unlike the real world, in Naylor's cartoon creation nobody ever gets hurt."

Naylor entered the Gothic realm in the Witch trilogies, about a young girl who suspects others of witchcraft. *Witch Water,* the second volume of the first trilogy, "presents with total believability the delicate, potentially volatile balance which exists in the sensitive heroine's mind between her world of escapist fantasy and her actual situation in ordinary reality," commented Sharon Leder in a review for *The Lion and the Unicorn.* Another venture by Naylor into the supernatural was the York trilogy, concerning a young man whose travels through time help him come to terms with his fears about a disease than runs in his family.

Naylor has received numerous awards and substantial acclaim for serious, issue-oriented works. In *The Keeper,* an adolescent boy tries to live a normal life while grappling with his father's mental illness. Naylor's inspiration for the book came after she had published *Crazy Love: An Autobiographical Account of Marriage and Madness,* dealing with her first

husband's schizophrenia and its effect on their relationship. "I began to think, hey, if I couldn't cope with this as a twenty-three-year-old woman, how would a thirteen-year-old boy handle it?" Naylor said in an interview for the American Audio Prose Library. Her exploration of this situation brought several favorable reviews. "This is a sensitively wrought novel with no happy ending but certainly with an affirmation of individual strength and emotional survival in the face of adversity," Denise M. Wilms wrote in *Booklist.*

Naylor has explored a variety of other difficult issues. *A String of Chances* focuses on a young girl, daughter of a fundamentalist minister, who finds her faith shaken after a cousin's baby dies. *Booklist* contributor Sally Estes found the characters well drawn and the situations absorbing. "Specific scenes and themes . . . all smoothly converge and interlock," she noted. "The effect is totally involving and moving." *The Dark of the Tunnel* tells the story of a teenage boy whose mother is dying of cancer; John R. Lord, reviewing for *Voice of Youth Advocates,* termed the book "one of the best adolescent novels dealing with death I have ever read." In *Booklist,* however, Stephanie Zvirin called the story "heavy-handed and uneven," although featuring "some genuine flashes of insight and emotion."

Moral questions are at the center of *Shiloh,* for which Naylor received the John Newbery Medal, the most prestigious award in children's literature. Marty, a young West Virginia boy, takes in a dog that has run away from an abusive master. He wants to protect the dog, but feels guilty about not returning it to its owner, and about the lies he tells to deal with the situation; he tries to figure out the right thing to do. "Without breaking new ground, Marty's tale is well told," observed a *Publishers Weekly* contributor, who described the book as "heartwarming." At least one critic, though, had a quibble with its selection for the Newbery award. "Surely there must have been a book more important than this agreeable but slight story," Jane Langton wrote in the *New York Times Book Review.* Langton pronounced *Shiloh* "a good book, not a great book."

Naylor's other works have exhibited great variety, from the comedy of *Beetles, Lightly Toasted,* about a boy who comes up with insect-based recipes in an effort to win a contest, to the nostalgia of *Maudie in the Middle,* concerning an early-twentieth-century girl, a middle child, seeking to distinguish herself in her family. The latter was inspired by the experiences of Naylor's mother, Lura Schield Reynolds, who is credited as co-author of the book.

Naylor has said many of her story ideas and characters have come from her relatives, as well as from her desire to live someone else's life for a while. "And so, because I want to know what it would be like to be a preacher or a bicycle courier or a motherless twelve-year-old or a bridge worker, I write," she noted in the *Something about the Author Autobiography Series.* She apparently has no shortage of ideas; in *How I Came to Be a Writer,* she commented, "On my deathbed, I am sure, I will gasp, 'But I still have five more books to write!'"

BIOGRAPHICAL/CRITICAL SOURCES:

BOOKS

Children's Literature Review, Volume 17, Gale (Detroit), 1989.
Naylor, Phyllis, *Crazy Love: An Autobiographical Account of Marriage and Madness,* Morrow (New York City), 1977.
Naylor, Phyllis, *How I Came to Be a Writer,* Atheneum (New York City), 1978, revised edition, Aladdin Books (New York City), 1987.
Something about the Author Autobiography Series, Volume 10, Gale, 1990.

PERIODICALS

Booklist, August, 1982, p. 1518; March 15, 1985, pp. 1051-52; October 1, 1985, pp. 264-65; April 1, 1986, p. 1144.
Chicago Tribune, January 28, 1992, section 1, p. 16.
Chicago Tribune Book World, March 2, 1986.
Lion and the Unicorn, fall, 1977, pp. 1111-15.
Los Angeles Times, November 1, 1986.
New York Times Book Review, December 2, 1979; November 2, 1986; May 10, 1992, p. 21.
Publishers Weekly, July 12, 1991, pp. 66-67; August 17, 1992, p. 501; October 17, 1994, p. 82; March 4, 1996, p. 67.
Quill and Quire, January, 1996, p. 45.
School Library Journal, January, 1986, p. 70; May, 1996, p. 114.
Voice of Youth Advocates, August, 1985, p. 188.
Washington Post, January 28, 1992, section E, p. 1.
Washington Post Book World, September 12, 1982; November 6, 1983; November 8, 1983; June 9, 1985; March 9, 1986; May 11, 1986; November

25, 1986; December 14, 1986, p. 8; May 10, 1987; January 7, 1996, p. 10.
Washington Post Magazine, August 13, 1995, p. 14.

OTHER

Phyllis Naylor Interview with Kay Bonetti (sound recording), American Audio Prose Library (Columbia, MO), 1987.*

—*Sketch by Trudy Ring*

*   *   *

NEWMAN, Shirlee P(etkin) 1924-

PERSONAL: Born February 16, 1924, in Brookline, MA; married Jackson J. Newman (an automotive dealer), June 25, 1946; children: Paul, Jeffrey. *Education:* Attended high schools in Massachusetts and California; also studied at Boston Center for Adult Education and Cambridge Centre for Adult Education. *Avocational interests:* Yoga, bird-watching, nature study, guitar, folk singing, bike riding.

ADDRESSES: Home—58B Charles River Rd., Waltham, MA 02154.

CAREER: Freelance writer; copywriter for advertising agencies in Los Angeles, 1941-45, and New York City, 1945-46; *Child Life Magazine,* associate editor, 1962-63; teacher of writing for children, Cambridge Center for Adult Education, Cambridge, MA, 1975-76, Lesley College, 1978-79, and Brandeis University, 1980-85.

WRITINGS:

Liliuokalani, Young Queen of Hawaii, Bobbs-Merrill (Indianapolis), 1960.
Yellow Silk for May Lee, Bobbs-Merrill, 1961.
(Adaptor) *Folk Tales of Latin America,* Bobbs-Merrill, 1962.
(Adaptor) *Folk Tales of Japan,* Bobbs-Merrill, 1963.
The Shipwrecked Dog, Bobbs-Merrill, 1963.
(With Diane Sherman) *About the People Who Run Your City,* illustrated by James David Johnson, Melmont (Chicago), 1963.
(With Sherman) *About Canals,* Melmont, 1964.
Marian Anderson: Lady from Philadelphia, Westminster (Philadelphia), 1966.
Ethel Barrymore: Girl Actress, Bobbs-Merrill, 1966.
The Story of Lyndon B. Johnson, Westminster, 1967.

Mary Martin on Stage, Westminster, 1969.
Tell Me, Grandma, Tell Me, Grandpa (picture book), illustrated by Joan Drescher, Houghton (Boston), 1979.
The Incas, F. Watts (New York City), 1992.
The Inuits, F. Watts, 1993.
The Creek, F. Watts, 1996.
The Pequots, F. Watts, in press.

Contributor to periodicals, including *American Girl, Book News, Calling All Girls, Good Housekeeping, Grade Teacher, Highlights for Children, Instructor, Jack and Jill, Saturday Evening Post, Scholastic,* and *Weekly Reader.*

SIDELIGHTS: Shirlee P. Newman has channelled a lifelong curiosity and enthusiasm into a series of nonfiction books for young readers which range over such varied topics as the workings of local government, Hawaiian princesses, former American presidents, famous actresses, and the ancient peoples of the Americas.

Newman first began writing professionally when her daughter began to tackle the articles in children's magazines as a beginning reader. Newman thought that she might be able to write magazine articles herself. She attended several classes in writing for children and then sat down to work. "After many long hours, days, weeks, months, of writing, re-writing, re-writing, re-writing, my work began to sell," she told *CA.* From a successful article writer, it was on to books and, in 1962, the associate editorship of *Child Life* magazine.

All of Newman's books have involved live research of one type or another: "From going through old houses, to windjamming on a high-masted schooner along the New England seacoast," explained Newman. Set in San Francisco's Chinatown, her 1961 novel *Yellow Silk for May Lee* made use of the author's own memories of living in the area as a young woman. "When I wrote the book many years later, I still read every scrap I could about Chinatown," she adds.

The Incas, which Newman published in 1992, is a study of the ancient South American civilization aimed at upper elementary and middle school students. Describing both the events of Incan history and the lifestyle of the Incas' modern-day descendants, Newman also delineates the culture's advanced road system, counting system, and calendar in a book that Merlyn Miller in *Voice of Youth Advocates* called "a springboard to future study."

In *The Inuits,* Newman turns her attention to the indigenous people of Alaska, northern Canada, and Greenland. From a discussion of such basic essentials as clothing, shelter, and transportation, she expands the reader's understanding of the development of Inuit culture by examining family life, the influence of contact with early explorers and missionaries, and the transformations that have come about in the Inuit lifestyle with the advent of modern technology and changing resources. Patricia Fry deemed the book "very readable, interesting and informative" in *CM: A Reviewing Journal of Canadian Materials for Young People.*

While Newman enjoys the investigations—both in libraries and in real life—that form the basis for her stories and nonfiction works, they don't compare to the satisfaction she gets from her readers. "The most fun of all my work," she told *CA,* "is receiving letters from boys and girls . . . knowing they're out there, reading my books."

BIOGRAPHICAL/CRITICAL SOURCES:

PERIODICALS

Booklist, December 1, 1993, p. 688.
Bulletin of the Center for Children's Books, September, 1979.
CM: A Reviewing Journal of Canadian Materials for Young People, September, 1992, p. 128.
Multicultural Review, March, 1993, p. 29.
School Library Journal, March, 1979, p. 128; August, 1992, p. 164.
Voice of Youth Advocates, August, 1992, p. 187.

*   *   *

NEWTON, David C.
  See CHANCE, John Newton

*   *   *

NOLAN, Dennis 1945-

PERSONAL: Born October 19, 1945, in San Francisco, CA; son of Arthur Thomas (an opera singer) and Helen (Fortier) Nolan; married Susan Christine Ericksen, January 28, 1967; married Lauren Ainsworth Mills, June 1, 1987; children: (first marriage)

Andrew William. *Education:* Attended College of San Mateo, 1963-65; San Jose State College (now University), B.A., 1967, M.A., 1968.

ADDRESSES: Home and office—Westhampton, MA 01027.

CAREER: San Mateo County Library, Belmont, CA, graphic artist, 1970-77; Canada Junior College, Redwood City, CA, art instructor, 1979-86; University of Hartford, West Hartford, CT, coordinator of illustration program in Hartford Art School, 1986—. Art instructor at College of San Mateo, 1982-86, and at San Jose State University, 1983-86. Work has been exhibited in one-man shows and in group shows.

AWARDS, HONORS: Outstanding Science Book Award, National Science Teachers Association, 1981, for *The Joy of Chickens,* and 1987, for *Step into the Night;* Pick of the List, American Booksellers, 1987, Top Twelve Books, *Christian Science Monitor,* 1987, and Prix de Zephyr, French Librarian Award, 1988, all for *The Castle Builder; Parents Choice* Magazine Top 15 Books, 1988, and Commonwealth Club of California award, 1988, both for *Step into the Night;* Notable Social Studies Books selection, 1988, for *Legend of the White Doe;* Golden Kite Picture Book Honor, 1990, for *Dinosaur Dream. Monster Bubbles: A Counting Book* was a Junior Literary Guild selection.

WRITINGS:

FOR CHILDREN; SELF-ILLUSTRATED

Big Pig (picture book), Prentice-Hall (Englewood Cliffs, NJ), 1976.
Monster Bubbles: A Counting Book (picture book), Prentice-Hall, 1976.
Alphabrutes (picture book), Prentice-Hall, 1977.
Wizard McBean and His Flying Machine (picture book), Prentice-Hall, 1977.
Witch Bazooza (picture book), Prentice-Hall, 1979.
The Joy of Chickens (nonfiction), Prentice-Hall, 1981.
The Castle Builder (picture book), Macmillan (New York City), 1987.
Wolf Child (picture book), Macmillan, 1989.
Dinosaur Dream (picture book), Macmillan, 1990.
(Reteller) *Androcles and the Lion,* Harcourt (San Diego), 1997.

ILLUSTRATOR

Charles Keller (compiler), *Llama Beans,* Prentice-Hall, 1979.

Bill Nygren, *Gnomes Color and Story Album,* Troubador Press, 1980.
Karen Schiller, *Bears Color and Story Album,* Troubador Press, 1982.
William Hooks, *The Legend of the White Doe,* Macmillan, 1988.
Joanne Ryder, *Step into the Night,* Four Winds (New York City), 1988.
Joanne Ryder, *Mockingbird Morning,* Four Winds, 1989.
Jane Yolen, *Dove Isabeau,* Harcourt, 1989.
Nancy Carlstrom, *Heather Hiding,* Macmillan, 1990.
Joanne Ryder, *Under Your Feet,* Four Winds, 1990.
Jane Yolen, *Wings,* Harcourt, 1991.
Nancy Carlstrom, *No Nap for Benjamin Badger,* Macmillan, 1991.
Ann Tompert, *Savina, the Gypsy Dancer,* Macmillan, 1991.
Maxinne Rhea Leighton, *An Ellis Island Christmas,* Viking (New York City), 1992.
T. H. White, *The Sword in the Stone,* Philomel Books (New York City), 1993.
Diane Stanley, *The Gentleman and the Kitchen Maid,* Dial (New York City), 1994.
Bruce Coville, reteller, *William Shakespeare's A Midsummer Night's Dream,* Dial, 1995.
Lauren A. Mills, *Fairy Wings: A Story,* Little, Brown (Boston), 1995.
Lauren A. Mills, *The Dog Prince,* Little, Brown, 1996.

FOR ADULTS; ILLUSTRATOR

Jim Barrett and others, editors, *"Sunset" Homeowner's Guide to Wood Stoves,* Lane, 1979.
David E. Clark and others, editors, *Gardeners Answer Book,* Lane, 1983.

SIDELIGHTS: Award-winning author and illustrator Dennis Nolan is known for his highly realistic acrylic paintings, though he has also used soft watercolors, such as those seen in Nancy Carlstrom's *No Nap for Benjamin Badger,* and experimented with a more fanciful, Arthur Rackham-like style in *Fairy Wings,* on which Nolan collaborated with Lauren Mills.

While still working as a graphic artist for the San Mateo County Library in Belmont, California, Nolan published his first self-illustrated picture book, *Big Pig,* in 1976. A silly poetic romp in which preschool readers can find all sorts of obese animals (like stout trouts, blimpy chimpies, and, on every page, a fat pig), *Big Pig* "is an ingenious but incongruous little book," according to one *Booklist* reviewer. Although the critic felt young readers would enjoy the book, he felt the intended audience would require help from an adult to understand all the words used in the text.

After spending much of the early 1980s as an art instructor at a California junior college, during which he worked on only a few children's books, Nolan actively began to pursue illustrating and writing again in the latter half of the decade. *The Castle Builder,* published in 1987, enters the world of childhood imagination as it tells of one young boy's day at the beach. The boy builds a sand castle and imagines himself to be its lord, Sir Christopher, a brave hero who defends his home against dragons and evil knights. When the tide comes in, however, the waves become a foe the boy can't defeat. His castle is washed away, but, undaunted, he vows to return to the beach and build a new one. A number of critics praised Nolan's picture book, including *School Library Journal* reviewer Shirley Wilton, who called it "a charming evocation of a child's world." Nolan's artwork was praised as well. For example, a *Publishers Weekly* critic wrote that the "photograph-like pictures in halftones . . . exhibit startling clarity." And Betsy Hearne of the *Bulletin of the Center for Children's Books* commented, "The duality of trompe l'oeil screened by a surface of dots serves the fantasy theme well."

In 1990 Nolan won a Golden Kite Picture Book Honor for his *Dinosaur Dream.* Returning to the world of childhood imagination that worked so well for him in *The Castle Builder,* Nolan once again brought dreams to life in this story about a modern boy who helps a baby apatosaurus find its way home. Wilbur is awakened one night when Gideon the dinosaur taps at his window. The boy, knowing immediately what must be done, resolves to return Gideon to the Jurassic Era. He manages to do this by simply walking back through time, with Gideon following him obediently like a puppy, past the Ice Age and back into the world of dinosaurs, while braving hazards like volcanoes and saber-tooth cats. When they at last arrive at their destination, Wilbur hugs Gideon and bids him a fond farewell. Throughout the story, Nolan leaves it up to the reader to decide whether this adventure is reality or merely a dream Wilbur is having after reading a book about dinosaurs before falling asleep. Although Cathryn A. Camper, a *School Library Journal* contributor, called the premise a "trite plot gimmick" and the conclusion "cloying," *Booklist* reviewer Leone McDermott called *Dinosaur Dream* "a dinosaur lover's delight." A *Publishers Weekly* commentator felt the story was clever, especially the role reversal

between Wilbur and Gideon that depicts the boy to be unexpectedly braver than his rather sheepish and cowardly dinosaur friend. She also considered the ending genuinely moving, adding that Gideon "ranks with the best of animal creations."

In his illustrating work, Nolan has teamed with such notable writers as William Hooks, Joanne Ryder, Jane Yolen, Nancy Carlstrom, and Ann Tompert. One of his most noted projects was the illustrations for Diane Stanley's *The Gentleman and the Kitchen Maid,* a well-received fantasy about the love between two figures in separate portraits hanging in a city art museum. A young art student who has come to copy the work of the Dutch masters becomes attuned to the plight of these unrequited lovers, and joins the two in a painting of her own making. "Hats off to Nolan for his thorough research and credible renderings of paintings in the style of artists ranging from Rembrandt to Picasso," commented a *Publishers Weekly* reviewer. Carolyn Phelan of *Booklist* called *The Gentleman and the Kitchen Maid* "an original," adding: "Nolan's sensitive watercolor illustrations make each portrait in the museum a definite character in the story." *School Library Journal* contributor Shirley Wilton also commented favorably on Stanley's and Nolan's effort in this work, asserting that "this lighthearted story is deftly told and handsomely illustrated."

More recently, Nolan has collaborated with his wife Lauren Mills on the illustrations for Mills's *Fairy Wings,* a tale about a wingless, ridiculed fairy who saves her fellow fairies from a wicked troll. Many commentators praised the artwork for this book. "Delicate, detailed watercolors add greatly to the book's appeal," noted *Booklist* reviewer Susan Dove Lempke. *School Library Journal* contributor Lisa Dennis similarly praised the "lovely illustrations, reminiscent of Arthur Rackham's ethereal style."

Nolan once told *CA:* "My grandparents were artists, as were my parents (my father was an operatic tenor). Art was not only encouraged but always around. Books have always been a large part of my life so the blending of two loves—art and books—seemed natural. As an illustrator I approach most of my projects with the visual problems foremost in my mind. The story generally moves along after the pictures have been visualized, at least in my mind if not on paper. Planning the illustrations for the lead-in, the climax, and the ending across a thirty-two page format is also a major concern. Most of my books are humorous, and I plan them in storyboard form somewhat like an animated film. In this way I can control the timing of the punch lines, surprises, and build-ups. I have found that varying my style and technical approach has kept me fresh for each new project."

BIOGRAPHICAL/CRITICAL SOURCES:

PERIODICALS

Booklist, April 15, 1976, p. 1192; February 15, 1978, p. 1010; December 1, 1989, p. 750; December 15, 1989, p. 834; March 15, 1990, p. 1443; October 15, 1990, p. 439; November 1, 1991, p. 330; January 15, 1994, p. 939; November 1, 1995, p. 478.

Bulletin of the Center for Children's Books, July, 1977, p. 178; January, 1988, p. 96; February, 1988, p. 110.

Kirkus Reviews, March 1, 1976, p. 253; January 15, 1977, p. 43; January 1, 1978, p. 1; August 15, 1989, p. 1248; October 1, 1989, p. 1483; February 15, 1990, p. 273; October 1, 1991, p. 1293.

Los Angeles Times Book Review, November 25, 1990, p. 18; December 16, 1990, p. 9.

Newsweek, December 3, 1990, p. 64.

Publishers Weekly, March 15, 1976, p. 57; January 17, 1977, p. 82; December 19, 1980, p. 52; August 14, 1987, p. 103; January 20, 1989, p. 147; July 28, 1989, p. 221; February 9, 1990, p. 60; October 26, 1990, p. 67; September 20, 1991, p. 132; November 22, 1993, p. 63; November 6, 1995, p. 94.

School Library Journal, April, 1976, p. 62; May, 1977, p. 54; February, 1978, p. 49; January, 1980, p. 60; January, 1988, p. 68; July, 1989, p. 75; December, 1989, p. 102; April, 1990, p. 110; July, 1990, p. 79; November, 1990, p. 96; August, 1994, p. 146; January, 1996, p. 90.

*   *   *

NORTH, Howard
  See TREVOR, Elleston

O

O'BRIEN, Darcy 1939-

PERSONAL: Born July 16, 1939, in Los Angeles, CA; son of George J. and Marguerite (Churchill) O'Brien (both film actors); married Ruth Ellen Berke, August 26, 1961 (divorced, 1969); married Suzanne Beesley, February 27, 1987; children: Molly Marguerite. *Education:* Princeton University, A.B., 1961; University of California, Berkeley, M.A., 1963, Ph.D., 1965; Pembroke College, Cambridge, graduate study, 1963-64. *Politics:* Independent. *Religion:* Roman Catholic.

ADDRESSES: Agent—c/o Robert Gottlieb, William Morris Agency, 1325 Avenue of the Americas, New York, NY 10019.

CAREER: Pomona College, Claremont, CA, instructor, 1965-66, assistant professor, 1966-70, associate professor, 1970-75, professor of English, 1975-78; University of Tulsa, Tulsa, OK, graduate professor of English, 1978—96.

MEMBER: Association of Literary Scholars and Critics, Authors Guild, P.E.N, Screen Writers Guild of America East, International Association of Crime Writers, American Irish Historical Society.

AWARDS, HONORS: Woodrow Wilson fellowship, 1961-62; Fulbright fellowship; University of Illinois Center for Advanced Study fellow, 1969-70; Mellon Foundation grant, 1973-74; Guggenheim fellowship, 1978-79; Ernest Hemingway Award, 1978, for *A Way of Life, Like Any Other*; Edgar Allan Poe Award, 1997, for *Power to Hurt*; inducted into the Oklahoma Writers Hall of Fame, 1997.

WRITINGS:

NONFICTION

The Conscience of James Joyce, Princeton University Press (Princeton, NJ), 1968.
W. R. Rodgers, Bucknell University Press (Cranbury, NJ), 1971.
Patrick Kavanagh, Bucknell University Press, 1975.
Two of a Kind: The Hillside Stranglers, New American Library (New York), 1985.
Reflections on Literature and the Law, McFarlin Library, University of Tulsa (Tulsa, OK), 1987.
Murder in Little Egypt, Morrow (New York), 1989.
A Dark and Bloody Ground, HarperCollins (New York), 1993.
Power to Hurt: Inside a Judge's Chambers: Sexual Assault, Corruption, and the Ultimate Reversal of Justice for Women, HarperCollins, 1996.

FICTION

A Way of Life, Like Any Other, Norton (New York), 1978.
The Silver Spooner, Simon & Schuster (New York), 1981.
Margaret in Hollywood, Morrow, 1991.

OTHER

Also author of *Moment by Moment,* 1978; contributor to *James Joyce Quarterly, New York, New York Times Magazine, The New Yorker,* and other publications.

WORK IN PROGRESS: The Hidden Pope, the true story of the continuing friendship between Pope John Paul II and Jerzy Kluger, a Jewish childhood friend, and how their friendship has transcended religious differences. Due for publication in April, 1998.

SIDELIGHTS: Darcy O'Brien was first published as a literary critic, then made his mark as a novelist, and finally has gone on to write several nonfiction books rated by numerous critics as among the best in the true-crime genre. His first novel, *A Way of Life, Like Any Other,* is a fictionalized account of his own boyhood as the son of two former Hollywood stars. "It's a half-comic, half-tragic memoir," O'Brien told Wayne Warga of the *Los Angeles Times.* "I used to say it was all made-up, but it's really half-autobiographical." Anthony Thwaite of the London *Observer* compared *A Way of Life, Like Any Other* with J. D. Salinger's *The Catcher in the Rye.* He found that O'Brien, like Salinger, wrote "with a humour which doesn't preclude seriousness; unlike Salinger, he stands back and looks at the boy from an unjudging but amused distance." A *New Yorker* critic described it as an "eccentric, cynical, and sometimes exceedingly funny first novel" and noted that "the story . . . conveys a great deal of feeling beneath a deceptively deadpan surface."

O'Brien's novel *Margaret in Hollywood* also drew on his inside knowledge of show business and its people. The fictional autobiography describes a feisty Kansas City girl's rise from vaudeville to Hollywood stardom in the 1920s. "The reader is treated to a polished, realistic story," observed Brad Hooper in *Booklist.* A *Publishers Weekly* writer called *Margaret in Hollywood* "a well-written, solid novel of character and situation," and called attention to the authenticity of O'Brien's portrayal of vaudeville, the theater, and the early movie industry. The reviewer did say, however, that the author's rendering of Margaret Spencer's story "fails to give her emotional appeal, and thus Margaret never earns the reader's strong attachment."

Commenting on the dramatic legacy left him by his parents, the author once told *CA:* "It took me too many years to realize how much I am the child of my parents, who were both fine actors. Now I see my fiction as a performing art, written to please an audience and myself. I do not know who or what that audience is, so I imagine an audience of my friends and family, assuming that among us we know best."

O'Brien first turned to recounting true-life crimes in 1985 when he published *Two of a Kind: The Hillside Stranglers.* It detailed the horrific crimes of Angelo Buono and Kenneth Bianchi, cousins who raped and murdered ten young women in Los Angeles in 1977-78. The book also outlined the prosecution of Buono and Bianchi, which was the longest trial in American history. "His probing, novelistic account . . . lays bare the frightening motives of these criminals," asserted a *Booklist* contributor. A *Kirkus Reviews* writer warned of "stupendously stomach-turning detail" about the crimes. *Publishers Weekly* found *Hillside Stranglers* "the definitive book" on the notorious case, and concluded: "O'Brien has done his research carefully . . . and the result is an outstanding true crime story."

The author's next true-crime book, *Murder in Little Egypt,* told another sordid tale, but Wendy Kaminer praised the author in the *New York Times Book Review* because he managed to reconstruct "this awful story for popular consumption without sensationalizing it." The central figure in *Little Egypt* is Dr. Dale Cavaness, a doctor who was something of a heroic figure in his hometown—despite his wife-beating, sadistic practical jokes on patients, heavy drinking, and more. Cavaness eventually killed two of his grown sons, at least in part for insurance money. *Kirkus Reviews* termed *Murder in Little Egypt* "engrossing and horrifying," and a *Booklist* writer praised: "O'Brien expertly stretches his reader's anticipation to near the breaking point in this masterful true-crime account."

By the time he wrote *A Dark and Bloody Ground,* O'Brien had established himself as "adept at analyzing crime by using sociological and cultural methods to create an integrated picture of the criminal and his world," declared a *Library Journal* reviewer. *A Dark and Bloody Ground* concerns members of a crime ring in the mountains of eastern Kentucky who robbed a local doctor of $2 million and murdered his daughter in the process. A *Kirkus Reviews* contributor found the portraits of the perpetrators "totally believable, even sympathetic" when seen in the context of their "lives impoverished at every level." The writer endorsed *A Dark and Bloody Ground* as a "first-rate—and lurid—true-crime chronicle." And a *Publishers Weekly* reviewer concurred that *A Dark and Bloody Ground* is "an arresting look into the troubled psyches of these criminals and into the depressed Kentucky economy that became fertile territory for narcotics dealers, theft rings and bootleggers."

Still more corruption and amorality provided the grist for *Power to Hurt: Inside a Judge's Chambers: Sexual Assault, Corruption, and the Ultimate Reversal of*

Justice for Women. This book offers the tale of David Lanier, a judge in a small Southern town. Lanier abused his power by sexually assaulting women in his soundproof, windowless chambers, then threatening his victims with dire consequences if they ever revealed his behavior. A *Kirkus Reviews* writer related: "O'Brien paints heroic portraits of the women involved . . . but he neglects fully to analyze Lanier. . . . What does emerge is a charged insight into the abuse of sex and power in the years between Anita Hill and Bob Packwood."

Darcy O'Brien recently told *CA*: "*Power to Hurt* has given me great satisfaction because of the impact it has had, on readers and on what was a gross miscarriage of justice. I never liked the term 'true crime' as a label for my books and was pleased when this one was also categorized under 'Current Affairs.' In it I describe not only human corruption but the courage of women who challenged a powerful, rapacious judge. Unfortunately, after beng convicted and sentenced to 25 years, Judge Lanier was freed by the highly controversial ruling of the U.S. Court of Appeals. This landmark case, involving the only conviction in history of a sitting judge on civil rights charges, was settled by the U.S. Supreme Court in a 9-0 vote in 1997. My book was cited to the Court as the definitive background to the case; civil rights and women's groups and U.S. attorneys have told me that it was instrumental in returning Lanier to jail.

"My real concern, whether in fiction or nonfiction, is with ethics, morality, and the conflict between good and evil. I am continuing these themes with my work-in-progress about Pope John Paul II, Catholicism, and Judaism."

BIOGRAPHICAL/CRITICAL SOURCES:

BOOKS

Contemporary Literary Criticism, Volume 11, Gale (Detroit), 1979.

PERIODICALS

Booklist, October 15, 1985, p. 294; February 1, 1989, pp. 901-02; January 15, 1991, p. 979; March 15, 1993, p. 1280-81.
Hudson Review, summer, 1978.
Kirkus Reviews, August 15, 1985, p. 861; December 1, 1988, pp. 1721-22; February 15, 1991, pp. 206-07; March 1, 1993, pp. 284-85; January 1, 1996, p. 48.
Library Journal, September 1, 1985, p. 210; March 15, 1991, p. 117; April 1, 1993, p. 116; February 15, 1996, p. 164; March 1, 1996, p. 92.
Listener, September 22, 1977.
Los Angeles Times, January 7, 1982.
New York, November 11, 1985, p. 106.
New Yorker, February 6, 1978; October 5, 1981.
New York Times Book Review, April 9, 1978, p. 14; March 12, 1989, p. 23; June 2, 1991, p. 20; April 28, 1996, pp. 22-23.
Observer, August 21, 1977.
People, March 1, 1982, p. 20; December 16, 1985, p. 34.
Publishers Weekly, August 23, 1985, p. 66; January 25, 1991, p. 47; March 15, 1993, p. 79; January 15, 1996, p. 453.
Saturday Review, August, 1981.
Sewanee Review, July, 1969.
Times Literary Supplement, April 24, 1969; October 21, 1977, p. 1249.

*　　*　　*

O'CONNOR, Francine M(arie) 1930-

PERSONAL: Born April 8, 1930, Springfield, MA; daughter of Wallace H. (a machinist) and Celestine (Morrison) Provost; married John F. O'Connor (an accountant), December 29, 1951; children: Margaret Anne, Kathryn Mary O'Connor Boswell, Timothy John. *Education:* Attended Washington University. *Religion:* Catholic.

*ADDRESSES: Home—*157 Crest Manor, House Springs, MO 63051. *Office—*Liguori Publications, One Liguori Dr., Liguori, MO 63057.

CAREER: Freelance writer, 1967-70; *St. Louis-Post Dispatch,* St. Louis, MO, book reviewer, 1970-75; *Liguorian* magazine, Liguori, MO, managing editor, 1975-93; Liguori Parish Educational Products, Liguori, associate editor, 1993—. Coordinator of children's church and communications director, parish council, Sts. Peter and Paul Parish.

MEMBER: Professed Secular Franciscan.

AWARDS, HONORS: Catholic Book Award, Catholic Press Association, 1992, for *ABC's Lessons of Love: Sermon on the Mount for Children;* Angel Award of Merit, 1995, for *ABC's of Christmas.*

WRITINGS:

"THE ABC'S OF FAITH" SERIES

ABC's of the Ten Commandments, illustrated by daughter, Kathryn Boswell, Liguori Publications (Liguori, MO), 1980, revised edition, 1989.

ABC's of the Sacraments . . . for Children, illustrated by Larry Nolte, Liguori Publications, 1981, revised edition, 1989.

ABC's of the Old Testament . . . for Children, illustrated by Kathryn Boswell, 1984, Liguori Publications, revised edition, 1989.

(With Kathryn Boswell) *ABC's of the Rosary,* Liguori Publications, 1984.

ABC's of the Mass . . . for Children, illustrated by Kathryn Boswell, Liguori Publications, 1988.

ABC's of Prayer . . . for Children, illustrated by Kathryn Boswell, Liguori Publications, 1989.

ABC's Lessons of Love: Sermon on the Mount for Children, illustrated by Kathryn Boswell, Liguori Publications, 1991.

ABC's of Christmas, illustrated by Bartholomew, Liguori Publications, 1994.

ABC's of Our Church, Liguori Publications, 1996.

OTHER

Stories of Jesus, Liguori Publications, 1982.

Special Friends of Jesus, Liguori Publications, 1986.

Wait and Wonder, Liguori Publications, 1991.

My Lenten Walk with Jesus, Liguori Publications, 1992.

You and God: Friends Forever—A Faith Book for Catholic Children, Liguori Publications, 1993.

ABC's for Teaching the Faith: Old Testament Program for Preschool/Kindergarten, Liguori Publications, 1995.

ABC's for Teaching the Faith: Meeting Jesus Program for Preschool/Kindergarten, Liguori Publications, 1996.

Questions and Answers for Children: Handing on the Faith, Regina Press, 1996.

The ABC's of Church, Liguori Publications, 1997.

Also author of "ABC's of Faith" column, *Liguorian* magazine, 1976—. Recorded the audio cassette "Joysongs," Liguori Publications, 1995, and wrote lyrics for the audio cassette "The ABC's in Song," music by Curtis Bell, Liguori Publications, 1996.

ADAPTATIONS: Several books from the "ABC's of Faith" series have been recorded as audio cassettes by Liguori Publications, including *ABC's of the Ten Commandments,* 1990, *ABC's of the Sacraments,* 1990, *ABC's of Prayer,* 1990, *ABC's of the Old Testament,* 1993, *ABC's of the Mass,* 1993, and *ABC's Lessons of Love,* 1993.

SIDELIGHTS: "I began my writing career in the 1960s, when I moved to the midwest from New England. Twelve hundred miles from home, friends, and family, I needed an outlet for the thoughts and feelings trapped inside my head," Francine M. O'Connor told *CA.* "At that time, I did not think of myself as a children's writer. In 1975, I was invited by the editor of *Liguorian* magazine to consider an editorial position with Liguori Publications. Soon after, it was decided that the magazine needed a children's column. Since the entire editorial staff at that time was made up of celibate clergy, I was given the assignment. My first "ABC's of Faith" column appeared in January 1976 and has run in every issue since. In 1979, in response to reader requests, the column was published in book form. Suddenly I became the resident children's author. For me, it was a perfect fit. While the learned clergy and theologians passed on the faith to our more sophisticated readers, I relished the opportunity to share my own simple faith with the little ones. Later books were written on assignment for Liguori Publications and other publishers. As for my inspiration, I did not have to look far from my home. My ten grandchildren have been my primary resource and major wellspring of inspiration through the years."

*   *   *

O'CONNOR, Karen 1938-
(Karen O'Connor Sweeney)

PERSONAL: Resumed maiden name legally in 1979; born April 8, 1938, in Chicago, IL; daughter of Philip K. (a business broker) and Eva (a homemaker; maiden name, Ennis) O'Connor; married John E. Sweeney (an attorney), June 11, 1960 (divorced November, 1979); married Charles R. Flowers (in customer service), April 9, 1983; children: (first marriage) Julie Bogart, James Sweeney, Erin Torr. *Education:* Clarke College, B.A., 1960; Institute of Children's Literature, diploma, 1977. *Politics:* Republican. *Religion:* Protestant. *Avocational interests:* Hiking, camping, reading, classical music.

ADDRESSES: Home and office—2050 Pacific Beach Dr., No. 205, San Diego, CA 92109. *Agent*—Julie

Castiglia, 1155 Camino Del Mar, Ste. 510, Del Mar, CA 92014.

CAREER: Elementary school teacher in North Hollywood, CA, 1960-61; Los Angeles City Schools, Los Angeles, CA, substitute teacher, 1963-66; writing instructor, Las Virgenes School District, 1976-80, University of California Extension, 1981—, Institute of Children's Literature, 1982—; writer. Has made presentations at school author fairs, teacher in-services, various professional groups, clubs, and national conferences.

MEMBER: American Society of Journalists and Authors (president of southern California chapter, 1979-80), Society of Children's Book Writers and Illustrators (southern California regional advisor, 1981-82).

AWARDS, HONORS: Certificate of Screening from Chicago International Film Festival, 1975, for *A Visit with "Don Juan in Hell";* California Press Women Nonfiction Book Award, 1980, for *Working with Horses: A Roundup of Careers,* and 1982, for *Maybe You Belong in a Zoo!: Zoo and Aquarium Careers;* Bookbuilders West Certificate of Merit, 1981, for *In Christ Jesus;* Notable Children's Trade Book in the Field of Social Studies and Outstanding Science Trade Book for Children, both 1982, for *Maybe You Belong in a Zoo!: Zoo and Aquarium Careers;* award from National Frederation of Press Women, 1982; Gold Medallion Award nomination, National Association of Christian Publishers, 1992, for *When Spending Takes the Place of Feeling.*

WRITINGS:

FOR CHILDREN

Special Effects: A Guide for Super-8 Filmmakers, F. Watts (New York City), 1980.
Working with Horses: A Roundup of Careers, photographs by Kelle Rankin, Dodd, Mead (New York City), 1980.
In Christ Jesus (activity books), Benziger, 1981.
Maybe You Belong in a Zoo!: Zoo and Aquarium Careers, photographs by Douglas K. Emry, Dodd, Mead, 1982.
Try These on for Size, Melody!, photographs by Emry, Dodd, Mead, 1983.
Sally Ride and the New Astronauts: Scientists in Space, F. Watts, 1983.
Contributions of Women: Literature ("Contributions of Women" series), Dillon Press (Minneapolis), 1983.

Sharing the Kingdom: Animals and Their Rights, Dodd, Mead, 1984.
Let's Take a Walk on the Beach, illustrated by Lois Axeman, Child's World (Elgin, IL), 1986.
(With Deborah Crowdy) *Let's Take a Walk in the City,* illustrated by Axeman, Child's World, 1986.
Garbage, Lucent Books, 1989.
Homeless Children, Lucent Books, 1989.
The Feather Book, Dillon Press, 1990.
San Diego, Dillon Press, 1990.
Dan Thuy's New Life in America, Lerner Publications, 1992.
The Herring Gull, Dillon Press, 1992.
The Green Team: The Adventures of Mitch and Molly, illustrated by Len Ebert, Concordia, 1993.
The Water Detectives: The Adventures of Mitch and Molly, illustrated by Len Ebert, Concordia, 1993.
Action Readers, Volume 1: *Junk-Food Finders,* Volume 2: *Little Kids' Olympics,* Volume 3: *French Toast and Dutch Chocolate,* Volume 4: *Service with a Smile,* illustrated by Glen Myers, Concordia, 1994.
A Kurdish Family, Lerner Publications, 1996.

FOR CHILDREN; UNDER NAME KAREN O'CONNOR SWEENEY

How to Make Money, illustrated by Carolyn Bentley, F. Watts, 1977.
Entertaining, illustrated by Yvette Santiago Banek, F. Watts, 1978.
Illustrated Tennis Dictionary for Young People, illustrated by Dave Ross, Harvey House (New York City), 1979.
Nature Runs Wild: True Disaster Stories, F. Watts, 1979.

FOR ADULTS

When Spending Takes the Place of Feeling, Thomas Nelson (Nashville), 1992, revised edition published as *A Woman's Place Is in the Mall and Other Lies,* 1995.
(With Charles R. Flowers) *52 Ways to Be a Better Step-parent,* Thomas Nelson, 1993.
Restoring Relationships with Your Adult Children, Thomas Nelson, 1993.
How to Hook Your Kids on Books: Create a Love for Reading That Will Last a Lifetime, Thomas Nelson, 1995.
Innovative Grandparenting: How Today's Grandparents Build Personal Relationships with Their Grandkids, Concordia (St. Louis), 1995.

Living the Healed Life: Surrounding Yourself with Belief, Joy, and Integrity, Thomas Nelson, 1996.

FOR ADULTS; UNDER NAME KAREN O'CONNOR SWEENEY

Everywoman's Guide to Family Finances, Major (Canoga Park, CA), 1976.
Improve Your Love Life, Major, 1976.
I Am a Compleat Woman: An Adventure in Self-Discovery, Wilshire (North Hollywood), 1978.

OTHER

A Visit with "Don Juan in Hell" (screenplay), North American Film Co., 1975.
Gold: The First Metal (screenplay), North American Film Co., 1978.

Also author of textbook lessons, flash cards, educational films, and a computer reading program. Work represented in anthologies, including *Metrovoices,* Glencoe Publishing Co.; *Strike up the Band,* Scott, Foresman Encore Readers; *The Complete Guide to Writing Nonfiction,* Writer's Digest Books, 1983; and *Tools of the Writing Trade,* HarperCollins, 1990. Contributor to periodicals, including *Crusader, Reader's Digest, Young Miss,* and *Seventeen.*

WORK IN PROGRESS: The Blessing Bag, a book about gratitude; *Intimacy: Getting Closer to Those You Love.*

SIDELIGHTS: Karen O'Connor once told *CA:* "I have wanted to be a writer ever since third grade . . . but I didn't realize that dream until almost thirty years later! After my own children were well into school, the little voice in the back of my head became very persistent indeed. 'Why don't you start writing?' it asked. 'You think about it. You talk about it. When are you going to do something about it?'

"One day I received a copy of a magazine for writers. I read it from front to back without looking up and suddenly I was hooked. I knew for sure that more than anything I wanted to become a writer.

"The next day I went to the library and brought home every book about writing that I could get my hands on. Then one day, I took the big step. I wrote my first article. Then a story. Then another article. I practiced for about three months. I wrote about what I knew (as all the books advised). I was a mother, a Camp Fire leader, a volunteer librarian and a former teacher. I spent most of my waking and sleeping hours with

children. . . . And so I wrote about them—mine and others—and the experiences I shared with them.

"Shortly after that I sold my first article to a small boys' magazine. It was called, 'A Trail of Tips for First-time Campers' and for that piece I earned the handsome sum of $12.50. But no sale since has given me more joy. The letter of acceptance still hangs in my office as a reminder of the day I turned professional."

More recently the author added: "Now that the dust has settled down and the kids have grown up, my thoughts turn to some of my new interests—the wilderness, animal rights, pollution, substance abuse recovery, and immigrants—topics I care about deeply, all of which have found their way into my writing world. *The Feather Book, Homeless Children, Garbage,* and *Sharing the Kingdom: Animals and Their Rights* are a few of the books I've written in recent years.

"And when I'm not writing, I'm trekking up and down mountain peaks with a group I belong to called Wednesday in the Wilderness. I also love to take long sunrise walks with my husband along the beach, attend yoga classes, play with my grandchildren, listen to classical music, and prepare vegetarian meals for my family and friends.

"I work six days a week. No two days are exactly alike, but they all add up to a week that includes writing and teaching. And I also spend some time each day in prayer and conversation with God. He has blessed me with a great gift and I praise Him for it. I cannot imagine a better life than the life of a writer, and I pray that I will be tapping away at this keyboard for years to come.

"As I review my life, one thing remains the same— my love of writing. It is truly the joy of my life. And next to writing, I love to work with student writers. Many people have helped build my career, and now it's my pleasure to pass on what I've learned."

*   *   *

O'MALLEY, Mary Dolling (Sanders) 1889-1974 (Ann Bridge)

PERSONAL: Born September 11, 1889, in Shenley, Hertfordshire, England; died March 9, 1974; daughter of James Harris and Marie (Day) Sanders; married Owen St. Clair O'Malley (a British Foreign Office official), October 25, 1913; children: Jane, John Patrick, Kate (Mrs. Paul Willert). *Education:* London School of Economics and Political Science, diploma, 1913. *Religion:* Roman Catholic.

CAREER: Writer, 1932-74. Member of prize committee, Prix Femina-Vie Heureuse, 1935-39; British Red Cross representative in Hungary, 1940-41; worked with Polish Red Cross, 1944-45; did relief work in France after World War II.

MEMBER: Society of Antiquaries of Scotland (fellow), Royal Horticulture Society (fellow), Wine and Food Society (fellow), Charity Organization Society (London; secretary, 1911-13), Wives Fellowship (central president, 1923-25).

AWARDS, HONORS: Atlantic Monthly prize, 1932, for *Peking Picnic.*

WRITINGS:

UNDER PSEUDONYM ANN BRIDGE

Peking Picnic, Little, Brown (Boston), 1932.
The Ginger Griffin (British Book Society selection), Little, Brown, 1934.
Illyrian Spring (British Book Society selection), Little, Brown, 1935.
The Song in the House (short stories), Chatto & Windus (London), 1936.
Enchanter's Nightshade (British Book Society selection), Little, Brown, 1937.
Four-Part Setting, Little, Brown, 1939.
Frontier Passage, Little, Brown, 1942.
Singing Waters (British Book Society and Literary Guild selection), Chatto & Windus, 1945, Macmillan (New York City), 1946.
And Then You Came, Chatto & Windus, 1948, Macmillan, 1949.
(With Susan Lowndes) *The Selective Traveller in Portugal* (nonfiction), Evans Brothers (London), 1949, Knopf (New York City), 1952, revised edition, McGraw (New York City), 1961.
The House of Kilmartin (juvenile), Evans Brothers, 1951.
The Dark Moment (Literary Guild selection), Macmillan, 1952.
A Place to Stand, Macmillan, 1953.
Portrait of My Mother (autobiography), Chatto & Windus, 1955, published as *A Family of Two Worlds: A Portrait of Her Mother,* Macmillan, 1955.

The Lighthearted Quest (also see below), Macmillan, 1956.
The Portuguese Escape (Literary Guild selection; also see below), Macmillan, 1958.
The Numbered Account (also see below), McGraw, 1960.
Julia Involved: Three Julia Probyn Novels (includes *The Lighthearted Quest, The Portuguese Escape,* and *The Numbered Account*), McGraw, 1962.
The Tightening String, McGraw, 1962.
The Dangerous Islands, McGraw, 1963.
Emergency in the Pyrenees, McGraw, 1965.
The Episode at Toledo, McGraw, 1966.
Facts and Fictions: Some Literary Recollections (autobiography) Chatto & Windus, 1968.
The Malady in Madeira, McGraw, 1969.
Moments of Knowing: Some Personal Experiences Beyond Normal Knowledge (autobiography), Hodder & Stoughton, 1970, published as *Moments of Knowing: Personal Experiences in the Realm of Extra-Sensory Perception,* McGraw, 1970.
Permission To Resign: Goings-On in the Corridors of Power (autobiography), Sidgwick & Jackson (London), 1971.
Julia In Ireland, McGraw, 1973.

SIDELIGHTS: Her marriage to a British Foreign Office official took Mary Dolling O'Malley to far-flung posts around the world, many of which appear in the novels she wrote under the pseudonym Ann Bridge. Besides such exotic settings as China, Spain and Hungary, the Bridge novels are noted, according to Pamela Cleaver in *Twentieth-Century Romance and Historical Writers,* for their "believable characters" and for always "exploring a human situation." "All Bridge's books . . . ,"Cleaver noted, "have a great deal of charm, many acute observations on life and people, and are very satisfying to read."

The Bridge novels usually concern upper-class characters and their troubled romantic relationships in far-off locales. China was a particularly favorite setting for Bridge, and one that she used in some of her most successful novels. In the prize-winning *Peking Picnic,* one of Bridge's best-known works, she tells the story of a group of Western tourists visiting a monastery outside of Peking. A run-in with bandits and the resulting hardships draws several of the party closer together. According to the critic for the *Boston Transcript,* "there is plenty of excitement in the story along with the realism, with the accurate picturing of a life strange and romantic to most readers." *Peking Picnic,* wrote Nathaniel Peffer in *Books,* "is written with a mature grace and some sensitiveness to the setting." "It is rare," Elizabeth Bibesco wrote in *New Statesman and Nation,* "to find such delicacy and insight, so many lights and shadows, never arresting the movement of the narrative. There is a perfect harmony between external and internal events." The *New York Times* critic concluded that *Peking Picnic* was "a finished work; the artistry of its style and its flawless construction mark it as the work of a mature artist."

Bridge returned to a Chinese setting with *Ginger Griffin,* the story of a young woman who spends a year with the British legation in Peking and encounters her first romantic entanglements. E. L. Buell in the *New York Times* wrote that Bridge "has her say with considerable authority and undeniable charm." Writing in *Saturday Review of Literature,* Lucille Douglass called *Ginger Griffin* "amusing, brilliant, and poignant."

In *Four-Part Setting* Bridge tells the tale of a group of Britishers on a camping trip in the Chinese mountains. Calling the novel "a bright, modern tale, woven in a cloth of many colors," D. B. Shapiro in *Books* summed it up as "a relaxing evening of romantic and sometimes exciting reading." The *Springfield Republican* critic found *Four-Part Setting* to be "written with delicacy, humor and beauty of style," while E. S. Hertell in *Churchman* judged the novel to contain "all that Miss Bridge's writing usually contains—a good plot, interesting characterizations, pleasant reading, and in addition, some rare insights into little-known sections of Chinese life." Olga Owens in *Boston Transcript* concluded that "Ann Bridge is one of the most graceful writers in existence. She represents true sophistication in its best sense."

BIOGRAPHICAL/CRITICAL SOURCES:

BOOKS

Twentieth-Century Romance and Historical Writers, third edition, St. James Press (Detroit), 1994.

PERIODICALS

Books, September 11, 1932, p. 5; October 29, 1939, p. 12.
Boston Transcript, September 21, 1932, p. 2; October 28, 1939, p. 1.
Churchman, December 1, 1939, p. 153.
New Republic, November 30, 1932, p. 73.
New Statesman and Nation, October 15, 1932, p. 4.
New York Times, September 11, 1932, p. 7; May 13, 1934, p. 7.
Saturday Review of Literature, May 19, 1934, p. 10.
Springfield Republican, December 3, 1939, p. 7E.*

P-Q

PACKARD, Edward 1931-

PERSONAL: Born February 16, 1931, in Huntington, NY; children: Caroline, Andrea, Wells. *Education:* Princeton University, B.A., 1953; Columbia Law School, LL.B., 1959.

ADDRESSES: Home—Box 720, Wainscott, NY 11975. *Agent*—Amy Berkower, Writers House, 21 West 26th St., New York, NY 10010.

CAREER: Lawyer, 1959-78. Author of children's books, 1975—. *Military Service:* U.S. Navy, 1953-56.

AWARDS, HONORS: Jeremiah Ludington Award, 1986.

WRITINGS:

"CHOOSE YOUR OWN ADVENTURE" SERIES

Sugarcane Island, illustrated by Barbara Carter, Vermont Crossroads Press, 1976.
Deadwood City, illustrated by Carter, Lippincott (Philadelphia), 1978.
The Cave of Time, illustrated by Paul Granger, Bantam (New York City), 1979.
The Mystery of Chimney Rock, illustrated by Granger, Bantam, 1979, published as *The Curse of the Haunted Mansion,* 1989.
Third Planet from Altair, illustrated by Barbara Carter, Lippincott, 1979, published as *Exploration Infinity,* Magnet, 1982, published as *Message from Space,* Bantam, 1989.
Your Code Name is Jonah, illustrated by Paul Granger, Bantam, 1980.

The Circus, illustrated by Granger, Bantam, 1981.
Who Killed Harlowe Thrombey?, Bantam, 1981.
The Forbidden Castle, Bantam, 1982.
Gorga, the Space Monster, Bantam, 1982.
Inside UFO 54-40, illustrated by Granger, Bantam, 1982.
Sunken Treasure, illustrated by Granger, Bantam, 1982.
Survival at Sea, illustrated by Granger, Bantam, 1982.
Jungle Safari, illustrated by Lorna Tomei, Bantam, 1983.
Help Your Shrinking, Bantam, 1983.
Underground Kingdom, Bantam, 1983.
Hyperspace, Bantam, 1983.
The Polar Bear Express, Bantam, 1984.
Mountain Survival, Bantam, 1984.
Supercomputer, Bantam, 1984.
You Are a Shark, Bantam, 1985.
Return to the Cave of Time, Bantam, 1985.
Ghost Hunter, Bantam, 1986.
The Great Easter Bunny Adventure, illustrated by Vincent Bell, Bantam, 1987.
Journey to the Year 3000, Bantam, 1987.
Space Vampire, Bantam, 1987.
A Day with the Dinosaurs, Bantam, 1988.
You Are a Monster, Bantam, 1988.
The Perfect Planet, Bantam, 1988.
Mutiny in Space, Bantam, 1989.
You Are a Superstar, Bantam, 1989.
You Are a Genius, Bantam, 1989.
The Worst Day of Your Life, Bantam, 1990.
Through the Black Hole, Bantam, 1990.
The Power Dome, Bantam, 1991, published as *Invaders from Within,* illustrated by Frank Bolle, Gareth Stevens Publishers (Milwaukee), 1995.
Skateboard Champion, Bantam, 1991.

Faster Than Light, Bantam, 1991.
Vampire Invaders, Bantam, 1991.
Kidnapped, Bantam, 1991.
Magic Master, Bantam, 1992.
Superbike, Bantam, 1992.
Viking Raiders, Bantam, 1992.
You Are Microscopic, Bantam, 1992.
The Luckiest Day of Your Life, Bantam, 1993.
Secret of the Dolphins, Bantam, 1993.
Roller Star, Bantam, 1993.
Dinosaur Island, Bantam, 1993.
Horror House, Bantam, 1993.
Reality Machine, Bantam, 1993.
Comet Crash, Bantam, 1994.
Soccer Star, Bantam, 1994.
Who Are You?, Bantam, 1994.
War with Mutant Spider Ants, Bantam, 1994.
Cyberspace Warrior, Bantam, 1994.
You Are an Alien, Bantam, 1995.
Sky Jam, Bantam, 1995.
Hostage!, Bantam, 1995.
Fright Night, Bantam, 1995.
Greed, Guns and Gold, Bantam, 1996.
Biting for Blood, Gareth Stevens, 1997.

"ESCAPE FROM TENOPIA" SERIES

Tenopia Island, Bantam, 1986.
Castle of Frome, Bantam, 1986.

"EARTH INSPECTORS" SERIES

America: Why Is There an Eye on the Pyramid of the One-Dollar Bill?, illustrated by Barbara Carter, McGraw (New York City), 1988.
Africa: Where Do Elephants Live Underground?, illustrated by Carter, McGraw, 1988.
Olympus: What Is the Secret of the Oracle?, McGraw, 1988.
Russia: What Is the Golden Horde?, illustrated by Carter, McGraw, 1989.

"SPACE HAWKS" SERIES

The Comet Masters, Bantam, 1991.
Space Fortress, Bantam, 1991.

OTHER

E.S.P. McGee, Avon (New York City), 1983.
Imagining the Universe: A Visual Journey (nonfiction), Berkley (New York City), 1994.
Night of the Werewolf, Bantam, 1995.

Packard's books have been translated into several foreign languages.

ADAPTATIONS: Deadwood City and *Third Planet from Altair* have been adapted for videocassette, Positive Image, 1982.

SIDELIGHTS: At volume number 170 and counting, Edward Packard's "Choose Your Own Adventure" series has been one of the most popular children's series in publishing history. Dubbed interactive fiction, such books pioneered the path that CD-ROM has followed, and have been called both a boon for reluctant readers and intellectual junk food no better than video games. Such books involve the reader directly in choosing options through the course of the book about where to go next, which plot twist they desire to follow, and which action would be most logical for them, and thus provide upwards of forty possible endings in some of Packard's most creative titles. It is, however, with this very structure of multiple plots that some critics take exception. Packard himself is aware of such criticisms. In an article on interactive fiction he wrote for *School Library Journal,* Packard conceded that branching multiple plots tended to be short, and therefore left less chance for character development and complex dramatic development. "Fast-paced action is the norm," he explained. "On the other hand, multiple plots afford the author the opportunity to depict alternative consequences and realities. Complexity may inhere in breadth rather than in length."

But whatever critics and educators may or may not say about interactive fiction, young readers have enthusiastically given the concept a thumbs up, and every major juvenile publisher has established its own series. As Packard pointed out in *School Library Journal,* however, such products are not interchangeable. There is a big difference between choosing to go through door one or two, or whether to entrust your safety to a character for which adequate development has not been reached. "If these books are to be exercises in decision-making . . . there should be motivation for each choice offered," so that readers have to weigh factors in favor of each choice. And there need to be consequences that are "consistent and plausible." Packard's subjects in his "Choose Your Own Adventure" series range from science to science fiction, from detective stories to detecting historical and natural truths, and reflect his own range of interests.

Born on Long Island, Packard wrote his first book at age twelve, an introduction to astronomy that was never published. From astronomy, his interest turned to meteorology, and he spent another year reading everything he could lay his hands on about that subject. "I read quite a bit as a kid," Packard once told *CA,* "but I wasn't what you'd call a bookworm. My favorite was *The Book of Knowledge,* an out-of-date . . . encyclopedia that was kept in the attic. It was wonderful. It had a marvelous section called 'Things to Make and Do,' lots of interesting puzzles and games, and lots of scientific material." It is exactly that sort of eclectic and playful knowledge that would later inform Packard's own books. At age fourteen he and some neighborhood kids made a movie, *Revenge on the Range,* which Packard shot with an eight millimeter camera. "Later on I often wondered why I didn't become more seriously interested in film and moviemaking," Packard told *CA.* "I think it was because I didn't see any relationship between what I had done and the films I'd seen in the theater."

But such youthful explorations stopped when Packard was sent off to boarding school at Andover, and from there to Princeton. "Princeton was not a good experience for me. I didn't have any clear goals. I fell into the Princeton social life. . . . Later on I regretted not having studied a simple discipline in depth. If I had it to do over again, I would probably major in literature." After graduation, Packard went into the Navy for three years, having gone to Princeton on a Navy scholarship. Commissioned a Naval officer, Packard's job was in public relations, most of which was spent trying "to get the captain promoted to admiral," according to Packard in *CA.* "The one good thing about the Navy for me was that I did a lot of my own reading. I read more literature there than during college." He also invented a board game, to keep boredom at bay. Once out of the Navy, Packard attended law school at Columbia and then practiced law for about the next twenty years, working during part of this time as counsel for RCA records.

Yet all the while there was a desire for something different in the back of his mind. Married with three children, Packard would read bedtime stories to his kids and often make up stories for them. And that is how he developed the idea for interactive stories. "If I were a better storyteller I wouldn't have come up with this idea," he recalled for *CA.* "I'd have been able to devise the endings by myself. Sometimes while telling my kids stories, I'd get stuck or feel too tired to go on. I would ask the kids, 'What do you think Pete would do now?' To some extent I was introducing the Socratic method of questioning for which law school training is famous. The kids loved it. The storytelling became lively and, of course, bedtime was often delayed while we worked out all the adventures the hero might have enjoyed or suffered if he/she had made a different decision."

In this manner, Packard wrote his first interactive work, *Sugarcane Island.* He then gave it to a literary agent to place for him, but after a year of trying there were no takers. Packard filed the story away in a drawer until one day five years later when he was feeling "moderately unconsciously unhappy" as a lawyer. He read an article about a new children's book publisher, Vermont Crossroads Press, whose co-owner, Ray Montgomery, was looking for innovative material. Packard sent along *Sugarcane Island,* which Vermont Crossroads subsequently published, and the rest is history. After the successful publication of this initial title, Bantam contracted for six more works, a contract that has since extended into the hundreds with sub-series included. Soon Packard was able to quit his law practice to devote his time to writing. The demand for his work was so high that he and Montgomery had to sub-contract writing to other authors.

Sugarcane Island, the first book in the popular series, finds the reader aboard a boat headed for the Galapagos Islands. The ship is wrecked and the 'you' in the narrative is then marooned on Sugarcane Island. "Now the excitement starts," a critic in *Publishers Weekly* noted in reviewing the book. On each page the reader has to make a choice that affects the possible ending. "Packard has an original idea," the *Publishers Weekly* reviewer added, concluding that readers could hardly resist trying out all the options and thus receiving "an exercise in thinking." Rex Benedict, writing in the *New York Times Book Review,* commented that the usual rule is to get the child "to turn the pages, preferably in the right direction, 1-2-3 and so on." But the first words of Packard's books are: "Do not read this book straight through from beginning to end." Benedict found that, in following the directions to turn to various pages as he made different choices, sometimes the reader found fortune, sometimes death. "Dead or alive," Benedict wrote, "you keep turning the pages. You become addicted."

Deadwood City has the reader as a stranger riding into town and faced with three initial choices: check out the saloon, the hotel, or the sheriff's office. Each selection will send the reader to a different page and from there more choices must be made. "Each choice has consequences," noted a *Publishers Weekly* commentator, "leading to further ramifications, so that the book can be a different adventure at each reading." Janet Mura, writing in *Voice of Youth Advocates,* remarked that such books as *Deadwood City* may "be helpful with unwilling readers." Reviewing Packard's third book, *The Cave of Time,* a critic for *Publishers Weekly* stated that Packard had come up with a "gimmicky but intriguing device" in allowing the reader to create her own story. "The brisk, inventive writing will undoubtedly lure kids . . . into making up dozens of different stories," the reviewer concluded. Other critics began to wonder about the negative aspects of the books, however. Writing in *School Library Journal,* Susan Cain declared that the format, "by definition, eliminates any chance for development of either character or plot line." As a result, Cain noted, the stories are "tedious the first time around, and if reread with the alternate options, they only get more so." A contributor in *Kirkus Reviews,* in a review of *Deadwood City,* found such books to be no more creative than video games, and concluded that there was another choice to be made: "Go along with Packard's gag or save your game-playing for the ones you plug into your TV set? Your move."

Many critics agree, however, that the best of such interactive books are not without value. They are, as Drew Stevens wrote in a *School Library Journal* review of *The Mystery of Chimney Rock,* "gimmicky maybe, fun definitely." Beyond that they could "be used in programming, book talks, creative writing and encouraging reluctant readers," concluded Carolyn Caywood in a *School Library Journal* review of *Inside UFO 54-40.* And Susan Williamson, writing in *Voice of Youth Advocates,* observed that the books have "appeal for readers of all ability levels" because of their emphasis on participation and concluded that "readers' choices and the resulting consequences are fertile ground for developing students' ability to predict outcomes or for group work on values clarification." Packard has created several sub-series to "Choose Your Own Adventure," including "Escape from Tenopia," which a *School Library Journal* critic described as a collective "chronicle of your attempt to escape after crash-landing on 'one of the most forbidding planets in the galaxy.'" Twenty years after the publication of his first "Choose Your Own Adventure," Packard continues to write for the series he created.

A non-series book for young readers and adults alike was *Imagining the Universe: A Visual Journey,* in which he brings distance and size in the universe down to comparisons with familiar objects. For ex-

ample, he uses the dimensions of a baseball stadium to lay out the solar system. "This rather elegant pictorial method works just as well when Packard creates time lines that equate time and distance on different scales," stated Donna Seaman in *Sci-Tech Books for Adults.* "The idea behind this book is a very good one," commented Gloria Levine in a *Kliatt* review.

In all his books Packard has employed the techniques and playfulness he learned while perusing *The Book of Knowledge* in his childhood attic, or while shooting an adolescent movie on the local golf course—the closest he could find to the open range on Long Island. His books are visual, told in scenes rather than chapters, and full of information of all sorts. There is also very often a message in his interactive books. "I think there is a very strong moral element in my books," Packard once remarked to *CA,* "but it's not tied up with the choices you make for endings, with rewards and things like that. Just because you choose the wise option in my book doesn't necessarily mean that things will go well from that point on. Choice operates in my books as it does in life: usually good judgement is rewarded, but not always. . . . The basic moral element in my books is the assumption that you, the reader, are a decent and caring person. 'You' never kill or assault anyone or act cruelly in my books. You may be guilty of a transgression—say, of not keeping a promise, or joining up in a dubious scheme to make some quick money—but these are things a weak person might do, a point made to the reader."

BIOGRAPHICAL/CRITICAL SOURCES:

PERIODICALS

Booklist, January 15, 1982, p. 651; July, 1982, p. 1438; December 1, 1994, p. 643.
Children's Book Watch, May, 1995, p. 2.
Kirkus Reviews, April 1, 1978, p. 375.
Kliatt, March, 1995, p. 39.
Library Journal, October, 1987, pp. 40-41.
New York Times, August 25, 1981.
New York Times Book Review, April 30, 1978, p. 43; January 25, 1981, p. 32.
Publishers Weekly, April 18, 1977, p. 62; May 22, 1978, p. 233; June 18, 1979, p. 94.
School Library Journal, September, 1978, p. 145; November, 1979, p. 68; September, 1980, p. 76; August, 1982, p. 120; March, 1983, p. 183; December, 1983, p. 31; May, 1984, p. 101; September, 1985, p. 153; January, 1986, p. 82; Sep-

tember, 1986, p. 152; October, 1987, p. 152; March, 1989, p. 177; August, 1990, p. 146.
Sci-Tech Books for Adults, December 1, 1994, p. 643.
Times Educational Supplement, April 4, 1980, p. 29; July 11, 1980, p. 28; October 1, 1981, p. 31.
Voice of Youth Advocates, April, 1982, p. 52; June, 1982, p. 40; August, 1986, p. 170; February, 1987, p. 295; June, 1987, p. 94; October, 1988, p. 185; June, 1989, p. 110; August, 1995, p. 146.

* * *

PALL, Ellen Jane 1952-
(Fiona Hill)

PERSONAL: Born March 28, 1952, in New York, NY; daughter of David B. (a scientist) and Josephine (an artist; maiden name, Blatt) Pall. *Education:* Attended University of Michigan, 1969-70; University of California, Santa Barbara, B.A., 1973. *Religion:* Jewish.

CAREER: Teacher of French in Glendale, CA, 1974; writer, 1975—.

MEMBER: Phi Beta Kappa.

WRITINGS:

NOVELS

Back East, David Godine (Boston), 1983.
Among the Ginzburgs, Zoland Books (Cambridge, MA), 1996.

NOVELS; UNDER PSEUDONYM FIONA HILL

The Trellised Lane, Berkley (New York City), 1975.
The Wedding Portrait, Berkley, 1975.
The Practical Heart, Berkley, 1975.
Love in a Major Key, Berkley, 1976.
Sweet's Folly, Berkley, 1977.
The Love Child, Putnam (New York City), 1977.
The Autumn Rose, Putnam, 1978.

SIDELIGHTS: Ellen Pall first made her mark in the publishing world with the Regency romances she wrote under the pseudonym Fiona Hill; nearly ten years later, she won the respect of critics with novels published under her own name. She began her literary career after graduating from college, when her father

agreed to support her financially for six months while she tried to write and sell a novel. Knowing that she could not complete a "serious" work of literature during that time, she determined to write a historical novel—specifically, a Regency romance. Pall described the genre in a *New York Times Book Review* article about her work: "Regency romances are a sunny and compact genre in which a lady and a gentleman meet, form indifferent opinions of each other, banter for 200 pages or so, kiss and agree to marry. They take place in the better drawing rooms of England and are written in a dense, slang-ridden version of the diction of their period, the years from 1811 to 1820 when the Prince Regent, the future George IV, reigned in place of his mad father—the eponymous Regency. . . . As much comedy as romance, a Regency makes its tickling assault on the imagination, not the senses."

In five months, Pall had finished her first book, which was soon published as *The Trellised Lane.* She hoped that her father would be sufficiently impressed to subsidize her work on a more serious novel. He was not. "Far from being moved to extend his literary patronage, he proudly, briskly, firmly and finally congratulated me on my good fortune in entering so congenial a profession, wished me luck and considered our joint experiment complete," she confided in the *New York Times Book Review* article. In order to support herself, she began another Regency. "Soon—alarmingly soon—writing Regencies was the only thing I really knew how to do," she confessed. The genre flourished, and "Fiona Hill" was soon promoted from paperback to hardcover. Pall, who was growing bored with her lucrative work, explained that "this meant my manuscripts had to be twice as long. Feeling like the girl in 'Rumpelstiltskin'—whose reward for having spun a room full of straw into gold was a larger room full of straw—I wrote on."

Ten years passed before Pall published a novel under her own name. When it happened, many reviewers rated *Back East* an unqualified success. It tells the story of Melanie Armour, a commercial songwriter who, after twelve years on the West Coast, leaves Los Angeles to return to her family in New York. She falls in love with a teenaged homosexual actor and, in another plot strand, visits her family's farm in Maine, where she enters into long-standing emotional struggles with her mother and brother. "Surprise follows surprise in the life of a heroine one cares about and wishes well," found a *Publishers Weekly* reviewer. A *Library Journal* contributor declared that "vivid characters coupled with a tightly structured plot . . . make this novel a pleasurable and moving experience." A *Kirkus Reviews* writer voiced some reservations, however. Describing Melanie's narration of the story as "arch but crisply stylish," the reviewer went on to say: "Unfortunately, first-novelist Pall gives relatively little space here to the promising family-material—which, treated so skimpily, emerges as contrived, caricatured, and unaffecting. . . . Weak, unfocused debut-fiction, then—but Pall's prose, though often just glib or smug/cute, is precise, shrewd, and brightly amusing enough to suggest better novels to come."

Pall's next novel, *Among the Ginzburgs,* again focused on family dynamics. In this book, a diverse group of siblings gathers at their old summer house to meet with the father who deserted them years before and who is now dying of leukemia. A *Library Journal* reviewer complained that "it is hard to feel too deeply for these characters," but other commentators, including Pulitzer Prize-winning playwright Wendy Wasserstein, were much more enthusiastic. Pointing out that much of the book consists of dialog, Wasserstein went on to say in the *New York Times Book Review:* "It's not the talk that gives this novel its honesty, but the insights that Ms. Pall . . . has about unspoken family ties. In dissecting the family's motivations, she breaks down her dramatic structure and is free to examine with absolute acuity the ever-expanding and contracting familial pull of brothers and sisters, husbands and wives." A *Publishers Weekly* critic was also emphatically positive, writing, "There are no villains or heroes in this perceptive, poignant examination of family" because Pall "digs deep to expose the sweetness and vulnerability that are at each one's core." She "puts a clever and always gentle twist on scenes that in less able hands would be cliched and melodramatic. Dialogue, characterizations, setting—all ring true in this mature, gracefully realized work."

Ellen Pall once told *CA:* "Why does anyone become a writer? I became a writer because I was moved by the things people do not say. I became a writer to impress my father. I became a writer because I *could* become a writer. I became a writer because I wrote well. I became a writer because writing became me."

BIOGRAPHICAL/CRITICAL SOURCES:

PERIODICALS

Horn Book, December, 1983, p. 740.
Kirkus Reviews, July 15, 1983, p. 784.

Library Journal, September 1, 1983, p. 1721; April 1, 1996, p. 119.
New York Times Book Review, April 30, 1989, p. 1; June 2, 1996, p. 24.
Publishers Weekly, July 22, 1983, p. 118; April 22, 1996, p. 61.
Washington Post Book World, July 14, 1996, p. 6.*

*   *   *

PARETSKY, Sara 1947-

PERSONAL: Born June 8, 1947, in Ames, IA; daughter of David Paretsky (a scientist) and Mary Edwards (a librarian); married Courtenay Wright (a professor), June 19, 1976; children: Kimball, Timothy, Philip. *Education:* University of Kansas, B.A., 1967; University of Chicago, M.B.A., 1977, Ph.D., 1977. *Avocational interests:* Baseball (Chicago Cubs), singing.

ADDRESSES: Home—1507 E. 53rd St., Chicago, IL 60615. *Agent*—Dominick Abel, 498 West End Ave., New York, NY 10024.

CAREER: Writer, 1986—. Urban Research Corp., Chicago, IL, publications manager, 1971-74; freelance business writer, 1974-77; Continental National America (CNA; an insurance company), Chicago, manager of advertising and direct mail marketing programs, 1977-86.

MEMBER: Private Eye Writers of America, Authors Guild, Sisters in Crime (founder and president, 1987-88), Crime Writers Association, Chicago Network.

AWARDS, HONORS: Award from Friends of American Writers, 1985, for *Deadlock;* named one of *Ms.* Magazine's Women of the Year, 1987; Silver Dagger award from Crime Writers Association, 1988, for *Blood Shot.*

WRITINGS:

"V. I. WARSHAWSKI" MYSTERIES

Indemnity Only, Dial (New York City), 1982.
Deadlock, Dial, 1984.
Killing Orders, Morrow (New York City), 1985.
Bitter Medicine, Morrow, 1987.

Blood Shot, Delacorte (New York City), 1988 (published in England as *Toxic Shock,* Gollancz [London], 1988).

Burn Marks, Delacorte, 1990.

Guardian Angel, Delacorte, 1992.

Tunnel Vision, Delacorte, 1994.

Windy City Blues, Delacorte, 1995 (published in England as *V. I. for Short,* Hamish Hamilton [London], 1995).

Three Complete Novels (contains *Indemnity Only, Blood Shot,* and *Burn Marks*), Wings (New York City), 1995.

OTHER

(Editor) *Beastly Tales: The Mystery Writers of America Anthology,* Wynwood Press (New York City), 1989.

(Editor) *A Woman's Eye* (collection of mystery stories), Delacorte, 1991.

(Editor) *Women on the Case: Twenty-Six Original Stories by the Best Women Crime Writers of Our Time,* Delacorte, 1996.

Work represented in anthologies, including *The Eyes Have It,* Mysterious Press (New York City), 1985, and *The Eyes Have It,* Volume 2, Mysterious Press, 1986. Contributor to periodicals, including *American Girl, Black Mask Quarterly,* and *Women: A Journal of Liberation.*

ADAPTATIONS: Indemnity Only was adapted into the film *V. I. Warshawski* starring Kathleen Turner and released in 1991.

SIDELIGHTS: Sara Paretsky is the creator of feminist V. I. Warshawski, a tough, street-smart private investigator—half Polish, half Italian—who inevitably uncovers murder and deceit in white-collar Chicago. Paretsky once told a *CA* interviewer that one of her motivations in creating Warshawski was "to try to combat some of the typical sexual stereotypes in literature." According to Paretsky, too many of the women characters in literature, not just in mysteries, are either predatory or helpless.

Paretsky had the idea for writing about a woman private eye for "three or four years" and made several false starts before finding the right path, she told *CA.* "At that time I was a middle manager for a large, multinational company," she recalled. "In 1979, I realized that I was trying to create a character who was aping the Raymond Chandler tradition, only in female form, and what I really wanted was a woman

who was doing what I was doing, which was trying to make a success in a field traditionally dominated by men. With that realization, I was able to find V. I.'s voice."

Warshawski was introduced in *Indemnity Only,* where she is hired to track a missing woman from the University of Chicago. Her investigation, however, leads first to the corpse of her client's murdered son. In investigating the killing and continuing her search for the woman, Warshawski unravels a scheme involving a union leader, a gangster, and quirky insurance agents, and she makes a surprising discovery about the identity of her client.

Critics accorded *Indemnity Only* respectable notices when it appeared in 1982. *New Republic* reviewer Robin W. Winks described the novel as "thoroughly convincing" and "gritty," and *Chicago Tribune Book World* critic William Brashler declared that "with the feisty Ms. Warshawski, Sara Paretsky . . . has the makings of an engaging sleuth." Jean M. White, writing in the *Washington Post Book World,* noted that Paretsky "writes smoothly within the bounds of convention" and added that she "writes with assurance about a milieu that she knows well."

In *Deadlock,* Warshawski decides to investigate the supposedly accidental death of her cousin, former hockey player Boom Boom Warshawski, who fell into a ship's propeller while working on the Chicago docks. Once into her probe, Warshawski acquaints herself with some of the more unsavory aspects of the shipping business, including despicable magnates and vicious thugs, and she becomes the target of violence and mayhem. Clues eventually implicate a wildly self-centered millionaire.

Deadlock earned Paretsky praise from numerous reviewers. "Good story, well told," summarized T. J. Binson in the *Times Literary Supplement.* Harriet Waugh, in her assessment for *Spectator,* agreed, deeming *Deadlock* "strongly plotted" and recommending Warshawski as "convincingly tough." And Alice Cromie wrote in the *Chicago Tribune Book World* that *Deadlock* is a "well-written mystery."

The third Warshawski novel, *Killing Orders,* finds the detective once again plunged into a world of danger and deceit. Here she is hired by one of her aunts—a church bookkeeper with whom she has had no communication in a decade—to solve the absence of five million dollars in stock certificates from a Chicago monastery. But with the investigation hardly under-way, the relative decides to abandon it. Soon after-wards, the missing funds suddenly appear at the mon-astery. Warshawski decides to investigate matters further, whereupon various thugs try to discourage her. One assailant splashes acid into her face, another torches her apartment. Undaunted, Warshawski pur-sues the case to its grim end, coming across a secret Catholic organization and a conspiracy that involves big business, organized crime, and the church.

With *Killing Orders* Paretsky drew further critical acclaim. A *New Yorker* reviewer praised the work as a "pretty good story" and commended the fullness of the Warshawski characterization, noting that "there are few private eyes anywhere about whom we are told so much." Likewise, *New Statesman* 's Joan Smith wrote that "the plot is first-class" and asserted that Warshawski is "a wholly successful character." She added that *Killing Orders* "restores politics to its rightful place in the mainstream private eye novel, and in doing so revitalizes the tradition." Newgate Callendar was still another enthusiast, writing in his *New York Times Book Review* column that the novel's ending is "exciting and even a bit scary." He also commended Paretsky for her courage in writing about church corruption, observing that she "seems willing to take on any institution, no matter how sacred."

Paretsky followed *Killing Orders* with *Bitter Medi-cine,* which has Warshawski uncovering corruption in the medical profession. The case begins when War-shawski agrees to drive a friend's son-in-law to a job interview. Accompanying them is the son-in-law's pregnant wife, who begins labor while waiting in the car. Warshawski drives the expectant mother to a nearby private hospital. Soon afterwards she learns that both mother and child have died. Aghast, War-shawski decides to investigate, and with the help of her own physician she finds major indications of malpractice at the facility. In doing so, she risks her life, and before the case is closed more murder and mayhem ensue.

As with previous Warshawski mysteries, *Bitter Medi-cine* was held in good standing by critics. Margaret Cannon, a reviewer for the Toronto *Globe and Mail,* deemed *Bitter Medicine* "a finely crafted and im-mensely readable book," and Callendar, in his *New York Times Book Review* appraisal, commended Par-etsky for her skills of narration and characterization. "The action moves logically along," he wrote, "and the characters are well drawn." James Kaufman,

writing in *Tribune Books,* expressed particular satis-faction with Paretsky's feats of characterization, and he declared that "with [*Bitter Medicine*], as with all good private-eye novels, what engages us is not so much the crime as . . . the detective." He ranked Warshawski with "today's best private eyes."

Blood Shot, the fifth Warshawski mystery, begins with the detective returning to her childhood neigh-borhood on Chicago's South Side, where she agrees to search for an old friend's hitherto unknown father. With the case hardly underway, however, the friend asks Warshawski to abandon it, fearful that a recent co-worker's murder is somehow related to the search. To the friend's chagrin, however, Warshawski contin-ues the investigation, and she eventually discovers that several despicable characters, including a chemi-cals magnate and a mobster, are polluting natural resources to exploit energy needs. In his assessment of *Blood Shot* for the *Chicago Tribune,* Paul Johnson described Warshawski as "one of the finest, if not *the* finest, of the female first-person shamuses who have appeared in print over the last decade." He noted Paretsky's "unpretentious prose style" and concluded that "what keeps us with Warshawski all the way is a dogged decency and an essential sweetness of char-acter behind her shrewdness." Particularly enthusias-tic about *Blood Shot* was Marilyn Stasio, who wrote in the *New York Times Book Review* that the novel constituted Paretsky's "best and boldest work to date in creating a criminal investigation that is a genuine heroic quest."

Burn Marks finds Warshawski investigating arson and political intrigue, while also being drawn into the life of her Aunt Elena, a troublesome, hard-drinking woman. To *Armchair Detective* contributor Guy Szu-berla, Warshawski's sense of responsibility to family members shows how she differs from detective fiction's most famous male private eyes. She is inde-pendent, he noted, but is still connected to a variety of people; she does not live the isolated existence of Dashiell Hammett's Sam Spade or Raymond Chand-ler's Philip Marlowe. The aid Warshawski offers Aunt Elena also indicates the detective's compassion for the downtrodden, Szuberla remarked. With this and the other Warshawski mysteries, he concluded, Paretsky has managed to "open the narrative bound-aries of the hard-boiled detective novel and transform its emotional center." *New Statesman and Society* reviewer Jo-Ann Goodwin added that the book's "plot is well constructed, with an ending that is both un-foreseen and convincing."

In *Guardian Angel,* Warshawski's sympathy for the underdog once again figures in the story. She is infuriated when an affluent couple from her neighborhood scheme to become guardians of another neighbor, an elderly, infirm woman whose dogs have created a nuisance. The two soon order the dogs euthanized, and Warshawski suspects they have designs on the woman's money as well. As Warshawski probes the couple's activities, she sees a possible relationship to another case she is investigating, this one regarding the disappearance of her downstairs neighbor's oldest friend. Both cases have connections with the law firm that employs Warshawski's ex-husband, Dick Yarborough.

"What moves [Warshawski] to action and involvement is not so much a need to prove herself as an extreme sensitivity to injustice, which she is always inclined to test for hidden neurotic motives," remarked *New York Times* critic Christopher Lehmann-Haupt in his review of *Guardian Angel.* He pronounced the book "the richest and most engaging yet of Ms. Paretsky's thrillers." *New York Times Book Review* contributor Vincent Patrick also was impressed by the novel, observing that "Ms. Paretsky deftly provides enough leads and loose ends to keep V. I. on a very busy schedule and us turning pages." Assessing *Guardian Angel* for Chicago *Tribune Books,* Dick Adler praised Paretsky for "her ability to zero in on the shadowy impulses that motivate some, but not all, human behavior." In *People,* Susan Toepfer declared *Guardian Angel*'s central mystery "difficult to follow, and intrinsically dull," but found Warshawski's appeal sufficient to recommend the book.

In *Tunnel Vision,* published in 1994, a system of tunnels beneath downtown Chicago has become flooded (such a disaster really happened in 1992). The flood threatens a homeless family living in the basement of Warshawski's office building, and she tries to assist them. Other threads in the story, all of which eventually come together, involve the murder of a wealthy woman and an investigation into the withdrawal of financing from a social service organization.

Several reviewers noted that *Tunnel Vision* reflects Paretsky's—and her heroine's—penchant for dealing with social issues. *New York Times* critic Lehmann-Haupt, however, found this manifested in stereotypes: "the poor, the weak, the young, the old, the female, the single and the black tend to be good, and the rich, the strong, the middle-aged, the married and the WASPish are likely to be evil." He deemed some

other elements of the book praiseworthy, though, especially Warshawski, who "remains an appealing character," complex and vulnerable. Added *Newsweek* reviewer Laura Shapiro: "In this, V. I.'s eighth adventure and a fine one, she wrestles with her motives—and then barges on, seeking justice the only way she knows."

Several short stories about Warshawski were collected under the title *Windy City Blues,* published in 1995. The plots include Warshawski's search for a musical manuscript that once belonged to her mother—a talented singer and half-Jewish refugee from Italy in the Fascist era—and the arrest of the detective's best friend, Dr. Lotty Herschel, for murder. Some reviewers thought the stories less effective than Paretsky's longer works. They "deliver little of the grit and passion on display in the Warshawski novels," asserted *New York Times Book Review* contributor Josh Rubins. For one thing, Rubins contended, "few of the stories . . . even try to sketch in the menacing, earthy textures of V. I.'s Chicago, or to suggest her flinty commitment to the city's underdogs." A *Publishers Weekly* critic also found the stories wanting; they "seem slight beside the broader canvases of Warshawski novels like *Blood Shot* and *Guardian Angel,*" the reviewer wrote. In a *Times Literary Supplement* piece, however, Natasha Cooper pronounced the collection's components "necessarily slight, but attractive."

Paretsky and some other women mystery writers, such as Sue Grafton and Patricia Cornwell, have created strong women protagonists in a genre once dominated by male authors and characters. But there are by no means too many women writing—or being portrayed in—detective fiction, according to Paretsky. "It's hard for me to think the field is crowded when we're still a very small minority in the genre as a whole," she told *CA.* Paretsky has sought to nurture women mystery writers and to scrutinize the portrayals of women characters in the genre by founding the group Sisters in Crime. She also has edited several anthologies of detection fiction by women. Her work certainly has struck a chord with many readers, especially women, and Paretsky has found the character of Warshawski to be an effective means of expressing her beliefs. "The things I want to say about law, society, women, seem to come naturally in her voice," she was quoted by *Newsweek* as saying. "There are women just beginning to be aware, who need strong role models."

BIOGRAPHICAL/CRITICAL SOURCES:

BOOKS

St. James Guide to Crime and Mystery Writers, 4th edition, St. James Press (Detroit), 1996.

PERIODICALS

Armchair Detective, spring, 1994, pp. 147-53.
Belles Lettres, spring, 1989, p. 15; summer, 1990, p. 36; spring, 1992, p. 22.
Chicago, March, 1986; January, 1989.
Chicago Tribune, June 2, 1985; July 16, 1987; September 29, 1988.
Chicago Tribune Book World, January 31, 1982.
Christian Science Monitor, April 13, 1984.
Clues: A Journal of Detection, spring-summer, 1995, pp. 77-87; fall-winter, 1995, pp. 1-15.
Cosmopolitan, March, 1990.
Entertainment Weekly, March 13, 1992, p. 47; February 19, 1993, p. 56; May 27, 1994, p. 79.
Forbes, February 13, 1984.
Globe and Mail (Toronto), October 12, 1982; June 20, 1987.
Los Angeles Times Book Review, April 1, 1984; October 13, 1991, p. 11; June 12, 1994, p. 8.
Ms., October, 1987; July-August, 1994, p. 78.
New Republic, March 3, 1982.
New Statesman, April 25, 1986, p. 27; September 4, 1987, p. 28.
New Statesman and Society, June 1, 1990, pp. 38-39; April 19, 1991, p. 37; June 5, 1992, p. 37.
Newsweek, July 13, 1987, p. 64; September 26, 1988, p. 73; May 14, 1990, p. 67; July 4, 1994, p. 67.
New Yorker, September 2, 1985, p. 87.
New York Times, January 27, 1992, p. C22; June 20, 1994, p. C18.
New York Times Book Review, April 29, 1982; March 18, 1984; September 15, 1985, p. 33; August 2, 1987, p. 29; October 9, 1988, p. 22; October 20, 1991, p. 36; March 31, 1992, p. 45; June 12, 1994, p. 42; October 8, 1995, p. 24.
People, March 16, 1992, pp. 23-24.
Playboy, March, 1990; July, 1994, p. 34.
Publishers Weekly, January 26, 1990, p. 406; December 6, 1991, p. 59; April 11, 1994, p. 57; August 28, 1995, p. 106; April 29, 1996, pp. 54-55.
Quill & Quire, January, 1989, p. 30.
Spectator, January 5, 1985, p. 21.
Times Literary Supplement, November 30, 1984; June 20, 1986, p. 683; October 21, 1994, p. 20; October 20, 1995, p. 24.

Tribune Books (Chicago), June 7, 1987, p. 6; February 2, 1992, p. 3; June 5, 1994, p. 8; November 5, 1995, p. 7.
USA Today, August 3, 1994, p. D2.
Washington Post Book World, February 21, 1982; March 18, 1984; June 16, 1985; July 19, 1987; June 19, 1994, p. 6; November 19, 1995, p. 6.
Women's Review of Books, July, 1989, p. 41; February, 1992.*

* * *

PARKHILL, John
See COX, William R(obert)

* * *

PARKINSON, C(yril) Northcote 1909-1993

PERSONAL: Born July 30, 1909, at Barnard Castle, County Durham, England; died March 9, 1993, in Canterbury, England; son of William Edward (an artist) and Rosemary (a musician; maiden name, Curnow) Parkinson; married Ethelwyn Edith Graves, 1943 (divorced, 1949); married Elizabeth Ann Fry (a writer), September 23, 1952 (died, 1983); married Iris Waters, 1985; children: (first marriage) Alison Barbara, Christopher Francis Graves; (second marriage) Charles Nigel Kennedy, Antonia Patricia Jane, Jonathan Neville Trollope. *Education:* Emmanuel College, Cambridge, B.A. (honors), 1932; King's College, London, Ph.D., 1935. *Politics:* Liberal. *Religion:* Church of England. *Avocational interests:* Painting, the stage, radio, television.

CAREER: Cambridge University, Emmanuel College, Cambridge, England, fellow, 1935-38; Blundell's School, Tiverton, Devon, England, senior history master, 1938-39; Royal Naval College, Dartmouth, England, master, 1939-40 and 1946; University of Liverpool, Liverpool, England, lecturer in naval history, 1946-50; University of Malaya, Singapore, Raffles Professor of History, 1950-58; Troy State University, Troy, AL, professor emeritus and honorary president, 1970-93. Visiting professor, Harvard University, 1958; George A. Miller Visiting Professor of History, University of Illinois at Urbana-Champaign, 1959-60; visiting professor of history, University of California, Berkeley, 1960. Chairman, Leviathan House, 1972-79. Lecturer. Seigneur of Fief d'Anneville and Fief des Mauxmarquis, Guernsey, Channel Islands. *Military service:* British Army, Queen's Royal Regiment, 1940-46; became major.

MEMBER: Royal Historical Society (fellow), Royal Commonwealth Society, Society for Nautical Research, Academie de Marine, U.S. Naval Institute, Army and Navy Club.

AWARDS, HONORS: Julian Corbett Prize, University of London, 1936; LL.D., University of Maryland, 1974; D.Litt., Troy State University, 1976.

WRITINGS:

Edward Pellew, Viscount Exmouth, Methuen (London), 1934.

Trade in the Eastern Seas, 1793-1813, Cambridge University Press (London), 1937, reprinted, Augustus Kelley, 1966.

(Editor) *The Trade Winds: A Study of British Overseas Trade during the French Wars, 1793-1815,* Allen & Unwin (London), 1948.

(Editor) *Portsmouth Point: The Navy in Fiction* (anthology), University of Liverpool Press (Liverpool), 1948, published as *Portsmouth Point: The British Navy in Fiction, 1793-1815,* Harvard University Press (Cambridge, MA), 1949.

Always a Fusilier: The War History of the Royal Fusiliers (City of London Regiment), 1939-1945, Low (London), 1949.

(Editor) *Samuel Walters, Lieutenant, R.N.,* University of Liverpool Press, 1949.

(Editor and translator) *The Journal of a Frenchman in Malayan Waters,* Royal Asiatic Society (Singapore), 1952.

The Rise of the Port of Liverpool, University of Liverpool Press, 1952.

War in the Eastern Seas, 1793-1815, Allen & Unwin, 1954.

Templer in Malaya, Eastern Universities Press (Singapore), 1954.

Britain in the Far East: The Singapore Naval Base, D. Moore (Singapore), 1955.

(With wife, Ann Parkinson) *Heroes of Malaya,* D. Moore, 1956.

Parkinson's Law, and Other Studies in Administration, Houghton (Boston), 1957 (published in England as *Parkinson's Law; or, The Pursuit of Progress,* J. Murray [London], 1958).

The Evolution of Political Thought, Houghton, 1958.

British Intervention in Malaya, University of Malaya Press (Singapore), 1960.

The Law and the Profits, Houghton, 1960.

In-Laws and Outlaws, Houghton, 1962.

East and West, Houghton, 1963.

Ponies' Plot, Houghton, 1965.

A Law unto Themselves: Twelve Portraits, Houghton, 1966.

Left Luggage: A Caustic History of British Socialism from Marx to Wilson, Houghton, 1967.

Mrs. Parkinson's Law, and Other Studies in Domestic Science, Houghton, 1968.

The Life and Times of Horatio Hornblower (biography), M. Joseph (London), 1970, Little, Brown, 1971.

The Law of Delay: Interviews and Outerviews, J. Murray, 1970, Houghton, 1971.

The Fur-Lined Mousetrap, Leviathan House, 1973.

(Editor) *Industrial Disruption,* Leviathan House, 1973.

Devil to Pay (novel), Houghton, 1973.

Incentives and Penalties, Ashwin Shah (Bombay), 1973.

Big Business, Little, Brown, 1974.

(With M. K. Rustomji) *How to Get to the Top without Ulcers, Tranquillisers, or Heart Attacks,* Macmillan (Delhi), 1974.

The Fireship (novel), Houghton, 1975.

(With Rustomji) *Watch Your Figures,* Macmillan (Delhi), 1976.

Gunpowder, Treason and Plot, Weidenfeld & Nicolson, 1976, St. Martin's, 1977.

Touch and Go (novel), Houghton, 1977.

The Rise of Big Business, Weidenfeld & Nicolson, 1977.

Britannia Rules: The Classic Age of Naval History, 1793-1815, Weidenfeld & Nicolson, 1977.

(With Nigel Rowe) *Communicate,* Prentice-Hall, 1978.

Dead Reckoning (novel), Houghton, 1978.

Jeeves: A Gentleman's Personal Gentleman, McDonald & Jane, 1979.

Parkinson: The Law, J. Murray, 1979, Houghton, 1980.

(With Herman Le Compte) *The Law of Longer Life,* Troy State University Press, 1980.

So Near So Far (novel), Houghton, 1981.

SIDELIGHTS: Though his professional specialty was naval history, C. Northcote Parkinson was also known for his historical novels of eighteenth-century sea adventure. But he was probably best known as the discoverer of a maxim called, appropriately enough, Parkinson's Law.

Parkinson's Law came to the public's attention in 1955 when an anonymous essay satirizing managerial bureaucracy in government and business appeared in the normally sedate London *Economist*. Entitled "How Seven Employees Can Be Made to Do the Work of One," the essay observed that work expands to fill the time available for its completion and that administrators make work for each other. Parkinson had come to this conclusion after learning that even though the number of British naval vessels decreased by more than two-thirds between 1914 and 1928, the number of admiralty officials nearly doubled during the same period.

The essay's dry, tongue-in-cheek humor proved to be extremely popular with readers in both Great Britain and the United States (*Fortune* magazine printed it in 1956), where a *New York Times* critic noted that the author's tone varied "from savage glee to coldly amused brutality." Eventually, Parkinson renounced his anonymity and became an instant celebrity, though for quite some time a few people continued to believe that he was just a creation of the *Economist*'s editors. Recalling his sudden success, the former professor wrote: "Many people had a sense of relief in finding that ideas, long vaguely present in the mind, had at last been put into words. Parkinson's Law had been discovered, remember, not invented, and the author could place himself (modestly, of course) on a level with Archimedes, Pythagoras, and Newton."

Parkinson expanded his ideas into a full-length collection of essays, a 1957 best-seller entitled *Parkinson's Law*. In prose that the *Atlantic*'s Phoebe Adams described as "pseudo-academic and quasi-official," the author poked fun at a variety of bureaucratic institutions. His findings on committees, for example, led him to conclude that five is the optimum number of members an effective group can have; larger groups must break into sub-committees of five or less to get the real work done. Observations he made at the typical executive meeting resulted in the development of Parkinson's Law of Triviality—the less something new is going to cost, the more time will be spent discussing it. On the subject of office decor, Parkinson discovered that the more luxurious the surroundings, the more stagnant the company. And as for cocktail parties, he noted that executives mingle (on schedule) from left to right.

Following his literary success, Parkinson left his position at the University of Malaya and headed for the United States, where he worked as a visiting professor and public speaker. He devised more laws through the years—expenditure rises to meet income, action

expands to fill the void created by human failure—but none matched the impact of the original. He came to admit that "the law changed the whole course of my life."

Parkinson preferred to talk about his career as a novelist. His first effort, *The Life and Times of Horatio Hornblower*, was a pseudo-biography of C. S. Forester's illustrious (but fictional) naval hero. Parkinson then invented an eighteenth-century naval hero of his own, Richard Delancey, whose adventures as an officer of the Royal Navy form the plots of the novels *Devil to Pay, The Fireship, Touch and Go*, and *Dead Reckoning*. In the course of his adventures Delancey fights during the American Revolution, the seige of Gibralter by the Spanish, and in the West Indies against the French. "In terms of their historical detail," wrote David Powell in *Twentieth-Century Romance and Historical Writers*, "the novels would be difficult to fault. Parkinson was scrupulous in his use of events and the presentation of facts. His knowledge of the naval world of the Napoleonic era was encyclopaedic; his understanding of ships and seamen, of politics, strategy and trade almost unrivalled. This solid bedding in the reality of the past gives the novels their appeal."

Delancey's nautical adventures began with the novel *Devil to Pay*, in which the seaman commands a cutter on a secret espionage mission to France, fights against smugglers along the English coast, and captains a privateer which is run aground on the French coast. Delancey manages to return to England with valuable intelligence data concerning the French military. J. T. Gilboy in *Best Sellers* noted that "Parkinson obviously knows his nautical jargon. The passages in which he describes ships shine with enthusiasm and respect for the vessels." Ed Murphy in *Library Journal* found that "Delancey is a worthy successor to [C. S. Forester's famous character] Horatio Hornblower. He shows all the competence, courage, and ingenuity of a Hornblower along with a bit more polish."

Speaking of the Delancey books as a whole, Powell concluded: "Parkinson's novels are faithful to their subject and their period. They display considerable invention and erudition, and they deserve to retain their (somewhat scholarly) place in the gallery of fictional contemporaries created in affectionate imitation of Forester's Hornblower. In chronicling the career of Richard Delancey, Parkinson has painted a realistic picture of the life of a sea-officer of his time."

In an interview with a *People* reporter, Parkinson said that he feels his major "philosophical contribution has been to show that the vacuum caused by silence fills up with nonsense, innuendo and abuse." Conceding that his laws have not had as much influence as he would have liked (especially in government), he theorizes that his "appalling variety of interests . . . may have limited my success in any one direction." Concluded Parkinson: "I've tried to be like the 16th century courtier who could do everything: play the lute, write a sonnet, ride into battle and partake in theological debate. It's just my nature, and I can only be myself."

BIOGRAPHICAL/CRITICAL SOURCES:

BOOKS

Twentieth-Century Romance and Historical Writers, third edition, St. James Press (Detroit, MI), 1994.

PERIODICALS

Atlantic, October, 1957.
Best Sellers, August 1, 1971; May 1, 1973, p. 33.
Books & Bookmen, November, 1975.
Christian Science Monitor, December 5, 1968; June 20, 1973, p. 11.
Economist, January 5, 1980.
Library Journal, March 1, 1973, p. 98.
New York Times, September 29, 1957; October 15, 1968; June 11, 1971.
New York Times Book Review, November 17, 1968; March 14, 1971; May 13, 1973, p. 38; June 22, 1975; May 4, 1980.
New York Times Magazine, July 10, 1960.
Observer, December 6, 1970.
People, October 16, 1978.
Punch, December 11, 1968.
Saturday Review, September 14, 1957.
Time, November 8, 1968; March 8, 1971; June 14, 1971.
Times Literary Supplement, January 26, 1967; June 8, 1973, p. 634.
Washington Post, June 18, 1971.

OBITUARIES:

PERIODICALS

New York Times, March 12, 1993, p. A19.
Times (London), March 11, 1993, p. 23.
Washington Post, March 12, 1993, p. B7.*

PATERSON, Katherine (Womeldorf) 1932-

PERSONAL: Born October 31, 1932, in Qing Jiang, China; daughter of George Raymond (a clergyman) and Mary (Goetchius) Womeldorf; married John Barstow Paterson (a clergyman), July 14, 1962; children: Elizabeth Po Lin, John Barstow, Jr., David Lord, Mary Katherine. *Education:* King College, A.B. (summa cum laude), 1954; Presbyterian School of Christian Education, M.A., 1957; Union Theological Seminary, New York City, M.R.E., 1962; postgraduate study at Kobe School of Japanese Language, 1957-60. *Politics:* Democrat. *Religion:* "Presbyterian Church in the United States." *Avocational interests:* Reading, swimming, tennis, sailing.

ADDRESSES: Home—Barre, VT. *Office*—c/o E. P. Dutton, 2 Park Ave., New York, NY 10016.

CAREER: Writer, 1966—. Public school teacher in Lovettsville, VA, 1954-55; Presbyterian Church in the United States, Board of World Missions, Nashville, TN, missionary in Japan, 1957-62; Pennington School for Boys, Pennington, NJ, master of sacred studies and English, 1963-65.

MEMBER: Authors Guild, Authors League of America, PEN, Children's Book Guild of Washington.

AWARDS, HONORS: American Library Association (ALA) Notable Children's Book, 1974, and Phoenix Award, Children's Literature Association, 1994, for *Of Nightingales That Weep;* ALA Notable Children's Book, 1976, National Book Award for Children's Literature, 1977, runner-up for Edgar Allan Poe Award (juvenile division), Mystery Writers of America, 1977, and American Book Award nomination (children's fiction paperback), 1982, all for *The Master Puppeteer;* ALA Notable Children's Book, 1977, John Newbery Medal, 1978, Lewis Carroll Shelf Award, 1978, and Michigan Young Reader's Award Division II runner-up, 1980, all for *Bridge to Terabithia;* ALA Notable Children's Book, 1978, National Book Award for Children's Literature, 1979, Christopher Award (ages 9-12), 1979, Newbery Honor Book, 1979, CRABbery (Children Raving About Books) Honor Book, 1979, American Book Award nominee (children's paperback), 1980, William Allen White Children's Book Award, 1981, Garden State Children's Book Award (younger division), New Jersey Library Association, 1981, Georgia Children's Book Award, 1981, Iowa Children's Choice Award, 1981, Massachusetts Children's Book Award (elementary), 1981, all for *The Great Gilly Hopkins;*

Hans Christian Andersen Award U.S. nominee, 1980, *New York Times* Outstanding Book List, 1980, Newbery Medal, 1981, CRABbery Honor Book, 1981, American Book Award nominee (children's hardcover), 1981, children's paperback, 1982, all for *Jacob Have I Loved;* Outstanding Books and Best Illustrated Books selection, *New York Times,* 1981, for *The Crane Wife,* illustrated by Suekichi Akaba and translated by Paterson from a retelling by Sumiko Yagawea; Parent's Choice Award, Parent's Choice Foundation, 1983, for *Rebels of the Heavenly Kingdom;* Irvin Kerlan Award "in recognition of singular attainments in the creation of children's literature," 1983; University of Southern Mississippi School of Library Service Silver Medallion, 1983, for outstanding contributions to the field of children's literature; Parent's Choice Award, Parent's Choice Foundation, and Notable Books list, *New York Times,* both 1985, both for *Come Sing, Jimmy Jo;* Laura Ingalls Wilder Award nominee, 1986; ALAN Award, 1987; Keene State College Award, 1987; Regina Medal Award, Catholic Library Association, 1988, for demonstrating "the timeless standards and ideals for the writing of good literature for children"; Best Illustrated list, *New York Times,* 1990, and Best Picture Books selection, *Boston Globe-Horn Book,* 1991, both for *The Tale of the Mandarin Ducks;* Irma S. and James H. Black Award, 1992, for *The King's Equal;* Scott O'Dell Award for Historical Fiction, Scott O'Dell Foundation, 1997, for *Jip: His Story.* Litt.D., King College, 1978; D.H.L., Otterbein College (Westerville, OH), 1980; Litt. D., St. Mary's of the Woods, 1981; Litt. D., University of Maryland, 1982; Litt. D., Shenandoah College, 1982; D.H.L., Washington and Lee University, 1982; D.H.L., Norwich University and Mount St. Vincent University, both 1990.

WRITINGS:

The Sign of the Chrysanthemum, illustrated by Peter Landa, Crowell (New York City), 1973.

Of Nightingales That Weep, illustrated by Haru Wells, Crowell, 1974.

The Master Puppeteer, illustrated by Haru Wells, Crowell, 1976.

Bridge to Terabithia, illustrated by Donna Diamond, Crowell, 1977.

The Great Gilly Hopkins, Crowell, 1978.

Angels and Other Strangers: Family Christmas Stories, Crowell, 1979 (published in England as *Star of Night: Stories for Christmas,* Gollancz [London], 1980).

Jacob Have I Loved, Crowell, 1980.

Rebels of the Heavenly Kingdom, Lodestar (New York City), 1983.

Come Sing, Jimmy Jo, Lodestar, 1985.

Park's Quest, Lodestar, 1988.

The Smallest Cow in the World, illustrated by Jane Clark Brown, Vermont Migrant Education Program, 1988.

The Tale of the Mandarin Ducks, illustrated by Leo and Diane Dillon, Lodestar, 1990.

Lyddie, Lodestar, 1991.

The King's Equal, illustrated by Vladimir Vagin, HarperCollins (New York City), 1992.

Flip-Flop Girl, Lodestar, 1994.

A Midnight Clear: Stories for the Christmas Season, Lodestar, 1995.

The Angel and the Donkey (retelling), illustrated by Alexander Koshkin, Clarion Books (New York City), 1996.

Jip: His Story, Lodestar, 1996.

Marvin's Best Christmas Present Ever, illustrated by Jane Clark Brown, HarperCollins, 1997.

Celia and the Sweet, Sweet Water, illustrated by Vladimir Vagin, Lodestar, 1998.

(With John Paterson) *Images of God,* illustrated by Alexander Koshkin, Clarion Books, in press.

Contributor of articles and reviews to periodicals; anthologized in *On the Wings of Peace;* co-editor of *The Big Book of Our Planet* and *The World in 1492.* Reviewer, *Washington Post Book World,* 1975—; member of editorial board, *Writer,* 1987—.

NONFICTION

Who Am I? (curriculum unit), CLC Press, 1966.

To Make Men Free (curriculum unit; includes books, records, pamphlets, and filmstrip), John Knox, 1973.

Justice for All People, Friendship, 1973.

Gates of Excellence: On Reading and Writing Books for Children, Lodestar, 1981.

(With husband, John Paterson) *Consider the Lilies: Flowers of the Bible,* Crowell Junior Books, 1986.

The Spying Heart: More Thoughts on Reading and Writing Books for Children, Lodestar, 1989.

A Sense of Wonder: On Reading and Writing Books for Children (includes *Gates of Excellence* and *The Spying Heart*), Plume (New York City), 1995.

TRANSLATOR

Sumiko Yagawa, *The Crane Wife,* Morrow, 1981.
Momoko Ishii, *Tongue-Cut Sparrow,* Lodestar, 1987.

Also translator of Hans Christian Andersen's *The Tongue Cut Sparrow,* for Lodestar.

ADAPTATIONS: The Great Gilly Hopkins was filmed by Hanna-Barbera, 1980; *Bridge to Terabithia* was filmed for PBS television, 1985, and adapted as a play with music, libretto by Paterson and Stephanie Tolan and music by Steve Liebman, French, 1992; *Jacob Have I Loved* was filmed for PBS, 1990. Several of Paterson's books, including *Bridge to Terabithia, The Great Gilly Hopkins, Angels and Other Strangers,* and *Jacob Have I Loved,* have also been adapted for audio cassette by Random House.

SIDELIGHTS: Two-time Newbery Medal winner Katherine Paterson writes of children in crisis, at the crossroads of major decisions in their lives. Her youthful protagonists turn "tragedy to triumph by bravely choosing a way that is not selfishly determined," according to M. Sarah Smedman in *Dictionary of Literary Biography.* "They embody the theme of redemption through sacrifice of oneself and one's ambitions," Smedman noted, "a theme that resounds convincingly, never cliched, never preached, always with the force of fresh discovery." Paterson's delicate touch with emotionally heavy topics such as death and familial jealousy sets her apart from other problem book authors. "The distinctive quality of Paterson's art," commented Smedman, "is her colorful concision. Whether she is narrating or describing, her mode is understatement, her style pithy. She dramatizes, never exhorts. . . . [She is] a major artist, skilled, discerning, and compassionate."

Smedman might also have added humorous. Paterson's wry understatement saves her work from sentimentality. In books such as *Bridge to Terabithia* and *Jacob Have I Loved,* she tackles serious themes head on, but always with compassion and strong storytelling skills. In others, such as *The Great Gilly Hopkins,* her humor and wit are showcased. Paterson establishes a powerful identification with the reader because she so strongly believes what she writes. "Why do I keep writing stories about children and young people who are orphaned or otherwise isolated or estranged?," Paterson asked in *Theory into Practice.* "It's because I have within myself a lonely, frightened child who keeps demanding my comfort. I have a rejected child, a jealous and jilted adolescent inside who demands, if not revenge, a certain degree of satisfaction. I am sure it is she, or should I say they, who keep demanding that I write for them."

Paterson often writes about children who are orphaned or estranged from their parents, teens who isolate themselves or who associate only with one or two close friends. These recurring situations reflect the instability of the author's childhood. "If I tell you that I was born in China of Southern Presbyterian missionary parents, I have already given away three chief clues to my tribal memory," Paterson once wrote in *Horn Book.* The third of five children, Paterson spent her early years in China, repatriating to the United States by the onset of World War II. Chinese being her first language, Paterson learned English with a distinct British accent, and dressed in missionary hand-me-downs—a sure recipe for ridicule from her classmates in North Carolina where the family resettled. Paterson, bereft of friends, found consolation in the school library and in books. Perennially the new kid in school—the family moved fifteen times in thirteen years—Paterson learned survival skills on the playground and delved even further into her private world of books and began writing her own stories. She was a self-confessed outsider and "weird" kid. "I'm sure there are plenty of fine writers who have overcome the disadvantage of a normal childhood and gone on to do great things," Paterson wrote in *Gates of Excellence: On Reading and Writing Books for Children.* "It's just that we weird little kids do seem to have a head start."

After high school, Paterson attended King College in Bristol, Tennessee, majoring in English literature. A year of teaching in a rural Virginia school followed, then a master's degree in education, and finally missionary work in Japan. Until that time her only contact with the Japanese had been with conquering soldiers when she was a child in war-torn China. But the four years she spent in Japan were a revelation for her, and she grew to love the country and its people. Paterson's experiences in Japan figured prominently in her first books, written several years later. In 1961 she returned to the United States, married, and began raising a family of four children, two of whom were adopted. Slowly she turned to writing as a private solace at the end of long and hectic days. Her literary career officially began with works for church school curricula. When finished with the project, she turned her hand to fiction, her first love. Seven years later, she had what she considered publishable material.

Paterson's first three books are historical fiction, set in Japan. The twelfth century and its civil wars are the setting for *The Sign of the Chrysanthemum* and *Of Nightingales That Weep,* while her third novel, *The Master Puppeteer,* is a mystery set in eighteenth-century Osaka during a great famine. All three books deal with teenagers who are either orphaned or have lost one parent and who must make it on their own in exceptionally difficult times. In *The Sign of the Chrysanthemum,* young Muna experiences the loss of his mother and tries without success to find his samurai father, whom he would know by the tatoo of a chrysanthemum on his shoulder. Although he does not find his father, in searching for him Muna travels a road of self-discovery that is not without its own rewards. Reviewing this first novel in *Horn Book,* Virginia Haviland noted that "the storytelling holds the reader by the quick pace of the lively episodes, the colorful detail, and the superb development of three important characters." Graham Hammond, writing in *Times Literary Supplement,* commented that "the book is about pain, wisdom, choosing, and growing up, but it is far from didactic." *Of Nightingales That Weep,* Paterson's second novel, deals with the fortunes of a young girl during the same period in Japan, and could, according to Margery Fisher of *Growing Point,* "satisfy adolescents and adults alike with its exotic flavour and mature handling of characters." Marcus Crouch, writing in *Junior Bookshelf,* noted his own initial reluctance to read a book dealing with twelfth-century Japan, but concluded that once started, the book was "hypnotically dominating."

Paterson's third novel, *The Master Puppeteer,* was her break-out book for which she won a National Book Award in 1977. Using the world of traditional Japanese puppet drama as a backdrop, Paterson wove a mystery around young Jiro and his best friend Kinshi, the son of a puppet master. Both boys are alienated from their fathers and find stability in their relationship with one another. Diana L. Spirt in her *Introducing More Books: A Guide for the Middle Grades,* described the book as "engrossing," and noted that "the author has blended a literate mix of adventure and Japanese history with a subtle knowledge of young people." Zena Sutherland, reviewing the novel in *Bulletin of the Center for Children's Books,* compared *The Master Puppeteer* to "intricate embroidery," and concluded with a terse, telling description: "good style, good story." The interplay of technique and content was also noted by Dora Jean Young in *School Library Journal.* "This novel . . . should be very popular for its combination of excellent writing and irresistible intrigue," Young declared.

Paterson turned to a contemporary rural American setting for her fourth novel, inspired by the death of

her son David's favorite friend, who was struck by lightning. In *Bridge to Terabithia,* Jess and Leslie are fifth-graders whose loneliness brings them together as fast friends. They build a secret hideout and call it the magical kingdom of Terabithia. Heavy rains make it impossible to go there for a time, but after returning from a trip, Jess learns that Leslie has drowned trying to get to their hideout. Thereafter, he builds his own monument to the young girl. A Newbery Award winning novel, *Bridge to Terabithia* is "an unromantic, realistic, and moving reaction to personal tragedy," according to Jack Forman in *School Library Journal.* Jill Paton Walsh, reviewing the work in the *Christian Science Monitor,* commends it as "tender and poetic without ever being sentimental, written in simple language which never fails to carry the emotional charge." A novel with a lighter touch is *The Great Gilly Hopkins,* a somewhat comic view of a spunky foster child and the foster mother who ultimately wins the girl's affection. The novel was the result of Paterson's own experiences as a foster mother for two months. "This is quite a book!," proclaimed Ellen M. Davidson in *Children's Book Review Service.* "It confronts racism, sexism, ageism, I.Q.ism and just about all the other prejudices of our society." However, Bryna J. Fireside in *New York Times Book Review* took Paterson to task for this very plenitude of issues. Fireside commented that the novel would have been better "without mixing up race relations, learning disabilities, the important relationships between young and old, *and* a terrific young girl who gamely comes to terms with her status as a foster child." Yet most reviewers—and awards committees—responded more favorably. Natalie Babbitt, reviewing the book in *Washington Post Book World,* concluded that *The Great Gilly Hopkins* "is a finely written story. Its characters linger long in the reader's thoughts after it is finished."

Smedman, writing in *Dictionary of Literary Biography,* described Paterson's next novel, *Jacob Have I Loved,* as the author's "most complex." A second Newbery Award winner, this novel examines the feelings of a twin for her tremendously talented sibling. Set on a Chesapeake island at the outset of World War II, the story is about Sara Louise—known as Wheeze—and her delicate and musically talented sister Caroline, as related from the adult Wheeze's retrospective point of view. Paul Heins, writing in *Horn Book,* commented that Paterson had again "written a story that courageously sounds emotional depths." *Christian Science Monitor* contributor Betty Levin dubbed the book "a breathtaking novel for older children and adults . . . a book full of humor and compassion and sharpness."

Paterson returned to Far Eastern settings for *Rebels of the Heavenly Kingdom,* set in nineteenth-century China. The story of a young peasant boy, Wang Lee, kidnapped by bandits, and his friendship with and growing love for Mei Lin, who helps to rescue him, the book is "on the epic scale," and was "skillfully crafted," according to *Publishers Weekly.* Mary Hobbs, writing in *Junior Bookshelf,* noted that the story "is beautifully told," and painlessly teaches the reader about details of "the traditional Chinese ways of life and thought."

Biblical and universal themes are at the heart of Paterson's books. Never preachy in tone, her stories nonetheless teach lessons—of humility, responsibility, and hope. As the author once wrote in *Horn Book,* "I have learned, for all my failings and limitations, that when I am willing to give myself away in a book, readers will respond by giving themselves away as well, and the book I labored over so long becomes in our mutual giving something far richer and more powerful than I could have ever imagined." Paterson elaborated on her artistic philosophy in an article for *The Writer,* where she explains: "I keep learning that if I am willing to go deep into my own heart, I am able miraculously to touch other people at the core. But that is because I do have a reader I must try to satisfy—that is the reader I am and the reader I was as a child. I know this reader in a way that I can never know a generic target out there somewhere. This reader demands honesty and emotional depth. She yearns for clear, rhythmically pleasing language. . . . And above all she wants characters who will make her laugh and cry and bind her to themselves in a fierce friendship."

Come Sing, Jimmy Jo and *Park's Quest* are two of Paterson's works that have been praised for the honesty, emotional depth, and character recognition that the author seeks to impart. The former relates the story of eleven-year-old James Johnson, a small, timid child taken from his grandmother and their quiet Appalachian mountain home to join his musician family on stage and on television. The family's agent, who has recognized the child's gifted voice, changes James's name to Jimmy Jo and propels him toward stardom—while James must learn to deal with all that fame offers, including difficulties among jealous family members and with schoolmates. "Paterson captures the subtleties of childhood friendships in

James's relationships with his classmates and records family interaction with a sensitive ear," noted *School Library Journal* contributor Cathryn A. Camper. A *Bulletin of the Center for Children's Books* reviewer similarly maintained that "Paterson creates strong characters and convincing dialogue, so that her story is effective even to those to whom the heavy emphasis on country music strikes no sympathetic chord." Denise M. Wilms of *Booklist* concluded that *Come Sing, Jimmy Jo* is "a rich, sensitive portrayal of growing up." *Park's Quest* is Paterson's tale of a boy's efforts to learn more about his father, who was killed in the Vietnam War. "In a multilayered novel filled with themes of reconciliation and renewal," wrote a *Kirkus Reviews* commentator, "[Paterson] draws parallels between a boy's quest for the family of his father, killed in Vietnam, and the Arthurian legends. . . . Park's quest is a fine journey of discovery, and the characters he meets are uniquely memorable." Many critics commented favorably on the author's skillful interweaving of Park's favorite reading matter—tales of Arthur and his knights—with the boy's own determination to solve the "mystery" of his father's life. The story is "a quest," according to Ethel L. Heins of *Horn Book,* "that will ultimately be fraught with emotional peril and stunning revelations." Heins added that *Park's Quest* "realistically presents a heroic response to a contemporary condition."

In addition to her longer juvenile and young adult novels, Paterson has written short stories for Christmas, gathered in *Angels and Other Strangers* and *A Midnight Clear,* and picture books, including the award winning *Tale of the Mandarin Ducks* along with *The Smallest Cow in the World, The King's Equal,* and *The Angel and the Donkey.* Two companion novels written in the 1990s are *Lyddie* and *Jip: His Story,* both set in New England in the middle to late nineteenth century. In the first of the novels, thirteen-year-old Lyddie is hired out as a servant after the failure of the family farm. She soon flees this situation for the mills of Lowell, Massachusetts, only to discover an even more grueling life in this new labor. She finds refuge in books and determines to get a college degree and pull herself out of her degrading existence. *Voice of Youth Advocates* contributor Mary L. Adams commented: "While the setting is interesting and authentic, the story and characterizations are Paterson at her best. Readers will carry the image of Lyddie with them for many years." Zena Sutherland, writing in *Bulletin of the Center for Children's Books,* noted that Paterson maintained her "usual fine job" in blending narrative with history in this book of "industrial oppression, workers' and women's rights, and prejudice." Elizabeth S. Watson of *Horn Book* concluded that this was "a superb story of grit, determination, and personal growth." Lyddie makes another appearance in *Jip: His Story,* when as a teacher she helps young Jip, the son of a runaway slave, to escape his impoverished life and the miserable conditions of a poor farm for a new start in Canada. *School Library Journal* contributor Ellen Fader noted that readers of *Jip* would be rewarded "with memorable characters and a gripping plot," adding that "Paterson's story resonates with respect for the Vermont landscape and its mid-19th-century residents, with the drama of life during a dark period in our nation's history, and with the human quest for freedom." Mary M. Burns of *Horn Book* praised Paterson's work as "an intense, third-person novel that maintains its riveting pace from the opening chapter to the final moment when the protagonist triumphs over adversity."

A tale with a more contemporary setting, *Flip-Flop Girl* is Paterson's story of distraught nine-year-old Vinnie, grieving for the death of her father. Forced to move to her grandmother's house, Vinnie is an outsider at school, her only friend the mysterious "Flip-Flop Girl" Lupe, whose own father is in jail for having killed her mother. The positive attention of Vinnie's male teacher helps matters for a time, though his simultaneous concern for Lupe and his later engagement to be married both come as a betrayal to Vinnie. A *Publishers Weekly* commentator noted that Paterson is "a master of rendering the intensity of childhood emotions," adding that in *Flip-Flop Girl* she explores "the impact of grief and the slow process of healing." Similarly, *Junior Bookshelf* reviewer Marcus Crouch maintained that "Paterson is always particularly good at exploring relationships and probing the minds of troubled children," noting that *Flip-Flop Girl* "is a beautifully planned and developed narrative which treats the minor pains and embarrassments of childhood with due seriousness." Ellen Fader, in *Horn Book,* concluded that "all children will discover parts of themselves in Vinnie, and, like Vinnie, will know more about themselves when they get to the conclusion of this powerful story."

For all the prizes and critical acclaim she has received, Paterson remains typically understated about her achievements. As she once commented in *Theory into Practice,* her aim, "like that of most writers of fiction, is to tell a story. My gift seems to be that I am one of those fortunate people who can, if she works hard at it, uncover a story that children will enjoy."

BIOGRAPHICAL/CRITICAL SOURCES:

BOOKS

Books for Children, Elsevier/Nelson, 1981.
Cary, Alice, *Katherine Paterson,* Learning Works (Santa Barbara, CA), 1997.
Children's Literature Review, Volume 7, Gale, 1984.
Cullinan, Mary, with Mary K. Karrer and Arlene M. Pillar, *Literature and the Child,* Harcourt, 1981.
Dictionary of Literary Biography, Volume 52: *American Writers for Children Since 1960,* Gale, 1986, pp. 296-314.
Peterson, Linda, and Marilyn Solt, *Newbery and Caldecott Medal and Honor Books: An Annotated Bibliography,* Twayne, 1982.
Schmidt, Gary D., *Katherine Paterson,* Twayne, 1994.
Spirt, Diana L., *Introducing More Books: A Guide for the Middle Grades,* R. R. Bowker, 1977, pp. 114-117.
Twentieth-Century Children's Writers, 4th edition, St. James Press (Detroit), 1995.

PERIODICALS

Booklist, May 1, 1985, p. 1257; September 1, 1990, p. 59; September 15, 1991, p. 169; December 15, 1993, p. 755; September 15, 1995, p. 171; March 1, 1996, p. 1189.
Books for Keeps, November, 1996, p. 11.
Bulletin of the Center for Children's Books, July-August, 1976, p. 181; June, 1985, pp. 191-192; April, 1988, pp. 164-65; September, 1990, pp. 14-15; February, 1991, p. 151; November, 1995, pp. 102-103; December, 1996, p. 147.
Children's Book Review Service, April, 1978, p. 89.
Children's Literature in Education, autumn, 1983.
Christian Science Monitor, May 3, 1978, p. B2; January 21, 1981, p. 17.
Growing Point, March, 1977, p. 3060.
Horn Book, October, 1975, p. 468; September, 1980, pp. 622-623; August, 1981; December, 1981; July-August, 1985, p. 456; July-August, 1988, pp. 496-497; November-December, 1990, pp. 753-54; May-June, 1991, pp. 338-339; March-April, 1994, pp. 200-201; November-December, 1995, pp. 729-730; November-December, 1996, pp. 739-40.
Junior Bookshelf, August, 1977, pp. 239-240; December, 1983, pp. 254-255; August, 1994, pp. 146-147; October, 1996, p. 205.
Kirkus Reviews, May 15, 1985, p. J53; March 1, 1988, p. 358; July 15, 1991, p. 933; December

15, 1993, p. 1596; October 1, 1995, p. 1435; January 1, 1996, p. 72.

New Advocate, fall, 1997, pp. 5-14.

New York Times Book Review, April 30, 1978, p. 54.

Publishers Weekly, May 6, 1983, p. 98; July 27, 1990, p. 233; July 12, 1991, p. 65; November 22, 1993, p. 64; February 12, 1996, p. 71.

School Library Journal, March, 1976, p. 117; November, 1977, p. 61; April, 1985, p. 91; May, 1988, p. 111; October, 1990, p. 111; January, 1992, p. 96; May, 1994, p. 117; March, 1996, p. 213; October, 1996, p. 124.

Theory into Practice, autumn, 1982, pp. 325-331.

Times Literary Supplement, September 19, 1975, p. 1056.

Voice of Youth Advocates, April, 1991, p. 34.

Washington Post Book World, May 14, 1978, pp. 1-2.

Writer, August, 1990, pp. 9-10.

* * *

PATRICK, Q.
See WHEELER, Hugh (Callingham)

* * *

PEARSON, Diane
See McCLELLAND, Diane Margaret

* * *

PERI ROSSI, Cristina 1941-

PERSONAL: Born November 12, 1941, in Montevideo, Uruguay; immigrated to Barcelona, Spain, 1972. *Education:* Licenciada in comparative literature. *Politics:*Leftist.

ADDRESSES: Home—Travessera de Les Corts 171, 4 piso la, Barcelona 08007, Spain. *Agent*—International Editors, Rambia de Cataluna 63, 3 piso, Barcelona 08007, Spain.

CAREER: Writer, 1963—. Teacher of literature in Montevideo, Uruguay; professor of comparative literature, Autonomous University of Barcelona. Writer for newspapers and magazines, including *Marcha;*

exiled from Uruguay, settled in Barcelona, Spain, 1972.

AWARDS, HONORS: Arca Prize, 1968; *Marcha* Prize, 1969; Inventarios Provisionales Prize, 1973, for *Diaspora;* City of Palma de Mallorca prize, 1976; Benito Perez Galdos Prize, 1980; City of Barcelona Prize, 1991.

WRITINGS:

Viviendo (short stories), Alfa (Montevideo), 1963.

El libro de mis primos (novel), Biblioteca de Marcha (Montevideo), 1969.

Los museos abandonados (short prose), Arca (Montevideo), 1969.

Indicios panicos (poetry and short prose), Nuestra America (Montevideo), 1970.

Evohe: poemas eroticos, Giron (Montevideo), 1971.

Descripcion de un naufragio (poetry), Lumen (Barcelona), 1975.

Diaspora (poetry), Lumen, 1976.

La tarde del dinosaurio (short stories), Planeta (Barcelona), 1976.

(Editor) Homero Aridjis, *Antologia,* Lumen, 1976.

Linguistica general (poetry), Prometeo (Valencia, Spain), 1979.

La rebelion de los ninos (short stories), Monte Avila (Caracas), 1980.

El museo de los esfuerzos inutiles (short stories and essays), Seix Barral (Barcelona), 1983.

La nave de los locos (novel), Seix Barral, 1984, translation by Psiche Hughes published as *The Ship of Fools,* Readers International (London), 1989.

Una pasion prohibida, Seix Barral, 1986, translation by Mary Jane Treacy published as *A Forbidden Passion,* Cleis (Pittsburgh, PA), 1993.

Europa despues de la lluvia (poetry), Banco Exterior de Espana (Madrid), 1987.

Solitario de amor (Grijalbo (Barcelona), 1988.

Cosmoagonias, Laia (Barcelona), 1988.

Babel barbara (poetry), Angria (Caracas), 1990.

Fantasias eroticas, Temas de Hoy (Madrid), 1991.

La ultima noche de Dostoievski, Mondadori (Madrid), 1992, translation by Laura C. Dail published as *Dostoevsky's Last Night,* Picador (USA), 1995.

SIDELIGHTS: An Uruguayan writer living in exile in Spain, Cristina Peri Rossi is the author of revolutionary poetry and prose. Her darkly humorous writings reflect a strong opposition to the inequities of class and sexual division and to the social and political repression that exist within dictatorial states. Themes of alienation, eroticism, and uncontrolled power dominate her works. "Her tales break down the logical interrelation of their parts and renounce all novelistic development and anecdotal mimesis in favor of the presentation of states of consciousness as images," wrote Hugo J. Verani in the *Dictionary of Literary Biography.* "The lyrical attitude, playful exploration of reality, metaphorical profusion, and digressive and cumulative forms are all signs of a poetic reality, a total experience intolerant of boundaries."

Peri Rossi's life as a political exile from her native Uruguay has influenced her writings. Her 1984 novel, *La nave de los locos,* translated as *The Ship of Fools,* is an unusual narrative which follows the exiled character Equis or Ecks (pronounced "X") on a never-ending journey, tracing his numerous encounters with women and his revelations about the lack of communication in the world. "The powerful sense of cultural alienation that the characters feel in the novel," explained Carol Gardner in the *Women's Review of Books,* "is clearly the product of the writer's own experience; it's a theme that recurs throughout her work written in exile." Verani agreed, calling the book "a lucid reflection on uprooting and displacement: in a troubled era, modern society subsists only fragmented and deprived of finality." "Around the image of the voyage," the *Dictionary of Literary Biography* contributor continued, "the novel presents successive stories of outcasts bereft of belongings and companions, symbolic figures in perpetual flight conscious of traveling without a fixed destination and alienated from society."

Equis is accompanied on part of his journey by fellow-passengers who are equally as lost and adrift as he is. La Bella Pasajera is a woman who exists only for the pleasure of others. Vercingetorix is a political prisoner who proves unable to come to terms with his own past—he was held in a polluted cement town whose inhabitants had nearly all deserted it. Gordon, a former lunar astronaut, spends his life bemoaning the fact that he can never return to the moon. Morris is an eccentric with a passion for collecting odd objects, such as pipes and maps. "Condemned to temporariness and wandering," Verani wrote, "Equis accepts precariousness as a form of survival. The other characters . . . are denied apparent individuality and psychological development. Exiled from themselves and from the world, they surpass geographic, political, and temporal barriers."

In her fiction, Peri Rossi also strives to escape traditional forms of storytelling in order to avoid what she sees as oversimplification of her art. "All her stories," Verani declared, "maintain a heterogeneous sense of invention as they alternate spontaneously between diverse motifs, never letting any one feature dominate—a creative propensity that rules out the possibility of reducing Peri Rossi's work to mere components cut off from its diverse and complex context." In *The Ship of Fools,* for instance, "she rejects traditional narrative form," writes Gardner. "The novel's shape (or shapelessness) is a critique of structure—of those comforting artistic visions that, while giving us refuge from chaos, also confine us (both men and women) to certain 'proper' roles." Dan Bellm, writing in the *Voice Literary Supplement,* commented, "*The Ship of Fools* is a mess in the finest sense—a glorious mess, baffling and alluring." Quoting from Peri Rossi's prose, the critic continued, "'We value in art the exercise of mind and emotion that can make sense of the universe without reducing its complexity.' That's hard to do, and that's what she's done."

Peri Rossi's 1992 novel *La ultima noche de Dostoievski,* translated and published in 1995 as *Dostoevsky's Last Night,* again plays with narrative expectations and modern themes. Verani commented that "the subversive potential of humor, irony, parody, and the absurd, distinctive traits of her literary practice, reaches a radical antimimetic and highly imaginative treatment" in the book. "The awareness of living at the end of a historical period . . . with its crumbling cities, unconscious fears and desires, and displaced and defamiliarized fantasies," the *Dictionary of Literary Biography* contributor added, ". . . moves in her fourth novel toward a playful and flippant takeoff on Fyodor Dostoyevsky's fascination with gambling that generates a relentlessly ironic, postmodern vision of humanity reduced to absurdity and undermines once again the very notion of representation and the reading experience."

Dostoevsky's Last Night is the story of Jorge, a magazine journalist who has a fascination with gambling. He plays Bingo European-style—not the church-basement American game, but a casino version in which "this simple game is played with jungle ferocity," according to *New York Times Book Review* contributor Erik Burns. Like the Russian writer Feodor Dostoevsky, Jorge rationalizes his addiction as a way of escaping the dullness of his job and his life. He says as much to his psychoanalyst Lucia, with whom he later falls in love. "For Jorge," noted *Atlanta Journal-Constitution* reviewer Candice Dyer, ". . . gambling is the grand passion, identifying him as an artiste whose risk-worshiping temperament sets him apart from the bourgeoisie who have taken 'society's precious path.'"

Critics agree that in her depiction of Jorge's obsession Peri Rossi presents a condemnation of the emptiness of modern life. Jorge "propitiates luck," Dyer explained, "with a mysticism that those who occasionally buy lottery tickets or brandish troll dolls at the bingo hall will recognize as their lark turned inexorably self-destructive." In her protagonist's speeches, Burns stated, Peri Rossi "convey[s] all too accurately the sensation of time and money being frittered away" on both empty psychoanalysis and on games of chance. *Booklist* contributor Donna Seaman declared that "Rossi dazzles us with acute and powerfully articulate observations about chance, desire, disorder, luck, literature and how" modern society has recategorized sin as compulsion and replaced ethics with psychology.

BIOGRAPHICAL/CRITICAL SOURCES:

BOOKS

Contemporary World Writers, 2nd edition, St. James Press (Detroit), 1993.
Dictionary of Literary Biography, Volume 145: *Modern Latin-American Fiction Writers,* Second Series, Gale (Detroit), 1994.
Peri Rossi, Cristina, *The Ship of Fools,* translated by Psiche Hughes, Readers International, 1989.

PERIODICALS

Atlanta Journal-Constitution, December 24, 1995, p. K10.
Booklist, July, 1995, p. 1861.
Los Angeles Times Book Review, July 23, 1995, p. 6.
New York Times Book Review, July 30, 1995, p. 14.
Voice Literary Supplement, May, 1989.
Woman's Review of Books, July, 1989, p. 37.
World Literature Today, winter, 1990, p. 79.

*   *   *

PETERS, Lawrence
  See DAVIES, L(eslie) P(urnell)

PHILIPS, Thomas
  See DAVIES, L(eslie) P(urnell)

*   *   *

PLAIDY, Jean
  See HIBBERT, Eleanor Alice Burford

*   *   *

PONSONBY, D(oris) A(lmon) 1907-
  (Doris Rybot, Sarah Tempest)

PERSONAL: Born March 23, 1907, in Devonport, Devon, England; daughter of Reginald Gordon (an Army officer) and Anne Marguerite (Almon) Ponsonby; married Francis John Chancellor Rybot (an Army officer), September 30, 1933 (died, 1979). *Education:* Attended Villabelle, Neuchatel, Switzerland. *Religion:* Anglican. *Avocational interests:* Animals.

ADDRESSES: Agent—Curtis Brown Ltd., 1 Craven Hill, London W2 3EP, England; and 575 Madison Ave., New York, NY 10022.

CAREER: Author. From 1928-37, worked as sub-editor, *Oxford Times,* Oxford, England, reporter, *Aldershot Gazette,* and freelance writer for *South China Morning Post* and *Hong Kong Herald.*

MEMBER: West Country Writers' Association.

WRITINGS:

The Gazebo, Hutchinson (London), 1945, published as *If My Arms Could Hold: A Vivid and Colorful Romance of Bath in the Time of Beau Nash,* Liveright (London), 1947.
Sophy Valentine, Hutchinson, 1946.
Merry Meeting, Hutchinson, 1948.
Strangers in My House, Hutchinson, 1948.
Call a Dog Hervey (biography), Hutchinson, 1949.
Bow Window in Green Street, Hutchinson, 1949.
Family of Jaspard, Hutchinson, 1950, published in two volumes as *The General* and *The Fortunate Adventure,* White Lion (London), 1971.
The Bristol Cousins, Hutchinson, 1951.
The Foolish Marriage, Hutchinson, 1952.
The Widow's Daughters, Hutchinson, 1953.

Royal Purple, Hutchinson, 1954.
Dogs in Clover, Hutchinson, 1954.
(With Lydia Ingleton under pseudonym Doris Rybot)
    The Popular Chow Chow (nonfiction), Popular
    Dogs Publishing Co. (London), 1954.
Conquesta's Caravan, Hutchinson, 1955.
Unhallowed House, Hutchinson, 1956.
*The Lost Duchess: The Story of the Prince Consort's
    Mother* (biography; Book Society recommenda-
    tion), Chapman & Hall (London), 1958.
So Bold a Choice, Hurst & Blackett (London), 1960.
(Under pseudonym Doris Rybot) *Romany Sister,* R.
    Hale (London), 1960.
(Under pseudonym Doris Rybot) *A Japanese Doll,* R.
    Hale, 1961.
A Living to Earn, Hurst & Blackett, 1961.
A Prisoner in Regent's Park (biography), Chapman &
    Hall, 1961.
The Orphans, Hurst & Blackett, 1962.
(Under pseudonym Doris Rybot) *My Kingdom for a
    Donkey* (nonfiction), Hutchinson, 1963.
Bells along the Neva, Hurst & Blackett, 1964.
The Jade Horse of Merle, Hurst & Blackett, 1966.
(Under pseudonym Doris Rybot) *A Donkey and a
    Dandelion* (nonfiction), Hutchinson, 1966.
An Unusual Tutor, Hurst & Blackett, 1967.
(Under pseudonym Sarah Tempest) *A Winter of Fear,*
    Hurst & Blackett, 1967.
The Forgotten Heir, Hurst & Blackett, 1969.
The Heart in the Sand, Hurst & Blackett, 1970.
Mr. Florian's Fortune, Hurst & Blackett, 1971.
(Under pseudonym Doris Rybot) *It Began before
    Noah* (nonfiction), M. Joseph (London), 1972.
Flight from Hanover Square, Hurst & Blackett, 1972.
The Gamester's Daughter, Hurst & Blackett, 1974.
The Heir to Holtwood, Hurst & Blackett, 1975.
An Unnamed Gentlewoman, Hurst & Blackett, 1976.
Kaye's Walk, Hurst & Blackett, 1977.
Sir William, Hurst & Blackett, 1978.
Exhibition Summer, R. Hale, 1982.
A Woman Despised, R. Hale, 1988.

SIDELIGHTS: D. A. Ponsonby specializes in romance novels set during the Regency Period of English history. "Her sense of period is accurate," writes Lornie Leete-Hodge in *Twentieth-Century Romance and Historical Writers,* "and her shrewd knowledge of people splendidly evokes the time in which the tales are set."

Ponsonby's stories often revolve around domestic matters, the marriage of family members, and the struggles of poor, working people trying to better themselves. In *The Widow's Daughters,* for example, Ponsonby tells the story of a woman attempting to marry off her four daughters to suitable gentlemen, and of the resulting conflicts she creates with her girls. Leete-Hodge calls the novel a "light-hearted story of a silly, scheming widow."

If My Arms Could Hold follows the divergent life-paths of three sisters in eighteenth-century England. "One was thrust reluctantly into the arms of an elderly admirer; one eloped with a scoundrel; and the third . . . lost her heart to a young man of wealth who . . . gives her an eighteenth-century brush off," Lisle Bell explains in the *New York Herald Tribune Weekly Book Review.* Barbara Bond of the *New York Times* writes that *If My Arms Could Hold* "reflects faithfully and enthusiastically the color, costumes and customs of England when Beau Nash ruled at Bath."

Family of Jaspard tells of Robert Jaspard's two illegitimate children who, when he brings them to live in his house with his wife and other children, disrupt his entire way of life. Although N. L. Rothamn in *Saturday Review of Literature* calls the novel "a comedy of manners, but it is not an engaging one," Isabelle Mallet in the *New York Times* states: "Generally we enjoy the book as a well-written, splendidly illustrated story of escape." The critic for *Springfield Republican* calls *Family of Jaspard* "a delightful 18th-century comedy of manners."

"The well-worn themes of regency novels," writes Leete-Hodge, "take on a new meaning under [Ponsonby's] narrative skill; the timelessness of her writing is its strong quality. Her sense of period and the fact that her stories can be read and re-read with ease makes them stand out in the morass of historical fiction. My regret is there are not more of them, though their exclusivity is another charm, making them novels to be treasured."

BIOGRAPHICAL/CRITICAL SOURCES:

BOOKS

Twentieth Century Romance and Historical Writers,
    3rd edition, St. James Press (Detroit), 1994.

PERIODICALS

Kirkus, February 15, 1947, p. 15; August 1, 1951, p.
    19.
New York Herald Tribune Weekly Book Review,
    March 9, 1947, p. 24.
New York Times, March 16, 1947, p. 22; November
    25, 1951, p. 5.

Saturday Review of Literature, November 24, 1951, p. 34.

Springfield Republican, November 25, 1951, p. 28A.

*   *   *

POPE, Dudley (Bernard Egerton) 1925-1997

PERSONAL: Born December 29, 1925, in Ashford, Kent, England; died April 25, 1997, in Marigot, St. Martin, French West Indies; son of Sydney Broughton (a classical scholar) and Alice (Meehan) Pope; married Kathleen Patricia Hall, March 17, 1954; children: Jane Clare Victoria. *Education:*Attended school in Ashford, England. *Politics:* Independent. *Religion:* Protestant.

CAREER: Evening News, London, England, naval correspondent, 1944-59; self-employed naval historian, 1959-97. *Wartime service:* British Merchant Navy, midshipman, 1941-43; invalided out.

MEMBER: Society for Nautical Research, Navy Records Society (councillor), Royal Temple Yacht Club.

WRITINGS:

NONFICTION

Flag 4: The Battle of Coastal Forces in the Mediterranean, William Kimber (London), 1954.

The Battle of the River Plate, William Kimber, 1956, published as *Graf Spee: The Life and Death of a Raider,* Lippincott (Philadelphia), 1957.

73 North: The Battle of the Barents Sea, Lippincott, 1957.

Decision at Trafalgar, Lippincott, 1959, published as *England Expects,* Weidenfeld & Nicolson (London), 1959.

At Twelve Mr. Byng Was Shot, Lippincott, 1962.

The Black Ship: Mutiny on the H. M. S. Hermion 1797, Weidenfeld & Nicolson, 1963, Lippincott, 1964.

Guns, Delacorte, 1965.

The Great Gamble, Simon & Schuster, 1972.

Harry Morgan's Way, Secker & Warburg (London), 1977, published as *The Buccaneer King: The Biography of Sir Henry Morgan,* Dodd, 1978.

Life in Nelson's Navy, U.S. Naval Institute Press (Annapolis), 1980.

The Devil Himself: The Mutiny of 1800, Secker & Warburg, 1987.

FICTION

Ramage, Lippincott, 1965.

Ramage and the Drum Beat, Weidenfeld & Nicolson, 1967, published as *Drumbeat,* Doubleday, 1968.

Triton Brig, Doubleday, 1969, published as *Ramage and the Freebooters,* Wedienfeld & Nicolson, 1969.

Governor Ramage RN, Simon & Schuster, 1973.

Ramage's Prize, Simon & Schuster, 1974.

Ramage and the Guillotine, Alison Press, 1975.

Ramage's Diamond, Alison Press, 1976.

Ramage's Mutiny, Alison Press, 1977.

Ramage and the Rebels, Alison Press, 1978, Walker, 1985.

Convoy, Alison Press, 1979.

The Ramage Touch, Alison Press, 1979, Walker, 1984.

Ramage's Signal, Alison Press, 1980, Walker, 1984.

Buccaneer, Secker & Warburg, 1981, Walker, 1984.

Ramage and the Renegades, Secker & Warburg, 1981.

Admiral, Secker & Warburg, 1982.

Ramage's Devil, Secker & Warburg, 1982.

Decoy, Secker & Warburg, 1983, Walker, 1984.

Ramage's Trial, Secker & Warburg, 1984.

Ramage's Challenge, Secker & Warburg, 1985.

Galleon, Secker & Warburg, 1986, Walker, 1987.

Ramage at Trafalgar, Secker & Warburg, 1986.

Corsair, Secker & Warburg, 1987.

Ramage and the Saracens, Secker & Warburg, 1988.

Ramage and the Dido, Secker & Warburg, 1989.

SIDELIGHTS: A prominent British naval historian and historical novelist, Dudley Pope expressed his love for the seafaring life in all of his written works. His novels featuring Lord Nicholas Ramage are set during the Napoleonic period and follow Ramage's adventures as a British sailor of the time. Pope's nonfiction accounts of British naval history drew critical praise for their combination of historical accuracy with clear, fluid writing and a compelling narrative pace. Arlene Moore, writing in the *Twentieth-Century Romance and Historical Writers,* explained that Pope possessed a comprehensive knowledge of British naval history which he used to good effect in both his fiction and nonfiction works. Moore stated that "one must acknowledge his vast store of historical information about the Royal Navy and its history. It is not the kind of knowledge that is found on tediously compiled note-cards. Pope has internalized so much of what he has learned that readers would find it difficult, if not impossible, to detect a false note within his writing."

Among Pope's most critically-acclaimed histories is *Graf Spee: The Life and Death of a Raider,* the story of a German pocket battleship during the Second World War that preyed successfully on Allied shipping until being hunted down and destroyed by the Royal Navy. Alfred Stanford in the *New York Herald Tribune Book Review* called the battle that sank the *Graf Spee* "one of the great naval engagements of all time" and Pope's account of the battle "a great contribution to the full understanding of this heroic sea fight." A *New Yorker* critic admitted that Pope's "account is by far the best" offered of this historic naval action. E. L. Beach of the *New York Times* claimed that "when the reader is through the book he will rightly feel that he has been through the battle as well."

73 North: The Defeat of Hitler's Navy tells the story of an Arctic convoy during the Second World War that defeated a larger German force and thus changed how German naval forces were deployed for the remainder of the war. A *Times Literary Supplement* critic called *73 North* "a clear and enthralling battle-narrative," while Richard Philbrick in the *Chicago Sunday Tribune* found it to be "an absorbing story and masterfully written history."

For *At Twelve Mr. Byng Was Shot,* Pope turned to an earlier period of British naval history to examine the execution of a naval officer for treason on what Pope argues were trumped-up charges. John Owen in the *New Statesman* called Pope's argument "an extremely competent and well-written piece of historical rehabilitation." Pope's study was praised for its thorough research of the incident in question and its clear narrative style. Charles Causley of *Spectator* described *At Twelve Mr. Byng Was Shot* as "a masterpiece of lucidity," while C. W. Weinberger in the *San Francisco Chronicle* called it "a model history covering, . . . in great detail and thoroughness, a comparatively small episode. . . . Pope's style and execution is masterly."

The Black Ship concerns the bloodiest mutiny in British naval history, which took place on board the frigate *Hermione* in the early eighteenth century. A *Times Literary Supplement* critic felt that "naval historians will indeed be grateful for Mr. Pope's extensive research and considerable narrative and descriptive skill." James Ball in *Best Sellers* praised Pope's historical accuracy: "It is tremendously detailed and yet tremendously accurate—even the conversations are exact."

In 1965 Pope ventured into seafaring fiction with the novel *Ramage,* in which the character Nicholas Ramage, a British naval lieutenant in the early 19th century, was first introduced. "Ramage," Moore explained, "is not a super-hero. He doubts, he ponders his decisions. He questions his perceptions and tries to be fair in a world that functioned on patronage, rank, and bribery."

Ramage's adventures are recorded in over a dozen novels in which the stalwart lieutenant rises through the ranks as he fights privateers, is shipwrecked, rides out tropical hurricanes, and defends himself in court against charges of cowardliness. Speaking of the novel *Governor Ramage, R.N.,* Moore explained that "tension and suspense do not resolve themselves until the last two or three pages, keeping the reader gripped by the story."

Pope lived year-round on the ocean-cruising ketch *Ramage.* From 1965 to his death in 1997, he did a great deal of sailing in the Baltic and crossed the Atlantic to cruise in the Caribbean.

BIOGRAPHICAL/CRITICAL SOURCES:

BOOKS

Twentieth-Century Romance and Historical Writers, 3rd edition, St. James Press (Detroit, MI), 1994.

PERIODICALS

Best Sellers, March 1, 1964, p. 23; February 15, 1968; April 15, 1969.
Chicago Sunday Tribune, January 27, 1957, p. 7; June 29, 1958, p. 7.
Guardian, June 1, 1962, p. 6.
Horn Book, October, 1965, p. 41.
Kirkus, March 15, 1958, p. 26.
Library Journal, February 1, 1957, p. 82; December 1, 1965, p. 90.
New Statesman, June 8, 1962, p. 63; June 11, 1965, p. 69.
New Yorker, January 26, 1957, p. 32; April 18, 1964, p. 40.
New York Herald Tribune Book Review, February 10, 1957, p. 6; June 15, 1958, p. 6; June 24, 1962, p. 9.
New York Times, January 27, 1957, p. 3; June 15, 1958, p. 6.

New York Times Book Review, May 20, 1962, p. 12.
San Francisco Chronicle, February 15, 1975, p. 21;
   July 8, 1962, p. 35.
Saturday Review, April 6, 1957, p. 40.
Spectator, July 20, 1956, p. 104; June 1, 1962, p.
   725.
Springfield Republican, March 17, 1957, p. 8C.
Times Literary Supplement, March 14, 1958, p. 141;
   November 21, 1963, p. 949.

OBITUARIES

New York Times, May 5, 1997, p. B11.*

*   *   *

PRONZINI, Bill 1943-
   (Jack Foxx, Alex Saxon; William Jeffrey, a
   joint pseudonym)

PERSONAL: Born April 13, 1943, in Petaluma, CA;
son of Joseph (a farm worker) and Helene (Guder)
Pronzini; married Laura Patricia Adolphson, May 15,
1965 (divorced, 1967); married Brunhilde Schier,
July 28, 1972 (marriage ended); married Marcia
Muller (a writer), 1992. *Politics:* Liberal Democrat.
Avocational interests: Sports, old movies and radio
shows, book collecting.

ADDRESSES: Home—P.O. Box 2536, Petaluma, CA
94953-2536. *Agent*—Dominick Abel, Dominick Abel
Literary Agency, 146 West 82nd Street #1B, New
York, N.Y. 10024.

CAREER: Petaluma Argus-Courier, Petaluma, CA,
reporter, 1957-60; writer, 1969—.

AWARDS, HONORS: Private Eye Writers of America
award for best novel, 1981 and 1983; lifetime achievement award, 1987.

WRITINGS:

CRIME NOVELS

The Stalker, Random House (New York City), 1971.
Panic!, Random House, 1972.
(Under pseudonym Alex Saxon) *A Run in Diamonds,*
   Pocket Books (New York City), 1973.
Snowbound, Putnam (New York City), 1974.
Games, Putnam, 1976.
(With Barry N. Malzberg) *The Running of Beasts,*
   Putnam, 1976.

(With Malzberg) *Acts of Mercy,* Putnam, 1977.
(With Malzberg) *Night Screams,* Playboy Press (New
   York City), 1979.
A Killing in Xanadu, Waves Press, 1980.
Masques, Arbor House (New York City), 1981.
(With John Lutz) *The Eye,* Mysterious Press (New
   York City), 1984.
Quincannon, Walker (New York City), 1985.
(With Marcia Muller) *Beyond the Grave,* Walker, 1986.
(With Muller) *The Lighthouse,* St. Martin's (New
   York City), 1987.
With an Extreme Burning, Carroll & Graf (New York
   City), 1994.
Blue Lonesome, Walker, 1995.

"NAMELESS DETECTIVE" SERIES

The Snatch, Random House, 1971.
The Vanished, Random House, 1973.
Undercurrent, Random House, 1973.
Blowback, Random House, 1977.
(With Collin Wilcox) *Twospot,* Putnam, 1978.
Labyrinth, St. Martin's, 1980.
Hoodwink, St. Martin's, 1981.
Scattershot, St. Martin's, 1982.
Dragonfire, St. Martin's, 1982.
Bindlestiff, St. Martin's, 1983.
Quicksilver, St. Martin's, 1984.
Nightshades, St. Martin's, 1984.
(With Marcia Muller) *Double,* St. Martin's, 1984.
Bones, St. Martin's, 1985.
Deadfall, St. Martin's, 1986.
Shackles, St. Martin's, 1988.
Jackpot, Delacorte (New York City), 1990.
Breakdown, Delacorte, 1991.
Quarry, Delacorte, 1992.
Epitaphs, Delacorte, 1992.
Demons, Delacorte, 1993.
Hardcase, Delacorte, 1995.
Sentinels, Carroll & Graf, 1996.

NOVELS UNDER PSEUDONYM JACK FOXX

The Jade Figurine, Bobbs-Merrill (Indianapolis),
   1972.
Dead Run, Bobbs-Merrill, 1975.
Freebooty, Bobbs-Merrill, 1976.
Wildfire, Bobbs-Merrill, 1978.

*NOVELS WITH JEFFREY M. WALLMANN; UNDER JOINT
   PSEUDONYM WILLIAM JEFFREY*

Duel at Gold Buttes, Leisure Books (New York City),
   1982.

Border Fever, Leisure Books, 1983.
Day of the Moon, R. Hale (London), 1983.

OTHER NOVELS

(With Malzberg) *Prose Bowl,* St. Martin's, 1980.
(With Jack Anderson) *The Cambodia File,* Doubleday (New York City), 1981.
The Gallows Land, Walker, 1983.
Starvation Camp, Doubleday, 1984.
The Last Days of Horse-Shy Halloran, M. Evans, 1987.
The Hangings, Walker, 1989.
Firewind, M. Evans, 1989.

SHORT STORY COLLECTIONS

Casefile: The Best of the "Nameless Detective" Stories, St. Martin's, 1983.
Graveyard Plots, St. Martin's, 1985.
Small Felonies: Fifty Mystery Short Stories, St. Martin's, 1988.
The Best Western Stories of Bill Pronzini, Swallow Press, 1990.

NONFICTION

Gun in Cheek: A Study of "Alternative" Crime Fiction, Coward, McCann, 1982.
(With Muller) *1001 Midnights: The Aficionado's Guide to Mystery and Detective Fiction,* Arbor House, 1986.
Son of Gun in Cheek, Mysterious Press, 1987.

EDITOR

(With Joe Gores) *Tricks and Treats,* Doubleday, 1976.
Midnight Specials: An Anthology for Train Buffs and Suspense Aficionados, Bobbs-Merrill, 1977.
Werewolf!: A Connoisseur's Collection of Werewolfiana, Arbor House, 1979.
The Edgar Winners: Thirty-third Annual Anthology of the Mystery Writers in America, Random House, 1980.
Voodoo!: A Chrestomathy of Necromacy, Arbor House, 1980.
Mummy!: A Chrestomathy of Crypt-ology, Arbor House, 1980.
The Arbor House Necropolis, Arbor House, 1981.
(With Malzberg and Martin H. Greenberg) *The Arbor House Treasury of Mystery and Suspense,* Arbor House, 1981.

(With Malzberg and Greenberg) *The Arbor House Treasury of Horror and the Supernatural,* Arbor House, 1981.
Creature!: A Chrestomathy of "Monstery," Arbor House, 1981.
Specter!: A Chrestomathy of "Spookery," Arbor House, 1982.
The Arbor House Treasury of Detective and Mystery Stories from the Great Pulps, Arbor House, 1983.
Wild Westerns, Walker, 1986.
(With Malzberg and Greenberg) *Mystery in the Mainstream,* Morrow, 1986.
(With Greenberg and Muller) *Lady on the Case,* Bonanza, 1988.
More Wild Westerns, Walker, 1989.
(with Jack Adrian) *Hard-Boiled: An Anthology of American Crime Stories,* Oxford University Press, 1995.

EDITOR WITH BARRY N. MALZBERG

Dark Sins, Dark Dreams: Crime in Science Fiction, Doubleday, 1978.
The End of Summer: Science Fiction of the Fifties, Ace Books, 1979.
Shared Tomorrows: Science Fiction Is Collaboration, St. Martin's, 1979.
Bug-Eyed Monsters, Harcourt, 1980.

EDITOR WITH MARTIN H. GREENBERG

The Arbor House Treasury of Great Western Stories, Arbor House, 1982.
The Lawmen, Fawcett (New York City), 1984.
The Outlaws, Fawcett, 1984.
The Reel West, Doubleday, 1984.
The Western Hall of Fame: An Anthology of Classic Western Stories Selected by the Western Writers of America, Morrow, 1984.
The Mystery Hall of Fame: An Anthology of Classic Mystery and Suspense Stories, Selected by the Mystery Writers of America, Morrow, 1984.
The Best Western Stories of Steve Frazee, Southern Illinois University Press (Urbana), 1984.
The Best Western Stories of Wayne D. Overholser, Southern Illinois University Press, 1984.
13 Short Mystery Novels, Greenwich House, 1985.
13 Short Espionage Novels, Bonanza, 1985.
Women Sleuths, Academy Chicago (Chicago), 1985.
Ethnic Detectives, Dodd, 1985.
Police Procedurals, Academy Chicago, 1985.
(And with Charles G. Waugh) *Murder in the First Reel,* Avon (New York City), 1985.
The Cowboys, Fawcett, 1985.

The Warriors, Fawcett, 1985.
The Second Reel West, Doubleday, 1985.
A Treasury of Civil War Stories, Bonanza, 1985.
A Treasury of World War II Stories, Bonanza, 1985.
The Railroaders, Fawcett, 1986.
The Third Reel West, Doubleday, 1986.
The Steamboaters, Fawcett, 1986.
Great Modern Police Stories, Walker, 1986.
101 Mystery Stories, Avenal, 1986.
Locked Room Puzzles, Academy Chicago, 1986.
Prime Suspects, Ivy, 1987.
(And Carol-Lynn Rossel Waugh) *Manhattan Mysteries,* Avenal, 1987.
Uncollected Crimes, Walker, 1987.
Suspicious Characters, Ivy, 1987.
The Horse Soldiers, Fawcett, 1987.
The Best Western Stories of Lewis B. Patten, Southern Illinois University Press, 1987.
The Cattlemen, Fawcett, 1987.
The Gunfighters, Fawcett, 1988.
The Texans, Fawcett, 1988.
Criminal Elements, Ivy, 1988.
13 Short Detective Novels, Bonanza, 1988.
Cloak and Dagger, Avenal, 1988.
The Mammoth Book of Private Eye Stories, Carroll & Graf, 1988.
Homicidal Acts, Ivy, 1989.
Felonious Assaults, Ivy, 1989.
The Californians, Fawcett, 1989.
The Best Western Stories of Loren D. Estleman, Swallow Press, 1989.
The Best Western Stories of Frank Bonham, Swallow Press, 1989.
The Arizonans, Fawcett, 1989.
New Frontiers, Volume 1, Tor Books, 1990.
New Frontiers, Volume 2, Tor Books, 1990.
The Northerners, Fawcett, 1990.
The Northwesterners, Fawcett, 1990.
The Best Western Stories of Ryerson Johnson, Swallow Press, 1990.
The Montanans, Fawcett, 1991.
The Best Western Stories of John Jakes, Ohio University Press, 1991.
The Best Western Stories of Les Savage, Jr., Ohio University Press, 1991.
Christmas Out West, Doubleday, 1991.
The Best Western Stories of Ed Gorman, Ohio University Press, 1992.
Combat! Great Tales of World War II, Signet, 1992.

EDITOR WITH MARCIA MULLER

The Web She Weaves, Morrow, 1983.
Child's Ploy, Macmillan, 1984.

Witches' Brew, Macmillan, 1984.
Chapter and Hearse, Morrow, 1985.
Dark Lessons, Macmillan, 1985.
Kill or Cure, Macmillan, 1985.
The Wickedest Show on Earth, Morrow, 1985.
The Deadly Arts, Arbor House, 1985.
She Won the West, Morrow, 1985.
Chapter and Hearse, Morrow, 1985.

Contributor to anthologies; also contributor of over three hundred short stories and articles to magazines, including *Argosy, Ellery Queen's Mystery Magazine,* and *Magazine of Fantasy and Science Fiction.* Pronzini's books have been translated into eighteen languages and published in more than thirty countries. His manuscripts are collected at the Mugar Memorial Library, Boston University.

ADAPTATIONS: Several of Pronzini's books have been adapted to film, including *The Jade Figurine, Snowbound* (Columbia Pictures), *Panic!* (Hal Wallis Productions), *Games* (Sara Films), *Night Screams* (Soge Films), and *The Lighthouse.* Short story "Liar's Dice" adapted into television movie *Tails You Live, Heads You're Dead,* USA Cable, 1995.

SIDELIGHTS: "Some mystery writers start big, with an instant classic," notes Edward D. Hoch in the *St. James Guide to Crime and Mystery Writers.* "Others, like Bill Pronzini, seem to improve from book to book, building a solid professional foundation." IN more than 50 published works, including the popular "Nameless Detective" series, Pronzini has established his reputation as a crafter of taut, engrossing thrillers.

A former newspaper reporter, Pronzini made his fiction debut in 1971 with *The Stalker,* about a group of ex-servicemen-turned robbers who are exterminated one by one as terror and suspicion grow among the survivors. "It's a classic situation and Pronzini does well by it," declares Hoch. *The Stalker* netted its author his first Mystery Writers of America award nomination.

But Pronzini's signature character was yet to emerge. The Nameless Detective, who was introduced in novel form in 1971's *The Snatch,* is a San Francisco sleuth whose everyman qualities more than make up for his lack of identity. In more than 20 stories to date, Nameless has survived an assassination attempt (in the short story "Private Eye Blues"), attended a pulp collectors' convention (*Hoodwink,* a Private Eye

Writers of America winner for best novel of 1981), and investigated a mystery connected with the internment of Japanese-Americans during World War II (*Quicksilver*).

Quicksilver, notes Hoch, "was followed by four more good Nameless novels, *Double, Nightshade, Bones,* and *Deadfall.* But nothing was to prepare the reader for the revelation and insight of his next case, recounted in *Shackles.* Here the detective is kidnapped and shackled to the wall of a remote mountain cabin, facing a slow death once a small quantity of food has run out. . . .The reader spends 90 days and nearly half the book with Nameless chained to that wall, and when he finally escapes and sets out to find his captor, he is a changed man in many ways."

Nameless did indeed return as an "older and wiser" private eye in the follow-up book, *Jackpot.* "When he is taunted by a younger, more powerful gang leader, the reader is full of sympathy for him," Hoch says. The book also examines Nameless' ongoing romance with longtime girlfriend Kerry (whom Nameless marries in 1985's *Hardcase*).

Aging his character throughout the series, Pronzini sets the "tough, terse, hardworking and honorable PI," as *Publishers Weekly* calls him, in late middle age in *Demons* (1993). In this episode, Nameless must overcome his reluctance to handle divorce cases to track down a philandering husband in a story that escalates into a hostage crisis. Citing the overall quality of the author's work, Wes Lukowsky in *Booklist* states that the Nameless series is one that, "taken in total, forms a multivolume novel with all the depth and character development of the best fiction."

Admiring notices also greeted the release of *Blue Lonesome,* a non-Nameless novel published in 1995. The plot opens with Jim Messenger, a single CPA, focusing his attention on anther solitary soul, a woman who dines alone at the same San Francisco eatery Messenger frequents. Her reported suicide leads the accountant into detective work as he seeks her identity and uncovers murder and a coverup in a small Nevada town. The author, according to a *Publishers Weekly* critic, adeptly uses "both the stark desert setting and knowledgeable digressions about jazz to evoke the loneliness at the heart of the tale." And to a *Rapport* reviewer, Pronzini shows he is "a fabulous craftsman, weaving a richly chromatic tale of midlife doldrums, an enigmatic crime, . . .and a

beautifully realized ensemble of characters that blossoms in the stark, still spaces of grit and sagebrush."

Pronzini and fellow thriller-writer Jack Adrian joined forces to edit 1995's *Hard-Boiled: An Anthology of American Crime Stories*—a work, says John Litwiler, that "traces the development of American noir fiction from its origins in the 1920s to the present." Writing in the *Chicago Tribune,* Litwiler adds that noir "is a specialized kind of crime fiction that [the book's] 17-page introduction attempts to define with incomplete success."

On the other hand, *Times Literary Supplement* critic David Flusfeder finds that the co-editors "give a good, brisk introductory history of the genre, even if they sometimes lapse into crassness or adopt a prissy tone. They take us from the first dime novel in 1860; to 1895, when *Argosy* magazine changed from smooth paper to cheaper wood pulp paper stock, thus giving birth to pulp fiction. . .[to the mid-century] and the golden age of the hard-boiled pulp magazine. The pulps lasted until the 1950s, when television saw them off. But the genre survives."

One more criticism of *Hard-Boiled* came from Litwiler: "There are no stories by the estimable Pronzini himself."

BIOGRAPHICAL/CRITICAL SOURCES:

BOOKS

St. James Guide to Crime and Mystery Writers, St. James Press (Detroit), 1996.

PERIODICALS

Booklist, September 1, 1993; June 5, 1995; November 1, 1995.
Chicago Tribune, November 12, 1995.
Los Angeles Times, March 12, 1981; August 14, 1985; October 24, 1985.
Los Angeles Times Book Review, October 20, 1985.
New York Times, April 24, 1987.
New York Times Book Review, March 2, 1980; September 13, 1987.
Publishers Weekly, August 2, 1993; August 28, 1995.
Rapport, volume 19, number 3, 1996.
Times (London), July 29, 1989.
Times Literary Supplement, December 29, 1995.
Village Voice Literary Supplement, February, 1984.
Washington Post Book World, January 18, 1981; April 18, 1982.

QUENTIN, Patrick
  See WHEELER, Hugh (Callingham)

* * *

QUIN-HARKIN, Janet 1941-
  (Janetta Johns)

PERSONAL: Born September 24, 1941, in Bath, England; immigrated to the United States in 1966; daughter of Frank Newcombe (an engineer) and Margery (a teacher; maiden name, Rees) Lee; married John Quin-Harkin (a retired sales manager), November 26, 1966; children: Clare, Anne, Jane, Dominic. *Education:*University of London, B.A. (with honors), 1963; graduate study at University of Kiel and University of Freiburg. *Religion:*Roman Catholic. *Avocational interests:* Tennis, travel, drama, music, sketching, and hiking.

ADDRESSES: Home and office—31 Tralee Way, San Rafael, CA 94903. *Agent*—Amy Berkower, Writers House, Inc., 21 West 26th St., New York, NY 10010.

CAREER: British Broadcasting Corp. (BBC), London, England, studio manager in drama department, 1963-66; writer, 1971—; teacher of dance and drama, 1971-76. Founder and former director of San Raphael's Children's Little Theater. Writing teacher at Dominican College, San Rafael, 1988-95.

MEMBER: Society of Children's Book Writers and Illustrators, Associated Authors of Children's Literature.

AWARDS, HONORS: Children's Book Showcase selection, Children's Book Council, Outstanding Books of the Year citation, *New York Times,* American Institute of Graphic Arts Children's Book Show citation, and Best Books of the year citation, *School Library Journal, Washington Post,* and *Saturday Review,* all 1976, all for *Peter Penny's Dance;* Children's Choice citation, 1985, for *Wanted: Date for Saturday Night.*

WRITINGS:

CHILDREN'S BOOKS

Peter Penny's Dance, illustrated by Anita Lobel, Dial (New York City), 1976.

Benjamin's Balloon, Parents' Magazine Press (New York City), 1979.
Septimus Bean and His Amazing Machine, illustrated by Art Cumings, Parents' Magazine Press, 1980.
Magic Growing Powder, Illustrated by Art Cumings, Parents' Magazine Press, 1981.
Helpful Hattie, illustrated by Susanna Natti, Harcourt (San Diego), 1983.
Three Impossible Things, Parents' Magazine Press, 1991.
Billy and Ben: The Terrible Two, illustrated by Carol Newsom, Bantam (New York City), 1992.

YOUNG ADULT NOVELS

Write Every Day, Scholastic (New York City), 1982.
(Under pseudonym Janetta Johns) *The Truth about Me and Bobby V.,* Bantam, 1983.
Tommy Loves Tina, Berkley/Ace (New York City), 1984.
Winner Takes All, Berkley/Ace, 1984.
Wanted: Date for Saturday Night, Putnam (New York City), 1985.
Summer Heat, Fawcett (New York City), 1990.
My Phantom Love, HarperCollins (New York City), 1992.
On My Own, HarperCollins, 1992.
Getting Personal: Becky, Silhouette Books (New York City), 1994.
The Apartment, HarperCollins, 1994.
The Sutcliffe Diamonds, HarperCollins, 1994.
The Boy Next Door, Bantam, 1995.

"SWEET DREAMS" SERIES

California Girl, Bantam, 1981.
Love Match, Bantam, 1982.
Ten-Boy Summer, Bantam, 1982.
Daydreamer, Bantam, 1983.
The Two of Us, Bantam, 1984.
Exchange of Hearts, Bantam, 1984.
Ghost of a Chance, Bantam, 1984.
Lovebirds, Bantam, 1984.
101 Ways to Meet Mr. Right, Bantam, 1985.
The Great Boy Chase, Bantam, 1985.
Follow That Boy, Bantam, 1985.
My Secret Love, Bantam, 1986.
My Best Enemy, Bantam, 1987.
Never Say Goodbye, Bantam, 1987.

"ON OUR OWN" SERIES

On Our Own, Bantam, 1986.
The Graduates, Bantam, 1986.

The Trouble with Toni, Bantam, 1986.
Out of Love, Bantam, 1986.
Old Friends, New Friends, Bantam, 1986.
Best Friends Forever, Bantam, 1986.

"SUGAR AND SPICE" SERIES

Flip Side, Ballantine, 1987.
Tug of War, Ballantine, 1987.
Surf's Up, Ballantine, 1987.
The Last Dance, Ballantine, 1987.
Nothing in Common, Ballantine, 1987.
Dear Cousin, Ballantine, 1987.
Two Girls, One Boy, Ballantine, 1987.
Trading Places, Ballantine, 1987.
Double Take, Ballantine, 1988.
Make Me a Star, Ballantine, 1988.
Big Sister, Ballantine, 1988.
Out in the Cold, Ballantine, 1988.
Blind Date, Ballantine, 1988.
It's My Turn, Ballantine, 1988.

"HEARTBREAK CAFE" SERIES

No Experience Required, Fawcett, 1990.
The Main Attraction, Fawcett, 1990.
At Your Service, Fawcett, 1990.
Catch of the Day, Fawcett, 1990.
Love to Go, Fawcett, 1990.
Just Desserts, Fawcett, 1990.

"FRIENDS" SERIES

Starring Tess and Ali, HarperCollins, 1991.
Tess and Ali and the Teeny Bikini, HarperCollins, 1991.
Boy Trouble for Tess and Ali, HarperCollins, 1991.
Tess and Ali, Going on Fifteen, HarperCollins, 1991.

"SENIOR YEAR" SERIES

Homecoming Dance, HarperCollins, 1991.
New Year's Eve, HarperCollins, 1991.
Night of the Prom, HarperCollins, 1992.
Graduation Day, HarperCollins, 1992.

"BOYFRIEND CLUB" SERIES

Ginger's First Kiss, Troll Communications, 1994.
Roni's Dream Boy, Troll Communications, 1994.
Karen's Perfect Match, Troll Communications, 1994.
Ginger's New Crush, Troll Communications, 1994.
Queen Justine, Troll Communications, 1995.
Roni's Two-Boy Trouble, Troll Communications, 1995.

No More Boys, Troll Communications, 1995.
Karen's Lesson in Love, Troll Communications, 1995.
Roni's Sweet Fifteen, Troll Communications, 1995.
Justine's Babysitting, Troll Communications, 1995.
The Boyfriend Wars, Troll Communications, 1995.

"TGIF!" SERIES

Sleepover Madness, Pocket Books, 1995.
Friday Night Fright, Pocket Books, 1995.
Four's a Crowd, Pocket Books, 1995.
Forever Friday, Pocket Books, 1995.
Toe-Shoe Trouble, Pocket Books, 1996.
Secret Valentine, Pocket Books, 1996.

SISTER, SISTER SERIES

Cool in School, Pocket Books, 1996.
You Read My Mind, Pocket Books, 1996.

Also author of *One Crazy Christmas and 5 to Come.*

OTHER

(Contributor) *Chandler Reading Program,* five volumes, edited by Lawrence Carillo and Dorothy McKinley, Noble & Noble, 1967-72.
Madam Sarah (adult historical novel), Fawcett, 1990.
Fool's Gold (adult historical novel), HarperCollins, 1991.
Amazing Grace (adult historical fiction), HarperCollins, 1993.
The Secrets of Lake Success (based on the NBC mini-series, created by David Stenn), Tor Books, 1993.
Trade Winds (based on the NBC mini-series, created by Hugh Bush), Schoolfield/Caribbean Productions, 1993.

Also author of several documentaries and four radio plays and scripts, including "Dandelion Hours," for the BBC, 1966. Many of Quin-Harkin's young adult novels, including *California Girl, Love Match, Ten-Boy Summer,* and *Daydreamer,* have been translated into other languages. Contributor to periodicals, including *Scholastic* and *Mother's Journal.*

SIDELIGHTS: Janet Quin-Harkin is the popular author of more than one hundred books, most of which are geared for teen readers. Quin-Harkin's series include "Sweet Dreams," "Sugar and Spice," "Heartbreak Cafe," and "On Our Own," among others, comprising books of standard length with a fixed group of characters involved in "the sort of lives that Middle America leads," as Quin-Harkin once said in describing her work. According to the author, the "Sweet Dreams" series opened up a new direction in publishing, providing books that were cheap enough for the readers themselves to purchase and thus making teen readers independent from the choices of parents and librarians. These were also books that were more upbeat than previous YA contributions, which dealt primarily, according to Quin-Harkin, with "the darker side of reality."

Criticized by some as lacking in substance, and praised by others as an encouragement to reading, teen books such as those Quin-Harkin has built a career on are an important part of juvenile publishing, accounting for hundreds of thousands of sales annually. Quin-Harkin's books tell what happens when a teen and her best friend break up, when a family moves or parents are divorced. And most often there are young men involved: guys a girl wants to date, or loves from afar, or beats at tennis. Quin-Harkin writes about the concerns of teenage girls of the 1980s and 1990s; relevance is her watchword. And she has built an enormous and faithful readership as a result.

Born in Bath, England, Quin-Harkin began writing for fun at an early age; she had published her first short story by sixteen. Her own teen years were quite placid, as she attended an all-girls school where academics rather than sports or romance were emphasized. The usual emotional upheavals of a young woman were thus largely postponed until Quin-Harkin attended college, earning a B.A. with honors from the University of London. For the first few years after graduation, Quin-Harkin worked for the British Broadcasting Corporation, as a studio manager and also a writer of radio and television plays. Such writings were "fairly highbrow," as the author described them. She then moved to Australia, where she met her husband while working for the Australian Broadcasting Company. The couple married in 1966 and moved to the United States. Settling in the San Francisco Bay area, Quin-Harkin balanced the role of mother and writer. She worked initially for a textbook company and helped develop new primary reading texts more relevant for contemporary urban children than the traditional primer stories of Dick and Jane.

Work on textbooks set Quin-Harkin to writing for herself again, and her first book was published in 1976. It was a long way from teen romance. *Peter Penny's Dance* was a picture book for children, in-

spired by the lyrics from an old English folk song: "I've come to claim a silver pound because I've danced the world around." Peter is a sailor who would rather dance a reel than scrub the decks, and sets off to dance around the world; he comes back in five years to claim the hand of his beloved Lavinia, the captain's daughter. Adventures greet him in France, Africa, China, and America, but Peter finally dances to the church to take Lavinia's hand. Everything about this first title was easy for Quin-Harkin: the story seemed to come of itself and the manuscript found a home on the second try. Zena Sutherland of the *Bulletin of the Center for Children's Books* called the tale "a bouncy, bonny book," and many critics praised the illustrations of Anita Lobel. Of the book's exciting conclusion, *Horn Book* reviewer Ethel L. Heins wrote: "In a splendid finale, reminiscent of *Around the World in Eighty Days,* Peter arrived back in England in the nick of time and skipped his way straight to the church and into the arms of his overjoyed bride." *Peter Penny's Dance* went on to win numerous awards. This early successful start, however, was followed by several years without sales as Quin-Harkin continued to raise her family while struggling to work at her craft. Then several early titles were sold to Parents Magazine Press: *Benjamin's Balloon, Septimus Bean and His Amazing Machine,* and *Magic Growing Powder.* Quin-Harkin was establishing a name as a picture book author.

In 1981 came a turning point in the author's career, when her agent called to ask if she could do a teen novel in a hurry. A trip to the local bookstore provided the author with a bundle of similar books which she studied carefully, and then she sat down to turn out sample chapters of her own teen fiction. These samples evolved into *California Girl,* the first in Bantam's "Sweet Dreams" series. In *California Girl,* Jenny is a sixteen-year-old swimmer with Olympic aspirations. When her coach moves to Texas, Jenny's family follows so that she can continue training. But Texas is a far cry from Jenny's former home state; here she is regarded as strange because of her devotion to her athletic dreams. She soon finds a friend, however: Mark is an injured football player who supports her swimming, helping her train, and the finale comes with Jenny competing in the Nationals for a berth in the Olympics. Along the way there is a crew of supporting characters: the scheming cheerleader who now wants her former boyfriend Mark back, Jenny's rather unsympathetic mother, and an empty-headed girl friend. Ella B. Fossum, writing in *School Library Journal,* thought the book was "a cut above the usual teenage love story" because of the added complications and insightful details of Jenny's Olympic aspirations, and Becky Johnson in *Voice of Youth Advocates* noted that "the story is fast-moving and the main character is serious-minded and independent." Johnson also felt, however, that the supporting cast of characters lacked meaningful depth: "This gets high marks for readability but could have had more realistic character development."

The second book in the series, *Love Match,* also involves an athletic theme, when Joanna refuses to try to ensure Rick's affection by allowing him to beat her at tennis. While *Bulletin of the Center for Children's Books* concluded that the book had "little substance" because of its formulaic plot—girl meets boy, loses boy, wins boy in the end—other reviewers, including Joe McKenzie in *School Library Journal,* commented that "readers will figure it all out early too, but many of them won't care," because of the sympathetic nature of the leading character, Joanna. This blend of sympathetic and generally well-drawn and independent main character along with a formula plot has formed the heart of much of Quin-Harkin's teen writing. Most of the titles fall into the category of escapist reading, "predictable but palatable," as Ilene Cooper of *Booklist* noted in a review of *Daydreamer,* a further title in the "Sweet Dreams" series. Maureen Ritter, however, writing in *Voice of Youth Advocates* about *Daydreamer,* emphasized the readability factor and noted that the book was "perfect for a hi/lo reader," and that aside from divorced parents, the main character, Lisa, "does not suffer from the traumas that most YA novel characters do; only the necessary conflicts needed for growth."

Other titles in the series have also earned mixed praise: formula plots that have just that twist of originality or individuality to set them apart. Kathy Fritts in *School Library Journal* noted that "funny scenes and a fast pace" set *101 Ways to Meet Mr. Right* "a notch above average," and Elaine Patterson, reviewing the same book in *Kliatt,* commented that "girls of all ages" would identify with the main character's "fears, fantasies, and flops" as she searches for the true love that is under her nose all the time. Critics may disagree about the relative merits of such books, but readers have pronounced them successes. One book in the "Sweet Dreams" series, *Ten-Boy Summer,* sold over half a million copies. In this work, central characters Jill and Toni determine to liven up their junior-year summer by breaking up with their respective boyfriends, betting on who will be the first to have dated ten boys. Sally Estes of *Booklist* found the book's premise "a bit farfetched, perhaps, but light

and lively enough to attract nondemanding readers of teenage romances." Similarly, Susan Levine wrote in *Voice of Youth Advocates* that *Ten-Boy Summer* "satisfies its requirements of a fast, uncomplicated, lightly romantic story with a happy ending."

Series writing has its pitfalls, according to Quin-Harkin, the largest of which is slipping into cliche. The author becomes so familiar with the set of characters that it is easy to use stock dialogue or responses instead of always being on guard to search for the most appropriate wording. Quin-Harkin generally writes a 200-page book every two months, and many of these are told in the first person. "On the whole, first person is very effective because it doesn't ever become overly dramatic," Quin-Harkin has noted, adding: "And of course, when you're first person, you're right there with the character and it's very immediate." Her experience in radio and television also informs her work, making for strong dialogue and pictorial writing. Quin-Harkin has said that she thinks in terms of scenes rather than chapters, a technique that gives her books a fast pace. Reaching back to her own feelings as a teenager for inspiration, Quin-Harkin has also used the experiences of her four children and their friends as they went through the teen years.

If cliche is one pitfall in series books, boredom for the writer can be another. According to Quin-Harkin, the "Sugar and Spice" series went on far longer than she wanted. The adventures of the two cousins, Chrissy and Cara, became somewhat stale after several books, but the series was so popular that Quin-Harkin was forced to go on with it, writing some twenty installments. Bouncy Chrissy is the cheerleader type from a small town in Iowa who has come to live in San Francisco with her serious, ballet-studying cousin, Caroline or Cara. *Flip Side* inaugurated the series and introduced the city cousin and country cousin in a situation in which they both yearn for the other's boyfriend but are too nice to do anything about it. *School Library Journal* contributor Kathy Fritts called the book "a winner," while Laurel Ibey, writing in *Voice of Youth Advocates,* concluded that everyone who read *Flip Side* would "find it full of fun!" Other adventures in the "Sugar and Spice" series take urban Cara to Chrissy's Iowa farm in *Nothing in Common,* about which Kathy Fritts asserted that a "fast pace, wonderful scenes of family and farm life, lots of action, and plenty of boy-girl mix and match make it a sure hit"; or have Cara finally decide to give up dancing in *The Last Dance,* which Juli Lund in *Voice of Youth Advocates* praised for the fact that it "did not have a perfect 'happy ending,' but instead realistically portrayed not-so-perfect actual life."

Other series books from Quin-Harkin include those from "On Our Own" and "Heartbreak Cafe," and do not suffer from claustrophobia as do the later titles of the "Sugar and Spice" series. "Heartbreak Cafe," for example, contains only six books and each is told from a different point of view of one of the people involved with the rundown cafe which is a hangout for teens with problems. With *No Experience Required,* Quin-Harkin featured heroine Debbie Leslie, whose parents have just divorced. Debbie manages to get a position at the Heartbreak Cafe, but Joe, the grandson of the owner, figures the wealthy kid won't last a month. Debbie sets out to prove him wrong and turns out to be one of Quin-Harkin's archetypal feisty and headstrong female characters. A *Publishers Weekly* reviewer, commenting on *No Experience Required,* noted that "Quin-Harkin's skilled storytelling effectively blends wry humor with universal concerns." The "On Our Own" series is a spin-off from "Sweet Dreams," following some of those main characters on their way into college. Jill has been accepted to an exclusive out-of-state school but Toni has to defer college plans because of her father's heart attack. Plagued by a miserable roommate, Jill is finally rescued by a visit from Toni, who tells the girl off. First-time college experiences inaugurated this mini-series, and a *Publishers Weekly* reviewer noted that such experiences "ring true." Other commentators found problems with the series: "Although worthwhile for the exposure of so many real problems of college freshmen, it is unfortunate that the shallow dialogue and narrative read so very quickly," concluded Sandra Dayton in a *Voice of Youth Advocates* review of *The Graduates.* Another *Voice of Youth Advocates* reviewer, Kaye Grabbe, objected to what she considered "little character development," noting that central character Jill "never seems like much of a real person."

A series geared at pre-teens is "Friends," which follows the relationship between two girls, Alison and Tess, over the four summers they spend together in a small resort town. Tess is newly arrived in the town in the first book of the series, *Starring Tess and Ali,* and Alison forms a quick friendship with her. Trouble arises, however, with remarks Tess makes about how overprotective Ali's mother is. Ali is upset by such remarks until she learns the root of them: Tess's mother has recently deserted the family and envy and spite are undoubtedly contributing to the girl's behav-

ior. A *Publishers Weekly* reviewer noted in a review of *Starring Tess and Ali* that younger readers might resent the "juvenile tone" of the book, but that Quin-Harkin had created a "compassionate protagonist whose heretofore compliant ways are undergoing thoughtful reevaluation."

Quin-Harkin has also written many non-series teen books, perhaps the best known being *Wanted: Date for Saturday Night,* in which the central problem is finding a date for shy Julie for the Freshman Formal. Along the way, Julie manages to join the "in" crowd, only to discover they are shallow and no fun. Reviews again were mixed. Carolyn Gabbard Fugate in *School Library Journal* found that "the characterizations of Julie and the minor characters are excellent," and concluded the book "a good, solid addition to a junior or senior high-school library." Zena Sutherland of *Bulletin of the Center for Children's Books,* however, concluded that the book had "a formula plot and cardboard characters," while Kaye Grabbe in *Voice of Youth Advocates* commented on the book's "improbable story" and "shallow characterizations." *Wanted: Date for Saturday Night* went on to win a Children's Choice award as well as a large readership.

Another stand-alone book from Quin-Harkin is *Summer Heat,* in which teen protagonist Laurie Beth, on the verge of graduating from high school, must choose between two suitors and two completely different lifestyles. A *Publishers Weekly* reviewer commented favorably on this title, noting that "love certainly plays an important role in [Laurie Beth's] decision—but so does her new-found sense of self-worth—and that's what makes this story so refreshing." Other of Quin-Harkin's non-series efforts include *The Sutcliffe Diamonds,* which romance readers will "devour," according to Elaine M. McGuire in *Voice of Youth Advocates;* and *The Apartment,* which a *Voice of Youth Advocates* contributor describes as a story of "three girls from very different backgrounds [who] share an apartment during a pivotal period in their lives."

A new direction for Quin-Harkin has been adult fiction dealing with historical settings: the California Gold Rush or Australia in the 1920s. Perhaps her teen readership will follow her on to a different level of writing, as well. But for now, each new series brings in a new generation of teen readers, as "Boyfriend Club" and "TGIF!," Quin-Harkin's most recent series contributions, hope to do. "I enjoy writing for children because it is a very positive medium," Quin-Harkin once told *CA.* "You can be optimistic, indulge in fantasy and have a happy ending. What's more, you don't have to introduce sex and violence to make it sell. Also, in common with many writers for children, I don't think I ever grew up." And there are thousands of teen readers hoping Quin-Harkin never does.

BIOGRAPHICAL/CRITICAL SOURCES:

BOOKS

Authors and Artists for Young Adults, Volume 6, Gale (Detroit), 1991, pp. 181-187.

PERIODICALS

Booklist, May 1, 1976, p. 1270; October 1, 1981, p. 189; January 15, 1982, p. 644; September 1, 1982, p. 37; May 15, 1983, p. 1221; February 1, 1984, p. 810; February 15, 1984, p. 862; June 15, 1984, p. 1474.
Bulletin of the Center for Children's Books, October, 1976, p. 30; March, 1982, p. 136; June, 1985, p. 192.
Horn Book, June, 1976, p. 281.

Kliatt, spring, 1982, p. 10; spring, 1983, p. 5; fall, 1985, p. 16.
New York Times Book Review, May 9, 1976, p. 12; November 14, 1976, p. 53; April 1, 1979, p. 37.
Publishers Weekly, July 25, 1986, pp. 192-193; December 22, 1989, p. 57; June 29, 1990, p. 103; May 24, 1991, p. 58.
School Library Journal, November, 1981, p. 110; March, 1982, p. 160; March, 1985, p. 181; September, 1985, p. 180; January, 1988, p. 95.
Times Educational Supplement, April 21, 1995, p. 16.
Voice of Youth Advocates, December, 1981, p. 34; December, 1982, p. 35; December, 1983, p. 281; June, 1985, p. 134; August-October, 1986, p. 156; December, 1986, p. 231; April, 1988. p. 35; October, 1994, p. 215; December, 1994, p. 279.
Wilson Library Bulletin, October, 1991, p. 102.

*   *   *

QUYTH, Gabriel
  See JENNINGS, Gary (Gayne)

R

RABE, David (William) 1940-

PERSONAL: Born March 10, 1940, in Dubuque, IA; son of William (a meatpacker) and Ruth (a department store worker; maiden name, McCormick) Rabe; married Elizabeth Pan (a laboratory technician), 1969 (marriage ended); married Jill Clayburgh (an actress), March, 1979; children: (first marriage) Jason. *Education:* Loras College, B.A., 1962; Villanova University, M.A., 1968.

ADDRESSES: Agent—Ellen Neuwald, Inc., 905 West End Ave., New York, NY 10025.

CAREER: Playwright. Worked various jobs, 1963-65; *New Haven Register,* New Haven, CT, feature writer, 1969-70; Villanova University, Villanova, PA, assistant professor, 1970-72, consultant, beginning 1972. *Military service:* U.S. Army, 1965-67; served in Vietnam.

MEMBER: Philadelphia Rugby Club.

AWARDS, HONORS: Rockefeller grant, 1967; Associated Press Award, 1970, for series of articles written on Daytop addict rehabilitation program; Obie Award for distinguished playwriting from *Village Voice,* Drama Desk Award, and Drama Guild Award, all 1971, all for *The Basic Training of Pavlo Hummel;* Elizabeth Hull-Kate Warriner Award from Dramatists Guild, 1971, *Variety* poll award, 1971, Outer Circle Award, 1972, and Antoinette Perry (Tony) Award for best play of 1971-72 season on Broadway, 1972, all for *Sticks and Bones;* New York Drama Critics Circle citation, 1972; New York Drama Critics Circle Award for best American play, 1976, for *Streamers;* National Institute and American Academy Award in Literature, 1976; Guggenheim fellowship, 1976.

WRITINGS:

PLAYS

Two Plays by David Rabe (contains *Sticks and Bones* [also see below; two-act], produced in New York City at Anspacher Theatre, November 7, 1971, produced on Broadway at John Golden Theatre, August 1, 1972; and *The Basic Training of Pavlo Hummel* [also see below], first produced in New York City at Newman Stage of The Public Theatre, May 20, 1971), Viking (New York City), 1973.

The Orphan (also see below), produced in New York City at Anspacher Theatre, April 18, 1973.

In the Boom Boom Room (three-act; produced on Broadway at Vivian Beaumont Theatre, November 8, 1973), Knopf (New York City), 1975, revised edition (produced in New York, 1986), Grove (New York City), 1986.

Burning, produced in New York, 1974.

Streamers (also see below; produced in New Haven at Long Wharf Theater, 1976; produced on Broadway at Mitzi Newhouse Theater, 1976), Knopf, 1977.

Goose and Tomtom (produced in New York, 1982), Grove, 1986.

Hurlyburly (also see below; three-act; produced in New York, 1984); Grove, 1985, revised edition (produced in Los Angeles, 1988), Grove Weidenfeld (New York City), 1990.

Sticks and Bones: A Play in Two Acts, Samuel French (New York City), 1987.

Those the River Keeps (produced in Princeton, NJ, 1991), Grove Weidenfeld, 1991, published with *Hurlyburly* as *Those the River Keeps and Hurlyburly: Two Plays,* Grove, 1995.
The Vietnam Plays, Volume 1: *The Basic Training of Pavlo Hummel* [and] *Sticks and Bones,* Volume 2: *Streamers* [and] *The Orphan,* Grove, 1993.

Also author of *The Crossing* (one-act).

SCREENPLAYS

Casualties of War, Columbia, 1989.
(With Robert Towne and David Rayfiel) *The Firm* (screenplay), Paramount, 1993.

Also author of *I'm Dancing as Fast as I Can,* 1982, and *Streamers,* 1983.

OTHER

Recital of the Dog (novel), Grove, 1993.
The Crossing Guard (novelization of the screenplay by Sean Penn), Hyperion Press (Westport, CT), 1995.

A collection of Rabe's manuscripts is housed at the Mugar Memorial Library, Boston University.

SIDELIGHTS: David Rabe tackles such difficult issues as war, drug addiction, and the abuse of women in plays noted for their lyrical language, black humor, and alienated characters. "David Rabe's corrosive portrait of American life," states *Contemporary Dramatists* contributor Mark W. Estrin, "evolves within a series of metaphoric arenas—living rooms, military barracks, disco bars—where his characters collide violently against each other, but where, primarily, the struggle with their own society-fostered delusions." Writing in the *Dictionary of Literary Biography,* James A. Patterson finds that Rabe's "best work is marked by intensity of confrontation and a penchant for lyrical, if obscene and often scatological language. He appears willing to use varied theatrical formats. He blends humor and fear expertly and shows no tendency toward sentimentality."

Though Rabe's award-winning plays *The Basic Training of Pavlo Hummel, Sticks and Bones,* and *Streamers* deal with the effects of the Vietnam war on his characters' lives, the playwright disavows an "antiwar" label. "I don't like to hear them called antiwar plays," he explained. "Works like that, like some of the social action plays of the thirties, are designed for

immediate effect. All I'm trying to do is *define the event* for myself and for other people. I'm saying, in effect, 'This is what goes on,' and that's all."

Like David in *Sticks and Bones,* Rabe returned home from Vietnam alienated from American society. "It wasn't just that I couldn't reach my family," he explained, "I couldn't reach *anybody.* People would listen attentively, but not understand a thing. It was the *impossibility* of understanding that got to me, caused not so much by a lack of awareness on the part of most people, but by the quality of what awareness there was." Rabe admitted he felt "tremendous hostility—no, *mistrust*—about the antiwar movement." "I agreed with the radicals intellectually, but I couldn't get emotionally involved because of the experience thing." He tried desperately to get a job as a Vietnam war correspondent to help change America's limited awareness of the war. Unsuccessful, he decided to resume graduate study at Villanova—where he also wrote his first two plays.

It was not until Joseph Papp, the director of the New York Shakespeare Festival's Public Theatre, read *The Basic Training of Pavlo Hummel* that the play was produced. The story of a "cipher" who dismally attempts to create a new identity for himself as a soldier, *Pavlo Hummel* was praised by Catharine Hughes as "one of the best to come out of America's Vietnam nightmare." But, Hughes pointed out, "Rabe does not make anything—apart from the hell and absurdity of war—*that* black and white. He avoids both easy sentimentality and facile point-scoring and . . . he realizes that horror and comedy, like tragedy and comedy, are seldom far apart. His Vietcong are no more heroic than his Americans (which by now seems almost refreshing)."

When *Sticks and Bones* joined *Pavlo Hummel* at the Anspacher in 1971, Rabe became the only playwright, other than Shakespeare, to have two plays performed concurrently in New York's Public Theatre. Director Papp enthusiastically praised his new talent: "He is the most important writer we've ever had. There's a great link between him and O'Neill, not so much in style but in that he's so painfully honest. I think he's in pain. He's dealing with things so deep."

Rabe's thrust on the American family in *Sticks and Bones* is made apparent by the names of his main characters: Ozzie, Harriet, David, and Rick. In contrast to the security provided by Harriet's fudge, Ozzie's possessions, and Rick's guitar, David, when he speaks, reminds his family of the atrocities of

Vietnam or his love for a "yellow girl." Henry Hewes gave this interpretation of the play's end: "Since David is unchangeable, the family must get rid of him and the memories he brought from the war. They do this by strangling the personification of the Vietnamese girl, who has been silently appearing throughout the play, and by helping David to kill himself. But the suggestion at the end of the play is that David will not entirely die, and that America will never quite exorcise the ghosts of Vietnam."

Variety objected to *Sticks and Bones* as "wordy and repetitious" and suffering from the inarticulateness of its hero. Despite these reservations, the reviewer applauded the "shattering impact" of Rabe's play—"a work of passion by a gifted writer." Clive Barnes cited "this interestingly flawed play" as being "far less confident in its style and texture" than *Pavlo Hummel,* claiming Rabe's inexperience must "take the rap" for "the occasionally ponderous symbolism." Nonetheless, *Sticks and Bones* "has a moral force that neither flinches nor sermonizes. This is surely all too unusual in our theater."

Once called "the Neil Simon of desperation and death," Rabe is unsure himself as to the roots of his pain. "I don't know where the pain comes from," he told *Newsweek.* "It can't be just the war." He took a lighter approach to his "fate" with another reviewer: "I didn't plan to be against the grain, you know. It just happened that way." As desperation and death are serious subjects, so is Rabe's devotion to the theatre. "Theater is very serious to me, and I'm serious about it," he said. "If I see a play that is totally frivolous, I almost get sick to my stomach. On the other hand, if *Sticks and Bones* is done right, it should be very funny. And its stylization should insulate the audience a little. If that doesn't happen, it can seem totally overbearing and self-righteous."

Rabe's third play, *The Orphan,* was an ambitious attempt to link modern violence with Greek mythology. John Simon believed the author's "parallel between the Manson 'family' and the House of Atreus preposterous." "Rabe hits out against both secular and religious authorities," Simon continued, "indeed, against God himself in the person of a slippery and unsavory Apollo; but, much as I sympathize with his thesis, it falls between parallels as surely as if they were stools." Walter Kerr saw unfulfilled possibilities in the play as he concluded, "If *The Orphan* were a cohesive work for the theatre, it would be one of the most despairing plays ever written."

Upon the production of *In the Boom Boom Room,* Rabe denied that his new play broke away from the pattern set in his earlier works. "It's not about the war," he noted, "but then *Sticks and Bones* wasn't either. . . . People are liable to think it's very different from what I've been doing but essentially it isn't." In Stanley Kauffmann's words, this play "is a semi-realistic, semi-expressionist work about a Philadelphia go-go girl, daughter of a casual criminal father and a vapid mother, sexual prey of dozens of men, how she got that way and how she declines to a new nadir." The theme, "the ravaging of a female-social-sexual victim" Kauffmann believed "so familiar that one *counts* on the familiarity," met a different interpretation from Marilyn Stasio: "The remarkable quality about David Rabe is his willingness to confront the alien culture of the Boom Boom Room and the level of society it represents. Not only does he face it head on, and attempt to understand and communicate the dynamics of the people who live in it, but he also finds amidst the wretchedness and ugliness a good deal of character and dignity."

Like Stasio, who felt *In the Boom Boom Room* lacked the vivid surrealism necessary to create "a dramatic vision of a woman's personal hell," many reviewers found some faults in the play but still gave praise to the total effect. Harold Clurman thought "the whole is uneven, at times forced and crude, but its power is unmistakable." In his *Commonweal* review Gerald Weales explained that "although much of *In the Boom Boom Room* is overextended and overexplained, at his best Rabe has an oblique style which is attractive because it suggests more than it defines, because it opens the audience to possibility."

Rabe returned to the backdrop of war and again found award-winning acclaim with *Streamers* in 1976. The barracks room set in a Virginia army camp was described as "a microcosm for some of the most explosive tensions in U.S. society—racial, sexual, social." In Rabe's story a homosexual (Richie), a professed anti-homosexual (Billy), and an indifferent black (Roger) make "considerable . . . adjustment to the sexual and racial differences in each other's personalities" until a newcomer (Carlyle), "a black draftee churning with bottled-up violence . . . becomes a human bomb that blasts the utopia into blood and death."

Weales found that in *Streamers* (the "most realistic of the Rabe plays") "it is obvious that Billy's interfering impulses, his failure to understand Richie or Carlyle, the violence hidden in his angry innocence provide a workable analogy for the American presence in Southeast Asia." "But," he continued, "Rabe clearly does not intend that his play should have a narrowly political reference." Clurman seemed to agree when he felt a "universal" inference invoked in *Streamers:* "Humanity is composed of poor forked animals caught in a trap of which they can never understand the exact identity or the way out." Among other criticism of *Streamers,* Kauffmann questioned the meaning of its title. "But what does it symbolize?" he asked. "What does the symbol of an unopened parachute mean to anything we have seen?" Weales had an answer: "*Streamers* offers a world . . . in which, eventually, everyone's parachute refuses to open."

Rabe's next play, *Goose and Tomtom,* ranks as one of his least successful works. The title characters are a pair of paranoid jewel thieves, living under the thrall of Lorraine, a streetwalker with plans to rule the world. Early in the play, Lorraine sticks pins into the arms of Goose and Tomtom to see which one is tougher. Both are so afraid of her that they never remove the pins, which become a running gag. Mel Gussow, reviewer for the *New York Times,* characterized *Goose and Tomtom* as a "vaudeville turn;" writing in the same newspaper, Wilborn Hampton termed the play "peculiar and slight." Gussow did give Rabe credit for trying something new, acknowledging that "one has to honor the attempt of a talented artist to break out of his mode," but he considered it "necessary to acknowledge the fact that 'Goose and Tomtom' lacks a light touch" and concluded that it "could be considered a long-delayed exploding cigar, a slow burn followed by a single anticlimactic pop."

Hampton declared that *Goose and Tomtom* had more serious flaws than simply not being funny enough. In his view, the play "works much too hard at trying to be shocking and violent. As a result, any dark humor is dissipated in its predictability." Warning that "throughout the play there is a lot of whacking and torture," he further criticized that "what is missing in all this mayhem is any kind of focus." He concluded that "the whole exercise, whether viewed as a comedic analysis of the decline of Western society or just as a spoof . . . is pointless."

New York contributor John Simon went so far as to say: "After *Goose and Tomtom,* I feared not just for David Rabe's talent, but even for his sanity." But he announced that Rabe redeemed himself with his next drama, the highly-praised *Hurlyburly. Hurlyburly* is set in Hollywood, and its chief characters are all men involved in the film industry. The action, such as it is, involves their drinking, drug abuse, loveless sex, and shallow philosophizing. Their talk goes on so incessantly that Rabe included lines such as "blah-blah-blah" and "rapateeta" to symbolize its meaninglessness. Although there is a great deal of humor in the play, it is really concerned with the breakdown of morals in modern society, as epitomized in Southern California. "The picture of Hollywood is bleak," observed Clive Barnes in the *New York Post.* "Zombie denizens seem preoccupied . . . 'with pharmaceutical experiments testing the parameters of the American dream.'" Barnes summed up: "Rabe has written a strange, bitterly funny, self-indulgent, important play. . . . I was entertained, horrified, intrigued, and disturbed by *Hurlyburly.*"

Robert Brustein analyzed the play's theme in depth in the *New Republic.* "What the play is about, I believe, is how the disintegration of American values has created a sense of anomie and a pronounced loss of purpose. Rabe's metaphor for this is cocaine." He further noted that *Hurlyburly* showed some marked stylistic changes from the playwright's earlier work— changes that in his opinion lifted Rabe's work to a new level. "Like [Eugene] O'Neill, who achieved greatness only when he adopted an unadorned Ibsenian realism, Rabe's style is now informed by the implicit *verismo* of David Mamet rather than the tendentious exhortations of Arthur Miller. . . . Besides displaying a dazzling new technique—not just a flawless command of dialogue, but an improved understanding of the nuances of human conflict—he has documented a chronicle of post-Vietnam War American life as pieced together from the shards of our shattered beliefs. Probing the social-metaphysical secrets revealed to only the most visionary playwrights, he has correctly seen that the plague of cocaine, which has infected virtually the entire entertainment industry, is less a disease than a symptom of a much larger malaise that is infecting virtually the entire country, thus giving us insights into our fall from grace, if not into our capacity for redemption." Not all critics were as wholehearted in their praise of *Hurlyburly,* however. Frank Rich admitted in the *New York Times* that the first half of the play "offers some of Mr. Rabe's most inventive and disturbing writing," but he complained that "it crash lands at midpoint." "Mr. Rabe remains a dynamic chronicler of the brutal games that eternally adolescent American men can play," Rich went on. "When his buddies aren't assaulting one another, they're on search-and-destroy missions against the No. 1 enemy—the women they invariably refer to as 'broads,' 'ghouls,' 'bitches' or worse." Rich declared that the play fails when it attempts to show its characters' softer sides. "The ensuing revelations aren't terribly revealing," he alleged, "and the tributes to the tough guys' previously hidden vulnerability are banal. . . . This is a paltry, amorphous payoff to the strong buildup."

Other reviewers, such as *Newsweek*'s Jack Kroll, had no reservations about calling *Hurlyburly* a virtual masterpiece. Kroll proclaimed it "a powerful permanent contribution to American drama" and "a challenging work. Starting out as a tough, funny play about some Hollywood wise guys, it swerves, darts and drives deep into a darkness shot through with the emergency lights of anxiety and despair. . . . The climax, with its casual, nutty, almost comedic violence, has a frightening inevitability. Rabe's vision of the wasteland may not be impeccably structured, but it has a savage sincerity and a crackling theatrical vitality. . . . This deeply felt play deserves as wide an audience as possible."

One of *Hurlyburly*'s characters, the self-destructive, emotional, would-be actor Phil, became the center of Rabe's next play, *Those the River Keeps*. This drama shows Phil in the years before the events of *Hurlyburly*. Having cut his ties with the East Coast mafia, Phil runs to California to realize his dream of acting, but he cannot escape the guilt he feels over his past crimes. When an old mobster associate shows up and urges Phil to join him on a hit mission, Phil is unable to turn him away. Rabe explained the major themes and metaphor of the title to Francis X. Clines of the *New York Times:* "Are there wounds in the past so strong that they'll pull you back no matter what you do? How do they seep into you unconsciously in indirect ways where you think you're doing one thing but really doing something else? What's the cut-off point where you can't get out?" *Those the River Keeps* was less well received than its predecessor. April Austin noted in *Christian Science Monitor* that "Phil's constant harping on the fact that life is essentially meaningless gets tiresome." She states that "Rabe needs to trim chunks of the dialogue, or risk turning off the audience he has wooed into Phil's corner." "Yet it's also true that, like David Mamet (his stylistic opposite)," declared Jeremy Gerard in *Variety,* "Rabe hears poetry in the stuttering attempts of ordinary people trying to connect." Austin allowed, however, that the play "is powered by funny and pugnacious one-liners. It's mostly the put-down kind of humor, but it's a welcome break from Phil's self-absorption. . . . It's an interesting, if not thoroughly engrossing, piece of theater."

Rabe drew on the experience of his Vietnam plays when he wrote the screenplay for the film *Casualties of War*. The film, which *Rolling Stone* critic Peter Travers called "flawed but overwhelming," is based on a 1969 nonfiction article about a squad of American soldiers who were courtmartialed for kidnaping, gang-raping, and then murdering a Vietnamese girl. The one member of the squad who did not participate in the rape and murder was a new arrival, Sven Ericksson, who later testified against the others. "The piece, published soon after in book form under the title *Casualties of War,*" Travers continued, "was both grim truth and a devastating metaphor for American imperialism." Some critics, however, felt that the film did not live up to the potential of either the director or the screenwriter. "In [Rabe's] screenplay all the characters seem familiar, not from life but from previous films or plays or novels," stated *New Republic* film reviewer Stanley Kauffman; "all of them are pushed around like charade figures to symbolize Quality A in conflict with Quality B. Following the story is less like watching a drama unfold than like watching a recipe being filled, a cup of bitterness, a spoonful of lust, a dash of remorse, etc." "Rabe champions the real Ericksson's point of view, which insists upon moral responsibility but which contradicts the film's social determinism," explained Gavin Smith in *Film Comment*. "A troubled discrepancy lies at this intersection of psychosocial behaviorism and humanist moralism that prevents the film from fully articulating a coherent point of view."

Rabe also was the coauthor of the screenplay adaptation of John Grisham's novel *The Firm*. *New York* movie critic David Denby found the film version of the story "exciting, well acted, and smartly written, but I find myself in the bizarre position of asking for a trashier approach." Denby believed that the film, by trying to insert a sense of morality in Grisham's amoral novel, succeeded only in making *The Firm* feel "priggish and self-deluded." "The movie tries to produce real emotions and even, God help us, a few real people," Denby explained. "The way [director Sydney] Pollack and company have adapted the material, it no longer makes sense. The movie retains Grisham's pop structure but denies the audience a pop payoff." "Sometimes you can't fight the power of pop; you just have to go with it," he concluded. "Instead, Pollack and his crew have turned a terrific piece of escapist fiction into an earnest seminar on the dangers of greed."

Rabe is also the author of two novels: *Recital of the Dog,* an original story, and *The Crossing Guard,* a novelization of the screenplay of the movie by Sean Penn. *Los Angeles Times Book Review* contributor Erika Taylor called the latter book "interesting to read," and concluded that "but the end of 'The Crossing Guard,' Rabe fully inhabits his sad, emotionally complex novel." Randall Short, writing in the *New York Times Book Review*, while acknowledging Rabe's status as "one of America's most distinguished playwrights [and] the possessor of a passionate moral imagination," felt that Rabe is out of his element in writing fiction rather than plays. He called the former book "uncomfortably reminiscent of a world-class pianist trying to impress his admirers by playing the violin." "It isn't that Mr. Rabc has difficulty with thc form of the novel," *New York Times* contributor Michiko Kakutani complained. "It's that he has abandoned the galvanic language and dark, sympathetic humor that made his finest plays so powerful and affecting."

Drawing the composite figure pervading Rabe's plays, T. E. Kalem summarized the playwright's "heroes": "In classic terms his protagonists are all undergoing initiation rites. But the lack of catharsis in his dramas means that after the initiation, no induction into full manhood occurs. Nothing like wisdom is reached, or even stoic serenity." If Kalem's assessment is accurate, then the unopened parachute of *Streamers* is an appropriate metaphor for the whole of Rabe's work.

BIOGRAPHICAL/CRITICAL SOURCES:

BOOKS

Beidler, Philip D., *American Literature and the Experience of Vietnam*, University of Georgia Press (Athens), 1982, pp. 85-136, 137-192.

Contemporary Dramatists, St. James Press (Detroit), 1993.

Contemporary Literary Criticism, Gale (Detroit), Volume 4, 1975; Volume 8, 1978; Volume 33, 1985.

Dictionary of Literary Biography, Volume 7: *Twentieth-Century American Dramatists*, Gale, 1981.

Hughes, Catharine, *Plays, Politics and Polemics*, Drama Book Specialists, 1973.

Kolin, Philip C., *David Rabe: A Stage History and a Primary and Secondary Bibliography*, Garland Publishing (New York City), 1988.

Simon, John, *Uneasy Stages: A Chronicle of the New York Theater, 1963-73*, Random House (New York City), 1975.

Zinman, Toby Silverman, *David Rabe: A Casebook*, Garland Publishing, 1991.

PERIODICALS

After Dark, August, 1972.
America, May 15, 1976.
Atlantic, December, 1976.
Boston Globe, July 18, 1990, p. 66; May 11, 1993, p. 29.
Chicago Tribune, August 1, 1985, section 5, p. 7; February 24, 1987, section 5, p. 5; March 7, 1991, section 1, p. 28; February 7, 1993, section 14, p. 6.
Christian Science Monitor, May 17, 1993, p. 12; February 8, 1994, p. 12.
Commentary, July, 1976.
Commonweal, December 14, 1973; May 21, 1976.
Critical Quarterly, spring, 1982, pp. 73-82.
Cue, December 4, 1971; December 3, 1973.
Entertainment Weekly, December 8, 1995, p. 63.
Film Comment, July-August, 1989, p. 49.
Interview, March, 1993, p. 84.
Library Journal, September 1, 1995, p. 209.
Los Angeles Magazine, January, 1989, p. 190; January, 1993, p. 125.
Los Angeles Times, February 6, 1985, section VI, p. 7; January 27, 1988, section VI, p. 6; November 17, 1988, section VI, p. 1; December 8, 1988, section VI, p. 1; December 11, 1988, p. C53; April 6, 1995, p. F10; September 20, 1995, p. F5.
Los Angeles Times Book Review, April 4, 1993, p. 7; December 10, 1995.
Nation, November 26, 1973; December 3, 1973; May 8, 1976; May 14, 1977.
National Review, August 9, 1993, p. 63.
New Republic, May 26, 1973; December 1, 1973; June 12, 1976; August 6, 1984, pp. 27-29; October 2, 1989, p. 26.
Newsday, March 2, 1972.
Newsweek, December 20, 1971; February 23, 1976; July 2, 1984, pp. 65, 67.
New York, September 17, 1973; July 16, 1984, pp. 42-45; July 12, 1993, p. 53.
New Yorker, May 29, 1971; March 11, 1972; May 3, 1976; May 2, 1977; August 21, 1989, p. 76; February 7, 1993, pp. 32-34; February 7, 1994, p. 32.
New York Post, March 11, 1972; June 22, 1984.
New York Sunday News, April 1, 1973.
New York Theatre Critics' Reviews, June 25, 1984, p. 235.
New York Times, May 30, 1971; November 3, 1971; November 8, 1971; December 12, 1971; April 19, 1973; April 29, 1973; November 9, 1973; May 8, 1977; May 8, 1982, p. 17; June 22, 1984,

p. C3; February 12, 1993, p. C31; January 30, 1994, section 2, p. 5; February 1, 1994, p. C13; April 19, 1995, p. C13.

New York Times Book Review, February 7, 1993, p. 21.

Publishers Weekly, November 16, 1992, p. 46; August 21, 1995, p. 48.

Rapport, 6, 1994, p. 26.

Rolling Stone, September 7, 1989, p. 31.

Saturday Review, November 27, 1971; April 17, 1976.

Time, May 3, 1975; May 9, 1977; August 21, 1989, p. 54.

Tribune Books (Chicago), January 3, 1993, p. 6; February 7, 1993, p. 6.

Variety, March 8, 1972; February 7, 1994, p. 60.

Village Voice, November 15, 1973.

Washington Post, July 9, 1990, p. B2; July 20, 1990, p. WW14.

World Literature Today, spring, 1994, p. 371.*

* * *

RANGER, Ken
See CREASEY, John

* * *

RATTRAY, Simon
See TREVOR, Elleston

* * *

RAY, Mary Lyn 1946-

PERSONAL: Born in 1946, in Monroe, LA. *Education:* Smith College, A.B., 1968; University of Delaware, M.A., 1970.

ADDRESSES: Home—Box 174, South Danbury, NH 03230.

CAREER: Writer and conservationist. Worked in museums for fifteen years; has also worked as a professional consultant in land protection and historic preservation.

AWARDS, HONORS: New Hampshire Conservationist of the Year, 1989; Calder Award finalist, Conservation Fund, 1991; named Citizen of the Year, Danbury Grange and New Hampshire State Grange, both 1995; Fiera di Bologna, Menzione d'Onore, for *Pumpkins;* American Bookseller Pick of the Lists citation, for *A Rumbly Tumbly Glittery Gritty Place;* Notable Children's Trade Book in the Field of Social Studies citation, National Council of Social Studies-Children's Book Council, for *Shaker Boy.*

WRITINGS:

PICTURE BOOKS

(Editor) Martha Wetherbee and Nathan Taylor, *Legend of the Bushwhacker Basket,* Martha Wetherbee Basket Shop (Sanbornton, NH), 1986.

Angel Baskets: A Little Story about the Shakers, illustrated by Jean Colquhoun, Martha Wetherbee Books (Sanbornton, NH), 1987.

(Editor) Wetherbee and Taylor, *Shaker Baskets,* Martha Wetherbee Basket Shop, 1988.

Pumpkins: A Story for a Field, illustrated by Barry Root, Harcourt (San Diego), 1992.

A Rumbly Tumbly Glittery Gritty Place, illustrated by Douglas Florian, Harcourt, 1993.

Alvah and Arvilla, illustrated by Barry Root, Harcourt, 1994.

Pianna, illustrated by Bobbie Henba, Harcourt, 1994.

Shaker Boy, illustrated by Jeanette Winter, Harcourt, 1994.

My Carousel Horse, Harcourt, 1995.

Mud, illustrated by Lauren Stringer, Harcourt, 1996.

Basket Moon, Little, Brown (Boston), 1998.

WORK IN PROGRESS: Picture books.

SIDELIGHTS: Mary Lyn Ray—a conservationist and author of books for children—was born in Louisiana and grew up in Little Rock, Arkansas. "But I never felt identity there," she told *CA.* "When I was very young, one of my favorite books was about an old farm in New Hampshire. If the idea was not already planted in me when I was born, the book—Tasha Tudor's *Snow Before Christmas*—planted it." Ray has lived in New England since 1964, when she first came east to attend college. In 1973 she began living in New Hampshire. In 1984 she came to South Danbury, the place she feels she has "always been coming to."

"I came here, to South Danbury, because I saw and felt a poetry in this place. A kind of scenery," Ray recalled for *CA.* "Everything I write is in some way informed by the memory and poetry I've found here. But I'm not just taking stories from this place. As it has become a part of me, I have had to risk opening myself to it. Everything I write is, in some way, from my life. And much comes directly from this old New Hampshire farm where I live."

When Ray bought her farmhouse, which is about 150 years old, it "hadn't been lived in for forty years before that," she told *CA*. "It had never had electricity or plumbing or running water, and squirrels and raccoons and foxes had taken it over." Room by room, she has restored plaster and painted, but has been careful to leave it "still an old house with old memories in it." A few years after she moved in, 160 acres of farmland surrounding her house were put up for sale. "I knew that I would buy the land to protect it from development," Ray said. "What I didn't know was how I would pay for it."

When Ray's sister jokingly suggested that she could plant pumpkins in the fields and sell them to come up with the necessary money, the idea came to Ray for her 1992 picture book, *Pumpkins*. In this story, a man worries that the field across from his home will be sold to developers. He sells almost everything he owns to try to raise money to buy the land himself, but he still does not have enough. So he plants pumpkin seeds. "The rain came and wet them, the sun came and warmed them. Soon the field was covered in pumpkins. And they grew and they grew and they grew." In the fall the man harvests 461,212 pumpkins—so many that he has to ship them around the world to sell them. Now he is able to buy the land, but he keeps one pumpkin for seeds. Pumpkins, he knows, would make him rich. But he chooses to give the seeds away, "because somewhere, someone might love another field pumpkins could save."

Ray herself didn't plant pumpkins. "Books have become my pumpkins," she told *CA*. She did, however, buy the land and protect it. "My commitment to saving this farm has encouraged neighbors to protect their land also—some 6,000 acres are now conservation land—and has sparked a larger project to create a greenway linking nine towns and three mountains in a preserve of thousands and thousands of acres. These numbers are dramatic; it's not everywhere that so much contiguous land can be protected. But everywhere something is possible, and that's what *Pumpkins* speaks to."

Ray has received several conservation awards for her work protecting New Hampshire's natural areas, but

"it has had a cost," she explained to *CA*. Because she wasn't planting pumpkins, she had to borrow all of the money from a bank, planning to repay the loan by allowing excavation of a lapsed gravel pit. The deposit of gravel turned out to be shallow. "Suddenly I held a loan I couldn't expect to pay. It hasn't been easy," she told *CA*. "But accepting the scar of the gravel pit was no easier. It was hard to walk there and look at it. Until a small story came that helped me see it differently." In *A Rumbly Tumbly Glittery Gritty Place* a child explores a gravel pit. For her it becomes "a place to watch machines in," "a beach without an ocean," "an album crossed with tracks of deer and bear who come at night." Ray noted to *CA* that the story has reminded her "of what children know, but we outgrow childhood and forget."

Other books by Ray also center around the people and places she's come to know in New Hampshire. For example, Ray was inspired to write *Alvah and Arvilla* after she attended the wedding of two of her neighbors. Since the couple ran a dairy farm, their honeymoon only lasted one night because they had to be home the following morning to milk the cows. In the story that grew from this, Alvah and Arvilla, who are farmers too, have been married for thirty-one years. But they've never taken a vacation due to the daily demands of running their farm. To achieve her dream of seeing the Pacific Ocean, Arvilla convinces her husband to pack up their belongings and all their animals to make the journey to California. After the unusual assortment of characters spends several days relaxing on the beach, they return home, where they spread sand they collected to make their own miniature beach. "And here Arvilla and Alvah and sometimes a cow or a cat or a dog lie and remember the ocean."

Pianna was also inspired by one of Ray's neighbors. Set in the early 1900s, Ray's book introduces an elderly woman named Anna as she looks back on her long life. Many of her best memories center around her beloved piano, which her parents bought for her when she was seven years old. Because no one else in town had a piano then, Anna had to ride the train 215 miles to Boston every week for a music lesson. As a young girl, she practiced so much that her brothers and sisters nicknamed her "Pianna." Over the years she got married and played for her husband and children, as well as at church and at social functions. "But mostly she played for herself." After her husband dies, her children move away, and times change, the piano continues to keep her company. "This is a story," Ray told *CA*, "about what endures. And finding it."

Despite her success as a writer for children, Ray grew up believing that she couldn't write. "I thought stories and characters and plots were something authors made up in their heads. I thought I wasn't smart enough—or, as it was called then, creative enough. I looked at blank paper and turned in blank paper," she recalled for *CA*. In graduate school, where she studied the history of American art and architecture, "something changed," she said. "Suddenly I began to see with my eyes, and to write what I saw. Becoming a writer was that simple." Still, she never thought that she could make up stories.

"Fiction, I thought, required a talent for invention which I didn't have," Ray told *CA*. "For another twenty years, I remained occupied with other work. Until stories, of themselves, began to come. I found out stories aren't something authors make up in their heads. Stories come to us, asking to be told. Like fish, maybe, they swim out of mystery and return to mystery. The responsibility of the writer is to receive them and give them voice, then let them go. I believe stories choose us. And because they choose us, they are very particular to us. We must each hear and tell our own."

BIOGRAPHICAL/CRITICAL SOURCES:

PERIODICALS

Booklist, October 15, 1992; December 1, 1993, p. 701; March 15, 1994, p. 1375; November, 1994.
Bulletin of the Center for Children's Books, July/August, 1994, p. 371; November, 1994, p. 101.
Christian Science Monitor, September 16, 1994; November 4, 1994.
Five Owls, November, 1994.
Horn Book, November/December, 1992, p. 719; November, 1994, p. 725; January, 1995, p. 55.
Kirkus Reviews, March 1, 1994, p. 309; September 15, 1994, p. 1279; October 15, 1994; March 1, 1996.
National Geographic, April, 1995, pp. 122-128.
New York Times Book Review, October 25, 1992.
Publishers Weekly, September 7, 1992, p. 93; October 25, 1993, p. 60; March 7, 1994; September 5, 1994, p. 110; October 17, 1994; May 6, 1996.
School Library Journal, March, 1993, p. 184; January, 1994, p. 97; May, 1994; November, 1994, p. 89; January, 1995; June, 1996.

REEMAN, Douglas Edward 1924-
(Alexander Kent)

PERSONAL: Born October 15, 1924, in Thames Ditton, Surrey, England; son of Charles Percival and Lilian (Waters) Reeman; married Winifred Isabella McGowan Melville, July, 7, 1958. *Education:* Attended local schools in England, 1928-39. *Avocational interests:* Has traveled extensively throughout the world, visiting Australia, Europe, Africa, and the United States.

ADDRESSES: Home—Blue Posts, Eaton Park Rd., Cobham, Surrey, England.

CAREER: Left school at sixteen and joined the Royal Navy, serving on destroyers and small craft in World War II from 1940-46; became lieutenant; member of Royal Naval Volunteer Reserve for ten years. Began writing short stories while serving from 1946-50 with the London Metropolitan Police, at first on the beat and later as detective in the Criminal Investigation Division. From 1950-60 he was a children's welfare officer for the London County Council, working in the poorer districts of London. He also has done book reviewing and held navigation classes for yachtsmen. Lecturer on juvenile problems and delinquency; script adviser for television and motion pictures. Governor, Foudroyant Trust. Director, Bolitho Maritime Productions Ltd. and Highseas Authors Ltd.

MEMBER: National Geographic Society, Navy League, Royal Navy Sailing Association, M.T.B. Officers Association, Society for Nautical Research, Maritime Preservation Society, British Sailors Society (president), Royal Society for the Protection of Birds (fellow), Savage Club (London), Officers' Club (London).

WRITINGS:

A Prayer for the Ship, Jarrolds (London), 1958, Putnam (New York City), 1973.
High Water, Jarrolds, 1959.
Send a Gunboat, Jarrolds, 1960, Putnam, 1961, published as *Escape from Santu,* Hamilton, 1962.
Dive in the Sun, Putnam, 1961.
The Hostile Shore, Jarrolds, 1962.
The Last Raider, Jarrolds, 1963, Putnam, 1964.
With Blood and Iron, Jarrolds, 1964, Putnam, 1965.
H.M.S. Saracen, Jarrolds, 1965, Putnam, 1966.
Path of the Storm, Hutchinson (London), 1966, Putnam, 1967.
The Deep Silence, Hutchinson, 1967, Putnam, 1968.

The Pride and the Anguish, Hutchinson, 1968, Putnam, 1969.

To Risks Unknown, Hutchinson, 1969, Putnam, 1970.

The Greatest Enemy, Hutchinson, 1970, Putnam, 1971.

Adventures in the High Seas: True Stories from Captain Bligh to the Nautilus, Walker (New York City), 1971.

Rendezvous: South Atlantic, Putnam, 1972.

Go in and Sink, Hutchinson, 1973.

The Destroyers, Putnam, 1974.

Winged Escort, Putnam, 1975.

Surface with Daring, Putnam, 1977.

Strike from the Sea, Morrow (New York City), 1978.

A Ship Must Die, Morrow, 1979.

Torpedo Run, Morrow, 1981.

Badge of Glory, Hutchinson, 1982, Morrow, 1984.

The First to Land (nonfiction), Morrow, 1984.

The Iron Pirate, Putnam, 1986.

The White Guns, Heinemann, 1989.

"RICHARD BOLITHO" SERIES; UNDER PSEUDONYM ALEXANDER KENT

To Glory We Steer, Putnam, 1968.

Form Line of Battle!, Putnam, 1969.

Enemy in Sight!, Hutchinson, 1970.

The Flag Captain, Putnam, 1971.

Sloop of War, Putnam, 1972.

Command a King's Ship, Putnam, 1973.

Signal: Close Action!, Putnam, 1974.

Richard Bolitho: Midshipman, Hutchinson, 1975, Putnam, 1976.

Passage to Mutiny, Putnam, 1976.

In Gallant Company, Putnam, 1977.

The Inshore Squadron, Hutchinson, 1977, Putnam, 1979.

Midshipman Bolitho and the Avenger, Putnam, 1978.

Captain Richard Bolitho, RN, Hutchinson, 1978.

Stand into Danger, Putnam, 1980.

Tradition of Victory, Hutchinson, 1981.

Success to the Brave, Hutchinson, 1983.

Colours Aloft!, Putnam, 1986.

Honour This Day, Heinemann (London), 1987.

With All Dispatch, Heinemann, 1988.

The Only Victor, Methuen (London), 1990.

Beyond the Reef, Heinemann, 1992.

Darkening Sea, Heinemann, 1993.

Bolitho, Heinemann, 1993.

SIDELIGHTS: Under the pseudonym Alexander Kent, Douglas Reeman writes novels about his popular character Richard Bolitho, a sea captain in the 18th-century British navy. Bolitho's adventures involve many of the major historical events of that period, including both the French and American Revolutions. As the series progresses, Bolitho moves up the ranks to eventually attain the rank of admiral. As Christopher N. Smith notes in *Twentieth-Century Romance and Historical Writers,* "Alexander Kent is this generation's outstanding author of naval romances. . . . Discerning critics have hailed Kent as the true heir to the highly successfully C. S. Forester [author of the Horatio Hornblower series of sea adventures]." Reeman's books have been translated into 22 languages and have sold over 12 million copies.

In the initial novel in the Bolitho series, *To Glory We Steer,* Bolitho is captain of a frigate operating in the West Indies at the close of the American Revolution. He must stifle an attempted mutiny and defeat a stronger French naval force in the area. Judson LsHaye in *Best Sellers* states: "The story is replete with cannonades, heroics, stiff-upper-lip sequences. It also provides a well-researched and convincing background of the matters of conduct and attendant crises aboard a warship of the British Navy circa 1782." Calling *To Glory We Steer* "a cutlass-and-cannon swashbuckler," Martin Levin in the *New York Times Book Review* claims that "if you're willing to follow the wake of [fictional sea captain Horatio] Hornblower into 18th-century seas, where a crew of shanghaied valiants kicks the stuffing out of all comers, you'll find a salty testament to the mystique and the brutality of the square rigger."

Bolitho's next adventure, *Form Line of Battle!,* again finds the captain battling French opponents, this time during the French Revolution. Critics particularly praised the character of Bolitho. G. E. Snow in *Best Sellers* writes that *Form Line of Battle!* is "a superb and stirring epic of 18th century naval warfare. . . . In this age of the anti-hero, Captain Richard Bolitho stands out as a welcome change—a strong, brooding but able man in the classical heroic mold." Similarly, Priscilla Wegars in *Library Journal* believes Bolitho "will be remembered as a hero who is both human and humane."

Kent's writing style, and his ability to depict exciting sea battles, has been praised by several critics. W. H. Archer in *Best Sellers* notes: "Kent exercises an admirably terse style, revealing a comprehensive knowledge of seafaring and of his period." Wegars finds that Kent's "18th-century sea battles are vividly depicted." Smith writes that, in addition to his "meticulously recorded detail" of British naval life of the time, Kent also excels at creating realistic scenes of naval battle. "Equally impressive," Smith writes, "are the battle scenes with their noise and confusion, their appalling carnage and the frightful suffering that follows even success in battle."

Kent's creation of Richard Bolitho has also been re-marked upon by critics who find the character to be fully-rounded and realistic. Smith remarks: "Since Alexander Kent places his tales within the grand pan-orama of war across the seven seas over several de-cades, we witness Bolitho as he faces up to a great variety of problems, in different situations. His re-sponse is always brave and ingenious, and his success is typically achieved against the odds, with scant help from his superiors." Smith concludes that the Bolitho series "dwells above all on the loneliness of a sensi-tive hero in a world of appalling cruelty and vio-lence." Virginia Borland in *Library Journal* finds that "for all who like adventure and sea battles; for all who would like to escape into the 18th Century—follow Bolitho, a cool captain." For avid readers of the series, Kent's British publisher Hutchinson pub-lishes *The Richard Bolitho Newsletter*.

Reeman told *CA:* "My main interest is in the sea, in ships, and in maritime history. I spend every avail-able moment, when not writing, on travel, research, and seeking out locations and situations for my books. I travel many thousands of miles per year, by sea whenever possible, for as my books are published throughout the world I feel I need to know better the people who read them. My hobbies, too, are con-nected with the sea: sailing, cruising, and exploring beaches are amongst them—wild birds too, in all forms and of all countries."

BIOGRAPHICAL/CRITICAL SOURCES:

BOOKS

Twentieth-Century Romance and Historical Writers, third edition, St. James Press (Detroit), 1994.

PERIODICALS

America, May 5, 1973.
Best Sellers, August 1, 1968, p. 28; June 15, 1969, p. 29; October 15, 1972, p. 32.
Books and Bookmen, August, 1969.
Book World, September 24, 1972.
Christian Science Monitor, December 3, 1975.
Library Journal, July, 1968, p. 93; July, 1969, p. 94; December 15, 1972, p. 97.
National Observer, January 13, 1973.

New York Times, February 16, 1965.
New York Times Book Review, March 3, 1968; July 14, 1968, p. 36; June 1, 1969, p. 24; May 24, 1970; October 15, 1972, p. 43.
Observer, August 13, 1972; November 24, 1974.
Saturday Review, November 9, 1968.
Times Literary Supplement, May 12, 1966; July 2, 1971.
Top of the News, June, 1968.

*   *   *

REEVE, Joel
See COX, William R(obert)

*   *   *

REILLY, William K.
See CREASEY, John

*   *   *

RENO, Clint
See BALLARD, (Willis) Todhunter

*   *   *

RILEY, Tex
See CREASEY, John

*   *   *

ROBBINS, Thomas Eugene 1936-
(Tom Robbins)

PERSONAL: Born in 1936 in Blowing Rock, NC; son of Katherine (Robinson) Robbins; married second wife, Terrie (divorced); children: (second marriage) Fleetwood Starr (son). *Education:* Attended Washing-ton and Lee University, 1950-52, Richmond Profes-sional Institute (now Virginia Commonwealth Univer-sity), and University of Washington.

ADDRESSES: Home—Box 338, LaConner, WA 98257. *Agent*—Pheobe Larmore, 228 Main St., Venice, CA 90291.

CAREER: Writer. *Richmond Times-Dispatch,* Richmond, VA, copy editor, 1960-62; *Seattle Times* and *Seattle Post-Intelligence,* Seattle, WA, copy editor, 1962-63; *Seattle Magazine,* Seattle, reviewer and art critic, 1964-68. Conducted research in New York City's East Village for an unwritten book on Jackson Pollock. *Military service:* U.S. Air Force; served in Korea.

WRITINGS:

UNDER NAME TOM ROBBINS

Guy Anderson (biography), Gear Works Press, 1965.
Another Roadside Attraction (novel), Doubleday (New York City), 1971.
Even Cowgirls Get the Blues (novel), Houghton (Boston, MA), 1976.
Still Life with Woodpecker (novel), Bantam (New York City), 1980.
Jitterbug Perfume (novel), Bantam, 1984.
Skinny Legs and All, (novel), Bantam, 1990.
Half-Asleep in Frog Pajamas (novel), Bantam, 1994.

ADAPTATIONS: Even Cowgirls Get the Blues was adapted for film by Gus Van Sant and released by Fine Line Features, 1994.

SIDELIGHTS: For all his influence on the West Coast literary scene, Tom Robbins told the *New York Times* in 1993 that his relatively small output of novels (six in over twenty-five years) is based on the fact that "I try never to leave a sentence until it's as perfect as I can make it. So there isn't a word in any of my books that hasn't been gone over 40 times."

Robbins was a critically admired but low-selling novelist until the mid-1970s, when his first two works of fiction, *Another Roadside Attraction* and *Even Cowgirls Get the Blues,* went into paperback editions. Only then did the books become accessible to students, and they took to the novels with an enthusiasm that made the author "the biggest thing to hit the 'youth market' in years," according to *New York Times Magazine* reporter Mitchell S. Ross. Much of Robbins's popularity among young readers, most critics agree, can be attributed to the fact that his novels encompass the countercultural "California" or "West Coast" school of writing, whose practitioners also

include the likes of Ken Kesey and Richard Braughtigan. In the words of R. H. Miller, writing in a *Dictionary of Literary Biography Yearbook* piece, the West Coast school emphasizes "the themes of personal freedom, the pursuit of higher states of being through Eastern mysticism, the escape from the confining life of urban California to the openness of the pastoral Pacific Northwest. Like the writings of his mentors, Robbins's own novels exhibit an elaborate style, a delight in words for their own sake, and an open, at times anarchical, attitude toward strict narrative form."

All of these qualities are evident in the author's first novel, *Another Roadside Attraction.* In this story, a collection of eccentrics with names like Plucky Purcell and Marx Marvelous gets involved with the mummified body of Jesus Christ, which somehow ends up at the Capt. Kendrick Memorial Hot Dog Wildlife Preserve, formerly Mom's Little Dixie Diner. As Ross sees it, the novel's plot "is secondary to the characters and tertiary to the style. [These characters] are nothing like your next-door neighbors, even if you lived in Haight-Ashbury in the middle '60s." Jerome Klinkowitz, digging deeper into the novel's meaning, declares in his book *The Practice of Fiction in America: Writers from Hawthorne to the Present* that in *Another Roadside Attraction* Robbins "feels that the excessive rationalization of Western culture since [17th-century philosopher Rene] Descartes has severed man from his roots in nature. Organized religion has in like manner become more of a tool of logic and control than of spirit. Robbins' heroine, Amanda, would reconnect mankind with the benign chaos of the natural world, substituting magic for logic, style for substance, and poetry for the analytical measure of authority." Klinkowitz also finds the author is "a master of plain American speech . . . and his greatest trick is to use its flat style to defuse the most sacred objects."

Robbins followed *Another Roadside Attraction* with what would become his best-known novel to date. In *Even Cowgirls Get the Blues,* the author "shows the same zest of his earlier book, but the plot is focused and disciplined, mostly because Robbins had learned by this time to use the structure of the journey as a major organizing principle in the narrative," according to Miller. This tale concerns one Sissy Hankshaw, an extraordinary hitchhiker due mainly to the fact that she was born with oversized thumbs. One of her rides takes her to the Rubber Rose Ranch, run by Bonanza Jellybean and her cowgirls, "whom Sissy joins in an attempt to find freedom from herself, as she participates in their communal search for that same freedom," as Miller relates. "They yearn for an open, sexual, unchauvinistic world, much like that of the Chink, a wizened hermit who lives near the ranch and who has absorbed his philosophy of living from the Clock people, a tribe of Indians, and from Eastern philosophy."

Again, plot takes a backseat to the intellectual forces that drive the characters on. To *Nation* critic Ann Cameron, *Even Cowgirls Get the Blues* shows "a brilliant affirmation of private visions and private wishes and the power to transform life and death. A tall tale and a parable of essential humanness, it is a work of extraordinary playfulness, style and wit." In his study *Tom Robbins,* author Mark Siegel sees two "major paradoxes in [the author's ideas]. One is the emphasis he places on individual fulfillment while he simultaneously castigates egotism. The second is his apparent devotion to Eastern philosophies in *Another Roadside Attraction,* although he warns against adopting Eastern religions in *Cowgirls.* Actually the two issues are closely related, both stemming from Robbins's notion that any truly fulfilling way of life must evolve from the individual's recognition of his true, personal relationship to the world. Thus, although Americans can learn from Oriental philosophies much about liberation from the ego, Western man must nevertheless find a way of liberation that is natural to him in his own world."

"Robbins has an old trunk of a mind," says Thomas LeClair in a *New York Times Book Review* piece on *Cowgirls.* "[He] knows the atmosphere on Venus, cow diseases, hitchhiking manuals, herbs, the brain's circuitry, whooping cranes, circles, parades, Nisei internment," adding that these visions "add up to a primitivism just pragmatic enough to be attractive and fanciful enough to measure the straight society." In Ross's opinion, the author's style "generates its own head of steam and dances past the plot, characters and clockwork philosophy. . . . Oddly, it is a style without a single voice. At times, Robbins booms out like a bard; the next instant he forces us to mourn the loss of the next Bob Hope to beautiful letters." Ross notes too that "a piling on of wisecracks is made to substitute for description."

Robbins's penchant for cracking wise represents a sore point in his next novel, *Still Life with Woodpecker,* according to Julie B. Peters. A *Saturday Review* writer, Peters states that in this tale of a princess's romance with an outlaw, the prose "is marbled with limping puns heavily splattered with recurrent motifs and a boyish zeal for the scatological." Taking a similar tack, *Commonweal* critic Frank McConnell points out that "a large part of the problem in reading Robbins [is that] he's so *cute:* his books are full of cute lines populated by unrelentingly cute people, even teeming with cute animals—frogs, chipmunks and chihuahuas in *Still Life with Woodpecker.* No one ever gets hurt very badly . . . , and although the world is threatened by the same dark, soulless business cartels that threaten the worlds of [Thomas] Pynchon, [Norman] Mailer, and our century, in Robbins it doesn't seem, finally, to matter. Love or something like it really does conquer all in his parables, with a mixture of stoned gaiety, positive thinking, and Sunday Supplement Taoism."

In telling the story of the unusual relationship between Princess Leigh-Cheri, heiress of the Pacific island of Mu, and good-hearted terrorist Bernard Micky Wrangle, alias Woodpecker, the author also frames the tale by a monologue "having to do with his [Robbins's] efforts to type out his narrative on a Remington SL-3 typewriter, which at the end fails him, and he has to complete the novel in longhand," says Miller, who also finds that the moral of *Still Life with Woodpecker* "is not as strong as that of the earlier two [novels], and while the plot seems more intricately interlaced, it has the complexity and exoticism of grand opera but little of its brilliance."

The generally disappointed reaction of critics to *Still Life with Woodpecker* left some writers wondering whether Robbins, with his free-form style, was addressing the needs of fiction readers in the upwardly mobile 1980s. The author answered his critics with *Jitterbug Perfume,* published in 1984. In this novel, Seattle waitress Priscilla devotes her life to inventing the ultimate perfume. The challenge is taken up in locales as varied as New Orleans and Paris, while back in Seattle, Wiggs Dannyboy, described by *Washington Post Book World* reviewer Rudy Rucker as "a Timothy Leary work-alike who's given up acid for immortality research," enters the scene to provide insights on the 1960s.

Comparing *Jitterbug Perfume* to the author's other works, Rucker notes that the first two novels were '60s creations—"filled with mushrooms and visions, radicals and police. *Still Life with Woodpecker* is about the '70s viewed as the aftermath of the '60s." And in *Jitterbug Perfume,* "Robbins is still very much his old Pan-worshipping self, yet his new book is lovingly plotted, with every conceivable loose end nailed down tight. Although the ideas are the same as ever, the form is contemporary, new-realistic craftsmanship. Robbins toys with the 1980s' peculiar love/hate for the 60s through his invention of the character Wiggs Dannyboy." To John House, the work "is not so much a novel as an inspirational fable, full of Hallmark sweetness, good examples and hope springing eternal." House, in a *New York Times Book Review* article, goes on to say that he finds Robbins's style "unmistakable—oblique, florid, willing to sacrifice everything for an old joke or corny pun." While *Jitterbug Perfume* "is still less exuberant than 'Cowgirls,'" according to Don Strachan in the *Los Angeles Times Book Review,* the former is still "less diminished than honed. The author may still occasionally stick his foot in the door of his mouth, as he would say in one of those metaphors he loves to mix with wordplay salads, but then he'll unfurl a phrase that will bring your critical mind to its knees."

Robbins greeted a new decade with a new novel. *Skinny Legs and All* takes on the 1990s Big Issues with the author's '60s verve. (Critic Joe Queenan said in the *New York Times Book Review* that the book "makes you want to dust off all those old Firesign Theater records and don those frayed, tie-dyed bell bottoms one last time.")

The story centers on Ellen Cherry Charles, waitress and would-be artist. She moves to New York City with her downscale husband, Boomer, hoping to break into the art world. It is Boomer, however, with his primitive trailer-art and homegrown wisdom ("If God didn't prefer for us to drink at night, he wouldn't have made neon"), who becomes the intelligentsia's darling. Along the way the reader meets overly enthusiastic evangelist Buddy Winkler, the Arab-and-Jewish restaurant partners Abu and Spike; the world's most erotic belly-dancer, who unfortunately for her sports-bar clientele will perform only during a Super Bowl kickoff; and a set of inanimate objects (spoon, sock, can of baked beans) that, thanks to reincarnation, suddenly becomes very animated.

Queenan finds all this funny—up to a point. Robbins is at his best, Queenan says, "when he is being snide, witty or downright juvenile. . . . But when [he] gets on his high horse, the results are pure bunkum." Charles Dickinson agrees. "Robbins is fed up with a lot of the things about this world and the people in it," notes the *Chicago Tribune* critic. "In fact, there

are times when it seems the only reason Robbins wrote this novel was to provide a framework for the delineation of his complaints; and that is the sole—but not unimportant—weakness in this book."

"I'm asking you to consider that hyperintelligent entities—agents of the overmind; aliens, if you will—could be abducting our frogs as part of a benign scheme to free us from the tyranny of the historical continuum and reunites our souls with the other-dimensional." That's just one of the propositions put forth in Robbins' 1994 novel, *Half Asleep in Frog Pajamas.* The story, written in the second-person, ostensibly covers four days in the life of Seattle stockbroker Gwen Mali—but as usual for a Robbins book, the plot serves only as a framework to parade such characters as Gwen's friend Q-Jo, a 300-lb psychic; lecherous businessman Jake Diamond, just back form a sabbatical in Timbuktu (and author of the aliens/frogs theory); straightman/foil Belford Dunn; and Andre, Belford's born-again monkey. ("It seems that Belford helped Andre find religion after the simian was caught helping a famous French their rob the rich of their jewels," explains *Chicago Tribune* reviewer Chris Petrakos.)

In assessing *Half Asleep,* critics generally stayed true to their view of Robbins: funny, but given to preachiness. To Petrakos, "the frequently hilarious mingling of characters and sensibilities in the early half of the book bogs down in later pages. The whole idea of a born-again monkey seems undeveloped, as is the character of the psychic. While there are great weird bits and lyrical observations, as there are in all Robbins' novels, there's not the kind of wild exhilaration that one might expect."

"My theory on Tom Robbins," says Karen Karbo, writing in the *New York Times Book Review,* "is that unless his work was imprinted on you when you were 19 and stoned, you'll find him forever unreadable." *Half Asleep,* she says, "is vintage Robbins, a recommendation for those of you who can stand it." *Washington Post's* Rudy Rucker was more accommodating in his evaluation: while he tires of the ceaseless ramblings of the Larry Diamond character, he advises like-minded readers "to indulge [the author] a little, as Robbins can still write phrases of mind-boggling beauty. On a foggy, rainy day in Seattle: 'Your building is surrounded by the soft, the gray, and the moist, as if it is being digested by an oyster.' On hearing some bad news: 'Your heart sinks like a roll of quarters in a wishing well.'"

BIOGRAPHICAL/CRITICAL SOURCES:

BOOKS

Contemporary Literary Criticism, Gale (Detroit), Volume 9, 1978, Volume 32, 1985, Volume 64, 1991.
Dictionary of Literary Biography Yearbook: 1980, Gale, 1981.
Klinkowitz, Jerome, *The Practice of Fiction in America: Writers from Hawthorne to the Present,* Iowa State University Press (Ames), 1980.
Nadeau, Robert, *Readings from the New Book on Nature: Physics and Metaphysics in the Modern Novel,* University of Massachusetts Press (Amherst), 1981.
Siegel, Mark, *Tom Robbins,* Boise State University Press, 1980.

PERIODICALS

Chicago Review, autumn, 1980.
Chicago Tribune, April 1, 1990, p. 3; November 17, 1994, p. 2.
Commonweal, March 13, 1981.
Detroit News, October 5, 1980, January 6, 1985.
Los Angeles Times Book Review, December 16, 1984; April 15, 1990; September 25, 1994. p. 3.
Nation, August 28, 1976, October 25, 1980.
New Boston Review, December, 1977.
New Republic, June 26, 1971.
New Statesman, August 12, 1977.
Newsweek, September 29, 1980.
New York Times, December 30, 1993.
New York Times Book Review, May 23, 1976; September 28, 1980; December 9, 1984; April 15, 1990, p. 12; October 30, 1994. p. 27.
New York Times Magazine, February 12, 1978.
Saturday Review, September, 1980.
Times Literary Supplement, October 31, 1980.
Washington Post, December 18, 1994, p. 5.
Washington Post Book World, October 25, 1980.*

* * *

ROBBINS, Tom
See ROBBINS, Thomas Eugene

* * *

ROBBINS, Wayne
See COX, William R(obert)

ROSS, Jonathan
See ROSSITER, John

* * *

ROSSITER, John 1916-
(Jonathan Ross)

PERSONAL: Born March 2, 1916, in Devonshire, England; married Joan Gaisford, February 21, 1942; children: Sally (Mrs. Rossiter-Smith). *Education:* Attended preparatory and military schools in Woolwich and Bulford, 1924-32. *Politics:* Conservative. *Religion:* "Still searching."

ADDRESSES: Home—3 Leighton Home Farm Court, Wellhead Lane, Westbury, Wiltshire BA13 3PT, England. *Agent*—Murray Pollinger Ltd., 222 Old Brompton Rd., London SW5 0BZ, England.

CAREER: Writer. British Police Service, Wiltshire, England, detective chief superintendent, 1939-69. Columnist, *Wiltshire Courier,* Swindon, 1963-64. *Military service:* Royal Air Force and Army, 1942-45; served in Glider Pilot Regiment; became Flight Lieutenant.

MEMBER: Crime Writers Association.

WRITINGS:

The Man Who Came Back, H. Hamilton (London), 1978, Houghton (Boston), 1979.
Dark Flight, Atheneum (New York City), 1981.

MYSTERIES

The Murder Makers, Cassell (London), 1970.
The Deadly Green, Cassell, 1970, Walker & Co. (New York City), 1971.
The Victims, Cassell, 1971.
A Rope for General Dietz, Constable (London), 1972.
The Manipulators, Cassell, 1973, Simon & Schuster (New York City), 1974.
The Villains, Cassell, 1974, Walker & Co., 1976.
The Golden Virgin, Constable, 1975, published as *The Deadly Gold,* Walker & Co., 1975.

MYSTERIES; UNDER PSEUDONYM JONATHAN ROSS

The Blood Running Cold, Cassell, 1968.
Diminished by Death, Cassell, 1968.

Dead at First Hand, Cassell, 1969.

The Deadest Thing You Ever Saw, Cassell, 1969, McCall (New York City), 1970.

The Burning of Billy Toober, Constable, 1972, Walker & Co., 1976.

Here Lies Nancy Frail, Saturday Review Press (New York City), 1972.

I Know What It's Like to Die, Constable, 1976, Walker & Co., 1978.

A Rattling of Old Bones, Constable, 1979, Scribner (New York City), 1982.

Dark Blue and Dangerous, Scribner, 1981.

Death's Head, Constable, 1982, St. Martin's (New York City), 1983.

Dead Eye, Constable, 1983, St. Martin's, 1984.

Dropped Dead, Constable, 1984, St. Martin's, 1985.

Burial Deferred, Constable, 1985, St. Martin's, 1986.

Fate Accomplished, St. Martin's, 1987.

Sudden Departures, St. Martin's, 1988.

A Time for Dying, St. Martin's, 1989.

Daphne Dead and Done For, Constable, 1990, St. Martin's, 1991.

Murder Be Hanged, Constable, 1992, St. Martin's, 1993.

The Body of a Woman, Constable, 1994, published as *None the Worse for a Hanging,* St. Martin's, 1995.

Murder! Murder! Burning Bright, Constable, 1996.

Contributor of drawings and articles on entomology to periodicals; contributor of cartoons to *Punch, Aeroplane,* and other magazines. Many of Rossiter's novels have been translated into German.

SIDELIGHTS: John Rossiter is best-known for the mystery novels he has written under the pseudonym Jonathan Ross, featuring British Detective Superintendent George Rogers. Under his own name, Rossiter has also written a series of police procedural novels about Roger Tallis. A former British police chief superintendent who spent thirty years with the force, Rossiter brings to his fiction an authority that is unique. Leo Fleming in *Best Sellers* finds that Rossiter's "writing bears the stamp of intimate experience with British police procedures; his style and vocabulary are reminiscent of the Victorian novelists rather unexpected in this genre . . . but nonetheless engrossing."

D. A. Miller, writing in the *St. James Guide to Crime and Mystery Writers,* describes Rossiter's character George Rogers as "an impatient, often irascible, emotionally vulnerable policeman with few illusions about himself or about mankind generally. He is highly intelligent, having the sort of sensitive, flexible, imaginative, and inquisitive mind useful for solving the puzzles his creator sets him." The Rogers novels, Miller believes, "are ingeniously and complexly plotted: switches in identity, false trails, and suspects who lie their heads off abound."

One of the earlier entries in the Rogers series, *The Deadest Thing You Ever Saw,* concerns a vengence-seeking vigilante who has targeted two murderers just released from prison for their crime. When one of the newly-released prisoners is found hanged, Rogers must try, against his own sensibilities, to protect the second killer from vengeance. The critic for the *Times Literary Supplement* finds that the novel "sympathetically spotlights a surprisingly large number of variously likeable policemen," while A. J. Hubin in the *New York Times Book Review* notes that Ross's "concealment of a killer's quite logical identity is deft, and he provides striking interplay of character."

Dark Blue and Dangerous is singled out in a *New Republic* review by Robin W. Winks for the high level of "craftsmanship" displayed by its author. Noting that the tone of the book is extremely hard-boiled, Winks goes on to say, "I was not a fan of his earlier books, but now they seem compelling." Reviewing the same book, Newgate Callendar of the *New York Times Book Review* points out that it is "solidly traditional," and even features the classic plot element of a staged re-enactment of the murder.

Ross's enjoyment of a good murder case is evident and contagious in another George Rogers mystery, *Death's Head,* according to Nick B. Williams, contributor to the *Los Angeles Times Book Review.* In this novel, the body of an alcoholic vagrant is found in a church, but it disappears by the time Rogers arrives on the scene. He intuitively links the incident with the report of a missing person—a butterfly breeder who deserted his wife. A *Publishers Weekly* reviewer praises the "well-drawn characters" and spare writing style of *Death's Head,* which, like many of Ross's mysteries, concentrates on the procedural aspects of detection.

Murder Be Hanged is yet another installment in the exploits of George Rogers. In this story, Rogers is recently divorced, and worried that his desire for golf seems to be growing stronger than his desire for women. The action begins when an ill-mannered young man, Willie Sloan, comes to Rogers to complain that his stepfather has threatened his mother, Rachel Horsbrugh. Gunshots are heard at Rachel's house soon after. Although it seems that someone is trying to kill her, everyone around her begins to die, while she survives. *Murder Be Hanged* drew mixed comment from reviewers. A *Publishers Weekly* reviewer finds that it "lacks tension," and remarks that even Roger's brief sexual attraction to Rachel is "not enough to spark this drab, generally predictable tale." Emily Melton is more enthusiastic, however. Writing in *Booklist,* she reports that *Murder Be Hanged* includes "one of the saddest and nastiest conclusions to a case in [Rogers's] career," and remarks that readers will find the "story has plenty to offer."

Rossiter once told *CA:* "The majority of my crime books are based on my experiences as a detective officer investigating murder and other serious crimes. My pilot training in Arizona was the background for the novel *The Murder Makers.* My residence in Spain was used to provide the background for the novels *A Rope for General Dietz* and *The Golden Virgin.*

"I believe that most successful writers have inside them a Walter Mitty-ish character trying to get out. Where they have not, they possess an arrogance requiring them to tell the world how it should be. Either defect (to which I own) will be a catalyst for the addictive compulsion a writer must have to sit out what is virtually a solitary exercise in his workshop for breast-beating. . . . The road for an aspiring writer is usually long and stony, all too often lined with the debris of rejections. He should never ask advice other than from a published writer; never an opinion from a relative or friend. Therein waits a self-dug black pit from which it is difficult to climb."

BIOGRAPHICAL/CRITICAL SOURCES:

BOOKS

St. James Guide to Crime and Mystery Writers, fourth edition, St. James Press (Detroit), 1996.

PERIODICALS

Best Sellers, November 1, 1970, p. 30; March 1, 1971; October 1, 1972.
Booklist, April 1, 1993, p. 1416; November 15, 1995, p. 537.
Books and Bookmen, September, 1971; August, 1972; February, 1984, p. 30.
Economist, November 6, 1971.
Library Journal, November 1, 1972, p. 97.
Los Angeles Times Book Review, July 31, 1983, p. 11.
National Review, April 20, 1971.

New Republic, August 22, 1981, p. 39.
New York Times Book Review, November 29, 1970, p. 61; April 18, 1971; October 1, 1972; October 8, 1972, p. 46; January 10, 1982, p. 29; December 2, 1984, p. 62.
Observer, September 13, 1970; January 8, 1984, p. 51.
Publishers Weekly, March 18, 1983, p. 54; September 15, 1989, p. 111; February 15, 1991, p. 77; February 22, 1993, p. 84; November 6, 1995, p. 85.
Punch, February 14, 1968.
Times Literary Supplement, September 26, 1968; December 11, 1969, p. 1431; May 26, 1972, p. 612; July 7, 1972; December 31, 1982, p. 1448.*

*   *   *

ROWBOTHAM, Sheila 1943-
(Sheila Turner)

PERSONAL: Born in 1943, in Leeds, England; daughter of Lancelot (in sales) and Jean (a clerical worker; maiden name, Turner) Rowbotham; children: William James Atkinson. *Education:* Oxford University, B.A., 1966. *Politics:* "Socialist Feminist."

ADDRESSES: Home—London, England. *Office*—Department of Sociology, Coupland II Building, University of Manchester, Oxford Road, Manchester M13 9PL, England.

CAREER: Teacher with Workers Educational Association at technical colleges and schools in England, 1964-79; *Black Dwarf* (socialist paper), London, staff writer, 1968-69; writer for *Red Ray* (socialist feminist paper), 1972-73; University of Amsterdam, visiting professor of women's studies, 1981-83; Greater London Council Economic Unit, London, research officer, 1983-86; World Institute for Development Economics Research, United Nations University, consultant to Women's Programme, 1987-91; Honorary Fellow in Women's Studies, University of North London; University of Manchester, Manchester, Simon Research Fellow, department of sociology, 1994—, five senior research fellows, department of sociology, 1996-2000.

WRITINGS:

Women's Liberation and the New Politics, Bertrand Russell Peace Foundation (Nottingham), 1971.

Women, Resistance, and Revolution: A History of Women and Revolution in the Modern World, Pantheon (New York City), 1972.

Hidden from History: Rediscovering Women in History from the 17th Century to the Present, Vintage (New York City), 1973, published as *Hidden from History: 300 Years of Women's Oppression and the Fight against It,* Pluto Press (London), 1973, third edition, 1977.

Women's Consciousness, Man's World, Penguin (Harmondsworth), 1973.

(Editor with Jean McCrindle) *Dutiful Daughters: Women Talk about Their Lives,* University of Texas Press (Austin), 1977.

(With Jeff Week) *Socialism and the New Life: The Personal and Sexual Politics of Edward Carpenter and Havelock Ellis,* Pluto Press, 1977.

A New World for Women: Stella Browne, Socialist Feminist, Pluto Press, 1978.

One Foot on the Mountain, Onlywoman Press (London), 1979.

(With Hilary Wainwright and Lynn Segal, *Beyond the Fragments: Feminism and the Making of Socialism,* [London], 1979, Alyson (Boston), 1981.

Dreams and Dilemmas: Collected Writings, Virago (London), 1983.

Friends of Alice Wheeldon, Pluto Press (Dover, NH), 1986.

The Past Is before Us: Feminism in Action since the 1960s, Beacon Press (Boston), 1989.

Women in Movement: Feminism and Social Action, Routledge (New York City), 1992.

Homeworkers Worldwide, Merlin Press (London), 1993.

(Editor with Swasti Mitter) *Dignity and Daily Bread: New Forms of Economic Organising among Poor Women in the Third World and the First,* Routledge, 1994.

(Editor with Mitter) *Women Encounter Technology: Changing Patterns of Employment in the Third World,* Routledge (London), 1995.

A Century of Women: The History of Women in Britain and the United States, Viking/Penguin (London), 1997.

Also author of political writings under pseudonym Sheila Turner.

SIDELIGHTS: "Any historian would admit that his material involves a process of selection," British novelist and literary critic Eva Figes once observed, "but he would perhaps be less ready to confess that this process can involve gross distortion of the truth. And yet until lately women have been consistently omitted: they have, apparently, no history." Such was the paradox that troubled feminist socialist Sheila Rowbotham in the early 1970s. An active member of the women's movement in England since the 1960s, Rowbotham realized very early the importance of a heritage for the "emerging woman." To this end she undertook to write several works that addressed women's absence from the panorama of history. Included among these works are *Women, Resistance, and Revolution: A History of Women and Revolution in the Modern World,* and her well-known opus, *Hidden from History: Rediscovering Women in History from the 17th Century to the Present.*

Born in Leeds, England in 1943, Rowbotham undertook the study of history at St. Hilda's College, Oxford before beginning her career as an economic historian and writer. Through her early work she is considered a pioneer in the British women's movement, which had beginnings distinct from its sister movement in the United States due to its primarily left wing, working-class origins. Where a nascent feminist consciousness in the United States was shaped by the Civil Rights Era, such would not be the case in Great Britain. In her essay "The beginnings of Women's Liberation in Britain," included in *Dreams and Dilemmas: Collected Writings,* Rowbotham notes that the British women's movement grew out of the working women's equal-work-for-equal-wage campaigns of the 1960s, gaining momentum as a result of the influx of news of similar activism in other nations. During her involvement in these equal wage campaigns, Rowbotham helped organize a landmark women's liberation conference at Ruskin College, Oxford; the first gathering of its kind in England, the conference was attended by over 500 people.

Rowbotham has since written numerous works that highlight the social, economic, and political contributions made to history by female figures. Her early books, which include *Hidden from History: 300 Years of Women's Oppression and the Fight against It,* are clearly Marxist in tenor. Intended as a general overview, 1973's *Hidden from History* reconstructs British history from a feminist perspective supplemented by class analysis. Commenting on the book, critics credited the author with the initiative to take the first major step in reevaluating the historical canon. "Miss Rowbotham has made a tremendous and unstinting effort to create history out of silence," wrote Monica Foot in the *Times Literary Supplement,* adding that the historian "is to be congratulated on at least trying to get women off their backs and into some kind of 'brave, responsible, thinking and diligent frame of mind.'"

Other works found Rowbotham similarly focused, although sometimes experimenting with different genres. *The Friends of Alice Wheeldon* is a dramatic portrait of the life of an early-20th century suffragette, one of three feminists to be imprisoned by the British government for their radical political activity. Far more radical in intent was 1978's *Beyond the Fragments: Feminism and the Making of Socialism,* in which, together with coauthors Hilary Wainwright and Lynn Segal, Rowbotham examines "the scope of power dynamics operating women's participation in socialist politics and a male-dominated left," according to *Feminist Writers* contributor Patricia Duncan.

As Third World Women became the subject of academic interest in the mid-1980s, Rowbotham turned her Marxist feminist scrutiny to their unique situation. The exploitation of many of these women as a cheap source of labor served as the focus of several works, including Rowbotham's coeditorship of *Dignity and Daily Bread: New Forms of Economic Organising among Poor Women in the Third World and the First,* released in 1994. Her 1992 overview of the modern feminist movement, *Women in Movement: Feminism and Social Action,* was described by Raka Ray in *Signs* as "a book so wide-ranging and so uncompromising in its refusal to accept easy answers that it is essential reading for anyone interested in women's political action."

BIOGRAPHICAL/CRITICAL SOURCES:

BOOKS

Abelove, Henry, and others, editors, *Visions of History: Conversations with Radical Historians,* Pantheon, 1984.
Feminist Writers, St. James Press (Detroit), 1996.
Humm, Maggie, editor, *Modern Feminisms: Political, Literary, Cultural,* Columbia University Press (New York City), 1992.
Wandor, Michelene, editor, *Once a Feminist: Stories of a Generation,* Virago, 1990.

PERIODICALS

American Scholar, autumn, 1973.
Books and Bookmen, August, 1973.
Canadian Literature, spring, 1996, pp. 189-92.
Economist, March 3, 1973.
New Statesman, November 15, 1974.

Newsweek, January 20, 1975.
New York Times Book Review, March 16, 1975.
Observer, January 20, 1974.
Signs, spring, 1995, pp. 766-79.
Times Literary Supplement, March 23, 1973; November 30, 1973; June 10, 1977.

*   *   *

RYBOT, Doris
    See PONSONBY, D(oris) A(lmon)

*   *   *

RYDEN, Hope

PERSONAL: Born in St. Paul, MN; daughter of Ernest E. (a minister) and Agnes (Johnson) Ryden. *Education:* Attended Augustana College, Rock Island, IL; University of Iowa, B.A.

ADDRESSES: Home—345 East 81st St., #7A, New York, NY 10028. *Agent*—N. S. Bienstock, 850 Seventh Ave., New York, NY 10019.

CAREER: Freelance documentary film producer, photographer, and writer. Drew Associates (affiliate of Time-Life Broadcast), New York City, film producer, 1960-64; Hope Ryden Productions, New York City, film producer, writer, and director, 1965; American Broadcasting Corp. (ABC-TV), New York City, feature producer for ABC-TV evening news, 1966-68. Member of board of directors, Defenders of Wildlife, 1977—, Society for Protective Animal Legislation, 1983—, and American Society for Protection of Animals, 1984—.

AWARDS, HONORS: "Oppie" Award for best book in Americana category, 1970, and *Library Journal* citation as one of the 100 best sci-tech titles, 1970, for *America's Last Wild Horses;* Screen Writers Guild nomination for best film documentary, 1970, for *Missing in Randolph;* New York Public Library citations for *God's Dog* and *America's Last Wild Horses;* Cine Golden Eagle award for *The Wellsprings;* Emmy Award, Clarion Award, and Society of the Silurians Award, all for *Angel Dust: Teenage Emergency;* Library of Congress Award, Notable Book award, Outstanding Science Book for Children award, Notable Book in Field of Social Studies award, and Children's

Choice award, all 1978, for *The Little Deer of the Florida Keys;* Humanitarian of the Year Award, American Horse Protection Association, 1979; Joseph Wood Krutch Award, Humane Society of the United States, 1981; Outstanding Achievement Award, Augustana College Alumni Association, 1981; Outstanding Science Book for Children award, 1983, for *Bobcat;* Books Can Develop Empathy award, 1990, for *Wild Animals of Africa ABC.*

WRITINGS:

NONFICTION; AND PHOTOGRAPHER

America's Last Wild Horses, Dutton (New York City), 1970, revised edition, Lyons & Burford (New York City), 1990.
The Wild Colt: The Life of a Young Mustang, Coward (New York City), 1972.
Mustangs: A Return to the Wild, Viking (New York City), 1972.
God's Dog: The North American Coyote, Coward, 1975.
The Wild Pups: The True Story of a Coyote Family, Putnam (New York City), 1975.
The Little Deer of the Florida Keys, Putnam, 1978, revised edition, Florida Classics Library, 1986.
Bobcat Year, Viking, 1981.
Bobcat, Putnam, 1983.
America's Bald Eagle, Putnam, 1985.
The Beaver, Putnam, 1986.
Wild Animals of America ABC, Lodestar (New York City), 1988.
Wild Animals of Africa ABC, Lodestar, 1989.
Lily Pond: Four Years with a Family of Beavers, Morrow (New York City), 1989.
The Raggedy Red Squirrel, Lodestar, 1992.
Your Cat's Wild Cousins, Lodestar, 1992.
Joey: The Story of a Baby Kangaroo, Tambourine (New York City), 1994.
Your Dog's Wild Cousins, Lodestar, 1994.
Out of the Wild: The Story of Domesticated Animals, Dutton, 1995.
ABC of Crawlers and Flyers, Clarion (New York City), 1996.
Wild Horse Summer, Clarion, 1997.

DOCUMENTARY FILMS; AND PRODUCER AND DIRECTOR

Susan Starr, produced by Drew Associates/Time-Life Films, 1962.
Jane, produced by Drew Associates/Time-Life Films, 1963.

Mission to Malaya, produced by Drew Associates/ABC-TV Network News, 1964.
Operation Gwamba, produced by Hope Ryden Productions and CBS-TV, 1965.
To Love a Child, broadcast by ABC-TV News, 1969.
Missing in Randolph, broadcast by ABC-TV news, 1970.
Strangers in Their Own Land: The Chicanos, broadcast by ABC-TV News, 1971.
The Wellsprings, broadcast by PBS-TV, 1976.
Beginning Again at Fifty, broadcast by CBS-TV, 1977.
The Forties: A Crossroad, broadcast by CBS-TV, 1977.
Angel Dust: Teenage Emergency, broadcast by CBS-TV, 1978.

OTHER

Backyard Rescue (fiction), Tambourine, 1994.

Contributor of articles to periodicals, including *Look, Children's Day, National Geographic, Reader's Digest, National Parks,* and *Conservation Magazine;* contributor of photographs to *National Geographic, Time, New York Times, Reader's Digest, Children's Day,* and other periodicals.

SIDELIGHTS: Hope Ryden is a photographer, filmmaker, and author best known for her nature books for children and young adults. She is especially noted for her works about North American animals like the coyote, beaver, bobcat, bald eagle, and Florida deer, which are illustrated with her own black-and-white photographs. For some of her books, including *Lily Pond: Four Years with a Family of Beavers* and *God's Dog: The North American Coyote,* Ryden spent years out in the field studying her subjects firsthand.

"I feel very little attention has been paid to North American wildlife," Ryden once commented. "Most people are more concerned with animals on other continents whose fate is beyond our control. Our own animals are exploited by commercial interests or removed if they have little or no commercial value and stand in the way of fuller exploitation of some other facet of nature. Though many people are enlightened regarding the balance of nature, the concept is not practiced in wildlife management. I wish to make this understood."

In a critically acclaimed 1978 story, *The Little Deer of the Florida Keys,* Ryden describes the plight of an endangered species. The rare miniature Key deer, once thought to be extinct, has been making a come-back since the establishment of the National Key Deer Refuge in 1957. Illustrated with both color and black-and-white photographs, the work explores the creatures' environment and behavior. Reviewing *The Little Deer of the Florida Keys,* Sarah Gagne of *Horn Book* stated that Ryden "skillfully creates tension by alternating an account of the deer's natural living habits with the story of its near extinction."

Another award-winning work, *Bobcat,* examines the lives of its solitary title creatures. Ryden includes information about the bobcat's mating habits, care of young, and hunting skills, and discusses natural selection and the evolution of a species. Though Zena Sutherland of the *Bulletin of the Center for Children's Books* felt that the text was "authoritative but diffuse in organization," a *Kirkus Reviews* critic deemed the work an "unusually interesting, intelligent, and smoothly knit introduction" to the life of the bobcat, adding that Ryden's photos "are truly illustrative and visually varied."

To research her 1989 book, *Lily Pond: Four Years with a Family of Beavers,* Ryden spent almost every night for four years observing a group of beavers living in a pond in New York state. During that time, the beaver family grew from four to six members and maintained a 150-foot-long, five-foot-high dam. The author became involved with the animals, bringing them food during a severe winter, helping them reconstruct the dam after vandals damaged it, and hand-feeding the elderly "Lily" before her death. "This is captivating natural history," remarked a *Publishers Weekly* reviewer, and *Booklist* contributor Mary Ellen Sullivan praised the author's "lively and perceptive prose" and "infectious passion" for her subjects.

In a more recent work, *Out of the Wild: The Story of Domesticated Animals,* Ryden traces the domestication of fifteen different animals, including dogs, cats, elephants, and pigs. Arranged chronologically, begin-

ning with the domestication of the dog some 15,000 years ago, *Out of the Wild* looks at the reasons why each animal proved useful to humans and discusses the methods scientists have used to unlock this information. Though some reviewers criticized Ryden for anthropomorphizing, especially in the introduction, most commentators felt she produced an informative, entertaining work. A *Kirkus Reviews* critic remarked that Ryden "speaks persuasively of the combined efforts of human and beast to bring each other out of the wild," and *Booklist* reviewer Mary Harris Veeder called *Out of the Wild* a "good treatment" of complicated issues.

BIOGRAPHICAL/CRITICAL SOURCES:

PERIODICALS

Appraisal: Science Books for Children, winter, 1986, pp. 31-32; summer, 1992, pp. 48-49; winter, 1995, p. 60; winter-spring, 1996, p. 52.
Booklist, September 1, 1981, p. 11; July, 1985, p. 1560; December 1, 1986, p. 581; November 15, 1989, p. 628; August, 1994, p. 2047; June 1, 1995, p. 1768.
Bulletin of the Center for Children's Books, September, 1972, p. 15; September, 1983, p. 16; April, 1988, p. 166.
Horn Book, October, 1978, pp. 541-543; November-December, 1989, p. 793; September-October, 1992, p. 601; May-June, 1994, pp. 336-337.
Kirkus Reviews, July 1, 1978, p. 693; March 1, 1983, p. 248; August 15, 1989, p. 1230; May 1, 1995.
New York Times Book Review, April 30, 1978, p. 47.
Publishers Weekly, September 11, 1981, p. 68; August 18, 1989, p. 46.
School Library Journal, January, 1976, pp. 40, 60; October, 1989, p. 108; September, 1994, p. 234; January, 1995, p. 110; July, 1995, p. 90.
Voice of Youth Advocates, October, 1985, pp. 279-280.

S

SARNA, Jonathan D(aniel) 1955-

PERSONAL: Born January 10, 1955, in Philadelphia, PA; son of Nahum Mattathias (a professor) and Helen Horowitz (a librarian) Sarna; married Ruth Langer (a professor), 1986; children: Aaron Yehuda, Leah Livia. *Education:* Hebrew College, Boston, MA, B.H.L. (with honors), 1974; Brandeis University, B.A. (summa cum laude), 1975, M.A. (Judaic studies), 1975; Yale University, M.A. (history), 1976, M.Phil., 1978, Ph.D., 1979.

ADDRESSES: Home—1215 Commonewalth Ave., West Newton, MA 02165; fax: 617-736-2070. *Office*—Department of Near Eastern and Judaic Studies, Brandeis University, Waltham, MA 02254. *E-mail*—sarna@binah.cc.brandeis.edu.

CAREER: American Jewish Historical Society, Wal-tham, MA, archivist, 1973-75, acting assistant librarian, 1976; America-Holy Land Project of American Jewish Historical Society and Institute for Contemporary Jewry, Waltham, researcher, 1975-77; Hebrew Union College-Jewish Institute of Religion, Cincinnati, OH, visiting lecturer, 1979-80, assistant professor, 1980-84, associate professor, 1984-88, professor of American Jewish history, 1988-90; Brandeis University, Waltham, MA, Joseph A. and Belle R. Braun Professor of American Jewish History, 1990—, chair of department of Near Eastern and Judaic Studies, 1992-95. Center for the Study of the American Jewish Experience, academic adviser, 1981-84, academic director, 1984-86, director, 1986-89. Visiting assistant professor at University of Cincinnati, 1983-84; visiting associate professor at Hebrew University, 1986-87.

Loewenstein-Weiner Fellow, American Jewish Archives, 1977. Lecturer at universities and to organizations. Director of applied research for Survivors of Hitler's Germany in Cincinnati Oral History Project, sponsored by American Jewish Archives and National Council of Jewish Women, 1980. Member of leadership council and Jewish education committee of Cincinnati Jewish Federation; member of board of directors of American Jewish Committee, Cincinnati Chapter, 1981-90; co-director of Kehilla: A Jewish Community Think Tank.

MEMBER: American Historical Association, Organization of American Historians, American Jewish Historical Society (archivist, 1973-75; librarian, 1976; director of academic council, 1992—), Immigration History Society, Association for Jewish Studies (director), Society for Historians of the Early American Republic, American Academy of Religion, Canadian Jewish Historical Society, Cincinnati Historical Society, Phi Beta Kappa.

AWARDS, HONORS: Seltzer-Brodsky Essay Prize from YIVO Institute, 1977, for "The American Jewish Response to Nineteenth-Century Christian Missions;" National Foundation for Jewish Culture fellowship, 1977-79; Memorial Foundation for Jewish Culture fellowship, 1977-79, 1982-83; Bernard and Audre Rapoport fellow at American Jewish Archives, 1979-80; National Jewish Book Award nomination, 1981, for *Jacksonian Jew: The Two Worlds of Mordecai Noah;* American Council of Learned Societies fellow, 1982; Lilly Endowment grant, 1984-93; Lady Davis Endowment, 1986-87; Pew Endowment grant, 1991-94; National Endowment for the Humanities senior fellowship, 1995-96.

WRITINGS:

(Editor) *Jews in New Haven,* Jewish Historical Society of New Haven (New Haven, CT), 1978.

Jacksonian Jew: The Two Worlds of Mordecai Noah, Holmes & Meier (New York City), 1981.

(Editor and translator) *"People Walk on Their Heads:" Moses Weinberger's Jews and Judaism in New York,* Holmes & Meier, 1982.

(Co-editor) *Jews and the Founding of the Republic,* Markus Wiener (New York City), 1985.

The American Jewish Experience: A Reader, Holmes & Meier, 1986.

(With Alexandra Shecket Korros) *American Synagogue History: A Bibliography and State-of-the-Field Summary,* Markus Wiener, 1988.

(With Nancy H. Klein) *The Jews of Cincinnati,* Center for the Study of the American Jewish Experience (Cincinnati), 1989.

JPS: The Americanization of Jewish Culture: A History of the Jewish Publication Society, 1888-1988, Jewish Publication Society (Philadelphia), 1989.

(With Janet Liss) *Yahadut Amerika/American Jewry: An Annotated Bibliography of Publications in Hebrew,* Hebrew University, 1991.

(Editor with Henry D. Shapiro) *Ethnic Diversity and Civic Identity: Patterns of Conflict and Cohesion in Cincinnati since 1820,* University of Illinois Press (Urbana), 1992.

(Editor with Daniel J. Elazar and Rela G. Monson) *A Double Bond: The Constitutional Documents of American Jewry,* University Press of America (Lanham, MD), 1992.

(Editor with Lloyd Gartner) *Yehude Artsot Ha-Berit,* Merkaz Shazar, 1992.

(Editor and author of foreword) Marshall Sklare, *Observing America's Jews,* Brandeis University Press (Waltham, MA), 1993.

(Consulting editor) Sondra Leiman, *America: The Jewish Experience,* Union of American Hebrew Congregations (New York City), 1994.

(Editor with Ellen Smith) *The Jews of Boston: Essays on the Occasion of the Centenary (1895-1995) of the Combined Jewish Philanthropies of Greater Boston,* Combined Jewish Philanthropies of Greater Boston (Boston), 1995.

(Editor with David G. Dalin) *Religion and State in the American Jewish Experience: A Documentary History,* University of Notre Dame Press (Notre Dame, IN), 1997.

Contributor to books, including Nathan W. Kaganoff, editor, *Guide to America-Holy Land Studies,* Volume I, Arno (New York City), 1980, Volume II, Praeger (New York City), 1982; David Gerber, editor, *The Encounter of Jew and Gentile in America: New Historical Perspectives,* University of Illinois Press, 1984; *Toward an American Jewish Culture: New Perspectives on Jewish Community,* National Foundation for Jewish Culture (New York City), 1993. Contributor to *American National Biography, Harper's Dictionary of Religion, Encyclopedia of Jewish Heritage and the Holocaust, Judaica Americana,* and *The Encyclopedia of Religion.*

General editor of "Masterworks of Modern Jewish Writing," eleven volumes, Markus Wiener, and of "Brandeis Series in American Jewish History, Culture and Life," seven volumes, Brandeis University Press; editor with Moses Rischin of "American Jewish Life" series, five volumes, Wayne State University Press. Editor of North American Judaism section, *Religious Studies Review,* 1984-89; member of editorial committee, *Queen City Heritage,* 1985—, and *Jewish Social Studies,* 1993—; member of editorial board, *American Jewish History,* 1988—, *Religion and American Culture,* 1989—, *Contemporary Jewry,* 1992—, and *Patterns of Prejudice,* 1994—. Contributor of articles and reviews to *Journal of American History, Library Journal, Hadassah Magazine, Gesher, American Jewish History, Moment, Sh'ma, Brandeis Review, Cincinnati Judaism Review, Spectator, Commentary, Midstream, Nation, Jewish Digest, Ethnicity,* and *Tradition;* also contributor to numerous newspapers.

WORK IN PROGRESS: Jewish-Christian Relations in the United States and *American Judaism: A History.*

SIDELIGHTS: A prominent scholar of the Jewish experience in America, Jonathan D. Sarna has written and edited a number of works detailing the history of Jewish communities in the United States. In such books as *Jews in New Haven, The Jews of Cincinnati,* and *The Jews of Boston: Essays on the Occasion of the Centenary (1895-1995) of the Combined Jewish Philanthropies of Greater Boston,* Sarna has examined the history of specific communities where Jewish immigrants to America have settled and prospered.

The Jews of Boston, edited by Sarna and Ellen Smith, is "the first comprehensive history of Boston's Jewish community," as J. Fischel describes it in *Choice.* The book covers some 350 years of Jewish presence in Boston, beginning with the arrival of the first Sephardic scholar from Holland in 1649. The foundation and development of local Jewish cultural and religious institutions is described, as well as the history of the community as a whole and the contributions made by that community to the cultural life of Boston. The book was published by the Combined Jewish Philanthropies of Greater Boston, the first such charitable organization to be founded by Jews in America.

Carol R. Glatt in *Library Journal* calls *The Jews of Boston* "engaging and lucid. . . . While numerous community histories have been published, this volume is in a class by itself—and will set the standard for all future works of this kind." Fischel concludes that *The Jews of Boston* provides "a wonderfully written historical perspective."

Sarna once told *CA:* "My interest in American Jewish history dates back to high school. Before then, I had already become fascinated by America's past (not surprising, considering that I am the first in my family to be born here), and I had been introduced to Jewish history which I learned from my father beginning when I was old enough to listen to stories.

"American Jewish history, which I discovered on my own as a teenager, synthesized these two interests and promised to explain something of the world which I was struggling to understand. Later, I realized that the field was still in its formative stages of development: filled with searching questions waiting to be asked and answered. Here was a frontier worth conquering, and I plunged in head first. As a high school senior I tried to write the history of American anti-Semitism.

"Being at Brandeis University as an undergraduate permitted me to work at the American Jewish Historical Society, located on the Brandeis campus. There I discovered the endless joys of grappling with primary sources, the raw materials of history, and I began to get a grasp of the history field as a whole. By the time I entered Yale, I had learned enough to know that I wanted to explore what seemed to me to be a central theme in American Jewish history: the effort to be American and Jewish at the same time. My study of Mordecai Noah, one of the first American Jews to be prominent in both the secular and Jewish communities, followed naturally, and the title summarizes the thesis: 'Jacksonian Jew' shows attempted synthesis, 'the *two* worlds of Mordecai Noah' demonstrates that tensions remained.

"My work on Mordecai Noah brought me into contact with early nineteenth-century sources of American Jewish history (by contrast, most recent work in the field dates to the post-1881 period), and this remains one important focus of my research. But I also discovered, while working on Noah, that no serious study of the interactions between Jews and non-Jews in this country had ever been written. This seemed to me to be a great challenge, and I have consequently been gathering material and formulating a conceptual scheme, which I hope one day will result in my writing a full-scale historical analysis of Jewish-Christian relations in the United States. In the meantime, I am focusing more narrowly on three issues: the relationship between Christian missionaries and American Jews, the nature of American anti-Semitism, and the culture of American Jews in its non-Jewish context.

"My approach to American Jewish history generally and to Jewish-Christian relations in particular has been heavily influenced by contemporary writings in history, religion, and social science, particularly those dealing with structural tensions, ambivalences, and historical complexity. American Jewish history must, in my opinion, be informed by the latest findings in American history and Jewish history. At the same time, the field must also be making creative strides of its own, from which others should be able to learn. Too often, American Jews have viewed themselves—and been viewed—only narrowly and in the present. One of my challenges as an American Jewish historian is to change this: to forge a field that speaks to current concerns while putting them in broader historical perspective, thereby shedding light on past and present at once."

BIOGRAPHICAL/CRITICAL SOURCES:

PERIODICALS

American Historical Review, April, 1987, p. 522.
Booklist, July, 1995, p. 1840.
Choice, February, 1990, p. 939; April, 1990, p. 1384; October, 1995, p. 356.
Christian Century, October 11, 1989, p. 916.
Journal of American History, March, 1990, p. 1355; September, 1990, p. 687; March, 1994, p. 1458.
Library Journal, November 1, 1989, p. 93; June 15, 1995, p. 81.

*   *   *

SAXON, Alex
See PRONZINI, Bill

SCHERTLE, Alice 1941-

PERSONAL: Born April 7, 1941, in Los Angeles, CA; daughter of Floyd C. (a real estate investor) and Marguerite (a teacher; maiden name, Soucie) Sanger; married Richard Schertle (a general contractor), December 21, 1963; children: Jennifer, Katherine, John. *Education:* University of Southern California, B.S. (cum laude), 1963.

ADDRESSES: Home—La Habra Heights, CA.

CAREER: Highland School, Inglewood, CA, elementary school teacher, 1963-65; writer, 1965—.

AWARDS, HONORS: Parents' Choice Picture Book award, 1989, and Christopher Award, 1990, both for *William and Grandpa;* Parents' Choice Picture Book award, 1991, for *Witch Hazel;* Best Books citation, *School Library Journal,* 1995, for *Advice for a Frog and Other Poems;* Notable Children's Books citations, American Library Association, 1996, for both *Advice for a Frog and Other Poems* and *Down the Road.*

WRITINGS:

FOR CHILDREN

The Gorilla in the Hall, illustrated by Paul Galdone, Lothrop (New York City), 1977.
The April Fool, illustrated by Emily Arnold McCully, Lothrop, 1981.
Hob Goblin and the Skeleton, illustrated by Katherine Coville, Lothrop, 1982.
In My Treehouse, illustrated by Meredith Dunham, Lothrop, 1983.
Bim Dooley Makes His Move, Lothrop, 1984.
Goodnight Hattie, My Dearie, My Love, Lothrop, 1985.
My Two Feet, Lothrop, 1985.
That Olive!, Lothrop, 1986.
Jeremy Bean's St. Patrick's Day, illustrated by Linda Shute, Lothrop, 1987.
Bill and the Google-Eyed Goblins, Lothrop, 1987.
Gus Wanders Off, illustrated by Cheryl Harness, Lothrop, 1988.
That's What I Thought, illustrated by John Wallner, Harper (New York City), 1988.
William and Grandpa, Lothrop, 1989.
Witch Hazel, illustrated by Margot Tomes, Harper, 1991.
Little Frog's Song, illustrated by Leonard Everett Fisher, HarperCollins, 1992.

How Now, Brown Cow? (poems), illustrated by Amanda Schaffer, Browndeer Press (San Diego), 1994.
Down the Road, illustrated by Margot Tomes, HarperCollins, 1994, illustrated by E. B. Lewis, Browndeer Press, 1995.
Maisie, illustrated by Lydia Dabcovich, Lothrop, 1995.
Advice for a Frog and Other Poems, illustrated by Norman Green, Lothrop, 1995.
Keepers, illustrated by Ted Rand, Lothrop, 1996.

"CATHY AND COMPANY" SERIES; ILLUSTRATED BY CATHY PAVIA

Cathy and Company and Mean Mr. Meeker, Children's Press (Chicago), 1980.
Cathy and Company and Bumper the Bully, Children's Press, 1980.
Cathy and Company and the Green Ghost, Children's Press, 1980.
Cathy and Company and the Nosy Neighbor, Children's Press, 1980.
Cathy and Company and the Double Dare, Children's Press, 1980.
Cathy and Company and Hank the Horse, Children's Press, 1980.

SIDELIGHTS: Alice Schertle is the author of a long list of engaging books for the read-aloud set. "I write children's books because I love them—always have," Schertle has stated. "The various seasons of my childhood are identified in my memory with the books that were important to me then. There was the year Mary Poppins floated into the lives of Jane and Michael Banks and me. And my sixth grade year I think I spent with the *Black Stallion* and *King of the Wind.*" As an adult helping to provide such moments to new generations of children, Schertle takes her work seriously; she asserted before the audience of the 1986 Writer's Conference in Children's Literature that "we who write for young children share the considerable responsibility and the wonderful opportunity of showing them that words can paint pictures too."

Schertle was born and raised in Los Angeles, California. "As a child, I could usually be found folded into some unlikely position (as often as not I was in a tree) either reading a story or trying to write one," she once told *CA.* "My writing was always very much influenced by the book I was reading at the moment. *The Wizard of Oz* and *Mary Poppins* inspired me to try my hand at fantasy. *The Black Stallion* led to a rash of horse stories. And after a summer of reading

Nancy Drew books, I churned out mysteries peppered with words like 'sleuth' and 'chum.'

"My early stories did have one thing in common: each got off to a roaring good start and ended abruptly somewhere in the middle. Those beginnings were always fun to write, but when it came to developing the plot and bringing it along to a logical conclusion, the whole thing began to smack of work. It still does, sometimes, but I've found it to be a very satisfying kind of work when the tale is told."

After graduating from the University of Southern California in 1963, Schertle married and began teaching elementary school students in Inglewood, California. Following the birth of her first child two years later, she left her teaching job to devote herself full time to raising what would soon be three children. It wasn't until 1975, when her kids had grown old enough to allow her some free time, that she began writing again. Her first book for children, *The Gorilla in the Hall,* a story about a young boy's vivid imagination, was published in 1975.

While her first read-aloud book received only mixed reviews from critics, Schertle's next book, *The April Fool,* was a winner. An amusing story about a curmudgeonly king's search for a pair of shoes that will not hurt his feet, *The April Fool* was described by *School Library Journal* reviewer Patt Hays as "a satisfying story." For Schertle, the story "almost seem[ed] to write itself, from beginning to end. . . . I started with 'Once there was a king whose feet hurt,' and wrote through to 'the end' with scarcely a hitch along the way."

Schertle has often gotten ideas for stories by keeping track of the activities of her three children. "*In My Treehouse* was inspired by my son's adventures in his own treehouse," she told *CA.* "As a child, I spent a good deal of time in trees, so I took John up on his invitation to join him in his house in a big fruitless mulberry. In fact, I did a lot of writing up there, though I find they're not making treehouses as big as they used to be." With *In My Treehouse,* Schertle translated the experience of being in her son's tree fort into a book about a young boy's love of being apart from the hustle and bustle of the world at large, and about gaining independence. And living with cats as well as children certainly provided Schertle the inspiration for *That Olive!,* a picture book about a mischievous kitty that Lucy Young Clem described in *School Library Journal* as "a hall-of-fame cat story."

Andy spends a lot of time looking for his cat, Olive, and Olive spends a lot of time playing hide-and-seek with Andy. Only the lure of tuna fish sandwiches brings the elusive Olive out into the open and into Andy's arms.

A book about making friends, *Jeremy Bean's St. Patrick's Day* features a first-grader whose excitement about his school's St. Patrick's Day party withers when he arrives at school and realizes that he has forgotten to put on the green sweater he so excitedly planned to wear the night before. The only one without green on, Jeremy is taunted by his classmates and finally hides in a closet, until the school principal discovers him there and loans him the use of his green bow tie for the party. Describing the book's "clear prose and sympathetic observation of small children and their concerns," a *Kirkus Reviews* critic praised *Jeremy Bean's St. Patrick's Day* as a good book about making friends, even with school principals.

The award-winning *William and Grandpa* is another book about the relationship between children and adults, and the friendships that can develop. When Willie comes to stay with his lonely grandfather, the two share a host of simple activities—singing songs, catching shadows, making shaving cream moustaches, and telling old stories about Willie's father—that bond them into a close and loving relationship. "The continuity of generations and the warm relationship between children and the elderly are communicated equally through story and pictures," noted Carolyn Caywood in *School Library Journal.*

Schertle's 1991 book, *Witch Hazel,* tells the story of Johnny, a young boy who is raised by his two grown brothers, Bill and Bart, after the death of his parents. Bill and Bart are farmers who can do without the young boy's help as they work their small farm. But they give their young brother some pumpkin seed and a branch of witch hazel; Johnny plants the seeds and makes a scarecrow lady out of the tree branch, dressing "her" in one of his mother's old dresses. When Bill and Bart leave Johnny and take their crop to market after the fall harvest, Johnny dreams that the scarecrow, "Witch Hazel," has tossed his huge orange pumpkin up into the sky, where it has remained, a full, round harvest moon. "Schertle's style combines poetic prose, terse dialogue, and the tight construction of the folk tale," explains Donnarae MacCann and Olga Richard in *Wilson Library Bulletin.* "You hurry along the plot line, but you stop to wonder at how unobtrusively Schertle turns a drama about an underdog into a poetic experience."

Sensitively capturing the many emotions common to a young read-aloud audience, Schertle continues to write books that are praised by reviewers for their sensitivity and perception. *Little Frog's Song* tells of the adventures and fears of a young frog who is washed from his lily pad during a fierce rain shower and must now find his way home. "The text . . . is a song, rich with images and the rhythm of repetition reminiscent of the writing of Margaret Wise Brown," commented Katie Cerra in *Five Owls*. Equally lyrical is Schertle's *How Now, Brown Cow?*, a collection of poetry. Everything from milking time to a cow's longing to jump the moon is covered in verses that a *Publishers Weekly* reviewer described as "by turns funny and tender, cheeky and thoughtful."

"When I talk to classes of children and tell them about the unfinished stories I used to write, they usually laugh and say they do the same thing," Schertle explained to *CA*. "Sometimes I suggest they try writing the last half of a story first, and then go back and write the beginning. That's something I occasionally do now with my books. Sometimes a funny, or exciting, or ridiculous situation will pop into my head, an idea that would make a good middle of a story. So I'll sit down and write about some characters who find themselves in that situation, though I haven't yet any idea how they got there or what will finally happen to them. Then comes the hard part—writing the beginning and the ending, and making the parts fit together smoothly and logically.

"One of the nicest things about being an author is that it gives me the opportunity to talk to classes of children about books and writing. I always tell them that the best way to learn to write is to read and read and read. It's advice I take myself. There's a tall stack of books precariously balanced on my bedside table, and a good many of them are children's books. One lifetime will never be long enough for me to read all the books I want to read, but it'll be fun to try."

Schertle makes her home on two acres of land in La Habra, California, along with her husband, three children, and "two dogs, four cats, eight chickens, two hives of bees, and assorted birds and butterflies. When I'm not feeding anybody or writing anything, I like to spend my time in my vegetable garden, where I spend a good deal of time trying to persuade the gophers and moles to live somewhere else. I find the garden quiet and peaceful, a good place to germinate seeds and ideas for stories."

BIOGRAPHICAL/CRITICAL SOURCES:

PERIODICALS

Booklist, September 15, 1994, p. 133.
Bulletin of the Center for Children's Books, June, 1977, p. 165; May, 1986.
Five Owls, April, 1992, pp. 76-77.
Horn Book, September/October, 1991, p. 589.
Kirkus Reviews, January 15, 1987, p. 132.
Los Angeles Times Book Review, April, 3, 1983.
New York Times Book Review, May 1, 1977, p. 42.
Publishers Weekly, June 27, 1986, p. 85; January 16, 1987, p. 73; May, 19, 1989, p. 82; September 5, 1994, pp. 110-111.
School Library Journal, October, 1981, p. 135; August, 1986, p. 87; August, 1989, p. 132; July, 1992, p. 64; April, 1995, p. 129.
Wilson Library Bulletin, March, 1992, p. 93.

*   *   *

SCHRAFF, Anne E(laine) 1939-

PERSONAL: Born September 21, 1939, in Cleveland, OH; daughter of Frank C. (a post office accountant) and Helen (a teacher; maiden name, Benninger) Schraff. *Education:* Pierce Junior College, A.A., 1964; San Fernando Valley State College (now California State University, Northridge), B.A., 1966, M.A., 1967. *Politics:* Independent. *Religion:* Roman Catholic. *Avocational interests:* Music, walking, travel, parish work.

ADDRESSES: Home—P. O. Box 1345, Spring Valley, CA 91979.

CAREER: Academy of Our Lady of Peace, San Diego, CA, teacher, 1967-77; writer, 1977—.

MEMBER: California Social Studies Council, Society of Children's Book Writers and Illustrators, International Reading Association.

WRITINGS:

(With brother, Francis N. Schraff) *Jesus Our Brother,* Liguori Publications (Ligouri, MO), 1968.
Black Courage: Sagas of Pioneers, Sailors, Explorers, Miners, Cowboys—Twenty-One Heroes of the American West, Macrae (New York City), 1969.

North Star, Macrae, 1972.

The Day the World Went Away, Doubleday (New York City), 1973.

(With Francis N. Schraff) *The Adventures of Peter and Paul: Acts of the Apostles for the Young,* Liguori Publications, 1978.

Faith of the Presidents, Concordia (St. Louis), 1978.

Tecumseh: The Story of an American Indian, Dillon (Minneapolis), 1979.

Christians Courageous, illustrated by Ned Ostendorf, Concordia, 1980.

(With Francis N. Schraff and Suzanne Hockel) *Learning about Jesus: Stories, Plays, Activities for Children,* illustrated by Jim Corbett, Liguori Publications, 1980.

You Can't Stop Me, So Don't Even Try, Perfection Form, 1980.

Caught in the Middle, Baker Book, 1981.

Who Do You Think You Are, Sam West?, Perfection Learning (Logan, IA), 1986.

Fifty Great Americans, J. Weston Walch, 1986.

The Sorceress and the Book of Spells, Berkley (New York City), 1988.

When a Hero Dies (with workbook), Perfection Learning, 1989.

Sparrow's Treasure (with workbook), Perfection Learning, 1989.

Maitland's Kid (with workbook), Perfection Learning, 1989.

A Song to Sing (with workbook), Perfection Learning, 1989.

The Great Depression and the New Deal: America's Economic Collapse and Recovery, foreword by Elliot Roosevelt, consulting editor, Barbara Silberdick Feinberg, F. Watts (New York City), 1990.

Summer of Shame, Perfection Learning, 1992.

The Darkest Secret, Perfection Learning, 1993.

The Shadow Man, Perfection Learning, 1993.

Women of Peace: Nobel Peace Prize Winners, Enslow Publishers (Springfield, NJ), 1994.

To Slay the Dragon, Perfection Learning, 1995.

Shining Mark, Perfection Learning, 1995.

Bridge to the Moon, Perfection Learning, 1995.

Power of the Rose, Perfection Learning, 1995.

American Heroes of Exploration and Flight, Enslow Publishers, 1996.

Beyond the Cherry Tree, J. Weston Walch, 1996.

Are We Moving to Mars?, John Muir Publications (Santa Fe), 1996.

Colin Powell: Soldier and Patriot, Enslow Publishers, 1997.

Coretta Scott King: Striving for Civil Rights, Enslow Publishers, 1997.

"PASSAGES READING PROGRAM" SERIES

Don't Blame the Children (with workbook), Perfection Form, 1978.

Please Don't Ask Me to Love You (with workbook), Perfection Form, 1978.

An Alien Spring (with workbook), Perfection Form, 1978.

The Vandal (with workbook), Perfection Form, 1978.

The Ghost Boy (with workbook), Perfection Form, 1978.

The Haunting of Hawthorne (with workbook), Perfection Form, 1978.

"RACEWAY DOUBLES READING PROGRAM" SERIES

That's What Friends Are For (with workbook and cassette), Perfection Form, 1981.

The Crook at Cleveland High (with workbook and cassette), Perfection Form, 1981.

The Coward (with workbook and cassette), Perfection Form, 1981.

Escape (with workbook and cassette), Perfection Form, 1981.

The Ghost of Sulphur Ridge (with workbook and cassette), Perfection Form, 1981.

Stranger at Windbreak Mountain (with workbook and cassette), Perfection Form, 1981.

Julia (with workbook and cassette), Perfection Form, 1981.

Jeremy (with workbook and cassette), Perfection Form, 1981.

You'll Never Get Out Alive (with workbook and cassette), Perfection Form, 1981.

The Journey (with workbook and cassette), Perfection Form, 1981.

Time of Terror (with workbook and cassette), Perfection Form, 1981.

Shearwaters (with workbook and cassette), Perfection Form, 1981.

"TALETWISTERS READING PROGRAM" SERIES

Fantastic Fortune, Perfection Form, 1982.

The Storm, Perfection Form, 1982.

The Most Amazing Amusement Park in the World, Perfection Form, 1982.

The Pirate House, Perfection Form, 1982.

Lost in the Wilds, Perfection Form, 1982.

The Wizard's Web, Perfection Form, 1982.

Mystery of Bat Cave, Perfection Form, 1982.

"CHOOSING YOUR WAY" SERIES

Choosing Your Way Through America's Past, illustrated by Steven Meyers, J. Weston Walch (Portland, ME), 1990.

Choosing Your Way Through Ancient History, J. Weston Walch, 1991.

Choosing Your Way Through Medieval History, J. Weston Walch, 1991.

Choosing Your Way Through World's Modern Past, J. Weston Walch, 1991.

"SILVER LEAF" SERIES

The Vampire Bat Girls Club, Perfection Learning, 1991.

El Zorrero and Son, illustrated by Helen Kunze, Perfection Learning, 1991.

In the Web of the Spider, Perfection Learning, 1991.

The Whispering Shell, Perfection Learning, 1991.

The Witch of Banneker School, Perfection Learning, 1991.

Mister Fudge and Missy Moran, Perfection Learning, 1991.

"TAKE TEN BOOKS" SERIES; EDITED BY LIZ PARKER

Nobody Lives Long in Apartment N-2, illustrated by Marjorie Taylor, Saddleback Publishing, 1992.

The Phantom Falcon, illustrated by Marjorie Taylor and Fujiko Miller, Saddleback Publishing, 1992.

Swamp Furies, edited by Liz Parker, illustrated by Marjorie Taylor, Saddleback Publishing, 1992.

"STANDING TALL" MYSTERY SERIES; EDITED BY CAROL NEWELL

As the Eagle Goes, Saddleback Publishing, 1995.

Beyond Glory, Saddleback Publishing, 1995.

Ghost Biker, Saddleback Publishing, 1995.

The Haunted Hound, Saddleback Publishing, 1995.

The Howling House, Saddleback Publishing, 1995.

Shadow on the Snow, Saddleback Publishing, 1995.

Terror on Tulip Lane, Saddleback Publishing, 1995.

The Twin, Saddleback Publishing, 1995.

The Vanished One, Saddleback Publishing, 1995.

Don't Look Now or Ever, Saddleback Publishing, 1995.

"PASSAGES TO SUSPENSE" SERIES

A Deadly Obsession (with workbook and software), Perfection Learning, 1996.

The Frozen Face (with workbook and software), Perfection Learning, 1996.

Like Father, Like Son (with workbook and software), Perfection Learning, 1996.

New Kid in Class (with workbook and software), Perfection Learning, 1996.

Rage of the Tiger (with workbook and software), Perfection Learning, 1996.

OTHER

Also author of interactive fiction for Homecomputer, 1984. Contributor of reviews to *Scholastic Teacher.*

SIDELIGHTS: Anne E. Schraff has written a number of fiction and nonfiction works for young adults, especially reluctant readers. Filled with mystery and suspense, many of her novels address common adolescent themes, such as divorce, friendship, death, and self-perception. Her nonfiction work covers major historical eras and events, along with the lives of both famous and obscure figures from the American west, science, religion, the military, and politics. Schraff once commented, "I've been motivated by a powerful desire to write that made it impossible to do otherwise."

Schraff's novels for reluctant readers include the "Passages Reading Program" series, the "Silver Leaf" series, and the "Taletwisters Reading Program" series. Most of the stories revolve around mysteries or science fiction involving young adult protagonists, such as the *Mystery of Bat Cave* and *Time of Terror.* Other stories focus on common situations or problems young adults face while growing up. For example, *Mister Fudge and Missy Moran* from the "Silver Leaf" series features eleven-year-old Missy who must decide with which divorced parent she wants to live. Schraff once explained that she began the "Passages Reading Program" series "to create exciting stories to interest reluctant teenaged readers who usually didn't read. Some letters from kids have told me my books were the first they ever read straight through. That pleased me greatly."

As a former high school teacher, Schraff has had a lot of experience in working with young adults. She once revealed to *CA* that "the hopes and dreams of hundreds of kids have been the stuff of which my books are made. My characters are composites of people I have known, a bit from one person, a piece from another." Typical of her writing process is *The Haunting of Hawthorne.* "One morning on my way to school," Schraff informed *CA,* "I saw a statue on a pedestal in an antique shop. The statue was of an intense young man in old-fashioned clothes. From that sight I told the story of a courageous high school principal who died rescuing his students in a long ago fire, only to return a hundred years later to save his beloved school and its modern students from the ravages of apathy and violence."

Schraff imparts the same enthusiasm for researching and writing nonfiction as she does fiction. "I love doing research and for me it's like detective work," Schraff once explained to *CA*. "When I come across a historic person who fascinates me, I cannot rest until I've told his or her story." Individual biographies penned by Schraff include *Tecumseh: The Story of an American Indian*, George Washington in *Beyond the Cherry Tree*, and *Colin Powell: Soldier & Patriot*. Inspiration to write *Tecumseh: The Story of an American Indian* came from the author's childhood travels around the country and "the pleasure of meeting many Indians and the special courage of these early Americans," Schraff commented.

Schraff's collective biographies include *Christians Courageous, Women of Peace: Nobel Peace Prize Winners*, and *American Heroes of Exploration and Flight. Women of Peace* tells the stories of nine women from around the world who were awarded the prestigious Nobel Peace Prize for their individual contributions toward social change. Jane Addams, Mother Teresa, and Daw Aung San Suu Kyi are among the prominent women covered. Julie Corsaro, writing for *Booklist*, appreciated Schraff's "clear, accessible [writing] style" and the way she "frankly discusses the tremendous sacrifices made by these women in their pursuit." *American Heroes of Exploration and Flight* features ten men and women, such as the Wright brothers, Sally Ride, and Jacqueline Cochran, who have made significant contributions in their respective fields. "Each bio . . . provides the most engaging highlights of the person's life, beginning with an exciting event to capture the readers' interest," noted Sandra L. Doggett in her review for *School Library Journal*.

In addition to biographies, Schraff has written about American and world history in her "Choosing Your Way" series. She has also written *The Great Depression and the New Deal: America's Economic Collapse and Recovery*, "a readable and objective look at a decade in which 'America would be changed forever,'" as reviewer David A. Lindsey noted in *School Library Journal*. Concerned that today's students don't know about or fully comprehend the Depression, Tom Pearson declared in the *Voice of Youth Advocates* that this work "is an interesting and well-written book which will help make the Great Depression easier for the average junior and senior high school student to understand."

Schraff has two objectives for her work, as she once explained to *CA:* "In my books, I hope to enable my readers to share the magic and adventure of life that I enjoyed in the books I devoured as a child. I also hope to convey the powerful beliefs that life is worth living and goodness is worth achieving."

BIOGRAPHICAL/CRITICAL SOURCES:

PERIODICALS

Booklist, January 1, 1995, p. 813.
School Library Journal, January, 1991, p. 120; September, 1994, p. 235; May, 1996, p. 136.
Voice of Youth Advocates, October, 1990, p. 251-252; June, 1996.

* * *

SCOTT, Warwick
  See TREVOR, Elleston

* * *

SHEPARD, Jim 1956-
  (Scott Eller, a joint pseudonym)

PERSONAL: Born December 29, 1956, in Bridgeport, CT; son of Albert R. and Ida (Picarazzi) Shepard. *Education:* Trinity College (Hartford, CT), B.A., 1978; Brown University, A.M., 1980.

ADDRESSES: Home—132 White Oaks Rd., Williamstown, MA 01267. *Office*—Department of English, Williams College, Williamstown, MA 01267. *Agent*—Liz Darhansoff, 1220 Park Ave., New York, NY 10028.

CAREER: University of Michigan, Ann Arbor, lecturer in creative writing, 1980-83; Williams College, Williamstown, MA, assistant professor, 1983-90, associate professor of English, 1990—; writer.

MEMBER: Phi Beta Kappa.

AWARDS, HONORS: Transatlantic Review Award, Henfield Foundation, 1979, for "Eustace."

WRITINGS:

NOVELS

Flights, Knopf (New York City), 1983.
Paper Doll, Knopf, 1987.
Lights out in the Reptile House, Norton (New York City), 1990.
Kiss of the Wolf, Harcourt (San Diego), 1994.

WITH WILLIAM HOLINGER; UNDER JOINT PSEUDONYM, SCOTT ELLER

Short Season, Scholastic (New York City), 1985.
21st Century Fox, Scholastic, 1989.

"THE JOHNSON BOYS" SERIES FOR YOUNG ADULTS; UNDER JOINT PSEUDONYM, SCOTT ELLER

The Football Wars, Scholastic, 1992.
First Base, First Place, Scholastic, 1993.
That Soccer Season, Scholastic, 1993.
Jump Shot, Scholastic, 1994.

OTHER

(Editor with Ron Hansen) *You've Got to Read This: Contemporary American Writers Introduce Stories That Held Them in Awe,* HarperPerennial (New York City), 1994.
(Editor with Amy Hempel) *Unleashed: Poems by Writer's Dogs,* Crown (New York City), 1995.
Batting against Castro (stories), Knopf, 1996.

Contributor to periodicals, including *Atlantic Monthly, Esquire, Harper's, New Yorker,* and *Redbook.*

SIDELIGHTS: Jim Shepard is the author of several teen sports stories, which he has co-written with William Holinger under the joint pseudonym Scott Eller, but much of his critical acclaim has been received for the novels he has penned solo. *Flights,* his first published work, is the story of a luckless adolescent boy, Biddy Siebert, who lives in Connecticut. Biddy's life is lonely and unpleasant. He seems to have no lasting relationships, and the few friendships he does maintain are undone when families move away. Biddy's home life is hardly more fulfilling, for his parents are given to tormenting each other. Judy, Biddy's mother, is weak and submissive to her husband, the domineering Walt. It is Biddy's father who becomes the catalyst for the boy's great adventure, for he encourages the youth's interest in airplanes. Walt Siebert brings his son books on aircraft and even

takes Biddy along when his friend offers a ride. Biddy, who sees himself as a failure, is inspired by the books and his flight, so he determines to steal the friend's plane and fly. For Biddy the theft and flight seems an opportunity for redemption. *Flights* was praised as a distinguished debut for its author. *Washington Post Book World* critic Tom Paulin deemed Shepard's work "subtle, brilliant, beautifully-wrought fiction." Another reviewer, Frederick Busch, described the novel in the *New York Times Book Review* as "well-made, well-written and splendidly imagined."

Shepard's second novel, *Paper Doll,* is about an American B-17 crew flying dangerous missions over Germany during World War II; it is told from the viewpoint of one of the plane's crew. The author returned to a more young-adult-oriented novel with *Lights out in the Reptile House,* a story about a youth's experiences in a country increasingly dominated by fascism. The novel's hero is fifteen-year-old Karel Roeder, who finds that his school work is becoming more and more devoted to subjects extolling the virtues of fascism and the fascist state. The meek, socially withdrawn Karel, who works at a zoo's reptile house, is in love with the rebellious Leda, who defies the state in its institutionalization and impending execution of her dyslexic brother. While Leda's family is subjected to scrutiny by local authorities, Karel finds that his own home life—he lives with a shiftless father—is disrupted by the state's presence. After Karel's father disappears, a soldier moves into his family's house. This menacing figure, Kehr, soon becomes Karel's personal tormentor, whereupon the hapless hero conspires to flee. As fear and suspicion spread throughout the community, so too does the presence of the fearful Civil Guard. It is this group, which counts the cruel Kehr among its members, that brings about the novel's key episode, the torching of the reptile house.

Since he began writing in the early 1980s, Shepard has been alternating between his solo ventures and his Scott Eller sport stories, which he writes because of his interest in athletics, an interest shared with his coauthor. The sports novels, which feature teens facing typical coming-of-age problems in plots generously peppered with play-by-play game action, are written with a more breezy approach that appeals to teen audiences looking for a light read. The novels Shepard writes under his own name, however, are much more intense, his more recent work, the highly praised *Kiss of the Wolf,* being no exception.

Kiss of the Wolf mixes the terror and intrigue of the thriller novel with the psychological drama of the strained relationship between a boy and his mother. Eleven-year-old Todd and his mother, Joanie, are deeply upset when Todd's father, Gary, abandons them and moves out west. Trying to fill the gap in her life, Joanie begins to see a man named Bruno, a used car salesman and suspicious character who seems to have connections with some pretty shady customers. The real trouble begins, however, on the night of Todd's confirmation party. Speeding off down a parkway after the festivities, Joanie does not see a pedestrian in time and hits him with her car. Horrified by what she has done, Joanie panics and drives off without reporting the incident to the police. Unwilling to confess her crime, she tries to persuade Todd to be quiet about what he has seen, too. "Altar boy Todd is deeply shocked by his mom's behavior and subsequent coverup," related a *Kirkus Reviews* contributor; "their rift is the heart of the novel." This isn't the end of their troubles, however, for it turns out that the dead man was an associate of Bruno's, and that he was supposed to be carrying money that is now missing. Bruno begins to suspect Joanie, and he goes after her with a vengeance. Richard Bausch contended in the *New York Times Book Review* that *Kiss of the Wolf* succeeds not only as a thriller, but on other levels as well: "We go through all the stages of Joanie's guilt, we are privy to all the nuances of feeling between her and the boy as their understanding of what has happened changes them, and we come to see the story as a parable of responsibility and absolution."

BIOGRAPHICAL/CRITICAL SOURCES:

BOOKS

Contemporary Literary Criticism, Volume 36, Gale, 1986, pp. 405-407.

PERIODICALS

America, December 3, 1983, p. 360.
Booklist, August, 1985, p. 1663.
Choice, February, 1986, p. 868.
Detroit News, February 1, 1987.
Kirkus Reviews, November 15, 1993, p. 1419.
Kliatt, November, 1992, p. 6.
Library Journal, July, 1985, p. 93; December, 1993, p. 177.
Newsday, February 18, 1990.
New York Times Book Review, October 9, 1983, pp. 15, 33; October 20, 1985; February 25, 1990, p.

27; February 20, 1994, p. 34; December 4, 1994, p. 71; February 12, 1995, p. 36.
Publishers Weekly, May 17, 1985, p. 98; November 15, 1993, p. 69.
School Library Journal, October, 1985, p. 171; March, 1989, p. 198; August, 1994, p. 184.
Sewanee Review, fall, 1986.
Voice of Youth Advocates, June, 1989, p. 100; October, 1990, p. 257.
Washington Post Book World, September 25, 1983, p. 4; February 11, 1990, p. 4.*

* * *

SHEPHERD, John
  See BALLARD, (Willis) Todhunter

* * *

SHOCKLEY, Ann Allen 1927-

PERSONAL: Born June 21, 1927, in Louisville, KY; daughter of Henry (a social worker) and Bessie (a social worker; maiden name, Lucas) Allen; married William Shockley in 1949 (divorced); children: William Leslie, Tamara Ann. *Education:* Fisk University, B.A., 1948; Western Reserve University (now Case Western Reserve University), M.S.L.S., 1959. *Politics:* Independent.

ADDRESSES: Office—Fisk University Library, 17th Avenue North, Nashville, TN 37203. *Agent*—Carole Abel, 160 West 87th Street, 7D, New York, NY 10024.

CAREER: Delaware State College, Dover, assistant librarian, 1959-60; Maryland State College (now University of Maryland Eastern Shore), Princess Anne, assistant librarian, 1960-66, associate librarian, 1966-69; Fisk University, Nashville, TN, associate professor of library science, 1970—, librarian for public services, 1975—, associate librarian for special collections and university archivist, 1980—. Lecturer at University of Maryland, 1968, and at Vanderbilt University and Jackson State College, both 1973; freelance writer.

MEMBER: Authors Guild, American Library Association (member of Black Caucus), Society of American

Archivists, Tennessee Archivists, Tennessee Literary Arts Association.

AWARDS, HONORS: American Association of University Women short story award, 1962; Fisk University faculty research grant, 1970; University of Maryland Library Administrators Development Institute fellowship, 1974; American Library Association Black Caucus Award, 1975, for editorship of Black Caucus newsletter, and 1992, for professional achievement; First Annual Hatshepsut Award for Literature, 1981; Martin Luther King Black Author's Award, 1982; Susan Koppelman Award, 1988; *OUTlook* Award, 1990, for pioneering contribution to lesbian and gay writing.

WRITINGS:

(With Sue P. Chandler) *Living Black American Authors: A Biographical Directory,* Bowker (New York City), 1973.
Loving Her (novel), Bobbs-Merrill (Indianapolis, IN), 1974.
(Editor with E. J. Josey, and contributor) *A Handbook of Black Librarianship,* Libraries Unlimited (Littleton, CO), 1977.
The Black and White of It (short stories), Naiad Press (Wetherby Lake, MO), 1980.
Say Jesus and Come to Me (novel), Avon (New York City), 1982.
(Editor) *Afro-American Women Writers, 1746-1933: An Anthology and Critical Guide,* G. K. Hall (Boston), 1988.

Short fiction and essays represented in anthologies, including *Impressions in Asphalt,* edited by Ruth T. Sheffey and Eugenia Collier, Scribner, 1969; *Out of Our Lives: A Selection of Contemporary Black Fiction,* edited by Quandra Prettyman Stadler, Howard University Press, 1975; *Lesbian Fiction,* edited by Elly Bulkin, Persephone Press, 1981; *Women Identified Women,* edited by Sandee J. Potter and Trudy E. Darty, Mayfield Publishing, 1982; *Home Girls: A Black Feminist Anthology,* edited by Barbara Smith, Kitchen Table: Women of Color Press, 1983; and *Between Mothers and Daughters,* edited by Susan Koppelman, Feminist Press, 1984.

Contributor of numerous short stories and articles to magazines, newspapers, and professional journals, including *Negro Digest, Umbra, Freedomways, Negro History Bulletin, Essence, Feminary, Azalea,* and *Phylon.* Editor of American Library Association Black Caucus newsletter, 1972-74.

SIDELIGHTS: Ann Allen Shockley is a writer and educator who addresses woman-centered and racial issues through her articles, short stories, and novels. In her capacity as a university librarian Shockley has expanded the number of works by women of color within U.S. public libraries, and these same pioneering efforts have extended to her fiction. "With publication of the novel *Loving Her* in 1974, Shockley earned the distinction of being the first writer to directly confront the strong homophobia prevalent in the black community by making a lesbian of color the main character in a lengthy work of fiction," according to Lynn MacGregor in *Feminist Writers.*

Born in 1927, Shockley graduated from Fisk University in 1948 before pursuing an M.S. in library science from Case Western Reserve University. After graduating in 1959, she spent the next decade working as a teacher and journalist, publishing both short stories and essays in a variety of periodicals. In 1969 she began her career as an archivist and librarian in Fisk University's Special Negro Collection. This position would inspire several of Shockley's nonfiction works, including 1973's *Living Black Authors: A Biographical Directory,* 1977's coeditorship of *Handbook of Black Librarianship,* and 1988's *Afro-American Women Writers (1746-1933): An Anthology and Critical Guide.* She has also published many articles on the subject in periodicals that include *Library Journal, Phylon,* and *Black World.*

Afro-American Women Writers highlights the work of black women from the Colonial Era through the Harlem Renaissance, a period during the early 1920s that witnessed a flowering of black literary talent. The book is divided into four sections: The Colonial period through the Civil War; Reconstruction; 1900 to the Harlem Renaissance; and the Renaissance itself. Including works from such diverse genres as poetry, autobiography, diaries, essays, novels, and short stories, *Afro-American Women Writers* was praised by a *Choice* reviewer as a "valuable resource for researchers and teachers of Afro-American literature" providing "an informative and readable discussion of the many long-forgotten and overlooked black women writers who lived and wrote between 1746 and 1933."

In addition to her nonfiction works, Shockley is also the author of the novels *Loving Her* and *Say Jesus and Come to Me,* as well as *The Black and White of It,* a collection of ten short stories published in 1980. Many of her short fictions focus on racism against African Americans, as well as on "the homophobia and sexism that have combined with racism to single out and oppress African American lesbians," according to MacGregor. "While Shockley has been criticized for depicting lesbian love affairs within her stories somewhat negatively," MacGregor adds, "those of her characters who act rather than react to the expectations of those around them, both black and white, are eventually rewarded by close, loving relationships."

Published in 1974, *Loving Her* was the first novel by a black woman to explore interracial lesbian love, the novel focuses on Renay as she leaves her abusive husband and finds a new relationship with Terry, a white woman of independent means. "As Shockley addresses Renay's personal growth," explained Helen R. Houston in *Dictionary of Literary Biography,* "she addresses the issues of unhappy, abusive, heterosexual relationships along with societal attitudes toward lesbians and black/white relationships. . . . The most tolerant and accepting of [Renay's relationship with Terry] are the homosexuals and the older women, never the 'normal' men."

Say Jesus and Come to Me also focuses on a lesbian relationship, this one between self-serving evangelist Myrtle Black and singer Travis Lee, who eventually begins to accept her lesbian identity. Resounding with echoes of gospel sermonizing, the novel openly satirizes the prejudices against gays and lesbians within the black church. As Shockley would tell Rita B. Dandridge in an interview for *Black American Literature Forum,* the purpose of *Say Jesus and Come to Me* was to "expose the conservatism and snobbishness of the black middle class and academicians, which I see all the time; black male oppression of women; the superior attitudes and opportunism of some white women towards black women in the women's liberation movement."

Pointed in its attack on social prejudices, Shockley's works have sometimes been criticized for their didacticism. However, other reviewers have found much to praise in her open portrayal of formerly taboo issues within the black community. As Houston noted, "Shockley continues to be ahead of her times and yet a part of tradition. Just as her nonfiction has been utilitarian . . . her fiction has been designed to fill the void of subjects not touched or explored and to continue to urge [social] institutions to bring their practice in line with their theories." Through her writing, Shockley has helped to expand the literary foundations in support of future black women writers.

BIOGRAPHICAL/CRITICAL SOURCES:

BOOKS

Dandridge, Rita B., editor, *Ann Allen Shockley: An Annotated Primary and Secondary Bibliography,* Greenwood Press (New York City), 1987.
Dictionary of Literary Biography, Volume 33: *Afro-American Fiction Writers after 1955,* Gale (Detroit), 1984.
Feminist Writers, St. James Press (Detroit), 1996.

PERIODICALS

Black American Literature Forum, spring/summer, 1987.
Choice, January, 1989, p. 802.
Los Angeles Times Book Review, July 4, 1982.

*   *   *

SHOWERS, Paul C. 1910-

PERSONAL: Born April 12, 1910, in Sunnyside, WA; son of Frank L. (a music teacher) and M. Ethelyn (a singer; maiden name, Walker) Showers; married Kay M. Sperry (a psychologist), August 5, 1946 (divorced, 1973); children: Paul Walker, Kate Barger (twins). *Education:* University of Michigan, A.B., 1931; New York University, post-graduate study, 1952-53. *Avocational interests:* Music, social history.

ADDRESSES: Home—101 Alma St., Apt. 408, Palo Alto, CA 94301-1049.

CAREER: Detroit Free Press, Detroit, MI, copyreader, 1937-40; *New York Herald Tribune,* New York City, copy desk staff member, 1940-41; *Sunday Mirror,* New York City, writer and copy editor, 1946; *New York Times,* New York City, member of Sunday department, 1946-76, assistant travel editor, 1949-61, copy editor of Sunday magazine, 1961-76; freelance writer, 1976—. *Military service:* U.S. Army, 1942-45; served on staff of *Yank* (army weekly), editor of Okinawa edition; became staff sergeant.

AWARDS, HONORS: Science award, New Jersey Institute of Technology, 1961, for *Find Out by Touching, The Listening Walk,* and *In the Night,* 1967, for

How You Talk, and 1968, for *A Drop of Blood, Before You Were a Baby,* and *Hear Your Heart.*

WRITINGS:

"LET'S READ AND FIND OUT" SERIES

Find Out by Touching, illustrated by Robert Galster, Crowell (New York City), 1961.

In the Night, illustrated by Ezra Jack Keats, Crowell, 1961.

The Listening Walk, illustrated by Aliki, Crowell, 1961, new edition, HarperCollins (New York City), 1991.

How Many Teeth?, illustrated by Paul Galdone, Crowell, 1962, revised edition illustrated by True Kelley, HarperCollins, 1991.

Look at Your Eyes, illustrated by Galdone, Crowell, 1962, revised edition, illustrated by Kelley, HarperCollins, 1993.

Follow Your Nose, illustrated by Galdone, Crowell, 1963.

Your Skin and Mine, illustrated by Galdone, Crowell, 1965, revised edition illustrated by Kathleen Kuchera, HarperCollins, 1991.

A Drop of Blood, illustrated by Don Madden, Crowell, 1967, revised edition, 1989.

How You Talk, illustrated by Galster, Crowell, 1967, revised edition illustrated by Megan Lloyd, HarperCollins, 1992.

(With wife, Kay M. Showers) *Before You Were a Baby,* illustrated by Ingrid Fetz, Crowell, 1968.

Hear Your Heart, illustrated by Joseph Low, Crowell, 1968.

A Baby Starts to Grow, illustrated by Rosalind Fry, Crowell, 1969.

What Happens to a Hamburger?, illustrated by Anne Rockwell, Crowell, 1970, revised edition, Harper (New York City), 1985.

Use Your Brain, illustrated by Rosalind Fry, Crowell, 1971.

Sleep Is for Everyone, illustrated by Wendy Watson, Crowell, 1974.

Where Does the Garbage Go?, illustrated by Loretta Lustig, Crowell, 1974, revised edition, illustrated by Randy Chewning, HarperCollins, 1994.

Me and My Family Tree, illustrated by Don Madden, Crowell, 1978.

No Measles, No Mumps for Me, illustrated by Harriet Barton, Crowell, 1980.

You Can't Make a Move without Your Muscles, illustrated by Barton, Crowell, 1982.

Ears Are for Hearing, illustrated by Holly Keller, Crowell, 1990.

Showers's works have been translated into Spanish, French, Dutch, Portuguese, and Japanese.

OTHER

Fortune Telling for Fun and Popularity, New Home Library (New York City), 1942, published as *Fortune Telling for Fun,* Newcastle (San Bernardino, CA), 1971, published as *Fortune Telling for Fun and Profit,* Bell (New York City), 1985.

Columbus Day, illustrated by Ed Emberly, Crowell, 1965.

Indian Festivals, illustrated by Lorence Bjorklund, Crowell, 1969.

The Bird and the Stars, illustrated by Mila Lazarevich, Doubleday, 1975.

The Moon Walker, illustrated by Susan Perl, Doubleday, 1975.

A Book of Scary Things, illustrated by Perl, Doubleday, 1977.

Contributor of articles and book reviews to the *New York Times Book Review;* contributor of humorous verse and short articles to *Life, Judge,* and *Ballyhoo.* Showers's manuscripts are included in the Kerlan Collection, University of Minnesota.

ADAPTATIONS: Many of Showers's books have been adapted by Crowell into filmstrips or educational videos.

SIDELIGHTS: Paul C. Showers worked for many years as a newspaperman—his career in journalism spanned thirty-nine years and encompassed newspapers in Detroit and New York City—before becoming an author of children's nonfiction. It was while he was on staff at the *New York Times* that Showers first tried his hand at writing a book for young readers. The year was 1960 and the American Museum of Natural History was preparing to launch a series of science-related books designed for the early grades. Showers's first title for the "Let's Read and Find Out" series, as it came to be called, was *Find Out by Touching;* the book's success encouraged him to continue writing juvenile nonfiction. Showers has since authored numerous other books on science-related topics in the direct and informal style that has won him praise from critics, teachers, and readers alike.

Graduating from the University of Michigan with the dream of becoming an actor and playwright, Showers found only bit parts and short-term work in "summer stock" theater. Discouraged by the lack of significant roles open to him, as well as by his inability to land a producer for his plays, the practical young man eventually realized that a career change was in order. During his years as an actor, he had supplemented his meager earnings by doing freelance writing for several national humor magazines, one of which was *Life*. In 1932 *Life* attempted to expand its circulation by including a novelty crossword feature, a gigantic "cockeyed" puzzle that covered an entire two-page spread. Showers recalled his transition to the field of publishing in an autobiographical essay in *Something about the Author Autobiography Series* (*SAAS*): "I had just sold a standard-size puzzle to *Life* when the decision was made to give the readers the biggest puzzle then on the market, and I was offered the job at fifty dollars a puzzle. At a time when T-bone steak was selling for twenty-eight cents a pound, an income of fifty dollars a month held definite potential, and I accepted." Constructing puzzles quickly became Showers's main occupation. "*Life* called its puzzle 'cockeyed' because the definitions were to be outrageously misleading and, whenever possible, funny. . . . All words had to be in the average reader's vocabulary; none could be used that required a hunt through the dictionary." Filling in the diagram was the easy part: "In a way it was fun. Thinking up the definitions was the dismaying part. Each month I had to rack my brains for suitably cockeyed definitions for a list of between 250 and 300 words. The only one I can now recall was for a four-letter word meaning 'A bender you can take the children on.' The answer was KNEE."

Showers's puzzlemaking career ended in 1936, after *Life* was bought by *Time* magazine. Wishing to remain in the publishing field, he took a job on the copy desk of the *Detroit Free Press* and learned how to edit reporters' written copy and compose headlines. Three years later he left the Midwest and headed to New York City, where a job with the *New York Herald-Tribune* awaited him. After the United States entered World War II, Showers served three years in the Army, returning home in 1945 to get married, raise a family, and work as an editor for the *New York Times*. He would remain at that prestigious newspaper for three decades, finally submitting his resignation on July 4, 1976. The date was not only of significance as the bicentennial anniversary of the signing of the Declaration of Independence; for Showers, it was "a once-in-a-lifetime opportunity to make my personal declaration of independence from the newspaper business to work at my own pace as a free-lance writer. That night the occasion was celebrated with a spectacular fireworks display over the Statue of Liberty in New York Harbor!"

Since his *Find Out by Touching* was published in 1961, Showers has made steady contributions to the efforts of parents and teachers to increase scientific literacy in young children. Through such entertaining books as *How Many Teeth?, Ears Are for Hearing, Follow Your Nose,* and *A Drop of Blood,* he has encouraged children's natural curiosity about the world around them, particularly about how their own body works. *Ears Are for Hearing,* for example, describes the way in which sound waves are translated into signals that the brain can interpret, while *How Many Teeth?* answers youngsters concerns about why their teeth keep falling out. In *The Listening Walk,* first published in 1961 and revised in 1991, Showers frames a discussion of the sense of hearing within the story of a girl and her father going for a walk. 1975's *The Bird and the Stars* uses a folk-rhyme format to introduce children to map reading, while *What Happens to a Hamburger?* explains how the food youngsters eat translates into strong bones, muscles to run fast, and energy enough to play all day. Society's concern with the ecosystem is addressed by Showers in the updated edition of his 1974 book *Where Does the Garbage Go?* A discussion of how garbage is sent on a path to a recycling plant, an incinerator, or to a local landfill site, the book was praised by *School Library Journal* reviewer Judith V. Lechner as "an enjoyable and useful introduction to the subject."

Each of Showers's "Let's Read and Find Out" titles—first published by Crowell—are based on topics suggested by the series' editorial staff. But once he has been given a topic, Showers has always had the freedom to compose his texts in an original manner, particularly taking into account the reading level of his audience. "I am less interested in writing about science than in putting together books that will appeal to kids who are still learning to read a new language (as kids in kindergarten and the first three grades are doing)," he once explained to *CA*.

Although they are elementary-level introductions to science, each of the "Lets Read and Find Out" books actually involves a great deal of work for their author. After thoroughly researching the subject at hand, Showers organizes all the information he has gathered in a way that he believes kids can best understand. "When I finally get down to the typewriter, I work out all sorts of sentence sequences, trying to be clear and specific and, when possible, amusing. It takes a lot of tries to work out a simple text that develops a new idea in [everyday] terms . . . and also repeats word combinations and groupings to give the struggling reader occasional patches of familiar ground," the author explains. He makes it a special point to include basic words and simple sentence structures; otherwise, the "inevitable [scientific] terminology" might discourage curious-minded young readers. Despite the use of elementary vocabulary and grammar, Showers also tries to present the subject matter with some degree of complexity; although a child might be a beginning-level reader, his or her questions usually involve more advanced concepts than a primary-grade reading vocabulary can express. For Showers, the task of bridging this gap between language and concept while keeping his texts interesting and engaging has been the greatest challenge in writing juvenile nonfiction.

In addition to the actual nuts and bolts of writing, being an author has its clandestine side as well: "When working on a book, I try, whenever possible, to eavesdrop on the conversation of kids, paying attention to the kinds of sentences they use when talking among themselves," Showers readily admitted to *CA*. The way four-to-eight year olds talk among themselves was a good measure for Showers in testing the readability of many of his books. "We lived in the suburbs and had a house and a garden with a swing in it," he explained in *SAAS*. "The swing was a magnet for the kindergarten set in our neighborhood, and when I was preparing to write a book, I would spend time on weekends working in the garden and eavesdropping on the swing crowd. . . . Later, when I sat at my typewriter, I would test each sentence I wrote against my recollection of those conversations. Is this how the kids would have phrased it? If I were talking to them instead of writing it down, is this the way I would say it?"

While repetition and simple sentence construction help in keeping beginning readers on track, they can often result in boring, simplistic texts, according to Showers. His success as a children's author can partially be explained by his efforts to add a little humor to his writing. "To relieve the monotony of the endless simplicities, I try mixing in jingles and phonic devices of one sort or another and, whenever possible, attempt to make a little joke," he noted.

Showers's success in writing for young readers has been demonstrated by the enduring popularity of many of his titles; whether his subject has been heredity, sleep, digestion, hearing, preventative medicine, sight, or blood and its function, his texts have remained popular with readers, sometimes running through several editions. Critics have been as enthu-

siastic about the author's nonfiction titles as have readers; in *Booklist* Denise Wilms commends Showers's *Ears Are for Hearing,* calling it "a fine introduction to a common curriculum topic," while *School Library Journal* contributor Denise L. Moll praises the 1989 revision of *A Drop of Blood* as "lively and highly readable, peppered with rhymes that reinforce the text."

Showers's ability to connect with young readers while answering basic questions about science makes his books notable in their field. In sparking the enthusiasm of young children to find out more about the world, he is also reminded of his own "early attempts to get sensible explanations about the world and its mysteries." While he recalled in *SAAS* that "As a small boy, I very soon learned never to expect intelligent answers from the grownups," Showers has made it his business as a children's author to point curious minds in the right direction on the pathway to scientific understanding.

BIOGRAPHICAL/CRITICAL SOURCES:

BOOKS

Children's Literature Review, Volume 6, Gale (Detroit), 1984, pp. 241-249.
Something about the Author Autobiography Series, Volume 7, Gale, 1989, pp. 285-298.

PERIODICALS

Booklist, September 1, 1974, p. 47; April 15, 1980, p. 1210; March 15, 1990, p. 1459; May 1, 1991, p. 1723; January 1, 1993, p. 807; March 15, 1994, p. 1369.
Horn Book, February, 1983, p. 83; September, 1990, p. 631.
Kirkus Reviews, November 15, 1970, p. 1253.
New York Times Book Review, November 7, 1965, p. 56.
School Library Journal, April, 1967, p. 64; August, 1985, p. 57; February, 1990, p. 85; July, 1991, p. 64; August, 1991, p. 162; March, 1992, p. 234; April, 1994, p. 122.

*   *   *

SLADE, Jack
See BALLARD, (Willis) Todhunter

SMITH, Caesar
  See TREVOR, Elleston

* * *

SMITH, Dave
  See SMITH, David (Jeddie)

* * *

SMITH, David (Jeddie) 1942-
  (Smith Cornwell, Dave Smith)

PERSONAL: Born December 19, 1942, in Portsmouth, VA; son of Ralph Gerald (a naval engineer) and Catherine (Cornwell) Smith; married second wife, Deloras Mae Weaver, March 31, 1966; children: (second marriage) David Jeddie, Jr., Lael Cornwell, Mary Margaret. *Education:* University of Virginia, B.A. (with highest distinction), 1965; College of William and Mary, graduate study, 1966; Southern Illinois University, M.A., 1969; Ohio University, Ph.D., 1976.

ADDRESSES: Office—Department of English, Louisiana State University, 43 Allen Hall, Baton Rouge, LA 70803. *Agent*—Timothy Seldes, Russell and Volkening Inc., 50 West 29th Street, New York, NY 10001.

CAREER: High school teacher of French and English, and football coach, in Poquoson, VA, 1965-67; instructor at Night School Divisions, College of William and Mary, Williamsburg, VA, Christopher Newport College, Newport News, VA, and Thomas Nelson Community College, Hampton, VA, all 1969-72; Western Michigan University, Kalamazoo, instructor, 1973-74, assistant professor of English, Cottey College, Nevada, MO, 1974-75; University of Utah, Salt Lake City, associate professor of English and director of creative writing, 1976-80; State University of New York at Binghamton, visiting professor of English, 1980-81; creative writing summer program staff, Bennington College, VT, 1980-87; University of Florida, Gainesville, associate professor of English, 1981-82; Virginia Commonwealth University, Richmond, professor of American Literature 1982-89; Louisiana State University, Baton Rouge, professor of American Literature, 1990—. Editor, *Sou'wester,* 1967-68; editor, founder, and publisher,

Back Door magazine, 1969-79; poetry editor, *Rocky Mountain Review,* 1978-80; poetry columnist, *American Poetry Review,* 1978-82; co-editor, *Southern Review,* 1990—. Has conducted poetry readings at colleges and universities. *Military service:* U.S. Air Force, 1969-72; became staff sergeant.

MEMBER: American Association of University Professors, Modern Language Association, Poetry Society of America, Poetry Society of Virginia, PEN, National Book Critics Circle, Associated Writing Programs, Writers in Virginia, Academy of American Poets, Phi Delta Theta.

AWARDS, HONORS: Fiction prize, *Miscellany,* 1972; Breadloaf Writer's Conference scholarship, summer, 1973; poetry prize, *Sou'wester,* 1973; *Kansas Quarterly Prize,* 1975; Borestone Mountain award, 1976; National Endowment for the Arts fellowship in poetry, 1976, 1981; Academy-Institute Award, American Academy and Institute of Arts and Letters, 1979; David P. Gardner Award, 1979; *Portland Review* poetry prize, 1979; *Prairie Schooner* poetry prize, 1980; Guggenheim fellowship, 1981; Lyndhurst fellowship, 1987-89; Virginia Prize in Poetry, 1988.

WRITINGS:

POETRY; UNDER NAME DAVE SMITH

Bull Island, Back Door Press (Poquoson, VA), 1970.
Mean Rufus Throw Down, Basilisk Press (Fredonia, NY), 1973.
The Fisherman's Whore, Ohio University Press (Athens, OH), 1974.
Drunks, Sou'wester (Edwardsville, IL), 1974.
Cumberland Station, University of Illinois Press (Urbana), 1977, reprinted in *Floating on Solitude,* University of Illinois Press, 1996.
In Dark, Sudden with Light, Croissant & Co. (Athens, OH), 1977.
Goshawk, Antelope, University of Illinois Press, 1979, reprinted in *Floating on Solitude,* University of Illinois Press, 1996.
Homage to Edgar Allan Poe, Louisiana State University Press (Baton Rouge), 1981.
Apparitions, Lord John (Northridge, CA), 1981.
Blue Spruce, Tamarack Editions (Syracuse, NY), 1981.
Dream Flights, University of Illinois Press, 1981, reprinted in *Floating on Solitude,* University of Illinois Press, 1996.
In the House of the Judge, Harper & Row (New York City), 1983.

Gray Soldiers, Stuart Wright (Winston-Salem, NC), 1983.

Southern Delights: Poems and Stories, Croissant & Co., 1984.

The Roundhouse Voices: Selected and New Poems, Harper & Row (New York City), 1985.

Three Poems, Words Press, 1988.

Cuba Night, Morrow (New York City), 1990.

Night Pleasures: New and Selected Poems, Bloodaxe Books (Newcastle upon Tyne, UK), 1992.

Fate's Kite: Poems 1991-1995, Louisiana State University Press, 1995.

Floating on Solitude: Three Volumes of Poetry, University of Illinois Press, 1996.

OTHER; UNDER NAME DAVE SMITH

Onliness (novel), Louisiana State University Press, 1981.

(Editor) *The Pure Clear Word: Essays on the Poetry of James Wright,* University of Illinois Press, 1982.

Local Assays: On Contemporary American Poetry, University of Illinois Press, 1985.

(Editor, with David Bottoms) *The Morrow Anthology of Younger American Poets,* Morrow, 1985.

(Editor and author of introduction) *The Essential Poe,* Ecco Press, 1990.

(Editor) *New Virginia Review,* New Virginia Review, Inc., 1986.

(Editor) *New Virginia Review Anthology Four,* New Virginia Review, Inc., 1986.

Poems represented in many anthologies, including *I Love You All Day: It Is That Simple,* edited by Philip Dacey and Gerald Knoll, Abbey Press, 1970, *Yearbook of Modern Poetry,* edited by Jeanne Hollyfield, Young Publications, 1971, *New Voices in American Poetry,* edited by Dave Allen Evans, Winthrop, 1973, *Heartland II,* edited by Lucien Stryk, Northern Illinois University Press, 1975, and *American Poets in 1976,* edited by William Heyen, Bobbs-Merrill, 1976. *The Colors of Our Age* was released as a sound recording, Watershed, 1988.

Contributor, sometimes under pseudonym Smith Cornwell, of short stories, poems, articles, and reviews to numerous popular and poetry magazines, including *American Poetry Review, Anteus, Nation, Southern Review, Shenandoah, New Yorker, Poetry, Poetry Northwest, Prairie Schooner,* and *Kenyon Review.*

SIDELIGHTS: David Smith, wrote friend and poet Robert DeMott in *Dictionary of Literary Biography,* is "the legitimate heir to the Romantic tradition in America." Like the Transcendentalists Henry David Thoreau and Ralph Waldo Emerson, Smith sees writing poetry as a redemptive act, as he told H. A. Maxon in *The Sam Houston Literary Review.* "In my life, poetry was very near a conversion. It was like a religious conviction had come into my life." Like Robert Penn Warren and James Dickey and other Southern poets, his poems tend to explore the Southern narrative heritage, including the occasionally grotesque, and express a distinct regional sense of place, such as the Virginia tidewater region in which many of his early poems are set, Maryland in *Cumberland Station,* and Wyoming and Utah in *Goshawk, Antelope.* The twenty books of poems that Smith has published range from full-length collections by university and New York publishers to limited edition chapbooks by small presses, an indication of the kind of broad-range appeal he has both to publishers and readers.

Smith's first book, *Bull Island* (1970), a limited edition chapbook published by his own Back Door Press, is structured around a journey back to the tidewater Virginia of his childhood, searching for a father figure. *Mean Rufus Throw Down* (1973), his second small press book, shows the poet beginning to explore domestic subjects as well as regional ones, alternating narrative poems with short imagist poems. *The Fisherman's Whore,* 1974, heralds both Smith's publication through university presses and notice by critics. Michael Heffernan, writing in *Commonweal,* praised its "fusion of poetry and prose," and Helen Vendler, in *Parnassus,* called Smith "a poet already capable of great control."

Cumberland Station (1977), the book that brought Smith substantial critical notice, is a circular quest in three movements: the first part, starting on the Virginia coast, concerns family origin and the historical past as he travels to the Cumberland, Maryland railroad station where his grandfather was a ticket-seller; the second part has the poet in exile, encountering midwest states, working hard to decode the parables they teach; and the final part brings the poet home to the coast, where, as Robert DeMott wrote, "the linked patterns of flowing images—boats, water, fish, rivers, music—capture the processional quality of Smith's vision." Dana Wier, in *Hollins Critic,* praised the book as "a celebration" and "a rich presentation of America's people, culture and landscape."

"It was not until his fourth collection, *Goshawk, Antelope,*" wrote Robert Phillips in *Hudson Review,* "that Dave Smith began to receive the wide critical attention his work deserves." The book, divided into four sections of about a dozen poems each, presents a number of poems that take on the starkness of the western landscape of Utah where Smith was teaching during this period. This collection, noted Michael McFee in *Parnassus,* shows "the mature Dave Smith," whose poems offer the "ambitious wordage" of "a poet of community and continuity" and "the complexity of shared experience."

In 1981, Smith published two new books. *Homage to Edgar Allan Poe* is a collection of brief poems, many less than a page, re-exploring family and sense of place, and the title sequence, in six sections, writes Phillips, "entwines Poe's personal history with Smith's." *Dream Flights* spreads seventeen poems that, as Thomas Swiss pointed out in *Sewanee Review,* "work through association, a complex linking that succeeds because of Smith's gift for creating a rich texture and backdrop for the action." *In The House of the Judge* (1983) received mixed reviews. Fred Chappell, in *Western Humanities Review,* criticized Smith's "heavy veneer of false elegance," and charged that "many of the lines are burdened with pronouns having unclear antecedents." Swiss, however, noted that "Smith is engaged with the literal and symbolic geographies of place," offering "less violence" and "less physical drama," so that this book has "a gentler touch." Following publication of *The Roundhouse Voices: Selected and New Poems* (1985), a volume which Helen Vendler in *New Yorker* called "a book too austerely thinned to give an adequate overview of his twenty years of poetic production," Smith published *Cuba Night.* Vendler singled out the book for its "Southern-gothic themes—family, memory, fear, fate, sex, violence," and indicated that, although Smith "walks a difficult line between the indignant and the overripe, . . . he manages a balance between the natural wrongness of life and the genuine rightness of art." Kathleen Norris, writing in *Library Journal,* called it "a deeply reflective, elegiac work full of . . . pleasurable music." *Night Pleasures: New and Selected Poems* published in 1993, was Smith's first collection to appear in Britain.

Smith once told *CA:* "Whatever I write in the future will have to conform to two principles: I want poetry whose clarity is pronounced and resonant and I want poetry whose validity will be proved to the extent the poems embody the true, durable, and felt experience of emotional life."

BIOGRAPHICAL/CRITICAL SOURCES:

BOOKS

Contemporary Authors Autobiography Series, Volume 7, Gale (Detroit), 1988.
Contemporary Literary Criticism, Gale, Volume 22, 1982, Volume 42, 1987.
Dictionary of Literary Biography, Volume 5: *American Poets since World War II,* Gale, 1980.
Evans, David Allan, editor, *New Voices in American Poetry,* Winthrop (Boston), 1973.
Hales, Corrine, editor, *Contemporary Poets, Dramatists, Essayists, and Novelists of the South,* Greenwood Press, 1994.
Harris, Alex, editor, *A World Unsuspected,* University of North Carolina Press, 1987.
Turner, Alberta, editor, *Poets Teaching,* Longman (New York City), 1980.
Vendler, Helen, *Part of Nature, Part of Us,* Harvard University Press, 1980, pp. 289-302.
Weigl, Bruce, editor, *The Giver of Morning: On the Poetry of Dave Smith,* Thunder City Press (Birmingham, AL), 1982.

PERIODICALS

America, July 10, 1982, p. 36; December 15, 1990, p. 490.
American Book Review, May, 1982, p. 7.
American Literature, December, 1982, p. 632; October, 1986, p. 481.
American Poetry Review, November, 1977, p. 46; January/February, 1978, pp. 15-19; January/February, 1982, p. 32-35.
Antioch Review, spring, 1982, p. 225.
Booklist, September 15, 1979, p. 89; June 15, 1981, p. 1330; November 115, 1981, p. 427; September 15, 1981, p. 88; December 15, 1982, p. 550; January 15, 1986, p. 728.
Chicago Review, autumn, 1977, pp. 123-126.
Choice, January, 1975, p. 1635; May, 1977, p. 379; January, 1982, p. 630; November, 1982, p. 430; January 1986, p. 745.
College Literature, spring, 1984, p. 200.
Commonweal, August 15, 1975, p. 346; January 6, 1978, p. 23; December 7, 1979, p. 701; March 11, 1983, p. 157.
Denver Quarterly, autumn, 1983, p. 123-138.
Georgia Review, spring, 1980, pp. 202-212; fall, 1982, p. 675; winter, 1985, p. 849.
Hollins Critic, October, 1977, p. 18.
Hudson Review, winter, 1974-75, pp. 611-614; spring, 1978, p. 211; summer 1980, p. 301; au-

tumn, 1981, p. 420; autumn, 1983, p. 589; summer, 1986, p. 345; winter, 1990, p. 598.

Journal of American Studies, August, 1983, p. 295.

Kenyon Review, spring, 1986, p. 113.

Kliatt Young Adult Paperback Book Guide, winter, 1982, p. 28.

Library Journal, February 15, 1974, p. 492; September 1, 1974, p. 2070; December 1, 1976, p. 2494; August, 1979, p. 1570; June 1, 1981, p. 1226; September 1, 1981, p. 1636; October 15, 1981, p. 2050; June 1, 1982, p. 1098; December 15, 1982, p. 2342; March 15, 1984, p. 598; August, 1985, p. 98; November 1, 1985, p. 100; February 1, 1990, p. 87; December, 1995, p. 116.

Nation, December 22, 1984, p. 687; October 5, 1985, p. 320.

New Criterion, December, 1985, p. 27-33.

New England Review, spring, 1982, p. 489; winter, 1983, p. 348; fall, 1991, p. 149.

New Leader, December 14, 1981, p. 16.

New Statesman and Society, July 30, 1993, p. 40.

New Yorker, June 30, 1980, p. 96; April 2, 1990, pp. 113-116.

New York Review of Books, November 7, 1985, p. 53.

New York Times Book Review, November 15, 1981, p. 14; April 18, 1982, p. 15; February 13, 1983, p. 15; January 12, 1986, p. 346.

North American Review, spring, 1977, p. 75; spring, 1980, p. 72.

Parnassus, fall-winter, 1975, pp. 195-205; spring-summer, 1977; fall-winter, 1980, p. 102; spring, 1983, p. 58; fall-winter, 1984, p. 154-182.

Poetry, August 1982, p. 293; February, 1984, p. 304; March, 1986, p. 346.

Poetry in Review, fall-winter, 1980, pp. 102-110.

Poetry Review, January-February, 1978, pp. 15-19.

Prairie Schooner, spring, 1974, p. 92; summer, 1984, p. 100.

Publishers Weekly, November 1, 1976, p. 73; June 25, 1979, p. 121; June 12, 1981, p. 50; August 7, 1981, p. 77; August 14, 1981, p. 50; December 17, 1982, p. 73; August 9, 1985, p. 72; January 5, 1990, p. 67; October 23, 1995, p. 64.

Sam Houston Literary Review, November, 1977, pp. 64-74.

Saturday Review, September 16, 1978, p. 42.

Sewanee Review, summer, 1980, p. 474; fall, 1982, p. 612; summer, 1983, p. 483; fall, 1983, p. 83; winter, 1989, pp. 543-555; spring, 1992, p. 311.

Southern Humanities Review, winter, 1987, p. 94; winter, 1991, p. 99.

Southern Review, spring, 1990, p. 456.

Sou'wester, spring-summer, 1974, pp. 56-64.

Stand, summer, 1988, p. 72; winter, 1993, pp. 77-80.

Sulfur, March, 1986, p. 175.

Three Rivers Poetry Journal, spring, 1977, pp 6-9.

Times Literary Supplement, November 27, 1981, p. 1388; May 22, 1987, p. 557; April 30, 1993, p. 23.

TriQuarterly, fall, 1985, p.p. 245-258.

Village Voice, May 5, 1980, p. 36; November 25, 1981, p. 47.

Virginia Quarterly Review, spring, 1980, p. 62; spring, 1982, p. 60; autumn, 1983, p. 135; winter, 1986, p. 27; summer, 1990, p. 99.

Washington Post Book World, October 4, 1981, p. 4; April 3, 1983, p. 10; January 5, 1986, p. 6.

Western Humanities Review, autumn, 1977, p. 371; autumn, 1983, p. 251; spring, 1987, p. 87.

Wilson Quarterly, winter, 1981, p. 158.

Yale Review, March, 1977, p. 407.*

—Sketch by Robert Miltner

*   *   *

SPELLMAN, Roger G.
See COX, William R(obert)

*   *   *

SPINNER, Stephanie 1943-

PERSONAL: Born November 16, 1943, in Davenport, IA; daughter of Ralph (in business) and Edna (Lowry) Spinner. *Education:* Bennington College, B.A., 1964. *Avocational interests:* Horses, painting, travel.

ADDRESSES: Home—Hickory Lane, Pawling, NY 12564.

CAREER: Children's book editor.

AWARDS, HONORS: Texas Bluebonnet Award, 1991, for *Aliens for Breakfast.*

WRITINGS:

Water Skiing and Surfboarding, Golden Press (New York City), 1968.

First Aid, Golden Press, 1968.

(Adaptor) *Popeye: The Storybook Based on the Movie,* Random House (New York City), 1980.

(Adaptor) *Dracula,* illustrated by Jim Spence, Random House, 1982.

Raggedy Ann and Andy and How Raggedy Ann Was Born, Bobbs-Merrill (Indianapolis), 1982.

(Adaptor) Carlo Lorenzini, *The Adventures of Pinocchio,* illustrated by Diane Goode, Random House, 1983.

The Mummy's Tomb, Bantam (New York City), 1985.

(With Jonathan Etra) *Aliens for Breakfast,* illustrated by Steve Bjorkman, Random House, 1988.

(With Jonathan Etra) *Aliens for Lunch,* illustrated by Steve Bjorkman, Random House, 1991.

Little Sure Shot: The Story of Annie Oakley, illustrated by Jose Miralles, Random House, 1993.

Aliens for Dinner, Random House, 1994.

(With Ellen Weiss) *Gerbilitis,* illustrated by Steve Bjorkman, HarperCollins (New York City), 1996.

(With Weiss) *Sing, Elvis, Sing,* illustrated by Steve Bjorkman, HarperCollins, 1996.

(With Weiss) *Born to Be Wild,* HarperCollins, 1997.

(With Weiss) *Bright Lights, Little Gerbil,* HarperCollins, 1997.

(With Weiss) *The Bird Is the Word,* HarperCollins, 1997.

EDITOR

Rock Is Beautiful: An Anthology of American Lyrics, 1953-1968, Dell (New York City), 1969.

Feminine Plural: Stories by Women about Growing Up, Macmillan (New York City), 1972.

Live and Learn: Stories about Students and Their Teachers, Macmillan, 1973.

Motherlove: Stories by Women about Motherhood, Dell, 1978.

SIDELIGHTS: Stephanie Spinner has written and edited a wide variety of works for both children and young adults. Her own books range from collections of essays on feminist topics to retellings of classic stories and humorous original chapter books. She has also edited the works of several prominent children's authors.

Spinner collaborated with Jonathan Etra on a series of three books about Richard Bickerstaff, a young science-fiction fan, and Aric, a tiny alien secret agent. The two characters meet for the first time in *Aliens for Breakfast,* published in 1988. In this story, Richard tries the new Alien Crisp cereal and finds Aric in his bowl. The alien soon informs his friend that they must work together to rid the world of a common enemy—a bad alien disguised as the cool new kid at

Richard's school. The heroes soon embark on a frantic search to find the one earthling household object that will prevent the evil alien from replicating himself and taking over the world. A *Booklist* reviewer praised the book for its "clever plotting, right-on characterization, and . . . jet-propelled pace."

In the first sequel, 1991's *Aliens for Lunch,* the greedy occupants of a distant planet have used up their resources of XTC-1000, the mysterious substance which makes desserts taste delicious. They threaten to steal the Earth's supply and doom the planet to eating bland desserts unless Richard and Aric can stop them. By chance, Richard stumbles upon the secret weapon that can repel the evil invaders: the celery sticks he always carries in his pocket. A writer for *Kirkus Reviews* appreciated the book's "brisk, imaginatively conceived action" and "rib-tickling dialogue," while Hazel Rochman noted in *Booklist* that "this is a story that will show smart new readers that books are fun." The intergalactic adventures of Richard and Aric continue in *Aliens for Dinner,* published in 1994, when they must save the Earth from being turned into a toxic amusement park by aliens that thrive on pollution.

BIOGRAPHICAL/CRITICAL SOURCES:

PERIODICALS

Booklist, May 15, 1978, p. 1478; February 15, 1984, p. 856; January 15, 1989; June 1, 1991; February 1, 1994, p. 98.

Bulletin of the Center for Children's Books, May 1973, p. 145; April 1984.

Kirkus Reviews, September 15, 1972, p. 1106; May 1, 1991.

Publishers Weekly, January 1, 1973, p. 57.

School Library Journal, August, 1982, p. 112; March, 1989; February 1994, p. 98.

*   *   *

SPRUILL, Steven G(regory) 1946-

PERSONAL: Born April 20, 1946, in Battle Creek, MI; son of John Chester (an engineer) and Arleen (a food service manager; maiden name, Camp) Spruill; married Nancy Lyon (a statistician), August 24, 1969. *Education:* Andrews University, B.A., 1968; Catholic University of America, M.A., 1979, Ph.D., 1981.

Avocational interests: Oil painting, piano playing, choral singing.

ADDRESSES: Home—123 North Park Dr., Arlington, VA 22203. *Agent*—Al Zuckerman, 21 West 26th St., New York, NY 10010.

CAREER: Hazleton Laboratories, Inc., Falls Church, VA, technical writer and editor, 1969-73; Washington Veterans Administration Hospital, Washington, DC, psychology intern, 1978-79; Mount Vernon Community Mental Health Center, Springfield, VA, psychology intern at Springfield Outpatient Unit, 1979-80; full-time writer, 1981—.

MEMBER: World Science Fiction Association (charter member, 1977—), Science Fiction and Fantasy Writers of America.

WRITINGS:

Keepers of the Gate (science fiction novel), Doubleday (New York City), 1977.
The Psychopath Plague (science fiction novel), Doubleday, 1978.
Hellstone (horror novel), Playboy, 1980.
The Janus Equation (science fiction novella), Dell (New York City), 1980.
The Imperator Plot (science fiction novel), Doubleday, 1983.
The Genesis Shield (novel), Tor (New York City), 1985.
The Paradox Planet (science fiction novel), Doubleday, 1988.
Painkiller (novel), St. Martin's (New York City), 1990.
Before I Wake (novel), St. Martin's, 1992.
My Soul to Take (novel), St. Martin's, 1994.
Rulers of Darkness (novel), St. Martin's, 1995.
Daughter of Darkness (novel), St. Martin's, 1996.

Also contributor of short stories to periodicals.

SIDELIGHTS: Steven Spruill's novels, which range from science fiction to thrillers, include elements of horror, suspense, and mystery. Common to his work is an attempt to present believable viewpoint characters grappling with extraordinary circumstances. Spruill comments in the *St. James Guide to Science Fiction Writers:* "Most of my novels are concerned with the bizarre, the complicated, the strange, and the psychological."

Spruill combines science fiction and mystery in his Elias Kane books, a series Arthur O. Lewis, writing for *St. James Guide to Science Fiction Writers,* calls "well-plotted, well-written and entertaining." The novels follow the adventures of Intergalactic Detective Elias Kane and his loyal sidekick, the alien Pendrake. Kane, a former Navy lieutenant, is portrayed as a highly-educated man possessing a photographic memory but subject to human foibles. Critics have noted a similarity between these works and Isaac Asimov's Elijah Baley series.

In the first two books, *The Psychopath Plague* and *The Imperator Plot,* Kane successfully uncovers the truth about a growing contamination that inspires people to violence and loses his true love while attempting to thwart an assassination plot. In *Paradox Planet,* the third installment in the series, Kane confronts his nemesis, ex-viceroy Richard Du Morgan. Narrow escapes, attempted murder, and puzzles follow one another "slickly in somewhat predictable fashion," according to a *Publishers Weekly* critic. A writer for *Kirkus Reviews,* however, compliments Spruill on "solid plotting and plenty of action."

Spruill began his transition to contemporary thrillers with *Painkiller,* a popular Literary Guild and Doubleday Book Club selection that met with mixed reviews. More successful was *Before I Wake,* a medical suspense novel called "first rate" by a reviewer for *Publishers Weekly.* In his thriller *My Soul to Take* Spruill explores the concept of microchip implantation to restore sight. Unexpected side effects develop for some individuals who begin to see future events. Ralph DeLucia, writing for *Library Journal,* finds fault with Spruill's characterization but allows that the book is "unusual and provocative." A writer for *Booklist* concurs and goes on to say that the author "knows how to portray people and develop a story naturally."

With *Rulers of Darkness* and *Daughter of Darkness* Spruill puts a twist on the vampire craze sweeping the horror and fantasy genres by calling his vampiric mutants "hemophages" and offering a scientific explanation for their unusual characteristics. An "intelligent and suspenseful thriller," according to Eric W. Johnson, writing for *Library Journal, Rulers of Darkness* follows Merrick Chapman, a detective in the near future with a secret—he is a hemophage himself, working to find and trap others of his kind. In this case, he is trailing the homicidal hemophage Zane, revealed to be Chapman's own son. A reviewer for

Publishers Weekly calls the novel's plot "intriguingly complex," and Lewis sums up the results of Spruill's labor as "an absorbing page-turner."

While some readers may regret Spruill's move from science fiction to suspenseful medical thrillers, Lewis points out that his entry into this field has in no way lessened the author's knack for telling "a good story." Praised by critics for his ability to utilize his professional expertise in his fiction, Steven Spruill deserves continued attention, according to Lewis.

Of his own work, Spruill has told *CA:* "As a novelist I'd like to do in another way what I attempt to do as a psychotherapist: to free a person for a few hours from the unhappier side of his life and turn him on to the constructive power of his mind."

BIOGRAPHICAL/CRITICAL SOURCES:

BOOKS

St. James Guide to Science Fiction Writers, St. James Press (Detroit), 1996.

PERIODICALS

Booklist, February 1, 1994, p. 995.
Kirkus Reviews, May 1, 1988, p. 659; December 15, 1993, p. 1549.
Library Journal, January, 1994, p. 165; July, 1995, p. 124.
Publishers Weekly, November 28, 1980, p. 47; May 6, 1988, p. 98; October 11, 1993, p. 84; December 13, 1993, p. 64; May 22, 1995, p. 47.

—Sketch by Meg Mac Donald

*   *   *

STAGGE, Jonathan
  See WHEELER, Hugh (Callingham)

*   *   *

STEVENSON, John P.
  See GRIERSON, Edward

STEWART, Mary (Florence Elinor) 1916-

PERSONAL: Born September 17, 1916, in Sunderland, Durham, England; daughter of Frederick Albert (a Church of England clergyman) and Mary Edith (Matthews) Rainbow; married Frederick Henry Stewart, 1945. *Education:* University of Durham, B.A. (first class honours), 1938, M.A., 1941. *Avocational interests:* Music, painting, the theatre, gardening.

ADDRESSES: Agent—c/o William Morrow & Co., 105 Madison Ave., New York, NY 10016.

CAREER: University of Durham, Durham, England, lecturer, 1941-45, part-time lecturer, 1948-55; writer, 1954—. *Military service:* Royal Observer Corps, World War II.

MEMBER: PEN, Royal Society of Arts (fellow).

AWARDS, HONORS: British Crime Writers Association Silver Dagger Award, 1961, for *My Brother Michael;* Mystery Writers of America Edgar Award, 1964, for *This Rough Magic;* Frederick Niven Literary Award, 1971, for *The Crystal Cave;* Scottish Arts Council Award, 1975, for *Ludo and the Star Horse;* fellow, Newnham College, Cambridge, 1986.

WRITINGS:

Madam, Will You Talk? (also see below), Hodder & Stoughton (London), 1955.
Wildfire at Midnight (also see below), Appleton (New York City), 1956.
Thunder on the Right, Hodder & Stoughton, 1957.
Nine Coaches Waiting (also see below), Hodder & Stoughton, 1958.
My Brother Michael (also see below), Hodder & Stoughton, 1960.
The Ivy Tree (also see below), Hodder & Stoughton, 1961, Mill (New York City), 1962.
The Moon-Spinners (also see below), Hodder & Stoughton, 1962.
Three Novels of Suspense (contains *Madam, Will You Talk?, Nine Coaches Waiting,* and *My Brother Michael*), Mill, 1963.
This Rough Magic (Literary Guild selection; also see below), Mill, 1964.
Airs above the Ground (also see below), Mill, 1965.
The Gabriel Hounds (Doubleday Book Club selection; *Reader's Digest* Condensed Book Club selection; Literary Guild alternate selection; also see below), Mill, 1967.

The Wind Off the Small Isles, Hodder & Stoughton, 1968.

The Spell of Mary Stewart (contains *This Rough Magic, The Ivy Tree,* and *Wildfire at Midnight*), Doubleday (New York City), 1968.

Mary Stewart Omnibus (contains *Madam, Will You Talk?, Wildfire at Midnight,* and *Nine Coaches Waiting*), Hodder & Stoughton, 1969.

The Crystal Cave (Literary Guild selection; also see below), Morrow (New York City), 1970.

The Little Broomstick (juvenile), Brockhampton Press (Leicester, England), 1971.

The Hollow Hills (also see below), Morrow, 1973.

Ludo and the Star Horse (juvenile), Brockhampton Press, 1974.

Touch Not the Cat (also see below), Morrow, 1976.

Triple Jeopardy (contains *My Brother Michael, The Moon-Spinners,* and *This Rough Magic*), Hodder & Stoughton, 1978.

Selected Works (contains *The Crystal Cave, The Hollow Hills, Wildfire at Midnight,* and *Airs above the Ground*), Heinemann (London), 1978.

The Last Enchantment (Literary Guild selection; also see below), Morrow, 1979.

A Walk in Wolf Wood, Morrow, 1980.

Mary Stewart's Merlin Trilogy (contains *The Crystal Cave, The Hollow Hills,* and *The Last Enchantment*), Morrow, 1980.

The Wicked Day, Morrow, 1983.

Mary Stewart—Four Complete Novels (contains *Touch Not the Cat, The Gabriel Hounds, This Rough Magic,* and *My Brother Michael*), Avenel Books (New York City), 1983.

Thornyhold, Morrow, 1988.

Frost on the Window and Other Poems, Morrow, 1990.

The Stormy Petrel, Morrow, 1991.

The Prince and the Pilgrim, Morrow, 1995.

Rose Cottage, Morrow, 1997.

Also author of radio plays, *Lift from a Stranger, Call Me at Ten-Thirty, The Crime of Mr. Merry* and *The Lord of Langdale,* produced by British Broadcasting Corporation, 1957-58. Stewart's works have been translated into sixteen languages, including Hebrew, Icelandic, and Slovak. The National Library of Scotland houses Stewart's manuscript collection.

ADAPTATIONS: The Moon-Spinners was filmed by Walt Disney in 1964.

SIDELIGHTS: Mary Stewart's writing career divides into two distinct parts. In her first period, according to Kay Mussell in the *St. James Guide to Crime and Mystery Writers,* Stewart "wrote a remarkable series of 10 popular novels of romantic suspense. . . . In her later phase, beginning in the late 1960s, Stewart's novels have been concerned with history and frequently with the occult. Her best-known work from this period is her four-volume series about King Arthur and Merlin." In the words of a *National Observer* critic, Stewart writes "like a magician, she conjures exotic moods and mysteries from mere words, her only aim to entertain."

Stewart explains in an article for *Writer* magazine: "I am first and foremost a teller of tales, but I am also a serious-minded woman who accepts the responsibilities of her job, and that job, if I am to be true to what is in me, is to say with every voice at my command: 'We must love and imitate the beautiful and the good.' It is a comment on our age that one hesitates to stand up and say this aloud."

While "predictability" is not a quality most authors would strive for, a *Christian Science Monitor* reviewer feels that this very trait is the secret of Stewart's success. Prior to 1970, for example, her plots followed a fairly consistent pattern of romance and suspense set in vividly depicted locales such as Provence, the Isle of Skye, the Pyrenees, Delphi, and Lebanon. Furthermore, notes the *Christian Science Monitor* reviewer, "Mrs. Stewart doesn't pull any tricks or introduce uncomfortable issues. Attractive, well-brought-up girls pair off with clean, confident young men, always on the side of the angels. And when the villains are finally rounded up, no doubts disturb us—it is clear that the best men have won again." The heroine of these stories is always "a girl displaying just the right combination of strengths and weaknesses. She may blunder into traps and misread most of the signals, but she will—feminine intuition being what it is—stumble onto something important. She will also need rescuing in a cliff-hanging finale." In short, the reviewer concludes, "it all makes excellent escape fiction."

"One of Stewart's finest qualities as a writer," Mussell writes, "is her extraordinary descriptive prose. Stewart's ability to evoke a highly specific time and place, through sensuous descriptions of locale, character, and food, provides an immediacy that is often lacking in mystery fiction. Her academic background in English literature lends thematic and dramatic elements in the epigrams to her chapters and the literary allusions within the works."

Anthony Boucher in the *New York Times Book Review* defines Stewart's fiction as belonging to "that special sub-species of mystery one might call the Cinderella-suspense novel." This sub-species, Boucher believes, "is designed by feminine authors for feminine readers; yet a male can relish such highpoints as *Jane Eyre* or *Rebecca.* Of current practitioners, I can't think of anyone (aside from du Maurier herself) who tells such stories quite as well as Mary Stewart."

Other critics have noted the same qualities in Stewart's writing. James Sandoe of the *New York Herald Tribune Book Review* calls *Madam, Will You Talk?* "a distinctly charming, romantic thriller . . . [that is] intelligently soft-boiled, pittypat and a good deal of fun." *My Brother Michael,* according to Francis Iles of the *Guardian,* is "the contemporary thriller at its very best." Speaking of the same novel, Christopher Pym of the *Spectator* comments: "Mary Stewart gives each of her admirable novels an exotically handsome (if somewhat rather travel-folderish) setting. . . . This [is] by a long chalk the best of them. . . . The Greek landscape and—much more subtle—the Greek character are splendidly done, in a long, charmingly written, highly evocative, imperative piece of required reading for an Hellenic cruise." Boucher, too, finds the book worthy of praise: "If the delightfully entertaining novels of Mary Stewart . . . have had a fault, it is that their plots are (in James Sandoe's useful term) Eurydicean—they cannot survive a backward glance. But in *My Brother Michael* even this flaw vanishes. . . . This detective adventure, rich in action and suspense, is seen through the eyes of a characteristic Stewart heroine; and surely there are few more attractive young women in today's popular fiction. . . . These girls are as far removed as you can imagine from the Idiot Heroine who disfigures (at least for men) so much romantic fiction."

After commenting on Stewart's overall achievement as a writer of romantic suspense novels, F. W. J. Hemmings concludes that it is "no wonder that Mary Stewart should be accounted 'very successful.' It is success well-earned, for there is nothing cheap in the writing and nothing machine-made in the devising. . . . Of course, the books do not pretend to offer anything but delight. . . . But they are the genuine triumphs of a minor art."

In 1970, Stewart turned to historical fiction. The main focus of this new interest was Arthurian England, especially as seen through the eyes of Merlin the magician. Liz Holliday in the *St. James Guide to Fantasy Writers* believes Stewart's Merlin character

"is an intriguing mixture of pragmatist and fey, believer and agnostic. He has visions, true dreams in which he sees what is and what is to come. These, he believes, come from a god: but he refuses to identify this god as being Christian, Mithraditic or of the Druidic, goddess-worshipping Old Faith. At the same time he is portrayed as a polymath, dedicated to understanding the world through scholarship in the fields of science, mathematics and engineering."

Unlike most other authors who have written about the legends of Camelot in terms of the Middle Ages, Stewart places her story in more historically accurate fifth-century Britain. Reviewing *The Crystal Cave,* the first of three books on Merlin, a *Best Sellers* critic writes: "Fifth century Britain and Brittany come to life in Miss Stewart's vigorous imagination. . . . Those who have read and enjoyed the many novels of Mary Stewart will not need to be told this is an expertly fashioned continually absorbing story, with a facile imagination fleshing out the legend of the parentage of the future King Arthur—and, too, of Merlin himself." A *Books and Bookmen* critic calls it "a highly plotted and rattling good yarn. Mary Stewart's evocation of an era of magic, as well as of bloodletting, is magnificently done. Her writing is virile, and of a very high quality indeed. Her descriptions of the countryside are often moving, also poetical."

Martin Levin of the *New York Times Book Review,* after reminding readers that little is actually known of Merlin's life, notes that "the author obligingly expands [Merlin's] myth into a first person history. . . . Cheerfully disclaiming authenticity, Miss Stewart . . . lightens the Dark Ages with legend, pure invention and a lively sense of history." A *Christian Science Monitor* reviewer, however, finds this type of "history" to be somewhat compromised by the author's emphasis on Merlin's magical powers. "There really is little 'magic' in the story," the reviewer begins, "and what there is rarely exceeds the familiar 'knowing before the event.' But the very uncertainty of its inclusion lends a certain falseness to an otherwise absorbing story, which has been carefully researched historically so that it is peripherally authentic." At any rate, the reviewer concludes, "*The Crystal Cave* evokes an England long gone and could prove an interesting guidebook to some of the less touristy attractions of the Cornish and Welsh countryside."

The Hollow Hills, a continuation of Merlin's story, was also fairly well-received. A *Publishers Weekly* critic calls it "romantic, refreshing and most pleasant reading. . . . Mrs. Stewart has steeped herself well in the folklore and known history of fifth century Britain and she makes of her feuding, fighting warlords lively and intriguing subjects." A *Best Sellers* critic writes: "All in all, this makes a smashing good tale. The suspense is superb and the reader is kept involved in the unwinding of the plot. Miss Stewart has taken the main lines of the Arthurian legend and has developed the basic elements in a plausible way."

Joseph McLellan of the *Washington Post Book World* finds the third Merlin book, *The Last Enchantment,* to be somewhat anti-climactic. "Having used two long, exciting novels to get Arthur on the throne," he writes, "Miss Stewart has reached the final volume of her trilogy and we can settle back expecting to hear the old stories told again with her unique touch. There is only one trouble with this expectation: Mary Stewart does not fulfill it, and she quite clearly never had any intentions of fulfilling it. Her story is not strictly about Arthur but about Merlin. . . . Strictly speaking, once Arthur is safely on the throne . . . Merlin's life work is over. He spends most of *The Last Enchantment* fading away as gracefully as he can manage. . . . [As a result of this shift in emphasis,] the role of Arthur in this volume is fitful and erratic; he is a powerful presence but not the central character."

Very much aware of the difficulties involved in gathering and making sense out of the confusing source material available on Merlin's life, McLellan praises Stewart for "the ingenuity of [her] effort," though he feels that the story's ultimate plausibility is somewhat in doubt. "She gives us . . . traditional materials," he notes, "but the treatment is her own, the emphasis shifted for her purpose, which is not simply to recast old material but to bring alive a long-dead historical epoch—not the Middle Ages of Malory but the Dark Ages of the original Arthur. This she does splendidly. Fifth-century Britain is caught in these pages, and while it may lack some of the exotic glitter of the imaginary 12th-century Britain that Arthur usually inhabits, it is a fascinating place."

Stewart followed her Merlin Trilogy with one last book based on the Arthurian legends, *The Wicked Day,* a tale told by Arthur's bastard son Mordred. According to Arthurian tradition, Mordred is the cause of Arthur's eventual downfall. He has a "bad reputation as Arthur's mean-spirited, traitorous, regicidal son," as Roy Hoffman explains in the *New York Times Book Review.*

But in Stewart's version of the story, Mordred is more a tragic figure in the drama than a conscious agent of destruction. "Stewart," Hoffman writes, "attempts to resurrect him as a compassionate young man who is helpless before fate." M. Jean Greenlaw in the *Journal of Reading* finds that "Stewart shapes a sense of the inevitable doom of Camelot, not by Mordred's desire but by the fateful actions of many men and women." Mary Mills in *School Library Journal* concludes that "Stewart has created flesh and blood characters out of legends, and in doing so has crafted a well-plotted and passionate drama." Holliday believes that "telling the tale from Mordred's point of view works splendidly. It allows his character to emerge as much more complex and sympathetic than it might otherwise have done. Here, Mordred is clearly as much a victim . . . as Arthur ever was, and his attempts to overcome the weakness of character that leads him to his final clash with his father make him an engaging, if not wholly likeable, character."

In an article for *Philological Quarterly,* Maureen Fries compares Stewart's treatment of Arthurian legend with that of T. H. White, the author of *The Once and Future King.* "Of all literary genres," Fries begins, "romance is perhaps the most irrational, focusing as it does upon the strange, the marvelous, and the supernatural. And of all the 'matters' of romance, that of Britain contains the most irrationalities." But Fries concludes that "in making over medieval romance into modern novels, T. H. White and Mary Stewart have not only coped, mostly successfully, with the irrationality of the Matter of Britain. They have also grasped and translated into a convincing modern, if diverse, idiom that rational core of truth about human psychology, and the human condition, which constitutes not only the greatness of the Arthurian legend but also its enduring appeal to readers of all centuries and all countries, and to writers of every time and every literary persuasion."

In the early 1980s Stewart continued writing medieval tales. *A Walk in Wolf Wood* concerns two modern-day children who are thrust backwards in time to the Middle Ages. "The eerie events that overtake [the children] become the vehicle for an incisive exploration of magic, savagery and the mis-uses of power," observes Mary Cadogan in the *Times Literary Supplement.* "The trappings of another time like jousts and hunts, terraces and towers, are vivid and atmospheric but not overdone."

Explaining her decision to switch from writing thrillers to historical fiction, Mary Stewart once told *CA:*

"I always planned that some day I would write a historical novel, and I intended to use Roman Britain as the setting. This is a period that I have studied over many years. But then, quite by chance, I came across a passage in Geoffrey of Monmouth's *History of the Kings of Britain,* which described the first appearance of Merlin, the Arthurian 'enchanter.' Here was a new story, offering a new approach to a dark and difficult period, with nothing known about the 'hero' except scraps of legend. The story would have to come purely from imagination, pitched somewhere between legend and truth and fairy-tale and known history. The setting would be imaginary, too, a Dark Age Britain in the unrecorded aftermath of the Roman withdrawal. I had originally no intention of writing more than one volume, but the story seized my imagination. . . . It has been a tough job and a rewarding one. I have learned a lot, not least that the powerful themes of the Arthurian 'Matter of Britain' are as cogent and real today as they were fourteen centuries ago. And Merlin's story has allowed me to return to my first avocation of all, that of poet."

BIOGRAPHICAL/CRITICAL SOURCES:

BOOKS

Contemporary Literary Criticism, Gale (Detroit), Volume 7, 1977; Volume 35, 1985.
Friedman, Lenemaja, *Mary Stewart,* Twayne (Boston), 1990.
Newquist, Roy, *Counterpoint,* Rand McNally, 1964.
St. James Guide to Crime and Mystery Writers, 4th edition, St. James Press (Detroit), 1996.
St. James Guide to Fantasy Writers, St. James Press, 1996.

PERIODICALS

Arthurian Interpretations, spring, 1987, pp. 70-83.
Best Sellers, October 1, 1967; July 15, 1970; July 15, 1973; November, 1976, p. 250.
Booklist, April 15, 1992, p. 1547.
Books and Bookmen, August, 1970.
Book Week, November 21, 1965.
Christian Science Monitor, September 28, 1967; September 3, 1970.
Guardian, February 26, 1960.
Harper's, September, 1970.
Journal of Reading, May, 1984, p. 741.
Kirkus Reviews, August 1, 1983, p. 840; July 15, 1991, p. 887.
Library Journal, June 15, 1973.
National Observer, October 23, 1967.
New Statesman, November 5, 1965.
New York Herald Tribune Book Review, May 27, 1956; October 5, 1958; March 8, 1959; March 4, 1962.
New York Times, March 18, 1956; September 9, 1956; May 18, 1958; January 18, 1959.
New York Times Book Review, April 10, 1960; January 7, 1962; October 24, 1965; October 15, 1967; August 9, 1970; July 29, 1973; September 2, 1979; January 1, 1984, p. 20.
Philological Quarterly, spring, 1977, pp. 259-265.
Publishers Weekly, September 16, 1988; July 12, 1991.
San Francisco Chronicle, October 21, 1956; May 22, 1960.
School Library Journal, March, 1984, p. 178.
Sunday Times Colour Supplement, June 13, 1976.
Time, January 5, 1968.
Times Educational Supplement, February 5, 1982, p. 28.
Times Literary Supplement, July 18, 1980, p. 806.
Washington Post Book World, March 31, 1968; September 15, 1976; July 22, 1979.
Writer, May, 1970, pp. 9-12, 46.*

*   *   *

STONE, Lesley
See Trevor, Elleston

*   *   *

STRICKLAND, Dorothy S(alley) 1933-

PERSONAL: Born September 29, 1933, in Newark, NJ; daughter of Leroy, Sr. (a factory worker) and Evelyn (a homemaker; maiden name, Daniels) Salley; married Maurice Raymond Strickland (an attorney), August 27, 1955; children: Mark, Maurice Randall, Michael. *Education:* Newark State College (now Kean College of New Jersey), B.S., 1955; New York University, M.A., 1958, Ph.D., 1971. *Politics:* Democrat. *Religion:* Catholic. *Avocational interests:* Traveling, gardening, reading.

ADDRESSES: Home—176 Elmwynd Dr., Orange, NJ 07050. *Office*—Rutgers University, 10 Seminary Place, New Brunswick, NJ 08903.

CAREER: East Orange Board of Education, East Orange, NJ, teacher, 1955-61, reading consultant and learning disabilities specialist, 1961-66; Jersey City State College, Jersey City, NJ, assistant professor of education, 1966-70; New York University, New York City, adjunct professor, 1969-73; Kean College of New Jersey, Union, NJ, assistant professor, 1970-72, associate professor, 1972-75, professor of early childhood education, 1975-80, chair of department, 1973-76; Columbia University Teachers College, New York City, Arthur I. Gates Professor of Education, 1980-90; Rutgers University, New Brunswick, NJ, State of New Jersey Professor of Reading, 1990—.

MEMBER: International Reading Association (president, 1978-79), National Council of Teachers of English (member of board of directors, 1975-78), National Committee for the Education of Migrant Children, National Association for the Education of Young Children.

AWARDS, HONORS: National Research Award, National Council of Teachers of English, 1972; Outstanding Teacher Educator in Reading Award, International Reading Association, 1985; Award for Outstanding Contribution to Education, National Association of University Women, 1987; elected into International Reading Association's Reading Hall of Fame, 1990; Distinguished Alumnus Award, New York University, 1990; Outstanding Alumnus Award, Kean College of New Jersey, 1990; Honorary Doctorate of Letters, Bank Street College, 1991; Rewey Bell Inglis Award, National Council of Teachers of English, for outstanding woman in English education, 1994.

WRITINGS:

(With Denny Taylor) *Family Storybook Reading,* foreword by Bernice E. Cullinan, Heinemann (Portsmouth, NH), 1986.

(With Joan T. Feeley and Shelley B. Wepner) *Using Computers in the Teaching of Reading,* foreword by George E. Mason, Columbia University Teachers College Press (New York City), 1987.

(With Eleanor R. Kulleseid) *Literature, Literacy, and Learning: Classroom Teachers, Library Media Specialists, and the Literature-Based Curriculum,* American Library Association (Chicago), 1989.

(With Lee Galda and Bernice E. Cullinan) *Language, Literacy and the Child,* Harcourt (San Diego), 1993.

EDITOR

World Congress on Reading, *The Role of Literature in Reading Instruction: Cross-Cultural Views,* International Reading Association (Newark, DE), 1981.

Listen Children: An Anthology of Black Literature, foreword by Coretta Scott King, illustrated by Leo and Diane Dillon, Bantam (New York City), 1982.

(With Eric J. Cooper) *Educating Black Children: America's Challenge,* Howard University, School of Education, Bureau of Educational Research, 1987.

(With Joan T. Feeley and Shelley B. Wepner) *The Administration and Supervision of Reading Programs,* Columbia University Teachers College Press, 1989.

(With Lesley Mandel Morrow) *Emerging Literacy: Young Children Learn to Read and Write,* International Reading Association, 1989.

(With Joan T. Feeley and Shelley B. Wepner) *Process Reading and Writing: A Literature-Based Approach,* Columbia University Teachers College Press, 1991.

(With son, Michael R. Strickland) *Families: Poems Celebrating the African American Experience,* illustrated by John Ward, Boyds Mills Press (Honesdale, PA), 1994.

OTHER

Senior author of *Treasury of Literature,* a reading program for kindergarten through eighth grade students published by Harcourt; contributor of articles to educational journals. Member of educational advisory boards of *Journal of Reading Instruction,* 1971-76, *Early Years,* 1972—, *Sprint,* 1974-76, and *Webster's New World Dictionary,* 1979.

SIDELIGHTS: A professor of education and former elementary school teacher, Dorothy S. Strickland is the editor of two collections of children's literature focusing on the experiences of African-American families, as well as the author of several publications concerning English education and reading instruction. In her first children's anthology, *Listen Children: An Anthology of Black Literature,* Strickland gathers poems, biographies, stories, folk tales, and speeches by prominent black figures, including Virginia Hamilton, Langston Hughes, Harriet Wheatley, and Maya Angelou, illustrated with block prints by Leo and Diane Dillon. The selections in this work showcase elements of the African-American experience and emphasize the important contributions black Americans have made to literature. Writing in *School Library Journal,* Hazel Rochman praises "the anthology's sense of strong individual identity rooted in the past and in the community."

In *Families: Poems Celebrating the African American Experience,* Strickland and her son Michael have selected poems written by African Americans that center on black children and relate the happy events of African-American family life. Featured in the collection is the poetry of Nikki Giovanni, Gwendolyn Brooks, and Eloise Greenfield, all of which "gets right inside a child's experience," according to Ilene Cooper, writing in *Booklist.* However, a critic in *Publishers Weekly* points out that although the initial poem written by the Stricklands celebrates racial diversity, the illustrations in the book feature only African-American children. Despite this, the critic goes on to say, "Teachers and parents will welcome the volume for its use of an African American cast."

BIOGRAPHICAL/CRITICAL SOURCES:

PERIODICALS

Booklist, August, 1982, p. 1526; February 15, 1995, p. 1087.
Children's Literature in Education, December, 1990, p. 261.
Kliatt, spring, 1982, p. 31.
Library Talk, November, 1994, p. 23.
Publishers Weekly, April 2, 1982, p. 79; November 28, 1994, p. 62.
School Library Journal, August, 1982, pp. 107-108.

* * *

SWEENEY, Karen O'Connor
  See O'CONNOR, Karen

* * *

SYMONS, Julian (Gustave) 1912-1994

PERSONAL: Born May 30, 1912, in London, England; died November 19, 1994, in Kent, England, of a heart attack (one source says cancer); son of Morris Albert (an auctioneer) and Minnie Louise (Bull) Symons; married Kathleen Clark, October 25, 1941;

children: Sarah Louise (deceased), Marcus Richard Julian. *Education:* Educated in state schools in England. *Politics:* "Left wing, with no specific party allegiance." *Avocational interests:* Cricket, football.

CAREER: Shorthand typist and secretary in London, 1929-41; advertising copywriter in London, 1944-47; full-time writer, beginning 1947. Founder and editor, *Twentieth Century Verse,* 1937-39; reviewer, *Manchester Evening News,* 1947-56, *London Sunday Times,* 1958-68. Member of council, Westfield College, University of London, 1972-75; visiting professor, Amherst College, Massachusetts, 1975-76. *Military service:* British Army, Royal Armoured Corps, 1942-44.

MEMBER: Crime Writers Association (co-founder and chair, 1958-59), Society of Authors (chair of committee of management, 1970-71), Mystery Writers of America, PEN, Detection Club (president, 1976-85), Royal Society of Literature, Conan Doyle Society (president, 1989-93), Writer's Guild.

AWARDS, HONORS: Crime Writers Association, Crossed Red Herrings Award for best crime story of the year, 1957, for *The Color of Murder,* special award, 1966, for *Crime and Detection,* Cartier Diamond Dagger Award, 1990; Mystery Writers of America, Edgar Allan Poe Award for best crime story of the year, 1961, for *The Progress of a Crime,* special award, 1973, for *Bloody Murder;* Grand Master of Swedish Academy of Detection, 1977, Danish Poe-Kluhben, 1979, and Mystery Writers of America, 1982; fellow, Royal Society of Literature, 1975.

WRITINGS:

NOVELS

The Immaterial Murder Case, Gollancz (London), 1945, Macmillan (New York City), 1957.
A Man Called Jones, Gollancz, 1947.
Bland Beginning, Harper (New York City), 1949, published in England as *Bland Beginning: A Detective Story,* Gollancz, 1949.
The 31st of February (also see below), Harper, 1950, published in England as *The Thirty-First of February: A Mystery Novel,* Gollancz, 1950.
The Broken Penny, Gollancz, 1952, Harper, 1953.
The Narrowing Circle, Harper, 1954, published in England as *The Narrowing Circle: A Crime Novel,* Gollancz, 1954.
The Paper Chase, Collins (London), 1956, published as *Bogue's Fortune,* Harper, 1957.

The Color of Murder, Harper, 1957.

The Gigantic Shadow, Collins, 1958, published as *The Pipe Dream,* Harper, 1959.

The Progress of a Crime (also see below), Harper, 1960.

The Plain Man, Harper, 1962, published in England as *The Killing of Francie Lake,* Collins, 1962.

The End of Solomon Grundy (also see below), Harper, 1964.

The Belting Inheritance, Harper, 1965.

The Julian Symons Omnibus (contains *The 31st of February, The Progress of a Crime,* and *The End of Solomon Grundy*), Collins, 1966.

The Man Who Killed Himself, Harper, 1967.

The Man Whose Dreams Came True, Harper, 1968.

The Man Who Lost His Wife, Harper, 1970.

The Players and the Game, Harper, 1972.

The Plot against Roger Rider, Harper, 1973.

A Three-Pipe Problem, Harper, 1975.

The Blackheath Poisonings: A Victorian Murder Mystery, Harper, 1978.

Sweet Adelaide: A Victorian Puzzle Solved, Harper, 1980.

The Detling Secret, Viking (New York City), 1982, published in England as *The Detling Murders,* Macmillan, 1982.

The Name of Annabel Lee, Viking, 1983.

A Criminal Comedy, Viking, 1985, published in England as *The Criminal Comedy of the Contented Couple,* Macmillan, 1985.

The Kentish Manor Murders, Viking, 1988.

Death's Darkest Face, Viking, 1990.

Something Like a Love Affair, Mysterious Press (New York City), 1992.

Playing Happy Families, Mysterious Press, 1995.

POETRY

Confusions about X, Fortune Press (London), 1939.

The Second Man, Routledge & Kegan Paul (London), 1943.

A Reflection on Auden, Poem-of-the-Month Club (London), 1973.

The Object of an Affair, and Other Poems Tragara Press (Edinburgh), 1974.

Seven Poems for Sarah, Tragara Press, 1979.

OTHER

(Editor) *An Anthology of War Poetry,* Penguin (London), 1942.

(Editor and author of introduction) Samuel Johnson, *Selected Writings of Samuel Johnson,* Grey Walls Press (London), 1949, British Book Centre (New York City), 1950.

A. J. A. Symons: His Life and Speculations (biography), Eyre & Spottiswoode (London), 1950.

Charles Dickens (biography), Roy (New York City), 1951, 2nd edition, Arthur Barker (London), 1969.

Thomas Carlyle: The Life and Ideas of a Prophet, Oxford University Press (New York City), 1952.

Horatio Bottomley: A Biography, Cresset Press (London), 1955.

(Editor) Thomas Carlyle, *Selected Works, Reminiscences and Letters,* Hart David (London), 1956, Harvard University Press (Cambridge, MA), 1957.

The General Strike: A Historical Portrait, Cresset Press, 1957, Dufour (Chester Springs, PA), 1963.

A Reasonable Doubt: Some Criminal Cases Re-examined, Cresset Press, 1960.

The Thirties: A Dream Resolved, Cresset Press, 1960, Dufour, 1963, revised edition, Faber, 1975, revised edition published as *The Thirties and the Nineties,* Carcanet (Manchester), 1990.

Murder, Murder (short story collection), Fontana Books (London), 1961.

The Detective Story in Britain, Longmans, Green (London), 1962.

Buller's Campaign, Cresset Press, 1963.

Francis Quarles Investigates (short story collection), Panther Books (London), 1965.

England's Pride: The Story of the Gordon Relief Expedition, Hamish Hamilton (London), 1965.

Critical Occasions, Hamish Hamilton, 1966.

A Pictorial History of Crime, Crown (New York City), 1966, published in England as *Crime and Detection: An Illustrated History from 1840,* Studio Vista (London), 1966.

(Editor) *A. J. A. Symons, Essays and Biographies,* Cassell (London), 1969.

Mortal Consequences: A History—from the Detective Story to the Crime Novel, Harper, 1972, revised edition published as *Bloody Murder,* Viking, 1985, published in England as *Bloody Murder: From the Detective Story to the Crime Novel: A History,* Faber, 1972, fourth edition, Pan (London), 1994.

(Editor and author of introduction) *Between the Wars: Britain in Photographs,* Batsford (London), 1972.

Notes from Another Country, London Magazine Editions (London), 1972.

(Editor and author of introduction) Wilkie Collins, *The Woman Who Wore White,* Penguin, (London) 1974, reprinted as *The Woman in White,* 1982.

(Editor) *The Angry Thirties,* Eyre & Spottiswoode (London), 1976.

Ellery Queen Presents Julian Symons' How To Trap a Crook and Twelve Other Mysteries, Davis (New York City), 1977.

The Tell-Tale Heart: The Life and Works of Edgar Allan Poe, Harper, 1978.

(Editor) *Verdict of Thirteen: A Detection Club Anthology,* Harper, 1979.

Conan Doyle: Portrait of an Artist, G. Whizzard (London), 1979; Mysterious Press, 1988.

(Editor) Edgar Allan Poe, *Selected Tales,* Oxford University Press (London), 1980.

The Modern Crime Story, Tragara Press, 1980.

(Editor and author of introduction) Agatha Christie, *The ABC Murders,* Collins, 1980.

(Editor and author of introduction) Freeman Wills Crofts, *The Loss of the Jane Vosper,* Collins, 1980.

(Author of commentary) Tom Adams, *Agatha Christie, the Art of Her Crimes: The Paintings of Tom Adams,* Everest House (New York City), 1981, published in England as *Tom Adams' Agatha Christie Cover Story,* introduction by John Fowles, Dragon's World (Limpsfield, Surrey, England), 1981.

(Author of preface) Arthur Conan Doyle, *The Complete Sherlock Holmes,* Abrams (New York City), 1981.

The Great Detectives: Seven Original Investigations, illustrated by Adams, Abrams, 1981.

Critical Observations, Ticknor & Fields (New Haven, CT), 1981.

(Editor) *A. J. A. Symons to Wyndham Lewis: Twenty-Four Letters,* Tragara Press, 1982.

The Tigers of Subtopia, and Other Stories (also see below), Viking, 1982.

Crime and Detection Quiz, Weidenfeld & Nicolson, 1983.

(Editor) *New Poetry 9,* Hutchinson (London), 1983.

(Editor) *The Penguin Classic Crime Omnibus,* Penguin, 1984.

1948 and 1984: The Second Orwell Memorial Lecture, Tragara Press, 1984.

(With A. J. Symons) *Two Brothers: Fragments of a Correspondence,* Tragara Press, 1985.

Dashiell Hammett (biography), Harcourt (San Diego, CA), 1985.

(Editor) Anton Chekov, *The Shooting Party,* translated by A. E. Chamot, Deutsch, 1986.

Makers of the News: The Revolution of Literature, Random House (New York City), 1987.

Oscar Wilde: A Problem in Biography, Yellow Barn Press (Council Bluffs), 1988.

(Editor) Wyndham Lewis, *The Essential Wyndham Lewis: An Introduction to His Work,* Deutsch (London), 1989.

Criminal Practices: Symons on Crime Writing 60's to 90's, Macmillan, 1994.

The Man Who Hated Television And Other Stories, G. K. Hall (Boston), 1995.

Also author of screenplay adaptation of his novel *The Narrowing Circle,* 1955, and of radio plays *Affection Unlimited,* 1968, and *Night Rider to Dover,* 1969, and of television plays *Miranda and a Salesman,* 1963, *The Witnesses,* 1964, *The Finishing Touch,* 1965, *Curtains for Sheila,* 1965, *Tigers of Subtopia,* based on the author's short story collection of the same title, 1968, *The Pretenders,* 1970, and *Whatever's Peter Playing At?,* 1974; editor, *New Poetry 9,* 1983. Editor, "Penguin Mystery" series, 1974-79. Contributor to *Times Literary Supplement, New York Times,* and other newspapers and magazines. Reviewer, *Manchester Evening News,* 1947-56, and *Sunday Times,* beginning 1958.

SIDELIGHTS: A staunch believer in the literary value of crime and detective novels, Julian Symons is best known as a novelist and critic of these genres, though he was also a respected historian, biographer, and poet—overall, "one of the most versatile men of letters of his generation, [who] impressively lived the vocation of freelance writer," in the words of *Dictionary of Literary Biography* contributor W. P. Kenney. Many of the English novelist's ideas about the crime fiction genre are expressed in his book, *Bloody Murder,* which traces the history of detective and crime novels over the past two centuries. Symons' "most important contribution to the study of the genre," attested Larry E. Grimes in the *Dictionary of Literary Biography,* "is his assertion that much of the focus in crime writing in the twentieth century has changed" from the "classical detective story" to the "crime novel." The detective story, explained Grimes, "is built around a great detective and upon a plot deception," while a crime novel "is based on the psychology of its characters, uses the lines of those characters (not methods, clues, and puzzles) as the basis of the story."

Symons has written novels that fall under both categories, but most of these works have one commonality: the author's interest in the surprising capability for violence that any person may release under the right circumstances. "The thing that absorbs me most in our age," remarked Symons in his introduction to *The Julian Symons Omnibus,* "is the violence behind respectable faces, the civil servant planning how to kill Jews most efficiently, the judge speaking with passion about the need for capital punishment, the quiet obedient boy who kills for fun. These are extreme cases, but if you want to show the violence that lives behind the bland faces most of us present to the world, what better vehicle can you have than the crime novel?"

Writing in the *St. James Guide to Crime & Mystery Writers,* George Woodcock noted his opinion that Symons was "one of the finest British writers of mysteries, the closest heir to either Dorothy L. Sayers or Agatha Christie." Yet the author himself was unsatisfied with his early work. "My first three crime stories, including the unfortunate [*The Immaterial Murder Case*]" he revealed in his *Contemporary Authors Autobiography Series* entry, "I look back on without pleasure. They were set in one orthodox pattern of the British crime story at that time, consciously light, bright, and determinedly 'civilized.' The fourth, *The Thirty-First of February. . . ,* is another matter. I must at this time have had some nascent ideas about doing all the things in the form of the crime story that one can do in a 'straight' novel, in the way of character development, and saying something about the form and shape of society." As with many of Symons' crime stories, *The Thirty-First of February* is not so much a murder mystery as it is a study in human psychology and sociology. The novel involves "Andy" Anderson, an advertising businessman who, after the apparently accidental death of his wife, is accused of her murder. His employers are completely unsympathetic to Anderson's situation and force him to return to work without a period for mourning, while also burdening him with an important account. At the same time, the police, who are certain Anderson is guilty, continually harass him. Though he is never convicted, the unrelenting pressures on him eventually lead to Anderson's insanity.

Similarly, the protagonist in *The Narrowing Circle,* David Nelson, is never convicted of the murder charges brought against him; but the events he experiences nevertheless effectively rob him of his sense of humanity. However, it is not so much the accusation of homicide that brings about Nelson's downfall; rather, as Grimes explained, it is his continued desire to climb up the social and financial ladder that "choke[s] off his ability to be human and know love." "A large part of the horror at the end of *The Narrowing Circle,*" wrote Steven R. Carter in *Armchair Detective,* "comes from the reader's awareness that

David Nelson is killing an essential part of himself by his decision to accept the sleazy material success which an ulcer-ridden entrepreneur offers him."

About the same time *The Color of Murder* was published, Symons was becoming an influential figure among crime writers. From 1958 to 1959 he was a chair of the Crime Writer's Association, and in 1958 he began work as a reviewer of mystery fiction for the *London Sunday Times. The Color of Murder* won the Crime Writer's Association Red Herrings Award in 1957, and in 1961 *The Progress of a Crime* won the Edgar Allan Poe Award. These books continue the pattern Symons previously established of using crime fiction as an instrument for social commentary. Like *The Thirty-First of February, The Color of Murder* ends with the insanity of an innocent man accused of a homicide. But in *The Progress of a Crime,* Symons reversed this plot so that the a guilty man is found innocent. Criticizing the misuse of force by the police, the desire of newspapers to capitalize on people's misfortunes in order to sell more papers, and lawyers who care only about winning their cases, *The Progress of a Crime* "is one of the truest and most sensible . . . English crime novels" of its time, opined *Spectator* critic Christopher Pym.

Discussing Symons's body of crime fiction, George Woodcock wrote in *St. James Guide to Crime & Mystery Writers* that in his best novels, "Symons was not really concerned to create the well-made detective story which works itself out as the intellectually satisfying solution of a complex puzzle through the right manipulation of given clues. His plots are often loose rather than tight, sometimes they are disconcertingly open and obvious, and often the denouements are deliberately anticlimactic. There is more than a little irony in his attitude to such matters, and he is quite capable of leaving a little fog of mystery unresolved to annoy the meticulous reader." Woodcock found one of the strongest points in the author's work to be the stamp of his own world view—the outlook "of a radical critic who looked on existing political and social orders with sardonic scepticism. Symons was concerned with how the crimes he portrayed reflected the decay of society, with the pretences of the cultural world, with politics and power as corrupting elements and, in his "Victorian' novels, with the hypocrisies of self-consciously "moral' societies. . . . In the end, it is not for the way he solved the details of crimes that Symons's novels are interesting, but rather for the way he found their causes in the minds of men and the shapes of societies."

Some of Symons' most complex novels were also among his best, according to a number of reviewers. *The Man Who Killed Himself,* for example, features a protagonist who creates a double identity to commit the perfect crime. One of his identities, Alan Brownjohn, murders his wife and then is, in turn, "murdered" by Major Easonby Mellon, Brownjohn's alter ego. William R. Evans, a *Best Sellers* critic, praised this novel as being "a brilliant portrait of a fascinating murderer along with an extremely ingenious and suspenseful plot." But, as Grimes revealed, *The Man Who Killed Himself* is not a simple murder mystery, "for Easonby/Brownjohn has plotted a perfect murder, not for murder's sake, but for the sake of freedom from an imperfect world." Grimes explained this in more detail in his comments about *The End of Solomon Grundy,* where he noted that in Symons' books the author portrays the world as a place where "one must either become a criminal or remain a hypocrite." Symons' characters are never all good or all evil; indeed, in some of his books it is difficult to find a character with whom the reader can sympathize completely.

The Players and the Game, another example of one of Symons' more intricate plots, is one such book that lacks sympathetic characters. As Leo Harris noted in *Books and Bookmen,* none of the people portrayed in this novel are "very nice." Symons' mysteries, Harris added, "have always the rebarbative surface of warts-and-all truthfulness, and he has a cold, perceptive, but not entirely unforgiving eye for human frailty." *The Players of the Game* tells two stories: one describes a business executive's journey toward self-destruction as he strives for success; the other is narrated by a character who calls himself "Dracula," and portrays a world in which criminal behavior is considered normal. "One of the most intriguing and unusual aspects of Symons' writing" that is illustrated in *The Players and the Game,* remarked Carter, "is his stress on games." Carter elucidated that "Symons has implied often that anyone might become a criminal by being subjected to too much pressure, by having insufficient outlets for release from pressure, or by surrendering to his fantasies."

Not long after *The Players of the Game,* Symons indulged his interest in the Victorian era by writing three novels set in late nineteenth-century England. These books include *The Blackheath Poisonings: A Victorian Murder Mystery, Sweet Adelaide: A Victorian Puzzle Solved,* and *The Detling Secret.* According to Symons in the *Contemporary Authors Autobiography Series,* he was "pleased" with the first book,

while the other two "seemed to me less good." William McPhearson echoed the author's assessment of *The Blackheath Poisonings,* praising the mystery as a "skillfully written, thoroughly researched and deftly plotted novel." As to Symons' other Victorian mysteries, critics have generally been more positive in their evaluations than the novelist himself.

One of these books, *Sweet Adelaide,* is based on an actual murder case in England. Still interested in studying how innocent-looking people can commit murder, Symons investigates the reasons why Adelaide Bartlett, a woman as infamous in England as Lizzie Borden is in the United States, could be driven into pouring liquid chloroform down her husband's throat. Bartlett was found not guilty, related Michael Malone in the *New York Times Book Review,* "by a jury that could not believe this demure little lady had either the will or the expertise" to kill her husband. Symons proposes, however, that she did possess these qualities, and proceeds to describe in his novel what could push a woman like Bartlett over the edge. *Los Angeles Times Book* critic Alan Cheuse lauded the writer's portrayal of Bartlett, saying that "Symons' masterly construction of Adelaide's mind—and journal—as she lives through years of suffering her husband's patronage of prostitutes . . . keep[s] us fascinated with each moment of this woman's inevitable slide toward murder." In *The Detling Secret,* Symons explored the more sinister impulses that lurk behind even civilized, upper-class members of society. A more traditional English mystery, critics have praised *The Detling Secret* for its authentic recreation of Edwardian England and the novelist's expert handling of plot. *New York Times Book Review* contributor Mary Cantwell praised the author's research, reporting that "Mr. Symons' use of period detail is both scrupulous and economical." And *Los Angeles Times* critic Carolyn See averred that as a murder mystery *The Detling Secret* "is simply perfect of its kind."

With *The Name of Annabel Lee,* Symons returned to contemporary settings for his novels, "having proved my ability to write such a story—at least to my own satisfaction," he said in *Contemporary Authors Autobiography Series.* Some critics gave this work a chilly reception, however. *Los Angeles Times* reviewer Art Seidenbaum, for one, felts that "the resolution of the mystery . . . leaves substance to be desired." But although Derrick Murdoch similarly believed that Symons' plot appears weak in this case, the reviewer noted in *Globe and Mail* that the novel succeeds in other ways. *The Name of Annabel Lee,* Murdoch wrote, "uses the form of the mystery novel to provide a sardonic study of the extent of modern decadence as scathing as his Victorian murder mysteries were of nineteenth-century injustice and hypocrisy." In a more light-hearted fashion, Symons' *A Criminal Comedy* also gibes capitalist society by painting "a savagely comic picture of Headfield [England] and its colour supplement *bourgeoisie*," according to T. J. Binyon's *Times Literary Supplement* review.

A Criminal Comedy has generally been well received by critics; but, more than this, to one *Time* contributor it also proved that Symons did not allow his story-telling powers to diminish over the years. "At 73," the reviewer declared, "Julian Symons has . . . published perhaps his best mystery ever." By this time, too, the author had long been a respected biographer and critic. Among other subjects, Symons' interest in mystery authors led him to write biographies of Edgar Allan Poe, Dashiell Hammett, and Sir Arthur Conan Doyle, whose famous creation, Sherlock Holmes, Symons honored with modern versions of the great detective in *A Three-Pipe Problem* and *The Kentish Manor Murders*. The author's biographies have received mixed reviews from critics, the most negative reactions being awarded to *The Tell Tale Heart: The Life and Works of Edgar Allan Poe*. For example, in a *New Republic* article Megan Marshall called Symons' biography of Poe "steadfastly superficial" and observed that the writer "fails to cover the full dimension of his subject." *Spectator* contributor Benny Green similarly commented that "what we get [in *The Tell Tale Heart*] is not so much a reassessment as a rearrangement" of Poe's life and work.

However, Symons' *Dashiell Hammett* and *Conan Doyle: Portrait of an Artist* were better received, although *Los Angeles Times* critic Carolyn See felt that Symons' English background puts him at a "cultural disadvantage" in interpreting Hammett's distinctly American works. One *Washington Post* contributor, on the other hand, states that the author wrote "with zestful, sometimes revisionist appreciation of the [Hammett] novels." Symons was more in his element when he talks about the much-admired Doyle; and though "this isn't a definitive work," according to Margaret Cannon in *Globe and Mail*, ". . . it's a carefully written, delightfully illustrated introduction" to Doyle.

But more than for his common interest in these giants of the crime fiction genre, Symons was unique in his fascination for lesser-known literary figures; and much of his critical writing focused on such writers as Wyndham Lewis, Frances Newman, James Branch

Cabell, and Peggy Hopkins Joyce. Indeed, in his *Makers of the New: The Revolution in Literature, 1912-1939*, Symons ranked Lewis with the likes of Ezra Pound, James Joyce, and T. S. Eliot. Some critics, like *Washington Post* contributor Charles Trueheart, felt that including Lewis among these authors is an "injustice." Even though some reviewers were puzzled by Symons' emphasis on these relatively minor writers, others saw his attention to such details as being a virtue. In a review of the author's *Critical Observations*, Valentine Cunningham wrote in the *Times Literary Supplement*: "Symons' greatest distinction as a critic . . . is [his] ungrudging affection for literary merit wherever it crops up. It's a critical versatility that rebuts the fixity of canons, without ever sinking into the flaccidities of a too liberal tastelessness."

Just as Symons tried to bring more obscure literary figures to public attention, he attempted throughout his career to elevate the status of crime fiction. "The crime story is a wonderfully literary form," he wrote in *Contemporary Authors Autobiography Series*. "In the hands of a good writer it can be used for anything from Kafkan ambiguity to raw slices of Zolaesque realism. A criminal theme is the sturdiest of backbones for a plot, and there is nothing intrinsically sensational or trivial about it—the sensationalism and triviality come, if they do, in the treatment." As for Symons himself, his work in the crime genre—especially as a device for social commentary—made a distinct impression. Grimes asserted: "No individual has done more in the postwar period to make crime stories into serious literature as has Julain Symons. He has documented a historical change in the crime-and-mystery genre, proposed a theory to account for the change, and subjected his theory to the test of writing. His many excellent novels and stories support the theory." Carter attested that Symons "has proven how flexible a vehicle [the mystery genre] is for presenting a personal vision of the stresses of modern western civilization."

Part of Symons' manuscript collection is housed at the Humanities Research Center, University of Texas at Austin.

BIOGRAPHICAL/CRITICAL SOURCES:

BOOKS

Contemporary Authors Autobiography Series, Volume 3, Gale (Detroit), 1986.

Contemporary Literary Criticism, Gale, Volume 2, 1974, Volume 14, 1980, Volume 32, 1985.

Dictionary of Literary Biography, Gale, Volume 87: *British Mystery and Thriller Writers since 1940,* 1989, Volume 155: *Twentieth-Century British Literary Biographers,* 1995.

Dictionary of Literary Biography Yearbook: 1992, Gale, 1993.

Scarte, Francis, *Auden and After: The Liberation of Poetry, 1930-1941,* Routledge & Kegan Paul, 1942.

St. James Guide to Crime and Mystery Writers, 4th edition, St. James Press (Detroit), 1996.

Symons, Julian, *The Julian Symons Omnibus,* Collins, 1966.

Walsdorf, John J. and Bonnie J. Allen, *Julian Symons,* Oak Knoll (New Castle, DE), 1996.

PERIODICALS

Armchair Detective, January, 1979.
Best Sellers, April 15, 1972.
Books and Bookmen, October, 1972.
Book World, May 28, 1972.
Detroit News, November 8, 1981.
Georgia Review, fall, 1972.
Globe and Mail (Toronto), January 28, 1984; January 16, 1988; April 9, 1988.
Los Angeles Times, February 14, 1983; November 2, 1983; April 8, 1985.
Los Angeles Times Book Review, October 19, 1980; September 14, 1986; January 24, 1988; July 10, 1988.
National Observer, January 5, 1970.
New Republic, August 26, 1978; September 2, 1978.
New Statesman, December 23, 1966; October 20, 1978.
Newsweek, February 14, 1983.
New Yorker, April 1, 1972.

New York Herald Tribune Book Review, June 22, 1958; November 4, 1962.
New York Times, October 23, 1949; November 9, 1952; April 24, 1955; June 29, 1958; July 3, 1978; January 10, 1986; November 6, 1987.
New York Times Book Review, July 21, 1965; January 8, 1967; May 14, 1967; December 9, 1973; July 9, 1978; February 4, 1979; November 16, 1980; December 13, 1981; March 20, 1983; January 29, 1984; May 5, 1985; January 10, 1988; August 14, 1988; January 1, 1995, p. 7.
Observer, July 23, 1978.
Publishers Weekly, July 2, 1982; October 25, 1985.
Spectator, October 26, 1951; July 29, 1960; August 11, 1973; June 29, 1974; March 22, 1975; November 11, 1978; January 19, 1980.
Time, February 14, 1983; February 24, 1986.
Times (London), November 19, 1981; May 13, 1982; September 22; 1983.
Times Literary Supplement, April 8, 1965; February 1, 1975; August 11, 1978; May 9, 1980; January 22, 1982; June 25, 1982; September 17, 1982; November 18, 1983; March 28, 1986; April 25, 1986; November 4, 1988; March 17, 1989.
Washington Post, December 26, 1978.
Washington Post Book World, July 9, 1978; November 2, 1980; March 17, 1985; March 16, 1986; January 3, 1988; August 21, 1988.

OBITUARIES

PERIODICALS

Chicago Tribune, November 27, 1994, Sec. 2, p. 8.
Los Angeles Times, November 24, 1994, p. A22.
New York Times, November 23, 1994, p. D19.
Time, December 5, 1994, p. 29.
Times (London), November 22, 1994, p. 23.
Washington Post, November 23, 1994, p. B6.*

T-V

TANNAHILL, Reay 1929-

PERSONAL: Born December 9, 1929, in Glasgow, Scotland; daughter of Hamish Cowan (a marine engineer) and Olive (Reay) Tannahill; married Michael Edwardes (an author), August 8, 1958 (divorced, 1983). *Education:* University of Glasgow, M.A., 1951.

ADDRESSES: Home—London, England. *Agent*—Gill Coleridge, RCW, 20 Powis Mews, London W11 1JN, England.

CAREER: Times Educational Supplement, London, England, reporter, 1952-56; Thames & Hudson, London, advertising manager, 1956-58; Folio Society, London, advertising consultant, 1958-62; writer, 1962—.

AWARDS, HONORS: Chianti Ruffino Antico Fattore award, 1988; Boots Romantic Novel of the Year, 1990, for *Passing Glory.*

WRITINGS:

NONFICTION

Regency England, Folio Society (London), 1964.
Paris in the Revolution, Folio Society, 1966.
The Fine Art of Food, Folio Society, 1968.
Food in History (Book-of-the-Month Club selection), Stein & Day (New York City), 1973.
Flesh and Blood: A History of the Cannibal Complex, Stein & Day, 1975.
Sex in History (Book-of-the-Month Club alternate selection), Stein & Day, 1980.

FICTION

A Dark and Distant Shore, St. Martin's (New York City), 1983.
The World, the Flesh, and the Devil, Crown (New York City), 1987.
Passing Glory, Crown, 1990.
In Still and Stormy Waters, Orion (London), 1992.

OTHER

Contributor to *Companion to Scottish Culture* (encyclopedia).

SIDELIGHTS: Reay Tannahill has had success with both nonfiction and fiction. Her studies of food and sex, published as *Food in History* and *Sex in History,* received favorable reviews in the 1970s and early 1980s, and her historical/romantic novels—including the best-selling *A Dark and Distant Shore*—have more recently earned a readership in the United Kingdom and America. *Twentieth-Century Romance and Historical Writers* contributor Pamela Cleaver cited Tannahill for an "encyclopedic" knowledge of social history that has contributed to her development as a fiction writer. As Cleaver put it, "The details [Tannahill] uses are well-chosen and skillfully integrated into her exciting historical novels, set mainly in Scotland."

Tannahill's 1973 nonfiction study, *Food in History,* was generally praised by the critics for its fresh and original examination of the significance of food and eating throughout history. *Sex in History,* published seven years later, reflects the author's interest in what she considers to be the other major preoccupation of human existence and its influence over the past centuries. It, too, was well-received, despite the observation of several reviewers that the topic of sex has been subjected to print and media overkill. *Time* magazine correspondent Eve Auchincloss called *Sex in History* a "levelheaded" and ". . . lively but never prurient history." Auchincloss continued of Tannahill: "She traces the roots of contraception, the long battle against venereal diseases and the attitudes that surround them, the changing mores of the West and the sometimes prudish Third World. She seems to have examined every sexual arena from the Garden of Eden to the harems of Asia and the Middle East to the screens of Hollywood. . . . Although Tannahill writes with what appears to be a feminist sensibility, she never indulges in special pleading." And though Auchincloss felt *Sex in History* to be "overfond of overstatement, and its survey is wider than it is deep," the critic concluded that Tannahill's book "is the most complete of its kind ever written. It is diligent, provocative and fascinating."

Recalling *Food in History* as a "charming, discursive and impressionistic study," L. S. Davis of the *Washington Post Book World* noted that *"Sex in History* is equally charming but, wisely, more businesslike. . . . Tannahill attacks [her subject] with tremendous verve." While admitting that "no such survey would be complete if it failed to inspire a quibble or two," Davis observed that "on the whole, Tannahill renders yeoman service to her subject." Nevertheless, the reviewer concluded, "because the book is so aptly, cleverly and lavishly illustrated, an argument is precisely what you're likely to get if you're incautious enough to try reading it on public transportation. It is a risk well worth taking. Sanity on the subject of sex is all too rare; wit is in even shorter supply, and an engaging style is about as commonplace as eyebrows on an egg. Three cheers and a tiger, therefore, for Reay Tannahill."

Since the early 1980s, Tannahill has turned her talents to fiction, creating a series of historical romances set in Scotland during different eras. Her first novel, *A Dark and Distant Shore,* reached the best-seller list in both hardback and paperback after being characterized as a cross between *Gone with the Wind* and *The Thorn Birds.* Covering many decades of the 19th century, *A Dark and Distant Shore* recounts the efforts of Vilia Cameron to regain her family's ancestral castle, Kinveil, and its mountainous Highland environs.

The award-winning *Passing Glory* follows the fortunes of two families, the Jardines, who work in a shipyard, and the Brittons, who own the facility. And

In Still and Stormy Waters features the machinations of two cousins, Rachel and Sophie Macmillan, who both seek to own Juran, another Scottish castle. Throughout her books Tannahill weaves her characters' personal stories with wider historical events, taking care to set her heroines carefully within the mores of their times.

According to Cleaver, Tannahill's descriptions "are evocative and all the books have a strong sense of place." The critic added: "Although she has attractive heroes, Tannahill's heroines dominate the books. These are women who, although very much of their times . . . have strong ambitions and almost modern feminist feelings." Cleaver concluded that all of Tannahill's historical fictions are "well written, richly textured, extremely readable and admirably researched. . . . To curl up with one of her sagas is both enjoyable and rewarding."

BIOGRAPHICAL/CRITICAL SOURCES:

BOOKS

Twentieth-Century Romance and Historical Writers, third edition, St. James Press (Detroit, MI), 1994, pp. 650-651.

PERIODICALS

Books and Bookmen, April, 1984, p. 29.
Chicago Tribune Book World, May 18, 1980.
Kirkus Reviews, April 1, 1983, p. 401.
Los Angeles Times, August 23, 1973; March 5, 1980.
Publishers Weekly, April 15, 1983, p. 42.
Time, March 3, 1980.
Times Literary Supplement, June 6, 1980.
Washington Post, August 11, 1973.
Washington Post Book World, February 24, 1980.

*   *   *

TATE, Ellalice
    See HIBBERT, Eleanor Alice Burford

*   *   *

TEMPEST, Sarah
    See PONSONBY, D(oris) A(lmon)

TENNANT, Emma (Christina) 1937-
(Catherine Aydy)

PERSONAL: Born October 20, 1937, in London, England; daughter of Christopher Grey (Lord Glenconner; a businessman) and Elizabeth (Lady Glenconner; maiden name, Powell) Tennant; married three times; children: (first marriage) Matthew, (second marriage) Daisy, (third marriage) Rose. *Education:* Attended St. Paul's Girls' School, London, England. *Avocational interests:*Walking.

ADDRESSES: Home—141 Elgin Cres., London W11, England.   *Office*—c/o Grafton Books Ltd., 77-85 Fulham Palace Rd., London W6 8JB England. *Agent*—A. D. Peters & Co., Ltd., 10 Buckingham St., London WC2N 6BU, England.

CAREER: Novelist, critic, and editor, 1960—. *Queen*, London, England, travel correspondent, 1963; *Vogue*, London, features editor, 1966; full-time novelist, 1973—.

MEMBER: Royal Society of Literature (fellow).

WRITINGS:

NOVELS

(Under pseudonym Catherine Aydy) *The Colour of Rain*, Weidenfeld & Nicolson (London), 1963, reprinted under name Emma Tennant, Faber (London), 1988.
The Time of the Crack, J. Cape (London), 1973, published as *The Crack*, Penguin (London), 1978.
The Last of the Country House Murders, J. Cape, 1975, Thomas Nelson (Nashville, TN), 1976.
Hotel de Dream, Gollancz (London), 1976.
The Bad Sister, Coward (New York City), 1978.
Wild Nights, J. Cape, 1979, Harcourt (New York City), 1980.
Alice Fell, J. Cape, 1980.
The Boggart (juvenile), illustrations by Mary Rayner, Granada (London), 1980.
The Search for Treasure Island (juvenile), illustrated by Andrew Skilleter, Puffin (New York City), 1981.
Queen of Stones, J. Cape, 1982.
Woman Beware Woman, J. Cape, 1983, published as *The Half-Mother*, Little-Brown (Boston, MA) 1985.
The Ghost Child (juvenile), illustrated by Charlotte Voake, Heinemann (London), 1984.
Black Marina, Faber, 1985.

The House of Hospitalities, Viking (London), 1987.
A Wedding of Cousins, Viking, 1988.
The Adventures of Robina, by Herself: Being the Memoirs of a Debutante at the Court of Queen Elizabeth II, Persea Books (New York City), 1988.
The Magic Drum, Viking, 1989.
Two Women of London: The Strange Case of Ms. Jekyll and Mrs. Hyde, Faber, 1989.
Faustine, Faber, 1992.
Pemberley; or, "Pride and Prejudice" Continued, St. Martin's (New York City), 1993, published in England as *Pemberley: A Sequel to Pride and Prejudice*, Hodder & Stoughton (London).
An Unequal Marriage; or, "Pride and Prejudice" Twenty Years Later, St. Martin's, 1994.
Tess, Flamingo (London), 1994.
Eleanor and Marianne, Simon & Schuster (New York City), 1996.

OTHER

(Contributor) *Women on Women*, Sidgwick & Jackson (London), 1974.
(Editor) *Bananas* (anthology), Quartet (London), 1977, reprinted, Charles River Books (Boston), 1988.
(Editor) *Saturday Night Reader*, W. H. Allen (London), 1979.
(Contributor) John Haffenden, editor, *Novelists in Interview*, Methuen, 1985.
(Contributor) Moira Monteith, editor, *Women's Writing: A Challenge to Theory*, St. Martin's, 1986.
The ABC of Writing (nonfiction), Faber, 1992.
(With Ann Davies) *Hooked Rugs*, Sterling Publishing Company (New York City), 1995.

Also author of *Sisters and Strangers*, 1990, and *Dare's Secret Pony*, 1992. Contributor to numerous periodicals, including *Guardian*. Founding editor, *Bananas* (literary magazine of the British Arts Council), 1975-78; general editor, *In Verse*, 1982—, and *Lives of Modern Women*, 1986-88.

WORK IN PROGRESS: Two novels: *Grandmother Sea* and a sequel to Margaret Mitchell's *Gone with the Wind*.

SIDELIGHTS: Emma Tennant's wide-ranging body of fiction offers a satirical but penetrating vision of conditions in modern England. Herself a descendant of Scottish nobility, Tennant turns a novelist's eye on the British upper class, with special emphasis on the uneasy relationships between men and women. "Fantasy, feminism, and political satire are combined in Emma Tennant's novels, which portray humanity's groping, fumbling quest of meaning and purpose today," writes Georgia L. Lambert in the *Dictionary of Literary Biography*. Lambert continues, "The difficulties of distinguishing between illusion and reality are exemplified by Tennant's often comic, dreamlike narratives and her stunning imagery. Her exploration of the imagination and her depiction of the passing of time show exciting originality, and she is a novelist who is inspiring followers of modern fiction."

Tennant's work defies easy categorization. Some of her novels are considered science fiction, others offer a mock Gothic atmosphere, and still others are indebted to Daniel Defoe, James Hogg, Robert Louis Stevenson, and Jane Austen. If any theme unites her fiction, it is the state of decay and disreputability plaguing her society in the wake of its grand empire days. *Times Literary Supplement* contributor Carol Rumens writes: "Large, faded country houses and hotels form an important part of the imaginative terrain of Emma Tennant. They seem to provide a metaphor both for the individual human consciousness and for historical change, particularly as it is played out between the generations." In the *London Review of Books,* Margaret Walters concludes that Tennant "has a caricaturist's skill in pinning down social types, and she brings them together in some splendid farcical set-pieces."

Tennant was born in London, the daughter of a wealthy titled businessman. Her father, Lord Glenconner, was of Scottish descent, but the family had long resided in or near London. Just before the outbreak of World War II, however, Lord Glenconner moved his wife and children to the relative safety of Peebleshire, Scotland, where he owned a manor house. In a piece for the *Contemporary Authors Autobiography Series* (*CAAS*), Tennant describes Glen House, the family seat, as "an unfashionable hideosity . . . with [a] labyrinthine basement, freezing halls, and elaborate staircases." It was there, Tennant continues, that she spent her early childhood. "And it is the landscape, both of those hills and burns and moors and of the inside of this surprising house itself, that informs a great deal of my work."

Thus Tennant grew up under the influence of Scottish fairy tales and legends and was especially inspired by the works of James Hogg, author of *The Confessions of a Justified Sinner.* Tennant writes: "As James Hogg knew—and described—it was only too probable that the idle walker would be transformed into a three-

legged stool, or a jay, or maybe even a hare. . . . This taking for granted of the magical and the mundane combined did a great deal to provide inspiration in my later years, when I came to understand that I would be a writer. The tales of possession by the devil, of the sinister double who takes over the *Confessions,* had been my earliest landscape. And it was as far from an English landscape, with its realism and irony, as it would be possible to find."

When Tennant was eight her family moved south again to their more comfortable homes in England. There she was raised in a genteel environment, doing "what was expected of a woman of class." At seventeen she had a formal debut, including a presentation at court. The experiences among high society provided Tennant with grist for her fiction—her first novel, *The Colour of Rain,* was written under the pseudonym Catherine Aydy when she was only twenty-four. Lambert describes the work as "a conventional third-person narrative that depicts the English upper-middle class way of life and shows the artificiality and shallowness in their lives and marriages." *Spectator* contributor Susanna Johnston writes: "Although there is an atmosphere of general malevolence in these 115 pages, the novel, at its birth, emerged alive and showing promise (subsequently borne out by the development of Miss Tennant's greater talent) as it shone an unsteady torch onto the spoilt ways of upper-crust high-livers."

More than ten years passed before Tennant published another novel, although she wrote constantly. In 1972 she became acquainted with several of England's notable science-fiction writers, including J. G. Ballard, John Sladek, and Michael Moorcock. These authors encouraged Tennant to use science fiction conventions to create surrealistic allegories about the hostile environment she perceived around her. The three novels she wrote between 1972 and 1975—*The Time of the Crack, The Last of the Country House Murders,* and *Hotel de Dream*—all offer portraits of England in crisis in the very near future. In these works, notes Harriet Waugh in *Spectator,* "the forces of reality and imagination are let loose on each other, and intermingle destructively."

Spectator correspondent Paul Ableman characterizes Tennant's three science-fiction works as "funny-satirical phantasies [that] show an increasing sureness of touch culminating in the authentically witty *Hotel de Dream.*" Ableman adds that, for a young author, Tennant "demonstrated an authority over satirical comedy rare in contemporary letters." In *Books and*

Bookmen, James Brockway observes that in Tennant's particular brand of science-fiction fantasy, "plenty of old English attitudes get murdered . . . and in her own wittily and elegantly lethal way, too."

Tennant writes in *CAAS* that after 1975, "my preoccupations as a writer had turned almost exclusively to the subject of the female psyche, whether pubescent or mature." In works such as *The Bad Sister, Wild Nights,* and *Woman Beware Woman,* Tennant makes the nature and role of women in society a central theme. While a departure from her earlier science fiction, these works abound in mystical and supernatural phenomena, especially the theme of the "double" and the myths and fairy tales that influence the female subconscious. *Spectator* reviewer Francis King observes that the novels are "primarily about the terrible damage that women can inflict on each other."

The Bad Sister, for instance, concerns a troubled young woman who murders her father and his legitimate daughter. Tennant's story is based on Hogg's *Confessions of a Justified Sinner,* but she substitutes a female character in the central role and then explores feminism carried to the extreme. In her *Village Voice* review of the novel, Sonia Jaffe Robbins writes that the central character's narrative "is a masterful emotional document, plunging us directly into her mind as she is driven mad by the fragmentation women often feel in trying to discover who they are. . . . In this story feminism is no answer, for all it denotes is fanaticism."

Some of Tennant's best-known work is her series of comic novels of manners, including *The House of Hospitalities, A Wedding of Cousins,* and *The Adventures of Robina, by Herself: Being the Memoirs of a Debutante at the Court of Queen Elizabeth II.* As the titles suggest, the novels offer a social history of the modern British upper class, sometimes from the point of view of its members and at other times from the point of view of a middle-class observer. *New York Times Book Review* correspondent David Sacks claims that in these satires of postwar British aristocracy, Tennant shows the reader "quite a crew: . . . rogues, boors and dimwits, the prey of pimps and con men, in love with bathroom humor and forever poor-mouthing amid ancestral splendors. Totally mercenary, they nevertheless harbor a medieval disdain for commerce, and so they are the worst gold diggers of all." Sacks adds: "Ms. Tennant knows her subject from the inside, . . . offering cruel insights into the mysteries of the ruling class." In the *Times Literary Supplement,*

Patricia Craig contends that with *The House of Hospitalities* and *A Wedding of Cousins,* Tennant "is attempting, and in the course of bringing off, . . . an indictment of upper-class exorbitance." Craig concludes that the works "[bristle] with astuteness and animation."

Dark comedy infuses the gothic-tinged *Magic Drum,* in which a female journalist struggles with her sanity while investigating a death at a writing colony. Called a "rattling good mystery" by Shena Mackay, writing for the *Times Literary Supplement,* the book drew less supportive reviews from others. Nicci Gerrard in *New Statesman and Society* criticizes the work as being ripe with "tortuously fearful sentiments" and "overwrought climaxes," a concern shared by *London Review of Books*'s Zachary Leader, who states that "the novel quickly dwindles into an uneasy satire of genre conventions." Mackay, nevertheless, asserts that the work remains an "entertaining, darkly comic whole."

Tennant's work continues to revisit the work of classical writers in *Faustine,* translating the ideas of Johann Wolfgang von Goethe into a contemporary, feminist setting. The work explores a middle-aged woman's rejuvenation as the result of her deal with the devil, which is revealed to the reader through her granddaughter's search for the truth about her grandmother's diabolically preserved image. According to Barbara Hardy, writing in *Times Literary Supplement,* "It is everywoman's story of youth's short span." Not all critics find Tennant successful in her treatment of feminist themes. John Sutherland in *London Review of Books* classifies the work as being in a subgenre of "feminist travesties of literary classics." Nevertheless he finds the work "as clever, enjoyable and tactfully self-revealing as anything Tennant has written." Similarly, Hardy concludes that this short novel is "so piercingly clear about the failure of 'attempts at idealism and brotherhood', that it could even be a heart-changer."

Based loosely on the Robert Louis Stevenson classic *Dr. Jekyll and Mr. Hyde,* Tennant's *Two Women of London: The Strange Case of Ms. Jekyll and Mrs. Hyde* concentrates on a cast of feminist characters in a contemporary setting haunted by the Notting Hill rapist. Judging the tale less frightening than the original, Mackay asserts that it is nevertheless a witty reworking that reflects "the Scottish obsession with duality." She states that the novel is "perceptive of modern mores and values, and, in its brilliant observation of its prey, has a horror of its own."

Jane Austen provides the inspiration for Tennant's later works, including *Pemberley; or, "Pride and Prejudice" Continued, An Unequal Marriage; or "Pride and Prejudice" Twenty Years Later,* and the *Sense and Sensibility* sequel *Eleanor and Marianne.* A sequel to Margaret Mitchell's *Gone with the Wind* was scheduled for release in 1997. The first two novels extrapolate on future events in the lives of classic lovers Elizabeth Bennet and Mr. Darcy. Taking place a year into their marriage, *Pemberley* revolves around Elizabeth's anxiety to provide her new husband with an heir. It also delves into her growing distrust of Darcy over a supposed affair with a mysterious Frenchwoman that may have produced an illegitimate son. Elizabeth is portrayed in great turmoil throughout the book, her preoccupations treated "with an openness that would horrify Austen," according to a *Kirkus Reviews* contributor. Delicate matters such as infertility and vaginal douches are even addressed in mixed company. Rachel Cusk, writing for the *Times Literary Supplement,* also comments on Tennant's bluntness: "Where Austen delicately fades out, Tennant tunes in and turns up the volume." Other critics praise her faithfulness to Austen's manner. In contrasting *Pemberley* with another Austen sequel, Robert Grudin, in the *New York Times Book Review,* compliments the author for her "utter mastery of Austen's style," owing the novel's "malaise" to Tennant's exploitation of material already present in *Pride and Prejudice.* Joyce R. Slater, reviewing for Chicago *Tribune Books,* goes so far as to claim the sequel is true enough to the original that it "smack[s] of deja vu."

As the subtitle suggests, *An Unequal Marriage; or, "Pride and Prejudice" Twenty Years Later* reaches two decades into the future where, according to a *Publishers Weekly* writer, Elizabeth is enmeshed in "a nicely snarled web of predicaments," not the least of which is the trouble her gambling teenage son, Edward, has caused. A wedding assembles a colorful cast of minor characters at the Darcy estate—both those familiar to Austenites and new creations provided by Tennant. While acknowledging the literary inventiveness of *Pemberley,* David Nokes, writing for *Times Literary Supplement,* takes exception to what he labels Tennant's "rambling cliche-ridden style," a style which a *Booklist* reviewer owes to the author's ability to infuse the novel with Austen's spirit and what the writer for *Publishers Weekly* calls "a creditable imitation of period diction" that is both sly and playful.

Written in epistolary form, the third of Tennant's Austen sequels, *Eleanor and Marianne,* is heralded by

Penelope Lively in the *Spectator* as a "cheerful, witty and nicely inventive read." Well-known Austen characters meet personal disaster in the form of abandonment, seduction, cannibals, madness, and New Age philosophies in what Lively suggests is a "larky tribute." A London *Times* reviewer fails to see humor in Tennant's work, calling the sequel "opportunistic . . . more burlesque than homage." In contrast, Lively maintains that the book provides the reader with "respectful and affectionate fun."

In addition to her fiction writing, Tennant has served as a magazine writer and as founding editor of *Bananas,* a respected English literary magazine. She has also edited several anthologies of women's writing. Brockway outlines the chief attractions of Tennant's own fiction, namely "the agility and ebullience of the humour, the sense of the absurd in human beings, . . . and, best of all, the stylish verve of the writing." In the *New Statesman,* Sara Maitland notes that, at its best, "Tennant's writing can sustain narrative, without losing its poetic quality." Likewise, Rumens cites Tennant for prose that is both "beautifully measured and graceful." One reads Emma Tennant, Rumens concludes, "for the pure pleasure of the style."

BIOGRAPHICAL/CRITICAL SOURCES:

BOOKS

Contemporary Authors Autobiography Series, Volume 9, Gale (Detroit, MI), 1989.
Contemporary Literary Criticism, Gale, Volume 13, 1980; Volume 52, 1989.
Contemporary Novelists, fifth edition, St. James Press (Chicago), 1991.
Dictionary of Literary Biography, Volume 14: *British Novelists since 1960,* Gale, 1983.
Twentieth-Century Science Fiction Writers, third edition, St. James Press, 1991.

PERIODICALS

Booklist, November 15, 1994, p. 580.
Books and Bookmen, September, 1975; January, 1977; December, 1982.
Chicago Tribune Books, December 25, 1994, section 14, p. 4.
Globe & Mail (Toronto), February 16, 1985.
Kirkus Reviews, October 1, 1993, p. 1224.
Library Journal, November 1, 1994, p. 112.
London Review of Books, October 13, 1988; June 22, 1989, p. 15; March 12, 1992, p. 23.

Los Angeles Times Book Review, November 7, 1993, p. 1.

New Review, March, 1975.

New Statesman and Society, July 28, 1978; September 18, 1987; June 9, 1989.

New York Review of Books, November 9, 1978.

New York Times, May 4, 1995.

New York Times Book Review, May 12, 1985; April 3, 1988; December 12, 1993, p. 11.

Observer, June 4, 1989, p. 47.

Publishers Weekly, March 16, 1992, p. 74; October 10, 1994, p. 63.

Spectator, February 1, 1975; July 24, 1976; July 22, 1978; September 22, 1979; November 26, 1983; October 10, 1987; March 12, 1988; April 6, 1996, p. 30.

Times (London), January 12, 1985; October 8, 1987; January 21, 1989; May 18, 1989; March 17, 1996, section 7, p. 8.

Times Educational Supplement, July 7, 1989, p. 27.

Times Literary Supplement, June 15, 1973; January 31, 1975; July 16, 1976; July 21, 1978; November 7, 1980; November 19, 1982; November 30, 1984; January 25, 1985; June 21, 1985; September 18-24, 1987; September 30, 1988; June 16-22, 1989, p. 669; March 6, 1992, p. 21; October 29, 1993, p. 19; December 2, 1994, p. 23.

Village Voice, October 16, 1978.

Washington Post Book World, November 21, 1993, p.5.*

*   *   *

TESSLER, Stephanie Gordon 1940-
(Jeffie Ross Gordon, a joint pseudonym)

PERSONAL: Born May 11, 1940, in Los Angeles, CA; daughter of Jack (a fireman) and Sylvia (a retail salesperson) Gordon; married Sidney E. Tessler (a business manager), August 6, 1961; children: Jonathan Adam, Todd Allyn, Jacklyn Paige. *Education:*California State University, Los Angeles, B.A.; attended UCLA and UCLA extension. *Politics:* Liberal conservative. *Religion:* Jewish. *Avocational interests:* Travel, movies, theater, reading, crossword puzzles, her dogs.

ADDRESSES: Office—1937 Pelham Ave. #2, Los Angeles, CA 90025. *Agent*—Ginger Knowlton, Curtis Brown Ltd., Ten Astor Pl., New York, NY 10003.

CAREER: Elementary and special education teacher, 1961-64; librarian, American Film Institute, 1975-76; emeritus professor, Santa Monica College, 1982-83; Writers Ink (a children's literature and editing service), Los Angeles, CA, partner, 1985—; Boyds Mills Press, Honesdale, PA, freelance senior editor, 1991—; Fox Broadcasting Co., Los Angeles, senior editor, *Fox Totally Kids* magazine, 1991—, and story editor/screenwriter for Fox's "Rimba's Island," 1994-95; writer for animation special, "Corduroy and the Snake," for Viacom, 1995-96.

MEMBER: Society Of Children's Book Writers and Illustrators (regional advisor, regional advisor chairperson, board member, 1987—), Southern California Council on Literature for Children and Young People, American Booksellers for Children, Southern California Children's Booksellers Association, Academy of Television Arts and Sciences.

AWARDS, HONORS: Choice honorable mention (with Judith Ross Enderle), *L.A. Parents,* 1991, for *Six Sleepy Sheep;* Children's Choice Book lists (all with Enderle), International Reading Association/Children's Book Council, 1982, for *Good Junk,* 1993, for *Two Badd Babies,* and 1995, for *Six Snowy Sheep;* Georgia Picture Storybook Award nominee (with Tessler), 1994-95, for *The Good-for-Something Dragon.*

WRITINGS:

"BAYSHORE MEDICAL CENTER" SERIES; WITH JUDITH ROSS ENDERLE

Andrea Whitman: Pediatrics, Walker & Co., (New York City), 1983.

Monica Ross: Maternity, Walker & Co., 1983.

Elizabeth Jones: Emergency, Walker & Co., 1984.

Gabriella Ortiz: Hot Line/Crisis Center, Walker & Co., 1984.

WITH ENDERLE; FOR CHILDREN

(Under joint pseudonym Jeffie Ross Gordon) *Rutabaga Ruby* (poetry), Curriculum Associates, 1989.

(Under joint pseudonym Jeffie Ross Gordon) *Hide and Shriek* (riddle book), Lerner (Minneapolis), 1991.

(Under joint pseudonym Jeffie Ross Gordon) *Six Sleepy Sheep,* illustrated by John O'Brien, Boyds Mills Press (Honesdale, PA), 1991.

Six Creepy Sheep, illustrated by John O'Brien, Boyds Mills Press, 1992.
(Under joint pseudonym Jeffie Ross Gordon) *Two Badd Babies,* illustrated by Cruse L. Demarest, Boyds Mills Press, 1992.
(Under joint pseudonym Jeffie Ross Gordon) *Muriel and Ruth,* Boyds Mills Press, 1992.
A Pile of Pigs, illustrated by Charles Jordan, Boyds Mills Press, 1993.
The Good-for-Something Dragon, illustrated by Les Gray, Boyds Mills Press, 1993.
(Under joint pseudonym Jeffie Ross Gordon) *Rebus Treasury II,* Boyds Mills Press, 1993.
Six Snowy Sheep, illustrated by John O'Brien, Boyds Mills Press, 1994.
What Would Mama Do?, illustrated by Chris L. Demarest, Boyds Mills Press, 1995.
Francis, the Earthquake Dog, illustrated by Brooke Scudder, Chronicle Books (San Francisco), 1996.
What's the Matter, Kelly Beans? Candlewick Press (Cambridge, MA), 1996.
Nell Nugget and the Cow Caper, illustrated by Paul Yalowitz, Simon & Schuster (New York City), 1996.
Here's Bobby: How a Cartoon Is Made, Celebration Press (Don Mills, ON, Canada), 1996.
Dear Timothy Tibbitts, illustrated by Carolyn Ewing, Marshall Cavendish (New York City), 1997.
Where Are You, Little Zack?, Houghton (Boston), 1997.

WITH ENDERLE; UNDER PSEUDONYM JEFFIE ROSS GORDON; FOR YOUNG ADULTS

Jacquelyn, Scholastic, Inc. (New York City), 1985.
A Touch of Genius, Silhouette (New York City), 1986.
The Journal of Emily Ross, Silhouette, 1986.
A Touch of Magic, Silhouette, 1987.
Nobody Knows Me, Silhouette, 1987.
Nora, Scholastic, Inc., 1987.
Gimme a Z, Silhouette, 1988.

OTHER

I Double Love You, Tempo Books, 1985.

Also author (with Enderle) of the "Read-a-Picture" series, Modern Publishing, 1989. Contributor of stories to *Highlights for Children.* Story writer and editor (with Enderle) for the first season of Fox TV's *Rimba's Island* series, and writer (with Enderle) for Viacom's *Corduroy Animation Specials.* Tessler's

books have been translated into French, Italian, Spanish, German, Danish, and Finnish.

WORK IN PROGRESS: (All with Judith Ross Enderle) *Six Sandy Sheep,* for Boyds Mills Press, and *Upstairs,* for Boyds Mills Press.

SIDELIGHTS: Stephanie Tessler has published young adult fiction under her own name and also under the name of Jeffie Ross Gordon, a joint pseudonym which she shares with Judith Ross Enderle. Tessler and Enderle also published together under both their names; books by the two have been translated into French, Italian, Spanish, German, Danish, and Finnish. "With my writing partner, Judith Ross Enderle, we've had over sixty books published—from young adult novels to picture books," Tessler told *Something about the Author (SATA).* "Judy and I have been lucky."

Tessler, like most writers for children, was herself an avid reader as a child. However, with Tessler, do not expect to find Goldilocks at the top of her favorites reading list. "I read the Red, the Blue, the Green . . . the every color fairy tales book," Tessler told *CA,* "and I read all the historical biographies I could find, along with *The Wizard of Oz, Mary Poppins,* and other books that became movies." Tessler, born and raised in Los Angeles, added: "I am a true child of California. I grew up working in the motion picture studios, but my favorite thing when I was a child was to sit with my dad and read the encyclopedia. My dad, who was a fireman and a great cook and a whiz bang crossword puzzle enthusiast, wanted to know about everything. He gave me that gift of curiosity, and I still love crosswords, encyclopedias, and want to know about everything. It was only appropriate then that the first piece I had published for children was an article for *Highlights for Children,* all about firemen and firetrucks. My dad would have been proud!"

Tessler's career got off the ground once her children were of school age and she had more time to devote to writing. She began with a writing course at UCLA taught by picture book author Sue Alexander and received further direction from middle-grade and young adult novelist Eve Bunting. During this time Tessler and Enderle met, became friends, and began their collaboration on both young adult and children's titles, including the award-winning *Two Badd Babies* and *Six Snowy Sheep.* From one of their teachers, Tessler learned that getting published would not be easy. "However," Tessler told *CA,* "together we have learned that there are two adages that hold true: If you want something bad enough, and work hard enough, you can achieve almost anything. Also, in our case, two heads *are* better than one. Though Judy and I have published separately, our most satisfying successes have come from joining our writing talents."

In addition to writing and editing children's literature, Tessler and Enderle have also written for Viacom and Fox television in children's programming. For Tessler, this has meant coming full circle back to her California childhood when she worked in motion picture studios. Now, in addition to her writing, she spends time at schools, working with the young people she writes for. "Judy and I have visited many schools and libraries," Tessler told *CA.* "We've met thousands of people, young and old. We've talked to and laughed with many talented future writers and enthusiastic readers in all grades. . . . Writing for young people is a great job. We recommend it."

BIOGRAPHICAL/CRITICAL SOURCES:

PERIODICALS

Bulletin of the Center for Children's Books, May, 1996, p. 299.
Kirkus Reviews, January 1, 1992, p. 52; August 1, 1992, p. 988.
Publishers Weekly, January 6, 1992, p. 65; January 4, 1993, p. 72; October 2, 1995, p. 72; June 3, 1996, p. 83.
Voice of Youth Advocates, December, 1986, p. 226; August, 1987, p. 125; October, 1988, p. 187.

* * *

THOMAS, Frances 1943-

PERSONAL: Born October 21, 1943, in Aberdare, South Wales; daughter of David Elwyn (a teacher) and Agnes (a teacher; maiden name, Connor) Thomas; married Richard Rathbone (a university professor), 1965; children: Harriet, Lucy. *Education:* Queen Mary College, London University, B.A. (with honors), 1965. *Politics:* Labour Party.

ADDRESSES: Home—London, England. *Agent*—David Higham Associates, 5-8, Lower John St., London W1R 4HA, England.

CAREER: Writer. Former school teacher; currently teaches dyslexic children at her home.

AWARDS, HONORS: Tir Na n-Og Prize, 1981, for *The Blindfold Track,* 1986, for *The Region of the Summer Stars,* and 1992, for *Who Stole a Bloater?;* Whitbread First Novel runner-up award, 1986, and Welsh Arts Council Fiction Prize, 1991, both for *Seeing Things.*

WRITINGS:

FOR YOUNG PEOPLE

The Blindfold Track (first novel in *Taliesin* trilogy), Macmillan (London), 1980.
Secrets, illustrated by L. Acs, Hamish Hamilton (London), 1982.
A Knot of Spells (second novel in *Taliesin* trilogy), Barn Owl Press, 1983.
Dear Comrade (for young adults), Bodley Head, 1983.
Zak (for young adults), Bodley Head, 1984.
The Region of the Summer Stars (third novel in *Taliesin* trilogy), Barn Owl Press, 1985.
Cityscape (for young adults), Heinemann, 1988.
Jam for Tea, Collins Educational, 1989.
The Prince and the Cave, Pont Books/WJEC Welsh History Project, 1991.
Who Stole a Bloater?, Seren Books, 1991.
The Bear and Mr. Bear, illustrated by Ruth Brown, Dutton's Children's Books, 1994, published in England as *Mr. Bear and the Bear,* Andersen Press, 1994.

FOR ADULTS

Seeing Things (novel), Gollancz, 1986.
The Fall of Man (novel), Gollancz, 1989.
Christina Rossetti: A Biography, Self Publishing Association, 1992, Virago, 1994.

ADAPTATIONS: Who Stole a Bloater? was dramatized by Jackanory on BBC television in 1993.

WORK IN PROGRESS: Supposing, a children's book, for Bloomsbury Books; *Pettifor's Angel,* a novel.

SIDELIGHTS: Welsh author Frances Thomas began her writing career, appropriately enough, with a historical fantasy set in her homeland. Referring to the Celtic epic, *The Mabinogion,* for inspiration, Thomas decided to write about the legend of Taliesin. *The Blindfold Track,* the first of Thomas's three books on the subject, follows the adventures of the boy Gwion, who is abandoned as a child, raised by a prince, and taught by Merlin the magician, eventually becoming the famed bard Taliesin. Margery Fisher of *Growing Point* wrote that in this retelling, Thomas depicts a "modern psychological view of a boy growing up" in a time now veiled in legend. Although *School Librarian* contributor Dennis Hamley felt that the dialogue was too "modern-sounding," *Junior Bookshelf* reviewer R. Baines called Thomas's first tale "a well-written, absorbing and enjoyable book." *The Blindfold Track* won the 1981 Tir Na n-Og Prize, and Thomas followed this success three years later with a sequel, *A Knot of Spells,* which tells how Taliesin leaves his position as the king of Powys's bard to protect the twin children of a queen who is dying in another Welsh kingdom. "The book mingles high politics and archaeology, military exploits and romantic affections," according to Fisher of *Growing Point,* who added that this time the magical elements of Taliesin's story are "subordinated" in favor of concentrating on the characters' relationships. In this complex tale, noted *Junior Bookshelf* contributor D. A. Young, an "enthusiasm for all things Welsh on the part of a reader" is helpful in maintaining interest in the involved storyline.

Thomas, who educates dyslexic children in her home, has also written other books for young readers that feature a present-day setting. *Dear Comrade* follows the written correspondences between Kate Bannister and Paul Miles as they slowly grow to love each other despite their completely opposing political views (he leans to the right, and she to the left). Kate and Paul argue about the law and other political matters, never coming to a consensus (though they do change their views a little), so that the reader must decide for himself who is in the right. Dennis Hamley, writing in *School Librarian,* found the two characters "convincing, funny and moving."

Thomas's next young adult novel is *Zak.* Told from the perspective of a teenager named Mark, *Zak* is about teens who are unhappy with who they are. Mark is bored silly by his life at school and at home, until a new kid named Zak comes to his school. Zak impresses everyone with his stories of living in Los Angeles with his father, whom he insists is a famous rock star. But when Mark visits Zak's home, he realizes the lies behind these stories. The book ends with Zak's disappearance and Mark going back to his original best friend and making amends. Young readers "will sympathise with the boredom and be enter-

tained by Mark's contempt for adults," Margaret Campbell said in *School Librarian.*

In *Cityscape* Thomas demonstrates again her ability to write in different genres: in this case, science fiction/fantasy. Fifteen-year-old Debra Stober discovers on her route to school that an old Jacobean mansion has doors that lead to cities in other worlds. She "travels" to a world in the future ruled by the Guardians, who suppress their people by denying them the right to read books. Debra becomes attracted to Cal, a handsome man who is leading a democratic rebellion that needs Debra's help because she knows how to read and write. By teaching these people to read, Debra gains a new sense of purpose and inner pride that inspires her to accept the dangerous mission of going to the Poison Tower where the Guardians have secreted away all the books. The Guardians are overthrown, but Debra is disillusioned when she later returns to the city to discover that Cal is becoming just as corrupt as the Guardians were. Debra rejects the other world in favor of her home, to which she returns to begin a relationship with a new boyfriend. "Among the proliferation of metaphors for growing up," commented Fisher of *Growing Point,* "the image of alternative cityscapes provides valid insights into teenage personality and problems."

In addition to novels like these, Thomas has written picture books for young children, including *Secrets* and the more recent *The Bear and Mr. Bear. Secrets* is a simple story about "the social need for discretion and self-control," according to *Growing Point* reviewer Margery Fisher. It tells how two boys seek out their own secret when a friend refuses to tell them her's. *The Bear and Mr. Bear* is a sensitive tale about a man who takes pity on a dancing bear that is abused by its trainer. He buys the bear and sets him loose on the grounds of his home. The man, who is called Mr. Bear by the town's children because of his grumpy disposition, empathizes with the sad bear, and man and animal find solace and comfort in each other's company. *School Library Journal* contributor Tom S. Hurlburt deemed the book a "heartfelt, uplifting story."

Having written historical fantasy, realistic young adult novels, fantasy for teens, and picture books for small children, Thomas has proven her diversity as a writer. She told *CA,* "For the last few years, I have divided my time between writing and teaching dyslexic children, which I do privately at home." Thomas continues to demonstrate her versatility by also writing novels for adults, and, in 1992, publishing her first biography for adults, *Christina Rossetti*.

BIOGRAPHICAL/CRITICAL SOURCES:

PERIODICALS

Booklist, January 15, 1995, pp. 938, 940.
Books for Keeps, November, 1987.
Books for Your Children, spring, 1985, p. 18; summer, 1995, p. 21.
Growing Point, September, 1980, p. 3767; January, 1983, pp. 4004-4005; May, 1984, p. 4263; January, 1989, pp. 5092-5093.
Junior Bookshelf, August, 1980, p. 201; February, 1983, p. 34; June, 1984, p. 146; February, 1985, pp. 49-50; December, 1988, pp. 297-98; February, 1995, p. 12.
Publishers Weekly, December 12, 1994, p. 62.
School Librarian, June, 1981, p. 157; June, 1983, p. 143; June, 1984, pp. 153-154; March, 1985, p. 63.
School Library Journal, March, 1995, p. 187.
Times Literary Supplement, November 25, 1983.

*   *   *

THOMAS, G. K.
See DAVIES, L(eslie) P(urnell)

*   *   *

THOMAS, Jane Resh 1936-

PERSONAL: Born August 15, 1936, in Kalamazoo, MI; daughter of Reed Beneval (a salesman) and Thelma (a teacher; maiden name, Scott) Resh; married Richard Thomas (a copywriter), November 13, 1961; children: Jason. *Education:* Bronson School of Nursing, R.N., 1957; attended Michigan State University, 1959-60; University of Minnesota, B.A. (summa cum laude), 1967, M.A., 1971.

ADDRESSES: Home—3121 44th Ave. S., Minneapolis, MN 55406.

CAREER: Worked as registered nurse, 1957-60; University of Minnesota at Minneapolis, instructor in English composition, 1967-80; freelance writer, 1972—; writing instructor for Split Rock Arts Pro-

gram, The Loft, and private workshops, 1974—; freelance editor of children's books, 1988-95; lecturer.

MEMBER: Phi Beta Kappa.

AWARDS, HONORS: Parent's Choice Award for fiction, for *Courage at Indian Deep;* American Booksellers Pick of the Lists citations, for *Wheels* and *Fox in a Trap;* Joan Fassler Award, 1989, American Library Association Notable Book citation, and Best of the Best for Children citation, all for *Saying Good-bye to Grandma;* British Children's Book Award Runner-up, for *The Princess in the Pigpen;* Consortium of Latin American Studies Programs' America's Children's and Young Adult Book Award—Commended List, 1994, for *Lights on the River.*

WRITINGS:

JUVENILE FICTION

Elizabeth Catches a Fish, illustrated by Joseph Duffy, Seabury (New York City), 1977.
The Comeback Dog, illustrated by Troy Howell, Clarion (New York City), 1981.
Courage at Indian Deep, Clarion, 1984.
Wheels, illustrated by Emily McCully, Clarion, 1986.
Fox in a Trap, illustrated by Troy Howell, Clarion, 1987.
Saying Good-bye to Grandma, illustrated by Marcia Sewall, Clarion, 1988.
The Princess in the Pigpen, Clarion, 1989.
Lights on the River, illustrated by Michael Dooling, Hyperion (New York City), 1994.
Daddy Doesn't Have to Be a Giant Anymore, illustrated by Marcia Sewall, Clarion, 1996.
Scaredy Dog, illustrated by Marilyn Mets, Hyperion, 1996.
Behind the Mask: The Life of Elizabeth I, Clarion, 1996, published as *Elizabeth the Great: Queen of the Golden Age,* Houghton (Boston), 1996.
Celebration!, Hyperion, 1997.

OTHER

Book critic for the *Minneapolis Star Tribune* and the Cleveland *Plain Dealer,* 1972—. Contributor of articles and reviews to periodicals, including *Horn Book* and *New York Times Book Review.*

WORK IN PROGRESS: Potluck Supper Fourth of July, illustrated by Raul Colon, for Hyperion; *Maggie's Eyes,* a picture book, for Hyperion; *Hunting for Bears,* a picture book, for Scholastic; *The Snoop,* a chapter book, for Kingfisher.

SIDELIGHTS: The children's books of Jane Resh Thomas are touched by the author's own life experiences, attitudes, and emotions. Both a dog from Thomas's childhood and one from her son's went into the making of *The Comeback Dog.* The Mexican migrant farm workers in *Lights on the River* were a familiar sight during Thomas's childhood on a Michigan farm. And though she did not realize it at the time, Thomas was writing about herself and her own difficult experiences when she told the story of Elizabeth in *The Princess in the Pigpen.* "The most surprising thing I have learned about writing fiction is the extent and subtlety of its connections to an author's own life," Thomas told *CA.* "Fiction writers 'make up' their stories, but not out of thin air. Even Rumpelstiltskin couldn't make something out of nothing, but spun gold from the common straw at his feet. And it is the common straw of everyday experience from which fiction writers spin their stories—the people and places they've known, their own unique perspectives and attitudes."

The majority of Thomas's childhood was spent in Kalamazoo, Michigan, on her grandparent's peach orchard and tree nursery farm near Lake Michigan, and at a cottage on Big Cedar Lake. Nature and exploring were common activities for Thomas, as was fishing with her father, who taught her the names of many of the natural elements around them. "When we were at home in Kalamazoo, my favorite place was the Washington Square Library, with its stone entryway, its fireplace and leaded windows, and what seemed like miles of books," Thomas once described for *CA.* And busy as Thomas's mother was raising four children with only financial support from her husband, she always found time to read to them. "I learned to love literature at her side," continued Thomas. "My family were uncommunicative people, and I relied on books, as I did on nature, not only to entertain but to sustain myself."

Desiring to be a writer since the age of seven, Thomas was at first discouraged by the responses of adults to the things she wrote. Overcoming this, she has since written a number children's books depicting sensitively drawn characters and accurately describing their experiences and emotions. The first, *Elizabeth Catches a Fish,* describes the seven-year-old title character's birthday present of a fishing rod and equipment as well as the excitement leading up to her

first fishing trip with her father. Barbara Karlin stated in *New York Times Book Review* that *Elizabeth Catches a Fish* is written "with vivid clarity and precision."

This same accuracy is found in the 1981 story *The Comeback Dog,* in which nine-year-old Daniel must deal with the recent death of his beloved dog Captain. Finding another dog near death at the side of the road, Daniel reluctantly brings it home and nurses it back to health. But Lady does not respond to his affections as Captain did, and when Daniel lets her off her leash she runs away. Reappearing a few weeks later and once again in need of Daniel's help, Lady slowly gains back her master's affections. A *Kirkus Reviews* contributor asserted that "once again . . . Thomas invests a youngish child . . . with real and satisfying skills, and writes a graceful, evocative prose." And Celia H. Morris concluded in *Horn Book* that *The Comeback Dog* is an "exceptionally gentle, poignant story."

Fox in a Trap, the sequel to *The Comeback Dog,* finds Daniel a bit older and more interested in the exciting life of his Uncle Pete, a sportsman and writer, than what he perceives to be his family's boring life on their farm. Upset that his father thinks he will dislike trapping small game, Daniel convinces his parents to allow Uncle Pete to teach him the trade and help set up a trapline. In the end, though, Daniel finds himself unable to kill the animals he catches and decides he is actually much more like his parents than he thought. In *School Library Journal,* Charlene J. Lenzen praised "Thomas's sound knowledge of farm life" and "her emotionally charged writing style." A *Booklist* reviewer similarly related that in *Fox in a Trap* Thomas "carefully manipulates the characters' changing emotions with believability."

Sensitivity and believable emotions merge again to create Thomas's 1988 realistic story *Saying Good-bye to Grandma.* Told through the eyes of seven-year-old Suzie, the book begins with a two-day journey to Grandpa's lakeside home for her grandmother's funeral. Once there, both the joys of being together as a family and the sorrows of the occasion intermingle as Suzie plays with her cousins and listens to her grandpa crying in the night. At first afraid that the funeral will take her grandma away forever, Suzie is comforted by her parents and able to participate in the ritual of saying good-bye. In the end she leaves her grandpa's house looking forward to visiting next summer and learning to fish and cook.

"The purpose of this slim, quiet picture book is to prepare young children for the experience of a close relative's funeral," as Anne Tyler described it in the *New York Times Book Review*. Pointing out the effectiveness of using Suzie as the narrator, Tyler added: "The tone is understated—not so much grief-stricken as stunned and uncertain, which seems exactly the emotion you'd expect from a child in these circumstances." Patricia Pearl similarly praised the first-person narrative in *School Library Journal,* stating that this book was an "exceptionally sensible and sensitive examination of a young girl's feelings about the death and funeral of her grandmother."

A departure from the realistic themes of her other books, Thomas's *The Princess in the Pigpen* introduces elements of fantasy. The daughter of a duke in the year 1600, nine-year-old Elizabeth and her mother are sick in bed when a sliver of sunlight in the young girl's room magically transports her ahead in time to a Black Hawk, Iowa, farm in 1988. Taken in by the McCormick family, Elizabeth sees a doctor for her fever and is cured, all the while struggling to understand the new world in which she finds herself. Only the McCormicks' daughter Anne believes Elizabeth's story of her true identity, and in the end helps her return to her mother with a cure for her illness. "The book's real drama lies in the many revelations Elizabeth finds in what we would call ordinary American society," remarked Patricia T. O'Conner in the *New York Times Book Review.* "Through her we learn that the things we take for granted—from female doctors to refrigerated food—are miracles indeed." A *Kirkus Reviews* contributor asserted that "Thomas develops her story with logic and gentle, compassionate humor," concluding that *The Princess in the Pigpen* is "an excellent venture into new territory by a fine author."

Back on more familiar ground, Thomas describes the life of a Mexican migrant farm worker family in *Lights on the River.* As the family travels from job to job in the old station wagon that is their home, young Teresa keeps memories of her real home in Mexico alive in her mind at all times. She longs for the happiness of her last Christmas dinner there, as well as the custom of floating candles down the river past other villages. As her family's situation continues to worsen, it is just such a candle given to Teresa by her grandmother that provides the memories of home needed to help the family through their rough times. "There's nothing heroic or sentimental about this poverty," stated Hazel Rochman in *Booklist.* Christine Heppermann, writing in *Five Owls,* also praised

the realism of *Lights on the River,* maintaining: "Expressed in terms children will understand, this just indictment of the deplorable conditions migrant workers in the U.S. endure also eloquently attests to the importance of family and connectedness."

Connections to her own family as well as all the other events that have shaped her life are the sparks that generate Thomas's stories and make them so realistic. "I have always recommended that the adult writers I teach write what haunts them, drawing on the satisfactions and troubles that they remember in their hearts and bellies," she continued for *CA.* "To do so is a dangerous thing, however, for writers who explore the unlit closets of their minds are always finding out things they didn't want to know."

BIOGRAPHICAL/CRITICAL SOURCES:

PERIODICALS

Booklist, November 1, 1986, p. 415; April 1, 1987, p. 1210; August, 1994, p. 2053.
Bulletin of the Center for Children's Books, November, 1977, p. 55; April 1, 1987, p. 1210; October, 1989, pp. 46-47.
Five Owls, December, 1994, pp. 37-38.
Horn Book, August, 1977, p. 436; August, 1981, p. 427.
Kirkus Reviews, June 15, 1981, p. 741; April 15, 1987, p. 645; August 1, 1988, p. 1158; October 15, 1989, p. 1537; September 15, 1994, p. 1284.
New York Times Book Review, May 1, 1977, p. 47; May 10, 1981, pp. 38-39; November 13, 1988, p. 48; April 22, 1990, p. 39.
Publishers Weekly, October 31, 1986, pp. 65-66; July 1, 1996, p. 60.
School Library Journal, December, 1986, p. 96; June-July, 1987, p. 102; February, 1989, p. 76.*

* * *

THUBRON, Colin (Gerald Dryden) 1939-

PERSONAL: Surname is pronounced *Thoo*-bron; born June 14, 1939, in London, England; son of Gerald Ernest (a brigadier in the British Army) and Evelyn (Dryden) Thubron. *Education:* Attended Eton College.

ADDRESSES: Home—Garden Cottage, 27 St. Ann's Villas, London W11 4RT, England.

CAREER: Hutchinson & Co. Ltd., London, England, member of editorial staff, 1959-62; British Broadcasting Corp. Television, London, freelance filmmaker, 1963-64; Macmillan Co., New York, NY, member of editorial staff, 1964; writer.

MEMBER: Royal Society of Literature (fellow).

AWARDS, HONORS: PEN Silver Pen Award, 1985, for *A Cruel Madness;* Thomas Cook Travel Award, and Hawthornden Prize, both 1988, both for *Behind the Wall: A Journey through China;* shortlist, Booker Prize, 1991, for *Turning Back the Sun.*

WRITINGS:

Mirror to Damascus, Heinemann (London), 1967, Little, Brown (Boston, MA), 1968, reprinted, Century Hutchinson (London), 1986, Penguin (New York City), 1996.

The Hills of Adonis: A Quest in Lebanon, Little, Brown, 1968, reprinted as *The Hills of Adonis: A Journey in Lebanon,* Atlantic Monthly Press (New York City), 1990.

Jerusalem, Little, Brown, 1969, reprinted, Century Hutchinson, 1986, Penguin, 1996.

Journey into Cyprus, Heinemann, 1975, reprinted, Penguin, 1986.

The God in the Mountain (novel), Heinemann, 1977, Norton (New York City), 1978.

Emperor (novel), Heinemann, 1978, reprinted, Penguin, 1991.

(With the editors of Time-Life Books) *The Venetians,* Time-Life (Alexandria, VA), 1980.

(With the editors of Time-Life Books) *The Ancient Mariners,* Time-Life, 1981.

The Royal Opera House, Covent Garden, Hamish Hamilton (London), 1982.

Among the Russians, Heinemann, 1983, published as *Where Nights Are Longest: Travels by Car through Western Russia,* Random House (New York City), 1984.

A Cruel Madness (novel), Heinemann, 1984, Atlantic Monthly Press, 1985.

Behind the Wall: A Journey through China, Heinemann, 1987, Atlantic Monthly Press, 1988.

The Silk Road: Beyond the Celestial Kingdom, with photographs by Carlos Navajas, Simon and Schuster (New York City), 1989.

Falling, Heinemann, 1989, Penguin, 1990.

Turning Back the Sun (novel), Atlantic Monthly Press, 1991.

The Lost Heart of Asia, HarperCollins (New York City), 1994.

Has also scripted and filmed three documentary motion pictures on Turkey, Morocco, and Japan for television in the United States and Britain.

WORK IN PROGRESS: A novel.

SIDELIGHTS: Colin Thubron told *CA:* "Motivation is hard. At first I wrote travel books out of a romantic love for Asia, and novels to discharge myself of personal unease. Now I'm less sure. In travel, I've become gripped by the harsh strangeness of other cultures, and try to understand and humanise them in my books. In fiction I've stayed obsessed by extreme states. The chief influences on my travel writing have been Freya Stark and Patrick Leigh Fermor; on my fiction, none that I know. I write always in solitude, in the Welsh hills, with no telephone, just pen and paper."

A veteran world traveler, Colin Thubron has written of his voyages in a series of books that are often considered superior to the average travelogue. The typical Thubron book is a blend of history, description, and personal observation; the author approaches each of his subjects with a perspective which, according to a *Choice* reviewer, goes "beyond the facade of the monuments and events" to evoke a "beautifully poetic but not romantic" portrait of the people and places he has come to know. In a *Times Literary Supplement* review of *Journey into Cyprus,* for example, David Hunt observes that "the book is mainly about people," adding that it "is full of the most fascinating conversations." Even though *Journey into Cyprus* focuses on "personalities and on village life," Hunt concludes that "it will also serve very well as a guide-book. The principal antiquities are poetically but accurately described, and history is so subtly interwoven into the narrative that by the end the reader has learnt painlessly all he needs to know of it." A *Times Literary Supplement* reviewer presents a similar assessment of *Mirror to Damascus:* "[Thubron's] narrative [exhibits] one great quality often missing from modern books of travel: its continual reference to the reality of another society and its actual people. His hosts and their relatives emerge as individuals, not as stereotypes." The critic concludes that "all this provides a pungent counterpoint of personal involvement and adventure to a solid account of the city's present flavour and past development, and the way Mr. Thubron has woven these elements together is a lesson for anyone who tries to combine entertainment with instruction."

"Colin Thubron's . . . book, *Among the Russians* [published in the United States as *Where Nights Are*

Longest: Travels by Car through Western Russia], can only serve to enhance his reputation," comments Fitzroy Maclean in the *Spectator*. "I enjoyed every page of it. It is well observed, well written and, unlike many books about Russia, gives proof of an unusual and penetrating insight into the character of the country and people." The book "is compiled from the notebooks of [Thubron's] extraordinary 10,000 mile journey across the Soviet Union in an old Morris Marina," describes *New Statesman* contributor Olga Semenova, "from Leningrad and the Baltic, to Moscow and central Russia, the Ukraine and Kiev, the Caucasus and Armenia. The result is a beautiful and poetic work, which captures much of the spirit of Russia." The critic notes that while "Thubron conveys the feel of places and their past with wonderful intensity," he also portrays "the ugliness and emptiness of modern Russian life, with its tawdry tower blocks, interminable queues and tension, radiating outwards from the Kremlin."

Although the former Soviet Union is a subject that has been studied and analyzed many times before, Nigel Ryan believes that "new" information is not the author's purpose. Writing in the *Times Literary Supplement,* Ryan suggests that "with [Thubron], one experiences the bewildering and disorientating contrasts of vast loneliness, of cruelty and indifference to human life on a horrifying scale, and of sudden extravagant gusts of personal warmth, generosity and desire to confide; of a deep national melancholia at odds with a fierce patriotism. If we have heard most of it before," states the critic, "we have seldom heard it so elegantly or powerfully put." Another difference, maintains Gail Pool of the *Christian Science Monitor,* is that "to a large degree, Thubron's journey through Russia is an exploration of attitudes, the Soviets' and his own. . . . If he is looking *at* everything, he is also looking *for* something, always moving beyond description to penetrate the texture of Russian life and compare it with his own world."

While some critics praise this personal angle in Thubron's work, *Washington Post Book World* contributor Joel Conarroe faults the author for bringing a biased attitude to his work: "Thubron is mesmerized by rampant alcoholism, by bribery, and by 'universal political hypocrisy.' About these and other matters he tends invariably to confuse first impressions with wisdom. . . . The author is himself quite willing to draw conclusions from skimpy evidence." The *Los Angeles Times*'s Richard Eder similarly believes that Thubron has not brought enough diverse elements to his account; he specifically cites as a "disabling de-

fect . . . that Thubron rarely is good at describing and conveying the particular quality of the people he meets. They blur into each other, and their conversations, whether official, dissident or simply private, have a uniformity rarely lightened by wit or individuality."

Other critics, however, praise the author for an honest, self-cognizant approach; Douglas Hill of the Toronto *Globe and Mail,* for example, claims that "what wins a reader over is Thubron's palpable honesty. . . . He gives the impression of complete candor, especially about himself, his enthusiasms, surprises and frustrations." The critic also observes that the author "makes quick but profound friendships; the connections he forges with the most unlikely people are explored sensitively, and they are often quite moving." *New York Times Book Review* contributor S. Frederick Starr echoes this opinion, writing that "the appeal of Mr. Thubron's account is deepened by his keen self-awareness, which pervades his narrative like an inner dialogue." The critic elaborates: "[Thubron] reports with surprise how he gradually ceased to be disappointed by the shortcomings he perceived in Soviet life and began to feel comforted by them. Then he stopped himself, realizing he had become like the Soviet visitor to the West who is at first disgusted and then smugly relieved by the flaws he observes around him." Starr also notes that Thubron, whom he calls "a subtle and humane writer," is able to "capture the fleeting words and gestures that define a culture." "Thubron is a limpid writer who has all the sharpness of eye . . . and can also present his version of Russia with a particular sweet-sour flavor," remarks Rosemary Dinnage in the *New York Review of Books,* adding that Thubron "has a novelistic gift for dialogue and settings." Citing Thubron's "fine writing," Ryan concludes that "the extraordinary dimensions [of the Soviet people] come through in *Among the Russians*. It is one of the best—and best written—travel books of recent years."

Thubron embarked on a similar voyage to prepare for *Behind the Wall: A Journey through China,* an account which *Times Literary Supplement* contributor Jonathan Mirsky claims that "many China specialists who disdain 'I saw China' books will wish they had written . . . [for it] contains remarkable insights into the country." After learning enough Mandarin Chinese to be able to travel without a guide, Thubron toured the country by fourth-class train, staying off the beaten tourist track and meeting many Chinese. "The result," writes Robin Hanbury-Tenison in *Spectator,* "is a rare first-hand account of a country seen through the eyes of one who has experienced what he describes and who is in a position to understand what he sees." The critic also comments that all the discomforts Thubron endured have produced "rich encounters, the special stuff of this author's writing. The world seems to be full of extraordinary people with amazing tales to tell, if a writer but puts himself in a position, however uncomfortable, to hear them." Because he was a lone British visitor, Thubron found himself approached by many Chinese, who found him a curiosity, as Patrick Taylor-Martin details in the *Listener*: "As an outsider, [Thubron] receives confidences from the Chinese, and throws much light on the mystery which still surrounds this nation of a billion uncomprehended people. Talking to him, people confess their sorrow at having no children, their longing to go to America to study medieval European art, [and] their hatred of communism," among other topics.

It is this personal aspect of *Behind the Wall* that impresses many critics. While Hanbury-Tenison observes that "the countryside through which [the author] travels for lonely months, the satanic industrial cities, the deserted but reviving temples he visits are vividly described," he maintains that "they come alive through the characters [Thubron] contrives to meet." "The distinction of his book is in the way, with conviction and elegance and humour, he describes through chance conversations, bits of history and visions of understanding the country's total *being*, its China-ness," claims Nicholas Wollaston in the *Observer*. "A travel book, to quote his own essay again, is one civilisation reporting on another: which is what this one does marvelously." And as with his other travelogues, Thubron brings a novelist's eye to his writing: "Thubron, as readers of his earlier books, especially the excellent *Among the Russians,* already know, is a wonderfully perceptive writer," notes Mirsky. Taylor-Martin similarly states that the author's "style is impeccable. The book is full of beautifully composed scenes, orchestrated as if for a novel, and exquisite passages of description. . . . It should be read for the intelligence and poetic insight which went into its making," concludes the critic. Calling *Behind the Wall* "an even better book than *Among the Russians,*" London *Times* contributor Victoria Glendinning notes that Thubron's "characteristic lyricism is in this book a controlled calligraphy of ideas and images, its richness cut by splashes of monosyllables. . . . At the end I turned to look—again, as I thought—at the pictures. There are none, except in the mind," adds the critic. "Writing as vivid as this needs no illustrations."

Having been praised for the intricate, lyrical descriptions in his travel books, it is not surprising that Thubron has turned his hand to fiction as well. Although his first two novels were not widely noticed, *A Cruel Madness,* his third, "sees Thubron in full possession of considerable talents as a novelist," claims *Times Literary Supplement* contributor Jayne Pilling, adding that "the book is a quietly extraordinary *tour de force.*" The novel begins as Daniel, a prep-school teacher who volunteers weekends at a local mental hospital, believes he sees on the grounds of the asylum a woman with whom he once had a brief but disastrous affair. As he painfully realizes she is a patient there, Daniel recalls his original passion for her, including passages from her point of view. As the novel progresses, however, the reader becomes aware that Daniel is untrustworthy as a narrator, that he is actually a patient at the asylum and that his visions and recollections may be delusions.

Although many books have been written about the illusory nature of human perception, *Los Angeles Times Book Review* contributor Sharon Dirlam believes that Thubron's book "isn't just another novel about madness and despair." Calling *A Cruel Madness* "spellbinding," the critic describes the novel as "a gripping tale of passion, however misspent, and the failure of an entire set of characters to come to grips with life seems not as distant from 'normal' as one might think, but simply a look deeper into the mind than most of us dare to probe." Pilling concurs, writing that "what is so impressive about *A Cruel Madness* is the way it transcends the conventional 'novelized' case history." The critic elaborates: "Thubron's descriptions of the hospital and its inmates are vividly convincing—fearfully so in their sad banality. The defences of a character traumatized by loss and separation—the madman's traditional cunning in weaving compulsive fictions—are appropriated by the novelist to impressive effect."

While *Washington Post Book World* contributor Stephen Koch also finds *A Cruel Madness* "an intriguing and sometimes rather moving novel about insanity and love, illusion and reality," he faults the author for the structure of the novel. In particular the critic dislikes what he terms "the absurdly simple device of omitting major pieces of information from an otherwise perfectly ordinary story. . . . This is what happens in *A Cruel Madness,* and I for one find it a cheap trick, an effort to make a story more portentous, merely because it is more perplexing." Other critics, however, find Thubron's use of Daniel's ambiguous narration very effective and well written; John

Wheatcroft, for example, states in the *New York Times Book Review* that "to experience this montage through Daniel's eyes and to hear through his ears echoes that are not perfectly congruent with what they supposedly repeat compels us to try to discover what actually has happened and what really is happening. As we do so," continues the critic, "all the apparently solid ground on which the narrative has built begins to shift, to reveal gaps and inconsistencies." "In such of his non-fiction as *Among the Russians,*" observes Francis King in the *Spectator,* "Mr. Thubron gives the impression of being the most rational and well-balanced of people. It is therefore all the more remarkable that he should have been able to enter so convincingly into a mind so disturbed. With a terrifying vividness, Mr. Thubron creates a phantasmagoric world in which . . . the demarcation between reality and delusion becomes harder to perceive." In its persuasive use of narrative, *A Cruel Madness* "brings to mind other novels set in the microcosmic world of a hospital," asserts Wheatcroft, including "Thomas Mann's *Magic Mountain,* Aleksandr Solzhenitsyn's *Cancer Ward,* Ken Kesey's *One Flew over the Cuckoo's Nest.* . . . Among such distinguished company, Mr. Thubron's novel holds its own," concludes the critic. And a *New Yorker* reviewer claims that Thubron's novel is "a study in madness so compelling that it is hard to believe we are not experiencing it at first hand," adding that *A Cruel Madness* is a "remarkable achievement."

Thubron's fifth novel, *Turning Back the Sun,* has been widely received as continuing on the path he had set for himself in his poetic travelogues and novels. Set in an unnamed country several critics likened to Australia with shades of South Africa or Argentina, the book centers on the conflict between white colonists and darker-skinned aborigines in a frontier desert town in the 1930s. A thousand miles away is the country's capital, the cosmopolitan center of the protagonist Rayner's upbringing until age nineteen, when a car crash killed his mother and subsequently brought an end to his ambitions for an easy life as a doctor to the city's wealthy denizens. Banished to the outback by the government for failing his exams, Rayner longs for the city, and feels an outsider among the townspeople; his nostalgia for an idealized past makes him spiritually akin to the aborigines, whose religion casts them as exiles from a paradise that existed before the white colonists came.

A lone remnant of Rayner's life in the city is Ivar, a schoolmate who polices the frontier town for the paramilitary government. Closer to Rayner's sensibilities is a local strip-tease dancer whose unwillingness to pander to her customers infuriates them and intrigues Rayner. A murder and the outbreak of a mysterious disease that afflicts the white population with a rash that turns their skin brown causes a breakdown in the uneasy truce between the whites and the aborigines, and sets the stage for the author's ruminations on colonialism and race. "If this sounds heavy going, in fact it is the opposite," remarks David Sacks in the *New York Times Book Review;* "the novel is crisply written and most enjoyable—as far as it goes."

Other critical reactions to *Turning Back the Sun* have been similarly mixed, though the book was shortlisted for Britain's most prestigious literary award, the Booker Prize. Thubron is accused of "flat predictability" in his characterization by Jennifer Howard in the *Washington Post,* who adds that "as an allegory of the perniciousness of colonialism, though, *Turning Back the Sun* is beautifully thought out . . . and lyrically delivered." Not surprising, given the stature of the author's travel writings, "The book's strongest suit is its remarkable setting," according to Sacks, who adds a paean to "Thubron's lucid, confident prose." Indeed, as in reviews of his travel writings, critics concur in their praise of the author's prose style, which adds a lyrical touch to what is otherwise an "existential allegory," according to Carolyn See in the *Los Angeles Times.*

Thubron returned to travel writing with the 1994 publication of *The Lost Heart of Asia,* a record of his trip through the former outposts of the Soviet Union in Central Asia, which when liberated from communist rule in 1991 became Turkmenistan, Uzbekistan, Tajikistan, Kazakhstan, and Kyrgyzstan. Armed with a rucksack and a knowledge of the Russian language that had stood him in his trek across the Soviet Union for his much-admired travelogue *Among the Russians,* Thubron travelled alone through a region that few Westerners have seen, among people who had rarely if ever encountered a Westerner before. "He was tolerated by everyone and confided in by many," remarks Dervla Murphy in her review in *The Spectator.* Indeed, the author's word-portraits of the people he met were often considered highly poetic: "These faces are not only intriguingly agile," writes Scott Malcomson in the *Times Literary Supplement,* "they are, for Thubron, astoundingly expressive. . . . We learn much about Central Asians from such eloquent faces."

While Malcomson condemns Thubron for failing to learn any of the Turkic languages native to Central

Asia, relying instead on his knowledge of Russian, the language of the region's latest colonizers, others note the sensitivity the writer brought to his subject, augmented greatly by his intimacy with the history of Central Asia as well as his travels in the Islamic Middle East and North Africa. Luree Miller observes in the *Washington Post* that Thubron "has a novelist's sensitivity and an historian's perception. One could not ask for a more rewarding travel companion through a little-known land." And, as in his novels and his earlier travelogues, Thubron's prose is singled out for special attention: "*The Lost Heart of Asia* is not a book to be read quickly," asserts Murphy. "On almost every page gleam burnished paragraphs, prose only in their form, in their sensibility pure poetry—and yet, in the precision of each detail, as exact as a photograph."

BIOGRAPHICAL/CRITICAL SOURCES:

PERIODICALS

America, April 1, 1989.
American Spectator, January, 1989.
Antioch Review, Spring, 1986.
Atlanta Journal and Atlanta Constitution, July 22, 1990, October 30, 1994.
Bestsellers, November, 1985.
Booklist, September 15, 1988, May 1, 1990, June 1, 1992, October 15, 1994.
Books, April, 1987, September, 1987, January, 1988, September, 1988, August, 1989, November, 1994.
British Book News, August, 1987.
Chicago Tribune, February 15, 1991.
Choice, December, 1968.
Christian Science Monitor, September 8, 1987.
Conn, October, 1987.
Contemporary Review, February, 1992, June, 1995.
Economist, July 23, 1988.
Far Eastern Economic Review, May 25, 1995.
Globe and Mail (Toronto), September 7, 1985.
Guardian Weekly, December 29, 1991.
Illustrated London News, vol. 278, 1990, vol. 279, 1991.
Journal of Asian Studies, May, 1989.
Kirkus Reviews, July 15, 1985, July 15, 1988, May 1, 1990, December 1, 1990, August 15, 1994.
Kliatt, January, 1996.
Library Journal, October 15, 1988, December, 1990, June 15, 1992, September 15, 1994.
Listener, September 22, 1977, September 24, 1987.
London Review of Books, October 1, 1987, September 28, 1989.

Los Angeles Times, April 4, 1984, July 2, 1992, p. E6, December 7, 1994.
Los Angeles Times Book Review, October 6, 1985, December 7, 1994, p. 6.
Middle East Journal, Autumn, 1991.
New Statesman, October 21, 1983.
New Statesman & Society, October 18, 1991, October 14, 1994, July 21, 1995.
New Yorker, October 7, 1985.
New York Review of Books, June 13, 1985, March 16, 1989.
New York Times Book Review, May 18, 1969, December 7, 1969, July 15, 1984, November 10, 1985, October 11, 1987, November 27, 1988, February 3, 1991, August 2, 1992, p. 6, November 13, 1994, December 4, 1994.
Observer, September 27, 1987, January 15, 1989, July 16, 1989, September 10, 1989, September 8, 1991.
Psychology Today, May, 1986.
Publishers Weekly, July 26, 1988, August 12, 1988, July 28, 1989, December 7, 1990, April 27, 1992, August 22, 1994, September 19, 1994.
Saturday Night, April, 1989.
Smithsonian, October, 1989.
Spectator, July 7, 1984, September 1, 1984, September 19, 1987, September 16, 1989, September 24, 1994, p. 44, December 10, 1994.
Times (London), December 15, 1983, July 25, 1985, September 17, 1987.
Times Educational Supplement, August 14, 1987, December 25, 1987, December 25, 1992, April 14, 1995, July 14, 1995.
Times Literary Supplement, December 21, 1967, October 31, 1968, June 6, 1975, December 30, 1977, June 22, 1984, September 7, 1984, September 11, 1987, September 8, 1989, September 6, 1991, September 30, 1994, p. 26.
Travel-Holiday, December, 1994.
Virginia Quarterly Review, Autumn, 1995.
Washington Post, August 4, 1992, p. E05.
Washington Post Book World, June 17, 1984, November 17, 1985, September 11, 1988, November 20, 1994, p. 5.

*   *   *

TOMPERT, Ann 1918-

PERSONAL: Born January 11, 1918, in Detroit, MI; daughter of Joseph (a farmer) and Florence (maiden name, Pollitt) Bakeman; married Robert S. Tompert (a social service employee), March 31, 1951. *Education:* Siena Heights College, B.A. (summa cum laude), 1938; Wayne State University, graduate study, 1941-46. *Politics:* "Independent with Republican leanings." *Religion:* Christian. *Avocational interests:* Reading new writers, collecting paperweights and milkglass, gardening, caning chairs, refinishing furniture, sewing, needlework.

ADDRESSES: Home—3900 Aspen Dr., #342, Port Huron, MI 48060.

CAREER: Teacher in elementary and junior and senior high schools in St. Clair Shores, East Detroit, Grosse Pointe, Marine City, and other cities in Michigan, 1938-59; writer, 1959—.

MEMBER: Society of Children's Book Writers and Illustrators, Children's Reading Round Table of Chicago, River District Hospital Auxiliary (life member; St. Clair, MI), Friends of the Port Huron Library, Port Huron Museum, Alpha Delta Kappa.

AWARDS, HONORS: Notable children's book citations, American Library Association and *School Library Journal,* 1976, Friend of American Writers citation, 1977, honors citation, Chicago Children's Reading Round Table, 1979, and "Best of the Best: 1966-1978," *School Library Journal,* 1979, all for *Little Fox Goes to the End of the World;* Irma Simonton Black award honor book, 1980, for *Charlotte and Charles;* Notable Children's Trade Book in the Field of Social Studies, Children's Book Council, 1988, for *The Silver Whistle,* 1990, for *Grandfather Tang's Story: A Tale Told with Tangrams;* "Pick of the List," American Booksellers Association (ABA), 1991, for *Savina, the Gypsy Dancer,* and 1993, for *Just a Little Bit;* Children's Reading Roundtable Service Award, 1994.

WRITINGS:

What Makes My Cat Purr?, Whitman Publishing (Racine, WI), 1965.
The Big Whistle, Whitman Publishing, 1968.
When Rooster Crowed, Whitman Publishing, 1968.
Maybe a Dog Will Come, illustrated by Frank Aloise, Follett, 1968.
A Horse for Charlie, Whitman Publishing, 1969.
The Crow, the Kite, and the Golden Umbrella, illustrated by Franklin Luke, Abelard-Schulman (New York City), 1971.
Fun for Ozzie, illustrated by Elizabeth Rice, Steck, 1971.

Hyacinth, the Reluctant Duck, illustrated by John Paul Richards, Steck, 1972.
It May Come in Handy Someday, illustrated by Bruce Cayard, McGraw (New York City), 1975.
Little Fox Goes to the End of the World, illustrated by John Wallner, Crown (New York City), 1976.
Little Otter Remembers and Other Stories, illustrated by John Wallner, Crown, 1977.
The Clever Princess, illustrated by Patricia Riley, Lollipop Power, Inc., 1977.
Badger on His Own, illustrated by Diane de Groat, Crown (New York City), 1978.
Three Foolish Tales, illustrated by Diane Dawson, Crown, 1979.
Charlotte and Charles, illustrated by John Wallner, Crown, 1979.
Nothing Sticks Like a Shadow, illustrated by Lynn Munsinger, Houghton (Boston), 1983.
The Greatest Showman on Earth: A Biography of P. T. Barnum, Dillon (Minneapolis), 1987.
Will You Come Back for Me?, illustrated by Robin Kramer, Whitman Publishing, 1988.
The Silver Whistle, illustrated by Beth Park, Macmillan (New York City), 1988.
Sue Patch and the Crazy Clocks, illustrated by Rosekrans Hoffman, Dial (New York City), 1989.
The Tzar's Bird, illustrated by Robert Rayevsky, Macmillan, 1990.
Grandfather Tang's Story: A Tale Told with Tangrams, illustrated by Robert Andrew Parker, Crown, 1990.
Savina, the Gypsy Dancer, illustrated by Dennis Nolan, Macmillan, 1991.
Just a Little Bit, illustrated by Lynn Munsinger, Houghton, 1993.
Bamboo Hats and a Rice Cake: A Tale Adapted from Japanese Folklore, illustrated by Demi, Crown, 1993.
A Carol for Christmas, illustrated by Laura Kelly, Macmillan, 1994.
The Jade Horse, the Cricket and the Peach Stone, illustrated by Winson Trang, Boyds Mills Press (New York City), 1996.
How Rabbit Lost His Tail, Houghton, 1997.

Contributor to children's magazines, including *Jack and Jill, Wee Wisdom,* and *Friend.* Contributor to *The Real Books of First Stories,* edited by Dorothy Haas, and *Sea Treasures,* edited by Ira E. Aaron. *Little Fox Goes to the End of the World* and *Little Otter Remembers and Other Stories* have been translated into Japanese. *Just a Little Bit* has been translated into French, German, and Japanese, *Nothing Sticks Like a Shadow* into French, and *Little Fox Goes to the End of the*

World and *Sue Patch and the Crazy Clocks* into Spanish.

SIDELIGHTS: Ann Tompert is the author of more than two dozen children's picture books, stories for the beginning reader, and folktales, including the award-winning *Little Fox Goes to the End of the World* and *Charlotte and Charles*. Although almost fifty years of age when her first book was published, Tompert had dreamed of being a writer from age twelve, modeling herself on Jo from *Little Women*. The necessities of life, however, intervened.

When Tompert was twelve, her mother died, and her father, a small farmer on the outskirts of Detroit, was left to care for Tompert and her two sisters. "I am just now realizing what a profound influence my father has had on me," she once told *CA*. "He did not let the fact that his formal education was limited to attendance at a typical rural school of the time hinder him in any way. He . . . would tackle any job because he did not fear failure. There was a stubbornness about him that helped him get things done in spite of what must have seemed insurmountable obstacles." As a child, Tompert helped her father sell vegetables at the roadside stand in front of their farm, and her sisters and she went with him whenever they were not in school. "An especially fond memory is of playing in the fields while my father mowed hay for the horses," Tompert recalled. Unaware of the fact that they were what might be today called "underprivileged," Tompert and her sisters invented their own fun rather than relied on toys. It was an upbringing that gave her a strong creative core and an optimistic approach to life.

Tompert left home for college at sixteen, majoring in English and still dreaming of becoming a writer. Practical concerns dictated that she work toward becoming a teacher, however, as it was "one of the few professions opened to women at that time," Tompert noted in *CA*. She continued to write during college, and upon graduation began her teaching career in a two-room schoolhouse. In 1940 she won an honorable mention and five dollars for a play she submitted to a writing contest. "That small success kept the spark of my desire alive during the next twenty years while I taught school in various parts of Michigan." In 1951 Tompert married and began working toward her masters in English part time. Finally, in 1959, she decided to devote herself to her dream of writing. "I was teaching first grade at the time," Tompert told *CA*, "and after reading hundreds of books to my pupils, I was convinced that I could write stories that

were just as good, if not better." So for the next three years she wrote and submitted stories and "built up one of the world's finest collections of rejection slips." Finally however, the stubbornness inherited from her father paid off. Her first story was accepted by *Jack and Jill*, and her writing career was underway.

Initially, Tompert wrote picture books for Whitman Publishing, a division of Western Publishing. "Many people do not consider this type of book worth mentioning," Tompert told *CA*, "although I do not understand why. Writing a manuscript for this type of book requires as much time, effort and talent as do manuscripts for hard-cover books." Many of these early books feature animal protagonists, a device she has continaued to use throughout her career. *Fun for Ozzie*, one of her first mainstream publications, tells the tale of a playful otter who tries hobbies enjoyed by other animals until he finally hits on the right one for him. Tompert's 1971 *The Crow, the Kite, and the Golden Umbrella* was inspired by a newspaper account of how the people in a Malaysian town were trying to cure themselves of a plague of crows. In Tompert's story, the town of Kota Kobis offers a golden umbrella to whomever can rid the town of the crows. Young Muda, who has a pet crow, constructs a kite with which to lure the other crows away. How Muda attempts to win the prize while at the same time keeping his own pet crow forms the crux of the story.

Tompert's own farm background provided some of the inspiration for her next title, *It May Come in Handy Someday*, in which an old man collects all sorts of paraphernalia that he thinks may come in handy on his farm. The old man neglects his garden while he scavenges, and the farm risks becoming engulfed in the junk until a passerby offers to tell the townspeople to come and take what they want. Zena Sutherland in *Bulletin of the Center for Children's Books* remarked upon the humor in the book as "the collected items get sillier as the pile grows and overflows."

With her next title, *Little Fox Goes to the End of the World*, Tompert began to hit her stride. Inspired by her own childish dream to follow a rainbow to the pot of gold, she originally wrote a story featuring a little boy's journey. An editor, however, suggested that she use an animal protagonist and Tompert thought of a fox, an animal she felt was sadly misunderstood by humans. The little fox in question is a bushy-tailed kit who wears jeans and sandals and who tells her mother what she would do if she set off to the end of the world. She relates all the adventures she would have, which involve bears with honey, banana-wielding monkeys, and mountain snows. Virginia Haviland commented in *Horn Book* that "it's all a whimsical and childlike game of pretend," while Cynthia Percak Infantino in *School Library Journal* concluded that "story hour audiences will relish Little Fox's escapades."

Tompert's ideas come from a variety of sources: the newspapers, personal experience, and her years of teaching young children. "For me," she once told *CA,* "ideas are everywhere, just waiting to be picked up. . . . The idea for a story is just the beginning, of course. It is somewhat like the first piece of a jigsaw puzzle. The rest of the pieces must be found and fitted into the right places before the picture is completed. Sometimes, the process goes quickly, but more often, it is a long series of trials and errors. When the story is finished, I know it has been worth the effort. And I know, too, that I can hardly wait to start on a new puzzle." For her next "puzzle," Tompert teamed up again with Wallner and employed an otter as the main character, as she had done with the earlier *Fun for Ozzie.* In *Little Otter Remembers and Other Stories,* the animal protagonist selects a gift for Mother Otter, searches for a lost pine cone, and goes to a sliding party with relatives. "The tone here is pleasantly warm," noted a reviewer for *Booklist,* and a contributor in *Publishers Weekly,* commenting on the success of the previous joint effort of Tompert and Wallner, remarked that "they now have another able contender for honors. . . ."

A cuddly animal also figures in *Badger on His Own,* in which Badger, tired of his father hounding him about turning cartwheels, sets up house in a new burrow. Befriended by Owl, Badger soon wonders if the bossy bird is any better than his parents. A *Booklist* reviewer concluded that the book's adult message "goes straight to the heart of most youngsters," while a critic in *Publishers Weekly* called it "a droll, original story." *Three Foolish Tales,* employing a story-within-the-story format, features Skunk, Raccoon, and Fox who vie for a purple umbrella, the prize for whomever can tell the most foolish tale. In the end it is Fox who makes the other two look foolish. A contributor in *School Library Journal* noted that the book had "a refreshing degree of wit," but a *Publishers Weekly* reviewer commented that Tompert often "expresses a grownup's hindsight," and that the book seemed geared more "to adults than to children."

With *Charlotte and Charles,* Tompert features human protagonists, though in this case they are two giants living on a lonely island. Normal-sized people come to settle the island, and at first Charlotte is happy about this, though Charles has his doubts. Such doubts are confirmed when the humans, out of a blind fear of difference, force the giants to flee to another island. "This is a highly readable story, almost an allegory of race relations and bigotry," noted Ruth K. MacDonald in *School Library Journal.* A nonsense tale is at the heart of Tompert's next title, *Nothing Sticks like a Shadow,* in which Rabbit, egged on by Woodchuck, tries futilely to outrun his shadow. Judith Gloyer, reviewing the book in *School Library Journal,* noted that it was "a well-rounded tale that hangs together from start to finish," and Barbara Ellerman in *Booklist* concluded that "librarians looking for lively Groundhog Day stories, will latch on to this with pleasure."

Tompert took a break from children's picture books with 1987's *The Greatest Showman on Earth: A Biography of P. T. Barnum,* written for a juvenile audience. Relatively longer in format than the author's previous works and illustrated with photographs, this biography covers the career of the showman who created the three-ring circus, among other achievements. Barnum was also something of a hoaxer and a minor fraud, who, as Tompert shows in her biography, also helped to create modern advertising. Todd Morning, in *School Library Journal,* called the book an "effective biography," though noting that the author's tendency to skip back and forth in time might confuse some young readers. "Tompert has assembled the facts of [Barnum's] life competently," a reviewer in *Bulletin of the Center for Children's Books* concluded.

Three books from 1988 deal with human protagonists and with themes ranging from the meaning of Christmas to the difficulties of adjusting to day care. In *The Silver Whistle,* set in Mexico, Miguel saves all year to buy a silver whistle to set on the altar as a gift to the Christ Child, but his savings go instead to save a burro being beaten by its master. In the end, it is the crude clay whistle that Miguel has fashioned that is the best altar gift of all. *Will You Come Back for Me?* examines four-year-old Suki's fear at being left for the first time at a day-care center. In the end the girl's fears are eased when her mother cuts out a red heart and gives Suki half of it: "When I leave you at Mrs. Clara's on Monday, I'll leave a part of my heart, too," the mother tells Suki. Both a multi-cultural story as well as a problem book, it is a tale "certain to calm the fears of little ones in the same situation as Suki," noted Ilene Cooper in *Booklist*. Tompert's *Sue Patch and the Crazy Clocks* tells the story of Sue who can fix anything until she is challenged by the king to set all the clocks in his huge palace to the same time. While she is first daunted by the challenge, in the end, logic prevails. "An entertaining story with whimsical logic to tickle minds and funny bones," stated a contributor in *Kirkus Reviews*.

A quartet of stories from the 1990s told in folktale and legend format are set from China to Russia to Japan. *Grandfather Tang's Story: A Tale Told with Tangrams* is about shape-changing fox fairies who compete against each other until they are finally reminded of their friendship by the danger a hunter presents. Employing the Chinese tangram, an ancient seven-piece puzzle that can be put together to tell a story, Tompert's book also relates the loving bond between an old man and his granddaughter and "will be valued by storytellers and listeners alike," according to Carolyn Noah in *School Library Journal*. *The Tzar's Bird* tells the story of a Russian king who is afraid of going to the edge of the world, a fear only increased by the threats of the witch Baba Yaga, the well-known figure from folklore. Ultimately the tzar, Prince Yaroslav, learns to overcome his fear of the unknown in this "lively story," as Denise Anton Wright characterized the book in *School Library Journal*. "Striking just the right balance between traditional folktales and modern morality tales, the text is filled with rich imagery," Wright noted. Another legend-like tale is *Savina, the Gypsy Dancer,* in which a gypsy girl captivates people with her marvelous dancing and ultimately arouses the jealousy and hatred of King Walid, who is fearful that such dancing might threaten his own power. In *Bamboo Hats and a Rice Cake: A Tale Adapted from Japanese Folklore,* Tompert adapted a Japanese folktale about a poor old couple who, wishing to have good luck in the New Year, are forced to trade the wife's wedding kimono for rice cakes that insure such luck. Once at the market, however, the old man, out of the goodness of his heart, makes trades that leave him worse off than before. "Kindness and generosity are the virtues celebrated in this pleasant adaptation," commented Nancy Vasilakis in a *Horn Book* review.

Tompert returns to animal protagonists with *Just a Little Bit,* the story of Mouse and Elephant who decide to go on a seesaw together. Mouse ends up needing the help of many other animals before they are able to go up and down, reinforcing the idea that help, even in small packages, can be of benefit in the aggregate. Mary M. Burns in *Horn Book* called the work "a charming tale of collaborative effort," and Harriett Fargnoli in *School Library Journal* noted that "repetitive phrasing, the parade of animal types, and the variety of the verb actions make this a beginning language pleaser." A mouse also figures in Tompert's *A Carol for Christmas,* set in Austria in 1818. This retelling of the origins of "Silent Night" is narrated by Jeremy, one of seventeen mouse children, who is present at the creation of the famous Christmas carol—he has slipped into the Pastor's pocket in search of cheese just as the man decides to take a walk in the night air in search of inspiration. Deborah Abbott in *Booklist* thought that "the story's crisp descriptive details add a sense of holiday magic" and concluded that the book was "a solid addition for Christmas collections."

In her many books, Tompert has managed to impart messages about kindness and cooperation, the evils of jealousy, and the power of friendship in a light manner. "I am very committed to the idea of fostering positive values in my books for children," she once explained. "We as a nation are so dedicated to preserving our physical environment and our quality of life (making ourselves safe from harm—auto safety, cancer research, pure food laws, etc.); yet, when it comes to dealing with our minds, anything and everything is permissible. I find this very disturbing, to say the least." In a letter to the editor of *Horn Book,* Tompert posited a question that sums up her efforts as a children's writer: "It seems to me that the media keep us well informed about 'how things are,'" she wrote. "Should not we writers consider presenting our readers with the possibilities of how things can be or perhaps should be?"

BIOGRAPHICAL/CRITICAL SOURCES:

PERIODICALS

Booklist, February 15, 1978, p. 1013; April 15, 1978, p. 1358; April 1, 1984, p. 1122; November 1, 1988, p. 488; October 15, 1994. p. 440.

Bulletin of the Center for Children's Books, October, 1969, p. 32; March, 1976, pp. 119-120; January, 1978, p. 87; April, 1980, p. 161; April, 1988, p. 171; May, 1991, p. 229.

Horn Book, September, 1976, pp. 616-617; July, 1989, p. 64; September/October, 1989, p. 548; January, 1990, p. 226; fall, 1991, p. 260; September/October, 1993, pp. 592-593; February, 1994, p. 79; spring, 1994, pp. 57, 111; spring, 1995, p. 59.

Kirkus Reviews, October 1, 1975, p. 125; August 1, 1976, p. 843; March 1, 1978, p. 241; February 15, 1980, p. 213; March 1, 1984, p. 111; September 1, 1988, p. 1329; October 15, 1989, p. 1538; April 15, 1990, p. 586; August 1, 1990, p. 1092; September 1, 1993, p. 1153; November 15, 1994, p. 1549.

New York Times Book Review, November 14, 1976, p. 39; July 1, 1990, p. 19.

Publishers Weekly, November 14, 1977, p. 66; February 27, 1978, p. 158; February 5, 1979, p. 95.

School Library Journal, December, 1976, pp. 51-52; May, 1979, p. 80; January, 1980, p. 62; May, 1984, p. 75; March, 1988, p. 210; April, 1988, p. 171; May, 1990, p. 92; November, 1990, p. 99; December, 1993, p. 95.

* * *

TRANTER, Nigel (Godwin) 1909-
(Nye Tredgold)

PERSONAL: Born November 23, 1909, in Glasgow, Scotland; son of Gilbert Tredgold (an insurance official) and Eleanor Anne (Cass) Tranter; married May Jean Campbell Grieve (died October, 1979); children: Frances May (Mrs. Robert Baker), Philip Nigel Lakin (died, 1966). *Education:* Attended schools in Edinburgh, Scotland. *Politics:* Liberal. *Religion:* Scottish Episcopal Church.

ADDRESSES: Home—Quarry House, Aberlady, East Lothian, Scotland.

CAREER: Accountant and inspector in family insurance company, Edinburgh, Scotland, 1929-39; full-time writer, 1946—. Broadcaster on own historical program, *Towers of Strength,* carried by Scottish Television, Border Television, and other programs on British Broadcasting Corp. (BBC-TV). Public lecturer. Chair, National Forth Road Bridge Committee. Trustee, Scottish Castles Preservation Trust. *Military service:* British Army, Royal Artillery, World War II; became lieutenant.

MEMBER: Society of Authors, National Book League, PEN (former Scottish president), Berwick and East Lothian Liberal Association (past president), East Lothian Wildfowlers Association (past president), East Lothian St. Andrew Society (chair), Fawside Castle Preservation Committee (former chair).

AWARDS, HONORS: Knight Commander of Order of St. Lazarus of Jerusalem; Officer, Order of the British Empire; M.A., University of Edinburgh.

WRITINGS:

NOVELS

Trespass, Moray Press (Edinburgh), 1937.
Mammon's Daughter, Ward, Lock (London), 1939.
Harsh Heritage, Ward, Lock, 1939.
Eagle's Feathers, Ward, Lock, 1941.
Watershed, Ward, Lock, 1941.
The Gilded Fleece, Ward, Lock, 1942.
Delayed Action, Ward, Lock, 1944.
Tinker's Pride, Ward, Lock, 1945.
Man's Estate, Ward, Lock, 1946.
Flight of Dutchmen, Ward, Lock, 1947.
Island Twilight, Ward, Lock, 1947.
Root and Branch, Ward, Lock, 1948.
Colours Flying, Ward, Lock, 1948.
The Chosen Course, Ward, Lock, 1949.
Fair Game, Ward, Lock, 1950.
High Spirits, Collins (London), 1950.
The Freebooters, Ward, Lock, 1950.
Tidewrack, Ward, Lock, 1951.
Fast and Loose, Ward, Lock, 1951.
Bridal Path, Ward, Lock, 1952.
Cheviot Chase, Ward, Lock, 1952.
Ducks and Drakes, Ward, Lock, 1953.
The Queen's Grace, Ward, Lock, 1953.
Rum Week, Ward, Lock, 1954.
The Night Riders, Ward, Lock, 1954.
There Are Worse Jungles, Ward, Lock, 1955.
Rio D'Oro, Ward, Lock, 1955.
The Long Coffin, Ward, Lock, 1956.
MacGregor's Gathering, Hodder & Stoughton (London), 1957.
The Enduring Flame, Hodder & Stoughton, 1957.
Balefire, Hodder & Stoughton, 1958.
The Stone, Hodder & Stoughton, 1958, Putnam (New York City), 1959.
The Man Behind the Curtain, Hodder & Stoughton, 1959.
The Clansman, Hodder & Stoughton, 1959.
Spanish Galleon, Hodder & Stoughton, 1960.
The Flockmasters, Hodder & Stoughton, 1960.
Kettle of Fish, Hodder & Stoughton, 1961.
The Master of Gray, Hodder & Stoughton, 1961.
A Drug on the Market, Hodder & Stoughton, 1962.
Gold for Prince Charlie, Hodder & Stoughton, 1962.
The Courtesan, Hodder & Stoughton, 1963.
Chain of Destiny, Hodder & Stoughton, 1964.
Past Master, Hodder & Stoughton, 1965.

A Stake in the Kingdom, Hodder & Stoughton, 1966.
Lion Let Loose, Hodder & Stoughton, 1967.
Cable from Kabul, Hodder & Stoughton, 1968.
Black Douglas, Hodder & Stoughton, 1968.
The Young Montrose, Hodder & Stoughton, 1972.
Montrose, Captain-General, Hodder & Stoughton, 1973.
The Wisest Fool, Hodder & Stoughton, 1974.
The Wallace, Hodder & Stoughton, 1975.
MacBeth the King, Hodder & Stoughton, 1978.
Margaret the Queen, Hodder & Stoughton, 1979.
David the Prince, Hodder & Stoughton, 1980.
True Thomas, Hodder & Stoughton, 1981.
The Patriot, Hodder & Stoughton, 1982.
Lord of the Isles, Hodder & Stoughton, 1983.
Unicorn Rampant, Hodder & Stoughton, 1984.
The Riven Realm, Hodder & Stoughton, 1984.
James, by the Grace of God, Hodder & Stoughton, 1985, Beaufort Books (New York City), 1986.
Rough Wooing, Hodder & Stoughton, 1986, Beaufort Books, 1987.
Columba, Hodder & Stoughton, 1987.
Cache Down, Hodder & Stoughton, 1987.
Flowers of Chivalry, Hodder & Stoughton, 1988.
Mail Royal, Hodder & Stoughton, 1989.
Warden of the Queen's March, Hodder & Stoughton, 1989.
Kenneth, Hodder & Stoughton, 1990.
Crusade, Hodder & Stoughton, 1991.
Children of the Mist, Hodder & Stoughton, 1992.
Druid Sacrifice, Hodder & Stoughton, 1993.
Tapestry of the Boar, Hodder & Stoughton, 1993.

"ROBERT THE BRUCE" TRILOGY

Robert the Bruce: The Steps to the Empty Throne (also see below), Hodder & Stoughton, 1969, St. Martin's (New York City), 1971.
Robert the Bruce: The Path of the Hero King (also see below), Hodder & Stoughton, 1970, St. Martin's, 1973.
Robert the Bruce: The Price of the King's Peace (also see below), Hodder & Stoughton, 1971, St. Martin's, 1973.
Robert the Bruce (trilogy; contains *The Steps to the Empty Throne, The Path of the Hero King, The Price of the King's Peace*), Hodder & Stoughton, 1985.

"STUART" TRILOGY

Lords of Misrule, Hodder & Stoughton, 1976.
A Folly of Princes, Hodder & Stoughton, 1977.
The Captive Crown, Hodder & Stoughton, 1977.

CHILDREN'S BOOKS

Spaniard's Isle, Brockhampton Press (Leicester), 1958.
Border Riding, Brockhampton Press, 1959.
Nestor the Monster, Brockhampton Press, 1960.
Birds of a Feather, Brockhampton Press, 1961.
The Deer Poachers, Blackie & Son (London), 1961.
Something Very Fishy, Collins (London), 1962.
Give a Dog a Bad Name, Collins, 1963, Platt (New York City), 1964.
Silver Island, Thomas Nelson (London), 1964.
Smoke across the Highlands, Platt, 1964.
Pursuit, Collins, 1965.
Fire and High Water, Collins, 1967.
Tinker Tess, Dobson (London), 1967.
To the Rescue, Dobson, 1968.

NONFICTION

The Fortalices and Early Mansions of Southern Scotland, 1400-1650, Moray Press, 1935.
The Fortified House in Scotland, Volume I: *South-East Scotland,* Oliver & Boyd (Edinburgh), 1962, Volume II: *Central Scotland,* Oliver & Boyd, 1963, Volume III: *Southwest Scotland,* Oliver & Boyd, 1965, Volume IV: *Aberdeenshire, Angus and Kincardineshire,* Oliver & Boyd, 1966, Volume V: *North and West Scotland and Miscellaneous,* W. & R. Chambers, 1970.
The Pegasus Book of Scotland, Dobson, 1964.
Portrait of the Borders, R. Hale (London), 1964.
Outlaw of the Highland: Rob Roy, Dobson, 1965.
Land of the Scots, Weybright, 1968.
(Editor) Philip Tranter, *No Tigers in the Hindu Kush,* Hodder & Stoughton, 1968.
The Queen's Scotland, Hodder & Stoughton, Volume I: *The Heartland, Clackmannanshire, Perthshire, and Stirlingshire,* 1971, Volume II: *The Eastern Counties,* 1972, Volume III: *The North East,* 1974, Volume IV: *Argyll and Bute,* 1977.
Portrait of the Border Country, R. Hale, 1972.
Portrait of the Lothians, R. Hale, 1979.
Nigel Tranter's Scotland: A Very Personal View, Drew, 1981, published as *Scotland: A Very Personal Review,* Penguin Books, 1983.
Scottish Castles: Tales and Traditions, Macdonald Publishers, 1982.
(With Michael Cyprien) *A Traveller's Guide to the Scotland of Robert the Bruce,* Historical Times, 1985.
The Story of Scotland, Routledge, 1987.

WESTERNS; UNDER NAME NYE TREDGOLD

Thirsty Range, Ward, Lock, 1949.
Heartbreak Valley, Ward, Lock, 1950.
The Big Corral, Ward, Lock, 1952.
Trail Herd, Ward, Lock, 1952.
Desert Doublecross, Ward, Lock, 1953.
Cloven Hooves, Ward, Lock, 1954.
Dynamite Trail, Ward, Lock, 1955.
Rancher Renegade, Ward, Lord, 1956.
Trailing Trouble, Ward, Lock, 1957.
Dead Reckoning, Ward, Lock, 1957.
Bloodstone Trail, Ward, Lock, 1958.

OTHER

Contributor of articles to all major Scottish magazines and newspapers.

ADAPTATIONS: Bridal Path was filmed under the same title; film rights to two other books have been sold.

SIDELIGHTS: Most of Nigel Tranter's fiction and nonfiction concerns Scottish history, antiquities and architecture. His *The Fortified House in Scotland,* for example, is a study of early domestic architecture while *Outlaw of the Highlands: Rob Roy* is a biography of one of Scotland's most colorful historical characters. His many novels dramatize noteworthy episodes in Scottish history. "To read Nigel Tranter's prolific output of historical novels," writes Pamela Cleaver in *Twentieth-Century Romance and Historical Writers,* "is to take a painless course in that subject. He is a scrupulous and indefatigable researcher, setting great store by accuracy, and he lovingly portrays Scottish scenery in a way that makes you feel he knows every moor, hill, and bern. His recipe for his books is to add romantic fiction to historical fact and mix invented characters with real people."

Tranter's historical novels range over a wide variety of topics. *Kenneth* tells of the battles between the Scots and marauding Viking raiders; *Crusade* depicts the Scottish involvement in the liberation of the Holy Land; and various other novels trace the rise of the house of Stuart. Cleaver notes that, although Tranter's invented characters are "sometimes two-dimensional," he can bring real historical figures "vividly to life. He gives us very engaging portraits of some monarchs."

Tranter describes himself as a moderate nationalist concerned with such internal matters as better roads in the Highlands, and with the larger problem of personal freedom and public rights. He told *CA:* "[I] have long worked for the reinstitution of a Scottish parliament for Scottish affairs. Since five hundred people will read a historical novel for every one who will read 'straight' history books, [I] seek to make readers more interested and concerned with Scotland's colourful and exciting history. [I] believe story-telling to be an essential need of man-kind and urge all who have the gift to use it."

BIOGRAPHICAL/CRITICAL SOURCES:

BOOKS

Twentieth-Century Romance and Historical Writers, third edition, St. James Press (Detroit), 1994.

PERIODICALS

Best Sellers, May 1, 1969, p. 29.
Booklist, April 1, 1959, p. 55.
Books and Bookmen, December, 1969; September, 1972; August, 1973.
Chicago Sunday Tribune, March 1, 1959, p. 9.
Kirkus, December 15, 1958, p. 26.
Library Journal, May 15, 1959, p. 84; April 1, 1969, p. 94.
Observer Review, May 17, 1970; March 30, 1974; June 27, 1976.
Times Literary Supplement, October 23, 1969; February 12, 1971; June 11, 1971; August 25, 1971.
Wisconsin Library Bulletin, May, 1959, p. 55.

*   *   *

TREDGOLD, Nye
See TRANTER, Nigel (Godwin)

*   *   *

TREMBLAY, Bill
See TREMBLAY, William Andrew

TREMBLAY, William (Andrew) 1940-
(Bill Tremblay)

PERSONAL: Born June 9, 1940, in Southbridge, MA; son of Arthur Achilles (a truck driver) and Irene (a lens grinder; maiden name, Fontaine) Tremblay; married Cynthia Ann Crooks (a radio producer), September 28, 1962; children: William Crooks, Benjamin Phillip, John Fontaine. *Education:* Attended Columbia University, 1957-58; Clark University, A.B., 1962, M.A., 1969; University of Massachusetts, M.F.A., 1972.

ADDRESSES: Home—3412 Lancaster Dr., Fort Collins, CO 80525. *Office*—Department of English, Colorado State University, Fort Collins, CO 80523.

CAREER: Leicester Junior College, Leicester, MA, assistant professor of English, 1967-70; Springfield College, Springfield, MA, instructor in English, 1972-73; Colorado State University, Fort Collins, assistant professor, 1973-78, associate professor, 1978-79, professor of creative writing, beginning 1983. Fulbright-Hays lecturer at Luso American Committee, Lisbon Portugal, 1979.

MEMBER: American Academy of Poetry, Associated Writing Programs (member of director's council, 1985-86), Western Literary Association, Rocky Mountain Modern Language Association, High Plains Arts Center.

AWARDS, HONORS: Hoyt Poetry Prize from Clark University, 1961 and 1962; National Endowment for the Arts fellow, 1985.

WRITINGS:

UNDER NAME BILL TREMBLAY; POETRY EXCEPT AS INDICATED

A Time for Breaking, Yellow Bus Press, 1970.
Crying in the Cheap Seats, University of Massachusetts Press (Amherst), 1971.
The Anarchist Heart, New Rivers Press (St. Paul, MN), 1977.
Home Front, Lynx House Press (Amherst, MA), 1978.
The Peaceable Kingdom, Four Zoas Press (Ashvelot Village, NH), 1979.
Second Sun, L'Epervier Press (Seattle, WA), 1985.

Duhamel: Ideas of Order in Little Canada, BOA Editions/Bookslinger (Brockport, NY), 1987.
The June Rise: The Apocryphal Letters of Antoine Janis (novel), Utah State University Press (Logan), 1994.

Also author of "The Next Level" (three-act play). Also author of scripts for radio and for educational television. Contributor of poems to literary journals, including *Chicago Review, Three Rivers Poetry Journal, Zahir,* and *Midwest Quarterly.* Poetry editor of *Colorado State Review* and Colorado State Review Press.

SIDELIGHTS: The poetry of William Andrew Tremblay inspires a range of critical reactions—with the term *urgency* mentioned more than once by reviewers. A former mill worker, the poet and teacher has used his working-class background as the basis for full-length works that explore modern issues. His poetry—published under the name Bill Tremblay—"has always struck a balance between unwavering surety of vision and sensitivity to subtle emotional nuance," in the opinion of *Bloomsbury Review* contributor Erika Lenz.

From his early collection *Crying in the Cheap Seats*—simultaneously decried as "elevated Rod McKuen verse" in *Choice* and recommended for its "integrity of real experience" in *Library Journal*—Tremblay presents a series of poems written from the perspective of "a man who is most alive in moments of crisis and confrontation," according to *Poetry* reviewer William Pitt Root. "Almost everything in this book has the feeling of urgency behind it, of a pressure that requires a counter-pressure to prevent a collapse."

With *The Anarchist Heart,* Tremblay "chose a full spectrum of life in America in the '70s as his subject," said *Prairie Schooner*'s Bob McNamara. "The urgency that runs through the book . . . grows out of the book's sense of itself, of what it is and what it's doing." While a *Choice* reviewer did not find every element of this collection noteworthy—"the big problem," stated the reviewer, "is getting the wheat out of the chaff"—he does recommend *The Anarchist Heart* for students and beginning poets who want to learn how to write from experience.

Tremblay returned to his milltown roots with the historical poems in *Duhamel: Ideas of Order in Little Canada.* Through his evocation of working-class New England in the 1950s, noted Bruce Shlain in his *New*

York Times Book Review critique, the poet "brings back the sights, smells and emotions of his boyhood." And in his story of a drunk-and-disorderly artist who rebels against a society that would stifle his impulse, Tremblay, concluded Shlain, "inspires awe and pity, but the book is ultimately no larger than the sum of its parts."

Tremblay departed from the poetry genre in 1995 to publish a historical novel. In *The June Rise: The Apocryphal Letters of Antoine Janis,* he "creates a character that subtly revises images of the Rocky Mountain West of the 1840s-70s," explained a writer for *Choice.* Janis, the title character, was a real-life trapper, trader, and liaison for the Lakota nation during the great migration west. Tremblay's Janis, who is forced to choose between living with his native wife on her reservation or remaining on his own homestead, "laments a paradise lost," a utopia of peaceful co-existence between Native American and settler. In an interview with Lenz, Tremblay recalled that his knowledge of and fascination with Janis goes back to the years when "my wife and our boys used to go to the Fort Collins museum. . . . They did a puppet show of the history of Fort Collins, called 'Move to Higher Ground.' And one time when I was standing around watching the rehearsal . . . one of the museum directors brought me into the Janis alcove." Tremblay elaborated that he was struck by his research into Janis's life and its parallels to his own family's history in America. "So I used Antoine as kind of a guide," reading into Janis' letters the portrait of a conflicted man who "was literate and not the stereotype of a bumpkin," a pioneer who loved the land even as he was made to choose what part of it would be his home. "What I tried to do," Tremblay explains, "was create a character who, in his own language, could reveal to a reader an unexpectedly rich inner life predicated on his dream life."

BIOGRAPHICAL/CRITICAL SOURCES:

PERIODICALS

Bloomsbury Review, July/August, 1995.
Choice, April, 1972, p. 218; November, 1977, p. 12; April, 1995, p. 1306.
Kirkus Reviews, September 1, 1994, p. 1161.
Library Journal, December 15, 1971, p. 409.
New York Times Book Review, January 25, 1987, p. 15.
Poetry, October, 1973, p. 55.
Prairie Schooner, summer, 1978, p. 207.*

TREVOR, Elleston 1920-1995
(Mansell Black, Trevor Burgess, T. Dudley-Smith, Roger Fitzalan, Adam Hall, Howard North, Simon Rattray, Warwick Scott, Caesar Smith, Lesley Stone)

PERSONAL: Name originally Trevor Dudley-Smith; born February 17, 1920, in Bromley, Kent, England; died of cancer, July 21, 1995, in Cave Creek, AZ; son of Walter and Florence (Elleston) Smith; married Jonquil Burgess, 1947 (died, 1986); married Chaille Anne Groom, 1987; children: (first marriage) Peregrine Scott (son). *Education:* Attended Yardley Court Preparatory School, 1928-32, Sevenoaks Public School, 1932-38.

CAREER: Apprentice racing-driver for two years prior to World War II. Writer, 1946-95. *Military service:* Royal Air Force, 1940-46.

AWARDS, HONORS: Edgar Award for *The Quiller Memorandum,* Mystery Writers of America, 1965; Grand Prix Litterature Policiere, 1965.

WRITINGS:

The Immortal Error, Swan (London), 1946.
Chorus of Echoes, Boardman (London), 1950.
Redfern's Miracle, Boardman, 1951.
Tiger Street, Boardman, 1951.
A Blaze of Roses, Harper (New York City), 1952, published in England as *The Fire-Raiser,* New English Library (London), 1970.
The Passion and the Pity, Heinemann (London), 1953.
The Big Pick-Up, Macmillan (New York City), 1955.
Squadron Airborne (Book Society recommendation), Heinemann, 1955, Macmillan, 1956.
The Killing-Ground, Heinemann, 1956, Macmillan, 1957.
Gale Force (Book Society recommendation), Heinemann, 1956, Macmillan, 1957.
The Pillars of Midnight, Heinemann 1957, Morrow (New York City), 1959.
Dream of Death, Brown and Watson (London), 1958.
The V.I.P., Heinemann, 1959, Morrow, 1960.
Silhouette, Swan, 1959.
The Mind of Max Doume, Swan, 1960.
The Billboard Madonna, Heinemann, 1960, Morrow, 1961.
The Burning Shore, Heinemann, 1961, Harper (New York City), 1962.
The Flight of the Phoenix, Harper, 1964.
The Second Chance, Consul (London), 1965.

Weave a Rope of Sand, Consul, 1965.
The Shoot, Doubleday (New York City), 1966.
The Freebooters, Doubleday, 1967.
A Place for the Wicked, Doubleday, 1968.
Bury Him among Kings, Doubleday, 1975.
Night Stop, Doubleday, 1975, published as *The Paragon*, New English Library, 1975.
The Theta Syndrome, Doubleday, 1977.
Blue Jay Summer, Dell (New York City), 1977.
Seven Witnesses, Remploy (London), 1977.
The Damocles Sword, Collins (London), 1981, Playboy Press (New York City), 1982.
The Penthouse, New American Library, 1983.
Death Watch, Beaufort (New York City), 1984.

UNDER PSEUDONYM MANSELL BLACK

Dead on Course, Hodder & Stoughton (London), 1951.
Sinister Cargo, Hodder & Stoughton, 1952.
Shadow of Evil, Hodder & Stoughton, 1953.
Steps in the Dark, Hodder & Stoughton, 1954.

UNDER PSEUDONYM TREVOR BURGESS

A Spy at Monk's Court, Hutchinson (London), 1949.
Mystery of the Missing Book, Hutchinson, 1951.
The Racing Wraith, Hutchinson, 1953.

UNDER PSEUDONYM T. DUDLEY-SMITH

Over the Wall, Swan, 1943.
Into the Happy Glade (children's book), Swan, 1943.
By a Silver Stream (children's book), Swan, 1944.
Double Who Double Crossed, Swan, 1944.
Escape to Fear, Swan, 1948.
Now Try the Morgue, Swan, 1948.

UNDER PSEUDONYM ROGER FITZALAN

A Blaze of Arms, Peter Davies (London), 1967.

UNDER PSEUDONYM ADAM HALL

The Volcanoes of San Domingo, Simon and Schuster (New York City), 1964.
The Quiller Memorandum, Simon and Schuster, 1965, published in Great Britain as *The Berlin Memorandum*, Collins, 1965.
The Ninth Directive, Heinemann, 1966, Simon & Schuster, 1967.
The Striker Portfolio, Simon & Schuster, 1969.
The Warsaw Document, Doubleday, 1970.
The Tango Briefing, Doubleday, 1973.

The Mandarin Cypher, Doubleday, 1975.
The Kobra Manifesto, Doubleday, 1976.
The Sinkiang Executive, Doubleday, 1978.
The Scorpion Signal, Collins, 1979, Doubleday, 1980.
The Sibling, Playboy Press (New York City), 1979.
Pekin Target, Collins, 1981, published as *The Peking Target*, Playboy Press, 1982.
Northlight, Berkley (New York City), 1985.
Quiller, Jove (New York City), 1985.
Quiller's Run, Jove, 1988.
Quiller K. G. B., Charter (New York City), 1989.
Quiller Barracuda, Morrow, 1990.
Quiller Bamboo, Morrow, 1991.
Quiller Solitaire, Morrow, 1993.
Quiller Meridian, Morrow, 1993.
Quiller Salamander, Otto Penzler Books (New York City), 1994.

UNDER PSEUDONYM HOWARD NORTH

Expressway, Doubleday, 1973.

UNDER PSEUDONYM SIMON RATTRAY

Knight Sinister, Boardman (London), 1951, Pyramid (New York City), 1971.
Queen in Danger, Boardman, 1952, Pyramid, 1971.
Bishop in Check, Boardman, 1953, Pyramid, 1971.
Dead Silence, Boardman, 1954, published as *Pawn in Jeopardy*, Pyramid, 1971.
Dead Circuit, Boardman, 1955, published as *Rook's Gambit*, Pyramid, 1972.
Dead Sequence, Boardman, 1957.

UNDER PSEUDONYM WARWICK SCOTT

Image in the Dust, Davies, 1951, published in United States as *Cockpit*, Lion (New York City), 1953.
The Domesday Story, Davies, 1952, published in United States as *Doomsday*, Lion, 1953.
Naked Canvas, Davies, 1954, Popular Library (New York City), 1955.

UNDER PSEUDONYM CAESAR SMITH

Heatwave, Wingate, 1957, Ballantine (New York City), 1958.

UNDER PSEUDONYM LESLEY STONE

Siren Song, W. H. Allen (London), 1985.
Riveria Story, W. H. Allen, 1987.

CHILDREN'S BOOKS

Wumpus, Swan, 1945.
Deep Wood, Swan, 1945, Longman (New York City), 1947.
Heather Hill, Swan, 1946, Longman, 1948.
More about Wumpus, Swan, 1947.
The Island of the Pines, Swan, 1948.
The Secret Travellers, Swan, 1948.
Where's Wumpus?, Swan, 1948.
Badger's Beech, Falcon (London), 1948.
The Wizard of the Wood, Falcon, 1948.
Badger's Moon, Falcon, 1949.
Ant's Castle, Falcon, 1949.
Mole's Castle, Falcon, 1951.
Sweethallow Valley, Falcon, 1951.
Challenge of the Firebrand, Jenkins (London), 1951.
Secret Arena, Jenkins, 1951.
Forbidden Kingdom, Lutterworth Press (London), 1955.
Badger's Wood, Heinemann, 1958.
The Crystal City, Swan, 1959.
Green Glades, Swan, 1959.
Squirrel's Island, Swan, 1963.

PLAYS

The Last of the Daylight, produced in Bromley, Kent, 1959.
Murder by All Means, first produced in Madrid, Spain, 1960, produced in England, 1961.
A Pinch of Purple, produced in Bradford, 1971.
A Touch of Purple (produced in Leatherhead, Surrey, and London, 1972), French (London), 1973.
Just before Dawn, produced in London, 1972.

Author of screenplay *Woman of Straw,* and a play titled *The Search,* produced in Bromley, England.

OTHER

Animal Life Stories: Rippleswim the Otter, Scamper-Foot Pine Marten, Shadow the Fox, three volumes, Swan, 1943-45.
Elleston Trevor Miscellany, Swan, 1944.

ADAPTATIONS: The Big Pick-Up was adapted as the film *Dunkirk,* produced by Ealing Studios and given a royal premiere. Some of Trevor's short stories have been adapted for radio and television plays, and his stage play, *The Search,* was adapted for British tele-

vision in 1963. *Flight of the Phoenix* and *The Quiller Memorandum* were filmed by 20th Century-Fox and released in 1966. Harold Pinter wrote the screenplay for the latter.

SIDELIGHTS: Elleston Trevor wrote the popular adventures of British secret agent Quiller under the pseudonym Adam Hall. Quiller—never given a first name—worked for a branch of the British government so secret it was not officially acknowledged to exist. His assignments took him throughout the world foiling Nazi plots, Soviet highjinx, drug smugglers, and Royal kidnappers in the far-flung corners of the globe. "Living only for the challenge of the mission, Quiller has no emotional or intellectual life independent of his work," explained R. Gordon Kelly in the *St. James Guide to Crime & Mystery Writers.* He is also, Kelly noted, "irascible, humorless, [and] suspicious of everyone." Speaking to Georgi Tolstiakov in *Armchair Detective,* Trevor explained: "Quiller is afraid of being a coward, afraid of not facing a challenge and so he faces it, he makes these challenges. He wants to improve himself. . . . Quiller pushes himself all the time."

The character of Quiller remained the same throughout the series. According to Newgate Callendar in the *New York Times Book Review,* Quiller "is an old pro and something of a superman—a karate expert, a phenomenal linguist, an agent who knows all the tricks." Hall's stories, explained another critic for the *New York Times Book Review,* were like "an elaborate chess game: check, sacrifice, discovered check, gambit material, predetermined opening moves." Speaking of *The Sinkiang Executive,* Robin Winks concluded in the *New Republic* that it was "stunningly well done, tense, elliptical, without a misplaced word."

Trevor first began writing while serving in the British Air Force during World War II, producing a novel a fortnight under a dozen pseudonyms. He told Tolstiakov: "During the War I had a publisher who happened to have a nice load of paper around. There was a paper shortage, but he happened to have a lot in his warehouse; so he was able to publish new writers."

Trevor once told *CA:* "There are two questions, often put to me, that have the same answer. 'Why do you write?' and 'What gave you the idea for this novel?' Answer: 'I don't know.'" As an illustration he points out that the word "Saigon" in a newspaper headline sent him on a train of thought that resulted in *The Burning Shore,* a novel about an imaginary town called Pasang.

"It is said that we read to escape. Some authors write to escape. (So this could be the answer to that first question: Why do I write?) But to escape just what? Not life—it's too darned interesting! To escape some imprisoning memory of infancy, maybe, such as we all have deep in the subconscious. Then why not take others along with me. . . ."

BIOGRAPHICAL/CRITICAL SOURCES:

BOOKS

St. James Guide to Crime & Mystery Writers, 4th edition, St. James Press (Detroit), 1996.

PERIODICALS

Armchair Detective, winter, 1996, pp. 80-84.
Best Sellers, February 1, 1964, p. 23; April 1, 1965, p. 25; December, 1978, p. 38.
Book Week, June 13, 1965, p. 19; September, 1975, p. 35.
Christian Science Monitor, January 14, 1967, p. 9; April 24, 1969, p. 13; October 3, 1973, p. 11.
Harper, July, 1965, p. 231; July, 1967, p. 235; October, 1971, p. 243.
Library Journal, January 15, 1964, p. 89; December 15, 1966, p. 91; August, 1971, p. 96; September 1, 1973, p. 98.
New Republic, April 7, 1979, p. 180.
New York Times Book Review, February 9, 1964, p. 26; March 28, 1965, p. 52; January 22, 1967, p. 36; March 23, 1969, p. 41; October 17, 1971, p. 30; October 26, 1975, p. 54; September 19, 1976, p. 47; June 25, 1978, p. 34.
Times Literary Supplement, December 8, 1966, p. 1157; October 1, 1976, p. 1260.

OBITUARIES:

PERIODICALS

Chicago Tribune, July 25, 1995, sec. 1, p. 10.*

* * *

TURNER, Clay
  See BALLARD, (Willis) Todhunter

TURNER, Sheila
  See ROWBOTHAM, Sheila

* * *

UPDYKE, James
  See BURNETT, W(illiam) R(iley)

* * *

VARDRE, Leslie
  See DAVIES, L(eslie) P(urnell)

* * *

VIORST, Judith 1931-

PERSONAL: Born February 2, 1931, in Newark, NJ; daughter of Martin Leonard (an accountant) and Ruth Jane (Ehrenkranz) Stahl; married Milton Viorst (a political reporter and writer), January 30, 1960; children: Anthony Jacob, Nicholas Nathan, Alexander Noah. *Education:* Rutgers University, B.A. (with honors), 1952; Washington Psychoanalytic Institute, graduate, 1981. *Religion:* Jewish.

ADDRESSES: Home—3432 Ashley Terrace N.W., Washington, DC 20008. *Agent*—Robert Lescher, 67 Irving Pl., New York, NY 10003.

CAREER: Poet, journalist, and writer of books for adults and children. Contributing editor, *Redbook* magazine.

MEMBER: Phi Beta Kappa.

AWARDS, HONORS: Emmy Award, 1970, for poetic monologues written for CBS television special, *Annie: The Women in the Life of a Man;* Silver Pencil Award, 1973, for *The Tenth Good Thing about Barney;* Penney-Missouri Award, 1974, for *Redbook* article; American Academy of Pediatrics Award, 1977, for *Redbook* article; American Association of University Women Award, 1980, for *Redbook* article; Christopher Award, 1988, for *The Good-bye Book.*

WRITINGS:

The Village Square (poems), Coward (New York City), 1965.
It's Hard to Be Hip over Thirty and Other Tragedies of Married Life (poems), World Publishing, 1968.
(With husband, Milton Viorst) *The Washington, D.C., Underground Gourmet,* Simon & Schuster (New York City), 1970.
People and Other Aggravations (poems), World Publishing, 1971.
Yes, Married: A Saga of Love and Complaint (collected prose pieces), Saturday Review Press, 1972.
How Did I Get to Be Forty and Other Atrocities (poems), Simon & Schuster, 1976.
Love and Guilt and the Meaning of Life, Etc., Simon & Schuster, 1979.
A Visit from St. Nicholas (to a Liberated Household), Simon & Schuster, 1979.
If I Were in Charge of the World and Other Worries: Poems for Children and Their Parents, Atheneum (New York City), 1981.
Necessary Losses, Simon & Schuster, 1986.
When Did I Stop Being Twenty and Other Injustices: Selected Poems from Single to Mid-Life, Simon & Schuster, 1987.
Forever Fifty and Other Negotiations, Simon & Schuster, 1989.
Murdering Mr. Monti (novel), Simon & Schuster, 1994.
Sad Underwear and Other Complications: More Poems for Children and Their Parents, illustrated by Richard Hull, Atheneum, 1995.

JUVENILE FICTION

Sunday Morning, Harper (New York City), 1968.
I'll Fix Anthony, Harper, 1969.
Try It Again, Sam: Safety When You Walk, Lothrop (New York City), 1970.
The Tenth Good Thing about Barney, Atheneum, 1971.
Alexander and the Terrible, Horrible, No Good, Very Bad Day, Atheneum, 1972.
My Mama Says There Aren't Any Zombies, Ghosts, Vampires, Creatures, Demons, Monsters, Fiends, Goblins, or Things, Atheneum, 1973.
Rosie and Michael, Atheneum, 1974.
(Contributor) *Free To Be . . . You and Me,* McGraw (New York City), 1974.
Alexander, Who Used to Be Rich Last Sunday, Atheneum, 1978.

The Good-bye Book, illustrated by Kay Chorao, Atheneum, 1988.
Earrings!, Atheneum, 1990.
The Alphabet from Z to A (With Much Confusion on the Way), illustrated by Hull, Atheneum, 1995.
Alexander, Who's Not (Do You Hear Me? I Mean It!) Going to Move, illustrated by Robin Preiss-Glasser, Atheneum, 1995.

JUVENILE NONFICTION

(Editor with Shirley Moore) *Wonderful World of Science,* Science Service, 1961.
Projects: Space, Washington Square Press (New York City), 1962.
One Hundred and Fifty Science Experiments, Step-by-Step, Bantam (New York City), 1963.
Natural World, Bantam, 1965.
The Changing Earth, Bantam, 1967.

OTHER

Also author of musical play, *Love and Shrimp.* Author of syndicated column for Washington Star Syndicate, 1970-72, and of regular column for *Redbook,* 1968—. Author of poetic monologues for television specials, including *Annie: The Women in the Life of a Man.* Contributor of poems and articles to *New York, New York Times, Holiday, Venture, Washingtonian,* and other periodicals.

WORK IN PROGRESS: An adult nonfiction book.

SIDELIGHTS: A wryly humorous poet and author, Judith Viorst has been described by a *Washington Post Book World* reviewer as "among the finest living authors for children." Much of the success that Viorst has achieved in her writings, whether it be her very popular books irreverently describing her life and family, her monthly column in *Redbook,* her contributions to numerous other periodicals, or her works for children, is due to the fact that Viorst "holds up a mirror to our lives so we can reflect and understand," to quote *Los Angeles Times Book Review* correspondent Barbara Karlin.

Viorst admitted that a writing career is something she had her eye on since the age of seven. "I always, always, always wanted to be a writer," she stated in an interview published in the *Chicago Tribune.* "I never wanted to be anything else—never. It never entered my mind that I was going to earn a living at it or be well-known as a result of it." Her first efforts, neatly printed poems mailed to various magazines, were promptly returned. Recalled Viorst, "[They were] terrible poems—about dead dogs, mostly." Her later works fared little better, meeting with what she describes as a "spectacular lack of success." All of them, she noted, were "deadly serious things. . . . Very grim. The meaning of life. Death. Pain. Lust. Suicide. That sort of thing."

One of Viorst's first "official" writing assignments came when she was hired as a stringer by the *New York Herald Tribune* to report on parties in Washington, DC. However, she reveals, "I could never recognize anyone famous. Milton [her husband] had to go everywhere with me." Eventually she began contributing poems to the newspaper's Sunday magazine section. In 1965 these poems were collected to form her first book, *The Village Square.* When her second collection of poetry, *It's Hard to Be Hip over Thirty and Other Tragedies of Married Life,* was published in 1968, the book was an instant bestseller establishing Viorst as one of the country's most popular writers of light verse.

While her verse may be termed "light," Viorst has disputed the notion that writing poems such as hers is effortless. "I slave over them," she told *CA.* "It always makes me feel embarrassed to say how hard I work on them because they are 'light verse' and yet it took me four years to write the twenty-four poems in *How Did I Get to Be Forty and Other Atrocities.*"

Readers have come to appreciate her labor, and reviewers point to Viorst's dedication to accurate portrayals of her thoughts as one of the major reasons for her success, especially in her books detailing the humorous side to everyday life. C. K. Carey wrote in a *Library Journal* review of *How Did I Get to Be Forty and Other Atrocities:* "Is there a reader . . . out there so self-assured, so together that she can't identify with Viorst's heroine? I doubt it. No one does it quite like Viorst; no one better expresses our daily discontents and unfulfilled fantasies." Carol Kleiman remarked in the *Chicago Tribune* that "as a poet, [Viorst] has a wonderful gift for convincing us in her first few stanzas that she always is cool and in charge of her life—then she wryly gets down to the truth, making us laugh aloud at the dichotomy."

Viorst gives much of the credit for her success to her husband and children, who usually serve as inspirations for her witty reflections on contemporary marriage and family life. Said the author: "Someone once remarked to me that if I hadn't gotten married, I might have written the great American novel, but I think if I hadn't gotten married, maybe I wouldn't have written anything. Milton and my life with him have given me the encouragement I needed to pursue writing. . . . I don't think it's a coincidence that I never had anything published before I was married to Milton." Recalling that early lack of self-confidence, Viorst remarked, "there was a time in my life when I was incapable of sending anything out until Milton said it was ready."

Viorst also told *CA:* "Married life is the rock on which I sit and do my work and the kids' role in this should not be dismissed. It is possible to find delight in just hanging around the kitchen while one kid is making a chicken sandwich and the other is tossing a napkin into the trash and missing. Milton and I are two people who know that family life is good, that it is better than most things going on in the universe."

Viorst's children have, of course, inspired their mother in more concrete ways. Many of the characters in her children's books are based on her three children and their experiences and problems. She explained: "Most of my children's books are for or about my own children, and mostly they're written to meet certain needs. For instance, when Anthony was mercilessly persecuting his younger brother I decided to write *I'll Fix Anthony* to cheer up Nick. When a lot of questions about death were being raised around our house, my struggle for a way to respond to those questions resulted in the Barney book. I observed that the concept of 'I'm having a bad day' seemed to help adults get through those bad days a little better and so I wrote about such a day for Alexander, who was having a lot of them. For Nick, who used to be scared of monsters and doubtful of his mother's infallibility (he's recovered from the former but not the latter), I wrote *My Mama Says.*"

It is books such as *I'll Fix Anthony* and *My Mama Says There Aren't Any Zombies, Ghosts, Vampires, Creatures, Demons, Monsters, Fiends, Goblins, or Things,* in addition to other favorites such as *Alexander and the Terrible, Horrible, No Good, Very Bad Day, Rosie and Michael,* and *The Tenth Good Thing about Barney* that have provided Viorst's readers with sensitive, tender, yet realistic stories with a consistent appeal. "Viorst is an author who can enter imaginatively into a child's difficulties without being either tactless or disablingly sympathetic," wrote a reviewer for the *Times Literary Supplement.*

In the *Dictionary of Literary Biography,* Douglas Street stated that Viorst "has shown herself to be a writer of talent and insight who has successfully combined entertainment and enrichment in her creations for the child audience. . . . Stories of her young sons, Anthony, Nicholas, and Alexander, show the sensitivity, humor, and timeliness readily accessible to American children today." Likewise, Barbara Karlin commented in the *Los Angeles Times Book Review* that the gifted Viorst "deftly zeroes in on the minor traumas and neuroses of childhood and lets us laugh at them."

In 1981, after her youngest son entered college, Viorst enrolled in classes at the Washington Psychoanalytic Institute. She explained in the *Chicago Tribune* interview: "I really wanted to keep doing what I was doing, which was writing about what goes on between people and inside people's heads. I wanted to pick up another source for writing about that. I wanted to expand the resources in my life. . . . Going back to school was really one of the great thrilling experiences in my life." She continued: "I had originally thought that I would just take everything I was learning and keep doing the same kind of writing I was doing and the writing would change somehow as a result of it. . . . [However,] psychoanalytic theory made me realize that everything I heard and saw could be better understood with it. And then I knew that I wanted to write more directly about it." As a result of these feelings, Viorst started thinking about writing about dealing with loss. In 1986 *Necessary Losses* was published.

Vic Sussman wrote in the *Washington Post Book World* that Viorst "brings an unusual perspective to *Necessary Losses,* a book that explores the painful separations we must continually undergo. . . . Yet while *Necessary Losses* glides above a landscape of heartache, it's never clinical or depressing. Viorst is, after all, a poet with a wonderful sense of humor and insight. She skillfully combines psychoanalytic theory, poetry (her own and others'), interviews, anecdotes, and her personal experiences into an instructive yet warm survey of the human journey." And Elinor Lenz stated in the *Los Angeles Times Book Review* that "there is much of value in this book—in Viorst's respect for the individual, in her emphatic detailing of the ways in which various people deal with the necessary losses in their lives, in her often poignant sketches of her own family relationships, and, though it may leave some readers unsatisfied, in her faith that self-understanding is better than self-delusion."

Viorst's sons may have departed the family home, but the author has not lacked for further themes and top-

ics related to childhood. *Sad Underwear and Other Complications: More Poems for Children and Their Parents* tackles both light and serious topics in the author's signature free-form verse style. Calling the poems in *Sad Underwear* "eminently, infectiously readable," *Washington Post Book World* contributor Michael Dirda commented that Viorst's works "make plenty happen—smiles, guffaws, even a few tears. . . . These are poems that parents can discuss with their kids, as well as laugh over." *School Library Journal* correspondent Amy Adler likewise cited *Sad Underwear* as "an inspired book of verse guaranteed to tickle the humerus again and again."

Nor has the author neglected the special concerns of older children. In the novel *Earrings!,* a determined little girl bargains, pines for, lusts after, and begs for pierced ears in which she could insert the earrings that have become her obsession. In a *New York Times Book Review* piece on the story, Kate Lynch noted: "Judith Viorst understands children. You can tell because she starts her new book the same way most youngsters start their sentences: 'I want.'. . . Viorst is a poet, and she writes about desire and frustration with insight and a musical ear. This book breathes with the roller-coaster rhythms of obsession . . . but since her characters are spoiled middle-class children, Ms. Viorst's mock-serious treatment of their problems adds a welcome element of humor and perspective to all her work." A boy who is faced with a family relocation serves as the hero in *Alexander, Who's Not (Do You Hear Me? I Mean It!) Going To Move.* The story follows Alexander through his last day of school and through the taunts of his brothers as he wrestles with the impending 1,000-mile move. Observing that this timely theme has been featured in many recent children's titles, a *Booklist* reviewer nonetheless praised Viorst's treatment for its "rare combination . . . of farce and immediacy and a wonderful empathy for the child's point of view."

In 1994 Viorst published her first novel for adults, entitled *Murdering Mr. Monti: A Merry Little Tale of Sex and Violence.* The farcical story introduces a Jewish matron and popular advice columnist named Brenda Kovner, who decides to murder a man who is threatening her family. "The plot is more improbable than a month's supply of supermarket tabloids, but the real point of the story is its wry look at the follies of superficial urbanites," declared Sharyn McCrumb in the *Washington Post Book World.* Viorst's "wit here is Ginsu-knife sharp," added the reviewer; "her observations on love and marriage, chilling." In the *New York Times Book Review,* Elinor Lipman concluded that *Murdering Mr. Monti* "has an endearing tendency to look over its own shoulder, to worry, to take its own pulse—to chart a romp with Jewish guilt."

The ability to express her feelings on a variety of topics and in a number of different genres is one of the reasons Viorst considers herself to be a very lucky woman. Commenting on her career, she remarked to *CA:* "It's a dream come true, exactly what I've always wanted to do. I have the freedom, the independence, the flexibility—following no one's schedule but my own, being able—while my kids were growing—to tailor my schedule to the needs of my household and three children. . . . My experiences have exceeded my expectations, and I do think these are the best years of my life. I know what I love. I have what I love. And I love what I have."

BIOGRAPHICAL/CRITICAL SOURCES:

BOOKS

Children's Literature Review, Volume 3, Gale (Detroit), 1978.
Dictionary of Literary Biography, Volume 52: *American Writers for Children since 1960: Fiction,* Gale, 1986.
Lanes, Selma G., *Down the Rabbit Hole,* Atheneum, 1971.

PERIODICALS

Booklist, January 1, 1973; November 15, 1976; March 1, 1986; August 1995, p. 1949.
Chicago Tribune, March 29, 1987; November 15, 1987; December 8, 1987.
Chicago Tribune Books, January 23, 1994, pp. 16-17.
Children's Book Review, April, 1973.
Horn Book, November/December, 1990, p. 741; May/June, 1994, p. 322.
House Beautiful, October, 1972.
Junior Literary Guild Catalogue, September, 1972; September, 1973.
Kirkus Reviews, September 15, 1972; July 15, 1974.
Library Journal, January 15, 1969; November 15, 1976; July 1986.
Life, December 17, 1971.
Los Angeles Times, January 7, 1988.
Los Angeles Times Book Review, September 16, 1984; April 27, 1986; March 27, 1988.
McCall's, September, 1969.
New Yorker, December 4, 1971.
New York Times Book Review, November 9, 1969; September 26, 1971; October 22, 1972; December 30, 1973; February 2, 1975; November 15, 1981; March 10, 1985; March 23, 1986; May 8, 1988; November 11, 1990, p. 40; January 23, 1994, p. 16; May 22, 1994, p. 30.
People, February 18, 1980.
Publishers Weekly, January 8, 1979; April 17, 1995, p. 60; September 11, 1995, p. 85.
Saturday Review, November 30, 1968.
Saturday Review/World, December 4, 1973.
School Library Journal, January, 1969; February, 1971; September, 1973; January, 1982; May, 1995, p. 116.
Times Literary Supplement, November 23, 1973.
Washington Post, May 31, 1979; June 8, 1986.
Washington Post Book World, December 29, 1968; November 5, 1972; December 5, 1976; May 14, 1978; May 11, 1986; April 5, 1987; January 16, 1994, p. 2; April 3, 1994, p. 10; June 4, 1995, p. 6.

W-Z

WADDY, Lawrence (Heber) 1914-

PERSONAL: Born October 5, 1914, in Sydney, Australia; son of Percival S. (a minister) and Etheldred (Spittal) Waddy; married first wife, Natalie (deceased); married Laurie Hermanson, October 7, 1972; children: (first marriage) Helena Lepovitz, Nerissa Wilson, Joanna. *Education:* Balliol College, Oxford University, B.A., 1937, M.A., 1945. *Politics:* Republican. *Religion:* Episcopalian. *Avocational interests:* Writing, directing, and acting for the theater.

ADDRESSES: Home—5910 Camino de la Costa, La Jolla, CA 92034.

CAREER: Winchester College, Winchester, Hampshire, England, chaplain and teacher of classics, 1938-42, 1946-49; Tonbridge School, Tonbridge, Kent, England, headmaster, 1949-62; British Broadcasting Corporation (BBC), London, education officer, religious broadcaster, and writer, 1962-63; The Bishop's School, La Jolla, CA, chaplain, associate in administration, and teacher, 1963-67; University of California, San Diego, lecturer in classics, 1969-80. Lecturer in classics, University of California, Berkeley, 1961. Honorary canon, Diocese of Rochester, England, 1961-63; honorary chaplain to Bishop of Rochester, 1963-67; vicar, Church of the Good Samaritan, 1970-74. *Military service:* Royal Naval Volunteer Reserve, chaplain, 1942-46.

AWARDS, HONORS: BBC production of his musical play, *Job*, was chosen as Britain's best religious program, 1963, and as a prize-winner at the Monte Carlo Film Festival, 1964.

WRITINGS:

PLAYS

The Prodigal Son (one-act; first produced in Coventry, England, at the Coventry Cathedral, 1963), Samuel French, 1963.
The Bible as Drama (includes *Job* [first produced on BBC, 1963], *Joseph, Good Friday, The Prodigal Son* [first produced on BBC television, 1963], and *The Wedding Feast* [first produced on BBC television, 1964]), Paulist/Newman, 1975.
Faith of Our Fathers, Morehouse, 1976.
Drama in Worship (includes *Jonah* [first produced on BBC television, 1964], *The Crafty Steward, Martin the Cobbler, God's Tumbler,* and *The Good Samaritan* [first produced on BBC television, 1963]), Paulist/Newman, 1978.
The Family of Man, first produced in La Jolla, CA, at Sherwood Auditorium, March, 1982.
Shakespeare Remembers, Players Press, 1994.
Florence Nightingale, Players Press, 1996.
Jonah, Players Press, 1996.

Musical scores for Waddy's plays are available from the author. Also author of thirteen radio plays for "The Witness" series of the Episcopal Church, 1964.

"EAGLE CITY" SERIES; NOVELS

Symphony, Lane & Associates, 1980.
Mayor's Race, Lane & Associates, 1980.

OTHER

Pax Romana and World Peace, Chapman & Hall, 1950.

A Parish by the Sea: A History of Saint James-by-the-Sea Episcopal Church, La Jolla, California, Saint James Bookshelf, 1988.
First Bible Stories, Paulist Press, 1994.

Contributor to periodicals, including *American Journal of Archaeology* and *Journal of Unconventional History.*

WORK IN PROGRESS: Two plays: *Paul of Tarsus* and *Eleanor Roosevelt;* children's stories; a novel about the abolition of guns; a novel about organ transplants.

SIDELIGHTS: Lawrence Waddy told *CA:* "I am a retired Episcopal minister and teacher. My interest in writing goes back a long way. I was an editor of my school magazine in England, and my education in the classics, history, and philosophy gave me a good deal of experience in writing papers, as well as Latin and Greek compositions.

"I began teaching in 1937 and was ordained deacon in 1940 (during the Battle of Britain), and priest in 1941. Early in 1942 I joined the British Navy as a chaplain and spent two years at sea. My first writing of any length occurred during four-hour watches in the cipher office of my cruiser, *HMS Jamaica.* I volunteered for this duty when we were at sea, and often it involved four uneventful hours in an office with a typewriter. On occasion, urgent signals came in, but usually they were routine, with gaps between them.

"For fun I began a novel about our situation, 'A Week in Iceland.' It was about two Navy officers who went ashore for an afternoon in Akureyri, the northernmost town in Iceland, and stumbled into a spy situation. A London publisher politely rejected it. Later I wrote another, 'Crime in a Cruiser,' about a murder which took place in a ship during one of the convoy operations.

"Writing these books gave me the feel of description and dialogue. When I came back from the war to teaching, to my surprise I was asked by Chapman and Hall to write a history of Rome, on the strength of my Oxford record. I said that I would do so if I could relate it to modern parallels. Result: *Pax Romana and World Peace,* which did quite well.

"In 1949 I became headmaster of a famous boarding school, Tonbridge, and for thirteen years I was too busy to write seriously; but in 1959, after a Greek cruise when I was a lecturer, I began to write songs which turned into a musical, *Isles of Greece.* It had one good amateur production in 1962. The text is horribly dated, but I still sing the songs in the shower.

"That led to a burst of song and play writing. A short musical, *The Prodigal Son,* written for my schoolboys, was accepted by the BBC for a TV play, and then published by Samuel French, all in 1963. In that year I moved to La Jolla, California, after one year of temporary work in the BBC's Schools department. During that year they accepted four more of my musicals.

"*Job* was very successful, being chosen as Britain's best religious program for 1963, and winning first prize in the Monte Carlo UNDA film festival. So I have been encouraged to write songs and plays ever since. Paulist Press later published two collections of plays.

"Apart from plays, I have written two published novels. This came about when my wife was president of the San Diego Symphony. I decided that a novel about a concert would be a good combination of fundraiser and publicity. It was, and I followed it with another novel published locally. All the time I was very busy acting and directing plays as part of my ministry.

"Now I am in a burst of writing with my first computer to help. Players Press has published three plays. My first children's book is out (*First Bible Stories*), and I am trying to publish a bigger collection of children's stories, as well as two novels."

*   *   *

WAINER, Cord
  See DEWEY, Thomas B(lanchard)

*   *   *

WALKER, George F. 1947-

PERSONAL: Born August 23, 1947, in Toronto, Ontario, Canada; son of Malcolm (a laborer) and Florence (Braybrook) Walker; married c. 1965 (marriage ended); married Susan Purdy (an actor); children: Renata, Courtney.

ADDRESSES: Agent—Great North Artists Management, Inc., 350 Dupont St., Toronto, Ontario M5V 1R5, Canada.

CAREER: Playwright. Factory Theatre Lab, Toronto, dramaturge, 1972-73, resident playwright, 1972-76. Has directed productions of his own work, including *Ramona and the White Slaves,* 1976, and *Rumours of Our Death,* 1980.

AWARDS, HONORS: Awarded five grants from Canada Council; Chalmers Award for Distinguished Playwriting nominations, 1977, for *Zastrozzi, The Master of Discipline,* and 1981, for *Theatre of the Film Noir;* Dora Award for directing, 1982, for *Rumours of Our Death;* Chalmers Award for Best New Canadian Play, 1985, and Governor General's Literary Award for drama, Canada Council, 1986, both for *Criminals in Love;* Dora and Chalmers Awards for Best New Canadian Play and Governor General's Award for English-language Drama, all 1988, all for *Nothing Sacred;* Chalmers Award for Best Play, 1989, for *Love and Anger;* Dora and Chalmers Awards for Best New Canadian Play, 1992, for *Escape from Happiness.*

WRITINGS:

PLAYS

Prince of Naples (produced in Toronto at Factory Theatre Lab, 1971; produced as a radio play by CBC-Radio, 1973), Playwrights Canada (Toronto), 1973.
Ambush at Tether's End (produced at Factory Theatre Lab, 1971; produced as a radio play by CBC-Radio, 1974), Playwrights Canada, 1974.
Sacktown Rag (produced at Factory Theatre Lab, 1972), Playwrights Canada, 1972.
Bagdad Saloon (produced in London at Bush Theatre, 1973), Playwrights Canada, 1973.
Demerit, produced at Factory Theatre Lab, 1974.
(And director) *Beyond Mozambique* (produced at Factory Theatre Lab, 1974), Playwrights Co-op, 1975.
(And director) *Ramona and the White Slaves,* produced at Factory Theatre Lab, 1976.
Gossip, produced in Toronto at Toronto Free Theatre, 1977.
Zastrozzi, The Master of Discipline: A Melodrama (produced at Toronto Free Theatre, 1977; produced at New York Shakespeare Festival, 1981), Playwrights Canada, 1977, second edition, 1991.
Three Plays by George F. Walker (contains *Bagdad Saloon, Beyond Mozambique,* and *Ramona and*

the White Slaves), Coach House Press (Toronto), 1978.
Filthy Rich (produced at Toronto Free Theatre, 1979; produced in New York City at 47th Street Theatre, 1985), Playwrights Canada, 1979.
(And director) *Rumours of Our Death,* produced at Factory Theatre Lab, 1980.
(And director) *Theatre of the Film Noir,* produced in Toronto at Adelaide Court Theatre, 1981.
Science and Madness, produced in Toronto at Tarragon Theatre, 1982.
(And director) *The Art of War: An Adventure* (produced at Toronto Workshop Productions, 1983), Playwrights Canada, 1982.
Criminals in Love (produced in Toronto at Factory Theatre, 1984), Playwrights Canada, 1984.
The Power Plays (contains *Gossip, Filthy Rich,* and *The Art of War*), Coach House Press, 1984.
Better Living, produced in Toronto at CentreStage, 1986.
Beautiful City, produced at Factory Theatre, c. 1987.
Nothing Sacred: Based on "Fathers and Sons" by Ivan Turgenev (produced in Los Angeles at Mark Taper Forum, 1988), Coach House Press, 1988.
Love and Anger (produced at Factory Theatre, 1989), Coach House Press, 1990.
Escape from Happiness (produced at Vassar College, 1991), InBook, 1992.
Shared Anxiety: Selected Plays (contains *Beyond Mozambique, Zastrozzi, The Master of Discipline, Theatre of the Film Noir, The Art of War, Criminals in Love, Better Living, Escape from Happiness,* and *Tough!*), Coach House Press, 1994.

Also author of *The East End Plays,* 1988. Works represented in anthologies, including *Now in Paperback: Canadian Playwrights of the 1970s,* edited by Connie Brissenden, Fineglow Plays (Toronto), 1973; and *The Factory Lab Anthology,* edited by Brissenden, Talonbooks (Vancouver), 1974.

TELEVISION PLAYS

Microdrama, Canadian Broadcasting Corp. (CBC-TV), 1976.
Strike, CBC-TV, 1976.
Sam, Grace, Doug, and the Dog, CBC-TV, 1976.
Overlap, CBC-TV, 1977.
Capital Punishment, CBC-TV, 1977.

RADIO PLAYS

The Private Man, CBC-Radio, 1973.
Quiet Days in Limbo, CBC-Radio, 1977.
Desert's Revenge, CBC-Radio, 1984.

OTHER

Contributor to periodicals, including *Descant.*

SIDELIGHTS: George Walker has been called a "playwright in progress" by critics. While enthusiastic about the compelling stories and fascinating characters created by one of Canada's leading dramatists, they have been baffled about how to categorize his work. Denis Johnston suggested in *Canadian Drama* that there is "no 'school' into which Walker may be conveniently slotted . . . partly because his work is so recent and his style is so distinctive, but also because his style continues to change."

Walker has been lauded as one of the writers who helped expand the scope of Canadian drama beyond naturalistic plays about rural and small town life into the fringes of realism with his distinguishing blend of Absurdism and pop culture references. His rise to popularity parallels the growth of the Canadian theatre scene throughout the 1970s and 1980s. While working as a cab driver in 1971, Walker submitted his first play, *Prince of Naples,* to the fledgling Factory Theater Lab in his native Toronto. The Lab had recently opened its doors as the first theatre in English-speaking Canada to devote itself entirely to Canadian plays, and this first production marked the beginning of a long and fruitful relationship for both playwright and producers: a majority of Walker's twenty-plus plays have premiered at the Factory Theater Lab, many directed by the author himself.

While helping to make Toronto a world-class theatre city, Walker has garnered several awards and accolades. He has won the prestigious Governor-General's Award for both *Criminals in Love* (1984) and *Nothing Sacred* (1988), as well as six Chalmers Awards for best new Canadian play and four Dora Awards, as both playwright and director, for Toronto theatre. *Love and Anger,* which opened the Factory Theatre Lab's 20th anniversary season in 1989, became the longest-running original play in Toronto theatrical history, lasting at the Lab for six months before transferring to the St. Lawrence Center and becoming the first original Canadian play to move directly from a non-profit to a commercial theatre.

Walker's plays have been noted for the way they process and often parody popular culture, especially B-movies and film noir detectives and damsels in distress. Critics have also found interest in the dark humor in his plays, and the constant struggle between the sometimes nebulous forces of good and evil, order

and chaos. It is not always easy to tell which side is winning, or deserves to. In *Zastrozzi, The Master of Discipline,* as elsewhere in Walker's work, the evil character is self-controlled and decisive while the good character is haunted by self-doubts to the point of ineffectiveness. Power, morality, and justice are not commonly recognized absolutes in Walker's world; they are all relative.

More than any other facet of his writing, however, it is his dialogue that has generated the most attention. Walker's verbal jousts have been compared to Tom Stoppard and his precision to that of Samuel Beckett, while the palpable, frightening menace in his words has drawn comparisons to Edward Albee and Harold Pinter, and his pop culture references are reminiscent of Sam Shepard.

Everything about a Walker play is defined by his characters' language. In his introduction to *Shared Anxiety,* a collection of eight of the playwright's works, Stephen Haff writes, "Nobody needs to decode a Walker play because his characters say what they mean and mean what they say. They speak with astonishing directness, telling us everything we need to know: who they are, who others are, what the situation is, how the world works, what they want, what's inside them, and how mixed up it all is."

The result is often dialogue with the intimation of soliloquy. While characters speak to one another, they sometimes seem to emerge, *sprecher*-like, through the fourth wall, fracturing psychological distance and engaging, challenging the audience to both think and feel. William, the Kafkaesque philosopher-bum in *Criminals in Love,* makes a forceful first impression with his cohorts in crime when he tells them, "I speak now from the heart of experience. I use words like destiny and fate and despair. I talk of the great abyss which beckons us all. I speak of the great underclass of our society, the doomed, the forgotten, the outcasts. I describe the fine line which separates the lands of function and dysfunction, I put it in terms which cover the spectrum. The political. The philosophical. The poetic. Occasionally I use the vernacular. . . . I describe the human condition."

William seems to be a stand-in for Walker himself, whose plays resonate with the political, the philosophical, the poetic and the vernacular. His earliest plays—*Prince of Naples, Ambush at Tether's End,* and *Sacktown Rag,* are now often dismissed as being too derivative of European Absurdists like Beckett and

Eugene Ionesco, yet these influences helped shape what was to come. "Existential comedy strung out along the border between the serious and the bizarre has for two decades been the specialty of George F. Walker," writes Jerry Wasserman in *Drama.*

Wasserman suggests that Walker's career progress through the late 1980s can be traced through three significant trilogies. *Three Plays* (1978) consists of *Bagdad Saloon, Beyond Mozambique,* and *Ramona and the White Slaves,* all of which are takes on B-movie plots and characters. *Bagdad Saloon* is a quirky, cartoonish work in which Arab terrorists kidnap American pop culture icons like Doc Halliday and Gertrude Stein in an attempt to discover the secret of mass appeal and popular success. Walker explores obsession in *Beyond Mozambique.* In this play, Rocco, the almost archetypal mad scientist, conducts human experiments in an old, run-down, colonial house surrounded by jungle. The plot is deadly serious, but the attitude and dialogue are ironic, self-mocking, and satirical. Rocco declares, for example, "There's something about committing crimes against humanity that puts you in touch with the purpose of the universe." In the last play of the loosely connected trilogy, *Ramona and the White Slaves,* Walker presents a murder mystery in an exotic locale. Ramona is the madam of a brothel in turn-of-the-century Hong Kong, and the play is about her various relationships with her children, their lovers, and a mysterious man who might be her missing husband. Writing for *Canadian Literature,* Chris Johnson called the part of Ramona "one of the most rewarding roles for an actress in Canadian drama, a striking presentation of the mother/whore dichotomy so central to Western erotic fantasy."

Walker's next series of plays actually centers on a single prominent character: Tyrone M. Power, an investigative reporter and, later, private eye who is the balding, middle-aged, anti-hero-protagonist of *The Power Plays* (1984). In this trilogy—*Gossip, Filthy Rich,* and *The Art of War*—Walker continues to exploit popular cinematography, but updates the settings to the here and now. Power begins this serio-comic detective spoof as a reporter investigating corruption in the art world of high society and ends as a hard-boiled, cynical Sherlock Holmes who has acquired his own nemesis, the international master criminal, General Hackman. When the chips are down, though, and Power has cornered Hackman, he cannot bring himself to shoot the arch-fiend, who escapes into the night, vowing to return again someday.

Although the trilogy met with popular success, some critics found *The Power Plays* inconsistent. "The two early plays amuse us with their convoluted murder plots," opined L. W. Conolly in *Canadian Literature,* "whereas *The Art of War,* while still amusing, poses troublesome questions about the nature of 'liberalism' in the face of autocratic power. *Gossip* and *Filthy Rich* are clever plays; *The Art of War* is an intelligent play, and it doesn't sit easily with the other two."

In his third trilogy, *The East End Plays,* Walker seemed to be moving even closer to the familiar. *Criminals in Love, Better Living,* and *Beautiful City* are all dramas that center on families and seem to take place in the playwright's own Eastside Toronto neighborhoods. *Criminals in Love* is probably Walker's most popular play to date. It is the story of Junior and Gail, teenage lovers who are forced into a terrorist conspiracy by Junior's Father, a clumsy thief who has never gotten away from the scene of a crime, his "Aunt" Wineva, a schizophrenic revolutionary, and his mysterious Uncle Ritchie, who never makes an appearance but manipulates everyone from behind the scenes.

As in most of Walker's plays, the line between serious social commentary and ironic self-satire is quite blurry in *Criminals in Love.* Before going to visit his father in prison, Junior bemoans his fate to Gail. He acknowledges that his father is a miserable failure, but nevertheless claims, "He's my destiny. I mean he's my family. I mean. . .he scares me. He's so ridiculous he's terrifying." From inside the prison, Junior's father coerces him into criminal activities with Wineva and Ritchie, and soon everyone is involved—Gail, her friend, Sandy, and William, a bum they meet on the street. By the end of the play, after a couple bungled robbery attempts and a near-miss explosion, the two young lovers are wanted felons, holed up in Junior's living room with the police surrounding the house.

Critics almost universally applauded the play, and rallied around its timely themes. In *Canadian Theatre Review,* Paul Walsh wrote, "*Criminals in Love* not only addresses the desires and anxieties of the '80s but accosts them with a relentless and uncompromising explication of the decade's terrifying epithet: 'No Future.'" Judith Rudakoff, writing for *Books in Canada,* opined, "In The East End Trilogy . . . the glorious orchestration of ideas and words reads as well as it plays. Walker's characters, from the ferociously ardent to the timidly uncertain, are genuine, memorable, and always in some way recognizable."

During the 1990s Walker's plays increasingly found their way to the United States, where they were produced in regional and university theatres, as well as on New York stages. His plays *Love and Anger* (1989), *Nothing Sacred* (1990), and *Escape from Happiness* (1991) all received multiple productions in the United States, while that country's playgoers also began to discover Walker's earlier work like *Zastrozzi* and *Beyond Mozambique*. William A. Henry III noted in *Time*. "Walker's work certainly travels. Although *Escape* was originally set in Toronto, [the director's] staging makes it feel entirely American, from the opening moment, when a battered TV onstage starts blaring *The Donna Reed Show,* to the snarling climax, when at least four people are pointing weapons at one another."

Perhaps Walker's work travels so well because it is so well-traveled. As Stephan Haff notes, "Wherever they are—an unspecified jungle, a crumbling prison in turn-of-the-century Italy, a graveyard in the Paris of 1945, a cliff in Nova Scotia, an alley, a kitchen, a park—Walker's characters are in our world because they give us their mighty effort to survive in words full, direct and present. . . . Walker's theatre offers a place where we can begin to acknowledge a community of emotion, where we can start to be brave *together,* to share life's struggle, its anxiety, its heartbeat."

BIOGRAPHICAL/CRITICAL SOURCES:

BOOKS

Contemporary Dramatists, fifth edition, St. James Press (Detroit), 1993.
Contemporary Literary Criticism, Gale (Detroit), Volume 44, 1987, Volume 61, 1990.
King, Bruce, editor, *Post-Colonial English Drama: Commonwealth Drama since 1960,* Macmillan (Toronto), 1992, pp. 82-96.
Walker, George F., *Shared Anxiety: Selected Plays,* Coach House Press (Toronto), 1994.
Wallace, Robert, and Cynthia Zimmerman, *The Work: Conversations with English-Canadian Playwrights,* Coach House Press, 1982, pp. 212-25.

PERIODICALS

Books in Canada, April 1980, p. 5; April 1982, p. 10; April 1985, pp. 11-14; April 1986, pp. 16-18; March 1989, p. 28; November 1992, p. 34; May 1995, 22.

Canadian Drama/L'Art Dramatique Canadien, Volume 10, number 2, 1984, pp. 195-206; Volume 11, number 1, 1985, pp. 141-49, 221-25.
Canadian Forum, August/September 1986, pp. 6-11.
Canadian Literature, summer 1980, pp. 82-103; spring 1987, 110-12; winter 1990, pp. 118, 164; spring 1993, pp.167-69.
Canadian Theatre Review, winter 1985, pp. 144-45.
Globe and Mail (Toronto), November 8, 1984, p. E5.
Los Angeles Times, June 14, 1985.
Maclean's, October 23, 1989, 76-77; October 3, 1994, p. 54.
Performing Arts in Canada, fall 1981, pp. 43-46.
Scene Changes, October 1975.
Theater, summer-fall 1991, pp. 78-85.
Theatrum, April 1985, pp. 11-14.
Time, March 8, 1993, pp. 71-72. *Times* (London), July 1, 1983.
University of Toronto Quarterly, summer 1975; fall 1986, pp. 65-66; fall 1989, pp.71-75.
Variety, December 12, 1984, p. 130; October 30, 1995, p. 178.
Village Voice, April 2, 1979.

* * *

WALLACE, David Foster 1962-

PERSONAL: Born February 21, 1962, in Ithaca, NY; son of James Donald (a teacher) and Sally (a teacher; maiden name, Foster) Wallace. *Education:* Amherst College, A.B. (summa cum laude), 1985; University of Arizona, M.F.A., 1987. *Politics:* "Independent." *Religion:* "No affiliation."

ADDRESSES: Agent—Frederick Hill Associates, 1842 Union St., San Francisco, CA 94123.

CAREER: Writer. Associate professor of English, 1993—.

AWARDS, HONORS: Whiting Writers' Award, Mrs. Giles Whiting Foundation, 1987; Residency Fellowship to the corporation of Yaddo, Saratoga Springs, NY, 1987, 1989; John Traine Humor Prize, *The Paris Review,* for "Little Expressionless Animals," 1988; inclusion of "Here and There" in *Prize Stories 1989: The O. Henry Awards,* edited by William Abrahams, 1988; National Endowment for the Arts Writer's Fellowship, 1989; Illinois Arts Council Award for Non-Fiction for "Fictional Futures and the Conspicuously Young," 1989; Quality Paperback Book Club's New

Voices Award in Fiction for *Girl with Curious Hair,* 1991; nomination of *Signifying Rappers* for Pulitzer Prize in Nonfiction, 1991; inclusion of "Forever Overhead" in *Best American Short Stories of 1992,* edited by Robert Stone, 1993; inclusion of "Three Protrusions" in *The Pushcart Prize XVIII,* edited by Bill Henderson, 1993; "Ticket to the Fair" named a Finalist for National Magazine Award, 1995; named Contributing Editor of *Harper's,* 1995; Lannan Foundation Award for Literature, 1996; selected as Judge for 1997 O. Henry Awards, 1997; "David Lynch Keeps his Head" named a finalist for National Magazine Award, 1997; "The String Theory" selected for *Best American Sportswriting 1997,* Houghton Mifflin, 1997; MacArthur Foundation Fellowship, 1997.

WRITINGS:

The Broom of the System, Viking, 1987.
Girl with Curious Hair (short stories and novellas; includes "Girl with Curious Hair," "Little Expressionless Animals," "My Appearance," "Westward the Course of Empire Takes Its Way," "Lyndon," "John Billy," and "Everything is Green"), Penguin, 1988, hardcover edition, Norton, 1989.
(With Mark Costello) *Signifying Rappers: Rap and Race in the Urban Present* (nonfiction), Ecco Press (New York City), 1990.
Infinite Jest, Little, Brown (Boston), 1996.
A Supposedly Fun Thing I'll Never Do Again: Essays and Arguments, Little, Brown, 1997.

Contributor of short fiction and nonfiction to numerous periodicals, including *Contemporary Fiction, Harper's,* and *The New Yorker.*

SIDELIGHTS: David Foster Wallace is the kind of writer whose talent leaves critics groping for the proper artistic comparison. Thomas Pynchon, John Irving, filmmaker David Lynch, and even comic David Letterman have all been invoked as readers tackle the sardonic humor and complicated style that have led Wallace to be cited as Generation X's first literary hero. Wallace, according to Frank Bruni in his *New York Times Magazine* profile, "is to literature what Robin Williams or perhaps Jim Carrey is to live comedy: a creator so maniacally energetic and amused with himself that he often follows his riffs out into the stratosphere, where he orbits all alone."

In his debut novel, *The Broom of the System,* Wallace uses a variety of writing techniques and points of view to create a bizarre, stylized world which, despite its strangeness, resonates with contemporary American images. Set in Cleveland on the edge of the state-constructed Great Ohio Desert (also known as G.O.D.), the story follows Lenore Beadsman's search for her ninety-two-year-old great-grandmother, also named Lenore Beadsman, who has disappeared from her nursing home. In attempting to find her childhood mentor, the younger Lenore encounters a bewildering assemblage of characters with names such as Rick Vigorous, Biff Diggerence, Candy Mandible, and Sigurd Foamwhistle. It is significant that the elder Lenore was a student of language philosopher Ludwig Wittgenstein, since *The Broom of the System* has been viewed as an elaborate exploration of the relationship between language and reality. Wallace orchestrates Lenore's coming of age through the use of innovative plotting and language. The character's search for her great-grandmother becomes the search for her own identity.

Critics praised the skill and creativity evident in Wallace's experimental bildungsroman. Rudy Rucker, writing in the *Washington Post Book World,* judged *The Broom of the System* to be a "wonderful book" and compared Wallace to novelist Thomas Pynchon. Despite finding the novel to be "unwieldy" and "uneven" in parts, *New York Times* reviewer Michiko Kakutani commended Wallace's "rich reserves of ambition and imagination" and was impressed by his "wealth of talents." *New York Times Book Review* critic Caryn James liked the novel's "exuberance" and maintained that it "succeeds as a manic, human, flawed extravaganza."

In Wallace's second work, a collection of short stories titled *Girl with Curious Hair,* the author employs a mix of facts, fiction, and his own distinctive use of language to make observations about American culture. "Little Expressionless Animals," one of several stories that deals with American television, reveals a plan by the producers of the game show *Jeopardy!* to oust a long-time champion because of their sensitivity to her continuing lesbian love affair. The difference between appearance and reality is the subject of "My Appearance," the story of an actress's tranquilizer-induced nervous ramblings while she is waiting to do a guest appearance on the David Letterman show. In the title story, "Girl with Curious Hair," a young, Ivy League-trained corporate lawyer reveals the roots of his sadistic sexual impulses when he reflects on a Keith Jarrett concert he once attended with a group of violent punk rockers.

To reviewers, Wallace's imagination and energy are enticing. "David Foster Wallace . . . proves himself a dynamic writer of extraordinary talent," asserted Jenifer Levin in the *New York Times Book Review,* commenting that "he succeeds in restoring grandeur to modern fiction." Writing in Chicago *Tribune Books,* Douglas Seibold commended Wallace's "irrepressible narrative energy and invention" claiming that, "as good a writer as he is now, he is getting better."

The buildup given to Wallace through his first books served as an appetizer to the hype that surrounded his 1996 novel, *Infinite Jest*—a work that, in the words of *Chicago Tribune* writer Bruce Allen, could "confirm the hopes of those who called Wallace a genius and, to a lesser extent, the fears of those who think he's just an overeducated wiseacre with a lively prose style." The book as released was massive—over 1,000 pages—and the publicity was no less so. The marketing unit of publishers Little, Brown piqued pre-publication interest by sending 4,000 influential booksellers and media outlets a series of six postcards. Each card "cryptically heralded the release of an at-first-unspecified book that gives 'infinite pleasure' with 'infinite style,'" writes Bruni. "And when blurbs to that effect became available from other authors and critics, Little, Brown put them on postcards and dispatched another series of three."

On the heels of that publicity, *Infinite Jest* became *de rigueur* as a book that literary fans bought and displayed, but would not—or could not—spend much time reading. Some of the reason lies in the volume's heft and some in Wallace's dense prose style, peppered for the occasion with numerous pharmacological references that are partly responsible for the novel's 900 footnotes.

Infinite Jest is set in the not-too-distant future, in a date unspecified except as "the Year of the Depend Adult Undergarment," corporate sponsors having taken over the calendar. The United States is now part of the Organization of North American Nations (read ONAN) and has sold off New England to Canada to be used as a toxic waste dump. Legless Quebecoise separatists have taken to terrorism in protest; what's more, President Limbaugh has just been assassinated. The book's title refers to a lethal movie—a film so entertaining that those who see it may be doomed to die of pleasure.

Into this fray steps the Incandenza brothers: tennis ace Hal, football punter Orin, and the less-gifted Mario. The boys have endured a tough childhood—their father "having committed suicide by hacking open a hole in a microwave door, sealing it around his head with duct tape and making like a bag of Orville Redenbacher," as *Nation* reviewer Rick Perlstein noted. The brothers's adventures in this bizarre society fuel the novel's thick and overlapping storylines. Readers looking for a traditional linear ending, however, are in for a surprise: Those who manage to "stay with the novel until the pages thin will come to realize that Wallace has no intention of revealing whether *les Assassins des Fauteuils Rollents* succeed or fail in their quest," Perlstein continued. "Nor whether . . . Orin will master his awful desires . . . or whether Hal Incandenza will sacrifice himself to the Oedipal grail. Readers will turn the last page, in other words, without learning anything they need to know to secure narrative succor."

For the most part, critical reaction to *Infinite Jest* mixed admiration with consternation. "There is generous intelligence and authentic passion on every page, even the overwritten ones in which the author seems to have had a fit of graphomania," said *Time*'s R. Z. Sheppard. Paul West, writing in the *Washington Post Book World,* came prepared for Pynchon but came away with the opinion that "there is nothing epic or infinite about [the novel], although much that's repetitious or long." As West saw it, "the slow incessant advance of Wallace's prose is winningly physical, solid and even, more personable actually than the crowd of goons, ditzes, inverts, junkies, fatheads and doodlers he populates his novel with."

Indeed, said Michiko Kakutani, "the whole novel often seems like an excuse for [the author] to simply show off his remarkable skills as a writer and empty the contents of his restless mind." Kakutani's *New York Times* review went on to laud "some frighteningly vivid accounts of what it feels like to be a drug addict, what it feels like to detox and what it feels like to suffer a panic attack." In the crowd of ideas and characters, the critic concluded, "somewhere in the mess, . . . are the outlines of a splendid novel, but as it stands the book feels like one of those unfinished Michelangelo sculptures: you can see a godly creature trying to fight its way out, but it's stuck there, half excavated, unable to break completely free."

Kakutani had more encouraging words for Wallace's 1997 release, *A Supposedly Fun Thing I'll Never Do Again: Essays and Arguments.* This nonfiction collection "is animated by [the author's] wonderfully exuberant prose, a zingy, elastic gift for metaphor and imaginative sleight of hand, combined with a taste for amphetaminelike stream-of-consciousness riffs." *Supposedly Fun Thing* covers Wallace's observations on cultural themes, such as the influence television has on new fiction. It also contains recollections of the author's childhood in the Midwest, thoughts on tennis (Wallace was a highly ranked player in his youth) and even a tour of the Illinois State Fair. While finding some aspects of the collection flawed, Kakutani ultimately praised *Supposedly Fun Thing* as a work that "not only reconfirms Mr. Wallace's stature as one of his generation's pre-eminent talents, but it also attests to his virtuosity, an aptitude for the essay, profile and travelogue, equal to the gifts he has already begun to demonstrate in the realm of fiction."

BIOGRAPHICAL/CRITICAL SOURCES:

BOOKS

Contemporary Literary Criticism, Volume 50, Gale, 1988.

PERIODICALS

Chicago Tribune, March 24, 1996.
Los Angeles Times, February 11, 1996; March 18, 1996.
Los Angeles Times Book Review, February 1, 1987.
Nation, March 4, 1996.
New York Times, December 27, 1986; February 13, 1996; February 4, 1997.
New York Times Book Review, March 1, 1987; November 5, 1989; March 3, 1996.
New York Times Magazine, March 24, 1996.
Time, February 19, 1996.
Tribune Books (Chicago), January 21, 1990.
Washington Post Book World, January 11, 1987; August 6, 1989; March 24, 1996.

* * *

WARD, Jonas
  See COX, William R(obert)

* * *

WEBER, Ken(neth J.) 1940-

PERSONAL: Last name is pronounced Wee-ber; born July 10, 1940, in Neustadt, Ontario, Canada; son of Milton J. (a merchant) and Viola (a homemaker; maiden name, Greib) Weber; married Rita Harcourt, June 26, 1965 (divorced January 1, 1978); married Cecile King (a teacher), December 24, 1979; children: Mary Pat, Michael, Sean, Stephen. *Education:* University of Toronto, B.A., 1963; University of Guelph, M.S., 1975. *Politics:* "Not if I can help it!"

ADDRESSES: Home—R.R. #1, Bolton, Ontario, Canada L7E 5R7. *Agent*—Stoddart Publications, 34 Lesmill Rd., Toronto, Ontario, Canada M3B 2T6.

CAREER: W. A. Porter High School, Scarborough, Ontario, teacher of special English, 1963-69; University of Toronto, Toronto, Ontario, assistant professor, 1969-75, associate professor of English, 1975-77, professor of special education, 1977-96.

WRITINGS:

Truth and Fantasy, Methuen (London), 1970.
Prose of Relevance, two volumes, Methuen, 1971.
(With Allan E. Eagle) *Selling,* McGraw (New York City), 1971.
Yes They Can, Methuen, 1974.
Thinklab, Science Research Associates (Palo Alto, CA), 1974.
Thinklab II, Science Research Associates, 1976.
Read and Think, two volumes, Methuen, 1977.
Yes They Can! A Practical Guide for Teaching the Adolescent Slow Learner, Methuen, 1978.
Insight: A Practical Approach to Language Arts, Books 1 and 2, Methuen, 1980.
The Teacher Is the Key: A Practical Guide for Teachers of Adolescents with Learning Difficulties, Methuen, 1982.
(With Doris Cowan) *Canadians All 4,* Methuen, 1983.
(Editor) *The Globe Modern Dictionary,* Globe, 1984.
(Editor) *The Puffin Canadian Beginner's Dictionary,* Penguin, 1984.
Mental Gymnastics for Adults: Quintessential Quizzes, Puzzles, Mindbenders, and Other Trivia, Methuen, 1984.
(Editor with Alvin Granowsky) *Fearon New School Dictionary,* D.S. Lake Publishers, 1987.
Five Minute Mysteries, Running Press (Philadelphia), 1988.
More Five Minute Mysteries, Running Press, 1991.
KIDZ Five Minute Mysteries, Running Press, 1994.

Further Five Minute Mysteries, Running Press, 1994.

Five Minute Trivia: Did the Corinthians Ever Write Back?, Stoddart Publications, 1995.

More KIDZ Five Minute Mysteries, Running Press, 1996.

Even More Five Minute Mysteries, Running Press, 1996.

Five Minute Mysteries have been translated into fourteen languages.

SIDELIGHTS: Ken Weber has stated: "The majority of my work has been for education, and most of that for, and on the subject of, 'slower' learners. I call them slower, not slow, since I'm convinced they are capable of more than they, and the rest of the world, believe. Most of the work has been directed to improving their thinking skills, since it is not their supposed lack of intelligence that causes their trouble, but rather their inefficient thinking styles."

*   *   *

WEIS, Margaret (Edith) 1948-
(Margaret Baldwin)

PERSONAL: Born March 16, 1948, in Independence, MO; daughter of George Edward (an engineer) and Frances Irene (Reed) Weis; married Robert William Baldwin, August 22, 1970 (divorced, 1982); married Donald Bayne Stewart Perrin (an author), May 5, 1996; children: (first marriage) David William, Elizabeth Lynn. *Education:* University of Missouri, B.A., 1970. *Politics:* Independent. *Religion:* "No formal."

ADDRESSES: Office—P.O. Box 1106, Williams Bay, WI 53191. *Agent*—Jonathon Lazear, Lazear Agency, 430 First Ave. N., Suite 416, Minneapolis, MN 55401. *Email*—mweis@mag7.com.

CAREER: Author and editor. Herald Publishing House, Independence, MO, advertising director, 1972-81, director of Independence Press trade division, 1981-83; TSR Hobbies, Inc., Lake Geneva, WI, editor of juvenile romances and other special product lines, 1983-86; freelance writer, 1987—. Former president and owner of Mag Force 7, Inc. (producer of trading card games).

MEMBER: Great Alkali Plainsmen (Kansas City, MO).

WRITINGS:

Fortune-Telling (nonfiction), Messner (New York City), 1984.

My First Book of Robots (nonfiction), F. Watts (New York City), 1984.

My First Book of Computer Graphics (nonfiction), F. Watts, 1984.

The Endless Catacombs (fantasy), illustrated by Jeff Easley, TSR (Lake Geneva, WI), 1984.

(Editor) *The Art of the Dungeons and Dragons Fantasy Game,* TSR (Lake Geneva, WI), 1985.

(With Janet Pack) *Lost Childhood: Children of World War II* (nonfiction), Messner, 1986.

(Editor with Tracy Hickman) *Leaves from the Inn of the Last Home: The Complete Krynn Source Book,* TSR, 1987.

(Editor with Tracy Hickman) *Love and War,* TSR, 1987.

(With Tracy Hickman) *DragonLance Adventures* (game source book), TSR, 1987.

(Editor) *A Dragon Lovers Treasury of the Fantastic,* Warner, 1994.

(With Tracy Hickman) *The Second Generation,* poetry by Michael Williams, illustrated by Ned Dameron, TSR, 1994.

(Editor and author of introduction) *Fantastic Alice,* Ace Books (New York City), 1995.

(Editor with Tracy Hickman) *The History of Dragon-Lance: Being the Notes, Journals, and Memorabilia of Krynn,* compiled by Maryls Heeszel, TSR, 1995.

(With husband, Don Perrin) *Knights of the Black Earth,* ROC (New York City), 1995.

(With Don Perrin) *The Doom Brigade,* TSR, 1996.

(With Tracy Hickman) *Star Shield Sentinels,* Del Rey (New York City), 1996.

(With Hickman) *Legacy of the Darksword,* Bantam, 1997.

The Soul Forge, TSR, 1997.

(Editor) *A Magic Lover's Treasury of the Fantastic,* Warner Books (New York City), 1998.

"DRAGONLANCE CHRONICLES"; WITH TRACY HICKMAN; POETRY BY MICHAEL WILLIAMS

Dragons of Autumn Twilight, illustrated by Denis Beauvais, TSR, 1984.

Dragons of Winter Night, TSR, 1984.

Dragons of Spring Dawning, illustrated by Jeffrey Butler, TSR, 1984.

Dragons of Summer Flame, illustrated by Larry Elmore, TSR, 1995.

"DRAGONLANCE LEGENDS" FANTASY NOVELS; WITH TRACY HICKMAN; POETRY BY MICHAEL WILLIAMS

Time of the Twins, TSR, 1985.
War of the Twins, TSR, 1985.
Test of the Twins, TSR, 1985.

"DARKSWORD TRILOGY"; WITH TRACY HICKMAN; PUBLISHED BY BANTAM

Forging the Darksword, 1988.
Doom of the Darksword, 1988.
Triumph of the Darksword, 1988.

"THE ROSE OF THE PROPHET TRILOGY"; WITH TRACY HICKMAN; PUBLISHED BY BANTAM

The Will of the Wanderer, 1989.
The Paladin of the Night, 1989.
The Prophet of Akran, 1989.

"STAR OF THE GUARDIAN" SCIENCE FICTION SERIES; PUBLISHED BY BANTAM

The Lost King, 1990.
King's Test, 1990.
King's Sacrifice, 1991.
Ghost Legion, 1993.

"DEATH'S GATE CYCLE" FANTASY SERIES; WITH TRACY HICKMAN; PUBLISHED BY BANTAM

Dragon Wing, 1990.
Elven Star, 1990.
Fire Sea, 1990.
Serpent Mage, 1990.
The Hand of Chaos, 1990.
Into the Labyrinth, 1993.
The Seventh Gate, 1994.

NONFICTION; UNDER PSEUDONYM MARGARET BALDWIN

The Boy Who Saved the Children (remedial reader for young adults; based on autobiography *Growing up in the Holocaust* by Ben Edelbaum), Messner, 1981.
(With Pat O'Brien) *Wanted! Frank and Jesse James: The Real Story* (young adult biography), Messner, 1981.
Kisses of Death: A Great Escape Story of World War II (remedial reader for young adults), illustrated by Norma Welliver, Messner, 1983.
My First Book: Thanksgiving (juvenile), F. Watts, 1983.

OTHER

Contributor to *The DragonLance Saga* by Roy Thomas (includes adaptations of *Dragons of Autumn Twilight* and *Dragons of Winter Night*), illustrated by Thomas Yeates with Mark Johnson, TSR, 1987. Also author of *Lasers,* F. Watts; author, with Gary Pack, of *Computer Graphics* and *Robots and Robotics,* both F. Watts. Author of graphic novels *A Fable of the Serra Angel,* Acclaim Comics, and (with David Baldwin) *Testament of the Dragon,* Teckno Books.

Creator of trading card games, including *Star of the Guardians* and *Wing Commander.* Weis's books have been translated into many languages, including French, Spanish, Japanese, German, Portuguese, Italian, Russian, Czech, Rumanian, Hebrew, Danish, and Finnish.

ADAPTATIONS: An audio recording was made of *Elven Star,* Bantam Audio, 1991.

WORK IN PROGRESS: Murder at the Exile Cafe, a mystery set in the "Star of the Guardians" universe; *Robot Blues,* a Mag Force 7 action-adventure science fiction novel with Don Perrin; two anthologies of stories, *Dragons of War* and *Dragons of Chaos;* editing the anthology, *The New Amazons,* for ROC.

SIDELIGHTS: A prolific and popular author, Margaret Weis is best known as the coauthor, with Tracy Hickman, of the many "DragonLance" fantasy adventures set in the imaginary world of Krynn. She began her career, however, by writing juvenile books, remedial readers, and nonfiction. Weis once commented, "I have always enjoyed writing—mainly, I believe, because I enjoy reading. But I did not seriously consider writing as a vocation during school; I wanted to be an artist. Several incidents caused me to change my mind, and they point out, I believe, how strong an effect good teachers can have on our lives. First, my high school English teacher, D. R. Smith, taught me how to write. Mr. Smith began by tossing out the curriculum intended for high school juniors. (He was forever in trouble with the school administrators. Aside from teaching me to write, the most important thing he taught me was to be my own person and stand up for my ideals.) Our class spent the first semester writing sentences. That's all. Just one sentence every day. We started out with simple sentences—a subject and verb. Then we were allowed to add an adjective. I remember the thrill, weeks later, when we could proudly put in an adverb. After sixteen weeks, Mr. Smith decided we were ready to move on. We wrote paragraphs—five sentences each.

We did that for the next sixteen weeks. I came to respect words in his class. I came to realize how critical every word—no matter how insignificant—is in writing. I saw how sentences joined together to form paragraphs. When we read books, in his class, we studied not only the literary content but how the writer created the effect he wanted by use of words and sentence structure. Mr. Smith showed me the door, but it still remained closed.

"I went to college, intending to make art my career. One day, however, my teacher for freshman English—a student teacher; I can't even remember her name—kept me after class, took me to the student union, and asked if I had considered studying writing. She told me about the University of Missouri's English program. (The university was one of the few in the 1960s to offer a creative writing program separate from journalism.) I have often thought this young woman should have been an army recruiter. If she had, I would no doubt have joined on the spot. I investigated the writing program, liked it, and switched my major. She gave me the key to the door.

"Finally, I met Dr. Donald Drummond, poet and professor. He showed me how the key opened the door. I entered and knew that I had come home. We wrote poetry in Dr. Drummond's class. They were grueling class sessions. The poet was required to read his work aloud, while his fellow poets sat, knives out, waiting to draw blood. Classes met at night, often for several hours. We came out battle-scarred, but we could write. Dr. Drummond was another unusual teacher. He began by giving us a long list of subjects we were under no circumstances to write about. These included: Love (with a capital 'L'), truth, beauty, death, and the Vietnam War. 'And,' he growled, 'if I get one poem about a daffodil you will flunk the semester!' Needless to say, I never have, and I never will, write about a daffodil."

What Weis has done, however, is become an internationally recognized author of fantasy and science fiction. The "DragonLance" books she wrote with Tracy Hickman have become even more popular with spin-off products like art books, trading cards, and role-playing games. In addition to these works, Weis has also written other well known series, including the "Death's Gate Cycle" fantasy books.

The "Death Gate" books, which Weis also wrote with Hickman, perhaps represent Weis's most complex works. The premise of the series is that two godlike races, the Sartan and the Patryns, have, through mutual enmity, caused the world to divide into four distinctive worlds separated by a magical labyrinth. The first four books in the series, *Dragon Wing, Elven Star, Fire Sea,* and *Serpent Mage,* describe the four different worlds. Evil serpents have come to threaten the existence of all four realms; by the last installment, *The Seventh Gate,* it becomes clear that the only way to defeat this threat is for the Sartan and Patryns to set aside their differences, cooperate, and combine their magic against a common enemy. In his *Booklist* review of the final volume, Roland Green noted that Weis and Hickman have demonstrated "complete mastery of the art of turning classic fantasy elements into equally classic well-told tales." A critic in *Voice of Youth Advocates* added that in the six previous books the coauthors had been "creating unique worlds, characters to believe in, and giving them dire circumstances to work through." With the seventh volume, the critic continued, "the message is what the reader wanted the characters to embrace all along. They all but say, 'there is that of God in all of us.'"

Most commentators and many loyal young readers appreciate Weis's fantasy epics and science fiction adventures; as *Voice of Youth Advocates* contributor Jennifer A. Fakolt noted in her review of *Ghost Legion,* "In much the same way as the Star Wars trilogy did, [Weis] captures our hearts and imaginations."

BIOGRAPHICAL/CRITICAL SOURCES:

PERIODICALS

Booklist, September 1, 1990, p. 32; November 1, 1993, p. 505; August, 1994, p. 2030; April 15, 1995, p. 1484.
Kirkus Reviews, January 1, 1993, p. 30; October 1, 1993, p. 1234; June 15, 1994, p. 812; March 15, 1995, p. 530.
Library Journal, February 15, 1993, p. 196; April 15, 1995, p. 119.
Publishers Weekly, October 18, 1993, p. 67; January 17, 1994, p. 420; July 25, 1994, p. 38; April 24, 1995, p. 64; November 6, 1995, p. 88.
Voice of Youth Advocates, December, 1993, p. 315; February, 1995, p. 352.

*   *   *

WELCH, Rowland
  See DAVIES, L(eslie) P(urnell)

WHEELER, Hugh (Callingham) 1912-1987
(Q. Patrick, Patrick Quentin, Jonathan Stagge)

PERSONAL: Born March 19, 1912, in London, England; died of heart and lung ailments, July 26, 1987, in Pittsfield, MA; naturalized U.S. citizen, 1942; son of Harold (a civil servant) and Florence (Scammell) Wheeler. *Education:* University of London, B.A., 1932.

CAREER: Novelist; playwright. *Military service:* Served in U.S. Army Medical Corps during World War II.

MEMBER: Dramatists Guild.

AWARDS, HONORS: Edgar Allan Poe Award, Mystery Writers of America, 1963, 1973; Antoinette Perry Award, 1973, for *A Little Night Music,* 1974, for *Candide,* and 1979, for *Sweeney Todd;* Vernon Rice Award, 1973; Drama Critics Circle Award, 1973, for *A Little Night Music,* 1974, for *Candide,* 1975, for *Pacific Overtures* (with John Weidmann), and 1979, for *Sweeney Todd;* Drama Desk Award, 1973, for *A Little Night Music,* 1974, for *Candide,* and 1979, for *Sweeney Todd;* Outer Critics Award, 1979, for *Sweeney Todd;* Hull-Warriner Award, 1981.

WRITINGS:

PLAYS

Big Fish, Little Fish (first produced in New York City at the ANTA Theatre, March 15, 1961), Random House (New York City), 1961, also published in *Broadway's Beautiful Losers,* edited by Marilyn Stasio, Delacorte (New York City), 1972.

Look: We've Come Through! (first produced in New York City at the Hudson Theatre on October 25, 1961), Dramatists Play Service (New York City), 1963, sound recording of Chicago Radio Theatre's production, All-Media Dramatic Workshop, 1976.

Rich Little Rich Girl (adaptation of a play by Miguel Mihura and Alvaro de Laiglesia), first produced in Philadelphia at the Walnut Street Theatre on November 14, 1964.

We Have Always Lived in the Castle (adaptation of the novel by Shirley Jackson; first produced in New York at the Ethel Barrymore Theatre on October 19, 1966), Dramatists Play Service, 1967.

MUSICALS

A Little Night Music (adaptation of a film by Ingmar Bergman, with music and lyrics by Stephen Sondheim; first produced in New York City at the Shubert Theatre on February 25, 1973), Dodd, Mead (New York City), 1974.

(With Joseph Stein) *Irene* (adaptation of the play by James Montgomery, with music by Harry Tierney, lyrics by Joseph McCarthy, adaptation by Harry Rigby), first produced in New York City at the Minskoff Theatre, on March 13, 1973.

Candide (adaptation of the novel by Voltaire, with music by Leonard Bernstein, lyrics by Richard Wilbur), first produced in New York City at Brooklyn Academy of Music, on December 20, 1973.

Truckload (with lyrics by Wes Harris), produced in New York City, 1975.

(With John Weidmann) *Pacific Overtures* (with music and lyrics by Sondheim), first produced in New York City at the Winter Garden Theatre on January 11, 1976.

Sweeney Todd (adaptation of play by Christopher Bond; music and lyrics by Sondheim), first produced on Broadway at Uris Theatre, March 1, 1979.

Silverlake (adaptation of a libretto by Georg Kaiser; music by Kurt Weill), produced in New York City, 1980.

The Student Prince (adaptation of the libretto by Dorothy Donelly; music by Sigmund Romberg), produced in New York City, 1980.

SCREENPLAYS

(With Peter Viertel) *Five Miles to Midnight,* United Artists, 1962.

Something for Everyone, National General, 1970.

(With Jay Presson Allen) *Cabaret,* Allied Artists, 1972.

(With Allen) *Travels with My Aunt,* Metro-Goldwyn-Mayer (MGM), 1972.

Also author of *The Snoop Sisters* (television play; with Leonard Stern), 1972, *A Little Night Music,* 1977, and *Nijinsky,* 1980.

NOVELS

The Crippled Muse, Hart Davis (London), 1951, Rinehart (New York City), 1952.

NOVELS UNDER PSEUDONYM Q. PATRICK, ALL WITH RICHARD WILSON WEBB

The Grindle Nightmare, Hartney (New York City), 1935, published as *Darker Grows the Valley,* Cassell (London), 1936.
Death Goes to School, Smith & Haas (New York City), 1936.
Death for Dear Clara, Simon & Schuster (New York City), 1937.
File on Fenton and Farr, Morrow (New York City), 1937.
File on Claudia Cragge, Morrow, 1938.
Death and the Maiden, Simon & Schuster, 1939.
Return to the Scene, Simon & Schuster, 1941 (published in England as *Death in Bermuda,* Cassell [London], 1941).
Danger Next Door, Cassell, 1951.
The Girl on the Gallows, Fawcett (New York City), 1954.

Also co-author of *Famous Trials.*

UNDER PSEUDONYM PATRICK QUENTIN

A Puzzle for Fools, Simon & Schuster, 1936.
Puzzle for Players, Simon & Schuster, 1938.
Puzzle for Puppets, Simon & Schuster, 1944.
Puzzle for Wantons, Simon & Schuster, 1945, published as *Slay the Loose Ladies,* Pocket Books (New York City), 1948.
Puzzle for Fiends, Simon & Schuster, 1946, published as *Love Is a Deadly Weapon,* Pocket Books, 1949.
Puzzle for Pilgrims, Simon & Schuster, 1947, published as *The Fate of the Immodest Blonde,* Pocket Books, 1950.
Run to Death, Simon & Schuster, 1948.
The Follower, Simon & Schuster, 1950.
Black Widow, Simon & Schuster, 1952 (published in England as *Fatal Woman,* Gollancz [London], 1953).
My Son, the Murderer, Simon & Schuster, 1954 (published in England as *The Wife of Ronald Sheldon,* Gollancz, 1954).
The Man with Two Wives, Simon & Schuster, 1955.
The Man in the Net, Simon & Schuster, 1956.
Suspicious Circumstances, Simon & Schuster, 1957.
Shadow of Guilt, Simon & Schuster, 1958.
The Green-Eyed Monster, Simon & Schuster, 1960.
The Ordeal of Mrs. Snow, Random House (New York City), 1962.
Family Skeletons, Random House, 1965.

MYSTERY NOVELS UNDER PSEUDONYM JONATHAN STAGGE

Murder Gone to Earth, Joseph (London), 1936, published as *The Dogs Do Bark,* Doubleday, 1937.
Murder or Mercy, Joseph, 1937, published as *Murder by Prescription,* Doubleday, 1938.
The Stars Spell Death, Doubleday, 1939 (published in England as *Murder in the Stars,* Joseph, 1940).
Turn of the Table, Doubleday, 1940 (published in England as *Funeral for Five*), Joseph, 1940.
The Yellow Taxi, Doubleday, 1942 (published in England as *Call a Hearse,* Joseph, 1942).
The Scarlet Circle, Doubleday, 1943 (published in England as *Light from a Lantern,* Joseph, 1943).
Death, My Darling Daughters, Doubleday, 1945 (published in England as *Death and the Dear Girls,* Joseph, 1946).
Death's Old Sweet Song, Doubleday, 1946.
The Three Fears, Doubleday, 1949.

STORY COLLECTIONS UNDER PSEUDONYM PATRICK QUENTIN

The Ordeal of Mrs. Snow and Other Stories, Gollancz, 1961, Random House, 1962.

Contributor of short stories and novelettes to national magazines under all three pseudonyms.

SIDELIGHTS: Until 1961, Hugh Wheeler wrote detective novels, published under three different pseudonyms; until about 1950, these were collaborative efforts, written with Richard Wilson Webb. So successful was the Wheeler/Webb partnership that Wheeler was able to support himself by writing and was able to live in a variety of places—including France, Italy, North Africa, Mexico, Brazil, and the West Indies.

A Puzzle for Fools, the first "Patrick Quentin" novel and which introduced the character of detective Peter Duluth, appeared as the initial volume in Simon and Schuster's "Inner Sanctum" mystery series. Both Patrick Quentin and Peter Duluth "made an immediate impression on readers and critics alike," according to R. E. Briney in the *St. James Guide to Crime & Mystery Writers.* Isaac Anderson in the *New York Times* found: "The background of the sanitarium with its slightly mad patients and its coldly scientific medical staff, makes an excellent setting for a mystery story, and the author has used it to the best advantage." Nicholas Blake, reviewing *A Puzzle for Fools* in *Spectator,* called it "exceptionally well done, the horrors are really blood-chilling, and the *denouement* is brilliant."

The Ordeal of Mrs. Snow and Other Stories gathers together twelve short stories written by the team under the name Patrick Quentin. The book won critical praise. Patrick Quentin, wrote the *Times Literary Supplement* critic, "is a master of the well-made mystery story. . . . [This collection] leaves no doubt about his high professional skill." Anthony Boucher in the *New York Times Book Review* called the stories "at once brilliant specimens of technical plotting and sensitive studies of human dilemmas." Briney stated that *The Ordeal of Mrs. Snow and Other Stories* "contains several stories that have established themselves as classics."

Reaction to *The Crippled Muse,* the one novel published under his own name, clarifies Wheeler's popular appeal. The *New York Herald Tribune Book Review* said: "He writes about people with maturity and he shows a particular understanding of the creative person. This, plus an amiable sort of humor, make his novel genuinely enjoyable despite its hackneyed structure." Similarly, Jocelyn Brooke in the *New Statesman and Nation* wrote that the book was, despite some "faults, intelligently written and easy to read." Briney labeled all of Wheeler's novels, written under his pseudonyms or not, to be "characterized by intricate plots, cleverly planted clues, and endings which legitimately surprise the reader."

In 1961, Wheeler turned to writing for the theater and was rewarded with Broadway productions of his first two plays. Not only did *Big Fish, Little Fish* star Jason Robards, Jr., but it was staged by Sir John Gielgud. Howard Taubman, who reviewed the play for the *New York Times,* found flaws—an occasional false ring in characterization, gratuitous wisecracking—but he also found "a current of honest feeling and human warmth" and felt that Wheeler had written with "beguiling integrity." *Look: We've Come Through* was staged by Jose Quintero and featured Burt Reynolds in a supporting role. Howard Taubman in the *New York Times* said that "the writing has the accuracy and unexpectedness of a thoughtful mind and appreciative ear."

Wheeler's first hit came in 1973 with *A Little Night Music,* which was based on an old Ingmar Bergman film, *Smiles of a Summer Night.* Marilyn Stasio thought Wheeler's adaptation "elegant," while Clive

Barnes considered it "uncommonly urbane and witty." *Sweeney Todd* also garnered critical praise. "As theatre, 'Sweeney Todd' is fascinating but also elitist in the extreme," Sylvia Drake commented in the *Los Angeles Times.* But Richard Eder compared it to Brecht-Weill's *Three-Penny Opera.* "There is more of artistic energy, creative personality and plain excitement in 'Sweeney Todd'. . . than in a dozen average musicals," he remarked.

BIOGRAPHICAL/CRITICAL SOURCES:

BOOKS

Contemporary Dramatists, 3rd edition, St. Martin's, 1982.
St. James Guide to Crime & Mystery Writers, 4th edition, St. James Press (Detroit), 1996.

PERIODICALS

Boston Transcript, October 3, 1936, p. 5.
Cue, March 3, 1973; March 2, 1979.
Los Angeles Times, March 2, 1979.
New Statesman and Nation, November 21, 1936, p. 12; November 10, 1951.
New York Herald Tribune Book Review, March 23, 1952.
New York Times, September 27, 1936, p. 22; November 2, 1952, p. 27; March 16, 1961; October 26, 1961; February 26, 1973; May 17, 1979.
New York Times Book Review, March 25, 1962, p. 20.
Saturday Review, April 26, 1952.
Spectator, November 20, 1936, p. 157.
Times Literary Supplement, September 8, 1961, p. 602.

OBITUARIES:

PERIODICALS

Chicago Tribune, July 30, 1987.
Los Angeles Times, August 1, 1987.
New York Times, July 28, 1987.
Washington Post, July 29, 1987.*

*   *   *

WIAT, Philippa
   See FERRIDGE, Philippa

WICK, Carter
  See WILCOX, Collin

*   *   *

WILCOX, Collin 1924-1996
  (Carter Wick)

PERSONAL: Born September 21, 1924, in Detroit, MI; died of cancer, July 12, 1996, in San Francisco, CA; son of Harlan C. and Lucille (Spangler) Wilcox; married Beverly Buchman, December 23, 1954 (divorced, 1964); children: Christopher, Jeffrey. *Education:* Antioch College, A.B., 1948. *Politics:* Democrat. *Religion:* None.

CAREER: Writer. Advertising copywriter in San Francisco, CA, 1948-50; Town School, San Francisco, teacher of art, 1950-53; Amthor & Co. (furniture store), San Francisco, partner, 1953-55; Collin Wilcox Lamps, San Francisco, owner, 1955-70. *Military service:* U.S. Army, 1943.

MEMBER: Mystery Writers of America (regional vice-president, 1975; member of board of directors, 1976), Sierra Club, Aircraft Owners and Pilots Association.

AWARDS, HONORS: Macavity Award, 1986.

WRITINGS:

The Black Door, Dodd (New York City), 1967.
The Third Figure, Dodd, 1968.
The Lonely Hunter, Random House (New York City), 1969.
The Disappearance, Random House, 1970.
Dead Aim, Random House, 1971.
Hiding Place, Random House, 1972.
Long Way Down, Random House, 1973.
Aftershock, Random House, 1975.
(Under pseudonym Carter Wick) *The Faceless Man,* Saturday Review Press (New York City), 1975.
The Third Victim, Dell (New York City), 1976.
Doctor, Lawyer, Random House, 1977.
(With Bill Pronzini) *Twospot,* Putnam (New York City), 1978.
The Watcher, Random House, 1978.
Power Plays, Random House, 1979.
Mankiller, Random House, 1980.
Spellbinder, Fawcett (New York City), 1981.

(Under pseudonym Carter Wick) *Dark House, Dark Road,* Raven House, 1982.
Stalking Horse, Random House, 1982.
Victims, Mysterious Press (New York City), 1984.
Night Games, Mysterious Press, 1985.
The Pariah, Mysterious Press, 1987.
Bernhardt's Edge, Tor Books (New York City), 1988.
Silent Witness, Tor Books, 1990.
A Death before Dying, Holt (New York City), 1990.
Hire a Hangman, Holt, 1991.
Except for the Bones, Tor Books, 1991.
Dead Center, Holt, 1992.
Switchback, Holt, 1993.
Find Her a Grave, Forge (New York City), 1993.
Full Circle, Forge, 1994.
Calculated Risk, Holt, 1995.

SIDELIGHTS: Collin Wilcox, according to Bill Pronzini in the *St. James Guide to Crime & Mystery Writers,* was "one of the few writers, (Ed McBain is another) who has been able to combine the portrayal of investigative police work with incisive psychological and sociological examinations of the people who live, love, and die in a major metropolitan city." Best known for his novels featuring the San Francisco homicide detective Frank Hastings, Wilcox also wrote about Alan Bernhardt, who works as a theatre director when not freelancing as a private investigator.

The Frank Hastings series displayed what a *Booklist* reviewer called "Wilcox's wry, winning way." Pronzini noted that the Hastings' books combined "straightforward police work and deep personal involvement" to good effect. In *The Lonely Hunter,* for example, Hastings is up against drug-dealers in the Haight-Ashbury district and finds that his own daughter, a runaway, is peripherally involved. *The Watcher* puts Hastings and his teenaged son in dangerous, isolated country in Northern California where they must survive the odds. Pronzini found the novel to be "a probing look at a father and son trying to bridge the generation gap." All of the Hastings books are "peopled with a rich cross-section of San Francisco's colorful and varied/individuals and lifestyles," as Pronzini described it.

Wilcox's novels about actor and detective Alan Bernhardt are also set in San Francisco but are less hard-boiled than the Hastings series. Bernhardt directs at the Little Theater and only works as a private investigator part-time. He is also "refreshingly non-violent and free from machismo," as Barry W. Gardner explained it in *Armchair Detective.* In *Find Her a Grave,* Bernhardt becomes involved in a Mafioso's attempt to bequeath a million dollars to his illegitimate daughter. The *Rapport* critic found the book to be an "energetic novel [that] bursts forth with an air of authenticity that is as suspenseful as it is chilling." Gardner concluded that "Wilcox is a veteran and proficient storyteller, and the third-person, multiple viewpoint narration is accomplished with terse and effective prose." Speaking of *Full Circle,* in which Bernhardt finds himself entangled in a ring of art thieves, Wes Lukowsky in *Booklist* claimed that "as always, Wilcox and Bernhardt deliver the goods. This is cleverly plotted and populated with a half-dozen self-serving, potentially lethal characters. A truly engrossing read."

BIOGRAPHICAL/CRITICAL SOURCES:

BOOKS

St. James Guide to Crime & Mystery Writers, fourth edition, St. James Press (Detroit), 1996.

PERIODICALS

Armchair Detective, November, 1994, pp. 116-117.
Booklist, April 1, 1982, p. 1007; December 1, 1994, p. 657.
Publishers Weekly, February 5, 1982, p. 383; October 24, 1994, p. 55; August 21, 1995, p. 50.
Rapport, Volume 18, number 2, p. 19.
Washington Post Book World, October 19, 1986.

OBITUARIES:

PERIODICALS

Los Angeles Times, July 19, 1996, p. A21.
New York Times, July 19, 1996, p. A20.
Washington Post, July 20, 1996, p. C6.*

*   *   *

WILLOUGHBY, Lee Davis
  See DEANDREA, William L(ouis)

*   *   *

YORK, Jeremy
  See CREASEY, John

YORKE, Margaret
  See LARMINIE, Margaret Beda

*   *   *

ZAHN, Timothy 1951-

PERSONAL: Born September 1, 1951, in Chicago, IL; son of Herbert William (an attorney) and Marilou (an attorney; maiden name, Webb) Zahn; married Anna L. Romo (a computer programmer), August 4, 1979; children: Corwin. *Education:* Michigan State University, B.A., 1973; University of Illinois at Urbana-Champaign, M.A., 1975, graduate study, 1975-80. *Avocational interests:* Listening to classical music (particularly nineteenth-century Romantic era), crossword puzzles, and martial arts.

ADDRESSES: Agent—Russell Galen, Scovil Chichak Galen Literary Agency Inc., 381 Park Avenue S., Suite 1020, New York, NY 10016-8806.

CAREER: Writer, 1980—.

MEMBER: Science Fiction Writers of America.

AWARDS, HONORS: Hugo Award nomination for best short story, World Science Fiction Convention, 1983, for "Pawn's Gambit"; Hugo Award for best novella, 1984, for *Cascade Point;* Hugo Award nomination for best short story, 1985, for "Return to the Fold."

WRITINGS:

SCIENCE FICTION

The Blackcollar, DAW Books (New York City), 1983.
A Coming of Age, Bluejay Books (New York City), 1984.
Cobra, Baen (New York City), 1985.
Spinneret, Bluejay Books, 1985.
Blackcollar: The Backlash Mission, DAW Books, 1986.
Cobra Strike, Baen, 1986.
Cascade Point and Other Stories, Bluejay Books, 1986, title novella published singly (bound with *Hardfought* by Greg Bear), Tor Books (New York City), 1988.
Triplet, Baen, 1987.
Cobra Bargain, Baen, 1988.

Deadman Switch, Baen, 1988.
Time Bomb and Zahndry Others (stories), Baen, 1988.
Warhorse, Baen, 1990.
Heir to the Empire, Bantam (New York City), 1991.
Distant Friends and Others (stories), Baen, 1992.
Cobras Two, Baen, 1992.
Dark Force Rising, Bantam, 1992.
The Last Command, Bantam, 1993.
Conquerors' Pride, Bantam, 1994.
Conquerors' Heritage, Bantam, 1995.
Conquerors' Legacy, Bantam, 1996.

Also author of *Starlord,* a three-part comic book, Marvel Comics, 1996-97. Contributor to anthologies, including *The 1983 Annual World's Best SF,* edited by Donald A. Wollheim, DAW, 1983, and *Alien Stars,* edited by Elizabeth Mitchell, Baen, 1985. Also contributor of numerous stories and novelettes to magazines, including *Analog Science Fiction/Science Fact, Ares, Fantasy and Science Fiction, Fantasy Gamer, Isaac Asimov's Science Fiction Magazine, Rigel,* and *Space Gamer.*

ADAPTATIONS: Heir to the Empire, Conquerors' Pride, and *Conquerors' Heritage* have all been recorded on audio cassette for Bantam; *Heir to the Empire, Dark Force Rising,* and *The Last Command* have been recorded on audio cassette by BDD audio; *Conquerors' Pride* and *Conquerors' Heritage* have been recorded on audio cassette by the Brilliance Corp. A comic book version of *Heir to the Empire* was published by Dark Horse Comics, 1996, illustrated by Olivier Vatine.

SIDELIGHTS: Timothy Zahn is an award-winning author whose military and action science fiction stories and books often deal with topics of appeal to adolescents and feature youthful protagonists. But as his Star Wars series demonstrates, Zahn is much more than a young adult writer. An adaptation of the George Lucas films, Zahn's trilogy are all bestsellers, not only bringing him financial success but also establishing him as one of the foremost science fiction writers of the day. Yet it was a near miss for Zahn, who began writing science fiction only as a hobby while studying for his real career as a physicist.

Growing up in Chicago, Zahn earned his B.A. at Michigan State and M.A. at the University of Illinois, where he also continued on with graduate studies. During this time he began writing science fiction stories, but it wasn't until he sold his first story, "Ernie," to *Analog Science Fiction/Science Fact* in 1979 that he began to wonder if writing could be

more than a hobby for him. He had resolved to take a year off from his studies and devote it to writing when his thesis advisor died in 1979, which would necessitate a new project under a new advisor. Instead of the latter course, Zahn decided to take his trial break, and published nine stories in one year. It was "enough to encourage me to continue," he once commented. In fact, there was no going back to academia for Zahn. Over the next few years, he published several dozen stories, becoming a regular contributor to *Analog Science Fiction/Science Fact,* and exploring the themes of militarism and the clash of cultures that would later inform his novels.

Zahn's first novel, *The Blackcollar,* was published in 1983, and posited an Earth dominated by an alien race, the Ryqril, who so oppress the remnant population of the planet that these humans rebel, with the help of a class of super-warriors who are not only trained in the martial arts, but who also have drug-enhanced reflexes. It is this same clash between Ryqrils and Blackcollar warriors that forms the centerpiece of a later Zahn book, *Blackcollar: The Backlash Mission.* Reviewing the first book in *Analog Science Fiction/Science Fact,* Tom Easton noted the "originality" in Zahn's debut novel, and also commented, regarding Zahn's style and use of detail, that "there is more realism here, and hence more satisfaction."

Psychic powers and a cautionary tale of generational competition inform Zahn's second novel, *A Coming of Age.* Mutational change among the children of the planet Tigris endows them with psychic powers between age five and the onset of puberty. At one point in Tigris's history, these supercharged children ruled the planet, though they largely misused their powers and proved violent. Now the adults, the Lost Generation, have developed new strategies to control them: child-rearing in large groups or hives, and deprivation of education among other restrictions. Out of this melange, Zahn creates a chase/detective story involving young Lisa, who does not want to lose her powers, a scientist who kidnaps his own son to experiment with a drug that could prolong the life of such telekinetic powers, and Detective Stanford Tirrell and his young assistant Tonio, who are on the trail of the kidnapper. Reviewing the book for *School Library Journal,* Penny Parker noted that "the story will interest SF readers, as well as young adults interested in stories in which young adults outsmart the adult characters." A reviewer for *Kirkus Reviews* also found Zahn's idea appealing, though wondering at the execution: "Unfortunately . . . Zahn turns this splendid notion into nothing more than a routine, kiddy-cops-and-baddies melodrama." Nancy Choice, however, writing in *Voice of Youth Advocates,* felt that *A Coming of Age* "successfully combines science fiction with a good detective story," and went on to say that the book should be recommended for the magazine's Best Books for Young Adults. A *Publishers Weekly* reviewer concurred: "Zahn has written an entertaining police procedural that should especially appeal to teenagers."

A serialized novel, *Spinneret* tells a story of Earth's first attempts at interstellar colonization. In a universe where aliens seemingly have snapped up all the good planets, Earthlings have to be content with Astra, a world so barren that no one else wants it. Astra, however, proves richer than anyone could imagine, yielding an ore that can be spun into a strong metallic thread. More of an old-fashioned space adventure than *A Coming of Age, Spinneret* was lauded by *Publishers Weekly* as one of "Zahn's best novels," and *Booklist* contributor Roland Green commented on the book's "excellent narrative technique, clear prose, and intelligent characterization." Hal Hoover, reviewing *Spinneret* in *Voice of Youth Advocates,* called the book "a first class sci-fi novel," and noted that Zahn "skillfully mixes espionage, archeology, human and alien psychology, and human rights psychology."

Zahn continued combining space adventures and militarism with a series of novels about more superhuman warriors, the Cobras, short for Computerized Body Reflex Armament. As with his Blackcollars, these Cobras are specially skilled soldiers with a technological edge: they have been programmed to react with deadly force to anything the sense as danger. Created to battle the Troft forces, they have no place in civilian society, and are banished to a far corner of the world where they can establish their own domain and protect settlers. The series is built around the Moreau clan, whose patriarch is Jonny Moreau, a young Cobra recruit in the first book, *Cobra.* Throughout the course of that book Jonny matures to become a leader of his people, and in the second of the series, *Cobra Strike,* he and his three sons must once again battle the Trofts and a strange group of humans who wish to use them as mercenaries. By the third book in the series, *Cobra Bargain,* a granddaughter, Justine, has decided to enter this all-male domain of action hero. While mentioning that Zahn's Cobra series provides "plenty of heart-stopping action," Diane G. Yates in *Voice of Youth Advocates* also noted that Zahn manages to avoid all-out war in these books, coming up with other more creative solutions to carnage. "The moral questions that [the Moreaus] struggle with are those that concern us all," Yates commented, "and to find a character in a military SF novel who agonizes over ethical questions is a refreshing change, and a welcome one."

In 1984 Zahn won a Hugo Award for his novella *Cascade Point,* about a spaceship that winds up in an alternate universe. This work was gathered with other published short stories for the 1986 publication, *Cascade Point and Other Stories.* Reviewing the collection for *Washington Post Book World,* Gregory Frost noted that "every story of Zahn's contains a novel idea," and *Booklist* reviewer Green remarked that the collection is "certainly high-quality work," though rather traditional in nature. Writing in *Voice of Youth Advocates,* Joni Bodart described the collection as "well-written, with believable situations, witty dialogue and engaging characters." Other short story collections include 1988's *Time Bomb and Zahndry Others,* and *Distant Friends and Others,* published in 1992.

Three other of Zahn's works of the late 1980s also rely less on militarism and adventure and more on psychological analysis of characters. *Triplet* is, according to Green in *Booklist,* "an intelligent, literate exploration of how science and magic coexist on three planets," while *Deadman Switch* is an examination of possible negative consequences of the death penalty. Death row is in the pilot's cabin on commercial ships bound for the world of Solitaire, whose territory can only be entered or exited by a spaceship navigated by a corpse—hence the use of convict pilots who will be executed upon entry to Solitaire. The 1990 work *Warhorse* is more of a return to Zahn's favorite theme of conflict between alien cultures, in this case an alien species who are biological engineers, Tampies, who think that all life is valuable. This belief structure comes into conflict with the rough and ready human colonists, and the Tampies' biologically-engineered spaceships—warhorses—act like updated Blackcollars or Cobras in the drama. "Zahn at his best," is how Roland Green described *Warhorse* in *Booklist.*

Zahn's career, already successful by most standards, went interstellar in 1991 with the introduction of his Star Wars series. Picking up the story five years after the point where George Lucas had left it with his final movie, *The Return of the Jedi,* Zahn has Han Solo and Princess Leia married and expecting twins. The evil Empire of Darth Vader has been defeated and Luke Skywalker continues to study the secrets of the Jedi. Trouble soon brews, however, when Grand

Admiral Thrawn, a former Empire warlord, attacks the Republic in the first book in the trilogy, *Heir to the Empire.* The adventures and escapades continue in volume two, *Dark Force Rising,* "a thundering melodrama with a satisfyingly complicated plot," according to *Kirkus Reviews.* A commentator reviewing this second book in *Publishers Weekly* noted that Zahn "adroitly" juggles plot twists and plot lines "to produce skillfully paced entertainment," while *Booklist* reviewer Green concluded that Zahn's adaptation was "one of the more remarkable pastiches of recent years." The trilogy was completed by *The Last Command,* with the ultimate vanquishing of Thrawn's forces by a small group led by Luke Skywalker who infiltrate the Grand Admiral's stronghold. Lisa Prolman commented in *Voice of Youth Advocates* that "Zahn's handling of the characters and plot create a work that readers will enjoy and is a joy to read," and noted that this final installment is a "thoroughly mesmerizing and satisfying continuation of the Star Wars saga." Each volume of the trilogy spent weeks on the *New York Times* bestseller list, with *Heir to the Empire* reaching number one.

Zahn, however, has not been resting on his laurels. The 1994 *Conquerors' Pride* initiated another trilogy, continued in *Conquerors' Heritage* and *Conquerors' Legacy.* Combining the theme of clashing cultures with a militaristic flavor, Zahn sets the first novel in the far future when humanity is facing difficulties and tensions both externally and from within. A new militaristic enemy attacks, and the son of an important statesman is captured after a space battle. *Booklist* reviewer Green commended Zahn for his "usual knack for swift pacing, plausible technology and characters, and a lived-in setting," all of which, Green commented, combine to make *Conquerors' Pride* both realistic and a page-turner. Interstellar war erupts in the second novel of the trilogy, *Conquerors' Heritage,* another "finely wrought space adventure," according to Green. The Zhirrzh, or alien race of conquerors of the title, battle the humans and their superweapons in this installment. The trilogy is completed with *Conquerors' Legacy.*

Despite his successful exploration of thought-provoking themes, Zahn is wary of dubbing himself anything more than a teller of tales. "I consider myself primarily a storyteller," he once remarked, "and as such have no major pulpit-thumping 'message' that I always try to insert in each story or book. If any theme crops up more than any other, it is my strong belief that there is no prison—whether physical, social, or emotional—that can permanently trap a person who truly wishes to break free of the bonds."

BIOGRAPHICAL/CRITICAL SOURCES:

BOOKS

Twentieth-Century Science Fiction Writers, 3rd edition, St. James Press (Detroit), 1992.

PERIODICALS

Analog Science Fiction/Science Fact, February, 1984, pp. 167-168; October, 1985, p. 182; November, 1985, pp. 182-83; August, 1986, pp. 178-79; November, 1986, p. 182; April, 1988, pp. 181-82.
Booklist, January 1, 1986, p. 662; May 1, 1986, p. 1288; August, 1987, p. 1722; March 15, 1990, p. 1420; April 1, 1992, p. 1413; September 1, 1994, p. 28; September 1, 1995, p. 48.
Christian Science Monitor, January 3, 1986, p. 18.
Fantasy Review, April, 1985, p. 31; May, 1985, p. 22; December, 1985, p. 26; March, 1986, p. 25.
Kirkus Reviews, November 1, 1984, p. 1025; April 1, 1992, p. 434.
Library Journal, April 15, 1992, p. 125.
Publishers Weekly, December 14, 1984, pp. 41-42; October 25, 1985, p. 61; March 21, 1987, p. 77; July 3, 1987, p. 58; March 23, 1992, p. 64.
School Library Journal, September, 1985, p. 155; February, 1992, p. 122.
Voice of Youth Advocates, August, 1985, p. 196; June, 1986, pp. 91-92; October, 1993, p. 237.
Washington Post Book World, May 25, 1986, p. 8.

*   *   *

ZUBROWSKI, Bernard 1939-
(Bernie Zubrowski)

PERSONAL: Born February 22, 1939, in Baltimore, MD; son of Anthony and Catherine Zubrowski. *Education:* Loyola College, Baltimore, MD, B.S., 1962; Boston College, M.S.T., 1967. *Avocational interests:* Sculpture.

ADDRESSES: Home—48 Warren St., Littleton, MA 04160. *Office*—Education Development Center, 55 Chapel St., Newton, MA 02158.

CAREER: U.S. Peace Corps, Bangladesh, elementary school English and science teacher, 1962-64; Education Development Center, Newton, MA, Peace Corps teacher trainer, 1966-67; African Primary Science program, Kenya, East Africa, designer and developer of curriculum guides, 1967-69; Children's Museum, Boston, MA, senior science developer, 1969-93; UNHCR Refugee Camp, Galang, Indonesia, curriculum developer, 1983; independent consultant, Paris, France, 1983; Exploratorium, San Francisco, CA, artist-in-residence, 1990; Education Development Center, Newton, project director, 1993—. *Exhibitions:* Children's Museum exhibits include *Water,* 1977-79, *Tools,* 1979-81, *Bubbles,* 1981—, *Raceways,* 1982—, *Water Lifting Machines,* 1984, *Tops and Yo-Yos,* 1988, *Salad Dressing Physics,* 1988—, and *Waves and Vibrations,* 1991—. Sculptures include *Ghost of Amelia Earhart,* Exploratorium, 1989-92, *Liquid Light,* Austin Children's Museum, 1993, and *Nested Circles,* Austin Children's Museum, 1993.

AWARDS, HONORS: Best Children's Books of 1979 Honorable Mention, New York Academy of Sciences, 1980, for *Bubbles: A Children's Museum Activity Book;* Best Children's Science Book Award, New York Academy of Sciences, 1982, for *Messing around with Water Pumps and Siphons;* Commonwealth Award, Interpretative Scientist Category, 1995.

WRITINGS:

CHILDREN'S BOOKS; UNDER NAME BERNIE ZUBROWSKI

Bubbles: A Children's Museum Activity Book, illustrated by Joan Drescher, Little, Brown (Boston), 1979.

Milk Carton Blocks: A Children's Museum Activity Book, illustrated by Otto Coontz, Little, Brown, 1979.

Ball-Point Pens: A Children's Museum Activity Book, illustrated by Linda Bourke, Little, Brown, 1979.

Messing around with Baking Chemistry, illustrated by Signe Hanson, Little, Brown, 1981.

Messing around with Water Pumps and Siphons, illustrated by Steve Lindblom, Little, Brown, 1981.

Messing around with Drinking Straw Construction, illustrated by Stefanie Fleischer, Little, Brown, 1981.

Raceways: Having Fun with Balls and Tracks, illustrated by Roy Doty, Morrow (New York City), 1985.

Wheels at Work: Building and Experimenting with Models of Machines, illustrated by Roy Doty, Morrow, 1986.

Clocks: Building and Experimenting with Model Time-pieces, illustrated by Roy Doty, Morrow, 1988.

Tops: Building and Experimenting with Spinning Toys, illustrated by Roy Doty, Morrow, 1989.

Balloons: Building and Experimenting with Inflatable Toys, illustrated by Roy Doty, Morrow, 1990.

Blinkers and Buzzers: Building and Experimenting with Electricity and Magnetism, illustrated by Roy Doty, Morrow, 1991.

Mirrors: Finding Out about the Properties of Light, illustrated by Roy Doty, Morrow, 1992.

Mobiles: Building and Experimenting with Balancing Toys, illustrated by Roy Doty, Morrow, 1993.

Structures, Cuisenaire Co. of America, 1993.

Inks, Food Colors, and Papers, Cuisenaire Co. of America (White Plains, NY), 1993.

Tops and Yo-Yos, Cuisenaire Co. of America, 1994.

Making Waves: Finding Out about Rhythmic Motion, illustrated by Roy Doty, Morrow, 1994.

Ice Cream Making and Cake Baking, Cuisenaire Co. of America, 1994.

Shadow Play: Making Pictures with Light and Lenses, illustrated by Roy Doty, Morrow, 1995.

Soda Science: Designing and Testing Soft Drinks, Morrow, 1997.

OTHER

Also author of African Primary Science Program Teacher's Guides, including *Construction with Grass, Making Paints, Colors, Liquids, Papers, Inks and Papers,* and *Tools Sink and Float.* Contributor of articles to periodicals, including *Technology Review, Journal of Research in Science Teaching, Day Care and Early Childhood Education,* and *School Science and Math.*

WORK IN PROGRESS: Learning to See, a video case study project to be published and distributed by Heinemann.

SIDELIGHTS: Bernard Zubrowski's educational science books enable children to perform their own experiments and activities while learning about the properties and functions of the subject of their experiments. While emphasizing the fun aspects of bubble-making in *Bubbles: A Children's Museum Activity Book,* Zubrowski also challenges his readers to think about how the bubbles are formed and the mathematical relationships they demonstrate. Cake ingredients and what they actually do are examined in *Messing around with Baking Chemistry,* several wheel machines are built and the principles of physics used to make them are described in *Wheels at Work: Building and Experimenting with Models of Machines,* and the creation of waves demonstrates rhythmatic motion in nature in *Making Waves: Finding out about Rhythmic Motion.*

In the majority of his books, Zubrowski provides an easily attainable list of materials for the activities, gives a step-by-step explanation for the construction of models and the actual conduction of the experiments, and also explains related scientific principles and properties. "Explicit instructions, experiments that evoke curiosity for further investigation, and a sense of play mark these two Children's Museum Activity Books," asserts Marybeth Franz in a *School Library Journal* review of *Bubbles* and *Ball-Point Pens: A Children's Museum Activity Book.* Karen M. Klockner, writing in *Horn Book,* similarly states: "In each book the text integrates questions with discussion and provides experiments which will help the reader learn answers as well as questions of his own." Zubrowski's books, concludes a *Bulletin of the Center for Children's Books* reviewer, "are evidence of the excellent results when subject knowledge is paired with experience in working with children who are doing experiments."

"Over the past twenty-five years I have been working with children in a variety of educational settings," Zubrowski told *CA.* "I have introduced to them and encouraged them to explore many kinds of interesting phenomena or assisted them in the construction of models of simple technologies. They have always reacted very positively and enthusiastically to these materials. It is my long-held view that children are not provided enough opportunities to activate their native curiosity and develop the skills and intellectual abilities for making sense of the world. Teachers in the formal education system certainly do not carry out many 'hands-on' activities and there aren't many parents that encourage this at home.

"Science activity books are one means for promoting and providing directions for this to happen. However, too many of them are superficial in their exposure to phenomena and in their explanations. Many of them are a collection of activities where there is something different on every page. The readers are not encouraged to carry out extended exploration, and attempt to know a phenomena in a deeper way. What I have tried to do over the past twenty years is to write activity books and science curriculum for elementary and middle school which show how this can be done. I try to balance engaging materials in the form of games and interesting explorations with careful scientific explanations. When certain kinds of phenomena are presented in an interesting manner and sequenced in a thoughtful way, children will continue to explore for weeks. All of the activities that I describe in my books were tried out in classrooms and museum programs a number of times before I decided on their suitability for publication. It is my hope that children will try out these activities at home under the supervision of parents, and that teachers will find them a useful supplementary resource in their teaching."

BIOGRAPHICAL/CRITICAL SOURCES:

PERIODICALS

Booklist, March 1, 1982, p. 901; July, 1992, p. 1936; July, 1994, p. 1942.
Bulletin of the Center for Children's Books, June, 1982; October, 1990, p. 50.
Horn Book, October, 1979, p. 553.
Kirkus Reviews, November 15, 1979, p. 1330; December 1, 1986, p. 1802.
School Library Journal, November, 1979, p. 83; February, 1987, pp. 86-87; August, 1994, p. 167.*

* * *

ZUBROWSKI, Bernie
See ZUBROWSKI, Bernard